HIGH COURT
CASE SUMMARIES

CONSTITUTIONAL LAW

Keyed to Chemerinsky's Casebook on
Constitutional Law,
3rd Edition

WEST.
A Thomson Reuters business

Thomson Reuters created this publication to provide you with accurate and authoritative information concerning the subject matter covered.
However, this publication was not necessarily prepared by persons licensed to practice law in a particular jurisdiction. Thomson Reuters does not
render legal or other professional advice, and this publication is not a substitute for the advice of an attorney. If you require legal or other expert
advice, you should seek the services of a competent attorney or other professional.

High Court Case Summaries and Thomson Reuters are registered trademarks used under license.
All rights reserved. Do not duplicate.

© West, a Thomson business, 2002, 2006
© 2010 Thomson Reuters
    610 Opperman Drive
    St. Paul, MN 55123
    1-800-313-9378
Printed in the United States of America

ISBN: 978-0-314-26632-3

Table of Contents

	Page
CHAPTER ONE. The Federal Judicial Power	**1**
Marbury v. Madison	5
District of Columbia v. Heller	7
Ex Parte McCardle	11
United States v. Klein	13
Plaut v. Spendthrift Farm, Inc.	15
Allen v. Wright	17
Massachusetts v. Environmental Protection Agency	21
Lujan v. Defenders of Wildlife	23
Singleton v. Wulff	27
Elk Grove Unified School Dist. v. Newdow	29
United States v. Richardson	31
Flast v. Cohen	33
Hein v. Freedom From Religion Foundation	35
Poe v. Ullman	37
Abbott Laboratories v. Gardner	39
Friends of the Earth, Incorporated v. Laidlaw Environmental Services	41
United States Parole Commission v. Geraghty	43
Baker v. Carr	45
Vieth v. Jubelirer	47
Powell v. McCormack	51
Goldwater v. Carter	53
Nixon v. United States	55
CHAPTER TWO. The Federal Legislative Power	**59**
McCulloch v. Maryland	65
Gibbons v. Ogden	69
United States v. E. C. Knight Co.	71
Carter v. Carter Coal Co.	73
Houston, East & West Texas Railway Company v. United States [the Shreveport Rate cases]	75
A.L.A. Schechter Poultry Corporation v. United States	77
Hammer v. Dagenhart	79
Champion v. Ames (The Lottery Case)	81
N.L.R.B. v. Jones & Laughlin Steel Corp.	83
United States v. Darby	85
Wickard v. Filburn	87
Heart of Atlanta Motel, Inc. v. United States	89
Katzenbach v. McClung, Sr. and McClung, Jr.	91
National League of Cities v. Usery	93
Garcia v. San Antonio Metropolitan Transit Authority	95
United States v. Lopez	99
United States v. Morrison	103
Pierce County, Washington v. Guillen	107
Gonzales v. Raich	109
New York v. United States	113
Printz v. United States	117
Reno v. Condon	121
United States v. Butler	123
Sabri v. United States	125
South Dakota v. Dole	127
United States v. Morrison	129
Katzenbach v. Morgan & Morgan	131
City of Boerne v. Flores	135

TABLE OF CONTENTS

	Page
Fitzpatrick v. Bitzer	139
Seminole Tribe of Florida v. Florida	141
Florida Prepaid Postsecondary Education Expense Board v. College Savings Bank and United States	145
Kimel v. Florida Board of Regents	149
Board of Trustees v. Garrett	153
Nevada Department of Human Resources v. Hibbs	155
Tennessee v. Lane	157
United States v. Georgia	159
Alden v. Maine	161

CHAPTER THREE. The Federal Executive Power — 165

Youngstown Sheet & Tube Co. v. Sawyer [The Steel Seizure Case]	167
United States v. Richard M. Nixon, President of the United States	169
William J. Clinton, President of the United States v. City of New York	171
A.L.A. Schechter Poultry Corporation v. United States	173
Panama Refining Co. v. Ryan	175
Whitman v. American Trucking Assn., Inc.	177
Immigration and Naturalization Service v. Jagdish Rai Chadha	179
Alexia Morrison, Independent Counsel v. Theodore B. Olson	181
United States v. Curtiss-Wright Export Corp.	183
Dames & Moore v. Regan, Secretary of the Treasury	185
Hamdi v. Rumsfeld	187
Boumediene v. Bush	191
Richard Nixon v. A. Ernest Fitzgerald	195
William Jefferson Clinton v. Paula Corbin Jones	197

CHAPTER FOUR. Limits on State Regulatory and Taxing Power — 199

Lorillard Tobacco Co. v. Reilly	205
Florida Lime & Avocado Growers, Inc. v. Paul, Director, Dept. of Agriculture of California	207
Pacific Gas & Electric Co. v. State Energy Resources Conservation & Development Commission	209
Hines, Secretary of Labor and Industry of Pennsylvania v. Davidowitz	211
H.P. Hood & Sons, Inc. v. Du Mond, Commissioner of Agriculture and Markets of New York	213
Aaron B. Cooley v. The Board of Wardens of the Port of Philadelphia	215
South Carolina State Highway Department v. Barnwell Brothers, Inc.	217
Southern Pacific Co. v. Arizona	219
City of Philadelphia v. New Jersey	221
C & A Carbone, Inc. v. Town of Clarkstown, New York	223
United Haulers Assn., Inc. v. Oneida–Herkimer Solid Waste Management Authority	225
Hughes v. Oklahoma	227
Hunt, Governor of the State of North Carolina v. Washington State Apple Advertising Commission	229
Exxon Corporation v. Governor of Maryland	231
West Lynn Creamery, Inc. v. Healy, Commissioner of Massachusetts Department of Food and Agriculture	233
State of Minnesota v. Clover Leaf Creamery Co.	235
Dean Milk Co. v. City of Madison, Wisconsin	237
Maine v. Taylor and United States	239
Loren J. Pike v. Bruce Church, Inc.	241
Bibb, Director, Department of Public Safety of Illinois v. Navajo Freight Lines, Inc.	243
Consolidated Freightways Corporation of Delaware v. Raymond Kassel	245
Western & Southern Life Insurance Co. v. State Board of Equalization of California	247
Reeves, Inc. v. William Stake	249
South-Central Timber Development, Inc. v. Commissioner, Department of Natural Resources of Alaska	251
Toomer v. Witsell	253
United Building and Construction Trades Council of Camden County v. Mayor and Council of the City of Camden	255
Lester Baldwin v. Fish and Game Commission of Montana	257
Supreme Court of New Hampshire v. Kathryn A. Piper	259

TABLE OF CONTENTS

	Page
CHAPTER FIVE. The Structure of the Constitution's Protection of Civil Rights and Civil Liberties	**261**
Barron v. Mayor and City Council of Baltimore	265
Slaughter-House Cases	267
Saenz v. Roe	269
Twining v. New Jersey	271
Duncan v. Louisiana	273
The Civil Rights Cases	275
Marsh v. Alabama	277
Jackson v. Metropolitan Edison Co.	279
Terry v. Adams	281
Evans v. Newton	283
Amalgamated Food Employees Union Local 590 v. Logan Valley Plaza, Inc.	285
Lloyd Corp. v. Tanner	287
Hudgens v. National Labor Relations Board	289
Shelley v. Kraemer	291
Lugar v. Edmondson Oil Co.	293
Edmonson v. Leesville Concrete Co.	295
Burton v. Wilmington Parking Authority	297
Moose Lodge No. 107 v. Irvis	299
Norwood v. Harrison	301
Rendell-Baker v. Kohn	303
Blum v. Yaretsky	305
Reitman v. Mulkey	307
Brentwood Academy v. Tennessee Secondary School Athletic Assn.	309
CHAPTER SIX. Economic Liberties	**311**
Allgeyer v. Louisiana	315
Lochner v. New York	317
Coppage v. Kansas	321
Muller v. Oregon	323
Adkins v. Children's Hospital	325
Weaver v. Palmer Bros. Co.	327
Nebbia v. New York	329
West Coast Hotel Co. v. Parrish	331
United States v. Carolene Products Co.	333
Williamson v. Lee Optical of Oklahoma, Inc.	335
BMW of North America, Inc. v. Gore	337
State Farm Mut. Automobile Ins. Co. v. Campbell	341
Philip Morris U.S.A. v. Williams	345
Home Building & Loan Association v. Blaisdell	347
Energy Reserves Group, Inc. v. Kansas Power & Light Co.	349
Allied Structural Steel v. Spannaus	351
United States Trust Co. v. New Jersey	355
Loretto v. Teleprompter Manhattan CATV Corp.	357
Pennsylvania Coal Co. v. Mahon	359
Miller v. Schoene	361
Penn Central Transportation Co. v. New York City	363
Lucas v. South Carolina Coastal Council	365
Dolan v. City of Tigard	367
Palazzolo v. Rhode Island	369
Tahoe-Sierra Preservation Council, Inc. v. Tahoe Regional Planning Agency	373
Hawaii Housing Authority v. Midkiff	375
Kelo v. City of New London	377
Brown v. Legal Foundation of Washington	381
CHAPTER SEVEN. Equal Protection	**383**
Romer v. Evans	391
United States Railroad Retirement Board v. Fritz	393
Railway Express Agency, Inc. v. New York	395
New York City Transit Authority v. Beazer	397

v

TABLE OF CONTENTS

	Page
United States Department of Agriculture v. Moreno	399
City of Cleburne, Texas v. Cleburne Living Center, Inc.	401
Dred Scott v. Sandford	403
Korematsu v. United States	405
Loving v. Virginia	407
Palmore v. Sidoti	409
Plessy v. Ferguson	411
Brown v. Board of Education (Brown I)	413
Johnson v. California	415
Washington v. Davis	417
McCleskey v. Kemp	419
City of Mobile v. Bolden	421
Palmer v. Thompson	423
Personnel Administrator of Massachusetts v. Feeney	425
Village of Arlington Heights v. Metropolitan Housing Development Corp.	427
Brown v. Board of Education (Brown II)	429
Swann v. Charlotte-Mecklenburg Board of Education	431
Milliken v. Bradley	433
Board of Education of Oklahoma City Public Schools v. Dowell	435
Parents Involved in Community Schools v. Seattle School District No. 1	437
Richmond v. J.A. Croson Co.	441
Adarand Constructors, Inc. v. Pena	443
Grutter v. Bollinger	445
Gratz v. Bollinger	449
Easley v. Cromartie	451
Frontiero v. Richardson	453
Craig v. Boren	455
United States v. Virginia	457
Geduldig v. Aiello	459
Orr v. Orr	461
Mississippi University for Women v. Hogan	463
Michael M. v. Superior Court of Sonoma County	465
Rostker v. Goldberg	467
Califano v. Webster	469
Nguyen v. Immigration and Naturalization Service	471
Graham v. Richardson	473
Foley v. Connelie	475
Ambach v. Norwick	477
Plyler v. Doe	479
Massachusetts Board of Retirement v. Murgia	481
CHAPTER EIGHT. Fundamental Rights Under Due Process and Equal Protection	**483**
Zablocki v. Redhail	489
Michael H. v. Gerald D.	493
Moore v. City of East Cleveland	497
Meyer v. Nebraska	501
Troxel v. Granville	503
Skinner v. Oklahoma	507
Griswold v. Connecticut	509
Eisenstadt v. Baird	513
Roe v. Wade	515
Planned Parenthood v. Casey	519
Gonzales v. Carhart	525
Maher v. Roe	529
Planned Parenthood v. Casey	531
Bellotti v. Baird	535
Cruzan v. Director, Missouri Department of Health	539
Washington v. Glucksberg	543
Lawrence v. Texas	547
Whalen v. Roe	551
Saenz v. Roe	553

	Page
Harper v. Virginia State Board of Elections	557
Kramer v. Union Free School District	559
Ball v. James	563
Crawford v. Marion County Election Board	565
Reynolds v. Sims	567
Bush v. Gore	571
Boddie v. Connecticut	575
United States v. Kras	577
M.L.B. v. S.L.J.	581
Lewis v. Casey	583
San Antonio Independent School District v. Rodriguez	587
Daniels v. Williams	591
County of Sacramento v. Lewis	593
DeShaney v. Winnebago County Department of Social Services	595
Town of Castle Rock v. Gonzales	599
Goldberg v. Kelly	601
Board of Regents v. Roth	605
Goss v. Lopez	607
Paul v. Davis	609
Mathews v. Eldridge	611

CHAPTER NINE. First Amendment: Freedom of Expression — 615

Turner Broadcasting System, Inc. v. Federal Communications Commission	629
Boos v. Barry	631
Republican Party of Minnesota v. White	633
City of Renton v. Playtime Theatres, Inc.	637
National Endowment for the Arts v. Finley	639
United States v. American Library Assn., Inc.	641
Near v. State of Minnesota ex rel. Olson	643
New York Times Company v. United States	645
Nebraska Press Association v. Stuart	647
Alexander v. United States	649
Watchtower Bible and Tract Society of New York, Inc. v. Village of Stratton	651
Thomas and Windy City Hemp Development Board v. Chicago Park District	653
City of Littleton, Colorado v. Z.J. Gifts D–4, L.L.C.	655
United States v. National Treasury Employees Union	657
West Virginia State Board of Education v. Barnette	659
Rumsfeld v. Forum for Academic & Institutional Rights, Inc.	661
McIntyre v. Ohio Elections Commission	663
Rust v. Sullivan	665
Legal Services Corp. v. Velazquez	667
Schenck v. United States	669
Frohwerk v. United States	671
Debs v. United States	673
Abrams v. United States	675
Gitlow v. New York	677
Whitney v. California	679
Dennis v. United States	681
Brandenburg v. Ohio	683
Chaplinsky v. New Hampshire	685
Gooding v. Wilson	687
R.A.V. v. City of St. Paul, Minnesota	689
Feiner v. New York	693
Beauharnais v. Illinois	695
Virginia v. Black	697
Roth v. United States	701
Paris Adult Theatre v. Slaton	703
Miller v. California	705
New York v. Ferber	707
Ashcroft v. The Free Speech Coalition	709
Young v. American Mini Theatres, Inc.	713

vii

TABLE OF CONTENTS

	Page
City of Erie v. Pap's A.M.	715
Stanley v. Georgia	717
Cohen v. California	719
Federal Communications Commission v. Pacifica Foundation	721
Sable Communications of California, Inc. v. Federal Communications Commission	723
Reno v. American Civil Liberties Union	725
Ashcroft v. American Civil Liberties Union	727
Virginia State Board of Pharmacy v. Virginia Citizens Consumer Council, Inc.	729
Bolger v. Youngs Drug Products Corp.	731
Central Hudson Gas v. Public Service Commission of New York	733
Friedman v. Rogers	735
Linmark Associates v. Township of Willingboro	737
44 Liquormart, Inc. v. Rhode Island	739
Lorillard Tobacco Co. v. Reilly	741
New York Times Co. v. Sullivan	743
Gertz v. Welch	745
Dun & Bradstreet, Inc. v. Greenmoss Builders, Inc.	747
Hustler Magazine v. Falwell	749
Cox Broadcasting Corporation v. Cohn	751
Florida Star v. B.J.F.	753
Bartnicki v. Vopper	755
United States v. O'Brien	757
Texas v. Johnson	759
Buckley v. Valeo	761
Nixon v. Shrink Missouri Government PAC	763
Randall v. Sorrell	765
First National Bank of Boston v. Bellotti	767
Hague v. Committee for Industrial Organization	769
Schneider v. New Jersey	771
Perry Education Assn. v. Perry Local Educators' Assn.	773
Police Department of Chicago v. Mosley	775
Hill et al. v. Colorado	777
Ward v. Rock Against Racism	779
Adderley v. Florida	781
Greer v. Spock	783
Lehman v. City of Shaker Heights	785
United States v. Kokinda	787
International Society for Krishna Consciousness, Inc. v. Lee	789
Arkansas Educational Television Commission v. Forbes	791
Parker v. Levy	793
Thornburgh v. Abbott	795
Shaw v. Murphy	797
Tinker v. Des Moines Independent Community School District	799
Bethel School District v. Fraser	801
Hazelwood School District v. Kuhlmeier	803
Morse v. Frederick	805
Garcetti v. Ceballos	807
National Association for the Advancement of Colored People v. Alabama, ex rel. Patterson	809
Board of Regents of the University of Wisconsin System v. Southworth	811
Roberts v. United States Jaycees	813
Hurley v. Irish-American Gay, Lesbian and Bisexual Group of Boston	815
Boy Scouts of America v. Dale	817
Minneapolis Star and Tribune Company v. Minnesota Commissioner of Revenue	819
Cohen v. Cowles Media Company	821
Branzburg v. Hayes	823
Red Lion Broadcasting Co. v. Federal Communications Commission	825
Miami Herald v. Tornillo	827
Richmond Newspapers, Inc. v. Virginia	829
Pell v. Procunier	831
Houchins v. KQED	833

TABLE OF CONTENTS

	Page
CHAPTER TEN. First Amendment: Religion	**835**
United States v. Seeger	839
United States v. Ballard	841
Employment Division, Department of Human Resources of Oregon v. Smith	843
Sherbert v. Verner	847
Church of the Lukumi Babalu Aye v. City of Hialeah	849
Cutter v. Wilkinson	851
Locke v. Davey	853
County of Allegheny v. American Civil Liberties Union Greater Pittsburgh Chapter	855
Larson v. Valente	859
Lemon v. Kurtzman	861
Rosenberger v. Rector and Visitors of the University of Virginia	863
Santa Fe Independent School District v. Doe	867
McCreary County v. American Civil Liberties Union of Kentucky	871
Van Orden v. Perry	873
Engel v. Vitale	875
Lee v. Weisman	877
Mitchell v. Helms	881
Zelman v. Simmons–Harris	885

Alphabetical Table of Cases

Abbott Laboratories v. Gardner, 387 U.S. 136, 87 S.Ct. 1507, 18 L.Ed.2d 681 (1967), 39

Abrams v. United States, 250 U.S. 616, 40 S.Ct. 17, 63 L.Ed. 1173 (1919), 675

Adarand Constructors, Inc. v. Pena, 515 U.S. 200, 115 S.Ct. 2097, 132 L.Ed.2d 158 (1995), 443

Adderley v. State of Fla., 385 U.S. 39, 87 S.Ct. 242, 17 L.Ed.2d 149 (1966), 781

Adkins v. Children's Hospital of the District of Columbia, 261 U.S. 525, 43 S.Ct. 394, 67 L.Ed. 785 (1923), 325

A.L.A. Schechter Poultry Corporation v. United States, 295 U.S. 495, 55 S.Ct. 837, 79 L.Ed. 1570 (1935), 77, 173

Alden v. Maine, 527 U.S. 706, 119 S.Ct. 2240, 144 L.Ed.2d 636 (1999), 161

Alexander v. United States, 509 U.S. 544, 113 S.Ct. 2766, 125 L.Ed.2d 441 (1993), 649

Allegheny, County of v. American Civil Liberties Union Greater Pittsburgh Chapter, 492 U.S. 573, 109 S.Ct. 3086, 106 L.Ed.2d 472 (1989), 855

Allen v. Wright, 468 U.S. 737, 104 S.Ct. 3315, 82 L.Ed.2d 556 (1984), 17

Allgeyer v. State of La., 165 U.S. 578, 17 S.Ct. 427, 41 L.Ed. 832 (1897), 315

Allied Structural Steel Co. v. Spannaus, 438 U.S. 234, 98 S.Ct. 2716, 57 L.Ed.2d 727 (1978), 351

Amalgamated Food Emp. Union Local 590 v. Logan Valley Plaza, Inc., 391 U.S. 308, 88 S.Ct. 1601, 20 L.Ed.2d 603 (1968), 285

Ambach v. Norwick, 441 U.S. 68, 99 S.Ct. 1589, 60 L.Ed.2d 49 (1979), 477

American Library Ass'n, Inc., United States v., 539 U.S. 194, 123 S.Ct. 2297, 156 L.Ed.2d 221 (2003), 641,

Arkansas Educ. Television Com'n v. Forbes, 523 U.S. 666, 118 S.Ct. 1633, 140 L.Ed.2d 875 (1998), 791

Arlington Heights, Village of v. Metropolitan Housing Development Corp., 429 U.S. 252, 97 S.Ct. 555, 50 L.Ed.2d 450 (1977), 427

Ashcroft v. American Civil Liberties Union, 542 U.S. 656, 124 S.Ct. 2783, 159 L.Ed.2d 690 (2004), 727

Ashcroft v. Free Speech Coalition, 535 U.S. 234, 122 S.Ct. 1389, 152 L.Ed.2d 403 (2002), 709

Baker v. Carr, 369 U.S. 186, 82 S.Ct. 691, 7 L.Ed.2d 663 (1962), 45

Baldwin v. Fish and Game Commission of Montana, 436 U.S. 371, 98 S.Ct. 1852, 56 L.Ed.2d 354 (1978), 257

Ball v. James, 451 U.S. 355, 101 S.Ct. 1811, 68 L.Ed.2d 150 (1981), 563

Ballard, United States v., 322 U.S. 78, 64 S.Ct. 882, 88 L.Ed. 1148 (1944), 841

Barron v. City of Baltimore, 32 U.S. 243, 7 Pet. 243, 8 L.Ed. 672 (1833), 265

Bartnicki v. Vopper, 532 U.S. 514, 121 S.Ct. 1753, 149 L.Ed.2d 787 (2001), 755

Beauharnais v. People of State of Ill., 343 U.S. 250, 72 S.Ct. 725, 96 L.Ed. 919 (1952), 695

Bellotti v. Baird, 443 U.S. 622, 99 S.Ct. 3035, 61 L.Ed.2d 797 (1979), 535

Bethel School Dist. No. 403 v. Fraser, 478 U.S. 675, 106 S.Ct. 3159, 92 L.Ed.2d 549 (1986), 801

Bibb v. Navajo Freight Lines, Inc., 359 U.S. 520, 79 S.Ct. 962, 3 L.Ed.2d 1003 (1959), 243

Blum v. Yaretsky, 457 U.S. 991, 102 S.Ct. 2777, 73 L.Ed.2d 534 (1982), 305

BMW of North America, Inc. v. Gore, 517 U.S. 559, 116 S.Ct. 1589, 134 L.Ed.2d 809 (1996), 337

Board of Educ. of Oklahoma City Public Schools, Independent School Dist. No. 89, Oklahoma County, Okl. v. Dowell, 498 U.S. 237, 111 S.Ct. 630, 112 L.Ed.2d 715 (1991), 435

Board of Regents of State Colleges v. Roth, 408 U.S. 564, 92 S.Ct. 2701, 33 L.Ed.2d 548 (1972), 605

Board of Regents of University of Wisconsin System v. Southworth, 529 U.S. 217, 120 S.Ct. 1346, 146 L.Ed.2d 193 (2000), 811

Board of Trustees of University of Alabama v. Garrett, 531 U.S. 356, 121 S.Ct. 955, 148 L.Ed.2d 866 (2001), 153

Boddie v. Connecticut, 401 U.S. 371, 91 S.Ct. 780, 28 L.Ed.2d 113 (1971), 575

Boerne, City of v. Flores, 521 U.S. 507, 117 S.Ct. 2157, 138 L.Ed.2d 624 (1997), 135,

Bolger v. Youngs Drug Products Corp., 463 U.S. 60, 103 S.Ct. 2875, 77 L.Ed.2d 469 (1983), 731

Boos v. Barry, 485 U.S. 312, 108 S.Ct. 1157, 99 L.Ed.2d 333 (1988), 631

Boumediene v. Bush, 553 U.S. 723, 128 S.Ct. 2229, 171 L.Ed.2d 41 (2008), 191

Boy Scouts of America v. Dale, 530 U.S. 640, 120 S.Ct. 2446, 147 L.Ed.2d 554 (2000), 817

Brandenburg v. Ohio, 395 U.S. 444, 89 S.Ct. 1827, 23 L.Ed.2d 430 (1969), 683

Branzburg v. Hayes, 408 U.S. 665, 92 S.Ct. 2646, 33 L.Ed.2d 626 (1972), 823

Brentwood Academy v. Tennessee Secondary School Athletic Ass'n, 531 U.S. 288, 121 S.Ct. 924, 148 L.Ed.2d 807 (2001), 309

Brown v. Board of Ed. of Topeka, Shawnee County, Kan., 347 U.S. 483, 74 S.Ct. 686, 98 L.Ed. 873 (1954), 413,

Brown v. Board of Educ. of Topeka, Kan., 349 U.S. 294, 75 S.Ct. 753, 99 L.Ed. 1083 (1955), 429

Brown v. Legal Foundation of Washington, 538 U.S. 216, 123 S.Ct. 1406, 155 L.Ed.2d 376 (2003), 381

Buckley v. Valeo, 424 U.S. 1, 96 S.Ct. 612, 46 L.Ed.2d 659 (1976), 761,

Burton v. Wilmington Parking Authority, 365 U.S. 715, 81 S.Ct. 856, 6 L.Ed.2d 45 (1961), 297

Bush v. Gore, 531 U.S. 98, 121 S.Ct. 525, 148 L.Ed.2d 388 (2000), 571

Butler, United States v., 297 U.S. 1, 56 S.Ct. 312, 80 L.Ed. 477 (1936), 123

C & A Carbone, Inc. v. Town of Clarkstown, N.Y., 511 U.S. 383, 114 S.Ct. 1677, 128 L.Ed.2d 399 (1994), 223

Califano v. Webster, 430 U.S. 313, 97 S.Ct. 1192, 51 L.Ed.2d 360 (1977), 469

Carolene Products Co., United States v., 304 U.S. 144, 58 S.Ct. 778, 82 L.Ed. 1234 (1938), 333

Carter v. Carter Coal Co., 298 U.S. 238, 56 S.Ct. 855, 80 L.Ed. 1160 (1936), 73

Castle Rock, Colo., Town of v. Gonzales, 545 U.S. 748, 125 S.Ct. 2796, 162 L.Ed.2d 658 (2005), 599

Central Hudson Gas & Elec. Corp. v. Public Service Commission of New York, 447 U.S. 557, 100 S.Ct. 2343, 65 L.Ed.2d 341 (1980), 733

Champion v. Ames, 188 U.S. 321, 23 S.Ct. 321, 47 L.Ed. 492 (1903), 81

Chaplinsky v. State of New Hampshire, 315 U.S. 568, 62 S.Ct. 766, 86 L.Ed. 1031 (1942), 685

Church of the Lukumi Babalu Aye, Inc. v. City of Hialeah, 508 U.S. 520, 113 S.Ct. 2217, 124 L.Ed.2d 472 (1993), 849

City of (see name of city)

Civil Rights Cases, 109 U.S. 3, 3 S.Ct. 18, 27 L.Ed. 835 (1883), 275

ALPHABETICAL TABLE OF CASES

Cleburne, Tex., City of v. Cleburne Living Center, 473 U.S. 432, 105 S.Ct. 3249, 87 L.Ed.2d 313 (1985), 401

Clinton v. City of New York, 524 U.S. 417, 118 S.Ct. 2091, 141 L.Ed.2d 393 (1998), 171

Clinton v. Jones, 520 U.S. 681, 117 S.Ct. 1636, 137 L.Ed.2d 945 (1997), 197

Cohen v. California, 403 U.S. 15, 91 S.Ct. 1780, 29 L.Ed.2d 284 (1971), 719

Cohen v. Cowles Media Co., 501 U.S. 663, 111 S.Ct. 2513, 115 L.Ed.2d 586 (1991), 821

Consolidated Freightways Corporation of Delaware v. Kassel, 455 U.S. 329, 102 S.Ct. 1496, 71 L.Ed.2d 187 (1982), 245

Cooley v. Board of Wardens of Port of Philadelphia, to Use of Soc for Relief of Distressed Pilots, Their Widows and Children, 53 U.S. 299, 12 How. 299, 13 L.Ed. 996 (1851), 215

Coppage v. State of Kansas, 236 U.S. 1, 35 S.Ct. 240, 59 L.Ed. 441 (1915), 321

County of (see name of county)

Cox Broadcasting Corp. v. Cohn, 420 U.S. 469, 95 S.Ct. 1029, 43 L.Ed.2d 328 (1975), 751

Craig v. Boren, 429 U.S. 190, 97 S.Ct. 451, 50 L.Ed.2d 397 (1976), 455

Crawford v. Marion County Election Bd., 553 U.S. 181, 128 S.Ct. 1610, 170 L.Ed.2d 574 (2008), 565

Cruzan by Cruzan v. Director, Missouri Dept. of Health, 497 U.S. 261, 110 S.Ct. 2841, 111 L.Ed.2d 224 (1990), 539

Curtiss-Wright Export Corporation, United States v., 299 U.S. 304, 57 S.Ct. 216, 81 L.Ed. 255 (1936), 183

Cutter v. Wilkinson, 544 U.S. 709, 125 S.Ct. 2113, 161 L.Ed.2d 1020 (2005), 851

Dames & Moore v. Regan, 453 U.S. 654, 101 S.Ct. 2972, 69 L.Ed.2d 918 (1981), 185

Daniels v. Williams, 474 U.S. 327, 106 S.Ct. 662, 88 L.Ed.2d 662 (1986), 591

Darby, United States v., 312 U.S. 100, 312 U.S. 657, 61 S.Ct. 451, 85 L.Ed. 609 (1941), 85

Dean Milk Co. v. City of Madison, Wis., 340 U.S. 349, 71 S.Ct. 295, 95 L.Ed. 329 (1951), 237

Debs v. United States, 249 U.S. 211, 39 S.Ct. 252, 63 L.Ed. 566 (1919), 673

Dennis v. United States, 341 U.S. 494, 71 S.Ct. 857, 95 L.Ed. 1137 (1951), 681

DeShaney v. Winnebago County Dept. of Social Services, 489 U.S. 189, 109 S.Ct. 998, 103 L.Ed.2d 249 (1989), 595

District of Columbia v. Heller, ___ U.S. ___, 128 S.Ct. 2783, 171 L.Ed.2d 637 (2008), 7

Dolan v. City of Tigard, 512 U.S. 374, 114 S.Ct. 2309, 129 L.Ed.2d 304 (1994), 367

Dun & Bradstreet, Inc. v. Greenmoss Builders, Inc., 472 U.S. 749, 105 S.Ct. 2939, 86 L.Ed.2d 593 (1985), 747

Duncan v. State of La., 391 U.S. 145, 88 S.Ct. 1444, 20 L.Ed.2d 491 (1968), 273

Easley v. Cromartie, 532 U.S. 234, 121 S.Ct. 1452, 149 L.Ed.2d 430 (2001), 451

E. C. Knight Co., United States v., 156 U.S. 1, 15 S.Ct. 249, 39 L.Ed. 325 (1895), 71

Edmonson v. Leesville Concrete Co., Inc., 500 U.S. 614, 111 S.Ct. 2077, 114 L.Ed.2d 660 (1991), 295

Eisenstadt v. Baird, 405 U.S. 438, 92 S.Ct. 1029, 31 L.Ed.2d 349 (1972), 513

Elk Grove Unified School Dist. v. Newdow, 542 U.S. 1, 124 S.Ct. 2301, 159 L.Ed.2d 98 (2004), 29

Employment Div., Dept. of Human Resources of Oregon v. Smith, 494 U.S. 872, 110 S.Ct. 1595, 108 L.Ed.2d 876 (1990), 843

Energy Reserves Group, Inc. v. Kansas Power and Light Co., 459 U.S. 400, 103 S.Ct. 697, 74 L.Ed.2d 569 (1983), 349

Engel v. Vitale, 370 U.S. 421, 82 S.Ct. 1261, 8 L.Ed.2d 601 (1962), 875

Erie, City of v. Pap's A.M., 529 U.S. 277, 120 S.Ct. 1382, 146 L.Ed.2d 265 (2000), 715

Evans v. Newton, 382 U.S. 296, 86 S.Ct. 486, 15 L.Ed.2d 373 (1966), 283

Ex parte (see name of party)

Exxon Corp. v. Governor of Maryland, 437 U.S. 117, 98 S.Ct. 2207, 57 L.Ed.2d 91 (1978), 231

F.C.C. v. Pacifica Foundation, 438 U.S. 726, 98 S.Ct. 3026, 57 L.Ed.2d 1073 (1978), 721

Feiner v. New York, 340 U.S. 315, 71 S.Ct. 303, 95 L.Ed. 295 (1951), 693

First Nat. Bank of Boston v. Bellotti, 435 U.S. 765, 98 S.Ct. 1407, 55 L.Ed.2d 707 (1978), 767

Fitzpatrick v. Bitzer, 427 U.S. 445, 96 S.Ct. 2666, 49 L.Ed.2d 614 (1976), 139

Flast v. Cohen, 392 U.S. 83, 88 S.Ct. 1942, 20 L.Ed.2d 947 (1968), 33

Florida Lime & Avocado Growers, Inc. v. Paul, 373 U.S. 132, 83 S.Ct. 1210, 10 L.Ed.2d 248 (1963), 207

Florida Prepaid Postsecondary Educ. Expense Bd. v. College Sav. Bank, 527 U.S. 627, 119 S.Ct. 2199, 144 L.Ed.2d 575 (1999), 145

Foley v. Connelie, 435 U.S. 291, 98 S.Ct. 1067, 55 L.Ed.2d 287 (1978), 475

44 Liquormart, Inc. v. Rhode Island, 517 U.S. 484, 116 S.Ct. 1495, 134 L.Ed.2d 711 (1996), 739

Friedman v. Rogers, 440 U.S. 1, 99 S.Ct. 887, 59 L.Ed.2d 100 (1979), 735

Friends of the Earth, Inc. v. Laidlaw Environmental Services (TOC), Inc., 528 U.S. 167, 120 S.Ct. 693, 145 L.Ed.2d 610 (2000), 41

Frohwerk v. United States, 249 U.S. 204, 39 S.Ct. 249, 63 L.Ed. 561 (1919), 671

Frontiero v. Richardson, 411 U.S. 677, 93 S.Ct. 1764, 36 L.Ed.2d 583 (1973), 453

Garcetti v. Ceballos, 547 U.S. 410, 126 S.Ct. 1951, 164 L.Ed.2d 689 (2006), 807

Garcia v. San Antonio Metropolitan Transit Authority, 469 U.S. 528, 105 S.Ct. 1005, 83 L.Ed.2d 1016 (1985), 95

Geduldig v. Aiello, 417 U.S. 484, 94 S.Ct. 2485, 41 L.Ed.2d 256 (1974), 459

Georgia, United States v., 546 U.S. 151, 126 S.Ct. 877, 163 L.Ed.2d 650 (2006), 159

Gertz v. Robert Welch, Inc., 418 U.S. 323, 94 S.Ct. 2997, 41 L.Ed.2d 789 (1974), 745

Gibbons v. Ogden, 22 U.S. 1, 6 L.Ed. 23 (1824), 69

Gitlow v. People of State of New York, 268 U.S. 652, 45 S.Ct. 625, 69 L.Ed. 1138 (1925), 677

Goldberg v. Kelly, 397 U.S. 254, 90 S.Ct. 1011, 25 L.Ed.2d 287 (1970), 601

Goldwater v. Carter, 444 U.S. 996, 100 S.Ct. 533, 62 L.Ed.2d 428 (1979), 53

Gonzales v. Carhart, 550 U.S. 124, 127 S.Ct. 1610, 167 L.Ed.2d 480 (2007), 525

Gonzales v. Raich, 545 U.S. 1, 125 S.Ct. 2195, 162 L.Ed.2d 1 (2005), 109

Gooding v. Wilson, 405 U.S. 518, 92 S.Ct. 1103, 31 L.Ed.2d 408 (1972), 687

Goss v. Lopez, 419 U.S. 565, 95 S.Ct. 729, 42 L.Ed.2d 725 (1975), 607

Graham v. Richardson, 403 U.S. 365, 91 S.Ct. 1848, 29 L.Ed.2d 534 (1971), 473

Gratz v. Bollinger, 539 U.S. 244, 123 S.Ct. 2411, 156 L.Ed.2d 257 (2003), 449

Greer v. Spock, 424 U.S. 828, 96 S.Ct. 1211, 47 L.Ed.2d 505 (1976), 783

Griswold v. Connecticut, 381 U.S. 479, 85 S.Ct. 1678, 14 L.Ed.2d 510 (1965), 509

Grutter v. Bollinger, 539 U.S. 306, 123 S.Ct. 2325, 156 L.Ed.2d 304 (2003), 445

Hague v. Committee for Indus. Organization, 307 U.S. 496, 59 S.Ct. 954, 83 L.Ed. 1423 (1939), 769

Hamdi v. Rumsfeld, 542 U.S. 507, 124 S.Ct. 2633, 159 L.Ed.2d 578 (2004), 187

ALPHABETICAL TABLE OF CASES

Hammer v. Dagenhart, 247 U.S. 251, 38 S.Ct. 529, 62 L.Ed. 1101 (1918), 79

Harper v. Virginia State Bd. of Elections, 383 U.S. 663, 86 S.Ct. 1079, 16 L.Ed.2d 169 (1966), 557

Hawaii Housing Authority v. Midkiff, 467 U.S. 229, 104 S.Ct. 2321, 81 L.Ed.2d 186 (1984), 375

Hazelwood School Dist. v. Kuhlmeier, 484 U.S. 260, 108 S.Ct. 562, 98 L.Ed.2d 592 (1988), 803

Heart of Atlanta Motel, Inc. v. United States, 379 U.S. 241, 85 S.Ct. 348, 13 L.Ed.2d 258 (1964), 89

Hein v. Freedom From Religion Foundation, Inc., 551 U.S. 587, 127 S.Ct. 2553, 168 L.Ed.2d 424 (2007), 35

Hill v. Colorado, 530 U.S. 703, 120 S.Ct. 2480, 147 L.Ed.2d 597 (2000), 777

Hines v. Davidowitz, 312 U.S. 52, 61 S.Ct. 399, 85 L.Ed. 581 (1941), 211

Home Bldg. & Loan Ass'n v. Blaisdell, 290 U.S. 398, 54 S.Ct. 231, 78 L.Ed. 413 (1934), 347

Houchins v. KQED, Inc., 438 U.S. 1, 98 S.Ct. 2588, 57 L.Ed.2d 553 (1978), 833

Houston, E. & W.T.R. Co. v. United States, 234 U.S. 342, 34 S.Ct. 833, 58 L.Ed. 1341 (1914), 75

H. P. Hood & Sons, Inc. v. Du Mond, 336 U.S. 525, 69 S.Ct. 657, 93 L.Ed. 865 (1949), 213

Hudgens v. N. L. R. B., 424 U.S. 507, 96 S.Ct. 1029, 47 L.Ed.2d 196 (1976), 289

Hughes v. Oklahoma, 441 U.S. 322, 99 S.Ct. 1727, 60 L.Ed.2d 250 (1979), 227

Hunt v. Washington State Apple Advertising Com'n, 432 U.S. 333, 97 S.Ct. 2434, 53 L.Ed.2d 383 (1977), 229

Hurley v. Irish–American Gay, Lesbian and Bisexual Group of Boston, 515 U.S. 557, 115 S.Ct. 2338, 132 L.Ed.2d 487 (1995), 815

Hustler Magazine v. Falwell, 485 U.S. 46, 108 S.Ct. 876, 99 L.Ed.2d 41 (1988), 749

I.N.S. v. Chadha, 462 U.S. 919, 103 S.Ct. 2764, 77 L.Ed.2d 317 (1983), 179

International Soc. for Krishna Consciousness, Inc. v. Lee, 505 U.S. 672, 112 S.Ct. 2701, 120 L.Ed.2d 541 (1992), 789

Jackson v. Metropolitan Edison Co., 419 U.S. 345, 95 S.Ct. 449, 42 L.Ed.2d 477 (1974), 279

Johnson v. California, 543 U.S. 499, 125 S.Ct. 1141, 160 L.Ed.2d 949 (2005), 415

Katzenbach v. McClung, 379 U.S. 294, 85 S.Ct. 377, 13 L.Ed.2d 290 (1964), 91

Katzenbach v. Morgan, 384 U.S. 641, 86 S.Ct. 1717, 16 L.Ed.2d 828 (1966), 131

Kelo v. City of New London, Conn., 545 U.S. 469, 125 S.Ct. 2655, 162 L.Ed.2d 439 (2005), 377

Kimel v. Florida Bd. of Regents, 528 U.S. 62, 120 S.Ct. 631, 145 L.Ed.2d 522 (2000), 149

Klein, United States v., 80 U.S. 128, 20 L.Ed. 519 (1871), 13

Kokinda, United States v., 497 U.S. 720, 110 S.Ct. 3115, 111 L.Ed.2d 571 (1990), 787

Kramer v. Union Free School Dist. No. 15, 395 U.S. 621, 89 S.Ct. 1886, 23 L.Ed.2d 583 (1969), 559

Kras, United States v., 409 U.S. 434, 93 S.Ct. 631, 34 L.Ed.2d 626 (1973), 577

Larson v. Valente, 456 U.S. 228, 102 S.Ct. 1673, 72 L.Ed.2d 33 (1982), 859

Lawrence v. Texas, 539 U.S. 558, 123 S.Ct. 2472, 156 L.Ed.2d 508 (2003), 547

Lee v. Weisman, 505 U.S. 577, 112 S.Ct. 2649, 120 L.Ed.2d 467 (1992), 877

Legal Services Corp. v. Velazquez, 531 U.S. 533, 121 S.Ct. 1043, 149 L.Ed.2d 63 (2001), 667

Lehman v. City of Shaker Heights, 418 U.S. 298, 94 S.Ct. 2714, 41 L.Ed.2d 770 (1974), 785

Lemon v. Kurtzman, 403 U.S. 602, 91 S.Ct. 2105, 29 L.Ed.2d 745 (1971), 861

Lewis v. Casey, 518 U.S. 343, 116 S.Ct. 2174, 135 L.Ed.2d 606 (1996), 583

Linmark Associates, Inc. v. Willingboro Tp., 431 U.S. 85, 97 S.Ct. 1614, 52 L.Ed.2d 155 (1977), 737

Littleton, Colo., City of v. Z.J. Gifts D–4, L.L.C., 541 U.S. 774, 124 S.Ct. 2219, 159 L.Ed.2d 84 (2004), 655

Lloyd Corp., Limited v. Tanner, 407 U.S. 551, 92 S.Ct. 2219, 33 L.Ed.2d 131 (1972), 287

Lochner v. New York, 198 U.S. 45, 25 S.Ct. 539, 49 L.Ed. 937 (1905), 317

Locke v. Davey, 540 U.S. 712, 124 S.Ct. 1307, 158 L.Ed.2d 1 (2004), 853

Lopez, United States v., 514 U.S. 549, 115 S.Ct. 1624, 131 L.Ed.2d 626 (1995), 99,

Loretto v. Teleprompter Manhattan CATV Corp., 458 U.S. 419, 102 S.Ct. 3164, 73 L.Ed.2d 868 (1982), 357

Lorillard Tobacco Co. v. Reilly, 533 U.S. 525, 121 S.Ct. 2404, 150 L.Ed.2d 532 (2001), 205, 741

Loving v. Virginia, 388 U.S. 1, 87 S.Ct. 1817, 18 L.Ed.2d 1010 (1967), 407

Lucas v. South Carolina Coastal Council, 505 U.S. 1003, 112 S.Ct. 2886, 120 L.Ed.2d 798 (1992), 365

Lugar v. Edmondson Oil Co., Inc., 457 U.S. 922, 102 S.Ct. 2744, 73 L.Ed.2d 482 (1982), 293

Lujan v. Defenders of Wildlife, 504 U.S. 555, 112 S.Ct. 2130, 119 L.Ed.2d 351 (1992), 23

Maher v. Roe, 432 U.S. 464, 97 S.Ct. 2376, 53 L.Ed.2d 484 (1977), 529

Maine v. Taylor, 477 U.S. 131, 106 S.Ct. 2440, 91 L.Ed.2d 110 (1986), 239

Marbury v. Madison, 5 U.S. 137, 2 L.Ed. 60 (1803), 5

Marsh v. State of Ala., 326 U.S. 501, 66 S.Ct. 276, 90 L.Ed. 265 (1946), 277

Massachusetts v. E.P.A., 549 U.S. 497, 127 S.Ct. 1438, 167 L.Ed.2d 248 (2007), 21

Massachusetts Bd. of Retirement v. Murgia, 427 U.S. 307, 96 S.Ct. 2562, 49 L.Ed.2d 520 (1976), 481

Mathews v. Eldridge, 424 U.S. 319, 96 S.Ct. 893, 47 L.Ed.2d 18 (1976), 611

McCardle, Ex parte, 74 U.S. 506, 19 L.Ed. 264 (1868), 11

McCleskey v. Kemp, 481 U.S. 279, 107 S.Ct. 1756, 95 L.Ed.2d 262 (1987), 419

McCreary County, Ky. v. American Civil Liberties Union of Ky., 545 U.S. 844, 125 S.Ct. 2722, 162 L.Ed.2d 729 (2005), 871,

McIntyre v. Ohio Elections Com'n, 514 U.S. 334, 115 S.Ct. 1511, 131 L.Ed.2d 426 (1995), 663

M'Culloch v. State, 17 U.S. 316, 4 L.Ed. 579 (1819), 65,

Meyer v. Nebraska, 262 U.S. 390, 43 S.Ct. 625, 67 L.Ed. 1042 (1923), 501

Miami Herald Pub. Co. v. Tornillo, 418 U.S. 241, 94 S.Ct. 2831, 41 L.Ed.2d 730 (1974), 827

Michael H. v. Gerald D., 491 U.S. 110, 109 S.Ct. 2333, 105 L.Ed.2d 91 (1989), 493

Michael M. v. Superior Court of Sonoma County, 450 U.S. 464, 101 S.Ct. 1200, 67 L.Ed.2d 437 (1981), 465

Miller v. California, 413 U.S. 15, 93 S.Ct. 2607, 37 L.Ed.2d 419 (1973), 705,

Miller v. Schoene, 276 U.S. 272, 48 S.Ct. 246, 72 L.Ed. 568 (1928), 361

Milliken v. Bradley, 418 U.S. 717, 94 S.Ct. 3112, 41 L.Ed.2d 1069 (1974), 433

Minneapolis Star and Tribune Co. v. Minnesota Com'r of Revenue, 460 U.S. 575, 103 S.Ct. 1365, 75 L.Ed.2d 295 (1983), 819

Minnesota v. Clover Leaf Creamery Co., 449 U.S. 456, 101 S.Ct. 715, 66 L.Ed.2d 659 (1981), 235

Mississippi University for Women v. Hogan, 458 U.S. 718, 102 S.Ct. 3331, 73 L.Ed.2d 1090 (1982), 463

Mitchell v. Helms, 530 U.S. 793, 120 S.Ct. 2530, 147 L.Ed.2d 660 (2000), 881

M.L.B. v. S.L.J., 519 U.S. 102, 117 S.Ct. 555, 136 L.Ed.2d 473 (1996), 581

ALPHABETICAL TABLE OF CASES

Mobile, Ala., City of v. Bolden, 446 U.S. 55, 100 S.Ct. 1490, 64 L.Ed.2d 47 (1980), 421

Moore v. City of East Cleveland, Ohio, 431 U.S. 494, 97 S.Ct. 1932, 52 L.Ed.2d 531 (1977), 497

Moose Lodge No. 107 v. Irvis, 407 U.S. 163, 92 S.Ct. 1965, 32 L.Ed.2d 627 (1972), 299

Morrison v. Olson, 487 U.S. 654, 108 S.Ct. 2597, 101 L.Ed.2d 569 (1988), 181

Morrison, United States v., 529 U.S. 598, 120 S.Ct. 1740, 146 L.Ed.2d 658 (2000), 103, 129

Morse v. Frederick, 551 U.S. 393, 127 S.Ct. 2618, 168 L.Ed.2d 290 (2007), 805

Muller v. State of Oregon, 208 U.S. 412, 28 S.Ct. 324, 52 L.Ed. 551 (1908), 323

National Ass'n for Advancement of Colored People v. State of Ala. ex rel. Patterson, 357 U.S. 449, 78 S.Ct. 1163, 2 L.Ed.2d 1488 (1958), 809

National Endowment for the Arts v. Finley, 524 U.S. 569, 118 S.Ct. 2168, 141 L.Ed.2d 500 (1998), 639

National League of Cities v. Usery, 426 U.S. 833, 96 S.Ct. 2465, 49 L.Ed.2d 245 (1976), 93

National Treasury Employees Union, United States v., 513 U.S. 454, 115 S.Ct. 1003, 130 L.Ed.2d 964 (1995), 657

Near v. State of Minnesota ex rel. Olson, 283 U.S. 697, 51 S.Ct. 625, 75 L.Ed. 1357 (1931), 643

Nebbia v. People of New York, 291 U.S. 502, 54 S.Ct. 505, 78 L.Ed. 940 (1934), 329

Nebraska Press Ass'n v. Stuart, 427 U.S. 539, 96 S.Ct. 2791, 49 L.Ed.2d 683 (1976), 647

Nevada Dept. of Human Resources v. Hibbs, 538 U.S. 721, 123 S.Ct. 1972, 155 L.Ed.2d 953 (2003), 155

New York v. Ferber, 458 U.S. 747, 102 S.Ct. 3348, 73 L.Ed.2d 1113 (1982), 707

New York v. United States, 505 U.S. 144, Nuclear Reg. Rep. P 20553, 112 S.Ct. 2408, 120 L.Ed.2d 120 (1992), 113

New York City Transit Authority v. Beazer, 440 U.S. 568, 99 S.Ct. 1355, 59 L.Ed.2d 587 (1979), 397

New York Times Co. v. Sullivan, 376 U.S. 254, 84 S.Ct. 710, 11 L.Ed.2d 686 (1964), 743

New York Times Co. v. United States, 403 U.S. 713, 91 S.Ct. 2140, 29 L.Ed.2d 822 (1971), 645

Nixon v. Fitzgerald, 457 U.S. 731, 102 S.Ct. 2690, 73 L.Ed.2d 349 (1982), 195

Nixon v. Shrink Missouri Government PAC, 528 U.S. 377, 120 S.Ct. 897, 145 L.Ed.2d 886 (2000), 763

Nixon v. United States, 506 U.S. 224, 113 S.Ct. 732, 122 L.Ed.2d 1 (1993), 55

Nixon, United States v., 418 U.S. 683, 94 S.Ct. 3090, 41 L.Ed.2d 1039 (1974), 169

N.L.R.B. v. Jones & Laughlin Steel Corp., 301 U.S. 1, 57 S.Ct. 615, 81 L.Ed. 893 (1937), 83

Norwood v. Harrison, 413 U.S. 455, 93 S.Ct. 2804, 37 L.Ed.2d 723 (1973), 301

O'Brien, United States v., 391 U.S. 367, 88 S.Ct. 1673, 20 L.Ed.2d 672 (1968), 757

Orr v. Orr, 440 U.S. 268, 99 S.Ct. 1102, 59 L.Ed.2d 306 (1979), 461

Pacific Gas and Elec. Co. v. State Energy Resources Conservation & Development Com'n, 461 U.S. 190, 103 S.Ct. 1713, 75 L.Ed.2d 752 (1983), 209

Palazzolo v. Rhode Island, 533 U.S. 606, 121 S.Ct. 2448, 150 L.Ed.2d 592 (2001), 369

Palmer v. Thompson, 403 U.S. 217, 91 S.Ct. 1940, 29 L.Ed.2d 438 (1971), 423

Palmore v. Sidoti, 466 U.S. 429, 104 S.Ct. 1879, 80 L.Ed.2d 421 (1984), 409

Panama Refining Co. v. Ryan, 293 U.S. 388, 55 S.Ct. 241, 79 L.Ed. 446 (1935), 175

Parents Involved in Community Schools v. Seattle School Dist. No. 1, 551 U.S. 701, 127 S.Ct. 2738, 168 L.Ed.2d 508 (2007), 437

Paris Adult Theatre I v. Slaton, 413 U.S. 49, 93 S.Ct. 2628, 37 L.Ed.2d 446 (1973), 703

Parker v. Levy, 417 U.S. 733, 94 S.Ct. 2547, 41 L.Ed.2d 439 (1974), 793

Paul v. Davis, 424 U.S. 693, 96 S.Ct. 1155, 47 L.Ed.2d 405 (1976), 609

Pell v. Procunier, 417 U.S. 817, 94 S.Ct. 2800, 41 L.Ed.2d 495 (1974), 831

Penn Cent. Transp. Co. v. City of New York, 438 U.S. 104, 98 S.Ct. 2646, 57 L.Ed.2d 631 (1978), 363

Pennsylvania Coal Co. v. Mahon, 260 U.S. 393, 43 S.Ct. 158, 67 L.Ed. 322 (1922), 359

Perry Educ. Ass'n v. Perry Local Educators' Ass'n, 460 U.S. 37, 103 S.Ct. 948, 74 L.Ed.2d 794 (1983), 773

Personnel Adm'r of Massachusetts v. Feeney, 442 U.S. 256, 99 S.Ct. 2282, 60 L.Ed.2d 870 (1979), 425

Philadelphia, City of v. New Jersey, 437 U.S. 617, 98 S.Ct. 2531, 57 L.Ed.2d 475 (1978), 221

Philip Morris USA v. Williams, 549 U.S. 346, 127 S.Ct. 1057, 166 L.Ed.2d 940 (2007), 345

Pierce County, Wash. v. Guillen, 537 U.S. 129, 123 S.Ct. 720, 154 L.Ed.2d 610 (2003), 107

Pike v. Bruce Church, Inc., 397 U.S. 137, 90 S.Ct. 844, 25 L.Ed.2d 174 (1970), 241

Planned Parenthood of Southeastern Pennsylvania v. Casey, 505 U.S. 833, 112 S.Ct. 2791, 120 L.Ed.2d 674 (1992), 519, 526, 531

Plaut v. Spendthrift Farm, Inc., 514 U.S. 211, 115 S.Ct. 1447, 131 L.Ed.2d 328 (1995), 15

Plessy v. Ferguson, 163 U.S. 537, 16 S.Ct. 1138, 41 L.Ed. 256 (1896), 411

Plyler v. Doe, 457 U.S. 202, 102 S.Ct. 2382, 72 L.Ed.2d 786 (1982), 479

Poe v. Ullman, 367 U.S. 497, 81 S.Ct. 1752, 6 L.Ed.2d 989 (1961), 37

Police Dept. of City of Chicago v. Mosley, 408 U.S. 92, 92 S.Ct. 2286, 33 L.Ed.2d 212 (1972), 775

Powell v. McCormack, 395 U.S. 486, 89 S.Ct. 1944, 23 L.Ed.2d 491 (1969), 51

Printz v. United States, 521 U.S. 898, 117 S.Ct. 2365, 138 L.Ed.2d 914 (1997), 117

Railway Exp. Agency v. People of State of N.Y., 336 U.S. 106, 69 S.Ct. 463, 93 L.Ed. 533 (1949), 395

Randall v. Sorrell, 548 U.S. 230, 126 S.Ct. 2479, 165 L.Ed.2d 482 (2006), 765

Rasul v. Bush, 542 U.S. 466, 124 S.Ct. 2686, 159 L.Ed.2d 548 (2004), 192

R.A.V. v. City of St. Paul, Minn., 505 U.S. 377, 112 S.Ct. 2538, 120 L.Ed.2d 305 (1992), 689

Red Lion Broadcasting Co. v. F.C.C., 395 U.S. 367, 89 S.Ct. 1794, 23 L.Ed.2d 371 (1969), 825

Reeves, Inc. v. Stake, 447 U.S. 429, 100 S.Ct. 2271, 65 L.Ed.2d 244 (1980), 249

Reitman v. Mulkey, 387 U.S. 369, 87 S.Ct. 1627, 18 L.Ed.2d 830 (1967), 307

Rendell-Baker v. Kohn, 457 U.S. 830, 102 S.Ct. 2764, 73 L.Ed.2d 418 (1982), 303

Reno v. American Civil Liberties Union, 521 U.S. 844, 117 S.Ct. 2329, 138 L.Ed.2d 874 (1997), 725

Reno v. Condon, 528 U.S. 141, 120 S.Ct. 666, 145 L.Ed.2d 587 (2000), 121

Renton, City of v. Playtime Theatres, Inc., 475 U.S. 41, 106 S.Ct. 925, 89 L.Ed.2d 29 (1986), 637

Republican Party of Minnesota v. White, 536 U.S. 765, 122 S.Ct. 2528, 153 L.Ed.2d 694 (2002), 633

Reynolds v. Sims, 379 U.S. 870, 85 S.Ct. 12, 13 L.Ed.2d 76 (1964), 567

Richardson, United States v., 418 U.S. 166, 94 S.Ct. 2940, 41 L.Ed.2d 678 (1974), 31

Richmond, City of v. J.A. Croson Co., 488 U.S. 469, 109 S.Ct. 706, 102 L.Ed.2d 854 (1989), 441

Richmond Newspapers, Inc. v. Virginia, 448 U.S. 555, 100 S.Ct. 2814, 65 L.Ed.2d 973 (1980), 829

ALPHABETICAL TABLE OF CASES

Roberts v. United States Jaycees, 468 U.S. 609, 104 S.Ct. 3244, 82 L.Ed.2d 462 (1984), 813

Roe v. Wade, 410 U.S. 113, 93 S.Ct. 705, 35 L.Ed.2d 147 (1973), 515

Romer v. Evans, 517 U.S. 620, 116 S.Ct. 1620, 134 L.Ed.2d 855 (1996), 391

Rosenberger v. Rector and Visitors of University of Virginia, 515 U.S. 819, 115 S.Ct. 2510, 132 L.Ed.2d 700 (1995), 863

Rostker v. Goldberg, 453 U.S. 57, 101 S.Ct. 2646, 69 L.Ed.2d 478 (1981), 467

Roth v. United States, 354 U.S. 476, 77 S.Ct. 1304, 1 L.Ed.2d 1498 (1957), 701

Rumsfeld v. Forum for Academic and Institutional Rights, Inc., 547 U.S. 47, 126 S.Ct. 1297, 164 L.Ed.2d 156 (2006), 661

Rust v. Sullivan, 500 U.S. 173, 111 S.Ct. 1759, 114 L.Ed.2d 233 (1991), 665

Sable Communications of California, Inc. v. F.C.C., 492 U.S. 115, 109 S.Ct. 2829, 106 L.Ed.2d 93 (1989), 723

Sabri v. United States, 541 U.S. 600, 124 S.Ct. 1941, 158 L.Ed.2d 891 (2004), 125

Sacramento, County of v. Lewis, 523 U.S. 833, 118 S.Ct. 1708, 140 L.Ed.2d 1043 (1998), 593

Saenz v. Roe, 526 U.S. 489, 119 S.Ct. 1518, 143 L.Ed.2d 689 (1999), 269, 553

San Antonio Independent School Dist. v. Rodriguez, 411 U.S. 1, 93 S.Ct. 1278, 36 L.Ed.2d 16 (1973), 587

Santa Fe Independent School Dist. v. Doe, 530 U.S. 290, 120 S.Ct. 2266, 147 L.Ed.2d 295 (2000), 867

Schenck v. United States, 249 U.S. 47, 39 S.Ct. 247, 63 L.Ed. 470 (1919), 669

Schneider v. State of New Jersey, Town of Irvington, 308 U.S. 147, 60 S.Ct. 146, 84 L.Ed. 155 (1939), 771

Seeger, United States v., 380 U.S. 163, 85 S.Ct. 850, 13 L.Ed.2d 733 (1965), 839

Seminole Tribe of Florida v. Florida, 517 U.S. 44, 116 S.Ct. 1114, 134 L.Ed.2d 252 (1996), 141

Shaw v. Murphy, 532 U.S. 223, 121 S.Ct. 1475, 149 L.Ed.2d 420 (2001), 797

Shelley v. Kraemer, 334 U.S. 1, 68 S.Ct. 836, 92 L.Ed. 1161 (1948), 291

Sherbert v. Verner, 374 U.S. 398, 83 S.Ct. 1790, 10 L.Ed.2d 965 (1963), 847

Singleton v. Wulff, 428 U.S. 106, 96 S.Ct. 2868, 49 L.Ed.2d 826 (1976), 27

Skinner v. State of Okl. ex rel. Williamson, 316 U.S. 535, 62 S.Ct. 1110, 86 L.Ed. 1655 (1942), 507

Slaughter-House Cases, 83 U.S. 36, 21 L.Ed. 394 (1872), 267

South Carolina State Highway Department v. Barnwell Bros., 303 U.S. 177, 58 S.Ct. 510, 82 L.Ed. 734 (1938), 217

South-Central Timber Development, Inc. v. Wunnicke, 467 U.S. 82, 104 S.Ct. 2237, 81 L.Ed.2d 71 (1984), 251

South Dakota v. Dole, 483 U.S. 203, 107 S.Ct. 2793, 97 L.Ed.2d 171 (1987), 127

Southern Pac. Co. v. State of Ariz. ex rel. Sullivan, 325 U.S. 761, 65 S.Ct. 1515, 89 L.Ed. 1915 (1945), 219

Stanley v. Georgia, 394 U.S. 557, 89 S.Ct. 1243, 22 L.Ed.2d 542 (1969), 717

State Farm Mut. Auto. Ins. Co. v. Campbell, 538 U.S. 408, 123 S.Ct. 1513, 155 L.Ed.2d 585 (2003), 341

Sturgis v. Honold, 60 U.S. 393, 19 How. 393, 15 L.Ed. 666 (1856), 403

Supreme Court of New Hampshire v. Piper, 470 U.S. 274, 105 S.Ct. 1272, 84 L.Ed.2d 205 (1985), 259

Swann v. Charlotte-Mecklenburg Bd. of Ed., 402 U.S. 1, 91 S.Ct. 1267, 28 L.Ed.2d 554 (1971), 431

Tahoe-Sierra Preservation Council, Inc. v. Tahoe Regional Planning Agency, 535 U.S. 302, 122 S.Ct. 1465, 152 L.Ed.2d 517 (2002), 373

Tennessee v. Lane, 541 U.S. 509, 124 S.Ct. 1978, 158 L.Ed.2d 820 (2004), 157

Terry v. Adams, 345 U.S. 461, 73 S.Ct. 809, 97 L.Ed. 1152 (1953), 281

Texas v. Johnson, 491 U.S. 397, 109 S.Ct. 2533, 105 L.Ed.2d 342 (1989), 759

The Florida Star v. B.J.F., 491 U.S. 524, 109 S.Ct. 2603, 105 L.Ed.2d 443 (1989), 753

Thomas v. Chicago Park Dist., 534 U.S. 316, 122 S.Ct. 775, 151 L.Ed.2d 783 (2002), 653

Thornburgh v. Abbott, 490 U.S. 401, 109 S.Ct. 1874, 104 L.Ed.2d 459 (1989), 795

Tinker v. Des Moines Independent Community School Dist., 393 U.S. 503, 89 S.Ct. 733, 21 L.Ed.2d 731 (1969), 799

Toomer v. Witsell, 334 U.S. 385, 68 S.Ct. 1156, 92 L.Ed. 1460 (1948), 253

Town of (see name of town)

Toyosaburo Korematsu v. United States, 323 U.S. 214, 65 S.Ct. 193, 89 L.Ed. 194 (1944), 405

Troxel v. Granville, 530 U.S. 57, 120 S.Ct. 2054, 147 L.Ed.2d 49 (2000), 503

Tuan Anh Nguyen v. I.N.S., 533 U.S. 53, 121 S.Ct. 2053, 150 L.Ed.2d 115 (2001), 471

Turner Broadcasting System, Inc. v. F.C.C., 512 U.S. 622, 114 S.Ct. 2445, 129 L.Ed.2d 497 (1994), 629

Twining v. State of N.J., 211 U.S. 78, 29 S.Ct. 14, 53 L.Ed. 97 (1908), 271

United Bldg. and Const. Trades Council of Camden County and Vicinity v. Mayor and Council of City of Camden, 465 U.S. 208, 104 S.Ct. 1020, 79 L.Ed.2d 249 (1984), 255

United Haulers Ass'n, Inc. v. Oneida-Herkimer Solid Waste Management Authority, 550 U.S. 330, 127 S.Ct. 1786, 167 L.Ed.2d 655 (2007), 225

United States v. _____ (see opposing party)

United States Dept. of Agriculture v. Moreno, 413 U.S. 528, 93 S.Ct. 2821, 37 L.Ed.2d 782 (1973), 399

United States Parole Commission v. Geraghty, 445 U.S. 388, 100 S.Ct. 1202, 63 L.Ed.2d 479 (1980), 43

United States R.R. Retirement Bd. v. Fritz, 449 U.S. 166, 101 S.Ct. 453, 66 L.Ed.2d 368 (1980), 393

United States Trust Co. of New York v. New Jersey, 431 U.S. 1, 97 S.Ct. 1505, 52 L.Ed.2d 92 (1977), 355

Van Orden v. Perry, 545 U.S. 677, 125 S.Ct. 2854, 162 L.Ed.2d 607 (2005), 873

Vieth v. Jubelirer, 541 U.S. 267, 124 S.Ct. 1769, 158 L.Ed.2d 546 (2004), 47

Village of (see name of village)

Virginia v. Black, 538 U.S. 343, 123 S.Ct. 1536, 155 L.Ed.2d 535 (2003), 697

Virginia, United States v., 518 U.S. 515, 116 S.Ct. 2264, 135 L.Ed.2d 735 (1996), 457

Virginia State Bd. of Pharmacy v. Virginia Citizens Consumer Council, Inc., 425 U.S. 748, 96 S.Ct. 1817, 48 L.Ed.2d 346 (1976), 729

Ward v. Rock Against Racism, 491 U.S. 781, 109 S.Ct. 2746, 105 L.Ed.2d 661 (1989), 779

Washington v. Davis, 426 U.S. 229, 96 S.Ct. 2040, 48 L.Ed.2d 597 (1976), 417

Washington v. Glucksberg, 521 U.S. 702, 117 S.Ct. 2258, 138 L.Ed.2d 772 (1997), 543

Watchtower Bible and Tract Society of New York, Inc. v. Village of Stratton, 536 U.S. 150, 122 S.Ct. 2080, 153 L.Ed.2d 205 (2002), 651

Weaver v. Palmer Bros. Co., 270 U.S. 402, 46 S.Ct. 320, 70 L.Ed. 654 (1926), 327

West Coast Hotel Co. v. Parrish, 300 U.S. 379, 57 S.Ct. 578, 81 L.Ed. 703 (1937), 331

Western and Southern Life Ins. Co. v. State Bd. of Equalization of California, 451 U.S. 648, 101 S.Ct. 2070, 68 L.Ed.2d 514 (1981), 247

West Lynn Creamery, Inc. v. Healy, 512 U.S. 186, 114 S.Ct. 2205, 129 L.Ed.2d 157 (1994), 233

West Virginia State Board of Education v. Barnette, 319 U.S. 624, 63 S.Ct. 1178, 87 L.Ed. 1628 (1943), 659

Whalen v. Roe, 429 U.S. 589, 97 S.Ct. 869, 51 L.Ed.2d 64 (1977), 551

ALPHABETICAL TABLE OF CASES

Whitman v. American Trucking Associations, 531 U.S. 457, 121 S.Ct. 903, 149 L.Ed.2d 1 (2001), 177

Whitney v. California, 274 U.S. 357, 47 S.Ct. 641, 71 L.Ed. 1095 (1927), 679

Wickard v. Filburn, 317 U.S. 111, 63 S.Ct. 82, 87 L.Ed. 122 (1942), 87,

Williamson v. Lee Optical of Oklahoma, 348 U.S. 483, 75 S.Ct. 461, 99 L.Ed. 563 (1955), 335

Young v. American Mini Theatres, Inc., 427 U.S. 50, 96 S.Ct. 2440, 49 L.Ed.2d 310 (1976), 713

Youngstown Sheet & Tube Co. v. Sawyer, 343 U.S. 579, 72 S.Ct. 863, 96 L.Ed. 1153 (1952), 167

Zablocki v. Redhail, 434 U.S. 374, 98 S.Ct. 673, 54 L.Ed.2d 618 (1978), 489

Zelman v. Simmons–Harris, 536 U.S. 639, 122 S.Ct. 2460, 153 L.Ed.2d 604 (2002), 885

CHAPTER ONE

The Federal Judicial Power

Marbury v. Madison
Instant Facts: Marbury (P) was a last-minute judicial appointee of outgoing President Adams, whose commission was not delivered to him before Adams left office; Jefferson, the incoming President, declined to deliver the commission.

Black Letter Rule: Where the Constitution, as interpreted by the Supreme Court, conflicts with laws or actions enacted by Congress, the Supreme Court may declare such laws or actions unconstitutional and invalid.

District of Columbia v. Heller
Instant Facts: Heller (P) was refused a registration certificate for a handgun, and he claimed that the District of Columbia (D) prohibition against handgun ownership was unconstitutional.

Black Letter Rule: Words and phrases in the Constitution are to be interpreted according to their normal and ordinary meanings as understood when the provision in question was adopted.

Ex Parte McCardle
Instant Facts: While appeal of a habeas corpus petition was pending on the Supreme Court's docket, Congress passed legislation eliminating the Supreme Court's appellate jurisdiction in habeas corpus cases.

Black Letter Rule: Although the Supreme Court's appellate jurisdiction is derived from the Constitution, Congress has the power to make exceptions and regulations to this jurisdiction.

United States v. Klein
Instant Facts: Congress passed a law terminating federal court jurisdiction in cases in which a claim was made for recovery of property seized by the United States during the Civil War and where the claimant used a presidential pardon to show he had not aided the enemy.

Black Letter Rule: Congress violated the separation of powers by passing a law rescinding the Supreme Court's appellate jurisdiction in claims cases supported by a presidential pardon and by infringing the president's exclusive power to pardon.

Plaut v. Spendthrift Farms, Inc.
Instant Facts: Congress passed legislation allowing cases on which the federal courts had rendered final decisions to be reopened in some situations.

Black Letter Rule: Legislation that directs the federal courts to reopen cases on which the courts have passed final judgment unconstitutionally violates the separation of powers.

Allen v. Wright
Instant Facts: Black parents sued the IRS for granting tax-exempt status to discriminatory private schools and thereby interfering with the desegregation of their public schools.

Black Letter Rule: Standing requires a plaintiff to allege a personal injury fairly traceable to the defendant's allegedly unlawful conduct and likely to be redressed by the requested relief.

Massachusetts v. Environmental Protection Agency
Instant Facts: Massachusetts (P) petitioned to determine whether the EPA (D) had the authority to refuse to regulate greenhouse gas emissions from cars, and the EPA (D) claimed that Massachusetts (P) lacked standing.

Black Letter Rule: When a party has been vested with a procedural right, that party has standing if there is some possibility that the requested relief will prompt the party causing the injury to reconsider the decision that allegedly harmed the other party.

Lujan v. Defenders of Wildlife

Instant Facts: When Congress passed a statute protecting endangered animals, it authorized any person to sue the administrative agency for violating it. When wildlife activists sued, the agency claimed they lacked standing.

Black Letter Rule: Congressional statutes cannot confer standing to plaintiffs who suffered no "actual" "injury in fact."

Singleton v. Wulff

Instant Facts: Abortion doctors sued to receive Medicaid payments through the state for abortions they had performed that were not "medically indicated."

Black Letter Rule: Persons may sue to protect a third party's right only when (1) the relationship between the parties is such that the person suing may advocate effectively for the right and (2) there are genuine obstacles to the third party asserting the right in court.

Elk Grove Unified School Dist. v. Newdow

Instant Facts: Newdow (P) challenged the Elk Grove Unified School District's (D) policy of student recitation of the Pledge of Allegiance in its public schools.

Black Letter Rule: Parents' prudential standing in federal court to challenge policies affecting the religious education of their children is determined by state domestic relations law.

United States v. Richardson

Instant Facts: A taxpayer sued to compel the CIA to release details of its expenditures pursuant to Article I, § 9 of the U.S. Constitution.

Black Letter Rule: Taxpayer status is not sufficient to confer standing to challenge the constitutionality of federal action unless the taxpayer alleges direct injury from the practice and not generalized grievances common to all members of the public.

Flast v. Cohen

Instant Facts: Taxpayers challenged federal funding for academic instruction, books and materials in private religious schools.

Black Letter Rule: Taxpayer status is sufficient to confer standing on an individual to bring suit in federal court to challenge the constitutionality of federal spending in violation of the First Amendment Free Exercise and Establishment clauses.

Hein v. Freedom From Religion Foundation

Instant Facts: The Freedom from Religion Foundation (P) claimed that the President's Faith–Based and Community Initiatives program violated the Establishment Clause, and Hein (D) claimed the Foundation (P) lacked standing.

Black Letter Rule: Taxpayers have standing to bring Establishment Clause challenges to a federal expenditure only if that expenditure is made pursuant to an explicit congressional authorization.

Poe v. Ullman

Instant Facts: A doctor and some of his patients challenged a Connecticut law that forbade medical personnel from disseminating information about contraception.

Black Letter Rule: The declaratory judgment of a state court upholding a statute on the books does not make the issue of that statute's constitutionality ripe for federal court determination when the state has not and likely will not prosecute under the statute.

Abbott Laboratories v. Gardner

Instant Facts: Drug Companies challenged a law that would have required them to print the generic name of a drug on all labels and advertisements containing the drug's trade name.

Black Letter Rule: A case is considered "ripe" for federal court resolution when (1) the issue(s) presented are appropriate for a judicial decision and (2) the parties would face hardship if the court declined to hear the case.

Friends of the Earth, Incorporated v. Laidlaw Environmental Services

Instant Facts: Defendant-polluter argued that its recent compliance with national standards and plant shutdown mooted a citizen suit alleging violations of the Clean Water Act.

Black Letter Rule: Defendant's voluntary cessation of actions that are the subject of a Complaint does not make the lawsuit moot unless there is no reasonable chance that the defendant can return to the actions.

United States Parole Commission v. Geraghty

Instant Facts: Federal prisoners were appealing a District Court's denial of their certification as a class when the named plaintiff's case became moot.

Black Letter Rule: Appeal of a lower court's denial of class certification does not become moot due to the mootness of the named plaintiffs case.

Baker v. Carr

Instant Facts: Tennessee voters seek a reapportionment of state assembly districts; the districts have not been reapportioned since 1901.

Black Letter Rule: The Guaranty Clause may not be used as a source of a constitutional standard for invalidating state action, but an equal protection claim may be so used where it does not implicate a political question.

Vieth v. Jubelirer

Instant Facts: Vieth (P) challenged state electoral districts established by the Pennsylvania General Assembly as unconstitutional political gerrymandering.

Black Letter Rule: When a legal claim has no judicially discoverable and manageable standards for resolving the issues presented, the claim is a nonjusticiable political question.

Powell v. McCormack

Instant Facts: The 90th Congress voted not to seat member-elect Powell due to his past improprieties.

Black Letter Rule: The political question doctrine does not bar the federal courts from deciding a case concerning Congress's powers to determine its membership when the text of the Constitution does not specifically commit the issue in the case to Congressional resolution.

Goldwater v. Carter

Instant Facts: In conjunction with normalizing U.S. relations with the Mainland Chinese government, President Carter terminated the United States treaty with Taiwan.

Black Letter Rule: The Senate's role in the termination of treaties is a nonjusticiable political question.

Nixon v. United States

Instant Facts: A federal judge, impeached by the Senate, challenged the constitutionality of the Senate's impeachment procedure.

Black Letter Rule: The judiciary may not review the Senate's trial of an impeached official.

Marbury v. Madison
(*Judicial Appointee*) v. (*Secretary of State*)
5 U.S. (1 Cranch) 137, 2 L.Ed. 60 (1803)

FEDERAL COURTS HAVE AUTHORITY TO REVIEW ACTS OF CONGRESS AND THE EXECUTIVE BRANCH AND TO INVALIDATE ACTS THAT VIOLATE THE CONSTITUTION

■ **INSTANT FACTS** Marbury (P) was a last-minute judicial appointee of outgoing President Adams, whose commission was not delivered to him before Adams left office; Jefferson, the incoming President, declined to deliver the commission.

■ **BLACK LETTER RULE** Where the Constitution, as interpreted by the Supreme Court, conflicts with the laws or actions of the other branches of government, the Supreme Court may declare such laws or actions unconstitutional and invalid.

■ **PROCEDURAL BASIS**
Direct claim to the Supreme Court asking for mandamus commanding delivery of a judicial commission.

■ **FACTS**
William Marbury (P) was appointed as a justice of the peace at the very end of John Adams' presidency. Thomas Jefferson, the incoming president, chose to disregard the appointments because formal commissions had not been delivered before the end of Adams' term. Marbury (P) and others took their case to the Supreme Court, seeking a writ of mandamus [order directing that an official perform an act] that would order Madison (D), Jefferson's Secretary of State, to deliver the commissions. John Marshall was Secretary of State under Adams, but had since been appointed Chief Justice of the Supreme Court by the time the Court heard the case [conflict of interest, maybe?]. The Court decided three separate issues.

■ **ISSUE**
(1) Does Marbury (P) have a right to the commission? (2) If so, and if that right has been violated, does Marbury (P) have a legal remedy? (3) Is the legal remedy a writ of mandamus issuing from the Supreme Court?

■ **DECISION AND RATIONALE**
(Marshall, J.) (1) Yes. As soon as the President signs the commission and the Secretary of State affixes the seal of the United States, the appointee has a vested legal right in the commission. To withhold the commission violates this legal right. (2) Yes. The government of the United States is one of laws and not of men, and the law must afford a remedy for violation of a vested legal right. There are cases in which the President, in accomplishing a legal political act, commits an injury to an individual. In these cases, the individual has no remedy. However, not every act of the President, or any of the great departments of government, constitutes such a case. The legality of an act of the head of a department [e.g., the Secretary of State] depends on the nature of the act. Where the heads of the departments merely execute the will of the President, or act in cases in which the President possesses a constitutional or legal right, the acts are only politically examinable, and cannot be examined by this Court. But where a duty is assigned to the head of the department by the Legislature, and individual rights depend on performance of that duty, an individual who is injured has a right to a remedy. (3) No. The answer to this question depends on (a) the nature of the writ applied for [mandamus], and (b) the power of the

Marbury v. Madison (Continued)

Supreme Court. (a) A mandamus is a proper remedy in this case. The Secretary of State was directed by law to do an act affecting the rights of individuals, and mandamus is the only appropriate remedy for violation of these rights. (b) By the Judiciary Act of 1789, the Supreme Court has the power to issue writs of mandamus to any persons holding office in the United States. However, this statute conflicts with Article III of the Constitution, which does not grant original jurisdiction to the Supreme Court over cases involving executive officers. This in turn creates a conflict between Congress and the Constitution. Either the Constitution is supreme, or it is on a level with ordinary legislative acts, and is alterable whenever Congress pleases. The idea of a written constitution is that it forms the fundamental and paramount law of the nation, and an act in conflict with the constitution must be void. It is emphatically the province and duty of the judiciary to say what the law is. If two laws conflict, the court must decide the case conformably with the Constitution. Also, the Constitution itself gives the judiciary jurisdiction over "all cases arising under the Constitution," supporting the Court's power to invalidate laws in conflict with the Constitution. The judge swears to discharge his duties in conformity with the Constitution, and according to the laws of the United States. In the Supremacy Clause of Article IV, the Constitution itself is first mentioned, and the laws of the land that are granted recognition are those made pursuant to the Constitution. Writ of mandamus denied.

Analysis:

Marbury has been widely criticized, although the doctrine of judicial review is now indisputably established. Most scholars, if not in agreement with Chief Justice Marshall's arguments, generally concur that Marshall's opinion in *Marbury* was shrewd and courageous. Some argue, however, that Marshall's assertions were statements *of* authority rather than arguments *for* authority. For example, one scholar has pointed out that the statement that it is the assigned duty of the Supreme Court to interpret the Constitution raises the question of why the judiciary's interpretation should trump the congressional interpretation. Also, just as the Court took an oath to uphold the Constitution, every government official takes a similar oath. It is important to recognize that the Court's opinion in *Marbury* reads the Constitution as setting the upper limits of the Supreme Court's jurisdiction. Thus, the Court could decline to grant *Marbury* relief by invalidating a statute on the grounds that it unconstitutionally expanded the Court's appellate jurisdiction.

■ CASE VOCABULARY

VESTED RIGHT: A right that is unconditional, that cannot be taken away from a party.

WRIT OF MANDAMUS: A writ requiring a lower court or government official to perform some duty or act.

District of Columbia v. Heller

(*Local Government*) v. (*Gun Owner*)
___ U.S. ___, 128 S.Ct. 2783 (2008)

CLAUSES IN A CONSTITUTIONAL AMENDMENT MUST BE READ TOGETHER

■ **INSTANT FACTS** Heller (P) was refused a registration certificate for a handgun, and he claimed that the District of Columbia (D) prohibition against handgun ownership was unconstitutional.

■ **BLACK LETTER RULE** Words and phrases in the Constitution are to be interpreted according to their normal and ordinary meanings as understood when the provision in question was adopted.

■ **PROCEDURAL BASIS**

Appeal from an order directing entry of summary judgment for Heller (P).

■ **FACTS**

District of Columbia (D) ordinances essentially prohibited the possession of handguns. In addition, no person could carry a handgun without a license, but the Chief of Police was authorized to issue licenses for one-year periods. Guns kept in a person's home were required to be stored in a way that made them inoperable. Heller (P) was a District of Columbia special police officer. He was authorized to carry a handgun while on duty at the Federal Judicial Center. Heller (P) applied to register a handgun to keep at home, but the District (D) refused. Heller (P) then filed suit in the district court seeking to enjoin the District (D) from enforcing its gun laws on Second Amendment grounds.

■ **ISSUE**

Did the District ordinance violate the Second Amendment?

■ **DECISION AND RATIONALE**

(Scalia, J.) Yes. Words and phrases in the Constitution are to be interpreted according to their normal and ordinary meanings as understood when the provision in question was adopted. Technical terms are not to be used. The Second Amendment is divided into two parts: the prefatory clause and the operative clause. The prefatory clause ("A well regulated Militia, being necessary to the security of a free State ...") announces a purpose. It does not limit the operative clause. A prefatory clause was common in other legal rights of the era, especially those that granted individual rights. Logic demands that there be some connection between the two.

The text of the operative clause ("the right of the people to keep and bear Arms, shall not be infringed") codifies a "right of the people." Other uses of the term "the people" refer to individual, not collective, rights. The phrase "keep and bear Arms" had the same meaning in the eighteenth century as today, and refers to the right to own weapons. The language applies to all instruments that constitute bearable arms, regardless of whether they existed in the eighteenth century. Bearing arms is not limited to carrying weapons while a member of an organized militia. "Keep and bear Arms" is not a unitary phrase, or a term of art with a solely military meaning.

District of Columbia v. Heller (Continued)

The prefatory clause does not limit the Second Amendment to members of state or federal military forces. The "militia" was defined as "all males physically capable of acting in concert for the common defense." When Article I of the Constitution speaks of the militia, the militia is assumed to be in existence. This is fully consistent with the ordinary definition of "militia" as including all able-bodied men. "Well regulated" implies nothing more than proper discipline and training. The prefatory clause fits perfectly with the operative clause. The history that the founding generation knew showed that tyrants eliminated a militia consisting of all able-bodied men by taking away the people's arms. It is therefore entirely sensible that the prefatory clause states the purpose for which the Amendment was adopted. It was not the only purpose, but the threat that the new federal government would destroy the citizen's militia was the reason the right was codified in the Constitution. Analogous arms-bearing rights in the state constitutions adopted before and immediately after the Second Amendment was adopted confirm this interpretation. The Second Amendment was interpreted as protecting an individual right unconnected with military service from immediately after its ratification to the end of the nineteenth century. When African Americans were routinely disarmed after the Civil War, those who opposed these actions frequently said that disarming was an infringement on the constitutional right to keep and bear arms. The post-Civil War Congress plainly understood that the Second Amendment protected an individual right to use arms for self-defense.

Precedent does not compel a different conclusion. The case of *United States v. Miller,* 307 U.S. 174 (1939), upheld against a Second Amendment challenge a conviction for transporting an unregistered short-barreled shotgun in interstate commerce. The basis for the Court's decision in that case was not bearing arms for nonmilitary use, but that the type of weapon carried was not eligible for Second Amendment protection. This holding suggests that the Second Amendment confers an individual right to keep and bear arms. That right, however, extends only to certain types of weapons. *Miller* should not be read for more than that proposition. The case was not an exhaustive discussion of the Second Amendment, and the Court heard only from the government, and not the respondent.

The right to bear arms is not unlimited. Commentators and courts have long held that the right is not a right to keep and carry any weapon whatsoever in any manner whatsoever and for whatever purpose. Nothing in the Court's opinion should be taken as casting doubt on longstanding prohibitions against gun ownership by certain individuals. The weapons protected by the Second Amendment are also those "in common use at the time." That limitation is fairly supported by the traditional prohibition against the carrying of "dangerous and unusual weapons." It may be that that a militia today, in order to be as effective as a militia in the eighteenth century, would require sophisticated arms that are highly unusual. The fact that modern developments limit the degree of fit between the prefatory clause and the protected right cannot change the Court's interpretation of that right.

The District (D) ordinance amounts to a complete prohibition against handgun ownership. The requirement that other guns be stored in a way that makes them inoperable effectively takes away the right to keep firearms for self-defense in the home. The ordinance cannot be read as making an exception for self-defense. In his dissent, Justice Breyer suggests an "interest-balancing" approach. The enumeration of the right takes from the government the power to decide on a case-by-case basis whether the right is really worth insisting upon .. The District (D) has various tools for combating its crime problem, but the absolute prohibition on possessing handguns is off the table. Affirmed.

■ DISSENT

(Stevens, J.) The Second Amendment does not protect the right to own a gun for all purposes. The history of the Amendment, and the Court's precedent, show that the purpose of the Amendment was to protect the right to bear arms for military purposes. The Court's holding in *United States v. Miller* was based on the absence of any evidence that possession of a short-barreled shotgun had a reasonable relationship to the preservation or efficiency of a well-regulated militia. The Court's holding in *Miller* was faithful to the text and purposes of the Second Amendment. The Amendment is based on a provision in the Virginia Constitution. That provision had a distinctly military purpose. When each word in the text is given its full effect, the Amendment is most naturally read as guaranteeing the right to keep and bear arms as a part of service in the militia.

The majority's interpretation of the text of the Amendment is incorrect. The prefatory clause of the Amendment should be read as a part of the Amendment as a whole, not merely as an introduction. The majority's interpretation of "the people" is limited to the subset of law-abiding, responsible citizens, but "the people" is not given such a limited reading when construing any other constitutional provision. The usual meaning of "bear arms" is "to serve as a soldier." The right announced today is not "enshrined" in the Constitution, but is a product of this law-changing opinion.

■ DISSENT

(Breyer, J.) The majority's view is not correct unless the District's (D) ordinance is unreasonable or inappropriate in Second Amendment terms. The ordinance focuses on the presence of handguns in high-crime urban areas. It represents a permissible legislative response to a serious, life-threatening problem. The law targets handguns, which are the weapon of choice for many criminals, and which are implicated in numerous firearm-related accidents and fatalities. The District's (D) judgment is open to question, but it is supported by substantial evidence.

Analysis:

The majority opinion and the two dissents show three complimentary theories of constitutional adjudication. Justice Scalia, writing for the majority, relies on a historical interpretation to determine the original intent of the Second Amendment. Justice Stevens would rely more heavily on precedent. Justice Breyer would emphasize deference to the judgment of the legislature.

■ CASE VOCABULARY

SECOND AMENDMENT: The constitutional amendment, ratified with the Bill of Rights in 1791, guaranteeing the right to keep and bear arms as necessary for securing freedom through a well-regulated militia.

Ex Parte McCardle
(*Imprisoned Newspaper Editor*)
74 U.S. (7 Wall.) 506, 19 L.Ed. 264 (1869)

CONGRESS MAY CREATE EXCEPTIONS AND REGULATIONS TO SUPREME COURT APPELLATE JURISDICTION

■ **INSTANT FACTS** While appeal of a habeas corpus petition was pending on the Supreme Court's docket, Congress passed legislation eliminating the Supreme Court's appellate jurisdiction in habeas corpus cases.

■ **BLACK LETTER RULE** Although the Supreme Court's appellate jurisdiction is derived from the Constitution, Congress has the power to make exceptions and regulations to this jurisdiction.

■ **PROCEDURAL BASIS**
Appeal of Circuit Court's denial of petition for habeas corpus.

■ **FACTS**
In 1867, Congress gave federal courts jurisdiction to grant habeas corpus where a person may be restrained in violation of federal law. The 1867 Act also authorized appeals to the Supreme Court in cases where circuit courts denied applications for a writ of habeas corpus. McCardle (P) was a Mississippi newspaper editor imprisoned for publishing "incendiary and libelous" articles tending to incite violence and impede Reconstruction. The Circuit Court denied McCardle's (P) petition for habeas corpus, so he appealed to the Supreme Court under the 1867 Act. The Court heard arguments in McCardle's (P) case. However, before the Court rendered a decision, Congress passed legislation that stripped the Court of jurisdiction to hear habeas corpus appeals.

■ **ISSUE**
May Congress repeal the Supreme Court's appellate jurisdiction?

■ **DECISION AND RATIONALE**
(Chase, C.J.) Yes. The Supreme Court's appellate jurisdiction is derived from the Constitution, but it is conferred "with such exceptions and under such regulations as Congress shall make." Congress had affirmatively described the Court's appellate jurisdiction, and any power not so described is negated. Thus, Congress grants the Court jurisdiction; it does not limit jurisdiction that the Constitution granted to the Court. We cannot inquire into Congress' motives for repealing the 1867 Act. Our only option here is to announce the fact that we do not have jurisdiction and dismiss the case. Note that Congress's repeal does not repeal the Court's entire appellate jurisdiction in habeas corpus cases. It only repeals jurisdiction over appeals from Circuit Courts under the 1867 Act. It does not affect jurisdiction that the Court previously had. Dismissed.

Analysis:
This case arose in the political context of post-Civil War Reconstruction Through the Military Reconstruction Act, Congress imposed a type of military rule on ten former Confederate states. The constitutionali-

Ex Parte McCardle (Continued)

ty of the Military Reconstruction Act was questionable, and Congress knew it. The Supreme Court had hinted in a previous case that it might strike down the Act, so Congress stripped the Supreme Court of the power to rule just as the Court was about to render a decision on McCardle's (P) petition. President Andrew Johnson vetoed Congress's repeal of jurisdiction, but Congress overrode the veto. Note that the effect of *McCardle* may have been minimal. In *Ex Parte Yerger,* another case challenging the Reconstruction Acts, Yerger filed a habeas corpus petition based on pre-1867 legislation. Under that legislation, the Court had jurisdiction through discretionary review by writ of certiorari. So the Court had discretionary review, but not appellate review. So too, McCardle (P) could have petitioned the Court for an original writ of habeas corpus, rather than appellate review of the Circuit Court's denial of his petition.

■ CASE VOCABULARY

HABEAS CORPUS: A judicial mandate to a prison official ordering that an inmate be brought to the court so it can be determined whether or not that person is imprisoned lawfully and whether or not he should be released from custody. A habeas corpus petition is a petition filed with a court by a person who objects to his own or another's detention or imprisonment. Latin for "you have the body."

United States v. Klein
(Federal Government) v. *(Property Owner/Claimant)*
80 U.S. 128 (1871)

CONGRESSIONAL LIMITATIONS ON JURISDICTION ARE INEFFECTIVE IF THEY VIOLATE THE SEPARATION OF POWERS

■ **INSTANT FACTS** Congress passed a law terminating federal court jurisdiction in cases in which a claim was made for recovery of property seized by the United States during the Civil War and where the claimant used a presidential pardon to show he had not aided the enemy.

■ **BLACK LETTER RULE** Congress violated the separation of powers by passing a law rescinding the Supreme Court's appellate jurisdiction in claims cases supported by a presidential pardon and by infringing the president's exclusive power to pardon.

■ **PROCEDURAL BASIS**
Appeal from federal Court of Claims ruling in favor of claimant for restoration of seized property.

■ **FACTS**
Just after the Civil War, in 1863, Congress passed a law that allowed individuals to sue the federal government in the Court of Claims to recover property seized during the war. To be successful, the claimant had to prove that he had not offered to give aid or comfort to the enemy. The U.S. Supreme Court ruled that a presidential pardon could be used as proof in these cases. As there were many of these pardons, Congress reacted to the Supreme Court's ruling by passing a bill which stated that, absent an explicit statement of innocence, pardons would have the effect of proving that the pardoned individual had aided the enemy. (Why else would he need a pardon? Hmmm?) The statute also provided that federal court jurisdiction over the case would terminate upon "proof of such a pardon." Klein (P) sued for recovery of property seized during the war and won the case in the Court of Claims. The pardon at issue in the case had been granted to an intestate to whom Klein (P) was the heir with regard to the property in question. The case was appealed to the U.S. Supreme Court.

■ **ISSUE**
Did Congress surpass its Constitutional authority when it enacted a law dismissing federal court jurisdiction on claims against the government supported by presidential pardons?

■ **DECISION AND RATIONALE**
(Chase, Chief Justice) Yes. The law in question violates the separation of powers for two reasons. First, the law surpasses Congressional power to create exceptions and regulations to the Supreme Court's appellate jurisdiction. Second, the law interferes with the Executive's exclusive power to pardon, a power granted without limit by the Constitution. The Constitution, in Article 3, section 2, vests judicial power exclusively within the federal courts, and gives the Supreme Court appellate jurisdiction, subject to exceptions and regulations made by Congress. Because Congress has already given the Supreme Court appellate jurisdiction over Court of Claims cases, this law has only the effect of directing particular outcomes of cases already pending. This is not a proper exercise by Congress of the power to create exceptions and regulations on appellate jurisdiction. Under the law at question, the Supreme Court has jurisdiction over a case until the existence of a pardon is established, then must dismiss due to lack of jurisdiction, effectively deciding the outcome of the case. If the Congress had decided to deny appeals

United States v. Klein (Continued)

of all Court of Claims cases, it could have done so. Here, however, the language of the statute shows that the intent of Congress was to nullify the effects of the presidential pardons.

Analysis:

The *Klein* case offers an interesting perspective on the relationship between the legislative and judicial branches. The practice of Congress passing legislation in response to an unpopular judicial ruling has been so common over the years that interest groups supporting such legislation speak of seeking a "legislative fix" to effectively overrule the Court. So, the natural question is why the Court struck down the attempted "fix" at issue in *Klein*. In its rationale, the Court emphasized two points. First, the language of the law seems to be result driven (disallow these claims) rather than concerned with articulating an exception to jurisdiction. Moreover, in *McCardle*, another decision written by Chief Justice Chase, the Court stated that it did not inquire into the motives of Congress. This may lend weight to the second point in the Court's rationale, the fact that this law would impact *pending* cases. Perhaps the Court could have passed over the jurisdiction question altogether and decided that the law was unconstitutional solely for the reason that it infringed on the president's power to issue pardons. By arguing as it did, however, the Court established precedent for the proposition that there are limits on Congressional power to create exceptions to federal jurisdiction under Article III, Section 2.

■ CASE VOCABULARY

INTESTATE: Someone who dies without a valid will.

PARDON: The act of a chief executive (President for federal pardons; Governor for state pardons) that negates a criminal offence and any penalties or other consequences of the offence.

Plaut v. Spendthrift Farm, Inc.

(Not Stated) v. (Not Stated)
514 U.S. 211, 115 S.Ct. 1447 (1995)

LEGISLATION REQUIRING FEDERAL COURTS TO REOPEN FINAL JUDGMENTS VIOLATES THE SEPARATION OF POWERS

■ **INSTANT FACTS** Congress passed legislation allowing cases on which the federal courts had rendered final decisions to be reopened in some situations.

■ **BLACK LETTER RULE** Legislation that directs the federal courts to reopen cases on which the courts have passed final judgment unconstitutionally violates the separation of powers.

■ **PROCEDURAL BASIS**

Appeal from the United States Court of Appeals.

■ **FACTS**

In a 1991 ruling, the Supreme Court held that a class action securities case filed under federal statutes had a limitation period of three years from the time of the alleged violation and one year from the time that the facts of the violation became known. Subsequently, Congress passed legislation [Section 27A(b)] stating that cases within the aforementioned class that were filed prior to the 1991 ruling could proceed if the case was permissible under the former law.

■ **ISSUE**

Does legislation that requires the federal courts to reopen cases upon which the courts have rendered a final decision violate the separation of powers doctrine?

■ **DECISION AND RATIONALE**

(Scalia, J.) Yes. Section 27A(b) violates the separation of powers doctrine because it requires the courts to decide that the law that applied to a completed case was different than the courts concluded it was. Prior to this case, the Supreme Court has held that two categories of cases are unconstitutional because they would have the federal courts act contrary to the judicial power articulated in Article III. The first case was *United States v. Klein,* which held unconstitutional legislation that prescribed the outcomes of cases pending in the federal courts. In *Robertson v. Seattle Audubon Soc,* however, the Court clarified that legislation that amends the applicable law is constitutional. The second case was Hayburn's Case, which held that Congress may not pass legislation that permits Executive review of federal court decisions. The law in the present case does not fall under either of these categories. Nevertheless, Section 27A(b) violates the separation of powers because it requires the courts to reopen cases on which a final judgment has already been rendered. This violates the Article III principle that the federal courts are empowered to "decide" cases. Article III establishes a judicial *department,* and vests the Supreme Court with the final voice on cases heard by the department. If the law is changed while cases are still being appealed, the higher courts are required to apply the new law. In this case, however, the last word had been given, and Congress cannot now require the federal courts to change that message. Section 27A(b) cannot be saved by the fact that it is a general law that would apply to

Plaut v. Spendthrift Farms, Inc. (Continued)

many cases. The violation is not based on favoritism or unfairness, but on the separation of powers. The Court of Appeals judgment is affirmed.

Analysis:

Although the Court distinguished *Hayburn's Case* from *Plaut,* the reasoning in *Plaut* is really not all that different. The basic problem in *Hayburn's Case* was that Congress passed legislation that directed the federal courts to decide Revolutionary War veterans' pension claims, but stated that the Secretary of War, an Executive Branch official, could ignore the courts' decisions. Thus, the courts' decision effectively becomes an *advisory opinion.* The federal courts are forbidden from issuing advisory opinions, however, because the federal courts are empowered only to decide "cases and controversies." We usually think of advisory opinions in contexts where no real controversy has yet arisen, such as the hypothetical situation where Congress, hoping to clear up ambiguity before passing a law, asks the courts whether such a law would be unconstitutional if adopted. *Plaut* is quite different from that scenario, since Congress passed the actual law, the actual controversy arose, and the courts decided it (in this case by saying "too late"). The problem the Court had with Section 27A(b) is that it would turn decisions already issued into advisory opinions by saying that even though the courts' reached final decisions based on the law at the time, those decisions could now be ignored.

■ CASE VOCABULARY

ADVISORY OPINIONS: A decision by a court that is not binding on the parties to the case or that may be ignored by those charged with enforcing the decisions.

Allen v. Wright
(IRS) v. (Black Parents)
468 U.S. 737, 104 S.Ct. 3315 (1984)

PARTY DOES NOT HAVE STANDING IN FEDERAL COURT ABSENT ALLEGATIONS OF DIRECT INJURY OR WHEN PARTY ALLEGES CAUSES TOO ATTENUATED FROM HIS INJURY

■ **INSTANT FACTS** Black parents sued the IRS for granting tax-exempt status to discriminatory private schools and thereby interfering with the desegregation of their public schools.

■ **BLACK LETTER RULE** Standing requires a plaintiff to allege a personal injury fairly traceable to the defendant's allegedly unlawful conduct and likely to be redressed by the requested relief.

■ **PROCEDURAL BASIS**
Appeal of judgment granting declaratory and injunctive relief in class action civil rights suit.

■ **FACTS**
Parents of black school children (parents) (P) sued the Internal Revenue Service (IRS) (D) in a nationwide class action for failing to carry out its statutory mandate to deny tax-exempt status to private schools that discriminated on the basis of race. The parents (P) argued that this failure amounted to federal support for segregated schools, which in turn interfered with federal and local desegregation efforts. The parents (P) did not allege that they applied to the discriminatory private schools, but only that their children attended public schools in need of desegregation, and that the IRS's (D) unlawful activities decreased the likelihood that their desegregation plans would be effective. The parents (P) sought relief requiring the IRS (D) to issue guidelines for properly carrying out its obligation. The IRS (D) argued that the parents (P) did not have standing to bring this action, because they had not properly alleged injury or redressability.

■ **ISSUE**
Did parents of minority children who attended public schools have standing to challenge IRS regulations for denying tax-exempt status to private schools that discriminated against racial minorities?

■ **DECISION AND RATIONALE**
(O'Connor, J.) No. Article III of the Constitution limits federal jurisdiction to "cases" and "controversies." The justiciability doctrines—standing, mootness, ripeness, political question, and the prohibition against advisory opinions—define the separation of powers with respect to the judicial branch, stating fundamental limits on the power of an unelected, unrepresentative federal judiciary. The question of standing is whether a litigant is entitled to have the court decide the merits of the case. Standing doctrine prohibits litigants from raising another person's rights, bars courts from adjudicating general grievances more appropriately addressed in the representative branches, and requires that a complaint fall within the zone of interests protected by the law invoked. In addition to these judicially self-imposed "prudential" limits on federal jurisdiction, standing also includes core components derived directly from the Constitution. The plaintiff's injury must be fairly traceable to the defendant's allegedly unlawful conduct and must be likely to be redressed by the requested relief. The injury must be "distinct and

palpable," and not "abstract," "conjectural" or "hypothetical." The dispute must be one "traditionally thought to be capable of resolution through the judicial process," and its adjudication must be consistent with the separation of powers. In this case the parents (P) allege two injuries: (1) direct harm from the mere fact of federal aid to discriminatory private schools, and (2) the impairment of their ability to have their schools desegregated. If the first claim of injury is a claim of right to have the government act in accordance with the law, this alone is insufficient to give standing. *Valley Forge Christian College v. Americans United for Separation of Church and State* [rejected claim of standing based on a "shared individuated right" to a government that does not violate the Establishment Clause]. Alternatively, if this claim is based on the stigmatizing injury caused by racial discrimination, it could afford a basis for standing, but only to those persons personally denied equal treatment by the discriminatory conduct. If the abstract injury asserted here was sufficient, a black person in Hawaii could claim injury based on the grant of a tax exemption to a discriminatory school in Maine. The parents' (P) second claim of injury, their diminished ability to have their children educated in racially desegregated schools, is sufficiently personal and concrete, but is not fairly traceable to the alleged unlawful conduct. The line of causation between the IRS's (D) grant of tax exemptions to some discriminatory schools and the desegregation efforts of the parents' (P) schools is attenuated at best. It is uncertain how many discriminatory schools are receiving tax exemptions, and whether there are enough in the parents' (P) communities to affect desegregation efforts at their schools. Moreover, it is entirely speculative whether withdrawal of a tax exemption would cause any particular school to change its policies, or whether such a change would cause particular parents to transfer their children to public schools, or whether school officials and parents in any particular community would reach these decisions in sufficient numbers to significantly affect the racial composition of their public schools. The independent decisions of third parties can be sufficient to break the chain of causation between the injury and the alleged unlawful conduct, especially where the third parties are as numerous as those in this case. While Congress may monitor the soundness of particular programs of the executive branch, this is not the role of the judiciary unless there is actual present or imminent injury caused by unlawful government action. A federal court is not the proper forum for general complaints about the way the government conducts its business. Judgment reversed, injunction vacated.

■ DISSENT

(Stevens, J.) The injury alleged by the parents (P) is adequate for standing and is presented in a way that is causally linked to the government activity in question. If, as the parents (P) allege, the IRS's (D) failure to deny tax-exempt status is effectively subsidizing the placement of white children into segregated private schools, the impact is the same as if their children were denied access to a public school. In the final analysis, the injury the parents (P) allege is the government subsidy of racial segregation. When a subsidy makes an activity more or less expensive, injury can be fairly traced to the subsidy because the subsidy increases or decreases the ability to engage in that activity. In this case, withdrawing the subsidy to discriminatory private schools would advance the process of desegregation because it would change the incentive structure facing white parents who seek such schools for their children. The parents' (P) injury in fact is fairly traceable to the IRS's (D) allegedly wrongful conduct. The purpose of standing analysis is to measure the plaintiff's stake in the outcome. The separation of powers, on the other hand, affects whether the court has the authority to provide the plaintiff with the outcome it seeks. The plaintiff's stake in the outcome is not diminished because a court has no authority to grant that outcome. If a plaintiff presents a nonjusticiable issue or seeks relief that a court may not award, then the complaint should be dismissed for those reasons, and not for lack of standing.

Analysis:

This opinion provides a good overview of the standing doctrine and its relation to separation of powers principles. Standing is one of the case or controversy doctrines, along with the doctrines concerning advisory opinions, mootness, ripeness, and political questions. Standing doctrines can be further broken down into constitutional and prudential categories, as the Court describes in *Allen*. Congress is free to override the prudential elements of standing, but may not override elements the Court finds are part of the constitutional "case or controversy" requirement. The most significant constitutional element is the "injury in fact" requirement for which *Allen* is often cited. More specifically, *Allen* demonstrates that standing will usually not be found where a litigant claims that tax incentives have caused a third party to injure him, since the causation component will usually be too attenuated. *Allen* also demonstrates that membership in a minority group is not alone sufficient to afford standing against conduct that denigrates that minority group. While the "stigmatizing injury" such conduct causes is sufficiently concrete, standing also requires litigants to have been personally denied equal treatment by the conduct.

■ CASE VOCABULARY

MOOTNESS DOCTRINE: Prohibits courts from deciding issues that are only abstract and do not involve a real dispute, or which have already been resolved.

POLITICAL QUESTION DOCTRINE: Requires courts to refrain from deciding issues which are more properly resolved by the other branches of government.

RIPENESS DOCTRINE: Requires courts to decide only issues which involve a real dispute and an actual injury, and not merely potential or speculative harm.

STANDING: The status of being qualified to assert legal rights in court because one has a sufficient stake in the outcome of the controversy

Massachusetts v. Environmental Protection Agency

(State) v. (Regulator)
549 U.S. 497, 127 S.Ct. 1438 (2007)

STATES RECEIVE SPECIAL CONSIDERATION WITH REGARD TO STANDING

Yes, you have standing to sue the EPA over failure to regulate greenhouse gases.

■ **INSTANT FACTS** Massachusetts (P) petitioned to determine whether the EPA (D) had the authority to refuse to regulate greenhouse gas emissions from cars, and the EPA (D) claimed that Massachusetts (P) lacked standing.

■ **BLACK LETTER RULE** When a party has been vested with a procedural right, that party has standing if there is some possibility that the requested relief will prompt the party causing the injury to reconsider the decision that allegedly harmed the other party.

■ **PROCEDURAL BASIS**

Appeal from a decision upholding the authority of the EPA (D) to refuse to issue regulations.

■ **FACTS**

Massachusetts (P), as well as other governments and private organizations, claimed that the EPA (D) abdicated its authority under the Clean Air Act (42 U.S.C. § 7401 *et seq.*) to regulate greenhouse gases, including carbon dioxide, from new motor vehicles. The petition of Massachusetts (P) asked whether the EPA (D) had the authority to regulate greenhouse gas emissions from new cars. If the EPA (D) had such authority, Massachusetts (P) asked whether the EPA's (D) stated reasons for refusing to issue regulations were consistent with the Clean Air Act. The EPA (D) argued that the Court could not address the issue unless at least one party had standing.

■ **ISSUE**

Did Massachusetts (P) have standing to bring its petition?

■ **DECISION AND RATIONALE**

(Stevens, J.) Yes. When a party has been vested with a procedural right, that party has standing if there is some possibility that the requested relief will prompt the party causing the injury to reconsider the decision that allegedly harmed the other party. Congress has given Massachusetts (P) the right to challenge the EPA's (D) actions, so Massachusetts (P) may assert that right without meeting all of the normal standards for redressability and immediacy.

States, like Massachusetts (P), are not normal litigants for federal jurisdictional purposes. When a state enters the Union, it surrenders some sovereign prerogatives. In some circumstances, the right of a state to regulate motor vehicle emissions may be preempted. This right is now lodged in the federal government. Congress has ordered the EPA (D) to protect Massachusetts (P) and others by prescribing standards for the emission of air pollutants from motor vehicles. Congress also recognized a procedural right to challenge rejection of a rulemaking petition as arbitrary and capricious. Given that procedural right and Massachusetts's (P) stake in protecting its quasi-sovereign interests, Massachusetts (P) is entitled to special solicitude in a standing analysis.

Massachusetts (P) has satisfied the requirements of standing. The EPA's (D) refusal to regulate greenhouse gas emissions poses an actual and imminent risk of harm to Massachusetts (P). There is also a substantial likelihood that the judicial relief requested will prompt the EPA (D) to take steps to reduce that risk.

Increases in greenhouse gases have been linked to a rise in global temperatures. The harms associated with this climate change are serious and well recognized, and include a rise in sea levels. If sea levels continue to rise, Massachusetts (P) could lose significant coastal territory. The fact that the risks of these harms are widely shared does not minimize the interest Massachusetts (P) has in this litigation. The severity of the injury will only increase over the course of the next century. The EPA (D) does not dispute the existence of a causal connection between human-made greenhouse gas emissions and global warming. The EPA's (D) refusal to regulate those emissions contributes to Massachusetts's (D) injuries.

The EPA (D) argued that its decision not to regulate greenhouse gases makes an insignificant contribution to Massachusetts's (P) injury. It alleged that there is no realistic possibility that issuing regulations would mitigate global warming, particularly because greenhouse gas emissions from developing nations are expected to offset any domestic decrease. In making this argument, the EPA (D) makes the erroneous assumption that a small incremental step can never be attacked in a federal court. That a first step may be tentative does not support a claim that federal courts lack the jurisdiction to determine whether that step conforms to the law. A reduction in domestic greenhouse gas emissions will slow the pace of global warming increases, no matter what happens elsewhere. Reversed.

■ DISSENT

(Roberts, J.) Massachusetts (P) bears the burden of alleging an injury that is fairly traceable to the EPA's (D) failure to issue new standards for motor vehicle greenhouse gas emissions, and that its injury is likely to be redressed by the prospective issuance of such standards. There is no authority to relax the standing requirements when the litigant is a state. The majority's "special solicitude" for Massachusetts (P) is an implicit concession that Massachusetts (P) cannot establish standing on traditional terms. The very concept of global warming seems inconsistent with the requirement that a litigant's injury be particularized. If the particular injury that threatens Massachusetts (P) is a loss of coastal land, that injury must also be actual and imminent, not conjectural and hypothetical. The injuries identified by Massachusetts (P) are pure conjecture. In addition, Massachusetts (P) cannot trace its alleged injury back to the fractional amount of global emissions that might have been limited by EPA (D) regulations. Redressability is also a problem. Any decreases in emissions produced by the standards requested by Massachusetts (P) are likely to be overwhelmed many times over by increases elsewhere in the world.

Analysis:

According to the majority, Massachusetts (P) has standing because of the threatened injury to its quasi-sovereign rights. Threatened injury to the citizens of Massachusetts (P) does not figure greatly in the majority's opinion. This would appear to take standing in this case out of the traditional view of the *parens patriae* doctrine. Parts of the majority opinion not reproduced in the casebook mention *parens patriae* only twice, and those mentions are in quotations from other authority.

■ CASE VOCABULARY

PARENS PATRIAE: The state regarded as a sovereign; the state in its capacity as provider of protection to those unable to care for themselves; a doctrine by which a government has standing to prosecute a lawsuit on behalf of a citizen, especially on behalf of someone who is under a legal disability to prosecute the suit. The state ordinarily has no standing to sue on behalf of its citizens, unless a separate, sovereign interest will be served by the suit.

Lujan v. Defenders of Wildlife

(Secretary of the Interior) v. (Environmental Protection Groups)
504 U.S. 555, 112 S.Ct. 2130, 119 L.Ed.2d 351 (1992)

CONGRESSIONAL STATUTES CANNOT GRANT STANDING TO CITIZENS NOT ACTUALLY INJURED IN FACT

■ **INSTANT FACTS** When Congress passed a statute protecting endangered animals, it authorized any person to sue the administrative agency for violating it. When wildlife activists sued, the agency claimed they lacked standing.

■ **BLACK LETTER RULE** Congressional statutes cannot confer standing to plaintiffs who suffered no "actual" "injury in fact."

■ **PROCEDURAL BASIS**

In statutory "citizen suit" seeking injunction, appeal from appellate judgment for plaintiff, seeking summary judgment.

■ **FACTS**

The *Endangered Species Act* ("*ESA*") requires federal agencies to consult with the Secretary of the Interior ("Secretary") (D) to "insure" federally-funded projects do not threaten endangered species. *ESA*'s regulations construed it as reaching projects overseas. Later, Secretary (D) made new regulations re-interpreting *ESA* to apply only to projects within the U.S. or on the high seas. *ESA* includes a "citizen suit" provision, that "any person may commence a civil suit on his own behalf . . . to enjoin any person, including the [U.S.] and any . . . government instrumentality or agency [who] is . . . in violation of any provision [of *ESA*]." Environmental protection groups, including Defenders of Wildlife ("Defenders") (P), sued Secretary (D), contending his regulation was illegal. Defenders (P) proposed several theories of standing to bring this claim. First, they alleged "injury in fact" because individual plaintiffs had personally visited potentially impacted foreign sites to view endangered animals and intended to do so again. Second, they proposed an "ecosystem nexus" that confers standing on any person who uses part of a "contiguous ecosystem" even if the damage done is quite distant from that person. Third, they proposed an "animal nexus" that confers standing on any person who wants to view or study endangered animals anywhere on the planet. Finally, fourth, they proposed a "vocational nexus" that confers standing whose profession is linked to endangered species affected by the Secretary's (D) decisions. On appeal, the Court of Appeals held Defenders (P) had standing because they suffered a "procedural injury," since *ESA*'s "citizen suit" provision grants all "persons" a "procedural right" to the consultation. [Secretary (D) appeals, seeking summary judgment on the issue of standing.]

■ **ISSUE**

Does the Constitution authorize Congress to pass legislation that creates "citizen suits" that confer standing on citizens who would not otherwise be able to allege "injury in fact"?

■ **DECISION AND RATIONALE**

(Scalia, J.) No. The irreducible constitutional minimum of standing contains three elements: (1) The plaintiff must have suffered an injury in fact—an invasion of a legally protected interest that is concrete and particularized and actual or imminent, rather than hypothetical. (2) There must be a causal connection between the injury and the conduct complained of, which is traceable to the act of the defendant, rather than a result of some action by a third party. (3) It must be likely, as opposed to merely speculative, that the injury will be redressed by a favorable decision. Defenders of Wildlife (P) has not satisfied the injury requirement, since they are not directly harmed by the present interpretation of the ESA. Even assuming that certain overseas agency-funded projects threaten endangered species, no facts indicate that damage to the species will inflict imminent injury on members of Defenders of Wildlife (P). That the members visited the areas before the projects proves nothing, and the intent to return to the places to see the wildlife is not enough, so long as the intentions are not accompanied by concrete plans. Defenders of Wildlife also propose a couple of novel standing themes: the "ecosystem nexus" approach, that anyone even remotely affected by damage to a contiguous ecosystem has standing, the "animal nexus" approach, where anyone interested in seeing the animals has standing, and the "vocational nexus" approach, where anyone with a professional interest in the animals may sue. However, standing is not created by an "ingenious academic exercise in the conceivable"—it is pure speculation and fantasy to say that anyone who observes or works with an endangered species, anywhere in the world, is appreciably harmed by a single project affecting some portion of that species with which he has no more specific connection. As to redressability, an injunction is unlikely to stop the projects that endanger certain species, since American aid to these projects usually makes up a very small percentage of the cost of the project. Furthermore, whether the funding agencies would even be bound by the Secretary's (D) regulation is an open question. Finally, the Court of Appeals found that Defenders of Wildlife (P) has standing because the organization suffered a procedural injury. A "citizen-suit" provision of the ESA allows a person to commence action against a government agency in violation of the ESA, regardless of whether there is actual injury. Defenders of Wildlife (P) asserts that the Secretary (D) failed to follow the ESA's interagency consultation provision. The Court of Appeals agreed, holding that the injury-in-fact requirement was satisfied by a congressional conferral of an abstract, self-contained "citizen-suit" right to have the Executive observe the procedures required by law. We reject this view. As Marshall said in *Marbury,* "the province of the court is, solely, to decide on the rights of individuals." Vindicating the public interest is the function of Congress and the Executive Branch. Congress may not convert the undifferentiated public interest in an Executive officer's compliance with a law into an individual right to sue. To do so would transfer from the President to the courts the President's constitutional duty to "take Care that the Laws be faithfully executed." We reject that vision of our role. In suits against the government, the concrete injury requirement must remain. Defenders of Wildlife (P) lacks standing to bring this action. Reversed.

■ DISSENT

(Blackmun, J.) First, I believe Defenders (P) raise genuine factual issues of injury and redressability, sufficient to survive summary judgment. Second, I question the Court's vague, overbroad rejection of "procedural injuries." Whatever it means, it should not mean that "procedural injuries" *as a class* are necessarily insufficient for standing, because most Governmental conduct can be termed "procedural." Also, the Court should defer to Congressional legislative mandates on executive agencies, since Congressional legislation often involves some procedural imposition on executive agencies' enforcement. Here, *ESA*'s "citizen suit" provisions do not transfer power from the Executive to the courts, so they do not violate *Art. III.*

Analysis:

Many professors view *Lujan* as a landmark in limiting Congressional conferral of standing. Under it, Congress cannot confer standing to plaintiffs who suffered no "injury in fact," defined as "actual or imminent" harm. "Injury in fact" is defined according to common law precedents. This *seems to* suggest that if an injury was previously viewed by courts as not "actual," (e.g., "generalized grievances"), then Congress cannot ever make it a cause of action. If this interpretation were followed, it would severely restrict Congress's ability to define statutory rights. But *Lujan*'s language contains an "out": Congress may recognize "actual" injuries that courts did not previously recognize as actionable. This interpretation allows courts to uphold "citizen suit" provisions on the ground that the injury is "actual," though not previously recognized. As evidence that the decision was somewhat controversial among the members of the Court, note that the Court's opinion is a plurality decision. In addition to the dissent noted above, Justices Kennedy and Stevens wrote concurring opinions that agreed with the Court's judgment, but disagreed with parts of its reasoning.

■ CASE VOCABULARY

"CITIZEN SUIT" [PROVISION]: Statutory provision allowing citizens injured by violations of a statute to sue.

"GENERALIZED GRIEVANCES" [DOCTRINE]: Judicial "standing" doctrine, which holds that, when government action affects (too) many people, no one person has standing to sue the government, because the proper remedy is to petition Congress to change the law.

INJUNCTION: Court order requiring/prohibiting an action.

"PROCEDURAL INJURY": Apparently, the disregard of a statutory procedure, which affects the plaintiff.

Singleton v. Wulff

(State Medicare Official) v. (Physicians)
428 U.S. 106, 96 S.Ct. 2868 (1976)

A PERSON MAY SUE TO PROTECT THE RIGHTS OF A THIRD PARTY WHEN THE INTERESTS OF THE PARTIES ARE SUFFICIENTLY CLOSE AND THERE ARE OBSTACLES TO THE THIRD PARTY ASSERTING HER RIGHTS

■ **INSTANT FACTS** Abortion doctors sued to receive Medicaid payments through the state for abortions they had performed that were not "medically indicated."

■ **BLACK LETTER RULE** Persons may sue to protect a third party's right only when (1) the relationship between the parties is such that the person suing may advocate effectively for the right and (2) there are genuine obstacles to the third party asserting the right in court.

■ **PROCEDURAL BASIS**

Appeal to U.S. Supreme Court of a motion to dismiss a case originally filed in the District Court for the Eastern District of Missouri.

■ **FACTS**

Missouri passed a statute that would provide benefits to a needy woman seeking an abortion only when the abortion was "medically indicated." Two Missouri doctors (P) who had performed such abortions, sued in federal court to have the law declared unconstitutional. The state Medicaid official (D) moved to dismiss the case. The doctors (P) opposed the motion, stating that they had performed non-medically indicated abortions, that they anticipated performing more such abortions, and that the Medicaid official (D) turned down all Medicaid applications associated with the abortions, citing as authority, the statute at issue in the case. The dismissal motion was appealed, eventually to the U.S. Supreme Court. The primary challenge on appeal did not concern the content of the statute, but rather the right of the physicians to file the suit. The Medicaid official (D) claimed that only the abortion patients had the right to challenge the abortion statute.

■ **ISSUE**

May physicians who performed abortions that were not compensated by the state sue to challenge the Medicaid statute that excluded abortions that are not "medically indicated"?

■ **DECISION AND RATIONALE**

(Blackmun, J.) Yes. Although the general rule is that a person cannot sue on behalf of a third party, the situations of the physicians (P) and patients in this case fit the exceptions to that general rule. The analysis of standing in this case begins with two questions: (1) do the physicians (P) allege an "injury in fact"? and (2) are the physicians (P) proper parties to bring this suit? The answer to both questions is yes. First, the physicians (P) allege injury in fact because they performed work for which the state Medicaid official (D) declined to pay them. Because of the circumstances in this case, the physicians (P) are proper advocates for a challenge to the Missouri statute denying Medicaid benefits for a class of abortions. Normally, the Courts will not allow a person to sue to protect the rights of a third party. The Court has adopted this rule for two reasons. First, the affected third party may choose not to assert her

Singleton v. Wulff (Continued)

right or may conclude that she can have the benefit of the right without litigating. In such cases, the courts should not litigate unnecessarily. Second, courts want the best possible advocate for a position and, in general, that would be the third party right-holder. When these two reasons do not apply, however, it may be proper for a person to assert the rights of a third party. This is such a case. First, the relationship between the physicians (P) and the patients is sufficiently close to make the physicians (P) effective proponents of the challenge to the Missouri statute. An indigent woman who might seek an abortion could not safely exercise her right to an abortion without access to her physician and Medicaid assistance to pay for that access. Second, genuine obstacles exist in this case to the woman bringing the case herself. For example, the woman might be scared off from the lawsuit because it would compromise her privacy. Furthermore, rights concerning pregnancy and abortion fit into the category of "capable of repetition yet evading review" since the case becomes "moot" once the pregnancy has advanced beyond the point where abortion is safe or practical. Although these obstacles could potentially be avoided through the use of pseudonyms or class action suits, physicians are representative enough of the position to advocate effectively. Thus, a physician may assert the rights of his or her patient to challenge government laws or actions restricting the patient's decision concerning abortion.

Analysis:

One of the most interesting aspects of the Court's opinion in *Singleton* is its recognition of the obstacles to an abortion patient bringing her case. These factors show the Court's sympathy to the special nature of abortion cases: the social stigmatization, the crisis nature and time constraints of the abortion decision, and the fact that the decision is a potentially reoccurring one. Even though the Court identified solutions to these obstacles, it allowed physician advocacy for the abortion right. The Court, it seems, was more concerned that physician advocacy corresponded to the underlying purposes of the exception to the third-party prohibition than to the strict language of the test. The *Singleton* decision is an example of an opinion that lays out the reasons behind a particular rule or exception and shows how the facts of the instant case fit these reasons. Still, it is worthwhile to question whether, if the Court had not wanted the case heard for substantive reasons, it could not have found reasons to consider the physicians to be inappropriate advocates. After all, the controversy that the court identified was that the physicians wanted to be paid for work they had already done. Could the argument be made that the financial interest of the doctors made their position essentially different from that of the patients? The Court, in this case, apparently did not think so.

Elk Grove Unified School Dist. v. Newdow

(School District) v. (Parent)
542 U.S. 1, 124 S.Ct. 2301 (2004)

FEDERAL COURTS ABSTAIN FROM RESOLVING STATE DOMESTIC RELATIONS ISSUES

■ **INSTANT FACTS** Newdow (P) challenged the Elk Grove Unified School District's (D) policy of student recitation of the Pledge of Allegiance in its public schools.

■ **BLACK LETTER RULE** Parents' prudential standing in federal court to challenge policies affecting the religious education of their children is determined by state domestic relations law.

■ PROCEDURAL BASIS

Certiorari to review a decision of the Ninth Circuit Court of Appeals invalidating a school policy.

■ FACTS

Initially an expression of patriotism, the Pledge of Allegiance was amended by Act of Congress in 1954 to include the words "under God." Under California law, every public school must begin the day with "appropriate patriotic exercises." To satisfy this requirement, the Elk Grove Unified School District (D) began its school day with a student recitation of the Pledge of Allegiance, allowing students with religious objections to abstain from the recitation. Newdow (P), an atheist, filed suit in California federal court "as a parent to challenge a practice that interferes with his right to direct the religious education of his daughter." The district court held that the school district's policy and the federal statute violated the Establishment Clause of the First Amendment. After the Ninth Circuit Court of Appeals issued an initial decision, the mother of Newdow's (P) daughter moved to intervene and dismiss the complaint. Although she and Newdow (P) shared physical custody over the daughter, the mother had exclusive legal custody of the child and claimed sole authorization to enforce her daughter's legal interests. Claiming the daughter to be a Christian who believed in God, she moved to dismiss Newdow's (P) complaint. The California Superior Court enjoined Newdow (P) from naming his daughter as a party to the lawsuit, without addressing Newdow's (P) Article III standing. The Ninth Circuit Court of Appeals then issued a second opinion, holding that Newdow (P) had Article III standing to challenge a government practice that interfered with his right to expose his daughter to his religious views notwithstanding the grant of sole legal custody to her mother. Elk Grove Unified School District (D) petitioned for certiorari.

■ ISSUE

Does a parent have standing in federal court to raise a constitutional challenge invoking issues of state domestic relations law?

■ DECISION AND RATIONALE

(Stevens, J.) No. In order to maintain a federal action, the party bringing the action must have standing. The standing question in this case is complicated by issues of parental rights established as a matter of state domestic relations law. Because domestic relations are deeply rooted as within the province of the states, federal courts are reluctant to intervene, "even when divorce, alimony, or child custody is not strictly at issue." Here, legal custody over the daughter is shared between Newdow (P) and the daughter's mother, but the mother held decision-making authority should the two disagree. Newdow (P) has the right to consult on the daughter's education, but the mother makes the ultimate decisions. His parental status is established as a matter of state law, and federal courts should not endeavor to decide a federal constitutional issue complicated by state domestic relations law. Because state law deprives Newdow (P) of legal custody of his daughter, Newdow (P) lacks standing.

■ DISSENT IN PART

(Rehnquist, C.J.) Although the school policy to recite the Pledge of Allegiance does not violate the Establishment Clause, Newdow (P) has standing to challenge the policy. Rather than abide by traditional Article III concepts of standing, the Court devises a new standing principle to avoid reaching the merits of a difficult case. Although the domestic relations exception to diversity jurisdiction requires federal abstention in deciding matters of "divorce, alimony, and child custody," this case is not based on diversity jurisdiction nor is the court asked to resolve such domestic relations issues. A substantial federal question exists, which demands the court's attention. The Ninth Circuit, with a better understanding of California domestic relations law, recognized Newdow's (P) state-law parental rights and acknowledged his Article III standing. The Court should defer to that judgment.

Analysis:

Unlike Article III standing, which ensures that a litigant presents a justiciable case or controversy for consideration, prudential standing assures that the case or controversy presented belongs to the litigant. Because state law had established that the decision-making authority over his daughter was held by her mother, Newdow (P) lacked prudential standing, although he presented a justiciable constitutional challenge.

■ CASE VOCABULARY

ABSTENTION: A federal court's relinquishment of jurisdiction when necessary to avoid needless conflict with a state's administration of its own affairs.

STANDING: A party's right to make a legal claim or seek judicial enforcement of a duty or right. To have standing in federal court, a plaintiff must show (1) that the challenged conduct has caused the plaintiff actual injury, and (2) that the interest sought to be protected is within the zone of interests meant to be regulated by the statutory or constitutional guarantee in question.

United States v. Richardson

(*Federal Government*) v. (*Taxpayer*)
418 U.S. 166, 94 S.Ct. 2940 (1974)

ABSENT DIRECT INJURY, TAXPAYER STATUS DOES NOT GIVE AN INDIVIDUAL STANDING TO CHALLENGE THE CONSTITUTIONALITY OF FEDERAL ACTION

■ **INSTANT FACTS** A taxpayer sued to compel the CIA to release details of its expenditures pursuant to Article I, § 9 of the U.S. Constitution.

■ **BLACK LETTER RULE** Taxpayer status is not sufficient to confer standing to challenge the constitutionality of federal action unless the taxpayer alleges direct injury from the practice and not generalized grievances common to all members of the public.

■ **PROCEDURAL BASIS**

Grant of certiorari for the purpose of determining standing.

■ **FACTS**

Richardson (P) brought suit to compel the CIA to release information about its expenditures, claiming that the secrecy of these expenditures was unconstitutional. Richardson (P) cited Article I, § 9, Clause 7, which states that for all appropriations made by Congress "a regular Statement and Account of the Receipts and Expenditures of all public Money shall be published from time to time." Richardson (P) claimed that he needed the information about the CIA's expenditures in order to participate meaningfully as a voter and to understand the actions of the federal government. The accounting procedures in the CIA accounting statute were similar to those for other agencies that dealt with sensitive matters.

■ **ISSUE**

Does an individual's status as a taxpayer give him standing to challenge the constitutionality of a statute regulating the CIA's financial accounting and reporting?

■ **DECISION AND RATIONALE**

(Burger, Chief Justice) No. Because his allegations do not fit the two-part test for taxpayer standing articulated in *Flast*, Richardson's (P) taxpayer status does not confer him standing to challenge the CIA reporting statute. *Frothingham v. Mellon* controls this case. There the plaintiff alleged that the Federal Maternity Act of 1921 violated the Fifth Amendment and that, if allowed to stand, the law would cause her income taxes to increase. The Court held that the plaintiff did not have standing because her alleged impacts were small and lacked the certainty and directness that would confer standing. *Flast v. Cohen* created an exception to *Frothingham's* general prohibition to taxpayer standing for taxpayers that could allege a case meeting a two-part test. First, the taxpayer needs to show that the federal action being challenged has been taken pursuant to Congress's taxing and spending authority. Second, the taxpayer must argue that the challenged action contravenes a "specific constitutional limit" on the government's authority. Even with this exception, the Court stated that taxpayers could not use the federal courts to air a "generalized grievance." Richardson's (P) claim does not satisfy either part of the *Flast* test. The challenged statute is regulatory in nature, not made pursuant to the taxing and spending power. Likewise, Richardson (P) does not allege that funds have been allocated in violation of a constitutional limit on the taxing and spending power, but rather looks to compel a release of information. Finally, the basis of Richardson's (P) claim, that he cannot adequately participate as a voter without the requested information, is an undifferentiated, generalized grievance, which he holds in common with the general public. In this sense, the present case is similar to *Ex Parte Levitt,* where the plaintiff alleged a genuine violation of the constitution but was denied standing because he could not show a direct impact unique to the plaintiff. We acknowledge that our decision to deny standing in this case may effectively make it impossible for this case to have judicial resolution. Those interested in changing the procedures at issue here may, therefore, pursue a political solution.

■ DISSENT

(Stewart, J.) This case is distinct from both *Frothingham* and *Flast* because in those cases the plaintiffs sought to have the Court strike down allegedly unconstitutional laws. Richardson's (P) claim is more on the order of a claim against the government for a duty owed. He claims that Article I, § 9, Clause 7 obligates the government to provide him with certain information regarding the expenditure of public finances. Imagine that Richardson (P) were claiming that a statute or constitutional provision obligated the government to pay him a sum of money. Now we can see that Richardson (P) is a plaintiff in a traditional, adversarial role in the type of disputes over rights and duties that the courts can resolve. With regard to standing to assert an alleged right, it should make no difference that Richardson (P) claims he is owed information rather than money.

Analysis:

Richardson is an interesting case to consider when reviewing the prohibition against generalized grievances. The majority opinion begins by simply citing to two precedents: the broad rule against taxpayer standing from *Frothingham,* and the narrow exception from *Flast.* Here the reasoning is straightforward; the opinion applies the facts of Richardson's claim to the *Flast* test and concludes that this case does not fit the exception. Then, however, the majority elaborates on the fact that Richardson's claim is a generalized grievance. The opinion states that when the generalized nature of the grievance makes it impossible to grant any plaintiff standing to bring the case, it is because the subject matter of the case was "committed" to a legislative or political resolution. But who was it that "committed" such subjects to the political branches, the Constitution or the courts? Different cases that apply the generalized grievance prohibition seem to give different answers to that question. The main interest of the dissent in Richardson lies in just how different justice Stewart's view of the basic dispute in the case is from the majority's view. For the dissent the question of whether every citizen has a right to receive the CIA's accounting information is a part of the merits of the case, not a reason to decline standing to the plaintiff.

Flast v. Cohen
(Not Stated) v. (Not Stated)
392 U.S. 83, 88 S.Ct. 1942 (1968)

TAXPAYER STATUS CONFERS STANDING TO CHALLENGE CONGRESSIONAL EXPENDITURES THAT VIOLATE SEPARATION OF CHURCH AND STATE

■ **INSTANT FACTS** Taxpayers challenged federal funding for academic instruction, books and materials in private religious schools.

■ **BLACK LETTER RULE** Taxpayer status is sufficient to confer standing on an individual to bring suit in federal court to challenge the constitutionality of federal spending in violation of the First Amendment Free Exercise and Establishment clauses.

■ **PROCEDURAL BASIS**

not stated

■ **FACTS**

Several individual taxpayers [the "Taxpayers"] (P) filed suit in federal District Court claiming that federal expenditures under the Elementary and Secondary Education Act of 1965 violated the First Amendment's Establishment and Free Exercise Clauses. The challenged expenditures were the purchase of books and materials and the funding of instruction in academic subjects for religious schools. The Taxpayers (P) claimed standing to bring their claim exclusively on their taxpayer status.

■ **ISSUE**

Does an individual's status as a taxpayer give that person standing to challenge Congressional expenditures in violation of the First Amendment Establishment and Free Exercise clauses?

■ **DECISION AND RATIONALE**

(Warren, Chief Justice) Yes. Because the Taxpayers (P) are challenging an exercise by Congress of its taxing and spending power and because they allege a violation of First Amendment separation of church and state, the Taxpayers (P) have a sufficient "personal stake" in the case to give them standing in federal court. The Taxpayers' (P) "personal stake" is the result of their taxpayer status. Although *Frothingham v. Mellon* has stood as a bar to taxpayer standing since 1923, standing should be determined on a case-by-case basis. The purpose of the standing requirement is to assure that the litigant has a sufficient personal stake to bring the case in a traditionally adversarial posture so that the courts may decide the controversy. Whether the nexus between a person's taxpayer status and his interest in a controversy will be sufficiently close to grant him standing can be determined through a two-part test. First, the taxpayer must be challenging an action taken by Congress under its Article I, § 8 taxing and spending power. In this case, the Taxpayers (P) are challenging a major funding program authorized under the Article I, § 8 power. Second, the taxpayer must allege that the challenged levies or expenditures violate specific constitutional limits on government power. Here, the Taxpayers (P) allege violations of the First Amendment Establishment and Free Exercise clauses. The Framers saw the connection between the power to tax and spend and religious liberty. They intended to prevent the

Flast v. Cohen (Continued)

government from using its power to favor a given religion or religious institution. The Framers intended the Establishment Clause as a limit on Congress's power to tax and spend.

■ DISSENT

(Harlan, J.) While the majority decision creates a two-part test to determine when taxpayer status gives a person a "personal stake" in the outcome of a case so as to confer standing on the taxpayer, neither of the two parts in their test really measures an individual's interest in the case. In the first part of the test, for example, why would a taxpayer be more interested in federal spending made pursuant to the taxing and spending power than in federal spending pursuant to a regulatory program? This is unclear since either direct funding or a regulatory scheme could be employed to help or hinder a particular religion. Likewise, in part two of the test, it is unclear why a taxpayer's interest In a case would vary according to which provision of the constitution was allegedly violated. The judiciary branch is not the only branch of the government with the power to check constitutional abuses of power and the judicial power needs to be exercised with restraint and prudence.

Analysis:

Flast is one of those rare cases that carves out an exception to a general rule that had seemingly stood the test of time. The Court has read *Flast* very narrowly, however, and has maintained a general prohibition against taxpayer standing. Knowing that, it is interesting to read *Flast* with an eye to whether the majority intended its opinion to apply only to a narrow class of church and state issues. In some ways, it is the dissent, with its concern over limited judicial resources, that provides the strongest suggestion that *Flast* might have radically overhauled the taxpayer standing landscape. Whatever its long-term impact, the *Flast* case raises important questions about aspects of constitutional law that are often taken for granted.

■ CASE VOCABULARY

ESTABLISHMENT: Actions by the government to recognize or aid a particular religion; the establishment of religion is barred by the First Amendment.

FREE EXERCISE: The ability of a person to hold (or not hold) whatever religious beliefs and engage (or refrain from engaging) in whatever religious practices she chooses; the First Amendment bars government action that would infringe on an individual's free exercise.

Hein v. Freedom From Religion Foundation

(Director of Office) v. (Taxpayer Group)
551 U.S. 587, 127 S.Ct. 2553 (2007)

TAXPAYERS DO NOT HAVE STANDING TO CHALLENGE EXECUTIVE BRANCH ACTIONS

■ **INSTANT FACTS** The Freedom from Religion Foundation (P) claimed that the President's Faith–Based and Community Initiatives program violated the Establishment Clause, and Hein (D) claimed the Foundation (P) lacked standing.

■ **BLACK LETTER RULE** Taxpayers have standing to bring Establishment Clause challenges to a federal expenditure only if that expenditure is made pursuant to an explicit congressional authorization.

■ PROCEDURAL BASIS

Appeal from a court of appeals holding that the Foundation (P) had standing as a taxpayer.

■ FACTS

The President's Faith–Based and Community Initiatives program (D) was established to help private and charitable community groups, including religious groups, compete for federal funds. The program was established by executive order. It was not funded through specific congressional appropriation, but through general Executive Branch appropriations. The Freedom from Religion Foundation (P) challenged the program (D) on Establishment Clause grounds. The Foundation (P) alleged that the program (D) held conferences that singled out religious organizations as being particularly worthy of federal funding. The Foundation (P) further alleged that the conferences sent a message to non-believers that they were "outsiders" and "not full members of the political community." The Foundation (P) asserted standing based on its members' status as federal taxpayers "opposed to the use of Congressional taxpayer appropriation to advance and promote religion." The court of appeals held that the Foundation (P) had standing to bring its action.

■ ISSUE

Did the Foundation (P) have standing?

■ DECISION AND RATIONALE

(Alito, J.) No. Taxpayers have standing to bring Establishment Clause challenges to a federal expenditure only if that expenditure is made pursuant to an explicit congressional authorization. Federal courts exist only to decide controversies that affect the rights of individuals. As a general rule, a taxpayer's interest in seeing that federal funds are spent in accordance with the Constitution does not give rise to the type of personalized injury required for Article III standing. The interests of a taxpayer are essentially the interests of the public at large. Deciding a case based solely on taxpayer standing would be assuming a position of authority over the acts of another, co-equal branch of government.

The case of *Flast v. Cohen,* 392 U.S. 83 (1968), made a narrow exception to the general prohibition against taxpayer standing. Under the rule of that case, a taxpayer will have standing to challenge the constitutionality of an expenditure if he or she shows that the challenged enactment exceeds specific constitutional limitations on the congressional taxing and spending power, not simply that the enact-

Hein v. Freedom From Religion Foundation (Continued)

ment is generally beyond the powers of Congress. The expenditures challenged in *Flast* were made pursuant to an express congressional mandate and a specific congressional appropriation. The taxpayers in that case could establish logical link between their status as taxpayers and the specific enactment challenged.

There is no link between a congressional action and the constitutional violation in this case. The expenditures were not made pursuant to a congressional authorization, but by executive discretion. Taxpayer standing has never been found under such circumstances. The Foundation (P) argues that it is arbitrary to draw a distinction between expenditures pursuant to congressional authorization and those made in the exercise of executive discretion, because the injury to taxpayers in both situations is the same. The holding in *Flast* was limited to challenges of congressional action. Extending *Flast* to executive branch actions would subject every federal action to Establishment Clause challenge by any taxpayer in federal court. It would also raise serious separation-of-powers concerns. The Foundation (P) sets out a parade of horribles that they claim could occur if *Flast* is not extended. None of those has happened, but if any of them did occur, Congress could quickly step in. The Court will not extend *Flast*, but it will not overrule it. Reversed

■ CONCURRENCE

(Scalia, J.) The plurality opinion sets out meaningless distinctions to differentiate this case from others. Either *Flast v. Cohen* should be applied consistently to all constitutional challenges to governmental expenditures, or the case should be overruled.

Cases that address taxpayer standing to raise Establishment Clause challenges to expenditures rely on two distinct types of injury: "wallet injury," or a claim that the taxpayer's tax burden is higher than it should be; and "psychic injury," the taxpayer's mental displeasure that money extracted from him or her is being spent unlawfully. Wallet injury does not satisfy the traceability and redressability requirements of standing. *Flast* invoked a peculiarly restricted version of psychic injury, permitting taxpayer displeasure to support standing only if the constitutional provision violated is a specific limitation on the taxing and spending power. The majority does not address whether psychic injury is consistent with Article III. The answer is no. *Flast* should be overruled.

■ DISSENT

(Souter, J.) The plurality opinion does not explain why the Foundation's (P) stake in the outcome here is any different because the challenged action is one taken by the executive branch, rather than the legislative branch. There is no question that taxpayer money in identifiable amounts is being spent on conferences alleged to promote religion. The Foundation (P) does not seek to extend *Flast*, but to apply it.

Analysis:

The distinction between expenditures made through executive discretion and expenditures made through congressional appropriation is a thin one, at best. All federal expenditures may be made only "in Consequence of Appropriations made by Law." U.S. Const. Art. I § , 9. Ultimately, every expenditure by any branch is traceable back to congressional action.

■ CASE VOCABULARY

ESTABLISHMENT CLAUSE: The First Amendment provision that prohibits the state and federal governments from establishing an official religion, or from favoring or disfavoring one view of religion over another.

Poe v. Ullman

(Married Couple) v. (Not Stated)
367 U.S. 497, 81 S.Ct. 1752 (1961)

ABSENT STATE PROSECUTION, THE EXISTENCE OF A STATUTE DOES NOT MAKE THE STATUTE'S CONSTITUTIONALITY RIPE FOR FEDERAL COURT REVIEW

■ **INSTANT FACTS** A doctor and some of his patients challenged a Connecticut law that forbade medical personnel from disseminating information about contraception.

■ **BLACK LETTER RULE** The declaratory judgment of a state court upholding a statute on the books does not make the issue of that statute's constitutionality ripe for federal court determination when the state has not and likely will not prosecute under the statute.

■ PROCEDURAL BASIS

Appeal from a declaratory judgment of Connecticut Supreme Court of Errors.

■ FACTS

Connecticut had a statute that prohibited individuals from using contraceptives and prohibited doctors and other medical personnel from giving any medical advice about contraception or contraceptives. A married couple and a married woman that sought medical advice about contraceptives brought, under the pseudonyms Paul and Paula Poe (P) and Jane Doe (P), a suit in Connecticut state court to have the anti-contraception statute clarified. The Connecticut Supreme Court of Errors ruled that the law forbade medical consultation even for married persons and in cases where contraception is indicated due to serious health problems. Paula Poe (P) had given birth three times to children who died shortly after their births due to genetic birth defects. The Poe's physician, Dr. Buxton (P), concluded that it would be medically advisable for Paula Poe (P) to use contraception to avoid the stress and danger of another pregnancy likely to end the same way. Another patient of Dr. Buxton (P), Jane Doe (P), a twenty-five year old married woman, had severe medical complications related to a recent pregnancy. Dr. Buxton (P) concluded that use of contraception was medically indicated for Jane Doe (P). Dr. Buxton (P) also brought a declaratory action in Connecticut, arguing that the statute unconstitutionally deprived him of liberty and property without due process. Although the anti-conception statute is eighty years old, it has produced only one criminal prosecution, a 1940 test case in which the information was dropped after the Supreme Court of Errors upheld the statute's constitutionality. Dr. Buxton (P), the Poe's (P) and Jane Doe (P) appealed the declaratory judgment of the Connecticut Supreme Court of Errors to the U.S. Supreme Court, claiming that the anti-conception statute violated the Fourteenth Amendment.

■ ISSUE

Does a declaratory judgment in state court that a state criminal statute would apply to a class of individuals make the issue of the statute's constitutionality ripe for federal court determination when the individuals in question have not been prosecuted under the statute?

■ DECISION AND RATIONALE

(Frankfurter, J.) No. Because the state has not chosen to enforce its anti-conception statute (and appears unlikely to do so), the issue of that statute's constitutionality is not ripe for determination by the

Poe v. Ullman (Continued)

federal courts. Even if the parties were to stipulate facts concerning possible prosecutions, it would not make the case ripe for federal court resolution because the reality of the situation is clearly different. For example, contraceptives are sold openly in Connecticut stores, yet no prosecutions have resulted. It is unlikely, therefore, that a prosecution would result from the giving of private medical advice.

■ DISSENT

(Douglas, J.) This case is ripe for resolution despite the fact that criminal prosecution is only potential. The medical consequences for the women in this case are severe. They have not been able to consult with a medical doctor about indicated treatments. To do so, or to use the recommended contraceptives, would be a crime that the State Attorney stated he will enforce. The 1940 prosecution noted by the majority closed a public clinic and led to State seizure of the clinic's equipment and literature. The majority's decision leaves these plaintiffs in a terrible predicament: break the law and face the penalties or try to avoid detection. This is an uncivilized way to conduct our medical consultations. The plaintiffs deserve a resolution of their issue.

Analysis:

The severity of the facts in this case serves to underscore how seriously the Court takes the issue of ripeness. The majority concludes that review of the Connecticut statute would be premature since there has been no enforcement. Should a court lower its ripeness threshold in cases, like this one, where the threat of harm from the law is significant? The dissent in *Poe* implies that the court could consider such facts. The majority opinion, on the other hand, seems to look exclusively to the likelihood of prosecution to determine whether it will decide the case. But neither the dissent nor the majority opinion outlines a clear test for determining when a controversy is ripe.

■ CASE VOCABULARY

DECLARATORY JUDGMENT: A court decision that states the rights or duties of parties, but does not provide for enforcement or remedy.

INFORMATION: The type of criminal charge used in states that do not have grand-jury indictment.

RIPENESS: The point in a dispute where the facts and adversity of the parties allow a court to render a meaningful resolution to the conflict; many courts decline to hear issues that are not "ripe" for their resolution.

Abbott Laboratories v. Gardner

(Pharmaceutical Company) v. *(FDA Commissioner)*
387 U.S. 136, 87 S.Ct. 1507 (1967)

A CASE IS "RIPE" WHEN IT INVOLVES A LEGAL ISSUE FOR THE COURT TO DECIDE AND THE PARTIES WOULD SUFFER IF THE COURT DECLINED TO HEAR THE CASE

■ **INSTANT FACTS** Drug companies challenged a law that would have required them to print the generic name of a drug on all labels and advertisements containing the drug's trade name.

■ **BLACK LETTER RULE** A case is considered "ripe" for federal court resolution when (1) the issue(s) presented are appropriate for a judicial decision and (2) the parties would face hardship if the court declined to hear the case.

■ **PROCEDURAL BASIS**

not stated

■ **FACTS**

In 1962, Congress passed legislation that required drug companies to print the "established name" [generic name] of any drug they sold in type "at least half as large" as the print used for the "proprietary name" [trade name] on labels and other materials. This intent of the legislation was to make sure that consumers and doctors knew when cheaper versions of identical drugs were available. Pursuant to this legislation, the Department of Health, Education and Welfare ["HEW"] (D) promulgated an order that applied the "established name" rule to labels, advertisements, and other printed materials referencing the drug. A number of drug companies and the Pharmaceutical Manufacturer's Association (P) sued in federal court to enjoin the HEW (D) order, arguing that the HEW Commissioner (D) exceeded his authority. The drug companies alleged that complying with the order would be very expensive. If they failed to comply, the companies faced fines and criminal penalties.

■ **ISSUE**

Is a case ripe for federal court determination prior to an enforcement action when it presents legal issues and the parties may suffer injury if the court fails to hear the case?

■ **DECISION AND RATIONALE**

(Harlan, J.) Yes. The federal courts should decide cases when two conditions are met: (1) the issue(s) in the case is currently appropriate for judicial decision, and (2) the parties will incur a hardship if the court declines to hear the case. In this case, the substantive issue is purely a legal one—whether the agency Commissioner (D) exceed his statutory authority—that is proper for the federal courts to decide. The high costs of compliance or non-compliance make it appropriate for the court to consider the case and to give a declaratory judgment. The court should hesitate to give declaratory judgments in administrative cases that are not ripe in order to allow the agency to make and apply its own decisions. In this case, however, the high costs and impacts that would arise if the court were to delay hearing the case outweigh the risks of a premature decision.

Abbott Laboratories v. Gardner (Continued)

Analysis:

This case is an interesting companion to *Poe.* In *Abbott,* the Court sets out a two-part test to determine ripeness. If the issue in the case is appropriate for judicial resolution, the Court will look at whether the parties will face a hardship if the courts cannot decide the case. After examining the rule in *Abbott*, it is tempting to go back to *Poe* and see where that case would have failed the *Abbott* test. The main difference between the cases seems to be that in *Poe* the law in question had been on the books a long time without much enforcement. Query whether if the law in *Poe* had been recently passed (as the drug law was in *Abbott*) the Court might have decided that case differently.

Friends of the Earth, Incorporated v. Laidlaw Environmental Services

(*Environmental Group*) v. (*"Former" Polluter*)
528 U.S. 167, 120 S.Ct. 693 (2000)

DEFENDANT'S VOLUNTARY CESSATION OF ACTION THAT IS BASIS FOR COMPLAINT WILL NOT MAKE A CASE MOOT UNLESS THERE IS NO REASONABLE CHANCE THAT DEFENDANT CAN RESUME THE ACTION

■ **INSTANT FACTS** Defendant-polluter argued that its recent compliance with national standards and plant shutdown mooted a citizen suit alleging violations of the Clean Water Act.

■ **BLACK LETTER RULE** Defendant's voluntary cessation of actions that are the subject of a Complaint does not make the lawsuit moot unless there is no reasonable chance that the defendant can return to the actions.

■ **PROCEDURAL BASIS**

not stated

■ **FACTS**

The environmental group Friends of the Earth (P) brought a citizen suit under the Clean Water Act alleging that Laidlaw Environmental Services ["Laidlaw"] (D) had violated the mercury discharge limits established by its National Pollutant Discharge Elimination System ["NPDES"] permit. During the course of the lawsuit (which went on for several years), Laidlaw (D) voluntarily achieved compliance with its NPDES permit and also closed its Roebuck facility. However, Laidlaw (D) retained its NPDES permit.

■ **ISSUE**

Does the defendant's voluntary compliance and plant closure make moot a citizen suit alleging violations of defendant's NPDES permit?

■ **DECISION AND RATIONALE**

(Ginsburg, J.) No. Laidlaw's (D) voluntary achievement of compliance and facility closure do not automatically moot this case. As a defendant claiming mootness as the result of its voluntary compliance, Laidlaw (D) bears the burden of proving to the trial court that there is no reasonable chance that it could resume its violations. The defendant's "heavy burden" to show that there is no reasonable chance that the violation could recur is the flipside of the standing burden that the plaintiffs have in bringing a lawsuit to enjoin violations. The plaintiff must show that if the litigation does not go forward, the defendant's behavior is likely to persist. One reason that the courts have standing requirements is to make sure that judicial resources are used to resolve "live" controversies between parties that have stakes in the outcome. Especially in cases like this one that have a duration of several years, it would be worse to absorb the "sunk costs" of all the litigation without reaching a concrete resolution of the dispute. The fact that Laidlaw (D) retained its polluter's permit is just one of the facts that the trial court will have to consider in order to determine whether there is any reasonable chance that Laidlaw's (D) violations could reoccur. The case is remanded.

Friends of the Earth, Incorporated v. Laidlaw Environmental Services (Continued)

Analysis:

This case is an example of the "voluntary cessation" exception to the mootness doctrine. It applies when a defendant stops doing the activity that produced the complaint in the case. The exception states that even though the challenged activity has ceased to exist, the court can still hear the case unless it is clear that the defendant cannot resume the activity. The standard of proof is very high for a defendant who wants to argue that his voluntary action has mooted the case. The defendant must show that there is "no reasonable chance" that he could start up the challenged behavior or activity again. Thus, shutting off a valve would not be sufficient, but creating a permanent barrier to the pipe's ability to flow probably would. This exception is especially important to the courts because it helps avoid the type of on-again/off-again dispute that ties up court resources without bringing finality to the case. In this sense, the voluntary cessation exception is similar to "wrongs capable of repetition but evading review." Although that category generally covers situations that have a short time-span, the practical effect is the same as with the defendant who stops long enough to make the lawsuit go away but then repeats the same behavior.

United States Parole Commission v. Geraghty

(Federal Parole Commission) v. (Federal Prisoner)
445 U.S. 388, 100 S.Ct. 1202 (1980)

APPEAL OF A TRIAL COURT'S DENIAL OF CLASS CERTIFICATION DOES NOT BECOME MOOT BECAUSE THE NAMED PARTY'S CASE BECAME MOOT

■ **INSTANT FACTS** Federal prisoners were appealing a District Court's denial of their certification as a class when the named plaintiff's case became moot.

■ **BLACK LETTER RULE** Appeal of a lower court's denial of class certification does not become moot due to the mootness of the named plaintiff's case.

■ **PROCEDURAL BASIS**

Appeal of a federal Court of Appeals decision to hear a challenge to a trial court's denial of class certification after the named plaintiff's case had become moot.

■ **FACTS**

Geraghty (P), a federal prisoner, filed suit in federal court to challenge the federal parole release guidelines. Geraghty (P) sought to be the named plaintiff to represent the class of all federal prisoners eligible for parole now or in the future. The District Court denied Geraghty's (P) request for class certification. The District Court granted summary judgment in favor of the federal parole board (D). Geraghty (P) appealed both decisions, but was released from prison while the appeal was pending. Other prisoners that would have been in the class moved to have themselves substituted as the named plaintiffs in the case.

■ **ISSUE**

May an appellate court consider a challenge to a district court's denial of class certification if the named plaintiff's case is moot?

■ **DECISION AND RATIONALE**

(Blackmun, J.) Yes. In a case such as this one where the dispute remains between members of the potential class and the defendant, the mootness of the named plaintiff's case does not prevent appellate courts from considering an appeal of the class certification denial. The fact that other prisoners moved to have themselves substituted for the named plaintiff underscores that the controversy is ongoing. Our decision in *Sosna v. Iowa* stated that a class action, once certified, does not become moot simply because the named plaintiff's case becomes moot. This was because, in that case, the state might have enforced the challenged statute against others in the class. In *Franks v. Bowman Transportation Co.* we held that even if the claim of the named plaintiff had no chance to reoccur, certification of a class prior to expiration of the named plaintiff's claim would avoid mootness. Other decisions noted the flexibility and uncertainty of mootness analyses. Courts need to hear cases between self-interested parties that will strongly advocate their positions. This is why the federal courts require plaintiffs to have a sufficient personal stake in the outcome of the case. Our decisions in the above mentioned class action cases show that the courts believe that named plaintiffs can continue to be strong advocates for a class even after the named plaintiffs' cases have become moot. Likewise, the

United States Parole Commission v. Geraghty (Continued)

named plaintiff can advocate for reversal of the denial of class certification even after his case becomes moot. If the Court of Appeals reverses the trial court and the class is certified, then the named plaintiff could represent the class just as he would under our *Sosna* decision.

Analysis:

United States Parole Commission v. Geraghty illustrates a third exception to the mootness doctrine in federal courts, namely, an exception for many class action lawsuits. The general rule is that when class members continue to have "live" controversies, the fact that the named plaintiff's case becomes moot does not make the entire class action moot. The specific rule in *Geraghty*—that an appeal of a denial of class certification is not mooted because the named plaintiff's case was mooted—is a logical extension of this general rule. If a defendant could dispose of a class action simply by settling with one named plaintiff, he might have much less incentive to discontinue the behavior that led to the lawsuit in the first place. One interesting point in the reasoning behind cases like *Geraghty* and *Sosna* is that the court concludes that a named plaintiff can continue to represent the class effectively after his case is mooted. Would the truth of this statement ever depend on the way that the plaintiff's attorney was to be paid, i.e., whether he had a contingency based on the recovery of the class versus a flat fee or other arrangements? There are many ethical and conflict-of-interest considerations that attorneys in class action suits must consider.

■ **CASE VOCABULARY**

CLASS ACTION: A lawsuit in which an individual (the "named plaintiff") brings a claim on behalf of a larger group of people with the same claim.

CLASS CERTIFICATION: The legal announcement by the court that it will recognize a class of plaintiffs for a class action lawsuit; if a court declines to certify a class of plaintiffs, the individuals may pursue their own claims.

Baker v. Carr
(Tennessee Voters) v. *(Tennessee State Assembly)*
369 U.S. 186, 82 S.Ct. 691, 7 L.Ed.2d 663 (1962)

CLAIMS THAT STATE APPORTIONMENT VIOLATES THE GUARANTY CLAUSE ARE NONJUSTICIABLE 'POLITICAL QUESTIONS,' BUT CLAIMS BASED ON VIOLATION OF EQUAL PROTECTION ARE JUSTICIABLE

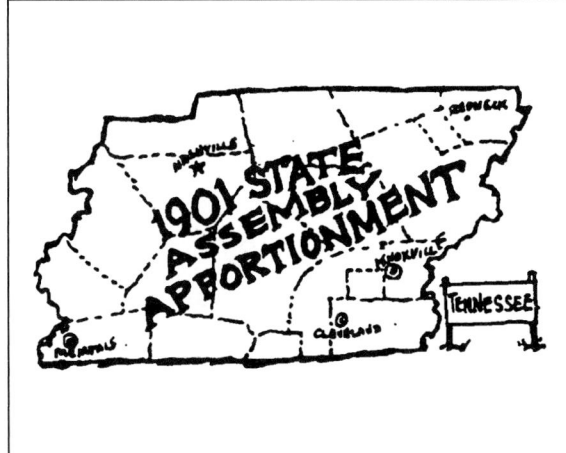

■ **INSTANT FACTS** Tennessee voters seek a reapportionment of state assembly districts; the districts have not been reapportioned since 1901.

■ **BLACK LETTER RULE** The Guaranty Clause may not be used as a source of a constitutional standard for invalidating state action, but an equal protection claim may be so used where it does not implicate a political question.

■ **PROCEDURAL BASIS**

Appeal from denial of injunction against elections and denial to order a reapportionment of assembly districts.

■ **FACTS**

Voters in Tennessee claimed that the apportionment of the Tennessee General Assembly violated their equal protection rights "by virtue of the debasement of their votes." The state constitution allocated representation based on population, but the assembly had not been reapportioned since 1901. Because of the malapportioned Assembly, the voters' group (P) contends that redress through changes in state law was difficult or impossible. They sought to enjoin any further elections under the 1901 apportionment, and asked a federal court either to direct elections at large or to decree an apportionment according to the most recent census figures. The lower court denied relief.

■ **ISSUE**

Does an equal protection claim complaining of the malapportionment of a state assembly constitute a non-justiciable political question, which the federal courts may not address?

■ **DECISION AND RATIONALE**

(Brennan, J.) No. This challenge to apportionment presents no non-justiciable "political question." The fact that the suit seeks protection of a political right does not mean that it is necessarily a political question. It has been argued that apportionment cases involve no federal constitutional right except one resting on Article IV, § 4, which guarantees a republican form of government. Based on a review of precedent, we hold that the case here neither rests upon nor implicates the Guaranty Clause. In Guaranty Clause and "political question" cases, it is the relationship between the judiciary and the coordinate branches of the Federal Government, and not the federal judiciary's relationship to the States, which gives rise to the "political question." Deciding whether a particular branch of government has constitutional authority over a measure, or whether an action exceeds constitutional authority, is a delicate exercise in constitutional interpretation, and is a responsibility of this Court as interpreter of the Constitution. In any case involving a political question is found (1) a constitutionally assigned duty or power to a branch of government; *or* (2) a lack of judicially manageable standards for resolving the

Baker v. Carr (Continued)

question; *or* (3) the impossibility of a court's deciding the issue without an initial policy determination of a kind clearly for non-judicial discretion; *or* (4) the impossibility of a court's undertaking independent resolution without expressing a lack of respect to other branches of government; *or* (5) an unusual need for adherence to a political decision already made; *or* (6) the potential for embarrassment from various pronouncements on a single issue by different departments of government. If none of these circumstances is present, the case should not be dismissed on the ground that it is a political question. The Supreme Court has refused to resort to the Guaranty Clause as a source of a constitutional standard for invalidating state action. As to this action, we note that none of the six circumstances listed above is present in the case. Judicial standards under the Equal Protection Clause are well developed, and the courts are given authority to decide whether a particular act reflects an arbitrary and capricious act of discrimination. This case involves the allocation of political power within a state, and the Tennessee Voters (P) could have added a claim under the Guaranty Clause, although the claim would have been futile. But just because a Guaranty Clause approach could not have succeeded does not mean that the voters cannot have their case heard on the equal protection claim. Reversed and remanded.

■ DISSENT

(Frankfurter, J.) The present case involves all of the elements that have made the Guaranty Clause case non-justiciable. It is, in effect, a Guaranty Clause claim masquerading under a different label. The gist of the complaint is the same regardless of the "equal protection" label. The voters are dissatisfied with Tennessee's basis of representation. They ask the Court to decide among competing bases of representation—really, among competing theories of political philosophy—in order to establish an appropriate frame of government for the State of Tennessee and thereby for all State of Tennessee and thereby for all the States of the Union. Apportionment is exceedingly complex, and does not lend itself to judicial determination. Furthermore, apportionment battles are overwhelmingly party or intra-party contests. It will add a great deal of friction to federal-state relations to involve the federal judiciary in this process.

Analysis:

Many people mistakenly believe that the Supreme Court always considers apportionment cases to contain nonjusticiable political questions, *Baker v. Carr* clarifies that it is not apportionment per se, but rather the Guaranty Clause that causes the Court trouble. The Guaranty Clause, said the majority, calls for Congress—not the courts—to determine the type of government that is established in a given state. The Court noted that this is why apportionment cases raised as alleged Guaranty Clause violations were refused on political question grounds. The claim in *Baker* was raised as a Fourteenth Amendment Equal Protection challenge. The Court found that the Constitution did not delegate decisions about Equal Protection to any other branch of government. Moreover, the Constitution and judicial precedent provided ample standards and guidelines for the courts to rule on Equal Protection issues. Thus, the issue presented in *Baker* was justiciable. Ultimately, the Court explained, arguments that cases involve political questions must be decided on a case-by-case basis.

■ CASE VOCABULARY

EQUAL PROTECTION CLAUSE: A Fourteenth Amendment clause providing that persons under the same circumstances shall be afforded the same constitutional rights.

GUARANTY CLAUSE: A clause in Article IV, § 4, providing that "the United States shall guarantee to every State in this Union a Republican Form of Government."

POLITICAL QUESTION: A question involving the use of discretionary authority by Congress or the Executive Branch.

Vieth v. Jubelirer

(North Carolina Resident) v. (State Official)
541 U.S. 267, 124 S.Ct. 1769 (2004)

POLITICAL GERRYMANDERING CLAIMS ARE NOT JUSTICIABLE

■ **INSTANT FACTS** Vieth (P) challenged state electoral districts established by the Pennsylvania General Assembly as unconstitutional political gerrymandering.

■ **BLACK LETTER RULE** When a legal claim has no judicially discoverable and manageable standards for resolving the issues presented, the claim is a nonjusticiable political question.

■ **PROCEDURAL BASIS**

Certiorari to review an undisclosed appellate decision.

■ **FACTS**

Following the 2000 census, Pennsylvania was entitled to nineteen Representatives in Congress, down two members from the previous election. The Republican-controlled General Assembly drew a new districting map under pressure from national Republicans to create Republican-favored districts, as retaliation for Democrat-favored districts created in other states. After the plan was adopted, Vieth (P) and other Pennsylvania Democrats challenged the plan as unconstitutional political gerrymandering.

■ **ISSUE**

Are political gerrymandering claims justiciable?

■ **DECISION AND RATIONALE**

(Scalia, J.) No. In *Davis v. Bandemer*, 478 U.S. 109 (1986), the Supreme Court held that political gerrymandering claims were justiciable but defined no standards under which such claims should be adjudicated. However, because political gerrymandering claims involve nonjusticiable political questions, *Bandemer* is overruled.

Although there are several tests for determining whether a political question exists, the Court has stated that "a lack of judicially discoverable and manageable standards for resolving" an issue calls for judicial abstention. When *Bandemer* was decided, six justices voted with the majority and three dissented. Of the six members of the majority, no agreement on the standard for adjudicating political gerrymandering claims was reached. Likewise, in the eighteen years since *Bandemer* was decided, lower courts have been unable to fashion a discernible and manageable standard applicable in such cases. Indeed, consideration of Vieth's (P) claims has garnered additional proposed standards from the Justices, demonstrating that there is no "judicially discoverable and manageable" standard for resolving political gerrymandering disputes. Although the day may come when a standard emerges, the Court cannot affirm merely because it does not know the standard to apply. Accordingly, such claims present nonjusticiable political questions.

■ **CONCURRENCE**

(Kennedy, J.) While the decision not to interfere in the political process by scrutinizing the district lines is correct in this case, the Court should have exercised caution in determining that no standard could

Vieth v. Jubelirer (Continued)

exist for sufficiently resolving the issues. The fact that no standard has developed in the eighteen years since *Bandemer* does not mean that no such standard may develop as society and the law progress. When important constitutional issues are raised, the Court should not foreclose the possibility that a standard could develop.

■ **DISSENT**

(Stevens, J.) The Court's insistence that there is no manageable standard by which to adjudicate gerrymandering cases ignores the fact that many different standards have been proposed by both judges and legislatures across the country. Differing views on the appropriate standard, many of which have been successful in managing gerrymanders, do not indicate that there is no manageable standard. Just as with racial gerrymandering, legislatures have a duty to treat all individuals equally and without preference. Applying these standards to political gerrymandering, district lines can be upheld only when the legislature points to some neutral justification unrelated to a desire to promote partisan strength.

■ **DISSENT**

(Souter, J.) Fairness requires more than districts drawn of equal numbers of voters, but rather requires that each voter's vote is equally meaningful. When districts are drawn to favor one political ideology over another, dissenting voters' votes are not equal to those of the majority. The reason there has been no development of a standard since *Bandemer*'s unworkable one was established is not because no workable standard exists, but rather because lower courts faced with gerrymandering cases have been bound to apply *Bandemer*'s unworkable standard.

Rather than overruling *Bandemer*, the Court should "make a fresh start" by adopting a manageable standard to guide lower courts. A plaintiff should be required to establish a prima facie case with five elements. First, the plaintiff must be a member of a "cohesive political group." Second, the plaintiff must demonstrate that the district plans ignore traditional considerations of contiguity, compactness, respect for political subdivisions, and geographic conformity. Third, there must be a specific correlation between the plan's deviations from such principles and the geographic division. Fourth, there must be a hypothetical district that will deviate less from traditional principles. Finally, the plaintiff must establish an intention to shape the district for political purposes. The burden would then shift to the defendant to justify the districting plan with other than partisan objectives. Based on this standard, political gerrymandering cases could be subject to judicial consideration.

■ **DISSENT**

(Breyer, J.) Political gerrymandering can promote democratic virtues to some, while simultaneously eroding democratic protections to others. When such a circumstance is proven, equal protection compels judicial scrutiny under the Constitution. Political gerrymandering artificially controls democratic elections by ensuring reelection of incumbents and making it difficult for minority voters to remove unwanted elected officials. While state and federal action can protect against such abuse, one should not rely upon the legislatures establishing self-serving voting districts for a remedy. Courts have developed district boundary lines in the past and should not be precluded from doing so in the future.

Analysis:

The stark differences among the justices illustrate the difficult questions often presented in cases deciding the justiciability of a claim. While the various dissenting justices appear willing to keep up the fight to develop a justiciable standard, the Court's plurality decision appears to foreclose that possibility. Just as Justice Souter pointed out, no manageable standard arose following *Bandemer* because the Court's decision prevented lower courts from exploring different standards. The Court's decision in *Vieth* seems to forever foreclose the possibility that such a standard will emerge.

■ CASE VOCABULARY

GERRYMANDERING: The practice of dividing a geographical area into electoral districts, often of highly irregular shape, to give one political party an unfair advantage by diluting the opposition's voting strength.

JUSTICIABILITY: The quality or state of being appropriate or suitable for review by a court.

POLITICAL QUESTION: A question that a court will not consider because it involves the exercise of discretionary power by the executive or legislative branch of government.

Powell v. McCormack

(*Member-elect of Congress*) v. (*Not Stated*)
395 U.S. 486, 89 S.Ct. 1944 (1969)

POLITICAL QUESTION DOCTRINE DOES NOT BAR THE COURTS FROM DECIDING WHETHER CONGRESS HAS POWER TO REFUSE TO SEAT A MEMBER-ELECT

■ **INSTANT FACTS** The 90th Congress voted not to seat member-elect Powell due to his past improprieties.

■ **BLACK LETTER RULE** The political question doctrine does not bar the federal courts from deciding a case concerning Congress's powers to determine its membership when the text of the Constitution does not specifically commit the issue in the case to Congressional resolution.

■ **PROCEDURAL BASIS**

Not stated.

■ **FACTS**

During the 89th Congress, Adam Clayton Powell, Jr. (P) served as Representative from New York's 18th District. Powell (P) was Chairman of the Committee on Education and Labor. A special subcommittee of the Committee on House Administration Investigated Powell (P) and produced a report citing evidence of illegal payments Powell (P) authorized to his wife and deceptive expense reports by Powell (P). Congress did not take action during the 89th Congress, although the Democratic caucus stripped Powell (P) of his Committee chairmanship. In 1966, voters reelected Powell (P) but Congress refused allow Powell (P) to take the oath of office, and after a report and a vote, decided not to seat Powell (P). Powell (P) sued to gain his seat in Congress. Congress (D) argued that the federal courts were barred from hearing the case due to the political question doctrine. Congress (D) argued that Article I, § 5 of the Constitution gives Congress (D) the sole authority to determine the qualifications for membership. Powell (P) argued that Article I, § 5 permitted Congress (D) to judge whether members-elect meet the membership qualifications outlined in the Constitution, but not the power to exclude those who met the stated qualifications.

■ **ISSUE**

Does the political question doctrine bar the federal courts from deciding the question of whether Congress, by majority vote, has the discretionary authority to deny a member-elect membership?

■ **DECISION AND RATIONALE**

(Warren, Chief Justice) No. Because the text of the Constitution does not commit to Congress a blanket authority to determine whether to seat a member-elect, the courts are not barred from deciding the issue. The rule to apply in this case is that the courts should refuse to decide cases in which the Constitution has explicitly committed the issue to the discretion of one of the other branches of government. Review of the documents and debates of the Framers of the Constitution leads to the conclusion that the phrase "be the Judge of the Qualifications of its own Members" in Article I, § 5 was not intended to give Congress authority to deny a seat to a duly elected member through a majority vote. This conclusion is consistent with the Framers' requirement that the House have a super-majority

Powell v. McCormack (Continued)

in order to expel a member. We agree with Powell (P) that Article I, § 5 demonstrably commits to Congress only the authority to judge the qualifications enumerated in the Constitution. For this reason, the political questions doctrine does not prevent the federal courts from deciding this case.

Analysis:

The federal courts consider issues of congressional self-governance to be political questions generally inappropriate for judicial resolution. Nevertheless, in *Powell* the Court was willing to step in and enjoin Congress from refusing to seat the plaintiff, a member-elect of the House. In determining whether the issue in *Powell* was a political question, the Court undertook a deep historical analysis of the Framers' intent for the key constitutional provision in the case—that Congress is empowered to be "the Judge of the Qualifications of its Members." The Court concluded that the Framers intended for Congress (indeed, for the Government as a whole) to give great deference to the will of the voters. Thus, the Court reasoned, the Framers did not intend to give Congress broad discretion to decide who it could or could not seat. The Court found further support for this position in other portions of the Constitution. Specifically, the Constitution calls for a two-thirds supermajority for Congress to expel a member. The Court reasoned that this provision is consistent with limitations on Congress's ability to keep members-elect from being seated. The Court's decision is consistent with the idea that to "judge" is to interpret the law as it is given or to announce what the law is.

Goldwater v. Carter

(*United States Senator*) v. (*United States President*)
444 U.S. 996, 100 S.Ct. 533 (1979)

THE ROLES OF THE SENATE AND PRESIDENT IN THE TERMINATION OF TREATIES IS A POLITICAL QUESTION THAT THE COURTS WILL NOT DECIDE

■ **INSTANT FACTS** In conjunction with normalizing U.S. relations with the Mainland Chinese government, President Carter terminated the United States treaty with Taiwan.

■ **BLACK LETTER RULE** The Senate's role in the termination of treaties is a nonjusticiable political question.

■ PROCEDURAL BASIS
Appeal from a decision of the federal Court of Appeals.

■ FACTS
In conjunction with actions recognizing the People's Republic of China, President Jimmy Carter terminated the United States treaty with Taiwan. The treaty was concerned with defense and other issues. The Senate debated a resolution that would have stated that Senate approval was required in the termination of this type of treaty. The Senate resolution never came to a vote. Some Members of Congress, led by Senator Barry Goldwater (P) sued, claiming that the President's actions were unconstitutional, because Article II, Section 2 requires the Senate to ratify treaties.

■ ISSUE
Is the proper role of the Senate in the rescission of treaties a question that the federal courts may resolve?

■ DECISION AND RATIONALE
(Rehnquist, J.) No. The issue of whether the Senate is required to rescind foreign treaties or to ratify the President's rescission is a political question beyond the scope of the federal courts. The issue is political because it involves a foreign policy decision of the President and a treaty involving potential commitments of military troops. The question of whether Congress is authorized to halt the President's decision is likewise political. Although the Constitution directs the Senate to ratify treaties, it says nothing as to the rescission or termination of treaties. The President and Congress should resolve the dispute among themselves. Because this case involves a nonjusticiable political question, the decision of the Court of Appeals is vacated and the case is remanded to the District Court with an order to dismiss the case.

■ CONCURRENCE
(Powell, J.) The case should be dismissed, but for the reason that it is not ripe. Neither the Executive nor the Legislature has yet asserted its authority. For prudential reasons, the federal courts should avoid encouraging litigation involving the division of power between the other two branches, unless or until those branches are at an irreconcilable stalemate over their powers or authorities under the constitution.

Goldwater v. Carter (Continued)

■ CONCURRENCE AND DISSENT

(Brennan, J.) This case is not ripe for judgment because Congress, as a body, has not voted on whether to challenge the President's decision to rescind the Taiwan treaty. The Court should not challenge the President on its own initiative. However, the majority is incorrect that the federal courts could never decide the issue. If this case were a ripe dispute, application of the three *Baker v. Carr* questions leads to the conclusion that the courts should decide the case. The first question from *Baker* is whether the text of the Constitution explicitly makes another branch of government responsible for resolving the dispute. In this case, it does not. No provision in the Constitution states that the President alone has the authority to rescind treaties, while there are provisions calling for the Senate's "advice and consent" in treaty making. The second *Baker* question is whether the dispute is beyond the court's judicial expertise. Again, the answer is no. The courts have principles for the interpretation of provisions in the Constitution. In deciding whether the Constitution requires the Senate to ratify a treaty rescission, we would not be reviewing the President's policy choices. Simply because an issue involves foreign policy does not make it a nonjusticiable political question. Finally, the third *Baker* question is whether the court should decline to address an issue for prudential reasons. This answer in this case is no. The prudential reasons militating in favor of the court declining political questions involves instances where there is a special need to avoid conflicting pronouncements from different branches of the government or to not upset a political decision. Those reasons are not present here. It is the duty of the court to interpret the Constitution and resolve stalemates in interpretation between the other two branches.

Analysis:

The majority has two primary reasons for considering Goldwater's challenge to the President a political question. First, the Court points out that the dispute is over the President's authority to dissolve a foreign treaty without Senate approval. This question, says the Court, involves foreign policy, and the courts will generally decline cases involving foreign policy issues. Although the Court said in *Baker v. Carr* that not every foreign policy issue is a "political question," the Court will, in general, avoid such cases when possible. The majority's second point is that the Constitution does not explicitly define the Senate's role in treaty dissolution. Thus, says the majority, the Executive branch and Senate should resolve the issue between them. Justice Powell's concurrence noted that since neither the Executive branch nor the Senate had asserted its authority or tried to resolve the dispute (either amicably or otherwise), the case simply was not ripe for decision. Powell's opinion does not pass judgment on whether the case presents a political question. While Justice Powell's Concurrence leaves that question unresolved, Justice Brennan's Concurrence in Judgment and Dissent are a kind of flipside to the majority opinion. To begin with, Brennan's opinion agrees with Powell's that the case simply is not ripe. Brennan is willing to go further than Powell, however, and declare that if this case were to become ripe, it would be exactly the type of dispute that the federal courts are duty-bound *to* resolve.

Nixon v. United States

(*Impeached Judge*) v. (*Government*)
506 U.S. 224, 113 S.Ct. 732 (1993)

FEDERAL COURTS ARE NOT AUTHORIZED TO REVIEW IMPEACHMENTS, WHICH THE CONSTITUTION EXPLICITLY CONFERS TO CONGRESS

■ **INSTANT FACTS** A federal judge, impeached by the Senate, challenged the constitutionality of the Senate's impeachment procedure.

■ **BLACK LETTER RULE** The judiciary may not review the Senate's trial of an impeached official.

■ PROCEDURAL BASIS

Appeal of Court of Appeals decision holding that challenge to impeachment conviction is nonjusticiable.

■ FACTS

Nixon (P) was a federal district court judge who was convicted of making false statements before a federal grand jury. The grand jury investigation arose from reports that Nixon (P) had accepted money in exchange for asking a district attorney to halt a prosecution. After his conviction, Nixon (P) refused to resign as judge and continued to collect his salary while in prison. The House of Representatives adopted articles of impeachment against Nixon (P) and presented them to the Senate. The Senate then invoked Impeachment Rule XI under which a committee of Senators is appointed to receive evidence and take testimony. After the Senate committee held an extensive hearing, it presented the Senate with a full transcript and a summary of the contested facts. Final arguments were held before the entire Senate. The Senate voted by more than the constitutionally required 2/3 majority to convict Nixon (P) and remove him from office. Nixon (P) sued the U.S. arguing that Senate Rule XI violated the Senate's constitutional authority to "try" all impeachments because it prohibited the whole Senate from taking part in the evidentiary hearing. The district court and the Court of Appeals for the District of Columbia Circuit held that Nixon's (P) claim was nonjusticiable. Nixon (P) appealed.

■ ISSUE

Is a challenge to a conviction on impeachment articles by the Senate justiciable?

■ DECISION AND RATIONALE

(Rehnquist, C.J.) No. A controversy is nonjusticiable if the Constitution commits the issue to another branch of government. Article I, section 3, clause 6 of the Constitution gives the Senate sole power to try all impeachments. Nixon (P) argues that "try" means that the procedure must be like a judicial trial and that, therefore, the Senate may not delegate to a committee the task of hearing witnesses' testimony. However, both in 1787 and today, "try" has a broader meaning than that. The word is not very precise and, therefore, does not limit the procedure the Senate may use to carry out its duties. This is in contrast to the three specific requirements that the Constitution does impose on the Senate, i.e., that the members must be under oath, that a 2/3 majority is required to convict, and that the Chief Justice [mel] presides when the President is tried. The word "sole" is of considerable significance. It means that only the Senate may determine whether someone should be acquitted or convicted of impeachment. Therefore, the courts have no part in the matter. Nixon (P) argues that "sole" means that the entire Senate, not a Senate committee, must conduct the trial. Clause 6 may be read this way, but this is not a natural reading. Nixon (P) does not offer any evidence from history or any commentary that suggests the possibility of judicial review of impeachment. The framers of the Constitution considered giving the judiciary power over impeachments, but decided against it for several reasons. First, the framers thought that the judiciary did not have the credit and authority of the legislature, which is the people's representative. Second, the framers believed that the judiciary was too small in number. Also, the framers recognized that, in addition to the impeachment proceeding, there would be a separate criminal trial that would involve the judiciary. The two proceedings remain separate in order to avoid any bias. Also, judicial review would be inconsistent with checks and balances because impeachment is the legislature's only check on the judicial branch. Nixon (P) argues that without judicial review, the Senate could usurp judicial power. However, two constitutional safeguards keep the Senate in check. First, the impeachment power is divided between the House and the Senate, with the House acting as the accusers and the Senate acting as the judges. Second, a 2/3 majority is required to convict. Also, judicial review would bring about a lack of finality over a long period of time, leading to uncertainty and possible illegitimacy to any successor. Judicial review would also present the problem of what type of relief would be available. Affirmed.

■ CONCURRENCE

(White, J.) I disagree that this matter is nonjusticiable. However, I concur in the judgment because the Senate fulfilled its constitutional obligation to try Nixon (P). The Senate has very wide discretion in carrying out its impeachment powers. However, to hold that the Senate's power is never reviewable could lead the Senate to be dismissive of its critical role in the impeachment process. Nonetheless, an issue is nonjusticiable if the Constitution has given one of the branches of government final responsibility for interpreting the scope and nature of a particular government function. There are few, if any, instances of this in the Constitution. The word "sole" is used to emphasize that only the Senate has the power to act as judge in the impeachment process and that only the House has the power to bring articles of impeachment. The House, not the judiciary, is the source of potential interference with the Senate. Allowing judicial review would promote checks and balances by ensuring that the Senate adhered to a minimal set of procedural standards in impeachment trials. The majority holds that the word "try" provides no identifiable textual limits. However, the word "try" presents no greater interpretive difficulties than other words that have been amenable to judicial construction. Rule XI is compatible with the Constitution's command that the Senate try all impeachments.

■ CONCURRENCE

(Souter, J.) Whether an issue is a political question requires a case-by-case inquiry. The Senate has broad boundaries for determining the procedures for trying someone for impeachment. This case is nonjusticiable because we should adhere to a political decision that was already made and because we should avoid the potential embarrassment of multiple decisions on a single question. However, judicial review may be necessary if the Senate acted in a way that seriously threatened the integrity of its decision, convicting, say, upon a coin toss.

Analysis:

As the concurrences suggest, this case was a rather easy one for the Supreme Court to refuse to hear because Nixon (P) received due process in the Senate. If his Senate hearing had been less comprehensive, as Justice Souter suggested, maybe the Court would have ruled that it could review the Senate's procedures. Or, if an official subject to impeachment is despised by over two-thirds of the Senate for political reasons, should the Court intervene on the assumption that the Senate's motives were improper in convicting the official? Note that other issues that the Court has ruled are nonjusticiable include regulation of the National Guard, issues regarding the Guarantee Clause of the Constitution, and issues of foreign relations, such as recognition of foreign governments and the President's ability to declare a war without Congressional authorization.

■ **CASE VOCABULARY**

IMPEACHMENT: The constitutional process whereby the House of Representatives may "impeach" (accuse of misconduct) high officers of the federal government for trial in the Senate.

NONJUSTICIABLE: A case that is not appropriate for judicial review.

CHAPTER TWO

The Federal Legislative Power

McCulloch v. Maryland

Instant Facts: Maryland (P) attempted to impose a tax on the federal bank. The bank's cashier, McCulloch (D) refused to pay the tax. Maryland (P) sued McCulloch (D), arguing that (1) the establishment of the bank is unconstitutional, and (2) the bank may be forced to pay state taxes.

Black Letter Rule: Under the Necessary and Proper Clause, Congress may enact legislation so long as its ends are legitimate under the Constitution and the legislation is appropriate and plainly adapted to those ends.

Gibbons v. Ogden

Instant Facts: Ogden (D) was granted an exclusive ferry operations license by New York State. Gibbons (P) began a competing ferry service and challenges Ogden's (D) exclusive license under the Commerce Clause.

Black Letter Rule: The federal commerce power extends to all commerce among and between the states and foreign nations, with only commerce having connections solely within a single state being unreachable under the commerce power.

United States v. E. C. Knight Co.

Instant Facts: A sugar refining company gained a monopoly in the industry by purchasing several other refineries.

Black Letter Rule: Manufacturing is separate from "commerce" because it occurs before any goods are transported in interstate commerce, and thus the federal government may not regulate manufacturing in and of itself.

Carter v. Carter Coal Co.

Instant Facts: Congress passed, pursuant to its commerce power, a law regulating the management-employee relations in the coal mining industry. The law is being challenged on the ground that Congress does not have the power to regulate such activities because they do not constitute "interstate commerce."

Black Letter Rule: Purely local activities, such as the negotiation of wages and working conditions, are outside of the Congress' realm of authority under the Commerce Clause.

Houston, East & West Texas Railway Company v. United States [The Shreveport Rate Cases]

Instant Facts: Due to state regulations of intrastate transport, a railway company charged much higher rates for interstate transport between Shreveport, Louisiana and certain Texas locations than it did for transport exclusively within Texas, leading the Interstate Commerce Commission to implement price controls.

Black Letter Rule: Congress has authority to regulate intrastate commerce where it has the potential to affect interstate commerce absent federal regulation.

A.L.A. Schecter Poultry Corporation v. United States

Instant Facts: Congress enacted a law governing wages, working conditions, and prices for poultry transported in interstate commerce. Wholesalers that purchase the chickens after they've arrived in-state challenge the law as unconstitutional.

Black Letter Rule: Once goods that have traveled in interstate commerce are sold or disposed of in the state of their final destination, they are no longer in interstate commerce and thus not subject to federal law.

Hammer v. Dagenhart

Instant Facts: A father wanting to put his two minor children to work in a cotton mill is suing on the ground that Congress' use of the commerce power to regulate child labor in the states by blocking the interstate transportation of child-made goods is unconstitutional.

Black Letter Rule: The commerce power does not allow Congress to regulate in areas traditionally left up to the states' police power, such as the area of child labor laws.

Champion v. Ames (The Lottery Case)

Instant Facts: The Federal Lottery Act prohibited interstate shipment of lottery tickets. It is being challenged as unconstitutional in that such shipments are not commerce.

Black Letter Rule: Congress may, pursuant to the Commerce Clause, prohibit the interstate shipment of items adjudged to be evil or pestilent in order to protect the commerce concerning all states.

N.L.R.B. v. Jones & Laughlin Steel Corp.

Instant Facts: A steel corporation whose operations span the continent is being sued by the government for violating the National Labor Relations Act for committing unfair labor practices.

Black Letter Rule: Congressional power to regulate interstate commerce extends to the regulation of intrastate activities that may burden or obstruct interstate commerce.

United States v. Darby

Instant Facts: A Georgia lumber company violated federal minimum wage/maximum hour laws. Its defense is that the federal government overreached its Commerce Clause authority in setting the standards.

Black Letter Rule: Congress has the authority, under the Commerce Clause, to exclude any article from interstate commerce, in judgment that they are injurious to the public health, morals or welfare.

Wickard v. Filburn

Instant Facts: Wickard (P) exceeded his allotted quota for wheat production, the excess amount to be used for his own consumption. He was fined by the government and seeks to have the quota ruled unconstitutional.

Black Letter Rule: Congress' commerce authority extends to all activities having a substantial effect on interstates commerce, including those that do not have such a substantial effect individually, but do when judged by their national aggregate effects.

Heart of Atlanta Motel, Inc. v. United States

Instant Facts: An Atlanta, Georgia motel wishes to continue its racially discriminatory operations in spite of the 1964 Civil Rights Act (Act) barring racial discrimination in public accommodations.

Black Letter Rule: Congress has the power, under the Commerce Clause, to regulate local activities that could reasonably be seen as exerting a substantial and harmful effect upon interstate commerce.

Katzenbach v. McClung, Sr. and McClung, Jr.

Instant Facts: The owners of a restaurant in Birmingham, Alabama continued to exclude Negro patrons from their restaurant dining area, in violation of the Civil Rights Act of 1964.

Black Letter Rule: Congress' commerce authority extends to any public commercial establishment selling goods that have moved in interstate commerce and/or serving interstate travelers.

National League of Cities v. Usery

Instant Facts: An amendment to the Fair Labor Standards Act extended wage and hour requirements to state employees. The States are seeking to have the regulations as applied to them declared unconstitutional.

Black Letter Rule: The Commerce Clause does not empower Congress to regulate states or local governments in their integral governmental functions.

Garcia v. San Antonio Metropolitan Transit Authority

Instant Facts: Application of the Fair Labor Standards Act to a city's mass transit system fuels a revisitation of National League of Cities v. Usery.

Black Letter Rule: Congress has full authority under the Commerce Clause to regulate the traditional, or core, functions of state and local governments notwithstanding the Tenth Amendment.

United States v. Lopez

Instant Facts: A 12th-grade student was convicted of violating the Gun–Free School Zones Act of 1990, which makes it a federal offense to possess a gun near a school.

Black Letter Rule: Congressional authority to regulate pursuant to the Commerce Clause extends to only those activities that rationally implicate (1) the channels of interstate commerce; (2) the instrumentalities of interstate commerce; or (3) activities having a substantial effect upon interstate commerce.

United States v. Morrison

Instant Facts: An alleged rape victim sought to sue her accused attackers under the federal Violence Against Women Act (Act or VAWA). The accused asserts that VAWA is an unconstitutional exercise of congressional authority.

Black Letter Rule: Congress may not, pursuant to the Commerce Clause, regulate a local activity solely on the basis that it has substantial effects on interstate commerce when viewed in its nationwide aggregate.

Pierce County, Washington v. Guillen

Instant Facts: Guillen (P) sought through discovery to obtain information from Pierce County, Washington (D), concerning accidents occurring at the intersection where his wife died.

Black Letter Rule: Under the Commerce Clause, Congress is empowered to regulate and protect the instrumentalities of interstate commerce, even though the threat may come only from intrastate commerce.

Gonzales v. Raich

Instant Facts: Raich (P) sought an injunction against enforcement of the federal Controlled Substances Act, insofar as that law prohibited her use of marijuana for medical purposes.

Black Letter Rule: Congress may regulate intrastate activity if there is a rational basis for concluding that the activity may have a substantial effect on interstate commerce.

New York v. United States

Instant Facts: Congress passed legislation requiring states to either provide for radioactive waste disposal or take title to waste generated within their borders. The legislation is being challenged as an unconstitutional exercise of federal power over the States.

Black Letter Rule: Congress does not have the authority to commandeer state governments by forcing them to implement particular regulations.

Printz v. United States

Instant Facts: The federal Brady Act required local law enforcement officials to temporarily administer its background check program. Two local law enforcement officers challenge the Brady Act's impressment of local law enforcement officials.

Black Letter Rule: Congress does not have authority to compel states to enact, enforce, or administer federal regulatory programs, and cannot circumvent this prohibition by conscripting state officials directly.

Reno v. Condon

Instant Facts: Congress passed legislation placing certain prohibitions on the dissemination of private information given states by individuals in applying for a driver's license. One State challenges the constitutionality of the legislation as it applies to states.

Black Letter Rule: States are required to comply with constitutionally valid legislation regulating state activities, even when compliance means incurring additional costs to be borne by the States.

United States v. Butler

Instant Facts: Congress attempted to regulate the quantity of local agricultural production through use of the taxing and spending powers. The regulation is challenged as being outside Congress's enumerated powers.

Black Letter Rule: Congress may not use the taxing or spending powers to force compliance in an area where the Constitution does not give Congress independent power to regulate.

Sabri v. United States

Instant Facts: Sabri (D) challenged a federal anti-bribery statute as facially unconstitutional.

Black Letter Rule: Under the Spending Clause, Congress is authorized to appropriate federal funds for the general welfare and use all rational means necessary and proper to further its spending power.

South Dakota v. Dole

Instant Facts: South Dakota (P) challenges a federal law withholding 5% of federal highway funds from any state with a drinking-age limit less than 21 years-of-age.

Black Letter Rule: Valid use of the Spending power is subject to three requirements: (1) It must be used for the general welfare; (2) Any conditions on receipt of funds must be unambiguous; and (3) Any conditions must be related to the federal interest in the particular national projects or programs being funded.

United States v. Morrison

Instant Facts: An alleged rape victim sought to sue her accused attackers under the federal Violence Against Women Act (Act or VAWA). The accused asserts that VAWA is an unconstitutional exercise of congressional authority.

Black Letter Rule: Congress's authority to regulate under the Fourteenth Amendment extends only to state activity, not activities of private individuals.

Katzenbach v. Morgan & Morgan

Instant Facts: New York voters are challenging a federal law prohibiting New York from enforcing its English literacy voting requirement.

Black Letter Rule: Section 5 of the Fourteenth Amendment authorizes Congress to enact remedial legislation prohibiting enforcement of state laws found to abrogate civil rights, even though such state laws are not unconstitutional.

City of Boerne v. Flores

Instant Facts: Flores (P), after the City of Boerne (D) denied a permit to expand the church, is suing under the Religious Freedom Restoration Act (RFRA).

Black Letter Rule: Section 5 of the Fourteenth Amendment gives Congress the power to enact laws as remedial measures and to prevent constitutional violations, but does not allow Congress to define the substantive scope of constitutional guarantees.

Fitzpatrick v. Bitzer

Instant Facts: Congress amended Title VII of the Civil Rights Act to allow a federal cause of action against state governments for employment discrimination. The provision is being challenged under the Eleventh Amendment.

Black Letter Rule: No constitutional provision prohibits Congress from providing for a private cause of action in the federal courts against a state government as a means of enforcing the guarantees of the Fourteenth Amendment.

Seminole Tribe of Florida v. Florida

Instant Facts: Congress passed a law allowing states to be sued for failing to negotiate in good faith with Indian tribes regarding the formation of gaming compacts between those parties. The law is challenged as a violation of the Eleventh Amendment's sovereign immunity.

Black Letter Rule: Congress may not, outside enforcement of Fourteenth Amendment Guarantees, authorize federal lawsuits against states in abrogation of the Eleventh Amendment's guarantee of state sovereign immunity.

Florida Prepaid Postsecondary Education Expense Board v. College Savings Bank and United States

Instant Facts: Congress enacted legislation providing a right to sue states in federal court over patent infringement. The legislation is challenged as beyond Congress's Fourteenth Amendment enforcement authority.

Black Letter Rule: For Congress's abrogation of State sovereignty pursuant to the Fourteenth Amendment to be constitutional, it must (1) show a history or pattern of unconstitutional activity by States giving rise to a need for remedial or preventive federal regulation, and (2) limit the scope of the remedy, making it proportionate to the constitutional violations giving rise to the need for enforcement.

Kimel v. Florida Board of Regents

Instant Facts: Congress extended coverage of federal age discrimination laws to the States using its 5 authority to enforce the Fourteenth Amendment. The extension is challenged as outside the scope of this authority.

Black Letter Rule: In order for Congressional legislation abrogating State sovereign immunity pursuant to § 5 of the Fourteenth Amendment to be valid, its substantive requirements must be congruent with and proportionate to the unconstitutional actions of the States.

Board of Trustees v. Garrett

Instant Facts: State employees sued the State of Alabama for disability discrimination in employment.

Black Letter Rule: The Americans with Disabilities Act does not hold state governments liable for employment discrimination on the basis of an employee's disability.

Nevada Department of Natural Resources v. Hibbs

Instant Facts: Hibbs (P) sued his government employer for wrongful discharge and violations of the Family and Medical Leave Act when he was fired while caring for his injured wife.

Black Letter Rule: State governments are liable for money damages for interfering or restraining state employees' exercise of their rights under the Family and Medical Leave Act of 1993.

Tennessee v. Lane

Instant Facts: Two disabled individuals sued the State of Tennessee (D) and several counties under Title II of the Americans with Disabilities Act of 1990.

Black Letter Rule: To abrogate the states' Eleventh Amendment immunity, Congress must have unequivocally expressed its intent to abrogate that immunity and do so under a valid grant of constitutional authority.

United States v. Georgia

Instant Facts: Goodman (P) brought an action against the state of Georgia (D) for violations of the Americans with Disabilities Act, and Georgia (D) claimed that the suit was barred by sovereign immunity.

Black Letter Rule: The enforcement power in the Fourteenth Amendment gives Congress the power to create a private right of action for violations of the Amendment.

Alden v. Maine

Instant Facts: Two probation officers sued their state employer in state court for violating federal employment laws. The State raises the state sovereign immunity defense.

Black Letter Rule: Congress does not possess the authority, under its Article I powers, to abrogate the States' sovereign immunity from suits in its own state courts.

McCulloch v. Maryland
(Federal Bank Cashier) v. *(State)*
17 U.S. (4 Wheat.) 316 (1819)

THE NECESSARY AND PROPER CLAUSE ALLOWS FOR A FEDERAL BANK WHICH IS IMMUNE FROM STATE CONTROLS

■ **INSTANT FACTS** Maryland (P) attempted to impose a tax on the federal bank. The bank's cashier, McCulloch (D) refused to pay the tax. Maryland (P) sued McCulloch (D), arguing that (1) the establishment of the bank is unconstitutional, and (2) the bank may be forced to pay state taxes.

■ **BLACK LETTER RULE** Under the Necessary and Proper Clause, Congress may enact legislation so long as its ends are legitimate under the Constitution and the legislation is appropriate and plainly adapted to those ends.

■ **PROCEDURAL BASIS**
Review by the United States Supreme Court of a judgment for a statutory penalty imposed on the bank by the State.

■ **FACTS**
The State of Maryland (P) imposed a tax on any bank operating within its territories without state authority. Maryland (P) attained a judgment against McCulloch (D), cashier for the Baltimore branch of the Bank of the United States, for issuing bank notes without payment of the state-imposed tax.

■ **ISSUE**
1) May Congress constitutionally establish/incorporate a national bank? 2) May a state impose restrictions/controls on federally established agencies against the federal government's directives?

■ **DECISION AND RATIONALE**
(Marshall, C.J.) 1) Yes. 2) No. With regard to the bank, an exposition of the Constitution, deliberately established by legislative acts ought not to be lightly disregarded. The bill establishing the Bank of the United States did not steal upon an unsuspecting legislature, and pass unobserved. Its principle was completely understood, and was opposed with equal zeal and ability. It would require no ordinary share of intrepidity, to assert that a measure adopted under these circumstances, was a bold and plain usurpation of state powers, to which the Constitution gave no authorization. Maryland (P) asserts that the Constitution and the powers it vests in the federal government emanates not from the people, but as the act of sovereign and independent states, i.e. that the powers of the general government are delegated by the states and must be exercised in subordination to the states. This is difficult to sustain. The document that became our Constitution was written by a convention of state delegates, chosen in each state by the people thereof, under recommendation of its legislature. Through this mechanism, the document was submitted to the people. They acted on it in the only feasible manner available, by assembling in convention. A nationwide popular referendum would have been unthinkable, even to a political dreamer. Of consequence, when they act, they act in their states. But the measures they adopt do not, on that account, cease to be the measures of the people themselves. The government thus proceeds directly from the people. The Constitution, when thus adopted, was of complete obligation, and bound the state sovereignties. The government of the Union then, is truly a government of the people. But this government is one of enumerated powers, i.e. it can exercise only the powers granted

McCulloch v. Maryland (Continued)

to it. It is, however, supreme within its sphere of action. This is evident in the document itself where it states that "this Constitution, and the laws of the United States, which shall be made in pursuance thereof," "shall be the supreme law of the land," to which members of state legislatures, and state officials, take an oath of fidelity. Its laws, therefore, when made in pursuance of the Constitution, form the supreme law of the land. Among these enumerated powers we do not find that of establishing a bank or creating a corporation. On the other hand, we do not find in the Constitution any phrase excluding incidental or implied powers. Indeed, for a constitution to include an accurate detail of all the subdivisions of which its great powers will admit, along with all the means by which they might be carried into execution, would be too complex to enact and administer. Its nature, therefore, requires that only its great outlines should be marked, its important objects designated, and the minor ingredients which compose those objects, be deduced from the nature of the objects themselves. So though we do not find the word "bank" in the Constitution, we do find the great powers, to lay and collect taxes; to borrow money; to regulate commerce, etc. Such powers imply the ordinary means of execution. That, for example, of raising revenue, and applying it to national purposes, is admitted to imply the power of conveying money from place to place, as circumstances may require. But it is denied that the government has its choice of means. However, the government which has a right to do an act, and has a duty of performing such act, must, according to the dictates of reason, be allowed to select the means. To this end, the Constitution provides the power to make "all laws which shall be necessary and proper, for carrying into execution the foregoing powers, and all other powers vested by this constitution, in the government of the United States ...." Maryland (P) would read the word "necessary" as controlling the whole sentence, and as limiting the right to pass laws for the execution of the granted powers, to such as are indispensable, and without which the power would be nugatory. That it excludes the choice of means, and leaves to Congress that which is most direct and simple. The word "necessary," however, has several meanings. In its usual sense, it implies no more than that one thing is convenient, or useful, or essential to another. To employ means necessary to an end is, therefore, understood as employing any means calculated to produce the end. This word, then, like others, is used in various senses; and, in its construction, the subject, the context, the intention of the person using them, are all to be taken into view. In the present context the subject is the execution of those great powers on which the welfare of a nation essentially depends. It must have been the intention of those who gave these powers to ensure their beneficial execution. Confining the choice of means to very narrow limits could not do this. The provision is made in a constitution, intended to endure for ages to come, and thus, to be adapted to the various crises of human affairs. Otherwise, the legislature would be deprived of the capacity to avail itself of experience, to exercise its reason, and to accommodate its legislation to circumstances. Additionally, this clause is found among the powers of Congress, not its limitations. Its terms purport to enlarge, not to diminish the powers vested in government. Had the intention been to make this clause restrictive, it would unquestionably have been so in form as well as in effect. Let the end be legitimate, let it be within the scope of the Constitution, and all means which are appropriate, which are plainly adapted to that end, which are not prohibited, but consist with the letter and spirit of the Constitution, are constitutional. The incorporation of the bank is constitutional. We turn now to the question of whether Maryland (P) may tax the bank. The states retain the power of taxation, a power that is not abridged by a grant of a similar power to the Union. This power is to be concurrently exercised by both governments. The Constitution, however, has the capacity to withdraw any subject from the action of even this power. For instance, the states are forbidden to collect taxes on imports and exports. Therefore, when a state's use of its taxing power is in its nature incompatible with the constitutional laws of the Union, it must give sway to the commands of the Constitution, which are supreme. A power to create implies a power to preserve. A power to destroy, if wielded by a different hand, is hostile to, and incompatible with these powers to create and preserve. Where such a repugnancy exists, that authority which is supreme must control. As we have seen, Congress had the authority to create the bank. The power to tax the bank, wielded by the states, is the power to destroy it. The Supremacy Clause allows the removal of all obstacles to its action within its own sphere, and to modify every power vested in subordinate governments, as to exempt its own operations from their own influence. A state may not trifle with the means properly employed by Congress in executing the powers conferred on it by the people of the United States. These powers are not given by the people of a single state, but by all of the people. Consequently, the people of a single state cannot confer a sovereignty which will extend beyond them, to the rest of the people of our nation. Only in the Congress are all of the people represented. The Congress alone, therefore, can be trusted with the power to control and deal with national concerns. The states thus have no power to retard, impede, or otherwise burden, the operation of the constitutional laws enacted by Congress to carry into execution the powers vested in the general government. This is the unavoidable consequence of that supremacy which the Constitution declares.

Analysis:

Notice Chief Justice Marshall's painstaking use of logic, including logical extensions outward from the text of the Constitution, in holding both that the bank is constitutional and that it may not be taxed by a state. First, he applies a presumption of constitutionality with regard to the bank's establishment, from the simple fact that Congress established it. How could the judgment of constitutionality from all of these learned men be mistaken, especially after so much debate? This presumption lives on today, as reflected in the Supreme Court's application of rational basis review. Second, he counters Maryland's (P) argument that the Constitution stems from the states by referencing the process by which it was adopted—through representatives from each state, chosen by the people of the states. One may question, however, the Chief Justice's assertion that a nationwide referendum could not be held. After all, what is a presidential election? Now, because the Constitution flows directly form the people, it, through the Supremacy Clause, trumps the laws of the several states. Moreover, narrow readings of the Constitution would render it useless in the face of changing times that call for flexible interpretations. A Constitution meant to be interpreted rigidly would necessarily have to cover the minutest details, leaving nothing to chance, and would thus be more similar to a legal code, rather than a broad governing document encompassing the general themes and ideals of governance.

■ CASE VOCABULARY

NUGATORY: Inoperative; useless.

Gibbons v. Ogden

(Ferryboat Operator) v. *(Ferryboat Operator)*
22 U.S. (9 Wheat.) 1 (1824)

SUPREME COURT INTERPRETS FEDERAL COMMERCE POWER BROADLY

■ **INSTANT FACTS** Ogden (D) was granted an exclusive ferry operations license by New York State. Gibbons (P) began a competing ferry service and challenges Ogden's (D) exclusive license under the Commerce Clause.

■ **BLACK LETTER RULE** The federal commerce power extends to all commerce among and between the states and foreign nations, with only commerce having connections solely within a single state being unreachable under the commerce power.

■ **PROCEDURAL BASIS**
Appeal to U.S. Supreme Court from New York State court's grant of injunction barring Gibbons (P) from competing with Ogden (D).

■ **FACTS**
Ogden (D) operated a ferry boat service between New York and New Jersey under an exclusive license granted by the New York legislature. Gibbons (P), holding a similar license granted by Congress, began competing with Ogden (D). Ogden (D) sought and received an injunction against Gibbons' (P) competing ferry service. Gibbons (P) appeals to the Supreme Court.

■ **ISSUE**
May a state legislate in the area of interstate commerce in a way that conflicts with federal law?

■ **DECISION AND RATIONALE**
(Marshall, C.J.) No. Before our Constitution was adopted, the States were sovereign and completely independent. But when these sovereigns got together and adopted our Constitution, the whole character in which the States appear underwent a change, the extent of which must be determined by a fair interpretation of the instrument effecting that change—our Constitution. The Constitution contains an enumeration of powers expressly granted by the people to their government. In the last of these, Congress is authorized "to make all laws which shall be necessary and proper" for the purpose. It also states, "Congress shall have power to regulate commerce with foreign nations, and among the several States, and with the Indian tribes." The subject to be regulated is commerce. It thus becomes necessary to settle the meaning of this word. Ogden (D) would have us limit it to traffic, and not admit that it encompasses navigation. This would restrict a general term applicable to many objects, to one of its significations. Of course, commerce is traffic, but it is much more: it is intercourse. The mind can scarcely come up with a system for regulating commerce between nations, which shall exclude laws concerning navigation. If commerce does not include navigation, our federal government can make no law respecting what constitutes American vessels, or where they shall be navigated, or how. Yet this power has been exercised from the commencement of the government. All America understands the word "commerce," to comprehend navigation; it was so understood, and must have been so understood, when the Constitution was framed. The power over commerce was one of the primary objects for which the people adopted their government, and so must have been contemplated in forming it. Any attempt to restrict it now surely comes too late. Thus, a power to regulate navigation is

Gibbons v. Ogden (Continued)

as expressly granted, as if that term had been added to the word "commerce." This power over commerce extends to commerce "with foreign nations, and among the several States, and with the Indian tribes." These words comprehend every species of commercial intercourse between the United States and foreign nations. Regarding commerce "among" the several States, the word "among" means intermingled with. Commerce among the States cannot stop at the external boundary line of each State, but may be introduced into the interior. Comprehensive as the word "among" is, it may very properly be restricted to that commerce which concerns more States than one. Therefore, the completely internal commerce of a State may be considered as reserved for the States itself. But, in regulating commerce with foreign nations, the power of Congress does not stop at jurisdictional lines of the several States. It would be a useless power if such were the case. If Congress has the power to regulate foreign commerce, that power must be exercised whenever the subject exists. If it exists within the States, if a foreign voyage may commence or terminate at a port within a State, then the power of Congress may be exercised within a State. Such power is the power to regulate; that is, to prescribe the rule by which commerce is to be governed. This power is complete in itself, may be exercised to its utmost extent, and has no limitations, other than those prescribed in the Constitution. The wisdom and the discretion of Congress, their identity with the people, and the influence which their constituents possess at elections, are, in this as in many other instances, the sole restraints on which they have relied to secure them from its abuse. They are the restraints on which the people must often rely, in all representative governments.

Analysis:

The Commerce Clause has two general purposes. First, it provides Congress with the authority to affirmatively regulate all commerce that is not exclusively founded and finished within the borders of a single state. Second, the commerce clause, without any affirmative declarations by Congress, acts as a limit on the exercise of state power in the interstate commerce arena. This is often called the dormant commerce clause. Both of these aspects are present in *Gibbons v. Ogden.* Though Chief Justice Marshall does not expressly state that Congress has the authority to license ferryboat operators in interstate commerce, this conclusion is surely implied by stating that Congress has plenary power in this arena. Possibly more importantly, the Chief Justice holds that by granting Ogden (D) an exclusive license to ferry passengers and cargo between New York and New Jersey, New York interferes with or burdens interstate commerce. *Gibbons* is one of the very first steps in giving "commerce" a broad definition, a trend that continues long after this decision.

■ **CASE VOCABULARY**

ANTERIOR: Before; prior to.

SIGNIFICATION: A single aspect of a broader whole, or concept.

United States v. E. C. Knight Co.

(Federal Government) v. (Sugar Monopoly)
156 U.S. 1, 15 S.Ct. 249 (1895)

COMMERCE DOES NOT INCLUDE THE MANUFACTURING OF GOODS MEANT TO TRAVEL IN INTERSTATE COMMERCE

■ **INSTANT FACTS** A sugar refining company gained a monopoly in the industry by purchasing several other refineries.

■ **BLACK LETTER RULE** Manufacturing is separate from "commerce" because it occurs before any goods are transported in interstate commerce, and thus the federal government may not regulate manufacturing in and of itself.

■ **PROCEDURAL BASIS**

[Not Stated]

■ **FACTS**

The American Sugar Refining Company (Knight)(D) purchased the stock of four Philadelphia sugar refineries. In so doing, Knight (D) acquired nearly complete control of the manufacturing of refined sugar within the United States. The United States (Government)(P) charged that the acquisition constituted illegal combinations in restraint of trade.

■ **ISSUE**

May Congress, pursuant to its commerce power, regulate the manufacturing of goods, before any have actually entered the stream of interstate commerce?

■ **DECISION AND RATIONALE**

(Fuller, C.J.) No. It cannot be denied that the power of a state to protect the lives, health and property of its citizens, and to preserve good order, within its boundaries, is a power originally and always belonging to the states exclusively. It is argued by the government (P) that the power to control the manufacturing of sugar is a monopoly over a necessity of life, to the enjoyment of which by a large part of the United States interstate commerce is indispensable. And that, therefore, the government (P), pursuant to its commerce power, may repress such a monopoly directly. But this argument cannot be logically confined to the necessities of life, but must include all articles of general consumption. It is true that the power over the manufacturing of something involves, to some extent, the power over its ultimate disposition. But this power of manufacture is secondary. Although the exercise of this power may result in bringing the operation of commerce into play, it does not control it, but effects it only incidentally and indirectly. Commerce succeeds to manufacture. It is not a part of it. The power to regulate commerce is independent of the power to regulate monopolies. It is thus vital that the independence of the commercial power and the police power be always recognized and preserved, and that acknowledged evils, however grave and urgent, had better be borne, than the risk be run of more serious consequences by resort to expedients of even doubtful constitutionality.

■ **DISSENT**

(Harlan, J.) The Court is correct in seeking to maintain the separateness of the federal commerce power and the police power of the states, to the end that the Union be strengthened and the autonomy of the

United States v. E. C. Knight Co. (Continued)

states be preserved. But it is equally true that the preservation of the just authority of the general government is essential as well to the safety of the states as to the attainment of the important ends for which it was formed. The Constitution should not, therefore, be subjected to an interpretation so rigid, technical, and narrow that those objects cannot be accomplished. It is the Constitution that invests Congress with the power to protect commerce among the states against burdens and exactions arising from unlawful restraints by whatever authority imposed. Any combination, therefore, that disturbs or unreasonably obstructs freedom in buying and selling articles manufactured to be sold to persons in other states affects, not incidentally, but directly, the people of all the states. The only true remedy lies in the hands of the government that represents all the people, exercising powers delegated by all, for the common benefit of all.

Analysis:

The majority opinion here represents a strict interpretation of interstate commerce, an opinion unbending to the practical considerations that would later shape constitutional interpretation under the Commerce Clause. Basically, the Court holds that until goods are actually moved in interstate commerce, they are not subject to regulation by the federal government. By so holding, the Court missed the big picture. By monopolizing the sugar refining industry, Knight (D) could charge much higher prices for its sugar, subject only to market realities such as the elasticity of demand for sugar. Specifically, what the Court missed is that by allowing the monopoly, the price of sugar will go up—a development that surely has an effect on interstate commerce. Justice Harlan recognized this point in his dissent when he criticized the majority for taking a "rigid, technical, and narrow" view of the issue.

■ CASE VOCABULARY

ELASTICITY OF DEMAND: The rate at which demand for something changes as its price is increased or decreased. When a shift in price causes very little change in the quantity demanded, the item is said to be inelastic.

MONOPOLY: Exclusive control over something.

Carter v. Carter Coal Co.
(Not Stated) v. (Mining Company)
298 U.S. 238, 56 S.Ct. 855 (1936)

LABOR/MANAGEMENT RELATIONS ARE PURELY LOCAL IN CHARACTER AND THUS NOT REGULABLE UNDER THE COMMERCE POWER

■ **INSTANT FACTS** Congress passed, pursuant to its commerce power, a law regulating the management-employee relations in the coal mining industry. The law is being challenged on the ground that Congress does not have the power to regulate such activities because they do not constitute "interstate commerce."

■ **BLACK LETTER RULE** Purely local activities, such as the negotiation of wages and working conditions, are outside of the Congress' realm of authority under the Commerce Clause.

■ **PROCEDURAL BASIS**
[Not Stated]

■ **FACTS**
Congress passed the Bituminous Coal Conservation Act of 1935 in order to stabilize the coal mining industry and promote its interstate commerce; to provide for the general welfare, etc. The act confers the power to fix the minimum/maximum price of coal, with variations as the board deems necessary and proper. The labor provisions require employees to be given the right to organize and bargain collectively, through representatives of their own choosing, free from interference, restraint, or coercion of employers in respect of their concerted activities.

■ **ISSUE**
Does the commerce power authorize Congress to legislate in the area of purely local activities, such as labor-management relations?

■ **DECISION AND RATIONALE**
(Sutherland, J.) No. When the federal government goes in the direction of taking over the power of the states we may find the states so despoiled of their powers, or so relieved of the responsibilities which possession of the powers necessarily enjoins, as to reduce them to little more than geographical subdivisions of the national domain. The Commerce Clause authorizes Congress to regulate only commerce. We must inquire, then—What is commerce? "Commerce," as used in the Constitution, is the equivalent of "intercourse for the purposes of trade," and includes transportation, purchase, sale, and exchange of commodities. The power to regulate commerce embraces the instruments by which it is carried on. However, that commodities produced or manufactured within a state are intended to be sold or transported outside the state does not render their production or manufacture subject to federal regulation under the Commerce Clause. Plainly, the incidents leading up to and culminating in the mining of coal do not constitute interstate commerce. The employment of men, the fixing of their wages, hours of labor, and working conditions—whether carried on separately or collectively—each and all constitute intercourse for the purposes of production, not of trade. Such is purely local in character. Extraction of coal form the mine is the aim and the completed result of local activities. Mining brings the subject matter of commerce into existence. Commerce disposes of it. All of this renders inescapable the conclusion that the effect of the labor provisions of the act primarily falls upon production and not upon

Carter v. Carter Coal Co. (Continued)

commerce; and confirms the further resulting conclusion that production is a purely local activity. Much stress is put upon the evils stemming from the struggle between labor and management in the mining industry, and the resulting strikes, irregularity of production and effect on prices; and it is insisted that interstate commerce is greatly affected thereby. But the conclusive answer is that the evils are all local evils over which the federal government has no legislative control. The relation of employer and employee is a local relation.

Analysis:

Carter is another case of historical interest that does not reflect the current philosophy of the Court. In *Carter,* the Court ruled that labor-management relations are a "purely local activity," and thus outside the scope of the commerce power. Purely local activities represent a subject matter over which the states have exclusive jurisdiction, unless it can be shown that they have a "direct effect" on interstate commerce. Here, the majority of the Court did not buy the government's argument that labor relations have such a direct effect on interstate commerce that they should fall within the sphere of subject matters reserved exclusively for the states under the Tenth Amendment. *Carter* thus represents the Court's intent to enforce the principle of federalism, as embodied in the Tenth Amendment, against what it saw as federal incursions into the states' domain in order to deal with economic upheaval. Whether the Court was willing to invalidate federal laws on the basis of the Tenth Amendment depended on whether the law infringed on a state interest.

■ CASE VOCABULARY

INSTRUMENTS: Items that facilitate interstate commerce, such as railroads, waterways, and highways, as well as the actual carriers of goods, such as trains and other vehicles.

Houston, East & West Texas Railway Company v. United States [the Shreveport Rate cases]

(Railway Carrier) v. (Government)
234 U.S. 342, 34 S.Ct. 833 (1914)

CONGRESS MAY REGULATE INTRASTATE ACTIVITIES IF DOING SO IS NECESSARY TO EFFECTUATE REGULATION OF INTERSTATE ACTIVITIES

■ **INSTANT FACTS** Due to state regulations of intrastate transport, a railway company charged much higher rates for interstate transport between Shreveport, Louisiana and certain Texas locations than it did for transport exclusively within Texas, leading the Interstate Commerce Commission to implement price controls.

■ **BLACK LETTER RULE** Congress has authority to regulate intrastate commerce where it has the potential to affect interstate commerce absent federal regulation.

■ **PROCEDURAL BASIS**

[Not Stated]

■ **FACTS**

The Houston, East & West Texas Railway Company (Railroad)(P) used a rates system that charged much higher rates, according to distance, for transport between Shreveport, Louisiana and several cities within Texas than it did for purely intrastate transport within Texas. Because this scheme made it much more expensive to ship through Shreveport, the commerce of Shreveport was injuriously affected. The Interstate Commerce Commission found that the interstate class rates out of Shreveport to named Texas points were unreasonable, and it established maximum class rates for this traffic. These rates were roughly equal to the rates fixed by the Texas Railroad Commission, and charged by the carriers for similar distances within the State. The Railroad (P) objects on the ground that the discrimination found by the Commission to be unjust arises out of the relation of intrastate rates, maintained under state authority, to interstate rates that have been upheld as reasonable, thus making the Commissions actions beyond its power under the Commerce Clause.

■ **ISSUE**

May Congress regulate intrastate commerce where it is found to affect interstate commerce?

■ **DECISION AND RATIONALE**

(Hughes, J.) Yes. It is the essence of the federal commerce power that, where it exists, it dominates. Interstate trade was not left to be destroyed or impeded by the rivalries of local government. Such parochialism was one of the chief evils the Framers intended to eradicate in adopting the Constitution. Congress is empowered to provide the law for the governance of interstates commerce; to enact all appropriate legislation for its protection and advancement; to adopt measures to promote its growth and insure its safety; to foster, protect, control, and restrain. Its authority, extending to these interstate carriers as instruments of interstate commerce, necessarily embraces the right to control their operations in all matters having such a close and substantial relation to interstate traffic that the control is essential to the security of that traffic. Congress, therefore, has the power to ensure that the agencies of interstate commerce shall not be used in such manner as to cripple, retard, or destroy it. The fact that

Houston, East & West Texas Railway Company v. U.S. [the Shreveport Rate cases] (Continued)

carriers are instruments of intrastate commerce, as well as of interstate commerce, does not derogate from the complete authority of Congress over the latter, or preclude the federal power from being used to prevent the intrastate operations of such carriers from being used to injure that which has been confided to federal care. Whenever the two are so closely related that the government of one involves the control of the other, it is Congress, not the state, which is entitled to set the final and dominant rule. Congress, in the exercise of its paramount power, may prevent the common instrumentalities of interstate and intrastate commercial intercourse from being used in their intrastate operations to the injury of interstate commerce.

Analysis:

Here the Court upholds the regulation of intrastate railroads because local rates for rail freight and other transport have a very close and significant effect on interstate railroad traffic. The theory that Congress could regulate activities having such a close and significant effect on interstate commerce was not extended beyond the railroad context. One of the cases the Court relied on in its *Shreveport Rate Cases* holding involved a federal railway safety law for vehicles used by interstate railroads only in intrastate traffic, as well as those used in interstate traffic. The applicable theory was that in order to effectively regulate the interstate vehicles, the intrastate vehicles had to be covered as well. Otherwise, it would have been possible for railroads to use vehicles only within one state and thus avoid the safety code. Similarly, here, the Texas railroads could effectively shut out Shreveport from competing for Texas shipments due to the two-tier rate structure. Such a scheme hampered interstate commerce much the same way protectionist tariffs hamper foreign trade.

■ CASE VOCABULARY

INTRASTATE COMMERCE: Commerce occurring solely within the borders of one state.

TARIFF: A tax on goods imported from foreign nations exacted by the importing nation.

A.L.A. Schechter Poultry Corporation v. United States
(*Chicken Wholesaler*) v. (*Government*)
295 U.S. 495, 55 S.Ct. 837 (1935)

ONCE GOODS REACH A STATE AND ARE SOLD TO WHOLESALERS THEY ARE NO LONGER IN INTERSTATE COMMERCE

■ **INSTANT FACTS** Congress enacted a law governing wages, working conditions, and prices for poultry transported in interstate commerce. Wholesalers that purchase the chickens after they've arrived in-state challenge the law as unconstitutional.

■ **BLACK LETTER RULE** Once goods that have traveled in interstate commerce are sold or disposed of in the state of their final destination, they are no longer in interstate commerce and thus not subject to federal law.

■ **PROCEDURAL BASIS**
Appeal to the Supreme Court after a conviction for violating the "Live Poultry Code."

■ **FACTS**
The "Live Poultry Code" (Code) was passed by Congress to assure quality poultry by preventing sellers from requiring buyers to purchase all chickens in a coop, including sick ones. The Code also required collective bargaining, prohibited child labor, and established a 40 our work week and a minimum wage. New York City imports more live poultry than anywhere else in the nation, 96% of which comes from other states. Three-fourths of this arrives by rail and is consigned to commission salespeople who sell the chickens to slaughterhouse operators. A.L.A. Schechter (Schechter)(D) runs slaughterhouses in New York City. Schechter (D) buys poultry for slaughter and resale, a process usually taking less than 24 hours. Schechter (D) does not sell poultry in interstate commerce. Schechter (D) was prosecuted for violating the Code's provisions relating to the hours and wages of its employees, as well as those relating to sales requirements.

■ **ISSUE**
Does the commerce power extend to goods moved in interstate commerce after they have arrived and been sold in their state of final destination?

■ **DECISION AND RATIONALE**
(Hughes, C.J.) No. Much is made of the fact that almost all of the poultry coming into New York comes from out of state. But the code provisions at issue here have nothing to do with the interstate transportation of poultry, or the transactions of the commission salespeople to whom it is consigned, or the sales made by these consignees to Schechter (D). Once Schechter (D) made its purchases and the poultry trucked to its slaughterhouses, the interstate transactions in relation to that poultry then ended. Schechter (D) held the poultry at its slaughterhouse markets for slaughter and local resale to dealers who in turn resold directly to consumers. Neither the slaughtering nor the sales by Schechter (D) were transactions in interstate commerce. The undisputed facts thus afford no basis for the argument that the poultry handled by Schechter (D) was in a "current" or "flow" of interstate commerce. The flow in interstate commerce had ceased. The poultry had come to a permanent rest within the state. It was not held, used, or sold by Schechter (D) in relation to any further transactions in interstate commerce and was not destined for transportation to other states. With regard to how far the federal government may

A.L.A. Schecter Poultry Corporation v. United States (Continued)

go in controlling intrastate transactions upon the ground that they "affect" interstate commerce, there is a necessary and well-established distinction between direct and indirect effects. The precise line to be drawn depends on individual facts, but the distinction is clear in principle. Direct effects are illustrated by the railroad cases. But where the effect is merely indirect, such transactions remain within the domain of state power. Otherwise the federal authority would embrace practically all the activities of the people and we would, for all practical purposes, have a completely centralized government.

Analysis:

The code at issue in *Schechter* was part of the National Industrial Recovery Act of 1933, a set of laws designed to help industry recover by increasing prices and stabilizing labor-management relations. The *Schechter* ruling evidenced the Supreme Court's willingness to invalidate such federal schemes designed to combat the panoply of problems with the national economy during the Great Depression. The Railroad Retirement Act of 1934 is another example. The Railroad Retirement Act dealt with the social welfare of railroad workers, which has nothing to do with commerce. Both of these examples show that the Court was analyzing the federal commerce power from a Tenth-Amendment standpoint, attempting to preserve certain areas for exclusive control by the states. The Court's unwillingness to read more flexibility into the Commerce Clause eventually led to Franklin Roosevelt's unsuccessful court-packing plan.

■ CASE VOCABULARY

CONSIGNMENT: The placing of an item for sale by another, acting as the owner's agent, in return for a certain percentage, or commission, of the sales price to be paid to the agent upon the item's sale.

Hammer v. Dagenhart
(Not Stated) v. (Not Stated)
247 U.S. 251, 38 S.Ct. 529 (1918)

CONGRESS MAY NOT USE THE COMMERCE POWER AS A PRETEXT FOR REGULATING EMPLOYMENT CONDITIONS WITHIN THE STATES

■ **INSTANT FACTS** A father wanting to put his two minor children to work in a cotton mill is suing on the ground that Congress' use of the commerce power to regulate child labor in the states by blocking the interstate transportation of child-made goods is unconstitutional.

■ **BLACK LETTER RULE** The commerce power does not allow Congress to regulate in areas traditionally left up to the states' police power, such as the area of child labor laws.

■ **PROCEDURAL BASIS**

Appeal to the Supreme Court after a bill was filed in federal district court seeking an injunction against enforcement of a federal law blocking interstate commerce in goods produced by child labor.

■ **FACTS**

Congress passed a law prohibiting the transportation in interstate commerce of goods manufactured in factories employing children under the age of fourteen, or between fourteen and sixteen, depending upon the number of hours these children were allowed to work. A father (P) seeking to put his two children to work seeks an injunction against enforcement of the law on the ground that it oversteps Congress' commerce power.

■ **ISSUE**

May Congress rely on the Commerce Clause in attempting to regulate local activities, such as child labor, by prohibiting the interstate transportation of goods manufactured through such local activities?

■ **DECISION AND RATIONALE**

(Day, J.) No. The thing intended to be accomplished by this statute is the denial of the facilities of interstate commerce to manufacturers who employ children within the prohibited ages. It does not, in its effect, regulate transportation among the states, but aims to set a national standard for the employment of children. The goods shipped are, of themselves, harmless. When offered for shipment, the labor of their production is over, and the mere fact that they were intended for interstate commerce transportation does not make their production subject to federal control under the commerce power. The production of articles intended for interstate commerce is a matter of local regulation. When the commerce begins is determined by its actual delivery to a common carrier for transportation, or the actual commencement of its transfer to another state. If it were otherwise, the states would be left with no authority over its local manufacturing concerns. It is asserted that the legislation is constitutional because it seeks to insulate from unfair competition other states where the evil of child labor has been recognized. There is, however, no power vested in Congress to require the states to exercise their police power so as to prevent possible unfair competition. The grant to Congress of power over the subject of interstate commerce enabled it to regulate such commerce, and not to give it authority to control the states in their exercise of the police power over local trade and manufacture. Police

Hammer v. Dagenhart (Continued)

regulations relating to the internal trade and affairs of the states have been uniformly recognized as within such state control. That regulation of child labor is an important issue is shown by the fact that every state has such regulations. But it is up to the states, not the federal government, to decide what regulation it needs and such regulation should be implemented. An opposite holding would sanction an invasion by the federal power of the control of a matter purely local in its character. The act is thus repugnant to the Constitution in two ways. It not only transcends the authority delegated to Congress over commerce, but also exerts a power as to a purely local matter to which the federal authority does not extend. To allow such a law to stand would practically destroy our system of government.

■ DISSENT

(Holmes, J.) If an act is within the powers specifically conferred upon Congress, it seems to me that it is not made any less constitutional because of the indirect effects that it may have, however obvious it may be that it will have those effects, and that we are not at liberty to hold it void upon such grounds. The statute in question is within the power expressly given to Congress if considered only as to its immediate effects and that, if invalid, it is so only upon some collateral ground. The statute confines itself to prohibiting the carriage of certain goods in interstate commerce. Congress is given power to regulate such commerce in unqualified terms. The power to regulate most assuredly includes the power to prohibit. I should have thought that the most conspicuous decisions of this Court had made it clear that the power to regulate commerce and other constitutional powers could not be cut down or qualified by the fact that it might interfere with the carrying out of the domestic policy of any state. The propriety of the exercise of a power admitted to exist should be for the consideration of Congress alone, without intrusions by this Court. Congress has the power to regulate the transportation of goods across state lines. This it did. Its motivation should not be part of the inquiry.

Analysis:

This case is a perfect example of congressional attempts to stop the "race to the bottom," where individual states, in order to provide themselves with a competitive advantage over other states, adopt a laissez faire approach to business and industry. By adopting child labor laws that are less restrictive than those of other, especially surrounding, states, a state makes it cheaper to do business within its borders. This principle can be seen in the context of environmental laws. Over the last third of the twentieth century, the state and federal governments began adopting more stringent environmental protection laws. Obviously, an industry that pollutes heavily, and thus incurs more costs in cleanup and pollution prevention, will save money by relocating to a state with less stringent pollution control laws. Many jurisdictions may be inclined to relax their laws in order to attract these industries, along with their concomitant jobs and tax base. To compete, other states are then forced to do the same. This is where the federal government's race to the bottom argument for a national minimum standard comes into play. In *Hammer*, the Court refused to buy this argument, though it had, and would, buy it in the past and future.

Champion v. Ames (The Lottery Case)
(Not Stated) v. (Not Stated)
188 U.S. 321, 23 S.Ct. 321 (1903)

CONGRESS MAY USE ITS COMMERCE POWER TO PROHIBIT THE INTERSTATE TRANSPORTATION OF GOODS THE SALE OF WHICH IS AGAINST PUBLIC POLICY

■ **INSTANT FACTS** The Federal Lottery Act prohibited interstate shipment of lottery tickets. It is being challenged as unconstitutional in that such shipments are not commerce.

■ **BLACK LETTER RULE** Congress may, pursuant to the Commerce Clause, prohibit the interstate shipment of items adjudged to be evil or pestilent in order to protect the commerce concerning all states.

■ **PROCEDURAL BASIS**
Supreme Court review of a criminal indictment under the Federal Lottery Act.

■ **FACTS**
The Federal Lottery Act (Act) barred the interstate shipment of lottery tickets. The prohibition applied to the mere carrying of lotto tickets across a state border. The Act is challenged as exceeding Congress' authority under the Commerce Clause.

■ **ISSUE**
Is the prohibition of the interstate shipment of items adjudged to be evil or pestilent within Congress' authority under the Commerce Clause?

■ **DECISION AND RATIONALE**
(Harlan, J.) Yes. It is insisted that the carrying of lotto tickets from one state to another by an express company engaged in carrying freight form state to state, although such tickets may be sealed in boxes, does not constitute commerce among the states within the meaning of the Commerce Clause. We are of the opinion that lottery tickets are subjects of traffic, and therefore are subjects of commerce. The regulation of the carriage of such tickets from state to state is thus a regulation of commerce among the several states. It is also said that Congress has the power to regulate, and that, by punishing those who carry lotto tickets from state to state, Congress has instead prohibited commerce, something it has no authority to do. But it must be remembered that the power of Congress to regulate commerce among the states is plenary. If a state, when considering legislation for the suppression of lotteries within its own borders, may take into account the evils that inhere in the raising of money through lotteries, why may not Congress? Besides, Congress, by its act, does not assume to interfere with traffic or commerce in lottery tickets carried on exclusively within the limits of any state, but has in view only commerce of that kind among the several states. The internal affairs of the states are thus left untouched. Just as a state may, for the purpose of guarding the morals of its own people, forbid all sales of lottery tickets within its limits, so Congress, for the purpose of guarding the people of the United States against the widespread pestilence of lotteries and to protect the commerce which concerns all states, may prohibit the carrying of lottery tickets from one state to another. The opposite holding would allow the purveyors of lotto tickets to undermine the declared policy of the states against the sale of these tickets. We

should hesitate long before adjudging that an evil of such appalling character, carried on through interstate commerce, cannot be met and crushed by the only power competent to that end.

Analysis:

In *Champion,* the Court holds that Congress has the authority, pursuant to the Commerce Clause, to both regulate and prohibit interstate commerce. Why was this not the case in *Hammer v. Dagenhart?* Remember in that case, Congress sought to prohibit the movement in interstate commerce of a class of goods produced through child labor. Congress did not seek to ban the use of child labor outright, just as in *Champion* it did not attempt to ban outright the sale of lottery tickets within a state. If Congress's power in this arena is plenary, why the different results? Some commentators assert that it is the "evil" nature of the goods. Lottery tickets were held to be, in and of themselves, evil or pestilent. The products produced through child labor were evil only insofar as the means by which they were produced. Once these products were made, the evil aspect—the child labor—was ostensibly over.

N.L.R.B. v. Jones & Laughlin Steel Corp.

(Government) v. (Steel Company)
301 U.S. 1, 57 S.Ct. 615 (1937)

CONGRESS MAY REGULATE LABOR-MANAGEMENT RELATIONS IN INTERSTATE INDUSTRIES

■ **INSTANT FACTS** A steel corporation whose operations span the continent is being sued by the government for violating the National Labor Relations Act for committing unfair labor practices.

■ **BLACK LETTER RULE** Congressional power to regulate interstate commerce extends to the regulation of intrastate activities that may burden or obstruct interstate commerce.

■ **PROCEDURAL BASIS**

Appeal to the Supreme Court from a denial of a petition to enforce a government order to end unfair labor practices.

■ **FACTS**

Jones & Laughlin Steel Corporation (J&L)(D) is a large, diversified and completely integrated steel producing enterprise with interests around the nation. J&L owns and/or controls coal mines, coke factories, iron mines, railroads and ships, all of which are used in the production and/or transportation of steel. The National Labor Relations Board (NLRB)(P) found that J&L (D) was guilty of unfair labor practices (ULP) in violation of the National Labor Relations Act (Act), by its discharge of several employees for their taking part in union activities. The NLRB (P) ordered J&L (D) to cease and desist its ULPs. To force compliance, the NLRB (P) sued for judicial enforcement of the order. The court of appeals denied the order on the ground that it was beyond the federal commerce power.

■ **ISSUE**

May Congress exercise its commerce power in the area of labor-management relations?

■ **DECISION AND RATIONALE**

(Hughes, C.J.) Yes. The Act is challenged in its entirety as an attempt to regulate all industry, thus invading the reserved powers of the States over their local concerns. We think it clear that the Act may be construed so as to operate within the sphere of constitutional authority. It covers interstate and foreign commerce, subjects left exclusively to the federal government. The Act also defines the term "affecting commerce": "The term 'affecting commerce' means in commerce, or burdening or obstructing commerce or the free flow of commerce, or having led or tending to lead to a labor dispute burdening or obstructing commerce or the free flow of commerce." This grant of authority does not extend to all industrial employees and their employers. It purports to reach only what may be deemed to burden or obstruct interstate commerce and, thus qualified, it must be construed as contemplating the exercise of control within constitutional bounds. Acts having such an effect are not rendered immune from federal control simply because they grow out of labor disputes. It is the effect upon commerce, not the source of the injury, which is the criterion. J&L (D) argues that its manufacturing employees are not subject to federal laws because manufacturing in itself is not commerce. However, congressional authority to protect interstate commerce is not limited to transactions deemed to be an essential part of the "flow" of interstate commerce. Burdens and obstructions may come from many sources. Congress' authority to deal with such burdens is plenary, and reaches to the source of the burden wherever it may lie. Thus, although the activities may be intrastate in character when separately considered, if they have such a close and substantial relationship to interstate commerce that their control is essential or appropriate to protect that commerce, Congress cannot be denied the power to exercise that control. In other words, the fact that the employees here concerned were engaged in production is not determinative. The question remains as to the effect upon interstate commerce of the labor practice involved. Given the breadth of J&L's (D) operations, a stoppage of those operations by industrial strife would have a most serious effect upon interstate commerce. Such effect would neither be indirect, or remote. Rather, it would be immediate and might be catastrophic. When industries organize themselves on a national scale, making their relation to interstate commerce the dominant factor in their activities, how can it be maintained that their industrial labor relations constitute a forbidden field into which Congress may not enter in order to protect interstate commerce?

■ DISSENT

(McReynolds, J.) Today the Court departs from well established principles found in *Schechter Poultry Corporation v. United States* and *Carter v. Carter Coal Co*. In each, the Labor Board formulated and then sustained a charge of unfair labor practices. These orders were declared invalid on the ground that production operations were not interstate commerce; that labor practices in the course of such operations did not directly affect interstate commerce; and that, consequently, none of the activities came within congressional power. Now, though differing in some respects, all manufacturing concerns procure raw materials from outside the state where they manufacture, fabricate within and then ship beyond the state. Manifestly that view of congressional power would extend it into almost every field of human industry.

Analysis:

Labor strife in the steel industry has a gigantic ripple effect on interstate commerce because of the important place steel occupies in the modern world. Automobiles, residences, buildings, and even the very computer being used to write these words include steel. This, however, is just a consideration of the finished product, to say nothing of all the individual workers involved in making the steel, as well as those involved in producing the products that use steel. A disruption at the source, that is, at the point where steel is produced, or at any prior point in the chain of production, can therefore have a devastating effect upon interstate commerce. Because this is a national problem, it demands a national solution. In *N.L.R.B. v. Friedman-Harry Marks Clothing Co.,* the Court upheld the application of the NLRA to even a relatively small clothing manufacturer that shipped clothing in interstate commerce. The Court noted that a strike in the New York clothing industry would have a severe effect on interstate commerce. This shows that an economic effect on interstate commerce, even if slight, gives Congress authority under the Commerce clause to regulate the activity.

■ CASE VOCABULARY

INTEGRATED: A business term describing the level of consolidation a corporation has in its industry. Full vertical integration occurs when a corporation owns or controls all aspects of the chains of production and distribution, including the raw materials that go into the finished product, all the way to the means of transporting the finished products to the buyers. Horizontal integration occurs when a corporation controls one aspect of production, such as when a company owns numerous steel mills, but not the coal or iron mines supplying the raw materials. One corporation can accomplish vertical and horizontal integration.

United States v. Darby

(*Government*) v. (*Lumber Producer*)
312 U.S. 100, 61 S.Ct. 451 (1941)

SUPREME COURT EXPRESSLY OVERRULES *HAMMER V. DAGENHART*

■ **INSTANT FACTS** A Georgia lumber company violated federal minimum wage/maximum hour laws. Its defense is that the federal government overreached its Commerce Clause authority in setting the standards.

■ **BLACK LETTER RULE** Congress has the authority, under the Commerce Clause, to exclude any article from interstate commerce, in judgment that they are injurious to the public health, morals or welfare.

■ **PROCEDURAL BASIS**

Appeal to the Supreme Court from a quashing of an indictment of an employer for unfair labor practices.

■ **FACTS**

Congress, through the Fair Labor Standards Act (Act), set up a comprehensive scheme for preventing the interstate shipment of certain products made in the United States under labor conditions (shown as wages and hours) which fail to conform to standards under the Act. Through the Act, Congress seeks to prevent the production of goods under conditions harmful to the maintenance of the minimum standards of living necessary for health and general well-being; and to prevent the use of interstate commerce as a means of competition in the distribution of goods so produced, and as the means of spreading and perpetuating such substandard labor conditions in the several states (i.e. Congress is exercising police powers). Darby (D), a Georgia lumber producer shipping lumber in interstate commerce, was indicted for violating the wage and hour standards of the Act.

■ **ISSUE**

May Congress exercise police powers by excluding from interstate commerce articles the production of which deteriorates the public health, morals or welfare of the nation?

■ **DECISION AND RATIONALE**

(Stone, J.) Yes. While manufacture is not of itself interstate commerce, the shipment of manufactured goods interstate is such commerce and the prohibition of such shipments by Congress is undoubtedly a regulation of the commerce. Congress, following its own vision of public policy, is free to exclude from the commerce articles whose use in the states for which they are destined it may conceive to be injurious to the public health, morals or welfare, even though the state has not sought to regulate their use. It is not a valid objection to such an assertion of congressional power to regulate commerce that its exercise is attended by the same incidents which attend the exercise of the police powers of the states. Congress' motive and purpose is immaterial and its regulations are valid so long as they do not infringe some constitutional prohibition. We therefore conclude that the Act's prohibitions are within Congress' commerce authority. The Court's conclusion in *Hammer v. Dagenhart*, that only those articles that are harmful or deleterious in and of themselves may be banned from interstate commerce, was not supported by any provision in the Constitution. It was novel then and has not been followed since. It

United States v. Darby (Continued)

therefore has little, if any, vitality and should be, and now is, overruled. There remains the question whether such restrictions on the production of goods for commerce are a permissible exercise of the commerce power. The federal commerce power extends to those activities intrastate which so affect interstate commerce or the exercise of the power of Congress over it as to make regulation of them an appropriate means to the attainment of a legitimate end—the exercise of the granted power of Congress to regulate interstate commerce. Congress may choose the means reasonably adapted to the attainment of the permitted end, even though they involve the control of intrastate activities. Our conclusion is unaffected by the Tenth Amendment. The Amendment states but a truism that all is retained which has not been surrendered. From the beginning and for many years the Amendment has been construed as not depriving the national government of authority to resort to all means for the exercise of a granted power which are appropriate and plainly adapted to the permitted end.

Analysis:

Remember the Court's ruling in *Hammer v. Dagenhart*, that Congress did not have the power, under the Commerce Clause, to prohibit child labor through a general ban on the shipment of its fruits. Was *Hammer* truly a ruling without support in prior and subsequent case law? In the *Lottery Case* the Court ruled that only those articles adjudged to be deleterious in and of themselves could be banned from interstate commerce. In *Schechter Poultry* (the Sick Chicken Case), the Court ruled that the commerce power did not extend past the initial sale once an article entered a state. In *E.C. Knight* the Court ruled that Congress could not regulate manufacturing because it is a local concern. The holding in *Carter v. Carter Coal* is directly on point for *Darby*. The Court held therein that Congress could not set wages and working conditions for miners, yet, after *Darby*, it has power to do so. Justice Stone's assertion thus seems somewhat disingenuous. The difference is in the Court's newfound ability to swallow the government's "race to the bottom" rationale. The result is that corporations have a harder time exploiting competition in attracting industry—which means jobs and a broader tax base—between states.

■ CASE VOCABULARY

PLENARY POWER: Complete power or authority.

Wickard v. Filburn
(Agriculture Secretary) v. *(Wheat Farmer)*
317 U.S. 111, 63 S.Ct. 82 (1942)

THE SUPREME COURT SETS A NEW OUTER BOUNDARY OF THE FEDERAL COMMERCE POWER

■ **INSTANT FACTS** Wickard (P) exceeded his allotted quota for wheat production, the excess amount to be used for his own consumption. He was fined by the government and seeks to have the quota ruled unconstitutional.

■ **BLACK LETTER RULE** Congress' commerce authority extends to all activities having a substantial effect on interstates commerce, including those that do not have such a substantial effect individually, but do when judged by their national aggregate effects.

■ **PROCEDURAL BASIS**
Appeal to the Supreme Court after a lower federal court granted an injunction against the enforcement of a statutory penalty.

■ **FACTS**
Congress, in passing the Agricultural Adjustment Act of 1938 (AAA), provided the federal government with authority to set national production quotas for agricultural commodities, including wheat. The purpose of this was to maintain price stability in the commodity markets by avoiding excess supplies and their concomitant obstructions to commerce. Wickard (P) was alloted 11.1 acres of wheat and a normal yield of 20.1 bushels per acre. Wickard (P) planted, however, 23 acres, and harvested from these 11.9 acres of excess acreage 239 bushels. His scheduled fine for the excess harvest was assessed at $117.11.

■ **ISSUE**
Does the commerce power extend to the regulation of the production of items not intended for distribution in the national market existing for such items?

■ **DECISION AND RATIONALE**
(Jackson, J.) Yes. It is urged that the Commerce Clause does not authorize Congress the powers it seeks to exercise here. This issue seems to be answered by our holding in *Darby*, but for the fact that the AAA extends federal regulation to production not intended in any part for commerce but wholly for consumption on the farm. Wickard (P) contends that such production is local in character, and its effects upon interstate commerce is at most "indirect." A review of the course of decision under the Commerce Clause makes plain, however, that questions of Congress' commerce power are not to be decided by reference to such nomenclature as "production" and "indirect," while foreclosing a consideration of the actual effects the activity has on interstate commerce. Whether the subject of regulation is termed "production," "consumption," or "marketing" is, therefore, not material for purposes of deciding the question of federal power before us. Even if an activity is local in nature, and therefore not regarded as commerce, it may still be reached by Congress if it exerts a substantial economic effect on interstate commerce, whether such an effect be "indirect" or "direct." Interstate commerce in wheat is large and important. The effect of consumption of homegrown wheat on interstate commerce is due to the fact that it constitutes the most variable factor in the overall consumption of the national wheat crop. Such home consumption appears to vary in an amount greater

than 20 per cent of average production. Government maintenance of the wheat price can be accomplished through controls on demand, or on supply. The AAA concentrates on controlling the wheat supply in order to control price. That Wickard's (P) own contribution for the demand for wheat may be trivial by itself is not enough to remove him from the scope of federal regulation where, as here, his contribution, taken together with those of many others similarly situated, is far from trivial. Congress' power to regulate commerce includes the power to regulate prices. It can hardly be doubted that a factor of such volume and variability as home-consumed wheat would have a substantial influence on price and market conditions. Even if we assume it is never marketed, it supplies a need of the man who grew it which would otherwise be reflected by purchases in the open market. Homegrown wheat in this sense competes with wheat in commerce. Such production, looked at cumulatively throughout the nation, has a substantial effect on commerce. This record leaves us no doubt that Congress may properly have considered that wheat consumed on the farm where grown, if wholly outside the scheme of regulation, would have a substantial effect in defeating and obstructing its purpose to stimulate trade therein at increased prices.

Analysis:

It is clear after *Wickard*, if it wasn't clear after *Darby*, that the Tenth Amendment is ineffective as a check on the federal commerce power. *Wickard* also set a new, broader standard for the exercise of the commerce power. How difficult is it to come up with an intrastate activity that doesn't, in some way, substantially affect interstate commerce when viewed in the national aggregate? As demonstrated in the 1960s civil rights cases, Congress has taken advantage of this vast broadening of its commerce authority. After *Wickard*, the only significant checks on the commerce power were specific guarantees, such as those in the Bill of Rights.

■ CASE VOCABULARY

AGGREGATE: In total; considering all similar production/consumption throughout the nation.

Heart of Atlanta Motel, Inc. v. United States

(*Discriminating Motel*) v. (*Government*)
379 U.S. 241, 85 S.Ct. 348 (1964)

RACIAL DISCRIMINATION IN PUBLIC ACCOMMODATIONS EXERTS A SUBSTANTIAL AND HARMFUL EFFECT UPON INTERSTATE COMMERCE

■ **INSTANT FACTS** An Atlanta, Georgia motel wishes to continue its racially discriminatory operations in spite of the 1964 Civil Rights Act (Act) barring racial discrimination in public accommodations.

■ **BLACK LETTER RULE** Congress has the power, under the Commerce Clause, to regulate local activities that could reasonably be seen as exerting a substantial and harmful effect upon interstate commerce.

■ **PROCEDURAL BASIS**

Declaratory judgment action appealed to the Supreme Court after a lower federal court issued an injunction prohibiting violation of the Act.

■ **FACTS**

Congress passed the Civil Rights Act of 1964 (Act) in order to ban racial discrimination in public accommodations. Testimony in support of the Act included evidence that such racial discrimination has the effect of making it much more difficult for racial minorities to find lodging and other accommodations while traveling from state to state. Further, that this has the concomitant effect of dissuading minorities from traveling interstate, which results in a substantially harmful effect on interstate commerce as a whole. In response to the Act, the Heart of Atlanta Motel (Heart)(P) filed a declaratory judgment action attacking the Act's constitutionality on the ground that it is beyond the federal commerce power. The case is before the Court on admissions and stipulations, some as follows: Heart (P) is a 216 room motel, readily accessible from two interstate highways and two state highways. Heart (P) advertises nationally; maintains over 50 billboards and highway signs within Georgia; approximately 75% of its guests are from out of state. Prior to the Act, Heart (P) refused to let rooms to Negroes, and it wishes to continue to follow this practice and, therefore, filed this suit.

■ **ISSUE**

May Congress exercise the commerce power by regulating local activities that are seen as exerting a substantial and harmful effect on interstate commerce?

■ **DECISION AND RATIONALE**

(Clark, J.) Yes. Our study of the legislative record brings us to the conclusion that Congress possessed ample power to pass the provisions of the Act at issue herein. The record of the Act's passage in each house is replete with evidence of the burdens that racial discrimination places upon interstate commerce: that our people have become increasingly mobile, with millions of people traveling from state to state; that Negroes in particular have been the subject of discrimination in transient accommodations; that these conditions had become so acute as to require the listing of available lodging for Negroes in a special guidebook. These exclusionary practices were found to be nationwide. The testimony indicated a qualitative as well as quantitative effect on interstate travel by Negroes. There was

Heart of Atlanta Motel, Inc. v. United States (Continued)

also evidence that these conditions stemming from racial discrimination had the effect of discouraging travel on the part of a substantial portion of the Negro community. Congress has often dealt with this interest in protecting interstate commerce. [The Court lists a number of Commerce Clause cases.] That Congress was legislating against moral wrongs in many of these areas rendered its enactments no less valid. Here, Congress was dealing with a moral problem. But this does not detract from the overwhelming evidence of the harmful effects of racial discrimination upon interstate commerce. It was this burden which empowered Congress to enact appropriate legislation. It is said that the operation of the motel here is of purely local character. Even if this were true, if it is interstate commerce that feels the pinch, it does not matter how local the operation which applies the squeeze. Thus, Congress may regulate the local incidents of interstate commerce, including within the states of origin and destination, which might have a substantial and harmful effect upon that commerce. We, therefore, conclude that the action of the Congress in the adoption of the Act as applied here to a motel which concededly serves interstate travelers is within the power granted it by the Commerce Clause of the Constitution. The means of removing obstacles to interstate commerce are up to Congress, with one caveat, that the means chosen by it must be reasonably adapted to the end permitted by the Constitution. We cannot say that its choice here was not so adopted.

■ CONCURRENCE

(Douglas, J.) Though I concur, I am somewhat reluctant here, to rest solely on the Commerce Clause. It is may belief that the right of people to be free of state action that discriminates against them because of race occupies a more protected position in our constitutional system than does the movement of cattle, fruit, steel and coal across state lines. The result reached by the Court is much more obvious when the facts are considered under the Fourteenth Amendment. For this Amendment deals with the constitutional status of the individual, not with the impact on commerce of local activities or vice versa. A decision based on the Fourteenth Amendment would have a more setting effect, doing away with much litigation surrounding these issues than is instigated under the Commerce Clause. Such a construction would put an end to all obstructionist strategies and finally close one door on a bitter chapter in American history.

Analysis:

The Court's opinion in *Heart of Atlanta* is well reasoned, at least partially due to the testimony Congress took when considering the Civil Rights Act of 1964. Congress knew the bar it had to meet in order to make the legislation constitutional, just as it surely knew the speed with which the Act would be challenged. The Act's constitutionality here flows from the fact that an inability to rely on finding accommodations while traveling from state to state is a substantial obstruction to the undertaking of such travel. When a significant percentage of the population is much less likely to travel interstate, even the purely economic ramifications are easy to recognize. People who travel spend money in local economies, without acting as a drain on public resources. A traveler is, therefore, someone who pays without also taking. Interestingly, had civil rights not been on just-assassinated president John F. Kennedy's legislative agenda, the Act may not have passed at all, but his successor, Lyndon Johnson, made a strong moral case for passing the agenda as a way of honoring JFK's memory.

Katzenbach v. McClung, Sr. and McClung, Jr.
(*Government*) v. (*Restaurant Owners*)
379 U.S. 294, 85 S.Ct. 377 (1964)

RESTAURANTS SERVING INTERSTATE TRAVELERS OR SERVING FOOD THAT HAS MOVED IN INTERSTATE COMMERCE ARE SUBJECT TO THE CIVIL RIGHTS ACT

■ **INSTANT FACTS** The owners of a restaurant in Birmingham, Alabama continued to exclude Negro patrons from their restaurant dining area, in violation of the Civil Rights Act of 1964.

■ **BLACK LETTER RULE** Congress' commerce authority extends to any public commercial establishment selling goods that have moved in interstate commerce and/or serving interstate travelers.

■ **PROCEDURAL BASIS**

[Not stated]

■ **FACTS**

The McClung's (Ollie's)(D) own Ollie's Barbecue, a restaurant located in Birmingham, Alabama, near both a state and an interstate highway. Ollie's (D) caters to a family and white-collar trade, with a takeout service for Negroes. Ollie's (D) purchases about $150,000 worth of food, 46% of which is meat purchased form a local supplier who procures it from out of state. The trial court below found that a substantial portion of the food Ollie's (D) sells has moved in interstate commerce. Ollie's (D) continued its racially discriminatory practices even after the Civil Rights Act of 1964 (Act), which bans such practices in public accommodations, went into effect on July 2, 1964.

■ **ISSUE**

Does a commercial enterprise serving the public fall within the reach of Congress' commerce authority when it sells goods a substantial portion of which have moved in interstate commerce?

■ **DECISION AND RATIONALE**

(Clark, J.) Yes. The basic holding in *Heart of Atlanta Motel* answers many of the contentions made by Ollie's (D). In this case we consider the Act's application to restaurants serving food a substantial portion of which has moved in commerce. Ollie's (D) Barbecue admits it is covered by the Act. There is no claim here that interstate travelers frequented the restaurant. The sole question, therefore, narrows down to whether the Act, as applied to a restaurant annually receiving about $70,000 worth of food which has moved in commerce, is a valid exercise of congressional power. We believe that the testimony heard by Congress on the effects of discrimination by restaurants afforded an ample basis for the conclusion that established restaurants in areas where such discrimination is practiced sell less interstate goods because of the discrimination; that interstate travel was obstructed directly by it; that business in general suffered, etc. True, the volume of Ollie's (D) food that has moved in interstate commerce was insignificant when compared with the total foodstuffs moving in commerce. But, as we held in *Wickard v. Filbum*, even though "appellee's own contribution to the demand for wheat may be trivial by itself is not enough to remove him from the scope of federal regulation where, as here, his contribution, taken together with that of many others similarly situated, is far from trivial." Therefore, so long as Ollie's (D) exerts a substantial economic effect on interstate commerce, it may be reached under the commerce power. Here, Congress has determined for itself that refusals of service to Negroes have imposed burdens both upon the interstate flow of food and upon the movement of products generally. So long as this Court, looking at the facts and testimony heard by Congress, can see a rational basis for finding a chosen regulatory scheme necessary to the protection of commerce, our investigation is at an end. The only remaining question—and one answered in the affirmative by these facts—is whether the particular restaurant either serves or offers to serve interstate travelers, or serves food a substantial portion of which has moved in interstate commerce. The Act, as here applied, we find to be plainly appropriate in the resolution of what Congress found to be a national commercial problem of the first magnitude.

Analysis:

Notice that the Court states that Congress had an ample basis for concluding that "established restaurants," in areas where racial discrimination is practiced, sold less interstate goods. When it refers to established restaurants, the Court is not necessarily referring to those restaurants that have racially discriminatory policies. Instead, the Court is saying that the existence of racially exclusive restaurants in a particular locale end up "rubbing off" on all of the other, non-discriminatory, restaurants in the area. Thus, a black traveler, knowing of one or two discriminatory restaurants in a town, will fail to stop in that town. This results in a loss of potential business for all restaurants in the town. When the aggregation principle is applied to such a situation, the sum total of the loss of interstate business in all such towns and cities most definitely reaches the "substantial effect on interstate commerce" standard.

National League of Cities v. Usery

(City Association) v. (Federal Government)
426 U.S. 833, 96 S.Ct. 2465 (1976)

CONGRESS DOES NOT HAVE AUTHORITY TO REGULATE THE STATES IN THEIR ROLE AS EMPLOYER

■ **INSTANT FACTS** An amendment to the Fair Labor Standards Act extended wage and hour requirements to state employees. The States are seeking to have the regulations as applied to them declared unconstitutional.

■ **BLACK LETTER RULE** The Commerce Clause does not empower Congress to regulate states or local governments in their integral governmental functions.

■ **PROCEDURAL BASIS**
Appeal to the Supreme Court after a federal appeals court ruled the federal scheme constitutional.

■ **FACTS**
The Fair Labor Standards Act (Act) requires covered employers to pay their employees a minimum hourly wage and to pay them overtime at time-and-a-half rates for hours worked in excess of forty. The Act was upheld in *United States v. Darby*. In 1974, Congress amended the Act to extend its coverage to employment by the States. The National League of Cities (P), a cooperative organization formed by many cities across the United States, sued the federal government in order to have the application of the Act to state and local governments declared unconstitutional.

■ **ISSUE**
Does the Commerce Clause grant Congress the authority to regulate the conduct of cities in their integral functions?

■ **DECISION AND RATIONALE**
(Rehnquist, J.) No. The National League of Cities (National)(P) contends that when Congress seeks to regulate directly the activities of States as public employers, it transgresses an affirmative limitation on the exercise of its commerce powers contained in the Constitution. There is no doubt that there are limits on Congress' power to override state sovereignty under the Commerce Clause. One undoubted attribute of state sovereignty is the States' power to set wages and other working conditions for their employees. The question to be resolved, then, is whether these determinations are functions essential to separate and independent existence, such that Congress may not abrogate the States' otherwise plenary power to make them. National (P), in its complaint, advanced estimates of substantial costs that will necessarily be incurred in complying with the Act. Judged solely in terms of increased dollar costs, these assertions show a significant impact on the functioning of the governmental bodies involved. [The Court lists a number of cities and their asserted potential new expenditures and budget cuts in complying with the Act.] Equally important is the Act's displacement of the States' considered policies regarding the manner in which they will structure delivery of those governmental services that their citizens require. Employment decisions, such as wages, hours, training requirements, etc., would be impossible under the Act's regulations. Our examination of the effect of the 1974 amendments to the

National League of Cities v. Usery (Continued)

Act satisfies us that both the minimum wage and the maximum hour provisions will impermissibly interfere with the integral governmental functions of these bodies. For example, the ability to structure employer-employee relationships in such areas as fire prevention, police protection, sanitation, public health, and parks and recreation, all activities typically performed by state and local governments. Should the Act be declared valid there would be little left of the States' separate and independent existence. This exercise of congressional authority does not comport with the federal system of government embodied in the Constitution. We hold that insofar as the challenged amendments operate to directly displace the States' freedom to structure integral operations in areas of traditional governmental functions, they are not within the authority granted Congress.

■ CONCURRENCE

(Blackmun, J.) I may misinterpret the Court's opinion, but it seems to me that it adopts a balancing approach, and does not outlaw federal power in areas such as environmental protection, where the federal interest is demonstrably greater and where state facility compliance with imposed federal standards would be essential. With this understanding, I join the Court's opinion.

■ DISSENT

(Brennan, J.) It is surprising that my Brethren should choose this bicentennial year of our independence to repudiate long-settled principles governing judicial interpretation of our Constitution: that the Constitution contemplates that restraints upon the exercise by Congress of its plenary commerce power lie in the political process and not in the judicial process. Instead, they purport to discover in the Constitution a restraint derived from sovereignty of the States on Congress' exercise of the commerce power. This is nothing more than a transparent cover for invalidating a congressional judgment with which they disagree.

DISSENT

(Stevens, J.) The Court holds that the federal government may not keep a State from paying a janitor a substandard wage. The principle on which this rests is difficult to see. The federal government may require the State to act impartially when it: hires and fires the janitor; withholds taxes; complies with safety regulations; forbids him from burning too much coal in the capitol furnace; prohibits him from driving the governor's limousine over 55 miles an hour, etc. Even though these and many other activities of the capitol janitor are activities of the State as State, I have no doubt that they are subject to federal regulation.

Analysis:

National League of Cities revived the Tenth Amendment as a check on Congress's asserted commerce power by providing a bubble of protection over state sovereignty in areas so integral to state and local governments that they are, in effect, state and local government. Core services of state and local governments are integral functions, such as fire and police protection, social services, street and highway repair, court services, etc. Provision of such services is the entire reason state and local governments exist. Justice Brennan states in his dissent that "the Constitution contemplates that restraints upon the exercise by Congress of its plenary commerce power lie in the political process and not in the judicial process." But just as there are implied powers in the Constitution, there are implied limits. The Constitution set up a federalist system, with the sovereignty of the States being a keystone of this system. Assuming these values, isn't there an implied limitation on the federal government's power to interfere in the most basic functions of state and local government?

Garcia v. San Antonio Metropolitan Transit Authority

(Not Stated) v. (City's Transit Authority)
469 U.S. 528, 105 S.Ct. 1005 (1985)

SUPREME COURT OVERRULES NATIONAL LEAGUE OF CITIES IN FAVOR OF THE ELECTORAL PROCESS AS A CHECK ON FEDERAL COMMERCE POWER

■ **INSTANT FACTS** Application of the Fair Labor Standards Act to a city's mass transit system fuels a revisitation of *National League of Cities v. Usery*.

■ **BLACK LETTER RULE** Congress has full authority under the Commerce Clause to regulate the traditional, or core, functions of state and local governments notwithstanding the Tenth Amendment.

■ **PROCEDURAL BASIS**

[Not Stated]

■ **FACTS**

The federal government applied the Fair Labor Standards Act (Act), which regulates hours, wage and overtime conditions for covered employers, to San Antonio's Metropolitan Transit Authority (MTA)(D). The MTA (D) objects to such an application on the ground that the Supreme Court's ruling in *National League of Cities* prohibits the federal government from regulating the States as States, in their traditional and core government functions, a category in which the MTA (D) claims it is included.

■ **ISSUE**

May Congress regulate a city's mass transit authority's employer-employee relations under the Commerce Clause?

■ **DECISION AND RATIONALE**

(Blackmun, J.) Yes. In *National League of Cities* we ruled that the Act could not be applied to state and local governments "in areas of traditional government functions," but we did not provide an explanation of how a "traditional" function is to be distinguished from a "nontraditional" function. Courts have struggled with this distinction ever since. The intervening years have convinced us that the attempt to draw such boundaries is not only unworkable, but is also inconsistent with the established principles of federalism. *National League of Cities* is, therefore, overruled. Under our federalist system, the States must be left open to engage in any activity that their citizens choose for the common weal, no matter how unorthodox anyone else—including the judiciary—deems state involvement to be. Attempts to apply a standard asking what is "traditional," "integral," or "necessary" when it comes to governmental functions inevitably invites an unelected federal judiciary to make decisions about which state policies it favors and which ones it dislikes. We therefore reject such an approach. If there be limits on the federal government's power to interfere with state functions—as undoubtedly there are—we must look elsewhere to find them, for they are not to be found in the language of the Commerce Clause. Further, we doubt that courts ultimately can identify principled constitutional limitations on the scope of Congress' commerce powers over the States merely by relying on a priori definitions of state sovereignty. Moreover, looking at the structure of the federal government, it is clear that its composition was designed in large part to protect the States from overreaching by Congress. This is shown by the States' indirect influence in federal elections through their ability to control electoral qualifications in Presidential elections. States have more direct influence in the Senate, where each State has equal representation. The effectiveness of the federal political process in preserving the States' interests is apparent even today in the course of federal legislation. The States have been very successful in garnering assistance from the federal government through general and program-specific grants in aid. This assistance has been a longstanding federal role. It has helped States fund services such as police and fire protection, education, public health and hospitals, parks and recreation, and sanitation. At the same time States have exercised their influence to receive such support, they have been able to exempt themselves from a wide variety of obligations imposed by Congress under the Commerce Clause. Even with the changes that have occurred in our system, such as the popular election of Senators, we are convinced that the fundamental limitation that the constitutional scheme imposes on the Commerce Clause to protect the "States as States" is one of process rather than one of result. Any substantive restraint on the exercise of Commerce Clause power must find its justification in the procedural nature of this basic limitation, and it must be tailored to compensate for possible failings in the national political process rather than to dictate a sacred province of State autonomy. Insofar as the present case is concerned, we see nothing in the Act's requirements, as applied to the MTA (D), that is unconstitutional. The principal and basic limit on federal commerce power is that inherent in all congressional action—the built-in restraints that our system provides through state participation in federal government action. Through the political process, the States are ensured that laws that unduly burden them will not be promulgated.

■ DISSENT

(Powell, J.) Because I believe this decision substantially alters the federal system embodied in the Constitution, I dissent. There have been few cases in which the principle of stare decisis and the rationale of recent decisions were ignored so abruptly. Our reasoning in National League of Cities, and the principle applied therein, has been reiterated consistently over the past eight years. Today's decision effectively reduces the Tenth Amendment to meaningless rhetoric when Congress acts pursuant to the Commerce Clause. This is so because the Court finds that National League of Cities "inevitably invites an unelected federal judiciary to make decisions about which state policies it favors and which one it dislikes." I note that it does not seem to have occurred to the Court that it—an unelected majority of five Justices—today rejects almost 200 years of the understanding of the constitutional status of federalism. In doing so, there is only a single passing reference to the Tenth Amendment. Today's decision radically departs from long-settled constitutional values and ignores the role of judicial review in our system of government, while failing to explain how the States' role in the electoral process guarantees that particular exercises of the Commerce Clause power will not infringe on residual state sovereignty. We recently noted "the hydraulic pressure inherent within each of the separate Branches to exceed the outer limits of its power." There is no reason offered why this pressure won't operate when Congress invokes its commerce power in the future. The States' political success in obtaining federal grants is not relevant to the question whether the political processes are the proper means of enforcing constitutional limitations. The States' role in our system of government is a matter of constitutional law, not of legislative grace. It is troubling that the Court today seems fine with allowing federal political officials, invoking the Commerce Clause, to be the sole judges of the limits of their own power. This is inconsistent with the fundamental principles of our constitutional system.

■ DISSENT

(Rehnquist, J.) I join both Justice Powell's and Justice O'Connor's thoughtful dissents. I do not think it incumbent on those of us in dissent to spell out further the fine points of a principle that will, I am confident, in time again command the support of a majority of this Court.

■ DISSENT

(O'Connor, J.) The Court today surveys the battle scene of federalism and sounds a retreat. I join Justice Powell's opinion. I also write to note my fundamental disagreement with the majority's views of federalism and the duty of this Court. Federalism cannot be reduced to the weak "essence" distilled by the majority today. There is more to federalism than the nature of the constraints that can be imposed on the States in the realm of authority left open to them by the Constitution. The central issue of federalism is whether any realm is left open to the States by the Constitution. The true "essence" of federalism is that the States as States have legitimate interests which the National Government is bound to respect even though its laws are supreme. The Court cannot abrogate its duty to ensure the federal government's compliance with its duty to respect the legitimate interests of the States. This duty remains, indeed, is all the more important, when the job of constitutional interpretation is so difficult, as it is here. Rather than embrace this duty, the Majority chooses to take the easy way out and leave protection of the States' interests to the political process.

Analysis:

Nine years before *Garcia*, the Court ruled in *National League of Cities* that the States are free from federal intrusion into their core, traditional functions, which signaled a revival of the Tenth Amendment as an affirmative check on the government's commerce power. Here, once again, the Tenth Amendment is dead in this regard. The Court asserts that an unelected federal judiciary should not be deciding which state functions are traditional. But don't Courts make these kind of normative decisions every day? Indeed, isn't making these decisions much of why courts exist? The Majority prefers to let the members of Congress make the decision here. The result is that where, before, the Judiciary performed its constitutionally appointed task of acting as a check on congressional power, now Congress has a free hand to meddle in the purely local affairs of state and local governments. While requiring the States to pay the federal minimum wage, along with overtime, etc., may not be an overly pervasive example of federal intrusion into traditionally local government functions, one can imagine examples that are. Imagine, for instance, a federally mandated affirmative action program in state and local government hiring. Would resorting to the political process be fruitful for those states whose popular majorities are opposed to such programs?

■ CASE VOCABULARY

A PRIORI: A logical reasoning process running from what is general and leading to the more specific.

WEAL: A sound, healthy or prosperous state.

United States v. Lopez
(*Government*) v. (*Criminal Defendant*)
514 U.S. 549, 115 S.Ct. 1624 (1995)

GUN-FREE SCHOOL ZONES ACT OF 1990 DECLARED AN UNCONSTITUTIONAL EXERCISE OF THE COMMERCE POWER

■ **INSTANT FACTS** A 12th-grade student was convicted of violating the Gun-Free School Zones Act of 1990, which makes it a federal offense to possess a gun near a school.

■ **BLACK LETTER RULE** Congressional authority to regulate pursuant to the Commerce Clause extends to only those activities that rationally implicate (1) the channels of interstate commerce; (2) the instrumentalities of interstate commerce; or (3) activities having a substantial effect upon interstate commerce.

■ **PROCEDURAL BASIS**

Appeal to the Supreme Court from the circuit court's reversal of a criminal conviction.

■ **FACTS**

Congress passed the Gun-Free School Zones Act of 1990 (Act or § 922), making it a federal offense "for any individual knowingly to possess a firearm at a place that the individual knows, or has reasonable cause to believe, is a school zone." A "school zone" is on the grounds of or within 1,000 feet of a school. The Act neither regulates a commercial activity nor contains a requirement that the possession be connected in any way to interstate commerce. Lopez (D), a 12th-grade student, was convicted of violating the Act by carrying a concealed .38-caliber handgun and five bullets into his high school.

■ **ISSUE**

Does the commerce power extend to regulation of activities having only a potential attenuated and distended effect upon interstate commerce?

■ **DECISION AND RATIONALE**

(Rehnquist, C.J.) No. The Constitution mandates a division of authority, which was adopted by the framers to ensure protection of our fundamental liberties. A healthy balance of power between the States and the Federal Government reduces the risk of tyranny and abuse from either front. [The Court reviewed a series of Commerce Clause decisions from *Gibbons* to the 1940s.] These decisions greatly expanded the authority of Congress. This doctrinal change partially reflects a view that earlier Commerce Clause cases artificially had constrained the authority of Congress to regulate interstate commerce. But even these modern expansions confirm that this power has outer limits shaped by the requirements of our dual federalist system. These limits require that there be some rational basis for concluding that a regulated activity sufficiently affects interstate commerce in order for the regulation to be valid. Consistent with this, we have identified three broad categories of activity that Congress may regulate under its commerce power. First is the use of the channels of interstate commerce. Second are the instrumentalities of interstate commerce. Third, Congress has the power to regulate those activities having a substantial relation to interstate commerce, i.e. those activities that substantially affect interstate commerce. We now consider § 922 in light of this framework. The first two categories above are not implicated here, so if § 922 is to be sustained, it must regulate an activity that substantially affects interstate commerce. In other words, where economic activity substantially affects interstate commerce, legislation regulating that activity will be sustained. The Act is a criminal statute that by its terms has nothing to do with "commerce." The Act is not an essential part of a larger regulation of economic activity. Further, the Act contains no jurisdictional element which would ensure, through case-by-case inquiry, that the firearm possession in question affects interstate commerce. When we look to congressional findings supporting any asserted effects on commerce we find none. The government (P) concedes that neither the statute nor its legislative history contain[s] express findings regarding any effects on commerce of gun possession in a school zone. In the courts, the government (P) argues that such firearm possession may result in a violent crime, which could affect the national economy in two ways. First, by imposing high financial costs upon society through insurance. Second, that violent crime dissuades individuals to travel into areas within the country where it occurs. The last argument is that guns threaten the learning environment, which handicaps the educational process. This, in turn, would have an adverse effect on the nation's well being. As a result, the government (P) argues, Congress could rationally have concluded that the Act substantially affects interstate commerce. Under the "violent crime" rationale, the commerce power would extend not only to all violent crime, but also to any activities that could lead to violent crime. Similarly, the "national productivity" reasoning would allow Congress to regulate any activity that it found was related to the economic productivity of individual citizens, such as family law. Under these theories, it is difficult to perceive any limitation on federal power. For example, if Congress can regulate activities adversely affecting the learning environment, then, a fortiori, it can also regulate the educational process directly. Admittedly, a determination whether an intrastate activity is commercial or noncommercial may in some cases result in legal uncertainty. But the Constitution mandates this uncertainty by withholding from Congress a plenary police power that would authorize enactment of every type of legislation. While these are not, and cannot be, precise formulations, we think they point the way to a correct decision in this case. Possession of a gun in a local school zone is in no sense an economic activity that might, through repetition elsewhere, substantially affect any sort of interstate commerce. It is true that some of our prior cases have taken long steps down that road, giving great deference to congressional action, but we decline here to proceed any further.

■ CONCURRENCE

(Kennedy, J.) Our struggle to define the extent to which the commerce power as our nation has changed, counsels great restraint before the Court invalidates a congressional act under the Clause. With this pause, I join the Court's opinion with the following observations on its holding. The history of our Commerce Clause jurisprudence teaches at least two lessons. First is the imprecision of content-based boundaries used without more to define the limits of the Commerce Clause. Second, and related, is that the Court has an immense stake in the stability of our Commerce Clause jurisprudence as it has evolved to this point. Stare decisis operates with great force in counseling against our disturbing the essential principles now in place respecting the commerce power. Also, let the political branches not forget that it is also their sworn obligation, in the first and primary instance, to preserve and protect the Constitution in maintaining the federal balance. At the same time, the absence of structural mechanisms to require those officials to undertake this principled task argues against a complete renunciation of the judicial role. The federal balance is too essential a part of our constitutional structure and plays too vital a role in securing freedom for us to admit inability to intervene when one or the other level of government has tipped the scales too far. The statute before us upsets the federal balance to a degree that renders it an unconstitutional assertion of the commerce power. Here neither the actors nor their conduct has a commercial character, and there is no commercial nexus to support the Act. In a sense, any conduct in this interdependent world of ours has an ultimate commercial origin or consequence. Should the commerce power be unlimited? When Congress attempts such an extension as is here evident, we must at least inquire whether the exercise of power seeks to intrude upon an area of traditional state concern. It is well established that education is a traditional concern of the States. There is a particularly important duty to make sure the federal-state balance is not destroyed in such an area. This allows states to remain the laboratories of experimentation, a role envisioned by the framers. Absent a stronger connection or identification with commercial concerns that are central to the Commerce Clause, the Act's interference contradicts the federal balance the framers designed and that this Court is obliged to enforce.

United States v. Lopez (Continued)

■ **CONCURRENCE**

(Thomas, J.) Although I join the majority, I write separately to demonstrate how far we have departed from the original understanding of the Commerce Clause, and to show that the result we reach today is by no means "radical." At the time of the framers, "commerce" consisted of selling, buying, and bartering, as well as transporting for these purposes. Also, the term was used in contradistinction to productive activities such as manufacturing and agriculture. Moreover, interjecting a modern sense of commerce into the Constitution generates significant textual and structural problems. For instance, "manufacturing" cannot replace "commerce." When a manufacturer produces a car, assembly cannot take place "with a foreign nation," or "with the Indian tribes." Manufacturing takes place at a discrete site. Agriculture and manufacturing involve production of goods; commerce encompasses traffic in such articles. There is also no support in the Constitution for the proposition that Congress has authority over all activities that "substantially affect" interstate commerce. Indeed, much if not all of Article I, § 8 would be surplusage if Congress were given authority over this broad of a range of activities. An Interpretation of Clause 3 that makes the rest of § 8 superfluous cannot be correct. Yet under this Court's interpretation, the power we have accorded Congress has swallowed Article I, § 8. Furthermore, if the "substantial effects" test is correct, why not apply it to other congressional powers? Congress could regulate all matters that "substantially affect" the Army and Navy, tax collection, bankruptcy, etc. My review of the case law indicates that the substantial effects test is but an innovation of the 20th century. It represents a dramatic departure in the 1930s from a century and a half of precedent. Apart from this, it suffers from the further flaw that it appears to grant Congress a police power over the Nation, in part as a result of the "aggregation principle." This principle is clever, but it has no stopping point. Allowing the use of such a formulation is akin to giving a Congress a blank check.

■ **DISSENT**

(Stevens, J.) The welfare of our future "Commerce with foreign Nations, and among the several States" is vitally dependent on the character of the education of our children. I therefore agree entirely with Justice Breyer's dissenting opinion. I also agree with Justice Souter's exposition of the radical character of the Court's holding. Congress's power to regulate commerce in firearms includes the power to prohibit possession of guns at any location because of their potentially harmful use; it necessarily follows that Congress may also prohibit their possession in particular markets. There is a substantial market for guns among school-age children. This justifies federal regulation.

■ **DISSENT**

(Souter, J.) In my view, the Act falls well within the scope of the commerce power as this Court has understood that power over the last half century. In concluding so, I apply three basic principles of Commerce Clause interpretation. First, the power to regulate commerce encompasses the power to regulate local activities insofar as they significantly affect interstate commerce. Second, when determining the effects of an activity, a court must consider the cumulative effect of all similar instances. Third, the Constitution requires us to judge the connections between a regulated activity and commerce, not directly, but at one remove, one degree of separation. Courts must, therefore, give Congress some leeway in making this determination. This because the Constitution delegates the commerce power directly to Congress, and because the determination requires an empirical judgment of a kind Congress is best suited for doing. The traditional words "rational basis" captures this leeway. We should therefore ask whether Congress could have had a rational basis for its conclusions. Here, the answer is yes. Numerous reports and studies make clear that Congress could reasonably have found the empirical connection that its law, implicitly or explicitly, asserts. These reports show that the problem of guns in and around schools is widespread and extremely serious, and include evidence linking guns to higher dropout rates and a drop in academic success. Congress thus could obviously have concluded that guns and learning are mutually exclusive. Next, Congress could have found, given the effect of education upon interstate and foreign commerce, that gunrelated violence in and around schools is a commercial, as well as human, problem. The violence-related facts, the educational facts, and the economic facts, taken together, make Congress's conclusion that gun possession in school zones has a substantial effect upon interstate commerce. Such a holding would not "obliterate" the "distinction between what is national and what is local." Nor would it logically extend to allowing Congress to regulate family law, or even any and all aspects of education. Congress must have a rational basis; it thus does not have a free hand. The majority's holding creates three serious legal problems. First, it

United States v. Lopez (Continued)

runs contrary to our modern Commerce Clause cases upholding congressional authority despite more attenuated connections to interstate commerce. Second is the Court's belief that it can reconcile its holding by distinguishing between "commercial" and non-commercial "transactions." This causes the same problems we encountered in attempting to employ nomenclature like "production," "indirect," and "direct" in earlier cases. Third, it threatens legal uncertainty in an area of law that, until now, seemed reasonably well settled. Congress has enacted numerous statutes that use the words "affecting commerce" to define their scope. What will happen with these? In sum, because Congress could have had a rational basis for concluding that guns have a harmful effect upon education, and thus interstate commerce, the Act should be upheld as a valid exercise of the commerce power.

Analysis:

As this and other Commerce Clause cases illustrate, the Court is sharply divided when it comes to the extent of, and proper way of interpreting, the Commerce Clause. When the activity has no direct connection with commerce, but is instead looked at as an activity traditionally regulated by the States, there is little chance its regulation will be upheld. This standard ensures that the States retain their proper place in the federal system, thus allowing them to fulfill their role as laboratories of experimentation. Gun possession in school zones is obviously undesirable. If the citizens of a particular state believe that such gun possession is undermining efforts to provide a good education to children, the state is perfectly free to ban gun possession around its schools. The other alternative—to apply an extremely deferential rational basis standard to Commerce Clause legislation—would go a long way toward allowing Congress a free hand.

■ CASE VOCABULARY

A FORTIORI: With even greater force.

RATIONAL BASIS: A standard of review that asks whether Congress could have (not does/did have) had a reasonable basis for reaching the conclusions necessary for its legislation to be constitutional.

United States v. Morrison
(*Government*) v. (*Accused Rapist*)
529 U.S. 598, 120 S.Ct. 1740 (2000)

THE SUPREME COURT RESTRICTS APPLICATION OF THE AGGREGATION DOCTRINE TO REGULATION OF ACTIVITIES THAT ARE ECONOMIC IN AND OF THEMSELVES

■ **INSTANT FACTS** An alleged rape victim sought to sue her accused attackers under the federal Violence Against Women Act (Act or VAWA). The accused asserts that VAWA is an unconstitutional exercise of congressional authority.

■ **BLACK LETTER RULE** Congress may not, pursuant to the Commerce Clause, regulate a local activity solely on the basis that it has substantial effects on interstate commerce when viewed in its nationwide aggregate.

■ **PROCEDURAL BASIS**
Appeal to the Supreme Court after the circuit court of appeals held that the VAWA is an unconstitutional exercise of the commerce power.

■ **FACTS**
Brzonkala (P1) sued her fellow university student, Morrison (D) under the Violence Against Women Act (Act or VAWA), alleging that he assaulted and raped her. The VAWA is a federal statute providing a federal civil remedy for victims of gender-motivated violence. Morrison (D) challenges the constitutionality of the Act. The United States (Government) (P2) intervened to defend the Act's constitutionality under the Commerce Clause.

■ **ISSUE**
May Congress regulate under the Commerce Clause local activities that are not economic in nature?

■ **DECISION AND RATIONALE**
(Rehnquist, C.J.) No. In the years since *NLRB v. Jones & Laughlin Steel Corp.* (1937), Congress has had considerably greater latitude in regulating conduct and transactions under the Commerce Clause than our previous case law permitted. *Lopez* [Gun-free School Zones Act declared to be an unconstitutional exercise of the commerce power] emphasized, however, that Congress's regulatory authority is not without effective bounds. Of the three broad categories in which Congress may properly exercise its commerce power, Brzonkala (P1) seeks to sustain the Act as a regulation of activity that substantially affects interstate commerce. We agree that if the Act is to be sustained, this is the category of activities—those substantially affecting interstate commerce—in which it must fit. Both Brzonkala (P1) and Justice Souter's dissent downplay the role that the economic nature the regulated activity plays in our Commerce Clause analysis. But a fair reading of *Lopez* shows that the noneconomic, criminal nature of the conduct at issue was central to our decision in that case. A second important consideration in *Lopez* was that the statute contained no express jurisdictional element which might limit its reach to a discrete set of firearms having an explicit connection with or effect on interstate commerce. Third, there were no express congressional findings regarding the effects upon interstate commerce of gun possession in a school zone. Finally, the purported link between gun possession and a substantial effect on interstate commerce was attenuated. Using these principles as reference points, the proper resolution of the present case is clear. Gender-motivated crimes of violence are not, in any

sense of the phrase, economic activity. Thus far in our Nation's history our cases have upheld Commerce Clause regulation of intrastate activity only where that activity is economic in nature. Like the statute in *Lopez*, VAWA contains no jurisdictional element establishing that the federal cause of action is in pursuance of Congress's power to regulate interstate commerce. And while VAWA is supported by numerous findings regarding the serious impact that gender-motivated violence has on victims and their families, the existence of such findings is not sufficient, by itself, to sustain the constitutionality of Commerce Clause legislation. In both this case and *Lopez*, Congress's findings are substantially weakened by its reliance on a method of reasoning that we have already rejected as unworkable if we are to maintain the Constitution's enumeration of powers. If accepted, this reasoning would allow Congress to regulate any crime as long as the nationwide, aggregated impact of that crime has substantial effects on employment, production, transit, or consumption. The same concern we had in *Lopez*, that Congress might use the Commerce Clause to completely obliterate the Constitution's distinction between national and local authority, seems equally well founded here. We accordingly reject the argument that Congress may regulate noneconomic, violent criminal conduct based solely on that conduct's aggregate effect on interstate commerce.

■ CONCURRENCE

(Thomas, J.) The majority correctly applies our decision in *Lopez* and I join it in full. I write separately to point out that the very notion of a "substantial effects" test is inconsistent with the original understanding of Congress's powers and with this Court's early Commerce Clause cases. By continuing to apply this rootless and malleable standard the Court has encouraged the view that the Commerce Clause has virtually no limits. Until we adopt a standard more consistent with the original understanding, Congress will continue appropriating state police powers under the guise of regulating commerce.

■ DISSENT

(Souter, J.) Our cases stand for the following propositions. That Congress has the power to legislate with regard to activity that, in the aggregate, has a substantial effect on interstate commerce. The fact of such a substantial effect is not an issue for the courts in the first instance, but for Congress, whose institutional capacity for gathering evidence and taking testimony far exceeds ours. The business of the courts is to review the congressional assessment simply for the rationality of concluding that a jurisdictional basis exists in fact. Applying these propositions here leads to only one conclusion. Unlike the statute at issue in *Lopez*, Congress assembled a mountain of data showing the effects of violence against women on interstate commerce. Congress explicitly stated the predicate for the exercise of its commerce power. The sufficiency of this evidence as providing a rational basis for its findings cannot be seriously questioned. Indeed, gender-based violence in the 1990s was shown to operate in a manner similar to racial discrimination in the 1960s in reducing the mobility of employees and their production and consumption of goods shipped in interstate commerce. Like racial discrimination, gender-based discrimination bars its victims from full participation in the national economy. We rejected this formalistic economic/noneconomic distinction in *Wickard*. But again, history seems to be repeating itself, for the theory of traditional state concern as grounding a limiting principle has been rejected previously. What the majority ultimately finds a way to ignore are the facts of integrated national commerce and a political relationship between States and Nation much affected by their respective treasuries and constitutional modifications adopted by the people. The federalism of the past is no more adequate to account for those facts today than the theory of laissez-faire was able to govern the national economy 70 years ago.

Analysis:

In *Morrison*, the Court strongly reaffirms its ruling and reasoning in *Lopez*. The significance of *Lopez* is the way it changed the standard applied to the federal regulation of intrastate activities. First, federal regulation of single state activities depends on whether such activities, when looked at as a class, substantially affect interstate commerce. Prior to *Lopez*, the Court had allowed such regulation without requiring that the effects on interstate commerce be "substantial." The second fundamental change wrought by the *Lopez* decision is the unwillingness of the Court to give blind deference to Congress's jurisdictional findings. Now, when the activity being regulated is not commercial in nature, true rational basis review will give way to a more searching scrutiny. Certain economic exigencies—the Great Depression, for example—led the Court to defer to Congress's judgment and allow an expansion of the commerce power. But, in light of current national and world economic realities, Congress's further attempts to expand its authority at the expense of state sovereignty and federalist principles finds little favor with a majority of the Court.

Pierce County, Washington v. Guillen

(County) v. (Decedent's Husband)
537 U.S. 129, 123 S.Ct. 720 (2003)

CONGRESS MAY REGULATE INTRASTATE ACTIVITY THAT AFFECTS INTERSTATE COMMERCE

■ **INSTANT FACTS** Guillen (P) sought through discovery to obtain information from Pierce County, Washington (D), concerning accidents occurring at the intersection where his wife died.

■ **BLACK LETTER RULE** Under the Commerce Clause, Congress is empowered to regulate and protect the instrumentalities of interstate commerce, even though the threat may come only from intrastate commerce.

■ **PROCEDURAL BASIS**

On interlocutory appeal to review an order compelling discovery.

■ **FACTS**

To improve highway safety throughout the nation, Congress adopted the Hazard Elimination Program. In exchange for federal highway expenditures, the Hazard Elimination Program required states to thoroughly and systematically survey public highways to identify potential dangers to motorists. The states grew concerned that such investigations may expose them to increased liability for accidents occurring after a site has been identified as dangerous, but before corrective measures can be taken. In response, Congress enacted 23 U.S.C. § 409, excluding any such state investigations from civil discovery and evidence in a civil trial. In 1996, Guillen's (P) wife died at an intersection on a public road in Pierce County, Washington. During the civil suit, Guillen (P) sought to obtain information on accidents at the intersection. Relying on § 409, the County (D) refused to comply with the discovery request. After Guillen (P) successfully moved to compel the disclosure, the County (D) filed an interlocutory appeal.

■ **ISSUE**

Is 23 U.S.C. § 409, excluding from evidence certain state investigations, a valid exercise of Congress's authority under the Commerce Clause?

■ **DECISION AND RATIONALE**

(Thomas, J.) Yes. Under the Commerce Clause, Congress is "empowered to regulate and protect the instrumentalities of interstate commerce . . . , even though the threat may come only from intrastate commerce." The Hazard Elimination Program was adopted to reduce hazardous road conditions affecting interstate commerce. In turn, § 409 was adopted to further meaningful state participation in the Program. Because Congress could reasonably believe § 409 to be necessary to further the Program's objectives, § 409 is within Congress's power under the Commerce Clause.

Analysis:

The Court's decision is controversial not because of its Commerce Clause analysis, but rather for the impact § 409 has on state sovereignty. While Congress undoubtedly has constitutional authority to regulate interstate highways, § 409 threatens state control over the administration of justice within its borders by insulating evidence from state discovery rules.

■ **CASE VOCABULARY**

INTERSTATE COMMERCE: Trade and other business activities between those located in different states, especially on a large scale involving transportation between citizens, states, and nations.

INTRASTATE COMMERCE: Commerce that begins and ends entirely within the borders of a single state.

Gonzales v. Raich

(U.S. Attorney General) v. (Marijuana Patient)
545 U.S. 1, 125 S.Ct. 2195 (2005)

CONGRESSIONAL REGULATION OF "INTERSTATE" COMMERCE MAY INCLUDE "INTRASTATE" ACTIVITIES

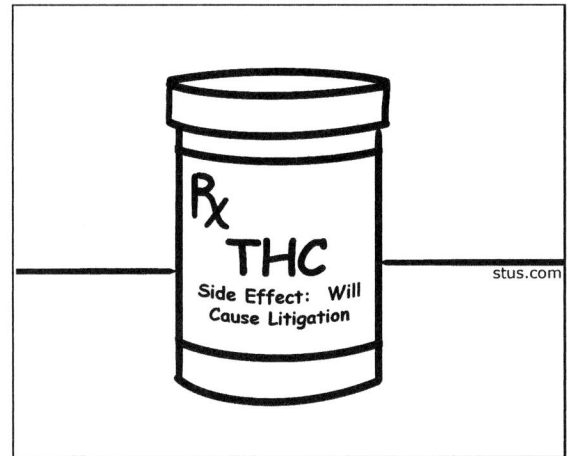

■ **INSTANT FACTS** Raich (P) sought an injunction against enforcement of the federal Controlled Substances Act, insofar as that law prohibited her use of marijuana for medical purposes.

■ **BLACK LETTER RULE** Congress may regulate intrastate activity if there is a rational basis for concluding that the activity may have a substantial effect on interstate commerce.

■ **PROCEDURAL BASIS**

Appeal from an order of the Ninth Circuit Court of Appeals granting injunctive relief.

■ **FACTS**

California passed laws permitting the use of marijuana for medical purposes. Raich (P) received a prescription of marijuana from her physician. She brought an action against the U.S. government (D) seeking injunctive and declaratory relief prohibiting enforcement of the federal Controlled Substances Act, 21 U.S.C. § 801 *et seq.*

■ **ISSUE**

Was the Controlled Substances Act, as applied to medical users of marijuana, a valid exercise of congressional power under the Commerce Clause?

■ **DECISION AND RATIONALE**

(Stevens, J.) Yes. Congress may regulate intrastate activity if there is a rational basis for concluding that the activity may have a substantial effect on interstate commerce. Raich (P) does not dispute that the enactment of the Controlled Substances Act was a valid exercise of congressional authority. She claims only that the application of the Act to the intrastate manufacture and possession of marijuana for medical purposes violates the Commerce Clause.

Precedent identifies three general types of authority Congress has pursuant to the Commerce Clause. The first allows Congress to regulate the channels of interstate commerce. The second allows Congress to regulate and protect the instrumentalities of interstate commerce, and the persons or things in interstate commerce. The third allows Congress to regulate activities that substantially affect interstate commerce. Case law has firmly established the power of Congress to regulate purely local activities that are part of an economic class of activities that have a substantial effect on interstate commerce. If Congress decides that the total incidence of a practice poses a threat to a national market, it may regulate all of the activity. When a general regulatory statute bears a substantial relation to commerce, the de minimis character of individual instances is of no consequence.

The case of *Wickard v. Filburn,* 317 U.S. 111 (1942), is relevant. In *Wickard,* the Court upheld application of a federal statute limiting wheat cultivation to a farmer who grew wheat for his own use. The Court

Gonzales v. Raich (Continued)

concluded that Congress had a rational basis for concluding that, when viewed in the aggregate, leaving home-consumed wheat outside the federal regulatory scheme would have a substantial effect on price and market conditions. There was also the concern that rising wheat prices could draw home-produced wheat into the interstate market, causing lower wheat prices. In this case, Congress had a rational basis for concluding that leaving home-consumed marijuana outside federal control would similarly affect price and market conditions. In addition, there was the concern that high demand in the interstate market for marijuana would draw home-produced marijuana into the interstate market. The Court is not concerned with whether Raich's (P) activities, taken in the aggregate, do have a substantial effect on interstate commerce, but only whether there is a rational basis for drawing that conclusion. It is not important that congressional regulation also takes in some intrastate activities.

The cases of *United States v. Lopez,* 514 U.S. 549 (1995), and *United States v. Morrison,* 529 U.S. 598 (2000), are distinguishable. In those two cases, the claim was that the entire statute was unconstitutional. Raich (P) concedes that the statute is constitutional, but is only unconstitutional as applied to her situation. If a class of activities may be regulated by Congress, the courts have no authority to excise as trivial individual instances of the class. In addition, the activities regulated by the Controlled Substances Act are essentially economic. Prohibiting the intrastate possession or manufacture of an article of commerce is a rational, and common, means of regulating commerce in that product.

Raich (P) also raises a substantive due process claim. This claim was not addressed by the Court of Appeals. There are other avenues of redress for Raich (P), including legislation or reclassification of marijuana. Reversed and remanded.

■ CONCURRENCE

(Scalia, J.) Activities that substantially affect interstate commerce are not themselves part of interstate commerce. The power to regulate those activities cannot come from the Commerce Clause alone. That power comes from the Necessary and Proper Clause. Where necessary to make a regulation of interstate commerce effective, Congress may regulate even those intrastate activities that do not themselves substantially affect interstate commerce. Even when the end is constitutional and legitimate, the means must be appropriate and plainly adapted to that end. The means must not be otherwise prohibited and must be consistent with the letter and spirit of the Constitution.

■ DISSENT

(O'Connor, J.) The "outer limits" of Commerce Clause authority are enforced to protect historic spheres of state sovereignty from excessive federal encroachment. This case exemplifies the role of the states as laboratories. The states' core police powers have always included the authority to define criminal law and protect the health, safety, and welfare of their citizens. California exercised that power, and came to is own conclusion on the issue of whether marijuana should be available to relieve severe pain and suffering. The rule announced by the majority allows Congress to regulate intrastate authority without check, provided there is some implication by legislative design that regulating intrastate activity is essential to the interstate regulatory scheme.

The courts must identify objective markers for confining the analysis in Commerce Clause cases. There are a number of objective markers available in this case. Both federal and state legislation draw a distinction between medical and non-medical uses of drugs. Moreover, because concerns about dual sovereignty animate Commerce Clause cases, it is relevant that this case involves the interplay of federal and state regulation in the area of criminal law and social policy, where "States lay claim by right of history and expertise." The majority's definition of economic activity is breathtaking. It includes any activity involving the production, distribution, and consumption of commodities. This broad definition threatens to sweep all of productive human activity into federal regulatory reach. Even assuming that economic activity is at issue in this case, the Government (D) has not shown that possession and use of homegrown marijuana for medical purposes has a substantial effect on interstate commerce. Similarly, there has been no showing that regulating such activity is necessary to an interstate regulatory scheme. A concern for dual sovereignty requires that a congressional excursion into the traditional domain of states be justified. Characterizing this case as being about the Necessary and Proper Clause does not change the analysis significantly.

◼ DISSENT

(Thomas, J.) The marijuana used by Raich (P) has never been bought or sold, has never crossed state lines, and has had no demonstrable effect on interstate commerce. If Congress can regulate this activity under the Commerce Clause, it can regulate virtually anything, and the federal government ceases to be one of limited and enumerated powers. Raich's (P) local cultivation and consumption of marijuana is not "Commerce . . . among the several States." The majority does not argue that Raich's (P) conduct is interstate commerce.

The Necessary and Proper Clause is not a warrant for Congress to enact any law with a conceivable connection to the exercise of an enumerated power. It is also, however, not a command to enact only laws that are absolutely indispensable to such an exercise of power. On its face, a ban in the intrastate production and possession of marijuana may be plainly adapted to stopping the interstate flow of marijuana. Raich (P) does not challenge the Controlled Substances Act on its face. She challenges it as applied to her conduct. Raich (P) is not subject to regulation because she is part of a subclass of marijuana users—local growers and users of state-authorized, medical marijuana—that does not undermine the interstate ban. California law sets her apart from other intrastate producers and users of marijuana.

Analysis:

On remand, the Ninth Circuit ruled against Raich's (P) substantive due process claim. The court held that she had not established that the right to use marijuana for medical purposes was "fundamental" and "implicit in the concept of ordered liberty." The court also held that Raich (P) could raise a defense of medical necessity, but only in the context of an individual criminal prosecution. The court did, however, express reservations as to whether that defense would be successful. *See Raich v. Gonzales,* 500 F.3d 850 (9th Cir. 2007).

◼ CASE VOCABULARY

NECESSARY AND PROPER CLAUSE: The clause of the U.S. Constitution permitting Congress to make laws "necessary and proper" for the execution of its enumerated powers. U.S. Const. art. I, § 8, cl. 18. The Supreme Court has broadly interpreted this clause to grant Congress the implied power to enact any law reasonably designed to achieve an express constitutional power. *McCulloch v. Maryland,* 17 U.S. (4 Wheat.) 316 (1819).

New York v. United States

(*State Government*) v. (*Federal Government*)
505 U.S. 144, 112 S.Ct. 2408 (1992)

CONGRESS MAY NOT COMMANDEER THE LEGISLATIVE PROCESS OF THE STATES IN ORDER TO FORCE THEM TO ADOPT A REGULATORY PROGRAM

■ **INSTANT FACTS** Congress passed legislation requiring states to either provide for radioactive waste disposal or take title to waste generated within their borders. The legislation is being challenged as an unconstitutional exercise of federal power over the States.

■ **BLACK LETTER RULE** Congress does not have the authority to commandeer state governments by forcing them to implement particular regulations.

■ **PROCEDURAL BASIS**

Appeal to the Supreme Court from dismissal of a declaratory judgment action seeking a nullification of congressional legislation.

■ **FACTS**

Congress passed the Low-Level Radioactive Waste Policy Amendments Act of 1985 (Act). The Act has three provisions regarding radioactive waste disposal: (1) monetary incentives for states to open their own waste cites; (2) access incentives allowing states without waste sites to be denied access to sites in other states; (3) a "take title" provision requiring states to take ownership of waste generated within its borders after January 1, 1996, if the state has been unable to arrange for proper disposal before that date. The take title provision would make states liable for all damages incurred by the waste generator or owner as a result of the State's failure to procure a disposal site. New York (P) and two of its counties are seeking to have the Act declared invalid as an impermissible invasion of state sovereignty, i.e. a violation of the Tenth Amendment.

■ **ISSUE**

May Congress force a state to adopt/enact a certain regulatory scheme?

■ **DECISION AND RATIONALE**

(O'Connor, J.) No. We live in a world of low level radioactive waste (waste). This waste is generated by the Government, by hospitals, by research institutions, and by various industries. In disposal, this waste must be isolated from humans for very long periods of time. The Act, based largely on a proposal submitted by the National Governor's Association, was designed to deal with this problem. The Act has been challenged as an impermissible invasion of state sovereignty by the Federal Government (Government) (D). The task of ascertaining the constitutional line between federal and state power has given rise to many of the Court's most difficult and celebrated cases. The questions that arise can be viewed in two ways. The first is to ask whether the legislation is authorized by one of the powers delegated to Congress in Article I of the Constitution. The other is to ask whether the exercise of power invades the province of state sovereignty reserved by the Tenth Amendment. In cases like this, involving the division of authority between federal and state governments, the two inquiries are mirror images of each other. The Tenth Amendment is thus essentially a tautology, but it does confirm that the power of

New York v. United States (Continued)

the Government (D) is subject to limits that may, in a given instance, reserve power to the States. This is the inquiry we face today. New York (P) does not question Congress's power to regulate the disposal of waste. Storage space for the waste is frequently sold between residents of different states. Congress has plenary power to regulate such interstate transactions. New York (P) contends only that the Tenth Amendment limits the power of Congress to regulate in the way it has chosen, i.e. by directing the states to regulate in this field. Most of our recent Tenth Amendment cases have concerned application of generally applicable laws to state governments. This case is different because it concerns whether Congress may direct or otherwise motivate the States to regulate in a particular field or a particular way. As an initial matter, Congress may not simply commandeer the legislative process of the States by directly compelling them to enact and enforce a federal regulatory program. This issue was debated by the framers, who explicitly chose a Constitution that confers upon Congress the power to regulate individuals, not states. We have consistently respected this choice. This is not to say that Congress may not hold out incentives to the States as a method of influencing a State's policy choices. Two of the methods Congress may use are of particular relevance here. First, under Congress's spending power it may attach conditions on the receipt of federal funds. Such conditions must bear some relationship to the purpose of federal spending. Second, where Congress has the authority to regulate private activity under the Commerce Clause, we have recognized Congress's power to offer States the choice of regulating that activity according to federal standards or having state law preempted by federal regulation, i.e. "cooperative federalism." By either of these methods, the residents of the State retain the ultimate decision as to whether or not the State will comply. By contrast, where the Government (D) compels States to regulate, the accountability of both state and federal officials is diminished. For when the Government (D) directs the States to regulate, it may be state officials who will bear the brunt of public disapproval, while the federal officials who devised the regulatory program may remain insulated from the electoral ramifications of their decision. Similarly, the state officials can simply pass the buck to the Government (D) when their constituents complain about a regulatory scheme. With these principles in mind, we turn to the three challenged provisions of the Act. [The Court upheld the monetary and access provisions of the Act, finding the first to be a permissible exercise of the spending power, and finding the second to be a permissible use of Congress's authority to encourage compacts among the States.] In the take title provision, Congress has crossed the line distinguishing encouragement from coercion. On the one hand, the Constitution would not permit Congress simply to transfer waste from generators to state governments. Standing alone, this would in principle be no different than a congressionally compelled subsidy from state governments to waste producers. The same is true for the provision making states liable for damages caused by the waste. This, alone, is simply an attempt to force states to assume liabilities of certain state residents. Either action commandeers state governments into the service of federal regulatory purposes. Both are thus inconsistent with the Constitution's division of authority between federal and state governments. The other alternative—regulating pursuant to Congress's direction—standing alone presents a simple command to state governments to implement legislation enacted by Congress. This the Constitution will not allow. Given that both alternatives, alone, are impermissible, it logically follows that Congress lacks the power to offer the States a choice between the two. The Government (D) emphasizes the amount of latitude provided the States under the Act in that it allows them a number of choices in dealing with the waste problem. This line of reasoning, however, only underscores the critical alternative a State lacks: A State may not decline to administer the federal program altogether. The Government (D) also argues that the constitutional barriers may be overcome where the federal interest is sufficiently important to justify state submission. However, no member of the Court has ever suggested that such a federal interest would enable Congress to command a state government to enact regulation. The Constitution simply does not contain such authority. Congress must legislate directly. Next, because the Act is the result of a bargain between the sited and non-sited states in which New York (P) was a willing participant, the Government (D) asks how the Act can be found an unconstitutional infringement of state sovereignty when state officials consented to its enactment. Such consent is immaterial, however, because the Constitution divides authority between the federal and state governments, not for the protection of the States, but for the protection of individuals. The framers felt that this federalist system would engender a healthy balance of power between the States and the Federal Government (D) thus reducing the risk of tyranny and abuse from either front. Where Congress exceeds its authority relative to the States, therefore, the departure from the constitutional plan cannot be ratified by the "consent" of state officials. We thus hold that, while there may be many constitutional methods of achieving regional self-sufficiency in waste disposal, the method Congress has chosen is not one of them.

■ CONCURRENCE AND DISSENT

(White, J.) [Justice White concurred in the upholding of the first two provisions under the Act.] The Court deems the take title provision unconstitutional under principles of federalism. Because I think the Court has mischaracterized the essential inquiry, misanalyzed the inquiry it takes, and undervalued the effect the seriousness of this problem should have on the constitutionality of the take title provision, I respectfully dissent from this aspect of its opinion. In its opinion, the majority leaves out much of the history that led to the Act. The Act is a result of the cooperative efforts of state leaders, who, when they reached a compromise, did not seek federal preemption or intervention, but rather congressional sanction of the interstate compromises they had reached. The seriousness of the problem being dealt with cannot be doubted. Only three disposal sites existed in the entire Nation. The three States possessing these sites faced the proposition of either continuing to be the Nation's dumping grounds or eliminating or reducing the amount of waste accepted for disposal. In response, the National Governors' Association Task Force embarked on finding a regional approach to the problem. The success of the compromise reached depended on the availability of stronger measures to guarantee compliance with the unsuited States' assurances that they would develop alternative disposal facilities. The bill that became the Act at issue here thus reflected hard-fought agreements among States as refereed by Congress, not congressional commandeering of the state legislatures. This distinction is key, and the Court's failure to see it affects its analysis of the take title provision's constitutionality. I am convinced that, seen as a term of an agreement between the States, this measure proves to be less constitutionally odious than the Court opines. First, the practical aspect of New York's (P) position is that other States with disposal sites must accept New York's (P) waste, whether they wish to or not. This impinges on the sovereignty of the other States. Moreover, it is utterly reasonable that in order to make the compromise work Congress would have to ratify some punitive measure as the ultimate sanction for noncompliance, a measure that takes effect only if a State fails to fulfill its acknowledged responsibilities under the Act. In addition, the Court's distinction between federal regulation of the States and private parties for general purposes, as opposed to regulation solely of the activities of States, has no support in our Tenth Amendment law. Never has the Court rested its holding on such a distinction. Nor is this distinction based on any defensible theory. An incursion into state sovereignty hardly seems more constitutionally acceptable if the federal statute commands specific action as to private parties as well. Given the lack of support for this position, it would be far more sensible to defer to a coordinate branch of government its decision to devise a national solution to this national problem. Though I disagree with the Court's holding, I do not read it as precluding Congress form adopting a similar measure under the Spending or Commerce Clauses. Congress could condition the receipt of federal funds on a State's willingness to take title. Similarly, should a State fail to establish a disposal facility by the deadline, Congress has the power under the Commerce Clause to regulate waste producers directly. Thus, should a State fail in this regard, Congress could keep all waste generated in New York (P) from being shipped out of the State. The ultimate irony of this decision is that in its formalistically rigid obeisance to "federalism," the Court gives Congress fewer incentives to defer to the wishes of the state officials in achieving local solutions to national problems, and instead, forces Congress to erect several additional hurdles to clear before achieving exactly the same objective.

■ CONCURRENCE AND DISSENT

(Stevens, J.) Under the Articles of Confederation, the Federal Government had the power to issue commands to the States. Because this proved ineffective, the framers empowered the new Federal Government (D) to exercise legislative authority over the individuals directly, even though this constitutes a greater intrusion into state sovereignty. The Constitution, therefore, enhanced, rather than diminished, the power of the Federal Government. The notion that Congress doesn't have the power to issue a simple command to state governments to implement legislation enacted by Congress is incorrect and unsound. There is no such limitation in the Constitution. Nor does the structure of the constitutional order or the values of federalism mandate such a formal rule. Indeed, the Government (D) regulates state-operated railroads, state school systems, state prisons, state elections, and many other state functions. I see no reason why Congress may not also command the States to enforce federal air and water standards or federal standards for waste disposal.

New York v. United States (Continued)

Analysis:

This case illustrates the different values the Justices place on federalism and the balance of power it strikes between the States and the federal government. The majority view represents a strict and formalistic adherence to federalism, unwilling to compromise the separation of power between state and federal governments. Much of the rationale behind this position is related to the accountability of elected officials, both national and local. The point the majority makes is that if the Federal Government is allowed to order states to enact regulations, the federal officials responsible may be able to evade accountability if local citizens disapprove of the regulation. Instead, local officials may be forced to take the heat for something they are not responsible for. On the other hand, if local officials decide to fashion their own regulations pursuant to a federal mandate, they may avoid accountability by simply pointing to the federal mandate as the culprit. Either way accountability is compromised. Justice Stevens's opinion that there is nothing in the Constitution limiting Congress's authority to command state governments to implement congressional legislation is troubling. The federal government is one of enumerated powers, and powers not conferred are, in effect, affirmatively denied. So the better question for Justice Stevens to ask is whether the Constitution confers such a power on Congress, not whether it has any limit on such power.

■ CASE VOCABULARY

TAUTOLOGY: The consideration of or inclusion of a variable twice in figuring causation or the end result.

Printz v. United States

(*Sheriff*) v. (*Federal Government*)
521 U.S. 898, 117 S.Ct. 2365 (1997)

CONGRESS IS NOT EMPOWERED TO REQUIRE STATE AND LOCAL LAW ENFORCEMENT OFFICIALS TO ADMINISTER FEDERAL REGULATIONS

■ **INSTANT FACTS** The federal Brady Act required local law enforcement officials to temporarily administer its background check program. Two local law enforcement officers challenge the Brady Act's impressment of local law enforcement officials.

■ **BLACK LETTER RULE** Congress does not have authority to compel states to enact, enforce, or administer federal regulatory programs, and cannot circumvent this prohibition by conscripting state officials directly.

■ **PROCEDURAL BASIS**

Appeal to the Supreme Court after the circuit court of appeals ruled the Brady Act constitutional in all respects.

■ **FACTS**

In 1993, Congress amended the Gun Control Act of 1968 by passing the Brady Handgun Violence Prevention Act (Brady). Brady requires the Attorney General to establish a national instant background check system by November 30, 1998, and creates interim provisions until the system goes online. Under these interim provisions, state and local law enforcement personnel must do background checks before issuing permits to purchase firearms. Under Brady, firearms dealers are required to forward Brady Forms to the local chief law enforcement officers (CLEOs), who are then obligated to make "reasonable efforts" within five days to determine whether the sales listed on the forms are lawful. Jay Printz and Richard Mack (CLEOs) (P) are chief local law enforcement officials who challenge the constitutionality of Brady's interim provisions.

■ **ISSUE**

May Congress compel state and local government officials to implement and administer federal regulatory programs?

■ **DECISION AND RATIONALE**

(Scalia, J.) No. Because the Constitution is silent on the issue, the answer to the CLEOs' (P) challenge must be sought in historical understanding and practice, in the structure of the Constitution, and in the jurisprudence of this Court. We treat these three sources in order. The CLEOs (P) contend that the practice at issue is, until very recently, unprecedented. The Government (D) asserts, to the contrary, that the earliest Congresses enacted similar statutes. This contention deserves attention, since early congressional enactments provide contemporaneous and weighty evidence of the Constitution's meaning. The Government (D) draws the Court's attention to statutes enacted by the first Congresses requiring state courts to record applications for citizenship, to transmit abstracts of citizenship applications and other naturalization records to the Secretary of State, and to register aliens seeking naturalization and issue certificates of registry. These early laws establish, at most, that the Constitution was originally understood to permit requiring state judges to enforce federal prescriptions, insofar as those prescriptions related to matters appropriate for the judicial power. Early statutes obligating state

Printz v. United States (Continued)

courts do not, however, imply a power of Congress to impress the state executive into its service. Indeed, these statute's existence with the absence of similar statutes regarding the state executives implies that such statutes were not within Congress's power. The absence of executive commandeering statutes continues into our present history as well, at least until very recent years. The Government (D) points to these recent enactments that require participation of state or local officials. Some are connected to federal funding measures, and can perhaps be more closely identified with the spending power; others, requiring only the provision of information to the Government (D), are not applicable to this issue, which is the forced participation of the States' executive in the actual administration of a federal program. Even if they were on point, they are of such recent vintage that they are no more probative than the statute before us of a constitutional tradition that lends meaning to the text. We turn next to the structure of the Constitution to try to find a principle that controls the present cases. Our Constitution established a system of dual sovereignty. Though the States surrendered many powers, they retained a residuary and inviolable sovereignty. This is reflected in the document's text, including the prohibition on any involuntary reduction or combination of a State's territory; the Judicial Power Clause; and the Privileges and Immunities Clause, which speak of the "Citizens" of the States; etc. Residual state sovereignty was also implicit, of course, in the Constitution's conferral upon Congress of only discrete, enumerated powers. This separation of the two spheres is one of the Constitution's structural protections of liberty, and recognition that a healthy balance of power between the States and the Federal Government (D) will reduce the risk of tyranny and abuse from either front. The other separation of powers under the Constitution—division into three coequal branches—is also upset by Brady.

The Constitution tasks the executive branch with enforcing the laws. Brady effectively transfers this function to thousands of CLEOs in the 50 States, who are left to implement the program without meaningful presidential control. Brady thus allows Congress to make an end run around the federal executive by vesting executive power in the CLEOs. Brady, therefore, runs counter to the maintenance of the federalist structure the framers put in place. We turn now to the prior jurisprudence of this Court. *New York v. United States* is instructive here. In that case, we held that the Federal Government (D) may not compel the States to enact or administer a federal regulatory program. The Government (D) seeks to distinguish *New York* on the ground that unlike the "take title" provisions invalidated there, the background-check provision of Brady does not require state legislative or executive officials to make policy, but instead issues a final directive to state CLEOs. This is an interesting assertion in that executive action that has virtually no policymaking component is rare. Is it really true that there is no policymaking involved in deciding, for example, what "reasonable efforts" shall be expended to conduct a background check? Were the Government's (D) contention true, such would serve only to further undermine Brady's constitutionality. It is hard to see how leaving the States with some policymaking discretion violates their sovereignty more than reducing them to puppets of a ventriloquist Congress. Finally, it is argued that because Brady serves very important purposes, is most efficiently administered by the CLEOs during the interim period, and places a minimal and temporary burden upon state officers, it should pass constitutional muster. These facts might be relevant if we were considering whether the incidental application to the States of a federal law of general applicability excessively interfered with their functioning. But when it is the law's only object to direct functioning of the state executive such a "balancing" analysis is inappropriate. A compromise of our governmental structure may not be balanced out by weighty concerns. We, therefore, adhere to this principle today and hold that the Federal Government (D) may not compel the States to enact or administer a federal regulatory program.

■ CONCURRENCE

(Thomas, J.) I join the Court's opinion in full, but write separately to emphasize that the Federal Government's authority under the Commerce Clause extends to the regulation of "commerce," and not to the regulation of wholly intrastate, point-of-sale transactions. Given this, Congress surely lacks the power to impress state law enforcement officers into administering and enforcing such regulations. In spite of this Court's broad reading of the commerce power, I continue to believe that we must "temper our Commerce Clause jurisprudence" and return to an interpretation better rooted in the Clause's original understanding. In addition, the Constitution places whole areas outside the reach of Congress's regulatory authority. The Second Amendment is an example. We have not had recent occasion to consider the nature of the substantive right safeguarded by the Second Amendment. If, however, the

Second Amendment is read to confer a personal right to "keep and bear arms," a colorable argument exists that the Federal Government's regulatory scheme, at least as it pertains to the purely intrastate sale or possession of firearms, runs afoul of that Amendment's protections. Because this argument was not raised, however, we need not address it.

■ DISSENT

(Stevens, J.) The majority's ruling is not supported by the Constitution's text, our Nation's early history, decisions of this Court, or a correct understanding of the basic structure of the Federal Government. This case does not implicate the issue—coercion of state legislatures—involved in *New York v. United States*. Nor do we need to even question whether local officials may be required to perform a federal function on a permanent basis. The issue presented by this case is remarkably similar to the question, heavily debated by the framers, whether Congress could require state agents to collect federal taxes. It is also similar to the question whether Congress could impress state judges into federal service to entertain and decide cases that they would prefer to ignore. Since the ultimate issue is one of power, we need to consider its implications in times of national emergency. Certain matters, such as the enlistment of air raid wardens, may require a national response before federal personnel can be made available to respond. If the Constitution allows for an appropriate federal response is there any authority proscribing the enlistment of state officers to make that response effective? More narrowly, what basis is there in any authority for concluding that it is the Members of this Court, rather than the elected representatives of the people, who should determine whether the Constitution contains the unwritten rule that the Court announces today? Brady is a response to what Congress described as an "epidemic of gun violence." Statistics show that the United States has the highest rate of gun violence among developed nations. The congressional decision to react to this, and the means chosen, warrants more respect than is accorded in today's unprecedented decision. Article I, § 8, grants Congress the power to regulate commerce. There can be no question this supports the regulation of commerce in handguns. When we additionally consider the Necessary and Proper Clause, there surely is adequate support for the temporary enlistment of local police officers in carrying out Brady's dictates. Furthermore, the Tenth Amendment imposes no restrictions on the exercise of these delegated powers because, as we have said before, it is a truism. Also, there is not a clause, sentence, or paragraph in the entire text of the Constitution that supports the position allowing local police officers to ignore a proper federal statutory command. The Articles of Confederation allowed for federal commands to the States. This method of governing proved unacceptable, not because it abrogated the sovereignty of the States, but because it was cumbersome and inefficient. Indeed, the historical record reflects an intent to enhance the power of the Federal Government (D) by allowing it to act through local officials in using the new authority to make demands of individual citizens. More specifically, during the Constitution debates, it was assumed that state agents would act as tax collectors for the federal government. As Alexander Hamilton explained in Federalist No. 27, the power of the government to act on "individual citizens"—included employing the ordinary magistracy of the States—was an answer to the problems faced by a central government that could act only directly upon the States in their political or collective capacities. Looking at the structural argument, the fact the framers intended to preserve the sovereignty of the several States simply does not speak to the question whether individual state employees may be required to perform federal obligations, such as registering young adults for the draft. Given the fact that Members of Congress are elected by the people of the several States, with each State having two senators, it is unrealistic to assume that they will ignore the sovereignty concerns of their constituents. Further, this case, unlike any precedent where the Court held that Congress exceeded its powers, merely involves the imposition of modest duties on individual officers. The Court seems to accept the fact that Congress could require private persons, such as hospital executives or school administrators, to provide arms merchants with relevant information about a prospective purchaser's fitness to own a weapon. A structural problem that vanishes when the statute affects private individuals as well as public officials is not much of a structural problem. Turning now to our prior jurisprudence, the take title provision at issue in *New York v. United States* was beyond Congress's authority to enact because it was "in principle . . . no different than a congressionally compelled subsidy form state governments to radioactive waste producers," and almost certainly a legislative act. The Brady provision, however, is more akin to a statute requiring local police officers to report the identity of missing children to the Department of Justice than it is to an offensive federal command to a sovereign state. We should,

Printz v. United States (Continued)

therefore, respect both Congress's policy judgment and its appraisal of its constitutional power with regard to this matter. Accordingly, I respectfully dissent.

Analysis:

There are three points at which a statute's constitutionality may be assessed. First, before Congress passes a statute, it assesses the constitutionality of the proposed legislation. If, in Congress's best judgment, the legislation passes constitutional muster, it may be enacted. Once Congress passes legislation, it goes to the President for consideration. Once again, the constitutionality of the legislation is assessed, and if it is found lacking, the President has the option of vetoing it. Obviously, the last potential hurdle a statute may have to pass is the Judiciary. The Supreme Court is usually the final arbiter of constitutionality, i.e., the last bulwark against a government attempting to exceed its enumerated powers.

■ CASE VOCABULARY

JURISPRUDENCE: The body of law, formed by precedent, a court relies on in deciding an issue.

Reno v. Condon

(*Attorney General*) v. (*South Carolina Attorney General*)
528 U.S. 141, 120 S.Ct. 666 (2000)

THE TENTH AMENDMENT DOES EXCUSE STATES FROM COMPLYING WITH FEDERAL REGULATIONS VALIDLY PROMULGATED UNDER THE COMMERCE CLAUSE

■ **INSTANT FACTS** Congress passed legislation placing certain prohibitions on the dissemination of private information given states by individuals in applying for a driver's license. One State challenges the constitutionality of the legislation as it applies to states.

■ **BLACK LETTER RULE** States are required to comply with constitutionally valid legislation regulating state activities, even when compliance means incurring additional costs to be borne by the States.

■ PROCEDURAL BASIS
Appeal to the Supreme Court of a suit initially filed in the federal district court.

■ FACTS
Congress passed the Driver's Privacy Protection Act of 1994 (DPPA), regulating the dissemination of personal information provided to states by driver's license applicants. The DPPA was passed in response to the widespread practice of states selling this private information to individuals and businesses. The DPPA generally prohibits any state DMV, or officer, employee, or contractor thereof, from "knowingly disclosing or otherwise making available to any person or entity personal information about any individual obtained by the department in connection with a motor vehicle record." The DPPA also regulates the resale and redisclosure of drivers' personal information by private persons who have obtained that information from a state DMV. South Carolina's [Condon (P) is South Carolina's Attorney General] law conflicts with the DPPA. Because of this conflict, Condon (P) filed suit in federal district court seeking to have the DPPA declared invalid under the Tenth and Eleventh Amendments.

■ ISSUE
May Congress regulate state activities that necessarily impose costs of compliance?

■ DECISION AND RATIONALE
(Rehnquist, C.J.) Yes. We of course begin with the time-honored presumption that the DPPA is a constitutional exercise of legislative power. The United States (Reno) (D) bases its Commerce Clause argument on the fact that the personal, identifying information that the DPPA regulates is a "thing in interstate commerce," and that the sale or release of that information in interstate commerce is therefore a proper subject of congressional regulation. We agree with this contention. The motor vehicle information which the States have historically sold is used by private, commercial parties to contact drivers with customized solicitation. Because drivers' information is, in this context, an article of commerce, its sale or release into the interstate stream of business is sufficient to support congressional regulation. This holding does not, however, necessarily mean the DPPA is valid. It still must not violate the principles of federalism contained in the Tenth Amendment. Condon (D) contends that the DPPA violates the Tenth Amendment by forcing the States to administer its complex provisions on a daily basis, thus making state officials the unwilling implementers of federal policy; forcing state employees to learn and apply the DPPA's substantive restrictions, thus consuming the States'

resources. We agree with Condon's (P) assertions that the DPPA will require time and effort on the part of state employees, but reject Condon's (P) argument that the DPPA violates the principles laid down in either *New York* or *Printz*. We think, instead, that *South Carolina v. Baker* is a more apt precedent. In that case, we upheld a federal statute prohibiting States from issuing unregistered bonds because the law "regulate[d] state activities," rather than "seek[ing] to control or influence the manner in which States regulate private parties." We further noted that "[s]uch commandeering is, however, an inevitable consequence of regulating a state activity. A federal regulation demands compliance. That a State wishing to engage in certain activity must take administrative and sometimes legislative action to comply with federal standards regulating that activity is a commonplace that presents no constitutional defect." The DPPA does not require the States in their sovereign capacity to regulate their own citizens. The DPPA regulates the States as the owners of databases. We accordingly conclude that the DPPA is consistent with the constitutional principles enunciated in *New York* and *Printz*. Condon (P) also asserts that the DPPA is invalid because it regulates the States exclusively. But we need not address this issue because the DPPA applies to private resellers as well and is, therefore, generally applicable.

Analysis:

The Court here avoids the issue of whether the DPPA would be valid if it applied to the states exclusively. The Court's opinions in *New York* and *Printz* provide guidance in evaluating this issue. In those cases, the Court was concerned with congressional attempts to hijack or commandeer the state legislative processes and executive officials. Specifically, in *Printz*, the enlistment of state officials in administering the Brady Act was seen as infringing upon the sovereignty of the states, as well as the discretion of local police officials. Other than the DPPA being "generally applicable," how does it differ from the Brady Act? It could possibly be distinguished on the ground that it is a direct regulation of "articles" in, or potentially in, interstate commerce, whereas the Brady Act sought to direct the manner in which access to such items was to be granted. One is a straight prohibition, while the other requires the exercise of discretionary control; one requires no thought, while the other does. Is this a valid distinction?

United States v. Butler
(*Government*) v. (*Cotton Company Receiver*)
297 U.S. 1, 56 S.Ct. 312 (1936)

CONGRESSIONAL EXERCISE OF AN ENUMERATED POWER IS LIMITED BY FEDERALIST CONCERNS

■ **INSTANT FACTS** Congress attempted to regulate the quantity of local agricultural production through use of the taxing and spending powers. The regulation is challenged as being outside Congress's enumerated powers.

■ **BLACK LETTER RULE** Congress may not use the taxing or spending powers to force compliance in an area where the Constitution does not give Congress independent power to regulate.

■ **PROCEDURAL BASIS**
Appeal to the Supreme Court from a decision invalidating the Agricultural Adjustment Act.

■ **FACTS**
After declaring a national crisis in agricultural production, Congress enacted the Agricultural Adjustment Act of 1933 (AAA). Under the AAA, the Secretary of Agriculture could contract with farmers to produce a limited amount of crops in exchange for benefit payments, the payments coming from an account funded by taxes imposed on producers for exceeding their production limits. Butler (P) attacks the tax on the ground that it is an integral part of an unconstitutional program to control agricultural production.

■ **ISSUE**
May the taxing and spending powers be used to purchase/force compliance with federal goals in an area of concern reserved to the States?

■ **DECISION AND RATIONALE**
(Roberts, J.) No. Article I, § 8, of the Constitution, vests sundry powers in the Congress, including the power "to lay and collect Taxes, Duties, Imposts and Excises, to pay the Debts and provide for the common Defence and general Welfare of the United States." The Government (D) concedes that the phrase "to provide for the general welfare" qualifies the power "to lay and collect taxes," and thus, there is no grant of power to regulate agricultural production upon the theory that such legislation would promote the general welfare. So it is clear, the Congress is expressly empowered to lay taxes to provide for the general welfare. The true and accurate interpretation of this phrase has been argued since our Nation's founding. Madison asserted that the power to tax and spend for the general welfare must be confined to the enumerated legislative fields, i.e. is qualified by the enumerated powers. However, this view creates a tautology, for it is implicitly clear that Congress may tax and spend for purposes of exercising its enumerated powers. Hamilton, on the other hand, maintained that the clause confers a power separate and distinct from those later enumerated, such that Congress has the substantive power to tax and spend, limited only by the requirement that it be for the general welfare. This Court has noticed the question, but has never found it necessary to decide which is the true construction. Mr. Justice Story, in his Commentaries, espoused the Hamiltonian view. Our review of these and other commentaries, as well as the legislative practice, leads us to conclude that the reading advocated by Mr. Justice Story is the correct one. Therefore, while the power to tax and spend is not unlimited, its confines are set in the clause that confers it, and not in those of § 8 which bestow and define the

legislative powers of Congress. The adoption of this broader construction still leaves some limits. Wholly apart from the question of the scope of the "general welfare," which we need not resolve here, there is another constitutional provision that prohibits enforcement of the AAA. The AAA invades the reserved rights of the States. Regulation and control of agricultural production is a matter beyond Congress's delegated powers. The tax, the appropriation of the funds raised, and the direction of their disbursement, are but parts of the whole plan. Congress has no power to enforce the commands of the AAA on the farmer directly. It follows that Congress may not indirectly accomplish those ends by taxing and spending to purchase compliance. Allowing a declaration of national concern to legitimate Congress's action would be the same as allowing Congress to ignore constitutional limitations upon its own powers and usurp those of the States any time it makes such a declaration. Congress may not make an end-run around the Constitution by using the taxing and spending powers. Otherwise, clause 1 of § 8 of article 1 would become the instrument for total subversion of the governmental powers reserved to the States.

■ DISSENT

(Stone, J.) There are certain propositions which should have controlling influence in determining the validity of the AAA. They are: (1) When considering the constitutionality of a statute, courts are concerned only with the power to enact statutes, not their wisdom, for while the constitutional exercise of power by the other two branches is subject to judicial restraint, the only check upon our own exercise of power is our own sense of self-restraint; (2) The power of Congress to levy an excise tax upon the processing of agricultural products is not questioned; (3) Given the current depressed state of the national market in agricultural commodities, there is no basis for saying that the expenditure of public money in aid of farmers is not within the power of Congress to levy taxes to "provide for the ... general welfare." Indeed, the opinion of the Court does not declare otherwise. (4) No question of an unauthorized delegation of power to the Secretary of Agriculture is presented. The fact the AAA was passed as a way to regulate agricultural production and is seen as an infringement of state power does not change the fact that it is completely within the enumerated powers of Congress. The AAA should thus be upheld.

Analysis:

Butler is still considered good law as far as its broad view of the General Welfare Clause. The concern of the majority was Congress's attempt to use its taxing and spending power to regulate, not only in an area outside of the enumerated powers, but within an area traditionally reserved for the States—agricultural production. In effect, lacking the authority to regulate agricultural production directly, pursuant to an explicitly enumerated power, Congress tried to make an end-run around this limitation by asserting its use of the taxing and spending powers was for the general welfare, and, therefore, valid. The Court did not necessarily disagree that the AAA used the taxing and spending powers for the general welfare. This issue was not addressed because, as the majority saw it, the AAA impinged on States' sovereignty, thus making the "general welfare" issue irrelevant.

■ CASE VOCABULARY

END-RUN: Taking an indirect route in reaching a goal because the most direct route, and usually the most proper route, is blocked in some way.

Sabri v. United States

(Briber) v. *(Federal Government)*
541 U.S. 600, 124 S.Ct. 1941 (2004)

CONGRESSIONAL ACTION MUST BE A RATIONAL MEANS TO A LEGITIMATE CONSTITUTIONAL END

■ **INSTANT FACTS** Sabri (D) challenged a federal anti-bribery statute as facially unconstitutional.

■ **BLACK LETTER RULE** Under the Spending Clause, Congress is authorized to appropriate federal funds for the general welfare and use all rational means necessary and proper to further its spending power.

■ PROCEDURAL BASIS
Certiorari to review a decision of the Eighth Circuit Court of Appeals in favor of the Government.

■ FACTS
Seeking to develop a hotel and retail structure in Minneapolis, Sabri (D) offered three separate bribes to a city councilman when he was uncertain whether he could comply with existing licensing and zoning laws. The councilman served as a member of a city council board charged with funding housing and economic development in Minneapolis, using federal funds. Sabri (D) was charged with violating 18 U.S.C. § 666(a)(2), providing criminal penalties for anyone who "corruptly gives, offers, or agrees to give anything of value to any person, with intent to influence or reward an agent of an organization . . . in connection with any business, transaction, or series of transactions . . . involving anything of value of $5,000 or more." Criminal liability requires that the organization receive more than $10,000 annually in federal benefits. Sabri (D) moved to dismiss the grand jury indictment, challenging the constitutionality of § 666(a)(2). Sabri (D) argued that the statute was facially unconstitutional because it failed to require a connection between federal funds and the alleged bribe. After the federal district court granted Sabri's (D) motion, the Eighth Circuit Court of Appeals reversed, holding that the statute was constitutional under the Necessary and Proper Clause in furtherance of Congress's spending power.

■ ISSUE
Is 18 U.S.C. § 666(a)(2) a valid exercise of congressional authority under Article I of the Constitution?

■ DECISION AND RATIONALE
(Souter, J.) Yes. Under the Spending Clause, Congress is authorized to appropriate federal funds for the general welfare. It may therefore act in all manners necessary and proper to ensure that federal expenditures are used for the general welfare. Bribes or kickbacks to local government agents certainly involve a federal interest when federal funds are appropriated, even if the specific transaction involves no federal funding. State or local money may be "siphoned off" for illegitimate purposes because federal benefits are otherwise available for use. It is the receipt of federal funds by the government agency that establishes the federal interest, not its specific connection to the alleged bribe. Congress may exercise any rational means to reach the legitimate aims of its spending power.

■ CONCURRENCE
(Thomas, J.) In approving § 666(a)(2) under the congressional spending power, the Court applies too liberal a standard. By invoking a rational means test, the Court deviates from the test established in

Sabri v. United States (Continued)

McCulloch v. Maryland. There, the Court required not that congressional action be a rational means to reaching a legitimate end, but rather that the law be "appropriate" and "plainly adapted" to the constitutional objective. "A statute can have a 'rational' connection to an enumerated power without being obviously or clearly tied to that enumerated power." Without a direct connection between federal expenditures and the alleged bribe, § 666(a)(2) is not clearly tied to the spending power. While the statute requires constitutional approval under the Commerce Clause, the Necessary and Proper Clause does not authorize it.

Analysis:

Importantly, *Sabri* substantially strengthens the federal government's regulation of state and local matters. By bestowing powers in connection with contributions of federal funds to state and local organizations, the Necessary and Proper Clause effectively grants the federal government carte blanche to regulate any matter directly or indirectly related to the contributions. Yet, despite these important federalist concerns, *Sabri* was a unanimous decision of the Court.

■ CASE VOCABULARY

FACIAL CHALLENGE: A claim that a statute is unconstitutional on its face—that is, that it always operates unconstitutionally.

NECESSARY AND PROPER CLAUSE: The clause of the U.S. Constitution permitting Congress to make laws "necessary and proper" for the execution of its enumerated powers. U.S. Const. art. I, § 8, cl. 18.

SPENDING POWER: The power granted to a governmental body to levy a tax; especially, the congressional power to levy and collect taxes as a means of effectuating Congress's delegated powers. U.S. Const. art. 1, § 8, cl. 1.

South Dakota v. Dole

(*State*) v. (*Secretary of Transportation*)
483 U.S. 203, 107 S.Ct. 2793 (1987)

SUPREME COURT ALLOWS CONGRESS LIBERAL USE OF THE SPENDING POWER

■ **INSTANT FACTS** South Dakota (P) challenges a federal law withholding 5% of federal highway funds from any state with a drinking-age limit less than 21 years-of-age.

■ **BLACK LETTER RULE** Valid use of the Spending power is subject to three requirements: (1) It must be used for the general welfare; (2) Any conditions on receipt of funds must be unambiguous; and (3) Any conditions must be related to the federal interest in the particular national projects or programs being funded.

■ FACTS

Congress passed legislation (§ 158) directing Dole (D), the Secretary of the Treasury, to withhold 5% of federal highway funds from any state that fails to set its legal age for alcohol consumption at 21 years. South Dakota (P) asserts that § 158 violates the constitutional limitations on congressional exercise of the spending power, as well as the Twenty-first Amendment to the Constitution.

■ ISSUE

May Congress use its spending power to regulate activities in areas reserved to the States?

■ DECISION AND RATIONALE

(Rehnquist, C.J.) Yes. Incident to the spending power, Congress may achieve its broad policy objectives by conditioning the receipt of federal funds upon compliance by the recipient with federal statutory and administrative directives. Such use of the spending power is, of course, not unlimited, but is subject to several general restrictions. The first limitation is that the exercise of the spending power must be in pursuit of the "general welfare." In considering whether this requirement is met, courts should defer substantially to the judgment of Congress. Second, any conditions must be set forth unambiguously, allowing the States to exercise their choice knowingly, cognizant of the consequences of their participation. Third, conditions on federal grants must be related to the federal interest in particular nationwide projects or programs. Here, the provision is unmistakably for the general welfare. The condition is also unambiguous, indeed, could not be more clearly stated. Third, the condition imposed is directly related to one of the main purposes for which highway funds are expended—safe interstate travel. We have also held that a perceived Tenth Amendment limitation on congressional regulations of state affairs did not, at the same time, limit the range of conditions legitimately placed on federal grants. Although we have also recognized that in some circumstances the financial inducement might be so coercive as to pass the point at which pressure turns into compulsion. This is not, however, the case here as only a relatively small percentage of highway funds are at stake. South Dakota's (P) contention that the success of the program proves its coercive nature is without merit. A conditional grant of money is not unconstitutional simply by the reason of its success in achieving the congressional objective.

■ DISSENT

(Brennan, J.) I agree with Justice O'Connor that a minimum drinking age law falls squarely within the ambit of those powers reserved to the States by the Twenty-first Amendment. Congress cannot condition receipt of funds in a manner that abridges this right.

South Dakota v. Dole (Continued)

■ DISSENT

(O'Connor, J.) I cannot agree that § 158 is a condition on spending reasonably related to the expenditure of federal funds. Rather, it is an attempt to regulate the sale of liquor, an attempt that lies outside Congress's power to regulate commerce because it falls within the ambit of § 2 of the Twenty-first Amendment, which reserves such regulation to the States. We have repeatedly said that Congress may condition grants under the spending power only in ways reasonably related to the purpose of the federal program. In my view, establishment of a national minimum drinking age is not sufficiently related to interstate highway construction to justify so conditioning funds appropriated for that purpose.

Analysis:

Justice O'Connor disagrees with the majority in this case. Justice O'Connor would require there to be a direct nexus between the funds' purpose and the conditions of their use, while the majority would require only a tangential relationship. Furthermore, the majority seems to be willing to let Congress be the "judge" of whether there exists the required reasonable relationship between the funds' purpose and the conditions. On another note, both Justices O'Connor and Brennan interpret the Twenty-first Amendment as reserving the regulation of alcohol exclusively to the States. Under this interpretation, Congress is absolutely foreclosed from exercising influence, in any way, on state regulation of the alcohol age limit.

United States v. Morrison

(Federal Government) v. (Assault Victim)
529 U.S. 598, 120 S.Ct. 1740 (2000)

CONGRESS MAY NOT REGULATE PRIVATE INDIVIDUALS PURSUANT TO THE FOURTEENTH AMENDMENT

■ **INSTANT FACTS** An alleged rape victim sought to sue her accused attackers under the federal Violence Against Women Act (Act or VAWA). The accused asserts that VAWA is an unconstitutional exercise of congressional authority.

■ **BLACK LETTER RULE** Congress's authority to regulate under the Fourteenth Amendment extends only to state activity, not activities of private individuals.

■ **PROCEDURAL BASIS**

Appeal to the Supreme Court after the circuit court of appeals held that the VAWA is an unconstitutional exercise of the commerce power.

■ **FACTS**

Brzonkala (P1) sued her fellow university student, Morrison (D) under the Violence Against Women Act (Act or VAWA), alleging that he assaulted and raped her. The VAWA is a federal statute providing a federal civil remedy for victims of gender-motivated violence. Morrison (D) challenges the constitutionality of the Act. The United States (Government)(P2) intervened to defend the Act's constitutionality under the Commerce Clause and the Fourteenth Amendment.

■ **ISSUE**

Does the Fourteenth Amendment provide Congress the authority to regulate the activities of private individuals?

■ **DECISION AND RATIONALE**

(Rehnquist, C.J.) No. The Government (P2) argues that VAWA is a constitutional exercise of Congress's remedial power under § 5 of the Fourteenth Amendment, which it expressly invoked as a source of authority to enact VAWA. The Government's (P2) argument is founded on an assertion that there is a pervasive bias in various state justice systems against victims of gender-motivated violence. A voluminous congressional record supports this assertion. Fourteenth Amendment analysis is well settled. The Amendment's language and purpose set certain limitations on the ways in which Congress may attack discrimination. These limitations are necessary to prevent upsetting the framer's carefully crafted balance of power between the States and the National Government. Foremost among these is the time-honored principle that the Fourteenth Amendment, by its very terms, prohibits only state action. It erects no shield against merely private conduct, however discriminatory or wrongful. This is the rule from *United States v. Harris* and the *Civil Rights Cases*, decided shortly after the Fourteenth Amendment was adopted. The Government's reliance on *United States v. Guest* as contrary authority is misplaced. In *Guest* the Court had no occasion to consider whether the Fourteenth Amendment authorizes legislation applicable to private individuals because "the indictment [charging private individuals with conspiring to deprive blacks of equal access to state facilities] in fact contain[ed] an express allegation of state involvement." The opinions of three Justices in *Guest* that Congress does have Fourteenth Amendment authority to regulate private individuals does not, therefore, have any force of law. The Act is not aimed at any state or state actor, but at individuals who have committed criminal acts motivated by gender bias. The Act is, therefore, unlike any of the § 5 remedies that we have previously upheld. Accordingly, we hold that the VAWA cannot be sustained under the Fourteenth Amendment.

■ **DISSENT**

(Breyer, J.) I write to express my doubts as to the Court's reasoning in rejecting the Fourteenth Amendment as a proper source of authority for enacting VAWA. The Court is correct in asserting that the Fourteenth Amendment does not authorize Congress to remedy the conduct of private persons. The Government's (P2) argument, however, is that Congress used § 5 to remedy the actions of state actors, namely, those States which, through discriminatory design or the discriminatory conduct of their officials, failed to provide adequate state remedies for gender-motivated violence. Though the private actors here in question did not violate the Constitution, this Court has held that Congress at least sometimes can enact remedial legislation prohibiting conduct that is not, itself, unconstitutional. Such action intrudes little upon either States or private parties. Given the relation between remedy and violation—the creation of a federal remedy to substitute for constitutionally inadequate state remedies—where is the lack of "congruence"?

Analysis:

The majority is correct in asserting that VAWA is distinguishable from all other legislation upheld under the Fourteenth Amendment. It is not aimed at state action and does not fit with any one of the proxies for state action the Court has allowed, such as cases holding private actions to have a "public function," thus allowing regulation, or the "nexus" cases, where state and private action are somehow linked. Another exception carved out by the Court is, arguably, more applicable. This is the government-encouraged/authorized private discrimination exception. The possible, though weak, argument is that by continually failing to adequately enforce state laws against gender motivated violence, the State is indirectly/implicitly encouraging or authorizing such criminal conduct. Such an argument suggests that states have a duty to enact and fully enforce criminal statutes, with a failure to do so being a breach of the duty, thus satisfying the Fourteenth Amendment's state action requirement.

Katzenbach v. Morgan & Morgan

(Federal Government) v. (New York Voter)
384 U.S. 641, 86 S.Ct. 1717 (1966)

CONGRESS HAS THE POWER PURSUANT TO THE FOURTEENTH AMENDMENT TO ENACT REMEDIAL LEGISLATION ENFORCING CONSTITUTIONAL RIGHTS

■ **INSTANT FACTS** New York voters are challenging a federal law prohibiting New York from enforcing its English literacy voting requirement.

■ **BLACK LETTER RULE** Section 5 of the Fourteenth Amendment authorizes Congress to enact remedial legislation prohibiting enforcement of state laws found to abrogate civil rights, even though such state laws are not unconstitutional.

■ **PROCEDURAL BASIS**

[Not Stated]

■ **FACTS**

Section 4(e) of the Voting Rights Act of 1965 (§ 4(e)) prohibits any state or local government from denying the right to vote to individuals who have completed the sixth grade at a public or private school in Puerto Rico, regardless of whether they can read and/or write in English. Morgan (P) challenges the constitutionality of § 4(e) because it is a pro tanto prohibition of the enforcement of the election laws of New York requiring an ability to read and write English as a condition of voting.

■ **ISSUE**

Does the Fourteenth Amendment authorize Congress to prohibit enforcement of state laws found to abrogate guaranteed civil rights, regardless of whether the state law is unconstitutional under some independent constitutional provision?

■ **DECISION AND RATIONALE**

(Brennan, J.) Yes. Morgan (P) asserts that, pursuant to § 5 of the Fourteenth Amendment, Congress may prohibit enforcement of a state law only if the judiciary determines that the state law is prohibited by the provisions of the Amendment Congress seeks to enforce. Thus, Morgan (P) asserts that unless a court first finds the New York literacy requirement unconstitutional under the Equal Protection Clause, Congress's ban on enforcement of the requirement cannot be sustained under § 5 of the Fourteenth Amendment. We disagree. Neither the language nor history of § 5 supports such a construction. Indeed, the grafting of such a requirement onto the Fourteenth Amendment would confine the legislative power in this context to the insignificant role of abrogating only those state laws that the judicial branch was prepared to adjudge unconstitutional, or of merely informing the judgment of the judiciary by particularizing the "majestic generalities" of § 1 of the Amendment. This case must, therefore, be decided without regard to whether New York's literacy requirement squares with the Equal Protection Clause. We are thus left only with the question of whether § 4(e) is, as required by § 5, appropriate legislation to enforce the Equal Protection Clause. By including § 5 the draftsmen sought to grant Congress, by a specific provision applicable to the Fourteenth Amendment, the same broad powers expressed in the Necessary and Proper Clause, Art. I, § 8, cl. 18. We are, therefore, left with considering whether § 4(e) may be regarded as an enactment to enforce the Equal Protection Clause,

Katzenbach v. Morgan & Morgan (Continued)

whether it is plainly adapted to that end, and whether it is not prohibited by but is consistent with the letter an spirit of the Constitution. There can be no doubt that § 4(e) may be regarded as an enactment to enforce the Equal Protection Clause. Congress specifically declared that § 4(e) was passed "to secure the rights under the fourteenth amendment of persons educated in American-flag schools in which the predominant classroom language was other than English." More specifically, § 4(e) may be viewed as a measure to secure for the Puerto Rican community nondiscriminatory treatment by government. Section 4(e) is "plainly adapted" to furthering these aims of the Equal Protection Clause. The practical effect of § 4(e) is to prohibit New York from denying the right to vote to large segments of its Puerto Rican community. Congress has thus prohibited the State from denying to that community the right that is "preservative of all rights." Section 4(e) thereby enables the Puerto Rican minority better to obtain "perfect equality of civil rights and the equal protection of the laws." It was well within Congress's authority to say this need for the vote warranted federal intrusion upon any state interests served by the English literacy requirement. It is enough that we perceive a basis upon which Congress might predicate a judgment that the application of New York's literacy test requirement to deny the right to vote to a person with a sixth grade education in Puerto Rican schools in which the language of instruction was other than English constituted an invidious discrimination in violation of the Equal Protection Clause. Reversed.

■ DISSENT

(Harlan, J.) I fail to see how § 4(e) can be sustained except at the sacrifice of the separation between the legislative and judicial function and the boundaries between federal and state political authority. By the same token, I think that the validity of the New York literacy test must be upheld. Our analysis here must begin with the established rule of law that the franchise is essentially a matter of state concern. We dealt with this question in *Lassiter v. Northampton Election Bd.* and resolved it unanimously in favor of the legitimacy of the state literacy requirement. In that case, we held that there is a "wide scope" for State qualifications of this sort. The same interests cited in *Lassiter* point toward upholding the rationality of the New York voting test. The pivotal question is what effect the added factor of a congressional enactment has on the straight equal protection argument dealt with above. The Court declares that because § 5 of the Fourteenth Amendment gives Congress the power to "enforce" the prohibitions of the Amendment by "appropriate" legislation, the proper test is one of rationality; that is, in effect, was Congress acting rationally in declaring the New York statute irrational? I believe the Court has confused the issue of how much enforcement power Congress possesses under § 5 with the distinct issue of what questions are appropriate for congressional determination and what questions are essentially judicial in nature. It is a judicial question whether the condition with which Congress seeks to deal is in truth an infringement of the Constitution, something that is the necessary prerequisite to bringing the § 5 power into play at all. Section 4(e), however, presents a significantly different type of congressional enactment. The proper question here is whether there has in fact been an infringement of the Equal Protection Clause in the first instance, i.e. whether a statute is so arbitrary or irrational as to offend the command of the Clause. That question is one for the judicial branch ultimately to determine. In view of our decision in *Lassiter*, I do not think it is open to Congress to limit the effect of that decision as it has undertaken to do by § 4(e). The Court reads § 5 of the Fourteenth Amendment as, in effect, giving Congress the power to define the substantive scope of the Amendment. Such a reading would also allow Congress to dilute equal protection and due process decisions of this Court. Such a reading abrogates the role of this Court and is tantamount to allowing the Fourteenth Amendment to swallow the States' constitutionally ordained primary authority in this field.

Analysis:

Section 1 of the Fourteenth Amendment states in pertinent part that "[n]o State shall make or enforce any law ... deny[ing] to any person within its jurisdiction the equal protection of the laws." Section 5 states that "[t]he Congress shall have power to enforce, by appropriate legislation, the provisions of this article." These provisions seem very clear. Section 1 provides a guarantee of the equal protection of the laws. Section 5 gives Congress power to enforce this guarantee. Therefore, according to the Amendment's plain meaning, unless the guarantee is being violated, there is no authority vested in Congress to remedy the violation. But this case goes further, authorizing Congress to enact remedial legislation, even when state laws infringing on Constitutional rights have not been found unconstitutional.

■ CASE VOCABULARY

PRO TANTO: As far as it lasts or goes.

City of Boerne v. Flores
(City) v. *(Archbishop)*
521 U.S. 507, 117 S.Ct. 2157 (1997)

CONGRESS MAY NOT USE THE FOURTEENTH AMENDMENT TO DEFINE THE SUBSTANTIVE SCOPE OF CONSTITUTIONAL RIGHTS

■ **INSTANT FACTS** Flores (P), after the City of Boeme (D) denied a permit to expand the church, is suing under the Religious Freedom Restoration Act (RFRA).

■ **BLACK LETTER RULE** Section 5 of the Fourteenth Amendment gives Congress the power to enact laws as remedial measures and to prevent constitutional violations, but does not allow Congress to define the substantive scope of constitutional guarantees.

■ **PROCEDURAL BASIS**

Appeal to the Supreme Court after the circuit court of appeals denied a constitutional challenge to the RFRA.

■ **FACTS**

The parishioners of St. Peter Catholic Church outnumbered the church's seating capacity. To remedy this, they, led by Archbishop Flores (P), decided to expand the church and sought a building permit from the City of Boeme (D) to do so. Boeme (D) denied the permit on the ground that the church is an historic landmark that, pursuant to a city ordinance, cannot be altered. Flores (P) sued Boeme (D) under various state laws and the Religious Freedom Restoration Act (RFRA). RFRA was enacted in 1993 and prohibits "[g]overnment" form "substantially burden[ing]" a person's exercise of religion even if the burden results from a rule of general applicability unless the government can demonstrate the burden "(1) is in furtherance of a compelling governmental interest; and (2) is the least restrictive means of furthering that compelling governmental interest." RFRA was passed in response to the Supreme Court's ruling in *Employment Div., Dept. of Human Resources of Oregon v. Smith*, wherein the Court held that laws burdening the exercise of religion are valid so long as they are generally applicable.

■ **ISSUE**

Does § 5 of the Fourteenth Amendment allow Congress to regulate state and/or local activities in a manner that defines the substantive scope of constitutional guarantees?

■ **DECISION AND RATIONALE**

(Kennedy, J.) No. The question we face is whether RFRA is a proper exercise of Congress's § 5 power "to enforce" by "appropriate legislation" the constitutional guarantee that no state shall deprive any person of "life, liberty, or property, without due process of law" nor any person "equal protection of the laws." We begin with the recognition that § 5 is a positive grant of legislative power. Laws that deter or remedy constitutional violations may fall within Congress's enforcement power even if the conduct prohibited is not in itself unconstitutional and intrudes into the States' sphere of legislative autonomy. This power is not unlimited though. It is limited to "enforc[ing]" the provisions of the Fourteenth Amendment, i.e. it is remedial. The Amendment's design and the text of § 5 are inconsistent with the notion that Congress may also decree the substance of the Amendment's restrictions on the States.

City of Boerne v. Flores (Continued)

Thus Congress may not alter the meaning of the Free Exercise Clause since this is not "enforcing" the Clause. The line between remedial measures and those that make a substantive change in the governing law is not easy to discern. Congress must have wide latitude in determining where it lies. But wherever it draws the line, there must always be a congruence and proportionality between the injury to be prevented or remedied and the means adopted to that end. Lacking such a connection, legislation may become substantive in operation and effect. [The Court goes into the history of the Amendment's enactment as support for its holding.] This position is also supported by our earlier cases. In the *Civil Rights Cases*, we ruled that Congress's enforcement power does not authorize Congress to pass general legislation upon the rights of the citizen, but corrective or remedial legislation. This Court since has not questioned such treatment of Congress's § 5 power. If Congress could define its own powers by altering the Fourteenth Amendment's meaning, no longer would the Constitution be "superior paramount law, unchangeable by ordinary means." We turn now to a consideration of RFRA's validity as § 5 enforcement legislation. It is said that RFRA is a reasonable means of protecting the free exercise of religion as defined in *Smith* by preventing and remedying laws enacted with the unconstitutional object of targeting religious beliefs and practices. While preventive laws may be appropriate remedial measures, there must be a congruence between means and ends, considered in the light of the evil presented. The greater the harm, the stronger the measures may be. But RFRA's legislative record lacks examples of modern instances of generally applicable laws passed because of religious bigotry. Indeed we can find no episodes occurring in the past 40 years. RFRA is so out of proportion to a supposed remedial or preventive object that it cannot be understood as responsive to, or designed to prevent, unconstitutional behavior. It appears, instead, to attempt a substantive change in constitutional protections. Sweeping coverage ensures RFRA's intrusion at every level of government, displacing laws and prohibiting official actions of almost every description, regardless of subject matter. Such vast reach and scope distinguish it from other measures passed under Congress's enforcement power, even in the area of voting rights. RFRA thus lacks the required proportionality or congruence between the means adopted and the legitimate end to be achieved and is, therefore, a considerable congressional intrusion into the States' traditional prerogatives and general autonomy to regulate for the health and welfare of their citizens. Congress's attempt, through RFRA, to redefine the substantive scope of our religious freedom guarantee also intrudes upon the fundamental role of the judiciary, for it is the judiciary that is tasked with ascertaining the scope of constitutional guarantees. When the political branches act against the background of a judicial interpretation of the Constitution already issued, it must be understood that in later cases and controversies the Court will treat its precedents with the respect due them under settled principles, including stare decisis, and contrary expectations must be disappointed. It is, therefore, this Court's precedent, not RFRA, which must control. Reversed.

■ DISSENT

(O'Connor, J.) The Court uses *Smith* as a yardstick for measuring the constitutionality of RFRA. Because I remain of the view that *Smith* was wrongly decided, I would use this case to reexamine the Court's holding there. If the Court were to correct the misinterpretation of the Free Exercise Clause set forth in *Smith*, it would simultaneously put our First Amendment jurisprudence back on course and allay the legitimate concerns of a majority of Congress who believed that *Smith* improperly restricted religious liberty. We would the be in a position to review RFRA in light of proper interpretation of the Free Exercise Clause.

■ DISSENT

(Souter, J.) The Court measures RFRA against the fee-exercise standard set forth in *Smith*. I have serious doubts about the precedential value of the *Smith* rule and its entitlement to adherence. In order to provide full adversarial consideration, this case should be set down for reargument permitting plenary reexamination of the issue. Until this happens, our free-exercise law remains marked by an intolerable tension, and the constitutionality of RFRA cannot now be soundly decided.

Analysis:

In *Smith*, discussed by the Court, two men were fired for using peyote. The state denied them unemployment benefits because peyote use, even in a religious context, was worker "misconduct" and disqualified the men for benefits. Smith and Black filed a lawsuit challenging the denial of benefits on the ground that it penalized them for exercising their religion. The Supreme Court ruled that generally applicable, religion-neutral laws that have the incidental effect of burdening a particular religious practice need not be justified by a compelling governmental interest. It is this ruling that Justices O'Connor, Breyer, and Souter would revisit, indeed, overrule. Consider the validity of Justice Kennedy's statement that there have been "no episodes occurring in the past 40 years," referring to the prevalence of laws motivated by religious bigotry. Is this true? What about *Church of the Lukumi Babalu Aye v. City of Hialeah* (1993), in which the city of Hialeah passed ordinances effectively forbidding the sacrifice of animals as practiced in the Santeria religion?

■ **CASE VOCABULARY**

RATIO DECIDENDI: The rule of law that a court bases its decision on in a particular case.

Fitzpatrick v. Bitzer
(Not Stated) v. (Not Stated)
427 U.S. 445, 96 S.Ct. 2666 (1976)

THE ELEVENTH AMENDMENT DOES NOT BAR CONGRESS FROM PROVIDING A CAUSE OF ACTION AGAINST STATES AS A MEANS OF ENFORCING THE FOURTEENTH AMENDMENT

■ **INSTANT FACTS** Congress amended Title VII of the Civil Rights Act to allow a federal cause of action against state governments for employment discrimination. The provision is being challenged under the Eleventh Amendment.

■ **BLACK LETTER RULE** No constitutional provision prohibits Congress from providing for a private cause of action in the federal courts against a state government as a means of enforcing the guarantees of the Fourteenth Amendment.

■ **PROCEDURAL BASIS**
Not Stated

■ **FACTS**
In 1972, Congress amended Title VII of the Civil Rights Act of 1964 authorizing federal courts to award money damages to a private individual against a state government found to have subjected that person to employment discrimination on the basis of "race, color, religion, sex, or national origin." The provision of a right to sue states in federal court is challenged as a violation of the Eleventh Amendment's grant of sovereign immunity to the States.

■ **ISSUE**
May Congress use its enforcement powers under § 5 of the Fourteenth Amendment to provide a federal cause of action against a state official or government in spite of the Eleventh Amendment's grant of sovereign immunity to the States?

■ **DECISION AND RATIONALE**
(Rehnquist, J.) Yes. The principal issue for the Court is whether, as against the shield of sovereign immunity afforded the State by the Eleventh Amendment, Congress has the authority to provide for such a cause of action against the states as a means of enforcing the substantive guarantees of the Fourteenth Amendment. We have examined the impact of the Fourteenth Amendment on the federal government-state government relationship in *Ex parte State of Virginia* (1880). In that case, we observed that the Thirteenth and Fourteenth Amendments "were intended to be ... limitations of the power of the States and enlargements of the power of Congress." In addressing the relationship between § 5 and the substantive provisions of the Fourteenth Amendment we said that "Congress is empowered to enforce [the prohibitions of the Fourteenth Amendment] ... against State action, however put forth, whether that action be executive, legislative, or judicial. Such enforcement is no invasion of State sovereignty. No law can be [such an invasion], which the people of the States have, by the Constitution of the United States, empowered Congress to enact." It is true that none of these cases examined the question of the relationship between the Eleventh Amendment and Congress's enforcement power under § 5. But we think that the Eleventh Amendment, and the principle of state sovereignty it embodies, is necessarily limited by the enforcement provisions of § 5 of the Fourteenth Amendment. When Congress acts under § 5, it is not only exercising legislative authority that is plenary within the

Fitzpatrick v. Bitzer (Continued)

terms of the constitutional grant, it is exercising that authority under one section of a constitutional Amendment whose other sections, by their own terms, embody limitations on state authority. We think that Congress may, in determining what is "appropriate legislation" for the purpose of enforcing the Fourteenth Amendment, provide for private suits against States or state officials, even though it may not do so in other contexts.

Analysis:

Here the Court construes two constitutional amendments, seemingly at odds with each other, in a way that preserves each, as much as possible, in their independent spheres. The logic behind the Court's holding is that in order for full effect to be given to the Fourteenth Amendment, which was adopted by the people. It necessarily must control the Eleventh Amendment's grant of sovereign immunity to the States. Otherwise, a very important tool in the Fourteenth Amendment's arsenal of enforcement would be rendered useless, marginalizing the Amendment itself. Implicit in the people's approval of the Fourteenth Amendment is an understanding that its enforcement must control any seemingly contradictory laws, including the Eleventh Amendment.

Seminole Tribe of Florida v. Florida
(*Indian Tribe*) v. (*State*)
517 U.S. 44, 116 S.Ct. 1114 (1996)

SUPREME COURT REAFFIRMS THE VITALITY OF THE ELEVENTH AMENDMENT BY OVERRULING PENNSYLVANIA V. UNION GAS CO.

■ **INSTANT FACTS** Congress passed a law allowing states to be sued for failing to negotiate in good faith with Indian tribes regarding the formation of gaming compacts between those parties. The law is challenged as a violation of the Eleventh Amendment's sovereign immunity.

■ **BLACK LETTER RULE** Congress may not, outside enforcement of Fourteenth Amendment Guarantees, authorize federal lawsuits against states in abrogation of the Eleventh Amendment's guarantee of state sovereign immunity.

■ **PROCEDURAL BASIS**

Appeal to the Supreme Court of an action filed in federal court after a motion to dismiss for lack of subject matter jurisdiction.

■ **FACTS**

Congress passed the Indian Gaming Regulatory Act (Act) in 1988 to provide a statutory basis for the operation and regulation of gaming by Indian Tribes. The Act requires that states negotiate in good faith with Indian Tribes to permit gambling on Native American reservations and authorizes suits against state governments in federal court to enforce the law. The Seminole Tribe of Florida (Seminoles)(P) sued the state of Florida (D), invoking jurisdiction under the Act, for failing to negotiate in good faith. Florida (D) moved to dismiss the complaint, arguing that the suit violated the State's sovereign immunity from suit in federal court.

■ **ISSUE**

May Congress abrogate the States' sovereign immunity under the Eleventh Amendment in an effort to enforce constitutional provisions falling outside the scope of the Fourteenth Amendment?

■ **DECISION AND RATIONALE**

(Rehnquist, C.J.) No. In order to determine whether Congress has properly abrogated the States' sovereign immunity we ask two questions: first, whether Congress has unequivocally expressed it's intent to abrogate immunity; and second, whether such abrogation is allowed by an affirmative grant of congressional authority. Congress's intent to abrogate must be obvious from a clear legislative statement. Here, we agree with the parties and the court below, as well as other courts, that Congress has, in the Act, provided an unmistakably clear statement of its intent to abrogate. Section 2710(d)(7)(A)(i) vests jurisdiction in "[t]he United States district courts . . . over any cause of action . . . arising from the failure of a State to enter into negotiations . . . or to conduct negotiations in good faith." We turn now to consider whether the Act was passed pursuant to a constitutional provision granting Congress the power to abrogate. We have previously found such authority under only two provisions of the Constitution. In *Fitzpatrick* we held that the Fourteenth Amendment had fundamentally altered the balance of state and federal power struck by the Constitution through § 1, which contains prohibitions expressly directed at the States, and § 5, expressly providing Congress with the power to "enforce, by appropriate legislation, the provisions of this article." Congress, therefore, has the authority, through

§ 5, to abrogate the immunity from suit guaranteed by the Fourteenth Amendment. The only other case upholding abrogation is *Pennsylvania v. Union Gas Co.*, in which we held that the Interstate Commerce Clause granted Congress the power to abrogate state sovereign immunity, stating that the power to regulate commerce would be "incomplete without the authority to render States liable in damages." However, the rationale for our *Union Gas* ruling was joined by only four justices, with Justice White joining these four in the result, but not in their rationale. In the time since this ruling, *Union Gas* has proved to be a solitary departure from established law. Reconsidering this decision, we conclude that none of the policies underlying stare decisis require our continuing adherence to its holding. The decision has been of questionable precedential value, with the plurality's rationale departing from our established understanding of the Eleventh Amendment and undermining the accepted function of Article III. *Union Gas* was thus wrongly decided and should be, and now is, overruled. In doing so, we reconfirm that the background principle of state sovereign immunity embodied in the Eleventh Amendment is not so ephemeral as to dissipate when the subject of the suit is an area, like the regulation of Indian commerce, that is under the exclusive control of the Federal Government. The Eleventh Amendment restricts the judicial power under Article III, and Article I cannot be used to circumvent the constitutional limitations placed upon federal jurisdiction. The Seminoles' (P) suit must, therefore, be dismissed for want of jurisdiction.

■ DISSENT

(Stevens, J.) This case is about the power of Congress to create a private federal cause of action against a State for violating a federal right. Breaking with the past, the Court holds that Congress has no power, with the narrow exception of that provided by § 5 of the Fourteenth Amendment. The importance of this ruling cannot be overstated. It prevents Congress from providing a federal forum for a broad range of actions, from those sounding in copyright and patent law, to those concerning bankruptcy, environmental law, and the regulation of our vast national economy. While there can certainly be no debate whether, in light of the Eleventh Amendment, Congress has the power to ensure that such a cause of action may be enforced in federal court by a citizen of another State. There can be no doubt, however, that Congress may provide such a cause of action to a citizen of the State being sued. The Court is obviously mistakenly applying a modern embodiment of the ancient doctrine of sovereign immunity, something that has nothing to do with the limit on judicial power contained in the Eleventh Amendment. The Amendment's dictates rest instead on concerns of federalism and comity that merit respect but are nevertheless subordinate to the plenary power of Congress.

■ DISSENT

(Souter, J.) The Court holds today for the first time since the founding of the Republic that Congress has no authority to subject a State to the jurisdiction of a federal court at the behest of an individual asserting a federal right. I choose to part company from the Court's ruling because I am convinced that its decision is fundamentally mistaken. The framers had no intent of creating state immunity from federal question jurisdiction or from suit by a non-citizen of the state being sued. The issue was debated, but until *Chisholm v. Georgia* was decided it was unclear whether there was any such immunity. The Court in that case ruled that a state defendant enjoyed no sovereign immunity from federal question jurisdiction, or from a federal suit by a non-citizen. The lack of debate among the framers over federal question immunity indicates a general understanding at the time that the States would have no immunity in such cases. The adoption of the Eleventh Amendment changed the result in *Chisholm* by eliminating citizen-state diversity jurisdiction over cases with state defendants. The Amendment, however, did not affect federal question jurisdiction. In *Hans v. Louisiana* the Court erroneously assumed that a State could plead sovereign immunity against a non-citizen suing under federal question jurisdiction, and for that reason held that a State must also enjoy the same protection in a suit by its own citizens. The error in this reasoning is underscored by its clear inconsistency with the Founder's hostility to the implicit reception of common law doctrine as federal law, and with the Founder's conception of sovereign power as divided between the States and the National Government. The Founders viewed the common law, when it was received into the new American legal system, as always subject to legislative amendment. But the Court ignores the reasons for this understanding, instead holding that a non-textual common law rule limits a clear grant of congressional power under Article I. The common law doctrine of sovereign immunity comprises two distinct rules, which are not always separately identified. The first is that the King, as the font of the law, is not bound by the law's provisions; the other provides that the King, as the font of justice, is not subject to suit in its own courts. The one limits the reach of substantive law; the other limits the jurisdiction of the courts. We are concerned only with the latter rule. While some colonial governments may have enjoyed immunity from jurisdiction, the scope of this governmental immunity in pre-Revolutionary America remains disputed. At any rate, the proposal to establish a National Government under the Constitution presented a prospect unknown to the common law at the time: a system dividing sovereignty, over even domestic matters, between the States and National Government, the latter to be vested with its own judicial power and supremacy of its laws. Considering the Eleventh Amendment now, its history and structure show that it reaches only to suits subject to federal question jurisdiction exclusively under the Citizen-State Diversity Clauses. The language in Article III providing for citizen-state diversity jurisdiction suggests to common sense that the text of the Eleventh Amendment addresses only diversity cases. If the framers had meant to bar federal question suits as well, they could not only have easily made their intentions very clear, but could simply have adopted the first post-*Chisholm* proposal, in the House of Representatives, that such a provision be adopted. Because neither text, precedent, nor history supports the majority's abdication of our responsibility to exercise our Article III jurisdiction, I would reverse the judgment of the Court of Appeals.

Analysis:

The Court holds in *Seminole Tribe of Florida* that Congress may not vest federal courts with jurisdiction over federal question suits against state governments, regardless of whether the plaintiff is from the would-be defendant state or some other state or nation. This rule is, of course, qualified by Congress's authority to enforce the substantive guarantees of the Fourteenth Amendment, as set forth in *Fitzpatrick v. Bitzer*. How does this ruling jibe with the text of the Eleventh Amendment? The Eleventh Amendment reads: "The Judicial power of the United States shall not be construed to extend to any suit in law or equity, commenced or prosecuted against one of the United States by Citizens of another State, or by Citizens or Subjects of any Foreign State." In plain English, this means that Congress may not vest jurisdiction in the federal courts over suits against States brought by citizens of a different state, or of another country. The Amendment thus does not address suits brought against a state by one of its own citizens.

■ CASE VOCABULARY

SOVEREIGN IMMUNITY: A government's immunity from being subject to suit, whether by its own citizens in its own courts, or in federal court, or otherwise.

Florida Prepaid Postsecondary Education Expense Board v. College Savings Bank and United States

(State) v. (Lender) & (Federal Government)

527 U.S. 627, 119 S.Ct. 2199 (1999)

CONGRESS MUST SHOW A PATTERN OF STATE VIOLATIONS OF THE FOURTEENTH AMENDMENT TO ABROGATE STATE SOVEREIGNTY

■ **INSTANT FACTS** Congress enacted legislation providing a right to sue states in federal court over patent infringement. The legislation is challenged as beyond Congress's Fourteenth Amendment enforcement authority.

■ **BLACK LETTER RULE** For Congress's abrogation of State sovereignty pursuant to the Fourteenth Amendment to be constitutional, it must (1) show a history or pattern of unconstitutional activity by States giving rise to a need for remedial or preventive federal regulation, and (2) limit the scope of the remedy, making it proportionate to the constitutional violations giving rise to the need for enforcement.

■ **PROCEDURAL BASIS**

Appeal of a federal patent infringement action to the Supreme Court after the court of appeals ruled the Patent Remedy Act constitutional.

■ **FACTS**

In 1992, Congress passed Patent and Plant Variety Protection Act (Act), amending the patent laws and expressly abrogating the States' sovereign immunity from claims of patent infringement. [The Act expressly says that states "shall not be immune" from federal patent infringement suits.] College Savings Bank (CSB)(P1) then sued the Florida Prepaid Postsecondary Education Expense Board (Prepaid)(D), a Florida State entity, in federal court for infringing upon CSB's (P1) patented financing methodology. Prepaid (D) challenges the Act as beyond Congress's Fourteenth Amendment enforcement authority.

■ **ISSUE**

May Congress properly use its Fourteenth Amendment enforcement authority to abrogate the States' sovereign immunity by providing a right to sue States in federal court for patent infringement?

■ **DECISION AND RATIONALE**

(Rehnquist, C.J.) No. It is claimed that the Act validly abrogated the States' sovereign immunity. To determine this proposition's merits we must answer two questions: First, whether Congress has unequivocally expressed its intent to abrogate the immunity; and second, whether Congress has acted properly within the constraints of its constitutional authority. It is very clear from the text of the Act that Congress intended to abrogate the States' sovereign immunity. Whether Congress has the power to do so, however, is another matter. Congress grounded the Act in three constitutional provisions: the Patent Clause, Art. I, § 8, cl. 8; the Interstate Commerce Clause, Art. I, § 8, cl. 3; and § 5 of the Fourteenth Amendment. *Seminole Tribe* makes clear that Congress may not abrogate state sovereign immunity pursuant to its Article I powers; hence the Act cannot be sustained under either the Commerce Clause or the Patent Clause. Congress does, as also held in *Seminole Tribe*, retain the authority to abrogate state sovereign immunity pursuant to the Fourteenth Amendment. Following *City of Boerne*, we must first identify the Fourteenth Amendment "evil" or "wrong" that Congress intended to remedy. CSB (P1) and the Government (P2) assert that the Act is needed to secure the Fourteenth Amendment's protections against deprivations of property by States without due process of law. The underlying conduct at issue is the unremedied patent infringement by the States. It is this conduct that must give rise to the Fourteenth Amendment violation that Congress sought to redress in the Act. But in passing the Act, Congress identified no pattern of patent infringement by the States, let alone a pattern of constitutional violations. Unlike the undisputed record of racial discrimination confronting Congress in the voting rights cases, Congress came up with little evidence of infringing conduct on the part of the States. At most, Congress heard testimony that patent infringement by States might increase in the future. Instead, only where the State provides no remedy, or only inadequate remedies, to injured patent owners for its infringement of their patent could a deprivation of property without due process result. The legislative record thus suggests that the Act does not respond to a history of widespread and persisting deprivation of constitutional rights. Though such a lack of support in the legislative record is not determinative, identifying the targeted constitutional wrong is still a critical part of our § 5 calculus because strong measures appropriate to address one harm may be an unwarranted response to another, lesser one. Here, there is scant support for concluding that States were depriving patent owners of property without due process. This shortfall makes the provisions of the Act so out of proportion to a supposed remedial or preventive object that they cannot be understood as responsive to, or designed to prevent, unconstitutional behavior. Indeed, Congress did nothing to limit the coverage of the Act to cases involving arguable constitutional violations, such as where a State refuses to even entertain a patent suit in its courts. Nor did Congress even attempt to confine the reach of the Act by limiting the remedy to certain types of infringement, such as infringement authorized pursuant to state policy. In *City of Boerne* we discussed with approval the various limits that Congress imposed in its voting right measures, and noted that where "a congressional enactment pervasively prohibits constitutional state action in an effort to remedy or to prevent unconstitutional state action, limitations of this kind tend to ensure Congress's means are proportionate to ends legitimate under § 5." The Act's indiscriminate scope offends this principle, and is particularly incongruous in light of the scant support for the predicate unconstitutional conduct that Congress intended to remedy. The Act, therefore, cannot be sustained under § 5 of the Fourteenth Amendment.

■ DISSENT

(Stevens, J.) The Constitution vests Congress with plenary authority over patents and copyrights. Nearly 200 years ago, Congress provided for exclusive jurisdiction of patent infringement litigation in the federal courts. In 1992, the Act clarified that jurisdictional grant by authorizing patent infringement actions against States. Given the absence of effective state remedies for patent infringement by States and the statutory preemption of such state remedies, the 1992 Act was an appropriate exercise of Congress's power under § 5 to prevent state deprivations of property without due process. Our decision in *City of Boeme* amply supports congressional authority to pass the Act, whether one assumes States seldom infringe patents, or that patent infringements potentially permeate an "unlimited range of state conduct." Instead, the majority relies entirely on perceived deficiencies in the evidence reviewed by Congress before it passed the clarifying [Act]. It is quite unfair for the Court to invalidate the Act based on an absence of findings supporting a requirement this Court had not yet articulated. Nevertheless, Congress did hear testimony about the inadequate state remedies for patent infringement when considering the Act. The legislative record references several cases of patent infringement involving States. In addition, Congress found that state infringement of patents was likely to increase. Even if state remedies might be available in theory, it would have been appropriate for Congress to conclude that they would not guarantee patentees due process in infringement actions against state defendants. State judges are likely to be inexperienced in the application of patent law and their decisions would not be reviewable in the Court of Appeals for the Federal Circuit. Finally, this Court has never mandated that Congress must find widespread and persisting deprivation of constitutional rights in order to employ its § 5 authority. It is thus not surprising that Congress would fail to compile an extensive legislative record analyzing the due process afforded patentees suing states. For these reasons, I am convinced that the Act should be upheld even if full respect is given to the Court's recent cases cloaking the States with increasing protection from congressional legislation.

Analysis:

In previous cases testing the limits of Congress's § 5 authority to enforce the substantive provisions of the Fourteenth Amendment, the Court extended deference to Congressional findings of constitutional violations justifying an abrogation of the states' Eleventh Amendment sovereign immunity. Yet here, such deference is lacking. What explains this shift? One may assert that there has not been a shift, that in *City of Boerne* the Court set forth a congruence requirement mandating that the scope of congressional abrogation of state sovereignty be in proportion to the evils being remedied, thus effectively requiring Congress to make findings reflecting a need for remedial measures under the Fourteenth Amendment. But the congruity or proportionality of the remedial measures is an inquiry separate from whether there are, or have been, persistent or potential constitutional violations.

■ CASE VOCABULARY

COPYRIGHT: An exclusive property right in any original work of an author allowing the, owner to control the dissemination of the work.

PATENT: An exclusive property right to an invention allowing the owner to control the use and/or disposition of the invention for a set number of years.

Kimel v. Florida Board of Regents

(*Employee*) v. (*State*)
528 U.S. 62, 120 S.Ct. 631 (2000)

CONGRESS MAY NOT USE ITS FOURTEENTH AMENDMENT AUTHORITY TO REMEDY AGE DISCRIMINATION IN EMPLOYMENT BY STATES

■ **INSTANT FACTS** Congress extended coverage of federal age discrimination laws to the States using its § 5 authority to enforce the Fourteenth Amendment. The extension is challenged as outside the scope of this authority.

■ **BLACK LETTER RULE** In order for Congressional legislation abrogating State sovereign immunity pursuant to § 5 of the Fourteenth Amendment to be valid, its substantive requirements must be congruent with and proportionate to the unconstitutional actions of the States.

■ PROCEDURAL BASIS

Appeal to the Supreme Court of a federal age discrimination suit against a State.

■ FACTS

[This is a group of companion cases in which state employees have sued their employers under the Age Discrimination in Employment Act of 1967 (ADEA). They will be referred to together, with the Kimel case being representative of all.] When first passed in 1967, the ADEA applied only to private employers. In 1974, Congress extended application of the ADEA's substantive requirements to the States. The ADEA makes it unlawful for an employer "to fail or refuse to hire or to discharge any individual or otherwise discriminate against any individual with respect to his [conditions of employment], because of such individual's age." The ADEA provides a private cause of action in federal court to enforce its provisions. The Florida Board of Regents (Florida)(D) challenges the ADEA, insofar as it abrogates state sovereign immunity, as an overstepping of Congress's authority under the Fourteenth Amendment.

■ ISSUE

May Congress abrogate the States' sovereign immunity pursuant to § 5 of the Fourteenth Amendment absent a sufficient finding of state constitutional violations to be remedied by the congressional enactment?

■ DECISION AND RATIONALE

(O'Connor, J.) No. In determining whether Congress has validly abrogated the States' Eleventh Amendment sovereign immunity from suits we must ask two questions. First, whether Congress unequivocally declared its intent to so abrogate that immunity; and second, whether Congress acted pursuant to a valid grant of constitutional authority. The first test is satisfied by the ADEA's clear authorization of employees to maintain actions for backpay "against any employer (including a public agency) in any Federal or State court of competent jurisdiction...." As for the next test, our cases show that § 5 of the Fourteenth Amendment is an affirmative grant to Congress of the authority to abrogate the States' sovereign immunity. Indeed, it is for Congress in the first instance to determine whether and what legislation is needed to secure the guarantees of the Fourteenth Amendment, and its conclusions are entitled to much deference. Congress's power in this regard includes the authority both to remedy and to deter violations of rights guaranteed by the Fourteenth Amendment by prohibiting a

Kimel v. Florida Board of Regents (Continued)

somewhat broader swath of conduct, including that which is not itself forbidden by the Amendment's text. This authority is, however, subject to some limits found within the Amendment itself. For example, Congress may not decree the scope of the Amendment's substantive restrictions on the States. Such is the province of the Judicial Branch. In analyzing these limits, we apply a "congruence and proportionality" test. Here, this leads us to the conclusion that the ADEA is not "appropriate legislation" under § 5. Initially, the substantive requirements the ADEA imposes on state and local governments are disproportionate to any unconstitutional conduct that could conceivably be targeted by the ADEA. We have considered claims of unconstitutional age discrimination under the Equal Protection Clause three times, and in each case we held that the age classifications at issue did not violate the Equal Protection Clause. Unlike governmental conduct based on race or gender, age classifications can, and most frequently do reflect a legitimate state interest, rather than reflecting any prejudice and/or antipathy. Older persons have not been subjected to a "history of purposeful unequal treatment such as would make them a discrete and insular minority." Indeed, all persons, if they live out their normal life spans, will experience old age. Accordingly, age is not a suspect classification under the Equal Protection Clause. States may, therefore, discriminate on the basis of age so long as the age classification in question is rationally related to a legitimate state interest.

Thus, under the Fourteenth Amendment, a State may rely on age as a proxy for other qualities, abilities, or characteristics that are relevant to the State's legitimate interests. Judged against this backdrop, it is clear that the ADEA is so out of proportion to a supposed remedial or preventive object that it cannot be understood as responsive to, or designed to prevent, unconstitutional behavior. The ADEA prohibits substantially more state employment decisions and practices than would likely be held unconstitutional under the applicable equal protection, rational basis standard. While this conclusion is certainly significant, it does not alone answer our § 5 inquiry. Our next determination must be whether the ADEA is an appropriate remedy, or reasonably prophylactic piece of legislation, or instead, merely an attempt to substantively redefine the States' legal obligations with respect to age discrimination. In evaluating the appropriateness of the ADEA's remedial measures, we must consider the depth and seriousness of the evil Congress seeks to remedy and prevent. Looking at the ADEA's legislative record, we conclude that Congress's extension of its coverage to the States was an unwarranted response to a perhaps inconsequential problem. Congress never identified any pattern of age discrimination by the States, much less any discrimination whatsoever that rose to the level of constitutional violation. Congress did make findings regarding discrimination by private employers, but this is beside the point. There were no such findings with respect to the States. A review of the ADEA's legislative record as a whole, then, reveals that Congress had virtually no reason to believe that state and local governments were unconstitutionally discriminating against their employees on the basis of age. Although such a lack of support is not, in itself, determinative of the § 5 inquiry, Congress's failure to uncover any significant pattern of unconstitutional discrimination here confirms that Congress had no reason to believe that broad prophylactic legislation was necessary in this field. Given this lack of evidence of discrimination by States, coupled with the ADEA's indiscriminate scope of regulation, we must hold that the ADEA is not a valid exercise of Congress's power under § 5 of the Fourteenth Amendment.

■ CONCURRENCE AND DISSENT

(Stevens, J.) Congress's power to regulate the American economy includes the power to regulate both the public and private sectors of the labor market. Neither the Eleventh Amendment nor the doctrine of sovereign immunity places any limit on that power. The Court's application of the ancient judge-made doctrine of sovereign immunity is supposedly justified as a freestanding limit on congressional authority, necessary to protect States' "dignity and respect" from impairment by the National Government. The framers did not, however, select the Judicial Branch as the constitutional guardian of those state interests. Rather, they designed important structural safeguards to ensure that the normal operation of the legislative process itself would adequately defend state interests from undue infringement. Federalism concerns do make it appropriate for Congress to speak clearly when it regulates state action. But when it does so, we can safely presume that Congress took the burdens the statute imposes on the States' sovereignty into account. Once Congress has made its policy choice, the sovereignty concerns of the several States are satisfied. There is nothing in the Constitution supporting the Court's conclusion that the judge-made doctrine of sovereign immunity limits Congress's power to authorize private parties to enforce federal laws against the States. Nor does the Eleventh Amendment support the Court's view. The Amendment only places a textual limitation on the diversity jurisdiction of the federal courts. Here, however, Kimel (P) is a citizen of the State he seeks to sue, i.e. diversity jurisdiction has not been invoked. Thus today's decision (relying as it does on *Seminole Tribe*) rests entirely on a novel judicial interpretation of the doctrine of sovereign immunity, which the Court treats as though it were a constitutional precept. I am unwilling to accept *Seminole Tribe* as controlling precedent. The Court's judicial activism manifested in cases like *Seminole Tribe* and others represents such a radical departure from the proper role of this Court that it should be opposed whenever the opportunity arises.

Analysis:

A number of Supreme Court opinions since 1897 have interpreted the Fourteenth Amendment's Due Process Clause to incorporate many of the Bill of Rights' amendments, thus making them applicable to the states, whereas before they were interpreted to apply to the federal government only. The Eleventh Amendment expressly extends to the states sovereign immunity from suits by non-citizens. The majority, under subheading it of its opinion and quoting *Seminole Tribe*, states that the Court has "long understood the Eleventh Amendment to stand not so much for what it says, but for the presupposition ... which it confirms." In other words, the majority cites the Eleventh Amendment as providing absolute immunity from suit, limited by the Fourteenth Amendment's enforcement clause. The common law doctrine of sovereign immunity was never incorporated, expressly or implicitly, into the Constitution.

■ CASE VOCABULARY

RATIONAL BASIS: The requirement under the Equal Protection Clause that a government classification bear some reasonable relation to the legitimate end sought in applying the classification at issue.

Board of Trustees v. Garrett

(State Actor) v. (Disabled Plaintiff)
531 U.S. 356, 121 S.Ct. 955 (2001)

STATES ARE NOT LIABLE UNDER THE ADA

■ **INSTANT FACTS** State employees sued the State of Alabama for disability discrimination in employment.

■ **BLACK LETTER RULE** The Americans with Disabilities Act does not hold state governments liable for employment discrimination on the basis of an employee's disability.

■ **PROCEDURAL BASIS**

Certiorari to review an undisclosed appellate decision.

■ **FACTS**

Garrett (P) was the nursing director at the University of Alabama in Birmingham Hospital. While she was undergoing cancer therapy, her supervisor required her to surrender her high-level position in exchange for a lower-paying one. She sued the Board of Trustees (D) for disability discrimination under the Americans with Disabilities Act (ADA).

■ **ISSUE**

Can a state government be held civilly liable for disability discrimination under the Americans with Disabilities Act?

■ **DECISION AND RATIONALE**

(Rehnquist, C.J.) No. Under the Americans with Disabilities Act, certain employers, including state governments, must refrain from discriminating against otherwise qualified individuals with disabilities and must make reasonable accommodations to enable disabled individuals to perform their jobs. Because the Eleventh Amendment confers upon the states sovereign immunity from civil liability, the Board of Trustees (D) can be liable under the ADA only if Congress unequivocally intended such a result under a valid grant of constitutional authority. Clearly, the plain language of the statute indicates congressional intent to bind state governments, and Congress may not abrogate sovereign immunity through its Article I powers. It may, however, pass such legislation in exercise of its enforcement powers under § 5 of the Fourteenth Amendment. The Court has established that legislation or state action treating individuals with disabilities differently than other individuals, if it exists, must meet the rational-basis review applicable to other social and economic legislation. "Thus, . . . States are not required by the Fourteenth Amendment to make special accommodations for the disabled, so long as their actions towards such individuals are rational."

To expose state governments to civil liability through a private right of action and satisfy constitutional scrutiny, Congress must identify a pattern of irrational state discrimination against the disabled. The legislative history of the ADA fails to demonstrate that Congress identified such a pattern. Without such historical discrimination, legislation seeking to hold states accountable for disability discrimination is not "congruent and proportional to the targeted violation." The ADA does not apply to state governments.

Board of Trustees v. Garrett (Continued)

■ CONCURRENCE

(Kennedy, J.) While the ADA achieves important social objectives, legislation seeking to remedy a state violation that has not been proven to exist does not pass constitutional muster.

■ DISSENT

(Breyer, J.) The legislative record contains substantial evidence of disability discrimination throughout local governments and society in general. It is illogical to assume that state governments are free from the stereotypical views perpetuating discrimination in general. Section 5 authorizes Congress to enact legislation to enforce constitutional equal protection guarantees, and the Equal Protection Clauses applies with equal force to state governments as it does to local governments and private employers.

Analysis:

The *Garrett* decision was limited to employment discrimination claims under Title I of the ADA. Under Title II of the statute, however, "no qualified individual with a disability shall, by reason of such disability, be excluded from participation in or be denied the benefits of the services, programs, or activities of a public entity, or be subjected to discrimination by any such entity." In *Tennessee v. Lane*, the Court determined that Title II was a valid exercise of § 5 power.

■ CASE VOCABULARY

AMERICANS WITH DISABILITIES ACT: A federal statute that prohibits discrimination—in employment, public services, and public accommodations—against any person with a disability ("a physical or mental impairment that substantially limits one or more of the major life activities."). 42 U.S.C. §§ 12101–12213.

ELEVENTH AMENDMENT: The constitutional amendment, ratified in 1795, prohibiting a federal court from hearing an action between a state and a person who is not a citizen of that state.

EQUAL PROTECTION: The constitutional guarantee under the 14th Amendment that the government must treat a person or class of persons the same as it treats other persons or classes in like circumstances.

RATIONAL–BASIS TEST: A principle whereby a court will uphold a law as valid under the Equal Protection Clause or Due Process Clause if it bears a reasonable relationship to the attainment of some legitimate governmental objective.

SOVEREIGN IMMUNITY: A government's immunity from being sued in its own courts without its consent. Congress has waived most of the federal government's sovereign immunity.

Nevada Department of Human Resources v. Hibbs

(State Agency) v. (State Employee)
538 U.S. 721, 123 S.Ct. 1972 (2003)

THE FMLA IS A PROPER EXERCISE OF CONGRESS'S § 5 POWER

■ **INSTANT FACTS** Hibbs (P) sued his government employer for wrongful discharge and violations of the Family and Medical Leave Act when he was fired while caring for his injured wife.

■ **BLACK LETTER RULE** State governments are liable for money damages for interfering or restraining state employees' exercise of their rights under the Family and Medical Leave Act of 1993.

■ **PROCEDURAL BASIS**
Certiorari to review an undisclosed lower court decision.

■ **FACTS**
Hibbs (P) worked for the Nevada Department of Human Resources (D). When his wife suffered serious injuries in a car accident, Hibbs (P) sought unpaid leave to care for her. The Department (D) authorized Hibbs (P) to take the full twelve weeks allowed under the Family and Medical Leave Act, to be used intermittently as needed over an eight-month period. When Hibbs (P) did not return to work, the Department (D) informed him that his statutory leave had been exhausted and demanded his return to work. When he refused to return, Hibbs (P) was terminated. Hibbs (P) sued the Department (D) and two of its officers in federal court for damages and injunctive relief.

■ **ISSUE**
Does the Family and Medical Leave Act of 1993 expose state governments to civil damages for a statutory violation?

■ **DECISION AND RATIONALE**
(Rehnquist, C.J.) Yes. When Congress abrogates the states' Eleventh Amendment sovereign immunity, it must do so unmistakably in the language of the statute and act pursuant to a valid exercise of its power under § 5 of the Fourteenth Amendment. Since the language of the Act itself clearly states that a "public agency" is covered by its terms, Congress's intent to apply the Act to state governments is unmistakably clear. The Act intends to eliminate gender-based classifications in private and public employment and therefore requires evidence of a pattern of constitutional violations in public employment to fall within Congress's § 5 powers.

The legislative record indicates a gender gap associated with employers' considerable maternity leave policies compared with scant evidence of paternity leave policies. These polices, patterned after state law, highlight the popular perception that women are better-suited or more inclined to fulfill child care duties than men. This sex-role stereotype places women's child-rearing duties ahead of the workplace. The states' participation in such gender-based discrimination is sufficiently patterned to warrant Congress's exercise of its § 5 powers.

Unlike in *Garrett* and *Kimel*, involving issues of disability and age discrimination, this case targets gender discrimination, which is subject to heightened constitutional scrutiny rather than the rational-basis review applicable there. Because the states bear a higher constitutional burden to justify gender classifications under heightened scrutiny, it is easier for Congress to establish a pattern of constitutional violations, as it was with the racial classifications targeted in *Katzenbach*.

Having properly exercised its § 5 powers, the monetary remedy employed is "congruent and proportional to the targeted violation."

■ DISSENT

(Scalia, J.) Congress's § 5 power may not be used to abrogate one state's immunity because of constitutional violations in other states. Rather than concentrate on the pattern of constitutional violations in each individual state, the Court treats states as a collective entity, binding even those with no history of constitutional violations. Section 5 power is prophylactic and cannot be extended to those states innocent of constitutional violations.

■ DISSENT

(Kennedy, J.) Although Congress identified historically disparate treatment of women in the private sector, it offered little evidence of such treatment in public employment. In fact, a majority of states had enacted family-leave legislation before the FMLA was enacted. Although the enforcement of such state legislation may support a disparate impact charge, it does not suffice to demonstrate a pattern of constitutional violations in state employment. The Court may not find a pattern of constitutional violation because the chosen methods to combat gender discrimination are less effective than what could have been adopted. Because these states have not committed or perpetuated purposeful discrimination, the remedy employed under the FMLA is not congruent and proportional to the constitutional violations asserted.

Analysis:

Hibbs concluded a seven-year period in which the Rehnquist Court generally favored states' rights in Eleventh Amendment cases. Often in close decisions, the Supreme Court consistently upheld states' Eleventh Amendment immunity under federal statutes dealing with disability discrimination, age discrimination, and labor standards. With the heightened scrutiny applied to gender classifications, however, the balance shifted against state immunity.

■ CASE VOCABULARY

FAMILY LEAVE: An unpaid leave of absence from work taken to have or care for a baby or to care for a sick family member.

INTERMEDIATE SCRUTINY: A standard lying between the extremes of rational-basis review and strict scrutiny. Under the standard, if a statute contains a quasi-suspect classification (such as gender or legitimacy), the classification must be substantially related to the achievement of an important governmental objective.

Tennessee v. Lane

(*State Government*) v. (*Paraplegic*)
541 U.S. 509, 124 S.Ct. 1978 (2004)

TITLE II OF THE ADA IS A VALID EXERCISE OF CONGRESS'S § 5 POWER

■ **INSTANT FACTS** Two disabled individuals sued the State of Tennessee (D) and several counties under Title II of the Americans with Disabilities Act of 1990.

■ **BLACK LETTER RULE** To abrogate the states' Eleventh Amendment immunity, Congress must have unequivocally expressed its intent to abrogate that immunity and do so under a valid grant of constitutional authority.

■ **PROCEDURAL BASIS**

Certiorari to review an undisclosed decision.

■ **FACTS**

Lane (P), a paraplegic, confined to a wheelchair, was charged with a crime. The courtroom in which Lane (P) was to appear to answer the charges was located on the courthouse's second floor. Because the courthouse had no elevator, Lane (P) crawled up the stairs to the courtroom. When he was asked to reappear, Lane (P) refused to crawl up the stairs or be carried by officers and was arrested and jailed for failing to appear. Jones (P), also a paraplegic, claimed to have lost income as a court reporter due to her inability to access many county courtrooms. Plaintiffs sued the State of Tennessee (D) and several counties for violations of Title II of the Americans with Disabilities Act of 1990.

■ **ISSUE**

Does Title II of the Americans with Disabilities Act of 1990 exceed Congress's power under § 5 of the Fourteenth Amendment?

■ **DECISION AND RATIONALE**

(Stevens, J.) No. Title II of the Americans with Disabilities Act of 1990 (ADA) ensures that "no qualified individual with a disability shall, by reason of such disability, be excluded from participation in or be denied the benefits of the services, programs or activities of a public entity, or be subjected to discrimination by any such entity," including state governments. To abrogate the states' Eleventh Amendment immunity, however, Congress must have "unequivocally expressed its intent to abrogate that immunity" and do so under "a valid grant of constitutional authority."

Here, the ADA expressly states that no state shall be immune from liability for any violation of the statute. To constitute a valid abrogation, then, Congress must have a valid constitutional grant of authority to abrogate the states' immunity. In Title I of the ADA, Congress sought to eradicate employment discrimination based on a qualified individual's disability. While Title II likewise strikes at disability discrimination, its reach extends far beyond employment, implicating such constitutional guarantees as the right to vote, the right to travel, and the right to access to the courts. Many of these rights are protected by the Fourteenth Amendment, but also involve Sixth Amendment protections. Therefore, for Title II to be a valid exercise of Congress's § 5 power, the remedies chosen must be appropriate to meet the constitutional violations sought to be redressed. When considering the

Tennessee v. Lane (Continued)

enactment of Title II, Congress collected considerable evidence and testimony demonstrating that individuals with disabilities had been deprived access to or participation in the court system because of physical inaccessibility of the buildings and other obstacles. From this evidence, Congress determined the need for a remedy for this historically unequal treatment.

Because the constitutional right to access to the courts is at issue, the Court need not consider whether Title II is a valid exercise of congressional authority as a whole, but rather only as it applies to court access. Having identified historically disparate treatment in the court system, Title II insists upon reasonable accommodations and the removal of physical barriers to ensure reasonable access to the courts. It does not, however, require states to fundamentally alter the services they offer or assure absolute access to and participation in the court system. The remedy employed is reasonably tailored to protect the right to court access without disrupting the entire court system. This remedy is reasonably targeted at reaching is constitutional aim.

■ CONCURRENCE

(Ginsburg, J.) Before exercising its § 5 power, Congress need not specifically identify those instances in which the constitutional violations it targets have occurred. Rather than point the finger at individual states, it suffices to identify a general existence of the constitutional violation and fashion a reasonable remedy to eradicate it wherever it occurs.

■ DISSENT

(Rehnquist, C.J.) In *Board of Trustees of Alabama v. Garrett*, the Court established that Congress lacked § 5 power to abrogate the states' Eleventh Amendment immunity under Title I of the ADA. In approving the application of Title II, the Court relies on much of the same evidence held insufficient in *Garrett*. The evidence provides little relevant proof of actual discrimination by state actors and therefore identifies few constitutional violations worthy of congressional protection. In any event, physical or architectural barriers do not create a constitutional violation. A defendant's right to access to the courts does not insist upon the "right to make his way into a courtroom without any external assistance." Title II application is unsupported by the necessary pattern of constitutional violations and is an invalid exercise of congressional power.

■ DISSENT

(Scalia, J.) The "congruence and proportionality" test used to monitor the validity of congressional action is an unworkable standard because it leaves Congress at the mercy of the arbitrary discretion of judges. The test should be replaced by a clearer standard that allows Congress to do what § 5 permits—"to enforce, by appropriate legislation." In so doing, Congress, not the courts, should determine what is appropriate and necessary to redress constitutional violations. Once Congress identifies an historical pattern of violations in specified States, reasonably tailors the remedy to target those state actors committing the violations, and otherwise acts within the Constitution, Congress's reasoned judgment of appropriate remedies should go unquestioned.

Analysis:

Interestingly, the Court recognized the myriad other constitutional rights that Title II implicates, but issued its decision on the only right before it—the right to access to the courts. Although the Court ultimately concluded that Title II was an appropriate exercise of Congress's § 5 power, claims of sovereign immunity appear to remain viable defenses if states demonstrate a lack of historical constitutional violations in other areas.

■ CASE VOCABULARY

AMERICANS WITH DISABILITIES ACT: A federal statute that prohibits discrimination—in employment, public services, and public accommodations—against any person with a disability ("a physical or mental impairment that substantially limits one or more of the major life activities."). 42 U.S.C. §§ 12101–12213.

United States v. Georgia

(*Intervenor*) v. (*Prison Authority*)
546 U.S. 151, 126 S.Ct. 877 (2006)

A STATE MAY BE SUED FOR SOME ADA VIOLATIONS

■ **INSTANT FACTS** Goodman (P) brought an action against the state of Georgia (D) for violations of the Americans with Disabilities Act, and Georgia (D) claimed that the suit was barred by sovereign immunity.

■ **BLACK LETTER RULE** The enforcement power in the Fourteenth Amendment gives Congress the power to create a private right of action for violations of the Amendment.

■ **PROCEDURAL BASIS**
Appeal from an order of the Fifth Circuit Court of Appeals dismissing Goodman's (P) complaint.

■ **FACTS**
Goodman (P), a paraplegic, was an inmate confined to a Georgia (D) state prison. Goodman (P) alleged that the conditions of his confinement violated the Americans with Disabilities Act, 42 U.S.C. § 12101. Georgia (D) claimed that his suit was barred by sovereign immunity. The District Court granted summary judgment in favor of Georgia (D), and the Eleventh Circuit Court of Appeals affirmed.

■ **ISSUE**
Was Goodman's (P) claim barred by sovereign immunity?

■ **DECISION AND RATIONALE**
(Scalia, J.) No. The enforcement power in the Fourteenth Amendment gives Congress the power to create a private right of action for violations of the Amendment. The enforcement power includes the power to abrogate state sovereign immunity by authorizing private suits for damages against a state. Title II of the Americans with Disabilities Act creates a cause of action for conduct that actually violates the Fourteenth Amendment. Title II, therefore, abrogates Georgia's (D) sovereign immunity.

It is not clear what conduct Goodman (P) claims violates Title II. Once Goodman's (P) complaint is amended, the lower courts will be best able to determine what alleged conduct of Georgia (D) violated Title II. The lower courts will also be able to determine whether the Title II violations were also conduct that violated the Fourteenth Amendment. If Georgia's (D) misconduct violated Title II but not the Fourteenth Amendment, the courts may then address whether Congress's purported abrogation of sovereign immunity as to that type of conduct is valid. Reversed and remanded.

Analysis:
It is important to recognize how limited the Court's decision is. There is no blanket holding that Title II of the ADA abrogates sovereign immunity for all purposes. In fact, there is no holding that Goodman's (P) suit is not barred by sovereign immunity. The Court is merely setting up rules for a case-by-case determination of the immunity question.

■ CASE VOCABULARY

AMERICANS WITH DISABILITIES ACT: A federal statute that prohibits discrimination—in employment, public services, and public accommodations—against any person with a disability ("a physical or mental impairment that substantially limits one or more of the major life activities"). 42 U.S.C.A. §§ 12101—12213. Under the ADA, major life activities include any activity that an average person in the general population can perform with little or no difficulty, such as seeing, hearing, sleeping, walking, traveling, and working. The statute applies to both private and governmental entities.

SOVEREIGN IMMUNITY: A government's immunity from being sued in its own courts without its consent; a state's immunity from being sued in federal court by its own citizens. Congress has waived most of the federal government's sovereign immunity.

Alden v. Maine

(Probation Officer) v. (State)
527 U.S. 706, 119 S.Ct. 2240 (1999)

THE STATES' SOVEREIGN IMMUNITY EXTENDS TO SUITS IN STATE COURTS

■ **INSTANT FACTS** Two probation officers sued their state employer in state court for violating federal employment laws. The State raises the state sovereign immunity defense.

■ **BLACK LETTER RULE** Congress does not possess the authority, under its Article I powers, to abrogate the States' sovereign immunity from suits in its own state courts.

■ **PROCEDURAL BASIS**

Appeal to the Supreme Court from the Maine Supreme Judicial Court after the suit was first filed in federal district court where it was dismissed, the dismissal being upheld by the federal appeals court.

■ **FACTS**

Alden (P), a Maine probation officer, filed suit against his employer, the State of Maine (D), in federal district court, alleging that Maine (D) had violated the overtime provisions of the Fair Labor Standards Act (Act or FLSA). The district court dismissed the suit based on state sovereign immunity. Alden (P) filed the same suit in the state trial court, where it was also dismissed on the same grounds, with the Maine Supreme Judicial Court affirming the dismissal.

■ **ISSUE**

Do any of Congress's enumerated powers under Article I authorize it to abrogate the States' sovereign immunity from suits in its own courts?

■ **DECISION AND RATIONALE**

(Kennedy, J.) No. We hold that the powers delegated to Congress under Article I of the Constitution do not include the power to subject nonconsenting States to private suits in state courts. The Eleventh Amendment expressly immunizes the States from suits in federal courts by citizens of other states or foreign countries. This is, however, something of a misnomer, for the sovereign immunity of the States neither derives from nor is limited by the terms of the Eleventh Amendment. Rather, such immunity is a fundamental aspect of the sovereignty which the States enjoyed before the ratification of the Constitution, and which they retain today. Although the Constitution gives the National Government broad, often plenary authority over matters within its recognized competence. Any doubt regarding the constitutional role of the States as sovereign entities is removed by the Tenth Amendment, which was enacted to quell concerns about the extent of national power. The doctrine that a sovereign could not be sued without its consent, well established in English law, was universal in the States when the Constitution was drafted and ratified. Indeed, the leading advocates of the Constitution unequivocally assured the people that the Constitution would not strip the States of sovereign immunity. Despite these assurances, this Court held, in *Chisholm v. Georgia*, that Article III authorized a private citizen of another State to sue the State of Georgia without its consent. This ruling shocked the country, especially the States. It might be asserted that *Chisholm* was correct and that the Eleventh Amendment was a deviation from the original understanding, but this seems unsupportable. The text and history of the Eleventh Amendment

Alden v. Maine (Continued)

also suggest that Congress acted not to change but to restore the original constitutional design. Given the *Chisholm* uproar, it is doubtful that if Congress meant to write a new immunity into the Constitution it would have limited that immunity to the narrow text of the Eleventh Amendment. It is more likely that the Constitution was understood to preserve the States' traditional immunity from private suits, since the Amendment dealt only with that immunity called into question in *Chisholm*. As a consequence, we have looked to history and experience, and the established order of things, rather than adhering to the mere letter of the Eleventh Amendment in determining the scope of the States' constitutional immunity from suit. In doing so, the Court has upheld States' assertion of sovereign immunity in many and varied contexts falling outside the letter of the Amendment. These holdings show a settled doctrinal understanding that sovereign immunity derives not from the Eleventh Amendment, but from the structure of the original Constitution itself. Turning to the merits of the case, Article I, § 8 grants Congress broad powers, while the Supremacy Clause makes federal law the supreme law of the land, binding all judges, including state judges. Alden (P) contends that these provisions mandate that Congressional legislation overrides the sovereign immunity of the States. But the Supremacy Clause enshrines as the "supreme Law of the Land" only those federal Acts that accord with the constitutional design. The Constitution does not foreclose a State from asserting immunity to claims arising under federal law merely because the law is federal. A contrary view is untenable. Although the States' sovereign immunity derives, at least in part, from the common-law tradition, the structure and history of the Constitution show that the immunity exists today by constitutional design. We must, therefore, look to history, practice, precedent, and structure of the Constitution in search of compelling evidence that derogation of the States' immunity from suits in state courts is inherent in the constitutional compact. We believe the founders' silence is explained by the simple fact that not even the Constitution's most ardent opponents suggested the document would strip the States of sovereign immunity. This suggests the principle was so well established that no one conceived it would be altered by the Constitution. In other words, by ratifying the Eleventh Amendment so quickly the people were expressing their outrage at the *Chisholm* ruling and were of the impression that enshrining State immunity from suits by noncitizens of the State being sued, the greater intrusions into State immunity—suits by the State's own citizens in federal or state court—were also prohibited as a natural consequence of banning the lesser evil. History also shows that while early Congresses enacted various statutes authorizing federal suits in state court, there have been no instances in which Congress purported to authorize suits against nonconsenting States in these fora. Furthermore, the theory and reasoning of our earlier cases suggest the States do retain a constitutional immunity from suit in their own courts. Next, in examining the structural imperatives of our Constitution we look both to the essential principles of federalism and to the special role of the state courts in the constitutional design. Our federalism requires that Congress treat the States in a manner consistent with their status as residuary sovereigns and joint participants in the governance of the Nation. The principle of sovereign immunity thus accords the States the respect owed them as members of the federation. Private suits against nonconsenting States present the indignity of subjecting a State to the coercive process of judicial tribunals at the instance of private parties, regardless of the forum. Moreover, the immunity of a sovereign in its own courts has always been understood to be within the sole control of the sovereign itself. The federal government retains such immunity in both state and federal courts. We are reluctant to conclude that the States are not entitled to a reciprocal privilege. Underlying the constitutional form are considerations of great substance. Private suits against nonconsenting states may threaten the States' financial integrity, possibly causing staggering burdens in effect giving Congress a power and leverage over the States that is not contemplated by our constitutional design. If the principle of representative government is to be preserved to the States, the balance between competing interests must be reached after deliberation by the political process established by the citizens of the State, not by judicial decree mandated by the federal government. Affirming the States' sovereign immunity does not bar all judicial review of state constitutional compliance. Rather, certain limits are implicit in the constitutional principle of the state sovereign immunity. For example, states may consent to suit, either on their own or in response to federal persuasion. The States have also consented to certain extents by ratifying the Constitution and the Fourteenth Amendment. The second important limit is that sovereign immunity does not protect lesser entities, such as municipal corporations or state officers. In sum, when Congress legislates in matters affecting the States, it may not treat these sovereign entities as mere prefectures or corporations. Congress must accord States the esteem due to them as joint participants in a federal system.

Alden v. Maine (Continued)

■ DISSENT

(Souter, J.) Today the Court holds that the Eleventh Amendment was understood as having been enhanced by a "background principle" of state sovereign immunity from suit, operating beyond its limited codification in the Amendment, which deals solely with federal citizen-state diversity jurisdiction. This conception is at odds with constitutional history and at war with the conception of divided sovereignty that is the essence of American federalism. The Court asserts that state immunity from suit stems from the common law and was enjoyed by the States prior to ratification, and retained after, confirmed by the Tenth Amendment. However, sovereign immunity at common law was not understood to be indefeasible or to have been given any such status by the Constitution, which does not mention it. Indeed, there is almost no evidence that the generation of the framers thought sovereign immunity was fundamental in the sense of being unalterable. The colonies did not enjoy sovereign immunity, it being a privilege understood in English law to be reserved for the Crown alone. Before the Declaration of Independence, none of the colonies were, or pretended to be, sovereign states. Several colonial charters, including those of Massachusetts, Connecticut, Rhode Island, and Georgia, expressly specified that the colony could sue and be sued. In 1776, the locus of sovereignty of the colonies was still an open question, as lacking a voice in parliament they had not consented to being taxed. In the same way, sovereign immunity from suit was also unsettled. Some of the new States simply converted their colonial charters, without immunity, while others understood themselves to be inheritors of the Crown's common law sovereign immunity. At the Constitutional convention, the notion of sovereign immunity was not an immediate subject of debate, and the sovereignty of a State in its own courts was not mentioned. It is clear that no one was espousing an indefeasible, natural law view of sovereign immunity. Even Madison and Marshall, emphatic supporters of sovereign immunity, did not indicate an adherence to any immunity conception outside the common law. After the close of the debates, the issue not settled, several state ratifying conventions proposed amendments and issued declarations that would have exempted States from subjection to suit in federal court. The Court's rationale for today's holding based on a conception of sovereign immunity as somehow fundamental to sovereignty or inherent in statehood fails for the lack of any substantial support for such a conception in the thinking of the founding era. But the Court has a backup argument; that sovereign immunity inheres in the structural basis in the Constitution's creation of a federal system. However, as we recognized in *U.S. Term Limits v. Thornton*, a system of multiple sovereignties is not the essential core of our constitutional order. Rather, it is the general scheme of delegated sovereignty as between the two component governments of the federal system. Under this correct interpretation, the State of Maine is not sovereign with respect to the national objective of FLSA. Nor does the fact that Maine created its own court system provide for sovereign immunity. These are courts of general jurisdiction required under the Supremacy Clause to enforce federal law, thus requiring the Maine courts to entertain this federal cause of action. The Court also relies on the "dignity and respect afforded a State, which the immunity is designed to protect," along with the many demands placed on a State's finances, to buttress its structural argument. Is there anything more inimical to the republican conception, which rests on the understanding that the government is not above its citizens, but of them? Dignity, for whatever its worth, is no justification for sovereign immunity. Nor is the fact that the United States may bring suit in federal court against a State for damages under FLSA. The federal government simply does not have enough resources to litigate each and every FLSA violation on behalf of the victims. The mass of accumulated rationales, each inadequate in itself, fails to justify today's ruling. For these reasons, I respectfully dissent.

Analysis:

In *Alden*, the majority finally brings all of its arguments in support of state sovereign immunity to bear in a clear and well-organized manner. The dissent attempts to refute each argument in kind. In the field of statutory interpretation there is a very powerful tool that goes by the Latin name *expressio unius est exclusio alterius*. It means that the inclusion of one thing without also including that which would naturally go along acts as an affirmative exclusion of that which would go along. Applied in the Eleventh Amendment context, since sovereign immunity of the states is dealt with by the Amendment, its failure to address anything other than federal diversity suits against states is a clear implication that the states

Alden v. Maine (Continued)

do not enjoy any broader immunity from suits. Both the majority and the dissenters fail to address this argument.

■ **CASE VOCABULARY**

MUNICIPAL CORPORATION: 1A political subdivision of a State, i.e. a city, town, etc., formed by state charter, having the power of self-governance.

RATIFICATION: Process by which the Constitution and amendments thereto are vested with legal force; the Constitution sets forth the manners in which amendments may be ratified.

CHAPTER THREE

The Federal Executive Power

Youngstown Sheet & Tube Co. v. Sawyer [The Steel Seizure Case]

Instant Facts: In order to prevent the (feared) interruption of supplies to troops in Korea, President Truman on the eve of a steelworkers' strike ordered the Secretary of Commerce (D) to take possession of the nation's largest steel mills and keep them operating.

Black Letter Rule: The President of the United States does not have the inherent authority to order the involuntary surrender of private property to the government.

United States v. Richard M. Nixon, President of the United States

Instant Facts: President Nixon (P) refused to turn over tapes of his surreptitiously recorded conversations that had been subpoenaed to assist in the prosecution of individuals in the Watergate break-in.

Black Letter Rule: Conversations between the President and his advisors are generally privileged, but the privilege is not absolute.

William J. Clinton, President of the United States v. City of New York

Instant Facts: President Clinton (D) used his newly acquired Line Item Veto power to cancel two items of congressional spending, and the intended recipients sued.

Black Letter Rule: The Line Item Veto Act is unconstitutional.

A.L.A. Schechter Poultry Corporation v. United States

Instant Facts: Congress delegated authority to an executive agency, which created criminal regulations that Schechter (D) was indicted for violating.

Black Letter Rule: Congress may not delegate law making authority to an executive agency without prescribing specific standards for exercise of that authority.

Panama Refining Co. v. Ryan

Instant Facts: Congress delegated to the President the power to restrict or prohibit the interstate and foreign transport of petroleum.

Black Letter Rule: It is a violation of the separation of powers for Congress to delegate law-making authority to the President without imposing standards or rules limiting that authority.

Whitman v. American Trucking Assn., Inc.

Instant Facts: American Trucking Association, Inc. (P) challenged the constitutionality of § 109(b)(1) of the Clean Air Act as an unconstitutional delegation of legislative power.

Black Letter Rule: Any congressional authorization of decision-making authority must establish an intelligible principle to which the person or body authorized to act is directed to conform.

Immigration and Naturalization Service v. Jagdish Rai Chadha

Instant Facts: Pursuant to a statute allowing for a one-house "veto" of administrative action, the House of Representatives passed a resolution overriding the Attorney General's decision to allow a deportable alien to remain in the United States.

Black Letter Rule: Legislative action is not legitimate unless there is bicameral approval and presentment to the President.

Alexia Morrison, Independent Counsel v. Theodore B. Olson

Instant Facts: The Independent Counsel was appointed by the Special Division of the D.C. Circuit Court of Appeals to investigate a high-ranking government official, and the official responded by claiming that the appointment of Independent Counsel was unconstitutional.

Black Letter Rule: Since the Independent Counsel is an inferior officer, a law giving judges the authority to appoint an Independent Counsel did not violate the Constitution.

United States v. Curtiss-Wright Export Corp.

Instant Facts: A weapons manufacturer (D) was convicted of selling arms to warring nations in South America in violation of an Executive Order that was promulgated pursuant to a Joint Resolution of Congress.

Black Letter Rule: The non-delegation doctrine does not bar Congress from delegating great authority and discretion to the President in the conduct of foreign affairs.

Dames & Moore v. Regan, Secretary of the Treasury

Instant Facts: The President ordered the dismissal of pending litigation against the government of Iran in U.S. courts and forced the claims into arbitration pursuant to an "executive agreement."

Black Letter Rule: The President has the power to settle claims by U.S. citizens against foreign governments, even without the consent of the U.S. citizens whose claims are compromised.

Hamdi v. Rumsfeld

Instant Facts: Hamdi (P) was detained indefinitely as an enemy combatant for allegedly forming an alliance with the Taliban while in Afghanistan.

Black Letter Rule: A citizen-detainee seeking to challenge his classification as an enemy combatant must receive notice of the factual basis for his classification and a fair opportunity to rebut the government's factual assertions before a neutral decisionmaker.

Boumediene v. Bush

Instant Facts: Boumediene (P) petitioned for a writ of habeas corpus to challenge his detention.

Black Letter Rule: If the privilege of habeas corpus is to be denied, Congress must act in accordance with the requirements of the Suspension Clause.

Richard Nixon v. A. Ernest Fitzgerald

Instant Facts: A cost-management expert for the Air Force was fired after he testified in front of Congress about cost overruns in certain military projects. President Nixon (D) claimed that he made the firing decision.

Black Letter Rule: The President of the United States is shielded by absolute immunity from civil damages liability for acts done in his official capacity as President.

William Jefferson Clinton v. Paula Corbin Jones

Instant Facts: President Clinton (D), accused of making inappropriate sexual advances toward a subordinate while Governor of Arkansas, sought to postpone the proceeding of a civil lawsuit until he left office.

Black Letter Rule: A sitting President does not enjoy temporary immunity from all civil lawsuits based on his unofficial acts taken prior to becoming President.

Youngstown Sheet & Tube Co. v. Sawyer [The Steel Seizure Case]

(Steel Manufacturers) v. (Secretary of Commerce)
343 U.S. 579, 72 S.Ct. 863 (1952)

THE PRESIDENT ACTING WITHOUT CONGRESSIONAL AUTHORITY MAY NOT SEIZE PRIVATE PROPERTY

■ **INSTANT FACTS** In order to prevent the (feared) interruption of supplies to troops in Korea, President Truman on the eve of a steelworkers' strike ordered the Secretary of Commerce (D) to take possession of the nation's largest steel mills and keep them operating.

■ **BLACK LETTER RULE** The President of the United States does not have the inherent authority to order the involuntary surrender of private property to the government.

■ PROCEDURAL BASIS

Appeal from injunction prohibiting the Secretary of Commerce from carrying out an Executive Order.

■ FACTS

During the Korean War, a strike by workers at the nation's largest steel mills was imminent. In order to prevent the strike, which the President feared would severely hamper the war effort, President Truman issued an Executive Order directing the Secretary of Commerce ("Secretary") (D) to take possession of most of the steel mills and keep them running. The Secretary (D) then ordered the presidents of the various steel companies to act as his operating managers for the steel mills, which they did under protest. Congress was twice informed of the President's and Secretary's (D) actions, but Congress remained silent on the matter. The companies (P) brought suit in federal court, arguing that the President acted outside of the scope of his constitutional authority. The Secretary (D) defended the President's actions, arguing that the President was acting within his power as chief executive and commander-in-chief of the nation's armed forces. The lower courts granted an injunction against the Secretary (D).

■ ISSUE

Was the President's Executive Order taking temporary possession of private property without the consent of the property owners unconstitutional?

■ DECISION AND RATIONALE

(Black, J.) Yes. If the President had power to issue this Executive Order, that power must come from either an act of Congress or from the Constitution. There is no statute that authorized the President to order the seizure of the steel mills. To the contrary, when considering the Taft-Hartley Act in 1947, Congress specifically rejected Executive seizure for less coercive methods of settling labor disputes, such as mediation and cooling-off periods. However, if these measures failed, Congress left union workers free to strike. Next, the Secretary (D) argues that the President had authority to order the seizure as commander-in-chief of the armed forces. However, the steel mills are not in the "theater of war." Under our constitutional scheme, taking possession of private property to prevent labor disputes

Youngstown Sheet & Tube Co. v. Sawyer [The Steel Seizure Case] (Continued)

is a job for the nation's lawmakers, not it's military authorities. Finally, the Secretary (D) argues that the seizure was within his constitutional authority as the nation's chief executive. The President has a limited role in the lawmaking process: He may recommend to Congress laws that he thinks wise, and he may veto laws passed by Congress that he thinks unwise. However, the President may not make laws, which is what he did here. The seizure order cannot stand. Affirmed.

■ CONCURRENCE

(Jackson, J.) As an analytical tool, it is useful to form three categories into which each of a President's actions may fall. (1) The President's actions have maximum force and authority when he acts pursuant to express or implied authorization by Congress. (2) When Congress is silent, the Constitution grants the President certain power to act independently or concurrently with Congress. The propriety of these actions will depend on the specific situation. (3) The President's power is at its lowest when he acts contrary to the will of Congress, expressed or implied. The seizure of the nation's steel mills falls within the third category, and as such is only valid if it falls outside of the powers of Congress and within the President's powers. While the President may command the armed forces, Congress alone has the authority to raise and supply the armed forces. The seizures were an exercise of authority without law.

■ CONCURRENCE

(Douglas, J.) Though the President can act quickly and the Congress by nature acts slowly and ponderously, expediency is not the hallmark of power—even in times of national crisis. The seizure of the steel plants was a taking under the Constitution, for which the government must pay compensation. It follows that since only Congress may raise money for such compensation, only Congress may condemn and take property. The President's actions were legislative.

■ CONCURRENCE

(Frankfurter, J.) Congress frequently acts to grant seizure power to the executive branch. However, in this instance, Congress made a conscious choice not to give seizure power to the President. Therefore, the President's seizure was unlawful, as surely as if Congress had specifically forbidden him to act.

■ DISSENT

(Vinson, J.) Legislative programs involve American troops in the war in Korea. The success of these programs requires a continued and sure supply of steel. The Constitution gives the President the power to act to carry out legislative programs, which is exactly what he was doing when he temporarily seized the steel mills.

Analysis:

The majority opinion takes a rigid approach to the functions of the various branches of government. However, the concurring opinions seem to advocate more flexibility and express a willingness to find executive powers even in the absence of constitutional or statutory provisions. In particular, note Justice Jackson's three-pronged approach to determining whether the President has the authority to act. Although Jackson's test was not the decision of the Court, it is the test that has been used most often in Judicial opinions—perhaps because it is more certain and easier to apply. Note also that this case involved the President acting in the context of a domestic dispute. In the field of foreign affairs, the President is much less restricted.

■ CASE VOCABULARY

EXECUTIVE ORDER: A decree from the President, usually directing executive officers to take certain actions.

TAKING: When the government seizes or substantially interferes with a private person's rights in property, the government must be acting for a public purpose and then must give just compensation to the owner.

United States v. Richard M. Nixon, President of the United States

(*U.S. President*) v. (*Special Prosecutor*)
418 U.S. 683, 94 S.Ct. 3090 (1974)

THE PRESIDENT IS NOT BEYOND THE REACH OF JUDICIAL PROCESS

■ **INSTANT FACTS** President Nixon (P) refused to turn over tapes of his surreptitiously recorded conversations that had been subpoenaed to assist in the prosecution of individuals in the Watergate break-in.

■ **BLACK LETTER RULE** Conversations between the President and his advisors are generally privileged, but the privilege is not absolute.

■ PROCEDURAL BASIS

Appeal from the District Court's denial of the President's (P) motion to quash a subpoena duces tecum.

■ FACTS

[Several of President Nixon's (P) associates were indicted on charges of conspiracy and obstruction of justice in the Watergate investigation, though the President (P) himself was not indicted. Formal criminal proceedings followed.] The District Court issued a subpoena duces tecum ordering the President (P) to produce the tape recordings of his conversations in one of the criminal cases. The President (P) brought this motion to quash the subpoena on the grounds of executive privilege and separation of powers. The District Court denied the President's (P) motion to quash, and the Supreme Court granted review.

■ ISSUE

Are the President's confidential communications subject to an absolute privilege?

■ DECISION AND RATIONALE

(Burger, J.) No. President Nixon (P) argues that all private conversations between himself and his advisors are absolutely privileged, claiming that his advisors may fear to speak candidly if they know that the conversations may later be used against them or their colleagues in a court of law. We agree that the President's (P) communications to his advisors are subject to general claims of confidentiality. However, this is based on a public policy ground, the need for candor, which may be outweighed by countervailing public policies. We also must reject absolute privilege based on the President's (P) separation of powers argument. Our government consists of three interdependent and coequal branches. The President (P) argues that properly served judicial process is an undue interference in his executive functioning. If we were to accept this argument we would gravely impair the role of the courts under Article III of the Constitution. Thus, while we recognize a need for a strong Presidential privilege, in this case we must weigh the importance of the general privilege of Presidential communications against the fair administration of criminal justice. The President (P) is not claiming privilege on the ground of a military or diplomatic secret. In addition, the tapes are to be reviewed in camera. It is unlikely that the President's (P) advisors will censor themselves on the slim chance that their conversations will become evidence in a criminal proceeding. On the other hand, the withholding of

United States v. Richard M. Nixon, President of the United States (Continued)

relevant information in a criminal trial will cut deeply into the guarantee of due process and gravely impair the basic function of the courts. When weighing the small and theoretical harm to the Presidential privilege against the great and concrete harm to the administration of justice in this case, we can only conclude that the President's (P) generalized interest in confidentiality cannot prevail over the fundamental demands of the criminal justice system. Affirmed

Analysis:

President Nixon obeyed the Court's order and turned over the tapes, and then resigned a few days later. The Court's decision has been criticized by some who claim that a fair reading of the Constitution supports the absolute privilege that Nixon claimed. While it is clear that even the President may be served with criminal process, it is not clear that he cannot claim absolute executive privilege. Notice the balancing act that the Court does—giving the President broad protection as a coequal branch of government, yet denying the President free reign to completely abuse his power. The Court specifically mentions that this is not a situation involving foreign affairs or military affairs. Since these would be matters that the Constitution specifically entrusts to the President, it seems that the Presidential privilege is even broader in these areas.

■ CASE VOCABULARY

ABSOLUTE PRIVILEGE: Some communications are thought to be so important that under no circumstances will a person be forced to testify about them. The rationale is that we want to encourage candor in these communications by assuring the speaker that no negative consequences will flow from speaking freely.

EXECUTIVE PRIVILEGE: The right of the President to keep his communications with his advisors confidential, based on the need of the President to receive candid advice from his advisors.

IN CAMERA: In Chambers. When the judge makes a preliminary examination of evidence outside of the presence of the parties.

SUBPOENA DUCES TECUM: A document issuing in the name of the court commanding the production of documents and things.

William J. Clinton, President of the United States v. City of New York

(City Government) v. (U.S. President)
524 U.S. 417, 118 S.Ct. 2091 (1998)

IF THE PRESIDENT WISHES TO EXERCISE HIS VETO POWER HE MUST VETO A BILL IN ITS ENTIRETY BEFORE SIGNING IT

■ **INSTANT FACTS** President Clinton (D) used his newly acquired Line Item Veto power to cancel two items of congressional spending, and the intended recipients sued.

■ **BLACK LETTER RULE** The Line Item Veto Act is unconstitutional.

■ **PROCEDURAL BASIS**
Appeal to the Supreme Court from the District Court's finding that a statute is unconstitutional.

■ **FACTS**
The Line Item Veto Act ("the Act") of 1996 purported to give the President (D) the power to cancel discrete provisions of certain spending and taxing bills after they have been signed into law. It sets out specific procedures that the President (D) must follow in making cancellations under the Act. Included is a procedure whereby the President (D) must notify the Congress of the cancellation, and the Congress will have the opportunity to resuscitate the cancelled measures by a majority vote. The President (D) used his line-item veto power to cancel an item of spending that would benefit only the State of New York (P) and also to cancel a tax break to farmers' cooperatives (P). It is undisputed that the President (D) complied with the Act, that the Congress properly enacted the Act, and that the taxing and spending provisions at issue fall within the Act.

■ **ISSUE**
May Congress grant the President the authority to cancel portions of legislation after it has been enacted?

■ **DECISION AND RATIONALE**
(Stevens, J.) No. In both legal and practical effect, the President (D) has amended two already enacted Acts of Congress by repealing a portion of each. "Repeal of statutes, no less than enactment, must conform with Art. I." *INS v. Chadha*. The President's (D) role in lawmaking is limited to initiating, influencing, and vetoing legislation. The President's (D) cancellation authority in a "line-item veto" differs from that of a constitutional veto. The constitutional veto takes place before the bill becomes law, whereas the statutory cancellation occurs after the bill becomes law. Therefore, it is a repeal, rather than a veto. In addition, the constitutional veto is of the entire bill, whereas the statutory cancellation is of only discrete parts. The power to enact statutes may only be exercised in accord with a single, finely wrought and exhaustively considered process. Historically, it is understood that the President must either approve all parts of a Bill or reject it in toto. While the Constitution is silent on the question of the President's (D) power to repeal or amend duly enacted statutes, we believe that the foregoing reasons compel the conclusion that constitutional silence is equivalent to an express prohibition. Affirmed.

William J. Clinton, President of the United States v. City of New York (Continued)

■ **CONCURRENCE**

(Kennedy, J.) Although the congressional attempt to curtail its persistent and excessive spending is laudable, the Constitution requires a stability that transcends the convenience of the moment. Our very Liberty is at stake when one or more of the branches seek to transgress the separation of powers: concentration of power in the hands of a single branch is a threat to liberty.

■ **DISSENT**

(Breyer, J.) The majority's reasoning is flawed because it assumes that the President (D) has been granted the authority to "repeal" or "amend" laws. Despite the name of the Act, Congress did not attempt to give the President (D) the true power to "veto" portions of already enacted legislation. The President (D) has simply followed the law as handed down by Congress, and in so doing left the statutes as they were written.

Analysis:

The majority based its ruling on the narrow ground that the Line Item Veto Act violated the constitutional procedures for enactment of legislation. However, the parties also argued about whether the Act violated the separation of powers. Consider whether a separation of powers argument is inapposite in this situation. Separation of powers concerns normally arise when one branch attempts to take over another branch's power for itself, thus aggrandizing itself at the other's expense. Here, however, the opposite is true; the question is whether the legislature was inappropriately giving power to the executive. Though not addressed by the majority, the dissent and concurrence do discuss separation of powers. The dissent reasoned that the power at issue in this case was executive and not legislative in nature because it resembled other traditional powers of the President to spend or not spend allocated funds and to change or not change tariff rates. Much of the debate in this case, though, centers on the conflict between practicality and efficiency on the one hand and constitutional requirements on the other hand. Many people believe that the line item veto is a useful tool for containing spending. In fact, it is a tool that is commonly used by the governors of many states to control the spending of the state legislatures.

■ **CASE VOCABULARY**

IN TOTO: In whole; in its entirety

LINE ITEM VETO: Legislation giving the chief executive (e.g., the President or the Governor) the power to void only part of spending bills passed by the legislature, rather than the choice to either sign the bill or veto the bills in their entirety.

A.L.A. Schechter Poultry Corporation v. United States

(*Agribusiness*) v. (*Federal Government*)
295 U.S. 495, 55 S.Ct. 837 (1935)

THE LEGISLATURE MAY NOT DELEGATE TO THE EXECUTIVE BRANCH THE UNFETTERED AUTHORITY TO MAKE LAW

■ **INSTANT FACTS** Congress delegated authority to an executive agency, which created criminal regulations that Schechter (D) was indicted for violating.

■ **BLACK LETTER RULE** Congress may not delegate law making authority to an executive agency without prescribing specific standards for exercise of that authority.

■ **PROCEDURAL BASIS**
Appeal from a criminal conviction.

■ **FACTS**
Under the National Industrial Recovery Act, Congress delegated to the President the authority to approve and implement as law codes that were suggested by various trade or industrial groups. One such code, actually approved and implemented, was the Code of Fair Competition for the Live Poultry Industry (Code), which prescribed labor and operational standards for poultry businesses in and around New York City. Schechter Poultry (D) was indicted and convicted for conspiracies and violations of the Code.

■ **ISSUE**
May Congress delegate unrestrained law making authority to the executive branch?

■ **DECISION AND RATIONALE**
(Hughes, J.) No. Congress cannot delegate unfettered authority to the President to make any laws that he thinks are desirable or necessary. Thus, we must examine the Nation Industrial Recovery Act (NIRA) to determine what limits Congress set for the President. First, the trade or industrial groups that propose codes must be "truly representative" of the industry members. However, this limit relates to the status of the initiators of new laws, not to the scope of the laws themselves. Second, the codes must not promote monopolies or be oppressive to small enterprises. However, this too leaves the scope of the laws to be enacted virtually unrestricted. In short, the NIRA sets up no specific standards for the President to apply in determining whether to accept or reject proposed codes, aside from the general aims of rehabilitation, correction, and expansion. This leaves the discretion of the President virtually unfettered. Thus, the code-making authority granted to the President is an unconstitutional delegation of power. Reversed.

Analysis:
Notice that the *Schechter Poultry* and *Panama Oil* cases, other cases invalidating legislation on the basis of the non-delegation doctrine, both involve New Deal legislation. Much New Deal legislation was heavily scrutinized and vulnerable to attack on constitutional grounds. The country was undergoing vast

economic, political, and social change at this time in history. It was also a time when the federal government was growing tremendously, both in its size and in its scope. The non-delegation doctrine, which worked well to preserve checks and balances in an era of limited government power and activity, would eventually give way to the modern administrative state.

Panama Refining Co. v. Ryan

(Oil Refiners) v. (Executive Officer)
293 U.S. 388, 55 S.Ct. 241 (1935)

CONGRESSIONAL DELEGATION OF POWER TO THE EXECUTIVE BRANCH MUST BE SPECIFIC AND LIMITED

■ **INSTANT FACTS** Congress delegated to the President the power to restrict or prohibit the interstate and foreign transport of petroleum.

■ **BLACK LETTER RULE** It is a violation of the separation of powers for Congress to delegate law-making authority to the President without imposing standards or rules limiting that authority.

■ **PROCEDURAL BASIS**

Appeal from denial of injunction.

■ **FACTS**

Congress enacted a provision in the National Industrial Recovery Act that gave the President the power to prohibit the transportation of petroleum products in excess of the amount permitted by state law. Based on this provision, the President promulgated an Executive Order making such a prohibition. [The Oil Refiners (P) brought suit to enjoin government officials from enforcing the Executive Order and implementing regulations. The District Court granted the injunction, but the Court of Appeals reversed.]

■ **ISSUE**

May Congress delegate unrestricted law-making authority to the President?

■ **DECISION AND RATIONALE**

(Hughes, J.) No. The law at issue contains nothing as to the circumstances and conditions under which the transportation of petroleum products should be forbidden. Nor was the President required to make any factual findings prior to issuing the prohibition. Rather, Congress simply left the matter to the President, without standard or rule, to be dealt with as he pleased. The Congress is not permitted to abdicate to others the essential legislative functions with which it is vested. The Constitution is flexible enough to allow the Congress to assign to certain administrative instrumentalities the ability to make subordinate rules—within prescribed limits—and to make certain factual determinations to which legislative enactments shall apply. However, if our constitutional system is to be maintained, the necessity of administrative authority cannot override the limitations on congressional authority to delegate. If we were to hold the legislation in question valid, Congress would be free to delegate authority at will to the President, another officer, or an administrative body. The delegation of authority was unlawful and invalid. Reversed.

Analysis:

Not yet a factor in the *Schechter Poultry* and *Panama Oil* cases was the rise of administrative agencies and the tremendous power that Congress entrusted to these agencies. The drafters of the Constitution

Panama Refining Co. v. Ryan (Continued)

had carefully separated the power of the government into three more-or-less competing branches and implemented a system of checks and balances to limit government power. The delegation of authority to a single agency that is insulated from political accountability is convenient, but the lack of checks and balances is of great concern to the Court. The non-delegation doctrine is an attempt by the Court to keep the constitutional structure of checks and balances solid by restricting the amount of lawmaking that an administrative agency is allowed to effect.

Whitman v. American Trucking Assn., Inc.

(*Administrator of the EPA*) v. (*Affected Business*)
531 U.S. 457, 121 S.Ct. 903 (2001)

EXECUTIVE ACTION INVOLVES A CERTAIN DEGREE OF ADMINISTRATIVE DISCRETION

■ **INSTANT FACTS** American Trucking Association, Inc. (P) challenged the constitutionality of § 109(b)(1) of the Clean Air Act as an unconstitutional delegation of legislative power.

■ **BLACK LETTER RULE** Any congressional authorization of decision-making authority must establish an intelligible principle to which the person or body authorized to act is directed to conform.

■ PROCEDURAL BASIS

Certiorari to review a decision of the District of Columbia Circuit Court.

■ FACTS

Under § 109(b)(1) of the Clean Air Act, the Administrator of the Environmental Protection Agency is required to establish National Ambient Air Quality Standards for certain identified air pollutants and review and revise such standards every five years as appropriate. In 1997, the EPA revised the standards for particulate matter and ozone. American Trucking Association (P) challenged the constitutionality of § 109(b)(1) as an improper delegation of legislative power to an administrative agency. Agreeing that the statute delegated legislative power to the EPA without an intelligible principle under which the EPA may act, the District of Columbia Circuit acknowledged that the statute could nonetheless be restrictively construed by the EPA so as to avoid unconstitutional delegation and remanded the matter to the EPA.

■ ISSUE

Does § 109(b)(1) of the Clean Air Act unconstitutionally delegate legislative power to the Administrator of the Environmental Protection Agency?

■ DECISION AND RATIONALE

(Scalia, J.) Yes. Article I, § 1 of the United States Constitution vests "[a]ll legislative Powers herein granted ... to a Congress of the United States." Because the Constitution does not permit the delegation of legislative power to a federal agency, any authorization of decision-making authority must establish "an intelligible principle to which the person or body authorized to [act] is directed to conform." When no such principle exists in congressional legislation, the constitutional violation cannot be cured by an administrative construction of its delegated authority in the most restrictive manner. It is for the courts, not the agency, to determine whether an unconstitutional delegation of legislative power exists.

Here, § 109(b)(1) demands that the EPA establish "ambient air quality standards the attainment and maintenance of which in the judgment of the Administrator, based on [established criteria] and allowing an adequate margin of safety, are requisite to protect the public health." Rarely has the Court invalidated federal legislation for lack of an intelligible principle to guide administrative decision-making. As with many other statutes the Court has reviewed, § 109(b)(1) falls "well within the outer limits of ...

Whitman v. American Trucking Assn., Inc. (Continued)

non-delegation precedents." Federal legislation need not establish "determinate criterion" that sufficiently limit administrative discretion. The statutory mandate to establish air pollutant standards that is no more or less than necessary to preserve the public health falls within the legitimate delegation of administrative discretion. Reversed.

Analysis:

With *Whitman*, the Court reaffirmed its long-standing precedents in the non-delegation doctrine. Generally affording wide latitude to the congressional delegation of administrative power, the Court has historically approved agency decision-making despite Article I's clear non-delegation language. As a practical matter, delegation to executive agencies is required to some degree in order to facilitate governmental efficiency.

■ CASE VOCABULARY

DELEGATION DOCTRINE: The principle (based on the separation-of-powers concept) limiting Congress's ability to transfer its legislative power to another governmental branch, especially the executive branch. Delegation is permitted only if Congress prescribes an intelligible principle to guide an executive agency in making policy.

LEGISLATIVE POWER: The power to make laws and to alter them at discretion; a legislative body's exclusive authority to make, amend, and repeal laws.

SEPARATION OF POWERS: The division of governmental authority into three branches—legislative, executive, and judicial—each with specified powers and duties on which neither of the other branches can encroach; the constitutional doctrine of checks and balances.

Immigration and Naturalization Service v. Jagdish Rai Chadha

(*Immigrant*) v. (*Federal Agency*)
462 U.S. 919, 103 S.Ct. 2764 (1983)

THE LEGISLATIVE VETO IS UNCONSTITUTIONAL

■ **INSTANT FACTS** Pursuant to a statute allowing for a one-house "veto" of administrative action, the House of Representatives passed a resolution overriding the Attorney General's decision to allow a deportable alien to remain in the United States.

■ **BLACK LETTER RULE** Legislative action is not legitimate unless there is bicameral approval and presentment to the President.

■ PROCEDURAL BASIS

Appeal from Court of Appeals' finding that a statute is unconstitutional.

■ FACTS

Chadha (P) was an alien who was lawfully admitted to the United States on a nonimmigrant student visa. He overstayed his visa, and the Immigration and Naturalization Service (INS) (D) initiated deportation proceedings against Chadha (P) in immigration court. [Both the INS (D) and the immigration court are within the Department of Justice, over which the Attorney General has ultimate authority.] The immigration judge found that Chadha (P) met the requirements set out in the Immigration and Nationality Act (the Act) for suspension of deportation. Pursuant to the Act, the Attorney General reported the suspension of deportation to Congress. Under the Act, either house of Congress had the option to pass a resolution to "veto" the Attorney General's determination that Chadha's (P) deportation should be suspended. The House of Representatives passed such a resolution, finding that Chadha (P) (along with five others) did not meet the statutory requirements for suspension of deportation. The House action was not submitted to the Senate or presented to the President.

■ ISSUE

Is the one-house "legislative veto" unconstitutional, even when authorized by a properly enacted statute?

■ DECISION AND RATIONALE

(Burger, J.) Yes. Congress may only exercise its legislative power of the federal government in accord with a single, finely wrought and exhaustively considered procedure. Nearly every legislative act, In order to have the force and effect of law, must be considered and passed by both houses of Congress and then presented to the President for his signature. The framers of the Constitution considered these bicameralism and presentment requirements to be essential. The President's participation in the legislative process was to protect the Executive Branch from Congress and to protect the people from congressional enactment of oppressive, improvident, and ill-considered laws. The division of Congress into two distinct bodies assured that laws would be enacted only after an opportunity for study and debate in separate settings. The first question we need to resolve here is whether Congress was taking "legislative" action. The Act allows one house of Congress to deport an alien who would otherwise be granted permanent residency. Thus, Congress has acted to alter the rights, duties, and legal status of Chadha (P). This is action that is legislative in character. Congress previously made a deliberate choice to delegate authority to the executive branch to determine which deportable aliens will be allowed to stay in this country under certain circumstances. This choice was considered by both houses of Congress and approved by the President. Congress must either abide by that delegation of authority or expressly revoke it. We also consider the structure of the Constitution. The Constitution explicitly allows one house of Congress to take unicameral action in only four instances, none of which are applicable here. Congress in this case has attempted to bypass the system of checks and balances instituted by the bicameralism and presentment requirements. Though this system often seems clumsy and inefficient, it is the way that our system endeavors to keep the people free from the arbitrary exercise of governmental power. The one-house legislative veto is unconstitutional. Affirmed.

■ CONCURRENCE

(Powell, J.) This case should have been decided on a narrower separation of powers ground. The House did not enact a general rule. Rather, it made its own determination that six people did not comply with certain statutory criteria. In doing so, the House did not make its own independent determination—it simply reviewed the findings of the INS (D). Thus it impermissibly assumed a judicial function.

■ DISSENT

(White, J.) The legislative veto, which is found in nearly 200 statutes, is an important tool that allows the President and Congress to resolve major political differences, assures the accountability of administrative agencies, and preserves congressional control over lawmaking. Congress has not used the legislative veto to aggrandize itself at the expense of other branches. The government of the United States has become an endeavor far beyond the contemplation of the framers. The Constitution should be interpreted with the flexibility to respond to contemporary needs.

Analysis:

Although the facts of *Chadha* are limited to the situation of a one-house legislative veto, the case has been read as imposing a general prohibition on all uses of the legislative veto. Subsequent cases hold that even a bicameral legislative veto is unconstitutional. The Supreme Court requires that every legislative act go through the process of bicameral passage and presentment. It is easy to see the attractiveness of the legislative veto. Congress allows the executive agency to take care of the day to day decision making but yet retains ultimate control over the outcome of those decisions. It should be no surprise that the legislative veto increased dramatically as the number and scope of administrative agencies increased. Despite the holding that the legislative veto is unconstitutional, Congress continues to pass laws containing legislative veto provisions.

■ CASE VOCABULARY

BICAMERAL REQUIREMENT: The Constitution divides the legislative branch into two houses, each of which must approve of all legislative acts (with four limited exceptions) by a majority vote before the legislation can become law.

LEGISLATIVE VETO: Mechanism whereby Congress delegates authority to an administrative or independent agency to act, but reserves the power review and nullify any particular action that the agency takes under this authority.

PRESENTMENT REQUIREMENT: The Constitution requires that all legislation, after passing both houses of Congress, be presented to the President before it may become law.

UNICAMERAL: An action taken by one house of Congress (either the House of Representatives or the Senate) without action by the other house.

Alexia Morrison, Independent Counsel v. Theodore B. Olson

(*Independent Counsel*) v. (*Subpoenaed Witness*)
487 U.S. 654, 108 S.Ct. 2597 (1988)

THE PRESIDENT DOES NOT HAVE EXCLUSIVE AUTHORITY TO APPOINT EXECUTIVE OFFICERS

■ **INSTANT FACTS** The Independent Counsel was appointed by the Special Division of the D.C. Circuit Court of Appeals to investigate a high-ranking government official, and the official responded by claiming that the appointment of Independent Counsel was unconstitutional.

■ **BLACK LETTER RULE** Since the Independent Counsel is an inferior officer, a law giving judges the authority to appoint an Independent Counsel did not violate the Constitution.

■ **PROCEDURAL BASIS**

Appeal from judgment in constitutional challenge to statute.

■ **FACTS**

The Ethics in Government Act created the position of independent counsel to investigate (and to prosecute when appropriate) high-ranking government officials for federal criminal violations. If the Attorney General receives information that a government official may have violated federal law, he is required by the Act to make a preliminary investigation and report to the Special Division [three judges] of the D.C. Circuit Court of Appeals. If the Attorney General believes that further investigation is warranted, the Special Division must appoint an independent counsel to investigate further and prosecute if necessary. Once appointed, the independent counsel can only be removed by the Attorney General for "good cause." Otherwise, the job of independent counsel terminates when she has completed all investigations or prosecutions. [Olson (D), the subject of an investigation, challenged the constitutionality of the Act after being subpoenaed by Morrison (P). The Court of Appeals held that the Act is unconstitutional.]

■ **ISSUE**

Does the Constitution require that the President exercise sole and exclusive control over the appointment of all executive officers?

■ **DECISION AND RATIONALE**

(Rehnquist, C.J.) No. The Appointments Clause, Art. II, § 2, cl. 2, divides executive officers into two classes: principal officers and inferior officers. The appointment of principal officers is for the President with the advice and consent of the Senate. However, for inferior officers the Congress may provide for appointment by the President alone, by the heads of departments, or by the Courts. Thus, this case turns upon whether the independent counsel is a "principal" or "inferior" officer. The independent counsel is clearly an inferior officer for several reasons. First, she is subject to removal by a higher executive branch official. Second, she is empowered by the Act to perform only certain, limited duties—namely the investigation and prosecution of specific crimes by specific government officials. Third, the office of independent is limited to the jurisdiction granted by the Special Division. Finally, her office is limited in tenure—it is temporary and for the limited purpose of accomplishing a single task. [Reversed.]

■ DISSENT

(Scalia, J.) Criminal investigation and prosecution are quintessentially executive functions. The President should have exclusive control over those functions. Today's decision deprives the President of a purely executive function, thereby substantially affecting the balance of powers.

Analysis:

Limitations on the appointment power of the President are a check on the power of administrative agencies. The Appointments Clause limits presidential appointments of principal officers only with the approval of the Senate. It also allows Congress to determine the method of appointment of inferior officers—Congress can leave that job up to the President alone, the heads of the Departments, or to the Judiciary. In *Morrison v. Olson,* note that it did not seem to bother the Court that Congress used a combination—both the Attorney General (Executive Officer) and the Judiciary (the Special Division made up of three judges of the D.C. Circuit Court of Appeals). However, the one limit is that Congress may not give appointment power to itself—the Constitution limits the grant of appointment power to the executive or judicial branches.

■ CASE VOCABULARY

EXECUTIVE FUNCTION: Carrying out and enforcing the laws.

INTERBRANCH APPOINTMENTS: Appointment of an officer to one branch by members of another branch; constitutionally permissible in some circumstances.

United States v. Curtiss-Wright Export Corp.

(Federal Prosecutor) v. (Arms Dealer)
299 U.S. 304, 57 S.Ct. 216 (1936)

THE PRESIDENT HAS BROAD AUTHORITY TO CONDUCT FOREIGN AFFAIRS

■ **INSTANT FACTS** A weapons manufacturer (D) was convicted of selling arms to warring nations in South America in violation of an Executive Order that was promulgated pursuant to a Joint Resolution of Congress.

■ **BLACK LETTER RULE** The non-delegation doctrine does not bar Con-gress from delegating great authority and discretion to the President in the conduct of foreign affairs.

■ PROCEDURAL BASIS
Appeal from District Court's finding that government action was unconstitutional.

■ FACTS
Congress passed a Joint Resolution authorizing the President to ban the sales of arms to countries involved in the Chaco border dispute [Bolivia and Paraguay], and the President immediately issued an Executive Order banning such sales. The Curtiss-Wright Export Corp. (Curtiss-Wright) (D) was indicted for conspiracy to sell fifteen machine guns to Bolivia in violation of the Joint Resolution and Executive Order. [The court below held that Congress had unconstitutionally delegated law making authority to the President.]

■ ISSUE
May Congress delegate law-making authority to the President in matters of foreign affairs?

■ DECISION AND RATIONALE
(Sutherland, J.) Yes. There is a fundamental difference in the role of government in foreign affairs as opposed to domestic affairs. For example, the doctrine that the federal government may only exercise those powers that are specifically enumerated in the Constitution applies to domestic affairs only. The concern was that the federal government could not usurp the power granted to the states. This concern is not present in the realm of foreign affairs. The federal government has both constitutional and inherent authority to conduct foreign affairs as it sees fit. Likewise, the roles of the legislative and executive branches are also different in the conduct of foreign affairs. The President is the United States' sole representative to foreign nations. In order to avoid embarrassment and achieve our foreign policy aims, the President must be afforded substantial discretion and wide latitude. In addition, the President is better able than Congress to judge the conditions that exist in foreign countries. The President has confidential sources of information [spies], as well as agents such as consular, diplomatic, and foreign affairs officers. [The delegation of authority was constitutional. Reversed.]

Analysis:
As this case underscores, the President has broad authority—even lawmaking authority—when it comes to foreign affairs. Technically, the power to conduct foreign affairs is shared between Congress and the

United States v. Curtiss-Wright Export Corp. (Continued)

President. The President has the power to recognize nations, negotiate treaties, and conduct other day-to-day dealings with foreign governments. Congress has certain limited powers to regulate commerce, maintain armies and declare war, and control the purse strings—which is important because it can control the budget of all of the executive agencies that the President depends on in gathering information and conducting foreign affairs on a day-to-day basis. This case demonstrates that there is a strong rationale for allowing the President wide latitude in the conduct of foreign affairs. So far, the other branches of government have acquiesced in the President's increasing power in the conduct of foreign affairs.

■ CASE VOCABULARY

EXECUTIVE ORDER: An order from the President having the force and effect of law and commanding certain actions to be taken.

INDICTMENT: Document whereby a grand jury, after considering evidence presented by the prosecution only, recommends charging a defendant with certain crimes.

Dames & Moore v. Regan, Secretary of the Treasury

(Contractor) v. (Executive Officer)
453 U.S. 654, 101 S.Ct. 2972 (1981)

AN EXECUTIVE AGREEMENT HAS THE SAME FORCE AND EFFECT AS A TREATY AND CAN ALTER THE RIGHTS OF U.S. CITIZENS

■ **INSTANT FACTS** The President ordered the dismissal of pending litigation against the government of Iran in U.S. courts and forced the claims into arbitration pursuant to an "executive agreement."

■ **BLACK LETTER RULE** The President has the power to settle claims by U.S. citizens against foreign governments, even without the consent of the U.S. citizens whose claims are compromised.

■ PROCEDURAL BASIS

Appeal from lower court's refusal to grant injunction preventing the enforcement of an executive order.

■ FACTS

On November 4, 1979, the U.S. Embassy in Iran was seized and U.S. diplomats were held hostage. In response, the President, pursuant to an act of Congress, froze all Iranian assets in the United States. In January 1981, the President signed an executive agreement that contained a provision terminating all legal proceedings against the Iranian government in U.S. courts and requiring U.S. citizens to arbitrate all claims against Iran. At the time, Dames & Moore (P) had claims pending against the government of Iran. Dames and Moore (P) brought suit for declaratory and injunctive relief against the United States (D) and Secretary of the Treasury (D), seeking to prevent enforcement of the Executive Orders and Treasury Department regulations implementing the executive agreement with Iran. Dames & Moore (P) claimed that the executive agreement was unconstitutional and beyond the President's power. [The lower court denied relief to Dames & Moore (P).]

■ ISSUE

Does the President have the unilateral authority to settle the claims of U.S. citizens against foreign nations?

■ DECISION AND RATIONALE

(Rehnquist, C.J.) Yes. The President has the power to terminate legal proceedings and settle pending claims of U.S. citizens against foreign governments where such action is necessary to the resolution of a major foreign policy dispute. International agreements settling claims by nationals of one state against the government of another are established international practice reflecting traditional international theory. In this country, there has been a longstanding practice of settling such claims by executive agreement without the advice and consent of the Senate. Congress has implicitly approved the practice of claim settlement by executive agreement. In 1949 Congress enacted the International Claims Settlement Act, which creates a procedure to implement future settlement agreements. By doing so, Congress placed its stamp of approval on such agreements. Congress has demonstrated its continuing acceptance of the President's claim settlement authority through its subsequent amendment of the Act. Prior cases of this Court also establish that the President has some measure of power to enter into

Dames & Moore v. Regan, Secretary of the Treasury (Continued)

executive agreements without obtaining the advice and consent of the Senate. Today's decision is narrow. The President does not necessarily possess plenary power to settle claims, even as against foreign governments. However, the President does have power to settle claims where, as here, settlement was necessary to resolve a major foreign policy dispute and Congress has acquiesced in the President's actions. [Affirmed.]

Analysis:

The debate in this case is whether the President can enter into "executive agreements" that are binding and have the force and effect of law. When the President acted unilaterally to take the claims of Dames & Moore (P) out of the hands of the U.S. courts and into binding arbitration, he clearly enacted an enforceable law (through his Executive Orders) that changed the parties' rights and relationships. As demonstrated in *INS v. Chadha*, all legislation is normally required to go through the process of enactment and presentment, not to mention that the Constitution requires the legislation start in Congress. This case, approving such a radical departure from the normal course of events, seems to establish quite clearly that the President had extraordinary power in matters of foreign affairs.

■ **CASE VOCABULARY**

DECLARATORY RELIEF: Asking the court to determine the legal rights and obligations of the parties, but not to award any monetary damages or to explicitly order either party to take any particular action.

EXECUTIVE AGREEMENT: An agreement between the United States and a foreign country which is identical to a treaty except that executive agreements need not be ratified by the Senate.

INJUNCTIVE RELIEF: One party asks the court to order that the other party take a certain course of action.

TREATY: An agreement between the United States and a foreign country, negotiated by the President, and which must be ratified by the Senate before becoming effective.

Hamdi v. Rumsfeld

(U.S. Citizen) v. (Secretary of Defense)
542 U.S. 507, 124 S.Ct. 2633 (2004)

INDIVIDUAL DUE PROCESS RIGHTS MUST BE BALANCED AGAINST NATIONAL SECURITY

■ **INSTANT FACTS** Hamdi (P) was detained indefinitely as an enemy combatant for allegedly forming an alliance with the Taliban while in Afghanistan.

■ **BLACK LETTER RULE** A citizen-detainee seeking to challenge his classification as an enemy combatant must receive notice of the factual basis for his classification and a fair opportunity to rebut the government's factual assertions before a neutral decisionmaker.

■ **PROCEDURAL BASIS**

Certiorari to review a decision of the Fourth Circuit Court of Appeals reversing a district court grant of a writ of habeas corpus.

■ **FACTS**

Hamdi (P) was an American citizen in Afghanistan. In 2001, the Northern Alliance detained Hamdi (P) for allegedly cooperating with the Taliban and surrendered him to the U.S. military. Hamdi (P) was transferred to a U.S. military brig in South Carolina, where he was indefinitely detained as an "enemy combatant" without formal charges or proceedings. Hamdi (P) filed a petition for a writ of habeas corpus, demonstrating that he had arrived in Afghanistan two months before the attacks on September 11, had received no military training, and was trapped there by the Northern Alliance's military invasion. The district court found the Government's (D) evidence insufficient to support Hamdi's (P) detention. On appeal, the Fourth Circuit Court of Appeals reversed, concluding that the evidence, if correct, supported Hamdi's (P) detention under a valid exercise of the President's war powers.

■ **ISSUE**

Does the President, under certain circumstances, have the authority to detain citizens declared by the government to be enemy combatants?

■ **DECISION AND RATIONALE**

(O'Connor, J.) Yes. In the context of this case, an enemy combatant is alleged by the government to be "part of or supporting forces hostile to the United States or coalition partners ... [who] engaged in an armed conflict against the United States." In 2001, Congress enacted the Authorization of Use of Military Force Resolution, enabling the President to use "all necessary and appropriate force" against those persons he determines to have assisted in the terrorist attacks of September 11. On its face, the Resolution authorizes Hamdi's (P) detention. However, 18 U.S.C. § 4001(a) precludes the detention of any citizen except by an Act of Congress. But because the detention of suspected combatants falls within the meaning of "necessary and appropriate force" under the Resolution, the requirements of § 4001(a) are satisfied by an Act of Congress as an important incident of war. So long as American troops are at battle in Afghanistan, Hamdi's (P) continued detention is lawfully authorized by the Resolution.

Hamdi v. Rumsfeld (Continued)

Due process, however, requires that Hamdi (P) be given an opportunity to have the disputes over his status as an enemy combatant heard in a proper forum. While the Government maintains a legitimate interest in removing enemy combatants from any military conflict as a matter of national security, erroneously detained persons possess equally important liberty interests. Therefore, "a citizen-detainee seeking to challenge his classification as an enemy combatant must receive notice of the factual basis for his classification, and a fair opportunity to rebut the Government's factual assertions before a neutral decisionmaker." These due process rights cannot, however, restrict the Government's (D) ability to administer a military conflict under exigent circumstances. In enemy combatant proceedings, the Government (D) may rely on hearsay statements to classify an individual if such evidence is the best available under the circumstances, and may be entitled to a presumption supporting its classification, so long as the presumption is rebuttable and the individual has a fair opportunity to present rebuttal evidence. This burden-shifting scheme balances the individual's due process right to challenge the Government's (D) classification while protecting the Government's (D) ability to make reasoned decisions during a time of war. Reversed and remanded.

■ DISSENT IN PART

(Souter, J.) Whether Hamdi (P) is declared an enemy combatant or not, the Resolution has not been shown to authorize his detention. Section 4001(a) does not, therefore, allow the Government (D) to detain him. Against the backdrop of § 4001(a), the prohibition against detention must be read broadly to place upon the Government (D) the burden of proving congressional authorization. Section 4001(a) envisions congressional checks on the Executive war powers. Yet, nothing in the Resolution manifestly authorizes the detention of suspected enemy combatants. When important liberty interests compete with national security, more than blanket authority to act as appropriate and necessary must be required under § 4001(a). The Government has demonstrated no such authority. Although Hamdi's (P) status as enemy combatant should be immaterial, by remanding the matter for consideration of his status, he is at least given the opportunity to present evidence that he is not an enemy combatant and rightfully avoid further detention.

■ DISSENT

(Scalia, J.) When the exigencies of war prevent the Government from instituting formal criminal charges against a citizen waging war against it, the Suspension Clause of the Constitution permits Congress to temporarily relax due process by suspending the writ of habeas corpus. It has not been argued, however, that the Resolution on which authority is based in this case is an exercise of the Suspension Clause. While suspension of the writ of habeas corpus may be necessary to enable the Government to fully interrogate enemy combatants, that determination is better suited for Congress, and the Constitution does not envision the Court's intervention in such areas.

■ DISSENT

(Thomas, J.) The Constitution affords the President considerable discretion to exercise his war powers according to his military expertise upon congressional authorization. Because the Executive Branch has exercised this judgment to declare Hamdi (P) an enemy combatant, the Court is ill suited to question this judgment. The Court's decision ignores the Executive Branch's fundamental interest in preserving national security. It is precisely this interest that should inspire the Court to refrain from questioning the constitutionality of the Government's (D) position, for sensitive information relating to the threat on the country remains exclusively in the President's possession.

Analysis:

The war on terror following the attacks of September 11 brought the debate between presidential war powers and individual civil rights to a head. It has been argued that, in times of international crisis threatening the safety of the country, the sacrifice of some individual rights for the benefit of the country as a whole is justified. The contrary view is that the value of national security is uniquely related to the individual liberties enjoyed under the law. Is the country better off as a safe police state than as a more vulnerable nation that upholds individual interests?

CASE VOCABULARY

DUE PROCESS: The conduct of legal proceedings according to established rules and principles for the protection and enforcement of private rights, including notice and the right to a fair hearing before a tribunal with the power to decide the case.

HABEAS CORPUS: A writ employed to bring a person before a court, most frequently to ensure that the party's imprisonment or detention is not illegal.

WAR POWER: The constitutional authority of Congress to declare war and maintain armed forces (U.S. Const. art. I, § 8, cls. 11–14), and of the President to conduct war as commander-in-chief (U.S. Const. art. II, § 2, cl. 1).

Boumediene v. Bush

(*Detainee*) v. (*President*)
553 U.S. 723, 128 S.Ct. 2229 (2008)

THE PRIVILEGE OF HABEAS CORPUS MAY NOT BE SUSPENDED WITHOUT AN ADEQUATE SUBSTITUTE REMEDY

■ **INSTANT FACTS** Boumediene (P) petitioned for a writ of habeas corpus to challenge his detention.

■ **BLACK LETTER RULE** If the privilege of habeas corpus is to be denied, Congress must act in accordance with the requirements of the Suspension Clause.

■ **PROCEDURAL BASIS**

Appeal from an order dismissing petitions for habeas corpus for a lack of jurisdiction.

■ **FACTS**

Boumediene (P) was one of several alien nationals designated as enemy combatants. They were detained at the U.S. Naval Station at Guantanamo Bay, Cuba. The detainees (P) petitioned for a writ of habeas corpus, and two district judges reached opposite conclusions on whether that remedy was available. While appeals were pending, Congress passed the Military Commissions Act (MCA), which provided in part that courts would have no jurisdiction to consider petitions for habeas corpus or any other lawsuits from prisoners determined to be detained as enemy combatants, or who were awaiting such a determination. The MCA was made applicable to any pending case relating to the detention of an alien detained by the U.S. (D) since September 11, 2001.

■ **ISSUE**

Was the MCA a valid suspension of the privilege of habeas corpus?

■ **DECISION AND RATIONALE**

(Kennedy, J.) No. If the privilege of habeas corpus is to be denied, Congress must act in accordance with the requirements of the Suspension Clause. The privilege—not "right"—of habeas corpus entitles a prisoner to a meaningful opportunity to demonstrate that he or she is being held unlawfully. The habeas court must also have the power to release the person whose detention is unlawful, although release need not be the only remedy available. Detention pursuant to an executive order, rather than after a criminal trial and conviction, makes the need for collateral review more pressing.

The U.S. (D) argued that Guantanamo Bay is outside its sovereign control. Questions of sovereignty are political questions. Pursuant to the lease agreement that covers Guantanamo Bay, Cuba holds legal sovereignty, while the U.S. (D) exercises "complete jurisdiction and control." Judicial notice is taken of the *de facto* sovereignty over the base held by the U.S. (D). *De jure* sovereignty is not the touchstone of habeas corpus jurisdiction. That being said, the argument of the U.S. (D) amounts to an argument that the Constitution may be waived by treaty, at least as it applies to noncitizens. The powers of the U.S. (D) are not absolute and unlimited when acting outside the nation's borders. The political branches do not have the power to switch the Constitution on and off at will.

Boumediene v. Bush (Continued)

The question of the extension of habeas corpus jurisdiction to enemy aliens convicted of violating the laws of war was addressed in *Johnson v. Eisentrager,* 339 U.S. 763 (1950). The prisoners in that case were detained in Germany during the post-World War II occupation. Although the Court denied access to the writ in that case, it did not do so solely because the prisoners were never within U.S. territory and were not subject to U.S. territorial jurisdiction. The opinion in *Eisentrager* was based on practical concerns of running the writ. In addition, the Court found it relevant that each prisoner was an enemy alien who had never been in the U.S., who was captured and held in military custody and held as a prisoner of war outside the U.S., and was tried and convicted by a military commission sitting outside the U.S. for war crimes committed outside the U.S. The Court's decision did not rest solely on sovereignty over the prison.

The reasoning of *Eisentrager* and other opinions of this Court on extra-territoriality lead to the conclusion that three factors are relevant in determining the reach of the Suspension Clause: the citizenship and status of the detainee and the adequacy of the process that made that determination; the nature of the sites where the apprehension and detention took place; and the practical obstacles in resolving the entitlement to the writ. In this case, the status of the detainees (P) is in dispute. They are not citizens, but they dispute that they are enemy aliens. Unlike in *Eisentrager,* they have not been tried. The detainees (P) in this case have some procedural protections, but those protections fall short of the mechanisms that would eliminate the need for habeas corpus review. Each detainee (P) is assigned a "personal representative" who is not that detainee's lawyer, or even his advocate. The government's (D) evidence is presumed valid, and while a detainee (P) is allowed to present "reliable" evidence, the ability to rebut the government's (D) evidence is limited by his confinement and his lack of counsel. Moreover, unlike the prisoners in *Eisentrager,* the detainees (P) here are being held at a secure U.S. (D) military facility. Guantanamo Bay is not a transient U.S. (D) possession.

Still, there are practical obstacles to holding the habeas corpus proceedings. The proceedings may require the government (D) to expend funds and may divert the attention of military personnel from other tasks. But these concerns are not dispositive. The government (D) has presented no credible arguments that the military mission of Guantanamo would be compromised if habeas corpus courts had jurisdiction to hear the detainees' (P) claims.

To determine the necessary scope of habeas corpus review, the mechanism for making the final designation of the petitioners' status as enemy combatants must be assessed. The most important deficiency in the procedure is the detainees' (P) inability to rebut the government's (D) claims that they are enemy aliens. Detainees do not have the assistance of counsel and may not know the most critical allegations relied upon by the government (D). Detainees may, in theory, examine witnesses, but there are no effective limits on hearsay. Even if the Court were to determine that the procedures are adequate, that would not end the inquiry. For the writ of habeas corpus, or its substitute, to function as a proper remedy in this context, the court that conducts the proceeding must have the means to correct errors that occurred during the proceeding. This includes some authority to assess the sufficiency of the evidence against the detainee, and the authority to admit and consider exculpatory evidence. The extent of the showing the government (D) must make is not an issue in this case. The statutes do not, however, permit a court of appeals to review or correct factual determinations. There is also no opportunity for a detainee to present exculpatory evidence that was not a part of the original record. By foreclosing consideration of additional evidence, the statute disadvantages the detainee by limiting collateral review to a record that may be inaccurate or incomplete. The U.S. (D) has not established that the statutory procedure for reviewing the detainees' (P) status is an adequate substitute for the writ of habeas corpus.

Practical considerations and exigent circumstances inform the definition and reach of the writ of habeas corpus. The writ is not available at the moment a prisoner is taken into custody. The U.S. (D) is allowed a reasonable period of time to determine a detainee's status before the courts will entertain a habeas corpus petition, but the instant case does not involve detainees who have been held for only a short period of time while awaiting determinations of their status. Reversed.

■ CONCURRENCE

(Souter, J.) The Court's opinion in *Rasul v. Bush,* 542 U.S. 466 (2004), leaves no doubt that the jurisdictional question in habeas corpus cases is the same in purely constitutional habeas corpus matters as in statutory cases. In addition, it is important to remember that some of the detainees (P) have been held in custody for as long as six years. The claim of the dissenters that the judiciary is inserting itself into cases that the military could handle in a reasonable period of time rings hollow.

■ DISSENT

(Roberts, C.J.) The majority rejects the statutory procedures out of hand without explaining what due process rights the detainees (P) possess, or how the statute does not protect those rights. No petitioner has attempted to avail himself of the statutory procedure. Habeas corpus is a procedural right. It is a mechanism for contesting the legality of executive detention. The political branches constructed a system that adequately protects the rights of the detainees (P). The procedures are set up as a means to challenge the government's (D) determination of the status of a detainee. The question is not how much process is provided; the question is whether basic process is provided. At a minimum, the Suspension Clause protects the writ as it existed in 1789. The common law courts abstained altogether from matters involving prisoners of war. The process provided the detainees (P) is thus more than sufficient.

For all its eloquence about the detainees' (P) right to the writ, the majority makes no effort to explain how the remedy prescribed will differ from the procedural protections the detainee's (P) now enjoy.

■ DISSENT

(Scalia, J.) The writ of habeas corpus does not run, and has never run, in favor of aliens abroad. The Suspension Clause thus has no application, and the majority's intervention in this military matter is entirely *ultra vires*.

America is at war with radical Islamists. The majority's opinion will make that war harder on us. This might be tolerable if necessary to preserve a time-honored legal principle vital to our constitutional Republic. It is, however, the majority's blatant abandonment of such a principle that produces their opinion. The Court held in *Hamdan v. Rumsfeld,* 548 U.S. 557 (2006), that the President (D) could return to Congress for the authority to conduct trials by military commission. It turns out they were just kidding. The majority decrees that no good reason to accept the judgment of the other two branches is "apparent." The majority imposes on our military commanders the impossible task of proving to civilian courts that evidence supports the confinement of each and every enemy prisoner.

Analysis:

At the time this decision was rendered, there were approximately 270 prisoners being detained at Guantanamo Bay. Many more had been detained there, but had been returned to their home countries. News reports said that around half of the prisoners were considered "too dangerous to release," but there was not enough evidence to charge them with an offense. Michael Abramowitz, *Administration Strategy for Detention now in Disarray,* Wash. Post, Jun. 13, 2008.

■ CASE VOCABULARY

ULTRA VIRES: Unauthorized; beyond the scope of power allowed or granted by a corporate charter or by law.

Richard Nixon v. A. Ernest Fitzgerald

(President) v. (Ex-Federal Employee)
457 U.S. 731, 102 S.Ct. 2690 (1982)

THE PRESIDENT IS IMMUNE FROM SUIT FROM HIS OFFICIAL ACTS

■ **INSTANT FACTS** A cost-management expert for the Air Force was fired after he testified in front of Congress about cost overruns in certain military projects. President Nixon (D) claimed that he made the firing decision.

■ **BLACK LETTER RULE** The President of the United States is shielded by absolute immunity from civil damages liability for acts done in his official capacity as President.

■ PROCEDURAL BASIS

Appeal from denial of motion for summary judgment.

■ FACTS

A. Ernest Fitzgerald (P) was fired from his job as a management analyst with the Air Force. The Air Force initially claimed that the firing was due to a reorganization and reduction in force, in which Fitzgerald's (P) job was eliminated. Approximately a year earlier, Fitzgerald (P) had appeared at a congressional hearing where, to the embarrassment of his superiors, he testified that there were massive cost-overruns on the development of a transport plane. In an internal memorandum written at around the time Fitzgerald (P) was fired, White House staff wrote that while Fitzgerald (P) was a "top-notch cost expert," he got "very low marks in loyalty." The recommendation in the memo was to "let him bleed." The firing attracted attention in the Congress and the press. At a news conference, President Nixon (D) claimed that he personally made the decision to fire Fitzgerald (P). The White House later issued a retraction of the statement, saying that the President (D) had confused Fitzgerald (P) with another employee. [Fitzgerald (P) brought suit, naming President Nixon (D) as one of the defendants. The President (D) moved for summary judgment on the ground of absolute immunity from suit, and the lower courts denied the motion.]

■ ISSUE

Does the President (D) have absolute immunity from suit for actions taken in his official capacity?

■ DECISION AND RATIONALE

(Powell, J.) Yes. As a matter of policy and principle, the President of the United States (D) is entitled to absolute immunity from liability in civil damages for his official acts. As is the case with prosecutors and judges—for whom absolute immunity is now established—a President must concern himself with matters likely to arouse the most intense feelings. In such situations, the President must be empowered with the maximum ability to deal fearlessly and impartially with the duties of his office. In addition, the high visibility of the President and far-reaching effects of his decision make him an easily identifiable target for suits for civil damages. Without absolute immunity, cognizance of this personal vulnerability could distract a President from his public duties, to the detriment of the nation and the office. Even with a rule of absolute immunity, there are still protections against presidential misconduct. There is the constitutional remedy of impeachment and vigilant oversight by Congress. The President is subject to

Richard Nixon v. A. Ernest Fitzgerald (Continued)

constant scrutiny by the press. Other incentives to avoid misconduct are the desire for reelection, the need to maintain the prestige of office, and the President's concern with his historical stature. Absolute immunity will not place the President above the law. It merely precludes a particular private remedy for alleged misconduct in order to advance compelling public ends. [Reversed.]

■ DISSENT

(White, J.) Reverting to the old notion that the King can do no wrong, today's decision places the President above the law. Whatever the President does, and however contrary to law he knows his actions to be, he may without fear of liability injure any person within or without the Government. Granting absolute immunity to the President for official acts is an abandonment of the most basic principle that the United States is a government of laws, and not of men.

Analysis:

This case gives the President absolute immunity for any action taken in his official capacity, and this immunity extends to the "outer parameters" of the President's authority. However, notice how narrow absolute immunity is. It only extends to civil actions for money damages—suits for injunctive relief may still be prosecuted, and the President can still be required to show cause in contempt proceedings. If the President is a lawyer, he may still be disbarred. Whether a President may be prosecuted criminally is still an open question. Immunity also only extends to the President's official acts. The immunity only extends as far as its rationale—to allow the President to make difficult decisions in the interest of the public good without fear of reprisal by a disgruntled few.

■ CASE VOCABULARY

ABSOLUTE IMMUNITY: The determination that candor and discretion in some jobs are so important that a person cannot be sued for actions taken within the scope of that job. Absolute immunity extends to the Presidency, judges, legislators speaking on the house floor, and attorneys making legal arguments to the court.

QUALIFIED IMMUNITY: Immunity against liability will be given for certain actions even though a person was harmed by those actions, but only if those actions are taken in good faith.

William Jefferson Clinton v. Paula Corbin Jones

(*President*) v. (*State Employee*)
520 U.S. 681, 117 S.Ct. 1636 (1997)

A SITTING PRESIDENT IS NOT IMMUNE FROM SUIT FOR UNOFFICIAL ACTS

■ **INSTANT FACTS** President Clinton (D), accused of making inappropriate sexual advances toward a subordinate while Governor of Arkansas, sought to postpone the proceeding of a civil lawsuit until he left office.

■ **BLACK LETTER RULE** A sitting President does not enjoy temporary immunity from all civil lawsuits based on his unofficial acts taken prior to becoming President.

■ **PROCEDURAL BASIS**
Appeal from denial of motion to postpone trial.

■ **FACTS**
In May 1991, Bill Clinton (D) was the governor of Arkansas. In 1992, Clinton (D) became President of the United States. In 1994, Paula Jones (P) filed suit against Clinton (D) based on events of May 8, 1991. The events took place at a hotel during an official conference. Clinton (D) was a speaker at the conference and Jones (P) was a state employee working at the reception desk. Jones (P) alleges that she was summoned by a state trooper to Clinton's (D) suite, where he made abhorrent sexual advances that she vehemently rejected. Jones (P) further claims that her supervisors at work subsequently dealt with her in a hostile and rude manner and changed her duties to punish her for rejecting those advances. Jones (P) filed suit seeking actual and punitive damages. [The District Court denied Clinton's (D) motion to dismiss, and the Court of Appeals determined that a trial in this matter should not be postponed until Clinton (D) leaves the presidency.]

■ **ISSUE**
Does the President have immunity from all suits against him while he occupies the office?

■ **DECISION AND RATIONALE**
(Stevens, J.) No. Clinton (D) claims that in all but the most exceptional cases, the Constitution affords the President temporary immunity from civil damages litigation arising out of events that took place before he took office. We cannot agree. For certain public officials (e.g., judges, legislators, and prosecutors), immunity serves the public interest by enabling them to perform official duties effectively without fear that a particular decision may give rise to personal liability. However, the sphere of protected action must be related closely to the immunity's justifying purposes. Here, Clinton (D) argues for a postponement of judicial proceedings (which amounts to a temporary immunity) on constitutional grounds. Clinton (D) contends that the President's powers and responsibilities are so vast and important that he must devote his undivided time and attention to his pubic duties. Thus, the argument goes, allowing this action to proceed would be tantamount to Judicial interference with the Executive Branch. Clinton (D) does not argue that the failure to postpone the trial will result in an aggrandizement of judicial power or a narrowing of executive power. Clinton's (D) argument rests on neither history or precedent. If the past is any indication, it seems unlikely that a deluge of civil litigation for past

William Jefferson Clinton v. Paula Corbin Jones (Continued)

wrongdoings will ever engulf the presidency. It is also settled law that the separation of powers doctrine does not bar every exercise of jurisdiction over the President. If the Judiciary may severely burden the President by reviewing his official conduct, and if it may direct appropriate process to the President himself, then it must follow that the federal courts have power to determine the legality of his unofficial conduct. We are not persuaded by Clinton's (D) claims that allowing this suit to go forward will result in harassing and frivolous litigation against future presidents, or that national security concerns might prevent the President from explaining a legitimate need for a continuance. The courts have tools and methods for dealing with both of these concerns. [Affirmed.]

Analysis:

Note the Court's unwillingness to extend executive immunity any further than necessary. This case is an example of the narrowness of the Court's decision in *Nixon v. Fitzgerald*. Immunity of any kind applies only to official acts of the President. The immunity ends when the rationale for immunity ends. Immunity is extended to official acts in order to encourage the President to act fearlessly for the public good. However, no such encouragement is needed for unofficial acts, and thus there is no immunity of any type in that regard.

■ CASE VOCABULARY

TEMPORARY IMMUNITY: Immunity from suit for a limited time. In this case, the President's request to postpone the trial was a "temporary immunity" from suit.

CHAPTER FOUR

Limits on State Regulatory and Taxing Power

Lorillard Tobacco Co. v. Reilly

Instant Facts: Massachusetts state regulations governing the advertising and promotion of tobacco products were challenged as preempted by federal regulations governing the advertising and promotion of cigarettes.

Black Letter Rule: When Congress expressly preempts state or local action on a specified matter, any conflicting state regulation must yield to federal law.

Florida Lime & Avocado Growers, Inc. v. Paul, Director, Dept. of Agriculture of California

Instant Facts: A Florida avocado producer challenged the constitutionality of a California statute that was more restrictive than federal regulations.

Black Letter Rule: When both a state and federal regulation can be satisfied, federal law does not preempt the state regulation.

Pacific Gas & Electric Co. v. State Energy Resources Conservation & Development Commission

Instant Facts: State law, which effectively placed a moratorium on construction of new nuclear power plants within the state, was not preempted by federal law that governed the regulation of safety aspects concerning nuclear power plants.

Black Letter Rule: State law is preempted if it stands as an obstacle to the accomplishment of the full purposes and objectives of Congress; however, the Court will not interfere where there is a permissible basis for the state law.

Hines, Secretary of Labor And Industry of Pennsylvania v. Davidowitz

Instant Facts: State alien registration law was challenged on the ground that the federal alien registration law occupied the field and therefore preempted the state law.

Black Letter Rule: If the federal government exercises superior authority in a particular field, and enacts a complete scheme of regulation, states cannot enact laws which conflict or interfere with, curtail or complement, the federal law, or enforce additional or auxiliary regulations.

H.P. Hood & Sons, Inc. v. Dumond, Commissioner of Agriculture and Markets of New York

Instant Facts: DuMond (D), a New York agriculture commissioner, denied Hood (P), a Boston milk distributor, a license to build a new milk distribution facility, and Hood (P) challenged the denial based on the dormant commerce clause.

Black Letter Rule: States may not enact laws that burden the exportation of local products in order to protect and advance local economic interests.

Aaron B. Cooley v. The Board of Wardens of the Port of Philadelphia

Instant Facts: State law required ships to hire local pilots to guide them through Port of Philadelphia, or pay a fine.

Black Letter Rule: The Congressional power to regulate commerce is not exclusive of all state powers to regulate commerce.

South Carolina State Highway Department v. Barnwell Brothers, Inc.

Instant Facts: Barnwell Brothers, Inc. (P) challenged state law prohibiting operation of trucks on state highways as an unconstitutional burden on interstate commerce.

Black Letter Rule: A state law placing width and weight limitations on trucks operating on state highways does not impose an unconstitutional burden on interstate commerce so as to violate the Commerce Clause.

Southern Pacific Co. v. Arizona

Instant Facts: Arizona (P) created a law limiting the number of railroad cars per train as a safety measure, and Southern Pacific Co. (D) asserted that the law violated the Commerce Clause.

Black Letter Rule: In deciding whether a state law created for its safety measures violates the Commerce Clause, the court will balance the benefits of the law against the burdens it imposes on interstate commerce.

City of Philadelphia v. New Jersey

Instant Facts: U.S. Supreme Court held that New Jersey (D) statute, which prohibited other states from disposing of solid and liquid waste in New Jersey (D), violated the Commerce Clause.

Black Letter Rule: State laws that regulate commercial activity may not, on their face or in effect, favor in-state interests over out-of-state interests.

C & A Carbone, Inc. v. Town of Clarkstown, New York

Instant Facts: Local ordinance, which required all waste to processed at local waste transfer facility before leaving town, was challenged as violating the Commerce Clause.

Black Letter Rule: State and local governments may not enact laws that favor local enterprise by prohibiting patronage of out-of-state competitors or their facilities.

United Haulers Assn., Inc. v. Oneida–Herkimer Solid Waste Management Authority

Instant Facts: United Haulers (P) claimed that an ordinance requiring trash to be hauled to a government-owned facility was unconstitutional.

Black Letter Rule: Laws that favor government operations, but that treat all private businesses equally, do not violate the Commerce Clause.

Hughes v. Oklahoma

Instant Facts: State law that prohibited the transportation of minnows outside the state violated the Commerce Clause.

Black Letter Rule: It is a violation of the Commerce Clause for states to enact laws that attempt to conserve natural resources for use by their own residents.

Hunt, Governor of the State of North Carolina v. Washington State Apple Advertising Commission

Instant Facts: North Carolina law was challenged by Washington State Apple Advertising Commission (P) on ground that it had a discriminatory impact, which caused it to violate Commerce Clause.

Black Letter Rule: A facially neutral state law is unconstitutional and violates the Commerce Clause if it has a discriminatory effect on interstate commerce.

Exxon Corporation v. Governor of Maryland

Instant Facts: Maryland (D) law, which prohibited petroleum producers and refiners from operating gas stations within the State, did not violate Commerce Clause.

Black Letter Rule: A state law that causes some business to shift from one interstate supplier to another does not impermissibly burden interstate commerce.

West Lynn Creamery, Inc. v. Healy, Commissioner of Massachusetts Department of Food and Agriculture

Instant Facts: Massachusetts (D) law, which imposed a tax on in-state milk sales, with the proceeds paid to local dairy farmers, was challenged on ground it violated the Commerce Clause.

Black Letter Rule: A state pricing order, which imposes a tax on the sale of local products, the proceeds of which are distributed as a subsidy to in-state producers of the product, discriminates against interstate commerce and thus is unconstitutional under the Commerce Clause.

State of Minnesota v. Clover Leaf Creamery Co.

Instant Facts: Minnesota (D) law banning the sale of milk in plastic nonreturnable, nonrefillable containers was challenged on the ground that it had a discriminatory purpose.

Black Letter Rule: A facially neutral state law will violate interstate commerce if the incidental burden imposed on interstate commerce is clearly excessive in relation to the putative local benefits.

Dean Milk Co. v. City of Madison, Wisconsin

Instant Facts: Dean Milk (P), upon being denied license to sell milk in Madison (D) because its pasteurization plants were more than 5 miles away, challenged City's milk plant ordinance on grounds that it violated the Commerce Clause.

Black Letter Rule: Where reasonable and adequate alternatives are available, a local health ordinance that places a discriminatory burden on interstate commerce violates the Commerce Clause.

Maine v. Taylor and United States

Instant Facts: Taylor (D), in defense of criminal charges, challenged Maine's law prohibiting the importation of live baitfish on the ground it violated the Commerce Clause.

Black Letter Rule: State statute that affirmatively discriminates against interstate commerce passes vigorous strict scrutiny test where it attempts to prohibit significant damage to State's environmental well-being.

Loren J. Pike v. Bruce Church, Inc.

Instant Facts: Bruce Church, Inc. (P) challenged Arizona (D) law that prevented the transportation of uncrated cantaloupes within the State on ground it violated Commerce Clause.

Black Letter Rule: Where a state statute regulates even-handedly to effectuate a legitimate local public interest, and its effects on interstate commerce are only incidental, it will be upheld unless the burden imposed on such commerce is clearly excessive in relation to the putative local benefits.

Bibb, Director, Department of Public Safety of Illinois v. Navajo Freight Lines, Inc.

Instant Facts: Navajo Freight Lines (P) challenged the constitutionality of Illinois' (D) mudguard law on ground that it interfered with interstate commerce.

Black Letter Rule: In determining whether a state's nondiscriminatory highway safety law violates the dormant Commerce Clause, the court will uphold the law unless the total effect of the law as a safety measure is so slight or problematical as not to outweigh the national interest in keeping interstate commerce free from interferences that seriously impede it.

Raymond Kassel v. Consolidated Freightways Corporation of Delaware

Instant Facts: Iowa's (D) statute banning trucks more than 60 feet in length from using state highways was challenged by Consolidated Freightways (P), which preferred 65-foot trucks, on ground that it violated Commerce Clause.

Black Letter Rule: Although state regulations concerning highway safety carry a strong presumption of validity, if the furtherance of safety is marginal or the burden on commerce is substantial, the regulations will be declared invalid under the Commerce Clause.

Western & Southern Life Insurance Co. v. State Board of Equalization of California

Instant Facts: Insurance company (P) challenged state law that imposed a retaliatory tax on out-of-state insurers on the ground that it violated the Commerce Clause.

Black Letter Rule: Congress, by its authority to regulate commerce among the several States, may give States the power to enact laws that restrict the flow of interstate commerce.

Reeves, Inc. v. William Stake

Instant Facts: When South Dakota (D) built a state-owned cement plant, which sold to private buyers, but later gave preferences to in-state buyers, Reeves (P), a long time buyer, challenged the policy under the Commerce Clause.

Black Letter Rule: States that are "market participants" in the buying or selling of goods, as opposed to "market regulators," are not bound by the Commerce Clause and thus may favor in-state interests.

South–Central Timber Development, Inc. v. Commissioner, Department of Natural Resources of Alaska

Instant Facts: Alaska (D) imposed a restriction on buyers of Alaska (D) timber that required them to process the timber in Alaska (D) before export.

Black Letter Rule: Although state-owned businesses may favor resident purchasers, they may not attach conditions to the sale of products that will burden interstate commerce.

Toomer v. Witsell

Instant Facts: Toomer (P) and other out-of-state commercial fishermen challenged South Carolina (D) law that imposed a higher license fee on out-of-staters based upon the Privileges and Immunities Clause.

Black Letter Rule: In determining whether a State law violates the Privileges and Immunities Clause, the court must determine whether the law discriminates against citizens of other States and, if so, whether there is substantial reason for the discrimination beyond the mere fact that they are citizens of other states.

United Building and Construction Trades Council of Camden County v. Mayor and Council of the City of Camden

Instant Facts: A municipal ordinance, which required 40% of employees working on city-funded projects be city residents, was challenged under Privileges and Immunities Clause.

Black Letter Rule: The Privilege and Immunities Clause prevents states (and cities) from discriminating against non-residents if: (i) the discrimination burdens a "fundamental" privilege (including "employment"), and (ii) there is no "substantial reason" for disparate treatment.

Lester Baldwin v. Fish and Game Commission of Montana

Instant Facts: Game hunters, Baldwin and others (P), challenged state law that imposed higher fees for hunting license on out-of-staters on ground it violated Privileges and Immunities Clause.

Black Letter Rule: State law, which imposes higher license fees for recreational hunting on out-of-state residents than in-state residents, is constitutional because recreational hunting is not a "fundamental right" entitled to protection under the Privileges and Immunities Clause.

Supreme Court of New Hampshire v. Kathryn A. Piper

Instant Facts: Non-resident attorney, Piper (P), challenged State Supreme Court Rule that required State's lawyers to be residents of the State on ground it violated Privileges and Immunities Clause.

Black Letter Rule: 1) The opportunity to practice law is a "fundamental right"; 2) there is no substantial reason for denying bar admission in the State to non-residents; and, 3) such discrimination does not bear a close relationship to the State's objectives.

Lorillard Tobacco Co. v. Reilly

(Tobacco Company) v. (State Official)
533 U.S. 525, 121 S.Ct. 2404 (2001)

FEDERAL CIGARETTE ADVERTISING REGULATIONS PREEMPT CONFLICTING STATE REGULATIONS

■ **INSTANT FACTS** Massachusetts state regulations governing the advertising and promotion of tobacco products were challenged as preempted by federal regulations governing the advertising and promotion of cigarettes.

■ **BLACK LETTER RULE** When Congress expressly preempts state or local action on a specified matter, any conflicting state regulation must yield to federal law.

■ **PROCEDURAL BASIS**

Certiorari to review an undisclosed appellate decision.

■ **FACTS**

The Massachusetts Attorney General promulgated state regulations to eliminate deception and unfairness in the marketing, sale, and distribution of tobacco products targeting child-users. The regulations established the use of self-service displays, the placement of tobacco products within consumers' reach, and certain advertising practices as unfair business practices. With the Federal Cigarette Labeling and Advertising Act (FCLAA), however, Congress established a federal scheme to regulate all advertising of cigarettes, expressly providing that "[n]o requirement or prohibition based on smoking and health shall be imposed under State law with respect to the advertising or promotion of any cigarettes the packages of which are labeled in conformity with the provisions of this chapter." Unlike the state regulations, the FCLAA does not apply to smokeless tobacco or cigars. The state regulations were challenged as preempted by the FCLAA.

■ **ISSUE**

Does the Federal Cigarette Labeling and Advertising Act preempt Massachusetts tobacco advertising regulations?

■ **DECISION AND RATIONALE**

(O'Connor, J.) Yes. When Congress expressly preempts certain matters, those matters falling outside the express preemption are implicitly not preempted. "[T]he historic police powers of the States [a]re not to be superseded by the Federal Act unless that [is] the clear and manifest purpose of the Act." But here, Congress expressly precluded any additional statements on cigarette packaging beyond those required by federal law, and any state regulation based on smoking and health with respect to the advertising and promotion of cigarettes. The FCLAA was enacted in response to Surgeon General warnings and increased medical evidence of the dangers of cigarette smoking, seeking to both inform the public of the dangers of cigarettes and protect the public from misleading advertising relating to the relationship between smoking and health. Like the FCLAA, the Massachusetts regulations, too, seek to protect young people from misleading advertising relating to smoking and health. Moreover, the Massachusetts limitations on the location, as opposed to the content, of cigarette advertisements do not save the state regulations from preemption. Congress included within the FCLAA a preemption

Lorillard Tobacco Co. v. Reilly (Continued)

provision to prevent state interference with its objectives, and did not limit its provisions to a certain specified location. The state regulations are preempted.

■ **DISSENT**

(Stevens, J.) When federal statutes seek to preempt matters traditionally within the police power of the states, Congress must provide clear, unambiguous language to that effect. If the statute is ambiguous, state regulations are not preempted. Here, the text of the FCLAA does not establish that Congress intended to preempt state regulation of the location of cigarette advertising. Congress's objective to inform and protect the public from the dangers of cigarette smoking necessarily required preemption of incompatible state regulation of the content of cigarette advertising. Cigarette advertising or labels varying from state to state would have required cigarette manufacturers to bear the extreme cost of preparing different packaging throughout the country. However, those concerns are not implicated by state limitations on the location of cigarette advertising. Instead, Congress sought a uniform regulatory scheme to control the content of cigarette advertising and labeling without intrusion on the historical police power of the states to govern land use and zoning. The FCLAA does not clearly and unambiguously preempt such state regulation.

Analysis:

Preemption arguments are carefully scrutinized to prevent Congress from intruding upon matters traditionally within the police power of the states. The need for nationally uniform standards or guidelines often justifies such an intrusion, but courts will attempt to construe preemption provisions as narrowly as possible to protect state powers while furthering congressional objectives.

■ **CASE VOCABULARY**

PREEMPTION: The principle (derived from the Supremacy Clause) that a federal law can supersede or supplant any inconsistent state law or regulation.

SUPREMACY CLAUSE: The clause in Article VI of the U.S. Constitution declaring that all laws made in furtherance of the Constitution and all treaties made under the authority of the United States are the "supreme law of the land" and enjoy legal superiority over any conflicting provision of a state constitution or law.

Florida Lime & Avocado Growers, Inc. v. Paul, Director, Dept. of Agriculture of California

(Avocado Grower) v. (Federal Agency)
373 U.S. 132, 83 S.Ct. 1210 (1963)

CONFLICT PREEMPTION REQUIRES IMPOSSIBLE COMPLIANCE WITH BOTH FEDERAL AND STATE REGULATIONS

■ **INSTANT FACTS** A Florida avocado producer challenged the constitutionality of a California statute that was more restrictive than federal regulations.

■ **BLACK LETTER RULE** When both a state and federal regulation can be satisfied, federal law does not preempt the state regulation.

■ PROCEDURAL BASIS

Certiorari to review the constitutionality of a California statute.

■ FACTS

Under California law, avocadoes are deemed mature if they have at least eight-percent oil content. Avocadoes not deemed mature under California law may not be transported and sold within the state. U.S. Department of Agriculture (D) marketing orders, however, do not use oil content as the measure of maturity. Florida Lime and Avocado Growers, Inc. (P) challenged the constitutionality of the California statute, given that they transport mature avocadoes under the federal regulations, but not satisfying California's requirements.

■ ISSUE

Is a state law conflicting with federal regulations governing interstate commerce preempted under the Supremacy Clause?

■ DECISION AND RATIONALE

(Brennan, J.) No. When compliance with both a state and federal regulation is impossible, the state regulation is preempted. However, the plaintiffs can comply with both the state and federal regulations simultaneously by allowing the avocadoes to remain on the trees until they reach the oil content required by California law. Although the two regulations are dissimilar, they are not inevitably conflicted.

Analysis:

Unlike express preemption, conflict preemption requires no explicit statement of congressional intent to supersede state law. Instead, conflict preemption arises when, by application, federal law completely occupies the field such that state law can never coexist. So long as both federal and state law can operate, both are enforceable.

Pacific Gas & Electric Co. v. State Energy Resources Conservation & Development Commission

(Utility Company) v. (State Energy Commission)
461 U.S. 190, 103 S.Ct. 1713 (1983)

STATE LAW PLACING MORATORIUM ON CONSTRUCTION OF NUCLEAR POWER PLANTS DOES NOT IMPEDE FEDERAL LAW'S OBJECTIVE OF DEVELOPING NUCLEAR ENERGY

■ **INSTANT FACTS** State law, which effectively placed a moratorium on construction of new nuclear power plants within the state, was not preempted by federal law that governed the regulation of safety aspects concerning nuclear power plants.

■ **BLACK LETTER RULE** State law is preempted if it stands as an obstacle to the accomplishment of the full purposes and objectives of Congress; however, the Court will not interfere where there is a permissible basis for the state law.

■ **PROCEDURAL BASIS**

Review by Supreme Court of lower court's decision concerning preemption of state nuclear regulatory law by federal Atomic Energy Act.

■ **FACTS**

California adopted a law that imposed a moratorium on the certification of nuclear energy plants until a demonstrated technology or means of disposal of high-level nuclear waste was in place. Pacific Gas & Electric Co. (P) sued California's State Energy Resources Conservation & Development Commission (D) and asserted that the state law was preempted by the federal Atomic Energy Act of 1954, and was therefore invalid under the Supremacy Clause.

■ **ISSUE**

Will a state law be preempted if it stands as an obstacle to the accomplishment of the full purposes and objectives of Congress?

■ **DECISION AND RATIONALE**

(White, J.) Yes. A state law will be preempted if it stands as an obstacle to the accomplishment of the full purposes and objectives of Congress; however, the Court will not interfere where there is a permissible basis for the state law. This case emerges from the intersection of the federal government's efforts to ensure that nuclear power is safe with the exercise of the state's traditional authority over the generation and sale of electricity. Pacific Gas & Electric Co. (P) asserts that the moratorium provision of the state Act is preempted by the federal Atomic Energy Act on three grounds. First, it regulates nuclear plant construction, allegedly predicated on safety concerns, and thus falls within a field controlled by the federal government. Second, it conflicts with decisions concerning nuclear waste disposal made by Congress and the Nuclear Regulatory Commission. And, third, it frustrates the goal of developing nuclear technology as a source of energy. As to the first ground, Congress intended that the federal government have authority to regulate safety with nuclear technology, but that the states retain their traditional responsibility in the field of regulating electrical utilities for determining questions of need, cost, and other related state concerns. The state law is thus not preempted on this ground because its purpose is not safety, but economics. [You can bet the true purpose is safety and environmental concerns, but disguised in economical terms to pass constitutional muster!] With respect to the second ground, the state law does not conflict with the federal rulings and regulations, which are aimed at ensuring that plants are safe, not that they are economical. Finally, with respect to the third ground, the primary purpose of the federal Atomic Energy Act was the promotion of nuclear power. The Court of Appeals is right, however, that the promotion of nuclear power is not to be accomplished "at all costs." Moreover, Congress has allowed the states to determine—as a matter of economics—whether a nuclear plant should be built. The decision of California to exercise that authority does not constitute, in itself, a basis for preemption. Therefore, Congress has left sufficient authority in the states to allow the development of nuclear power to be slowed for economic reasons. Given this statutory scheme, it is for Congress to rethink the division of regulatory authority in light of its possible exercise by the states to undercut a federal objective. The courts should not assume the role which our system assigns to Congress. Thus, the state law is not preempted.

Analysis:

In its conclusion, the Court Invites Congress to enact laws or clarify existing laws to prevent the states from having laws that stop the construction of nuclear plants on economic grounds. The court determined that a state's economic reasons do not conflict with the federal law's purpose of ensuring safety. The case demonstrates how the courts must determine the federal objective and whether, or at what point, the state law interferes with achieving the goal. The court characterized the federal government's objective in the Atomic Energy Act quite narrowly, thereby avoiding preemption of the state law, which obviously limited the broad purpose of promoting nuclear energy. The court offered a broad interpretation of the state statute—focusing on the economic basis—rather than limiting its purpose to safety, which would have resulted in preemption.

■ CASE VOCABULARY

AMICI: Plural of amicus curiae, a "friend of the court" brief, submitted by Interested non-parties.

Hines, Secretary of Labor and Industry of Pennsylvania v. Davidowitz

(State Government) v. *(Alien)*
312 U.S. 52, 61 S.Ct. 399 (1941)

SUPREME COURT DECLARES THAT CONGRESS INTENDED FOR FEDERAL GOVERNMENT TO OCCUPY THE FIELD OF IMMIGRATION REGULATION

■ **INSTANT FACTS** State alien registration law was challenged on the ground that the federal alien registration law occupied the field and therefore preempted the state law.

■ **BLACK LETTER RULE** If the federal government exercises superior authority in a particular field, and enacts a complete scheme of regulation, states cannot enact laws which conflict or interfere with, curtail or complement, the federal law, or enforce additional or auxiliary regulations.

■ **PROCEDURAL BASIS**

Review by United States Supreme Court of lower court's decision concerning preemption of state alien registration law by federal law.

■ **FACTS**

The State of Pennsylvania (D) passed an Alien Registration Act, which required among other things that aliens register annually, provide information, and carry a registration card to be exhibited to police or others or be subject to criminal prosecution. The following year, the federal government enacted the Alien Registration Act, which provided for a single registration and other detailed requirements. The federal Act did not require that aliens carry a registration card to be exhibited to police or others, and only the willful failure to register constituted a criminal offense. The Supreme Court reviewed the matter to determine whether the state Act was preempted by the federal Act.

■ **ISSUE**

If the federal government has exercised superior authority in a particular field can the states enact laws which conflict or interfere with, curtail or complement, the federal law, or enforce additional or auxiliary regulations?

■ **DECISION AND RATIONALE**

(Black, J.) No. The supremacy of the national power in the general field of foreign affairs, including the power over immigration, naturalization and deportation, is made clear by the Constitution and recognized by the authors of The Federalist in 1787. [So why is this case before the court?] Pursuant to the Supremacy Clause, when the national government by treaty or statute has established rules and regulations concerning the rights, privileges, obligations or burdens of aliens, the treaty or statute is the supreme law of the land. Where the federal government, in the exercise of its superior authority in this field, has enacted a complete scheme of regulation and has therein provided a standard for the registration of aliens, states cannot, inconsistently with the purpose of Congress, conflict or interfere with, curtail or complement, the federal laws, or enforce additional or auxiliary regulations. Congress has provided a standard for alien registration in a single integrated and all-embracing system in order to

Hines, Secretary of Labor and Industry of Pennsylvania v. Davidowitz (Continued)

obtain the information deemed to be desirable in connection with aliens. It has plainly manifested a purpose to do so in such a way as to protect the personal liberties of law-abiding aliens through one uniform national registration system, and to leave them free from the possibility of inquisitorial practices and police surveillance that might not only affect our international relations but might also generate the very disloyalty which the law has intended guarding against.

■ DISSENT

(Stone, J.) Assuming, as the Court holds, that Congress could constitutionally set up an exclusive registration system for aliens, I think it has not done so and that it is not the province of the courts to do that which Congress had failed to so. The Judiciary of the United States should not assume to strike down a state law which is immediately concerned with the social order and safety of its people unless the statute plainly and palpably violates some right granted or secured to the national government by the Constitution or similarly encroaches upon the exercise of some authority delegated to the United States for the attainment of objects of national concern.

Analysis:

This is one of the early leading cases wherein the Supreme Court established the traditional preemption test. When Congress has enacted laws that are intended to occupy the field, state law is preempted. Note that the case involves *implied* preemption, since the federal Act did not expressly state that it preempted all other laws. Thus, the Court was required to determine whether Congress, in enacting the law, intended to occupy the field of alien registration. In finding such intent, the court acknowledged the existence of numerous treaties and International practices, which are aimed at preventing injurious discrimination against aliens. It commented that the regulation of aliens is so intimately blended and intertwined with responsibilities of the national government that the federal act is supreme. Justice Stone dissented and questioned whether Congress even had the power to exclusively regulate aliens.

■ CASE VOCABULARY

SOJOURNING: Temporarily residing in a place.

H.P. Hood & Sons, Inc. v. Du Mond, Commissioner of Agriculture and Markets of New York

(Boston Milk Distributor) v. (N.Y. Agriculture Commissioner)
336 U.S. 525, 69 S.Ct. 657 (1949)

LOCAL EMBARGO INVALIDATED BASED UPON DORMANT COMMERCE CLAUSE

■ **INSTANT FACTS** DuMond (D), a New York agriculture commissioner, denied Hood (P), a Boston milk distributor, a license to build a new milk distribution facility, and Hood (P) challenged the denial based on the dormant commerce clause.

■ **BLACK LETTER RULE** States may not enact laws that burden the exportation of local products in order to protect and advance local economic interests.

■ **PROCEDURAL BASIS**

Review by United States Supreme Court of decision rejecting challenge to State's denial of license for new plant based upon the Commerce Clause.

■ **FACTS**

In Boston, 90% of its milk came from outside Massachusetts. Hood (P) was a Boston milk distributor, who received milk from New York producers through various New York plants. Hood (P) sought to build a new plant in New York, but the New York Agriculture Commissioner (D) denied Hood (P) a license for the new plant on the grounds that issuance of the license would tend to destroy competition in a market already adequately served. Hood (P) challenged the license denial on the ground that it violated the dormant Commerce Clause.

■ **ISSUE**

May a state deny a license for a new plant to acquire and ship milk in interstate commerce on the grounds that such limitation on interstate business will protect and advance local economic interests?

■ **DECISION AND RATIONALE**

(Jackson, J.) No. We hold that a state may not enact laws that burden the exportation of local products in order to protect and advance local economic interests. As [that very smart, wise and famous] Justice Cardozo emphasized in the *Baldwin v. G.A.F. Seelig, Inc.* case, the State may not promote its own economic advantages by curtailment or burdening of interstate commerce. He stated, "neither the power to tax nor the police power may be used by the state of destination with the aim and effect of establishing an economic barrier against competition with the products of another state or the labor of its residents." Our system, fostered by the Commerce Clause, is that every farmer and every craftsman shall be encouraged to produce by the certainty that he will have free access to every market in the Nation, that no home embargoes will withhold his export, and no foreign state will by customs duties or regulations exclude them. Likewise, every consumer may look to the free competition from every producing area in the Nation to protect him from exploitation by any. Such was the vision of the founders; such has been the doctrine of this Court which has given it reality. The State (D), however, insists that denial of the license for a new plant does not restrict or obstruct interstate commerce,

H.P. Hood & Sons, Inc. v. DuMond, Commissioner of Agriculture and Markets of New York (Continued)

because Hood (P) has been licensed at its other plants without condition or limitation as to the quantities it may purchase, and thus all that is being denied is local convenience. The weakness of this contention is that a buyer has to buy where there is a willing seller, and the peculiarities of the milk business necessitate a location with a receiving and cooling station for nearby produces. There has been no showing that Hood (P) can obtain such supplies through existing facilities; rather there was a finding that he experienced some difficulty in obtaining the product.

Analysis:

This case reflects the traditional argument justifying the need for a dormant Commerce Clause. The court discusses the historical reasons, looking at the desire of the Forefathers to federalize regulation of foreign and interstate commerce and prevent state laws that interfered therewith. Thus, embargoes that promote local economic objectives—such as retaining domestic resources for local consumption—are not permitted under the principle of the dormant Commerce Clause. Note that some justices are critical of the dormant Commerce Clause and assert that there is no textual basis in the Constitution to support such an interpretation of the Clause. The Court continues to struggle with competing policy considerations as to whether there should be a dormant Commerce Clause, and when it should apply.

■ CASE VOCABULARY

EMBARGO: Restrictions on the import or export of goods or things for a specific purpose.

Aaron B. Cooley v. The Board of Wardens of the Port of Philadelphia

(Ship Master) v. (Pennsylvania Shipping Authority)
53 U.S. (12 How.) 299 (1851)

SUPREME COURT ESTABLISHES "THE SELECTIVE EXCLUSIVENESS TEST" FOR JUDICIAL REVIEW OF STATE REGULATION OF COMMERCE

■ **INSTANT FACTS** State law required ships to hire local pilots to guide them through Port of Philadelphia, or pay a fine.

■ **BLACK LETTER RULE** The Congressional power to regulate commerce is not exclusive of all state powers to regulate commerce.

■ **PROCEDURAL BASIS**

Review by Supreme Court of Commerce Clause challenge to state law.

■ **FACTS**

A Pennsylvania law required ships entering or leaving the port of Philadelphia to hire a local pilot to guide them through the harbor, or pay a fine of half the pilotage fee. [Since the money goes to the retired pilots fund, the pilots must have had a say in the drafting of the legislation.] Although not stated in the edited version of the case, apparently Cooley (P) challenged the law's constitutionality, contending that the Commerce Clause's provision that Congress could regulate commerce gave Congress exclusive jurisdiction over commerce, so that Congress could not re-grant that authority to Pennsylvania, and any Pennsylvania law regulating commerce is void.

■ **ISSUE**

Is the Congressional power to regulate commerce exclusive of all state powers to regulate commerce?

■ **DECISION AND RATIONALE**

(Justice not stated) No. We think the regulation concerning half-pilotage fees is an appropriate part of a general system of regulations of this subject. Other states and countries have also found it necessary to make similar regulations. At the same time the law is imposed on certain vessels, there is another class of vessels for which it does not apply. The legislative discretion has been constantly exercised, based upon differences in both the character of the trade, and the tonnage of the vessels. We do not perceive anything in this system, which would cause us to declare it to be other than a fair exercise of legislative discretion.

Analysis:

This case is recognized for establishing "the selective exclusiveness test," which provides that if the subject of the regulation requires national uniformity, then Congressional power is exclusive. However, if the subject matter is of a purely local concern, then the state may regulate the subject, providing there are no competing federal regulations. Some scholars have noted that this test does not determine

Aaron B. Cooley v. The Board of Wardens of the Port of Philadelphia (Continued)

whether a subject is appropriately a local or national concern. Simply because there are no federal statutes governing a particular concern does not necessarily imply that the federal government is not interested, or meant to leave the concern to the states. Note that in the early case of *Gibbons v. Ogden,* the test was police power versus commerce power, whereas in *Cooley* the focus is on the local versus national subject matter of the regulation.

■ CASE VOCABULARY

PILOTAGE: The guiding of ships in and out of harbors by licensed pilots.

South Carolina State Highway Department v. Barnwell Brothers, Inc.

(State) v. (Trucking Co.)
303 U.S. 177, 58 S.Ct. 510 (1938)

STATE REGULATIONS LIMITING WIDTH AND WEIGHT OF TRUCKS OPERATED ON STATE HIGHWAYS DO NOT VIOLATE COMMERCE CLAUSE

■ **INSTANT FACTS** Barnwell Brothers, Inc. (P) challenged state law prohibiting operation of trucks on state highways as an unconstitutional burden on interstate commerce.

■ **BLACK LETTER RULE** A state law placing width and weight limitations on trucks operating on state highways does not impose an unconstitutional burden on interstate commerce so as to violate the Commerce Clause.

■ **PROCEDURAL BASIS**

Review by United States Supreme Court of challenge to state law imposing width and weight limitations for trucks traveling on state highways on ground that it violated Commerce Clause.

■ **FACTS**

South Carolina (D) passed a law that prohibited trucks that exceeded certain width and weight limitations on its state highways. Barnwell Brothers, Inc. (P) challenged the law as an unconstitutional burden on interstate commerce, in violation of the Commerce Clause. [Better to challenge the law than buy smaller trucks.]

■ **ISSUE**

Does a state law placing width and weight limitations on trucks operating on state highways impose an unconstitutional burden on interstate commerce?

■ **DECISION AND RATIONALE**

(Stone, J.) No. Few subjects of state regulation are so peculiarly of local concern as is the use of state highways. The local highways are built, owned, and maintained by the state, and the state has a primary and immediate concern in their safe and economical administration. The present regulations, if they are to accomplish their end, must be applied alike to interstate and intrastate traffic both moving in large volume over the highways. Our decisions have held that a state may impose nondiscriminatory restrictions with respect to the character of motor vehicles moving in interstate commerce as a safety measure and as a means of securing the economical use of its highways. The courts cannot act as Congress does [although they often try] when it determines when and how much the state regulatory power shall yield to the larger interests of a national commerce. Since the adoption of one weight or width regulation, rather than another, is a legislative, not a judicial choice, its constitutionality is not to be determined by weighing in the judicial scales the merits of the legislative choice and rejecting it if the evidence appears to favor a different standard. The regulatory measures taken by South Carolina (D) are within its legislative power, and they do not violate the Commerce Clause.

South Carolina State Highway Department v. Barnwell Brothers, Inc. (Continued)

Analysis:

This 1938 case is demonstrative of the Supreme Court's shift to a balancing approach for determining whether state regulation violates the Commerce Clause. Such an approach examines the benefits of a law against the burdens that it places on interstate commerce. Recall that previous tests consisted of the rigid police power test used in *Gibbons v. Ogden* and "the Selective Exclusiveness Test" of *Aaron B. Cooley v. The Board of Wardens of the Port of Philadelphia*, which focused on the subject matter of the local regulation. Compare the holding of this case with that of *Southern Pacific Co. v. Arizona*, wherein the court invalidated a state law limiting the length of trains operating in the state because the burdens on interstate commerce outweighed the state's asserted safety need for the law.

■ CASE VOCABULARY

INTERSTATE: Between different states.

INTRASTATE: Within the boundaries of one state.

Southern Pacific Co. v. Arizona

(Railroad Company) v. *(State)*
325 U.S. 761, 65 S.Ct. 1515 (1945)

A STATE LAW THAT PUTS A SIGNIFICANT BURDEN ON INTERSTATE COMMERCE, YET PROVIDES NO REAL IMPROVEMENT IN SAFETY, WILL BE FOUND TO VIOLATE THE COMMERCE CLAUSE

■ **INSTANT FACTS** Arizona (P) created a law limiting the number of railroad cars per train as a safety measure, and Southern Pacific Co. (D) asserted that the law violated the Commerce Clause.

■ **BLACK LETTER RULE** In deciding whether a state law—created for its safety measures—violates the Commerce Clause, the court will balance the benefits of the law against the burdens it imposes on interstate commerce.

■ **PROCEDURAL BASIS**

Review by United States Supreme Court of challenge to state law imposing car length limitations for trains traveling through state on ground that it violated Commerce Clause.

■ **FACTS**

The Arizona Train Limit Law of 1912 prohibited the operation of trains of more than 14 passenger or 70 freight cars, and authorized the state to recover a money penalty for each violation. The Supreme Court was required to determine if the law placed an unconstitutional burden on interstate commerce [Visualize the hassle invovled if train companies had to stop at state borders and shorten their trains for the trip across the state.]

■ **ISSUE**

Are the benefits of a purported state safety-measure law limiting the length of trains outweighed by the burdens on interstate railroad commerce?

■ **DECISION AND RATIONALE**

(Stone, J.) Yes. As this Court has previously recognized, in the absence of conflicting legislation by Congress, there is a residuum of power in the state to make laws governing matters of local concern which nevertheless in some measure affect interstate commerce or even, to some extent, regulate it. When the regulation of matters of local concern is local in character and effect, and its impact on the national commerce does not seriously interfere with its operation, and the consequent incentive to deal with them nationally is slight, such regulation has been generally held to be within state authority. We must determine: (1) the nature and extent of the burden which the state regulation of interstate trains, adopted as a safety measure, imposes on interstate commerce, and (2) whether the relative weights of the state and national interests involved are such as to make inapplicable the rule that the free flow of interstate commerce and its freedom from local restraints in matters requiring uniformity of regulation are interests safeguarded by the Commerce Clause from state interference. The findings show that the operation of long trains is standard practice over the main lines of the U.S. railroads, and that, if the length of trains is to be regulated at all, national uniformity in the regulation adopted, such as only Congress can prescribe, is practically indispensable to the operation of an efficient and economical national railway system. Outside of Arizona, Southern Pacific (D) runs a substantial proportion of long

Southern Pacific Co. v. Arizona (Continued)

trains, but because of the state's Train Limit Law, it is required to haul over 30 % more trains in Arizona than would otherwise have been necessary. The record shows a definite relationship between operating costs and the length of trains, the increase in length resulting in a reduction of operating costs per car. There is no doubt that the state law imposes a serious burden on the interstate commerce conducted by Southern Pacific (D). It materially impedes the movement of its interstate trains through that state and interposes a substantial obstruction to the national policy proclaimed by Congress, to promote adequate, economical and efficient railway transportation service. Enforcement of the state law results in an impairment of uniformity of efficient railroad operation because the railroads are subjected to regulation that is not uniform in its application. [Just imagine if each state had a different train limit law.] We think, as the trial court found, that the state law, viewed as a safety measure, affords at most slight and dubious advantage, if any, over unregulated train lengths, because it results in an increase in the number of trains and train operations and the consequent increase in train accidents of a character generally more severe than those due to slack action. Its undoubted effected on the commerce is the regulation, without securing uniformity, of the length of trains operated in interstate commerce, which lack is itself a primary cause of preventing the free flow of commerce by delaying it and by substantially increasing its cost and impairing its efficiency.

Analysis:

At first blush, it is difficult to reconcile the holding in this case with *South Carolina State Highway Department v. Barnwell Brothers, Inc.* However, the evidence concerning the relationship of the state law and the safety requirements was much stronger in *Barnwell Brothers* than in this case. In addition, the court in *Barnwell* noted, "few subjects of state regulation are so peculiarly of local concern as is the use of state highways." Here, however, the court was persuaded by the economic burden involved in complying with the state law, the lack of uniform application of regulation among the states concerning train car length, and the impediment to the free flow of commerce, all of which balanced against the slight safety advantage afforded by the state law.

City of Philadelphia v. New Jersey

(Out-of-State City) v. (State)
437 U.S. 617, 98 S.Ct. 2531 (1978)

NEW JERSEY STATUTE PROHIBITING OUT-OF-STATE WASTE DISPOSAL IN NEW JERSEY LANDFILLS VIOLATES THE COMMERCE CLAUSE

■ **INSTANT FACTS** U.S. Supreme Court held that New Jersey (D) statute, which prohibited other states from disposing of solid and liquid waste in New Jersey (D), violated the Commerce Clause.

■ **BLACK LETTER RULE** State laws that regulate commercial activity may not, on their face or in effect, favor in-state interests over out-of-state interests.

■ **PROCEDURAL BASIS**

Appeal to U.S. Supreme Court in Commerce Clause challenge of state statute.

■ **FACTS**

New Jersey (D) passed a state statute that prohibited the importation of most "solid or liquid waste which originated or was collected outside the territorial limits of the State..." until the State Commissioner determined that it could be imported without endangering the public health, safety, and welfare. [Does New Jersey (D) think its garbage is better than other states' garbage?] The City of Philadelphia (P), and several out-of-state cities, challenged the statute on the grounds that it violated the Commerce Clause, and that "valueless" waste is not entitled to constitutional protection.

■ **ISSUE**

Is it a violation of the Commerce Clause for one state to prohibit others from selling and transporting legitimate articles of commerce within its borders?

■ **DECISION AND RATIONALE**

(Stewart, J.) Yes. All objects of interstate trade deserve protection under the Commerce Clause, including such waste as is at issue here. [This means garbage has constitutional rights too.] The question is whether New Jersey's (D) law is constitutionally permissible under the Commerce Clause. Where simple economic protectionism is effected by state legislation, a virtually per se rule of invalidity has been erected. Thus, we must determine whether the statute is a protectionist measure, or a law directed to legitimate local concerns, with effects upon interstate commerce that are only incidental. The expressed purpose of the law is to protect the local environment and the public health, safety, and welfare of its residents. New Jersey (D) may pursue those ends by slowing the flow of all wastes into the State's landfills, even though interstate commerce may incidentally be affected. However, New Jersey (D) may not accomplish those purposes by discrimination against articles of commerce coming from outside the State unless there is some reason, apart from their origin, to treat them differently. The statute on its face, as well as in its effect, violates the principle of nondiscrimination. It imposes solely on out-of-state commercial interests the full burden of conserving the State's remaining landfill space, which clearly is impermissible under the Commerce Clause.

City of Philadelphia v. New Jersey (Continued)

■ DISSENT

(Rehnquist, C.J.) Under our precedents, New Jersey (D) should be free to prohibit importation of solid waste for reasons of health and safety. Just because New Jersey (D) must continue to dispose of its own waste does not mean it may not bar importation of even more waste into the State. Because past precedents establish that the Commerce Clause does not present New Jersey (D) with such a Hobson's choice, I dissent.

Analysis:

Note that the state statute involved in this case is a facially discriminatory law—the very language of the law discriminated, through distinction, against out-of-staters. The law permitted waste from inside New Jersey to be disposed of in the state's landfills, but prohibited waste from other states. In such a case, there is a strong presumption that the law violates the Commerce Clause, unless it can be shown that it is necessary to achieve a very important purpose. Although the law here is discriminatory, the majority and dissent have differing views on whether such law is justified. As the majority commented, there may come a time when New Jersey (D) will need to export its waste to Pennsylvania or New York, and those states may then claim the right to close their borders. Note that in *C&A Carbone, Inc. v. Town of Clarkstown*, the court is faced with the issue of whether the law was actually discriminatory.

■ CASE VOCABULARY

APPELLEE: Party who is responding to an appeal, rather than initiating it.

ECONOMIC PROTECTIONISM: Policies designed to protect local businesses from outside competition.

HOBSON'S CHOICE: Derived from old English wherein a stable owner required the customer to take the next available horse rather than giving him a choice; modem day definition is where one is faced with a dilemma but has no choice.

PER SE: Alone or by itself.

C & A Carbone, Inc. v. Town of Clarkstown, New York

(Waste Processing Company) v. (Town)
511 U.S. 383, 114 S.Ct. 1677 (1994)

LOCAL ORDINANCE REQUIRING ALL WASTE TO BE PROCESSED AT LOCAL TRANSFER STATION VIOLATES THE COMMERCE CLAUSE

■ **INSTANT FACTS** Local ordinance, which required all waste to processed at local waste transfer facility before leaving town, was challenged as violating the Commerce Clause.

■ **BLACK LETTER RULE** State and local governments may not enact laws that favor local enterprise by prohibiting patronage of out-of-state competitors or their facilities.

■ PROCEDURAL BASIS

Review by United States Supreme Court of local mandatory waste processing ordinance for determination of whether it violates the Commerce Clause.

■ FACTS

The Town of Clarkstown, New York, (P) entered into a consent decree with the State of New York to close its landfill and build a new solid waste transfer station on the site. In order to finance the building of the site, the Town (P) adopted an ordinance requiring all non-hazardous solid waste generated or brought into the town be processed at the transfer station, for an above market fee. Violators could be punished by a fine and jail if they did not comply. C & A Carbone, Inc., (D) a company engaged in processing of solid waste, was caught trying to avoid the ordinance by trucking waste that had not been processed at the local transfer station. [It didn't do it just once, it was caught under surveillance doing it 6 more times!]

■ ISSUE

May state and local governments enact laws that favor local enterprise by prohibiting patronage of out-of-state competitors or their facilities?

■ DECISION AND RATIONALE

(Kennedy, J.) No. We hold that state and local governments may not enact laws that favor local enterprise by prohibiting patronage of out-of-state competitors or their facilities. The rationale for the rule against discrimination in interstate commerce is to prohibit state or local municipal laws whose object is local economic protectionism. Clarkstown (P) claims that its ordinance does not discriminate because it does not differentiate solid waste on the basis of its geographic origin. All solid waste, regardless of origin, must be processed at the designated transfer station before it leaves the town. [It's an equal opportunity town when it comes to garbage.] Unlike the statute in *City of Philadelphia v. New Jersey* [New Jersey statute prohibiting out-of-state waste disposal in New Jersey landfills violates the Commerce Clause], the ordinance erects no barrier to the import or export of any solid waste but requires only that the waste be channeled through the designated facility. What makes garbage a profitable business is not its own worth but the fact that its possessor must pay to get rid of it. The article of commerce is not so much the solid waste itself, but rather the service of processing and disposing of it. With respect to this stream of commerce, the ordinance discriminates, for it allows only the favored operator to process waste that is within the limits of the town. The ordinance is no less discriminatory because in-state or in-town processors are also covered by the prohibition. The vice of laws of this sort is that they bar the import of the processing service. They hoard solid waste, and the demand to get rid of it, for the benefit of the preferred processing facility. The ordinance here squelches competition in the waste-processing service altogether, leaving no room for investment from the outside. Clarkstown's (P) ordinance does not fall within the narrow exception to the rule, such as where a municipality can show that it has no other means to advance a legitimate local interest. Arguments must be rejected absent the clearest showing that the unobstructed flow of interstate commerce itself is unable to solve the local problem. The Commerce Clause presumes a national market free from local legislation that discriminates in favor of local interests. Clarkstown (P) has any number of nondiscriminatory alternatives for addressing the health and environmental problems alleged to justify the ordinance, the most obvious of which would be uniform safety regulations. The ordinance here is a financing measure, and by itself, revenue generation is not a local interest that can justify discrimination against interstate commerce. Thus, because the ordinance attains its financial goal by depriving competitors, including out-of-state firms, of access to a local market, it violates the Commerce Clause.

■ DISSENT

(Souter, J.) Previous cases have held that the "negative" or "dormant" Commerce Clause makes local legislation unconstitutional when it discriminates against out-of-state or out-of-town businesses. The difference between the local ordinance here and other local laws that discriminate is that this law does not differentiate between all local and all out-of-town providers of a service, but instead between the one entity responsible for ensuring that the job gets done and all others entities regardless of their location. The measure thus falls outside the class of measures that the Commerce Clause has barred States from enacting against each other. The majority is greatly extending the Clause's dormant reach, which causes me to dissent.

Analysis:

This case is another example of a facially discriminatory law, in that it favored a local company, to the exclusion of others. The Court noted that discrimination existed even though both out-of-state and in-state processors were required to have their waste processed at the favored company. The majority and dissent were divided, however, on whether the law was actually discriminatory. Recall that in *City of Philadelphia v. New Jersey,* the majority and dissent agreed that the law was discriminatory, but differed on whether the law was justified. Here, Justice Souter emphasized the fact that the law differentiated between only the one operator and all others, including those within the state as well as out-of-staters. Nevertheless, the majority relied upon the fact that the law favored the local processor and prohibited patronage of out-of-state competitors.

■ CASE VOCABULARY

CONSENT DECREE: A binding agreement by the parties that is sanctioned by the court.

United Haulers Assn., Inc. v. Oneida–Herkimer Solid Waste Management Authority

(Trash Haulers) v. (Public Benefit Corporation)
550 U.S. 330, 127 S.Ct. 1786 (2007)

DISCRIMINATION IN FAVOR OF GOVERNMENT-OWNED ENTERPRISES IS CONSTITUTIONAL

■ **INSTANT FACTS** United Haulers (P) claimed that an ordinance requiring trash to be hauled to a government-owned facility was unconstitutional.

■ **BLACK LETTER RULE** Laws that favor government operations, but that treat all private businesses equally, do not violate the Commerce Clause.

■ **PROCEDURAL BASIS**

Appeals from orders of the court of appeals sustaining the constitutionality of ordinances.

■ **FACTS**

The Oneida–Herkimer Solid Waste Management Authority (D) was a public benefit corporation set up to manage solid waste in Oneida (D) and Herkimer (D) counties. In order to fund the cost of a waste facility operated by the Authority (D), the two counties (D) enacted "flow control" ordinances. These ordinances required all solid waste generated within the counties to be hauled to the facility managed by the Authority (D). Private waste haulers were required to obtain permits to collect waste.

United Haulers (P), an association of solid waste management companies, claimed that the ordinances violated the Commerce Clause of the Constitution. The Haulers (P) argued that the case of *C & A Carbone v. Clarkstown,* 511 U.S. 383 (1994), did not draw a distinction between laws that discriminate in favor of private businesses and those that discriminate in favor of public entities.

■ **ISSUE**

Did the counties' (D) ordinances violate the Commerce Clause?

■

(Roberts, C.J.) No. Laws that favor government operations, but that treat all private businesses equally, do not violate the Commerce Clause. The majority in *Carbone* did not address the distinction between private business and public operations because it was not an issue in that case. To determine whether a law violates the so-called "Dormant" Commerce Clause, the first question is whether the law discriminates, on its face, against interstate commerce. Discrimination, in this context, means that a law benefits in-state economic interests and burdens out-of-state interests. Discriminatory laws are invalid, absent a showing that the state has no other means to advance a legitimate local purpose.

The flow control ordinances at issue here benefit a public facility, but treat all private companies exactly the same. Compelling reasons justify treating laws such as these differently from laws favoring particular private businesses. Government is vested with the responsibility of protecting the health, safety, and welfare of its citizens. Laws that favor particular businesses are often simple economic protectionism. Laws that favor local governments could be directed towards any number of other legitimate goals. The

United Haulers Assn., Inc. v. Oneida–Herkimer Solid Waste Management Authority (Continued)

counties' (D) flow control ordinances allow the counties (D) to pursue particular waste management policies, while allocating the costs of those policies as they deem best. Treating public and private entities the same would lead to unprecedented interference by the courts with state and local government. The dormant Commerce Clause is not a roving license for courts to determine the proper activities of state and local government. Waste disposal is typically and traditionally a function of local government. The most palpable harm caused by the ordinances—more expensive trash removal—is likely to fall on those who voted for the ordinances. When the burden of state regulation falls on interests outside the state, it is unlikely that it will be alleviated by the operation of local political restraints.

No disparate impact on out-of-state as opposed to in-state businesses has been detected. Any arguable burden does not exceed the public benefits of the ordinances. Affirmed.

■ CONCURRENCE

(Scalia, J.) The negative Commerce Clause is a judicial invention. There are no grounds for reading the Commerce Clause as doing anything other than authorizing Congress to regulate commerce.

■ CONCURRENCE

(Thomas, J.) *Carbone* was decided incorrectly. The negative Commerce Clause has no basis in the Constitution and has proven unworkable in practice.

■ DISSENT

(Alito, J.) The ordinances in this case are essentially identical to the ordinance invalidated in *Carbone*. The public-private distinction is both illusory and without precedent. Discriminatory legislation has never been treated with greater deference because the favored entity was a government-owned enterprise. Similarly, the Court has never suggested that discriminatory legislation favoring a state-owned enterprise is entitled to favorable treatment.

Analysis:

The Court relied on the holding in this case the next term in *Kentucky v. Davis*. In that case, the Court upheld a Kentucky law that exempted interest payments on only Kentucky-issued municipal bonds from state income tax. Interest payments on out-of-state municipal bonds were subject to the income tax. The majority opinion emphasized the language in *United Haulers* that gave particular deference to government decisions regarding traditional government functions.

■ CASE VOCABULARY

DORMANT COMMERCE CLAUSE: The constitutional principle that the Commerce Clause prevents state regulation of interstate commercial activity even when Congress has not acted under its Commerce Clause power to regulate that activity.

Hughes v. Oklahoma

(Not Identified) v. (State)
441 U.S. 322, 99 S.Ct. 1727 (1979)

SUPREME COURT HOLDS THAT OKLAHOMA'S LAW PROHIBITING THE TAKING OF MINNOWS OUTSIDE THE STATE VIOLATES THE COMMERCE CLAUSE

■ **INSTANT FACTS** State law that prohibited the transportation of minnows outside the state violated the Commerce Clause.

■ **BLACK LETTER RULE** It is a violation of the Commerce Clause for states to enact laws that attempt to conserve natural resources for use by their own residents.

■ **PROCEDURAL BASIS**

Review by United States Supreme Court of state law for determination of whether it violates the Commerce Clause.

■ **FACTS**

Oklahoma (P) enacted a statute that provided "no person may transport or ship minnows for the sale outside the State which were seined or procured within the waters of this State." The law was challenged on the ground that it violated the Commerce Clause.

■ **ISSUE**

Is it a violation of the Commerce Clause for states to enact laws that attempt to conserve natural resources for use by their own residents?

■ **DECISION AND RATIONALE**

(Brennan, J.) Yes. The burden is on the challenging party to show that the statute at issue discriminates, but when discrimination against commerce is demonstrated, the burden falls on the state to justify it both in terms of the local benefits flowing from the statute and the unavailability of nondiscriminatory alternatives adequate to preserve the local interests at stake. This Court will determine for itself the purpose of the challenged statute, and is not bound by the legislature or the courts of the state. [That's why it's called the *Supreme* Court.] The statute before us on its face discriminates against interstate commerce. It overtly blocks the flow of interstate commerce at the State's borders. We reject Oklahoma's (P) argument that the statute serves a legitimate local purpose as a conservation measure. The State places no limits on the number of minnows that can be taken by licensed dealers, nor does it limit the number of minnows that can be disposed of within the State. Yet, it forbids the transportation of the minnows outside the State for sale. The statute is certainly not a last ditch attempt at conservation after nondiscriminatory alternatives have proved unfeasible. It is rather a choice of the most discriminatory means even though nondiscriminatory alternatives would seem likely to fulfill the State's purported legitimate local purpose more effectively.

Analysis:

The Supreme Court rejected the purported purpose of the statute in this case as a conservation measure, and noted that there was no showing that nondiscriminatory alternatives had been attempted

Hughes v. Oklahoma (Continued)

and failed. The statute would have had a better chance at survival had there been limitations on the number of minnows that could be taken by those within the state. Rather, the limitation was placed on transporting them outside the state, thereby allowing the state's residents to keep the minnows for themselves. Accordingly, the facially discriminatory law failed to pass constitutional muster.

Hunt, Governor of the State of North Carolina v. Washington State Apple Advertising Commission

(North Carolina) v. (Washington State Apple Growers)
432 U.S. 333, 97 S.Ct. 2434 (1977)

DISCRIMINATORY IMPACT OF STATE LAW—NEUTRAL ON ITS FACE—VIOLATES COMMERCE CLAUSE

■ **INSTANT FACTS** North Carolina law was challenged by Washington State Apple Advertising Commission (P) on ground that it had a discriminatory impact, which caused it to violate Commerce Clause.

■ **BLACK LETTER RULE** A facially neutral state law is unconstitutional and violates the Commerce Clause if it has a discriminatory effect on interstate commerce.

■ **PROCEDURAL BASIS**

Review by U.S. Supreme Court of constitutionality of state law, challenged on the ground that it violated the Commerce Clause.

■ **FACTS**

North Carolina (D) enacted a statute requiring all closed apple containers to bear "no grade other than the applicable U.S. grade," which is set by the U.S. Department of Agriculture (USDA). The State of Washington, the largest apple-producing state, utilized an alternate grading system, which was equivalent or superior to the grades adopted by the USDA. The Washing State Apple Advertising Commission (P), [representing a whole lot of apples] challenged the statutes' constitutionality, contending it burdened interstate commerce by requiring the Washington apple producers to alter their containers, discontinue preprinted containers, or repackage apples shipped to North Carolina (D), at substantial cost. North Carolina (D) defended its statute on the ground that it was intended to prevent fraud in the apple marketing industry.

■ **ISSUE**

Can a facially neutral state law be unconstitutional and in violation of the Commerce Clause if it has a discriminatory effect on interstate commerce?

■ **DECISION AND RATIONALE**

(Burger, C.J.) Yes. The challenged statute has the practical effect of not only burdening interstate sales of Washington apples, but also discriminating against them in various ways. First, a consequence of the law is the raising of costs of doing business in North Carolina for Washington apple producers, while leaving those of their North Carolina counterparts unaffected. This disparate effect results from the fact that North Carolina apple producers were not forced to alter their marketing practices in order to comply with the law. Second, the law has the effect of stripping away from the Washington apple industry the competitive and economic advantages it has earned for itself through its expensive inspection and grading system. Third, by prohibiting Washington apple producers from marketing apples under their State's grades, it has a leveling effect, which insidiously operates to the advantage of local apple producers. [The locals were sick and tired of hearing about those great tasting Washington apples!]

Hence, with free market forces at work, Washington sellers would normally enjoy a distinct market advantage vis-à-vis local producers in those categories where the Washington grade is superior. The effect of the statute, however, requires that the otherwise superior grades to be marketed under their inferior USDA counterparts. Such "downgrading" offers the North Carolina apple industry the very sort of protections against competing out-of-state products that the Commerce Clause was designed to prohibit. The statute does little to eliminate the problems of deception and confusion in the marketing of foodstuffs, and directs its primary efforts, not at consumers at large, but at apple wholesalers and brokers. Finally, nondiscriminatory alternatives are readily available, such as permitting state grades along with the applicable USDA label.

Analysis:

The state statute at issue is one that is considered to be facially neutral, but with a discriminatory effect or impact. By raising the cost to market and sell apples in North Carolina, the law discriminates against the out-of-state Washington apple producers who must change their grading labels in order to compete with the local producers who do not have to make any changes. The court rejected the defense argument that the law was one to prevent consumer fraud by noting that those to whom the law applied were wholesalers and brokers who were knowledgeable in the field. There were other means to accomplish the purpose of the law without discrimination. Thus, even though the law imposes the same requirements on out-of-state and in-state apple producers, its discriminatory effect results in a negative impact on interstate commerce, thereby violating the Commerce Clause.

■ CASE VOCABULARY

VIS-A-VIS: French for "face to face."

Exxon Corporation v. Governor of Maryland
(Out-of-State Petroleum Refiner) v. (State)
437 U.S. 117, 98 S.Ct. 2207 (1978)

STATE LAW PROHIBITING OIL COMPANIES FROM OPERATING GAS STATION UPHELD, EVEN THOUGH THOSE AFFECTED WERE MOSTLY FROM OUT-OF-STATE

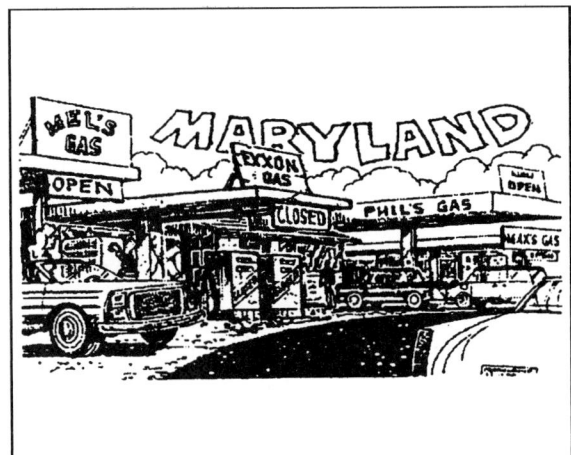

■ **INSTANT FACTS** Maryland (D) law, which prohibited petroleum producers and refiners from operating gas stations within the State, did not violate Commerce Clause.

■ **BLACK LETTER RULE** A state law that causes some business to shift from one interstate supplier to another does not impermissibly burden interstate commerce.

■ **PROCEDURAL BASIS**

Review by U.S. Supreme Court of constitutionality of state law, challenged on the ground that it placed a burden on interstate commerce in violation of the Commerce Clause.

■ **FACTS**

Exxon (P), a petroleum producer and refiner, sells to independent retailers in Maryland (D) and also owns company-operated gas stations in the State. Maryland (D) passed a law that prohibited producers or refiners of petroleum products from operating retail gas stations within the state—supposedly to correct inequities in the distribution and pricing of gasoline that favored company-operated stations during the oil shortages in the early 1970's. However, no petroleum products are produced or refined in Maryland (D), so those affected by the law are mostly out-of-state entities. Exxon (P) [not happy about having to close its company owed stations] challenged the law on the grounds that it had a discriminatory effect, which resulted in the law being in violation of the Commerce Clause.

■ **ISSUE**

Does a state law that causes some business to shift from one interstate supplier to another impermissibly burden interstate commerce so as to violate the Commerce Clause?

■ **DECISION AND RATIONALE**

(Stevens, J.) No. All gasoline in Maryland (D) originates out-of-state. The statute does not alter the flow of gasoline into Maryland (D). It does not discriminate among out-of-state producers or refiners. The law does not favor in-state refiners in comparison to out-of-state refiners, because there are no in-state refiners. Just because the burden of the law falls upon some out-of-state companies does not, by itself, establish discrimination against interstate commerce. The Commerce Clause protects the interstate market, not particular Interstate firms, from prohibitive or burdensome regulations. Although the consuming public may be injured by the loss of the high volume, low-priced stations operated by the independent refiners, that argument relates to the wisdom of the statute, not to its burden on commerce. [Meaning, its up to Maryland's (D) legislature to draft a better law.] Thus, we hold that a state law that causes some business to shift from one interstate supplier to another does not impermissibly burden interstate commerce.

Exxon Corporation v. Governor of Maryland (Continued)

■ DISSENT

(Blackmun, J.) I dissent because the Court's opinion fails to condemn impermissible discrimination against interstate commerce in retail gasoline marketing. The law's effect is to protect in-state retail gas station dealers from the competition of the out-of-state business. This protectionist discrimination is not justified by any legitimate state interest that cannot be vindicated by more even-handed regulation. The law therefore violates the Commerce Clause.

Analysis:

Why did the Court find no discrimination in this case when it did find discrimination in *Hunt, Governor of the State of North Carolina v. Washington State Apple Advertising Commission*? The Court distinguished the two cases by noting that Maryland's (D) law does not create any barriers against interstate independent dealers; it does not prohibit the flow of interstate goods, place added costs upon them, or distinguish between in-state and out-of-state companies in the retail market. In *Hunt,* however, the state statute raised the cost of doing business for out-of-state apple producers and favored in various ways the in-state market. Justice Blackmun was of the opinion that Maryland's (D) statute did have a discriminatory effect—even though it was neutral on its face—because it excluded mostly out-of-state gasoline retailers while providing protection from competition to the locals. It is often difficult for courts to determine whether a law has a discriminatory effect or a legitimate, non-discriminatory objective.

■ CASE VOCABULARY

COMPLAINT: The first document usually filed with the court in a civil matter that states the particulars of that being demanded by the suing party.

West Lynn Creamery, Inc. v. Healy, Commissioner of Massachusetts Department of Food and Agriculture

(Milk Producer) v. (State)
512 U.S. 186, 114 S.Ct. 2205 (1994)

STATE'S MILK TAX SUBSIDY VIOLATES INTERSTATE COMMERCE

■ **INSTANT FACTS** Massachusetts (D) law, which imposed a tax on in-state milk sales, with the proceeds paid to local dairy farmers, was challenged on ground it violated the Commerce Clause.

■ **BLACK LETTER RULE** A state pricing order, which imposes a tax on the sale of local products, the proceeds of which are distributed as a subsidy to in-state producers of the product, discriminates against interstate commerce and thus is unconstitutional under the Commerce Clause.

■ PROCEDURAL BASIS

Review by United States Supreme Court of State tax subsidy law for determination of whether it violates the Commerce Clause.

■ FACTS

Massachusetts (D) enacted a pricing order, which taxed all milk sales in the state, regardless of whether it was produced in-state or out-of-state. The proceeds from the tax were distributed to the in-state dairy farmers as a subsidy. West Lynn Creamery, Inc. (P), a milk dealer who buys 97% of its raw milk from out-of-state milk producers, challenged the law on the ground that it violated the Commerce Clause. Massachusetts (D) argues that the law is constitutional because it utilizes lawful means—a nondiscriminatory tax and a direct subsidy. [But those local farmers are making money from the tax.]

■ ISSUE

Does a state pricing order, which imposes a tax on the sale of local products, the proceeds of which are distributed as a subsidy to in-state producers of the product, discriminate against interstate commerce?

■ DECISION AND RATIONALE

(Stevens, J.) Yes. We hold that Massachusetts (D) pricing order discriminates against interstate commerce and thus is unconstitutional under the Commerce Clause. Massachusetts (D) argues that the milk order is constitutional because it is a product of two independently lawful regulations: 1) the subsidies to the Massachusetts (D) dairy farmers are valid exercises of state power, and 2) the tax that provides the money for the subsidy is nondiscriminatory. We disagree. The pricing order is funded principally from taxes on the sale of milk produced in other States. By so funding the subsidy, Massachusetts (D) not only assists local farmers, but burdens interstate commerce. This violates the cardinal principle that a State may not benefit in-state economic interests by burdening out-of-state competitors. By conjoining a tax and a subsidy, Massachusetts (D) has created a program more dangerous to interstate commerce than either part alone. When a nondiscriminatory tax is coupled with a subsidy to one of the groups hurt by the tax, a State's political processes can no longer be relied upon to prevent legislative abuse, because one of the in-state interests which would otherwise lobby against the tax has been mollified [in other words, reap the benefits from the tax in a big way] by the subsidy. Instead of opposing the tax that raises the price for milk, the powerful group of local dairy

West Lynn Creamery, Inc. v. Healy, Comm'r of Mass. Dep't of Food & Agriculture (Continued)

farmers supported the tax. The purpose and effect of the pricing order—diversion of the market share to local dairy farmers—necessarily injures out-of-state farmers. Preservation of local industry by protecting it from the rigors of interstate competition is the hallmark of the economic protectionism that the Commerce Clause prohibits.

Analysis:

Although this case concerns the Commerce Clause, note that the Court considered how the law affected the political process. It observed that farmers who would normally lobby against a tax that increased the price of milk (and hence reduced the demand) were in favor of it because of the subsidy. As a result, "a State's political processes can no longer be relied upon to prevent legislative abuse." The law was enacted because of a state of emergency within Massachusetts as a result of local farmers being forced out of the dairy business due to lower-cost producers in neighboring states. Nevertheless, the economic emergency did not justify economic protectionism.

■ CASE VOCABULARY

SUBSIDY: A financial contribution made by the government to a group or organization whose services or goods are in the public interest.

State of Minnesota v. Clover Leaf Creamery Co.

(State) v. (Creamery)
449 U.S. 456, 101 S.Ct. 715 (1981)

LAW BANNING PLASTIC MILK CONTAINERS IS NOT A "CLEARLY EXCESSIVE BURDEN" ON OUT-OF-STATE INTERESTS

■ **INSTANT FACTS** Minnesota (D) law banning the sale of milk in plastic nonreturnable, nonrefillable containers was challenged on the ground that it had a discriminatory purpose.

■ **BLACK LETTER RULE** A facially neutral state law will violate interstate commerce if the incidental burden imposed on interstate commerce is clearly excessive in relation to the putative local benefits.

■ PROCEDURAL BASIS

Review by U.S. Supreme Court of constitutionality of state law in action seeking to enjoin its enforcement.

■ FACTS

Minnesota (D) enacted a statute banning the retail sale of milk in *plastic* nonreturnable, nonrefillable containers. However, the sale of milk in non-plastic containers such as paperboard cartons was permitted even if they were nonreturnable or nonrefillable. [Sounds like someone didn't like plastic.] The express purpose of the statute was to address the problem of solid waste management in the State. Clover Leaf Creamory Co. (P) filed suit to enjoin the enforcement of the statute. The district court found that contrary to the statute's express purpose, the actual basis for it was to promote the economic interest of certain segments of the local dairy and pulpwood industry and the plastics industry. The district court found the statute null, void, and unenforceable. The U.S. Supreme Court reviewed the matter to determine whether the statute violated the Commerce Clause.

■ ISSUE

Can a facially neutral state law violate interstate commerce if the incidental burden imposed on interstate commerce is clearly excessive in relation to the putative local benefits?

■ DECISION AND RATIONALE

(Brennan, J.) Yes. If a state law purporting to promote environmental purposes is in reality simple economic protectionism, a virtually per se rule of invalidity applies. *Philadelphia v. New Jersey* [New Jersey statute, which prohibited other states from disposing of solid and liquid waste in New Jersey, violated the Commerce Clause.] Even if a statute regulates evenhandedly, and imposes only incidental burdens on interstate commerce, the courts must strike it down if the burden imposed on such commerce is clearly excessive in relation to the putative local benefits. A state law may constitute "economic protectionism" on proof either of discriminatory effect or of discriminatory purpose. Clover Leaf Creamery (P) argues the statute has a discriminatory purpose because of the lower court's finding that the actual basis for it was to promote the economic interest of certain segments of the local dairy and pulpwood industry and the plastics industry. However, the statute regulates evenhandedly by prohibiting all milk retailers from selling their products in plastic, nonreturnable milk containers, without

State of Minnesota v. Clover Leaf Creamery Co. (Continued)

regard to whether the milk, the containers, or the sellers are from outside the State. Since the statute does not discriminate between interstate and intrastate commerce, the issue is whether the incidental burden imposed on interstate commerce is clearly excessive in relation to the putative local benefits. We conclude that it is not. The burden imposed in interstate commerce is minor, since milk products may continue to move freely across the State border, and changes in packaging will be only a slight inconvenience. Pulpwood producers are the only Minnesota industry likely to benefit significantly from the statute at the expense of out-of-state firms. The degree of burden on the out-of-state plastic industry has been exaggerated. Even if this industry is burdened more heavily than the State's pulpwood industry, this burden is not "clearly excessive" in light of the substantial state interest in promoting conservation of energy and other natural resources and easing solid waste disposal problems, which we have already reviewed in the context of equal protection analysis.

Analysis:

This case demonstrates a number of principles. First, there can be Interference with interstate commerce if the law in question does not differentiate between interstate and intrastate commerce but has a discriminatory purpose. The district court rejected the statute's expressly stated purpose and concluded that its true purpose was to promote certain local industries. But since most out-of-state dairies packaged their products in more than one type of container, there would only be a slight inconvenience to conform to the requirements of the law. Without a discriminatory objective, there could be no violation of the Commerce Clause. The Court therefore concluded that the environmental purpose of the law was proper, and it was not for a discriminatory purpose such as hoarding resources for the economic benefit of the in-state entities.

■ CASE VOCABULARY

ENJOIN: The result of having an injunction issued by the court to prohibit or restrain an act.

PUTATIVE: Supposedly, allegedly.

Dean Milk Co. v. City of Madison, Wisconsin

(*Milk Distributor*) v. (*City*)
340 U.S. 349, 71 S.Ct. 295 (1951)

STATES MUST CONSIDER REASONABLE ALTERNATIVES WHEN ENACTING LAWS INTENDED TO PROTECT PUBLIC HEALTH BUT WHICH ALSO BURDEN COMMERCE

■ **INSTANT FACTS** Dean Milk (P), upon being denied license to sell milk in Madison (D) because its pasteurization plants were more than 5 miles away, challenged City's milk plant ordinance on grounds that it violated the Commerce Clause.

■ **BLACK LETTER RULE** Where reasonable and adequate alternatives are available, a local health ordinance that places a discriminatory burden on interstate commerce violates the Commerce Clause.

■ **PROCEDURAL BASIS**

Appeal to U.S. Supreme Court to determine constitutionality of state statute in action involving denial of license to sell products within state.

■ **FACTS**

The City of Madison, Wisconsin (D) passed an ordinance barring pasteurized milk that had not been processed within five miles of the City. Dean Milk (P), a milk distributor, bought its milk from farms in Illinois and Wisconsin and pasteurized it at two plants, 65 and 85 miles from Madison. Dean Milk (P) was denied a license to sell milk in Madison (D) solely because of the distance of the plants from Madison. Dean Milk's (P) farms and plants were licensed and inspected by Chicago public health officials, who operated under a rating and inspection system similar to Madison's (D). Dean Milk (P) sued and challenged the ordinance on the ground that it placed a burden on interstate commerce in violation of the Commerce Clause.

■ **ISSUE**

Does a local health ordinance that places a discriminatory burden on interstate commerce violate the Commerce Clause when reasonable and adequate alternatives are available?

■ **DECISION AND RATIONALE**

(Justice Name Not Stated) Yes. The practical effect of the ordinance is that it excludes from distribution in Madison (D) milk that is produced and pasteurized in Illinois. It thus places an economic barrier protecting a major local industry against competition from outside the State, which is clearly discrimination against interstate commerce. Even in the exercise of its power to protect the health and safety of its people, the state cannot enact such a law if reasonable nondiscriminatory alternatives, adequate to conserve legitimate local interests, are available. It appears that reasonable and adequate alternatives are available. If Madison (D) wishes to use its own officials for inspection of the milk, it could charge the actual and reasonable cost of such inspection to the importing entities. [They probably will then sue to challenge the imposition of the fee.] To permit Madison (D) to adopt a regulation not essential for the protection of local health interests and placing a discriminatory burden on interstate commerce would invite a multiplication of preferential trade areas destructive of the very purpose of the Commerce Clause. The regulation must yield to the principle that one state in its dealings with another may not place itself in a position of economic isolation.

Dean Milk Co. v. City of Madison, Wisconsin (Continued)

Analysis:

This case establishes the "reasonable alternatives" doctrine used in the analysis of Commerce Clause issues. If there are reasonable alternatives that would have a less discriminatory effect, the law will be held unconstitutional. Madison's (D) argument that the ordinance was necessary to safeguard the health and well-being of its citizens fails because it employs means that are more restrictive than necessary to achieve the goal of the ordinance. The Court cites to an example of charging out-of-state milk producers for having their products inspected by local inspections, rather than absolutely barring them from selling milk within the City.

Maine v. Taylor and United States

(State) v. (Bait Importer)
477 U.S. 131, 106 S.Ct. 2440 (1986)

SUPREME COURT UPHOLDS PATENTLY DISCRIMINATORY STATE LAW

■ **INSTANT FACTS** Taylor (D), in defense of criminal charges, challenged Maine's law prohibiting the importation of live baitfish on the ground it violated the Commerce Clause.

■ **BLACK LETTER RULE** State statute that affirmatively discriminates against interstate commerce passes vigorous strict scrutiny test where it attempts to prohibit significant damage to State's environmental well-being.

■ **PROCEDURAL BASIS**

Review by U.S. Supreme Court of constitutionality of a state statute challenged in a federal criminal proceeding by way of motion to dismiss an indictment.

■ **FACTS**

A law in Maine (D-Intervenor), enacted to protect the State's fisheries from parasites and nonnative species, prohibited the importation of live baitfish. Taylor (D) operated a bait business in Maine and imported into the State live "golden shiners," a species of minnow often used for live bait. A federal grand jury indicted Taylor (D) for violating and conspiracy to violate a federal law, which made it a federal crime to import, receive, or purchase in interstate commerce any fish possessed, transported or sold in violation of any State law. Taylor (D) moved to dismiss the indictment on the ground that Maine's (D-Intervenor) statute was an unconstitutional burden on interstate commerce. [And a burden on Taylor (D) who'll go to jail if the statute is constitutional.] Maine (D-Intervenor) intervened to defend the validity of its statute.

■ **ISSUE**

Does a State statute that affirmatively discriminates against interstate commerce pass the vigorous strict scrutiny test where it attempts to prohibit significant damage to the State's environmental well-being?

■ **DECISION AND RATIONALE**

(Blackmun, J.) Yes. Maine's (D-Intervenor) statute directly restricts interstate trade by blocking all inward shipments of live baitfish. However, this alone does not render the statute unconstitutional. States have authority under their general police powers to regulate matters of legitimate local concern even though interstate commerce may be affected. [And minnows are of local concern to the residents of Maine.] In determining whether the State has overstepped its role, we must distinguish between those statutes that burden interstate commerce only incidentally (which will violate the Commerce Clause only if the burdens are clearly excessive in relation to the putative local benefits) and those statutes that affirmatively discriminate against interstate commerce (which are subject to more demanding scrutiny.) In this case, expert scientific testimony revealed that live baitfish imported into the State posed significant threats to Maine's unique and fragile fisheries. Although justification for discrimination against interstate commerce is subject to the strictest scrutiny, it is the responsibility of the district courts, rather than appellate courts, to make such fact-finding determinations. After reviewing the expert testimony in this case, we cannot say that the District Court clearly erred in finding that substantial scientific uncertainty surrounds the effect that baitfish parasites and nonnative species could have on Maine's fisheries. We agree with the District Court that Maine (D-Intervenor) has a legitimate interest in guarding against imperfectly understood environmental risks, despite the possibility that they may ultimately prove to be negligible. The constitutional principles underlying the Commerce Clause cannot be read as requiring Maine (D-Intervenor) to sit idly by and wait until potentially irreversible environmental damage has occurred or until the scientific community agrees, on what disease organisms are or are not dangerous before it acts to avoid such consequences.

■ DISSENT

(Stevens, J.) There is something fishy about this case. Maine (D-Intervenor) is the only State that blatantly discriminates against out-of-state baitfish by flatly prohibiting their importation. Such stark discrimination requires rigorous justification by the State and the burden is on the State to supply such justification. If there is ambiguity about whether feasible alternatives exist that would make a total ban unnecessary, such ambiguity should defeat, rather than sustain, the discriminatory measure. If Maine (D-Intervenor) wishes to rely on its interest in ecological preservation, it must show that interest, and the infeasibility of other alternatives, with far greater specificity.

Analysis:

In this case, there is no doubt that the law discriminates against interstate commerce—importing of live baitfish into the state from other states is prohibited. As a result, the strict scrutiny test must be applied. The Court held that the district court's findings of fact would not be disturbed on appeal. In other words, the high court felt that the trial court did its job of weighing the expert witness testimony and concluding that there was valid justification for the law in order to prevent possible environmental damage. The dissent felt that because there was scientific uncertainty concerning the true effect on Maine's fisheries if the law were not enforced, Maine (D-Intervenor) had not met its burden of showing the statute's legitimate public purpose. The majority, however, noted that Maine (D-Intervenor) should not have to wait until there is irreversible environmental damage before it can enact a ban on imports.

■ CASE VOCABULARY

INDICTMENT: Document whereby Grand Jury recommends charging one with a crime.

INTERVENED: Third party joins into lawsuit.

Loren J. Pike v. Bruce Church, Inc.

(*Arizona Official*) v. (*Cantaloupe Company*)
397 U.S. 137, 90 S.Ct. 844 (1970)

SUPREME COURT DEVELOPS TEST FOR DETERMINING WHETHER NON-DISCRIMINATORY STATE LAWS VIOLATE THE DORMANT COMMERCE CLAUSE

■ **INSTANT FACTS** Bruce Church, Inc. (P) challenged Arizona (D) law that prevented the transportation of uncrated cantaloupes within the State on ground it violated Commerce Clause.

■ **BLACK LETTER RULE** Where a state statute regulates even-handedly to effectuate a legitimate local public interest, and its effects on interstate commerce are only incidental, it will be upheld unless the burden imposed on such commerce is clearly excessive in relation to the putative local benefits.

■ **PROCEDURAL BASIS**

Review by Supreme Court of order issued pursuant to state law barring transport of uncrated cantaloupe in action seeking to enjoin the order as unconstitutional.

■ **FACTS**

Arizona law requires that all cantaloupes grown in Arizona and offered for sale must be packed in closed standard containers approved by government officials. Loren J. Pike (D), Arizona's official in charge of enforcing the law, issued an order prohibiting Bruce Church, Inc. (P), a cantaloupe farming company, from transporting uncrated cantaloupes from its Arizona ranch to its California packing shed facility, 31 miles away. Cantaloupes, a highly perishable fruit, must be immediately harvested, processed, packed, and shipped in order to prevent spoilage. These processing and packaging functions can only be performed in packing sheds. The closest packing shed available to Bruce Church, Inc. (P) was in its California facility, and none was available in Arizona. It thus faced imminent loss of its anticipated annual cantaloupe crop in the amount of $700,000 unless the order was enjoined. [That's a lot of cantaloupes.] Accordingly, Bruce Church, Inc. (P) filed suit in federal court to enjoin the order on the ground that it was unconstitutional because it violated the Commerce Clause.

■ **ISSUE**

Can a nondiscriminatory state law violate the dormant Commerce Clause?

■ **DECISION AND RATIONALE**

(Stewart, J.) Yes. Where a state statute regulates even-handedly to effectuate a legitimate local public interest, and its effects on interstate commerce are only incidental, it will be upheld unless the burden imposed on such commerce is clearly excessive in relation to the putative local benefits. If a legitimate local purpose is found, then it becomes a question of degree. The extent of the burden that will be tolerated will of course depend on the nature of the local interest involved, and on whether it could be promoted as well with a lesser impact on interstate activities. The purpose of the Act in question here is simple to protect and enhance the reputation of growers within the State, a surely legitimate State interest. However, the State's (D) interest in having the company's (P) cantaloupes identified as originating in Arizona cannot constitutionally justify the requirement that the company (P) build and operate an unneeded $200,000 packing plant in the State. We have previously held that the Commerce Clause forbids a State from requiring business operations to be performed in the home State that could

Loren J. Pike v. Bruce Church, Inc. (Continued)

more efficiently be performed elsewhere, even where the State is pursuing a clearly legitimate local interest. The State's (D) interest in the matter before us now is minimal at best. [It's just a self-promoting campaign to promote State cantaloupes and disguised as a law.] We thus hold that the State (D) cannot be permitted to require the company (P) to go into a local packing business solely for the sake of enhancing the reputation of their producers within its borders.

Analysis:

This often-cited case sets forth the analysis used by the Court in determining whether a non-discriminatory state law—one in which in-staters and out-of staters are treated equally—violates the dormant Commerce Clause. If the state law imposes an undue burden on interstate commerce, it may violate the Commerce Clause. In reaching its decision, the court will weigh the state's interest in protecting the health, safety, and economic well-being of its citizens and its environment versus the burden placed on interstate commerce. Some members of the Court have expressed their opinion that the dormant Commerce Clause should not even apply to laws that are nondiscriminatory, and that the balancing test used is too subjective.

Bibb, Director, Department of Public Safety of Illinois v. Navajo Freight Lines, Inc.

(State) v. (Trucking Company)
359 U.S. 520, 79 S.Ct. 962 (1959)

SUPREME COURT STRIKES DOWN ILLINOIS' SPLASH GUARD LAW DUE TO BURDEN ON INTERSTATE MOVEMENT OF TRUCKS

■ **INSTANT FACTS** Navajo Freight Lines (P) challenged the constitutionality of Illinois' (D) mudguard law on ground that it interfered with interstate commerce.

■ **BLACK LETTER RULE** In determining whether a state's nondiscriminatory highway safety law violates the dormant Commerce Clause, the court will uphold the law unless the total effect of the law as a safety measure is so slight or problematical as not to outweigh the national interest in keeping interstate commerce free from interferences that seriously impede it.

■ **PROCEDURAL BASIS**

Review by Supreme Court of constitutionality of state law in action seeking to enjoin its enforcement.

■ **FACTS**

Illinois (D) law required trucks and trailers traveling within the State to be equipped with a certain type of rear fender mudguard having detailed specifications. These contoured mud guards differed from conventional or straight mud flaps—which were legal in at least 45 states—and Illinois (D) contended that they had a decided safety factor in that they prevented the throwing of debris into passing or following vehicles. Navajo Freight Lines, Inc. (D), an interstate motor carrier company, challenged the constitutionality of the Act, claiming that it violated the Commerce Clause and its enforcement should therefore be enjoined. The District Court agreed and declared it to be in violation of the Commerce Clause. The District Court concluded that the contour mud flap possessed no advantage over the conventional or straight mud flaps and that their use creates hazards previously unknown, such as decreasing the effectiveness of brakes, and being susceptible of being hit by other trucks. Moreover, the court found that carriers would be required to equip all their trailers with the mud guard, since it is impossible for them to determine which of its equipment will be used in a particular area, or on a particular day. The cost to the carrier (P) to install the mudguards on all trucks it owned ranged from $4,500 to $45,840, and maintenance and replacement costs would be substantial. [Sounds like this law is doomed.]

■ **ISSUE**

Does a state's nondiscriminatory highway safety law violate the dormant Commerce Clause where the total effect of the law as a safety measure is slight and it seriously interferes with interstate commerce?

■ **DECISION AND RATIONALE**

(Douglas, J.) Yes. In determining whether a state's nondiscriminatory highway safety law violates the dormant Commerce Clause, the court will uphold the law unless the total effect of the law as a safety measure is so slight or problematical as not to outweigh the national interest in keeping interstate commerce free from interferences that seriously impede it. The power of the State to regulate the use of its highways is broad and pervasive. Safety measure laws carry a strong presumption of validity when challenged. In addition to the evidence presented below concerning the lack of advantages of the contour mud flap and its own potential hazards, we note that Arkansas requires trailers operating within its borders to have the straight or conventional mud flaps. Thus, vehicles equipped with Illinois (D) required contoured mud flaps would not comply with Arkansas law, and vice versa. Trailers operating in both States would have to interchange mudguards, causing significant operational delays and costs. It was also found that the Illinois (D) law seriously interferes with the "interline" operations of motor carriers—the process of interchanging of trailers between an originating carrier and another carrier when the latter serves an area not served by the former, without unloading or reloading of cargo. Thus, certain carriers may be required to cease interlining with those carriers who do not equip their trailers with contour mud flaps. We conclude that the heavy burden that the Illinois (D) law places on the interstate movement of trucks and trailers passes the permissible limits even for safety regulations. Thus, the law [clearly and without doubt] violates the dormant Commerce Clause.

Analysis:

Although the power of the states to regulate the use of their highways is very broad, the special and conflicting requirements of the mud guard design in this case significantly interfered with interstate commerce and thus violated the Commerce Clause. The Court also relied upon the findings of the district court that the alleged safety benefit of the contoured guards was slight, if any, and noted that they might even create their own set of safety hazards for the public. This decision is in line with *Southern Pacific Co. v. Arizona ex rel. Sullivan,* wherein the court invalidated a state law limiting the length of trains operating in the state because the burdens on interstate commerce outweighed the state's asserted safety need for the law. There too, there was only a slight safety advantage afforded by the state law.

Consolidated Freightways Corporation of Delaware v. Raymond Kassel

(State Agency) v. (Interstate Trucking Co.)
455 U.S. 329, 102 S.Ct. 1496 (1982)

COURT IMPOSES LIMIT ON DEFERENCE TO HIGHWAY SAFETY REGULATIONS

■ **INSTANT FACTS** Iowa's (D) statute banning trucks more than 60 feet in length from using state highways was challenged by Consolidated Freightways (P), which preferred 65-foot trucks, on ground that it violated Commerce Clause.

■ **BLACK LETTER RULE** Although state regulations concerning highway safety carry a strong presumption of validity, if the furtherance of safety is marginal or the burden on commerce is substantial, the regulations will be declared invalid under the Commerce Clause.

■ **PROCEDURAL BASIS**

Review by U.S. Supreme Court after trial of matter challenging constitutionality of state statute based on the Commerce Clause.

■ **FACTS**

Iowa (D) by statute restricts the length of trucks traveling on its highways to a maximum of 60 feet. Consolidated Freightways Corp. ("Consolidated") (P), a large nationwide common carrier, favors using 65-foot long "double" (or "twin") trucks, which have larger capacity and two detachable trailers. Consolidated (P), desiring to use the 65-foot trucks in Iowa, challenged the law on the ground that it violated the Commerce Clause because it burdened interstate commerce. Interstate 80 through Iowa is the principal east-west route linking New York, Chicago, and the west coast, and interstate 35 is a major north-south route. Iowa (D) defended the law as a reasonable safety measure, contending that the 65-foot doubles are more dangerous than the 55-foot singles. [Aren't all of them dangerous?] After trial in the District Court, the court concluded that that twin is as safe as the semi, and thus there is no valid safety reason for barring twins from Iowa's (D) highways.

■ **ISSUE**

May a state highway regulation offering only marginal safety benefits be an unconstitutional burden on interstate commerce?

■ **DECISION AND RATIONALE**

(Powell, J.) Yes. We conclude that the Iowa (D) truck-length limitations unconstitutionally burden interstate commerce. Iowa (D) failed to present any persuasive evidence that 65-foot doubles are less safe than 55-foot singles. Moreover, Iowa's (D) law is out of step with the laws of all other Mid-western and Western States. It thus substantially burdens the interstate flow of goods by truck. In the absence of congressional action to set uniform standards, some burdens associated with state safety regulations must be tolerated. [This is a wake-up call to Congress to enact uniform laws on the subject.] Nevertheless, where, as here, the State's safety interest has been found to be illusory, and its regulations impair significantly the federal interest in efficient and safe interstate transportation, the state law cannot be harmonized with the Commerce Clause. Iowa's (D) law may in fact aggravate, rather than ameliorate, the problems of highway accidents since it requires either driving more (small) trucks, or driving longer distances around Iowa (D) in large trucks. In the latter case, Iowa's (D) law would shift the incident of accidents from Iowa (D) to neighboring states. Because Iowa (D) has imposed this burden without any significant countervailing safety interest, its statute violates the Commerce Clause.

■ DISSENT

(Rehnquist, J.) The Court has overstepped our limited authority to review state legislation under the Commerce Clause and seriously intrudes upon the fundamental right of the States to pass laws to secure the safety of their citizens. The plurality neglects to note that both Pennsylvania and New Jersey, through which Interstate 80 runs before reaching New York, also ban 65-foot doubles. Thus, Iowa (D) is not an oddity standing alone to block commerce carried in 65-foot doubles. A "sensitive consideration" of the safety purpose in relation to the burden on commerce is required. When engaging in such a consideration the Court does not directly compare safety benefits to commerce costs and strike down the legislation if the latter can be said in some vague sense to "outweigh" the former. The purpose of the "sensitive consideration" is to determine if the safety justification is merely a pretext for discrimination against interstate commerce. It will be if the safety benefits from the law are demonstrably trivial while the burden on commerce is great. There can be no doubt that Iowa's (D) statute is a valid safety regulation that is entitled to the strongest presumption of validity against Commerce Clause challenges.

Analysis:

Once again, the Supreme Court has declared a non-discriminatory law to be unconstitutional. The Court weighed the purported safety purpose against the interference with interstate commerce, and found that the law offered no real safety benefit (and perhaps would even increase the incidence of accidents), yet burdened commerce. The Court traditionally accorded some deference to states' safety regulations (of any type), but the amount of deference varied; highway safety regulations received more deference than railroad regulations. This traditional deference was under the "sensitive consideration," as defined by Justice Rehnquist in his dissent. *Kassel* now seems to reject the "sensitive consideration" as the proper level of deference. Nominally, *Kassel* still gives deference, but less. The Court notes that it will presume the regulation is constitutional, upon finding (i) the safety justification is not mere pretext, and (ii) the burden on interstate commerce is not vastly greater than the benefit to state safety.

■ CASE VOCABULARY

PLURALITY: A quantity that is not a majority, but which gets more votes than any other does.

PRETEXT: A non-truth asserted to hide the truth.

SENSITIVE CONSIDERATION: Judicial standard applied when analyzing whether state statute's asserted safety justification is merely a pretext for discrimination against commerce.

Western & Southern Life Insurance Co. v. State Board of Equalization of California

(*Insurance Co.*) v. (*State*)
451 U.S. 648, 101 S.Ct. 2070 (1981)

EXCEPTION TO DORMANT COMMERCE CLAUSE EXISTS IF CONGRESS AUTHORIZES STATE LAW

■ **INSTANT FACTS** Insurance company (P) challenged state law that imposed a retaliatory tax on out-of-state insurers on the ground that it violated the Commerce Clause.

■ **BLACK LETTER RULE** Congress, by its authority to regulate commerce among the several States, may give States the power to enact laws that restrict the flow of interstate commerce.

■ **PROCEDURAL BASIS**

Review by U.S. Supreme Court of challenge to state statute on Commerce Clause grounds.

■ **FACTS**

California (D) enacted a law that imposed a retaliatory tax on out-of-state insurers doing business in California, when the insurer's State of incorporation imposes higher taxes on California insurers doing business in that State than California would otherwise impose on that State's insurers doing business in California. [An eye for an eye.] Congress had passed a law giving the States authority to tax insurance companies. Western & Southern Life Insurance Co. (P) challenged the statute on Commerce Clause grounds.

■ **ISSUE**

May Congress give States the power to enact laws that restrict the flow of interstate commerce?

■ **DECISION AND RATIONALE**

(Brennan, J.) Yes. Congress, by its authority to regulate commerce among the several States, may give States the power to enact laws that restrict the flow of interstate commerce. We have long recognized that the Commerce Clause contains an implied limitation on the power of the States to interfere with or impose burdens on interstate commerce. However, our decisions, do not limit the authority of Congress to regulate commerce among the several States as it sees fit. In the exercise of this plenary authority, Congress may confer upon the States an ability to restrict the flow of interstate commerce that it would not otherwise enjoy. If Congress declares that that States may regulate an aspect of interstate commerce, then any action taken by the State within the scope of this authority is proper and not subject to Commerce Clause challenge [even if it hugely discriminates against interstate commerce]. Congress, in passing the McCarren-Ferguson Act, removed all Commerce Clause limitations on the States' authority to regulate and tax the business of insurance. Nevertheless, Western & Southern (P) still asserts that the Act does not permit California (D) to impose anti-competitive state taxation that discriminates against out-of-state insurers. We disagree. There is no such limitation in the language or the history of the Act. The Act expressly provides, "The business of insurance . . . shall be subject to the laws of the several States which relate to the regulation or taxation of such business." [You can't be any clearer than that.]

Analysis:

This case demonstrates one of the exceptions to the Commerce Clause—congressional approval. If Congress has specifically approved the state law, there can be no dormant Commerce Clause violation, even if the state law is clearly discriminatory. But Congress must have acted in order to indicate its approval of the state law, so the commerce power is not "dormant." Thus, if the Supreme Court were to rule that a particular state law violated the dormant Commerce Clause, Congress could enact a law that authorizes the law, thereby effectively overruling the Supreme Court. This case was not a difficult one for the Court, since the federal statute clearly gave states the power to enact laws regarding the business of insurance, without any limitations.

■ CASE VOCABULARY

AMICUS CURIAE: A "friend of the court" brief, submitted by interested non-parties.

PLENARY AUTHORITY: A broad authority (here, granted to Congress to enact laws concerning commerce).

Reeves, Inc. v. William Stake

(*Out-of-State Cement Buyer*) v. (*South Dakota Official*)
447 U.S. 429, 100 S.Ct. 2271 (1980)

STATES ACTING AS "MARKET PARTICIPANTS" MAY FAVOR IN-STATE CUSTOMERS WITHOUT VIOLATING COMMERCE CLAUSE

■ **INSTANT FACTS** When South Dakota (D) built a state-owned cement plant, which sold to private buyers, but later gave preferences to in-state buyers, Reeves (P), a long time buyer, challenged the policy under the Commerce Clause.

■ **BLACK LETTER RULE** States that are "market participants" in the buying or selling of goods, as opposed to "market regulators," are not bound by the Commerce Clause and thus may favor in-state interests.

■ PROCEDURAL BASIS

Review by U.S. Supreme Court of State's policy that favors in-state buyers of goods on Commerce Clause grounds, in action seeking injunctive relief.

■ FACTS

Responding to cement shortages, South Dakota (D) built and operated a cement plant selling to both in-state and out-of-state buyers for 50 years. When plant difficulties and a booming construction industry caused the plant to be unable to meet all orders, the State (D) implemented a policy [previously in effect a very long time ago] that gave preference to private in-state buyers. Longtime out-of-state buyer Reeves, Inc. (P) [who was denied cement and had nowhere else to go for it] sued South Dakota (D) on the ground that the preferential policy violated the Commerce Clause.

■ ISSUE

May a State, which produces goods for sale to private buyers, give preference to in-state buyers?

■ DECISION AND RATIONALE

(Blackmun, J.) Yes. When states become "market participants" by buying or selling goods, their commercial activities are not bound by the Commerce Clause, and may favor in-state interests. The basic distinction between States as market participants and States as market regulators makes good sense and sound law. The Commerce Clause is applicable primarily to state taxes and regulatory measures that impede free private trade in the national marketplace. There is no limit on the ability of the States to operate freely in the free market. Any restraint in this area should come from Congress rather than from the courts. South Dakota (D), as a seller of cement, unquestionably fits the "market participant" exception to the Commerce Clause.

■ DISSENT

(Powell, J.) South Dakota's (D) policy that in times of shortage the State cement plant must turn away out-of-state customers until all orders from within the state are filled, represents precisely the kind of economic protectionism that the Commerce Clause was intended to prevent. While I agree with the Court that South Dakota (D) may provide cement for its public needs without violating the Commerce Clause, I cannot agree that it may withhold its cement from interstate commerce in order to benefit those within the State. If the State enters into the private market and operates a commercial enterprise

Reeves, Inc. v. William Stake (Continued)

for the advantage of its private citizens, it may not evade the constitutional policy against economic Balkanization. The creation of a free national economy was a major goal of the States when they resolved to unite under the Federal Constitution. The decision today cannot be reconciled with that purpose.

Analysis:

The Supreme Court in this case utilizes the "market participant" exception to the Commerce Clause. As long as the state is discriminating in favor of its own citizens while conducting market transactions—in this case a state owned cement plant—there is no violation of the Commerce Clause. However, when the state is acting as a regulator rather than a participant, the Commerce Clause will apply. Justice Powell in his dissent argued that the state was engaging in protectionist policies because it operated a commercial enterprise for the advantage of its private citizens. There is a fine line between what constitutes market participation and what constitutes economic protectionism. An example of the State acting as a regulator would be if its policy required privately owned cement plants within the state to sell exclusively to in-state residents.

■ **CASE VOCABULARY**

BALKANIZATION: Division of territories into small hostile states.

STATE SOVEREIGNTY: A state's right to be its own supreme authority.

South-Central Timber Development, Inc. v. Commissioner, Department of Natural Resources of Alaska

(Alaska Timber Co.) v. (Alaska)
467 U.S. 82, 104 S.Ct. 2237 (1984)

THE MARKET PARTICIPANT EXCEPTION IS LIMITED TO THE PARTICULAR MARKET IN WHICH THE STATE IS A PARTICIPANT

■ **INSTANT FACTS** Alaska (D) imposed a restriction on buyers of Alaska (D) timber that required them to process the timber in Alaska (D) before export.

■ **BLACK LETTER RULE** Although state-owned businesses may favor resident purchasers, they may not attach conditions to the sale of products that will burden interstate commerce.

■ **PROCEDURAL BASIS**

Review by U.S. Supreme Court of state law on Commerce Clause grounds in action seeking injunctive relief.

■ **FACTS**

Alaska (D) gave notice that it would sell a large quantity of Alaska timber. As a condition of the sale, Alaska (D) required that the buyer of the timber partially process the timber in Alaska (D) before shipping it out of the State. The purpose of the requirement was to protect Alaska (D) timber processors, develop new industries, and derive revenue from the timber resources. South-Central Timber Development, Inc. (P), an Alaska (D) corporation that purchases and ships timber out of state for processing, filed suit seeking an injunction to prevent enforcement of the in-state processing requirement on the ground that it violated the Commerce Clause. Alaska (D) responded that the requirement was exempt from Commerce Clause scrutiny because of the "market participant" exception.

■ **ISSUE**

May a State, acting as a market participant, impose conditions on "down-stream" market participants without violating the dormant Commerce Clause?

■ **DECISION AND RATIONALE**

(White, J.) No. If a State is acting as a market participant, rather than as a market regulator, the dormant Commerce Clause places no limitations on its activities. The precise contours of the market participant doctrine have yet to be established; it has only been applied in three cases of this Court to date. Alaska (D) participates in the timber market, by imposing conditions down-stream in the timber-processing market. It is clear that Alaska (D) is more than merely a seller of timber [rather, it's regulating who and where the timber will be processed]. A seller usually has no say over, and no interest in, how the product is to be used after sale. Here, however, payment for the timber does not end the obligations of the purchaser. He cannot do as he pleases with it; instead, he is obligated to deal with a stranger to the contract after completion of the sale. The limit of the market-participant doctrine must be that it allows a State to impose burdens on commerce within the market in which it is a participant, but allows it to go no further. The State may not impose conditions that have a substantial regulatory effect outside of that

South-Central Timber Dev't, Inc. v. Comm'r, Dep't of Natural Resources of Alaska (Continued)

particular market. Thus, Alaska (D) may not avail itself of the market-participant doctrine to immunize its down-stream regulation of the timber-processing market in which it is not a participant.

■ DISSENT

(Rehnquist, J.) The line between participation and regulation is what we are trying to determine [and it's not easy]. Alaska (D) is merely paying the buyer of the timber indirectly, by means of a reduced price, to hire Alaska (D) residents to process the timber. Alaska (D) could accomplish the same result in different ways. For example, it could sell its timber only to those companies that maintain active primary-processing plants in Alaska (D), or it could directly subsidize the primary-processing industry within the State. Finally, it could even pay to have the logs processed and then enter the market only to sell processed logs. It is unduly formalistic to conclude that the one path chosen by Alaska (D) as best suited to promote its concerns is the path forbidden it by the Commerce Clause.

Analysis:

This case demonstrates that there is a limitation to the market participant exception to the dormant Commerce Clause. By imposing conditions "down-stream," Alaska (D) went beyond the market in which it was participating. The Court rejected Alaska's (D) argument that it was merely subsidizing the local timber processing plants. Critics of the market participant exception assert that protectionism should not be permitted at all, regardless of whether the state is acting as a market participant or a regulator, and moreover, there is no clear distinction between when the state is acting as a regulator and a market participant. Defenders of the doctrine argue that the citizens of a state should be permitted to recoup the benefits of the taxes that they pay. Note that the dissent in this case was unconcerned about the down-stream conditions, arguing that Alaska (D) had not Improperly shifted the cost to out-of-state persons or entities.

■ CASE VOCABULARY

MARKET PARTICIPANT DOCTRINE: If the state is acting as a market participant (e.g., selling products) instead of as a regulator, it may favor its own citizens over others (and its activities are not limited by the Commerce Clause.)

PROSPECTUS: A writing distributed to prospective buyers that provides details concerning what is being offered for sale, often used by corporations before offering to sell stock in the corporation.

Toomer v. Witsell

(Out-of-State Fishermen) v. (South Carolina Official)
334 U.S. 385, 68 S.Ct. 1156 (1948)

PRIVILEGES AND IMMUNITIES CLAUSE INVALIDATES STATE'S DISCRIMINATORY COMMERCIAL FISHING LAW

■ **INSTANT FACTS** Toomer (P) and other out-of-state commercial fishermen challenged South Carolina (D) law that imposed a higher license fee on out-of-staters based upon the Privileges and Immunities Clause.

■ **BLACK LETTER RULE** In determining whether a State law violates the Privileges and Immunities Clause, the court must determine whether the law discriminates against citizens of other States and, if so, whether there is substantial reason for the discrimination beyond the mere fact that they are citizens of other states.

■ **PROCEDURAL BASIS**

Review by U.S. Supreme Court to determine whether State law violated Privileges and Immunities Clause in action seeking to enjoin enforcement of law.

■ **FACTS**

South Carolina (D) enacted a statute that imposed a license fee for out-of-state commercial shrimp boats that was 100 times greater than the license fee imposed on residents of the State. [If allowed, we know which state would have the lowest shrimp prices.] Toomer (P) and other fishermen, all out-of-state residents, filed suit to enjoin the law on the ground that it violated the Privileges and Immunities Clause of the United States Constitution. Toomer (P) contended that the purpose of the statute was not to conserve shrimp, but to exclude non-residents and thus create a commercial monopoly for South Carolina (D) residents.

■ **ISSUE**

Does a state law that discriminates against out-of-staters violate the Privilege and Immunities Clause where its purpose is to conserve natural resources but creates a commercial monopoly for the States' residents by excluding non-residents?

■ **DECISION AND RATIONALE**

(Vinson, J.) Yes. The primary purpose of the Privileges and Immunities Clause was to help fuse into one Nation a collection of independent, sovereign States, to insure to a citizen of State A who ventures into State B the same privileges which the citizens of State B enjoy. One of the privileges that the clause guarantees to citizens of State A is that of doing business in State B on terms of substantial equality with the citizens of that State. The Privileges and Immunities Clause is not absolute. It does bar discrimination against citizens of other States where there is no substantial reason for the discrimination beyond the mere fact that they are citizens of other States. But it does not preclude disparity of treatment in the many situations where there are perfectly valid independent reasons for it. We must therefore determine whether reasons do exist and whether the degree of discrimination bears a close relation to them, keeping in mind that States should have considerable leeway in analyzing the local evils and in prescribing appropriate cures. The South Carolina (D) statute clearly discriminates against non-residents, and there is little doubt that the practical effect is virtually exclusionary. Even if we agree

Toomer v. Witsell (Continued)

that the purpose of the statute is to conserve the State's shrimp supply and to head off an impending threat of excessive trawling [for you non-fishermen out there that means using a large fishing net, usually dragged behind a boat, to catch fish], it cannot be assumed that any means adopted to attain valid objectives necessarily squares with the Privileges and Immunities Clause. The purpose of the Clause is to outlaw classifications based on the fact of non-citizenship unless there is something to indicate that non-citizens constitute a peculiar source of the evil at which the statute is aimed. Thus, the statute must be held unconstitutional.

Analysis:

If a statute is obviously discriminatory against non-citizens, it will be held unconstitutional unless there is some substantial reason beyond the mere fact of non-citizenship. The Court indicated that even if there was a valid purpose for the law, not just any means could be used to obtain the objectives. Rather, there must be a correlation between the non-citizens and attaining the desired objectives. Here, the court concluded that there was no evidence that non-citizens were a "peculiar source of the evil." Note that this case is an example of a common Privileges and Immunities Clause challenge based upon discrimination against out-of-staters with respect to their ability to earn their livelihood.

■ CASE VOCABULARY

PRIVILEGES AND IMMUNITIES CLAUSE: Contained in Art. IV, § 2 of the United States Constitution and provides: "The Citizens of each State shall be entitled to all Privileges and Immunities of Citizens in the several States."

United Building and Construction Trades Council of Camden County v. Mayor and Council of the City of Camden

(Trade Organization) v. (City)

465 U.S. 208, 104 S.Ct. 1020 (1984)

TWO-STEP ANALYSIS USED TO DETERMINE WHETHER LOCAL ORDINANCE VIOLATES PRIVILEGES AND IMMUNITIES CLAUSE

■ **INSTANT FACTS** A municipal ordinance, which required 40% of employees working on city-funded projects be city residents, was challenged under Privileges and Immunities Clause.

■ **BLACK LETTER RULE** The Privilege and Immunities Clause prevents states (and cities) from discriminating against non-residents if: (i) the discrimination burdens a "fundamental" privilege (including "employment"), and (ii) there is no "substantial reason" for disparate treatment.

■ PROCEDURAL BASIS

Review by U.S. Supreme Court of decision, certified for direct appeal by State Supreme Court following administrative proceeding, concerning Privileges and Immunities challenge to city ordinance

■ FACTS

The city of Camden (D), New Jersey passed a municipal ordinance requiring 40% of the contractors working on city-funded projects to be residents of Camden (D). [Camden's (D) reasoning is that non-Camden residents who work on city projects are the source of the evil at which the statute is aimed.] United Building & Construction Trades Council (P) challenged the ordinance under the Privileges and Immunities Clause, contending that it discriminated against out-of-staters seeking employment. Camden (D) contended that the Privileges and Immunities Clause (i) applies only to laws passed by states, not cities, (ii) does not prohibit discrimination solely on the basis of municipal residency, and (iii) does not prohibit discriminatory laws which also discriminate against in-state residents (i.e., New Jersey citizens residing outside Camden (D).)

■ ISSUE

Will a local ordinance violate the Privileges and Immunities Clause if it discriminates against non-residents by burdening a "fundamental" privilege, such as employment, and there is no substantial reason for the disparate treatment?

■ DECISION AND RATIONALE

(Rehnquist, J.) Yes. The Privilege and Immunities Clause prevents states (and cities) from discriminating against non-residents if: (i) the discrimination burdens a "fundamental" privilege (including "employment"), and (ii) there is no "substantial reason" for disparate treatment The Clause applies to municipal ordinances as well as State laws, since cities derive their legislative authority from the State. The Clause forbids discrimination based upon municipal residency as much as that based on state residence, since a person who is not residing in a state city is, *ipso facto,* not residing in any of its cities. While it is true that New Jersey residents living outside the City of Camden (D) are disadvantaged by the ordinance as much as out-of-state citizens, and have no Privileges and Immunities claim, this denial of claims should not be applied to the out-of-state residents. The New Jersey residents at least can remedy the discrimination against them by voting against it, while out-of-state residents have no such vote, and deserve greater protection. The pursuit of a common calling [a job] is one of the most fundamental of the privileges protected by the Clause. The conclusion that Camden's (D) ordinance discriminates against a protected privilege does not end our inquiry, for the Clause does not preclude discrimination against citizens of other States where there is a "substantial reason" for the difference in the treatment. Camden (D) sets forth various reasons for the need for the ordinance—to increase the number of employed persons living in the City, to stop middle class flight, and to stop non-residents from "living off" Camden (D) without "living in" Camden (D). We are unable, however, to determine from the record before us whether there is substantial reason for the discriminatory ordinance. There was no trial or findings of fact, and the matter was certified for appeal after a brief administrative proceeding. It would be inappropriate for us to make factual findings. Therefore, we remand the case to the New Jersey Supreme Court for determination of the best method for making the necessary factual findings. [In other words, they passed the buck back to the State.]

Analysis:

Although the Court was unable to make a definitive ruling on the constitutionality of the ordinance due to an incomplete factual record, it set forth a two-step analysis to be used to determine whether a state or local ordinance violates the Privileges and Immunities Clause First, the court must determine if the statute or ordinance discriminates against out-of-state residents on a matter of fundamental concern. The Court held here that "employment" is a matter of fundamental concern. Second, the court must determine if there is a substantial reason for the discriminatory statute or ordinance treating in-staters and out-of-staters differently. The case also made clear that the Privileges and Immunities Clause applies to residency restrictions imposed by local governments as well as the state. Without such a holding, the states could escape the requirements of the Clause by having each city impose residency requirements, thereby excluding all out-of-state residents.

■ **CASE VOCABULARY**

ADMINISTRATIVE PROCEEDINGS: A trial-type hearing before a board, commission, or agency, etc.

FINDINGS OF FACT: Court weighs the evidence and makes a determination as to the facts.

IPSO FACTO: Latin for, by the fact itself.

REMAND: Sending the case back to the same court from which it came, such as after reversal on appeal and further proceedings ordered.

Lester Baldwin v. Fish and Game Commission of Montana

(Hunters) v. (State)
436 U.S. 371, 98 S.Ct. 1852 (1978)

RECREATIONAL HUNTING DOES NOT CONSTITUTE A FUNDAMENTAL INTEREST ENTITLED TO PROTECTION UNDER THE PRIVILEGES AND IMMUNITIES CLAUSE

■ **INSTANT FACTS** Game hunters, Baldwin and others (P), challenged state law that imposed higher fees for hunting license on out-of-staters on ground it violated Privileges and Immunities Clause.

■ **BLACK LETTER RULE** State law, which imposes higher license fees for recreational hunting on out-of-state residents than in-state residents, is constitutional because recreational hunting is not a "fundamental right" entitled to protection under the Privileges and Immunities Clause.

■ **PROCEDURAL BASIS**
Review by U.S. Supreme Court of state law challenged on Privileges and Immunities Clause ground in action for declaratory and injunctive relief, and reimbursement.

■ **FACTS**
Baldwin (P), a Montana resident and hunting guide (whose customers are usually non-residents who come to Montana to hunt), and four out-of-state hunters, brought suit challenging Montana's (D) law that imposed higher hunting license fees on out-of-state hunters than imposed on residents of Montana (D). Baldwin (P) contends that the law violates the Privileges and Immunities Clause because it imposes unreasonable burdens on citizens of other states.

■ **ISSUE**
Does a state law that makes a distinction between residents and non-residents concerning recreational hunting threaten a "fundamental right" entitled to protection under the Privileges and immunities Clause?

■ **DECISION AND RATIONALE**
(Blackmun, J.) No. We note that there are situations when a state citizenship or residency may be used by a State to distinguish among persons. For example, the right to vote or seek elective office within a state may be tied to an individual's state residency without violating the Privileges and Immunities Clause. Only with respect to those "privileges" and "immunities" bearing upon the vitality of the Nation as a single entity must the State treat all citizens, resident and nonresident, equally. Thus, we must determine whether the distinction made by Montana (D) between residents and nonresidents in establishing access to big-game hunting threatens a basic right in a way that offends the Privileges and Immunities Clause. Elk (and other big game) hunting is a recreation and a sport, and is not a means to the nonresident's livelihood. [Baldwin (P) making his living as a hunting guide disagrees.] The desire to share in limited supply of big game within Montana (D) does not fall within the purview of the Privileges and Immunities Clause. Equality in access to Montana elk (and other game) is not basic to the maintenance or well-being of the Union. The non-residents are not deprived of a means of a livelihood by the system or of access to any part of the State (D) to which they may seek to travel. Whatever rights or activates may be "fundamental" under the Privileges and Immunities Clause, we hold that elk hunting by nonresidents in Montana (D) is not one of them.

Lester Baldwin v. Fish and Game Commission of Montana (Continued)

Analysis:

This case demonstrates that the Privileges and immunities Clause is limited to protecting "fundamental rights" that involve economic interests, such as one's livelihood, and civil rights. Thus, not all forms of discrimination against out-of-state residents are protected. Only those that bear on the "vitality of the Nation as a single entity" will be subject to protection. Recall that in *Toomer v. Witsell*, "commercial" fishermen successfully challenged a state law that imposed higher license fees on out-of-staters operating commercial shrimp boats, based upon the Privileges and Immunities Clause. The commercial fishermen's livelihoods were affected by the law, whereas here the Court concluded the out-of-state hunters' livelihood was not affected. However, one of the plaintiffs, Baldwin (P), was a hunting guide and earned a living at it. Thus, his livelihood was affected.

■ **CASE VOCABULARY**

DECLARATORY: As in *Declaratory Relief*—Action merely to have court declare one's rights, such as under a contract or to specific property.

Supreme Court of New Hampshire v. Kathryn A. Piper

(State Supreme Court) v. (Non-Resident Attorney)
470 U.S. 274, 105 S.Ct. 1272 (1985)

PRACTICE OF LAW IS A FUNDAMENTAL RIGHT ENTITLED TO PROTECTION UNDER THE PRIVILEGES AND IMMUNITIES CLAUSE

■ **INSTANT FACTS** Non-resident attorney, Piper (P), challenged State Supreme Court Rule that required State's lawyers to be residents of the State on ground it violated Privileges and Immunities Clause.

■ **BLACK LETTER RULE** 1) The opportunity to practice law is a "fundamental right"; 2) there is no substantial reason for denying bar admission in the State to non-residents; and, 3) such discrimination does not bear a close relationship to the State's objectives.

■ **PROCEDURAL BASIS**

Review by U.S. Supreme Court of State Supreme Court Rule limiting bar admission to State residents on Privileges and Immunities Clause ground.

■ **FACTS**

Piper (P), a resident of Vermont, took the bar examination in neighboring New Hampshire [she actually lives about 400 yards from New Hampshire's border] and passed. The Rules of the Supreme Court of New Hampshire limit bar admission to state residents, and thus Piper (P) would have to establish residence in New Hampshire prior to being sworn in as an attorney licensed to practice in that State. Piper (P) sued the Supreme Court of New Hampshire (D) [let's hope if she wins she never has a case before them] contending that the Rule violates the Privileges and Immunities Clause.

■ **ISSUE**

Does the practice of law constitute a "fundamental right" subject to protection under the Privileges and Immunities Clause?

■ **DECISION AND RATIONALE**

(Powell, J.) Yes. Like the occupations considered in our prior cases, the practice of law is important to the national economy, and there is nothing in these cases suggesting that it should not be viewed as a privilege under the Privileges and Immunities Clause. In addition to the lawyer's role in the national economy, out-of-state lawyers often represent persons who raise unpopular claims, and representation by nonresident counsel may be the only means available for the vindication of federal rights. We thus conclude that the opportunity to practice law is a "fundamental right." The Clause is not "absolute." [This means discrimination is sometimes legal.] It does not preclude discrimination against nonresidents where (i) there is a substantial reason for the difference in treatment; and (ii) the discrimination practiced against nonresidents bears a substantial relationship to the State's objective. We conclude that there is no evidence to support New Hampshire's (D) justifications for its Rule. We do not agree that nonresidents would be less likely to keep abreast of local rules and procedures, and there is no reason to believe that a nonresident lawyer will conduct his practice in a dishonest or unethical manner. Finally, there is no merit to the contentions that a nonresident member of the bar would be unavailable for court proceedings or to do pro bono work. Thus, New Hampshire (D) neither advances a "substantial reason" for its discrimination against nonresident applicants to the bar, nor demonstrates that the discrimination practiced bears a close relationship to its proffered objectives.

■ DISSENT

(Rehnquist, J.) The Court's decision will be surprising because it so clearly disregards the fact that the practice of law is fundamentally different from other occupations because it does not readily translate across state lines. The State (D) has a substantial interest in creating its own set of laws that correspond to its own local interests. A residency law such as the one before us could exist in order for the State (D) to have an interest in maximizing the number of resident lawyers for the purpose of increasing the quality of the pool from which its lawmakers could be drawn. A State should be able to decide that a trial court should not have to add to its present scheduling difficulties the uncertainties and added delays fostered by counsel who might reside 1,000 miles away from New Hampshire (D). Thus, New Hampshire (D) has more than enough substantial reasons to conclude that its lawyers should also be residents. I would hold that the Rule does not violate the Privileges and Immunities Clause.

Analysis:

The Court held in this case that the practice of law is a fundamental right that is protected by the Privileges and immunities Clause. Lawyers are vital to the nation. After concluding that the practice of law was a fundamental right entitled to protection, the Court determined whether a substantial reason existed for the rule excluding nonresidents from the bar. The opinion rejects each of New Hampshire's (D) justifications for the rule, whereas the dissenting justice sets forth examples of why a state could have substantial justification for denying non-residents admission to practice.

■ CASE VOCABULARY

PRO BONO: Latin meaning, "for the public good" and referring to providing legal services without charge.

PRO HAC VICE: Latin meaning, "for a certain occasion or purpose", and referring to a lawyer admitted in one state being admitted to the bar of another state on a temporary basis in order to work on a certain case within that state.

CHAPTER FIVE

The Structure of the Constitution's Protection of Civil Rights and Civil Liberties

---

Barron v. Mayor and City Council of Baltimore

Instant Facts: A wharf owner sued the City for taking his property without just compensation in violation of the Fifth Amendment.

Black Letter Rule: The Bill of Rights applies only to the federal government, not to state and local governments.

Slaughter–House Cases

Instant Facts: Butchers challenged the constitutionality of a state law giving a monopoly to a particular slaughterhouse.

Black Letter Rule: The Thirteenth and Fourteenth Amendments apply only to former slaves.

Saenz v. Roe

Instant Facts: California (D) paid residents who had lived in the state for less than 12 months lower welfare benefits than it paid other residents.

Black Letter Rule: Under the Privileges or Immunities Clause, a State must provide the same benefits to new residents as it does to other residents.

Twining v. New Jersey

Instant Facts: A law providing that a jury may draw an unfavorable inference from a criminal defendant's failure to testify was challenged under the Due Process Clause of the Fourteenth Amendment.

Black Letter Rule: Provisions of the Bill of Rights may apply to the States under the Due Process Clause of the Fourteenth Amendment if the provisions are necessary for due process of law.

Duncan v. Louisiana

Instant Facts: A man charged with simple battery, punishable by up to two years in prison, was denied the right to a jury trial and claimed he was therefore denied due process of law.

Black Letter Rule: The Sixth Amendment right to a jury trial is fundamental and is applicable to the states pursuant to the Due Process Clause of the Fourteenth Amendment.

The Civil Rights Cases

Instant Facts: Owners of theaters and hotels were prosecuted for discriminating against African Americans.

Black Letter Rule: Under the Fourteenth Amendment, Congress does not have the power to pass laws prohibiting discrimination by private citizens.

Marsh v. Alabama

Instant Facts: A Jehovah's Witness was arrested for trespass after attempting to distribute religious literature in a privately-owned town.

Black Letter Rule: A private entity that acts like a governmental body and performs a public function is subject to the Constitution.

Jackson v. Metropolitan Edison Co.

Instant Facts: A customer of an electric company claimed the company performed a public function and therefore could not shut off her electricity without adequate notice and a hearing pursuant to the Due Process Clause of the Fourteenth Amendment.

Black Letter Rule: The actions of a private entity are not considered state action unless there is a sufficiently close nexus between the State and the challenged action.

Terry v. Adams

Instant Facts: A private political party that excludes members based on race, and that controls the ultimate outcome of elections, was held to be engaging in state action for purposes of the Fifteenth Amendment.

Black Letter Rule: A private political party that controls the outcome of elections engages in state action thereby making it subject to the Fifteenth Amendment.

Evans v. Newton

Instant Facts: A will provision leaving land for a park for whites only was challenged under the Equal Protection Clause of the Fourteenth Amendment.

Black Letter Rule: Operating a park constitutes a public function; thus the owner is subject to the Fourteenth Amendment.

Amalgamated Food Employees Union Local 590 v. Logan Valley Plaza, Inc.

Instant Facts: After a shopping center owner barred union members from picketing on its property, the union claimed the shopping center served a public function and that its First Amendment rights prevailed.

Black Letter Rule: Shopping centers serve a public function and, therefore, the First Amendment applies.

Lloyd Corp. v. Tanner

Instant Facts: Anti-war demonstrators told to leave a shopping center sued the shopping center owners for violating their First Amendment rights.

Black Letter Rule: There are no First Amendment rights in a private shopping center if the speech at issue is not related to the activities at the shopping center.

Hudgens v. National Labor Relations Board

Instant Facts: Labor union members picketing in a privately-owned mall claimed their First Amendment rights to free speech were violated when they were threatened with criminal trespass prosecution.

Black Letter Rule: The First Amendment does not apply to people entering privately-owned shopping centers.

Shelley v. Kraemer

Instant Facts: A black person bought property in violation of a restrictive covenant providing that only whites could own or occupy the property. White neighbors sued to enforce the covenant.

Black Letter Rule: Judicial enforcement of a private agreement constitutes state action for purposes of the Fourteenth Amendment.

Lugar v. Edmondson Oil Co.

Instant Facts: A debtor sued a creditor for violating his due process rights when the creditor obtained an ex parte writ of attachment and had a sheriff seize the debtor's property.

Black Letter Rule: Using the court and government officials to seize property without due process of law involves state action for purposes of the Fourteenth Amendment.

Edmonson v. Leesville Concrete Co.

Instant Facts: An injured construction worker suing for negligence claimed that allowing the defendant to exclude jurors based on their race violated his equal protection rights under the Fourteenth Amendment.

Black Letter Rule: When a private litigant in a civil action makes peremptory challenges based on the jurors' race, he or she violates the Equal Protection Clause of the Fourteenth Amendment.

Burton v. Wilmington Parking Authority

Instant Facts: A black man was denied service in a restaurant located in a government-owned building.

Black Letter Rule: When a State becomes entangled in a private party's actions so that the State and the private party have a symbiotic relationship, the private party must comply with the Fourteenth Amendment.

Moose Lodge No. 107 v. Irvis

Instant Facts: When a black man was denied service by a private club, he sued to revoke its state-issued liquor license.

Black Letter Rule: A private club that obtains a state liquor license does not necessarily engage in state action for purposes of the Fourteenth Amendment.

Norwood v. Harrison

Instant Facts: School children claimed their rights under the Equal Protection Clause of the Fourteenth Amendment were violated by a state program that provided free textbooks to racially discriminatory private schools.

Black Letter Rule: Under the Equal Protection Clause of the Fourteenth Amendment, a State may not provide aid to private institutions that practice racial discrimination.

Rendell–Baker v. Kohn

Instant Facts: Private school employees sued the private school for violating their constitutional rights, alleging that the private school was a state actor because it was publically funded and performed a public function.

Black Letter Rule: Publically-funded and regulated private organizations are not state actors under the Fourteenth Amendment unless the government compels or influences their actions.

Blum v. Yaretsky

Instant Facts: Medicaid patients claimed the State could be held liable for the failure of private nursing homes to provide them adequate notice of decisions to transfer or discharge them.

Black Letter Rule: The State is not liable for decisions made by private parties which the State did not coerce or significantly encourage.

Reitman v. Mulkey

Instant Facts: Prospective renters were denied an apartment based on their race. They challenged a state constitutional provision that barred all laws prohibiting racial discrimination in housing.

Black Letter Rule: A state constitutional provision that bars laws prohibiting discrimination involves the State in discrimination in violation of the Fourteenth Amendment.

Brentwood Academy v. Tennessee Secondary School Athletic Assn.

Instant Facts: Brentwood Academy (P) claimed civil rights violations after the Tennessee Secondary School Athletic Association (D), a non-profit organization regulating high school athletics, disciplined it for rule violations.

Black Letter Rule: State action may be found if there is such a close nexus between the state and the challenged action that seemingly private behavior may be fairly treated as that of the state itself.

Barron v. Mayor and City Council of Baltimore
(*Wharf Owner*) v. (*City*)
32 U.S. (7 Pet.) 243 (1833)

BILL OF RIGHTS APPLIES ONLY TO FEDERAL GOVERNMENT, NOT TO STATES

■ **INSTANT FACTS** A wharf owner sued the City for taking his property without just compensation in violation of the Fifth Amendment.

■ **BLACK LETTER RULE** The Bill of Rights applies only to the federal government, not to state and local governments.

■ PROCEDURAL BASIS
Not stated.

■ FACTS
Barron (P) owned a wharf. He sued the City of Baltimore (the "City") (D), claiming that the City (D) ruined his wharf by diverting streams and making the water too shallow for boats. Barron (P) claimed the City (D) took his property without just compensation in violation of the Takings Clause of the Fifth Amendment.

■ ISSUE
Does the Fifth Amendment apply to state and local governments?

■ DECISION AND RATIONALE
(Marshall, C.J.) No. The Constitution was designed for the federal government, not for the states. Each state has its own constitution, with its own limitations on government power. The limitations on power in the Fifth Amendment apply only to the federal government. History is clear that many people opposed the Constitution. People feared that the powers granted to the government would be abused. Therefore, amendments were enacted to guard against the encroachments of the federal government, not the states. The amendments do not have any language indicating that they apply to the states. Therefore, the takings clause of the Fifth Amendment limits only the federal government, not the states.

Analysis:
At the time this opinion was written, the case was likely decided correctly. The drafters of the Bill of Rights did intend to make them applicable only to the federal government. As Chief Justice Marshall explained, the states had their own constitutions that checked their powers. It was not until the Fourteenth Amendment was ratified in 1868 that the Bill of Rights was made applicable, at least selectively, to the states.

■ CASE VOCABULARY
TAKINGS CLAUSE: A clause of the Fifth Amendment prohibiting the government from taking private property for public use without just compensation.

Slaughter-House Cases

(*Butchers*) v. (*State of Louisiana*)
83 U.S. (16 Wall.) 36 (1873)

THIRTEENTH AND FOURTEENTH AMENDMENTS APPLY ONLY TO FORMER SLAVES

■ **INSTANT FACTS** Butchers challenged the constitutionality of a state law giving a monopoly to a particular slaughterhouse.

■ **BLACK LETTER RULE** The Thirteenth and Fourteenth Amendments apply only to former slaves.

■ **PROCEDURAL BASIS**

Appeal of decision of state supreme court upholding the constitutionality of a state law.

■ **FACTS**

Louisiana (D) passed a law giving a monopoly in the New Orleans slaughterhouse business to the Crescent City Livestock Landing and Slaughter-House Company (D). The Butchers' Benevolent Association of New Orleans (P) sued, arguing that the law violated the Thirteenth and Fourteenth Amendments because it created involuntary servitude, deprived them of their property without due process, denied them equal protection, and abridged their privileges and Immunities.

■ **ISSUE**

Do the Thirteenth and Fourteenth Amendments make the Bill of Rights applicable to the states?

■ **DECISION AND RATIONALE**

(Miller, J.) No. The legislature has the right and the duty to determine where slaughtering should be conducted. We are now called upon to interpret the Thirteenth and Fourteenth Amendments for the first time. The questions presented here are the most important this Court has ever faced. With respect to the Thirteenth Amendment, slavery was the main cause of the South seceding from the country and of the Civil War. When the war was over and the federal government regained full authority, the emancipation of the slaves was guaranteed in the Constitution, rather than being based only on the proclamation of President Lincoln or the result of the war. To apply the Thirteenth Amendment to all servitudes, rather than just to slavery, requires a great effort. The obvious purpose of the Thirteenth Amendment was to abolish African slavery. Similarly, the Fourteenth Amendment was designed to protect the newly freed slaves from onerous discrimination. While only the Fifteenth Amendment [gave blacks the right to vote] specifically refers to black slaves, the Thirteenth and Fourteenth Amendments were also designed to remedy the grievances of blacks. On the other hand, the Amendments do not apply only to blacks. They forbid enslaving any race, such as Mexicans or Chinese. The language is "No State shall make or enforce any law which shall abridge the privileges or immunities of citizens of the United States." If this clause were meant to protect a citizen of a state against his own state's legislation, then the drafters would have used that language, as they did in the previous sentence. The clause protects only the privileges and immunities of the citizens of the United States, not of the citizens of the states. The fourth article of the Constitution states that "The citizens of each State shall be entitled to all the privileges and immunities of citizens of the several States." Both these clauses protect the same thing. That clause has been interpreted as protecting those rights that are fundamental, such as the right to acquire and possess property and to pursue and obtain happiness and safety. The privileges and immunities of citizens of the States are within the power of the States. The Fourteenth Amendment was not intended to bring the entire domain of civil rights, previously belonging to the States, to the federal government. If it were, Congress could pass laws limiting States' legislative powers. In addition, this Court would be a perpetual censor of all state legislation. But this interpretation would subject the States to the control of Congress and radically change the entire relationship between the States and the federal government and between these governments and the people. We are certain no such result was intended by Congress when it drafted these Amendments nor by the states when they ratified them. Because the privileges and immunities at issue here are left to state governments to protect, we need not here define the privileges and immunities of citizens of the United States. But we do suggest that some of these privileges and immunities include the right to assert any claim one has against the government, to transact business with the government, to seek the government's protections, and to freely access seaports, land offices, and courts. Nonetheless, the rights claimed by the butchers (P) are not privileges and immunities of citizens of the United States within the meaning of the Fourteenth Amendment. Likewise, under no construction of the Due Process Clause of the Fourteenth Amendment can the restraint imposed by Louisiana (D) upon the butchers' (D) trade be considered a deprivation of property within that clause. Similarly, the Equal Protection Clause was intended to prohibit discriminatory laws against newly emancipated slaves. We doubt whether any state action that did not directly discriminate against Negroes would violate the Fourteenth Amendment. It was clearly intended to protect that race in that emergency. Affirmed.

■ DISSENT

(Field, J.) The first clause of the Fourteenth Amendment provides that citizens of a State are also citizens of the United States residing in that State. The fundamental rights, privileges, and immunities belong to all citizens of the United States, and are not dependent on citizenship of any State. These rights are affected by the States, but are not derived from state power. The Fourteenth Amendment assumes that certain privileges and immunities exist and that they may not be abridged by the States. If the Amendment only protects those privileges and immunities that existed before it was adopted, then it was a vain and idle enactment. But if the Amendment refers to the natural and inalienable rights which belong to all citizens, then it has a profound significance.

Analysis:

It is important to remember that this case arose immediately after the end of the Civil War, soon after the Fourteenth Amendment was ratified. The majority's narrow interpretation is based on this historical context, and ignores the Amendment's broad language Since this opinion, however, the Court has rejected the framers' intent and has used the language of the Due Process Clause to protect the right to marry, to use contraception, and to obtain an abortion. Similarly, the Equal Protection Clause has been applied to prohibit discrimination based on race, gender, and alienage. However, the Court's narrow interpretation of the privileges and immunities clause had not been disturbed until 1999 in the case of *Saenz v. Roe*, in which the Court held that the state must provide the same benefits to new residents as to other citizens.

Saenz v. Roe

(California) v. *(Newly Arrived Citizens)*
526 U.S. 489, 119 S.Ct. 1518 (1999)

COURT APPLIES PRIVILEGES OR IMMUNITIES CLAUSE FOR NEARLY FIRST TIME IN HISTORY

■ **INSTANT FACTS** California (D) paid residents who had lived in the state for less than 12 months lower welfare benefits than it paid other residents.

■ **BLACK LETTER RULE** Under the Privileges or Immunities Clause, a State must provide the same benefits to new residents as it does to other residents.

■ **PROCEDURAL BASIS**

Appeal of district court ruling striking down state law as unconstitutional.

■ **FACTS**

In 1992, California (D) enacted a law limiting the welfare benefits available to new residents. A family that has resided in California (D) for less than 12 months may receive only the amount payable by the State in which the family previously resided. Roe (P), representing a class of newly arrived citizens to California (D), challenged the law on equal protection grounds.

■ **ISSUE**

Does a statute providing lower benefits to families who have lived in a State for less than 12 months violate the Privileges or Immunities Clause?

■ **DECISION AND RATIONALE**

(Stevens, J.) Yes. A statute providing lower benefits to families who have lived in a State for less than 12 months violates the Privileges or Immunities Clause of the Fourteenth Amendment ["All persons born or naturalized in the United States, and subject to the jurisdiction thereof, are citizens of the United States and of the State wherein they reside. No State shall make or enforce any law which shall abridge the privileges or immunities of citizens of the United States"]. The right to equal benefits is protected by the new resident's status as a citizen of the State and as a citizen of the United States. Despite different opinions in the *Slaughter-House Cases* [Thirteenth and Fourteenth Amendments apply only to former slaves], it has always been understood that the Privileges or Immunities Clause protects the right to travel. Neither the rational basis test nor an intermediate standard should apply here. California (D) argues that affected citizens have already completed their travel, and so its welfare scheme affects the right to travel only incidentally. But the right to travel includes a citizen's right to be treated equally after residing in a new state. The scheme may not be justified on the ground that it deters welfare applicants from migrating to California (D). The evidence indicates that the number of such persons is small and does not justify a burden on those without such motive.

■ **DISSENT**

(Rehnquist, C.J.) This Court has relied on the Privileges or Immunities Clause only once before, and that decision was overruled five years later. I believe California's (D) law is reasonable and is a good-faith residency requirement.

Saenz v. Roe (Continued)

■ DISSENT

(Thomas, J.) The majority attributes a meaning to the Privileges or Immunities Clause that the framers did not intend. The *Slaughter-House Cases* sapped the Clause of any meaning. However, I believe the demise of the Privileges or Immunities Clause has contributed to the current disarray of our Fourteenth Amendment jurisprudence. In an appropriate case, we should reevaluate the Clause's meaning. We should also consider whether the Clause should displace some of our Fourteenth Amendment jurisprudence. However, I fear that, as the majority applied it, the Privileges or Immunities Clause will become yet another tool for inventing new rights.

Analysis:

Following *Shapiro v. Thompson*, in which the Court struck down state laws requiring new residents to live within a state for one year before being eligible for welfare benefits, the Court's holding here is not surprising. What is surprising is the fact that the Court invalidated California's (D) law under the Privileges or Immunities Clause, rather than under the Equal Protection Clause. Note that, unlike the Due Process Clause and the Equal Protection Clause, the Privileges or Immunities Clause protects only U.S. citizens. Thus, theoretically, a state could impose a durational residency requirement, like the one at issue here, on lawfully resident aliens. However, such a law could still be invalidated under the Equal Protection Clause.

■ CASE VOCABULARY

STANDARD OF REVIEW: The Supreme Court applies different levels of scrutiny depending on the group that a challenged law affects. This different levels of scrutiny are called strict scrutiny (for suspect classifications), intermediate scrutiny (for quasi-suspect classifications), and rational review (for all other classifications).

Twining v. New Jersey

(*Criminal Defendant*) v. (*State*)
211 U.S. 78, 29 S.Ct. 14 (1908)

PROVISIONS OF THE BILL OF RIGHTS MAY APPLY TO STATES IF THEY ARE PART OF DUE PROCESS OF LAW

■ **INSTANT FACTS** A law providing that a jury may draw an unfavorable inference from a criminal defendant's failure to testify was challenged under the Due Process Clause of the Fourteenth Amendment.

■ **BLACK LETTER RULE** Provisions of the Bill of Rights may apply to the States under the Due Process Clause of the Fourteenth Amendment if the provisions are necessary for due process of law.

■ **PROCEDURAL BASIS**

Appeal of criminal conviction based on violation of civil rights.

■ **FACTS**

New Jersey (P) law provided that a jury may be instructed that it may draw an unfavorable inference from a criminal defendant's failure to testify. Twining (D) challenged this law under the Due Process Clause and the Privileges and Immunities Clause of the Fourteenth Amendment.

■ **ISSUE**

Does the Fourteenth Amendment make the right against self-incrimination applicable to the States?

■ **DECISION AND RATIONALE**

(Moody, J.) No. When the Constitution was drafted, the exemption from compulsory testimony was part of the common law and was an important privilege. It was not included in the original Constitution, but was included in the Bill of Rights. Every State except New Jersey (P) and Iowa have included the right in their constitutions, and New Jersey (P) and Iowa include it in their laws. Civil rights considered fundamental and inalienable were left untouched by the Privileges and Immunities Clause of the Fourteenth Amendment. Twining (D) claims the compelled self-incrimination was a denial of due process of law. It is possible that some of the personal rights safeguarded by the Bill of Rights against national action may also be safeguarded against state action under the Due Process Clause of the Fourteenth Amendment because they are included in the conception of due process of law. Due process of law may be determined by looking at the law of England before our ancestors emigrated and by asking whether something is a fundamental principle of liberty and justice which inheres to the very idea of a free government. The right against self-incrimination does not rate as an immutable principle of justice which is the inalienable possession of every citizen of a free government. It does not rank with the right to a hearing before condemnation, the immunity from arbitrary power not acting by general laws, and the inviolability of private property.

Analysis:

In *Twining,* although the Court held that the specific right at issue was not enforceable against the states, the case is significant because it was the first time the Court held that provisions of the Bill of

Twining v. New Jersey (Continued)

Rights could be applied to the States if the provisions were incorporated into the Due Process Clause of the Fourteenth Amendment. Thus, the debate centers on what rights are necessary for due process, and are therefore incorporated into the Due Process Clause and applicable to the states, and which ones are not. The debate involves three issues: the framers' Intent, the relationship of the states to the federal government, and the proper role of the judiciary in choosing which rights should be incorporated. The Court has expressly held that the First Amendment's protection of free speech and the Sixth Amendment's right to counsel in a capital case are applicable to the states. But while the Court has never agreed that the entire Bill of Rights is incorporated in the Due Process Clause, it has over time held almost all of the individual provisions to be incorporated.

■ **CASE VOCABULARY**

DUE PROCESS OF LAW: The idea that laws and legal proceedings must be fair. The Fourteenth Amendment guarantees that the government cannot take away a person's basic rights to life, liberty or property, without due process of law.

Duncan v. Louisiana

(Batterer) v. *(State)*
391 U.S. 145, 88 S.Ct. 1444 (1968)

SUPREME COURT HOLDS THAT SIXTH AMENDMENT RIGHT TO JURY TRIAL IS APPLICABLE TO STATES

■ **INSTANT FACTS** A man charged with simple battery, punishable by up to two years in prison, was denied the right to a jury trial and claimed he was therefore denied due process of law.

■ **BLACK LETTER RULE** The Sixth Amendment right to a jury trial is fundamental and is applicable to the states pursuant to the Due Process Clause of the Fourteenth Amendment.

■ PROCEDURAL BASIS

Appeal of criminal conviction based on denial of jury trial.

■ FACTS

Duncan (D) was convicted of simple battery, a misdemeanor. Duncan (D) had requested a jury trial, but his request was denied because, in Louisiana (P), jury trials are allowed only where sentences of capital punishment or hard labor may be imposed. Duncan (D) claimed the denial of a jury trial violated his Fourteenth Amendment right to due process of law.

■ ISSUE

Does the Fourteenth Amendment Due Process Clause make the Sixth Amendment right to a jury trial applicable to the States?

■ DECISION AND RATIONALE

(White, J.) Yes. Under the Fourteenth Amendment, the States may not "deprive any person of life, liberty, or property, without due process of law." To determine what constitutes due process of law, this Court has looked to the Bill of Rights for guidance. For example, the Court has held that the Due Process Clause protects the right to compensation for property taken by a state, the First Amendment rights of speech, press, and religion, the Fourth Amendment right to be free from unreasonable searches and seizures, the Fifth Amendment right to be free of compelled self-incrimination, the Sixth Amendment rights to counsel, public counsel, confrontation of opposing witnesses, and compulsory process of witnesses. This Court has based its determination as to whether a Fifth or Sixth Amendment right is applicable to the States under the Fourteenth Amendment on whether the right is a "fundamental principle of liberty and justice which lie at the base of all our civil and political institutions," whether it is "basic in our system of jurisprudence," and whether it is a "fundamental right, essential to a fair trial." We believe that trial by jury in criminal cases is fundamental to our scheme of justice. A jury trial is meant to prevent oppression by the government, such as a corrupt or overzealous prosecutor or a biased, eccentric judge. The right to a jury trial reflects the reluctance to trust a judge with power over a citizen's life or liberty and fear of arbitrary law enforcement. The right to a jury trial is protected under the Due Process Clause of the Fourteenth Amendment and must therefore be respected by the States.

Duncan v. Louisiana (Continued)

■ CONCURRENCE

(Black, J.) I believe that the entire Fourteenth Amendment, including the Due Process Clause and the Privileges and Immunities Clause, make the entire Bill of Rights applicable to the States. What greater "privilege" of American citizenship can there be than those protected by the Bill of Rights? I am not bothered by the fact that applying the Bill of Rights to the States interferes with federalism by preventing the States from trying novel experiments. I do not believe that the States should be able to experiment with the protections provided by the Bill of Rights. Although I believe that the drafters intended total incorporation of the Bill of Rights to the States, I have supported selective incorporation. Selective incorporation keeps judges from roaming at will regarding policies outside the Bill of Rights and has already made most of the Bill of Rights applicable to the States.

Analysis:

This case summarizes the results of the selective incorporation approach. Indeed, through constant selective incorporation, the total incorporationists have nearly won the war. Nearly all of the Bill of Rights guarantees pertaining to criminal proceedings have been imposed on the states. Only five provisions do not apply to the states; the Second Amendment right to bear arms, the Third Amendment prohibition on having soldiers quartered in one's home, the Fifth Amendment right to a grand jury indictment, the Seventh Amendment right to a jury trial in a civil case, and the Eighth Amendment's prohibition of excessive fines. While the other rights set forth in the Bill of Rights do apply to the states, they sometimes apply in a different form. For example, while a 12-person jury is required in federal criminal cases, a state criminal case may have only six jurors. In addition, while a unanimous jury is required to convict in a federal criminal case, states may allow a conviction based on a 10–2 jury vote.

■ CASE VOCABULARY

SELECTIVE INCORPORATION DOCTRINE: The view that provisions of the Bill of Rights should be selectively applicable to the States under the Due Process Clause of the Fourteenth Amendment, as opposed to complete incorporation.

The Civil Rights Cases

(*Accommodations Owners*) v. (*U.S.*)
109 U.S. 3, 3 S.Ct. 18 (1883)

FOURTEENTH AMENDMENT DOES NOT PROHIBIT DISCRIMINATION BY PRIVATE CITIZENS

■ **INSTANT FACTS** Owners of theaters and hotels were prosecuted for discriminating against African Americans.

■ **BLACK LETTER RULE** Under the Fourteenth Amendment, Congress does not have the power to pass laws prohibiting discrimination by private citizens.

■ PROCEDURAL BASIS
Appeal from criminal convictions for violation of federal civil rights statute.

■ FACTS
The Civil Rights Act of 1875 subjects any person who denies another person full and equal enjoyment of inns, public transportation, theaters, and other places of amusement to criminal prosecution. Stanley (D) and Nichols (D) were charged with refusing to allow persons of color to stay at their inns. Ryan (D) and Singleton (D) were charged with denying African-Americans entry to theaters.

■ ISSUE
Under the Fourteenth Amendment, does Congress have the power to pass laws prohibiting discrimination by private citizens?

■ DECISION AND RATIONALE
(Bradley, J.) No. The Fourteenth Amendment prohibits only state action. The Amendment gives Congress the power to enforce the Fourteenth Amendment by appropriate legislation. This legislation may correct the effects only of prohibited state action. The Amendment does not give Congress the power to regulate private rights. The Civil Rights Act makes no reference to any violation of the Fourteenth Amendment by the States. It does not correct any constitutional wrong committed by the States. Therefore, it steps into the domain of local jurisprudence. If this law were permitted, it is difficult to see where it would stop.

■ DISSENT
(Harlan, J.) The majority opinion is too narrow and artificial. It sacrifices the spirit of the Fourteenth Amendment by looking only at the words. The Court ignores the full effect that the Amendment was intended to have.

Analysis:
As this case clearly states, the general rule is that the Constitution applies only to state action. However, there are a few exceptions. First, the Thirteenth Amendment prohibits slavery by private citizens. In addition, Congress has passed laws that prohibit discrimination in employment and public accommoda-

The Civil Rights Cases (Continued)

tions. Under the "public functions exception" to the state-action doctrine, a private entity must comply with the Constitution if it is performing a task that has traditionally been performed by the government, such as operating a company-owned town or running elections. The majority here creates a clear, bright-line rule: The Fourteenth Amendment is inapplicable unless there is overt state action. Justice Harlan's dissent would have allowed Congress to prevent private discrimination. However, the line that he draws is not very clear.

■ CASE VOCABULARY

STATE ACTION: Government (federal, state, or local) legislation or action, including the actions of executive and judicial officers.

Marsh v. Alabama

(Jehovah's Witness) v. (State)
326 U.S. 501, 66 S.Ct. 276 (1946)

CONSTITUTION APPLES TO PRIVATE ENTITY THAT ACTS LIKE A GOVERNMENT BODY

■ **INSTANT FACTS** A Jehovah's Witness was arrested for trespass after attempting to distribute religious literature in a privately-owned town.

■ **BLACK LETTER RULE** A private entity that acts like a governmental body and performs a public function is subject to the Constitution.

■ PROCEDURAL BASIS

Appeal of criminal conviction to U.S. Supreme Court challenging constitutionality of application of state statute.

■ FACTS

The Gulf Shipbuilding Corporation (Gulf) owned the town of Chickasaw, Alabama, including the streets, sidewalks, sewers, and a business block. The town was freely accessible and used by the general public. It was indistinguishable from any other town, except for the fact that Gulf held the title. Gulf paid the town's policeman. Marsh (D), a Jehovah's Witness, attempted to distribute religious literature in Chickasaw. She was warned that she could not distribute the literature without a permit, and that she would not be issued a permit. She refused to leave the sidewalk and Chickasaw. She was arrested and charged with violating Alabama's (P) anti-trespassing statute. Marsh (D) argued that applying the statute to her violated the First and Fourteenth Amendments. Marsh (D) was convicted.

■ ISSUE

Is the Constitution applicable to the actions of a privately-owned town?

■ DECISION AND RATIONALE

(Black, J.) Yes. If Chickasaw were a municipal corporation, clearly Marsh's (D) conviction would have to be reversed. Neither a State nor a municipality may bar the distribution of religious or political literature on its sidewalks. The fact that a private corporation runs the town is irrelevant. It is not the same, as Alabama (P) argues, as the right of a homeowner to regulate his guests. The more an owner opens up his property to the public, the more the Constitution is applicable. Even if Chickasaw is privately-owned, the channels of communication must remain free. Chickasaw functions like any other town. Many people in the U.S. live in company-owned towns. These people are free citizens of their State and of the U.S., and must be informed to make good decisions. When we balance the Constitutional rights of property owners against those of people to enjoy free speech, the latter occupies a preferred position. The fact that the property was privately-owned does not justify restricting fundamental liberties. Alabama's (P) attempt to punish Marsh (D) cannot stand. Reversed.

Analysis:

This case is significant because it established the "public function" test. Under this test, a private entity engaging in an activity that has traditionally and exclusively been performed by the government is held to be subject to the Constitution. Because the government could engage in nearly any activity, it is sometimes difficult to determine whether a function is a public one. Note that in *Marsh*, the Court balances Gulf's constitutional rights against Marsh's (D) First Amendment right to free speech.

■ CASE VOCABULARY

MUNICIPAL CORPORATION: A city, town, village, etc., that operates under a corporate charter granted by the state.

Jackson v. Metropolitan Edison Co.

(Customer) v. (Public Utility)
419 U.S. 345, 95 S.Ct. 449 (1974)

SUPREME COURT REQUIRES SUFFICIENTLY CLOSE NEXUS BETWEEN STATE AND CHALLENGED ACTION TO FIND STATE ACTION

■ **INSTANT FACTS** A customer of an electric company claimed the company performed a public function and therefore could not shut off her electricity without adequate notice and a hearing pursuant to the Due Process Clause of the Fourteenth Amendment.

■ **BLACK LETTER RULE** The actions of a private entity are not considered state action unless there is a sufficiently close nexus between the State and the challenged action.

■ PROCEDURAL BASIS

Appeal in action for damages in Fourteenth Amendment Due Process Clause claim.

■ FACTS

Metropolitan Edison Co. (Metropolitan) (D) is a privately-owned corporation with an exclusive license from the State of Pennsylvania to deliver electricity to a certain service area. It is subject to extensive state regulation. It has the right to discontinue service to any customer on reasonable notice who fails to pay bills. Catherine Jackson (P) received electricity from Metropolitan (D) until her account was terminated for failure to pay bills. A new account was opened under the name of James Dodson, another occupant of Jackson's (P) home. After Dodson left the residence, no payments were made. Jackson (P) claimed she received no bills during this period. After Metropolitan's (D) employees visited Jackson (P) a couple of times to inquire about Dodson's whereabouts and to check the meter, Jackson (P) requested that an account be opened in the name of her 12-year-old son, Robert. Four days later, without further notice to Jackson (P), Metropolitan (D) disconnected her service. Jackson (P) sued Metropolitan (D) claiming that Metropolitan (D) was serving a public function and, therefore, could not disconnect her electricity without adequate notice and a hearing pursuant to the Due Process Clause of the Fourteenth Amendment. The trial court held for Metropolitan (D). Jackson (P) appealed.

■ ISSUE

Is operating a public utility state action?

■ DECISION AND RATIONALE

(Rehnquist, J.) No. It is well established that private action is immune from the Fourteenth Amendment. However, it is not easy to determine whether particular conduct is private or state action. Metropolitan (D) is a private company but its business is subject to extensive state regulation. However, extensive government regulation does not make conduct state action. We must look at whether there is a sufficiently close nexus between the State and the challenged action so that the action of the private actor may be fairly treated as that of the State itself. First, the fact that Metropolitan (D) may have had a monopoly does not determine whether Metropolitan's (D) actions were state action. Second, the fact that Metropolitan (D) performed an essential public service required under Pennsylvania law to be supplied on a reasonably continuous basis does not make Metropolitan's (D) business a public

Jackson v. Metropolitan Edison Co. (Continued)

function. Metropolitan (D) is not exercising a power traditionally associated with the government, such as eminent domain. Pennsylvania law requires utilities to provide continuous service; it does not require the State to do so. We decline Jackson's (P) invitation to expand the public function doctrine to include all businesses "affected with the public interest." Doctors, lawyers, and grocers are all regulated by the government and provide essential goods and services affected with the public interest, yet we do not believe they are state actors. Thus, we find that Metropolitan (D) is not a state actor merely because it was a heavily regulated, privately-owned utility, enjoying a partial monopoly in supplying electricity and terminated Jackson's (P) service in a manner that was permissible under state law. The State of Pennsylvania is not sufficiently connected with Metropolitan's (D) actions to make Metropolitan (D) subject to the Fourteenth Amendment.

■ DISSENT

(Marshall, J.) I find state action here based on the fact that Metropolitan (D) has a monopoly, is extensively regulated, receives state cooperation in myriad ways, and has received state approval for its mode of service termination. Our prior cases found state action based on these factors. I disagree with the majority on three separate grounds. First, the State need not "order" an action to make it state action. We have previously held that state authorization and approval is enough. Second, the majority gives short shrift to the extensive Interaction between Metropolitan (D) and the State. Third, the State has approved Metropolitan's (D) termination procedures. The fact that Metropolitan (D) provides an essential public service that is often supplied by governments weighs heavily for me. The Court admits that state action might be present if the activity were traditionally associated with the government. But it undercuts its position by stating that the activity is not a public function if the State does not require that it be governmentally operated.

Analysis:

Here the Court determines whether an activity is a public function based on whether the activity has traditionally and exclusively been performed by the government. It also looks at whether there is a sufficiently close nexus between the state and the challenged activity. This is very different, and much narrower, than the test used in *Marsh v. Alabama*, where the Court weighed the constitutional rights of the private property owner against those of the Jehovah's Witness. Under the Court's holding here, there are very few public functions that subject a private actor to constitutional limitations. Running elections and operating towns appear to be the only two activities that qualify as public functions.

Terry v. Adams

(Not stated) v. (Not stated)
345 U.S. 461, 73 S.Ct. 809 (1953)

PRIVATE ORGANIZATION'S PRIMARY ELECTION CONSTITUTES PUBLIC FUNCTION

■ **INSTANT FACTS** A private political party that excludes members based on race, and that controls the ultimate outcome of elections, was held to be engaging in state action for purposes of the Fifteenth Amendment.

■ **BLACK LETTER RULE** A private political party that controls the outcome of elections engages in state action thereby making it subject to the Fifteenth Amendment.

■ PROCEDURAL BASIS
Appeal of action claiming violation of civil rights.

■ FACTS
The Jaybird Democratic Association (Jaybird) is a political party whose members are all white. Jaybird endorses candidates and holds primary elections. Jaybird's expenses are paid for by the candidates for office in its primaries. With few exceptions, all successful Jaybird candidates have entered Democratic primaries and the general elections and won without opposition. Jaybird has been the dominant political group in the county since 1889. Jaybird's president admitted that the purpose of the party was to exclude blacks from voting and to escape the Fifteenth Amendment's command that all citizens may vote, regardless of their race. Jaybird argues that the Fifteenth Amendment does not apply to it because it is not regulated by the State and is not a political party, but a self-governing voluntary club.

■ ISSUE
Does a private political party that controls elections engage in state action, thereby making it subject to the Fifteenth Amendment?

■ DECISION AND RATIONALE
(Black, J.) Yes. The Fifteenth Amendment bans racial discrimination in voting by the government. It is clear that barring blacks from voting would be unconstitutional if done by the county. Jaybird produces the equivalent of a prohibited election. For a State to allow this defeats the purposes of the Fifteenth Amendment. The county-operated primary in which the Jaybird candidate runs ratifies this unconstitutional result. It is immaterial that the State does not control the Jaybird primary. The Jaybird primary is the only part of the election that determines who governs in the county. The total effect strips blacks of every vestige of influence in selecting their local officials.

Analysis:
About ten years before *Terry*, in *Smith v. Allwright*, the Court held that running elections is a state function and that a primary system established by a state political party that included only whites violated the Fifteenth Amendment. The difference in *Terry* is that Jaybird held private pre-primary elections to determine who would run in the state-sponsored primary. Note that there is no majority

Terry v. Adams (Continued)

opinion in *Terry*. However, the Justices agreed that, although there had been no formal connection between Jaybird and the state, holding an election is a public function that subjected Jaybird to the Fifteenth Amendment. Note also that the Court relies on state ratification of Jaybird's activities by allowing Jaybird's candidates to run in (and win) the county elections, which raises the issue of state encouragement or support of private action.

Evans v. Newton

(*White Park Managers*) v. (*City*)
382 U.S. 296, 86 S.Ct. 486 (1966)

OPERATING A PARK IS A PUBLIC FUNCTION; BLACKS MAY NOT BE CONSTITUTIONALLY EXCLUDED

■ **INSTANT FACTS** A will provision leaving land for a park for whites only was challenged under the Equal Protection Clause of the Fourteenth Amendment.

■ **BLACK LETTER RULE** Operating a park constitutes a public function; thus the owner is subject to the Fourteenth Amendment.

■ **PROCEDURAL BASIS**

Appeal by intervenors in case alleging that enforcing a will provision violates the Fourteenth Amendment.

■ **FACTS**

In his will, Senator Bacon devised land to the City of Macon, Georgia (D), to be used as a park for whites only. He wanted the park to be controlled by an all-white Board of Managers (P). The City (D) kept the park segregated for a few years, but then let blacks use it, claiming that it could not constitutionally manage the park on a segregated basis. Members of the Board of Managers (P) sued the City (D) and the residuary beneficiaries of Bacon's estate (D) asking that title to the park be transferred to private people so that it can be used only by whites. The City (D) argued that it could not legally enforce racial segregation in the park. Several black Macon citizens (P) intervened, asking the court to refuse to appoint private trustees. Other Bacon heirs intervened asking that the park revert to the Bacon estate. The City (D) then resigned as trustee. The trial court appointed private trustees. The black intervenors appealed to the Supreme Court of Georgia, which affirmed the trial court's decision and held that Bacon had the right to give his property to whites only.

■ **ISSUE**

Does operating a park constitute a public function subjecting the owner to the Fourteenth Amendment?

■ **DECISION AND RATIONALE**

(Douglas, J.) Yes. It is not always easy to determine whether something is state action or private action. If a testator wanted to leave a school for the use by one race only, and the State was not involved in supervising, controlling, or managing the school, there would be no constitutional violation. However, this park is different. For years, the City (D) maintained it and granted it a tax exemption. This momentum as a public facility is not dissipated ipso facto by appointing private trustees. If the City (D) remains entwined in managing the park, it remains subject to the Fourteenth Amendment. Where the tradition of municipal control becomes firmly established, substituting private trustees does not transfer the park from the public to the private sector. Even a private park provides a municipal service. A golf club, social center or school may be racially oriented. However, a park is more like a fire department that serves the entire community. Mass recreation in parks is plainly in the public domain. State courts that aid private parties to perform a public function on a segregated basis implicate the State.

Analysis:

The Court here based its decision on two interesting grounds. First, the Court discussed the unique municipal nature of parks and the fact that operating a park is an essential public function that cannot be delegated to a private party to avoid constitutional restrictions. The Court also discussed the fact that state action may exist if the judiciary enforces actions by private citizens that would be unconstitutional if done by the state. Thus the Court held that any state court that helps the private trustees operate the park on a segregated basis implicates the state. It is interesting to note what happened to Bacon's land after this case was decided. The trial court terminated the trust and allowed the land to revert to Bacon's heirs to use for purposes other than a park. In *Evans v. Abney,* the Supreme Court held that terminating the trust and returning the land to the heirs was not unconstitutional because it was not based on any racial restrictions.

■ CASE VOCABULARY

DEVISE: To assign or transmit property by a will.

IPSO FACTO: Latin for "by the fact itself" or "by the very nature of the deed."

RESIDUARY BENEFICIARY: A person entitled to the remainder of an estate after the payment of all debts, charges, devises, and bequests.

TESTATOR: A person who makes a will.

Amalgamated Food Employees Union Local 590 v. Logan Valley Plaza, Inc.

(Union) v. (Shopping Center Owner)
391 U.S. 308, 88 S.Ct. 1601 (1968)

COURT HOLDS SHOPPING CENTER SERVES PUBLIC FUNCTION; FIRST AMENDMENT RIGHTS PREVAIL

■ **INSTANT FACTS** After a shopping center owner barred union members from picketing on its property, the union claimed the shopping center served a public function and that its First Amendment rights prevailed.

■ **BLACK LETTER RULE** Shopping centers serve a public function and, therefore, the First Amendment applies.

■ PROCEDURAL BASIS

Appeal in case against property owner alleging violation of First Amendment rights.

■ FACTS

Logan Valley Plaza, Inc. (Logan) (D) owned a mall occupied by Weis Markets, Inc. (Weis) (D), a supermarket, and Sears, Roebuck and Co. (Sears). The mall was open to the public. Weis (D) employed only nonunion employees. Weis (D) posted a sign outside its building prohibiting trespassing or soliciting by anyone other than its employees. Amalgamated Food Employees Union Local 590 (Amalgamated) (P) began picketing Weis (D) in Weis's (D) parcel pickup area and parking lot.

■ ISSUE

Does operating a shopping center constitute a public function subjecting the owner to the First Amendment?

■ DECISION AND RATIONALE

(Marshall, J.) Yes. Peaceful picketing in a location open to the public is generally protected by the First Amendment. If the property were owned by a municipality, Amalgamated (P) could not be barred from exercising its First Amendment rights there. In *Marsh v. Alabama,* we held that a privately-owned business block may be treated for First Amendment purposes as if it were publically owned. The business block in *Marsh* is strikingly similar to the shopping center here. We see no reason why the result here should be different than the result in *Marsh* just because the property surrounding the mall is not privately owned. The roadways and sidewalks leading through the mall are the functional equivalent of streets and sidewalks in a normal town. All we hold here is that because the shopping center is a community business block and is freely accessible to the public, the State may not use its trespass laws to exclude people wishing to exercise their First Amendment rights. Logan (D) may make reasonable regulations governing the exercise of First Amendment rights on its property and prevent interference with the use of the property, so long as those regulations are like those a government body may impose. The more an owner opens his property for public use, the more the owner's rights become limited by the rights of those who use it.

Amalgamated Food Employees Union Local 590 v. Logan Valley Plaza, Inc. (Continued)

Analysis:

This case is the first of a series of three addressing First Amendment rights in shopping centers. Here, the Court held that a private shopping center is like the company town in *Marsh*, so, as in *Marsh*, the First Amendment applies. In *Lloyd Corp. v. Tanner,* the Court distinguished *Amalgamated* and held that there are no First Amendment rights in a shopping center if the speech does not relate to the store owners' activities. Finally, in *Hudgens v. National Labor Relations Board,* the Court simplified the issue and flatly held that the First Amendment does not apply to shopping center owners. So, the Court overruled *Amalgamated.*

Lloyd Corp. v. Tanner

(Shopping Center Owner) v. (Handbill Distributors)
407 U.S. 551, 92 S.Ct. 2219 (1972)

FREE SPEECH RIGHTS DO NOT EXIST IN SHOPPING CENTER IF SPEECH IS NOT RELATED TO ACTIVITIES AT SHOPPING CENTER

■ **INSTANT FACTS** Anti-war demonstrators told to leave a shopping center sued the shopping center owners for violating their First Amendment rights.

■ **BLACK LETTER RULE** There are no First Amendment rights in a private shopping center if the speech at issue is not related to the activities at the shopping center.

■ PROCEDURAL BASIS

Appeal in First Amendment rights case of ruling against property owner.

■ FACTS

Lloyd Corp., Ltd. (Lloyd) (D) owns a shopping center containing about 50 acres bounded by four public streets. Several other public streets with adjacent sidewalks cross the shopping center. The shopping center has parking facilities, private sidewalks, escalators, gardens, an auditorium, and a skating rink. Lloyd (D) has a strictly enforced policy prohibiting people from distributing handbills within the mall. Five young people (collectively Tanner) (P) [hippies!] distributed invitations to a meeting to resist the draft and the Vietnam War. The lower courts held in favor of Tanner (P).

■ ISSUE

Does operating a shopping center constitute a public function subjecting the owner to the First Amendment?

■ DECISION AND RATIONALE

(Powell, J.) No. This case is distinguishable from *Amalgamated Food Employees Union Local 590 v. Logan Valley Plaza, Inc.* [shopping centers serve a public function and, therefore, the First Amendment applies]. The holding in that case was limited to picketing that was directly related to the use to which the shopping center property was being put. In addition, the picketers there had no other reasonable opportunities to convey their message to their intended audience. Here, the handbills had no relationship to the shopping center. Tanner (P) could have distributed them on any public street or park. Tanner (P) also could have distributed them to mall patrons on public sidewalks and streets as the patrons left the mall, which is what Tanner (P) did when he was asked to leave the mall. Therefore, where adequate alternative avenues of communication existed, it would have been an unwarranted infringement of Lloyd's (D) property rights to require it to yield to Tanner's (P) First Amendment rights. It must be remembered that the First and Fourteenth Amendments apply only to state action. Property does not lose its private character merely because the public is invited to use it. A free-standing store is not public merely because the public is invited to shop there. The fact that the shopping center is large does not change this analysis. Reversed.

Analysis:

This case distinguishes *Amalgamated* and holds that under these facts, people do not have First Amendment rights in a private shopping center. Note that the case is very fact specific. The Court does not just look generally at whether a shopping center serves a public function. Instead, the Court bases its holding largely on the content of the communication. Note also that under the First Amendment, a state may not regulate speech based on its content. This is a key basis for the holding in the next case, *Hudgens v. National Labor Relations Board,* where the Court flatly held that a shopping center does not serve a public function and the First Amendment is inapplicable.

■ CASE VOCABULARY

DEDICATION: The appropriation of property to public use.

Hudgens v. National Labor Relations Board

(*Shopping Center Owner*) v. (*Picketers*)
424 U.S. 507, 96 S.Ct. 1029 (1976)

PEOPLE ENTERING PRIVATELY-OWNED SHOPPING CENTER HAVE NO FIRST AMENDMENT RIGHTS

■ **INSTANT FACTS** Labor union members picketing in a privately-owned mall claimed their First Amendment rights to free speech were violated when they were threatened with criminal trespass prosecution.

■ **BLACK LETTER RULE** The First Amendment does not apply to people entering privately-owned shopping centers.

■ **PROCEDURAL BASIS**

Appeal of administrative decision by National Labor Relations Board.

■ **FACTS**

A group of labor union members (P) engaged in peaceful picketing in a privately-owned shopping center owned by Scott Hudgens (D). The union members (P) were protesting the failure of the Butler Shoe Co., a company with a store in the shopping center, to agree to union demands in contract negotiations. Hudgens' agent (D) threatened the picketers (P) with arrest for criminal trespass if they did not leave the mall and the parking lot. The picketers (P) left, came back, were threatened again, and left for good.

■ **ISSUE**

Does operating a shopping center constitute a public function subjecting the owner to the First Amendment?

■ **DECISION AND RATIONALE**

(Stewart, J.) No. The constitutional guarantee of free speech applies only against the government. While some members of the Court may think that *Amalgamated Food Employees Union Local 590 v. Logan Valley Plaza, Inc.* [shopping centers serve public function and, therefore, First Amendment applies] was rightly decided, that holding was rejected in *Lloyd Corp. v. Tanner* [no First Amendment rights in shopping center if speech at issue is not related to shopping center activities]. If a shopping center were the functional equivalent of a municipality, then the content of the speech would not be relevant as it was in *Lloyd*. Municipalities are not permitted to discriminate in the regulation of expression based on the content of that expression. Accordingly, if the respondents in *Lloyd* did not have a First Amendment right to distribute handbills protesting the Vietnam War, the union members here did not have a First Amendment right to enter the shopping center to advertise their strike against the Butler Shoe Co.

Analysis:

Here the Court put to rest the conflict between *Amalgamated* and *Lloyd*. The Court expressly overruled *Amalgamated* and held, finally, that operating a shopping center does not involve a public function and, therefore, the First Amendment is inapplicable. Note that states are free to pass laws protecting the free

Hudgens v. National Labor Relations Board (Continued)

speech rights of persons entering shopping centers. For example, in *PruneYard Shopping Center v. Robins*, the Supreme Court held that a state may expand its protection of civil liberties beyond those provided by the federal Constitution. It is only the First Amendment of the federal Constitution that is not applicable to private shopping center owners.

Shelley v. Kraemer
(*Black Property Buyers*) v. (*White Neighbors*)
334 U.S. 1, 68 S.Ct. 836 (1948)

JUDICIAL ENFORCEMENT OF DISCRIMINATORY PRIVATE AGREEMENT CONSTITUTES STATE ACTION FOR FOURTEENTH AMENDMENT PURPOSES

■ **INSTANT FACTS** A black person bought property in violation of a restrictive covenant providing that only whites could own or occupy the property. White neighbors sued to enforce the covenant.

■ **BLACK LETTER RULE** Judicial enforcement of a private agreement constitutes state action for purposes of the Fourteenth Amendment.

■ **PROCEDURAL BASIS**
Appeal of judgment for injunctive relief in Fourteenth Amendment equal protection claim.

■ **FACTS**
In 1911, 30 property owners signed an agreement stating that for the next 50 years they would not sell or rent their property to anyone who was not white. In 1945, Shelley (D), a black person, bought a parcel covered by the restrictive covenant with no actual knowledge of it. Owners of other parcels covered by the covenant (collectively Kraemer) (P) sued Shelley (D) seeking an injunction divesting Shelley (D) from title to the property and revesting title in the immediate grantor. The lower court held in favor of Kraemer (P).

■ **ISSUE**
Is judicial enforcement of a restrictive covenant state action for purposes of the Fourteenth Amendment?

■ **DECISION AND RATIONALE**
(Vinson, C.J.) Yes. The Fourteenth Amendment protects the right to acquire, enjoy, own, and dispose of property. The restrictive covenant at issue here would clearly be unconstitutional if imposed by statute. However, these are private agreements. Participation by the state consists of judicially enforcing the agreements. The purposes of the agreements were obtained by judicial enforcement. This Court has long held that judicial action is considered state action for purposes of the Fourteenth Amendment. This is true even in cases in which the issue was not the procedural unfairness of the judicial proceedings. The actions of state courts in enforcing substantive common law rights may violate the Fourteenth Amendment even if the proceedings rigorously conformed with due process. In any event, it has never been suggested that state court action is immune from the Fourteenth Amendment. Here, there has been state action in enforcing the restrictive covenants, and this action has denied Shelley (D) equal protection. If there were no state action here, Shelley (D) would not have been prevented from fully enjoying property rights available to other members of the community.

Analysis:
It makes sense that judicial action should be considered state action for Fourteenth Amendment purposes. It certainly is considered state action for procedural purposes. Otherwise, state courts could

Shelley v. Kraemer (Continued)

discriminate and deny certain races due process of law. However, here the Court took a further leap and held that, while private people are free to discriminate with impunity, they cannot use the courts to enforce their discrimination. The breadth of this holding is infinite. Nearly all private activity can be made the subject of a court case. If state courts cannot enforce discriminatory private agreements, then private individuals cannot engage in racial discrimination. An agreement that is unenforceable is the functional equivalent of no agreement at all. Later Court cases suggest that there is a limit to what is state action under *Shelley*. For example, if a property owner has another person removed from his property for racial reasons, judicial enforcement of the trespass laws would not violate the Fourteenth Amendment because the trespass laws are racially neutral.

Lugar v. Edmondson Oil Co.

(*Debtor*) v. (*Creditor*)
457 U.S. 922, 102 S.Ct. 2744 (1982)

USING COURT AND SHERIFF TO EXECUTE ATTACHMENT MAY VIOLATE DEBTOR'S DUE PROCESS RIGHTS

■ **INSTANT FACTS** A debtor sued a creditor for violating his due process rights when the creditor obtained an ex parte writ of attachment and had a sheriff seize the debtor's property.

■ **BLACK LETTER RULE** Using the court and government officials to seize property without due process of law involves state action for purposes of the Fourteenth Amendment.

■ **PROCEDURAL BASIS**

Appeal of judgment for damages in civil rights action.

■ **FACTS**

Lugar (P) owed money to a supplier, Edmondson Oil Co. (Edmondson) (D). In a state action, Edmondson (D) sued Lugar on the debt. As part of that action, Edmondson (D) sought an ex parte writ of attachment of Lugar's (P) property, alleging only its belief that Lugar (P) was disposing of his property to defeat his creditors. The court granted the writ of attachment, which the County Sheriff then executed, causing Lugar's (P) property to be sequestered. The court later held a hearing on the propriety of the attachment. The court dismissed the attachment based on Edmondson's (D) failure to establish the proper statutory grounds. Lugar (P) then sued Edmondson (D) for acting with the State to deprive him of his property without due process of law. The Court of Appeals held in favor of Edmondson (D).

■ **ISSUE**

Does obtaining and executing an ex parte writ of attachment constitute state action under the Fourteenth Amendment?

■ **DECISION AND RATIONALE**

(White, J.) Yes. The state action requirement recognizes the fact that generally speaking only governments can violate the Constitution. It also protects the State from responsibility for conduct for which they cannot be blamed. This requires courts to respect the limits of their own power against state governments and private interests. To fairly attribute conduct involving the deprivation of a right to the State, we apply a two-part approach. First, the deprivation must be caused by the exercise of a right or privilege created by the State. Second, the responsible party must be a state actor. Here, the procedural scheme by which Edmondson (D) obtained the writ of attachment is the product of state action. Edmondson's (D) joint participation with the State to seize the property made Edmondson (D) a state actor for purposes of the Fourteenth Amendment. The Court of Appeals was wrong in holding that something more than using state officials was required to invoke state action. Edmondson (D) was acting under color of law in participating in the deprivation of Lugar's (P) rights. Reversed.

Lugar v. Edmondson Oil Co. (Continued)

Analysis:

This case reflects the broad holding in *Shelley v. Kraemer*. Here, the Court held that the involvement of the court and county sheriff in enforcing a writ of attachment amounted to state action. On the other hand, in *Flagg Brothers, Inc. v. Brooks*, the Court held that no state action existed when a warehouseman sold a debtor's goods when the debtor failed to pay the storage charges, even though a state law permitted the sale. Taking a debtor's property is not a public function. If a creditor takes the property on its own, no state action is involved. However, if, as in *Lugar*, the creditor obtains the assistance of government officials, state action is involved. The use of pre-judgment writs of attachment is not uncommon in disputes between debtors and creditors.

■ CASE VOCABULARY

EX PARTE: Latin for "by or for one party" or "by one side." Refers to situations in which only one party appears before a judge. Sometimes judges issue temporary orders ex parte when there is an emergency.

LEVY: To seize or attach property by judicial order.

WRIT OF ATTACHMENT: A pre-judgment judicial command to the sheriff or other officer to seize any property, credit, or right, belonging to the defendant, wherever it may be found, to satisfy the demand which the plaintiff has against him.

Edmonson v. Leesville Concrete Co.

(Injured Construction Worker) v. (Negligent Employer)
500 U.S. 614, 111 S.Ct. 2077 (1991)

RACE-BASED PEREMPTORY CHALLENGES BY PRIVATE LITIGANT VIOLATE FOURTEENTH AMENDMENT

■ **INSTANT FACTS** An injured construction worker suing for negligence claimed that allowing the defendant to exclude jurors based on their race violated his equal protection rights under the Fourteenth Amendment.

■ **BLACK LETTER RULE** When a private litigant in a civil action makes peremptory challenges based on the jurors' race, he or she violates the Equal Protection Clause of the Fourteenth Amendment.

■ PROCEDURAL BASIS
Appeal of judgment in negligence action for damages.

■ FACTS
Edmonson (P) was a black construction worker. He sued Leesville Concrete Co. (Leesville) (D) in federal court for negligence after he was injured on a job site when a Leesville (D) employee permitted a truck to roll backward and pin Edmonson (P) against some equipment. During voir dire, Leesville (D) used two peremptory challenges to remove blacks from the jury. Pursuant to *Batson v. Kentucky* [equal protection prohibits prosecutors in criminal cases from using race-based peremptory challenges], Edmonson (P) asked the trial court to require Leesville (D) to set forth a race-neutral reason for striking the jurors. The trial court denied the request, holding that *Batson* does not apply to civil cases. The jury rendered a verdict for Edmonson (P) and assessed his damages at $90,000, but also held that Edmonson (P) was 80% at fault, thereby awarding him only $18,000.

■ ISSUE
Does excluding jurors based on their race in a civil action constitute state action?

■ DECISION AND RATIONALE
(Kennedy, J.) Yes. We held in *Powers v. Ohio* that when a prosecutor excludes jurors based on race, the excluded jurors' equal protection rights are violated. Excluded jurors are harmed no less in civil trials. However, that an act is unconstitutional when committed by a government official does not mean it is unconstitutional when committed by a private litigant. In *Lugar v. Edmondson Oil Co.* [using court and government officials to seize property involves state action], we applied a two-step analysis. First, we look at whether the constitutional deprivation resulted from the exercise of a right or privilege deriving from state authority. Second, we look at whether the private party charged with the deprivation is a state actor. Here, the first step is satisfied. Peremptory challenges have no significance outside a court of law. They are not constitutionally required, and are permitted only by law. Here, the challenges were authorized by a federal statute allowing each party three peremptory challenges. To determine whether the actor is a state actor, we look at the following three factors: (1) the extent to which the actor relies on governmental assistance and benefits; (2) whether the actor is performing a traditional government function; and (3) whether the injury is aggravated uniquely by governmental authority.

Edmonson v. Leesville Concrete Co. (Continued)

Here, we hold that Leesville's (D) exercise of peremptory challenges was state action. State action is present when private parties make extensive use of state procedures assisted by state officials. Without government assistance, the jury trial system would not exist. The court summons jurors, subjects them to public examination, and discharges them. Without a judge's participation, the peremptory challenge system serves no purpose. By enforcing a discriminatory peremptory challenge the court significantly involves itself with invidious discrimination. Reversed.

Analysis:

The Court here thoroughly examined of the entanglement of state action in the jury selection process. A simpler way to look at the jury selection issue is as a public function. Jury selection is a traditional government function to which the Fourteenth Amendment applies. State and federal statutes allow the government to delegate that function to private litigants. The private litigants must abide by the Fourteenth Amendment as the government would if it did not delegate the duty. Indeed, the second factor the Court examined, whether the actor is performing a traditional government function, is the traditional public function analysis. A year after deciding *Edmonson,* the Court ruled in *Georgia v. McCollum* that the same analysis and holding apply to a criminal defendant's use of race-based peremptory challenges. While a criminal defendant is the government's adversary in a criminal trial, the court assists and enforces the defendant's discriminatory actions.

■ CASE VOCABULARY

PEREMPTORY CHALLENGE: A limited number of challenges each side in a trial can use to eliminate potential jurors without stating a reason.

PETIT JURY: The ordinary trial jury whose duty it is to find facts, as opposed to the grand jury who decides to indict.

VOIR DIRE: French for "to speak the truth." The process by which judges and lawyers select a petit jury from among those eligible to serve, by questioning them to determine their knowledge of the facts of the case and a willingness to decide the case only on the evidence presented in court.

Burton v. Wilmington Parking Authority

(Black Customer) v. (State Agency)
365 U.S. 715, 81 S.Ct. 856 (1961)

LESSEE FROM STATE MUST COMPLY WITH FOURTEENTH AMENDMENT

■ **INSTANT FACTS** A black man was denied service in a restaurant located in a government-owned building.

■ **BLACK LETTER RULE** When a State becomes entangled in a private party's actions so that the State and the private party have a symbiotic relationship, the private party must comply with the Fourteenth Amendment.

■ **PROCEDURAL BASIS**

Appeal of action for declaratory and injunctive relief.

■ **FACTS**

The Eagle Coffee Shoppe, Inc. (Eagle) refused to serve Burton (P), solely because he is black. The building in which Eagle is located is a parking garage owned and operated by the Wilmington Parking Authority (the Authority) (D), an agency of the State of Delaware. Eagle admitted that serving blacks would injure its business. The Authority's (D) statutory purpose is to provide adequate parking facilities to relieve the city's parking crisis. The Authority (D) is given broad powers, including purchasing and leasing land and facilities as necessary for financing the facilities. Here, to finance its debt service, the Authority (D) entered into long-term leases with various tenants, including Eagle, in its protected garage building. The building had signs indicating the public character of the building and flew state and national flags.

■ **ISSUE**

When a State becomes entangled in a private party's actions so that the State and the private party have a symbiotic relationship, must the private party comply with the Fourteenth Amendment?

■ **DECISION AND RATIONALE**

(Clark, J.) Yes. The Equal Protection Clause of the Fourteenth Amendment applies only to state action. Here, the building was publically owned and was dedicated to public use. The building was financed with public money. Eagle and the Authority (D) derived mutual benefits from their relationship. Eagle's customers had a convenient place to park, and the presence of Eagle created an increased demand for the Authority's (D) parking facilities. Eagle's alleged increased profits based on its discrimination contributed to the Authority's (D) financial success. In addition, Eagle was an integral part of a public building, indicating the degree of state participation in discriminatory action. It is ironic that in one part of a public building all persons have equal rights, while in another portion, a Negro is a second-class citizen. In its lease with Eagle, the Authority (D) could have expressly required Eagle to discharge its responsibilities under the Fourteenth Amendment. A State may not abdicate its responsibilities. By its inaction, the State made itself a party to Eagle's discrimination. The State's interdependence with Eagle makes it a joint participant in the challenged activity, which cannot be considered to be "purely private." We hold that when a State leases public property in the manner and for the purposes shown here, the lessee must comply with the Fourteenth Amendment.

Burton v. Wilmington Parking Authority (Continued)

Analysis:

The Court's decision here is not based on any single factor, but on the totality of the circumstances indicating the entanglement between Eagle and the Authority (D). The Authority (D) and Eagle were held to have a "symbiotic relationship" that deemed Eagle a state actor. This is similar to *Evans v. Newton*, where the Court held that a park could not be racially segregated, even if it was privately owned, because the government was intimately involved in its operation. Here, Eagle's location and status as a government lessee made it appear as though the government authorized its discriminatory practices. The Authority (D) and Eagle also mutually benefitted from their relationship. Thus the Authority (D) benefitted from Eagle's discrimination.

Moose Lodge No. 107 v. Irvis
(*Private Club*) v. (*Black Man*)
407 U.S. 163, 92 S.Ct. 1965 (1972)

GRANTING LIQUOR LICENSE DOES NOT IMPLICATE STATE IN PRIVATE DISCRIMINATION

■ **INSTANT FACTS** When a black man was denied service by a private club, he sued to revoke its state-issued liquor license.

■ **BLACK LETTER RULE** A private club that obtains a state liquor license does not necessarily engage in state action for purposes of the Fourteenth Amendment.

■ **PROCEDURAL BASIS**

Appeal of action for injunctive relief.

■ **FACTS**

Moose Lodge No. 107 (Moose Lodge) (D), the Harrisburg, Pennsylvania, branch of a national fraternal organization, is a private club. It operates in its own privately-owned building and does not receive public funds. Only members and their guests are permitted in the lodge. Moose Lodge (D) is licensed to serve alcoholic beverages by the Pennsylvania Liquor Control Board (the Board) (D). Moose Lodge (D) refused to serve Irvis (P), a black man. Irvis (P) sued Moose Lodge (D) and the Board (D), seeking an injunction requiring the Board (D) to revoke Moose Lodge's (D) liquor license. Irvis (P) argued that granting Moose Lodge (D) a liquor license amounts to state involvement in discriminatory activity in violation of the Equal Protection Clause of the Fourteenth Amendment.

■ **ISSUE**

Is a private club that is licensed by the State to serve alcohol required to abide by the Fourteenth Amendment?

■ **DECISION AND RATIONALE**

(Rehnquist, J.) No. Private discrimination does not violate the Equal Protection Clause if the private entity receives any state benefit or service. Otherwise, since state services include providing electricity, water, and police and fire protection, all private activity would be considered state activity. The State must have "significant" involvement in the discrimination in order to violate the Fourteenth Amendment. There is no symbiotic relationship like the one in *Burton v. Wilmington Parking Authority* [state entanglement in private party's actions creating symbiotic relationship indicate state action]. Moose Lodge (D) owns its own building and clearly proclaims that it is not open to the public. Moose Lodge (D) does not perform a public function or service. The Board (D) does not establish or enforce the Moose Lodge's (D) membership policy. There is no suggestion that Pennsylvania law discriminates against minorities in their ability to apply for club licenses or to be served liquor in places of public accommodation. The state regulations do not foster or encourage discrimination. They do not make the State Moose Lodge's (D) partner. We therefore hold that the Board's (D) regulatory scheme does not implicate the State in Moose Lodge's (D) discriminatory guest policies to make Moose Lodge's (D) actions equal to state action.

Moose Lodge No. 107 v. Irvis (Continued)

■ DISSENT

(Douglas, J.) The mere granting of a state license does not make a private club a public enterprise. However, Pennsylvania has a pervasive regulation scheme with regard to liquor licenses. Regulation § 113.09 provides that every club licensee shall adhere to all of the provisions of its constitution and by-laws. This regulation requires Moose Lodge (D) to adhere to the racially discriminatory provisions of its constitution. Therefore, § 113.09 compels Moose Lodge (D) to discriminate and is, thus, an invidious form of state action. Moreover, there is a quota system for liquor licenses in Pennsylvania. In fact, no more liquor licenses may be issued in Harrisburg. This state-enforced scarcity of licenses restricts the ability of blacks to obtain liquor. A group desiring to form a nondiscriminatory club and serve liquor must buy a license from an existing group and likely pay a monopoly price. This is assuming that an existing group would even be willing to sell its license, because without it a group may not survive. Thus, Pennsylvania is putting the weight of its liquor license, a highly valued asset, behind racial discrimination.

Analysis:

This case distinguishes and narrows *Burton*. The Court seems to apply a quantitative analysis, adding up the number of connections between the State and Moose Lodge (D) and determining that the number is substantially less than in *Burton*. Although the Moose Lodge (D) was subjected to extensive government regulation, the Court held that the government did not endorse, approve of, or benefit from the Moose Lodge's (D) discrimination. Because there appears to be no bright line rule regarding when private activity is sufficiently entangled with the government to constitute state, action, reasonable justices are free to disagree. In his dissent. Justice Douglas stated his belief that the state regulation did constitute sufficient state entanglement, whereas the majority disagreed.

Norwood v. Harrison

(School Children) v. *(State)*
413 U.S. 455, 93 S.Ct. 2804 (1973)

STATE MAY NOT PROVIDE SUBSIDIES TO DISCRIMINATORY PRIVATE ORGANIZATION

■ **INSTANT FACTS** School children claimed their rights under the Equal Protection Clause of the Fourteenth Amendment were violated by a state program that provided free textbooks to racially discriminatory private schools.

■ **BLACK LETTER RULE** Under the Equal Protection Clause of the Fourteenth Amendment, a State may not provide aid to private institutions that practice racial discrimination.

■ **PROCEDURAL BASIS**

Appeal of class action challenging statute as violating the Equal Protection Clause of the Fourteenth Amendment.

■ **FACTS**

For over 30 years, the State of Mississippi (D) purchased textbooks and loaned them to private and public schools, regardless of the schools' racial discrimination. A class action on behalf of all Mississippi students (P) alleged that by supplying textbooks to students attending discriminatory private schools, the State (D) provided financial aid to racially segregated schools and impeded the progress of fully desegregating public schools.

■ **ISSUE**

Does providing a government subsidy to a discriminatory private organization violate the Fourteenth Amendment?

■ **DECISION AND RATIONALE**

(Burger, J.) Yes. The State is not required to provide assistance to private schools equivalent to that provided to public schools. This Court has consistently held that state tuition grants to racially discriminatory private schools are unconstitutional. Free textbooks are also a form of financial assistance. When a state bears the cost of textbooks, it supports private schools' racial discrimination. The State (D) argues that its textbook loan program is a sincere effort to foster quality education for all Mississippi children. However, good intentions do not negate the State's (D) involvement in violating a constitutional duty. The Equal Protection Clause would be a sterile promise if we looked only at the goals of the disputed action. A State may not give significant aid to institutions that practice racial or other invidious discrimination.

Analysis:

In this case, Mississippi (D) was giving financial assistance to private parties whose activities would violate the Fourteenth Amendment if the government engaged in them. The Court does not hold that the private schools could not segregate, only that the State (D) could not provide the segregated schools any direct aid. The Court did not hold that the State (D) could not provide indirect general aid, such as police and fire protection. It is interesting to note that in an earlier case, *Board of Education v.*

Norwood v. Harrison (Continued)

Allen, the Court held that a state could provide textbooks to private religious schools that were not racially discriminatory. Note that the Court here upheld a challenge to government aid to segregated private schools in Mississippi, a state with a long history of invidious discrimination. However, government subsidies to private organizations are not always a basis for finding state action, as other cases demonstrate.

Rendell-Baker v. Kohn

(*School Counselor*) v. (*Private School*)
457 U.S. 830, 102 S.Ct. 2764 (1982)

PRIVATE SCHOOL IS NOT A STATE ACTOR MERELY BECAUSE IT IS PUBLICALLY FUNDED AND REGULATED

■ **INSTANT FACTS** Private school employees sued the private school for violating their constitutional rights, alleging that the private school was a state actor because it was publically funded and performed a public function.

■ **BLACK LETTER RULE** Publically-funded and regulated private organizations are not state actors under the Fourteenth Amendment unless the government compels or influences their actions.

■ **PROCEDURAL BASIS**

In civil rights action, appeal of wrongful discharge judgment for the employer.

■ **FACTS**

The New Perspectives School (New Perspectives) (D) is a nonprofit private school located on private property in Massachusetts. Kohn (D) is its director. New Perspectives (D) specializes in dealing with special needs students who are usually referred by public schools or by the state mental health department. When schools refer students to New Perspectives (D), their school boards pay for the students' education. New Perspectives (D) also receives funds from other government agencies, with public funds accounting for at least 90% of its operating budget. To be eligible for tuition funding, New Perspectives (D) must comply with various regulations involving record-keeping, student-teacher ratios, and maintaining written job descriptions. Rendell-Baker (P) was a counselor at New Perspectives (D) who supported a proposal allowing the student-staff council greater responsibilities. Kohn (D) opposed the proposal and fired Rendell-Baker (P). Kohn (D) fired five other teachers (P) when they wrote a letter to the editor of a local newspaper supporting students' right to picket the home of the president of New Perspectives' (D) board. Rendell-Baker and the five other teachers (collectively Rendell-Baker) (P) sued for wrongful termination, alleging that New Perspectives (D) violated their First Amendment right of free speech without due process under the Fourteenth Amendment.

■ **ISSUE**

Is a private school that receives state financial assistance a state actor for purposes of the Fourteenth Amendment?

■ **DECISION AND RATIONALE**

(Burger, C.J.) No. New Perspectives (D) is no different than any other private business that depends on government contracts. Acts of private contractors do not become state action merely because they are performing public contracts. State regulation did not influence New Perspectives' (D) decision to discharge Rendell-Baker (P). In fact, there was very little regulation regarding personnel matters. Rendell-Baker (P) argues that New Perspectives (D) is a state actor because it performs a public function. However, we must look at whether the function has been "traditionally the exclusive

Rendell-Baker v. Kohn (Continued)

prerogative of the state." While educating maladjusted students is a public function, it is not within the state's *exclusive* province.

■ DISSENT

(Marshall, J.) I believe that the nexus between Massachusetts and New Perspectives (D) is substantial. The State delegates its duty to educate special needs children to New Perspectives (D), New Perspectives (D) receives almost all its funds from the State, and New Perspectives (D) is heavily regulated. New Perspectives' (D) financial dependence on the State indicates state involvement. The State could exercise complete control over the school by threatening to withdraw its financial support. New Perspectives (D) exists solely to fulfill the State's statutory obligation. Unlike private contractors, New Perspectives (D) is closely supervised by the State and is performing the State's statutory duty.

Analysis:

Here the Court substantially limits its state action doctrine. The Court held that private organizations are not state actors merely because they receive nearly all of their funds from public sources or because they are regulated by the government. More government involvement is required: specifically, coercion over or encouragement of the substance of the disputed action. This "hands off" policy reflects a backing away from civil rights protection and a less aggressive approach to private behavior. Note too that the Court looks only narrowly at the disputed action, i.e., firing employees, which was not highly regulated by the state. If the challenged action had involved something more regulated, such as record-keeping, it is possible that the Court may have found state action.

Blum v. Yaretsky

(State) v. (Medicaid Patients)
457 U.S. 991, 102 S.Ct. 2777 (1982)

PRIVATE NURSING HOMES' DECISIONS TO TRANSFER MEDICAID PATIENTS NOT STATE ACTION

■ **INSTANT FACTS** Medicaid patients claimed the State could be held liable for the failure of private nursing homes to provide them adequate notice of decisions to transfer or discharge them.

■ **BLACK LETTER RULE** The State is not liable for decisions made by private parties which the State did not coerce or significantly encourage.

■ PROCEDURAL BASIS
Appeal of civil rights class action for damages and injunctive relief.

■ FACTS
Congress established the Medicaid program to provide federal funds to states that reimburse certain medical costs incurred by the poor. New York (D) provides Medicaid assistance to people who receive care in private nursing homes, designated as either "skilled nursing facilities" (SNF's) or "health-related facilities" (HRF's). HRF's provide less extensive and less expensive medical care than SNF's. New York (D) reimburses nursing homes chosen by Medicaid patients. To obtain Medicaid, a person must meet income eligibility standards and must seek medically necessary services. To ensure the latter, nursing homes must establish a utilization review committee (URC) to periodically assess whether each patient's continued stay at the home is justified. Yaretsky (P) and Cuevas (P) were Medicaid patients at an SNF in New York City. The nursing home's URC determined that they should be transferred to a lower level of care at a HRF. In response, New York officials (D) prepared to reduce or terminate payments to the nursing home. State social service officials affirmed this decision. Yaretsky (P) and Cuevas (P) sued individually and on behalf of a class of Medicaid-eligible residents of New York nursing homes. They sued the Commissioners of the New York Department of Social Services and the Department of Health (D). They alleged that they did not receive adequate notice of the URC decisions or of their right to appeal, and that this violated the Due Process Clause of the Fourteenth Amendment. They sought damages and an injunction ordering New York (D) to adopt regulations prohibiting the transfer or discharge of Medicaid patients without adequate notice. The Court of Appeals held for Yaretsky (P) and Cuevas (P). It held that state action was present in the nursing homes' transfer or discharge decisions because New York (D) responded to the decisions by adjusting the patients' Medicaid benefits.

■ ISSUE
Is the State responsible for the actions of private nursing homes that receive Medicaid funds?

■ DECISION AND RATIONALE
(Rehnquist, J.) No. Yaretsky (P) and Cuevas (P) concede that state officials do not make the decisions to discharge or transfer patients. They seek to hold state officials responsible for the actions of private parties. This is different from cases in which the defendant is a private party and the plaintiff claims the private party is a state actor. First, the mere fact that a business is subject to state regulation does not make it a state actor. There must also be a close nexus between the State and the challenged action.

Second, a State can normally be held responsible for a private decision only when it has coerced or encouraged it. Mere approval or acquiescence is not sufficient. Third, the nexus may be present if the private entity exercises powers that are traditionally exclusively those of the State. The Court of Appeals decided this case incorrectly because Yaretsky (P) and Cuevas (P) are not challenging the adjustment of benefits. They are challenging their discharge or transfer without adequate notice or hearings. New York's (D) response of adjusting benefits does not render it responsible for those actions. There is no suggestion that the nursing home's decisions were influenced by New York's (D) obligation to adjust the benefits. Yaretsky (P) and Cuevas (P) claim that New York (D) affirmatively commands the summary discharge or transfer of Medicaid patients who are thought to be inappropriately placed in their nursing facilities. However, our review of the statutes and regulations does not support this claim. We conclude that Yaretsky (P) and Cuevas (P) have failed to show state action here. Reversed.

■ DISSENT

(Brennan, J.) For the Fourteenth Amendment to have any effect, we must look carefully at the subtle ways in which a State may influence private action. We must make a realistic and delicate appraisal of the State's involvement in the total context of the challenged action. The level-of-care decisions at issue here are based not on the exercise of independent professional judgment, but on New York's (D) desire to save money. The two levels of care, HRF and SNF, are based not on any medical model, but on the government's cost-containment policies. Shifting nursing home residents from one level of care to another, usually from one facility to another, rarely makes medical sense. In addition, New York (D) precisely prescribes the standards by which the private nursing homes are to make their decisions. The degree of interdependence between New York and the nursing home is far more than it was between the State and the restaurant in *Burton v. Wilmington Parking Authority* [when state is entangled in private party's actions so that state and private party have symbiotic relationship, private party is state actor]. Here, New York (D) subsidizes nearly all the nursing home's expenses and pays the medical expenses of more than 90% of its residents. It also provides the nursing home a profit. The residents are completely dependent on New York (D) for their support and placement. The nursing home provides food, clothing, shelter, and health care, and is the functional equivalent of a State.

Analysis:

The majority here considers whether the actual decision to discharge or transfer a Medicaid patient is made by a private party or by the state. Viewed at so narrowly, the Court's decision makes sense. However, as Justice Brennan points out, the reality is much more complex. While it is true that the nursing home makes the decisions, the state defines the relevant standards and even penalizes nursing homes that fail to discharge or transfer patients in compliance with those standards. As Justice Brennan described the facts, it seems hard to imagine a case with more entanglement between the State and a private party.

Reitman v. Mulkey

(Landlord) v. (Prospective Renters)
387 U.S. 369, 87 S.Ct. 1627 (1967)

STATE CONSTITUTIONAL PROVISION THAT BARS LAWS PROHIBITING DISCRIMINATION UNCONSTITUTIONALLY INVOLVES STATE IN DISCRIMINATION

■ **INSTANT FACTS** Prospective renters were denied an apartment based on their race. They challenged a state constitutional provision that barred all laws prohibiting racial discrimination in housing.

■ **BLACK LETTER RULE** A state constitutional provision that bars laws prohibiting discrimination involves the State in discrimination in violation of the Fourteenth Amendment.

■ **PROCEDURAL BASIS**

In civil rights action, appeal from state supreme court holding that state law violates the Fourteenth Amendment Equal Protection Clause.

■ **FACTS**

In 1964, California voters passed Proposition 14 which prohibits any state agency from limiting any person's right to decline to sell or rent residential property to any other person for any reason. Proposition 14 became part of Article 1, § 26 of the California constitution. The Mulkeys (P) sued Reitman (D) when Reitman (D) refused to rent them an apartment solely on account of their race. Reitman (D) moved for summary judgment claiming that Proposition 14 protected his right to refuse to rent to them. The California Supreme Court held that Proposition 14 involved the State in racial discrimination in the housing market, and was therefore invalid.

■ **ISSUE**

Does a state constitutional provision barring laws prohibiting private racial discrimination in housing unconstitutionally involve the state in the discrimination?

■ **DECISION AND RATIONALE**

(White, J.) Yes. The California Supreme Court did not hold that it was unconstitutional to repeal the anti-discrimination laws. It first rejected the idea that California was required to have a statute prohibiting racial discrimination in housing. It then held that § 26 was intended to authorize private racial discrimination in housing, repeal existing anti-discrimination laws, and create a constitutional right to discriminate. Third, the court held that § 26 would encourage and significantly involve the State in private racial discrimination. The California court reasonably held that § 26 would have a wider impact than just to repeal existing statutes. The right to discriminate was not embodied in the State's basic charter, and was immune from all legislative, executive, or judicial regulation. We accept the California court's holding that § 26 would involve the State in private racial discrimination to an unconstitutional degree.

■ **DISSENT**

(Harlan, J.) While this decision seems favorable, I believe that in the long run it may actually handicap progress in racial matters. Through the proposition process, California has remained neutral in private

Reitman v. Mulkey (Continued)

racial discrimination in housing. All that has happened is that California has effected a pro tanto repeal of its prior statutes forbidding discrimination. This is no more unconstitutional than if California had not passed the laws at all. The fact that the repeal was accompanied by a constitutional provision prohibiting future enactments of anti-discrimination laws does not affect the constitutionality of what California has done. Section 26 is not an affirmative call to discriminate. Section 26 is permissive rather than coercive and should not be struck down without persuasive evidence of an invidious purpose or effect. Every act of private discrimination is either forbidden by state law or permitted by it. This is very different from prior cases where state agencies were actively involved in discrimination or where fostering discrimination was an obvious purpose of a state enactment. To be unconstitutional, the state involvement must be affirmative and purposeful. Drawing lines regarding discrimination is best left to legislatures rather than to courts. This decision may inhibit flexibility in the legislative process. By refusing to accept the decision of the people of California, the Court has taken on powers and responsibilities left elsewhere by the Constitution.

Analysis:

The Court here gives great deference to the California Supreme Court's holding, rather than articulating a specific legal principle on which its opinion is based. Basically, the Court holds that there is state action if there is any state encouragement of private actions. This seems contrary to *Blum v. Yaretsky*, where the Court held that state coercion or significant encouragement is required in order for there to be state action. One commentator, Professor Charles Black, has defended the Court's opinion here on the ground that § 26 made it more difficult for minorities to achieve legislative remedies for discrimination in the housing market. Section 26 would require California to amend its constitution, a relatively difficult task, before minorities could seek legislative protection of housing rights. Thus, § 26 would violate the Fourteenth Amendment because it restricted minorities' ability to seek favorable legislation based solely on their race.

Brentwood Academy v. Tennessee Secondary School Athletic Assn.

(*Private School*) v. (*Interscholastic Athletic Association*)
531 U.S. 288, 121 S.Ct. 924 (2001)

EVEN PRIVATE ASSOCIATIONS CAN BE STATE ACTORS

■ **INSTANT FACTS** Brentwood Academy (P) claimed civil rights violations after the Tennessee Secondary School Athletic Association (D), a non-profit organization regulating high school athletics, disciplined it for rule violations.

■ **BLACK LETTER RULE** State action may be found if there is such a close nexus between the state and the challenged action that seemingly private behavior may be fairly treated as that of the state itself.

■ PROCEDURAL BASIS

Certiorari to review an undisclosed appellate decision.

■ FACTS

The Tennessee Secondary School Athletic Association (D) was a non-profit organization formed to regulate interscholastic sports among its public and private school members. Although membership is voluntary, no alternative athletic association existed in the state, resulting in the membership of nearly all the state's public schools. The Association's (D) voting membership is made up of nine-person committees of high school principals, vice principals, and other school administrators. Association (D) members are not paid by the state for their participation, but they are eligible to join the state's retirement system for employees. The Association (D) establishes and enforces rules for student-athlete eligibility, coaching requirements, and other matters governing interscholastic athletic competitions, and has long been recognized and endorsed by the Tennessee Board of Education.

In 1997, the Association (D) initiated a regulatory enforcement proceeding against Brentwood Academy (P), a private parochial school, for the improper recruitment of athletes. Following an Association vote by a board comprised entirely of public school administrators, Brentwood Academy (P) was placed on probation, banned from post-season participation for two years, and fined. Brentwood (P) filed suit under 42 U.S.C. § 1983, claiming violations of the First and Fourteenth Amendments.

■ ISSUE

Does a statewide association incorporated into an interscholastic athletic competition among public and private secondary schools engage in state action when it enforces a rule against a member school?

■ DECISION AND RATIONALE

(Souter, J.) Yes. Although the Fourteenth Amendment applies only to state action, "state action may be found if, though only if, there is such a 'close nexus between the State and the challenged action' that seemingly private behavior 'may be fairly treated as that of the State itself.'" When the challenged action results from the coercive power, significant encouragement, or willing participation of the state or its agents, state action has been found. Similarly, when a private entity has been delegated a clearly public function, its actions have been found to be entwined with government policies or control. Here,

Brentwood Academy v. Tennessee Secondary School Athletic Assn. (Continued)

the Association's (D) private character is "overborne by the pervasive entwinement of public institutions and public officials." Its membership is comprised largely of public schools, and Association (D) policies and procedures are shaped and enforced by public school administrators. It is an organization of public schools performing a public function, entwined with the state government. The Association (D) engaged in state action.

■ DISSENT

(Thomas, J.) Never before has the Court found state action by mere entwinement. Instead, the Court has always insisted that the private actor perform a public function, be created or encouraged by the government, or act in a close relationship with the government. The Association's (D) actions cannot be attributed to the State. It is a privately formed corporation with private rules and membership. No state law requires the membership of public schools, although a majority of the State's schools have opted to join. And the fact that the board members enforcing the Association's (D) rule happened to be public school administrators at the time does not make their decision state action. Rule enforcement is not an act traditionally delegated to the state, and the state has never undertaken to engage in that act. Likewise, there is no symbiotic relationship between the Association (D) and the state such that the state can fairly be said to control the Association's (D) actions. Yet, rather than follow these established considerations, the Court finds state action based on an undefined concept of state "entwinement" with private conduct. In so doing, the Court threatens to convert any private conduct with even minimal state connections into state action.

Analysis:

The entwinement principle used by the Court in *Brentwood* operates like a statutory catch-all provision. Rather than point to articulable connections between private conduct and the government, entwinement enables courts to view the totality of the circumstances to determine whether the closeness required for state action exists. As Justice Thomas stresses, entwinement potentially converts many private activities into state action.

■ CASE VOCABULARY

STATE ACTION: Anything done by a government; especially, in constitutional law, an intrusion on a person's rights (especially civil rights) either by a governmental entity or by a private requirement that can be enforced only by governmental action (such as a racially restrictive covenant, which requires judicial action for enforcement).

CHAPTER SIX

Economic Liberties

Allgeyer v. Louisiana

Instant Facts: State of Louisiana banned all foreign corporations from doing business in the state unless it had a place of business and an agent within the state.

Black Letter Rule: Liberty, as used in the Fourteenth Amendment, means not just the right of a citizen to be free from physical restraint, but also free to enjoy all faculties and to use them in all lawful ways.

Lochner v. New York

Instant Facts: Owner of bakery charged with violating state law restricting number of hours bakery employees could work challenged law on due process grounds.

Black Letter Rule: Legislation enacted using a state's police powers that interferes with an individual's right to contract must directly relate to the goal of protecting public health or safety and must have an appropriate and legitimate end.

Coppage v. Kansas

Instant Facts: Employer convicted of violating state law that prohibited conditioning employment on not joining a union challenged the constitutionality of the law.

Black Letter Rule: The freedom of contract includes the right to make contracts affecting personal employment without arbitrary interference by the state.

Muller v. Oregon

Instant Facts: Employer convicted of violating law that restricted the number of hours women could work in certain types of jobs challenged the constitutionality of the law under the Fourteenth Amendment.

Black Letter Rule: The general right to contract in relation to one's business is not absolute, but instead is subject to reasonable restrictions placed upon that right by government.

Adkins v. Children's Hospital

Instant Facts: Employee sued employer for not paying her in accordance with the state's minimum wage law.

Black Letter Rule: Freedom of contract is the general rule and the exercise of legislative authority to infringe upon that freedom the exception that must be justified by the existence of exceptional circumstances.

Weaver v. Palmer Bros. Co.

Instant Facts: Manufacturer of blankets, sued for violating law that prohibited manufacturing blankets with shoddy, challenged constitutionality of law.

Black Letter Rule: Laws aimed at protecting public health must be the only reasonable way to eliminate a known health risk.

Nebbia v. New York

Instant Facts: Grocer convicted of selling milk at prices lower than price set by state regulatory agency challenged the constitutionality of the price control.

Black Letter Rule: State price controls are constitutional if they are nondiscriminatory and bear a reasonable relationship to a proper legislative purpose.

West Coast Hotel Co. v. Parrish

Instant Facts: Employee sued employer to recover difference between her actual wages and the minimum wage state law required that she be paid.

Black Letter Rule: Regulation that is reasonable in relation to its subject and is adopted in the interests of the community satisfies the due process clause of the Fourteenth Amendment.

United States v. Carolene Products Co.

Instant Facts: Company indicted for violating federal law prohibiting the shipping of adulterated milk products across interstate lines challenged constitutionality of the law.

Black Letter Rule: When reviewing legislation, the existence of facts supporting the legislation is to be presumed and such legislation shall not be pronounced unconstitutional unless it is of such character as to preclude the assumption that it rests upon some rational basis.

Williamson v. Lee Optical

Instant Facts: Optician brought suit to have law prohibiting him from dispensing lenses or fitting lenses in frames without a prescription from a licensed ophthalmologist or optometrist and to enjoin state officials from enforcing the law.

Black Letter Rule: Economic legislation will be upheld so long as there is any conceivable justification for it.

BMW of North America, Inc. v. Gore

Instant Facts: Consumer who purchased automobile from retailer brought suit for damages upon finding that the vehicle had been repainted prior to sale without consumer's knowledge.

Black Letter Rule: A punitive damages award that can fairly be characterized as grossly excessive in relation to a state's legitimate interests in punishing unlawful conduct and deterring repetition of such conduct is arbitrary and violates the due process clause of the Fourteenth Amendment.

State Farm Mut. Automobile Ins. Co. v. Campbell

Instant Facts: After State Farm (D) failed to settle claims against Campbell (P) for its policy limits, Campbell obtained a judgment for $1 million in compensatory damages and $145 million in punitive damages.

Black Letter Rule: In evaluating the appropriateness of a punitive damages award, a court must weigh the reprehensibility of the defendant's conduct, the disparity between the actual harm caused and the amount of the punitive damages awarded, and the difference between the punitive damages awarded and the civil penalties imposed under state law.

Philip Morris U.S.A. v. Williams

Instant Facts: Williams (P) was awarded punitive damages after his attorney argued that Philip Morris's (D) actions would harm others.

Black Letter Rule: An award of punitive damages based on a desire to punish the defendant for harming persons not before the court is an unconstitutional taking of property without due process.

Home Building & Loan Association v. Blaisdell

Instant Facts: Borrower took advantage of a state law that permitted borrowers to ask for extensions of the time in which they were to pay back their mortgages, and bank brought lawsuit challenging the constitutionality of the law.

Black Letter Rule: A state may impose temporary conditions on the creditor-debtor relationship so long as there is an emergency, the legislation is addressed to a legitimate end and the relief afforded is proportional and reasonable.

Energy Reserves Group, Inc. v. Kansas Power & Light Co.

Instant Facts: State enacted legislation that precluded natural gas supplier from charging prices established in contract with buyer.

Black Letter Rule: A state may enact legislation that infringes on the contractual rights of parties so long as the substantial impairment is justified by a significant and legitimate purpose.

Allied Structural Steel v. Spannaus

Instant Facts: State enacted legislation that required employers to pay pension benefits to employees whose benefits had not yet vested.

Black Letter Rule: A state may not unilaterally change the contractual obligations of parties to a pension fund absent a reasonable justification.

United States Trust Co. v. New Jersey

Instant Facts: State enacted legislation that repealed a prior statute that prohibited the use of toll revenues to subsidize railroad passenger service.

Black Letter Rule: Legislation abdicating a government's obligations will only be upheld if it is both reasonable and necessary to serve the purposes claimed by the government.

Loretto v. Teleprompter Manhattan CATV Corp.

Instant Facts: Landlord challenged law requiring him to allow a cable company to install cable facilities on his property without compensation.

Black Letter Rule: Any permanent physical intrusion by the government or authorized by the government constitutes a taking for which just compensation must be paid.

Pennsylvania Coal Co. v. Mahon

Instant Facts: Landowner sued coal company for violating state law prohibiting mining under homes.

Black Letter Rule: Land use regulation that goes too far will be recognized as a taking.

Miller v. Schoene

Instant Facts: State entomologist ordered all red cedar trees within certain vicinity of apple orchards destroyed in order to stop spread of disease that was killing the orchards.

Black Letter Rule: In extreme exigent circumstances, the state may chose to destroy one property without paying just compensation in order to save another, so long as the taking is necessary to protect the health, safety, moral or general welfare of the public.

Penn Central Transportation Co. v. New York City

Instant Facts: Owner of Grand Central Station in New York City claimed a law declaring the station a landmark and thus precluding any building on top of it constituted a regulatory taking.

Black Letter Rule: A land use regulation that does not deprive a property owner of all uses of the property does not constitute a taking.

Lucas v. South Carolina Coastal Council

Instant Facts: State law preventing building on beachfront property precluded landowner from building the homes he had planned on his property.

Black Letter Rule: Government regulation that deprives a property owner of all economically beneficial use constitutes a taking for which just compensation must be paid.

Dolan v. City of Tigard

Instant Facts: City conditioned building permit for expansion of store on owner's granting city land for use as a flood plain and building of a public walkway.

Black Letter Rule: Permit conditions will only be upheld where there is an essential nexus between the legitimate state interest and the government shows that some sort of individualized determination has been made that the required dedication is related both in nature and extent to the impact of the proposed development.

Palazzolo v. Rhode Island

Instant Facts: Palazzolo's (P) petition for approval of development plans for his coastal property was denied because state regulations restricted the development of coastal wetlands.

Black Letter Rule: When a regulation denies all economically beneficial or productive use of property, the Takings Clause requires just compensation to the landowner.

Tahoe–Sierra Preservation Council, Inc. v. Tahoe Regional Planning Agency

Instant Facts: Property owners in the Lake Tahoe area were prohibited from undertaking any development of their property for thirty-two months in order to get a handle on the development needs of the area to preserve its natural beauty.

Black Letter Rule: A regulation that prohibits economic use of land for an extended but finite period of time does not constitute a taking requiring that the owner of the property be compensated.

Hawaii Housing Authority v. Midkiff

Instant Facts: State agency initiated program that took property from concentrated landowners without compensation and resold it to others in order to dilute number of landowners.

Black Letter Rule: What constitutes public use for purposes of the Takings Clause is determined by the legislature, whose determination will be upheld except in the most narrowest of cases.

Kelo v. City of New London

Instant Facts: The City of New London (P) used eminent domain to acquire Kelo's (D) house for a private development project.

Black Letter Rule: "Public purpose" is defined broadly, and deference must be given to legislative judgments on this question.

Brown v. Legal Foundation of Washington

Instant Facts: Brown (P) demanded just compensation for state use of interest earned on his private funds in an IOLTA account.

Black Letter Rule: Just compensation is measured by the property owner's loss rather than the government's gain.

Allgeyer v. Louisiana

(Resident) v. (State)
165 U.S. 578, 17 S.Ct. 427 (1897)

SUPREME COURT RULES THAT STATE CANNOT PREVENT WHAT FEDERAL CONSTITUTION ALLOWS

■ **INSTANT FACTS** State of Louisiana banned all foreign corporations from doing business in the state unless it had a place of business and an agent within the state.

■ **BLACK LETTER RULE** Liberty, as used in the Fourteenth Amendment, means not just the right of a citizen to be free from physical restraint, but also free to enjoy all faculties and to use them in all lawful ways.

■ **PROCEDURAL BASIS**

Appeal from Louisiana Supreme Court's ruling upholding law banning foreign corporations from doing business within the state without a place of business and agent located therein.

■ **FACTS**

The state of Louisiana (D) passed a law conditionally banning foreign corporations from doing business within its borders. Under the law, a foreign corporation can only do business within the state of Louisiana (D) if it has one or more known places of business and an authorized agent within the state. In this case, the state of Louisiana (D) applied this rule against Atlantic Mutual Insurance Company, an insurance company whose business is confined within the state of New York. The only act of which the state of Louisiana (D) complains, however, is the mailing of a letter from the New York insurance company (D) to a Louisiana resident, Allgeyer (P). The letter was a notice to the resident of property to be covered by an insurance contract entered into in the state of New York and which was to be carried out within the state of New York.

■ **ISSUE**

May a state prohibit a foreign corporation from doing any kind of incidental business within the state?

■ **DECISION AND RATIONALE**

(Peckham, J.) No. There is no doubt that a state can impose such conditions as it sees fit on the ability of foreign corporations to do business within its borders and may prohibit such corporations from doing any business within the state unless the state complies with those conditions. The question, here, however, is whether the state can stretch its definition of doing business so as to apply its penal provisions of a statute conditioning the right to business within a given state so broad as to encompass the mere sending of a letter to a resident. Here, the contract at issue was made outside the jurisdiction of the state of Louisiana (D) and was to be performed outside the state's borders. The act of which Louisiana (D) complains was the mere sending of a letter to a resident of the state notifying them of the property to which the contract, which had already been entered into, attached. The Supreme Court of Louisiana held that the sending of the letter constituted an act done to effect an insurance contract and, as such, was an act of business by that company within the state of Louisiana (D) by a company that had not complied with the conditions put upon such transactions by the state (D). Construed in this

Allgeyer v. Louisiana (Continued)

way, we find the statute unconstitutional in that it deprives Allgeyer of its liberty without due process of law. The word liberty in the Fourteenth Amendment to the U.S. Constitution refers not only to the right of every citizen to be free from physical restraint, but also to be free to enjoy all of his faculties and to use them in all lawful ways. In addition, liberty includes the right to live and work where one wants, to earn a livelihood by any lawful means by pursuing whatever calling or vocation one wishes to pursue and to enter into all contracts that may be proper, necessary and essential to carrying out these purposes. It is thus clear that a citizen has a right, guaranteed by the federal constitution, to enter into a contract for insurance with a company outside the borders of his/her state or to do any act necessary to carry out that contract. To deprive a citizen of this right without due process of law is illegal, and it is not sufficient due process to simply enact the statute, because the mere enactment of the statute has no more effect than to deprive a citizen of the right to do that which the federal constitution gives him. We do not mean to say that the right of the states to enact legislation in the legitimate exercise of its police or other powers as it may deem proper is limited or otherwise interfered with—however, in enacting legislation, the states must take care not to infringe upon those rights that the federal constitution guarantees. Here, Atlantic Mutual, which conducted no business within the state of Louisiana (D) and did not subject itself to the laws of that state, had the right to enter into a contract to sell insurance to Louisiana (D) residents, such as Allgeyer (P), even if the property insured was within the state of Louisiana (D), and residents of the state (D) also have the right to seek insurance from companies outside their state's borders. Any statute that prohibits a company or a resident from entering into such contracts, or from mailing notification required by such a contract within the state, is an improper statute which violates the Fourteenth Amendment's protection of liberty. Reversed.

Analysis:

This case represents another battle between the federal government and the state government. The state wants to restrict certain business practices within its borders, and to apply those conditions as broadly as possible, while the federal constitution prohibits it from doing so in some cases like the one here. More importantly, this case represents the Court's willingness to use the Due Process Clause of the Fourteenth Amendment to protect the freedom to contract, a freedom that, at least in this case, is a constitutionally protected interest. The due process infirmity here also was not the typical due process violation that is seen in modern law (lack of notice and a hearing, or procedural due process). Rather, the Court's use here was the true beginning of the use of substantive due process, the principle that there are interests so protected that they cannot be infringed upon by state law without great justification.

■ **CASE VOCABULARY**

AGENT: One who acts on behalf of another.

FOREIGN CORPORATION: A business entity incorporated in another state.

Lochner v. New York

(Bakery Owner) v. *(State)*
198 U.S. 45, 25 S.Ct. 539 (1905)

HIGH COURT FROWNS ON STATE'S ATTEMPT TO SET MAXIMUM HOURS LIMIT FOR BAKERY EMPLOYEES

■ **INSTANT FACTS** Owner of bakery charged with violating state law restricting number of hours bakery employees could work challenged law on due process grounds.

■ **BLACK LETTER RULE** Legislation enacted using a state's police powers that interferes with an individual's right to contract must directly relate to the goal of protecting public health or safety and must have an appropriate and legitimate end.

■ PROCEDURAL BASIS
Appeal from conviction by state court for violating maximum hours labor act.

■ FACTS
The State of New York (D) passed a law limiting the number of hours an employee of a bakery may work to no more than sixty hours per week or ten hours per day. Lochner (P), the owner of a bakery, was convicted of violating this statute, which was a misdemeanor, for allowing his employees to exceed the maximum hours limit. Lochner (P) appealed his conviction.

■ ISSUE
Is a state law setting the maximum hours employees can work in a given field a valid and reasonable exercise of that state's police powers?

■ DECISION AND RATIONALE
(Peckham, J.) No. Clearly this statute infringes upon the right to contract enjoyed by both the bakery owner and employees. It has been recognized that the right to make a contract in relation to one's business is protected by the Fourteenth Amendment to the U.S. Constitution. A state does have, however, certain police powers that may, in the right circumstance, justify passing a law that restricts this right. As a result, all property and liberties are held subject to the reasonable conditions that may be imposed by government. Therefore, the state has the power to limit the ability of its citizens to make certain kinds of contracts, and if the restriction is a valid exercise of the state's police powers, the Fourteenth Amendment offers no protection from such a restriction. When such a law is passed and a citizen challenges the state's right to pass such a law, as is the case here, it falls to the courts to determine which right prevails: the right of the state to exercise its police powers or the right of the citizen to contract as he sees fit. This Court has previously recognized, in *Holden v. Hardy*, the right of the state of Utah to restrict the number of hours mine employees may work as a valid exercise of the police power. The restriction was upheld because of the kind of work being done, the characteristics of which made it reasonable to restrict the maximum number of hours a man could spend working in a mine. That case aside, it must be conceded that there is a limit to the exercise of a state's police power. Otherwise, the Fourteenth Amendment would be rendered superfluous. It necessarily follows that the exercise of the police power must be more than a mere pretext. Thus, in a case such as this where a

state's exercise of the police power is challenged on grounds that it infringes a protected liberty, the issue arises whether the law is a fair, reasonable and appropriate exercise of the police power or whether it is an unreasonable, unnecessary and arbitrary interference with individual liberty? If the law is valid, regardless of whether this Court would have passed such a law, it is a valid law. Here, however, the law in question is not a valid exercise of the state of New York's (D) police power because there is no reasonable ground for interfering with an individual's liberty by setting the hours that individual may work simply because he/she works in a bakery. Such a law does not involve the safety, morals or the general welfare of the public. There is no assertion that bakers as a class are in need of special protection or are so incapable of protecting their own rights while bargaining for employment that this law is necessary. Moreover, there is nothing in this law that serves to insure the marketing of clean and wholesome bread. If this law is valid, it must be because it relates to the protection of the public's health, and there must be more than a mere allegation that the law is aimed at protecting the health of bakers. The law must have a more direct relation as a means to an end and the end itself must be legitimate and appropriate. All labor carries with it the seeds of unhealthiness, and bakers are not subject to these seeds more than any other profession. Thus, unlike the mining industry that has special characteristics that justify limiting the hours miners may work, bakers are no different than any other trade or occupation. Thus, if a state could limit the hours of bakers, it could do so for everyone else as well, even if such a result would limit the ability of individuals to provide for themselves and their families. A law such as the one at issue is not, by any means of the term, a health law. Rather, it appears to have been passed with other motives that do not justify the illegal interference with an individual's freedom to contract. While this Court hesitates to overturn the decisions of legislators, we are justified in doing so when the character of the law and the subject matter at which it is aimed makes it apparent that the law was passed, not as a valid exercise of the police powers, but for some other means. The police powers may not be used as a pretext for passing laws, and it is the duty of this court to intervene when the legislature oversteps its bounds. Reversed.

■ DISSENT

(Holmes, J.) Today the majority imposes its own view of the nation's economic policy, that of laissez-faire, on the state of New York (D). In my view, the constitution was not meant to be a tool by which courts impose and/or favor an economic theory of any kind. Rather, a law should only be struck down when it can be said that a rational and fair man necessarily would admit that the law proposed would infringe fundamental principles that have been understood by the traditions of our people and our law. It is not for this court to strike down a law for infringing on an economic policy that the nation itself has not adopted. Because men of rational minds could not find this law to be unreasonable, I would uphold it.

■ DISSENT

(Harlan, J.) In striking down the state of New York's (D) law restricting the number of hours a baker may work, the majority overlooks the fact that this law reflects a belief by the people of New York (D) that bakers who work more than sixty hours a week or more than ten hours a day are subject to health hazards by virtue of their labor. While I do not disagree with the majority on the law, I strongly disagree that this law was passed as a mere pretext of protecting the public's health. I think there is more than substantial evidence to support the position of the state of New York (D) that bakers in particular are in need of some protection since by agreeing to work more than sixty hours a week or ten hours a day, they endanger their health more so than those in a professional field. Bakers breath air that is not pure and clean and, as a lot, are palefaced and of more delicate health than any others. I would thus uphold the law, there being no evidence that it is plainly inconsistent with the constitution.

Analysis:

This case is said to have begun the substantive due process era of the Supreme Court, known as the *Lochner* era. During this time, the Supreme Court used the Fourteenth Amendment to strike down hundreds of laws aimed at restricting the economic liberties of individuals in all sorts of areas, including maximum hours, minimum wage, unionizing, and general consumer protection laws. This era marked the Supreme Court's intervention in many areas in an effort to protect the laissez-faire economy. It was an era in which the Court applied a heightened strict scrutiny test to determine whether a law infringed upon an economic liberty, and as with most strict scrutiny cases, not many laws passed. Note that Justice Holmes' dissent called for a more rational basis test, the kind of test applied to these types of laws in modern times.

■ CASE VOCABULARY

LAISSEZ-FAIRE: An economic principle that favors no government interference with the marketplace.

MISDEMEANOR: A crime punishable by a small fine and no more than six months in jail.

POLICE POWERS: The exercise by the state of its right to legislate for the protection of its citizens' health, safety, morals and general welfare.

Coppage v. Kansas

(Employer) v. (State)
236 U.S. 1, 35 S.Ct. 240 (1915)

CONSTITUTION ALLOWS EMPLOYERS TO CONDITION EMPLOYMENT ON EMPLOYEE NOT JOINING A UNION

■ **INSTANT FACTS** Employer convicted of violating state law that prohibited conditioning employment on not joining a union challenged the constitutionality of the law.

■ **BLACK LETTER RULE** The freedom of contract includes the right to make contracts affecting personal employment without arbitrary interference by the state.

■ **PROCEDURAL BASIS**

Appeal from conviction by state court for violating state law precluding conditioning employment on not joining a union.

■ **FACTS**

Coppage (P), an employer in the state of Kansas (D), was convicted upon an information charging him with violating a state law that made it a crime for any employer to condition an offer of employment upon the prospective employee promising not to join a union.

■ **ISSUE**

Is a state law precluding an employer from conditioning an offer of employment on the employee promising not to join a union a valid and reasonable exercise of that state's police powers?

■ **DECISION AND RATIONALE**

(Pitney, J.) No. This law necessarily precludes an employer and employee from entering into a contract for employment terminable by will by which the employer agrees to hire the employee, and the employee agrees not to join a union. In a previous case, *Adair v. United States,* this Court struck down an identical federal law because it was an improper invasion on the personal liberty and right of property guaranteed by the Fifth Amendment, which provides, as does the Fourteenth Amendment, that no person shall be deprived of liberty or property without due process of law. In that case, we said that it is not within the government's function to compel any person to employ another against his will or to compel anyone to work for another against his will. Unless *Adair* be overruled, then it is controlling upon this court, and as we are not inclined to overrule *Adair,* its holding must control the outcome of this case. There being a freedom to contract protected by the Fourteenth Amendment, granting both parties the right to bargain for employment on the conditions they deem appropriate, has not each the right to stipulate to the terms of that employment? The employee is just as free to seek employment elsewhere where there is no condition imposed regarding joining a union as the employer is to only offer employment to those willing to be bound by such a condition. This freedom is chief among those liberties protected by the constitution, and if the right is interfered with arbitrarily by the state legislature, as it has been here, such a law can only be upheld if it is a valid exercise of the state's police powers. There being no such exercise here, the law must be declared unconstitutional. Reversed.

Analysis:

Here we have a simple application of the substantive due process we saw in *Lochner*, only without a claim that the law was aimed at protecting the health, safety, morals, or general welfare of the public. It is easy to see the court's theory at work in this opinion: an employer and employee have the right to bargain for the terms of employment without state interference, and if the employer only wanted to hire those willing not to join a union, any employee that did not want to make such a promise could seek employment elsewhere or choose not to be employed. The theory is simple enough, but consider the implications of such a rule in an economy where employment is hard to come by and all employers could place such a condition on employment, thereby putting all employees at risk. In true *Lochner* fashion, the court simply assumed that freedom to contract and right to employment were fundamental protected liberties with which all were vested before the constitution was ever written, thus prohibiting any interference with those liberties without substantial justification.

■ CASE VOCABULARY

INFORMATION: A document filed by a prosecutor indicating the charges with which one is charged; an informal recitation of charges filed directly by the prosecutor as opposed to an indictment handed down by a grand jury.

SINE QUA NON: An indispensable thing, an essential condition or element.

TERMINABLE AT WILL: A policy of employment law that deems any employment to be at the will of either the employer or the employee, with either free at any time and for any reason to terminate employment.

Muller v. Oregon

(*Employer*) v. (*State*)
208 U.S. 412, 28 S.Ct. 324 (1908)

HIGH COURT DECLARES WOMEN IN NEED OF SPECIAL PROTECTION

■ **INSTANT FACTS** Employer convicted of violating law that restricted the number of hours women could work in certain types of jobs challenged the constitutionality of the law under the Fourteenth Amendment.

■ **BLACK LETTER RULE** The general right to contract in relation to one's business is not absolute, but instead is subject to reasonable restrictions placed upon that right by government.

■ **PROCEDURAL BASIS**

Not stated.

■ **FACTS**

The state of Oregon (D) passed a law restricting the number of hours a woman could work in any mechanical establishment, factor or Laundromat to no more than ten hours a day. Muller (P) was convicted of violating that law.

■ **ISSUE**

Is a state law setting the maximum number of hours a woman could work in certain types of jobs a valid and reasonable exercise of that state's police powers?

■ **DECISION AND RATIONALE**

(Brewer, J.) Yes. In the brief filed on behalf of the state of Kansas (D) by Louis D. Brandels, there appears a large amount of data tending to show that long hours of labor are dangerous for women, especially because of their physical differences, maternal function, rearing and education of children and maintenance of the home. We have no doubt that the general right to contract in relation to one's business matters is part of the liberty protected by the Fourteenth Amendment. That right is not absolute, however. A state may, if necessary to protect health, safety, morals or general welfare of its citizens, pass a law restricting the right to contract. Here, there can be no doubt that this is such a law. Healthy mothers are essential to insuring the offspring of our population, making the physical well-being of women of utmost public concern. Women have always been dependent upon man and have been looked upon by the court as needing special protection as she struggles for subsistence in a world where she is not equal with her brother. As such, legislation to protect women is necessary to secure equality of right and such legislation may be upheld, even if it is not necessary for men. Even were all restrictions on political, persona and contractual rights taken away, women would still not be on equal footing with men and would still be in need of special protection. The restriction imposed by the law in question here is not imposed merely for the benefit of women but also for the benefit of all society. The differences between men and women in all aspects justify a difference in legislation and while the health of men may not need to be so protected, the health of women does. Affirmed.

Muller v. Oregon (Continued)

Analysis:

Here the Court was convinced that women were in need of special protection, since they could not insure their own health through standard employment contracts. Interestingly, however, despite the court's use of the differences between men and women in upholding Oregon's (D) law, ten years later, in *Bunting v. Oregon*, the same Court upheld a law limiting the total number of hours men or women could work in the manufacturing industry. That law was upheld on the grounds that it was in the public's interest to protect the health of those working in that particular industry. It is also interesting to note that several years later, in *Adkins v. Children's Hospital*, the court struck down a minimum wage law for women, finding that women were not so different as to justify setting the amount of money a woman must make. This opinion is also famous for the "Brandels brief", which paved the way for other attorneys in these types of cases to file similar briefs establishing with all kinds of scientific data the need for a given law.

■ CASE VOCABULARY

BRANDEIS BRIEF: A detailed brief, filled with social science data, seeking to show the need for a specific law.

Adkins v. Children's Hospital

(*Employee*) v. (*Employer*)
261 U.S. 525, 43 S.Ct. 394 (1923)

STATES MAY NOT SET MINIMUM WAGE FOR WOMEN

■ **INSTANT FACTS** Employee sued employer for not paying her in accordance with the state's minimum wage law.

■ **BLACK LETTER RULE** Freedom of contract is the general rule and the exercise of legislative authority to infringe upon that freedom the exception that must be justified by the existence of exceptional circumstances.

■ **PROCEDURAL BASIS**
Not stated.

■ **FACTS**
The District of Columbia passed a law setting the minimum wage women and children could earn in the District.

■ **ISSUE**
Is a state law setting the minimum wage a woman must earn a valid and reasonable exercise of that state's police powers?

■ **DECISION AND RATIONALE**
(Sutherland, J.) No. That there is a freedom to contract that includes contracts for employment is no longer an issue. It has been recognized in numerous opinions of this court and there can no longer be any question that such a right exists and that the Fourteenth Amendment protects it. In making such contracts, the parties have equal right to bargain for whatever terms they see fit. That said, there is no such thing as an absolute right. However, the freedom to so contract is the general rule and restraint upon that right the exception. Legislation infringing upon the freedom to contract can thus only be sustained by the presence of exceptional circumstances. Here, there has been no such showing. The inequality of the sexes as explained in *Muller v. Oregon*, has continued, but to a diminished intensity. These differences have almost all but disappeared. While the physical differences are still present, and may be properly taken into account in some cases, such as those fixing a maximum number of hours, the doctrine that women of mature age require restrictions upon their liberty to contract that could not lawfully be imposed upon men no longer holds up. To allow such restrictions would ignore all implications from present day laws that have accorded women emancipation from similar restrictions on her freedom to contract. Further, there is no set amount that can be determined that equals the cost of living a woman worker needs to maintain her in good health. What is a great amount to some, will be too little to another. Additionally, the relation between earnings and morals is not capable of standardization. Thus, as a means of safeguarding morals, the current law is inadequate. The law here takes into account only the necessities of one party to the contract, but it completely ignores those necessities of the employer who may not be able to pay a set minimum amount without jeopardizing his business. The law thus arbitrarily shifts a burden to the employer that should, on all accounts, be borne by all of society. The law is therefore unconstitutional. Reversed.

Adkins v. Children's Hospital (Continued)

Analysis:

The key here is that the court did not believe that setting a minimum wage law for women was necessary to protect the health, safety, morals, and general welfare of society as a whole and, even if remotely related, that the minimum wage was not a legitimate and adequate end to protecting these goals. Thus, unlike in *Muller*, the differences between men and women in society did not justify treating women differently and infringing upon a woman's freedom to contract for employment by any terms she may desire, including working for less. Notice that the Court did not overrule *Muller*. Rather, the Court recognized that, in some circumstances, the differences, mostly physical in nature, may justify treating women differently and infringing upon their freedom to contract in order to protect their health and thus the welfare of society as a whole.

■ CASE VOCABULARY

COST OF LIVING: An index used to determine the lowest amount of money on which an individual can meet his everyday needs: food, shelter and clothing. As the cost of securing these necessities goes up, so does the index.

Weaver v. Palmer Bros. Co.

(*Consumer*) v. (*Manufacturer*)
270 U.S. 402, 46 S.Ct. 320 (1926)

STATE CANNOT BAN BLANKETS THAT "MAY BE" SUBSTANDARD BECAUSE THEY ARE NOT "DANGEROUS"

■ **INSTANT FACTS** Manufacturer of blankets, sued for violating law that prohibited manufacturing blankets with shoddy materials, challenged constitutionality of law.

■ **BLACK LETTER RULE** Laws aimed at protecting public health must be the only reasonable way to eliminate a known health risk.

■ **PROCEDURAL BASIS**

Not stated.

■ **FACTS**

Palmer Bros. Co. (D) manufactures comfortables filled with materials known as shoddy. The law in question prohibits the selling of comfortables made with shoddy materials.

■ **ISSUE**

Is a state law prohibiting a manufacturer from using shoddy in his products a valid and reasonable exercise of that state's police powers?

■ **DECISION AND RATIONALE**

(Butler, J.) No. There is no dispute here that shoddy may be rendered harmless by disinfection or sterilization. Further, while there is evidence that the shoddy materials may carry some disease-carrying bacteria, such bacteria can only be transferred by direct contact and it is undisputed that the bacteria do not live long enough to be transferred to the consumer of the comfortable. Thus, even in the absence of disinfection or sterilization, there is little or no danger to the health of consumers. It necessarily follows that this law prohibiting the use of shoddy is not a valid exercise of the state's power to pass laws to protect the health of the public. There being little or no danger, the law is unreasonable and arbitrary. Reversed.

■ **DISSENT**

(Holmes, J.) It is not our job as jurists to second-guess the legislature. We ought to presume the law is valid and then test it from there. Here it is admitted that it is impossible to distinguish between comfortables made from shoddy and those that are not. If the legislature regarded the danger of shoddy as great and inspection and tagging as inadequate remedies, we ought to have upheld the law as aimed at preventing the spread of disease.

Analysis:

Justice Holmes advocated in this case for a different test than that used by the court in the *Lochner* era. Had the Court followed his test, this law clearly would have been upheld, as would many others. Justice

Weaver v. Palmer Bros. Co. (Continued)

Holmes was trying to get the court to apply a lower standard of review to insure that policy decisions were made by the legislature and not the courts. The majority, however, applying the substantive due process analysis used at that point in time, found the law unreasonable because there was no danger to the public, especially if sterilization were used. Underlying this opinion is the belief that consumers, like all individuals, enjoyed a freedom to contract that allowed them to purchase whatever product they wanted and that permitted manufacturers to conduct their businesses as they saw fit, so long as the public health was not endangered.

■ CASE VOCABULARY

COMFORTABLES: A type of blanket, commonly referred to as a comforter.

SHODDY: Scraps of fabric obtained from cutting tables in factories and secondhand garments and rags.

Nebbia v. New York

(Grocer) v. (State)
291 U.S. 502, 54 S.Ct. 505 (1934)

BAD MILK CONSTITUTES HEALTH RISK JUSTIFYING STATE REGULATION

■ **INSTANT FACTS** Grocer convicted of selling milk at prices lower than price set by state regulatory agency challenged the constitutionality of the price control.

■ **BLACK LETTER RULE** State price controls are constitutional if they are nondiscriminatory and bear a reasonable relationship to a proper legislative purpose.

■ PROCEDURAL BASIS
Appeal of conviction for violating price control law.

■ FACTS
The state of New York (D) enacted legislation that created a Milk Control Board whose job was to oversee and to set the minimum and maximum retail prices of milk to be charged by stores to consumers for consumption off the premises. The board fixed nine cents as the minimum price. Nebbia (P), a grocery store owner, was convicted of selling milk for less than the minimum price.

■ ISSUE
Is a state law setting the minimum price of a product a valid and reasonable exercise of that state's police powers?

■ DECISION AND RATIONALE
(Roberts, J.) Yes. The issue here is whether the federal constitution prohibits a state from establishing price controls. The law here was enacted to protect farmers who were seeing their milk sold for prices far below the cost of production, resulting in farmers and their families living in dire straits and forced to take public aid similar to unemployment benefits. There is no doubt that milk and its characteristics justify regulation. Milk is essential to diet and cannot be stored for long. Safeguards are thus necessary and, as a consequence, the milk industry has long been subjected to a myriad of regulations rivaled only by the railroad industry. We recognize that the general rule is that both consumers and grocers are free to contract absent governmental interference. But the right is not absolute. Equally fundamental is the right of the government to regulate in the common interest, even when it infringes on economic liberties. Here, the legislature saw that the milk industry was in danger of leaving dairy farmers too poor to continue producing milk without receiving more subsidies. The unrestricted competition among grocers and other retailers and the normal law of supply and demand was incapable of correcting the problem. In order to address these concerns and insure the continued availability of milk, the board created certain price controls. In light of the circumstances, those controls were reasonable and rationally related to the purpose for which they were designed. Accordingly, a state is free to adopt whatever economic policy it may reasonably deem necessary to promote public welfare and to enforce that policy by legislation. If the laws passed have a reasonable relation to a proper legislative purpose, the requirements of due process are satisfied. Such is the case here. Affirmed.

Nebbia v. New York (Continued)

Analysis:

Many saw this case as a signal that the *Lochner* era was coming to an end. Although the court did not so state, and appeared to apply the same rule of law, most observers believed that the opinion indicated a switch to a rational basis review, with the courts deferring to the legislature on issues of policy rather than scrutinizing all laws to be sure they served an adequate and legitimate purpose. Further, the opinion appears to relax the definition of legitimate purposes at which legislation may be aimed. If nothing else, this opinion certainly represented a departure from *Lochner* insofar as it left the decision of what economic policy to choose up to the states.

■ **CASE VOCABULARY**

AGRICULTURAL AND MARKET LAW: The entire codification of all laws regulating the milk industry.

LAW OF SUPPLY AND DEMAND: An economic principle that provides that as supply increases and demand decreases, it results in a market where the price of the product will be less and vice versa.

MALADJUSTMENTS: A decrease in the price that results in negative effects on the supplier.

West Coast Hotel Co. v. Parrish

(*Employer*) v. (*Employee*)
300 U.S. 379, 57 S.Ct. 578 (1937)

COURT FLIPS AND NOW RULES THAT MINIMUM WAGE LAWS FOR WOMEN ARE CONSTITUTIONAL

■ **INSTANT FACTS** Employee sued employer to recover difference between her actual wages and the minimum wage state law required that she be paid.

■ **BLACK LETTER RULE** Regulation that is reasonable in relation to its subject and is adopted in the interests of the community satisfies the due process clause of the Fourteenth Amendment.

■ **PROCEDURAL BASIS**

Not stated.

■ **FACTS**

West Coast Hotel Co. (P) ("Hotel") owns and operates a hotel in Washington state. Hotel (P) employed Elsie Parrish (D) as a chambermaid. Ms. Parrish (D) brought the action below against Hotel (P) to recover the difference between the wages she had been paid and the state's minimum wage requirement. Under the wage law of the state of Washington, women were to be paid no less than $14.50 per each workweek consisting of 48 hours. Hotel (P) challenged the constitutionality of the minimum wage law.

■ **ISSUE**

Is a state law setting the minimum wage a woman can earn a valid and reasonable exercise of that state's police powers?

■ **DECISION AND RATIONALE**

(Hughes, J.) Yes. Those challenging minimum wage laws such as the one at issue here do so on the grounds that such laws infringe upon the freedom to contract. But where is this freedom? The constitution does not speak of it. Rather, it speaks of liberty and prohibits the deprivation of that liberty without due process of law. Even in prohibiting such deprivation, however, the constitution does not recognize an absolute and uncontrollable liberty. The liberty safeguarded in the constitution is liberty in a social organization that requires the protection of law against evils that threaten the health, safety, morals and welfare of the people. It is thus subject to the restraints of due process, and regulation that is reasonable in relation to its subject and is adopted in the interests of the community is due process. That such regulations include those aimed at the contractual relationships between employer and employee is undeniable. Further, the legislature has wide discretion in deciding what is necessary to protect the public health, safety, morals and general welfare. In this regard, we believe the decision in *Adkins* [holding that minimum wage laws for women are unconstitutional insofar as they infringe on the freedom to contract without sufficient justification] was incorrect because it is impossible to reconcile that decision with the well settled principles regarding liberty and due process set forth above. If the protection of women is a legitimate state end, how can it be said that establishing a minimum wage is not an admissible means to that end? Women are in a class that receives the least amount of pay, their

West Coast Hotel Co. v. Parrish (Continued)

bargaining power is relatively weak and they are often victims of those who would take advantage of them. One need not cite a myriad of statistics to show what is apparent and of common knowledge. To remedy this and to prevent sweating systems, the legislature of Washington was free to enact the legislation in question. Further, the adoption of similar legislation across the nation indicates both the presence of the evil women face in the marketplace and the means adapted to protect against that evil. The legislative response to this evil cannot be regarded as arbitrary or capricious, and that is all we need to decide. The law in question is thus valid and constitutional.

Analysis:

In overruling *Adkins*, where the court previously held a similar law unconstitutional because it impermissibly infringed on the freedom to contract, the Court here has taken an entirely new approach, one that defers to the legislature in regard to deciding how best to remedy evil that threatens the public's health, safety, morals, or general welfare. In this opinion, the Court does not appear to concede that there is a fundamental freedom to contract protected by the Fourteenth Amendment, stating that such a freedom is not discussed in the Constitution. Also, note that the Court seems to accept that there are infirmities inherent in women that require certain protections, an idea that the court previously disputed in *Adkins*. The key here is to recognize the new test applied by the Court, that of simply looking to see if a law is arbitrary or capricious without regard to whether the law is aimed at a legitimate purpose or uses adequate and reasonable means to reach that purpose.

■ CASE VOCABULARY

SWEATING SYSTEM: The exploiting of workers at wages so low as to be insufficient to meet the bare cost of living.

United States v. Carolene Products Co.
(*Government*) v. (*Manufacturer*)
304 U.S. 144, 58 S.Ct. 778 (1938)

COURT APPLIES RATIONAL BASIS TEST AND UPHOLDS BAN ON FILLED MILK

■ **INSTANT FACTS** Company indicted for violating federal law prohibiting the shipping of adulterated milk products across interstate lines challenged constitutionality of the law.

■ **BLACK LETTER RULE** When reviewing legislation, the existence of facts supporting the legislation is to be presumed and such legislation shall not be pronounced unconstitutional unless it is of such character as to preclude the assumption that it rests upon some rational basis.

■ PROCEDURAL BASIS
Appeal of indictment for violation of federal law.

■ FACTS
Carolene Products (D) was indicted on charges of shipping Milnut across interstate lines in violation of a federal law that prohibits shipment in interstate commerce of skimmed milk compounded with any fat other than milk fat.

■ ISSUE
Is a state law prohibiting certain types of milk products from being sold a valid and reasonable exercise of that state's police powers?

■ DECISION AND RATIONALE
(Stone, J.) Yes. Simply put, the prohibition of Carolene Product's (D) product does not infringe the Fifth Amendment. This Court has previously so held in *Hebe Co. v. Shaw* [holding that a state law forbidding the manufacture and sale of condensed skimmed milk mixed with coconut oil was not unconstitutional]. We see no persuasive reason for departing from that ruling here. In doing so, we might rest our decision on the presumptive constitutionality of the law alone. In reviewing a law such as this, the existence of facts supporting the law is to be presumed and such a law shall not be pronounced unconstitutional absent a showing that there is no rational basis to support it. However, evidence also supports our decision. Numerous scientists and other experts testified about the effects of a product like Carolene Product's (D) on the public's health and how that effect is enhanced when an inferior product is indistinguishable from a good product. Although not relevant to this case, we note that when the existence of a rational basis depends on facts outside the sphere of judicial notice, those facts may properly be made a matter of judicial inquiry and the law predicated upon such facts challenged upon a showing that the facts no longer exist. However, the law must be upheld if any set of facts, whether known to the legislature or not, supports the law. Here, there is no question that the law is supported by facts and that there is thus a rational basis for it. Affirmed.

Analysis:
This is the case that is said established the rational basis test for economic due process cases. Note the language used: "must presume the existence of facts" and "any set of facts, whether known to the

United States v. Carolene Products Co. (Continued)

legislature or not." Such language indicates a strong deference to the legislature, the likes of which was not seen prior to this time. In this case, it became undeniably clear that the *Lochner* era was dead. Perhaps even more important is a footnote that appeared in the case, which stated, "[t]here may be narrower scope for operation of the presumption of constitutionality when legislation appears on its face to be within a specific prohibition of the Constitution, such as those of the first ten Amendments, which are deemed equally specific when held to be embraced by the Fourteenth." This has been called the most famous footnote in all of constitutional law. Clearly it set the groundwork for the standard the Court would apply to all constitutional challenges under the Fourteenth Amendment, applying the rational basis test unless a specific enumerated right or protected class of individuals was implicated.

■ **CASE VOCABULARY**

FILLED MILK ACT: The law in question that prohibits shipment of skimmed milk mixed with any type of fat other than milk fat.

MILNUT: A compound of condensed skimmed milk and coconut oil.

Williamson v. Lee Optical of Oklahoma, Inc.

(State Representative) v. (Optician)
348 U.S. 483, 75 S.Ct. 461 (1955)

FROM NOW ON, ALL ECONOMIC REGULATIONS PRESUMED CONSTITUTIONAL

■ **INSTANT FACTS** Optician brought suit to have law prohibiting him from dispensing lenses or fitting lenses in frames without a prescription from a licensed ophthalmologist or optometrist and to enjoin state officials from enforcing the law.

■ **BLACK LETTER RULE** Economic legislation will be upheld so long as there is any conceivable justification for it.

■ PROCEDURAL BASIS

Appeal from declaratory judgment finding state law unconstitutional.

■ FACTS

Oklahoma enacted a law that prohibited anyone from fitting lenses to a face or duplicating or replacing into frames lenses or other optical appliance, except with a written prescription from a licensed ophthalmologist or optometrist. Lee Optical (D) brought suit to have the law declared unconstitutional, since as an optometrist, Mr. Lee (D) was in the business of doing what the law prohibited.

■ ISSUE

Is a state law prohibiting individuals from fitting or replacing lenses without a prescription from a licensed eye doctor a valid and reasonable exercise of that state's police powers?

■ DECISION AND RATIONALE

(Douglas, J.) Yes. The effect of Oklahoma's law is to prevent an optician from fitting or replacing lenses without a prescription. Although the trial court conceded that the law was a valid exercise of the state's right to regulate the examination of eyes, it balked at the idea that a state could require a prescription before an optician could simply replace a lost lense or fit old lenses into new frames. The trial court thus held that such a requirement was not reasonably and rationally related to the health and welfare of the people and declared the law unconstitutional. We agree that the law may exact a needless and wasteful requirement, but it is for the legislature, not the courts, to balance the advantages and disadvantages of such legislation. There are numerous reasons the legislature could have concluded this law was necessary. It could have recognized that in some cases, a prescription is absolutely imperative in order to insure the lenses are fit correctly so as to correct the defect in the vision. Or it may have determined that the number of times a prescription was needed justified requiring one in every case. Or it may have concluded that an eye examination is so important as to require each new eyeglass purchase with one. Even if the law is not logically consistent with its aims, it is enough that there is an evil at hand that needs to be corrected and that it might be thought that the measure enacted was a rational way to correct it. If the people are unhappy with the decisions of their legislature on these issues, they shall take their concerns to the polls, not to the courts. Reversed.

Williamson v. Lee Optical of Oklahoma, Inc. (Continued)

Analysis:

This case illustrates the total abdication of the *Lochner* era and further emphasizes the level of deference the courts will give to legislatures when reviewing economic legislation. Here, it didn't matter what the reason was for passing the law. All that was required to uphold the law was a finding that there was some rational reason for it. It didn't even matter that the reason may not have been one the legislature relied upon. In cases following this one, the court continued to demonstrate how unlikely it was that an economic legislation would be found unconstitutional. Although no economic legislation has been held unconstitutional since *Williamson,* the court has not entirely abdicated economic substantive due process as some may have thought. In recent years, the doctrine reared its ugly head in the most unusual of places. Consider *BMW v. Gore,* in which the court used the doctrine to strike a punitive damages award, finding that the action of the state in granting the award was unjustified.

■ CASE VOCABULARY

OPHTHALMOLOGIST: An eye doctor that handles all areas of the care of eyes.

OPTICIAN: A qualified artisan qualified to grind lenses and to fill prescriptions for eyeglasses.

OPTOMETRIST: An eye doctor that examines the eyes for refractive error and recognizes but does not treat eye diseases.

BMW of North America, Inc. v. Gore

(*Distributor*) v. (*Consumer*)
517 U.S. 559, 116 S.Ct. 1589 (1996)

COURT RESURRECTS ECONOMIC SUBSTANTIVE DUE PROCESS IN STRIKING PUNITIVE DAMAGES AWARD

■ **INSTANT FACTS** Consumer who purchased automobile from retailer brought suit for damages upon finding that the vehicle had been repainted prior to sale without consumer's knowledge.

■ **BLACK LETTER RULE** A punitive damages award that can fairly be characterized as grossly excessive in relation to a state's legitimate interests in punishing unlawful conduct and deterring repetition of such conduct is arbitrary and violates the due process clause of the Fourteenth Amendment.

■ **PROCEDURAL BASIS**

Appeal from Alabama Supreme Court's affirmance but reduction of jury's verdict imposing award of punitive damages.

■ **FACTS**

In January 1990, Dr. Ira Gore (D) purchased a black BMW sports sedan for $40,750.88 from an authorized dealer in Birmingham, Alabama. After driving the car for nine months without any problems, Dr. Gore (D) took the car to "Slick Finish", an independent detailer, to make the car look "snazzier". Employees at Slick Finish discovered that the car had been repainted. Convinced he had been cheated, Dr. Gore (D) brought suit against BMW (P), the American distributor. It was Dr. Gore's (D) theory that BMW (P) failed to disclose the car had been repainted prior to sale. At trial, BMW (P) acknowledged it had a policy of selling a car as used if it required repairs exceeding three percent of the cars price, but if the repairs did not exceed this baseline, the car was sold as new without disclosure of any of the repairs. Since the cost of repainting Dr. Gore's (D) car was less than three percent of its value, the repainting was never disclosed. Dr. Gore (D), however, asserted that his car was worth $4,000 less than it would have been had it not been repainted. Further, Dr. Gore (D) asserted that since 1983, BMW (P) had sold 983 refinished cars as new. On this basis, Dr. Gore (D) sought punitive damages equal to $4,000 per car. The jury returned a verdict in Dr. Gore's (D) favor, awarding him $4,000 in compensatory damages and $4 million in punitive damages. The award of punitive damages was based on a finding that the nondisclosure policy constituted gross and malicious fraud. On appeal, the Alabama Supreme Court rejected BMW's (P) claim that the award exceeded a constitutionally permissible amount. It did, however, rule in BMW's (P) favor that the amount of punitive damages had been improperly calculated. The court then reduced the punitive damages award to $2 million. BMW (P) then appealed to this court.

■ **ISSUE**

May a state constitutionally impose any amount of economic sanctions in the form of punitive damages?

■ **DECISION AND RATIONALE**

(Stevens, J.) No. Punitive damages may properly be awarded to further a state's legitimate interests in punishing and deterring unlawful conduct. Most states require only that the damages be reasonably necessary to vindicate these interests. Thus, only when an award is grossly excessive in relation to these interests will it be said to be so arbitrary as to be in violation of the Fourteenth Amendment. We thus first begin with an examination of the state of Alabama's interests in punishing and deterring BMW's (P) conduct. No one doubts that the states have a right to protect its residents from such fraudulent behavior. But each state need not do so in the same way as other states. The diversity alone of rules regarding disclosure of the kind found unlawful in this case indicates that reasonable minds will differ on how best to protect citizens from such harm. It follows from the principles of state sovereignty and comity that a state may not impose economic sanctions on violators of its laws with the intent of changing the tortfeasor's' lawful conduct in other states. By attempting to alter BMW's (P) national policy, Alabama has infringed upon the policy choices of many other states where its conduct would be lawful. Thus, the economic penalties a state such as Alabama imposes, whether it be through legislative fines or punitive damages, must be supported only by a desire to protect its own residents and on deterring conduct within its own borders. The due process clause of the constitution requires that a person receive fair notice not only of the conduct that will subject him to punishment, but also of the severity of the penalty. Three reasons lead us to conclude that the punitive damages award in this case, even as reduced by the Alabama Supreme Court, is excessive. First, none of the aggravating factors indicative of reprehensible conduct is present in this case. Second, the ratio to the actual harm is more than 500 to 1. While it is impossible to set a specific ration that will always be deemed excessive, clearly 500 to 1 is a ration that more than raises a judicial eyebrow. Third, comparing the possible criminal or civil penalties for the conduct here with the award also shows its excessiveness. The maximum civil penalty for this conduct is $2,000, and the most other states impose is $10,000. Thus, the sanction here was clearly excessive and as such, is unconstitutional. The fact that the award prompted changes in policy sheds no light on the question of whether a lesser award would have deterred the conduct. Reversed.

■ DISSENT

(Scalia, J.) In my opinion, this area is of no concern to us from a constitutional standpoint and the majority's opinion today opens the door for constitutional scrutiny of a subject that has no business being included in constitutional doctrine. It is clear that the appeals process, which furnishes a defendant with the right to judicial review of any award of damages, punitive or otherwise, is sufficient to protect any due process interests implicated in this case. The Fourteenth Amendment is not a substantive guarantee against unfairness. By deciding as it has today, the majority has opened the door for all kinds of challenges to the fairness of any award, which will lead to an enormous amount of litigation challenging such awards on constitutional grounds when the constitution should not be involved at all. By the majority's view today, any challenge to anything seen as unfair would implicate constitutional analysis. Since I do not believe such analysis is warranted in this or any other case where a claim of unfairness is raised, I would uphold the award.

Analysis:

Whether this opinion represents a revival of economic substantive due process in areas other than economic legislation is unclear. What is clear, however, is that the Court will limit a state's right to impose burdens that will have an effect on another state, as was the case here. Interestingly, the Court's test could easily have been framed in some other language, rather than the Constitution or the Fourteenth Amendment. However, in framing the analysis as one of due process, the Court seems to be indicating that substantive due process is not dead. Some legal observers have said that in focusing the inquiry on what notice was given, the Court was really applying a tortured version of procedural due process, and not substantive due process. In any case, the idea of comity and the right of one state to act outside its borders is important. More important, however, is that this case notwithstanding, the Court had not used the Due Process Clause of the Fourteenth Amendment to invalidate any economic legislation since 1937.

■ CASE VOCABULARY

COMPENSATORY DAMAGES: Actual damages aimed at making the victim whole again.

PUNITIVE DAMAGES: Damages imposed solely to punish a tortfeasor for committing the tort, usually aimed at motivating the tortfeasor to change its ways.

STARE DECISIS: Following the previous decisions of the court, precedent.

STATE SOVEREIGNTY AND COMITY: A principle that recognizes that each state is its own independent government and that one state cannot impose its policy or goals on another state or impose burdens on the interstate market out of respect for the effect of doing so on other states.

TORTFEASOR: One who commits a tort.

State Farm Mut. Automobile Ins. Co. v. Campbell

(Insurance Company) v. (Insured)
538 U.S. 408, 123 S.Ct. 1513 (2003)

PUNITIVE DAMAGES AWARDS MUST BE WEIGHED AGAINST THE COMPENSATORY DAMAGES

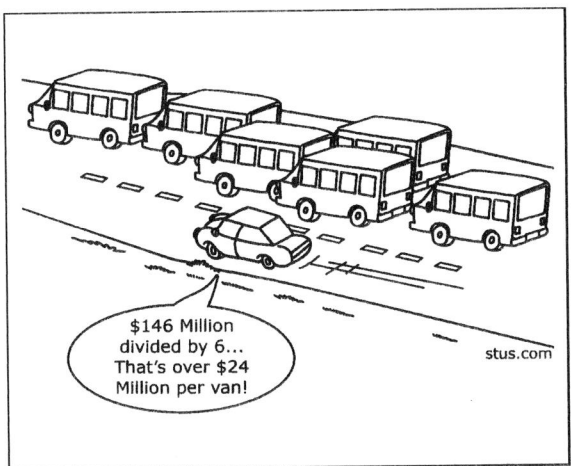

■ **INSTANT FACTS** After State Farm (D) failed to settle claims against Campbell (P) for its policy limits, Campbell obtained a judgment for $1 million in compensatory damages and $145 million in punitive damages.

■ **BLACK LETTER RULE** In evaluating the appropriateness of a punitive damages award, a court must weigh the reprehensibility of the defendant's conduct, the disparity between the actual harm caused and the amount of the punitive damages awarded, and the difference between the punitive damages awarded and the civil penalties imposed under state law.

■ PROCEDURAL BASIS

Certiorari to review the excessiveness of a punitive damages verdict.

■ FACTS

Campbell (P) held an automobile policy with State Farm Mutual Automobile Insurance Co. (D). While traveling in Utah, Campbell (P) decided to pass six vans traveling slowly in front of him. As Campbell (P) was driving in the wrong direction, Ospital was forced onto the shoulder to avoid a head-on collision. In the process, Ospital lost control of his vehicle, collided with a vehicle driven by Slusher, and died. Slusher became permanently disabled. An investigation of the incident determined that Campbell's (P) unsafe pass had caused Ospital's death and Slusher's injuries. Nonetheless, State Farm (D) decided to contest liability and declined offers from Ospital's estate and Slusher to settle both claims for its total policy limit of $50,000. At trial, a jury found Campbell (P) liable for the accident and returned a verdict for $185,849. State Farm (D) refused to pay the verdict in excess of its $50,000 policy limits and refused to post a supersedeas bond required for Campbell's (P) appeal. Campbell (P) subsequently obtained independent counsel and appealed the verdict. During the appeal, Campbell (P) agreed to pursue a bad faith action against State Farm (D) in exchange for an agreement by Ospital's estate and Slusher not to seek satisfaction of the judgment against Campbell (P). Ospital's estate and Slusher agreed to accept ninety percent of any proceeds received from State Farm (D) in the bad faith suit. The Utah Supreme Court denied Campbell's (P) appeal from the wrongful death judgment, and State Farm (D) subsequently agreed to pay the full amount of the judgment against him. Campbell (P) then commenced his bad faith suit. A jury awarded Campbell $2.6 million in compensatory damages and $145 million in punitive damages. After the trial court reduced the compensatory damages award to $1 million and the punitive damages to $25 million, the Utah Supreme Court reinstated the $145 million punitive damages verdict. State Farm (D) sought a writ of certiorari.

■ ISSUE

When compensatory damages are $1 million, is an award of $145 million in punitive damages against a defendant excessive in violation of the Due Process Clause of the Fourteenth Amendment?

■ DECISION AND RATIONALE

(Kennedy, J.) Yes. Unlike compensatory damages, which serve to compensate an injured person for the wrongful conduct of another, punitive damages are aimed at deterrence and retribution against the

State Farm Mut. Automobile Ins. Co. v. Campbell (Continued)

wrongdoer. The Due Process Clause does not permit "the imposition of grossly excessive or arbitrary punishments on a tortfeasor." Because punitive damages serve a purpose similar to criminal sanctions, but without the procedural protections accompanying criminal punishment, a court must weigh the reprehensibility of the defendant's conduct, the disparity between the actual harm caused and the amount of the punitive damages awarded, and the difference between the punitive damages awarded and the civil penalties imposed under state law. Weighing these factors, the jury's $145 million punitive damages award was excessive.

First, State Farm's (D) conduct cannot be considered so reprehensible as to justify the award. In gauging a defendant's conduct, a court should consider whether the harm caused was physical rather than economic, whether the defendant acted with reckless disregard for the health and safety of others, whether the plaintiff was financially vulnerable, whether the conduct involved a repetitive pattern or an isolated incident, and whether the conduct was intentional. Here, while State Farm's (D) handling of Campbell's (P) insurance claims is not laudable, its conduct does not justify such an excessive punitive damages award. Rather than focusing on the particular conduct of the case, the award focuses on State Farm's (D) nationwide handling of claims. A state court, however, has no authority to punish a defendant for conduct that occurred outside its territorial limits and involving parties who were directly affected by the out-of-state conduct. A defendant's dissimilar conduct, bearing no relation to the harm involved in a particular lawsuit, may not be taken into account when determining punitive damages. Due process does not permit a court to award a party punitive damages merely because the defendant may have caused some harm to others who were not proper parties to the litigation.

Second, although there is no bright-line ratio between the amount of punitive damages and the harm caused to a plaintiff, an award 145 times the actual harm suffered is excessive. Generally, anything over a single-digit ratio calls for close judicial scrutiny. Likewise, as the compensatory damages award increases, the appropriate proportion to the punitive damages award decreases, since a larger ratio is unnecessary to serve the purposes of deterrence and retribution. Here, the 145:1 ratio between the punitive award and the compensatory award is unreasonable given the $1 million compensatory damages award for emotional distress.

Finally, the $145 million punitive damages award is grossly in excess of the maximum civil penalty of $10,000 imposed under Utah law. Under this factor, the punitive damages award is again excessive. Because a punitive award more closely approximating the compensatory award would be an adequate and rational punishment for the defendant's conduct, the award is excessive. Reversed and remanded.

■ DISSENT

(Scalia, J.) The Due Process Clause affords no protections against "excessive" or "unreasonable" punitive damages awards.

■ DISSENT

(Thomas, J.) The Constitution does not "constrain the size of punitive damages awards."

■ DISSENT

(Ginsburg, J.) The field of punitive damages lies entirely within the prerogative of the states. While the punitive damages award in this case may be excessive, it should be addressed through state tort reform legislation, but the Court should not substitute its judgment for that of the state courts. The state court could have determined that State Farm's national scheme to deny benefits to its consumers had an adverse impact on Utah residents. In second-guessing the state's determination on the trial record, the Court affords no respect to the states and inappropriately threatens to create a bright-line test for determining the appropriateness of a punitive damages award.

Analysis:

The Court's fascination with the appropriate ratio between the compensatory damages and punitive damages is interesting. If punitive damages serve a separate and distinct purpose from compensatory damages, why should the amount of compensatory damages affect the amount of punitive damages? If a defendant commits intentional conduct worthy of punishment, should it matter whether the compensatory damages were substantial or not?

■ CASE VOCABULARY

BAD FAITH: Dishonesty of belief or purpose.

COMPENSATORY DAMAGES: Damages sufficient in amount to indemnify the injured person for the loss suffered.

PUNITIVE DAMAGES: Damages awarded in addition to actual damages when the defendant acted with recklessness, malice, or deceit.

SUPERSEDEAS BOND: A bond that suspends a judgment creditor's power to levy execution, usually pending appeal.

Philip Morris U.S.A. v. Williams

(*Cigarette Maker*) v. (*Smoker*)
549 U.S. 346, 127 S.Ct. 1057 (2007)

TOBACCO COMPANIES ARE NOT LIABLE FOR PUNITIVE DAMAGES FOR HARMING NON-PARTIES

■ **INSTANT FACTS** Williams (P) was awarded punitive damages after his attorney argued that Philip Morris's (D) actions would harm others.

■ **BLACK LETTER RULE** An award of punitive damages based on a desire to punish the defendant for harming persons not before the court is an unconstitutional taking of property without due process.

■ PROCEDURAL BASIS

Appeal from an order of the Oregon Supreme Court affirming a judgment for Williams (P).

■ FACTS

Williams (P) was a heavy cigarette smoker. After his death, his widow (P) sued Philip Morris (D), the manufacturer of his favorite brand, for negligence and deceit. At trial, Williams's (P) lawyer told the jury to consider others injured by Philip Morris (D) in awarding damages. Philip Morris (D) requested an instruction that the jury could consider the extent of the harm suffered by others in awarding punitive damages, but could not punish Philip Morris (D) for the harm suffered by non-parties. The trial court refused to give such an instruction. Instead, the jury was instructed that punitive damages are awarded "to punish misconduct and to deter misconduct." The jury was also told that punitive damages "are not intended to compensate [Williams (P)] or anyone else for damages caused by [Philip Morris's (D)] conduct." The jury awarded $821,000 as compensatory damages for deceit, and about $79.5 million as punitive damages. Philip Morris (D) claimed that there was a significant likelihood that a portion of the award represented punishment for having harmed others. It argued that such punishment was prohibited by the Due Process Clause. The Oregon Supreme Court rejected this argument.

■ ISSUE

Did awarding punitive damages for harm to non-parties violate due process?

■ DECISION AND RATIONALE

(Breyer, J.) Yes. An award of punitive damages based on a desire to punish the defendant for harming persons not before the court is an unconstitutional taking of property without due process. Threatening a defendant with punishment for harm to a non-party denies the defendant of an opportunity to defend against the charge. It also adds a nearly standardless dimension to the calculation of punitive damages. The jury does not know how many victims there were, or how seriously and under what circumstances they were injured. The risks of arbitrariness, uncertainty, and lack of notice will be magnified.

There is also no authority supporting an award of punitive damages for harming others. It is appropriate to consider the potential harm caused by the defendant. That potential harm, however, is harm to the plaintiff. Williams (P) argues that showing harm to others is relevant to the question of reprehensibility. Evidence of harm to others may show that the conduct posed a substantial risk of harm to the public and was therefore particularly reprehensible. A jury may not go further than this and use punitive damages to punish for harm to non-parties.

It is particularly important that states avoid procedures that unnecessarily deprive juries of proper legal guidance. The Due Process Clause requires that juries are not asking the wrong question. The Oregon Supreme Court applied the wrong constitutional standard. Application of this standard may lead to the need for a new trial or an adjustment in the amount of punitive damages, so the Court will not consider whether the award was constitutionally grossly excessive. Judgment vacated and remanded.

■ DISSENT

(Stevens, J.) There is no reason why an interest in punishing a wrongdoer for harm to non-parties should not be taken into consideration when assessing a sanction for reprehensible conduct. Punitive damages are a sanction for the public harm caused or threatened by a defendant. The distinction the majority draws between using harm to others to assess the reprehensibility of conduct and to punish directly is elusive.

■ DISSENT

(Thomas, J.) The Constitution does not constrain the size of punitive damages awards.

■ DISSENT

(Ginsburg, J.) The inquiry as to the reprehensibility of Philip Morris's (D) conduct focuses on the harm Philip Morris (D) "was prepared to inflict on the smoking public at large." The majority identifies no evidence introduced and no charge delivered inconsistent with that inquiry. More deference should be given to state courts that try to adhere to the Court's precedent.

Analysis:

The jury's verdict is broken down into compensatory and punitive damages, but the punitive damages are not divided into punishment for harm to Williams (P) and for harm to others. The majority is speculating that the jury's award could have been based on an improper motive. There is no way of knowing, since the jury's deliberations remain a secret. Counsel's argument could have been passed off as merely a rhetorical flourish. As noted in the casebook, the Supreme Court of Oregon affirmed the award on remand, and the U.S. Supreme Court granted certiorari. The writ of certiorari was later dismissed as improvidently granted. See *Philip Morris U.S.A., Inc. v. Williams*, 129 S. Ct. 1436 (2009).

■ **CASE VOCABULARY**

PUNITIVE DAMAGES: Damages awarded in addition to actual damages when the defendant acted with recklessness, malice, or deceit.

Home Building & Loan Association v. Blaisdell
(Lender) v. (Borrower)
290 U.S. 398, 54 S.Ct. 231 (1934)

COURT UPHOLDS STATE'S ATTEMPT TO HELP DEBTORS

■ **INSTANT FACTS** Borrower took advantage of a state law that permitted borrowers to ask for extensions of the time in which they were to pay back their mortgages, and bank brought lawsuit challenging the constitutionality of the law.

■ **BLACK LETTER RULE** A state may impose temporary conditions on the creditor-debtor relationship so long as there is an emergency, the legislation is addressed to a legitimate end and the relief afforded is proportional and reasonable.

■ PROCEDURAL BASIS
Action by lender challenging the constitutionality of law allowing debtors the right to an extension of the redemption period during the Depression.

■ FACTS
In 1933, during the Depression, Minnesota enacted a law that authorizes a district court, upon application to the court by the debtor, to extend the period of redemption from foreclosure sales for such additional time as the court deems just, with the debtor responsible for paying the reasonable rental value of the property during the extended period. Aside from the extension of time, no other part of the debtor-creditor relationship has been affected.

■ ISSUE
May a state constitutionally enact temporary legislation that alters the creditor-debtor contractual relationship?

■ DECISION AND RATIONALE
(Hughes, J.) Yes. Home Building & Loan Association (P) challenges the validity of the Minnesota law on the grounds that it violates the Contracts Clause in the U.S. Constitution. In determining the constitutionality of the challenged law, we must consider the effect of the stated emergency on the state's power to enact such a law. First, we note that the existence of an emergency alone does not expand or create any lawmaking power on the part of the states. It may, however, furnish the occasion for exercising a power the state already has. The question thus becomes in light of the emergency that existed here, was this law a valid exercise of Minnesota's police power? Regardless of whether a law has the affect of abrogating or modifying a contractual relationship, the state still maintains the power to pass legislation to safeguard the vital interests of its people. However, the state's power is not absolute, otherwise the Contracts Clause, which recognizes a certain right in the people to be free to contract as they wish, would be meaningless. But, on the same note, the Contracts Clause cannot be read to preclude any legislation that affects contractual relationships. Thus, while a state cannot adopt a policy that destroys or totally repudiates a contract or denies people of the means to enforce such contracts, it does not follow that the state cannot impose such conditions as it deems necessary to protect the interests of the community. The state's power to place such temporary conditions on contracts in the presence of an emergency is thus inferred in every contract. And if the power exists to give temporary relief to citizens

Home Building & Loan Association v. Blaisdell (Continued)

in times of great natural disasters, it cannot disappear when the urgent public need arises from economic or other causes. It is not enough to say that the need itself was not foreseen a century ago or that what the Constitution meant to the framers it must still mean today. The Constitution was not meant to be a rigid brick that never changes. Rather, the Constitution was intended to last for ages, and as the ages came and went, the Constitution must be interpreted in the modern times and be adapted to the trials of those times. We must thus consider Minnesota's law in light of these considerations. In doing so, we find that an emergency existed, the legislation was addressed to a legitimate end, the relief afforded was justified by the emergency and a reasonable response to it, the conditions imposed were not unreasonable and the legislation itself was temporary. As such, it does not violate the Contracts Clause. Whether or not it is a wise policy does not concern us, the fact remains the law is constitutional.

Analysis:

This case indicates a shift in constitutional theory among the majority of justices. Note that the Court prefaces its holding with statements that the Constitution was not meant to be interpreted as black letter law, but rather must be adapted to modern times. This was important, because the Contracts Clause states that no state shall pass a law that impairs the obligation of contracts. In the face of such clear language, the Court needed a way to find a power in the states to help address an emergency situation, such as the one here, where thousands were losing their homes because of the great loss suffered during the Depression. Here, the law clearly modified existing contractual obligations. However, it did so only slightly and it did so only temporarily. In light of the emergency and the great risk to the people, the Court had little trouble finding that the law was a valid exercise of a state's police powers.

■ CASE VOCABULARY

FORECLOSURE: A judicial procedure by which the holder of a deed of trust takes possession of property securing a debt in order to collect that debt.

MORTGAGE: A loan secured by real property.

PERIOD OF REDEMPTION: The time in which a debtor has to pay the full amount owed on a mortgage in order to avoid foreclosure.

Energy Reserves Group, Inc. v. Kansas Power & Light Co.

(Seller) v. (Buyer)
459 U.S. 400, 103 S.Ct. 697 (1983)

PRICE CONTROLS ON NATURAL GAS UPHELD

■ **INSTANT FACTS** State enacted legislation that precluded natural gas supplier from charging prices established in contract with buyer.

■ **BLACK LETTER RULE** A state may enact legislation that infringes on the contractual rights of parties so long as the substantial impairment is justified by a significant and legitimate purpose.

■ PROCEDURAL BASIS
Not stated.

■ FACTS
Energy Resources Group (P) entered into a contract with Kansas Power & Light (D) by which Energy (P) would sell natural gas to Kansas Power (D) at a price that fluctuated as the market price for natural gas changed. Subsequently, the state of Kansas adopted a law that froze natural gas prices, thereby prohibiting any price increases, in order to comply with prices set by federal authorities. As a result, the state law prevented Energy (P) from charging more for its gas, even though its contract allowed them to do so.

■ ISSUE
May a state enact price controls that have the effect of substantially impairing contractual obligations?

■ DECISION AND RATIONALE
(Blackmun, J.) Yes. First, we must determine whether Kansas' law operates as a substantial impairment on contractual obligations. It is the severity of the impairment that determines the scrutiny that this Court applies to the challenged law. Regulation that restricts a party's reasonable expectations does not necessarily work a substantial impairment. To determine the extent of the impairment, we must consider whether the industry has been regulated in the past. If the legislation constitutes a substantial impairment, the legislation is not necessarily unconstitutional. However, to be valid, the law must have a significant and legitimate public purpose behind it. That purpose need not be directed at an emergency or temporary situation, however. If such a legitimate purpose is present, then we must decide whether the impairment is reasonable. In making this last determination, courts defer to the legislature unless the state itself is a contracting party. Here, the parties were operating in a heavily regulated industry. In fact, they used the regulated prices as the guideline in their escalator clause. Further, the contract itself expressly recognized that it was subject to regulations. To say now, as Energy (P) does, that foreseeable price regulations should not alter a contract the parties knew was subject to regulation and specifically to price regulation in order to protect some absolute right to freedom of contract is illogical. Such a result cannot be permitted. As a result, this court does not believe the law here constitutes a substantial impairment on the parties' contractual obligations. Even if we assume it is a substantial impairment, however, the law is based upon a significant and legitimate state interest and it is reasonably related to that purpose. As such, it is constitutional.

Analysis:

In this case, the Court clarifies the standard it will apply in order to determine the constitutionality of economic legislation that infringes upon an individual's freedom to contract in the post-*Lochner* era. Basically, it applies a three-part test. First, it determines if the legislation works a substantial impairment on the parties' contractual obligations. If so, the Court next determines whether the legislation serves a significant and legitimate goal. Finally, the Court looks at whether the legislation is reasonable in light of that goal. It is the second and third requirements that change if the government itself is a party to the contract. In that instance, a higher scrutiny is applied, and the Court will not defer to the legislature's policy decisions. If the government is not a contracting party, however, the courts defer to the legislature and only invalidate a law that does not meet the rational basis test.

■ CASE VOCABULARY

ESCALATOR CLAUSE: A contractual provision that provides for the increase in the price to be paid under the contract in correlation with an outside indicator, such as market price.

Allied Structural Steel v. Spannaus

(*Employer*) v. (*State Representative*)
438 U.S. 234, 98 S.Ct. 2716 (1978)

STATE LAW AMENDED PENSION PLAN FOUND TO BE UNCONSTITUTIONAL

■ **INSTANT FACTS** State enacted legislation that required employers to pay pension benefits to employees whose benefits had not yet vested.

■ **BLACK LETTER RULE** A state may not unilaterally change the contractual obligations of parties to a pension fund absent a reasonable justification.

■ **PROCEDURAL BASIS**

Suit by employer seeking declaration that the law was unconstitutional.

■ **FACTS**

In 1974, Allied Structural Steel Co. (P) ("Allied"), whose principal place of business was in Illinois, maintained an office with 30 employees in the state of Minnesota. Under the company's general pension plan, which was qualified under § 401 of the Internal Revenue Code, salaried employees were entitled to retire at age 65, and if they did so, they would receive 1% of their average monthly earnings multiplied by the number of years of employment. Employees could also receive pension benefits, payable in full at age 65, if they had worked for the company for 15 years or more and had reached the age of 60, were at least 55 and the sum of the employee's age and years of service was at least 75 or was less than 55 but the sum of the employee's age and years of service was at least 80. Once an employee satisfied any of these conditions, his pension plan benefits were vested. Those employees whose employment was terminated prior to age 65 who did not meet one of these three conditions did not receive pension benefits. Allied (P) was the sole contributor to the plan and funded it based upon its actuarial predictions of eventual payout needs. Any contributions made by Allied (P) were irrevocable, but it was not required to make any type of contribution to the plan under the plan agreement. Further, Allied (P) retained an unrestricted right to amend the plan agreement and was free to terminate it at any time. If terminated, the assets of the pension trust fund would go first to those already retired and receiving benefits, next to those eligible for retirement and finally to those covered employees whose rights had not vested. In April 1974, Minnesota enacted a law that subjected private employers of more than 100 employees, at least one of whom was a Minnesota resident, that provided pension benefits to its employees with a § 401 plan to a pension funding charge if the employer terminated the plan or closed its office in the state. During the summer of 1974, Allied (P) began closing its Minnesota office. On July 31, it discharged all of its 30 employees, at least nine of which did not have vested pension benefits but had worked for the company for at least 10 years. On August 8, the state notified Allied (P) that it owed a pension funding charge of approximately $185,000. Allied (P) brought this suit challenging the constitutionality of the law requiring it to pay the charge.

■ **ISSUE**

May a state enact legislation that alters an employer's obligations under a pension plan?

Allied Structural Steel v. Spannaus (Continued)

■ DECISION AND RATIONALE

(Stewart, J.) No. There is no doubt that the Minnesota act in question substantially altered the relationship between Allied (P) and its employees by superimposing pension obligations upon the company beyond those it had voluntarily assumed. It does not necessarily follow, however, that the act violates the Contracts Clause of the US Constitution. Although used with much greater force and meaning prior to the emergence of the Fourteenth Amendment, the Contracts Clause is not superfluous. If it is to retain any meaning at all, however, it must be read to impose some limits on the power of states to abrogate existing contractual obligations. Thus, we must apply a three-part test. First, does the law work a substantial impairment? If not, the inquiry ends here and the law is constitutional. If so, the inquiry continues and the purpose and nature of the legislation is subjected to a higher scrutiny. Here, the plan satisfied all federal requirements and Allied (P) had no reason to anticipate that its employees rights could vest except in accordance with the terms of the plan. Allied (P) funded the plan based on the expectation that benefits would vest only in accordance with the plan. The effect of the instant law was thus severe in that it retroactively modified Allied's (P) obligations under the plan. Furthermore, the law here does not even come close to that upheld in *Home Building & Loan Association v. Blaisdell* [state law extending time for debtor to redeem property and to avoid foreclosure upheld as valid exercise of police powers as reasonable response to economic emergency]. While there is no requirement that the state's power be exercised only to deal with an emergency, the existence of an emergency and the temporary nature of legislation enacted to handle that emergency often will justify interfering with existing contractual rights to the extent attempted here. In this case, however, there is no emergency and the legislation is not temporary in nature. In fact, this law was not even enacted to deal with a broad social or economic problem at all. Further, its narrow aim was only directed at those who had already obligated themselves by contract to provide pension benefits. As such, the law only affects existing contractual obligations of employers. Therefore, it is a violation of the Contracts Clause and must be struck down.

■ DISSENT

(Brennan, J.) Today the majority greatly expands the Contracts Clause beyond any meaning previously ascribed to it. Because the law the majority strikes down today only imposed new, additional obligations on a class of persons, any constitutional problem must derive not from the Contracts Clause but from the Due Process Clause. Minnesota's law was designed to remedy a serious social problem, the deprivation of pension benefits to those employees who had worked many years for one company that subsequently ceases to operate. The law addresses this problem by requiring employers to pay employees who had worked for at least 10 years pension benefits and to pay those benefits out of money deposited into the fund by employees or the employer that will not have to be paid out. For this reason, the law merely imposes an additional obligation on the employer, it does not modify existing obligations. As such, there is no violation of the Contracts Clause. In holding otherwise today, the majority has made the Contracts Clause into something that protects all contract-based expectations, including those that the obligations of an employer to its employees will not be legislatively enlarged beyond those set forth in any agreement.

Analysis:

Here, the Court seems to use a more detailed analysis in finding that Minnesota's law improperly interferes with existing contractual obligations. Notice that the Court does not even give much consideration to the reasons for the enactment of the law. Instead, if focuses on the impairment the law works. This is also the main focus of Justice Brennan's dissent, since he believes the law does not work any impairment on Allied's (P) contractual obligations. Most observes have viewed this case as an anomaly, especially since all other Contracts Clause cases involving interference with private contracts have not resulted in a finding of unconstitutionality. The Court did, however, in *United States Trust Co. v. New Jersey,* hold a law repealing a statute that prohibited use of toll revenues to subsidize railroad passenger service unconstitutional as violating the Contracts Clause. In doing so, the Court indicated that an even higher scrutiny will apply to laws modifying the obligations, however created, of the government itself.

■ CASE VOCABULARY

§ 401—INTERNAL REVENUE CODE: The section of the tax laws that outlines the criteria for tax-deferred retirement plans.

ACTUARIAL PREDICTIONS: A mathematical calculation used to determine the amount of money needed on a future date.

DEFERRED ANNUITIES: A contract under which payments are made beginning at a certain age for as many years as purchased.

DESUETUDE: No longer in use.

GENERAL PENSION PLAN: A standard retirement plan.

PENSION FUNDING CHARGE: A charge, to be paid by purchasing deferred annuities, assessed under Minnesota's state law if the pension funds of a company are not sufficient to cover full pensions for all employees who had worked for the company for at least 10 years.

PENSION TRUST FUND: A trust established for the benefit of employees, the benefits of which are paid upon their retirement.

VESTED: Irrevocable, permanent.

United States Trust Co. v. New Jersey

(Not Stated) v. (State)
431 U.S. 1, 97 S.Ct. 1505 (1977)

CONTRACTS CLAUSE PRECLUDES GOVERNMENT FROM REPEALING LEGISLATION

■ **INSTANT FACTS** State enacted legislation that repealed a prior statute that prohibited the use of toll revenues to subsidize railroad passenger service.

■ **BLACK LETTER RULE** Legislation abdicating a government's obligations will only be upheld if it is both reasonable and necessary to serve the purposes claimed by the government.

■ PROCEDURAL BASIS
Not stated.

■ FACTS
In 1962, both New Jersey and New York enacted legislation that prohibited the use of toll revenues in subsidizing railroad passenger service. The law was meant to assure bondholders that the toll funds would be used solely to pay off the debt. Ten years later, however, during the energy crisis of 1970, the states adopted legislation repealing the 1962 laws.

■ ISSUE
May a state enact legislation that abdicates its own obligations?

■ DECISION AND RATIONALE
(Blackmun, J.) No. As with any challenge to legislation on the grounds that it violates the Contracts Clause, we must first determine whether the legislation at issue impaired the states' obligations to their bondholders. It has long been held that the Contracts Clause limits the power of the states to modify their own contracts as well as those between private parties. But it does not prevent the states from repealing or amending statutes generally, or from enacting new legislation with retroactive effects. Here, the obligation itself was created by statute. Here, the trial court found that the covenant in the 1962 legislation constituted a valid contract with the bondholders. Given the trial court's findings, we have no doubt that the 1962 law has been properly characterized as a contractual obligation. It is not always unconstitutional, however, for new legislation to affect pre-existing contracts. During the early years when the Contracts Clause was seen as an absolute bar to any legislation that impaired contracts, that view was supported by the belief that remedies and contractual obligations were two completely separately things. Although this distinction is not always clear and is now obsolete, its use can be seen as a more particularized review of the nature and purpose of the challenged law and the parties' reasonable expectations under their respective agreements. Generally, even in a case such as this where legislation clearly impairs a contractual obligation, the law will be upheld if it reasonably serves a legitimate purpose. Ordinarily, courts will defer to the legislature in looking at whether the law reasonably serves a legitimate purpose. However, when the challenged legislation impairs a state's own obligations, a higher test is required. In such a case, the courts will not defer to the legislature. Mass transportation and energy conservation are lofty and important goals. But such a broad purpose cannot sustain a law such as this. A state cannot refuse to honor its obligation simply because it wishes to

spend the money elsewhere. It is argued that the states' plan for encouraging users of private cars to shift to public transportation is a more specific purpose. However, we do not believe the repeal of the prior law was necessary to facilitate this purpose. As such, it was also an unreasonable means to achieve the states' admitted purpose. A less drastic approach could have been used. As such, the law repealing the states' obligation to use toll revenues for other purposes than subsidizing mass transportation efforts was unconstitutional.

■ DISSENT

(Brennan, J.) Today's decision, like that in Allied Structural Steel, rejects longstanding law on the Contracts Clause and molds the clause into something much more than it was intended to be. Here, the state was faced with an energy crises and in response, attempted to shift money around to try to deal with that crisis in a reasonable and necessary way. Thus, the Contracts Clause is not implicated. Further, the majority today ignores an underlying principle of our democracy, that each generation of representatives not be bound by the acts of their predecessors. Because I believe the majority's foray into policymaking today is unwarranted and unwise, I dissent.

Analysis:

For the first time, the Court here applied a tougher test than that typically used in Contracts Clause cases. In this case, because the repeal substantially impaired a contractual obligation of the state itself, the Court refused to defer to the legislature in determining whether the law was reasonable and necessary. In this respect, the Court reached back to its prior law on impermissible interference with contracts that permeated the *Lochner* era. As Justice Brennan's dissent points out, however, there is a strong argument favoring the state's ability to do what it did here: this was a policy decision and, as such, disagreement with it should be left to the voters and not the courts.

■ CASE VOCABULARY

BONDHOLDER: One who purchases a note from the government that will be paid off at some later date.

COVENANT: A promise or obligation.

SUBSIDIZE: A government payment meant to share the expense of an action that serves the public good.

Loretto v. Teleprompter Manhattan CATV Corp.
(*Homeowner*) v. (*Cable Company*)
458 U.S. 419, 102 S.Ct. 3164 (1982)

ANY PHYSICAL INTRUSION BY GOVERNMENT REQUIRES COMPENSATION

■ **INSTANT FACTS** Landlord challenged law requiring him to allow a cable company to install cable facilities on his property without compensation.

■ **BLACK LETTER RULE** Any permanent physical intrusion by the government or authorized by the government constitutes a taking for which just compensation must be paid.

■ **PROCEDURAL BASIS**

Appeal from New York Court of Appeal's holding that small physical intrusion did not amount to a taking.

■ **FACTS**

Prior to 1973, Teleprompter Manhattan CATV Corp. (D) ("TMCC") routinely obtained permission from property owners before installing cable equipment on their property. To facilitate tenant access to cable television, however, the New York legislature enacted legislation that precluded a landlord from interfering with the installation of cable television facilities on his property. The landlord was permitted to require the cable company or the tenant to bear the cost of installation and to indemnify him for any damages caused by the installation. The statute provided for payment of $1 as nominal compensation to the landlord for the inconvenience.

■ **ISSUE**

May the state authorize a small but permanent physical intrusion onto a private landowner's property without paying just compensation?

■ **DECISION AND RATIONALE**

(Marshall, J.) No. The New York Court of Appeals ruled that insofar as the statute in question serves the legitimate public purpose of promoting rapid development of important communication services, it was a proper exercise of the state's police power. We have no reason to doubt that finding. The question here is, however, whether this valid law so frustrates individual property rights so as to constitute a taking requiring the payment of just compensation. It has long been recognized that a physical intrusion by the government is a severe and unusually serious characteristic for purposes of the Takings Clause. When physical intrusion reaches the point of permanency, however, a taking has occurred, regardless of the reason for the intrusion. In all cases, the character of the government's action, not its purpose, is the determinative factor. Long ago we held that where real estate is actually invaded so as to destroy or impair the usefulness of the property, a taking has occurred requiring just compensation. In fact, courts have never denied a taking in a situation where there is an actual physical invasion of property. It is the actual fixing of property to private property that amounts to a permanent physical occupation of that property and thus constitutes a taking. While the purpose and extent of the occupation will be an important factor in determining the amount of compensation due, they have no bearing on whether a taking occurred. Reversed.

Loretto v. Teleprompter Manhattan CATV Corp. (Continued)

■ DISSENT

(Blackmun, J.) This Court's prior case law on the Takings Clause illustrate only one clear point: that there is no set rule for determining when a taking has occurred. In complete disregard for our prior case law, the majority today has fashioned a per se rule that draws a tenuous distinction between permanent intrusions, which are always takings, and temporary ones, which require a balancing test like the one we have always used. Because I believe the Court's adopting of this per se rule reduces our constitutional analysis to a mere dispute over the formalities, I dissent.

Analysis:

There are generally four questions that arise in every takings case: (1) is there a taking, (2) is it property, (3) if there is a taking of property, was it for public use, and (4) was just compensation paid? Here we are concerned with the threshold issue, was there a taking? Finding that TMCC (D) permanently placed a structure on private property for public use, the Court determined there was a taking. But the real meat of this decision is not the ultimate outcome, but the means by which the Court reached that outcome. In this case, for the first time, the Court held that any permanent physical occupation of private property for public use constituted a taking, no matter the reason for or extent of the occupation. This was a big departure from prior takings cases, in which the issue of whether or not there was a taking was decided on an ad hoc basis.

■ CASE VOCABULARY

APPROPRIATION: To take possession of.

CATV: Cable television.

INDEMNIFY: To pay on behalf of someone else.

Pennsylvania Coal Co. v. Mahon
(Coal Company) v. (Homeowner)
260 U.S. 393, 43 S.Ct. 158 (1922)

REGULATORY RESTRICTIONS ON PROPERTY CAN RESULT IN A TAKING

■ **INSTANT FACTS** Landowner sued coal company for violating state law prohibiting mining under homes.

■ **BLACK LETTER RULE** Land use regulation that goes too far will be recognized as a taking.

■ **PROCEDURAL BASIS**

Review of state court ruling upholding state law.

■ **FACTS**

The Mahons (D), owners of the property in question, brought suit to enjoin Pennsylvania Coal Co. (P) from mining under their home in such a way as to cause subsidence of the surface of their home. The Mahons (D) obtained title to the surface of the property only by deed from Pennsylvania Coal Co. (P). In the deed, the Mahons (D) expressly waived any claim for damages arising from the mining for coal. However, the Mahons (D) claim whatever rights Pennsylvania Coal Co. (P) had were extinguished by the Kohler Act, passed in 1921 by the state of Pennsylvania. The act precludes the mining of coal in such a way as to cause subsidence of any structure used for human habitation. Pennsylvania Coal Co. (P) has challenged the constitutionality of the act.

■ **ISSUE**

Does a land use regulation that restricts the use of property constitute a taking?

■ **DECISION AND RATIONALE**

(Holmes, J.) Yes. Some values, including ownership of property, are enjoyed with the implied limitation that such enjoyment must sometimes yield to the police power. Otherwise, government would be useless. However, there must also be a limit on the state's power. The key is deciding when the state has exercised its power in such a way as to deprive an individual of liberty or due process. In this instance, one factor to consider is the extent of the diminution. When it reaches a certain magnitude, there must be an exercise of eminent domain and payment of just compensation, or else the act is unconstitutional. The issue is thus one of degree that can only be decided on a case by case basis. In reviewing such cases, however, the greatest of deference is to be given to the legislature. Here, there is no doubt a public interest in every purchase and sale of real estate. However, this interest is not so great as to warrant the kind of interference that has occurred here. The possibility of damage to a limited number of homes does not justify the substantial impairment inflicted by this act. As such, the statute cannot be sustained as a valid exercise of police power. However, the protection of property presupposes that property may be wanted for public use, but provides that private property cannot be so used without payment of just compensation. Here, assuming an exigency exists, we still do not see how the taking of the coal company's rights to mine the coal is constitutional absent payment of just compensation. Having chosen to risk purchasing only the surface rights of their property, the Mahons

Pennsylvania Coal Co. v. Mahon (Continued)

(D) cannot now claim that their risk of danger is greater than the rights they bought or the protection to which Pennsylvania Coal Co. (P) is entitled under the Constitution. Reversed.

■ DISSENT

(Brandeis, J.) Here, the owner of property has the right to use his land, but that use is not absolute. He may not use it so as to create a danger to himself or others, and the risk of subsidence here is great and poses a substantial threat to the public as a whole. As such, the Kohler act was a valid exercise of the state's police power. In my view, restrictions imposed for the health, safety, morals or general welfare of the public can never constitute a taking.

Analysis:

All takings cases arise out of the Fifth Amendment, which provides that private property shall not be taken for public use without just compensation. Notice that the taking here occurred not by the damage to the surface rights, but by the act's restrictions on the rights obtained by the coal company (P). The majority concluded that it was not a reasonable step to deprive the coal company (P) of its rights to mine the coal as it saw fit simply to protect those few homeowners who took the risk that such mining would occur. In this respect, the majority and dissent seem to be in disagreement over whether or not the purpose of the taking is a factor in determining whether a taking has occurred, although both consider it. Notice that justice Brandeis seems to support a categorical rule that would preclude the finding of a taking in any case where regulation was enacted using a state's police powers. Note the test used for determining whether a regulatory taking has occurred: an ad hoc analysis that begins with looking at the degree of the taking or the diminution of the property by virtue of the regulation. As is usually the case when the Court applies a case-by-case analysis, identifying when a regulation will constitute a taking is difficult.

■ CASE VOCABULARY

DEED: The document by which real property is transferred.

DIMINUTION: A decrease in value.

EMINENT DOMAIN: The power of government to condemn property for public use.

SUBSIDENCE: The underlying support.

Miller v. Schoene

(*Landowner*) v. (*State Entomologist*)
276 U.S. 272, 48 S.Ct. 246 (1928)

STATES EMPOWERED TO SAVE ONE PROPERTY BY DESTROYING ANOTHER

■ **INSTANT FACTS** State entomologist ordered all red cedar trees within certain vicinity of apple orchards destroyed in order to stop spread of disease that was killing the orchards.

■ **BLACK LETTER RULE** In extreme exigent circumstances, the state may chose to destroy one property without paying just compensation in order to save another, so long as the taking is necessary to protect the health, safety, moral or general welfare of the public.

■ PROCEDURAL BASIS

Appeal of Virginia Supreme Court's decision upholding state regulation that authorized destruction of red cedar trees without payment of just compensation.

■ FACTS

Acting under a Virginia statute that authorized him to do so, the state entomologist (D) ordered the Millers (P) to cut down a large number of ornamental red cedar trees growing on their property as a means of eradicating the communication of rust that the trees were infected with to nearby apple orchards. Neither the statute nor the order permitted payment of just compensation for the loss of the trees.

■ ISSUE

Does the destruction of one property in order to save another that is of more vital importance to the general community under exigent circumstances constitute a taking?

■ DECISION AND RATIONALE

(Stone, J.) No. The statute at issue here presents a comprehensive scheme for the eradication of cedar rust. The only method for controlling the disease is the destruction of all red cedar trees subject to the infection located within a certain vicinity of apple trees. Traditionally, the red cedar tree has no special meaning to the state of Virginia and has only a nominal, ornamental value. By contrast, Virginia is famous for its apple orchards and one of its largest exports is apples. Thus, it is clear the state was faced with a choice of preserving the small number of red cedar trees near apple orchards and losing its apple trees, or destroying the red cedar trees. When faced with such a choice, a state does not exceed its constitutional powers by deciding to destroy the trees in favor of the apple orchards, which, in the legislature's judgment, have more value to the community as a whole. When that choice is, as it was here, unavoidable, the exercise of the state's power does not constitute a taking.

Analysis:

Here, the Court seems to reach the opposite result that it did in *Pennsylvania Coal Co. v. Mahon.* In *Mahon*, the Court held that a regulation precluding a coal company from mining for coal under a

Miller v. Schoene (Continued)

residential home constituted a taking of the coal company's subsurface mineral rights. Why then is it not a taking when the government authorized the destruction of trees upon private property in order to save apple orchards? *Mahon* has been seen as declining to adopt the per se rule, advocated by Justice Brandeis in his dissent, that the Court seems to adopt here: that being that in the exercise of the state's police power, there can be no taking. Since the Court flatly rejected a per se rule in *Mahon*, however, most legal observers attempt to distinguish the two cases on the basis that, while there is no per se rule for every exercise of the state's police power, there will be no taking when the government is faced with a public emergency that necessitates the taking, as was the case here but not in *Mahon*.

■ CASE VOCABULARY

CEDAR RUST: An infectious plant disease that destroys fruit and foliage of apple trees.

ENTOMOLOGIST: A specialized field within zoology that deals solely with insects.

Penn Central Transportation Co. v. New York City
(Landowner) v. (State)
438 U.S. 104, 98 S.Ct. 2646 (1978)

STATE'S REFUSAL TO PERMIT BUILDING ON TOP OF LANDMARK SITE CONSTITUTIONAL

■ **INSTANT FACTS** Owner of Grand Central Station in New York City claimed a law declaring the station a landmark and thus precluding any building on top of it constituted a regulatory taking.

■ **BLACK LETTER RULE** A land use regulation that does not deprive a property owner of all uses of the property does not constitute a taking.

■ **PROCEDURAL BASIS**

Appeal of state commission's denial of a building permit.

■ **FACTS**

Penn Central Transportation Co. (P) ("Penn Central") owns Grand Central Station, one of New York's oldest and most famous buildings. Built in 1913, it is regarded not only as an ingenious feat of engineering but also as a magnificent example of French beaux-arts style. In 1968, Penn Central (P) entered into a 50 year renewable lease with UGP Properties, Inc., under which UGP would construct a multistory office building on top of the existing terminal. When Penn Central and UGP applied for the building permit, however, their request was denied as being inconsistent with the New York's landmark preservation law. This action followed.

■ **ISSUE**

Does a land use regulation that precludes some but not all uses of private property constitute a taking?

■ **DECISION AND RATIONALE**

(Brennan, J.) No. The Fifth Amendment has been held to prevent the government from imposing upon an individual a burden that more properly should be borne on society as a whole. In years of regulatory takings jurisprudence, however, the court has been unable to fashion any kind of formula for determining when justice requires society rather than the individual to bear the burden of regulatory restrictions on private property. The courts decisions have, however, identified several factors that aid in making such a determination. Among those are the economic impact of the regulation, the extent of interference on the property being affected and the character of the government's action. Generally speaking, a taking may be more readily found where there is a physical invasion of property by the government. A taking may also be found when a regulatory restriction goes too far. However, the court has upheld land use regulations that called for the outright destruction of property and zoning laws that prohibit a certain type of use on private property. Takings challenges to such zoning laws have always been denied even though the law restricted the property owner from putting the property to the beneficial use it had previously been put to. Here, Penn Central (P) argues that any substantial restriction on the use of property constitutes a taking. With that we cannot agree. Otherwise, cities would become virtually powerless to enact any type of land use regulation, regulation that is both necessary and an implied limitation on land ownership. We thus reject the contention that diminution in property value alone is sufficient to establish a taking. Here, the law does not interfere in any way with

Penn Central Transportation Co. v. New York City (Continued)

the present uses of the terminal. It does not interfere with Penn Central's (P) primary expectation of use of the primary parcel. More importantly, the law does not restrict Penn Central's (P) ability to earn a profit from operation of the terminal. Therefore, we conclude that the application of New York's landmark preservation act does not operate as a taking of Penn Central's (P) property. Affirmed.

■ DISSENT

(Rehnquist, J.) In my opinion, the landmark designation imposed upon Penn Central (P) also imposes a substantial burden upon it to bear the cost of foregoing future development that could be hugely profitable. The desire to preserve landmarks is admirable, but insofar as it is seen as an act for the public good, the burden of so preserving should fall on society as a whole for whom the designation is made, not the landowner.

Analysis:

The most important aspect of this case is the statement by the majority that proving a decrease in the value of property, by itself, is insufficient to establish that a taking has occurred. A secondary principle that has arisen from this case, one of the most memorable takings cases of all time, is that when evaluating the effect on the property, the court must look at the whole parcel, not just the piece that the property owner is concerned with. Finally, notice how this case falls in line with *Miller v. Schoene*. In both cases, the protection of the general welfare of the public is an overriding concern that leads the Court to find that no taking occurred. In this case, however, the Court has a much more compelling reasoning for reaching that conclusion: namely, that the law, while preventing some use of the property, has not precluded all beneficial use.

■ CASE VOCABULARY

RENEWABLE LEASE: A lease agreement that is renewable at one party's option after a set number of years.

SUBLEASE: A lease of the property by a lessee to a third party.

Lucas v. South Carolina Coastal Council

(*Property Owner*) v. (*State agency*)
505 U.S. 1003, 112 S.Ct. 2886 (1992)

SECOND PER SE RULE ADDED TO REGULATORY TAKINGS LAW

■ **INSTANT FACTS** State law preventing building on beachfront property precluded landowner from building the homes he had planned on his property.

■ **BLACK LETTER RULE** Government regulation that deprives a property owner of all economically beneficial use constitutes a taking for which just compensation must be paid.

■ PROCEDURAL BASIS

Appeal of South Carolina Supreme Court's ruling overturning trial court's decision that regulation constituted a taking.

■ FACTS

In the late 1970s, Lucas (P) and others began extensive residential development of the Isle of Palms. In 1986, Lucas (P) purchased the two lots at issue for his own personal use. The lots, located 300 feet from the beach, were completely vacant and were not considered to be in a "critical area". Accordingly, Lucas (P) was not required to seek a building permit before commencing any development activity on the lots. It was Lucas' (P) intention to build homes to rent on the property. In 1988, however, the South Carolina legislature passed the Beachfront Management Act, which precluded all construction of occupiable structures on any land seaward of a line drawn 20 feet landward and parallel to the baseline, without exception. The restriction covered Lucas' (P) property. Upon bringing this action, Lucas (P) did not take issue with the validity of the act itself. Rather, he argued that the act completely extinguished any value his property had thereby constituting a taking that, in the absence of just compensation, was unconstitutional.

■ ISSUE

Does a land use regulation that deprives a property owner of all economically beneficial use of his property constitute a taking?

■ DECISION AND RATIONALE

(Scalia, J.) Yes. Prior to our decision in *Pennsylvania Coal Co. v. Mahon*, which established that a taking could occur by virtue of regulation and not just upon a permanent physical occupation of property, Lucas' (P) case would be easy to resolve. Since *Mahon*, however, we have struggled to define when a regulatory taking occurs. There is no set formula, rather, we have engaged in ad hoc analysis that has left many land use regulators in the lurch. There are two situations, however, where we have recognized a taking as a matter of law. First, where there is any physical occupation of private property for public use, a taking has occurred. Second, where regulation denies a property owner of all economically beneficial or productive use, a taking has also occurred. This second rule, which we have not before justified, stems from the fact that total deprivation of beneficial use is the equivalent of a physical occupation of land. The rule is also justified by the fact that when a land use regulation deprives an owner of all beneficial use of his property, it is more likely that the land is being forced into public use

Lucas v. South Carolina Coastal Council (Continued)

under the guise of an emergency necessitating the need to eradicate a public harm. The trial court here found that as a result of the act in question, Lucas' (P) lots were rendered valueless. We agree. When a landowner shows that a regulation has left him with no beneficial use, the state may only resist paying just compensation where they can establish that the nature of the property itself impliedly puts the possibility of such devastating regulation in the owner's title. Since the trial court did not reach this issue, we remand this action back to it for further consideration. We note, however, that to win, South Carolina (D) must show more than mere allegations or a violation of the maxim *sic utere tuo ut alienum non laedas*. Rather, South Carolina (D) must identify background principles of nuisance and property law that prohibit the uses Lucas (P) intends to put his property to. Reversed and Remanded.

■ DISSENT

(Blackmun, J.) Today, the majority "launches a missile to kill a mouse". Rather than simply determining the issue upon which we granted review, whether South Carolina (D) must pay compensation to Lucas (P), the majority carves out a new categorical rule ignoring all prior takings jurisprudence that advocates an ad hoc approach. Further, the court states that only when a state can show that all use would be precluded under common law principles of nuisance can it regulate in such a way as to deny an owner of all beneficial uses of the property. Such a per se rule is dangerous and uncalled for. I would instead follow the ad hoc analysis we have always followed rather than creating a new rule.

Analysis:

Expounding on the principle set forth in *Penn Central*, the Court actually establishes a second per rule in regulatory takings law: that a regulation that deprives a landowner of all economically beneficial or productive use of his property constitutes a taking as a matter of law. It then recognizes an exception to that rule, allowing states to so deprive a landowner only in situations where the common law of nuisance would have had the same effect. Essentially then, the exception is very narrow. Not surprisingly, the current trend is for litigants to claim a total deprivation. Despite Justice Blackmun's warning in his dissent, however, there are very few cases that will result in a total deprivation of use.

■ CASE VOCABULARY

BEACHFRONT MANAGEMENT ACT: South Carolina legislation regulating the use of beachfront property.

IPSE DIXIT: A mere assertion, wholly unsupported.

ISLE OF PALMS: A barrier island located east of Charleston, South Carolina.

REGULATORY TAKING: The deprivation of use of property by operation of state law to such a degree as to require payment of just compensation.

SIC UTERE TUO UT ALIENUM NON LAEDAS: literally, "each one must so use his own so as not to injure his neighbor"

SUBDIVISION: A grouping of single-family residential homes.

Dolan v. City of Tigard

(*Property Owner*) v. (*Municipality*)
512 U.S. 374, 114 S.Ct. 2309 (1994)

CONDITIONAL BUILDING PERMIT EXAMINED BY HIGH COURT

■ **INSTANT FACTS** City conditioned building permit for expansion of store on owner's granting city land for use as a flood plain and building of a public walkway.

■ **BLACK LETTER RULE** Permit conditions will only be upheld where there is an essential nexus between the legitimate state interest and the government shows that some sort of individualized determination has been made that the required dedication is related both in nature and extent to the impact of the proposed development.

■ PROCEDURAL BASIS

Appeal from decision of Oregon Supreme Court upholding permit conditioned on deeding portion of property over to city for public use.

■ FACTS

In 1973, Oregon enacted a comprehensive land use management program that required all Oregon cities and counties to adopt new plans that were consistent with the goals of the program. Pursuant to the state's requirement, the city of Tigard (D) adopted a plan that requires 15% open space and landscaping requirements within its central business district. To accomplish this, the city (D) limits total site coverage to 85%, including parking, with the remaining going to a pedestrian/bicycle pathway. Additionally, in accordance with the city's (D) drainage control plan, certain areas along Fanno Creek could not be developed. Florence Dolan (P) owns a plumbing and electrical store in the central business district of the city of Tigard (D). She submitted a proposal for an expansion of her store to the city (D), which the city granted conditioned on her dedicating a portion of her property lying within the Fanno Creek flood plain to the city (D) and constructing a pathway along an additional 15 foot strip. The total conditions cover approximately 7,000 square feet, or 10%, of Ms. Dolan's (P) property. Ms. Dolan (P) brought the instant action, claiming the conditions constituted an impermissible taking of her property.

■ ISSUE

May a municipality impose conditions on a building permit that result in taking of private property for public use without paying just compensation?

■ DECISION AND RATIONALE

(Rehnquist, J.) Yes. In this case, had the city simply required Ms. Dolan (P) to dedicate a portion of her property for public use, a taking would have occurred. However, having placed the dedication as a condition to a building permit, the takings issue is not easy to determine. We have long ago recognized that a land use regulation does not effect a taking if it substantially advances legitimate state interests and does not deny an owner economically viable use of his land. But this is not a standard land use regulation, in that it applies only to Ms. Dolan's (P) land and requires her to turn over a portion of her property as a condition to receiving a building permit rather than restricting a use of her property. In this case, Ms. Dolan (P) does not challenge the authority of the city (D) to exact some conditions regarding dedication of her property. Rather, she challenges the showing the city (D) has made to justify the

Dolan v. City of Tigard (Continued)

conditions in this case. When evaluating this challenge, we must first determine whether an essential nexus exists between the state's interests and the permit conditions. Here, the conditions imposed relate to legitimate goals: the prevention of flooding and preservation of open space in a crowded business district. The question thus becomes whether the conditions are proportional to these goals. The showing necessary to meet this second burden has varied among the different states. In some, a generalized showing that the connection is necessary is enough. In others, a specific and uniquely attributable test is used. Still in others, a reasonable relationship must be shown. In our view, the reasonable relationship test is the closest to what our constitution requires, but we believe "rough proportionality" is the better phrase. Under the test we adopt here now, the city (D) must show that some sort of individualized determination has been made that the required dedication is related both in nature and extent to the impact of the proposed development. Reversed and remanded.

■ DISSENT

(Stevens, J.) The facts of this case and the result reached today are not so important as the rule of law established as a means of reaching that result. In my view, it is sufficient to merely adapt our existing tests for reviewing regulatory takings challenges so that the owner, not the government, bears the burden of showing disproportionality and that grants the required deference to the government in deciding what is necessary. In changing the burden so that it rests on the government, the majority has not only created a new area of takings jurisprudence, but has increased the already substantial problems that exist in land use planning.

Analysis:

In this opinion, the Court establishes yet another test to determine whether a regulatory taking has occurred. In this instance, however, the nexus test applies only in those situations where a government conditions a building permit on the dedication of private property for public use. In those narrow circumstances, the court must not only determine if an essential nexus (connection) exists between the state's interest and the conditions imposed, but also whether the government can establish that the conditions are roughly proportionate to the stated goals. This is an interesting twist in takings law insofar as it places the burden, in part, on the government to show that its actions were reasonable, rather than on the party challenging the law to show that the government acted unreasonably.

■ CASE VOCABULARY

DEDICATION: A grant of private property to the government.

FLOODPLAIN: An area of land that is prone to flooding.

SPECIFIC AND UNIQUELY ATTRIBUTABLE TEST: A requirement by which local government must demonstrate that its conditions are directly proportional to the need in order to validly impose conditions in building permits that require property be turned over to the government for public use.

UNCONSTITUTIONAL CONDITIONS: The constitutional doctrine that recognizes that the government may not require a person to give up a constitutional right.

Palazzolo v. Rhode Island

(*Property Owner*) v. (*State Government*)
533 U.S. 606, 121 S.Ct. 2448 (2001)

ENVIRONMENTAL CONCERNS JUSTIFY LIMITATIONS ON DEVELOPMENT

■ **INSTANT FACTS** Palazzolo's (P) petition for approval of development plans for his coastal property was denied because state regulations restricted the development of coastal wetlands.

■ **BLACK LETTER RULE** When a regulation denies all economically beneficial or productive use of property, the Takings Clause requires just compensation to the landowner.

■ **PROCEDURAL BASIS**

Certiorari to review a decision of the Rhode Island Supreme Court.

■ **FACTS**

In 1959, Palazzolo (P), as principal of Shore Gardens, Inc. (SGI), purchased three vacant lots along Rhode Island's Atlantic coastline. The lots were largely salt marsh due to tidal flooding, requiring significant landfill to support permanent construction. In 1962, SGI submitted a proposal to the Rhode Island Division of Harbors and Rivers to dredge an adjacent pond and fill the property for development. After that application was denied, SGI presented another proposal, in 1966, to develop a private beach club on the property. That proposal was denied because of adverse environmental impacts. In 1971, Rhode Island (D) enacted legislation creating the Rhode Island Coastal Resources Management Council, which adopted regulations designating marshes as "coastal wetlands" on which development was greatly limited. In 1978, SGI's corporate charter was revoked and title to the property was transferred to Palazzolo (P) as the sole shareholder. In 1983, Palazzolo (P) renewed his initial 1962 proposal to the Council, which denied the proposal as threatening to the state's waters and wetlands. A renewed private beach club proposal was likewise denied because the proposal did not serve "a compelling public purpose which provides benefits to the public as a whole as opposed to individual or private interests." Palazzolo (P) sued the state (D) in state court, challenging the Council's regulations as a taking without just compensation in violation of the Fifth and Fourteenth Amendments. The Superior Court ruled against Palazzolo (P). On appeal, the Rhode Island Supreme Court affirmed, finding that his takings claims were not ripe, that he lacked standing to challenge state regulations predating his 1978 acquisition of the property, and that he continued to maintain economic value in the property.

■ **ISSUE**

Does a regulation significantly restricting the use of land for environmental concerns constitute a total taking such that the Fifth Amendment requires just compensation to the landowner?

■ **DECISION AND RATIONALE**

(Kennedy, J.) No. Generally, when a regulation "denies all economically beneficial or productive use of land," the Takings Clause requires just compensation to the landowner. When the regulation merely limits the beneficial use of the landowner's property, however, a taking may occur, but consideration must also be given to such factors as the economic effect on the land, the interference with reasonable

Palazzolo v. Rhode Island (Continued)

investment-backed expectations, and the nature of the government action involved. The state (D) argues that Palazzolo (P) has no ripe claim because the regulations at issue were enacted before he obtained legal title from SGI, placing him on notice that the land was subject to developmental restrictions. However, a landowner facing an unconstitutional state regulation has no less a right to challenge the regulation because it preceded his personal interest in the land than his predecessor in interest. The regulation is as unconstitutional as to one as it is to the other, and the state (D) may not avoid constitutional requirements merely by placing citizens on notice of the unconstitutional regulation.

Application of the regulation to Palazzolo's (P) property, however, does not deprive him of total beneficial use of the land. The parties agreed that, the regulations notwithstanding, the development value of the land is $200,000. While the state may not avoid its duty to compensate a deprived landowner based merely on the existence of some small token interest in the property, the remaining interest is significant enough here such that the regulation does not effectuate a total taking. Because the state courts did not consider the factors set forth in *Penn Central* to determine whether the partial deprivation of use constitutes a taking, the matter is remanded for application of those factors. Affirmed in part, reversed in part, and remanded.

■ CONCURRENCE

(O'Connor, J.) Although Palazzolo's (P) notice of the regulation at the time he took title does not bar his takings claim, the timing of his interest must be considered in evaluating the *Penn Central* factors. Because the interference with investment-backed expectations is an important factor in a partial takings case, the timing of the plaintiff's title is particularly relevant. Notice of regulatory limitations at the time title is passed helps establish the plaintiff's reasonable expectations for the use of the property.

■ CONCURRENCE

(Scalia, J.) The fact that a property restriction existed at the time a landowner acquired title should have no bearing on whether just compensation is due. If the regulation is unconstitutional, notice of its requirements is simply irrelevant. A state cannot avoid just compensation by claiming a landowner's investment-backed expectations are unreasonable simply because he had been put on prior notice of the constitutional violation.

■ CONCURRENCE IN PART

(Stevens, J.) While a takings claim is not lost because a regulation was adopted before a landowner took title to the property, a landowner may not assert a taking of property that predated his interest in the property. Here, Palazzolo (P) is the wrong party to challenge the regulation. When it was adopted, the regulation prohibited the fill of wetlands on the property. At that time, Palazzolo (P) had no interest in the property. Although Palazzolo's (P) petitions to fill the property had been denied after he acquired title, the agency decisions merely reinforced the pre-interest regulations and decisions made relative to the property. And although Palazzolo (P) could challenge any new takings of his property, he does not by extension obtain the right to challenge his predecessors' constitutional rights merely by obtaining title to the property.

■ DISSENT

(Breyer, J.) While the takings effect of the regulations depends on the owner's investment-backed expectations, the regulations do not present a significant Takings Clause issue. If a regulation is generally applicable and is directed at preventing substantial public harm, no taking occurs. The regulations at issue satisfy these criteria.

Analysis:

A physical governmental intrusion upon land occurs at the time the actual intrusion occurred. Thus, a subsequent landowner acquiring the property with notice of the intrusion is generally unable to claim a taking. A regulatory taking, however, occurs at the time the regulation is enforced, and a landowner acquiring title with notice of the regulation is not barred from claiming a taking if the regulation was not previously enforced. Looking to the landowner's investment-backed expectations, one may easily understand the reasons for the distinction, for without enforcement of the regulation, the landowner's expectations are more justifiable.

■ CASE VOCABULARY

EMINENT DOMAIN: The inherent power of a governmental entity to take privately owned property, especially land, and convert it to public use, subject to reasonable compensation for the taking.

INVERSE CONDEMNATION: An action brought by a property owner for compensation from a governmental entity that has taken the owner's property without bringing formal condemnation proceedings.

JUST COMPENSATION: Under the Fifth Amendment, a fair payment by the government for property it has taken under eminent domain—usually the property's fair market value, so that the owner is no worse off after the taking.

RIPENESS: The circumstance existing when a case has reached, but has not passed, the point when the facts have developed sufficiently to permit an intelligent and useful decision to be made.

TAKING: The government's actual or effective acquisition of private property either by ousting the owner and claiming title or by destroying the property or severely impairing its utility.

Tahoe-Sierra Preservation Council, Inc. v. Tahoe Regional Planning Agency

(*Landowner Association*) v. (*Interstate Planning Board*)
535 U.S. 302, 122 S.Ct. 1465 (2002)

A MORATORIUM ON DEVELOPMENT IS NOT A TAKING

■ **INSTANT FACTS** Property owners in the Lake Tahoe area were prohibited from undertaking any development of their property for thirty-two months in order to get a handle on the development needs of the area to preserve its natural beauty.

■ **BLACK LETTER RULE** A regulation that prohibits economic use of land for an extended but finite period of time does not constitute a taking requiring that the owner of the property be compensated.

■ PROCEDURAL BASIS
Certiorari to review an undisclosed decision.

■ FACTS
Due to a lack of adequate regional planning, the area around Lake Tahoe became overdeveloped. The clarity of the lake became threatened with algae fed by the run-off from paved areas. The Tahoe Regional Planning Agency (TRPA) (D) was established to study the problem and create goals to preserve the area. To help in the planning process, the TRPA (D) imposed a thirty-two-month moratorium on all development. The Tahoe–Sierra Preservation Council (P) brought suit, alleging that the ban on development constituted an unconstitutional taking of the property.

■ ISSUE
Does a moratorium on all development constitute an unconstitutional regulatory taking for which the landowners are entitled to compensation?

■ DECISION AND RATIONALE
(Stevens, J.) No. When the government physically takes possession of private property for public use, a taking has clearly occurred for which just compensation is due. Yet, a property owner can be equally deprived of his property when government regulations limit the purposes for which the property can be used. Treating all land-use regulations as Fifth Amendment takings, however, would undermine governmental objectives designed to further matters of public interest by demanding compensation to the objects of the regulations. Accordingly, the compensation due for a regulatory taking depends on the extent that the government action deprives the landowner of his value in the property.

When the regulation amounts to a total taking of all economic value, as in *Lucas v. South Carolina Coastal Council*, just compensation is clearly required. In the absence of a total taking, however, *Penn Central* determines the proper analysis for value taken. An estate in real property is determined by both its physical boundaries and the time dominion is extended over the parcel. A temporary restriction on use of property cannot logically render a parcel valueless. The ultimate question is whether the Takings Clause concepts of "fairness and justice" are served by hard and fast rules, or on a case-by-case inquiry as described in *Penn Central*. It cannot be stated enough that a delay in the use of property is not compensable. While a rule that allows compensation for deprivations of use for more than a year may be reasonable, this rule should be made by the legislatures. In a case where regulation only temporarily affects the development of land, the rationale set forth in *Penn Central* should be followed. Affirmed

■ DISSENT

(Rehnquist, C.J.) Plaintiffs have been prohibited from building anything on their land for nearly six years. Such an extensive restriction on the use of property contravenes all traditional land-use planning methods. The Court has always recognized that the ability to use one's property is subject to limits. In *Lucas*, the Court held that a prohibition on all "economically beneficial use of the coastal land" came within the Court's rule on taking. Here, a ban on all economic development for six years is not a typical state property-law restriction. A moratorium is generally used only for interim control over land and prohibits only certain development—restaurants, commerce, etc. In those circumstances, there are other uses to which owners can put the land in order to make profitable use of it. The majority worries that granting compensation to owners would lead to compensation for delays in granting permits or other administrative hold-ups; however, in those cases, at least the permits will eventually issue if the appropriate procedures are followed. In this case, no matter what actions the landowners took, they were prevented from making any use of their property.

Analysis:

The plaintiffs in this case, unlike the property owner in *Lucas v. South Carolina Coastal Council*, had not been told they would never be permitted to build on their land again. They are asked to wait patiently while representatives from the surrounding area take the time to make a careful development plan—one that would hopefully slow development to the point that the property around Lake Tahoe would continue to be aesthetically pleasing. In that respect, the moratorium could be seen as adding value to the landowners' property.

■ CASE VOCABULARY

TAKINGS CLAUSE: The Fifth Amendment provision that prohibits the government from taking private property for public use without fairly compensating the owner.

Hawaii Housing Authority v. Midkiff

(State Agency) v. *(Landowner)*
467 U.S. 229, 104 S.Ct. 2321 (1984)

LAND TAKEN IN ORDER TO BREAK UP A MONOPOLY CAN BE RESOLD TO INDIVIDUALS, AND THE TAKING WILL STILL BE DEEMED TO BE FOR A PUBLIC USE

■ **INSTANT FACTS** State agency initiated program that took property from concentrated landowners without compensation and resold it to others in order to dilute number of landowners.

■ **BLACK LETTER RULE** What constitutes public use for purposes of the Takings Clause is determined by the legislature, whose determination will be upheld except in the most narrowest of cases.

■ **PROCEDURAL BASIS**

Not stated.

■ **FACTS**

When the Hawaiian islands were originally settled by Polynesian immigrants, their economy developed around the feudal land tenure system. As a result, the ali'l nui controlled the land and assigned it for development to certain subchiefs, who handed it down to lower ranking officials who oversaw those working the land. All of the land was held at the will of the ali'l nui. There was no private ownership of land. In the early 1800s, when American settlers began to arrive, repeated attempts were made to divide up ownership of the land. These efforts were largely unsuccessful, and the land remained in the hands of only a few. By the mid 1960s, the Hawaiian legislature discovered that while the state owned 49% of the land, 47% of the remaining land was owned by only 72 private fee simple owners. The concentrated land ownership resulted in a skewed real estate market, inflated prices and thus was injuring the public tranquility and welfare. To remedy the situation, the legislature enacted the Land Reform Act of 1967. Under the act, the state would condemn the land, and resell it to the lessees on the land, with the money paid by the lessees going to the landowners as compensation.

■ **ISSUE**

Does the Fifth Amendment prohibit a state from taking land, with just compensation, for resale to private lessees?

■ **DECISION AND RATIONALE**

(O'Connor, J.) No. The starting point for our analysis is whether or not the actions of the state of Hawaii constitute a taking for public use. In *Berman v. Parker*, we held that a redevelopment plan in the District of Columbia that called for exercise of the eminent domain power, payment of just compensation and possible resale of the areas condemned to private parties was a permissible taking. In that case we said what constitutes a taking for public use would depend on the facts of the individual case, but noted that the public use requirement is coterminous with the scope of a state's police powers and that in reviewing what constitutes a public use, courts should defer to the legislature's determinations. While the courts play a role in reviewing such decisions, that role is extremely narrow. While the Fifth Amendment prohibits a state from taking private property for public use without just compensation, and

Hawaii Housing Authority v. Midkiff (Continued)

by extension, would prohibit the taking of private party for anything other than public use even with compensation, where the exercise of the eminent domain power is rationally related to a conceivable public purpose, the takings clause is satisfied. Applying these principles to the facts here, we have no trouble finding Hawaii's plan constitutional.

Analysis:

There has not been much challenge to takings based on an alleged non-public use. As a result, almost anything the legislature says is a public use will be upheld as a public use, much like under the rational basis test for economic legislation used after the *Lochner* era. If the courts can find a reasonable public use, even if it is not the use the legislature came up with, the taking will be upheld. Keep in mind, however, that even where just compensation is paid, if private property is taken for private use and not public use, the taking is still unconstitutional.

■ CASE VOCABULARY

ALI'L NUI: An island high chief.

COTERMINOUS: Having the same boundaries.

FEE SIMPLE: The absolute owner of property.

FEUDAL LAND TENURE SYSTEM: Where those who live and work on the land do so at the behest and as a guest of the landowner.

LAND REFORM ACT OF 1967: State law that created a mechanism for condemning residential real estate for transfer to existing lessees on the land condemned.

LESSEES: One leasing the land from the owner.

OLIGOPOLY: A situation where a few control the whole.

Kelo v. City of New London

(*Homeowner*) v. (*Using Eminent Domain*)

545 U.S. 469, 125 S.Ct. 2655 (2005)

ECONOMIC DEVELOPMENT IS A "PUBLIC PURPOSE"

■ **INSTANT FACTS** The City of New London (P) used eminent domain to acquire Kelo's (D) house for a private development project.

■ **BLACK LETTER RULE** "Public purpose" is defined broadly, and deference must be given to legislative judgments on this question.

■ **PROCEDURAL BASIS**

Appeal from an order of the Supreme Court of Connecticut upholding the condemnation of property.

■ **FACTS**

Kelo (D) owned a home in the Fort Trumbull area of New London (P). The Fort Trumbull area was targeted for economic redevelopment. A redevelopment plan was drawn up that included creation of a park and the building of a research center for Pfizer Inc. The development plan was projected to create more than one thousand new jobs, to increase tax revenue, and to revitalize an economically distressed city. Kelo (D) refused to sell her house for the redevelopment project, and New London (P) instituted condemnation proceedings.

■ **ISSUE**

Was taking the property for development a "public purpose?"

■ **DECISION AND RATIONALE**

(Stevens, J.) Yes. "Public purpose" is defined broadly, and deference must be given to legislative judgments on this question. It has long been accepted that the government may not take property from one party for the sole purpose of transferring it to another private party. It is also well-established that a government may transfer property from one private party to another for a future use by the public. The taking at issue here is not being done to confer a private benefit on a particular private party. It is being done pursuant to a "carefully considered" redevelopment plan. There is no evidence of an improper purpose.

It is true that the condemned land will not be opened for use by the general public. The definition of "use by the public" has, however, been broadened to mean a "public purpose." Public purpose has been defined broadly. The Court has refused to evaluate claimed public uses in isolation, and has held that the Constitution does not require that redevelopment be accomplished in a piecemeal fashion. The Court has also deferred to a legislative judgment that reducing the concentration of land ownership was a valid public purpose. The mere fact that property would be immediately transferred to private parties did not diminish the public character of the taking.

New London's (P) determination that the Fort Trumbull area was in need of economic rejuvenation is entitled to deference from the Court. The economic development plan was developed after thorough deliberation, and is a comprehensive plan for the neighborhood. Given the nature of the plan, and the

Kelo v. City of New London (Continued)

limited scope of the Court's review, it is appropriate to resolve the challenges of the individual property owners in light of the entire plan. The plan unquestionably serves a public purpose, so the takings challenged here satisfy the public use requirement of the Fifth Amendment.

Kelo (D) urges adoption of a rule that economic development does not qualify as a public use. Promoting economic development is, however, a traditional and long accepted function of government. There is also no principled way of distinguishing economic development from other public purposes the Court has recognized. A government's pursuit of a public purpose will often benefit individual private parties. The hypothetical presented by Kelo (D) of a taking of property to transfer it to an owner who will make a better use of the property and pay more taxes is not presented here. Kelo (D) also argues that the Court should adopt a rule that requires a "reasonable certainty" the expected benefits will accrue. Such a rule would be a departure from precedent. Debates about the wisdom of takings are not for the federal courts to resolve.

There is nothing to prevent states from adopting stricter rules on the exercise of the power to take property. In this case, the Court's authority extends only to determining that the takings are for a "public use," within the meaning of the Fifth Amendment. Affirmed.

■ CONCURRENCE

(Kennedy, J.) The deferential standard of review echoes the rational basis test used to review economic regulation under the Due Process and Equal Protection Clauses. Appling the rational basis test should strike down takings that are clearly shown to benefit only a particular private party, with only incidental or pretextual public justifications.

■ DISSENT

(O'Connor, J.) Allowing takings when incidental public benefits are a by-product of the private use of property erodes the distinction between public and private use of property. The public use requirement limits the scope of a government's power to take property. Legislative determinations of public use are given a great deal of deference, but the courts still have a check on the interpretation of public use.

Takings for economic development are unconstitutional. In this case, the property taken is not claimed to be a source of any social harm that would make condemnation appropriate. By upholding the economic development plan, the Court "significantly expands the meaning of public use" to include any legislative plan that provides a secondary benefit to the public. Any property may now be taken for the benefit of another private party, but the fallout from this decision will not be random. The beneficiaries are likely to be citizens with disproportionate political influence and power, including large corporations and developers. The government now has license to transfer property from those with fewer resources to those with more.

■ DISSENT

(Thomas, J.) If takings for economic development are for a public use, any taking is. The Public Use Clause has effectively been erased from the Constitution. The public Use Clause provides a meaningful limit to a government's eminent domain power. There is no justification for giving almost insurmountable deference to a legislative determination of "public use."

Analysis:

The Court's opinion caused an enormous outcry of opposition. Literally hundreds of bills to limit or prohibit takings for economic development were introduced in state legislatures. Bills to prohibit such takings were even introduced in states that already prohibited the practice. Interestingly, the development that spurred the taking of Kelo's (D) house never materialized. The property, as of early 2010, remains a vacant lot.

■ **CASE VOCABULARY**

EMINENT DOMAIN: The inherent power of a governmental entity to take privately owned property, especially land, and convert it to public use, subject to reasonable compensation for the taking.

TAKINGS CLAUSE: The Fifth Amendment provision that prohibits the government from taking private property for public use without fairly compensating the owner.

Brown v. Legal Foundation of Washington

(Legal Client) v. (Charitable Legal Organization)
538 U.S. 216, 123 S.Ct. 1406 (2003)

IOLTA ACCOUNTS ARE NOT TAKINGS REQUIRING JUST COMPENSATION

■ **INSTANT FACTS** Brown (P) demanded just compensation for state use of interest earned on his private funds in an IOLTA account.

■ **BLACK LETTER RULE** Just compensation is measured by the property owner's loss rather than the government's gain.

■ PROCEDURAL BASIS
Certiorari to review an undisclosed decision.

■ FACTS
The Washington Supreme Court, as opposed to the state legislature, required interest on lawyers' trust accounts (IOLTA) to be used to pay for legal services for the needy. Under the rules, all client funds that cannot bear net interest for the client must be deposited in an IOLTA account. In *Phillips v. Washington Legal Foundation*, the Supreme Court held that interest generated in an IOLTA account is the private property of the owner of the principal. Brown (P) claimed the Washington requirement constitutes an unlawful taking of private property without just compensation.

■ ISSUE
Does the required use of interest on lawyers' trust accounts (IOLTA) for charitable purposes constitute an unlawful taking without just compensation?

■ DECISION AND RATIONALE
(Stevens, J.) No. Under the Fifth Amendment, private property may not be taken for public use without just compensation. As is clear from its language, the Fifth Amendment does not forbid the taking of private property, but merely requires just compensation when such a taking occurs. "[T]he 'just compensation' required by the Fifth Amendment is measured by the property owner's loss rather than the government's gain." The interest earned on a client's principle in an IOLTA account is the client's private property and, therefore, the state's charitable use of that interest constitutes a taking under the Fifth Amendment. However, because the interest earned in an IOLTA account is interest that would otherwise not be earned by the client, the loss to the property owner is nothing. Having suffered no loss, no compensation is due to the client.

■ DISSENT
(Scalia, J.) The measure of just compensation due to a private property owner is its market value. Although the IOLTA interest may not have accrued absent the state rule requiring client funds to be deposited in such an interest-bearing account for the benefit of the state, the interest earned properly belongs to the principal's owner. Once the state takes the money and gives it to the Legal Foundation of Washington, the property has value. Whether just compensation is measured by the owner's loss or

Brown v. Legal Foundation of Washington (Continued)

the government's gain, compensation is required. The gain to the government is identical to the owner's loss—the value of the interest earned. The Court embraces "Robin Hood Taking," in which the government takes from the rich to give to the poor. Brown (P) should be paid the market value of his taken property.

Analysis:

All fifty states use IOLTA accounts in various forms. Often dedicated to financing free legal assistance to the underprivileged, IOLTA accounts generate millions of dollars each year. Whether the state's possession of IOLTA interest is a taking or not, it is instrumental in ensuring competent legal representation to many who otherwise may not be able to afford it.

■ CASE VOCABULARY

JUST COMPENSATION: Under the Fifth Amendment, a fair payment by the government for property it has taken under eminent domain—usually the property's fair market value, so that the owner is no worse off after the taking.

CHAPTER SEVEN

Equal Protection

Romer v. Evans

Instant Facts: An Equal Protection challenge was brought against a popularly ratified amendment to Colorado's constitution, which made it unlawful for government entities and political subdivisions to explicitly ban discrimination on the basis of sexual orientation.

Black Letter Rule: A law declaring that it shall be more difficult for one group of citizens than for all others to seek aid from the government is, in the most literal sense, a denial of equal protection of the laws.

United States Railroad Retirement Board v. Fritz

Instant Facts: A retired railroad worker filed suit challenging the Railroad Retirement Act of 1974, legislation which made the plaintiffs ineligible for certain retirements benefits granted to other workers, on the ground that the statute made a distinction disallowed by equal protection.

Black Letter Rule: The rational basis test requires only that there be plausible reasons for the challenged legislation, regardless of the actual reasons behind the law.

Railway Express Agency, Inc. v. New York

Instant Facts: A national delivery company sought to challenge a New York City traffic regulation which prohibited advertisements on the side of vehicles, claiming that the regulation was in violation of equal protection because it did not apply to delivery vehicles which advertised the delivery service itself.

Black Letter Rule: Where the government chooses to regulate a particular activity, the regulation will not be held invalid simply because it is not applicable to every form of that activity.

New York City Transit Authority v. Beazer

Instant Facts: A group of former and current employees of the New York City Transit Authority filed a suit challenging the Transit Authority's rule disallowing any employees from partaking in methadone treatment.

Black Letter Rule: An exclusionary scheme which is not directed against any individual or category of person, but rather represents a policy choice made by government, is not unconstitutional so long as it does not circumscribe a class of persons characterized by some unpopular trait or affiliation.

United States Department of Agriculture v. Moreno

Instant Facts: A group of individuals who were excluded from the federal government's food stamp program because they lived with unrelated persons challenged their exclusion from the program on the ground that the rule barring unrelated households from the program was wholly unrelated to the purpose of the statute.

Black Letter Rule: Even under rational basis scrutiny, a challenged classification must rationally further some legitimate governmental purpose.

City of Cleburne, Texas v. Cleburne Living Center, Inc.

Instant Facts: Acting pursuant to municipal zoning ordinance requiring permits for such homes, a Texas city denied a special use permit for the operation of a group home for the mentally retarded.

Black Letter Rule: Because legislative or regulatory classifications based on mental retardation are neither suspect nor "quasi-suspect" their validity should be determined pursuant to a rational basis review.

Dred Scott v. Sandford

Instant Facts: After being taken by his owner to Illinois, a free-state under the Missouri Compromise, a slave sought to prevent his extradition to Missouri, a slave state, by the administrator of the slave owner's estate.

Black Letter Rule: The word "citizen" as used by the Constitution does not include slaves.

Korematsu v. United States

Instant Facts: A Japanese–American appealed his conviction for failing to comply with a federal military order excluding Japanese–Americans from certain parts in the western-half of the United States.

Black Letter Rule: Military necessity and national security may justify placing legal restrictions on a single racial group.

Loving v. Virginia

Instant Facts: An interracial couple appealed their convictions for breaking Virginia's miscegenation statute.

Black Letter Rule: Legislation which restricts the freedom to marry solely on the basis of racial classification violates the Equal Protection Clause of the Fourteenth Amendment.

Palmore v. Sidoti

Instant Facts: Sidoti (D) petitioned for custody of his daughter after his ex-wife, who had previously been granted custody, began living with a black man.

Black Letter Rule: Courts may not use private racial bias as a justification for official court action.

Plessy v. Ferguson

Instant Facts: A man asserted an equal protection challenge against his conviction for violating a Louisiana statute which required railway companies to maintain separate accommodations for whites and blacks.

Black Letter Rule: The Fourteenth Amendment does not withhold from states the power to permit or require the separation of races.

Brown v. Board of Education (Brown I)

Instant Facts: Several minor children in Kansas, South Carolina, Virginia and Delaware challenged the denial of their admission to schools attended by whites pursuant to laws permitting or requiring segregation.

Black Letter Rule: States may not segregate public schools on the basis of race.

Johnson v. California

Instant Facts: Johnson (P) claimed that California's (D) practice of segregating new inmates by race was a violation of equal protection violation.

Black Letter Rule: All racially based classifications imposed by the government are subject to strict scrutiny, including classifications made by prison authorities.

Washington v. Davis

Instant Facts: Two black police officers and two black applicants to the District of Colombia's police department sought to challenge the department's application process as discriminatory on the basis of race on several grounds, including that certain written tests had a discriminatory impact on blacks.

Black Letter Rule: A facially neutral law or official act will be declared unconstitutional only if there is proof that the law or act has a discriminatory purpose.

McCleskey v. Kemp

Instant Facts: A black man convicted of murder appealed his death sentence on equal protection grounds, claiming that the state administered the death penalty in a discriminatory manner against blacks.

Black Letter Rule: Statistical evidence indicating a risk that race plays a role in capital sentencing determinations does not alone prove a violation of equal protection.

City of Mobile v. Bolden

Instant Facts: A group of black citizens of Mobile, Alabama filed suit in federal district court claiming that the city's commission form of government was maintained in violation of the Fifteenth Amendment's prohibition against race-based interference with the right to vote.

Black Letter Rule: The Fifteenth Amendment does not entail the right to have black candidates elected but prohibits only purposefully discriminatory denial or abridgment by government of the freedom to vote "on account of race, color, or previous condition of servitude."

Palmer v. Thompson

Instant Facts: A group of black citizens files suit against the city of Jackson, Mississippi challenging the city council's decision to close public pools rather than operate them on a segregated basis as a violation of Equal Protection.

Black Letter Rule: A legislative act does not violate equal protection merely because it was motivated by a discriminatory purpose.

Personnel Administrator of Massachusetts v. Feeney

Instant Facts: A female state employee who was passed over for promotion by several less qualified male applicants who had served in the armed forces filed an equal protection suit challenging the state personnel office's stated preference for veterans.

Black Letter Rule: To be deemed purposefully discriminatory, a government act must have been taken because of, not merely in spite of, its adverse effects upon an identifiable group.

Village of Arlington Heights v. Metropolitan Housing Development Corp.

Instant Facts: A real estate developer filed suit in federal court alleging that the decision of the defendant municipality to deny a rezoning request for low-and moderate-income housing was racially discriminatory and in violation of the Fourteenth Amendment.

Black Letter Rule: Where there is proof that a discriminatory purpose was a motivating factor in the decision, the judicial deference usually accorded to government action is no longer warranted.

Brown v. Board of Education (Brown II)

Instant Facts: After issuing its decision in Brown I, the Supreme Court set the case for re-argument to determine the question of how to remedy school segregation.

Black Letter Rule: The Federal District Courts which first heard the cases involved in Brown I are to employ their full equitable power to ensure and oversee the full implementation of the constitutional principles announced therein.

Swann v. Charlotte–Mecklenburg Board of Education

Instant Facts: A black student and others filed a petition in federal District Court seeking relief from the failure of the Charlotte School to desegregate in an expedient manner consistent with Brown I.

Black Letter Rule: Once it has been shown that school officials have failed to comply with the constitutional principles announced in Brown v. Board of Education, district court's have at their discretion broad equitable powers which they may employ to remedy the violation.

Milliken v. Bradley

Instant Facts: A federal district court in Michigan ordered a multidistrict, area-wide remedy to address the racial segregation in only one of the 53 school districts in the metropolitan Detroit area.

Black Letter Rule: Before the boundaries of separate and autonomous school districts may be set aside by consolidating the separate units for remedial purposes or by imposing a cross-district remedy, it must first be shown that there has been a constitutional violation within one district that produces a significant segregative effect in another district.

Board of Education of Oklahoma City Public Schools v. Dowell

Instant Facts: A group of black students and their parents filed a claim seeking to reopen a desegregation case closed ten years earlier on the ground that their local school district had not achieved unitary status.

Black Letter Rule: A desegregation decree should be dissolved after local authorities have made a sufficient showing of constitutional compliance with the court order.

Parents Involved in Community Schools v. Seattle School District No. 1

Instant Facts: Seattle School District (D) used race as a factor is assigning children to schools.

Black Letter Rule: Use of race as a factor in school assignments, unless it is to remedy past segregation or used as one of a range of factors, violates the Equal Protection Clause.

Richmond v. J.A. Croson Co.

Instant Facts: After losing its bid on a public project due to its inability to procure satisfactory bids from minority subcontractors, a construction company filed suit against the city of Richmond, Virginia to challenge that city's ordinance requiring that 30% of subcontractors on public projects be owned by minorities.

Black Letter Rule: A city may use its spending powers to remedy private discrimination if it identifies that discrimination with the particularity required by the Fourteenth Amendment.

Adarand Constructors, Inc. v. Pena

Instant Facts: A highway construction company filed suit against the federal government challenging the Department of Transportation's policy favoring minority subcontractors as a violation of equal protection under the Due Process Clause of the Fifth Amendment.

Black Letter Rule: All racial classifications, imposed by whatever federal, state, or local government, must be analyzed by a reviewing court under strict scrutiny.

Grutter v. Bollinger

Instant Facts: Grutter (P), a white law school applicant, brought suit to challenge the University of Michigan Law School's (D) policy of relying on an applicant's race in the admissions decision.

Black Letter Rule: Racial classifications must be narrowly tailored to achieving a compelling state interest.

Gratz v. Bollinger

Instant Facts: Gratz (P) was denied admission to the University of Michigan's College of Literature, Science, and the Arts in favor of minority candidates.

Black Letter Rule: University admissions policies must take race into account, if at all, only on a case-by-case, individualized basis.

Easley v. Cromartie

Instant Facts: A three-judge district court panel held that the North Carolina legislature's 12th Congressional District's boundaries were unconstitutionally established using race as a predominant factor.

Black Letter Rule: When racial identification correlates highly with political affiliation, the party attacking the legislatively drawn boundaries must show that the legislature could have achieved its legitimate political objectives in alternative ways that are comparably consistent with traditional districting principles.

Frontiero v. Richardson

Instant Facts: A female lieutenant in the U.S. Air Force filed suit against the Armed Forces claiming that the statute creating the presumption that the wives of servicemen were "dependent" for the purpose of obtaining increased living allowances but requiring servicewomen to prove their husbands were "dependent" for such purposes was a violation of equal protection under the Fifth Amendment.

Black Letter Rule: Gender-based classifications are inherently suspect and must be subjected to strict scrutiny.

Craig v. Boren

Instant Facts: A male between the ages of 18 and 21 and a licensed vendor of 3.2% beer filed an action in federal district court challenging the constitutionality of Oklahoma statutes prohibiting the sale of "nonintoxicating" 3.2% beer to males under the age of 21 and to females under the age of 18.

Black Letter Rule: Gender classifications must serve important governmental objectives and must be substantially related to achievement of those objectives.

United States v. Virginia

Instant Facts: A female applicant seeking admission to the all-male Virginia Military Institute, a public university, filed a claim against the state of Virginia challenging the school's policy against admitting women.

Black Letter Rule: State's must proffer an exceedingly persuasive justification for gender classifications which categorically excludes women from education opportunities.

Geduldig v. Aiello

Instant Facts: A group of women filed a claim against the state of California challenging its disability insurance system on the ground that the denial of benefits for pregnancy related disability worked a discrimination against women in violation of equal protection.

Black Letter Rule: Discrimination on the basis of pregnancy is not in itself a violation of equal protection.

Orr v. Orr

Instant Facts: A man in a divorce proceeding sought to challenge upon equal protection grounds a state law which provided that men, but not women, could be required to pay alimony upon divorce.

Black Letter Rule: A state may not enact a statute requiring only men to pay alimony upon divorce.

Mississippi University for Women v. Hogan

Instant Facts: A male applicant denied admission to an all-female state-sponsored nursing school sought to challenge the school's exclusion of men.

Black Letter Rule: A state may designate an educational opportunity to members of only one-sex if the state seeks to remedy actual past discrimination related to the educational opportunity.

Michael M. v. Superior Court of Sonoma County

Instant Facts: A 17-year-old male sought to challenge his conviction for the statutory rape of a 16-year-old female on the ground that the statute under which he was convicted violated equal protection because it was only applicable to men.

Black Letter Rule: States may enact laws making it a crime for a man to have sex with an underage female in an effort to address teen pregnancy and teen sex.

Rostker v. Goldberg

Instant Facts: An equal protection challenge was brought against the Military Selective Service Act which requires only men between the ages of 18 and 26 to register for possible eventual conscription into the Armed Services.

Black Letter Rule: Congress does not violate equal protection by authorizing the president to require only males to register for selective service.

Califano v. Webster

Instant Facts: An equal protection claim was brought against the federal government to challenge provisions of Social Security Act that allowed women to exclude three more lower earning years in the computation of the retirement benefits.

Black Letter Rule: Reduction of the disparity in economic condition between men and women caused by the long history of discrimination is a governmental interest sufficiently important to justify a gender based classification.

Nguyen v. Immigration and Naturalization Service

Instant Facts: Nguyen (D), a Vietnamese-born child of an unmarried American man and Vietnamese woman, faced deportation after two felony convictions in the United States.

Black Letter Rule: To withstand an equal protection challenge, a gender-based classification must be substantially related to achieving an important governmental objective.

Graham v. Richardson

Instant Facts: A resident alien living in Arizona sought to challenge a state law which prohibited resident aliens who had lived in the state less than 15 years from receiving welfare benefits.

Black Letter Rule: A State's desire to preserve limited welfare benefits for its own citizens is inadequate to justify the exclusion of resident aliens from receiving a portion of those benefits.

Foley v. Connelie

Instant Facts: A resident alien sought to challenge the denial of his admission to a state police force on the ground that the exclusion of aliens violated the Equal Protection Clause.

Black Letter Rule: A state may, consistent with the Constitution, confine participation in its police force to citizens of the United States.

Ambach v. Norwick

Instant Facts: Two resident alien women filed suit against the state of New York seeking to invalidate a statute which restricted public school teacher certification to citizens of the United States.

Black Letter Rule: Public school teachers come well within the "governmental function" exception to the rule requiring strict scrutiny for classifications based on alienage.

Plyler v. Doe

Instant Facts: Several undocumented alien children filed an equal protection challenge, aiming to invalidate a state law which denied them free public education.

Black Letter Rule: If a state chooses to deny the benefit of free public education to undocumented alien children it must do so in order to further some substantial state interest.

Massachusetts Board of Retirement v. Murgia

Instant Facts: A police officer forced into retirement sought to challenge a state law requiring uniformed state police officers to retire at the age of 50 on the grounds that it violated equal protection.

Black Letter Rule: Classifications based on age need only be rationally related to a legitimate state purpose.

Romer v. Evans

(Governor of Colorado) v. *(Not Provided)*
517 U.S. 620, 116 S.Ct. 1620 (1996)

SUPREME COURT INVALIDATES A STATE LAW AS IRRATIONAL LEGISLATION PURSUANT TO THE FOURTEENTH AMENDMENT'S GUARANTEE OF EQUAL PROTECTION

■ **INSTANT FACTS** An Equal Protection challenge was brought against a popularly ratified amendment to Colorado's constitution, which made it unlawful for government entities and political subdivisions to explicitly ban discrimination on the basis of sexual orientation.

■ **BLACK LETTER RULE** A law declaring that it shall be more difficult for one group of citizens than for all others to seek aid from the government is, in the most literal sense, a denial of equal protection of the laws.

■ **PROCEDURAL BASIS**

Appeal to the United States Supreme Court challenging a decision of the Colorado Supreme Court, which affirmed the trial court's decision to enjoin the enforcement of an amendment to the state's constitution on equal protection grounds.

■ **FACTS**

In 1992, the Constitution of the State of Colorado (D) was amended by popular referendum to provide that "Neither the State of Colorado (D), through any of its branches or departments, nor any of its agencies, political subdivisions, municipalities or school districts, shall enact, adopt or enforce any statute, regulation, ordinance or policy whereby homosexual, lesbian or bisexual orientation, conduct practices or relationships shall constitute or otherwise be the basis of or entitle any person or class of persons to have or claim any minority status quota preferences, protected status or claim of discrimination." The history of the amendment suggested that it was ratified in an effort to invalidate ordinances enacted in several municipalities that banned discrimination on the basis of sexual orientation in such matters as housing, employment, education, public accommodations and health services.

■ **ISSUE**

Consistent with the Fourteenth Amendment's guarantee of Equal Protection, may a state amend its constitution to provide that gays cannot be considered a group entitled to legislation or other government action prohibiting discrimination on the basis of sexual orientation?

■ **DECISION AND RATIONALE**

(Kennedy, J.) No. A law declaring that in general it shall be more difficult for one group of citizens than for all others to seek aid from the government is, in the most literal sense, a denial of equal protection of the laws. The State of Colorado (D) argues that its constitution does nothing more than place gays in the position of all other persons, that it only denies gays any special rights not afforded to others. We disagree. The amendment withdraws from homosexuals, but no others, specific legal protection from the injuries caused by discrimination, and it forbids government action banning such discrimination. While the protection from discrimination in areas of housing and employment, to name two for example, are taken for granted by most citizens, the amendment in question attempts to withhold such protection from gays. Since gays are not a suspect class, nor are gays being denied any fundamental right, the amendment need only bear a rational relation to some legitimate government purpose in order to pass constitutional muster. Under this inquiry, the amendment fails for two reasons: (1) It imposes a broad and undifferentiated disability on a single named group; and (2) it is so broad as to call into doubt any of the justifications proffered in its defense. In searching for a link between the ends sought and the legislation enacted, we find that the classification of homosexuals is both too broad and too narrow. It identifies persons by a single trait then denies them protection across the board, resulting in a denial of the right to seek specific protection from the law. Furthermore, any law of this type raises the inference that it was enacted out of mere animosity toward the class of persons affected, a motivation which makes classification such as the one at issue here invalid under the Fourteenth Amendment. We also believe that the amendment bears no legitimate purpose. Colorado has classified gays and denied them protection for the mere reason that they are gay. This a state may not do. For all of the foregoing reasons, the amendment acts as an unconstitutional deprivation or Equal Protection. Affirmed.

■ DISSENT

(Scalla, J.) The amendment to the Colorado Constitution is nothing more than an attempt to preserve sexual mores, an objective which has been specifically approved by this Court. We have previously held that a state may, consistent with the Constitution, make it a crime to engage in homosexual activity. If criminalizing homosexuality is permissible, so too should be legislation which disfavors homosexuals. The Court is also mistaken in its attempt to frame the amendment at issue as a denial of equal treatment. Today the Court holds that it is a denial of equal protection when a group is singled out and made to resort to a more difficult level of political decision-making in order to garner legislation in its favor than is required of the general population. Until today, this principle was unheard of.

Analysis:

The gist of the Court's opinion in *Romer* was that a state may not enact legislation that classifies a particular group of citizens on the basis of one characteristic and imposes upon them a political burden not applicable to the general citizenry. In other words, what made the legislation at issue unconstitutional was not necessarily that it denied gays the right to protection from discrimination on the basis of sexual orientation. Rather, the constitutional violation stemmed from the fact that the law required gays to amend Colorado's Constitution before they could gain protection aimed at eradicating discrimination on the basis of sexual orientation. Although the particular point at issue in this case was whether the Colorado Constitution violated the Equal Protection Clause of the Fourteenth Amendment, this case serves the more broad purpose of providing a rare example of the Court's willingness to strike down legislation subject to the lowest level of constitutional scrutiny—the rational basis test.

■ CASE VOCABULARY

SUSPECT CLASSIFICATION: Any legislation which seeks to group persons on the basis of race, national origin, alienage and gender

United States Railroad Retirement Board v. Fritz
(Government) v. (Retired Railroad Worker)
449 U.S. 166, 101 S.Ct. 453 (1980)

UNDER RATIONAL BASIS REVIEW, THE ACTUAL PURPOSE BEHIND THE CHALLENGED LEGISLATION IS IRRELEVANT SO LONG AS SOME LEGITIMATE PURPOSE CAN BE CONCEIVED TO JUSTIFY THE LAW

■ **INSTANT FACTS** A retired railroad worker filed suit challenging the Railroad Retirement Act of 1974, legislation which made the plaintiffs ineligible for certain retirements benefits granted to other workers, on the ground that the statute made a distinction disallowed by equal protection.

■ **BLACK LETTER RULE** The rational basis test requires only that there be plausible reasons for the challenged legislation, regardless of the actual reasons behind the law.

■ **PROCEDURAL BASIS**
Appeal to the U.S. Supreme Court from a decision of the Southern District of Indiana, which held unconstitutional a section of the Railroad Retirement Act of 1974.

■ **FACTS**
In 1974 Congress enacted the Railroad Retirement Act (Act) to restructure the railroad retirement system. Up to that point all eligible railroad workers would receive both social security and railroad retirement benefits and an accompanying "windfall" benefit. The Act changed all of that to ensure the solvency of the railroad retirement fund. The Act divided workers, present and former, into various groups. First, those with less than 10 years railroad experience would not be eligible for the windfall. Second, those already receiving windfall benefits would continue to do so. Third, those who qualified for the windfall as of January 1, 1975, the "changeover date," but had not retired would not receive benefits unless they were "connected" to the railroad system in 1974 or had completed 25 years of railroad service as of the changeover date. Finally, those who failed to meet either the "connection" or 25-year service requirements would be entitled to a lesser windfall if they had qualified for social security prior to their leaving the railroad system. The statute was challenged on the ground that the "current connection" requirement was an arbitrary distinction in violation of Equal Protection.

■ **ISSUE**
Does the rational basis standard of judicial review require a court to take into account the actual purposes behind challenged legislation?

■ **DECISION AND RATIONALE**
(Rehnquist, J.) No. The rational basis test requires only that there be plausible reasons for the challenged legislation, regardless of the actual reasons behind the law. This rule is particularly applicable in cases such as this, where Congress must draw lines somewhere. The United States Railroad Retirement Board (D) argues that the legislation was enacted to provide benefits to career railroad workers. The "current connection" test is not an arbitrary means of determining who is a career railroad worker. Congress could assume that those who had a current connection with the railroad industry in 1974, or those who returned to the industry prior to retirement, were more likely to be career railroad workers. Reversed.

United States Railroad Retirement Board v. Fritz (Continued)

■ DISSENT

(Brennan, J.) The standard applied by the court today virtually immunizes social and economic legislative classifications. This court has frequently stated that it is the actual purpose behind the challenged legislation which must be scrutinized, and not the post hoc justifications proffered by government attorneys. Thus, the rational basis test requires that the challenged classification be rationally related to achievement of an actual legitimate governmental purpose.

Analysis:

As do many constitutional issues, this case involves a difficult choice between two alternatives. The holding that any conceivable legislative purpose is sufficient under rational basis scrutiny carries with it the benefit that courts are not placed in the position of guessing the intent of legislators. Such an inquiry is often difficult in light of the fact that legislators act for different purposes and there is rarely one "true" purpose behind a law. However, the problem with this less exacting standard of review is that, as the dissent points out, it makes legislation immune from attack. After all, it is almost always possible to come up with some plausible and legitimate purpose to defend legislation under constitutional attack.

Railway Express Agency, Inc. v. New York

(Delivery Business) v. (State)
336 U.S. 106, 69 S.Ct. 463 (1949)

UNDER RATIONAL BASIS SCRUTINY, LEGISLATION WILL NOT BE HELD UNCONSTITUTIONAL MERELY BECAUSE IT IS UNDERINCLUSIVE

■ **INSTANT FACTS** A national delivery company sought to challenge a New York City traffic regulation which prohibited advertisements on the side of vehicles, claiming that the regulation was in violation of equal protection because it did not apply to delivery vehicles which advertised the delivery service itself.

■ **BLACK LETTER RULE** Where the government chooses to regulate a particular activity, the regulation will not be held invalid simply because it is not applicable to every form of that activity.

■ **PROCEDURAL BASIS**

Appeal to the United States Supreme Court challenging the decision of the New York Court of Appeals, which upheld a conviction and fine for a traffic violation.

■ **FACTS**

Railway Express Agency, Inc. (Railway) (D) was convicted and fined for violating a New York City (P) traffic regulation which prohibited vehicles containing advertisements. Railway (D) challenged its conviction on the ground that the regulation violated equal protection because it expressly did not apply to "business notices upon business delivery vehicles, so long as such vehicles [were] engaged in the usual business or regular work of the owner and not used merely...for advertising."

■ **ISSUE**

Does government regulation violate equal protection merely because it does not apply to every activity of the same type sought to be regulated?

■ **DECISION AND RATIONALE**

(Douglas, J.) No. Where the government chooses to regulate a particular activity, the regulation will not be held invalid simply because it is not applicable to every form of that activity. Railway (D) argues that basing the regulation's primary exclusion on the identity of the owner of the vehicle is not justified by the aim of the regulation. In other words, the fact that a particular sign is placed on a delivery truck not owned by the person choosing to advertise does not create any more traffic problems than when a person chooses to advertise on their own delivery truck. Assuming that this is the true aim of the statute, the argument is untenable. The local authorities could have decided that the traffic problems associated with those who advertised others' businesses were different in kind or degree from the traffic problems associated with persons choosing to advertise their own business. It is no requirement of equal protection that all evils of the same genus be eradicated or none at all. Affirmed.

■ **CONCURRENCE**

(Jackson, J.) This Court often invokes the Due Process Clause of the Fourteenth Amendment to strike down regulations enacted by municipalities to deal with local activities. In contrast to the Due Process Clause, which frequently disables government from dealing with the subject at issue, the Equal Protection Clause prohibits government from making arbitrary and unreasonable distinctions between

Railway Express Agency, Inc. v. New York (Continued)

its citizens. Because we are more likely to find arbitrariness in the regulation of the few, I am more receptive to attacks on local ordinances grounded in equal protection than challenges based on due process. I do not think that differences in treatment under law should be approved because of differences unrelated to the legislative purpose. The Equal Protection Clause ceases to fulfill its purpose if it can be avoided by any conceivable difference that can be pointed out between those subject to regulation and those free from it.

Analysis:

When strictly scrutinizing legislation challenged on equal protection grounds, courts often strike down legislation that is underinclusive—legislation that does not apply to every person engaged in the activity sought to be regulated. However, as the court makes clear in *Railway Express,* underinclusiveness is not fatal under the rational basis test. Thus, the fact that the state chose to reduce a perceived danger by regulating only a few of those who were purportedly responsible for the danger—in this case, delivery trucks advertising other businesses—did not alone make the regulation violative of equal protection.

■ CASE VOCABULARY

UNDERINCLUSIVENESS: The failure of some regulation to apply to all persons engaged in the activity which the government seeks to regulate.

New York City Transit Authority v. Beazer

(*Municipal Agency*) v. (*Dismissed Employee*)
440 U.S. 568, 99 S.Ct. 1355 (1979)

RATIONAL BASIS REVIEW WILL TOLERATE OVERINCLUSIVE LEGISLATION

■ **INSTANT FACTS** A group of former and current employees of the New York City Transit Authority filed a suit challenging the Transit Authority's rule disallowing any employees from partaking in methadone treatment.

■ **BLACK LETTER RULE** An exclusionary scheme which is not directed against any individual or category of person, but rather represents a policy choice made by government, is not unconstitutional so long as it does not circumscribe a class of persons characterized by some unpopular trait or affiliation.

■ **PROCEDURAL BASIS**

Appeal to the United States Supreme Court challenging the holding of the Second Circuit Court of Appeals, which affirmed the decision of the District Court striking down the defendant Transit Authority's rule prohibiting employment of methadone users as unconstitutional.

■ **FACTS**

The New York Transit Authority (Authority) (D) enacted a policy which prohibited the hiring of narcotics users, which was read to include those undergoing methadone treatment for heroin addiction. Two former employees of, and two applicants rejected by, the Authority sought to challenge to rule on the ground that it violated the Equal Protection Clause because it failed to distinguish between methadone users who successfully refrained from using heroin and all other methadone users.

■ **ISSUE**

May a city agency enact a blanket exclusion from employment against all persons undertaking methadone treatment?

■ **DECISION AND RATIONALE**

(Stevens, J.) Yes. An exclusionary scheme which is not directed against any individual or category of person, but rather represents a policy choice made by government, is not unconstitutional so long as it does not circumscribe a class of persons characterized by some unpopular trait or affiliation. Beazer (P) challenges the rule on the ground that successful methadone users—usually those who have completed one-year of treatment—should not be included in the class of narcotic users because they do not pose the same threat to safety as the latter. However, the District Court found that as many as 30% of "successful" methadone users regressed to using heroin again. Thus, the Authority (D) merely chose to distinguish between users and non-users, rather than drawing its distinction at the one-year line. Any other rule would have been less precise and more costly. Accordingly, the policy that postponed employment eligibility until completion of the methadone program was rational. We must also keep in mind that we cannot fault the Authority for not proving the unemployability of "successful" methadone users. Under rational basis review, it is those who challenge the exclusion who bear the burden of proving that drawing the distinction elsewhere would be as effective and efficient. The Authority did not violate equal protection by enacting a blanket exclusion from employment against persons undertaking

New York City Transit Authority v. Beazer (Continued)

methadone treatment, without any regard to the ability of particular methadone users to do their job safely. Reversed.

■ DISSENT

(White, J.) The Court ignores the fact that the District Court found that "successful" methadone users can be easily identified through normal procedures and, for many jobs, are as employable as non-users. Thus the blanket exclusion too broadly furthers the rule's stated objective—the efficient screening of unemployable persons. For that reason the rule violates the Equal Protection Clause.

Analysis:

Whereas *Railway Express* stands for the broad proposition that regulation will not fail equal protection scrutiny merely because it is underinclusive, the decision here makes it clear that overinclusiveness is also not dispositive under rational basis review. Accordingly, the fact that the reach of the rule at issue included persons who did not exhibit the trait the Authority was seeking to exclude—i.e., unemployability due to narcotic use—did not make the regulation unconstitutional. The Court reasoned that drawing the bright-line at use/no use was at least as efficient, and no more imprecise, than basing the distinction on whether the employee had completed some level of methadone treatment.

■ CASE VOCABULARY

METHADONE: A synthetic narcotic used in the treatment of heroin addiction.

United States Department of Agriculture v. Moreno

(*Government Agency*) v. (*Person Ineligible for Food Stamps*)
413 U.S. 528, 93 S.Ct. 2821 (1973)

CLASSIFICATIONS MAY BE SO IRRATIONAL AS TO FAIL RATIONAL BASIS SCRUTINY

■ **INSTANT FACTS** A group of individuals who were excluded from the federal government's food stamp program because they lived with unrelated persons challenged their exclusion from the program on the ground that the rule barring unrelated households from the program was wholly unrelated to the purpose of the statute.

■ **BLACK LETTER RULE** Even under rational basis scrutiny, a challenged classification must rationally further some legitimate governmental purpose.

■ **PROCEDURAL BASIS**

Appeal to the U.S. Supreme Court challenging the decision of the District Court, which held that federal legislation barring unrelated households from its food stamp program violated equal protection.

■ **FACTS**

In 1971, Congress amended § 3(e) of the Food Stamp Act to provide that eligible households did not include groups of unrelated persons. The Department of Agriculture accordingly amended its regulations to provide that a household would be ineligible if it included at least one person unrelated to the other members. Since eligibility for the program was based on households rather than individuals, a number of people became ineligible for the program because they happened to live with unrelated persons. For example, Jacinta Moreno (P), a 56-year old diabetic, became ineligible because she lived with an unrelated person who helped care for her and with whom Moreno (P) shared living expenses.

■ **ISSUE**

May a statute be invalidated pursuant to a rational basis review if it classifies persons in a manner which is irrelevant to the stated purpose of the act?

■ **DECISION AND RATIONALE**

(Brennan, J.) Yes. Even under rational basis scrutiny, a challenged classification must rationally further some legitimate governmental purpose. The stated policy of the Food Stamp Act is to provide for the nutritional requirement of needier segments of society. The fact that unrelated persons live as one economic unit is in no way related to this purpose. Thus, for the classification to withstand scrutiny it must be related to some other purpose of the statute. The scant legislative history which exits suggest that the classification was created to prohibit hippies and their communes from participating in the program. However, this is not a legitimate government interest. The Government (D) argues that the amendment should be upheld as rationally related to the legitimate interest in minimizing fraud in the administration of the program. It argues that Congress may have believed that unrelated households either were more likely than related ones to fail to report other sources of income or were relatively unstable, making it difficult to detect such abuses. Even if we accepted the prevention of fraud as the purpose behind the law, it is clear that the classification is not rationally related to that concern. The fact that the statute contains other provisions, including criminal penalties, aimed at preventing fraud casts

United States Department of Agriculture v. Moreno (Continued)

doubt that § 3(e) was rationally aimed at preventing the same abuses. Furthermore, the classification does not rationally further even this tenuous purpose. Affirmed.

■ **DISSENT**

(Rehnquist, J.) Today the Court oversteps it bounds. Our role is merely to determine whether there is any rational basis which would support Congress' decision to withhold food stamps from unrelated persons living together. Surely, the statute passes this minimal inquiry. It is not unreasonable to assume that Congress could deny food stamps to households formed for the very purpose of taking advantage of the program. The fact that Congress may have chosen a method which sweeps too many people under the purview of the regulation bears no weight under rational basis review.

Analysis:

This case serves as a good illustration of the notion that rational basis scrutiny is a malleable standard, often deferential, sometimes critical. If, as many cases suggest, rational basis scrutiny involves an inquiry that merely asks whether Congress could have had some reasonable basis for the classification, then one must agree with the dissent. However, other cases have suggested that such a deferential standard makes rational basis scrutiny meaningless by deferring too much to legislative action. Contrast the majority's efforts to question the "true" intent behind the statute with the Court's later holding in *Fritz*. The Court states here that provisions of the Food Stamp Act other than that under review in this case make it unlikely that the statute's purpose was to prevent fraud. The Court's subsequent decision in *Fritz* makes evident that such an inquiry is not appropriate under the rational basis test. In any event, the Court's opinion appears to suggest that the term "rational relation" is coterminous with a likely relation.

City of Cleburne, Texas v. Cleburne Living Center, Inc.

(Local Government) v. (Home for Mentally Retarded)
473 U.S. 432, 105 S.Ct. 3249 (1985)

UNSUBSTANTIATED FEARS OR NEGATIVE ATTITUDES AIMED AT SOME GROUP ARE NOT PERMISSIBLE BASES FOR CLASSIFYING MEMBERS OF THAT GROUP SEPARATE FROM THE GENERAL POPULATION

■ **INSTANT FACTS** Acting pursuant to municipal zoning ordinance requiring permits for such homes, a Texas city denied a special use permit for the operation of a group home for the mentally retarded,.

■ **BLACK LETTER RULE** Because legislative or regulatory classifications based on mental retardation are neither suspect nor "quasi-suspect" their validity should be determined pursuant to a rational basis review.

■ **PROCEDURAL BASIS**

Appeal to the U.S. Supreme Court challenging the holding of the Court of Appeals for the Fifth Circuit, which held that mental retardation was a "quasi-suspect" classification warranting intermediate scrutiny.

■ **FACTS**

Clebume Living Center, Inc. (CLC) (P) applied to the city of Cleburne, Texas (City) for a special use permit to operate a group home for the mentally retarded. After the City Council (D) held a public hearing on the application, it voted 3 to 1 to deny the permit.

■ **ISSUE**

Are regulatory classifications based on mental retardation "quasisuspect" classifications warranting intermediate scrutiny?

■ **DECISION AND RATIONALE**

(White, J.) No. Because legislative or regulatory classifications based on mental retardation are neither suspect nor "quasi-suspect" their validity should be determined pursuant to a rational basis review. First, the fact is that the mentally retarded require special needs, have a reduced ability to function in the everyday world and are diverse with respect to their relative abilities. Accordingly, states have a legitimate interest in dealing with and providing for them. Second, recent legislation, both state and federal, has shown greater sympathy for the plight of this group, obviating the need for enhanced judicial scrutiny. Requiring legislators to justify their decision could lead to government inaction in this area. Third, the fact that legislators have responded to the needs of the mentally retarded indicates that they are not a politically powerless group. Fourth, if the mentally retarded were deemed a quasi-suspect class, such a determination would also have to apply to groups such as the disabled or infirm. The Court is unwilling to go so far. For these reasons, any challenged classification based on mental retardation is to be subjected to rational basis scrutiny. Nevertheless, we find that the City's (D) refusal to grant the CLC (P) a special use permit fails even this inquiry. There simply is no rational basis for believing that the CLC's (P) proposed home would threaten the city's legitimate interests. The attitudes of the citizens who would neighbor the group home are irrelevant since negative attitudes and fears are not a permissible basis for treating the mentally retarded differently from other groups. The same is true

City of Cleburne, Texas v. Cleburne Living Center, Inc. (Continued)

of the City's (D) fear that the home proximity to a junior high school may lead to harassment on the part of the students. The fact that the home would be a on a 500-year flood plain also fails to provide a meaningful distinction between the CLC and any other group home. Finally, the City's (D) concern as to the number of potential residents also provides no justification for the denial since the lower courts found that the permit would have been granted to a fraternity house, dormitory, nursing home and a host of other group dwellings.

Analysis:

This case serves as an example that rational basis review does not always serve as a judicial rubber stamp. The Court found itself in a difficult position. The majority was aware that legislation aimed at the mentally retarded is not only legitimate, but often desirable. Accordingly, the Court did not want to make mental retardation a *quasi-suspect* class. However, the Court was also aware that the motives behind the City's (D) decision to deny the permit were irrational. Plainly, the Court here undertakes a type of review that exceeds the traditional rational basis test and approaches an intermediate level of scrutiny. This case serves to substantiate the notion that the levels of review are really more on a sliding scale than in distinct categories.

■ CASE VOCABULARY

QUASI-SUSPECT: Term used for a classification which is not expressly subject to heightened scrutiny, but which, according to some, deserves close attention.

SPECIAL USE PERMIT: Authorization from a zoning board to use property for a purpose for which it is not particularly zoned.

Dred Scott v. Sandford

(*Slave*) v. (*Estate Administrator*)
60 U.S. (19 How.) 393 (1856)

THE SUPREME COURT HOLDS THAT NEGROES ARE NOT CITIZENS UNDER THE U.S. CONSTITUTION

■ **INSTANT FACTS** After being taken by his owner to Illinois, a free-state under the Missouri Compromise, a slave sought to prevent his extradition to Missouri, a slave state, by the administrator of the slave owner's estate.

■ **BLACK LETTER RULE** The word "citizen" as used by the Constitution does not include slaves.

■ **PROCEDURAL BASIS**

Not provided.

■ **FACTS**

As a result of the Missouri Compromise, the state of Missouri was admitted to the union as a slave-state and Illinois (along with all northern states) was made a free-state. Thereafter, Dred Scott (P), a slave, was taken by his owner, John Emerson, from Missouri into Illinois. When Emerson died in Illinois, the administrator of his estate, John Sandford (D), sought to make Scott (P) part of the estate. Scott (P) filed suit seeking his freedom.

■ **ISSUE**

Consistent with the Constitution, can a slave become a member of the political community entitled to all the rights, privileges and immunities appertaining thereto?

■ **DECISION AND RATIONALE**

(Taney, C.J.) No. The word "citizen" as used by the Constitution does not include slaves. In fact, at the time the Constitution was drafted, slaves were considered a subordinate and inferior class of beings. The plight of this population is unlike that of the Indian, who although made subject to the white race and legislation enacted by Congress, have been treated as members of a different government. That is not the case with the descendants to those persons imported to the United States as slaves. The language of Declaration of Independence stating that "all men are created equal," clearly was not intended to apply to slaves. The fact of the matter is that slaves have never been thought of as citizens. Thus, a mere act of Congress is insufficient to make members of this class into citizens of the United States.

Analysis:

The *Dred Scott* case has been considered by some as one of the five most unfortunate decisions ever handed down by the U.S. Supreme Court. Ironically, the decision indirectly led to the freeing of slaves. In many ways the decision limited the federal government's ability to deal with the slave issue, and the corresponding tensions between North and South, in a conciliatory fashion. The *Dred Scott* decision

Dred Scott v. Sandford (Continued)

became central to the issues that eventually led to the Civil War. In 1865, the United States ratified the Thirteenth Amendment to the Constitution, which expressly made slavery unlawful. Three years later, the Fourteenth Amendment overturned *Dred Scott* by granting citizenship to all persons born in the United States.

■ CASE VOCABULARY

MISSOURI COMPROMISE: Congressional act which divided the nation between slave states in the South and free states in the North.

Korematsu v. United States

(Convicted Japanese-American) v. (Government)
323 U.S. 214, 65 S.Ct. 193 (1944)

SUPREME COURT UPHOLDS A RACIAL CLASSIFICATION SUBJECTED TO STRICT SCRUTINY

■ **INSTANT FACTS** A Japanese-American appealed his conviction for failing to comply with a federal military order excluding Japanese-Americans from certain parts in the western-half of the United States.

■ **BLACK LETTER RULE** Military necessity and national security may justify placing legal restrictions on a single racial group.

■ PROCEDURAL BASIS
Not Provided.

■ FACTS
In May of 1942, the U.S. Army issued an order which excluded all persons of Japanese ancestry from the West Coast. The order was issued pursuant to Congressional authority granted to the Executive Branch to decide who should and should not remain in threatened areas. The exclusion was deemed necessary to handle the presence of an unascertained number of disloyal Japanese-Americans. Korematsu (D) was convicted of failing to comply with the order by remaining in San Leandro, California.

■ ISSUE
May a racial classification survive strict scrutiny on the basis of military need or national security?

■ DECISION AND RATIONALE
(Black, J.) Yes. Military necessity and national security may justify placing legal restrictions on a single racial group. The fact that the military authorities have concluded that it is impossible to segregate disloyal Japanese-Americans from those who are loyal justifies the exclusion. Furthermore, there was some evidence that there in fact existed within the United States disloyal Japanese. While the hardships endured by those made subject to the order are severe, we must keep in mind that hardships are a part of war, and are endured to differing degrees by different citizens. Korematsu (D) was excluded from his home not because of animosity toward his race but because we are at war with Japan, and the military authorities decided that the order was necessary to secure our borders.

■ DISSENT
(Murphy, J.) While military necessity may justify a racial classification, such a need must be supported by evidence. Just as any act of Congress or Executive Order, a military order drawn on racial lines must be subjected to the proper judicial inquiry. The test is whether the deprivation is reasonably related to a public danger that is so "immediate, imminent and impending" as to not permit the ordinary constitutional process. The fact that the order deprived Japanese-Americans fundamental rights is unquestioned. However, no "immediate, imminent and impending" danger has been proffered to justify the order. Instead, the Commanding General's Final Report is filled with instances of racial bias. The military has inferred the potential guilt of over 100,000 citizens from the fact that a few are suspected to

Korematsu v. United States (Continued)

be disloyal to the nation. No reason has been given why these citizens cannot be dealt with on an individual basis by holding investigations and hearings to determine their loyalty. There was no evidence that espionage was out of control. Furthermore, no Japanese-Americans have been found guilty of treason.

■ DISSENT

(Jackson, J.) The fact is that Korematsu has been convicted of a crime because of who his parents are. Were he of Italian or German descent, he would be free to remain in his home. The Constitution forbids the military from executing an order such as the one which led to the conviction.

Analysis:

The existence of a compelling interest alone does not justify a violation of equal protection. The classification chosen must be necessary to fulfill the objective sought. In this case, the threat of espionage was the danger the government sought to avoid. Nevertheless, the Court failed to require the government to show why internment was the only means of handling the question of espionage. Furthermore, the Court ignored the fact that the order was both overinclusive and underinclusive— underinclusive in the sense that the order did not apply to Americans of German and Italian descent, and overinclusive in that it applied to Japanese-Americans who were not suspected of espionage.

Loving v. Virginia

(*Interracial Married Couple*) v. (*Government*)
388 U.S. 1, 87 S.Ct. 1817 (1967)

THE FACT THAT A RACIAL CLASSIFICATION BURDENS BOTH WHITES AND MINORITIES EQUALLY DOES NOT INDICATE THAT THERE IS NO VIOLATION OF EQUAL PROTECTION

■ **INSTANT FACTS** An interracial couple appealed their convictions for breaking Virginia's miscegenation statute.

■ **BLACK LETTER RULE** Legislation which restricts the freedom to marry solely on the basis of racial classification violates the Equal Protection Clause of the Fourteenth Amendment.

■ **PROCEDURAL BASIS**

Appeal to the U.S. Supreme Court challenging the decision of the Supreme Court of Virginia which upheld two convictions based on the State's ban against interracial marriages.

■ **FACTS**

In 1958, Mildred Jeter (P), a black woman, and Richard Loving, a white man, were married in the District of Colombia. Shortly thereafter, the Lovings (P) moved to and began to reside in Virginia. In January of 1959, the Lovings (P) pled guilty to violating Virginia's (D) ban on interracial marriages. Their one year sentences were suspended on the condition that the two not return together to Virginia for 25 years. In 1963, the Lovings (P) filed a motion in Virginia (D) state court to set aside their sentence on the ground that the statute violated the Fourteenth Amendment. The Supreme Court of Appeal upheld the statute and affirmed the Lovings' (P) convictions.

■ **ISSUE**

Do statutes which ban interracial marriages violate the Equal Protection Clause of the Fourteenth Amendment?

■ **DECISION AND RATIONALE**

(Warren, C.J.) Yes. Legislation which restricts the freedom to marry solely on the basis of racial classification violates the Equal Protection Clause of the Fourteenth Amendment. In upholding the constitutionality of Virginia's (D) miscegenation statute the state's Supreme Court held that state's legitimate interest lay in preserving racial integrity, and preventing "the corruption of blood," "a mongrel breed of citizens," and "the obliteration of racial pride." The court went on to hold that marriage was within the sole province of the States, free from the intervention of the federal government. The State (D) argues that the provisions are constitutional because they apply equally to whites and blacks. However, we reject the notion that the mere "equal application" of a statute containing racial classifications makes those classifications consistent with the Fourteenth Amendment. It is clear these statutes are subject to strict scrutiny. The State of Virginia (D) has no legitimate interest in enforcing its ban on interracial marriages. The fact that the state does not prohibit interracial marriages between persons not of the white race is proof that their purpose is to preserve the idea of White Supremacy. Reversed.

Analysis:

The Court here rejects the notion that equal application of race based statutes takes such classifications out of the purview of the Fourteenth Amendment. The Court's decision in this case rests heavily on the assumption that the purpose of the Fourteenth Amendment was to eliminate racial discrimination. However, the decision to hold anti-miscegenation statutes unconstitutional could be criticized for a couple of reasons. First, there is no indication that the drafters of the Fourteenth Amendment intended to make these laws unconstitutional. Second, there is some strength to Virginia's (D) argument that equal protection requires only equal application, not desegregation. However, the fact that legislation drawn on racial lines must undergo strict scrutiny may have sounded the death knell for the Virginia (D) statute. The Court's decision to strike down anti-miscegenation statutes was based on its belief that these statutes have no legitimate purpose, except to maintain the notion that blacks are inferior to whites.

■ CASE VOCABULARY

MISCEGENATION: Interracial marriage.

Palmore v. Sidoti

(Ex–Wife) v. (Ex–Husband)
466 U.S. 429, 104 S.Ct. 1879 (1984)

CUSTODY DETERMINATIONS MAY NOT BE BASED ON POTENTIAL RACIAL BIAS AGAINST THE CHILD

■ **INSTANT FACTS** Sidoti (D) petitioned for custody of his daughter after his ex-wife, who had previously been granted custody, began living with a black man.

■ **BLACK LETTER RULE** Courts may not use private racial bias as a justification for official court action.

■ PROCEDURAL BASIS
Certiorari to review a state court judgment modifying a custody determination.

■ FACTS
After Palmore (P) and Sidoti (D) were divorced, Palmore (P) was awarded custody of the couple's daughter. When Palmore (P), a white woman, began cohabiting with a black man, whom she later married, Sidoti (D) petitioned to modify the custody determination due to changed circumstances. Making no findings concerning Sidoti's (D) allegations of improper care, the court granted the modification. Citing the societal pressures the daughter is likely to face from her mother's mixed-race relationship, the court granted Sidoti (D) custody.

■ ISSUE
May a court consider private racial bias and the possible injury caused by them when determining the custodial placement of a child?

■ DECISION AND RATIONALE
(Burger, C.J.) No. Although matters of domestic relations are usually within the powers of the states, the state court judgment here invokes a matter of considerable constitutional importance. While a child living in a mixed-race household may indeed endure societal pressure and private bias, the Constitution cannot permit a state court to give way to such influences. "The Constitution cannot control such prejudices but neither can it tolerate them." Having previously determined the best interests of the child to be served in Palmore's (P) custody, the court cannot give way to racial classifications merely because of societal pressures.

Analysis:
In custody disputes, courts are called upon to determine the best interests of the child. Such a custody determination may be modified if circumstances change such that the initial determination is called into question. Here, the lower court no doubt sought to protect the child from any potential psychological trauma caused by a mixed-race household. Yet, the court's use of race-conscious speculation, while perhaps well intentioned, is not appropriate grounds for modification.

Plessy v. Ferguson

(Black Man) v. (State Judge)
163 U.S. 537, 16 S.Ct. 1138 (1896)

SUPREME COURT HOLDS THAT THE FOURTEENTH AMENDMENT DOES NOT REQUIRE THE DESEGREGATION OF SOCIETY

■ **INSTANT FACTS** A man asserted an equal protection challenge against his conviction for violating a Louisiana statute which required railway companies to maintain separate accommodations for whites and blacks.

■ **BLACK LETTER RULE** The Fourteenth Amendment does not withhold from states the power to permit or require the separation of races.

■ PROCEDURAL BASIS
Not Provided.

■ FACTS
Plessy (D), who was one-eighth black and seven-eighths white, was forcibly removed by police from a coach which, pursuant to Louisianan law, was reserved for whites. Plessy (D) was imprisoned and convicted of violating the Louisiana statute providing, in pertinent part, that, "No person or persons shall be permitted to occupy seats in coaches, other than the ones assigned to them, on account of the race they belong to." Plessy (D) challenged the statute on grounds that it was a violation of equal protection.

■ ISSUE
Does the Equal Protection Clause of the Fourteenth Amendment restrict states from segregating citizens based on race?

■ DECISION AND RATIONALE
(Brown, J.) No. The Fourteenth Amendment does not withhold from states the power to permit or require the separation of races. The power of states to require the separation of races is well established. Laws prohibiting interracial marriages and the establishment of separate schools for white and black children are just two examples. Plessy's (D) argument rests on the assumption that segregation brandishes blacks as inferior to whites. However, the statute at issue carries no such implication. If his argument is correct, then whites would be deemed inferior to blacks if blacks were ever to gain dominant power in the legislature and enact a similar provision. It is doubtful that whites would acquiesce in this assumption. The fact remains that social prejudices cannot be overcome by legislation. If one race is inferior socially to the other, the Constitution cannot place them on equal social footing.

■ DISSENT
(Harlan, J.) Louisiana's policy of forced segregation is inconsistent with equality of rights and personal liberty. Although the law applies equally to whites and blacks, it is common knowledge that it was enacted more to exclude blacks from occupying "white" coaches than vice versa. If a white man and a black man choose to occupy the same accommodations, government should be powerless to stop

Plessy v. Ferguson (Continued)

them on the grounds of race. Whether whites are superior to blacks is of no consequence. All men are equal in the eyes of the law. There is no accounting for class or race. In my opinion, this case will someday prove as pernicious as this Court's decision in *Dred Scott* [U.S. Supreme Court holds that slaves are not "citizens," as defined by the Constitution]. The segregation of citizens on the basis of race is wholly inconsistent with the notions of civil freedom and equality before the law.

Analysis:

Justice Harlan's dissent in this case proved to be prophetic. Indeed, *Plessy* was, and is, regarded along with *Dred Scott* as one of the worst decisions handed down by the U.S. Supreme Court. The ramifications of *Plessy* were far-reaching. The Court's implication that separate was not necessarily unequal led to the systematic and institutional segregation of whites and blacks, particularly in the South, for the entire first half of the twentieth century. It was not until the Court's decision in *Brown v. Board of Education* that *Plessy* was expressly overruled.

Brown v. Board of Education (Brown I)

(*Black Student*) v. (*School Board*)
347 U.S. 483, 74 S.Ct. 686 (1954)

U.S. SUPREME COURT DISAVOWS THE NOTION OF "SEPARATE BUT EQUAL"

■ **INSTANT FACTS** Several minor children in Kansas, South Carolina, Virginia and Delaware challenged the denial of their admission to schools attended by whites pursuant to laws permitting or requiring segregation.

■ **BLACK LETTER RULE** States may not segregate public schools on the basis of race.

■ **PROCEDURAL BASIS**

Appeal from state court decisions upholding the segregation of schools.

■ **FACTS**

Black school children in four states challenged the denial of their admission to public schools reserved solely for whites. The cases came to the Supreme Court on separate appeals, but were consolidated by the Court, as they all presented the same issue—the legality of racial segregation in public schools.

■ **ISSUE**

May states require or permit that public schools be segregated on the basis of race?

■ **DECISION AND RATIONALE**

(Warren, J.) No. States may not segregate public schools on the basis of race. We ordered reargument in this case to clarify the circumstances surrounding the ratification of the Fourteenth Amendment. However, the history behind the amendment and the circumstances existing at that time prove inconclusive with respect to the issue before us. Also providing us with little guidance was the fact that public education in this country was in its infancy at that time the Fourteenth Amendment was adopted Although the amendment is prohibitory in its language, it contains an implication of a positive right to the exemption of blacks from unfriendly legislation aimed at them solely on the basis of their race. Our decision in this case must turn on the effect which segregation has on public education. Today, public education is perhaps the most important function of state and local governments. One cannot be expected to succeed in today's society if denied the opportunity of an education. We believe that segregation solely on the basis of race deprives minority children of the right to an equal education, with regard to the condition of the facilities provided to them. Segregation has a harmful impact on school-aged children. It gives children a feeling of inferiority, which in turn, affects their motivation to learn. Accordingly, we thus conclude that the doctrine of "separate but equal" is wholly inapplicable in the area of public education. Separate schools are inherently unequal Thus, to the extent it is inconsistent with our holding today, *Plessy v. Ferguson* [the Fourteenth Amendment does not withhold from states the power to permit or require the separation of races] is overruled.

Analysis:

Despite the language in *Brown* purporting to limit its scope to public education, the Court has unanimously and consistently applied the principle elucidated in *Brown* in other contexts. The decision is somewhat unusual in that it relies more on social psychology than established principles of law. In fact, many have criticized much of the data on which the decision was based. While some have applauded the Court for coming to some consensus on the notion that segregation was unconstitutional in the context of public schooling, others have criticized the decision for unnecessarily restricting itself to the area of public education. Despite this criticism, it is clear that courts have expanded the notion that the doctrine of "separate but equal" is a violation of equal protection in virtually every area of civic life.

Johnson v. California

(Inmate) v. *(Corrections Authority)*
543 U.S. 499, 125 S.Ct. 1141 (2005)

PRISONS MAY HAVE GOOD REASONS TO SEGREGATE INMATES

■ **INSTANT FACTS** Johnson (P) claimed that California's (D) practice of segregating new inmates by race was a violation of equal protection violation.

■ **BLACK LETTER RULE** All racially based classifications imposed by the government are subject to strict scrutiny, including classifications made by prison authorities.

■ PROCEDURAL BASIS

Appeal from an order affirming summary judgment in favor of California (D).

■ FACTS

The California Department of Corrections (D) housed new inmates and transferees from other facilities in reception centers. Pursuant to an unwritten policy, the Corrections Department (D) based its cell assignments predominantly on race. There was practically no chance that an inmate would be assigned a cellmate of a different race. The Corrections Department (D) instituted this policy to prevent racial violence by prison gangs. Prison officials testified that racial conflict would result if the inmates were not segregated by race. Johnson (P) was an African–American inmate in the custody of the Department of Corrections (D). When he was first incarcerated, and every time he was transferred to a new institution, he was assigned an African–American cellmate. Johnson (P) brought suit to challenge the segregation policy.

■ ISSUE

Is the practice of segregating inmates by race per se unconstitutional?

■ DECISION AND RATIONALE

(O'Connor, J.) No. All racially based classifications imposed by the government are subject to strict scrutiny, including classifications done by prison authorities. Under strict scrutiny, the Department of Corrections (D) has the burden of proving that racial classifications are narrowly tailored to further compelling governmental interests. Here, it is possible that the Department (D) could meet that burden.

Racial classifications raise fears that they are motivated by an invidious purpose. Without strict scrutiny, there is no way of deciding whether a classification is due to illegitimate notions of racial inferiority or simple racial politics. Racial classifications receive strict scrutiny even if the classification imposes an equal burden or benefit on all races. The notion that separate could be equal was rejected in *Brown v. Board of Education,* 347 U.S. 483 (1954). Racial classifications threaten to stigmatize individuals due to their race, and threaten to incite racial hostility. By insisting that inmates be housed only with other inmates of the same race, it is possible that further hostility could be bred and that racial and ethnic divisions will be reinforced.

The Department of Corrections (D) urges a standard of review that defers to the needs of prison administration. The right to be free from racial discrimination is not, however, a right that need

Johnson v. California (Continued)

necessarily be compromised for prison administration. Racial discrimination is especially pernicious in the justice system. The government's power is strongest in the prison system, and stringent judicial review of racial classification is necessary to guard against invidious discrimination. Deference to the expertise of prison administrators does not require a more relaxed level of scrutiny. Strict scrutiny does not, however, prevent the Department of Corrections (D) from addressing the compelling interest in prison safety. It does not mean that the racial classifications are necessarily invalid. Indeed, no determination is made on that issue. Prisons are dangerous places, and the special circumstances they present may justify some racial classifications. Reversed.

■ **DISSENT**

(Stevens, J.) Segregating prisoners by race violates the Equal Protection Clause. The Department of Corrections (D) had ample opportunity to justify its policy, but it did not do so. The policy uses an inmate's race as a proxy for gang membership, and gang membership as a proxy for violence. The Department of Corrections (D) has offered no empirical evidence to justify this proposition. There is also no evidence that the Department of Corrections (D) attempted any alternative means of curbing violence.

■ **DISSENT**

(Thomas, J.) Strict scrutiny is not applicable here. Deference should be given to the reasonable judgments of the officials experienced in running the nation's prisons. The majority decides this case without addressing the problems that racial violence poses in prisons.

Analysis:

A few months after the opinion in this case was issued, the Department of Corrections (D) agreed to end racial segregation of inmates. Although the *agreement* came quickly, the *practice* did not end quickly. The Department (D) ultimately developed a system that automatically segregated only those inmates who had been involved in racial violence in the past. The Department (D) began implementing this new system in 2008.

■ **CASE VOCABULARY**

STRICT SCRUTINY: The standard applied to suspect classifications (such as race) in equal protection analysis and to fundamental rights (such as voting rights) in due-process analysis. Under strict scrutiny, the state must establish that it has a compelling interest that justifies and necessitates the law in question.

Washington v. Davis

(*Mayor of Washington, D.C.*) v. (*Applicants to Police Department*)
426 U.S. 229, 96 S.Ct. 2040 (1976)

SUPREME COURT REQUIRES PROOF OF DISCRIMINATORY INTENT BEFORE A LAW WHICH IS RACIALLY NEUTRAL ON ITS FACE WILL BE DEEMED A SUSPECT CLASSIFICATION

■ **INSTANT FACTS** Two black police officers and two black applicants to the District of Colombia's police department sought to challenge the department's application process as discriminatory on the basis of race on several grounds, including that certain written tests had a discriminatory impact on blacks.

■ **BLACK LETTER RULE** A facially neutral law or official act will be declared unconstitutional only if there is proof that the law or act has a discriminatory purpose.

■ **PROCEDURAL BASIS**

Appeal to the U.S. Supreme Court challenging the decision of the District Court, which granted a motion for summary judgment and shifted the burden of disproving discrimination onto the defendant.

■ **FACTS**

In order to be admitted into the District of Colombia Metropolitan Police Department 17-week training program for police officers, prospective applicants were required to take a written test, known as "Test 21," and earn a grade of at least 40 out of 80. Test 21 was used generally throughout the federal service and was designed to test verbal ability, vocabulary, reading and comprehension. In 1970, two black applicants who had failed to meet department requirements were permitted to intervene in a case filed against the D.C. Chief of Police (D) and others. The rejected applicants challenged the application process on the ground that it worked a discrimination against blacks. At trial, the validity of Test 21 came the court on a motion for summary judgment. The court found that there was no discriminatory purpose behind Test 21, but that the test was unrelated to job performance and had a "highly discriminatory impact in screening out black applicants." The court also found that (1) the number of black police officers did not correlate with the percentage of black citizens, (2) a larger number of blacks fail Test 21, and (3) Test 21 has not been validated to measure job performance. Thus, the court granted the motion for summary judgment and shifted the burden of proof.

■ **ISSUE**

Does a facially neutral law or official act a violate equal protection merely because it has a discriminatory impact?

■ **DECISION AND RATIONALE**

(White, J.) No. A facially neutral law or official act will be declared unconstitutional only if there is proof that the law or act has a discriminatory purpose. Of course, discriminatory intent need not be present on the face of the law. Discriminatory intent may be inferred from all the surrounding circumstances, including the fact that there has been a discriminatory impact. However, discriminatory impact alone will not support a finding of invidious discrimination. We find it difficult to accept the proposition that an exam intended to determine the communicative ability of applicants can be discriminatory and deny equal protection simply because a greater proportion of blacks fail to qualify. Furthermore, the Constitution does not prohibit the government from seeking to enhance the verbal ability of its employees. Thus, the test is both racially neutral on its face and seeks to further a legitimate governmental purpose. A rule which holds invalid a statute designed to serve neutral ends if it benefits or burdens one race more than another would be far-reaching and would raise serious questions about a whole range of statutes that may be more burdensome to the poor and the average black than to an affluent white.

■ DISSENT

(Brennan, J.) Sound policy considerations support the view that the department prove that Test 21 either measures job-related skills or predicts job performance. It is obvious that a written examination does not become job-related simply because it relates to some test given in the future. The Court's holding today implies that employers could justify testing based on its relation to further testing, rather than to on-the-job performance.

Analysis:

For the first time, the Court held in *Washington v. Davis* that a discriminatory purpose must be shown before a law race-neutral on its face will be deemed a violation of the equal protection guarantee. At the heart of the debate between discriminatory purpose and discriminatory impact lies the issue of what the Equal Protection Clause is aimed at ensuring. The Court's decision here seems to imply that the Clause ensures only some sort of procedural fairness. However, critics of the purposeful discrimination requirement argue that the Equal Protection Clause seeks to guarantee certain results for all citizens. Aside from the debate between purpose and impact, the Court also makes clear that purposeful discrimination may be inferred from the totality of the circumstances. While rejecting the notion that discriminatory impact alone is sufficient to infer a violation of equal protection, the Court makes clear that such an impact may serve as evidence of a discriminatory purpose.

McCleskey v. Kemp

(Convicted Murderer) v. (Superintendent, Georgia Diagnostic and Classification Center)
481 U.S. 279, 107 S.Ct. 1756 (1987)

SUPREME COURT REJECTS AN EQUAL PROTECTION CHALLENGE TO THE ADMINISTRATION OF THE DEATH PENALTY BASED SOLELY ON STATISTICAL EVIDENCE OF A DISPARATE TREATMENT BETWEEN BLACK AND WHITE DEFENDANTS

■ **INSTANT FACTS** A black man convicted of murder appealed his death sentence on equal protection grounds, claiming that the state administered the death penalty in a discriminatory manner against blacks.

■ **BLACK LETTER RULE** Statistical evidence indicating a risk that race plays a role in capital sentencing determinations does not alone prove a violation of equal protection.

■ **PROCEDURAL BASIS**

Appeal to the U.S. Supreme Court from a holding of the Court of Appeals affirming the decision of the District Court, which denied a petition for writ of habeas corpus.

■ **FACTS**

McCleskey (P), a black man, was charged and convicted of murder by shooting a police officer during the commission of an armed robbery. After the jury found McCleskey (P) guilty, it heard arguments concerning the appropriate sentence. McCleskey (P) offered no mitigating evidence and the jury recommended that the death penalty be imposed. The court followed the jury's recommendation and sentenced McCleskey (P) to death. McCleskey (P) then filed a writ of habeas corpus in federal court challenging his sentence on several grounds, including that the death penalty in Georgia is administered in a manner inconsistent with the Fourteenth Amendment's guarantee of equal protection. McCleskey (P) based his equal protection claim on a statistical study, the Baldus Study, which indicated generally that black defendants were more likely to be sentenced to death than their white counterparts, as were defendants in cases where the victim was white compared to defendants in cases where a black person was killed.

■ **ISSUE**

Does statistical evidence indicating a risk that race plays a role in capital sentencing determinations prove a violation of equal protection?

■ **DECISION AND RATIONALE**

(Powell, J.) No. Statistical evidence indicating a risk that race plays a role in capital sentencing determinations does not alone prove a violation of equal protection. To prevail under the Equal Protection Clause, McCleskey (P) was required to prove that decision makers in his case acted with a discriminatory purpose. However, as proof he offered only the data from the Baldus Study, with no other evidence specific to his case. Were we to accept the study as proof of purposeful discrimination the validity of virtually every capital case in Georgia where a defendant was black and the victim was white would be called into question. Each decision to impose the death penalty is made by a jury of the defendant's peers. Prosecutors are traditionally given wide discretion and to require them to justify their

McCleskey v. Kemp (Continued)

decisions to pursue capital cases years after they were made would be improper. To require explanation of these decision we would demand exceptionally clear proof of impropriety. Furthermore, there is a legitimate, unrebuttable explanation for the sentence: McCleskey (P) committed a crime for which the death penalty is a statutory and constitutionally permitted penalty. McCleskey (P) argues that the state as a whole has acted in a manner inconsistent with the Equal Protection Clause by maintaining a system it knows is being applied in a discriminatory fashion. However, purposeful discrimination means something more than knowledge or awareness of a particular outcome. To succeed in his claim, McCleskey (P) would have to show that the legislature adopted the death penalty to further some discriminatory purpose. We refuse to infer such a purpose from the Baldus Study. Affirmed.

■ DISSENT

(Brennan, J.) The fact remains that before McCleskey (P) was sentenced to death the two most important factors in the outcome of the sentencing phase were the color of his skin and that of his victim. The Baldus Study makes clear that over one-half of the defendants in cases where a black person was killed would not have been sentenced to death if their victim had been black. Furthermore, prosecutors pursue the death penalty in 70% of black defendant/white victim cases, but only 19% of the time in white defendant/black victim cases. Perhaps more enlightening are the circumstances surrounding executions in Georgia since our last decision upholding the constitutionality of the state's death sentence. Six of the 7 persons executed since that decision were black, and all of their victims were white. However, only 9.2 percent of the homicides in the state involved black defendants and white victims. This evidence establishes that race plays a role in the administration of Georgia's death penalty. We agree that numbers alone cannot validate McCleskey's (P) claim. When the statistical evidence is viewed in light of Georgia's history of a race-conscious criminal justice system and this Court's express recognition and denouncement of such a system, it indicates that McCleskey (P) is not grasping at straws. The Court's decision today ignores the influence of the past, but more importantly, it does nothing to address the apparent racial injustice occurring in the administration of Georgia's death penalty.

Analysis:

As this case illustrates, the Court's steadfast insistence on showing a discriminatory purpose is often outcome determinative. Where no such purpose is shown, government action is subject to a rational basis test and need not be justified by officials. As a long line of cases has made clear, the rational basis test is intended to defer heavily to government decisions, which means that claims of discrimination often fail. The problem with requiring a showing of purposeful discrimination independent of a discriminatory impact is that most discrimination is subtle, with the decision-maker often unaware of his or her own prejudice.

■ CASE VOCABULARY

BALDUS STUDY: Statistical study showing that the death penalty in Georgia was administered in a discriminatory fashion.

WRIT OF HABEAS CORPUS: Petition by a state prisoner to a federal court to review his or her conviction.

City of Mobile v. Bolden

(*Local Government*) v. (*Black Citizens*)
446 U.S. 55, 100 S.Ct. 1490 (1980)

SUPREME COURT EXTENDS THE PURPOSEFUL DISCRIMINATION REQUIREMENT TO CLAIMS BROUGHT UNDER THE FIFTEENTH AMENDMENT'S PROHIBITION AGAINST RACE-BASED INTERFERENCE WITH THE RIGHT TO VOTE

■ **INSTANT FACTS** A group of black citizens of Mobile, Alabama filed suit in federal district court claiming that the city's commission form of government was maintained in violation of the Fifteenth Amendment's prohibition against race-based interference with the right to vote.

■ **BLACK LETTER RULE** The Fifteenth Amendment does not entail the right to have black candidates elected but prohibits only purposefully discriminatory denial or abridgment by government of the freedom to vote " on account of race, color, or previous condition of servitude."

■ **PROCEDURAL BASIS**

Appeal to the U.S. Supreme Court challenging the holding of the Eleventh Circuit Court of Appeals which upheld the District Court's judgment that the at-large electoral system in Mobile, Alabama violated the Fifteenth Amendment.

■ **FACTS**

A group of black citizens filed a class-action suit against the City of Mobile, Alabama (D), claiming that the city's at-large electoral system violated the Fifteenth Amendment. The City of Mobile (D) maintained a system of government whereby three Commissioners exercised all legislative, executive and administrative duties within the city. As required by a state law enacted in 1911, the Commissioners were elected at large. In other words, the city itself acted as, essentially, one large district from which all the candidates received their votes. The class-action suit claimed that this system interfered with black citizens' right to vote. As proof of discrimination, it was shown that no black had ever been elected to the Commission and that the Commission discriminated against blacks in municipal employment and that Alabama had a history of racial discrimination. Despite finding that blacks in Mobile (D) vote without hindrance, the District Court found a Fifteenth Amendment violation and the Court of Appeals affirmed.

■ **ISSUE**

Where it is found that minorities vote without hindrance, may a Fifteenth Amendment violation nevertheless be inferred from the fact that a proportionate number of minority candidates have failed to hold office?

■ **DECISION AND RATIONALE**

(Stewart, J.) No. The Fifteenth Amendment does not entail the right to have black candidates elected but prohibits only purposefully discriminatory denial or abridgment by government of the freedom to vote "on account of race, color, or previous condition of servitude." We have consistently held that multimember legislative districts are not unconstitutional per se. However, they may be found to violate the Fourteenth Amendment if maintained to invidiously minimize or cancel the votes of minorities. Our cases have held that a showing of discriminatory purpose is essential to any claim brought under the Fifteenth Amendment. The fact that no black has been elected to the Commission alone does not

City of Mobile v. Bolden (Continued)

render a system of government unconstitutional. That the Commission discriminates in municipal employment may form the basis of some other constitutional claim, but it only serves as tenuous evidence of the constitutional validity of an electoral system. The lower courts also placed too much emphasis on Alabama's history of discrimination. Past discrimination cannot condemn governmental action that itself is not unlawful. Reversed.

■ **DISSENT**

(White, J.) In rejecting the conclusion reached by the lower courts that there existed purposeful discrimination in the maintenance of Mobile's (D) governmental system, the Court ignores the principle that discrimination can be inferred from objective factors, which alone do not constitute an equal amendment violation. Both the District Court and Court of Appeals acknowledged that Bolden (P) and the others bore the burden of producing evidence supporting a conclusion of discriminatory intent. Both lower courts found that the evidence provided raised the inference of purposeful discrimination and that should be enough.

Analysis:

The decision rendered by the Court in *Mobile* establishes a stringent standard for proving purposeful discrimination under the Fifteenth Amendment. As Justice White points out in his dissent, however, it is well settled that intent must be inferred from objective factors. While the Court is probably correct that each of the factors relied on by the district court in its findings do not alone raise the inference of discrimination, the Court fails to acknowledge that, when viewed together, the factors may reasonably raise such an inference. Furthermore, such inferences are usually within the sole province of the trial court. The impact of the Court's holding was severely blunted by the congressional amendments to the Voting Rights Act of 1965. That statute eliminates the need for proof in discriminatory purpose when an election system is challenged under the statute as racially discriminatory.

■ **CASE VOCABULARY**

FIFTEENTH AMENDMENT: Post-Civil War Amendment which prohibits race-based interference with the right to vote.

Palmer v. Thompson
(Black Citizens) v. (Mayor of Jackson, Mississippi)
403 U.S. 217, 91 S.Ct. 1940 (1971)

SUPREME COURT INDICATES THAT A SHOWING OF DISCRIMINATORY IMPACT MAY BE NECESSARY TO SUCCEED ON AN EQUAL PROTECTION CLAIM

■ **INSTANT FACTS** A group of black citizens files suit against the city of Jackson, Mississippi challenging the city council's decision to close public pools rather than operate them on a segregated basis as a violation of Equal Protection.

■ **BLACK LETTER RULE** A legislative act does not violate equal protection merely because it was motivated by a discriminatory purpose.

■ **PROCEDURAL BASIS**

Appeal to the U.S. Supreme Court challenging the holding of the Court of Appeals which affirmed the decision of the District Court denying the plaintiffs' request for an injunction on account that there was no constitutional violation.

■ **FACTS**

After being forced to desegregate public facilities, the city of Jackson, Mississippi (D) closed its public pools. Stating that the pools could not be operated safely and economically on an integrated basis, the council closed four city-owned pools and surrendered its lease on a fifth. Palmer (P) and a group of black citizens of Jackson (D) filed suit on equal protection grounds, to force the city to reopen and operate the pools on a desegregated basis. The District Court held that there was no denial of equal protection. The Court of Appeals affirmed.

■ **ISSUE**

May an act of local government, race-neutral on its face, be held invalid under Fourteenth Amendment merely due to the race-based motives behind it?

■ **DECISION AND RATIONALE**

(Black, J.) No. A legislative act does not violate equal protection merely because it was motivated by a discriminatory purpose. It is important to note that nothing in the Constitution imposes a duty on States to operate swimming pools. This case does not involve a situation where facilities are held open for whites, but not blacks, nor is it a case where local officials have maintained separate pools for members of each race. Instead, the decision to close pools is based on the motives of those who made it. But motives alone cannot form the basis of a successful equal protection claim. First, it is often difficult to ascertain the true motive behind an act of government. Officials often act for different reasons. Furthermore, were we to strike down the decision based on motives, nothing would stop those who voted in favor of closing pools from re-closing them under the guise of a different purpose. This Court does not have the power to require local government to open swimming facilities closed for any reason, sound or unsound. Affirmed.

■ **DISSENT**

(Douglas, J.) May a state close its schools to avoid desegregation? Nothing in the Constitution requires them to provide public schooling. It is difficult to imagine that a federal court could order a city to levy

Palmer v. Thompson (Continued)

taxes and operate a public school. Although a State may discontinue any of its municipal services, it may not do so for the purpose of perpetuating a system of segregation. It could be the case that the closing of pools has a greater impact on poor blacks than on poor whites. Beyond that, the decision to close pools has taught blacks in Mississippi that, if they protest segregation, they risk losing even segregated public facilities.

Analysis:

While the Court has never expressly stated that a plaintiff must prove a discriminatory impact to be successful on an equal protection claim, this case seems to indicate that such a showing is required. The Court states that it is often futile to attempt to discern the motives behind government action, yet that is exactly was is required of a plaintiff who must prove purposeful discrimination. That notwithstanding, the decision, broadly construed, could be read to stand for the proposition that substantive equality is sufficient to cure procedural inequality.

Personnel Administrator of Massachusetts v. Feeney

(*Government*) v. (*State Employee*)
442 U.S. 256, 99 S.Ct. 2282 (1979)

SUPREME COURT NARROWS THE DEFINITION OF DISCRIMINATORY PURPOSE

■ **INSTANT FACTS** A female state employee who was passed over for promotion by several less qualified male applicants who had served in the armed forces filed an equal protection suit challenging the state personnel office's stated preference for veterans.

■ **BLACK LETTER RULE** To be deemed purposefully discriminatory, a government act must have been taken because of, not merely in spite of, its adverse effects upon an identifiable group.

■ **PROCEDURAL BASIS**

Not provided.

■ **FACTS**

On several instances, Helen Feeney (P), an employee of the State of Massachusetts (D), scored higher on civil service exams than had men who were hired or promoted instead. Those men were rated higher than Feeney (P) solely on account of their status as veterans. Consequently, Feeney (P) filed suit against Massachusetts' Personnel Administrator (D), claiming that the preference for hiring and promoting veterans acted to discriminate against women in a manner inconsistent with the Equal Protection Clause.

■ **ISSUE**

Does the government's awareness of the discriminatory impact of certain legislation suggest that such legislation was enacted for a discriminatory purpose?

■ **DECISION AND RATIONALE**

(Stewart, J.) No. To be deemed purposefully discriminatory, a government act must have been taken because of, not merely in spite of, its adverse effects upon an identifiable group. It is undeniable that the preference for hiring veterans has a disparate negative impact on women. However, such a policy is grounded in legitimate objectives, such as the desire to reward veterans and promote service in the military. Furthermore, the effect of the preference is attributable mostly to federal regulations limiting the number of women who serve in the U.S. Armed Forces. It is true that the Massachusetts (D) legislature was aware that its policy preferring veterans would have an adverse impact on women. However, such knowledge is insufficient to establish purposeful discrimination. A discriminatory purpose implies more than volition or intent as awareness of consequences. Nothing suggests that the preference was enacted for the purpose of harming women. In fact, the act also applies to veteran women. Reversed.

Analysis:

The Court here provides a definition of "intent" for purposes of the Fourteenth Amendment that differs significantly from the definition of intent in other areas of the law. Whereas the criminal and civil law

Personnel Administrator of Massachusetts v. Feeney (Continued)

often presume that a person intends the foreseeable consequences of his actions, the Court here requires something more to prove purposeful discrimination. The Court requires that the governmental act under scrutiny was motivated by an intent to discriminate before an equal protection violation will be found. Note, however, that it is one thing to say that the presumption of intent does not follow from the mere knowledge of discriminatory impact, but it is a wholly different thing to say that knowledge of discriminatory impact does not lead, at least in part, to an inference of intent.

■ **CASE VOCABULARY**

DISCRIMINATORY INTENT: In the context of equal protection, to act with the purpose of imposing adverse conditions on a particular group.

Village of Arlington Heights v. Metropolitan Housing Development Corp.

(Local Government) v. (Real Estate Developer)
429 U.S. 252, 97 S.Ct. 555 (1977)

SUPREME COURT PROVIDES PLAINTIFFS WITH A FRAMEWORK FOR PROVING DISCRIMINATORY IMPACT UNDER THE FOURTEENTH AMENDMENT

■ **INSTANT FACTS** A real estate developer filed suit in federal court alleging that the decision of the defendant municipality to deny a rezoning request for low- and moderate-income housing was racially discriminatory and in violation of the Fourteenth Amendment.

■ **BLACK LETTER RULE** Where there is proof that a discriminatory purpose was a motivating factor in the decision, the judicial deference usually accorded to government action is no longer warranted.

■ **PROCEDURAL BASIS**

Appeal to the U.S. Supreme Court challenging the holding of the Seventh Circuit Court of Appeals reversing the decision of the District Court.

■ **FACTS**

In 1971, the Metropolitan Housing Development Corporation (MDHC) (P) applied to the Village of Arlington Heights, Illinois (Village) for the rezoning of a 15 acre parcel from single-family to multiple-family use. With the use of federal funds, the MDHC (P) planned to build low- to medium-income housing. The Village (D) denied the request. MDHC (P) then filed suit in federal court alleging that the denial was racially discriminatory and violated the Fourteenth Amendment.

■ **ISSUE**

To succeed on a Fourteenth Amendment equal protection claim, must the plaintiff show that the challenged action was motivated solely by race?

■ **DECISION AND RATIONALE**

(Powell, J.) No. Where there is proof that a discriminatory purpose was one motivating factor in the decision, the judicial deference usually accorded to government action is no longer warranted. The determination of whether discrimination was a motivating factor demands a sensitive inquiry into both circumstantial and direct evidence of intent. Sometimes there emerges a clear pattern from the effect of state action, unexplainable on grounds other than race, even when regulation appears neutral on its face. Absent such a pattern, however, Courts must take other factors into consideration. The historical background of the decision, including substantive and procedural departures from the norm, is often relevant. Also relevant may be the legislative or administrative history. Keeping this in mind, we find that MDHC (P) failed to meet its evidentiary burden. There is nothing about the sequence of events which raises suspicion. The zoning rule had remained as such since 1959. The Village (D) has been, and remains, committed to single-family homes as the dominant residential use of land. The rezoning request underwent the usual procedures. In fact, the Village (D) went as far as to accommodate MDHC (P) and permit it to supplement its presentation.

Village of Arlington Heights v. Metropolitan Housing Development Corp. (Continued)

Analysis:

The Court in *Arlington* sets forth an approach for determining the existence of a discriminatory intent under the Fourteenth Amendment. The important thing to note from the framework provided by the Court is its focus on procedure. In elucidating the particular types of evidence that will give rise to an inference of discrimination, it is clear that the Court sees the Equal Protection Clause as a guarantee of procedural fairness. For example, the Court states that procedural irregularities are important in determining the existence of discrimination. Consequently, the Court focuses on the fact that the decision to deny the permit in this case occurred in the ordinary course of city business to reason that no discriminatory motive existed.

Brown v. Board of Education (Brown II)
(*Black Student*) v. (*School Board*)
349 U.S. 294, 75 S.Ct. 753 (1955)

FEDERAL DISTRICT COURTS RETAIN JURISDICTION OF SCHOOL SEGREGATION CASES TO ENSURE THAT SCHOOL DISTRICT TAKE APPROPRIATE STEPS TO ENSURE THE INTEGRATION OF PUBLIC SCHOOLS

■ **INSTANT FACTS** After issuing its decision in *Brown I,* the Supreme Court set the case for re-argument to determine the question of how to remedy school segregation.

■ **BLACK LETTER RULE** The Federal District Courts which first heard the cases involved in *Brown I* are to employ their full equitable power to ensure and oversee the full implementation of the constitutional principles announced therein.

■ **PROCEDURAL BASIS**

Rehearing of the case *Brown v. Board of Education* addressing the question of appropriate remedies.

■ **FACTS**

After issuing its decision in *Brown I* [states may not segregate public schools on the basis of race], the Supreme Court set the case for re-argument to determine the question of how to remedy school segregation, the result of which was the decision in *Brown II.*

■ **ISSUE**

What is the appropriate remedy for a violation of the constitutional principles invalidating public school segregation?

■ **DECISION AND RATIONALE**

(Warren, C.J.) The Federal District Courts which first heard the cases involved in *Brown I* are to employ their full equitable power to ensure and oversee the full implementation of the constitutional principles announced therein. However, school authorities have the primary responsibility for elucidating, assessing and solving the varied problems presented by desegregation. The courts are to consider whether the actions of these authorities are taken in good faith. The implementation of the principles announced in *Brown I* [states may not segregate public schools on the basis of race] may require the elimination of obstacles. Accordingly, courts may take into account the public interest in ordering their systematic and effective elimination. Courts are to require that the defendants make a prompt and reasonable start to full compliance. If more time is required, the local schools districts carry the burden of proving such a necessity. In making the determination of whether more time is indeed required, courts should consider various factors, including the physical conditions of schools, transportation of students, and personnel among others. Reversed and remanded.

Analysis:

This case highlights the fact that courts are ill-equipped to ensure particular substantive outcomes. In fact, the Court actually states that school officials—the very persons responsible for perpetuating segregation in public schools—are to have the primary authority for implementing systematic racial integration. Furthermore, although the Court was attempting to fashion a flexible remedy, placing within the district courts the jurisdiction to ensure compliance with *Brown II*, this only led to volumes of litigation on the issue, as local officials fiercely resisted integration.

Swann v. Charlotte-Mecklenburg Board of Education

(*Black Student*) v. (*School Board*)
402 U.S. 1, 91 S.Ct. 1267 (1971)

U.S. SUPREME COURT ANNOUNCES THAT FEDERAL COURTS HOLD VAST EQUITABLE POWERS TO TAILOR REMEDIES AIMED AT ENSURING THE INTEGRATION OF PUBLIC SCHOOLS

■ **INSTANT FACTS** A black student and others filed a petition in federal District Court seeking relief from the failure of the Charlotte School to desegregate in an expedient manner consistent with *Brown I*.

■ **BLACK LETTER RULE** Once it has been shown that school officials have failed to comply with the constitutional principles announced in *Brown v. Board of Education,* district court's have at their discretion broad equitable powers which they may employ to remedy the violation.

■ **PROCEDURAL BASIS**
Not provided.

■ **FACTS**
In 1965, a federal District Court approved a plan for the desegregation of public schools in Mecklenburg County, North Carolina (County) (D). However, as of 1969, that school system remained largely segregated, with approximately two-thirds of black students attending virtually all-black public schools. Swann (P) filed a petition in federal court seeking acceleration of the planned desegregation. As a result of the failure of school officials to comply with its order, the District Court fashioned a remedy which implemented quotas, required a substantial reduction in the number of all-black schools, gerrymandered school districts and employed busing as techniques for expediting the desegregation of County (D) schools.

■ **ISSUE**
May federal district courts employ broad equitable powers to fashion a plan for desegregation once it has been shown that school officials have failed to do so?

■ **DECISION AND RATIONALE**
(Burger, C.J.) Yes. Once it has been shown that school officials have failed to comply with the constitutional principles announced in *Brown v. Board of Education* [states may not segregate public schools on the basis of race], district court's have may employ broad equitable powers to remedy the violation. The only limits to the use of the equitable power of federal courts are those contained in the Constitution. However, judicial authority enters only when local authority defaults. This case presents us with the issue of student assignment, and there are essentially four problem areas. First, we find that the District Court was well within its jurisdiction to make use of racial quotas as a starting point for determining the approximate racial balance schools needed to achieve. Second, in cases where their remain some schools which are all-white or all-black, there is a presumption that school assignments are discriminatory. Third, within certain limits, courts have the power to gerrymander in order to break-up single-race districts. Finally, courts may require school district to employ bus transportation where assignment of children to their nearest school fails to bring about desegregation. Thus, the techniques used by the District Court in this case were within its equitable powers; implementation of the plan is within the capacity of school authorities. Affirmed.

Analysis:

The Court in this case discusses the precise scope of the power of district courts to bring about an end to school segregation. First the court notes that courts are powerless until a constitutional violation has been established and school authorities fail to adequately remedy the situation after being given the opportunity to do so. Nevertheless, once a court determines that its intervention is required, this case makes clear that the remedial powers of federal courts in school desegregation cases are broad. While refusing to provide district courts with rigid guidelines, the Court expressly authorizes the proper use of what were important desegregation tools, including busing, gerrymandering school districts, and racial quotas.

■ CASE VOCABULARY

BUSING: The practice of transporting (usually by bus) students from one district to another in an effort to desegregate schools or school districts.

GERRYMANDER: To draw district lines with an odd shape in the hopes of achieving a particular composition of residents.

Milliken v. Bradley

(*Governor of Michigan*) v. (*Black Student*)
418 U.S. 717, 94 S.Ct. 3112 (1974)

SUPREME COURT SETS A LIMIT ON THE REMEDIAL POWER OF COURTS IN DESEGREGATION CASES

■ **INSTANT FACTS** A federal district court in Michigan ordered a multidistrict, area-wide remedy to address the racial segregation in only one of the 53 school districts in the metropolitan Detroit area.

■ **BLACK LETTER RULE** Before the boundaries of separate and autonomous school districts may be set aside by consolidating the separate units for remedial purposes or by imposing a cross-district remedy, it must first be shown that there has been a constitutional violation within one district that produces a significant segregative effect in another district.

■ **PROCEDURAL BASIS**

Appeal to the U.S. Supreme Court challenging the decision of the Sixth Circuit Court of Appeals, which held that the District Court was authorized to implement a metro-wide order as a cure to the segregation in one district.

■ **FACTS**

In an effort to remedy the *de jure* segregation of schools in one of 53 school districts in the Detroit area, a district court judge directed school officials to submit desegregation plans encompassing the entire Detroit metropolitan area, despite the fact that the outlying school districts were not parties to the action and despite the fact that there had been no claim that these outlying districts had committed constitutional violations.

■ **ISSUE**

May a federal court impose a multi-district, area-wide remedy to a single-district de jure segregation problem, absent any finding that the other included school districts have failed to operate unitary school systems within their districts, the boundary lines of any affected school district were established with the purpose of fostering racial segregation in public schools, and the included districts committed acts which effected segregation within the other districts?

■ **DECISION AND RATIONALE**

(Burger, C.J.) No. Before the boundaries of separate and autonomous school districts may be set aside by consolidating the separate units for remedial purposes or by imposing a cross-district remedy, it must first be shown that there has been a constitutional violation within one district that produces a significant segregative effect in another district. Specifically, it must be shown that racially discriminatory acts of the state or local school districts, or of a single school district have been a substantial cause of inter-district segregation. However, without an inter-district violation having inter-district effect, there is no constitutional wrong calling for such a remedy. The record in this case shows that *de jure* segregation existed only in the Detroit schools, not the outlying areas. Reversed.

■ **DISSENT**

(White, J.) The Court's holding today cripples the ability of the federal judiciary to perform the task of devising effective remedies aimed at ending *de jure* segregation. Acts of segregation will go unreme-

Milliken v. Bradley (Continued)

died, not because no remedy is available, but because the Court considers inter-district remedies administratively inconvenient. The Court appears to ignore two crucial points: First, it is the duty of the State of Michigan to ensure its schools are desegregated. Second the Fourteenth Amendment addresses the States, not school districts.

Analysis:

The Court here imposes a severe restriction on the ability of district judges to end area-wide segregation. The Court prohibits federal judges from including in their remedies school districts not shown to have committed a constitutional violation. Such proof is often difficult to obtain, because urban-suburban racial segregation is often the result of a host of policies. In fact, the inability of courts to fashion far-reaching remedies in the absence of such evidence has led to *de facto* segregation in many urban areas. The Court bases its position on the principle that a court-imposed remedy can apply only to those who have shown to violate the constitution. However, as the dissent points out, the Fourteenth Amendment is aimed at the states, and school authorities derive their power from the states. Thus, the argument goes, when one school district violates the Constitution, it is in fact the state that must answer. Accordingly, a multi-district remedy is not unconstitutional.

■ **CASE VOCABULARY**

DE JURE SEGREGATION: Segregation imposed or permitted by law.

Board of Education of Oklahoma City Public Schools v. Dowell

(School Board) v. (Black Student)
498 U.S. 237, 111 S.Ct. 630 (1991)

SUPREME COURT IMPOSES A TEMPORAL LIMIT ON FEDERAL COURT DESEGREGATION ORDERS

■ **INSTANT FACTS** A group of black students and their parents filed a claim seeking to reopen a desegregation case closed ten years earlier on the ground that their local school district had not achieved unitary status.

■ **BLACK LETTER RULE** A desegregation decree should be dissolved after local authorities have made a sufficient showing of constitutional compliance with the court order.

■ **PROCEDURAL BASIS**

Appeal to the U.S. Supreme Court challenging the holding of the Court of Appeals which reversed the District Court's decision to refuse to reopen a desegregation case closed ten years earlier.

■ **FACTS**

In 1961, a group of black students (P) filed suit against the Board of Education of Oklahoma City Public Schools (Board) (D) seeking the end of *de jure* segregation in that area. In 1972, after finding that efforts to desegregate Oklahoma City schools were unsuccessful, the District Court order the Board (D) to adopt the "Finger Plan," which essentially assigned students to particular schools. In 1977, the District Court terminated its decree on the ground that the plan had worked to achieve a "unitary" school system. In 1985, the Board adopted a plan to assign students to neighborhood schools. A group of students and parents filed a claim with the District Court seeking to reopen the case, but were denied relief. The Court of Appeals reversed.

■ **ISSUE**

May a court reinstate a desegregation decree even after it has been shown that local authorities have been in full compliance for some time?

■ **DECISION AND RATIONALE**

(Rehnquist, C.J.) No. A desegregation decree should be dissolved after local authorities have made a sufficient showing of constitutional compliance with the court order. Requiring federal courts to limit the time in which they exercise control over public schools systems recognizes the importance of local control over those systems. In deciding whether a sufficient showing of compliance was made, the District Court should ascertain whether the Board (D) complied in good faith with the desegregation decree and whether the vestiges of past segregation have been eliminated to the extent practicable. Reversed and remanded.

■ **DISSENT**

(Marshall, J.) From the time of its admission to the Union until 1972, 18 years after this Court decided *Brown v. Board of Education* [states may not segregate public schools on the basis of race], Oklahoma maintained segregated schools. Intervention by federal courts ended this system. The question now is

Board of Education of Oklahoma City Public Schools v. Dowell (Continued)

whether the Board (D) should be permitted to return schools to their one-race status after having complied with the original decree. Certainly, *Brown* did not require only 13 years of desegregation. The Court ignores the fact that the threat of the reemergence of one-race schools is a relevant vestige of *de jure* segregation. I believe that desegregation decrees should not be dissolved until there no longer remains the threat of "resegregation."

Analysis:

This case was the first of a series of three in which the Supreme Court intimated that the end of federal court supervision of public schools was near. At issue in these cases is a struggle between the inherent value in having local officials control the administration of schools and the need to ensure that the goals of *Brown I* are met in full. Federal courts have begun to withdraw their jurisdiction over these cases. After this case was decided, the Court announced that an order should end after compliance has been achieved, even if the same district is subject to other orders that remain in place. Three years later, the Supreme Court ordered the end of federally supervised desegregation in Kansas City, Missouri.

■ CASE VOCABULARY

UNITARY STATUS: Having achieved school desegregation to the extent possible.

Parents Involved in Community Schools v. Seattle School District No. 1

(Parents' Group) v. (School District)

551 U.S. 701, 127 S.Ct. 2738 (2007)

ASSIGNING STUDENTS TO SCHOOLS BY RACE VIOLATES EQUAL PROTECTION

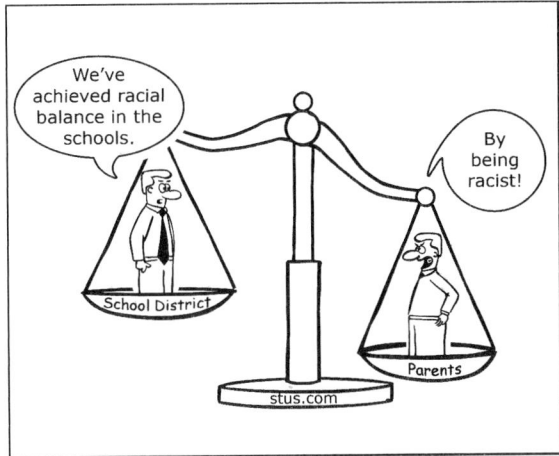

■ **INSTANT FACTS** Seattle School District (D) used race as a factor is assigning children to schools.

■ **BLACK LETTER RULE** Use of race as a factor in school assignments, unless it is to remedy past segregation or used as one of a range of factors, violates the Equal Protection Clause.

■ PROCEDURAL BASIS

Appeals from orders of the Ninth and Sixth Circuit Courts of Appeals sustaining school integration plans.

■ FACTS

Seattle School District (D) and Jefferson County Public Schools (D) operated school assignment plans that used race as a factor. Seattle (D) had never operated segregated schools. Jefferson County (D) was found to have maintained a segregated school system in 1973, but the desegregation decree was dissolved in 2000 when the court found that Jefferson County (D) was a unitary district. The Seattle (D) plan described students as white or nonwhite. Students were allowed to state a preference for which high school they would attend. If too many students chose a particular school, and the school was not within ten percentage points of Seattle's (D) white/nonwhite composition, preference was given to students who would help the school achieve racial balance. The Jefferson County (D) plan called for schools to have student bodies that were between fifteen and fifty percent black. Students were assigned to elementary schools based on available space within the schools and on the racial guidelines. The plans in each district were challenged on equal protection grounds. Both plans were sustained.

■ ISSUE

Were the school desegregation plans constitutional?

■ DECISION AND RATIONALE

(Roberts, C.J.) No. Use of race as a factor in school assignments, unless it is to remedy past segregation or used as one of a range of factors, violates the Equal Protection Clause. In order to satisfy the strict scrutiny standard of review, the school assignment plans must be narrowly tailored to meet a compelling government interest. The only two compelling interests recognized by the Court in the context of racial classifications in schools have been remedying past segregation and promoting diversity in higher education. The Seattle School District (D) has not shown that it was ever segregated, nor that it was subject to a court-ordered desegregation decree. Jefferson County (D) was a segregated district, but once it achieved unitary status the vestiges of past segregation were eliminated. The

Parents Involved in Community Schools v. Seattle School District No. 1 (Continued)

Constitution is not violated by racial imbalance, without more. Remedying past segregation cannot be relied upon to justify the two plans at issue here.

The interest in promoting diversity was approved in the context of higher education in *Grutter v. Bollinger,* 539 U.S. 306 (2003). In that case, race was not the only factor considered. The admissions program in that case focused on each applicant as an individual, not as a member of an ethnic group. In the present cases, however, race is not considered as one of several factors. When race is used, it is decisive by itself. It is also used in a mechanistic way, with students being classified as white/nonwhite in Seattle (D), or black/other in Jefferson County. The holding in *Grutter* also relied on considerations unique to higher education. The present cases are not governed by *Grutter.*

Seattle (D) and Jefferson County (D) also assert that their plans help to reduce racial concentration in schools and to help ensure that racially concentrated housing patterns do not prevent nonwhite students from having access to the most desirable schools. They argue that the diversity they seek is racial diversity, so it makes sense to promote that interest by relying on race alone. The Court has, however, repeatedly condemned efforts to achieve a racial balance as illegitimate. Racial balance is not to be achieved for its own sake. Accepting racial balance as a compelling state interest would justify imposing racial proportionality throughout American society. Racial balancing is not transformed from "patently unconstitutional" to a compelling state interest simply by relabeling it "racial diversity." The plans have a minimal effect on school enrollment, so it can hardly be said that the use of racial classifications is necessary to achieve the stated goals of the districts (D).

Justice Breyer's dissent comes down to an argument that the end justifies the means. He urges deference to the districts (D) on the issue of racial integration. Such deference is at odds with equal protection jurisprudence. Government action dividing the people by race is inherently suspect. Racial classifications promote notions of racial inferiority and lead to racial hostility. The holding in *Brown v. Board of Education,* 347 U.S. 483 (1954), was clear that according differential treatment based on race violates the Fourteenth Amendment. What do the racial classifications at issue here do, if they do not afford unequal treatment based on race? The districts (D) have not met the burden of demonstrating that such unequal treatment should be allowed again, for whatever reason. Reversed.

■ CONCURRENCE

(Thomas, J.) Neither Seattle (D) nor Jefferson County (D) is threatened with resegregation. Neither is constitutionally compelled or permitted to undertake race-based remediation. The relationship between racial mixing and improved educational results for black children is a tenuous one. The dissent attempts to marginalize the notion of a color-blind Constitution.

■ CONCURRENCE

(Kennedy, J.) Diversity, depending on its meaning and definition, is a compelling educational goal a school district may pursue. The plurality opinion is too dismissive of the legitimate interest government has in ensuring that all people, regardless of race, have equal opportunities. State and local school authorities are not constitutionally mandated to accept the status quo of racial isolation in schools. The goal of bringing together students of different races may be pursued by means other than labeling students by race.

■ DISSENT

(Stevens, J.) The Chief Justice's reference to *Brown v. Board of Education* is ironic. The Chief Justice states that, before *Brown,* "schoolchildren were told where they could and could not go to school based on the color of their skin." Only black schoolchildren were so ordered. There are no stories of white schoolchildren struggling to attend black schools.

■ DISSENT

(Breyer, J.) The plans at issue here are narrowly tailored to serve compelling interests. The distinction between de jure segregation of school systems and de facto segregation caused by housing patterns is meaningless in the present context. Real-world efforts to substitute racially diverse schools for schools that are, for whatever reason, racially segregated are complex. A long line of precedent allows local school boards to use race-conscious criteria to achieve positive race-related goals, even if the

Constitution does not compel it. It is appropriate to consider context when scrutinizing racial classifications. The context here is that racial classifications are not being used to stigmatize or exclude. Instead, the classifications are used to bring the races together.

The principal interest advanced in these cases has three elements. First, there is an interest in setting right the consequences of prior segregation. Second, there is an educational interest in overcoming the adverse educational effects of highly segregated schools. Third, there is a democratic interest in producing an educational environment that reflects the "pluralistic society" in which our children will live. The plans before the Court are narrowly tailored to achieve these objectives. Several factors, taken together, lead to a conclusion that the use of race-conscious criteria here passes even the strictest "tailoring" test. Race-conscious criteria only help set the outer bounds of broad ranges. They are only one part of plans that depend primarily upon other, nonracial elements. To use race in this way is not to set a forbidden "quota." Second, broad-range limits on voluntary school choice plans are less burdensome than other race-conscious restrictions the Court has previously approved. Third, the manner in which the districts (D) developed these plans reflects "narrow tailoring."

The plurality, or at least those who follow Justice Thomas's "color-blind" approach, may feel confident that, to end invidious discrimination, one must end all governmental uses of race-conscious criteria, including those with inclusive objectives. By way of contrast, I do not claim to know how best to stop harmful discrimination. Until today, the Court understood the Constitution as affording the people, acting through their elected representatives, freedom to select the use of "race-conscious" criteria from among their available options.

Analysis:

The harm identified by the plurality is the harm of the racial classifications themselves. It is assumed that, because there is no judicial decree mandating desegregation, racial imbalance in the schools is not an issue for the districts (D) to address. The plurality opinion does not allow school districts to take their own steps to prevent segregation, but requires them to wait until a court orders the remedy.

■ CASE VOCABULARY

COMPELLING–STATE–INTEREST TEST: A method for determining the constitutional validity of a law, whereby the government's interest in the law and its purpose is balanced against an individual's constitutional right that is affected by the law. Only if the government's interest is strong enough will the law be upheld. The compelling-state-interest test is used, for example, in equal-protection analysis when the disputed law requires strict scrutiny.

Richmond v. J.A. Croson Co.

(City) v. (General Contractor)
488 U.S. 469, 109 S.Ct. 706 (1989)

SUPREME COURT ANNOUNCES AFFIRMATIVE ACTION PLANS ARE SUBJECT TO STRICT SCRUTINY

■ **INSTANT FACTS** After losing its bid on a public project due to its inability to procure satisfactory bids from minority subcontractors, a construction company filed suit against the city of Richmond, Virginia to challenge that city's ordinance requiring that 30% of subcontractors on public projects be owned by minorities.

■ **BLACK LETTER RULE** A city may use its spending powers to remedy private discrimination if it identifies that discrimination with the particularity required by the Fourteenth Amendment.

■ **PROCEDURAL BASIS**

Appeal to the U.S. Supreme Court challenging the holding of the Fourth Circuit Court of Appeals, which, after having its initial ruling vacated by the Supreme Court, reversed the District Court's decision to uphold an city-enacted affirmative action plan.

■ **FACTS**

In 1983, the city of Richmond, Virginia (D) adopted an ordinance which essentially required that at least 30% of the dollar value of a public project be set aside for businesses which were certified Minority Business Enterprises (MBEs). MBE was a company in which blacks, Hispanics, Orientals, Indians, Eskimos or Aleauts had a majority ownership interest. At the time that the ordinance was adopted there existed no evidence that either the city of Richmond (D) or general contractors had discriminated against minority subcontractors in the past.. Instead, city officials relied on the fact that the general population of Richmond (D) was 50 percent black, but only 0.67 percent of the Richmond's (D) prime construction contracts had been awarded to minority businesses in the 5-year period from 1978 to 1983. City officials also found that a variety of contractors' associations had virtually no minority businesses within their membership. After the plan was implemented, the J.A. Croson Company (Croson) (P) was initially awarded a public contract to install plumbing fixtures. When Croson (P) was unable to procure sufficient minority subcontractors, it requested from, and was denied a waiver by, the City (D). City officials then informed Croson (P) that the project would be rebid. Shortly thereafter, Croson (P) filed suit.

■ **ISSUE**

May a local government justify maintenance of a policy of affirmative action in awarding public project contracts in an effort to remedy prior discrimination where there is no precise evidence of prior purposeful discrimination?

■ **DECISION AND RATIONALE**

(O'Connor, J.) No. A city may use its spending powers to remedy private discrimination if it identifies that discrimination with the particularity required by the Fourteenth Amendment. In this case, the city of Richmond (D) relies on our holdings which have stated that race-based remedial efforts to eradicate prior discrimination are appropriate. What Richmond (D) ignores, however, is that it is Congress to whom the Fourteenth Amendment gives broad powers to redress the effect of society-wide discrimina-

Richmond v. J.A. Croson Co. (Continued)

tion. That is not to say that state and local governments have no interest in eradicating the effects of private discrimination. However, if local governments wish to remedy discrimination with the use of affirmative action plans they must prove that such plans are necessary and that they are addressing actual past discrimination. In other words, such measures are subject to strict judicial scrutiny. We feel that Richmond has failed to meet its burden. The mere recitation that a classification is aimed at remedying prior discrimination is insufficient. The Constitution requires proof of discrimination. The 30% quota is not tied to any injury suffered by anyone. There is no evidence presented by the city which identifies discrimination in Richmond's (D) construction industry. Furthermore, the inclusion of non-black minorities is arbitrary. There is absolutely no evidence which gives rise to a suspicion that Hispanics, Eskimos, Orientals or Aleuts have suffered discrimination by Richmond's (D) construction industry. There is also no evidence that the city of Richmond (D) narrowly tailored its remedy. First, there was no consideration of non-race measures to combat the perceived discrimination. Second, the 30% quota was only an effort at racial balancing, not tailored to any goal.

■ CONCURRENCE

(Stevens, J.) I disagree with the premise that a government decision based on race is never permissible except as a remedy for a past wrong. Nevertheless, I agree that the policy at issue here is unconstitutional.

■ CONCURRENCE

(Scalia, J.) I agree that Richmond's (D) affirmative action policy is unconstitutional. However, I disagree with the notion that a racial classification may be justified if aimed at ameliorating the effect of past discrimination. Instead, States may act by race only to eliminate their own maintenance of a system of unlawful racial classification. Of course a State is free to undo the effects of past discrimination in many other ways. In this case, for example, Richmond (D) could have adopted an ordinance preferring small businesses.

■ DISSENT

(Marshall, J.) The essence of the Court's holding is that Richmond failed to catalog adequate findings of past discrimination. However, there appears to be no lack of proof. City officials relied on statistics showing that minority businesses have played a grossly disproportionately minor role in city projects and that few if any such businesses have belonged to trade associations. More disturbing is the Court's attack on race-based remedies in general and the adoption of strict scrutiny to review such measures. Racial classifications drawn for the purpose of remedying the effect of discrimination are simply not as pernicious as those based on the inferiority of one race to another.

Analysis:

In *J.A. Croson,* the Supreme Court adopts strict scrutiny as the appropriate level of review for racial classifications aimed at remedying past discrimination—*i.e.,* affirmative action. The Court is clear that a state or local governmental body has a compelling interest in remedying past discrimination. However, the Court requires that classifications aimed at fulfilling that interest must be justified by particularized instances of prior discrimination. An interesting point to note is Justice O'Connor's statement that while the Fourteenth Amendment provides Congress with broad powers to eliminate racial discrimination, local authorities are more restricted. This would seem to suggest that remedial efforts enacted by Congress are subject to a lower standard of review.

■ CASE VOCABULARY

MINORITY BUSINESS ENTERPRISE: Under federal regulations, a Minority Business Enterprise, for purposes of public bidding, is a business in which some or several minority groups hold at least a majority interest.

Adarand Constructors, Inc. v. Pena

(*Subcontractor*) v. (*U.S. Secretary of Transportation*)
515 U.S. 200, 115 S.Ct. 2097 (1995)

SUPREME COURT HOLDS THAT STRICT SCRUTINY IS APPLICABLE TO FEDERAL AFFIRMATIVE ACTION PROGRAMS

■ **INSTANT FACTS** A highway construction company filed suit against the federal government challenging the Department of Transportation's policy favoring minority subcontractors as a violation of equal protection under the Due Process Clause of the Fifth Amendment.

■ **BLACK LETTER RULE** All racial classifications, imposed by whatever federal, state, or local government, must be analyzed by a reviewing court under strict scrutiny.

■ **PROCEDURAL BASIS**

Appeal to the U.S. Supreme Court challenging the ruling of the Tenth Circuit Court of Appeals which upheld the use of race-based presumptions in subcontractor compensation clauses under intermediate scrutiny.

■ **FACTS**

Adarand Constructors, Inc. (P), a construction company not certified as a small disadvantaged business, filed a claim against the U.S. Department of Transportation (DOT) (D), alleging that certain DOT (D) policies favoring minorities were a violation of equal protection under the Due Process Clause of the Fifth Amendment. DOT (D) policies required general contractors to presume that socially and economically disadvantages individuals included blacks, Hispanics, Native Americans and other minorities. Adarand (P) claimed that, as a result of subcontractor compensation clauses that provided additional compensation if the general contractor hired certified businesses, it lost a subcontract on a highway construction project to a certified competitor.

■ **ISSUE**

Are affirmative action plans subject to strict scrutiny review when they are the result of a federally mandated policy?

■ **DECISION AND RATIONALE**

(O'Connor, J.) Yes. All racial classifications, imposed by whatever federal, state, or local government, must be analyzed by a reviewing court under strict scrutiny. In *Metro Broadcasting, Inc. v. Federal Communications Commission* we held that congressionally approved affirmative action plans were to be reviewed under intermediate scrutiny. That decision marked a significant departure from Supreme Court jurisprudence. First, it ignored the reasons proffered in *Richmond v. J.A. Croson Co.* [Supreme Court strikes down the city of Richmond's affirmative action plan for public projects under a strict scrutiny review] as to why strict scrutiny is required of all racial classifications, even those deemed "benign." Second, *Metro Broadcasting* rejects the well-settled principle that requires congruence between standards applicable to federal and state governments for racial classifications. Thus, to the extent it is inconsistent with our ruling today, *Metro Broadcasting* is overruled. Accordingly, both Federal and State racial classifications must be narrowly tailored to serve a compelling governmental interest, which may

Adarand Constructors, Inc. v. Pena (Continued)

include the need to obviate the effects of prior discrimination. Because our decision today changes the playing field somewhat, we remand the case to the Court of Appeals for proceedings consistent with our holding today.

■ CONCURRENCE

(Scalia, J.) Although I agree with the ruling of the Court, I disagree that a government can have a compelling interest in discriminating against one race to make up for prior discrimination. There are no debtor and creditor races under our Constitution. The Constitution focuses on individuals, not groups.

■ CONCURRENCE

(Thomas, J.) I disagree with the dissent's presumption that there is a racial paternalism exception to the principle of equal protection. In fact there is little difference between a law which subjugates a race and one which distributed benefits on the basis of race in order to achieve some current notion of equality. The paternalism of affirmative action is a direct contradiction to the principle of inherent equality that underlies our Constitution. Furthermore, affirmative action stamps minorities with a mark of inferiority—incapable of competing without government assistance.

■ DISSENT

(Stevens, J.) The Court today assumes that there is no difference between a decision by the majority to impose a burden on members of a minority race and a decision to provide a benefit to that minority with corresponding burdens on the majority. There is a difference. Invidious discrimination is oppressive; remedial race-based classifications foster equality. The need for consistency does not justify obliterating this important difference. I also believe that application of strict scrutiny to congressionally approved affirmative action is unwarranted. The fact is that congressional mandates reflect the will of the entire nation. Local programs, on the other hand, may have consequences on persons who were unable to participate in the local political process.

Analysis:

This decision gets at the heart of the judicial debate over affirmative action. Justice Thomas artfully points out that strict scrutiny is required, due to the impact affirmative action has on the very persons it seeks to benefit. He points out that affirmative action stigmatizes minorities. Some commentators have argued that affirmative action goes so far as to breed racial resentment and foster further discrimination. The other side of the argument, as espoused by justice Stevens, is that affirmative action is not invidious discrimination, and that it seeks to foster equality. Thus, according to Justice Stevens, the Constitution requires a less exacting standard of review in affirmative action cases. There may in fact may be a difference between a decision by the majority to benefit the minority at the expense of itself, and a decision to burden the minority simply because they are the minority. However, Justice Scalia does well to counter this argument by pointing out that the Constitution overridingly aims at protecting individuals, not groups, from government action.

Grutter v. Bollinger

(White Law School Applicant) v. (University Official)
539 U.S. 306, 123 S.Ct. 2325 (2003)

EDUCATIONAL DIVERSITY IS A COMPELLING STATE INTEREST

■ **INSTANT FACTS** Grutter (P), a white law school applicant, brought suit to challenge the University of Michigan Law School's (D) policy of relying on an applicant's race in the admissions decision.

■ **BLACK LETTER RULE** Racial classifications must be narrowly tailored to achieving a compelling state interest.

■ **PROCEDURAL BASIS**

Certiorari to review an undisclosed appellate decision.

■ **FACTS**

The University of Michigan Law School's admissions policy required school officials to consider the grades, personal statements, personal recommendations, and other scholastic criteria in accepting candidates for school admission. The policy also emphasized the inclusion of candidates from racial or ethnic groups historically victimized by discrimination to foster racial and ethnic diversity in the student body. Grutter (P), a white candidate with exceptional academic credentials, brought suit when her application was denied because the school's policy relied upon race.

■ **ISSUE**

May a law school use race as a factor in student admissions?

■ **DECISION AND RATIONALE**

(O'Connor, J.) Yes. Under *Regents of the University of California v. Bakke*, student body diversity serves a compelling state interest that can justify the use of race in the admissions process. To withstand a constitutional challenge, however, a race-based admissions policy must be narrowly tailored to achieve that compelling state interest. Here, the University's (D) policy strives for educational and social diversity to enhance the educational benefits to its students. The Court will defer to the University's (D) assessment, developed from its expertise in such matters. Racial diversity exposes students to different perspectives to which they may otherwise not be exposed and strengthens classroom discussion of important legal and social issues. With law schools in particular, university graduates move on to assume high-ranking positions in business and government, for which a diverse education serves the interests of many Americans.

To be narrowly tailored to its compelling interest, a law school may not use an applicant's race to meet a predetermined quota, but may use race as a "plus" when admitting an otherwise eligible applicant. While the policy strives for an undefined mass of minority students, resort to some numerical calculation does not convert an admissions policy into a quota system. The University (D) does not use a mechanical formula for admitting successful applicants, but instead uses a highly individualized review of the student's accomplishments to determine his or her acceptance. While race is a factor, so too are such diversity characteristics as fluency in several languages and unique life experiences that may

Grutter v. Bollinger (Continued)

contribute to the educational culture. The University (D) has considered various race-neutral admissions alternatives, but in the end those alternatives would sacrifice racial diversity, academic quality, or both. The University's (D) admissions policy survives strict scrutiny.

■ CONCURRENCE

(Ginsburg, J.) Despite values and ideals of equal opportunity, minority children continue to receive substandard educations in comparison to their nonminority peers. Some minority students are nonetheless able to meet the educational criteria demanded of colleges and universities. As the educational opportunities for minority students continue to improve, one may hope that affirmative action programs, including race-based admissions policies, will be largely unnecessary.

■ DISSENT IN PART

(Scalia, J.) The goals of multiculturalism and cross-racial understanding, while laudable aims, are not educational, but rather societal. They are lessons of life that go untested in law school curriculums. They are the same lessons that are taught in Boy Scout troops and corporate settings. While such aims may make good citizens, the Court's decision fails to reach a clear constitutional conclusion to the issue, making future challenges certain.

■ DISSENT IN PART

(Thomas, J.) Under a strict-scrutiny analysis, the desire for racial diversity and improved education are not compelling state interests that justify a policy of racial discrimination. The goal of having an elite law school is not a pressing public necessity. Even if it were, the University (D) has failed to demonstrate a cognizable interest worthy of constitutional protection. Because few of the law school's (D) graduates remain in the state to practice law, the enhanced educational setting allegedly resulting from racial diversity does little to advance the interests of Michigan residents. Moreover, the University (D) could achieve racial diversity without considering the applicant's race merely by setting minimum admissions standards and accepting all students who achieve them. There is no evidence that racial diversity in fact improves educational results, and the majority's deference to the University's (D) views is misguided when other reasonably contrary views call them into question. By implementing a race-conscious admissions policy, the University (D) satisfies its desire for an aesthetically pleasing student body to enable it to claim elite status, but does a disservice to those students admitted because of their race. Many of these students are admitted with dreams of obtaining a law degree from a prestigious school, only to find failure in the face of competition among the student body. Yet, had these students attended a less-elite school with other students of like caliber, their legal education may very well have been enhanced, and their successes more easily achieved.

■ DISSENT

(Rehnquist, C.J.) Although the University (D) claims to seek racial diversity in its student body, its policy is not narrowly tailored to achieving this result. Of the minority students admitted to the University (D) over a five-year span, most have been African–American. If racial diversity is the goal, the admissions policy fails by excluding other minority groups, such as Native Americans and Hispanics. Because the policy in practice serves mainly to ensure the admission of African–American applicants, it is a naked attempt at unconstitutional racial balancing.

■ DISSENT

(Kennedy, J.) If race-conscious admissions policies are to survive a true strict-scrutiny standard, the Court may not defer to the views of the University (D) to determine proper educational objectives. Institutional deference deprives the educational system of the opportunity for "new and fairer ways to ensure individual consideration."

Analysis:

Opponents of affirmative action programs taking race, gender, or other personal characteristic into account often question whether they achieve their intended objectives. Although affirmative action generally seeks to afford opportunities that may have traditionally been denied to a specific class of individuals in order to diminish the effects discrimination has historically had on these individuals, some may argue that by conferring special benefits on account of an individual's race or gender, such programs actually compound the problem by identifying the individual's beliefs and viewpoints with their physical characteristics. A focus on life experiences arguably provides more diversity than one's physical attributes.

■ CASE VOCABULARY

COMPELLING–STATE–INTEREST TEST: A method for determining the constitutional validity of a law, whereby the government's interest in the law is balanced against the individual's constitutional right to be free of the law. Only if the government's interest is strong enough will the law be upheld. The compelling-state-interest test is used most commonly in equal-protection analysis when the disputed law requires strict scrutiny.

STRICT SCRUTINY: The standard applied to suspect classification (such as race) in equal-protection analysis and to fundamental rights (such as voting rights) in due-process analysis. Under strict scrutiny, the state must establish that it has a compelling state interest that justifies and necessitates the law in question.

Gratz v. Bollinger

(*White University Applicant*) v. (*University Official*)
539 U.S. 244, 123 S.Ct. 2411 (2003)

A POINT SYSTEM EMPHASIZING MINORITY STATUS VIOLATES EQUAL PROTECTION

■ **INSTANT FACTS** Gratz (P) was denied admission to the University of Michigan's College of Literature, Science, and the Arts in favor of minority candidates.

■ **BLACK LETTER RULE** University admissions policies must take race into account, if at all, only on a case-by-case, individualized basis.

■ **PROCEDURAL BASIS**

Certiorari to review an undisclosed appellate decision.

■ **FACTS**

Gratz (P) and Hamacher (P) were white candidates for admission to the University of Michigan's College of Literature, Science, and the Arts. After both were denied admission, they filed a class action suit against the University (D) for its past and current discriminatory admission policies. The University (D) considered various factors in granting candidates admission, one of which was race. Considering black, Hispanic, and Native American candidates to be "underrepresented minorities," the University (D) admitted "virtually every qualified . . . applicant" from these groups. Under its revised scoring system, a candidate must accumulate 100 points to gain admission, with points awarded based on the high school grade point average, standardized test scores, the academic quality of the student's high school, the strength of the high school curriculum, resident status, alumni relationships, the personal essay, and leadership skills. Under this scoring system, minority candidates received twenty points by virtue of their minority status.

■ **ISSUE**

Does the University of Michigan's use of racial preferences in undergraduate admissions violate the Equal Protection Clause and Title VI of the Civil Rights Act of 1964?

■ **DECISION AND RATIONALE**

(Rehnquist, C.J.) Yes. Although racial classifications may be used to remedy past discrimination, such classifications require strict scrutiny under the Equal Protection Clause. To withstand this scrutiny, the University's (D) admissions policy must be narrowly tailored to further compelling government interests. The awarding of one-fifth of the necessary points to gain admission by virtue of minority status is not narrowly tailored to further the compelling government interest of racial and ethnic diversity. The University's (D) system does not judge each applicant on an individualized basis, but rather threatens to render the applicant's race the decisive factor in granting admission. The policy does not survive strict scrutiny.

■ **CONCURRENCE**

(O'Connor, J.) If race is to be used as a consideration in the admissions decision, it must be on a case-by-case, individualized basis. With the University's (D) point system, even the most gifted non-minority academic leader earns far fewer points for his or her achievements than a less gifted minority candidate. Such a mechanical use of an applicant's race does not withstand constitutional scrutiny.

■ DISSENT

(Ginsburg, J.) Discrimination and economic disadvantage continue to plague America's minority population. Race is a suspect classification in constitutional jurisprudence not because classification on that basis is entirely impermissible, but because of its historic use as a tool of discrimination. The Constitution does not forbid the use of classifications to even the score for those who suffer racial inequality. The University's (D) admissions policy is nothing more than a constitutionally permissible affirmative action plan to ensure minority participation in higher education.

Analysis:

The fatal blow to the University's admissions policy was the quantification of each student's admissibility, giving a specific value based on the applicant's race. By attributing specific points to race, less-qualified minority candidates are mechanically and systematically admitted ahead of better-qualified white candidates. While the University (D) could admit a minority candidate over an equally qualified white candidate, it must, according to the Court, do so after an individualized review of their comparable qualifications.

■ CASE VOCABULARY

AFFIRMATIVE ACTION: A set of actions designed to eliminate existing and continuing discrimination, to remedy lingering effects of past discrimination, and to create systems and procedures to prevent future discrimination.

REVERSE DISCRIMINATION: Preferential treatment of minorities, usually through affirmative-action programs, in a way that adversely affects members of a majority group.

Easley v. Cromartie

(*Governor*) v. (*State Citizen*)
532 U.S. 234, 121 S.Ct. 1452 (2001)

LEGISLATIVE DETERMINATIONS ARE ENTITLED TO DEFERENCE IN DISTRICT BOUNDARY CHALLENGES

■ **INSTANT FACTS** A three-judge district court panel held that the North Carolina legislature's 12th Congressional District's boundaries were unconstitutionally established using race as a predominant factor.

■ **BLACK LETTER RULE** When racial identification correlates highly with political affiliation, the party attacking the legislatively drawn boundaries must show that the legislature could have achieved its legitimate political objectives in alternative ways that are comparably consistent with traditional districting principles.

■ **PROCEDURAL BASIS**
Certiorari to review a three-judge district court decision for the plaintiff.

■ **FACTS**
A three-judge District Court held that the North Carolina legislature's 12th Congressional District's boundaries were unconstitutionally established using race as a predominant factor.

■ **ISSUE**
Did the District Court err in finding race to be a predominant factor in the legislature's districting plan?

■ **DECISION AND RATIONALE**
(Breyer, J.) Yes. Plaintiffs challenging a legislature's motive in establishing voting district boundaries bear a demanding burden of proof. It is insufficient to establish that race was a motive in the legislative plan, but rather race must be the predominant factor motivating the legislative decision. Plaintiffs must show that a facially neutral plan "is unexplainable on grounds other than race."

Here, the district court concluded that race, rather than politics, predominated in the legislature's districting plan. Because racial identification and political affiliation are highly correlated in North Carolina, the shape of the district, the division of towns and counties, and the high black voter population in the district do not establish race as the predominant factor as a matter of law. The evidence simply does not establish race as the predominant factor motivating the districting plan. "[W]here majority-minority districts (or the approximate equivalent) are at issue and where racial identification correlates highly with political affiliation, the party attacking the legislatively drawn boundaries must show at the least that the legislature could have achieved its legitimate political objectives in alternative ways that are comparably consistent with traditional districting principles." The district court erred in finding that the plaintiffs met this burden.

■ **DISSENT**
(Thomas, J.) On appeal, the Court must review the district court's decision for clear error. This standard does not permit the Court to substitute its factual determinations for those of the district court, which is in a better position to review the record, consider the testimony of witnesses, and render a sound factual judgment. Yet, the Court overrules the district court's factual conclusions because they were not

Easley v. Cromartie (Continued)

subjected to intermediate review and the trial was not lengthy. These reasons, however, do not change the standard of review or give the Court more authority than it otherwise possesses. The district court has considered the evidence presented and reached its decision. The Court should not have disturbed it.

Analysis:

The Court's "predominant factor" standard confirms the extremely heavy burden one has in challenging racial gerrymandering. Surprisingly, the Court does not prohibit state legislatures from considering race in drawing voting districts, but rather requires that race not be the only or predominant factor motivating the legislature. Unlike many other instances in which the Court has condemned consideration of racial stereotype, the Court permits it to a limited degree here.

Frontiero v. Richardson

(Female Air Force Lieutenant) v. (Secretary of Defense)
411 U.S. 677, 93 S.Ct. 1764 (1973)

SUPREME COURT IS INITIALLY UNABLE TO DETERMINE LEVEL OF JUDICIAL SCRUTINY FOR GENDER-BASED CLASSIFICATIONS

■ **INSTANT FACTS** A female lieutenant in the U.S. Air Force filed suit against the Armed Forces claiming that the statute creating the presumption that the wives of servicemen were "dependent" for the purpose of obtaining increased living allowances but requiring servicewomen to prove their husbands were "dependent" for such purposes was a violation of equal protection under the Fifth Amendment.

■ **BLACK LETTER RULE** Gender-based classifications are inherently suspect and must be subjected to strict scrutiny.

■ **PROCEDURAL BASIS**

Direct appeal from the U.S. District Court for the Middle District of Alabama to the U.S. Supreme Court challenging the District Court's decision to uphold the constitutionality of a gender-based classification enacted by Congress.

■ **FACTS**

Sharron Frontiero (P), a lieutenant in the U.S. Air Force (D), was denied her application for increased quarters allowances and medical and dental benefits for her husband because she failed to demonstrate that her husband was dependent on her for more than one-half of his support, as required by federal statute. Frontiero (D) then filed a claim against the Government (D) in federal court, contending that the statute was unconstitutional because servicemen were not required to show that their wives were dependent for any part of the servicemen's income.

■ **ISSUE**

Are gender classifications subject to strict scrutiny?

■ **DECISION AND RATIONALE**

(Brennan, J.) Yes. Gender-based classifications are inherently suspect and must be subjected to strict scrutiny. As a result of antiquated notions regarding the role of men and women, there are countless statutes laden with stereotyped distinctions between the sexes. In fact, women were denied the franchise until 1920, 50 years after blacks were franchised. Nevertheless, the fact remains that discrimination against women remains pervasive throughout our society. Furthermore, since sex is an immutable characteristic, the imposition of burdens on members of a particular sex goes against our notion of individual responsibility. The statute at issue here classifies members of the military solely on the basis of sex and serves no purpose other than administrative convenience. For the statute to survive, the Government (D) must show that it is cheaper to provide all married men with increased benefits than it would be to determine which married servicemen and women actually require those benefits.

■ **CONCURRENCE**

(Stewart, J.) I concur that the statute is an invidious discrimination in violation of the Constitution.

Frontiero v. Richardson (Continued)

■ CONCURRENCE

(Powell, J.) I agree that the statute at issue is unconstitutional. However, I find myself unable to join the portion of the Court's opinion requiring gender-based classifications to be subjected to strict scrutiny. Our holding does not require a finding that sex is a suspect classification requiring heightened scrutiny.

Analysis:

In *Frontiero*, an eight-member Court was unable to agree on the level of scrutiny applicable to gender-based classifications. Justice Brennan's plurality opinion, which was joined in by only three other members of the Court, characterized sex as a suspect classification that warranted strict scrutiny. However, Justice Powell, joined by Chief Justice Burger and Justice Blackmun, felt that the Court need not determine which level of scrutiny was applicable to gender-based classifications. Despite the inability of the Court to reach an agreement in *Frontiero,* the case foreshadowed the adoption of some level of heightened scrutiny for gender-based classifications.

Craig v. Boren

(*Male Plaintiff*) v. (*Governor of Oklahoma*)
429 U.S. 190, 97 S.Ct. 451 (1976)

SUPREME COURT HOLDS THAT GENDER-BASED CLASSIFICATIONS ARE SUBJECT TO INTERMEDIATE SCRUTINY

■ **INSTANT FACTS** A male between the ages of 18 and 21 and a licensed vendor of 3.2% beer filed an action in federal district court challenging the constitutionality of Oklahoma statutes prohibiting the sale of "nonintoxicating" 3.2% beer to males under the age of 21 and to females under the age of 18.

■ **BLACK LETTER RULE** Gender classifications must serve important governmental objectives and must be substantially related to achievement of those objectives.

■ **PROCEDURAL BASIS**

Direct appeal to the U.S. Supreme Court from the District Court for the Western District of Oklahoma upholding the constitutionality of a gender-based classification and dismissing the complaint.

■ **FACTS**

Oklahoma (D) had enacted two statutes which interacted to prohibit the sale of "nonintoxicating" 3.2% beer to males under the age of 21 and to females under the age of 18. A male between the ages of 18 and 21 and a licensed vendor of 3.2% beer filed suit in federal court challenging the constitutionality of the statutes on the ground that they arbitrarily distinguished between men and women.

■ **ISSUE**

Are statutes which discriminate between men and women subject to heightened scrutiny?

■ **DECISION AND RATIONALE**

(Brennan, J.) Yes. Gender classifications must serve important governmental objectives and must be substantially related to achievement of those objectives. The proffered objective underlying the statutes at issue is the enhancement of traffic safety, which of course is an important function of local governments. The state of Oklahoma (D) offered statistical evidence it felt supported the classification. For example, an analysis of arrests for 1973 showed that the number of arrests of men between 18 and 21 for driving under the influence substantially exceeded the number of women in that age group. Second, a disproportionate number of youths between 17 and 21 were killed in traffic accidents. Third, a random survey revealed that young males were more inclined to drink and drive than their female counterparts. Fourth, FBI statistics noted an increase in arrests for driving under the influence. Finally statistics from other states supported the findings made in Oklahoma. Assuming the validity of these figures, we believe that they do not support the classification at issue. The studies show that 2% of males between the ages of 18 and 21 were arrested for driving under the influence, while only .8% of women in that group were arrested for the same offense. Though not insignificant, this statistical disparity does not justify a gender-based classification. Again ignoring the methodological problems associated with these studies, they simply do not support the statutes as enacted. No study measures the use and dangerousness of 3.2% beer. There is also no statistical support relating to relation between age-sex differentials and the increase in driving under the influence arrests. For these reasons,

Craig v. Boren (Continued)

we find the Oklahoma statutes constitute a denial of equal protection to males between the ages of 18 and 21.

■ DISSENT

(Rehnquist, J.) The Court improperly applies an intermediate level of scrutiny to gender-based classifications. Instead, such classifications should be subject to a rational basis review. Neither the language of the Equal Protection Clause nor our prior cases support the heightened level of scrutiny adopted by the Court today. Furthermore, the standard appears difficult to apply in practice. How does a court determine what objectives are "important" and whether the classification "substantially" furthers them. The Court's casual dismissal of the statistical evidence offered is troubling. First, studies indicated that males between 18 and 21 were 18 times more likely to be arrested for driving under the influence than females of that age. Second, 92% of all national DUI arrests were males. Third, more than 75% of the drivers under 20 in Oklahoma (D) are males who drive 50% more than their female counterparts. Fourth, 80% of males under twenty profess a preference for drinking beer, while only 60% of females claim that same preference. The Court today holds legislatures to too strict a standard when relying on statistical evidence in their decision making.

Analysis:

This case is important for two purposes. First, it established intermediate scrutiny as the appropriate level of review for gender-based classifications. The Court announced that in order to pass such scrutiny, a classification had to substantially further important government objectives. The Court has consistently reaffirmed intermediate scrutiny as the appropriate level of review. Even those cases striking down gender-base classifications prior to the decision in *Craig*, it is apparent that the Court was applying some heightened level of scrutiny, and not the deferential rational-basis review. This case is also important for showing that gender-based classifications that burden men, and not just those that negatively affect women, are subjected to heightened scrutiny.

■ CASE VOCABULARY

INTERMEDIATE SCRUTINY: A level of judicial review which is less deferential than the rational basis standard, less exacting than strict scrutiny, and which specifically requires that the challenged legislation be substantially related to important government objectives.

United States v. Virginia

(Federal Government) v. (State Government)
518 U.S. 515, 116 S.Ct. 2264 (1996)

SUPREME COURT REQUIRES AN "EXCEEDINGLY PERSUASIVE JUSTIFICATION" TO SUPPORT GENDER-BASED CLASSIFICATIONS

■ **INSTANT FACTS** A female applicant seeking admission to the all-male Virginia Military Institute, a public university, filed a claim against the state of Virginia challenging the school's policy against admitting women.

■ **BLACK LETTER RULE** State's must proffer an exceedingly persuasive justification for gender classifications which categorically excludes women from educational opportunities.

■ **PROCEDURAL BASIS**

Appeal to the United States Supreme Court from a decision of the Fourth Circuit Court of Appeals, which upheld the constitutionality of an all-male public military institution.

■ **FACTS**

Among its 15 public institutions of higher education, the state of Virginia (D) maintained the Virginia Military Institute (VMI) as an all-male military school. VMI (D) provides cadets with a unique educational opportunity based on an "adversarial method" of training. The purpose of this training was to impart on students a strong moral code and instill physical and mental discipline. That VMI (D) had the largest per-student endowment of all public universities in the country evinced the school's success in developing civilian and military leaders. After the Fourth Circuit ruled that VMI's (D) policy of excluding women was in violation of equal protection, the state of Virgina (D) proposed a parallel program for women at Mary Baldwin College. However, many of the features which made VMI (D) such a unique opportunity were absent from the program at Mary Baldwin College, not to mention the fact that VMI (D) conferred a wider range of degrees and employed a more educated faculty than did Mary Baldwin.

■ **ISSUE**

Can a state constitutionally deny to capable and willing women certain public educational opportunities?

■ **DECISION AND RATIONALE**

(Ginsburg, J.) No. State's must proffer an exceedingly persuasive justification for gender classifications which categorically exclude women from educational opportunities. Virginia (D) has failed to meet this burden. Its assertion that single-sex education provides important education benefits and contributes to diversity in educational approaches must be dismissed. Virginia (D) has not proved that VMI (D) has been maintained as an all-male school in an effort to diversify educational opportunities within the state. Our cases establish that the justification proffered in defense of a gender-based classification must be an actual purpose, not a post hoc rationalization. Virginia (D) also claims that the admission of women into VMI (D) would modify the school's adversarial method to such an extent that neither sex would benefit from the transformation. In other words men would be deprived of the opportunities currently available to them and women would fail to realize the benefits of those currently available opportunities.

United States v. Virginia (Continued)

However, this notion is one which is hardly proved, and is no different than many of the "self-fulfilling prophecies" once used to deny rights or opportunities. Surely VMI's (D) goal of producing "citizen-soldiers" is one that can accommodate women. Turning to the issue of whether Virginia's (D) parallel program at Marry Baldwin College sufficiently remedies the constitutional violation, we find that it does not. The proper remedy for an unconstitutional exclusion aims to "eliminate the discriminatory effects of the past" and to "bar like discrimination in the future." Virginia (D) has taken the opposite route—it has chosen to perpetuate and leave unchanged VMI's (D) exclusionary policy. Admittedly the parallel program does not come near to "the entirely militaristic experience of VMI (D)," a failure which Virginia has sought to justify on the ground that the parallel program is designed for women who do not expect to pursue military careers. This justification is inappropriate in light of the fact that only 15% of VMI (D) graduates pursue a career in the Armed Forces. The only proper remedy is one that does not exclude women from the educational opportunity afforded at VMI (D) simply because of their sex.

■ DISSENT

(Scalia, J.) The Court today rejects the factual findings of the lower courts, ignores established precedent and rejects the history of our people. First, the Court today ignores the fact that there exist "gender-based developmental differences" supporting the exclusion of women from the adversative method and supporting the notion that all-male composition is essential to VMI's unique experience. Second, the majority drastically revises this Court's established standards for reviewing sex-based classifications. Finally, the decision today gives little credence to the national long history of supporting all-male military institutions. The Court has essentially written into the Constitution notions of current societal preferences.

Analysis:

This case is interesting from the standpoint that the court appears to require a level of scrutiny for gender-based classifications that exceeds the intermediate level announced in *Craig v. Boren*, but that does not, on the surface, purport to reach the level of strict scrutiny applicable to race-based classification. Justice Ginsburg's opinion states that sex-based classifications are valid only when there is an "exceedingly persuasive justification." However, the majority's opinion in *Craig* clearly states that gender classifications must serve important governmental objectives and must be substantially related to achievement of those objectives. Nothing in *Craig* appears to require "exceedingly persuasive justifications." Nevertheless, *Virginia* appears to leave us with this definition of intermediate scrutiny.

■ CASE VOCABULARY

ADVERSATIVE METHOD: A philosophy of instruction, employed at Virginia Military Institute, which aims at developing physical and mental discipline.

EXCEEDINGLY PERSUASIVE JUSTIFICATION: The burden imposed on the government if it wishes to support a gender-based classification

Geduldig v. Aiello

(*Insured Women*) v. (*Director, California Department of Human Resources Development*)
417 U.S. 484, 94 S.Ct. 2485 (1974)

A STATUTE IS NOT VIOLATIVE OF EQUAL PROTECTION MERELY BECAUSE IT FAILS TO ACCOUNT FOR BIOLOGICAL DIFFERENCES BETWEEN THE SEXES

■ **INSTANT FACTS** A group of women filed a claim against the state of California challenging its disability insurance system on the ground that the denial of benefits for pregnancy related disability worked a discrimination against women in violation of equal protection.

■ **BLACK LETTER RULE** Discrimination on the basis of pregnancy is not in itself a violation of equal protection.

■ **PROCEDURAL BASIS**

Not provided.

■ **FACTS**

The state of California (D) administered a disability insurance system that paid benefits to persons in private employment who were temporarily unable to work because of disabilities not covered by workmen's compensation. The program defined "disability" to exclude certain disabilities arising from pregnancy. The program also excluded disabilities of less than 8 days in duration and those lasting more than 26 weeks. To be eligible for the program an employee must have contributed 1% of his salary to the fund. The program was completely self-supporting and never required otherwise public funds. The rationale behind excluding pregnancy-related disabilities was the extraordinary cost associated with them.

■ **ISSUE**

Does discrimination on the basis of pregnancy amount to invidious discrimination under the Equal Protection Clause?

■ **DECISION AND RATIONALE**

(Stewart, J.) No. Discrimination on the basis of pregnancy is not in itself a violation of equal protection. The classification in this case is challenged on the basis of the underinclusiveness of the set of risks covered by the disability program. This Court has held that a State may regulate one step at a time. Particularly with respect to social welfare programs, so long as the line drawn by the State is rationally supportable, the courts will not interpose their judgment as to the appropriate stopping point. It is clear that the costs associated with the inclusion of pregnancy-related disabilities into the program would require state subsidy, a higher rate of contribution or lower benefits for those insured. The State has a legitimate interest in maintaining the self-supporting nature of the program. There is no risk from which men are protected and women are not, and vice versa. The program classifies citizens into two groups: pregnant women and non-pregnant persons. The first of these groups is composed entirely of women, the second is a combination of both sexes. Thus, the benefits provided accrue to both sexes.

■ **DISSENT**

(Brennan, J.) By singling out for less favorable treatment a gender-linked disability peculiar to women, California (D) has created a double standard for disability compensation: Men may recover for all

Geduldig v. Aiello (Continued)

disabilities associated with only their sex, women may not recover for an important disability associated with theirs. In effect, one set of rules is applicable to women and another to men, and this constitutes sex discrimination.

Analysis:

By holding that classifications made on the basis of pregnancy are not subject to heightened scrutiny, the Court makes an implicit distinction between gender-based classifications and gender-related ones. The former are subject to intermediate scrutiny, the latter need only pass the rational basis test to be upheld. The Court reasoned that it made no sense to deem a classification as discriminating against women if women were included in both groups. That rationale has been expressly invoked in subsequent Supreme Court cases where a classification was merely gender-related. The distinction made by this case notwithstanding, the impact of the holding was lessened by statute when the Pregnancy Discrimination Act was enacted, which expressly prohibits discrimination on the basis of pregnancy.

■ CASE VOCABULARY

PREGNANCY DISCRIMINATION ACT: Federal legislation which prohibits discrimination on the basis of pregnancy.

Orr v. Orr

(*Husband*) v. (*Wife*)
440 U.S. 268, 99 S.Ct. 1102 (1979)

CLASSIFICATIONS BENEFITING WOMEN MAY NOT BE JUSTIFIED ON THE STEREOTYPE OF WOMEN BEING ECONOMICALLY DEPENDENT ON MEN

■ **INSTANT FACTS** A man in a divorce proceeding sought to challenge upon equal protection grounds a state law which provided that men, but not women, could be required to pay alimony upon divorce.

■ **BLACK LETTER RULE** A state may not enact a statute requiring only men to pay alimony upon divorce.

■ **PROCEDURAL BASIS**

Appeal to the U.S. Supreme Court challenging the decision of the Alabama Court of Civil Appeals upholding the constitutionality of the State's alimony statute.

■ **FACTS**

A man in a divorce proceeding sought to challenge an Alabama statute which provided that husbands, but not wives, could be required to pay alimony.

■ **ISSUE**

May a state provide that only men may be required to pay alimony to their ex-spouses?

■ **DECISION AND RATIONALE**

(Brennan, J.) No. A state may not enact a statute requiring only men to pay alimony upon divorce. We first note that gender classifications may not be justified on the reinforcement of the stereotype that wives play a dependent role to the husband in the allocation of family responsibilities. The opinion of the Alabama Court of Civil Appeals suggests that the statute was designed for the wife of a broken marriage who needs financial assistance. This justification could be read to mean that the statute is aimed at helping needy spouses, using sex as a proxy for need. It could also be read to imply that the statute seeks to compensate women for past discrimination during marriage, which has left them unprepared to fend for themselves after marriage. Certainly, a state has an important interest in fulfilling either of these goals. The question remains whether the classifications substantially furthers these objectives. Using sex as a proxy for need does not. Needy males could be helped along with needy females. The hearings regularly undertaken to determine the relative financial condition of the parties can be used to determine which spouse is in fact needy. Thus, the gender based distinction does not actually further the proffered state interest. In fact, the statute may have the opposite effect by forbidding the court to order that a financially secure wife pay alimony to a needy husband. Reversed.

Analysis:

The Court in this case makes clear that gender-based stereotypes may not serve to justify classifications based on sex, even when the classification benefits women. Implicit in the Court's holding is that

Orr v. Orr (Continued)

the state cannot have an interest in providing merely for women after divorce. However, the Court holds that an interest in providing for spouses left unprepared by marriage or in providing for needy spouses are government interests sufficiently important to justify a gender-based classification. Nevertheless, the Court strikes down the Alabama statute on the ground that it fails to further these goals. The statute was underinclusive in two senses. First it failed to provide for needy or unprepared men. Second, the statute failed to require financially stable wives to pay alimony.

Mississippi University for Women v. Hogan

(State Nursing School) v. (Male Applicant)
458 U.S. 718, 102 S.Ct. 3331 (1982)

SUPREME COURT HOLDS UNCONSTITUTIONAL A STATE STATUTE PROHIBITING MALE ENROLLMENT IN A PUBLIC SCHOOL FOR NURSES

■ **INSTANT FACTS** A male applicant denied admission to an all-female state-sponsored nursing school sought to challenge the school's exclusion of men.

■ **BLACK LETTER RULE** A state may designate an educational opportunity to members of only one-sex if the state seeks to remedy actual past discrimination related to the educational opportunity.

■ **PROCEDURAL BASIS**

Not Provided.

■ **FACTS**

As its name suggests, the Mississippi University for Women (MUW) (D) was an all-female university founded and sponsored by the State of Mississippi. Joe Hogan (P), a registered nurse who held no nursing degree, sought admission to the School of Nursing in an effort to earn a baccalaureate degree. However, Hogan (P) was denied admission solely on the basis of his sex.

■ **ISSUE**

May a state-sponsored nursing school deny admission to males?

■ **DECISION AND RATIONALE**

(O'Connor, J.) No. A state may designate an educational opportunity to members of only one-sex if the state seeks to remedy actual past discrimination related to the educational opportunity. Although it maintains that the exclusion of men from MUW's School of Nursing (D) is aimed at remedying past discrimination against women, the state of Mississippi has not proved that women have lacked opportunities in the field of nursing. In fact, in the year preceding the school's opening, 94% of nursing degrees conferred in the state of Mississippi were earned by women. It is clear that MUW's (D) policy does not seek to remedy past discrimination, but only to perpetuate the stereotyped view of nursing as a woman's job. The exclusion of males is also invalid because the state has failed to show that the classification substantially furthers the purported interest. MUW (D) actually permits men to attend classes as auditors, dispelling the notion that the presence of men harms female students.

■ **DISSENT**

(Powell, J.) The Court today ignores the fact that Mississippi affords abundant coeducational opportunities to men and women and the preferences of over 40,000 women who attend MUW (D). Hogan's (P) only real complaint is that he must travel to attend a state-sponsored school. However, the Constitution does not grant the right to attend school in one's own backyard. The Court errs in applying heightened scrutiny to a narrowly utilized classification that provides women with alternate choices. Mississippi's

Mississippi University for Women v. Hogan (Continued)

accommodation of student choices is legitimate because it is completely consensual and it is important for it gives students the right to choose what is best for themselves.

Analysis:

As in *Orr v. Orr*, the Court here strikes down a gender-based classification premised on a stereotype as to the role of men and women in society. Justice O'Connor's opinion holds that a state may not engage in gender classification that perpetuates common stereotypes regarding the role of men and women. Thus, it is clear that the Court is concerned with the institutional and governmental propagation of these stereotypes, and not really the constitutional harm done to the male plaintiffs in each case. One interesting aside is that, after graduating third in her class from Stanford Law School, Justice O'Connor was able to obtain employment only as a secretary at the elite law firms to which she applied.

Michael M. v. Superior Court of Sonoma County

(Convicted Minor) v. (State)
450 U.S. 464, 101 S.Ct. 1200 (1981)

SUPREME COURT UPHOLDS A STATUTORY RAPE LAW APPLICABLE ONLY TO MEN

■ **INSTANT FACTS** A 17-year-old male sought to challenge his conviction for the statutory rape of a 16-year-old female on the ground that the statute under which he was convicted violated equal protection because it was only applicable to men.

■ **BLACK LETTER RULE** States may enact laws making it a crime for a man to have sex with an underage female in an effort to address teen pregnancy and teen sex.

■ **PROCEDURAL BASIS**

Appeal to the U.S. Supreme Court challenging the California Supreme Court's decision to strike down as unconstitutional the state's statutory rape law.

■ **FACTS**

In 1978, Michael M. (D), a 17-year-old male, was charged with statutory rape for having sex with a 16-year-old female. Michael M. (D) was convicted under California Penal Code § 261.5, which made it unlawful for a male to have sex with a female under the age of 18 who was not his wife. Prior to trial, Michael M. (D) sought to set aside the information on the grounds that the statute was unconstitutional under the Equal Protection Clause. The trial court and the state appellate court upheld the validity of the statute, but the California Supreme Court held that it discriminated on the basis of sex because only women could be victims and only men could be convicted.

■ **ISSUE**

Does a statutory rape law violate equal protection if it is applicable only to men who have sex with underage women?

■ **DECISION AND RATIONALE**

(Rehnquist, J.) No. States may enact laws making it a crime for a man to have sex with an underage female in an effort to address teen pregnancy. Although the actual or primary purpose of a statute is often difficult to ascertain, the prevention of teen pregnancy was the justification offered by the State (P), and accepted by the California Supreme Court, in support of § 261.5. Although there may have indeed been other purposes behind the statute, the finding of the California Supreme Court is, of course, accorded great deference. Since most of the harmful consequences of teen pregnancy fall on the female, a legislature may elect to punish only males who suffer few of the consequences of their conduct. Thus, the law acts to equalize the deterrents. Furthermore, we find there is significant merit to the State's (P) assertion that a gender-neutral statute would not serve as adequately because females may be less likely to report violations if they are subject to prosecution.

■ **DISSENT**

(Brennan, J.) The Court today places too much attention on the asserted statutory goal without considering whether the classification substantially furthers that goal. The State (P) has failed to prove

Michael M. v. Superior Court of Sonoma County (Continued)

that its statute more effectively deters underage sexual intercourse than a gender-neutral statute would. First, the fact that other states have enacted gender-neutral statutes belies the assertion that such law would be virtually incapable of enforcement. Second, even if gender-neutral statutes were more difficult to enforce, the State (P) has not shown that they would not deter underage women from engaging in sexual intercourse.

■ DISSENT

(Stevens, J.) States have legitimate interests in reducing venereal disease and teen pregnancy. However, those interests alone do not justify a statute which punishes only one-half of the participants in the activity which increase the risk the state seeks to reduce. In my mind, the fact that a women bears most of the risk the state seeks to reduce is a reason for applying the statute to her, rather than allowing her to assume the risk. Would a parent forbid their son and authorize their daughter to engage in an act that is particularly harmful to the daughter? That is the effect of the statute in this case.

Analysis:

It is clear that the plurality opinion issued by the Court in *Michael M.* paid only lip service to the application of intermediate scrutiny. First, Justice Rehnquist accepts the prevention of teen pregnancy as the purpose of the statute without any in-depth analysis. Heightened scrutiny requires the state to prove that the purpose that supports the classification is actually the one behind the statute. Justice Rehnquist is right that ascertaining the "actual" purpose is difficult, but that is exactly what heightened scrutiny is all about. Heightened scrutiny is reserved for only a few types of classifications, because it requires courts to undertake a difficult task. However, the fact that heightened scrutiny may be taxing does not justify its inapplicability in gender-based discrimination cases. Second, as Justice Brennan's dissent points out, the plurality merely accepts the notion that the statute substantially furthers the stated statutory interest.

■ CASE VOCABULARY

STATUTORY RAPE: As opposed to common law rape, a crime where an person, usually (but not always) an adult, engages in sexual activity with a minor

Rostker v. Goldberg

(Not Provided) v. (Not Provided)
453 U.S. 57, 101 S.Ct. 2646 (1981)

SUPREME COURT UPHOLDS THE APPLICATION OF SELECTIVE SERVICE ONLY TO MEN

■ **INSTANT FACTS** An equal protection challenge was brought against the Military Selective Service Act which requires only men between the ages of 18 and 26 to register for possible eventual conscription into the Armed Services.

■ **BLACK LETTER RULE** Congress does not violate equal protection by authorizing the president to require only males to register for selective service.

■ **PROCEDURAL BASIS**

Not Provided.

■ **FACTS**

Pursuant to its Constitutional power over the Armed Services, Congress enacted the Military Selective Service Act, which, in pertinent part, empowers the president to require the registration of every male citizen and resident alien between the ages of 18 and 26. The purpose of the act was to provide a pool of capable of persons for any eventual conscription which may be required.

■ **ISSUE**

Is it a violation of equal protection to authorize the president to require the registration of men, but not women, for selective service?

■ **DECISION AND RATIONALE**

(Rehnquist, J.) No. Congress does not violate equal protection by authorizing the president to require only males to register for selective service. This case involves decisions affecting the military, an area in which this Court has traditionally shown extreme deference to Congress. The interest in supporting and raising armies is an "important government interest," as defined by our previous cases. Obviously, Congress was not only aware of its decision to exclude women from registration, but reflected and debated the issue considerably. The purpose of registration is to fulfill needs of the nation in the case of a draft. Congress determined that such draft would call heavily on combat troops. Women are not eligible for combat. Consequently, the registration of women would not fulfill the interest selective service was designed to serve. The exemption of women is closely related to the asserted congressional purpose in enacting the statute.

■ **DISSENT**

(White, J.) I assume that the exclusion of women from combat does not itself violate the Constitution. The Court today gives too much deference to Congress. There is no indication that Congress concluded that every position in the military must be filled by combat-ready men. Certainly, females, as they have in the past, play an important role during war, despite the ineligibility for combat. The exclusion of women from registration could be justified if it were found that the non-combat positions could be filled adequately by female volunteers. However, Congress made no such findings. Simply

Rostker v. Goldberg (Continued)

put, there is no proof that Congress made the type of findings necessary to justify a gender-based classification as the one here.

Analysis:

The Court here foregoes the type of intermediate scrutiny applicable to gender-based classifications and exhibits the usual hesitancy to decide matters pertaining to military affairs. The Court fails to require the showing of a substantial fit between the classification and the stated interest. As the dissent points out, heightened scrutiny requires some proof that the women would not be needed in time of war or that the cost of registering women would be prohibitive. But the Court appears satisfied with a mere assertion that such is the case.

■ CASE VOCABULARY

CONSCRIPTION: Compulsory enrollment for military service.

Califano v. Webster

(Not Provided) v. (Not Provided)
430 U.S. 313, 97 S.Ct. 1192 (1977)

GENDER CLASSIFICATIONS WHICH BENEFIT WOMEN ARE PERMISSIBLE IF THEY REMEDY PAST DISCRIMINATION

■ **INSTANT FACTS** An equal protection claim was brought against the federal government to challenge provisions of Social Security Act that allowed women to exclude three more lower earning years in the computation of the retirement benefits.

■ **BLACK LETTER RULE** Reduction of the disparity in economic condition between men and women caused by the long history of discrimination is a governmental interest sufficiently important to justify a gender based classification.

■ **PROCEDURAL BASIS**

Appeal to the U.S. Supreme Court challenging the decision of the Court of Appeals, which invalidated certain provisions of the Social Security Act on equal protection grounds.

■ **FACTS**

Section 215 of the Social Security Act provides that insurance benefits are to be computed on the basis of the wage earner's "average monthly wage" during the "elapsed years" during which the wage earner's wages were highest. Under § 215(b)(3), male wage earners would have three more "elapsed years" than a similarly situated female wage earner. In other words, women could exclude three more low-wage years than men in order to increase their insurance benefits.

■ **ISSUE**

May the government enact a gender based classification in an effort to remedy past economic disparity between men and women arising as a result of prior discrimination aimed at women?

■ **DECISION AND RATIONALE**

(Per Curiam) Yes. Reduction of the disparity in economic condition between men and women caused by the long history of discrimination is a governmental interest sufficiently important to justify a gender based classification. The disparate treatment of men and women authorized by statute is not the result of archaic stereotypes. Instead, the more favorable treatment given to women in this case is a direct result of Congress' desire to redress our society's long history of disparate treatment of women. The statute achieves this very goal. Insurance benefits are based on past earnings, which occurred in an environment hostile to women in the workplace. Thus, the statute directly remedies prior discrimination.

Analysis:

A remedial purpose will justify a gender classification if it directly serves that purpose. The Court here makes a point to reject the idea that the gender-based classification was premised on stereotypes, because, as *Orr v. Orr* shows, statutes that perpetuate such archaic notions are viewed with suspicion. Instead, the Court upholds the validity of a legislative effort to remedy economic disparity between men and women that resulted from discrimination in the labor market.

Nguyen v. Immigration and Naturalization Service

(Deported Criminal) v. (Government Agency)
533 U.S. 53, 121 S.Ct. 2053 (2001)

BASIC BIOLOGICAL DIFFERENCES BETWEEN MEN AND WOMEN FACTOR INTO AN EQUAL PROTECTION ANALYSIS

■ **INSTANT FACTS** Nguyen (D), a Vietnamese-born child of an unmarried American man and Vietnamese woman, faced deportation after two felony convictions in the United States.

■ **BLACK LETTER RULE** To withstand an equal protection challenge, a gender-based classification must be substantially related to achieving an important governmental objective.

■ PROCEDURAL BASIS
Certiorari to review an undisclosed decision of the Fifth Circuit Court of Appeals.

■ FACTS
Nguyen (P) was born in Vietnam in 1969 to an American man and a Vietnamese woman, who were unmarried. After lawfully moving to the United States later in life, Nguyen (P) was convicted of two felonies. The United States Immigration and Naturalization Service (INS) (D) initiated deportation proceedings and ultimately ordered Nguyen's (P) deportation. While Nguyen (P) appealed the deportation order, his father obtained a parentage order from a state court establishing Nguyen (P) as his son, and supporting Nguyen's (P) claim of American citizenship. Nguyen's (P) appeal was nonetheless dismissed for failure to comply with 8 U.S.C. § 1409(a), which governs the citizenship of children born outside the country to an unwed American father and foreign mother. Nguyen (P) appealed the dismissal to the Fifth Circuit Court of Appeals, challenging the constitutionality of the statute under the Equal Protection Clause.

■ ISSUE
Does 8 U.S.C. § 1409(a), the federal statute governing the citizenship of children born outside the country to an unwed American father and foreign mother, violate the Equal Protection Clause?

■ DECISION AND RATIONALE
(Kennedy, J.) No. Under 8 U.S.C. § 1409(a), a child born outside of the United States to a citizen father and an alien mother who are unmarried is an American citizen if: (1) he can provide clear and convincing evidence of his blood relationship with the father, (2) the father was an American national at the time of birth, (3) the father agrees to financially support the child, (4) the child is legitimated in his place of residence or domicile, (5) the father acknowledges paternity, and (6) paternity has been established by court order. When the child is born under similar circumstances to an American mother and an alien father, however, American citizenship is established upon proof of blood relationship and the mother's nationality at the time of birth. The statute, therefore, demands additional showings based upon the gender of the citizen parent.

To withstand an equal protection challenge, a gender-based classification must be substantially related to achieving an important governmental objective. Here, the statute is substantially related to two important governmental objectives. First, the government has a legitimate interest in ensuring the parent-child relationship exists before granting citizenship. With mothers, the fact of birth establishes such a relationship. With fathers, however, additional steps need to be taken to ensure paternity. Because men and women are not similarly situated in such instances, and the statute is substantially related to achieve its objective in both instances. Second, the government has an important interest in ensuring the development of a meaningful relationship between the parent and the child. With mothers, this relationship inures in the birth itself. Having conceived, carried, and delivered the child, the parental bond has been given the opportunity to develop. Not so with unwed fathers. Given the time between conception and birth, an unwed father may not believe, or even know, that he is the child's biological father. As a result, even upon proof of paternity, the parent-child relationship may not develop sufficiently to create a traditional family environment. The statute need not ignore this reality nor the basic biological differences of men and women in such circumstances.

■ DISSENT

(O'Connor, J.) Under heightened scrutiny, one seeking to justify a gender-based classification bears the burden of proving the importance of the governmental objective allegedly furthered and the substantial relationship between the means chosen to reach it. The INS (D) has failed to do so, and the Court failed to demand it. In highlighting its first governmental interest, the Court neither explains why the assurance of a biological relationship is important nor queries whether it in fact is an objective of the federal statute. Regardless, the Court improperly justifies the importance of the statute in achieving this objective. Just as the act of birth provides clear and convincing evidence of a blood relationship between mother and child, DNA evidence establishes the relationship between father and child. No additional demands need be made upon a father when such scientific evidence is available. Likewise, the Court failed to inquire as to whether the statute was intended to ensure the opportunity for a meaningful family relationship. While it is questionable whether such a purpose is "important" in any event, the statute treats differently a mother who is, by nature, present at birth and a father who is, by choice, present at birth. The opportunity for a meaningful relationship is presumed with the former, but the father requires an additional showing merely because of his gender. The biological differences between men and women do not justify such distinctions.

Analysis:

While the Court's focus on biological differences has some appeal in the context of childbirth, Justice O'Connor's reasoning is also convincing. Hypothetically, if an unwed American mother gives birth overseas and places the child for adoption, she has had the "opportunity" for a traditional parent-child relationship and has elected to forgo it. The Court's reasoning would grant the child citizenship status nonetheless. Yet, a child of an unwed American man who knowingly disclaims the same opportunity would not gain citizenship. Further, the offspring of a mother unwilling to unite with the child could conceivably gain citizenship without the mother's cooperation, with proper proof, but a father's acquiescence is needed under the statute, despite any scientific evidence of paternity.

Graham v. Richardson

(State Administrator) v. (Resident Alien)
403 U.S. 365, 91 S.Ct. 1848 (1971)

SUPREME COURT APPLIES STRICT SCRUTINY TO CLASSIFICATIONS BASED ON ALIENAGE

■ **INSTANT FACTS** A resident alien living in Arizona sought to challenge a state law which prohibited resident aliens who had lived in the state less than 15 years from receiving welfare benefits.

■ **BLACK LETTER RULE** A State's desire to preserve limited welfare benefits for its own citizens is inadequate to justify the exclusion of resident aliens from receiving a portion of those benefits.

■ PROCEDURAL BASIS

Not Provided.

■ FACTS

Pursuant to federal regulations, the State of Arizona (D) distributes welfare benefits to its citizens. Section 46-233 of the Arizona Revised Statutes provided that only U.S. Citizens and resident aliens who had lived in the state more than 15 years could receive those benefits. In 1969, Carmen Richardson (P), a resident alien of 13 years, was totally disabled. As a result she became eligible for government assistance, except for the 15-year statutory residency requirement for aliens. Richardson (P) filed suit to challenge the requirement.

■ ISSUE

Does the Equal Protection Clause prevent states from conditioning welfare benefits upon U.S. citizenship or length of residency?

■ DECISION AND RATIONALE

(Blackmun, J.) Yes. A State's desire to preserve limited welfare benefits for its own citizens is inadequate to justify the exclusion of resident aliens from receiving a portion of those benefits. The Fourteenth Amendment provides that no State shall "deny to any person within its jurisdiction the equal protection of the laws." It is long settled that the term "person" includes both citizens and resident aliens. Thus, classifications based on alienage are inherently suspect and subject to strict scrutiny, for aliens are a prime example of a "discrete and insular" minority for which heightened scrutiny is appropriate. The state of Arizona (D) claims that it has a special interest in preserving limited public funds for its own citizens. This Court has often upheld laws which treat aliens differently because they were necessary to protect special interests of citizens. But, as we have held, the saving of welfare costs cannot justify an otherwise invidious discrimination.. Accordingly, the statute is unconstitutional.

Analysis:

The Court in this case either reiterates and establishes several propositions. First, it notes that the term "person" as used in Fourteenth Amendment applies to aliens. Also, the Court announces a second

Graham v. Richardson (Continued)

"suspect" classification under the Equal Protection Clause. *Graham* clearly establishes that classifications based on alienage are a form of invidious discrimination and, as such, they are subject to strict scrutiny. Finally, in applying strict scrutiny, the Court rejects the notion that financial concerns can justify classifications based on alienage.

■ CASE VOCABULARY

ALIENAGE: The status of being from a country other than the one in which a person resides.

Foley v. Connelie

(Resident Alien) v. (State Administrator)
435 U.S. 291, 98 S.Ct. 1067 (1978)

SUPREME COURT HOLDS THAT THE RATIONAL-BASIS TEST IS APPLICABLE WHEN A STATE SEEKS TO EXCLUDE ALIENS FROM THE DEMOCRATIC PROCESS

■ **INSTANT FACTS** A resident alien sought to challenge the denial of his admission to a state police force on the ground that the exclusion of aliens violated the Equal Protection Clause.

■ **BLACK LETTER RULE** A state may, consistent with the Constitution, confine participation in its police force to citizens of the United States.

■ **PROCEDURAL BASIS**

Not Provided.

■ **FACTS**

Edmund Foley (P), a resident alien living in New York, applied for an appointment as a State Trooper, a position filled on the basis of competitive exams. However, pursuant to a New York statute, only U.S. citizens were eligible to sit for the exam. Foley (D) filed suit challenging the statute as an unlawful classification based on alienage.

■ **ISSUE**

May a state constitutionally limit the appointment of members of its police force to U.S. citizens?

■ **DECISION AND RATIONALE**

(Burger, C.J.) Yes. A state may, consistent with the Constitution, confine participation in its police force to citizens of the United States. Although our cases reflect the application of strict scrutiny of classifications based on alienage, this Court has never held that all such legislation is inherently invalid, or that all limitations on aliens are suspect. In order to preserve the meaning and value of citizenship, and the concept of political community that results, we have recognized that a State may exclude aliens from participation in the democratic process. Accordingly, a State need only justify its classification by a showing of some rational relationship between the interest sought to be protected and the limiting classification. Thus, States may reserve for U.S. citizens important non-elective governmental positions in which officers participate directly in the formulation, execution or review of broad public policy. We believe that a police officer is precisely this type of position. The police are vested with wide discretionary powers, such as the invasion of privacy and the power to forcefully enter private residencies, which can significantly affect members of the pubic. This type of discretionary power only makes reasonable the presumption that a citizen will be more familiar with and sympathetic to American traditions. Since citizenship clearly bears a rational relationship to the special demand of the particular position, the classification is valid under the Constitution. The State may reasonably presume that citizens are more familiar with and sympathetic to American traditions.

■ **DISSENT**

(Marshall, J.) State troopers do not perform functions which place them in this narrow exception to the rule prohibiting discrimination of aliens. It is true that a policeman executes public policy, but he dos so

Foley v. Connelie (Continued)

in the same sense that a firefighter executes the public policy of extinguishing fires or a sanitation worker ensures the streets are kept clean. The phrase "execution of broad public policy" which is the cornerstone of the exception cannot mean simply the carrying out of government programs. The discrimination in this case seems based on a notion that aliens are not trustworthy or disloyal. This presumption must be rejected as an improper basis for the classification. However, even if the Court were willing to accept the premise that aliens are disloyal or not trustworthy, it is up to the state to prove that such characterization is true.

Analysis:

This case illustrates the lone exception to the general rule that classifications based on alienage are suspect and deserving of strict scrutiny. In applying the rule that a state may discriminate against aliens in the democratic process and the execution of public policy, the Court holds that police officers occupy a type of position that qualifies for the exception. The decision in this case is even more troubling for a reason discussed in the dissent. Assuming *arguendo* that police do fit within the narrow execution of public policy exception, the classification must still survive rational basis scrutiny. The justification seems tenuous in this case. Nevertheless, Justice Rehnquist writes that it is reasonable for states to presume that citizens will more faithfully execute the laws than resident aliens.

Ambach v. Norwick

(*State Commissioner of Education*) v. (*Resident Alien*)
441 U.S. 68, 99 S.Ct. 1589 (1979)

COURT HOLDS THAT STATES MAY PREVENT ALIENS FROM HOLDING TEACHING POSITIONS

■ **INSTANT FACTS** Two resident alien women filed suit against the state of New York seeking to invalidate a statute which restricted public school teacher certification to citizens of the United States.

■ **BLACK LETTER RULE** Public school teachers come well within the "governmental function" exception to the rule requiring strict scrutiny for classifications based on alienage.

■ PROCEDURAL BASIS
Not Provided.

■ FACTS
Ms. Norwick (P), a Scottish-born resident alien, and Ms. Dambach (P), a Finnish-born resident alien, both sought certification to teach in the public schools of the State of New York (D). However, New York (D) had enacted a statute which prohibited public school teacher certification of any person who was not a United States citizen, unless such person manifested an intent to apply for naturalization.

■ ISSUE
May a state refuse to employ as elementary and secondary school teachers aliens who are eligible for United States citizenship but who refuse to seek naturalization?

■ DECISION AND RATIONALE
(Powell, J.) Yes. Public school teachers come well within the "governmental function" exception to the rule requiring strict scrutiny for classifications based on alienage. In making this determination we must look to the role of public education and the discretion teachers possess in fulfilling that role. The importance of public schools in preparing people to become citizens and the preserving societal values is well recognized. Through the presentation of materials and the example they set, teachers influence the attitudes of students toward government the political process, and civic duties. A State may properly regard all teachers as having an obligation to promote civic virtues and understanding in the classes, regardless of the subject taught. Consequently, the Constitution requires only that a citizenship requirement applicable to teaching in the public schools bear a rational relationship to a legitimate state interest. The restriction enacted by the state of New York (D) is carefully framed to serve its purpose, as it bars only those person who have demonstrated their unwillingness to obtain U.S. citizenship. Thus, it is Ms. Norwick (P) and Ms. Dambach (P) who chose to classify themselves.

■ DISSENT
(Blackmun, J.) It seems absurd to say that at the elementary and secondary school levels that a Frenchman cannot teach French, or that an Englishwoman may not teach English grammar. There has been no showing that either Ms. Norwich (P) or Ms. Dambach (P) are not otherwise qualified to teach in pubic school. Each has been in this country for 12 years and is married to a U.S. citizen. The

Ambach v. Norwick (Continued)

classification is irrational. Is it better to employ a poor teacher than an fully capable resident-alien teacher. The State (D) may undertake other measures to decide who is and is not a good teacher without having to classify persons based on alienage.

Analysis:

As illustrated by this decision and that in *Foley v. Connelie*, the Supreme Court has carved a large exception into the rule prohibiting classifications. In doing so, it has applied the rational basis test to scrutinize statutes that prohibit non-citizens from public employment. Originally, the exception was aimed only at those positions involving the "execution of broad public policy" and that are integral to the democratic process. However, it seems that the Court has strayed from that rationale in holding that police officers, teachers, and even probation officers qualify for the exception. The Court in this case argues that a state may rationally conclude that teachers are integral to the formation of civic values in their students.

Plyler v. Doe

(*School Superintendent*) v. (*Undocumented Alien Children*)
457 U.S. 202, 102 S.Ct. 2382 (1982)

SUPREME COURT SUBJECTS A STATE'S CLASSIFICATION OF UNDOCUMENTED ALIENS TO A HEIGHTENED FORM OF THE RATIONAL-BASIS TEST

■ **INSTANT FACTS** Several undocumented alien children filed an equal protection challenge, aiming to invalidate a state law which denied them free public education.

■ **BLACK LETTER RULE** If a state chooses to deny the benefit of free public education to undocumented alien children it must do so in order to further some substantial state interest.

■ **PROCEDURAL BASIS**

Not provided.

■ **FACTS**

The State of Texas (D) had enacted a statute which prohibited children who resided in the State (D) as undocumented aliens from enrolling in the state's public schools. The law was challenged on the ground that, in violation of the Equal Protection Clause, it worked a discrimination against these children.

■ **ISSUE**

May a state deny to undocumented school-age children the free public education that it provides to children who are citizens of the United States or legally admitted citizens?

■ **DECISION AND RATIONALE**

(Brennan, J.) No. If a state chooses to deny the benefit of free public education to undocumented alien children it must do so in order to further some substantial state interest. First, we reject Texas' (D) argument that the Fourteenth Amendment is not applicable in this case because undocumented aliens are not "person[s] within its jurisdiction," as that phrase is employed in the Equal Protection Clause. As we have previously held, aliens are certainly "persons," and it is clear that the framers of the Fourteenth Amendment intended to use the phrase "within the jurisdiction" to mean within the borders of. Undocumented aliens may not be treated as a "suspect class" because their illegal presence is not Constitutionally irrelevant. Nor is education a fundamental right being denied to these children. Therefore, no compelling necessity is required to justify a classification based on undocumented status. However, this case presents some very important issues. Lax enforcement of our immigration laws has created a "shadow population" of illegal immigrants. This population is encouraged to remain as a source of cheap labor, but its members are denied the benefits made available to other citizens. While controlling illegal immigration is a legitimate state interest, in this particular case, we have a state law which is aimed at withholding benefits from a class of persons who have no control over their unlawful conduct—children who are illegally brought to this country by their parents. Thus, it is difficult to conceive a rational justification for withholding from them the benefits of a free education. Although clearly not a Constitutional or fundamental "right," public education is clearly something more than a mere "benefit." Public education is vital to the maintenance of a democratic political system, as it

Plyler v. Doe (Continued)

provides children with the tools necessary to become adult citizens. The denial of public education to these children also acts an unreasonable obstacle to advancement on the basis of individual merit—one of the fundamental goals underlying the Equal Protection Clause. The denial of a basic education will handicap these children for the remainder of their lives. We disagree with the fact that their mere status of being an illegal alien provides the state with a rational basis upon which to deny public education to these children. The fact is that these children may never be deported, and it is fully within the power of Congress to offer them citizenship at some point in the future. There is no discernable national policy supporting the denial of public education to the children of undocumented aliens. We also reject Texas' (D) argument that a concern for the preservation of resources justifies the denial of public education. There is nothing in the record which supports either the view that illegal immigrants pose a significant burden on the State's (D) coiffeurs or that claim that the exclusion of undocumented aliens is likely to improve the overall quality of education in the State.

■ **DISSENT**

(Burger, C.J.) I agree that the decision to deny these children an education is wrong. However, the members of this Court are not "Platonic Guardians" with the authority to strike down legislation they find disagreeable. Noble motives aside, the decisions of this Court must be based in the Constitution. The majority acknowledges that these children are neither a suspect class nor is public education a fundamental right. Thus, the sole question is whether a concern for state resources provides a legitimate reason to differentiate between those in this country lawfully and undocumented aliens. Yet, with its decision today, the Court has created a quasi-suspect class and quasi-fundamental-rights analysis. The fact remains that Texas (D) has a legitimate interest in conserving its resources and a classification aimed at excluding those within its borders illegally is not irrational.

Analysis:

As pointed out by the dissent, the Court in this case undertakes a constitutional analysis heretofore unknown. The majority refuses to hold that undocumented aliens, because of their status as illegal immigrants, are a suspect class entitled to heightened scrutiny. The majority also holds that public education is not a fundamental right, the denial of which must be scrutinized closely. The Court states that Texas (D) may justify the denial of public education to undocumented children only upon a showing of a *substantial* state interest. Clearly, the word substantial implies something more than the *legitimate* state interest of the rational basis test. In the majority's view, the fact that undocumented children have no control over their presence, combined with the fundamental importance education plays in our society, were enough to require Texas (D) to furnish some substantial justification for the classification.

■ **CASE VOCABULARY**

PLATONIC GUARDIANS: A type of "philosopher king" whose mission to guard the ideal of Plato's utopian Republic.

Massachusetts Board of Retirement v. Murgia

(State Agency) v. (50-Year Old Police Officer)
427 U.S. 307, 96 S.Ct. 2562 (1976)

SUPREME COURT HOLDS THAT RATIONAL BASIS REVIEW SHOULD BE USED TO SCRUTINIZE AGE DISCRIMINATION

■ **INSTANT FACTS** A police officer forced into retirement sought to challenge a state law requiring uniformed state police officers to retire at the age of 50 on the grounds that it violated equal protection.

■ **BLACK LETTER RULE** Classifications based on age need only be rationally related to a legitimate state purpose.

■ **PROCEDURAL BASIS**

Not Provided.

■ **FACTS**

The state of Massachusetts (D) enacted a statute providing that uniformed state police officers "shall be retired...upon [their] attaining age fifty." When Robert Murgia (P), a state police officer, turned 50, the Massachusetts Board of Retirement (D) forcibly retired him. Murgia (P) then filed an equal protection claim challenging his forced retirement.

■ **ISSUE**

May a state force its police officers to retire at a certain age?

■ **DECISION AND RATIONALE**

(Per Curiam) Yes. Classifications based on age need only be rationally related to a legitimate state purpose. Those over the age of 50 are not a suspect class, nor is employment as a police officer a fundamental right. Under the rational-basis analysis, it is clear that the law is constitutional. By requiring retirement at age 50, the legislature is seeking to ensure that those charged with protecting the public are physically prepared to perform their job. Clearly, the law is rationally related to a legitimate interest.

■ **DISSENT**

(Marshall, J.) Contrary to language in our prior decisions, the court holds that the right to work is not a fundamental right under the Equal Protection Clause. While agreeing that the elderly have suffered discrimination in the country, the Court refuses to designate them a suspect class. More so than young people, the elderly suffer greatly from the deprivation of a job. They often find it difficult to obtain work thereafter. Furthermore, it takes away the right to contribute to society. The elderly have been subjected to repeated and arbitrary discrimination in employment and they are a class who merits judicial attention. While the state has a legitimate, indeed compelling, interest at stake, the means chosen are inadequate to justify the forced retirement of those who have obtained the age of 50. The state already undertakes to test the physical fitness of its officers. This is a perfectly capable means of determining who is, and who is not, capable of protecting the public.

Massachusetts Board of Retirement v. Murgia (Continued)

Analysis:

The Court in this case refuses to apply any level of heightened scrutiny to classifications drawn on the basis of age. In fact, the case serves as an example of the most deferential form of the rational basis test. The Court merely accepts that there is a rationale connection between ensuring the physical fitness of police officers and forcing their retirement at age 50. As is proper under the rational-basis test, no analysis is undertaken to determine whether, indeed, there is some correlation between attaining the age of 50 and a physical deterioration. Of course, the impact of this case is somewhat softened by federal legislation prohibiting discrimination on the basis of age in a number of areas, including employment.

CHAPTER EIGHT

Fundamental Rights Under Due Process and Equal Protection

Zablocki v. Redhail

Instant Facts: A Wisconsin man challenged a state statute disallowing persons who are in arrears on child support payments the opportunity to obtain a marriage license and enter into a valid marriage.

Black Letter Rule: When a statutory classification significantly interferes with the exercise of a fundamental right such as the right to marry, it cannot be upheld unless it is supported by sufficiently important state interests and is closely tailored to effectuate only those interests.

Michael H. v. Gerald D.

Instant Facts: A man who used a blood test to establish that he was the natural father of a certain child challenged a state court's denial of his request for parental and visitation rights, which denial was based on a California presumption that a child born to a married woman living with her husband is the child of that marriage.

Black Letter Rule: In order to receive the protections of substantive due process under the Fourteenth Amendment, an asserted liberty interest must be both a fundamental interest and one that has traditionally been protected by American society.

Moore v. City of East Cleveland

Instant Facts: A grandmother filed an appeal after she was sentenced to five days in jail for allowing two of her grandsons to live with her in her home, which living arrangement violated a city ordinance.

Black Letter Rule: The right of both immediate and extended family members to live together is a fundamental right protected by principles of substantive due process.

Meyer v. Nebraska

Instant Facts: A school teacher was prosecuted for teaching reading to a young student in German, in contravention of a state law which prohibited teaching certain subjects in a language other than English.

Black Letter Rule: The Constitution provides that the government may not, under the guise of protecting the public interest, interfere with a person's liberty by legislative action that is arbitrary or without reasonable relation to some legitimate governmental purpose.

Troxel v. Granville

Instant Facts: Two children's paternal grandparents filed suit seeking visitation rights when the children's mother told the grandparents' that she was going to limit their access to the children.

Black Letter Rule: Parents have a fundamental right to make decisions concerning the care and control of their children, and any state interference with that right will be closely scrutinized by the courts.

Skinner v. Oklahoma

Instant Facts: Objections arose when the State of Oklahoma (P) attempted to use its Habitual Criminal Sterilization Act to authorize the sterilization of an individual who had thrice been convicted of theft-related felonies (one of which involved the theft of chickens).

Black Letter Rule: Any law requiring the sterilization of certain persons is reviewed with strict scrutiny lest invidious discriminations are made in violation of the constitutional guaranty of equal protection.

Griswold v. Connecticut

Instant Facts: A birth control counselor was convicted of a misdemeanor for providing advice about contraception to married couples in violation of a Connecticut statute.

Black Letter Rule: There exists a constitutional right of privacy, implied from the penumbras of the Bill of Rights, that cannot be invaded by government action absent a showing that the government action at issue is necessary to accomplish a compelling governmental interest.

Eisenstadt v. Baird

Instant Facts: A lecturer at Boston University was arrested and charged with a violation of a Massachusetts criminal statute for exhibiting contraceptives during a lecture and giving certain contraceptives to one attendee following the completion of the lecture.

Black Letter Rule: If the right of privacy means anything, it is the right of the individual, married or single, to be free from unwarranted governmental intrusion into matters so fundamentally affecting a person as the decision whether to carry or conceive a child.

Roe v. Wade

Instant Facts: A pregnant woman challenged a Texas criminal abortion law that permitted abortion only when a continuation of the pregnancy would place the life of the mother in jeopardy.

Black Letter Rule: Criminal abortion statutes that only permit the termination of pregnancy when the life of the mother is in danger are unconstitutional.

Planned Parenthood v. Casey

Instant Facts: A family planning clinic challenged the constitutionality of a Pennsylvania law placing certain restrictions on a woman's right to obtain an abortion.

Black Letter Rule: The state can regulate and place restrictions on abortion so long as those regulations do not impose an undue burden on the woman's ability to make the abortion decision; when an undue burden results, the regulations are unconstitutional.

Gonzales v. Carhart

Instant Facts: Carhart (P) challenged the federal Partial–Birth Abortion Ban Act of 2003 as facially unconstitutional.

Black Letter Rule: Laws that place restrictions on abortion that express respect for the life of the unborn are valid, provided the laws do not unduly burden a woman's right to obtain an abortion.

Maher v. Roe

Instant Facts: A Connecticut regulation which allowed the State to fund childbirths but not abortions was challenged in federal court.

Black Letter Rule: The Constitution does not require the government to subsidize abortions, even when it chooses to subsidize childbirth.

Planned Parenthood v. Casey

Instant Facts: A constitutional challenge was brought against a Pennsylvania abortion law that contained a spousal notification requirement.

Black Letter Rule: Spousal notification requirements in abortion laws are unconstitutional because they place an undue burden upon a woman's ability to obtain an abortion.

Bellotti v. Baird

Instant Facts: A Massachusetts law which regulated the access of minors to abortions was challenged as being unconstitutional.

Black Letter Rule: If the State chooses to require a pregnant minor to obtain one or both parents' consent to an abortion, it also must provide an alternative procedure whereby authorization for the abortion can be obtained without parental consent.

Cruzan v. Director, Missouri Department of Health

Instant Facts: The parents of a patient who had long been in a vegetative state sought court permission to have their daughter's life terminated when the hospital in which their daughter was staying refused to discontinue life-saving treatment without a court order.

Black Letter Rule: When a guardian seeks to discontinue lifesaving nutrition and hydration or other lifesaving medical treatment for an incompetent person, the State may require that the guardian show by clear and convincing evidence that the person would have wanted such a termination of her life.

Washington v. Glucksberg

Instant Facts: A group of doctors challenged the constitutionality of a Washington ban on physician assisted suicide.

Black Letter Rule: The Fourteenth Amendments does not create a constitutionally protected right to participate in physician-assisted suicide; nor does it prohibit states from making it a crime to assist another person in committing suicide.

Lawrence v. Texas

Instant Facts: Lawrence (D) was convicted of deviate sexual intercourse with another man in violation of a state statute.

Black Letter Rule: State laws criminalizing homosexual relations violate substantive due process.

Whalen v. Roe

Instant Facts: A lawsuit challenged the right of the New York Department of Health to record and store in a central computer certain information related to the issuance of medical prescriptions by New York physicians.

Black Letter Rule: The disclosure of private medical information to medical personnel, insurance companies, and public health agencies does not per se amount to an impermissible and unconstitutional invasion of privacy.

Saenz v. Roe

Instant Facts: A lawsuit challenged a California law which limited the welfare benefits of new California residents to that amount which they would have received in the state they most recently moved from.

Black Letter Rule: The constitutionally-protected right to travel embraces the citizen's right to be treated equally in her new State of residence.

Harper v. Virginia State Board of Elections

Instant Facts: A dispute arose over a Virginia poll tax which required residents to pay $1.50 in order to vote in state elections.

Black Letter Rule: A State violates the Equal Protection Clause whenever it makes the payment of a fee a precondition to voting.

Kramer v. Union Free School District

Instant Facts: A citizen challenged a New York law which precluded certain persons from voting in school district elections.

Black Letter Rule: Laws which limit the ability of certain persons to vote in various governmental elections are unconstitutional unless they are narrowly tailored and necessary to achieve a compelling state interest.

Ball v. James

Instant Facts: A group of registered voters living within the geographic boundaries of a water district filed suit challenging a district voting scheme which limited their ability to vote in district elections.

Black Letter Rule: In certain situations, states may limit the right to vote in a particular election to only those voters who are primarily affected by or have a special interest in the outcome of the election.

Crawford v. Marion County Election Board

Instant Facts: Indiana (D) enacted a statute that required voters to show a picture ID at the polls, and Crawford (P) claimed the statute was an unconstitutional burden on voting rights.

Black Letter Rule: Evenhanded restrictions on the right to vote that are related to voter qualifications and that protect the integrity and reliability of the electoral process are valid.

Reynolds v. Sims

Instant Facts: A constitutional challenge was levied against Alabama's legislative districting scheme on the ground that it violated equal protection by not apportioning its districts according to population and thereby resulted in less-populated districts having more representation in the state legislature than more populous districts.

Black Letter Rule: The Equal Protection Clause requires that all voters be awarded the opportunity for equal participation in the election of state legislators.

Bush v. Gore

Instant Facts: Following the 2000 presidential election, the Florida Supreme Court ordered certain counties to manually count ballots for inclusion in the vote total.

Black Letter Rule: Once a state vests voting rights in its citizens, it must afford each person's vote equal treatment under the Equal Protection Clause.

Boddie v. Connecticut

Instant Facts: An indigent citizen challenged a Connecticut law which made the payment of a court fee a prerequisite to accessing the judicial system for the purpose of obtaining a divorce.

Black Letter Rule: The Due Process Clause prohibits the States from denying individuals seeking dissolution of their marriages access to the courts based solely on the person's inability to pay court fees.

United States v. Kras

Instant Facts: An indigent person challenged a federal law which required him to pay a filing fee in order to file for bankruptcy.

Black Letter Rule: The principle set forth in Boddie that the government may not make the payment of a court fee a prerequisite to accessing the courts for the purpose of obtaining a divorce does not apply in cases involving the payment of fees as a prerequisite to initiating no-asset bankruptcy proceedings.

M.L.B. v. S.L.J.

Instant Facts: A mother whose parental rights were terminated challenged a Mississippi requirement that she pay for trial transcripts before her appeal would be permitted to proceed past the initial stages.

Black Letter Rule: States may not deny appellate review of a decision finding a biological parent to be unfit simply because of the parent's inability to pay for the appeal.

Lewis v. Casey

Instant Facts: A group of Arizona prisoners filed a class action lawsuit seeking remediation for their perceived inability to access the court system.

Black Letter Rule: A subpar prison law library or legal assistance program does not per se place an unconstitutional limitation on a prisoner's right of access to the courts.

San Antonio Independent School District v. Rodriguez

Instant Facts: A class of lower-income persons challenged Texas' system for financing public education.

Black Letter Rule: The right to acquire a public education is not a constitutionally guaranteed fundamental right; therefore, laws affecting that right are subject only to rational basis scrutiny.

Daniels v. Williams

Instant Facts: A state prisoner who slipped and fell on a pillow filed an equal protection-based lawsuit against the correctional officer who had negligently left the pillow on the ground.

Black Letter Rule: The negligent act of a government official which causes unintended loss or injury to life, liberty, or property, while actionable at law, does not generally implicate the Due Process Clause.

County of Sacramento v. Lewis

Instant Facts: A lawsuit alleging a violation of due process was filed when a teenager was killed as a result of a high-speed chase with the police.

Black Letter Rule: In emergency situations involving law enforcement officials, negligence and recklessness will not create a constitutional deprivation; only conduct that "shocks the conscience" can create a due process deprivation, and to reach that level, there must be evidence of intent to harm.

DeShaney v. Winnebago County Department of Social Services

Instant Facts: An abused child and his mother filed suit against Winnebago County after it was discovered that a father who had been repeatedly beating his child was permitted by the County Department of Social Services to retain custody of the child despite warnings from hospitals and others that abuse was taking place.

Black Letter Rule: The Due Process Clause protects against deprivations of life, liberty, and property by arbitrary government action; nowhere does the language of the Clause require the State to protect the life, liberty, and property of its citizens against invasions by private actors.

Town of Castle Rock v. Gonzales

Instant Facts: Castle Rock (D) police officers did not enforce a restraining order against Gonzales's (P) estranged husband, and he murdered her three children.

Black Letter Rule: An individual who has obtained a restraining order against another does not have a constitutionally protected property interest in the enforcement of that order when there is probable cause to believe it was violated.

Goldberg v. Kelly

Instant Facts: A group of citizens facing the potential loss of financial aid without notice or a hearing filed suit seeking to have those procedures be provided.

Black Letter Rule: The extent to which procedural due process must be afforded in a particular situation is influenced by the extent of the loss suffered, and depends on whether the aggrieved party's interest in avoiding that loss outweighs the governmental interest in summary adjudication.

Board of Regents v. Roth

Instant Facts: A government employee who had signed a one-year employment contract filed suit when his employer chose not to rehire him following the completion of the one year.

Black Letter Rule: A person is not deprived of liberty or property in violation of the Fourteenth Amendment when he is not hired or rehired for a government job but remains free to seek other employment.

Goss v. Lopez

Instant Facts: A group of high school students filed suit against their respective administrators for suspending them without the opportunity for a hearing on the issue.

Black Letter Rule: Having chosen to extend the right to an education to certain persons, a State cannot withdraw that right from a single person on grounds of misconduct absent fundamentally fair procedures to determine whether the misconduct has occurred.

Paul v. Davis

Instant Facts: A suspected shoplifter filed suit when his face appeared on a law enforcement flier bearing the words "Active Shoplifters" and the mug shots of various persons known or believed to be shoplifters.

Black Letter Rule: The Fourteenth Amendment's guarantee against deprivations of liberty or property without due process does not apply to governmental actions which have the effect of harming a persons' reputation.

Mathews v. Eldridge

Instant Facts: A state disability benefit recipient filed suit when the state decided to stop providing him with the benefits he had been receiving.

Black Letter Rule: An identification of the specific dictates of due process generally requires consideration of three distinct factors: (1) the private interest that will be affected by the official action; (2) the risk of an erroneous deprivation of such interest through the procedures used, and the probable value, if any, of additional or substitute procedural safeguards; and (3) the Government's interest, including the function involved and the fiscal and administrative burdens that the additional or substitute procedural requirement would entail.

Zablocki v. Redhail
(*Milwaukee County Clerk*) v. (*Marriage License Applicant*)
434 U.S. 374, 98 S.Ct. 673 (1978)

THE RIGHT TO MARRY IS A FUNDAMENTAL RIGHT

■ **INSTANT FACTS** A Wisconsin man challenged a state statute disallowing persons who are in arrears on child support payments the opportunity to obtain a marriage license and enter into a valid marriage.

■ **BLACK LETTER RULE** When a statutory classification significantly interferes with the exercise of a fundamental right such as the right to marry, it cannot be upheld unless it is supported by sufficiently important state interests and is closely tailored to effectuate only those interests.

■ **PROCEDURAL BASIS**
Not stated.

■ **FACTS**
In the early 1970's, Wisconsin had in effect a statute, § 245.10, which provided that any person with child support obligations had to get the permission of a court to marry. The statute further provided that persons in arrears on child support payments would not be given judicial permission to obtain marriage licenses or enter into valid marriages. Specifically, the statute required that such persons could not be granted permission to marry unless proof of compliance with the support obligation was provided and the person was able to demonstrate that the children covered by the support order "are not then and are not likely thereafter to become public charges." On September 27, 1974, Redhail (P) applied for a marriage license in Milwaukee County, but because he was in arrears on child support owed to a child born out of wedlock two years earlier, the County Clerk (D) denied Redhail's (P) application. Redhail (P) was $3,700 behind on his payments and the child was a public charge in that she was receiving state assistance. Redhail (P) filed suit against the Clerk (D) following the denial of his application.

■ **ISSUE**
Can a state place a restriction on marriage such that persons who owe child support and are not current in their payments cannot obtain marriage licenses and therefore cannot marry?

■ **DECISION AND RATIONALE**
(Marshall, J.) No. In evaluating the constitutionality of § 245.10 under the Equal Protection Clause, we must first look to the nature of the classification and the individual interests affected thereby to determine what level of justification must be presented in support of the statute. Because our past decisions have made it clear that the right to marry is of fundamental importance, and since the classification at issue here significantly interferes with the exercise of that right, we believe that a "critical examination" of the classification and the State's interests in support of that classification must occur. The seminal case in the area of the right to marry is *Loving v. Virginia,* which holds that the right to marry is of fundamental importance. Other decisions such as *Griswold v. Connecticut* establish that the right to marry is part of the fundamental "right of privacy" implicit in the Due Process Clause. It is not surprising that the decision to marry has been determined to be of equal importance to decisions regarding procreation, childbirth, child rearing, and familial relationships. And as the facts of this case show, it would make no sense to recognize a right of privacy with respect to these other matters of

family life, yet not recognize that right with respect to the decision to enter the relationship which forms the basis of the family. In reaching this decision we are not suggesting that every state regulation that affects the right to marry is subject to rigorous scrutiny. To the contrary, reasonable regulations that do not significantly interfere with the decision to marry may legitimately be imposed. The statutory classification at issue here, however, interferes both directly and substantially with the right to marry because under the statute people like Redhail (P) may never be able to obtain the necessary court order because they either lack the financial means to meet their obligations or they cannot prove that their children will not become public charges. Such persons are absolutely prevented from marrying. And even those who can meet the statute's requirements suffer a serious intrusion into their freedom of choice in an area in which we have held such freedom to be fundamental. When a statutory classification significantly interferes with the exercise of a fundamental right, it cannot be upheld unless it is supported by sufficiently important state interests and is narrowly tailored to effectuate only those interests. Zablocki (D) asserts that two interests are served by the statute: (1) the requirement that a person get court permission to marry provides the State with an opportunity to counsel the person as to the necessity of fulfilling support obligations; and (2) the welfare of certain children will be protected. These are legitimate and substantial interests. However, the means chosen to effectuate these interests unnecessarily impinges on the right to marry. As originally drafted, the statute was merely intended to establish a method of giving persons with pending child support obligations some degree of counseling before they entered into new marriages and incurred additional support obligations. The statute as enacted, however, does not require any counseling and therefore cannot be justified as a means for ensuring that the desired persons get counseling. The "collection device" rationale similarly does not justify the statute's broad infringement of the right to marry. In some cases the statute merely prevents a person from marrying and does so without delivering any money to the person's prior children. More importantly, the State already has numerous other means for collecting support obligations (wage assignments, contempt proceedings, criminal penalties, etc.) that do not infringe upon the right to marry. Finally, there is some thought that § 245.10 protects the ability of marriage applicants to meet existing support obligations by preventing them from incurring new ones. But the challenged provision is grossly over and underinclusive in this respect. It is underinclusive in that it does not limit the incursion of new financial commitments other than those arising out of a new marriage, and overinclusive in that it is always possible that the marriage will increase a person's financial situation and allow for improved payment of past obligations. In sum, the statutory classification created by § 245.10 cannot be justified by the interests advanced in support of it, and is therefore unconstitutional.

■ CONCURRENCE

(Stewart, J.) The statute does not violate the guarantees of the Equal Protection Clause. The Equal Protection Clause does not deal with substantive rights, but with invidiously discriminatory classifications. The issue in this case is not one of discriminatory classifications, but of unwarranted encroachment on the constitutionally protected freedom to marry. The Wisconsin statute is unconstitutional because it goes beyond the bounds of permissible state regulation of marriage and invades the sphere of liberty protected by the Due Process Clause. The State is certainly free to place restrictions on people's ability to marry. However, as it does so, there are limits to which the State must adhere. This law goes beyond those limits. The State has legitimate interests in collecting delinquent support payments, and as applied to those who can afford to meet the statute's financial requirements, the law is a superior method of advancing that objective. However, some simply cannot afford to meet the statute's financial requirements, and to deny these people permission to marry penalizes them for their financial status. Insofar as the law applies to indigents, it is an irrational means of achieving these objectives.

■ DISSENT

(Rehnquist, J.) The right to marry is not a "fundamental right" that triggers strict scrutiny. I think that the proper level of scrutiny under the Equal Protection Clause and the Due Process Clause is rational basis scrutiny. Under that level of scrutiny, the statute, which seeks to assure that parents provide for their children, is a permissible exercise of state power.

Analysis:

Zablocki v. Redhail stands for the proposition that the right to marry is a fundamental right, and, as such, government regulations that directly and substantially interfere with that right will be subjected to heightened scrutiny under the Equal Protection Clause. However, as the opinion makes clear, not all regulations that affect the right to marry will be subjected to such a rigorous scrutiny; only those that impose a direct and substantial interference with the right are reviewed with that degree of care. For example, a law that prohibits siblings from marrying one another will not be subject to an increased level of scrutiny as it does not directly and substantially interfere with the right of any persons to marry. It simply interferes with the right of certain people to marry each other. By holding that not all regulations are subject to strict scrutiny, *Zablocki* leaves the issue of marriage and equal protection not fully resolved as future courts will have to decide which regulations constitute a direct and substantial restraint on marriage and which do not.

■ CASE VOCABULARY

ENUMERATED RIGHTS: Rights specifically listed or granted to the people in the text of the Constitution.

FUNDAMENTAL RIGHT: A constitutional right deemed so important and fundamental to life and liberty that a substantial infringement of that right is reviewed with strict scrutiny.

INVIDIOUSLY DISCRIMINATORY CLASSIFICATION: An offensive or otherwise objectionable discrimination based on some sort of classification (gender, race, etc.).

RATIONAL BASIS SCRUTINY: A method of scrutinizing the government interference of certain rights under which the means employed to effect the purpose of the infringement must rationally or reasonably be related to a legitimate end.

STRICT SCRUTINY: A method of scrutinizing the government interference of certain rights under which the means employed to effect the purpose of the infringement must be necessary to the achievement of a compelling government interest.

SUBSTANTIVE DUE PROCESS: A principle of constitutional law which requires that if the government wishes to interfere with a constitutional right, it must have and be able to demonstrate a purpose sufficient to justify interference with that right.

Michael H. v. Gerald D.

(Natural Father) v. (Father Listed on Birth Certificate)
491 U.S. 110, 109 S.Ct. 2333 (1989)

TO RECEIVE PROTECTION UNDER THE DUE PROCESS CLAUSE AN ASSERTED LIBERTY INTEREST MUST BE ROOTED IN HISTORY AND TRADITION

■ **INSTANT FACTS** A man who used a blood test to establish that he was the natural father of a certain child challenged a state court's denial of his request for parental and visitation rights, which denial was based on a California presumption that a child born to a married woman living with her husband is the child of that marriage.

■ **BLACK LETTER RULE** In order to receive the protections of substantive due process under the Fourteenth Amendment, an asserted liberty interest must be both a fundamental interest and one that has traditionally been protected by American society.

■ **PROCEDURAL BASIS**

Appeal to the United States Supreme Court of a California state court decision denying a natural father parental and visitation rights with respect to his child.

■ **FACTS**

Michael H. (P) brought a state court action in California to establish paternity and visitation rights with respect to a little girl, Victoria, who he claimed was his biological daughter through an adulterous affair with Carole D. Through a guardian ad litem, Victoria filed a similar suit. At the time the California courts were making decisions in the matter, Victoria was living with her mother and her mother's husband, Gerald D. (D), who was married to Carole at the time of Victoria's conception, was listed as Victoria's father on her birth certificate, and who had always claimed to be her father. Blood tests showed a 98.07% probability that Michael (P) was the natural father. California law, however, established a presumption that a child born to a married woman living with a husband who is neither impotent or sterile, is the child of that marriage. Relying on that presumption, which could only be rebutted in very limited circumstances, the California courts rejected Michael's (P) claims. He appealed to the United States Supreme Court, which granted certiorari and took up the case.

■ **ISSUE**

Are there any restrictions on what type of interests can receive constitutional protection under the Due Process Clause of the Fourteenth Amendment?

■ **DECISION AND RATIONALE**

(Scalia, J.) Yes. Michael (P) is seeking to be declared Victoria's father so that he can obtain visitation and possibly custody rights. In support of his claim, Michael (P) challenges the constitutionality of California's presumption of legitimacy. In so doing, he first asserts that principles of procedural due process prevent California from terminating his interest in his relationship with Victoria without affording him an opportunity to demonstrate his paternity. This claim derives from a misconception of the nature of the California statute. While it is phrased as a presumption, the statute is actually the implementation of a substantive rule of law which excludes inquiries into a child's paternity that would be destructive of familial integrity. Michael (P) also contends, as a matter of substantive due process, that because he has established a parental relationship with Victoria, protection of Gerald's (D) marriage to Carole is an

Michael H. v. Gerald D. (Continued)

insufficient state interest to support termination of that relationship. This argument is based on the assertion that Michael (P) has a constitutionally protected liberty interest in his relationship with Victoria. It is an established part of our constitutional jurisprudence that the term "liberty" in the Due Process Clause extends beyond freedom from physical restraints. In an attempt to guide interpretation of the Clause, we have insisted that to be a "liberty" interest, an interest must be both "fundamental" and one traditionally protected by society. This insistence that the asserted liberty interest be rooted in history and tradition is evident in our cases according constitutional protection to certain parental rights. Michael (P) reads the seminal case of *Stanley v. Illinois* and subsequent cases as establishing that biological fatherhood plus an established parental relationship creates a liberty interest. Such a reading, however, distorts the rationale of those cases as they rest not on such isolated factors, but upon the respect traditionally accorded to relationships within the unitary family. Thus, the legal issue in the present case is whether the relationship between persons in the situation of Michael (P) and Victoria has been treated as a protected family unit or has otherwise been given special protection in our legal tradition. It is impossible to find that it has, and, in fact, our traditions have protected the marital family against the type of claim that Michael (P) asserts. Michael (P) wishes to be declared Victoria's natural father and to be given parental prerogatives. What he must establish, therefore, is not that our society has traditionally allowed a natural father in his circumstances to establish paternity, but that it has traditionally accorded such a father parental rights (or at least has not traditionally denied them). Even if the law in all states had always been that anyone can challenge the marital presumption, that would not advance Michael's (P) claim. What counts is whether the states in fact award substantive parental rights to the natural father of a child born into an extant marital union that wishes to embrace the child.

We are not aware of any authority that has done so. This is not the stuff of which fundamental rights qualifying as liberty interests are made. Justice Brennan asserts that our decision "squashes" the liberty that consists of "the freedom not to conform." Such a position reflects the erroneous view that there is only one side to this controversy when in fact there is not. To provide protection to an adulterous natural father is to deny protection to a marital father, and vice versa. If Michael (P) has a "freedom not to conform" (whatever that means), Gerald (D) must equivalently have a "freedom to conform." Our disposition does not choose between these two freedoms, but leaves that to the people of California. Justice Brennan's approach chooses one of them as the constitutional imperative, and does so with no apparent basis other than the unconventional is to be preferred. Finally, with respect to Victoria's claims, we have never had occasion to decide whether a child has a liberty interest in maintaining a filial relationship. We need not do so here, however, because even assuming that such a right exists, Victoria's position fails as the claim that a state must recognize multiple fatherhood has no support in history or tradition. Affirmed.

■ DISSENT

(Brennan, J.) Five members of the Court refuse to foreclose the possibility that a person such as Michael H. (P) can have a constitutionally protected interest in a relationship with a child such as Victoria. The plurality would agree that the "liberty" that is protected by the Due Process Clause encompasses more than a freedom from bodily restraint. However, it fears that unless limitations are placed on that concept, judges will substitute their own preferences for those of elected officials. For this reason, the plurality seeks to make "tradition" a key limitation. What it fails to see, however, is that "tradition" has as elusive a definition as "liberty," and that there is much room for disagreement on when a tradition becomes firm enough to be relevant to a definition of liberty. Unfortunately, the plurality supplies no objective means by which one might make such determinations. Furthermore, it is ironic that an approach so dependant on tradition would reject clear precedent. In deciding as it does, the plurality acts as though common law legal treatises are the sole source for constitutional principles. Had we followed this approach in other cases, such as *Ingraham v. Wright* [upholding a right to not be subject to corporal punishment in school—an interest not traditionally protected by society], our results would have been vastly different. That we did not apply such a principle of tradition in these other cases shows the novelty of the plurality's interpretation. The plurality is also misguided as it ignores the good reasons for limiting the role of "tradition" in interpreting the Constitution's deliberately capacious language. The plurality ignores the fact that the original reasons for the conclusive presumption of paternity are out of place in a world in which blood tests can prove virtually beyond any doubt who sired a particular child, and therefore basically ignores the possibility that the world can change. In construing the Fourteenth Amendment to offer shelter only to those interests specifically protected by historical practice, moreover, the plurality ignores the fact that we are not an assimilative, homogeneous society, but a facilitative, pluralistic one in which we must be willing to abide someone else's unfamiliar or even repellant practice because the same tolerant impulse protects our own idiosyncrasies. Even if we can agree, therefore, that "family" and "parenthood" are part of the good life, it is absurd to assume that we can agree on the content of those terms and it is destructive to pretend that we do. in a community such as ours, "liberty" must include the freedom not to conform. The plurality today squashes this freedom by requiring specific approval from history before protecting anything in the name of liberty. In short, I cannot accept an interpretive method that does not recognize that times change and does not see that sometimes a rule outlives its foundations. On four prior occasion we have concluded that although an unwed father's biological link to his child does not, in and of itself, guarantee him a constitutional stake in his relationship with that child, such a link combined with a substantive parent-child relationship will do so. We have that here.

Analysis:

In an effort to limit the subjectivity of the Court's analysis of Justice Scalia tries to link substantive due process to history and tradition, granting a recognition of liberty to only those deeply-rooted rights that were historically granted special protection. Justice Scalia's approach, however, could not muster the full support of the Court. Even Justice O'Connor, who claimed to otherwise fully support the opinion, suggested that Justice Scalia's reasoning was not entirely consistent with the Court's past cases, and that it might not be useful in every future case. The dissent in *Michael H.* is more directly critical of Justice Scalia's standard. Justice Brennan emphasizes that what constitutes "tradition" is not always clear. Scalia's approach has also been criticized as offering too little protection for the rights of minorities, who have traditionally received no special protections from society. As it stands today, history and tradition are important considerations to which the Court will look in making substantive due process determinations.

■ CASE VOCABULARY

GUARDIAN AD LITEM: A legal guardian appointed to appear in court on behalf of a minor child.

Moore v. City of East Cleveland

(Family Matriarch) v. (City Government)
431 U.S. 494, 97 S.Ct. 1932 (1977)

THE GOVERNMENT HAS NO RIGHT TO DECIDE WHICH RELATIVES MAY LIVE TOGETHER AND WHICH MAY NOT

■ **INSTANT FACTS** A grandmother filed an appeal after she was sentenced to five days in jail for allowing two of her grandsons to live with her in her home, which living arrangement violated a city ordinance.

■ **BLACK LETTER RULE** The right of both immediate and extended family members to live together is a fundamental right protected by principles of substantive due process.

■ **PROCEDURAL BASIS**

Appeal to the United States Supreme Court of a woman's criminal conviction for violating a city ordinance by living with two of her grandsons at the same time.

■ **FACTS**

During the 1970's, the city of East Cleveland, Ohio, had in effect an ordinance which limited the occupancy of certain dwellings to members of a single family. More than just placing limits on occupancy, however, the ordinance also set forth a specific definition of "single family" and provided criminal penalties for anyone violating the single family dwelling ordinance. At the time, Inez Moore (D) lived within the boundaries of East Cleveland. Living with her were her son Dale Moore, and her grandsons Dale Moore Jr. and John Moore Jr. The grandsons were not brothers, but cousins. In 1973, the City of Cleveland (P) informed Inez (D) that she was living in violation of the ordinance as the group with which she was living did not fall within the statutory definition of "single family." Specifically, John Jr. was singled out as the illegal occupant of the home. When Inez (D) refused to evict her grandson, she was prosecuted, found guilty, and sentenced to a fine of $25 and five days in jail. Inez (D) appealed the conviction on grounds that the single family ordinance under which she was prosecuted was unconstitutional.

■ **ISSUE**

Is a municipal housing ordinance which limits occupancy of certain dwellings to members of a single family and then defines family as only a few categories of related individuals one which survives scrutiny under the Due Process Clause of the Fourteenth Amendment?

■ **DECISION AND RATIONALE**

(Powell, J.) No. The City (P) argues that our decision in *Village of Belle Terre v. Boraas* [upholding a limitation on the types of groups who could occupy a single family dwelling] requires us to uphold the ordinance in question. But the ordinance in question is very different from the one in *Belle Terre.* Specifically, the ordinance there—which we upheld because it promoted "family needs" and "family values"—affected only unrelated individuals, and allowed persons who were related by blood, adoption, or marriage to live together. The East Cleveland (P) ordinance, on the other hand, seeks to regulate the family itself, predetermining which family members may live together and which may not. Specifically, it makes a grandmother's choice to live with two grandsons a crime. When a city undertakes such an intrusive regulation of the family, the usual judicial deference to the legislature, which we applied in *Belle Terre,* is inappropriate. This Court has long recognized that freedom of personal choice in matters of marriage and family life is one of the liberties protected by the Due Process Clause. The family is not beyond regulation, but when the government intrudes on choices concerning family living arrangements, this Court must examine carefully the importance of the governmental interests advanced and the extent to which they are served by the challenged regulation. When thus examined, this ordinance cannot survive. The City (P) seeks to justify the ordinance as a means of preventing overcrowding, minimizing traffic and parking congestion, and avoiding an undue financial burden on East Cleveland's school system. Although these are legitimate goals, the ordinance serves them marginally at best. For example, the ordinance permits any family consisting only of husband, wife, and unmarried children to live together, even if the family has six licensed drivers, each with his or her own car. At the same time it forbids an adult brother and sister to share a household, even if both faithfully use public transportation. The City (P) further suggests that any constitutional right to live together as a family extends only to the nuclear family. But unless we dose our eyes to the basic reasons that certain rights associated with the family have been protected by the Fourteenth Amendment's Due Process Clause, we cannot avoid applying these precedents to the family choice involved in this case. Understanding those reasons requires careful attention to this Court's function under the Due Process Clause. There are risks when the judicial branch gives enhanced protection to certain substantive liberties without the guidance of the more specific provisions of the Bill of Rights. In this regard, there is reason for concern lest the only limits to such judicial intervention become the predilections of those who happen to be on the Court. History counsels caution and restraint, but it does not counsel abandonment, nor does it require cutting off any protection of family rights at the boundary of the nuclear family. Appropriate limits on substantive due process come from careful respect for the teachings of history and solid recognition of the basic values that underlie our society. Our decisions establish that the Constitution protects the sanctity of the family precisely because the institution of the family is deeply rooted in this Nation's history and tradition. Ours is by no means a tradition limited to respect for the bonds uniting the members of the nuclear family. The tradition of uncles, aunts, cousins, and grandparents sharing a household with parents and children has roots equally deserving of constitutional recognition. For whatever reason, it has been common for close relatives to draw together and participate in the duties and satisfactions of a common home. The choice of relatives in this degree of kinship to live together may not lightly be denied by the state. Moore's (D) conviction is reversed.

■ DISSENT

(Stewart, J.) The existence of ties of kinship in the present case does not elevate Moore's (D) claims of associational freedom and privacy to a level invoking constitutional protection. The ordinance does not impede anyone's choice to have children, and it does not dictate how children are to be raised. It also does not prevent parents and children from living together. The City (P) might have chosen a different definition of "family," but any definition would produce hardships in some cases without materially advancing the legislative purpose. Unless we are to use our power to interpret the Constitution as a general grant of authority to correct inequity wherever it surfaces, the fact that this ordinance causes hardship to Moore (D) is no reason to hold it unconstitutional. It is not for us to rewrite the ordinance, or to substitute our judgment for the discretion of the prosecutor who initiated the proceedings.

Analysis:

In addition to setting forth certain rules of law and the principle that a choice of family members to live together is a fundamental right, the Court's decision here is useful in that it demonstrates the process of substantive due process analysis. There are four general issues that need to be addressed when determining whether there has been a violation of constitutional rights such that the Court needs to step in. The first step is to determine whether the right that has allegedly been violated is a fundamental right. In this case, it was determined that the right to live with one's extended family is a fundamental right. The second step, then, is to determine whether the right was infringed upon. In *Moore* it is clear that the majority decided that the right at issue was infringed upon by the City's giving Moore the choice of either go to jail or evict one of her grandsons. An infringement having been found, the third step in fundamental rights analysis is to determine whether the government's action is justified by a constitutionally sufficient purpose. Also referred to as the "compelling interest test," it is clear that in this case the majority rejected the City's assertions that the law's alleged relief of traffic and school budgetary concerns was a compelling interest. Clearly these interests could be served by less-intrusive laws, meaning the government action in *Moore* was not justified by a constitutionally sufficient purpose. Finally, the fourth step in fundamental rights analysis involves a determination of whether the government action that infringes upon the claimant's rights is sufficiently related to that constitutionally sufficient purpose. In *Moore,* of course, this step is irrelevant as the East Cleveland ordinance was determined to not serve a constitutionally sufficient purpose.

■ CASE VOCABULARY

NUCLEAR FAMILY: A family that consists solely of a couple and their dependent children.

Meyer v. Nebraska

(School Teacher) v. (State of Nebraska)
262 U.S. 390, 43 S.Ct. 625 (1923)

THE CONSTITUTION PROTECTS A TEACHER'S RIGHT TO TEACH A FOREIGN LANGUAGE AND A PARENT'S RIGHT TO HAVE A CHILD LEARN THAT LANGUAGE

■ **INSTANT FACTS** A school teacher was prosecuted for teaching reading to a young student in German, in contravention of a state law which prohibited teaching certain subjects in a language other than English.

■ **BLACK LETTER RULE** The Constitution provides that the government may not, under the guise of protecting the public interest, interfere with a person's liberty by legislative action that is arbitrary or without reasonable relation to some legitimate governmental purpose.

■ **PROCEDURAL BASIS**

Appeal to the United States Supreme Court of a criminal conviction for teaching a student in a language other than English.

■ **FACTS**

In April of 1919, Nebraska (P) passed a criminal statute which prohibited school teachers from "teach[ing] any subject to any person in any language [other] than the English language." Teachers were also prohibited from teaching a foreign language as its own subject to children who had not yet completed the eighth grade. The statute further provided that any violation thereof was a misdemeanor punishable by a fine of not less than $25 and not more than $100, and by incarceration of up to thirty days in the county jail. Meyer (D), a teacher at the Zion Parochial School, was charged with a violation of the statute when he used German to teach the subject of reading to Raymond Parpart, a ten year-old child. Meyer (D) appealed his conviction to the United States Supreme Court.

■ **ISSUE**

Does the Constitution permit a state to prohibit the teaching of children in languages other than English?

■ **DECISION AND RATIONALE**

(McReynolds, J.) No. While this Court has not attempted to define with exactness the term "liberty" as used in the Fourteenth Amendment, certain things have been found to fall within the purview of that concept. In addition to the right to be free from physical restraint, liberty also encompasses the right to contract, to work, to learn, to marry, to establish a home and raise children, to worship as one desires, and generally to enjoy those privileges long recognized as essential to the pursuit of happiness. The Constitution provides that the government may not, under the guise of protecting the public interest, interfere with a person's liberty by legislative action that is arbitrary or without reasonable relation to some legitimate governmental purpose. Furthermore, a determination by the Legislature of what constitutes a proper exercise of police power is subject to supervision by the courts. Mere knowledge of the German language is not harmful. Meyer taught German in school as a part of his occupation. His right to do so, and the right of parents to engage him to so instruct their children, is within the liberty of the Fourteenth Amendment. The legislature desires to foster a homogeneous people with certain American ideals, and there is nothing wrong with that desire. However, the means which they adopted exceeded the limitations that the Constitution places upon the State to exercise its police power and, in doing so, violated Meyer's (D) rights. Reversed.

Analysis:

Meyer, which was decided well before *Zablocki, Michael H.,* and *Moore*, is an important case because it lays the groundwork for the more recently decided family rights-related cases. Specifically, in *Meyer* the Supreme Court held that the Constitution does not permit government interference with a parent's right to make education-related decisions, such as a decision to have a child study a foreign language. That general acceptance of a parental right to make decisions regarding the upbringing of a child has expanded into other family-related areas. Even more important, however, is the fact that *Meyer* is one of the first cases to accept a very broad reading of the term "liberty." Specifically, Justice McReynolds writes that liberty "denotes not merely freedom from bodily restraint but also the right of the individual to contract, to engage in any of the common occupations of life, to acquire useful knowledge, to marry, establish a home and bring up children, to worship God according to the dictates of his own conscience, and generally to enjoy these privileges long recognized at common law as essential to the orderly pursuit of happiness by free men." This broad definition of the constitutional term "liberty" has been seized upon by modem Courts that have sought to expand the term to include other unenumerated rights.

Troxel v. Granville

(Paternal Grandparents) v. *(Mother)*
530 U.S. 57, 120 S.Ct. 2054 (2000)

A FIT PARENT'S DECISION REGARDING THE RAISING OF A CHILD SHOULD BE ACCORDED A PRESUMPTION OF VALIDITY AND BE GIVEN SOME WEIGHT WHEN THAT DECISION IS SUBJECTED TO JUDICIAL REVIEW

■ **INSTANT FACTS** Two children's paternal grandparents filed suit seeking visitation rights when the children's mother told the grandparents' that she was going to limit their access to the children.

■ **BLACK LETTER RULE** Parents have a fundamental right to make decisions concerning the care and control of their children, and any state interference with that right will be closely scrutinized by the courts.

■ **PROCEDURAL BASIS**

Appeal to the United States Supreme Court of a Washington Supreme Court decision holding unconstitutional a Washington statute which, by its broad language, allowed grandparents to obtain court-ordered visitation with grandchildren.

■ **FACTS**

In June 1991, Brad Troxel and Tommie Granville (D) ended a relationship that had produced two children—Isabelle and Natalie. Until May of 1993, when he committed suicide, Brad regularly took the children to see his parents, Jenifer and Gary Troxel (P). Shortly after Brad's death, however, Tommie (D) told the Troxels (P) that their access to the girls would be limited to one short visit per month. In December of 1993, the Troxels (P) filed suit, seeking visitation rights with the children. The Troxels' (P) claim for visitation rights was based on Washington Revised Code § 26.10.160(3), which permitted "any person" to petition for visitation rights "at any time," and allowed the petitioned court to grant such visitation so long as it was determined to be in the best interest of the child.

■ **ISSUE**

Is a statute which allows any person to petition a court for visitation rights with a child and then gives the petitioned court wholesale authority to decide the issue without giving any weight to the position of the child's parents constitutional?

■ **DECISION AND RATIONALE**

(O'Connor, J.) No. The liberty interest at issue in this case—the interest of parents in the care, custody, and control of their children—is one of the oldest of the fundamental liberty interests recognized by this Court. The Washington statute, as applied in this case, unconstitutionally infringes on that fundamental parental right. Section 26.10.160(3) is breathtakingly broad, allowing "any person" to petition the court for visitation "at any time," and giving the court the power to grant such visitation any time it determines that such visitation "may serve the best interest of the child." The language effectively permits any third party seeking visitation to subject any decision by a parent concerning visitation to state court review. The law contains no requirement that a court accord the parents' decision any presumption of validity or any weight. Instead, the Washington statute places the best-interest determination solely in the hands of the judge. Should the judge disagree with the parents' decision, the judge's view prevails. Thus, in practical effect, a court can disregard and overturn a fit custodial parent's decision concerning visitation whenever a third party affected by that decision files a visitation petition. The Superior Court's order granting visitation in this case was not founded on any special factors that might justify the State's interference with Granville's (D) fundamental right to make decisions regarding her daughters. This fact, along with other factors, compels our conclusion that § 26.10.160(3), as applied, violates the Due Process Clause. First, there has been no allegation that Granville (D) is an unfit parent. This is important because there is a presumption that fit parents act in their children's best interest. So long as a parent adequately cares for his or her children, there will generally be no reason for the State to inject itself into familial decisions. Second, when the court intervened in this case it gave no special weight to Granville's (D) determination of what was in her daughters' best interest. If a fit parent's decision of the kind at issue here becomes subject to judicial review, the court must accord at least some special weight to the parent's own determination. Finally, it is important to note that Granville (D) did not attempt to completely cut off visitation, but simply attempted to limit it to less than what the Troxels (P) wanted. When all of these things are considered, it becomes apparent that the visitation order issued in this case was an unconstitutional infringement on Granville's (D) fundamental right to make decisions concerning the care and control of her children. Accordingly, we hold that § 26.10.160(3), as applied in this case, is unconstitutional. It should be noted that our decision does not define the precise scope of the parental due process right in the visitation context. Nor do we consider the issue of whether the Due Process Clause requires all non-parental visitation statutes to include a showing of harm or potential harm to the child as a condition precedent to granting visitation. In this respect, the constitutionality of any standard for awarding visitation turns on the specific manner in which the standard is applied. Affirmed.

■ CONCURRENCE

(Souter, J.) The Washington Supreme Court invalidated the statute in question based on the text of the statute alone, not on its application to a particular case. It's ruling rested on two independently sufficient grounds. The second of these grounds—the determination that the statute sweeps too broadly and is therefore unconstitutional as it authorizes "any person" at "any time" to petition for visitation rights subject only to a free-ranging best-interests-of-the-child standard—is adequate grounds to hold the statute unconstitutional. Consequently, there is no need to decide whether a showing of harm to the child is required to justify the entering of a disputed visitation order. Neither is it necessary for us to consider the precise scope of a parent's rights with regard to third party visitation of a child or to address the specific application of the statute by the trial court.

■ CONCURRENCE

(Thomas, J.) I agree that this Court's recognition of a fundamental right of parents to direct the upbringing of their children resolves this case. The opinions of the plurality, Justice Kennedy, and Justice Souter recognize such a right, but curiously none articulates the appropriate standard of review. I would apply strict scrutiny to infringements of fundamental rights, and because the State of Washington lacks even a legitimate governmental interest in this case, I would affirm the judgment below.

■ DISSENT

(Stevens, J.) The Court today wisely declines to endorse either the holding or the rationale of the Washington Supreme Court. In my opinion, the Court should never have even granted certiorari in this case. Given the problematic character of the trial court's decision and the uniqueness of the statute at issue, there was no need to review a state supreme court judgment that merely requires the legislature to draft a better statute. Having decided to address the issue, however, we should have at least addressed the federal questions presented and not danced around them.

■ DISSENT

(Scalia, J.) While it is entirely appropriate to argue in legislative chambers or in electoral campaigns that the state has no power to interfere with parents' authority over child rearing, I do not believe that the power which the Constitution confers upon me as a judge entitles me to deny legal effect to laws that infringe upon rights not enumerated in the Constitution. If we embrace this enumerated right, we will be ushering in a new regime of judicially and federally prescribed family law. I have no reason to believe that federal judges will be better at this than state legislatures; and state legislatures have the great advantages of doing harm in a more circumscribed area, of being able to correct their mistakes more quickly, and of being removable by the people.

■ DISSENT

(Kennedy, J.) The first flaw the Washington Supreme Court found in the statute is that it allows an award of visitation to a non-parent without a finding that harm to the child would result if visitation were withheld. In my view, this theory is too broad to be correct as it appears to contemplate that the best-interests-of-the-child standard may not be applied in any visitation case. I acknowledge the possibility that visitation cases arise where the best-interests-of-the-child standard would give insufficient protection to the parent's constitutional right to raise the child without undue intervention by the state; but it is quite a different matter to say that a harm-to-the-child-standard is required in every instance. Given the error of this conclusion that the best-interests-of-the-child standard is never appropriate in third-party visitation cases, the Washington court should have the first opportunity to reconsider the case. The judgment now under review should be vacated and remanded on the sole ground that the harm ruling that was so central to the Washington court's decision was error.

Analysis:

When the Court's decision in *Troxel* was first published, many people misconstrued the holding of the decision, taking it to mean that grandparents have no visitation rights. While the effect of the *Troxel* decision was to limit the Troxels' right to visit their grandchildren, its holding was something entirely different from a prohibition of grandparent visitation. Specifically, the central holding of *Troxel* is an affirmation of the holdings of prior cases such as *Meyer*, in which the Court determined that parents have a fundamental right to control the upbringing of their children. The problem with the Washington statute at issue in this case was not that it allowed grandparents to petition for visitation rights, but that it completely disregarded the fundamental right that parents have to make decisions regarding their children.

■ CASE VOCABULARY

BEST-INTERESTS-OF-THE-CHILD STANDARD: Standard often applied in children-related family law cases in which a court will make the decision which best furthers the needs and interests of the child involved in the case.

Skinner v. Oklahoma
(Habitual Criminal) v. (Attorney General of Oklahoma)
316 U.S. 535, 62 S.Ct. 1110 (1942)

LAWS WHICH CREATE CONSPICUOUSLY ARTIFICIAL CLASSIFICATIONS ARE UNCONSTITUTIONAL

■ **INSTANT FACTS** Objections arose when the State of Oklahoma (P) attempted to use its Habitual Criminal Sterilization Act to authorize the sterilization of an individual who had thrice been convicted of theft-related felonies (one of which involved the theft of chickens).

■ **BLACK LETTER RULE** Any law requiring the sterilization of certain persons is reviewed with strict scrutiny lest invidious discriminations are made in violation of the constitutional guaranty of equal protection.

■ PROCEDURAL BASIS
Appeal to the United States Supreme Court of an Oklahoma Supreme Court affirmation of a decision authorizing the sterilization of a habitual criminal offender.

■ FACTS
In 1935, Oklahoma (P) passed the Habitual Criminal Sterilization Act, which permitted the State to sterilize certain "habitual criminals," or criminals who had been convicted of at least three felonies involving moral turpitude and sentenced to a term of imprisonment on the third conviction. The Act made distinctions between which felonies applied and which did not. For example, grand theft and armed robbery were crimes for which a person could be sterilized while embezzlement was not. Skinner (D) was convicted of his third felony in 1934 (armed robbery), and in 1936 the Attorney General of Oklahoma (P) instituted sterilization proceedings against him. Skinner (D) challenged the Act as unconstitutional. A jury trial was had in which it was decided that a vasectomy could be performed without detriment to Skinner's (D) general health. The trial judge, who had instructed the jury that Skinner's (D) crimes had involved moral turpitude, then ordered that a vasectomy be performed. The Supreme Court of Oklahoma affirmed the trial court's ruling and Skinner (D) appealed to the United States Supreme Court.

■ ISSUE
Can a State implement a criminal sterilization law which makes arbitrary distinctions between the types of criminals that can be sterilized under the law without running afoul of the Constitution?

■ DECISION AND RATIONALE
(Douglas, J.) No. The legislation at issue here involves one of mankind's basic civil rights—procreation. The power to sterilize, if exercised, may have subtle, far-reaching, and devastating effects. There is no redemption for the individual whom the law touches. He is forever deprived of that basic liberty. When a state attempts to use a sterilization law, strict scrutiny is essential lest invidious discriminations are made in violation of the constitutional guaranty of just and equal laws. Sterilization of those who have thrice committed grand larceny with immunity for those who are embezzlers is an unmistakable discrimination. We have not the slightest basis for inferring that the line has any significance in eugenics nor that the inheritability of criminal traits follows the neat legal distinctions which the law has marked between those two offenses. Furthermore, the crimes rate the same in terms of fines and imprisonment.

Skinner v. Oklahoma (Continued)

Only when it comes to sterilization are the penalties different. The Equal Protection Clause would be meaningless if such conspicuously artificial lines could be drawn. Reversed.

■ CONCURRENCE

(Stone, J.) The Equal Protection Clause is not the appropriate means for reaching the decision that has been reached. If Oklahoma may sterilize criminals on the assumption that their criminal propensities are inheritable, I doubt that equal protection requires it to apply the measure to all criminals or none. I think the real question is whether the wholesale condemnation of a class to such an invasion of personal liberty, without opportunity to any individual to show that his is not the type of case which would justify resort to it, satisfies the demands of due process.

Analysis:

Skinner is a landmark case for a number of reasons. First, in finding that some rights deserve special judicial protection from the legislative process, *Skinner* helped to establish the basis for fundamental rights analysis under the Equal Protection Clause. In this respect, *Skinner* was one of the first cases to point out that there exist some fundamental interests that the government cannot take away without meeting a very significant burden. Second, *Skinner* also holds that the right to procreate is a right deserving of special constitutional significance—a fundamental interest or right. Putting these two ideas together, in *Skinner* the Court held that the fundamental right of procreation deserves special judicial protection to the degree of strict scrutiny analysis. *Skinner* has also been cited as support for the proposition that the government cannot control a person's right to decide what should be done with his or her own reproductive capabilities. In this sense, it has been teamed with *Roe v. Wade* to support a woman's right to abortion.

■ CASE VOCABULARY

EUGENICS: The study of the use of selective breeding to improve human genetics.

HABITUAL CRIMINAL (OKLAHOMA): A criminal who has been convicted of three or more felonies involving moral turpitude.

INIMICAL: Hostile or unfriendly.,

MORAL TURPITUDE: Dishonest and unjust conduct which reflects a lack of morals.

PROCREATION: To have or produce offspring.

STERILIZATION: The process through which a person is made unable to reproduce.

VASECTOMY: The surgical removal of the male vas deferens (a duct through which sperm travels).

Griswold v. Connecticut
(*Director of Planned Parenthood*) v. (*State of Connecticut*)
381 U.S. 479, 85 S.Ct. 1678 (1965)

A BROAD CONSTITUTIONAL RIGHT OF PRIVACY PROTECTS CERTAIN INTIMATE ASPECTS OF OUR PERSONAL LIVES FROM GOVERNMENTAL INTRUSION

■ **INSTANT FACTS** A birth control counselor was convicted of a misdemeanor for providing advice about contraception to married couples in violation of a Connecticut statute.

■ **BLACK LETTER RULE** There exists a constitutional right of privacy, implied from the penumbras of the Bill of Rights, that cannot be invaded by government action absent a showing that the government action at issue is necessary to accomplish a compelling governmental interest.

■ **PROCEDURAL BASIS**

Appeal to the United States Supreme Court of a defendant's state court conviction for violating an anti-contraception law.

■ **FACTS**

In 1961, Connecticut had in effect a law which provided that "[a]ny person who uses any drug, medicinal article or instrument for the purpose of preventing conception shall be fined not less than fifty dollars or imprisoned not less than sixty days nor more than one year or be both fined and imprisoned." (The use of contraceptives for the prevention of disease was not banned by the statute.) At the same time, Connecticut also had in effect an aiding and abetting statute which applied to those who assisted or counseled another in the commission of a crime. Griswold (D), the executive director of the Planned Parenthood League of Connecticut, was arrested for aiding and abetting a violation of the anti-contraception law when he gave information about contraceptives to married couples at a clinic where he worked. Griswold (D) appealed his conviction.

■ **ISSUE**

Does the Constitution provide a right to privacy that is protected from government intrusion?

■ **DECISION AND RATIONALE**

(Douglas, J.) Yes. We are not a super-legislature that sits to determine the wisdom of laws that address economic, commercial, and social issues. This law, however, operates directly on an intimate relation of husband and wife and their physician's role in one aspect of that relation. Neither the Constitution nor the Bill of Rights mentions the right of association of people, the right to educate a child as one sees fit, and the right to study a foreign language. Yet the First Amendment has been construed to include these rights, made applicable to the States by the Fourteenth Amendment. The foregoing cases suggest that specific guarantees in the Bill of Rights have penumbras, formed by emanations from those guarantees that help give them life and substance. Various guarantees create zones of privacy. The present case concerns a relationship lying within the zone of privacy created by several fundamental constitutional guarantees. And it concerns a law which, in forbidding the use of contraceptives rather than regulating their manufacture or sale, seeks to achieve its goals by a means that has a destructive impact upon the marital relationship. Such a law cannot stand in light of the principle that a "governmental purpose to

Griswold v. Connecticut (Continued)

control or prevent activities constitutionally subject to state regulation may not be achieved by means which sweep unnecessarily broadly and thereby invade the area of protected freedoms." We deal with a right of privacy older than the Bill of Rights—marriage. It is an association for as noble a purpose as any involved in our prior decisions. Connecticut's law unnecessarily infringes upon that right and is therefore unconstitutional. Reversed.

■ **CONCURRENCE**

(Goldberg, J.) The Connecticut law at issue today unconstitutionally intrudes upon the right of marital privacy. This conclusion that the concept of liberty embraces the right of marital privacy despite the fact that this right is not mentioned explicitly in the Constitution is supported both by this Court's prior decisions and by the Ninth Amendment. The Ninth Amendment reads: "The enumeration in the Constitution, of certain rights, shall not be construed to deny or disparage others retained by the people." This Amendment was proffered to quiet fears that a bill of specifically enumerated rights could not be sufficiently broad to cover all essential rights and that the specific mention of certain rights would be interpreted as a denial that others were protected. To hold that a right so fundamental and deeply-rooted in our society as the right of privacy in marriage may be infringed because that right is not guaranteed in so many words by the first eight amendments is to ignore the Ninth Amendment. In determining which rights are fundamental, judges must look to the "traditions and (collective) conscience of our people" to determine whether a principle is "so rooted ... as to be ranked as fundamental." The inquiry is whether a right involved "is of such a character that it cannot be denied without violating those 'fundamental principles of liberty and justice which lie at the base of all our civil and political institutions.'" Applying these tests demonstrates that the right of privacy is a fundamental personal right. While it may shock some to hold that the Constitution protects the right of marital privacy, it is far more shocking to believe that the personal liberty guaranteed by the Constitution does not include protection against totalitarian dictations of family size. The state interest in safeguarding marital fidelity can be served by a more discriminately-tailored statute which does not sweep unnecessarily broadly, such as those statutes already in existence in Connecticut which prohibit adultery and fornication. Finally, it should be noted that the Court's holding today does not interfere with a State's proper regulation of sexual promiscuity or misconduct. It simply protects against abridgment of the constitutional right to privacy in the marital relation.

■ **CONCURRENCE**

(Harlan, J.) The proper inquiry in this case is whether the Connecticut statute infringes upon the Due Process Clause. While this inquiry may be aided by resort to one or more of the provisions of the Bill of Rights, it is not dependent on them or any of their radiations. The Due Process Clause stands on its own. Judicial self-restraint in this area will be achieved only by continued insistence upon respect for the teachings of history and the basic values that underlie our society, as well as an appreciation of federalism and separation of powers. The continued recognition of these values will go farther towards keeping judges from roaming at large in the constitutional field than will the interpolation into the Constitution of an artificial restriction on the content of the Due Process Clause.

■ **CONCURRENCE**

(White, J.) As applied to married couples, Connecticut's law deprives people of "liberty" without due process of law. The statute is said to serve the State's policy against promiscuous or illicit sexual relationships. While this is a legitimate legislative goal, I fail to see how the ban on the use of contraceptives by married couples in any way reinforces the State's ban on illicit sexual relationships. Connecticut does not bar the importation or possession of contraceptives, and possession of such devices to prevent disease is clearly legal. The only way Connecticut seeks to limit or control the availability of such devices is through its general aiding and abetting statute. In these circumstances one is rather hard pressed to explain how the ban on use by married persons in any way prevents use of such devices by persons engaging in illicit sexual relations and thereby contributes to the policy against such relationships. Furthermore, the statute has too significant an effect on the freedoms of married persons and is therefore unconstitutional.

■ DISSENT

(Black, J.) The law at issue is as offensive to me as it is to the majority. Despite this fact, however, I cannot agree with the majority decision. The Court talks of a constitutional "right of privacy" as though there is some constitutional provision forbidding any law to be passed which might abridge the "privacy" of individuals. But there is not. There are guarantees in certain specific constitutional provisions which are designed in part to protect privacy at certain times and places with respect to certain activities. But it belittles these provisions to talk of them as though they protect nothing but "privacy." For these reasons, I get nowhere in this case by talk about a constitutional "right of privacy" as an emanation from one or more constitutional provisions. I like my privacy as well as the next person, but I am nevertheless compelled to admit that government has a right to invade it unless prohibited by some specific constitutional provision. This brings me to the arguments made by the concurring opinions. Neither the Due Process Clause nor the Ninth Amendment, nor both together, could under any circumstances be a proper basis for invalidating the Connecticut law. Justice Goldberg has adopted the recent discovery that the Ninth Amendment as well as the Due Process Clause can be used by this Court as authority to strike down all state legislation which it thinks violates "fundamental principles of liberty and justice," or is contrary to the "traditions and conscience of our people." One would certainly have to look far beyond the language of the Ninth Amendment to find that the framers vested in this Court any such awesome veto powers over law-making, either by the States or by the Congress. Furthermore, I do not agree that this Court must keep the Constitution in tune with the times. The framers knew the need for change and provided for it by allowing the addition of constitutional amendments. In short, I cannot rely on the Due Process Clause or the Ninth Amendment or any natural law concept as a reason for striking down this law.

■ DISSENT

(Stewart, J.) I think this law is silly for a number of reasons. However, we are not asked to say whether we think this law is unwise. We are asked to hold that it violates the Constitution, and that I cannot do. It is the essence of judicial duty to subordinate our own personal views and ideas of what legislation is wise and what is not. If the law at issue does not reflect the standards of the people of Connecticut, they can freely exercise their true Ninth and Tenth Amendment rights to persuade their elected representatives to repeal it. That is the constitutional way to take it off the books.

Analysis:

In *Griswold,* the Supreme Court concluded that the Constitution recognizes and protects a broad right of personal privacy, which right shields the use of contraceptives by married persons from governmental intrusion. As the many concurrences and dissents illustrate, the Court experienced some difficulty in defining a precise constitutional basis for invalidating the law at issue. Justice Douglas, writing for the Court, focused on constitutional penumbras, finding that a right of privacy can be implied from other rights explicitly enumerated in the Constitution. The concurring justices found alternative constitutional bases to support their conclusions. Justice Goldberg's novel approach attempted to ground a marital privacy right within the text of the Ninth Amendment, which provides that the enumeration of certain rights in the Constitution shall not be construed to deny other rights retained by the people. This novel approach drew significant criticism from Justice Black and Justice Stewart in their dissents. As a reading of the legislative history of the Ninth Amendment shows, the Amendment was intended to be a limitation on the federal government and federal power, not state power.

■ CASE VOCABULARY

CONTRACEPTIVE: A birth control device.

PENUMBRA: A shadowed area between complete darkness and illumination; as used in *Griswold,* it signifies those powers that may be implied from or necessarily attached to those powers expressly mentioned in the Constitution.

Eisenstadt v. Baird

(Not Stated) v. (Distributor of Contraceptives)
405 U.S. 438, 92 S.Ct. 1029 (1972)

THE RIGHT TO ACCESS CONTRACEPTIVES MUST BE THE SAME FOR MARRIED AND UNMARRIED PERSONS

■ **INSTANT FACTS** A lecturer at Boston University was arrested and charged with a violation of a Massachusetts criminal statute for exhibiting contraceptives during a lecture and giving certain contraceptives to one attendee following the completion of the lecture.

■ **BLACK LETTER RULE** If the right of privacy means anything, it is the right of the individual, married or single, to be free from unwarranted governmental intrusion into matters so fundamentally affecting a person as the decision whether to carry or conceive a child.

■ **PROCEDURAL BASIS**

Appeal to the United States Supreme Court of a defendant's Massachusetts state court criminal conviction for the exhibition and distribution of contraceptives.

■ **FACTS**

William Baird (D) was convicted of a felony when, in contravention of state law, he displayed contraceptives during a lecture to a group of students at Boston University and then gave a package of vaginal foam to a female student. The law under which he was convicted made it a crime to give away "any drug, medicine, instrument or article whatever for the prevention of conception," unless the person giving away the contraceptive was a physician or a pharmacist acting at a physician's direction and the recipient was married. Under the law contraceptives could be distributed to unmarried persons for the purpose of preventing the spread of disease, but not for the purpose of contraception. Baird (D) appealed his conviction.

■ **ISSUE**

Is there a difference between married and unmarried persons such that a state can legitimately pass a law that permits the distribution of contraceptives to married persons but makes their distribution to unmarried persons illegal?

■ **DECISION AND RATIONALE**

(Brennan, J.) No. The Massachusetts law at issue stems from an 1879 law which prohibited, without exception, the distribution of contraceptives. The purpose of that law was to preserve chastity and to encourage continence and moral virtue. Such a deterrence of premarital sex, however, may not reasonably be regarded as the purpose of the current version of the law. It would be unreasonable to assume that Massachusetts has prescribed pregnancy (a result of the inability to use contraceptives) as punishment for fornication. If the statute cannot be upheld as a deterrent to fornication or as a health measure, can it be sustained as a prohibition on contraception? No. Whatever the rights of the individual to access contraceptives may be, the rights must be the same for married and unmarried persons. If, under *Griswold,* the distribution of contraceptives to married persons cannot be prohibited, a ban on distribution to unmarried persons would be equally impermissible. The marital couple is not an independent entity, but is an association of two individuals each with a separate intellectual and

Eisenstadt v. Baird (Continued)

emotional makeup. If the right of privacy means anything, it is the right of the individual, married or single, to be free from unwarranted governmental intrusion into matters so fundamentally affecting a person as the decision whether to carry or conceive a child. Even if *Griswold* is read not to be a bar to a prohibition on the distribution of contraceptives, the State cannot, consistent with the Equal Protection Clause, outlaw distribution to unmarried but not to married persons. In each case the evil, as perceived by the State, would be identical, and the underinclusion would be invidious. Reversed.

■ DISSENT

(Burger, J.) I see nothing in the Constitution that even vaguely suggests that contraceptives must be available in the open market. I do not challenge *Griswold,* despite its tenuous moorings to the text of the Constitution, but I cannot view it as controlling authority for this case. The Court in *Griswold* was confronted with a statute flatly prohibiting the use of contraceptives, not one regulating their distribution. I simply cannot believe that the limitation on the class of lawful distributors has significantly impaired the right to use contraceptives in Massachusetts. By relying on *Griswold* in the resent case, the Court has passed beyond the penumbras of the specific guarantees into the uncircumscribed are of personal predilections.

Analysis:

Eisenstadt v. Baird is the case that led the Court from *Griswold* to *Roe v. Wade.* In addressing a ban on the distribution of contraceptives in which marriage was not a factor, the Court in *Eisenstadt* held that the right of privacy "is the right of the individual, married or single, to be free from unwarranted governmental intrusion into matters so fundamentally affecting a person as the decision whether to bear or beget a child." In turning the focus of the right of privacy in the direction of the the right to make decisions regarding bearing children, *Griswold* could no longer be read as simply holding that a state may not prohibit a married couple's use of contraceptives. Instead, the cases are read to hold that a woman has a right to determine whether or not she wants to bear children at all.

■ CASE VOCABULARY

CONTINENCE: An abstention or refraining from sexual intercourse.

PERSONAL PREDILECTIONS: A personal preference or liking for something.

Roe v. Wade

(Pregnant Woman) v. *(Texas County Attorney)*
410 U.S. 113, 93 S.Ct. 705 (1973)

THE CONSTITUTIONAL GUARANTEE OF PRIVACY INCLUDES A QUALIFIED RIGHT TO OBTAIN AN ABORTION

■ **INSTANT FACTS** A pregnant woman challenged a Texas criminal abortion law that permitted abortion only when a continuation of the pregnancy would place the life of the mother in jeopardy.

■ **BLACK LETTER RULE** Criminal abortion statutes that only permit the termination of pregnancy when the life of the mother is in danger are unconstitutional.

■ **PROCEDURAL BASIS**

Not stated.

■ **FACTS**

Texas Penal Code Art. 1196 made it a crime to obtain an abortion unless it was necessary to save the life of the mother. Jane Roe (P) challenged the constitutionality of the statute, arguing that the law improperly infringed upon a woman's right to obtain an abortion whenever she so desired.

■ **ISSUE**

Does a woman have a constitutional right to obtain an abortion during the early stages of a pregnancy?

■ **DECISION AND RATIONALE**

(Blackmun, J.) Yes. Today we must attempt to resolve the abortion controversy by constitutional measurement. In doing so, we place emphasis on medical and medical-legal history and what that history reveals about the abortion procedure over the centuries. At common law, at the time of the adoption of our Constitution, and throughout the major portion of the 19th century, abortion was viewed with less disfavor than under most American statutes currently in effect. At least with respect to the early stage of pregnancy, and very possibly without such limitation, the opportunity to make this choice was present in this country well into the 19th century. Even later, the law continued for some time to treat less punitively an abortion procured in early pregnancy. This history is significant. In reaching our decision, we must also look at the justifications advanced in support of criminal abortion laws. In the present case, two justifications of the enactment of such laws are advanced. The first is a concern with abortion as a medical procedure. When most criminal abortion laws were first enacted, and prior to the development of antisepsis, the procedure was hazardous for the woman. Medical data presented to the Court, however, indicates that abortion in early pregnancy, prior to the end of the first trimester, is now relatively safe. Consequently, any interest of the State in protecting the woman from an inherently hazardous procedure has largely disappeared. Of course, important state interests in the areas of health and medical standards do remain. The State has a legitimate interest in seeing that abortions are performed under circumstances that ensure maximum safety for the patient. Moreover, the risk to the woman increases as her pregnancy continues. Thus, the State retains a definite interest in protecting the woman's own health and safety when an abortion is proposed at a late stage of pregnancy. The

Roe v. Wade (Continued)

other reason advanced today is the State's interest in protecting prenatal life. Some of the argument for this justification rests on the theory that a new human life is present from the moment of conception. It is argued that only when the life of the pregnant mother herself is at stake, balanced against the life she carries within her, should the interest of the embryo or fetus not prevail. It is with these interests that this case is concerned. The Constitution does not explicitly mention any right of privacy, but in a line of decisions going back to the late nineteenth century, the Court has recognized that a right of personal privacy does exist under the Constitution. This right, whether it be founded in the Fourteenth Amendment's concept of personal liberty (our view), or in the Ninth Amendment's reservation of rights to the people (the District Court's view), is broad enough to encompass a woman's decision to terminate her pregnancy. The State would impose significant detriment upon the pregnant woman by denying her the choice to receive an abortion. Maternity or additional offspring may force the woman into a distressful life. Mental and physical health may be taxed by child care. There is also the distress associated with an unwanted child and the difficulties of unwed motherhood. On the basis of such elements, Roe (P) argues that the woman's right to an abortion is absolute at all times during a pregnancy. The Court's decisions recognizing a right of privacy, however, also acknowledge that some state regulation in areas protected by that right is appropriate. As noted, a State may properly assert important interests in safeguarding health, in maintaining medical standards, and in protecting potential life. At some point in pregnancy, these respective interests become sufficiently compelling to sustain regulation of the factors that govern the abortion decision. The privacy right involved, therefore, cannot be said to be absolute. We therefore conclude that the right of personal privacy includes the abortion decision, but that this right is not unqualified and must be considered against important state interests in regulating abortions. Texas (D) argues that a fetus is a "person" within the language and meaning of the Fourteenth Amendment. However, the Constitution does not define "person" in so many words. This, together with the observation that throughout the major portion of the 19th century prevailing legal abortion practices were far freer than they are today, persuades us that the word "person," as used in the Fourteenth Amendment does not include the unborn. The pregnant woman cannot be isolated in her privacy. She carries and embryo, and later a fetus. As we have intimated above, it is reasonable for a State to decide that at some point in time another interest, that of the threat of the mother or that of potential human life, becomes significantly involved. The woman's privacy is no longer sole and any right of privacy she possesses must be measured accordingly. Texas (D) urges that, apart from the Fourteenth Amendment, life begins at conception and is present throughout pregnancy, and that the State therefore has a compelling interest in protecting that life from conception. We need not resolve the difficult question of when life begins. When those trained in respective disciplines of medicine, philosophy, and theology are unable to arrive at any consensus, the judiciary is not in a position to speculate as to the answer. In view of all this, we do not agree that, by adopting one theory of life, Texas may override the rights of the pregnant woman that are at stake. We repeat, however, that the State does have important and legitimate interests that grow in substantiality as the woman approaches term and, at a point during pregnancy, each becomes "compelling." With respect to the State's important and legitimate interest in the health of the mother, the "compelling" point, in the light of present medical knowledge, is at approximately the end of the first trimester. It follows that, from and after this point, a State may regulate the abortion procedure to the extent that the regulation reasonably relates to the preservation and protection of maternal health. This might include regulations as to who can perform abortions and where abortions can be performed. This means, on the other hand, that for the period of pregnancy prior to this "compelling" point, the woman is free to determine, without regulation by the State, that her pregnancy should be terminated. If that decision is reached, the judgment may be effectuated by an abortion free of interference by the State. With respect to the State's interest in potential life, the "compelling" point is at viability. This is because at that point the fetus presumably has the capability of meaningful life outside the mother's womb. If the State is interested in protecting fetal life after viability, it may go so far as to proscribe abortion during that period, except when it is necessary to preserve the life or health of the mother. Measured against those standards, the Texas law at issue sweeps too broadly and is therefore unconstitutional.

■ DISSENT

(Rehnquist, J.) I have difficulty concluding that this case involves the right of privacy. A transaction resulting in an abortion is not "private" in the ordinary usage of the word. Nor is the "privacy" that the Court finds here even a distant relative of the freedom from searches and seizures protected by the

Fourth Amendment, which the Court has referred to as embodying the right to privacy. The test traditionally applied in the area of social and economic legislation is whether a law has a rational relation to a valid state objective. The Due Process Clause undoubtedly places a limit on legislative power to enact laws such as that at issue today, but the Court's sweeping invalidation of any restrictions on abortion during the first trimester is impossible to justify under that standard, and the weighing of compelling factors that the Court's opinion apparently substitutes for the established test is far more appropriate to a legislative judgment than to a judicial one. The decision to break pregnancy into three distinct terms and to outline the permissible restrictions the State may impose in each, for example, partakes more of judicial legislation than it does of a determination of the intent of the drafters of the Fourteenth Amendment. The fact that a majority of states have had restrictions on abortion for at least a century is a strong indication that the right to an abortion is not so "rooted in the traditions and conscience of our people as to be ranked as fundamental." Even today, when society's views on abortion are changing, the very existence of the debate is evidence that the right to an abortion is not universally accepted. To reach its result, the Court has had to find within the scope of the Fourteenth Amendment a right that was apparently completely unknown to the drafters of the Amendment. As early as 1821, the first state law dealing directly with abortion was enacted by the Connecticut Legislature. By the adoption of the Fourteenth Amendment in 1868, there were at least 36 laws enacted by state or territorial legislatures limiting abortion. First enacted in 1857, Texas' law has remained substantially unchanged, and was therefore in effect at the time of the ratification of the Fourteenth Amendment. There apparently was no question concerning the validity of this provision or of any of the other state statutes when the Fourteenth Amendment was adopted. The only conclusion possible from this history is that the drafters did not intend to have the Fourteenth Amendment withdraw from the States the power to legislate with respect to this matter.

Analysis:

One of the more controversial holdings in the history of the modern Supreme Court, *Roe v. Wade* is also one of the more significant and far-reaching decisions in its effect on the law of fundamental rights and substantive due process and the right of privacy. In holding as it does, the Court finds that the right of privacy contained in the penumbras of the Fourteenth Amendment is extremely broad, encompassing a woman's prima facie right to terminate her pregnancy. One major criticism that has been levied against the decision in *Roe* involves Justice Blackmun's determination of when each of the enumerated state interests becomes sufficiently compelling to override the pregnant woman's right to privacy and bodily autonomy. Justice Blackmun notes that there is widespread disagreement as to when life begins, yet he delineates strict time periods when the various conflicting interests become entitled to governmental protection. *Roe* has also been criticized as a modern example of *Lochnerizing,* or the permitting of extensive judicial intervention into state legislative schemes. Many have argued that the Court went outside of its judicial function and transformed itself into a legislature. Justice Rehnquist agrees that the Court went too far, noting in his dissent that "[t]he decision to break pregnancy into three distinct terms and to outline the permissible restrictions the State may impose in each, for example, partakes more of judicial legislation than it does of a determination of the intent of the drafters of the Fourteenth Amendment."

■ CASE VOCABULARY

ANTISEPSIS: The use of antiseptics to stop the growth and multiplication of microorganisms.

EMBRYO: A human fetus in its first eight weeks of development.

FETUS: An unborn child.

PRENATAL LIFE: Life prior to birth.

TRIMESTER: A period of three months.

VIABILITY: The time at which a fetus is capable of living on its own outside of the mother's womb.

Planned Parenthood v. Casey

(Family Planning Clinic) v. (Governor of Pennsylvania)
505 U.S. 833, 112 S.Ct. 2791 (1992)

THE SUPREME COURT REAFFIRMS A WOMAN'S RIGHT TO AN ABORTION BUT HOLDS THAT THE *ROE V. WADE* TRIMESTER SYSTEM IS NO LONGER THE LAW

■ **INSTANT FACTS** A family planning clinic challenged the constitutionality of a Pennsylvania law placing certain restrictions on a woman's right to obtain an abortion.

■ **BLACK LETTER RULE** The state can regulate and place restrictions on abortion so long as those regulations do not impose an undue burden on the woman's ability to make the abortion decision; when an undue burden results, the regulations are unconstitutional.

■ **PROCEDURAL BASIS**

Not stated.

■ **FACTS**

In 1982, Pennsylvania enacted the Abortion Control Act, which, as amended in later years, contained the following requirements: (1) a woman seeking an abortion must provide her informed consent prior to the procedure; (2) she must be provided with certain information at least 24 hours before the procedure is to take place; (3) minors seeking an abortion must obtain either the informed consent of one of her parents or the permission of a judge; (4) married women must notify their husbands of the intent to obtain an abortion; and (5) facilities performing abortions must meet certain reporting requirements. The Act also provided an exception to some of the above requirements for medical emergencies.

■ **ISSUE**

Should the essential holding of *Roe v. Wade* be retained and affirmed?

■ **DECISION AND RATIONALE**

(O'Connor, J.) Yes. Our post-*Roe* decisions have cast some doubt on the meaning and reach of its holding. As a result, state and federal courts, as well as legislatures, need guidance as they seek to address this subject in conformance with the Constitution. As such, it is imperative that we review the principles that define the rights of women and the legitimate authority of the State with respect to abortion. After considering the fundamental constitutional questions resolved by *Roe*, principles of institutional integrity, and the rule of stare decisis, we conclude that the essential holding of *Roe v. Wade* should be reaffirmed. Constitutional protection of the woman's decision to terminate her pregnancy derives from the Due Process Clause. The Constitution promises that there is a realm of personal liberty which the government may not enter. Marriage is not mentioned in the Bill of Rights, but the Court was no doubt correct in finding that it is protected by the substantive component of the Due Process Clause. Neither the Bill of Rights nor the specific practices of States at the time of the adoption of the Fourteenth Amendment marks the outer limits of the substantive sphere of liberty which the Fourteenth Amendment protects. In this vein, our law affords constitutional protection to personal decisions relating to marriage, procreation, contraception, family relationships, child rearing, and

Planned Parenthood v. Casey (Continued)

education, and recognizes "the right of the individual, married or single, to be free from unwarranted governmental intrusion into mattes so fundamentally affecting a person as the decision whether to bear a or beget a child." These matters are central to the liberty protected by the Fourteenth Amendment. At the heart of liberty is the right to define one's own concept of existence, of meaning, of the universe, and of the mystery of human life. Beliefs about these matters could not define the attributes of personhood were they formed under compulsion of the State. These considerations begin our analysis of the abortion issue but cannot end it, for abortion is a unique act fraught with consequences for others. Though abortion is conduct, it does not follow that the State is entitled to proscribe it in all instances. That is because the liberty of the woman is at stake in a sense unique to the human condition. The mother who carries a child to full term is subject to anxieties, to physical constraints, to pain that only she must bear. That these sacrifices have been endured by woman from the beginning cannot alone be grounds for the State to insist she make the sacrifice. Her suffering is too personal for the State to insist upon its own vision of the woman's role. In short, the reservations any of us may have in reaffirming the central holding of *Roe* are outweighed by the explication of individual liberty we have given combined with the force of stare decisis. We now turn to stare decisis. To determine whether stare decisis requires us to follow a prior holding, we may inquire whether that prior holding has been found unworkable; whether the rule's limitation on state power could be removed without serious inequity to those who have relied upon it or significant damage to the stability of the society governed by it; whether the law's growth in the intervening years has left the holding a doctrinal anachronism discounted by society; and whether the holding's premises of fact have so far changed as to render it irrelevant or unjustifiable in dealing with the issue it addressed. Although *Roe* has engendered opposition, it has in no sense proven "unworkable." Furthermore, for two decades of economic and social development, people have organized intimate relationships and made life choices in reliance on the availability of abortion. The ability of women to participate equally in the economic and social life of the Nation has been facilitated by their ability to control their reproductive lives. No evolution of legal principle has left *Roe*'s doctrinal footings weaker than they were in 1973. No development of constitutional law has since made *Roe* a mere survivor of obsolete constitutional thinking. Advances in maternal health care allow for abortions safe to the mother later in pregnancy than was true in 1973, and advances in neonatal care have advanced viability to a point somewhat earlier. But these facts go only to the scheme of time limits on the realization of competing interests and have no bearing on the validity of *Roe*'s central holding. The soundness or unsoundness of that constitutional judgment in no sense turns on when viability occurs, and whenever it does occur, the attainment of viability may continue to serve as the critical fact, just as it has done since *Roe* was decided. In short, no change in *Roe*'s factual underpinning has left its central holding obsolete, and none supports an argument for overruling it. For these reasons, stare decisis dictates that we uphold the central holding of *Roe*. We also conclude that the line between the State's interests and the mother's right to an abortion must continue to be drawn at viability, so that before that time the woman has a right to choose to terminate her pregnancy. The reason is viability is the time at which there is a realistic possibility of maintaining and nourishing a life outside the womb, so that the independent existence of the second life can be the object of state protection that now overrides the rights of the woman. *Roe* established a trimester framework to govern abortion regulations. It was erected to ensure that the woman's right to choose not become so subordinate to the State's interest in promoting fetal life that her choice exits in theory but not in fact. We do not agree, however, that the trimester approach is necessary to accomplish this objective. A framework of this rigidity is unnecessary and has sometimes contradicted the State's permissible exercise of its powers. Though the woman has a right to obtain an abortion before viability, it does not follow that the State is prohibited from taking steps to ensure that this choice is thoughtful and informed. Even in the earliest stages of pregnancy, the State may enact rules and regulations designed to encourage her to know that there are arguments in favor of continuing pregnancy. "The Constitution does not forbid a State or city, pursuant to democratic processes, from expressing a preference for normal childbirth." *Webster v. Reproductive Health Services.* States are free to enact laws to provide a reasonable framework for a woman to make a decision that has such profound and lasting meaning. We therefore reject the trimester framework, which we do not consider to be part of the essential holding of *Roe*. Measures aimed at ensuring that a woman's choice contemplates the consequences for the fetus do not necessarily interfere with the right recognized in *Roe*. Not every law which makes a right more difficult to exercise is, ipso facto, an infringement of that right. Numerous forms of state regulation might have the incidental effect of increasing the cost or decreasing the availability of abortion. The fact that a law which serves a valid purpose has the incidental effect of making it more difficult or more expensive to procure an abortion cannot be enough to invalidate it. Only where state regulation imposes an undue burden on a woman's ability to make this decision does the power of the State reach into the heart of the liberty protected by the Due Process Clause. The very notion that the State has a substantial interest in potential life leads to the conclusion that not all regulations must be deemed unwarranted, and not all burdens on the right to decide whether to terminate a pregnancy will be undue. In our view, the undue burden standard is the appropriate means of reconciling the State's interest with the woman's constitutionally protected liberty. A finding of undue burden is a shorthand for the conclusion that a state regulation has the purpose or effect of placing a substantial obstacle in the path of a woman seeking an abortion of a nonviable fetus. Unless it has that effect on her right of choice, a State law designed to persuade her to choose childbirth over abortion will be upheld if reasonably related to that goal. Regulations designed to foster the health of a woman seeking an abortion are valid if they do not constitute an undue burden.

■ **CONCURRENCE AND DISSENT**

(Blackmun, J.) Three years ago, in *Webster v. Reproductive Health Services*, four members of this Court appeared poised to overturn our decision in *Roe v. Wade*. I do not underestimate the significance of today's joint opinion. Yet I remain steadfast in my belief that the right to reproductive choice is entitled to the full protection afforded by this Court before *Webster*. And I fear for the darkness as four Justices anxiously await the single vote necessary to extinguish the light. State restrictions on abortion violate a woman's right of privacy. Compelled continuation of a pregnancy infringes upon a woman's right to bodily integrity by imposing substantial physical intrusions and significant risks of physical harm. When the State restricts a woman's right to terminate her pregnancy, it deprives her of the right to make her own decision about reproduction and family planning—critical life choices that this Court long has deemed central to the right of privacy. Furthermore, restrictive abortion laws deprive a woman of basic control over her life. Restrictions on abortion also implicate constitutional guarantees of gender equality by forcing women to accept the "natural" status and incidents of motherhood—a conception of women's role that has triggered the protection of the Equal Protection Clause. The Court has held that limitations on the right of privacy are permissible only if they survive "strict" constitutional scrutiny. In my view, application of this analytical framework is no less warranted than when it was approved by the Court in *Roe*. Strict scrutiny of state limitations on reproductive choice still offers the most secure protection of the woman's right to make her own reproductive decisions, free from state coercion. No majority of this Court has ever agreed upon an alternative approach. Furthermore, the factual premises of the trimester framework have not been undermined, and the *Roe* framework is far more administrable, and far less manipulable, than the "undue burden" standard adopted by the joint opinion. In sum, the trimester framework should not be disturbed. Finally, I must mention that I am disturbed at the Chief Justice's opinion, and hope that when I retire my successor will not be the single vote needed to overturn *Roe*. The selection process may very well turn on that issue.

■ **CONCURRENCE AND DISSENT**

(Rehnquist, J.) The joint opinion, following its newly-minted variation on stare decisis, retains the outer shell of *Roe v. Wade*, but beats a wholesale retreat from the substances of the case. *Roe* was wrongly decided, and it can and should be overruled consistent with our traditional approach to stare decisis in constitutional cases. In terming the right to an abortion as "fundamental," the *Roe* majority read the earlier opinions upon which it was based much too broadly. Unlike marriage, procreation, and contraception, abortion "involves the purposeful termination of a potential life." The abortion decision must therefore "be recognized as sui generis, different in kind from the others that the Court has protected under the rubric of personal or family privacy and autonomy." One cannot ignore the fact that a woman is not isolated in her pregnancy, and that the decision to abort necessarily involves the destruction of a fetus. Nor do the historical traditions of the American people support the view that the right to terminate a pregnancy is "fundamental." The common law made abortion after "quickening" an offense. At the time of the adoption of the Fourteenth Amendment, statutory prohibitions or restrictions on abortion were commonplace. By the turn of the century virtually every State had a law prohibiting or restricting abortion, and by the middle of the present century an overwhelming majority of States prohibited abortion unless necessary to preserve the life or health of the mother. On this record, it can scarcely be said that any deeply-rooted tradition of relatively unrestricted abortion in our history

Planned Parenthood v. Casey (Continued)

supports the classification of the right to abortion as "fundamental." Both in view of this history and our decided cases dealing with substantive liberty under the Due Process Clause, it is apparent that the Court was mistaken in *Roe* when it classified a woman's decision to terminate her pregnancy as a "fundamental right" that can be abridged only in a manner which withstands strict scrutiny.

■ CONCURRENCE AND DISSENT

(Scalia, J.) The States may permit abortion on demand, but the Constitution does not require it. A State's choice between two positions on which reasonable people can disagree is constitutional even when it intrudes upon "liberty" in the absolute sense of the term. The issue in these cases is not whether the power of a woman to abort her unborn child is a "liberty" in the absolute sense. The issue is whether it is a liberty protected by the Constitution. It is not. I reach this conclusion because of two simple facts: (1) the Constitution says absolutely nothing about abortion, and (2) the longstanding traditions of American society have permitted it to be legally proscribed. The Court's description of the place of *Roe* in the social history of the United States is unrecognizable. Not only did *Roe* not resolve the deeply divisive issue of abortion; it did more than anything else to nourish it by elevating it to the national level where it is infinitely more difficult to resolve. *Roe*'s mandate for abortion on demand destroyed the compromises of the past, rendered compromise impossible for the future, and required the entire issue to be resolved uniformly at the national level. To portray *Roe* as a statesmanlike settlement of a divisive issue is not accurate. *Roe* famed into life an issue that has inflamed our national politics and has obscured with its smoke the selection of Justices to this Court. We should get out of this area where we have no right to be and where we do neither ourselves nor the country any good by remaining.

Analysis:

Nineteen years after its decision in *Roe v. Wade*, a very divided Supreme Court in *Casey* again directly confronted the issue of whether women have a fundamental right to have an abortion and the extent to which a state may constitutionally burden any such right. *Casey* substantially alters the *Roe* approach by throwing out *Roe*'s trimester framework and the strict scrutiny requirements, and, in their place, providing an entirely new standard for judging the constitutionality of abortion regulation by states. Both Justice Blackmun, who authored *Roe* and here would have maintained the trimester framework and strict scrutiny approach, and Chief Justice Rehnquist, who dissented in *Roe* and here would have overturned that decision in favor of a mere rational relationship scrutiny of state abortion regulations, strongly criticize the joint opinion's "undue burden" standard as too indefinite. Many commentators have agreed, pointing to the inconsistency of the joint opinion itself as to what constitutes a substantial obstacle. For example, the joint opinion permitted Pennsylvania to impose a 24-hour waiting period on a woman, even though there was evidence that this might greatly burden women who had to travel long distances from a rural area to obtain an abortion. At the same time, the opinion struck down a husband notification provision on the belief that this might put many women at risk of spousal abuse. The Court never gives any clear reasoning as to how many people have to be affected or what other threshold must be reached before a regulation's burden becomes "undue."

■ CASE VOCABULARY

DOCTRINAL ANACHRONISM: A doctrine that is out of place in current times.

IPSO FACTO: Latin phrase meaning "by the fact itself," or "as a result of the fact."

NEONATAL CARE: Care given to a newborn baby.

QUICKENING: Common law term that denoted the time of the first movement of a fetus of its own accord within the mother's womb.

RUBRIC: A heading or classification.

SUI GENERIS: Something unique or peculiar.

STARE DECISIS: Latin phrase meaning "to stand by things decided," which refers to the principle of law that courts follow precedent when applicable.

Gonzales v. Carhart
(*Attorney General*) v. (*Physician*)
550 U.S. 124, 127 S.Ct. 1610 (2007)

PROTECTING THE DIGNITY OF HUMAN LIFE JUSTIFIES REGULATION OF ABORTIONS

We're back for another round in the eternal match between the left and right over abortion. The last round, over a federal ban on partial-birth abortions with no exception for a women's health risk, went to the right.

■ **INSTANT FACTS** Carhart (P) challenged the federal Partial–Birth Abortion Ban Act of 2003 as facially unconstitutional.

■ **BLACK LETTER RULE** Laws that place restrictions on abortion that express respect for the life of the unborn are valid, provided the laws do not unduly burden a woman's right to obtain an abortion.

■ PROCEDURAL BASIS
Appeal from a decision finding a federal statute unconstitutional.

■ FACTS
In 2000, the Court decided the case of *Stenberg v. Carhart*, 530 U.S. 914, which held unconstitutional a Nebraska statute that outlawed a certain type of late-term abortion. After that decision, Congress enacted the Partial–Birth Abortion Ban Act of 2003, 18 U.S.C. § 1531. The Act prohibited a type of abortion performed in the second trimester of pregnancy, known as "intact D & E." In passing the Act, Congress made factual findings stating, among other things, that intact D & E was a "gruesome and inhumane procedure that is never medically necessary." The Act also contained an exception for procedures necessary to save the *life* of the mother. There was no exception for preserving the *health* of the mother. The Act also defined the prohibited procedure with specificity, and stated that the prohibition applied only to intact D & Es done intentionally. Carhart (P), a physician, brought a pre-enforcement challenge to the Act. Carhart (P) contended that the Act was facially unconstitutional.

■ ISSUE
Is the Partial–Birth Abortion Ban Act of 2003 unconstitutional?

■ DECISION AND RATIONALE
(Kennedy, J.) No. Laws that place restrictions on abortion that express respect for the life of the unborn are valid, provided the laws do not unduly burden a woman's right to obtain an abortion. An undue burden exists if the law places substantial obstacles in the woman's path to obtaining an abortion before the fetus attains viability.

The Act is not void for vagueness, because the prohibited procedures are defined in explicit terms. First, the Act only applies when a living fetus is delivered vaginally. Second, the delivery must be performed to defined anatomical landmarks. Third, the physician who performs the abortion must perform an overt act, other than completion of the delivery, that kills the fetus. Fourth, the Act contains scienter requirements for all of the prohibited acts. The Act provides physicians of "ordinary intelligence" a reasonable opportunity to know what conduct is prohibited. Unlike the Nebraska law found unconstitutional in *Stenberg,* the Act defines the line between potentially criminal conduct and lawful abortion. In addition, the Act requires proof of intent before liability may be imposed. Scienter requirements will eliminate vagueness concerns. The Act also establishes minimum guidelines to govern law enforce-

Gonzales v. Carhart (Continued)

ment. The specificity of the Act means also that the Act does not impose an undue burden on the right to receive an abortion based on its overbreadth. Procedures other than intact D & Es are not prohibited.

The purpose of the Act was not to place a substantial obstacle in the path of a woman seeking an abortion. The Act states its purpose as serving the government's legitimate interests in respecting the dignity of human life, in regulating the integrity of the medical profession, and in safeguarding the emotional health of the mother. In enacting the legislation, it was reasonable for Congress to think that intact D & E's "undermine[ ] the public's perception of the appropriate role of a physician during the delivery process, and pervert[ ] the process during which life is brought into the world."

The Act considerably limits the use of intact D & Es even to preserve the health of the mother. These limits would be unconstitutional if they were certain to present significant health risks to the mother. However, the Act's creation of risks is a factual question. Both sides of the question are equally supported by medical evidence. Legislators are given wide discretion when there is medical and scientific uncertainty. Considerations of marginal safety are within the competence of the legislature, as long as the regulation is rational and made in pursuit of rational ends. As long as there are safe alternatives to an intact D & E, the Act is not facially unconstitutional. The proper means for challenging the Act's lack of exceptions is by an as-applied challenge. The Act is open to a proper as-applied challenge. Facial attacks to the Act should not have been entertained at all.

■ CONCURRENCE

(Thomas, J.) The Court's abortion jurisprudence, including *Roe v. Wade,* 410 U.S. 113 (1973), and *Planned Parenthood v. Casey,* 505 U.S. 833 (1992), has no basis in the Constitution.

■ DISSENT

(Ginsburg, J.) The majority applauds federal intervention to ban a procedure the American College of Obstetricians and Gynecologists finds to be necessary under certain circumstances. Legal challenges to abortion do not rest on some generalized notion of privacy. They are centered on a woman's autonomy to determine her life's course, and thus to enjoy equal citizenship. It is for this reason that the Court has consistently required that restrictions on abortion safeguard a woman's health.

The Act does not further the asserted governmental interest of protecting the life of the fetus, because the Act attacks merely the method of abortion. The Act also was not designed to protect the lives or health of pregnant women. The majority finds the Act constitutional because Carhart (P) failed to show it would be unconstitutional in a large fraction of relevant cases. The very purpose of the health exception is to protect women in the exceptional cases. The absence of a health exception burdens the women for whom it is relevant: those women who, in their doctors' opinions, require an intact D & E because other procedures would put their health at risk.

The majority's allowance of only an as-applied challenge to the Act jeopardizes women's health and puts doctors in an untenable position. Even if exceptions to the ban were carved out through piecemeal litigation, women whose circumstances were unanticipated in prior litigation could be left unprotected. The majority continues to chip away at a right declared again and again to be central to women's lives.

Analysis:

The majority opinion makes reference to the medical and scientific uncertainty surrounding intact D & Es. In her dissent, Justice Ginsburg differs with this assessment. She notes that the lower federal courts that considered the Act held full trials, in which both parties were allowed to present their best evidence. The trial courts all rejected the congressional findings that the intact D & E was an unsafe procedure, and found that the congressional findings in support of the Act were unreasonable and not supported by the evidence.

■ CASE VOCABULARY

AS–APPLIED CHALLENGE: A lawsuit claiming that a law or governmental policy, though constitutional on its face, is unconstitutional as applied, usually because of a discriminatory effect; a claim that a statute is unconstitutional on the facts of a particular case or to a particular party.

FACIAL CHALLENGE: A claim that a statute is unconstitutional on its face—that is, that it always operates unconstitutionally.

OVERBREADTH DOCTRINE: The doctrine holding that if a statute is so broadly written that it deters free expression, then it can be struck down on its face because of its chilling effect—even if it also prohibits acts that may legitimately be forbidden. The Supreme Court has used this doctrine to invalidate a number of laws, including those that would disallow peaceful picketing or require loyalty oaths.

SCIENTER: A degree of knowledge that makes a person legally responsible for the consequences of his or her act or omission; the fact of an act's having been done knowingly, especially as a ground for civil damages or criminal punishment.

VOID FOR VAGUENESS: Establishing a requirement or punishment without specifying what is required or what conduct is punishable, and therefore void because violative of due process.

Maher v. Roe
(Not Stated) v. (Not Stated)
432 U.S. 464, 97 S.Ct. 2376 (1977)

ROE V. WADE DOES NOT PRECLUDE THE STATE FROM MAKING VALUE JUDGMENTS THAT FAVOR CHILDBIRTH OVER ABORTION

■ **INSTANT FACTS** A Connecticut regulation which allowed the State to fund childbirths but not abortions was challenged in federal court.

■ **BLACK LETTER RULE** The Constitution does not require the government to subsidize abortions, even when it chooses to subsidize childbirth.

■ PROCEDURAL BASIS
Appeal to the United States Supreme Court of a lower court decision which held that a state regulation that allows for the funding of childbirth but not abortion is unconstitutional in light of *Roe v. Wade.*

■ FACTS
In the mid-seventies, the Connecticut Welfare Department had in effect a regulation which precluded the use of state Medicaid benefits to fund abortions except in those situations in which an abortion was medically necessary. That regulation was challenged in federal court. Those challenging the regulation argued that Connecticut should have to accord equal treatment to abortion and childbirth.

■ ISSUE
Does the Constitution require states to pay for nontherapeutic abortions when they make the decision to pay for childbirth?

■ DECISION AND RATIONALE
(Powell, J.) No. The Constitution does not obligate States to pay the medical expenses of indigents, including pregnancy-related expenses. But when a State decides to pay for some such expenses, the manner in which it dispenses benefits is subject to constitutional limitations. This case does not involve a discrimination against a suspect class. This Court has never held that financial need alone identifies a suspect class for purposes of equal protection analysis. Accordingly, the central question in this case is whether the regulation "impinges upon a fundamental right explicitly or implicitly protected by the Constitution." *Roe v. Wade* did not declare an unqualified "constitutional right to an abortion." Rather, *Roe* protects the woman from unduly burdensome interference with her freedom to decide whether to terminate her pregnancy. It implies no limitation on the authority of a State to make a value judgment favoring childbirth over abortion, and to implement that judgment by the allocation of public funds. The Connecticut regulation at issue places no obstacles in the pregnant woman's path to an abortion. An indigent woman who desires an abortion is not disadvantaged as a consequence of Connecticut's decision to fund childbirth. The State may have made childbirth a more attractive alternative, but it has not imposed any restrictions on access to abortions that were not already there. Additionally, the indigency is neither created nor affected by the regulation. Simply put, the regulation does not impinge upon the fundamental right recognized in *Roe.* This conclusion does not signal a retreat from *Roe,* but simply recognizes that there is a difference between direct state interference with a protected activity

and state encouragement of an alternative activity consonant with legislative policy. We are not unsympathetic to the difficulties of the indigent, but "the Constitution does not provide judicial remedies for every social and economic ill." States have a wide latitude in choosing among competing demands for limited public funds. Our conclusion is not based on a weighing of the wisdom or social desirability of the Connecticut regulation, for courts do not strike down laws "because they may be unwise, improvident, or out of harmony with a particular school of thought." When an issue involves policy choices as sensitive as those implicated by public funding of nontherapeutic abortions, the appropriate forum for their resolution is the legislature. Reversed.

■ DISSENT

(Brennan, J.) As a result of the Court's decision, many indigent women will feel they have no choice but to carry their pregnancies to term because the State will pay for the associated medical services, even though they would have chosen an abortion if the State had also provided funds for that procedure. This disparity in funding clearly operates to coerce indigent pregnant women to bear children they would not otherwise choose to have, and just as clearly, this coercion can only operate upon the poor, who are uniquely the victims of this form of financial pressure.

Analysis:

The first of a handful of abortion funding cases, *Maher v. Roe* held that while the government cannot restrict a woman's right to receive an abortion under the circumstances set forth in *Roe v. Wade* and its progeny, it does not have to pay for those abortions. This is true even when the entity at issue chooses to make public funds available to subsidize childbirth. Additionally, the *Maher* majority held that local governments can pass legislation that encourages women to choose childbirth over abortion. Calling it an attack on the holding of *Roe v. Wade*, the dissenters expressed disgust at what they perceived as an erosion of the constitutional right to an abortion and the treatment of indigents as a non-suspect class. The majority, however, made a distinction between giving a woman the opportunity to seek an abortion and the state paying for that procedure, and in doing so held that because the law at issue does not place significant obstacles in the way of a woman seeking to receive an abortion, it is not unconstitutional. Because the majority determined that the right to receive funding for an abortion (as opposed to the right to get an abortion) was not a fundamental right, a rational basis standard of review was applied to the ordinance and it was determined that, under that standard, the ordinance was constitutional.

■ CASE VOCABULARY

NONTHERAPEUTIC ABORTION: An abortion that is not medically necessary to preserve the life or health of the mother.

Planned Parenthood v. Casey

(Family Planning Clinic) v. (Governor of Pennsylvania)
505 U.S. 833, 112 S.Ct. 2791 (1992)

THE STATE CANNOT REQUIRE A MARRIED WOMAN TO NOTIFY HER SPOUSE OF HER INTENT TO OBTAIN AN ABORTION

■ **INSTANT FACTS** A constitutional challenge was brought against a Pennsylvania abortion law that contained a spousal notification requirement.

■ **BLACK LETTER RULE** Spousal notification requirements in abortion laws are unconstitutional because they place an undue burden upon a woman's ability to obtain an abortion.

■ **PROCEDURAL BASIS**

Not stated.

■ **FACTS**

Section 3209 of Pennsylvania's abortion law provided that before an abortion could be performed, the physician performing the procedure had to obtain from the patient a signed statement indicating that she had informed her spouse of her plan to terminate her pregnancy. Spousal consent was not required. The law had some exceptions, including cases of medical emergency, inability to locate the spouse, spousal sexual assault, and pregnancy as a result of infidelity. Additionally, the law did not require spousal consent when the woman indicated that notifying her husband would cause either him or someone else to inflict bodily injury upon her. Physicians who performed an abortion without obtaining the proper consent form would, by law, lose their license to practice medicine. Such physicians were also liable to the husband for damages.

■ **ISSUE**

Are laws which require spousal notification of an intent to obtain an abortion constitutional?

■ **DECISION AND RATIONALE**

(O'Connor, J.) No. The majority of women notify their partners of their decision to obtain an abortion. Where the husband is the father, the primary reason women do not notify their husbands is that the husband and wife are experiencing marital difficulties, often accompanied by violence. These findings are supported by studies of domestic violence and reinforce what common sense would suggest: in well-functioning marriages, spouses discuss important decisions such as whether to bear a child, but in situations in which there is regular physical and psychological abuse, women have good reasons for not wanting to inform their husbands of a decision to obtain an abortion. These women, who have good reason to fear additional abuse, are not exempted from the notification requirement in the law at issue. As such, the spousal notification requirement is likely to prevent a significant number of women from obtaining an abortion. It does not merely make abortions a little more difficult to obtain; for many women, it will impose a substantial obstacle. Respondents point out that the notification requirement imposes almost no burden at all upon the vast majority of women seeking abortions. They argue that since some of these women will be able to notify their husbands without adverse consequences or will qualify for one of the exceptions, the statute affects fewer than one percent of women seeking abortions. For this reason, it is asserted, the statute cannot be invalid on its face. We disagree. The analysis does not end with the one percent of women upon whom the statute operates; it begins there. Legislation is measured for consistency with the Constitution by its impact on those whose conduct it affects. This conclusion is not inconsistent with our decisions upholding parental notification or consent requirements. Those enactments are based on the assumption that minors will benefit from consultation with their parents. We cannot adopt a parallel assumption about adult women. We recognize that a husband has a significant interest in the growth of a fetus that he helped to create. If these cases concerned a State's ability to require the mother to notify the father before taking some action with respect to a living child, it would be reasonable to conclude that the father's interest in the welfare of the child is equal to the mother's interest. Before birth, however, things are different. Regulation with respect to the child a woman is carrying will have a far greater impact on the mother's liberty than the father's. The Court has held that "when the wife and the husband disagree on this decision, the view of only one of the two ... can prevail. Inasmuch as it is the woman who physically bears the child and who is the more directly and immediately affected by the pregnancy ... the balance weighs in her favor." The Constitution protects individuals, men and women alike, from unjustified state interference, even when that interference is enacted for the benefit of their spouses. The Court held in *Planned Parenthood v. Danforth* (1976) that the Constitution does not permit a State to require ?? married woman to obtain her husband's consent before undergoing an abortion. The principles that guided the Court in *Danforth* guide us today. For the great many women who are victims of abuse, a spousal notification requirement enables the husband to wield a veto over his wife's decision. Whether the prospect of notification itself deters such women from seeking abortions, or whether the husband, through physical force, psychological pressure, or economic coercion, prevents his wife from obtaining an abortion, the notice requirement will often be tantamount to the veto found unconstitutional in *Danforth*. The husband's interest in the life of the child his wife is carrying does not permit the State to empower him with this troubling degree of authority over his wife; women do not lose their constitutionally protected liberty when they marry. These considerations confirm our conclusion that the provision at issue is invalid.

■ CONCURRENCE AND DISSENT

(Rehnquist, J.) The State has a legitimate interest in protecting the interests of a father and the potential life of a fetus, and the spousal notification requirement is reasonably related to advancing those state interests. By providing that a husband will usually know of his spouse's intent to have an abortion, the provision makes it more likely that the husband will participate in deciding the fate of his unborn child. This participation might, in some cases, result in a decision to proceed with the pregnancy when the mother originally sought an abortion. The State also has a legitimate interest in promoting the integrity of the marriage relationship. The spousal notification requirement is a rational attempt to improve truthful communication between spouses and to encourage collaborative decision-making, and thereby fosters marital integrity. Petitioners argue that the notification requirement does not further any such interest; they assert that the majority of wives already notify their husbands of such decisions, and the remainder have excellent reasons for keeping their decisions secret. In the first case, they argue, the law is unnecessary, and in the second it will only serve to foster marital discord. The spousal notification provision will admittedly be unnecessary in some circumstances, and possibly harmful in others, but "the existence of particular cases in which a feature of a statute performs no function ordinarily does not render the statute unconstitutional." The Pennsylvania Legislature was in a position to weigh the benefits and adverse effects of the statute, and presumably concluded that the provision would be beneficial. Whether this was a wise decision or not, I cannot say that it was irrational, and therefore conclude that the spousal notification provision is not unconstitutional.

Analysis:

Since the Supreme Court decided *Roe* in 1973, state legislatures have made numerous attempts to place restrictions on access to abortions. One such effort involved the imposition of spousal notice and consent requirements—requirements that a woman must either obtain her husband's consent or notify him of her intent to get an abortion before she can actually terminate a pregnancy. The first significant decision to address these issues, as referenced in Justice O'Connor's opinion, was *Planned Parenthood v. Danforth* (1976), which addressed the constitutionality of a Missouri law that included a spousal consent requirement. The Court concluded that a spousal veto that precludes a woman from exercising a fundamental constitutional right is inappropriate, and on that basis struck down the Missouri law. The present case addresses a less-restrictive version of the Missouri law; Pennsylvania did not require spousal consent, but attempted to require spousal notification. As Justice O'Connor's opinion indicates, a majority of Justices determined that such a notification requirement placed an "undue burden" on a woman's ability to access an abortion, and on that basis struck down the requirement.

Bellotti v. Baird

(Not Stated) v. (Not Stated)
443 U.S. 622, 99 S.Ct. 3035 (1979)

STATES CANNOT GIVE PARENTS AN ABSOLUTE VETO POWER OVER A MINOR'S DECISION TO OBTAIN AN ABORTION

■ **INSTANT FACTS** A Massachusetts law which regulated the access of minors to abortions was challenged as being unconstitutional.

■ **BLACK LETTER RULE** If the State chooses to require a pregnant minor to obtain one or both parents' consent to an abortion, it also must provide an alternative procedure whereby authorization for the abortion can be obtained without parental consent.

■ **PROCEDURAL BASIS**

Appeal to the United States Supreme Court of a legal challenge to a Massachusetts law governing the access of minors to abortion.

■ **FACTS**

In the late 1970's, Massachusetts had in effect a law which provided that an unmarried girl under eighteen years of age could not get an abortion without either her parents' permission or the consent of a judge. The law also imposed criminal penalties on persons performing abortions on minors who did not receive one of the two forms of consent. The law was challenged as being an unconstitutional restriction on a woman's right to obtain an abortion.

■ **ISSUE**

Can a State give parents an absolute veto over a minor child's decision to obtain an abortion?

■ **DECISION AND RATIONALE**

(Powell, J.) No. A child, merely on account of his minority, is not beyond the protection of the Constitution. However, the unique role of the family in our society requires that constitutional principles be applied with sensitivity and flexibility to the special needs of parents and children. There are three reasons that the constitutional rights of children cannot be equated with those of adults: the peculiar vulnerability of children; their inability to make critical decisions in an informed and mature manner; and the importance of the parental role in child rearing. Central to many theories on child-rearing, and deeply rooted in our Nation's history and tradition, is the belief that the parental role implies a substantial measure of authority over one's children. With these principles in mind, we consider the specific constitutional questions presented by these appeals. In the law at issue, Massachusetts has attempted to reconcile the constitutional right of a woman to terminate a pregnancy with the special interest of the State in encouraging an unmarried pregnant minor to seek the advice of her parents in making the important decision whether or not to bear a child. In *Planned Parenthood of Central Missouri v. Danforth* (1976), we held that a State cannot lawfully authorize an absolute parental veto over the decision of a minor to terminate her pregnancy. However, parental notice and consent are qualifications that typically may be imposed by the State on a minor's right to make important decisions. As such, a State may reasonably determine that, with respect to the abortion decision, parental consultation is in the best interest of the minor. But we are concerned here with a constitutional right to seek an abortion. The abortion decision differs from other decisions that may be made during minority. The need to preserve the constitutional right and the unique nature of the abortion decision requires a State to act with particular sensitivity when it legislates to foster parental involvement in this matter. The pregnant minor's options are much different from those facing a minor in other situations. A pregnant adolescent cannot preserve for long the possibility of aborting, which effectively expires in a matter of weeks from the onset of the pregnancy. Moreover, the potentially severe detriment facing a pregnant woman (health concerns, unwanted motherhood, financial concerns, etc.) is not mitigated by her minority. In sum, there are few situations in which denying a minor the right to make an important decision will have consequences so grave and indelible. Yet an abortion may not be the best choice for the minor. The circumstances in which this issue arises will vary widely. In a given case, alternatives to abortion may be feasible and relevant to the minor's best interests. Nonetheless, the abortion decision is one that simply cannot be postponed, or it will be made by default with far-reaching consequences. For these reasons, "the State may not impose a blanket provision . . . requiring the consent of a parent or person in loco parentis as a condition for abortion of an unmarried minor during the first 12 weeks of her pregnancy." *Planned Parenthood v. Danforth*. Although such deference to parents may be permissible with respect to other choices facing a minor, the unique nature and consequences of the abortion decision make it inappropriate to give a parent such a veto power.

We therefore conclude that if the State decides to require a pregnant minor to obtain one or both parents' consent to an abortion, it also must provide an alternative procedure whereby authorization for the abortion can be obtained. A pregnant minor is entitled in such a proceeding to show either: (1) that she is mature enough and well enough informed to make her abortion decision independently of her parents' wishes; or (2) that even if she is not able to make this decision independently, the desired abortion would be in her best interests. The proceeding must assure that a resolution of the issue will be completed with anonymity and sufficient expedition to provide an effective opportunity for an abortion to be obtained. In sum, the procedure must ensure that the provision requiring parental consent does not amount to the "absolute, and possibly arbitrary, veto" found impermissible in *Danforth*. We conclude, therefore, that under state regulations such as that undertaken by Massachusetts, every minor must have the opportunity to go directly to a court without first consulting or notifying her parents.

■ CONCURRENCE

(Stevens, J.) Massachusetts requires the consent of both of a woman's parents. It does provide an alternative, but that alternative gives a judge an absolute veto power of the minor's decision. In Massachusetts, then, the State has imposed an "absolute limitation on the minor's right to obtain an abortion." The provision of an absolute veto to a judge is troubling. It is inherent in the right to make the abortion decision that the right may be exercised without public scrutiny and in defiance of the contrary opinion of the sovereign or other third parties. The need to commence judicial proceedings imposes a burden at least as great as that imposed on the minor child by the need to obtain parental consent. Moreover, once this burden is met, the only standard provided for the judge's decision is the best interest of the minor. That standard provides little guidance to the judge, and his decision may very likely reflect personal and societal values whose enforcement upon the minor is fundamentally at odds with privacy interests underlying the constitutional protection afforded to her decision.

Analysis:

Bellotti v. Baird stands for the proposition that while a state can require that a minor get some sort of special permission before she terminates a pregnancy, parents cannot be given an absolute veto power over a minor child's decision to obtain an abortion. As such, when a minor's parents do not agree that an abortion should be performed or when the minor does not wish to tell her parents about the pregnancy, she must be provided with an alternative method of gaining permission. That method is through a court order, which *Bellotti* holds will be given either when the minor can demonstrate the requisite maturity to make the abortion decision, or when the court finds that an abortion is in the minor's best interest. If either of these findings is made, the abortion can be performed without parental consent and notification. *Bellotti* also makes it clear that states cannot make the judicial bypass

Bellotti v. Baird (Continued)

procedure so lengthy and complicated that it effectively precludes the minor from pursuing that option in time to have the abortion. The procedure must be such that the minor has ready access to the courts.

■ **CASE VOCABULARY**

IN LOCO PARENTIS: Latin phrase meaning "in the place of a parent," denoting the existence of a temporary guardian for a child.

Cruzan v. Director, Missouri Department of Health

(*Coma Patient's Parents*) v. (*State of Missouri*)
497 U.S. 261, 110 S.Ct. 2841 (1990)

THE CONSTITUTION GRANTS COMPETENT PERSONS THE RIGHT TO ACCEPT OR REFUSE LIFE-SAVING MEDICAL TREATMENT

■ **INSTANT FACTS** The parents of a patient who had long been in a vegetative state sought court permission to have their daughter's life terminated when the hospital in which their daughter was staying refused to discontinue lifesaving treatment without a court order.

■ **BLACK LETTER RULE** When a guardian seeks to discontinue lifesaving nutrition and hydration or other lifesaving medical treatment for an incompetent person, the State may require that the guardian show by clear and convincing evidence that the person would have wanted such a termination of her life.

■ **PROCEDURAL BASIS**

Appeal to the United States Supreme Court of a Missouri Supreme Court decision not to permit an incompetent person's parents to authorize the hospital to cease measures aimed at sustaining the patient's life.

■ **FACTS**

On January 11, 1983, Nancy Cruzan (P) entered a vegetative coma as a result of an automobile accident. She remained in a coma for approximately three weeks until she entered an unconscious state in which she was able to orally ingest some nutrition. Surgeons later implanted a gastrostomy feeding and hydration tube into her body, doing so with the consent of her then husband. Subsequent rehabilitative efforts proved unavailing, and for a significant period of time, Cruzan (P) remained in a persistent vegetative state, a condition in which a person exhibits motor reflexes but evinces no indications of significant cognitive function. After it had become apparent that she had no chance of regaining her mental faculties, Cruzan's parents (P) asked hospital employees to terminate the artificial nutrition and hydration procedures. All agreed that doing so would cause her death. The hospital refused to honor the request without court approval, so Cruzan's parents (P) went to court. At trial, the Cruzans (P) presented evidence of statements made by their daughter to a housemate a year prior to her accident to the effect that she would not want to live as a vegetable. The statements did not, however, go specifically to the withdrawal of medical treatment. The parents (P) received that approval from a Missouri trial court, but that court's decision was reversed by the Missouri Supreme Court.

■ **ISSUE**

Does a person have a right to refuse medical treatment?

■ **DECISION AND RATIONALE**

(Rehnquist, J.) Yes. At common law, the touching of another without consent or legal justification was a battery. This notion of bodily integrity is embodied in the requirement that informed consent is generally required before medical treatment can be administered. The logical corollary of this doctrine is that the patient generally possess a right to not consent, or to refuse treatment. The principle that a competent person has a constitutionally-protected liberty interest in refusing unwanted medical treatment can be inferred from our prior decisions, but determining that a person has this kind of "liberty interest" does not end the inquiry. Whether a person's constitutional rights have been violated "must be determined by balancing his liberty interests against the relevant state interests." An incompetent person is not able to make an informed and voluntary choice to exercise a hypothetical right to refuse treatment. Such a "right" must be exercised for her by some sort of surrogate. Missouri (D) has recognized that under certain circumstances a surrogate may act for the patient in electing to have hydration and nutrition withdrawn, but it has established a procedural safeguard to assure that the action conforms to the wishes expressed by the patient while competent. This safeguard is the requirement of proof by clear and convincing evidence of intent to have treatment withdrawn. Whether Missouri's (D) clear and convincing evidence requirement comports with the Constitution depends in part on what interests the State may property seek to protect in this situation. Missouri (D) relies on its interest in the protection and preservation of human life. We do not think a State is required to remain neutral in the face of an informed and voluntary decision by a physically able adult to starve to death. But in the context presented here, a State has more particular interests at stake. The choice between life and death is a deeply personal decision of obvious finality. Missouri (D) may legitimately seek to safeguard the personal element of this choice through the imposition of heightened evidentiary requirements. Not all incompetent patients will have loved ones available to serve as surrogate decision-makers, and even where family members are present, there will be unfortunate instances in which family members will not act in the patient's best interest. A State is entitled to guard against potential abuses in such situations. In our view, Missouri (D) has permissibly sought to advance these interests through the adoption of a clear and convincing standard of proof. The interests at stake in the instant proceedings are more substantial than those involved in a run-of-the-mill civil dispute. But not only does the standard of proof reflect the importance of a particular adjudication, it also serves as "a societal judgment about how the risk of error should be distributed between the litigants." The more stringent the burden of proof a party must bear, the more that party bears the risk of an erroneous decision. Missouri (D) may permissibly place an increased risk of an erroneous decision on those seeking to terminate an incompetent individual's life-sustaining treatment because an erroneous decision to withdraw such treatment cannot be corrected. In sum, we conclude that a State may apply a clear and convincing evidence standard in proceedings where a guardian seeks to discontinue nutrition and hydration of a person in a persistent vegetative state. The Supreme Court of Missouri held that the testimony adduced at trial did not amount to clear and convincing proof of the patient's desire to have hydration and nutrition withdrawn. Looking at the record, we cannot say that the Supreme Court of Missouri committed constitutional error in reaching that conclusion. Cruzan's parents (P) alternatively contend that Missouri (D) must accept the substituted judgment of close *family* members even in the absence of the requisite degree of proof. There is no doubt that Cruzan's parents (P) are loving parents, and if the State were required to repose a right of substituted judgment with anyone, the Cruzans (P) would surely qualify. But the Due Process Clause does not require the State to repose judgment on these matters with anyone but the patient herself. There is no automatic assurance that the view of close family members will necessarily be the same as the patient's would have been had she been confronted with the prospect while competent. All of the reasons for allowing Missouri (D) to require clear and convincing evidence of the patient's wishes lead us to conclude that the State may choose to defer only to those wishes, rather than confide the decision to close family members. Affirmed.

■ CONCURRENCE

(O'Connor, J.) The State's imposition of medical treatment on an unwilling competent adult necessarily involves some form of restraint and intrusion, and may burden that individual's liberty interests as much as any other state coercion. The artificial provision of nutrition and hydration implicates identical concerns. Requiring a competent adult to endure such procedures against her will burdens the patient's liberty, dignity, and freedom to determine the course of her own treatment. Accordingly, the liberty guaranteed by the Due Process Clause must protect an individual's decision to reject life-sustaining medical treatment. Today the Court does not decide the issue whether a State must also give effect to the decisions of a surrogate decision-maker. In my view, such a duty may well be constitutionally required to protect the patient's liberty interest in refusing medical treatment. Few individuals provide explicit oral or written instructions regarding their intent to refuse medical treatment should they become incompetent. States which decline to consider any evidence other than such instructions may frequently fail to honor a patient's intent. Such failures might be avoided if the State considered an equally probative source of evidence: the patient's appointment of a proxy to make health care decisions on her behalf. Today's decision does not preclude a future determination that the Constitution requires the States to implement the decisions of a patient's duly appointed surrogate. Nor does it prevent States from developing other approaches to protecting an incompetent individual's liberty interest in refusing medical treatment. No national consensus has yet emerged on the best solution for this difficult problem. Today we decide only that one State's practice does not violate the Constitution; the more challenging task of crafting appropriate procedures for safeguarding incompetents' liberty interests is entrusted to the States.

■ CONCURRENCE

(Scalia, J.) This case demonstrates the difficult questions presented by the increasing power of science to keep the human body alive. States have begun to grapple with these problems through legislation. I am concerned from the tenor of today's opinions that we are poised to confuse that enterprise as we have confused the enterprise of abortion—requiring it to be conducted against a background of federal constitutional imperatives that are newly crafted from Term to Term. While I agree with the Court's analysis, I would have preferred that we announce that the federal courts have no business in this field, but that it should be controlled by the States, which are as well or better equipped to address these issues than the members of this Court. When it is demonstrated by clear and convincing evidence that a patient no longer wishes certain measures to be taken to preserve her life, it is up to the citizens of Missouri to decide, through their elected representatives, if that wish will be honored. It is quite impossible (because the Constitution says nothing about the matter) that those citizens will decide upon a line less lawful than the one we would choose; and it is unlikely (because we know no more about "life and death" than they do) that they will decide upon a line less reasonable.

■ DISSENT

(Brennan, J.) Nancy Cruzan (P) lives in "a twilight zone of suspended animation where death commences while life, in some form, continues." Cruzan (P) previously expressed her wish to forgo continuing medical care under circumstances such as these. Her family, friends, and a guardian ad litem are convinced that this is what she would want. And yet the Missouri Supreme Court has determined that this irreversibly vegetative patient will remain a passive prisoner of medical technology for perhaps the next thirty years. Today the Court, while tentatively accepting that there is some degree of constitutionally protected liberty interest in avoiding unwanted medical treatment, including life-sustaining treatment, affirms that Court's decision on the ground that a State may require "clear and convincing" evidence of Cruzan's (P) prior decision to forgo life-sustaining treatment in *order* to ensure that her actual wishes are honored. Because I believe that Cruzan (P) has a fundamental right to be free of unwanted artificial nutrition and hydration, which right is not outweighed by any interests of the State, and because I find that the improperly biased procedural obstacles imposed by the Missouri Supreme Court impermissibly burden that right, I respectfully dissent. Whatever a State's interests in mandating life-support treatment under other circumstances, there is no good to be obtained here by Missouri's (D) insistence that Cruzan (P) remain on life-support if it is her wish not to do so. Society as a whole will not be benefitted by her receiving medical treatment. No third party's situation will be improved, and no harm to others will be averted. The State's general interest in life must accede to Cruzan's (P) particularized and intense interest in self-determination in her choice of medical treatment. There is simply nothing to be gained by superseding her decision.

Analysis:

The issue in *Cruzan* is the right of the state of Missouri (D) to refuse to cease administering life sustaining nutrition to Nancy Cruzan unless it is shown by clear and convincing evidence that death was her wish. The case, however, stands for much more than the proposition that a state can require the family of a person in a persistent vegetative state to meet a certain evidentiary standard before the person's life is terminated. *Cruzan*, through the declarations of a majority of Justices, stands for the proposition that legally competent persons most likely have a right, protected by the Constitution, to refuse lifesaving medical treatment, including hydration and nutrition. Specifically, Justice Rehnquist, Justice O'Connor, and the members of the dissent all seem to recognize such a right, and would apparently do so if the question came before the Court. To put it another way, the Court seems to say

Cruzan v. Director, Missouri Department of Health (Continued)

that there exists a constitutionally protected right to die. Prior to the *Cruzan* decision in 1990, it was not clear whether any such right existed, so in that sense *Cruzan* is a significant case.

■ CASE VOCABULARY

CLEAR AND CONVINCING EVIDENCE: Evidence indicating that the proposition to be proved is reasonably certain or highly probable; the "clear and convincing" standard is greater than "preponderance of the evidence" but less than "beyond a reasonable doubt."

COGNITIVE FUNCTION: Brain function that allows or permits a person to reason, think, and judge.

SURROGATE DECISION-MAKERS: One who is authorized to make a decision for another.

Washington v. Glucksberg

(State of Washington) v. (Physician Willing to Assist with Patient Suicide)
521 U.S. 702, 117 S.Ct. 2258 (1997)

THERE IS NO FUNDAMENTAL RIGHT TO COMMIT SUICIDE

■ **INSTANT FACTS** A group of doctors challenged the constitutionality of a Washington ban on physician assisted suicide.

■ **BLACK LETTER RULE** The Fourteenth Amendments does not create a constitutionally protected right to participate in physician-assisted suicide; nor does it prohibit states from making it a crime to assist another person in committing suicide.

■ PROCEDURAL BASIS

Appeal to the United States Supreme Court of a lawsuit challenging the constitutionality of a Washington ban against physician-assisted suicide.

■ FACTS

Washington law provides: "A person is guilty of promoting a suicide attempt when he knowingly causes or aids another person to attempt suicide." The law further provides that promoting suicide is a felony, punishable by up to five years in prison and a $10,000 fine. Harold Glucksberg (P), a physician who practices in Washington, and a group of other doctors who regularly treat terminally ill patients, as well as three ill, pseudonymous plaintiffs, filed suit in federal district court seeking a declaration that the above law is unconstitutional.

■ ISSUE

Does the Fourteenth Amendment prohibit states from making it a crime to assist another person in the commission of suicide?

■ DECISION AND RATIONALE

(Rehnquist, J.) No. Glucksberg (P) asserts "the existence of a liberty interest protected by the Fourteenth Amendment which extends to a personal choice by a mentally competent, terminally ill adult to commit physician assisted suicide." We begin today by examining our Nations' history, legal traditions, and practices. In almost every State, it is a crime to assist a suicide. These assisted-suicide bans are not innovations, but are longstanding expressions of commitment in the preservation of human life. Indeed, condemnation of suicide and assisted suicide are consistent themes in our philosophical, legal, and cultural heritage. In recent years, assisted-suicide bans have been reexamined and, generally, reaffirmed. During this time, public concern and democratic actions sharply focused on how best to protect dignity and independence at the end of life, with the result that there have been many significant changes in state laws. At the same time, however, voters and legislators continue to reaffirm prohibitions on assisting suicide. We have "always been reluctant to expand the concept of substantive due process because guideposts for responsible decision making in this unchartered area are scarce and open-ended." We must therefore "exercise the utmost care whenever we are asked to break new ground in this field," lest the liberty protected by the Due Process Clause be subtly transformed into the policy preferences of the members of this Court. Our established method of substantive due process analysis has two primary features. First, we have regularly observed that the Due Process Clause specially protects those fundamental rights and liberties which are "deeply rooted in this Nation's history and tradition," and "implicit in the concept of ordered liberty," such that "neither liberty nor justice would exist if they were sacrificed." Second, we have required a "careful description" of the asserted fundamental liberty interest. It is these principles that we use in assessing the right asserted today. In doing so, we are again confronted with an almost universal tradition that has long rejected the asserted right, and continues to reject it today. To hold for Glucksberg (P), we would have to reverse centuries of legal doctrine and practice, and strike down the considered policy choice of almost every State. Glucksberg (P) contends that in *Cruzan* we "acknowledged that competent, dying persons have the right to direct the removal of life-sustaining medical treatment and thus hasten death," and that the constitutional principle behind recognizing that decision applies to a choice to hasten an impending death by physician-assisted suicide. The right assumed in *Cruzan*, however, was not simply deduced from abstract concepts of personal autonomy, but was based on common-law rules and long legal tradition protecting the decision to refuse unwanted medical treatment. The decision to commit suicide with the assistance of another may be just as personal and profound a decision, but it has never enjoyed similar legal protection. Indeed, the two acts are quite distinct. This being the case, our decision must be that the asserted right to assistance in committing suicide is not a fundamental liberty interest protected by the Due Process Clause. But we are not done. The Constitution also requires that Washington's assisted-suicide ban be rationally related to a legitimate government interest. This requirement is unquestionably met here. First, Washington (D) has an "unqualified interest in the preservation of human life." The State also has an interest in protecting the integrity and ethics of the medical profession, something which might be undermined by blurring the time-honored line between healing and harming. Second, the State has an interest in protecting vulnerable groups from abuse, neglect, and mistake. The State's interest here goes beyond protecting the vulnerable from coercion; it extends to protecting disabled and terminally ill people from prejudice, negative and inaccurate stereotypes, and "societal indifference." Finally, the State may fear that permitting assisted suicide will start it down the road to voluntary and perhaps even involuntary euthanasia. Washington (D), like most other States, reasonably ensures against this risk by banning, rather than regulating, assisted suicide. These various interests are unquestionably important and legitimate, and Washington's (D) ban on assisted suicide is at least reasonably related to their promotion and protection.

■ CONCURRENCE

(O'Connor, J.) I agree that there is no generalized right to commit suicide. But Glucksberg (P) asks us to address a narrower question of whether a mentally competent person experiencing great suffering has a constitutionally protected interest in controlling the circumstances of an imminent death. I see no need to address that question in the context of the challenges before us today. There is no dispute that dying patients in Washington (D) and New York can obtain medication to relieve their suffering, even when taking the medication may hasten their deaths. The difficulty in defining terminal illness and the risk that a dying patient's request for assistance in ending his or her life might not be truly voluntary justifies the prohibitions on assisted suicide we uphold here. Determining the parameters of those prohibitions is properly left up to the States.

■ CONCURRENCE

(Stevens, J.) The Court observes that our holding today is fully consistent with a continuation of the vigorous debate about the "morality, legality, and practicality of physician-assisted suicide." There is also room, however, for debate about the constitutional limits on the power of the States to punish the practice. The Court has decided that Washington's statute is not invalid "on its face," or that it is valid in most cases in which it might be applied. That holding, however, does not foreclose the possibility that some applications of the statute might well be invalid. Just as our conclusion that capital punishment is not always unconstitutional did not preclude later decisions holding that it is sometimes impermissibly cruel, so is it equally clear that a decision upholding a general statutory prohibition of assisted suicide does not mean that every possible application of the statute would be valid. A State that has authorized the death penalty and thereby has concluded that the sanctity of human life does not require that it always be preserved, must acknowledge that there are situations in which an interest in hastening death is legitimate. Indeed, not only is that interest sometimes legitimate, but there are times when it is entitled to constitutional protection.

■ CONCURRENCE

(Breyer, J.) I agree that the critical question in these cases is whether "the 'liberty' specially protected by the Due Process Clause includes a right" of the sort that Glucksberg (P) asserts. I do not agree, however, with the formulation of that claimed liberty interest as a "right to commit suicide with another's assistance." I would not reject Glucksberg's (P) claim without considering a different formulation, one for which there is greater legal support. That formulation would use words to the effect of a "right to die with dignity," and would encompass a combination of personal control over the manner of death, professional medical assistance, and the avoidance of unnecessary and severe physical suffering. Glucksberg (P) argues that one can find a "right to die with dignity" by examining the protection the law has provided for related interests involving personal dignity, medical treatment, and freedom from state-inflicted pain. I do not believe, however, that this Court need now decide whether such a right is "fundamental" because the avoidance of severe physical pain would have to constitute an essential part of any successful claim and because the laws before us do not force a dying person to undergo that kind of pain. Rather, the laws do not prohibit doctors providing patients with drugs sufficient to control pain despite the risk that those drugs themselves will kill. Under these circumstances, the laws at issue overcome any remaining significant interests and would be justified regardless.

Analysis:

In *Glucksberg* the Court refused to extend its ruling in *Cruzan* that a mentally competent adult has the right to refuse life-saving medical treatment to hold that a mentally competent adult has the right to take affirmative steps to die. Chief Justice Rehnquist applies the standard substantive due process and equal protection analysis that the Supreme Court has used since the end of the *Lochner* era. In doing so, he first considers whether the ability to commit suicide is a fundamental right. If it is, the Court must determine whether it serves a compelling state interest and whether the statute is narrowly tailored to serve that interest (strict scrutiny analysis). If the ability to commit suicide is not a fundamental right, the statute is presumed constitutional. A person challenging the law would then have to show that there was no conceivable state of facts under which the statute might be rationally related to any legitimate government interest (rational basis analysis). In *Glucksberg*, the Court held that there was no fundamental right to commit suicide, and used a rational basis standard to find that the Washington law did not violate substantive due process.

Lawrence v. Texas

(Homosexual Man) v. *(Prosecuting Authority)*
539 U.S. 558, 123 S.Ct. 2472 (2003)

THE REGULATION OF SEXUAL EXPRESSION VIOLATES THE FUNDAMENTAL RIGHT OF PRIVACY

■ **INSTANT FACTS** Lawrence (D) was convicted of deviate sexual intercourse with another man in violation of a state statute.

■ **BLACK LETTER RULE** State laws criminalizing homosexual relations violate substantive due process.

■ **PROCEDURAL BASIS**

Certiorari to review the constitutionality of a state statute.

■ **FACTS**

On a report of a weapons disturbance, Houston police entered Lawrence's (D) dwelling, where they discovered him having sexual relations with another man. The two men were arrested, charged, and convicted for violating a Texas statute prohibiting "deviate sexual intercourse with another individual of the same sex."

■ **ISSUE**

Does a statute prohibiting private sexual intercourse between consenting homosexual adults violate the Due Process Clause?

■ **DECISION AND RATIONALE**

(Kennedy, J.) Yes. The right of privacy includes the right to make decisions regarding the marital relationship. That right has been expanded beyond marital relations to include the right of unmarried individuals to decide whether to conceive a child. At its core, the right of privacy involves the right to be free from unwarranted government intrusion into fundamental personal decisions and liberty interests. Statutes prohibiting a certain type of sexual expression deprive individuals of more than a chosen sexual behavior. They infringe upon fundamental personal relationships in private homes between consenting adults. The Constitution protects individual choices to express their personal feelings with intimate conduct.

Laws against homosexual behavior do not have "ancient roots" that make homosexual contact any less of a fundamental right than intimate conduct in general. Historical sodomy laws were not enforced against homosexuals in particular, but against society in general. Further, sodomy laws have not historically been enforced against consenting adults acting in private. Not until relatively recently in our country's history have states sought to specifically prohibit homosexual activity, and the more recent trend is toward abolishing such laws. Although in *Bowers v. Hardwick*, 478 U.S. 186 (1986), the Court held that state laws prohibiting homosexual relations withstand constitutional scrutiny, the Court should have acknowledged this growing recognition of homosexual rights.

While an appropriately tailored statute prohibiting homosexual relations may survive equal-protection scrutiny, the inevitable violations of individual liberty interests violate due process. The criminalization of homosexual conduct creates a public stigma and carries other consequences. Because these consequences bear an important relationship to the liberty interests of consenting adults, *Bowers* is overruled, and state laws criminalizing homosexual contact between consenting adults in private violate the Due Process Clause.

■ CONCURRENCE

(O'Connor, J.) The statute in *Bowers* presented a different issue than presented in this case. In *Bowers*, the statute criminalized sodomy for all individuals, while the Texas statute here punishes only homosexual conduct. Because the statute targets one class of individuals over another, it suffices to strike down the Texas statute as violating the Equal Protection Clause. *Bowers*, however, should not be overruled.

■ DISSENT

(Scalia, J.) Under the majority's approach to stare decisis, an erroneous decision should be overruled if its foundation has been eroded by subsequent decisions, there has been "substantial and continuing" criticism of the decision, and there has been no societal reliance on the decision counseling against overruling it. Accepting those factors, the Court should overrule *Roe v. Wade*, which it has vehemently declined to do. Even accepting this approach, there has been overwhelming societal reliance on *Bowers'* direction that moral offenses involving sexual behavior are supported by the Constitution. Courts have accepted this approach to sustain laws proscribing bigamy, same-sex marriages, adultery, and obscenity, among others. Reliance on the *Bowers* decision thus supports stare decisis even under the majority's misguided approach.

While the Texas statute undoubtedly deprives individual liberty interests, the Due Process Clause does not prohibit all denials of liberty. Under a due-process review, only those rights that are "deeply rooted in this Nation's history and tradition" are fundamental and raise compelling state interests. Although the Court points to the lack of historical targeting of homosexual sodomy, the Court ignores that sodomy has been criminalized in general throughout American history, and it matters not whether those laws specifically targeted one class of citizens. Because sodomy has long been criminalized, there is no historical right to such conduct that is deeply rooted in American history and tradition. Moreover, an "emerging awareness" of a protected liberty interest to engage in sexual activity by consenting adults in private does not establish a fundamental right.

In concluding that the Texas law is not rationally related to a legitimate state interest, the majority surmises that the state has no legitimate interest in regulating immoral and unacceptable sexual activity. Yet, laws against bigamy, fornication, adultery, and incest support the same moral agenda, and one cannot imagine successful constitutional challenges to such regulations.

Neither does the Texas statute violate the Equal Protection Clause, for it treats all individuals alike, regardless of gender. The statute does not punish men differently than women, but rather punishes both equally, not because of their gender, but because of the gender of their partner and the activities in which they engage.

■ DISSENT

(Thomas, J.) The Constitution contains no general right of privacy that compels the Court to strike down the Texas statute. Nonetheless, the law at issue should be legislatively repealed because it "does not appear to be a worthy way to expend valuable law enforcement resources."

Analysis:

The Court's decision has largely been criticized as results-oriented, without any logical resort to legal doctrine. In such an ideologically divisive topic as homosexual rights, it is easy to understand the Court's temptation to reach the desired outcome, using broad legal principles to justify its decision. Although the Justices are bound by oath to uphold the Constitution, is it possible that personal beliefs could creep into certain Court decisions?

■ CASE VOCABULARY

SODOMY: Oral or anal copulation between humans, especially those of the same sex.

SUBSTANTIVE DUE PROCESS: The doctrine that the Due Process Clauses of the Fifth and Fourteenth Amendments require legislation to be fair and reasonable in content and to further a legitimate governmental objective.

Whalen v. Roe

(Not Stated) v. (Not Stated)
429 U.S. 589, 97 S.Ct. 869 (1977)

THE RIGHT TO PRIVACY GUARANTEED BY THE FOURTEENTH AMENDMENT DOES NOT PRECLUDE THE STATE FROM COLLECTING INFORMATION REGARDING THE USE OF PRESCRIPTION DRUGS BY ITS CITIZENS

■ **INSTANT FACTS** A lawsuit challenged the right of the New York Department of Health to record and store in a central computer certain information related to the issuance of medical prescriptions by New York physicians.

■ **BLACK LETTER RULE** The disclosure of private medical information to medical personnel, insurance companies, and public health agencies does not per se amount to an impermissible and unconstitutional invasion of privacy.

■ **PROCEDURAL BASIS**

Appeal to the United States Supreme Court of a right-to-privacy lawsuit filed against the State of New York in federal court.

■ **FACTS**

In the early 1970s, a special commission formed by the New York Legislature determined that the state's drug-control laws were deficient in several respects. For example, the commission found that under the law as it existed in 1970, there was no way to prevent the use of stolen or altered prescriptions, no way to prevent dishonest pharmacists from continuing to refill expired prescriptions, no way to prevent drug users from simultaneously obtaining prescriptions from a number of doctors, and no way to prevent doctors from over-prescribing certain drugs. In an attempt to overcome these problems, legislation was drafted which provided that copies of all prescriptions for certain types of drugs had to be sent to the New York State Department of Health. When received, the Department would then enter the identity of the physician, the pharmacy, the drug and dosage, and the name, address, and age of the patient into a computer. The law also included certain safeguards to protect against inappropriate disclosure of or access to the recorded information. Shortly after its inception, the law was challenged on grounds that it violated the right of privacy of those whose information was recorded.

■ **ISSUE**

Can a state, consistent with the Constitution, record in a centralized computer the names and addresses of all persons who have obtained certain prescription drugs for which there is both a lawful and unlawful market?

■ **DECISION AND RATIONALE**

(Stevens, J.) Yes. Our prior cases demonstrate that States have been given wide latitude in experimenting with potential solutions to problems of local concern. The statute challenged in this case represents such an attempt. There is nothing unreasonable in the assumption that the patient-identification requirement might aid in the enforcement of laws designed to minimize the misuse of dangerous drugs, for the requirement could reasonably be expected to both have a deterrent effect on potential violators

Whalen v. Roe (Continued)

and aid in the investigation of instances of apparent abuse. Appellees contend that the statute invades a constitutionally protected "zone of privacy." There are at least two different kinds of privacy interests recognized by the law. One is the individual interest in avoiding disclosure of personal matters, and the second is the interest in independence in making certain important decisions. We are persuaded that the New York program does not pose a sufficiently grievous threat to either interest to establish a constitutional violation. With respect to the issue before us today, public disclosure of patient information can come about in two ways: (1) Health Department employees may fail to maintain proper security; and (2) a patient or doctor may be accused of a violation and the stored data offered in evidence in a related judicial proceeding. Neither of the other two possibilities provides a proper ground for attacking the statute. There is no support for an assumption that the security provisions of the statute will be administered improperly, and the mere possibility that judicial supervision of the evidentiary use of information will provide inadequate protection against unwarranted disclosures is surely not a sufficient reason for invalidating the program. It is true that private information must be disclosed to the authorized employees of the Department of Heath. Such disclosures, however, are not meaningfully distinguishable from a host of other invasions of privacy associated with health care. Disclosures of private medical information to medical personnel, insurance companies, and public health agencies is an essential part of modern medical practice. Requiring similar disclosures to state representatives responsible for the health of the community does not automatically amount to an impermissible invasion of privacy. We are not unaware of the threat to privacy implicit in the accumulation of vast amounts of personal information in computerized data banks or other government files. The right to collect and use such data for public purposes is typically accompanied by a concomitant duty to avoid unwarranted disclosures. Recognizing that in some circumstances that duty may have its roots in the Constitution, New York's statutory scheme nevertheless has a proper concern with and protection of the individual's interest in privacy. We therefore need not decide any question which might be presented by the unwarranted disclosure of accumulated private date by a system that did not contain comparable security provisions. We simply hold that this record does not establish an invasion of any right or liberty protected by the Fourteenth Amendment.

Analysis:

As the most prominent of the Supreme Court decisions addressing the issue of government collection and retention of personal information, *Whalen* stands for the proposition that the constitutional right to privacy discussed in *Griswold*, *Roe*, and other Fourteenth Amendment cases does not preclude the government from having access to certain personal information that citizens may or may not be willing to share. With respect to the potential ramifications of completely limiting government access to personal information, *Whalen* is a logical decision. Imagine, for example, if the government was wholly prohibited from accessing any part of its citizens' personal financial information. Such a result would make it impossible to collect taxes in a systematic and uniform way, and would therefore limit the government's ability to fund the programs that we want and need the government to fund. A balance needs to be struck between the individual's right to privacy and the government's need to know, and *Whalen* makes an effort to strike that balance. Furthermore, as the majority opinion indicates, the government does have a duty to keep certain information private. From the tenor of the majority and concurring opinions in *Whalen*, it is apparent that if the New York law at issue did not contain the safeguards against unwarranted disclosure that it did in fact have, the Court would likely have gone the other way.

■ CASE VOCABULARY

CONCOMITANT DUTY: An accompanying duty.

Saenz v. Roe

(Not Stated) v. (Not Stated)
526 U.S. 489, 119 S.Ct. 1518 (1999)

THE PRIVILEGES OR IMMUNITIES CLAUSE REQUIRES STATES TO PAY THE SAME WELFARE BENEFITS TO NEW STATE RESIDENTS AS THEY PAY TO LONG-TERM RESIDENTS

■ **INSTANT FACTS** A lawsuit challenged a California law which limited the welfare benefits of new California residents to that amount which they would have received in the state they most recently moved from.

■ **BLACK LETTER RULE** The constitutionally-protected right to travel embraces the citizen's right to be treated equally in her new State of residence.

■ **PROCEDURAL BASIS**

Not stated.

■ **FACTS**

The Social Security Act authorizes States to fund various welfare programs and provides some federal tax dollars for those programs. In 1992, the California Legislature decided that a reduction in its vast welfare budget was needed. In order to effect this reduction, the legislature enacted § 11450.03 of the Welfare and Institutions Code, which limited payments made to first-year residents of the State to the amount of benefits they would have received had they stayed in the state from which they moved to California. Because California was one of the more generous states when it came to making welfare payments, the statute meant that first-year residents generally received lower welfare payments than other welfare recipients.

■ **ISSUE**

Can a State, consistent with the Constitution, place limits on the amount of welfare benefits a new resident may receive?

■ **DECISION AND RATIONALE**

(Stevens, J.) No. The word "travel" is not found in the Constitution, and yet the "constitutional right to travel from one State to another," "a virtually unconditional personal right," is firmly embedded in our jurisprudence. *Shapiro v. Thompson* (1969). In *Shapiro*, we reviewed the constitutionality of three statutory provisions that denied welfare assistance to residents of Connecticut, the District of Columbia, and Pennsylvania, who had resided in those jurisdictions less than one year. In doing so, we noted that the Court had long "recognized that the nature of our Federal Union and our constitutional concepts of personal liberty unite to require that all citizens be free to travel throughout the length and breadth of our land uninhibited by statutes, rules, or regulations which unreasonably burden or restrict this movement." We squarely held that it was "constitutionally impermissible" for a State to enact durational residency requirements for the purpose of inhibiting the migration by needy persons into the State. We further held that a classification that had the effect of imposing a penalty on the exercise of the right to travel violated the Equal Protection Clause "unless shown to be necessary to promote a compelling governmental interest." The "right to travel," discussed in a handful of prior cases, embraces the right

Saenz v. Roe (Continued)

of a citizen of one State to enter and leave another State, the right to be treated as a welcome visitor rather than an unfriendly alien when temporarily present in the second State, and, for those who elect to become permanent residents of a new State, the right to be treated like other citizens of that State. Given that § 11450.03 imposed no obstacle to respondents' entry into California, the State is correct when it argues that the statute does not directly impair the exercise of the right to free interstate movement. For the purposes of this case, therefore, we need not identify the source of that particular right in the text of the Constitution. The second component of the right to travel is expressly protected by the text of the Constitution. Article IV, § 2, provides: "The Citizens of each State shall be entitled to all Privileges and Immunities of Citizens of the several States." Thus, by virtue of a person's state citizenship, a citizen of one State who travels in other States, intending to return home at the end of his journey, is entitled to enjoy the "Privileges and Immunities of Citizens in the several States" that he visits. In this respect, the Privileges or Immunities Clause bars "discrimination against citizens of other States where there is no substantial reason for the discrimination beyond the mere fact that they are citizens of other States." At issue in this case is the third aspect of the right to travel—the right of newly arrived citizens to the same privileges and immunities enjoyed by other citizens of the same State. That right is protected not only by the new arrival's status as a state citizen, but also by her status as a citizen of the United States: as the Fourteenth Amendment states, "No State shall make or enforce any law which shall abridge the privileges or immunities of citizens of the United States." Despite differing views on the coverage of the Privileges or Immunities Clause of the Fourteenth Amendment, it has always been understood that this Clause protects this third component of the right to travel. That newly arrived citizens "have two political capacities, one state and one federal," adds special force to their claim that they have the same rights as others who share their citizenship. Neither mere rationality nor some intermediate standard of review should be used to judge the constitutionality of a rule that discriminates against some State citizens because they have been domiciled in the State for less than a year. Because this case involves discrimination against citizens who have completed their interstate travel, the State's argument that its welfare scheme affects the right to travel only "incidentally" is beside the point. Were we concerned solely with actual deterrence to migration, we might be persuaded that a partial withholding of benefits constitutes a lesser incursion on the right to travel than an outright denial of all benefits. But since the right to travel embraces the citizen's right to be treated equally in her new State of residence, the discriminatory classification is itself a penalty. California has advanced an entirely fiscal justification for its multi-tiered scheme: § 11450.03 will save the State approximately $10.9 million a year. The question is whether the State may accomplish that end by the discriminatory means it has chosen, and the answer is "no." The Citizenship Clause of the Fourteenth Amendment, which is a limitation on the power of the National Government, expressly equates citizenship with residence: "That Clause does not provide for, and does not allow for, degrees of citizenship based on length of residence." Neither the duration of a person's residence, nor the identity of their prior State of residence, has any relevance to their need for benefits. Nor do these factors bear any relationship to the State's interest in making an equitable allocation of funds. Moreover, the fact that Congress approved durational residence requirements in the 1996 amendment to the Social Security Act does not save § 11450.03, as Congress may not authorize States to violate the Fourteenth Amendment.

■ **DISSENT**

(Rehnquist, J.) The Court today breathes new life into the previously dormant Privileges or Immunities Clause—a Clause relied upon in only one other decision, *Colgate v. Harvey* (1935), which was overruled five years later. It uses this Clause to strike down a reasonable measure falling under the head of a "good-faith residency requirement." Much of the Court's opinion is sound. For example, the right to travel clearly embraces the right to go from one place to another, and prohibits States from impeding that movement. But I cannot see how the right to become a citizen of another State is a necessary "component" of the right to travel. A person is no longer "traveling" when he finishes his journey to a State which he plans to make his home. Furthermore, the right to travel and the right to become a citizen are distinct, their relationship is not reciprocal, and one is not a "component" of the other. In holding as it does, the Court ignores a State's need to assure that only persons who establish a bona fide residence receive the benefits provided to current residents of the State. If States can require individuals to reside in-state for a year before exercising the right to educational benefits (*Starns v. Malkerson*), the right to terminate a marriage (*Sosna v. Iowa*), or the right to vote in primary elections (*Rosario v. Rockefeller*), then States may surely do the same for welfare benefits. There is no material difference between a one-year residence requirement applied to the level of welfare benefits given out by a State, and the same requirement applied to the level of tuition subsidies at a state university. The durational residence requirement challenged here is a permissible exercise of the State's power to "assur[e] that services provided for its residents are enjoyed only by residents."

Analysis:

Based on precedent set by prior cases, the outcome of *Saenz v. Roe* is not a surprise. Somewhat surprising, however, is the way that the Court reached that outcome—by way of the Privileges or immunities Clause. The right of persons to travel freely from state to state without hindrance has long been recognized by the Supreme Court. The seminal case in this area, cited by Justice Stevens in his opinion for the majority, is *Shapiro v. Thompson* (1969). Addressing the unconstitutionality of a durational residency requirement for those seeking welfare benefits, the majority opinion in *Shapiro* states: "Since the classification here touches on the fundamental right of interstate movement, its constitutionality must be judged by the stricter standard of whether it promotes a compelling state interest. Under this standard, the waiting-period requirement clearly violates the Equal Protection Clause." *Shapiro*, then, stands for the proposition that states must have a very good reason for imposing classifications that hinder interstate travel. The Court's decision in this case is even more clearly foreshadowed in *Memorial Hospital v. Maricopa County* (1974), which addressed the constitutionality of a law requiring one year of in-county residency in order for a person to receive non-emergency hospitalization or medical care at county expense. In holding that law unconstitutional, the Court wrote that its prior decisions "stand for the proposition that a classification which operates to penalize those persons . . . who have exercised their constitutional right of interstate migration, must be justified by a compelling state interest."

■ CASE VOCABULARY

DURATIONAL RESIDENCE REQUIREMENT: Requirement that a person live in a certain location (generally a state) for a pre-determined period of time before things such as welfare and other government benefits become available.

PRIVILEGES OR IMMUNITIES CLAUSE: Portion of the Fourteenth Amendment which prohibits states from passing laws that abridge the privileges or immunities of United States Citizens.

Harper v. Virginia State Board of Elections
(Voter) v. *(State of Virginia)*
383 U.S. 663, 86 S.Ct. 1079 (1966)

STATE POLL TAXES ARE UNCONSTITUTIONAL

■ **INSTANT FACTS** A dispute arose over a Virginia poll tax which required residents to pay $1.50 in order to vote in state elections.

■ **BLACK LETTER RULE** A State violates the Equal Protection Clause whenever it makes the payment of a fee a precondition to voting.

■ **PROCEDURAL BASIS**
Not stated.

■ **FACTS**
Section 173 of the Virginia Constitution directed the State to impose an annual poll tax of $1.50 on every resident 21 years of age or older. A group of Virginia residents (P) challenged that portion of the State's Constitution as being unconstitutional under the federal Constitution.

■ **ISSUE**
Are poll taxes constitutional?

■ **DECISION AND RATIONALE**
(Douglas, J.) No. The Equal Protection Clause prevents the States from fixing voter qualifications which invidiously discriminate. In this regard, a State violates the Equal Protection Clause whenever it makes the affluence of the voter or payment of any fee an electoral standard—voter qualifications have no relation to wealth or the payment of any tax. It is argued that if a State can demand a fee for a driver's license, it can demand an equal poll tax for voting. But the interest of the State when it comes to voting is limited to the power to fix qualifications. Wealth, like race, creed, or color, is not germane to one's ability to participate intelligently in the electoral process. As such, the requirement of fee paying causes an "invidious" discrimination that runs afoul of the Equal Protection Clause. Where fundamental rights and liberties are asserted under the Equal Protection Clause, classifications which might invade them must be closely scrutinized and carefully. Because the right to vote is too precious and too fundamental to be so burdened or conditioned, those principles apply here.

Analysis:
Before the 1960's, the Supreme Court showed great deference toward state regulations of voter qualifications. One reason for that deference was the Constitution itself, which expressly delegates to the states the power to establish their own qualifications for voting in both state and federal elections. *Harper* is the beginning of a change in the Court's deferential policy in this area and opened the door to more active supervision of state voting schemes. The Court's decision is based on two modes of analysis: fundamental rights and suspect classifications. In its opinion, the Court notes that classifica-

tions based on wealth, like those based on race, are traditionally disfavored. While this equal protection analysis is important to the Court's decision in subsequent decisions on voting rights and restrictions have focused on the fundamental rights aspect of this case, and have made it clear that because citizen voting is essential to our system of democratic, representative government, the right to vote is a fundamental right.

■ CASE VOCABULARY

POLL TAX: A fee that must be paid before a person is permitted to vote.

Kramer v. Union Free School District

(State Citizen) v. (Local School District)
395 U.S. 621, 89 S.Ct. 1886 (1969)

OWNING LAND OR HAVING CHILDREN ENROLLED IN PUBLIC SCHOOL CANNOT BE MADE A PREREQUISITE TO VOTING IN SCHOOL DISTRICT ELECTIONS

■ **INSTANT FACTS** A citizen challenged a New York law which precluded certain persons from voting in school district elections.

■ **BLACK LETTER RULE** Laws which limit the ability of certain persons to vote in various governmental elections are unconstitutional unless they are narrowly tailored and necessary to achieve a compelling state interest.

■ **PROCEDURAL BASIS**

Appeal to the United States Supreme Court of a federal lawsuit challenging a state limitation on the right of certain persons to vote in school district elections.

■ **FACTS**

Section 2012 of the New York Education Law provided that in certain school districts, a person could vote in school district elections only if he or she either owned or leased taxable real property within the district, or was a parent of a child enrolled in local public schools. Kramer (P), a bachelor who did not fit into either category, filed suit against the Union Free School District (D) claiming that § 2012 denied him equal protection of the law in violation of the Fourteenth Amendment.

■ **ISSUE**

Can a State lawfully allow only landowners and people with children enrolled in public school to vote in school district elections?

■ **DECISION AND RATIONALE**

(Warren, J.) No. In addition to Kramer (P), the statute at issue affects a number of persons. For example, the statute disenfranchises seniors living with their children; clergy, military personnel, and others who have no children and live on tax-exempt property; and parents who neither own nor lease qualifying property and whose children are either too young to attend school or choose to attend private school. We therefore turn to the question of whether the exclusion is necessary to promote a compelling state interest. The School District (D) argues that the State has a legitimate interest in limiting the franchise in school district elections to those primarily interested in and directly affected by such elections, namely property tax payers and parents of the children enrolled in the district's schools. The District (D) argues that it is necessary to limit the franchise to those primarily interested in school affairs because "the ever increasing complexity of the many interacting phases of the school system and structure make it extremely difficult for the electorate fully to understand the whys and wherefores of the detailed operations of the school system." We need express no opinion as to whether the State in some circumstances might limit the exercise of the franchise to those primarily interested in or affected by the election, for, assuming arguendo that New York legitimately might limit the franchise in these school district elections to those primarily interested in school affairs, close scrutiny of the § 2012 classifications demonstrates that they do not accomplish this purpose with sufficient precision. Whether

Kramer v. Union Free School District (Continued)

classifications allegedly limiting the franchise to those primarily interested deny equal protection to those excluded depends on whether all who are excluded are in fact substantially less interested or affected than those the statute includes. In other words, the classifications must be tailored so that the exclusion of Kramer (P) and members of his class is necessary to achieve the articulated state goal. Section 2012 does not meet this standard of precision. The classifications in § 2012 permit inclusion of many persons who have, at best, a remote and indirect interest in school affairs and, on the other hand, exclude others who do have such an interest. Nor does the District (D) offer any justification for the exclusion of seemingly interested and informed residents. In short, the requirements of § 2012 are not sufficiently tailored to limit the franchise to those primarily interested in school affairs to justify the denial of the franchise to Kramer (P) and members of his class.

■ **DISSENT**

(Stewart, J.) In *Lassiter v. Northampton County Election Board* (1959), we upheld a North Carolina literacy requirement applicable to voters in all state and federal elections. In doing so, we held that "[t]he States have long been held to have broad powers to determine the conditions under which the right of suffrage may be exercised, absent . . . the discrimination which the Constitution condemns." In the present case, Kramer (P) is not the victim of any such discrimination. The traditional test of a statute's validity under the Equal Protection Clause holds that a legislative classification is invalid only "if it rest[s] on grounds wholly irrelevant to achievement of the regulation's objectives." The premise of our decision in *Lassiter* was that a state may constitutionally impose voting requirements reasonably "designed to promote intelligent use of the ballot." A similar premise underlies the proposition consistently endorsed by this Court that a state may exclude nonresidents from participation in elections as residence requirements help ensure that voters have a substantial stake in the outcome of elections and an opportunity to become familiar with the candidates and issues. In this case, New York has determined that local education policy is best left to those who have direct and definable interests in that policy, and unless this Court is willing to claim a monopoly of wisdom regarding the sound operation of school systems in the fifty states, I see no way to justify the conclusion that the legislative classification involved here is not rationally related to a legitimate legislative purpose. Under any equal protection standard, short of doctrinaire insistence that universal suffrage is somehow mandated by the Constitution, Kramer's (P) claim must be rejected. It should also be emphasized that "the franchise" referred to by the majority deals not with a general election, but with a limited, special-purpose election. Kramer (P) is eligible to vote in all state, local, and federal elections, and is fully able, therefore, to participate in the process by which the requirements for school district voting may be changed and in those by which the levels of state and federal financial assistance to the District (D) are determined. He is in no way locked into any self-perpetuating status of exclusion from the electoral process.

Analysis:

While one might think it would be nearly impossible for a state to constitutionally limit an election to interested voters, there are two cases. *Salyer Land Co. v. Tulare Lake Basin Water Storage District* (1973) and *Ball v. James* (1981), in which the Court upheld state statutes permitting only landowners to vote in water storage district elections. In those cases, the Court noted that the water storage district had very limited authority in the governmental sense. The Court in both cases also concluded that because the district at issue had a specific purpose that had a disproportionate effect on landowners, the state could allow only landowners to vote in the election. While those exceptions do exist, it should be noted that *Kramer* does present a generally applicable rule that property ownership requirements, except in narrow circumstances, are invalid when used as restrictions on the right to vote.

■ **CASE VOCABULARY**

ARGUENDO: Latin phrase meaning "for the sake of argument."

DISENFRANCHISE: To deprive a person of a constitutional right, such as the right to vote.

DOCTRINAIRE: A strict application of a given approach that is employed despite its practical difficulties.

FRANCHISE: A constitutional right or privilege, such as the right to vote.

RIGHT OF SUFFRAGE: The right to vote.

Ball v. James

(Not Stated) v. (Not Stated)
451 U.S. 355, 101 S.Ct. 1811 (1981)

NOT ALL VOTING SCHEMES ARE SUBJECT TO THE ONE-PERSON-ONE-VOTE PRINCIPLE OF *REYNOLDS V. SIMMS*

■ **INSTANT FACTS** A group of registered voters living within the geographic boundaries of a water district filed suit challenging a district voting scheme which limited their ability to vote in district elections.

■ **BLACK LETTER RULE** In certain situations, states may limit the right to vote in a particular election to only those voters who are primarily affected by or have a special interest in the outcome of the election.

■ **PROCEDURAL BASIS**

Appeal to the United States Supreme Court of a lawsuit challenging the constitutionality of a water district's voting scheme.

■ **FACTS**

The Salt River Project Agricultural Improvement and Power District, formed as a governmental entity in 1937, stores and delivers untreated water to landowners on approximately 236,000 acres of central Arizona. It subsidizes its water operations by selling electricity, and is the source of electricity for hundreds of thousands of people. Under an existing statutory scheme, the legislature permitted the district to limit voting for its directors to those who own land within the district. The scheme also apportioned voting power according to the number of acres owned. The constitutionality of the law was challenged.

■ **ISSUE**

Can the narrow function of a local government body and the special relationship of one class of citizens to that body release it from the strict demands of the one-person, one-vote principles of the Equal Protection Clause?

■ **DECISION AND RATIONALE**

(Stewart, J.) Yes. In *Reynolds v. Simms*, we upheld the one-person, one-vote principle. However, we recognized a significant exception to that principle in *Salyer Land Co. v. Tulare Lake Basin Water Storage District* (1973). At issue in *Salyer* was the constitutionality of a voting scheme for electing a water district's directors under which only landowners could vote and voting power was apportioned according to the assessed value of one's property. We recognized that the Tulare District did exercise "some typical governmental powers," but concluded that it had "relatively limited authority," because its primary purpose was to acquire, store, and distribute water for farming in the Tulare Lake Basin. We also noted that the financial burdens of the district fell on the landowners in proportion to the benefits they received. In short, in *Salyer* we held that the strictures of *Reynolds* did not apply to the Tulare District and simply inquired whether the statutory voting scheme bore some relevancy to the statutes objectives. We determined that it did. The services currently provided by the Salt River District (D) are more diverse and affect more people than those of the Tulare District. Nevertheless, a careful

Ball v. James (Continued)

examination of the Salt River District (D) reveals that, under the principles of *Salyer*, these distinctions do not amount to a difference of constitutional significance. First, the District (D) does not exercise the sort of governmental powers that invoke the strict demands of *Reynolds*. It cannot impose ad valorem property taxes or sales taxes; cannot enact laws governing the conduct of citizens; and does not administer any of the normal functions of government. Second, even the District's (D) water functions are relatively narrow. It does not own, sell, or buy water, nor does it control its use. The District (D) simply stores water and delivers it through project canals. The functions of the Salt River District (D) are of the narrow, special sort which justifies a departure from the popular-election requirement of *Reynolds*. Furthermore, the voting landowners are the only residents of the District (D) whose lands are subject to liens to secure District bonds and the acreage-based taxing power of the District. Voting landowners are also the only residents who have ever committed capital to the District. In short, the voting scheme for the District (D) is constitutional because it bears a reasonable relationship to its statutory objectives. The subscriptions of land which made the District (D) possible might well have never occurred had the subscribing landowners not been assured a special voice in the conduct of the District's (D) business. On that basis, the State could rationally limit the vote to landowners and make the weight of their vote dependant on the number of acres they own since that number reasonably reflects the relative risks they incurred as landowners and the distribution of the benefits and the burdens of the District's water operations. Reversed.

■ DISSENT

(White, J.) In concluding that the District's (D) voting scheme is constitutional, the Court misapplies the limited exception recognized in *Salyer*. Nothing in *Salyer* changed the relevant constitutional inquiry. Although the water district in that case exercised certain governmental authorities, its purposes were quite narrow. The district had an insubstantial effect on nonvoters, and its burdens fell entirely on the landowners. In the present case, the District (D) clearly exercises substantial governmental powers. It is a municipal corporation which, pursuant to the Arizona Constitution, are "political subdivisions of the State, and vested with all the rights, privileges and benefits, and entitled to the immunities and exemptions granted municipalities and political subdivisions." The District's (D) bonds are tax exempt, and its property is not subject to state or local property taxation. It also has the power of eminent domain, has been given the power to enter into a wide range of contractual arrangements to secure energy sources, and is authorized to control the use and source of energy generated by the District (D). This broad authorization transcends the limited functions of the agricultural water storage district involved in *Salyer*. The purpose and authority of the Salt River District (D) are of extreme public importance. The District (D) affects the lives of thousands of citizens who, because of the present voting scheme, are unable to participate in any meaningful way in the conduct of the District's (D) operations. The limited exception recognized in *Salyer* does not save this voting arrangement.

Analysis:

Ball v. James stands for the proposition that in certain situations, states may limit the right to vote in a particular election to only interested voters or those voters who are primarily affected by the election. If an election is determined to be one of "special interest," the government can limit the right to vote to only those who are primarily affected by the election so long as it can show a reasonable basis for the limitation. The Court has not provided a set method for determining whether or not an election is a "special interest" election, meaning cases will have to be determined on an individual basis until more guidance is provided. The second way in which a governmental entity can limit the right of certain persons to vote in particular elections is to overcome the burdens imposed by strict scrutiny. Specifically, in *Hill v. Stone*, the Supreme Court wrote: "[A]s long as the election in question is not one of special interest, any classification restricting the franchise on grounds other than residence, age, and citizenship cannot stand unless the district or State can demonstrate that the classification serves a compelling state interest."

■ CASE VOCABULARY

AD VALOREM TAXES: A tax imposed at a rate proportional to the value of the item or property that is being taxed.

Crawford v. Marion County Election Board

(Citizen) v. *(Election Administrator)*
553 U.S. 181, 128 S.Ct. 1610 (2008)

REQUIRING PHOTO IDs DOES NOT INTERFERE WITH THE RIGHT TO VOTE

■ **INSTANT FACTS** Indiana (D) enacted a statute that required voters to show a picture ID at the polls, and Crawford (P) claimed the statute was an unconstitutional burden on voting rights.

■ **BLACK LETTER RULE** Evenhanded restrictions on the right to vote that are related to voter qualifications and that protect the integrity and reliability of the electoral process are valid.

■ **PROCEDURAL BASIS**

Appeal from an order finding a challenged statute constitutional.

■ **FACTS**

An Indiana statute, known as the "Voter ID Law," required voters to present picture identification when voting. The law applied to in-person voting, but did not apply to absentee ballots submitted by mail. An indigent voter, or a voter with a religious objection to being photographed, was allowed to cast a provisional ballot. That ballot would be counted only if the voter signed an affidavit within ten days following the election. A voter who was unable to present photo identification on election day could file a provisional ballot that would be counted if he or she brought identification to the circuit county clerk's office within ten days. No photo identification was required to register to vote. Free photo identification was offered to qualified voters who could establish their residence and identity. Crawford (P) challenged the law as an unconstitutional interference with the right to vote, but the lower courts denied his challenge.

■ **ISSUE**

Was the "Voter ID Law" unconstitutional?

■ **DECISION AND RATIONALE**

(Stevens, J.) No. Evenhanded restrictions on the right to vote that are related to voter qualifications and that protect the integrity and reliability of the electoral process are valid. The state (D) identified three interests that arguably justify the Voter ID Law. Each of these interests is relevant to protecting the integrity and reliability of the electoral process. These interests are deterring and detecting voter fraud, modernizing election procedures, and safeguarding voter confidence.

The only kind of voter fraud that the Voter ID Law addresses is in-person voter impersonation. There is no evidence of any such fraud actually occurring in Indiana. It is true, however, that flagrant examples of such fraud in other parts of the country have been documented. Not only is the risk of voter fraud real, it could affect the outcome of a close election. There is no question about the legitimacy or importance of the state's (D) interest in counting only the votes of eligible voters.

Two recently enacted federal statutes have made it necessary for states to modernize their election procedures. The requirements of the National Voter Registration Act of 1993 (NVRA) increased the number of registered voters and also restricted the ability of states to remove names from the lists of

Crawford v. Marion County Election Board (Continued)

registered voters. The Help America Vote Act (HAVA) imposed new identification requirements on individuals registering to vote for the first time who submit their applications by mail. If the voter is casting his ballot in person, he or she must present local election officials with written identification. HAVA also authorized the casting of provisional ballots by challenged voters. Neither HAVA nor NVRA required the enactment of the Voter ID Law, but they do indicate that Congress believes that photo identification is one effective method of establishing a voter's qualifications, and that the integrity of elections is enhanced through improved technology.

The interest in protecting public confidence in the integrity and legitimacy of government is closely related to the state's (D) interest in preventing voter fraud. Public confidence in the integrity of the electoral process also has an independent significance, because it encourages citizen participation in the democratic process.

States use different methods to identify voters at the polls. A photo identification requirement imposes some burdens on voters that other methods of identification do not. The burdens are imposed on those who are eligible to vote but who do not have photo identification that complies with the law. The fact that most voters have some form of acceptable identification would not save the statute if the state (D) required voters to pay a tax or a fee to obtain a new photo identification. The photo identification cards issued by the state (D) are, however, free. For most voters who need them, the inconvenience of obtaining a free card does not qualify as a substantial burden on the right to vote. A limited number of persons could face a heavier burden. The severity of that burden is mitigated by the fact that eligible voters without photo identification may cast provisional ballots that will ultimately be counted.

Crawford (P) argues that partisan considerations motivated the Legislature to enact the Voter ID Law. A nondiscriminatory law that is supported by neutral justifications is not invalid because partisan interests may have been behind the votes of some legislators. Affirmed.

■ CONCURRENCE

(Scalia, J.) The special burden that the voter-identification law may impose on some voters is irrelevant. The burden is minimal and justified. The law should be upheld.

■ DISSENT

(Souter, J.) The Voter ID Law threatens to impose nontrivial burdens on the voting rights of many citizens. A significant percentage of those individuals are likely to be deterred from voting. A state may not burden the right to vote merely by invoking abstract interests. A state must make a particular, factual showing that threats to its interests outweigh the impediments it imposes. There was no such justification here. The burden likely to be imposed by the Voter ID Law is serious, and a significant number of voters is likely to be affected.

Analysis:

There are many other voting-related laws besides the one at issue in this case. The National Voter Registration Act, 42 U.S.C. §§ 1973gg *et seq.*, is sometimes known as the "Motor Voter Law." Its purpose was to make voter registration easier by requiring states to offer voter registration when a person receives or renews a driver's license, or when he or she applies for government benefits. It also requires states to allow mail-in registration, as well as individual voter registration drives. The Help America Vote Act, Pub. L. No. 107–252, established minimum standards for the administration of elections.

Reynolds v. Sims

(*Not Stated*) v. (*Not Stated*)
379 U.S. 870, 85 S.Ct. 12 (1964)

FULL AND EFFECTIVE PARTICIPATION IN STATE GOVERNMENT REQUIRES THAT EACH CITIZEN HAVE AN EQUALLY EFFECTIVE VOICE IN THE ELECTION OF THE STATE LEGISLATURE

■ **INSTANT FACTS** A constitutional challenge was levied against Alabama's legislative districting scheme on the ground that it violated equal protection by not apportioning its districts according to population and thereby resulted in less-populated districts having more representation in the state legislature than more populous districts.

■ **BLACK LETTER RULE** The Equal Protection Clause requires that all voters be awarded the opportunity for equal participation in the election of state legislators.

■ **PROCEDURAL BASIS**

Appeal to the United States Supreme Court of a federal district court decision holding Alabama's state legislative apportionment scheme unconstitutional.

■ **FACTS**

In 1961, a group of citizens (P) filed suit challenging Alabama's legislative apportionment scheme. Specifically, they claimed that under the Alabama Constitution, legislative apportionment was to be governed by population, and reapportionment was to take place every ten years. The citizens (P) further claimed that no reapportionment had occurred since 1900. Under the challenged scheme, a number of counties were given a much more diluted voting power than their less-populated counterparts. For example, Bullock county, population 13,462, elected two representatives to the Alabama House, whereas Mobile County, population 314,301, elected just three. Other discrepancies existed as well, all of which were claimed to perpetuate a violation of equal suffrage and equal protection.

■ **ISSUE**

Does a state legislative apportionment scheme under which unevenly-populated districts each elect the same number of representatives to the state legislature violate equal protection?

■ **DECISION AND RATIONALE**

(Warren, J.) Yes. The Constitution protects the right of all qualified citizens to vote in state and federal elections. This right is fundamental, meaning any alleged infringement must be carefully scrutinized. Under this standard, constitutional concerns would certainly be raised by an allegation that otherwise qualified voters had been prohibited from voting for members of a state legislature. And, if a State should provide that the votes of citizens of one part of the State should be given two, five, or ten times the weight of votes of citizens in another part of the State, it could hardly be said that some significant vote dilution had not occurred. In the present case, the resulting discrimination against voters living in disfavored areas is easily demonstrable. Their right to vote is simply not the same as those living in a favored part of the State. Weighting the votes of citizens differently merely because of where they happen to reside is forbidden by the Constitution. The basic aim of legislative apportionment is to achieve a fair and effective representation for all citizens, so we must therefore conclude that the Equal Protection Clause guarantees the opportunity for equal participation by all voters in the election of state legislators. It is true that the complexions of society change, often with amazing rapidity, but the basic principle of representative government remains, and must remain, unchanged—the weight of a citizen's vote cannot be made to depend on where he lives. We hold that as a basic constitutional standard, the Equal Protection Clause requires that the seats in both houses of a bicameral state legislature must be apportioned on a population basis. Simply stated, an individual's right to vote for state legislators is unconstitutionally impaired when its weight is substantially diluted when compared with votes of citizens living in other parts of the State. One of the proposed plans considered by the District Court resembles the scheme of legislative representation followed in the federal Congress. Under this plan, each of Alabama's 67 counties is allotted one senator, and no counties are given more than on Senate seat. This is analogous to the allocation of two Senate seats to each state in the federal Congress. The system of representation in the two Houses of the federal Congress is one ingrained in our Constitution. Arising from unique historical circumstances, it is based on the consideration that in establishing our type of federalism a group of formerly independent States bound themselves together under one national government. Admittedly, the original thirteen states surrendered some of their sovereignty in agreeing to join together, but at the head of our constitutional system remains the concept of separate and distinct governmental entities which have delegated some, but not all, of their formerly held powers to the single national government. Political subdivisions of States—counties, cities, or whatever—never were and never have been considered sovereign entities. Rather, they have been traditionally regarded as subordinate governmental instrumentalities created by the State to assist in the carrying out of state governmental functions. Thus, we conclude that a plan that apportions seats in the Alabama Legislature the way the federal Senate is apportioned cannot be sustained by recourse to the federal analogy. The Equal Protection Clause requires that a State make an honest and good faith effort to construct districts as nearly of equal population as is practicable. Mathematical exactness is hardly a workable constitutional requirement, but efforts to come close must be made. Affirmed.

■ DISSENT

(Harlan, J.) In holding that seats in the Alabama legislature are proportioned in violation of the Constitution, today's decision has the effect of placing a basic aspect of state political systems under the pervasive overlordship of the federal judiciary. Had the Court examined the matter more closely, it would have found that the Equal Protection Clause was never intended to inhibit the States in choosing any democratic method they pleased for the apportionment of their legislatures. This is shown by the language of the Fourteenth Amendment, by the understanding of those who proposed and ratified it, and by the political practices of the States at the time the Amendment was adopted. It is further confirmed by numerous state and congressional actions since the ratification of the Fourteenth Amendment, and by the common understanding of the Amendments as evidenced by subsequent constitutional amendments and decisions. The Court's failure to consider any of these matters cannot be excused by any concept of "developing" constitutionalism. It is meaningless to speak of constitutional "development" when both the language and history of the controlling provisions of the Constitution are wholly ignored. Since it can be shown that state legislative apportionments are wholly free constitutional limitations, the Court's action now bringing them within the purview of the Fourteenth Amendment amounts to nothing less than an exercise of the amending power. The complaints in these cases should have been dismissed because what has been alleged shows no violation of any constitutional right.

Analysis:

One of the more significant cases in recent history, *Reynolds v. Sims* establishes the "one person, one vote" principle that now governs the apportionment of state legislative districts and other voting issues. The purpose of that principle is to lessen the effects of vote dilution by making each voter's ballot equal in weight. Two years before *Reynolds*, the Supreme Court decided *Baker v. Carr* (1962), in which it first found reapportionment cases to be justiciable under the Equal Protection Clause. In *Baker*, the Court held that the debasement of a person's vote by malapportionment violates the Equal Protection Clause. That same principle was applied in *Reynolds* and its five companion cases, and in each case led to the invalidation of the apportionment scheme at issue.

■ **CASE VOCABULARY**

VOTE DILUTION: The placement of a limitation on the effectiveness of a person's vote.

Bush v. Gore

(Presidential Candidate) v. *(Presidential Candidate)*
531 U.S. 98, 121 S.Ct. 525 (2000)

FAILURE TO ESTABLISH A STATEWIDE RECOUNT PROCESS VIOLATES EQUAL PROTECTION

■ **INSTANT FACTS** Following the 2000 presidential election, the Florida Supreme Court ordered certain counties to manually count ballots for inclusion in the vote total.

■ **BLACK LETTER RULE** Once a state vests voting rights in its citizens, it must afford each person's vote equal treatment under the Equal Protection Clause.

■ **PROCEDURAL BASIS**

Certiorari to review a decision of the Florida Supreme Court ordering a manual recount of presidential votes.

■ **FACTS**

The day after the 2000 Presidential Election, the State of Florida announced that Bush (P) had received fewer than 2000 popular votes more than his opponent, Gore (D). Pursuant to state law, an automatic machine recount was held, which showed Bush (P) to be the winner, though by fewer votes than the initial count. Gore (D) then filed suit under Florida's state election protest statute seeking manual recounts in several counties. Interpreting Florida's election statute, the Florida Supreme Court defined the meaning of "legal votes" and ordered a manual recount of votes in those counties that had not yet completed a recount, including "undervotes"—those ballots for which no vote had been recorded by voting machines due to "hanging chads" that were incompletely perforated from the paper ballot—to determine the intent of the voters on each ballot. Bush (P) filed an emergency application with the U.S. Supreme Court to stay the order.

■ **ISSUE**

When a state court orders a statewide election recount, must the court's recount procedure assure equal protection and fundamental fairness?

■ **DECISION AND RATIONALE**

(Per curiam.) Yes. Under the electoral college system, the private individual's constitutional right to vote in a presidential election depends upon the state legislature's use of a statewide process to choose the members of the electoral college. Although history now favors the appointment of electoral college members by the citizens, states do hold the power to appoint the members without a public vote. Once a state enfranchises its citizens with the right to vote, however, that right becomes fundamental, and the state must afford equal weight to each vote by all citizens. Similarly, equal protection requires that a state choosing to later disenfranchise its citizens must do so on equal grounds so as to value each person's vote equally.

By ordering a manual recount, the Florida Supreme Court determined that the intent of the voters must be discerned even though the voting machines were unable to record their votes. No standard has been established to ensure that the method employed to discern the intent of the voter satisfies the

Bush v. Gore (Continued)

Equal Protection Clause. Here, Florida counties utilized different standards on recount to determine what constitutes a legal vote to be counted in the certified vote totals. The Florida Supreme Court failed to establish appropriate guidelines and standards to be applied statewide. Furthermore, the Florida recount procedure calls for a manual examination of "undervotes"—those ballots that were insufficiently marked for detection by voting machines—but makes no provision for the examination of "overvotes"—those ballots that were unrecognizable because more than one vote was registered by the machine. In allowing undervotes to count while excluding overvotes from the election results, the court's procedure treats one citizen's erroneous vote over another, although the intent of each voter may be equally discernable. Accordingly, what constitutes the legal vote of a citizen in one county does not apply in a neighboring county, and equal protection has not been preserved by the recount procedure.

Because all votes appointing members of the electoral college cannot be counted and certified by December 12, as required by federal statute, and the state recount procedure is unconstitutional, the decision of the Florida Supreme Court is reversed and remanded for further proceedings.

■ CONCURRENCE

(Rehnquist, C.J.) Although comity and federalism generally require the Court to respect the state's distribution of powers among its branches, the state's role in the presidential election maintains a uniquely federal character. In carrying out its constitutional prerogative, the Florida legislature established a carefully crafted procedure for counting ballots and determining what a legal vote is. The Florida Supreme Court, in ordering a manual recount, deviated from that legislative directive by authorizing the counting of improperly marked ballots. In a presidential election, the clearly expressed intent of the legislature must prevail.

Further, although the state legislature authorizes state courts to provide relief as "appropriate under such circumstances," the authority conferred must be understood to comply with the cut-off date for electoral college member appointment as provided by federal statute. Because the state court departed from the legislative scheme and cannot possibly meet the deadlines of the federal statute, the decision ordering a recount must be reversed.

■ DISSENT

(Stevens, J.) While federal statutes or the U.S. Constitution may require federal court intervention into state affairs, the meaning of state election laws must be left to the determination of state courts. State legislatures and state appellate jurisdiction are both created by the state constitution, and nothing in the U.S. Constitution frees the legislature from appellate jurisdiction over its decisions. The only motive for invoking federal review is a lack of confidence in the state court's ability to impartially decide the recount procedure.

■ DISSENT

(Souter, J.) The December 15 statutory deadline does not mandate that states select electors when they are unable to do so. Moreover, the Florida Supreme Court was called upon to interpret a state statute and acted reasonably in doing so. The court provided definitions for terms that were lacking in the statute, to reasonably apply its interpretation of the statutory intent to the election. Finally, while the differing approaches among Florida counties raise equal protection concerns, there is no reason to presume that the state cannot successfully achieve a recount under properly established standards by the deadline established by federal statute, even if the state were held to it. The matter should be remanded to establish such standards and conduct the recount.

■ DISSENT

(Ginsburg, J.) The Constitution provides that the states shall operate as a republican form of government, and nothing in Article II, providing that state legislators must direct the appointment of electors, can be understood to interfere with the states' governmental regime. By reversing the Florida Supreme Court's interpretation of a state statute, the Court does nothing more than substitute its own interpretation for that of the state court. "Federal courts should defer to state high courts' interpretations of their state's own law." Additionally, the recount procedure as proposed by the Florida Supreme Court is no less fair than the original election procedures such that it triggers an equal protection violation. Finally, even if the recount offends equal protection, the Court should not dismiss the valid votes cast by

Florida voters merely because of the passing of the December 12 deadline. The statute does not so require.

■ DISSENT

(Breyer, J.) This case should not be considered because it involves only the constitutional allocation of power, not the deprivation of any constitutional right. Although the election of the President is a matter of national importance, the importance is political, not legal. The Constitution and federal statutes establish a procedure for reviewing electoral disputes and place that responsibility with the state courts. The federal electoral statute vests Congress with the power to count electoral votes and determine what is a legal vote, but does not bestow any right of review on the Supreme Court. The decision to delegate electoral responsibilities to Congress, rather than the Court, expresses the desire that a body elected by the people consider matters relating to presidential elections. The Court should have exercised judicial restraint and denied certiorari.

Analysis:

Many commentators speculate that the Bush decision will have little constitutional significance in the future, declaring the decision less of a constitutional decision than a political statement of the Court's conservative members to ensure George Bush's election. Yet, following the Bush decision, lawsuits have been filed across the country challenging election results as unconstitutional, relying principally on the Court's constitutional reasoning.

■ CASE VOCABULARY

ELECTORAL COLLEGE: The body of electors chosen from each state to formally elect the U.S. President and Vice President by casting votes based on the popular vote.

ENFRANCHISE: To grant voting rights or other rights of citizenship to (a person or class).

SUFFRAGE: The right or privilege of casting a vote at a public election.

Boddie v. Connecticut

(*Indigent Person*) v. (*State of Connecticut*)
401 U.S. 371, 91 S.Ct. 780 (1971)

THE DUE PROCESS CLAUSE REQUIRES THAT ALL PERSONS BE AFFORDED AN OPPORTUNITY TO GO TO COURT TO OBTAIN A DIVORCE

■ **INSTANT FACTS** An indigent citizen challenged a Connecticut law which made the payment of a court fee a prerequisite to accessing the judicial system for the purpose of obtaining a divorce.

■ **BLACK LETTER RULE** The Due Process Clause prohibits the States from denying individuals seeking dissolution of their marriages access to the courts based solely on the person's inability to pay court fees.

■ **PROCEDURAL BASIS**

Not stated.

■ **FACTS**

Boddie (P), an indigent welfare recipient living in the state of Connecticut, filed suit challenging a state law which required the payment of a court fee prior to obtaining a divorce. Despite the fact that the fee was around $60, Boddie (P) and many others were still unable to pay it. And because he did not have the required amount of money, Boddie (P) was not permitted to file for divorce.

■ **ISSUE**

Can a state, without running afoul of the Constitution, make payment of a court fee a prerequisite to obtaining a divorce?

■ **DECISION AND RATIONALE**

(Harlan, J.) No. Marriage involves interests of basic importance in our society. It is not surprising, then, that the States have seen fit to oversee many aspects of that relationship. One important aspect of that control for the purposes of this case is the fact that two consenting adults may not divorce and mutually liberate themselves from the constrains of legal obligations that go with marriage without invoking the State's judicial machinery. Because resort to state courts is the only way to dissolve a marriage, we think Boddie's (P) plight is akin to that of a defendant faced with exclusion from the only forum effectively empowered to settle his dispute. As our prior cases demonstrate, due process requires, at a minimum, that absent a countervailing state interest of overriding significance, persons forced to settle their claims of right and duty through the judicial process must be given a meaningful opportunity to be heard. Drawing upon this principle, we conclude that the States's refusal to admit indigent persons to its courts, the sole means for obtaining a divorce, must be regarded as a denial of due process. The arguments for this kind of fee are that the State's interest in the prevention of frivolous litigation is substantial, its use of court fees and costs to allocate scarce resources is rational, and its balance between the defendant's right to notice and the plaintiff's right to access is reasonable. None of these considerations is sufficient to override Boddie's (P) interest in having access to the only avenue open for dissolving an untenable marriage. Not only is there no necessary connection between a litigant's assets and the seriousness of his motives in bringing suit, but there are other alternatives for conserving

Boddie v. Connecticut (Continued)

the time of courts and protecting parties from frivolous litigation. The State's asserted interest in its fee requirements as a mechanism of resource allocation was offered and rejected in *Griffin v. Illinois* (1956), in which we struck down a requirement that all persons, including the indigent, obtain a transcript in order to appeal a conviction, which requirement blocked the access of certain defendants to the judicial process. Here the State (D) invariably imposes the costs as a measure of allocating judicial resources, so the rational of *Griffin* applies in this case. In holding as we do, we go no further than necessary to dispose of the case before us. We do not decide that access for all individuals to the courts is a right that is, in all circumstances, guaranteed by the Due Process Clause, for in the case before us this right is the exclusive precondition to the adjustment of a fundamental human relationship. The requirement that Boddie (P) resort to the judicial process is entirely a state-created matter. Thus we hold only that a State may not preempt the right to dissolve this legal relationship without affording all citizens access to the means it has prescribed for doing so.

■ DISSENT

(Black, J.) In this country, marriage and divorce are wholly under state control and always have been. This is because states have particular interests in the kinds of laws regulating their citizens when they enter into, maintain, and dissolve marriages. The Court here holds, however, that Connecticut has so little control over the marriages and divorces of its own citizens that it is without power to charge them nominal initial court costs when they are without ready money to put up those costs. The Court holds that the state law requiring payment of costs is barred by the Due Process Clause. The Court is wrong. Civil lawsuits are not like criminal prosecutions. In civil cases the government is not usually involved as a party, and there is no deprivation of life, liberty, or property as punishment for crime. Our Federal Constitution, therefore, does not place civil disputes on the same level as it places criminal trials. There is consequently no reason that in civil cases the government should be hampered by the strict due process rules the Constitution has provided to protect those charged with a crime.

Analysis:

In *Boddie*, the Supreme Court addresses the issue of filing fees and access to the courts in civil proceedings, holding that while there is not a general right of access to the courts, certain limitations on access are violative of the constitutional guarantee of due process of law. The Court had previously addressed the issue of access to the courts and indigence in the criminal arena, holding in *Griffin v. Illinois* (1956) that a state could not deny an indigent criminal defendant the right to appeal his or her conviction simply because the defendant could not pay the costs of obtaining a trial transcript. The right of access in civil proceedings, however, had not yet been significantly addressed before the Court decided *Boddie*. As the opinion indicates, the Court found that when the judicial process provides the only means of settling a dispute affecting a fundamental matter such as marriage, an inflexible fee that prevents indigent persons from settling those disputes (i.e., getting a divorce) violates due process.

■ CASE VOCABULARY

JUDICIAL IMPRIMATUR: Judicial approval.

United States v. Kras

(*United States Government*) v. (*Indigent Person*)
409 U.S. 434, 93 S.Ct. 631 (1973)

THE GOVERNMENT CAN CONSTITUTIONALLY MAKE THE PAYMENT OF A FEE A PREREQUISITE TO INITIATING BANKRUPTCY PROCEEDINGS

■ **INSTANT FACTS** An indigent person challenged a federal law which required him to pay a filing fee in order to file for bankruptcy.

■ **BLACK LETTER RULE** The principle set forth in *Boddie* that the government may not make the payment of a court fee a prerequisite to accessing the courts for the purpose of obtaining a divorce does not apply in cases involving the payment of fees as a prerequisite to initiating no-asset bankruptcy proceedings.

■ **PROCEDURAL BASIS**

Appeal to the United States Supreme Court of a federal district court decision which held that a filing fee requirement for bankruptcy filings is unconstitutional in light of *Boddie v. Connecticut.*

■ **FACTS**

Robert William Kras (P), an unemployed father of two, attempted to file for bankruptcy in the Eastern District of New York on May 28, 1971. When he was unable to come up with the required filing fee, his petition was denied. Kras (P) was unable to come up with the filing fee because of extreme poverty. In addition to supporting his wife and two children, Kras (P) also supported his mother and her six year-old child. All six lived in the same small apartment and the financial support that they received from the government was only enough to cover their rent and living expenses. Kras' (P) wife did not work because she chose to care for the couple's eight month old child. Kras (P) had tried diligently to find work, but was repeatedly unable to do so. Kras (P) was unable to find work, in part, because of an accusation of theft on the part of a prior employer and a debt of $1000 owed to that employer. Kras owed other debts as well, totaling $6,428.69.

■ **ISSUE**

Is it unconstitutional to impose a filing fee as a precondition to filing for bankruptcy?

■ **DECISION AND RATIONALE**

(Blackmun, J.) No. Kras (P) contends that his case falls within the purview of *Boddie.* The Government (D) disagrees, arguing that the fee requirements are a reasonable exercise of Congress' plenary power over bankruptcy. We agree with the Government (D). *Boddie* was based on the notion that a State cannot deny access, because of indigence, to a judicial proceeding that is "the only effective means of resolving the dispute at hand." Throughout the opinion there is constant reference to Connecticut's exclusive control over the establishment and dissolution of the marital relationship and the fact that "marriage involves interests of basic importance in our society." In light of these considerations, we concluded that resort to the judicial process in a divorce situation was "no more voluntary . . . than that of the defendant called upon to defend his interests in court." Furthermore, the appellants in *Boddie* and Robert Kras (P) stand in materially different postures. The denial of access to the judicial forum in *Boddie* touched directly on the marital relationship and on the association interests that surround the establishment and dissolution of that relationship, interests of fundamental importance under the Constitution. In *Boddie*, the filing fee impaired appellants' freedom to pursue other protected associational activities. Kras' (P) alleged interest in the elimination of his debt burden, although important, does not rise to the same constitutional level. If Kras (P) is not discharged in bankruptcy, his position will not be materially altered in any constitutional sense, and will effect no change with respect to basic necessities. No fundamental interest is gained or lost in a discharge in bankruptcy. Nor is the Government's control over the establishment or dissolution of debts nearly so exclusive as Connecticut's (D) control over the marriage relationship. This is because bankruptcy is not the only method available to a debtor for the adjustment of his legal relationship with his creditors. Additionally, there is no constitutional right to obtain a discharge of one's debts in bankruptcy. The Constitution merely authorizes Congress to "establish . . . uniform Laws on the subject of Bankruptcies." The rational basis for the fee requirement is readily apparent, and Congressional power over bankruptcy is plenary and exclusive. General Order No. 35(4) permits payment of the filing fees in installments, which over an available nine-month period would come to $1.28 per week. Despite Kras' (P) poverty, this much available revenue should be within his reach when the adjudication in bankruptcy has stayed collection and has brought to a halt whatever harassment, if any, he may have sustained from creditors, including the charges of fraud to which he is allegedly subject. We decline to extend the principle of *Boddie* to the no-asset bankruptcy proceeding. Reversed.

■ **DISSENT**

(Stewart, J.) *Boddie* held that a statute requiring the payment of a filing fee as a prerequisite to a divorce action was unconstitutional as applied to indigents unable to pay the fee. The violation of due process seems to me equally clear in the present case. The debtor, like the married plaintiffs in *Boddie*, originally entered into his contract freely and voluntarily. But it is the Government that continues to enforce that obligation; that debt is effective only because the judicial machinery is there to collect it through garnishment, attachment, and the panoply of other creditor remedies. In the unique situation of the indigent bankrupt, the Government provides the only effective means of his ever being free of these Government-imposed obligations. As in *Boddie*, there are no "recognized, effective alternatives." While the creditors of a bankruptcy with assets might well desire to reach a compromise settlement, that possibility is foreclosed to the truly indigent as the assetless bankrupt has nothing to offer his creditors. Unless the Government provides him access to the bankruptcy court, Kras (P) will remain in the totally hopeless situation he now finds himself. The Government (D) has thus truly pre-empted the only means for the indigent bankrupt to get out from under a lifetime burden of debt.

■ **DISSENT**

(Marshall, J.) Justice Stewart makes clear the majority's failure to distinguish this case from *Boddie*. I add only some words on the extraordinary route by which the majority reaches its conclusion. The majority notes that the minimum amount Kras (P) must pay each week is only $1.28, which it says he can do with some minor lifestyle changes. I cannot agree that it is so easy for the poor to come up with even this amount of money. The 1970 Census found that over 800,000 families had annual incomes of less than $1,000, or $19.23 a week. I see no reason to require such families to sacrifice over 5% of their annual income as a prerequisite to getting a discharge in bankruptcy. No one who has had close contact with poor people can fail to understand how close to the margin of survival many of them are. It is perfectly proper for judges to disagree about what the Constitution requires, but it is disgraceful for an interpretation of the Constitution to be premised upon unfounded assumptions about how people live.

Analysis:

United States v. Kras is a case of constitutional significance because, among other things, it shows how far the Supreme Court is willing (or unwilling) to extend the general principles set forth in *Boddie v. Connecticut*. *Boddie* left it unclear how far that decision might reach, and what other filing fees and court access limitations, if any, it would preclude. *Kras* provides some information in that respect as it makes it clear that the presence of a fundamental right is required to make filing fees unconstitutional. Specifically, because bankruptcy is not a fundamental right, the government can require the payment of filing and other court fees as a prerequisite to the filing of a bankruptcy petition. In so holding, *Kras* significantly limits the *Boddie* decision.

M.L.B. v. S.L.J.
(Biological Mother) v. (Biological Father)
519 U.S. 102, 117 S.Ct. 555 (1996)

STATES MUST PROVIDE AN INDIGENT PARENT WITH TRIAL TRANSCRIPTS AT NO CHARGE WHEN THOSE TRANSCRIPTS ARE NEEDED TO FACILITATE AN APPEAL OF A TERMINATION OF PARENTAL RIGHTS

■ **INSTANT FACTS** A mother whose parental rights were terminated challenged a Mississippi requirement that she pay for trial transcripts before her appeal would be permitted to proceed past the Initial stages.

■ **BLACK LETTER RULE** States may not deny appellate review of a decision finding a biological parent to be unfit simply because of the parent's inability to pay for the appeal.

■ **PROCEDURAL BASIS**

Appeal to the United States Supreme Court of a Mississippi state court decision denying a mother the opportunity to appeal a parental rights termination action because of her inability to pay the costs of the appeal.

■ **FACTS**

During an eight-year marriage, M.L.B. (the wife) and S.L.J. (the husband) had two children. Following a divorce and a subsequent remarriage, S.L.J. (P), who had been given custody of the children, filed suit seeking a termination of M.L.B.'s (D) parental rights. In the same action, he sought to have his new wife, J.P.J., become the children's adopted mother. The Chancery Court found for S.L.J. (P) and terminated M.L.B.'s (D) parental rights. M.L.B. (D) sought to appeal the decision, but was unable to do so because Mississippi law required her to pay in advance certain record preparation fees, such as the preparation of the trial transcript. Because she could not pay the estimated $2,352.36, M.L.B.'s (D) appeal was dismissed. M.L.B. (D) challenged the dismissal on the grounds that the Due Process and Equal Protection Clauses of the Fourteenth Amendment prevent the State of Mississippi from requiring indigent persons to pay record preparation fees as a prerequisite to an appeal of a termination of parental rights.

■ **ISSUE**

May a State, consistent with the Fourteenth Amendment, condition appeals from trial court decrees terminating parental rights on the affected parent's ability to pay record preparation fees?

■ **DECISION AND RATIONALE**

(Ginsburg, J.) No. Choices regarding marriage, family life, and raising children are associational rights "of basic importance in our society," and are therefore protected by the Fourteenth Amendment against unwarranted state usurpation. Guided by precedent, we turn to the classification issue this case presents. We do not question the general rule that fee requirements are ordinarily examined only for rationality. But our cases solidly establish two exceptions to this general rule: (1) the basic right to participate in political processes as voters and candidates cannot be limited to those who can pay for a license; and (2) nor may access to judicial processes in criminal or quasi-criminal actions turn on ability

M.L.B. v. S.L.J. (Continued)

to pay. We place decrees forever terminating parental rights in the category of cases in which the State may not "bolt the door to equal justice." S.L.J. (P) argues that we will open floodgates if we do not rigidly restrict the second exception to only criminal cases. But parental status termination decrees are not ordinary civil actions. Termination decrees "wor[k] a unique kind of deprivation" as they involve the authority of the State "to destroy permanently all legal recognition of the parental relationship." We are therefore satisfied that the label "civil" should not entice us to leave undisturbed the Mississippi courts' disposition of this case. Reversed.

■ DISSENT

(Thomas, J.) Today the majority holds that the Fourteenth Amendment requires Mississippi to provide M.L.B. (D) a free transcript because her civil case involves a fundamental right. It also seeks to limit the reach of its holding to the type of case we confront here, but I do not think that the new-found constitutional right to free transcripts in civil appeals can be effectively restricted to this type of case. Inevitably, there will be greater demands for free assistance in all manner of civil cases involving interests that cannot, based on the test established today, be distinguished from the admittedly important interest at issue here. The cases on which the majority relies, primarily cases requiring appellate assistance for indigent criminal defendants, were questionable when decided, and have, in my view, since been undermined. Even accepting those cases, however, I am of the view that the majority takes them too far. This is a civil, not a criminal, action, an important distinction under the law. If all that is required to trigger the right to a free appellate transcript is that the interest at stake appear to be as fundamental as the interest of a convicted misdemeanant, several kinds of civil suits involving interests that seem equally fundamental, such as paternity, custody, and divorce suits, leap to mind. In brushing aside the distinction between criminal and civil cases, the Court has eliminated the last meaningful limit on the free-floating right to appellate assistance.

Analysis:

In *M.L.B.*, the majority places great significance on whether the right at issue in a particular lawsuit (or a lawsuit that a person wishes to file or appeal) is a constitutionally protected right (though not necessarily a fundamental right). When the right is protected by the Constitution, access to the courts cannot be precluded by a requirement that all persons, including the indigent, pay initial filing or transcript fees. This is why *Boddie*, which addressed the right to marry, *M.L.B.*, which addressed a termination of parental rights, and *Little v. Streater* (1981), which involved a paternity action, came out as they did—the rights addressed in each of these cases were found to be constitutionally protected rights (though, again, not necessarily fundamental rights in the equal protection sense). *M.L.B.* also indirectly raises the issue of wealth-based classifications. The Supreme Court has held that wealth-based classifications are not examined using strict scrutiny analysis, but a rational basis test. However, when the wealth-based classification affects fundamental or other important rights, the Court has applied the stricter standard in protection of those important rights.

■ CASE VOCABULARY

MISDEMEANANT: A person who has been convicted of a misdemeanor.

Lewis v. Casey

(Not Stated) v. (Not Stated)
518 U.S. 343, 116 S.Ct. 2174 (1996)

A PRISONER CANNOT PURSUE A CLAIM OF A DENIAL OF ACCESS TO THE COURTS UNLESS HE OR SHE HAS SUFFERED ACTUAL INJURY

■ **INSTANT FACTS** A group of Arizona prisoners filed a class action lawsuit seeking remediation for their perceived inability to access the court system.

■ **BLACK LETTER RULE** A subpar prison law library or legal assistance program does not per se place an unconstitutional limitation on a prisoner's right of access to the courts.

■ **PROCEDURAL BASIS**

Appeal to the United States Supreme Court of a lower federal district court decision imposing very strict standards on the Arizona Department of Corrections (ADOC) with respect to prison law libraries and legal assistance programs.

■ **FACTS**

In 1990, a group of twenty-two Arizona Department of Corrections (ADOC) inmates (P) filed a class action lawsuit "on behalf of all adult prisoners who are or will be incarcerated by the State of Arizona" alleging deprivations of their right to access to the courts. In holding for the inmates (P), the District Court found what it perceived were substantial shortcomings in the ADOC system. A number of those shortcomings involved prison libraries, and included matters involving the training of library staff, the updating of legal materials, and the availability of photocopying services for inmates. The District Court also found that two groups of inmates were particularly affected by the ADOC's shortcomings in that their access to both legal materials and the courts was even more severely limited than normal: inmates in solitary confinement and those who do not speak English. To alleviate the shortcomings that it believed it had discovered, the District Court created a very detailed program to assist inmates in the filing of lawsuits (a program that went so far as to regulate noise levels in prison law libraries) and then imposed its program on all ADOC prisons.

■ **ISSUE**

Does the existence of a subpar law library per se limit the ability of prisoners to access the courts in violation of the Constitution?

■ **DECISION AND RATIONALE**

(Scalia, J.) No. The doctrine of standing requires that an inmate alleging a violation of his rights must show actual injury. Courts exist to provide relief to claimants who have suffered or will imminently suffer actual harm; it is not the role of courts to shape institutions of government in such fashion as to comply with the laws and the Constitution. That is the role of th political branches of government. The right at issue today is not the right to a law library or to legal assistance. *Bounds v. Smith* (1977) established no such right. The right that *Bounds* acknowledged was the right of access to the courts. In other words, prison law libraries and legal assistance programs are only a means for ensuring a reasonable opportunity to present claims to the courts. Because *Bounds* did not create an abstract, freestanding right to a law library or legal assistance, an inmate cannot establish relevant actual injury simply by establishing that his prison's law library or legal assistance programs is subpar. Under *Bounds*, "meaningful access to the courts is the touchstone," and the inmate must therefore demonstrate that the alleged shortcomings in the library or legal assistance program hindered his efforts to pursue a legal claim. Although *Bounds* itself made no mention of an actual-injury requirement, it can hardly be thought to have eliminated that constitutional prerequisite, as actual injury is apparent on the face of almost all of the opinions in the line of cases on which *Bounds* relied. Furthermore, several statements in *Bounds* went beyond the right of access recognized in earlier cases, statements that appear to suggest that the State must enable the prisoner to discover grievances and to litigate effectively once in court. These elaborations upon the right of access have no antecedent in our pre-*Bounds* cases, and we now disclaim them. Finally, the injury requirement is not satisfied by just any type of frustrated legal claim. *Bounds* does not guarantee inmates the wherewithal to transform themselves into litigating engines capable of filing everything from shareholder derivative actions to slip-and-fall claims. The tools it requires to be provided are simply those needed in order to attack a sentence, directly or collaterally, and in order to challenge the conditions of confinement. Impairment of any other litigating capacity is simply one of the incidental consequences of conviction and incarceration. There is one additional reason that the district court's ruling cannot stand. In *Turner v. Safley* (1987), we held that prison regulations that impinge on inmates' constitutional rights are valid if reasonably related to "legitimate penological interests." Under rational basis review, the district court's decision cannot stand. Reversed.

■ CONCURRENCE

(Thomas, J.) Federal judges are to decide cases—they do not run state prisons. Yet, too frequently federal district courts effect wholesale takeovers of state correctional facilities and run them by judicial decree. In the present case, the District Court imposed a statewide decree on the ADOC, dictating in excruciatingly minute detail a program to assist inmates in the filing of lawsuits. Such gross overreaching simply cannot be tolerated. Principles of federalism and separation of powers dictate that exclusive responsibility for administering state prisons resides with the State. In *Bounds*, we recognized a duty to provide prison inmates with law libraries or other legal assistance at state expense, an obligation that is part of a loosely defined "right of access to the courts." While the Constitution may guarantee state inmates an opportunity to bring suit to vindicate their constitutional rights, I find no basis in the Constitution for any claimed right to have the government finance the endeavor.

■ DISSENT

(Stevens, J.) In recent decades, this Court has repeatedly held that the convicted felon's loss of liberty is not a total loss. Even convicted criminals retain some of the liberties enjoyed by all who live outside prison walls. The well-established right of access to the courts is one of these aspects of liberty that States must affirmatively protect. Without the ability to access the courts, prisoners and free citizens alike would be deprived of the first, and often the only, line of defense against constitutional violations. Finally, it must be mentioned that the Court's view of the standing requirements is excessively strict. There is a constitutional right to effective access, and if a prisoner alleges that he personally has been denied that right, he has standing to sue.

Analysis:

Until the Supreme Court decided the present case, the seminal case in the area of prisoner access to courts was *Bounds v. Smith* (1977), which is referenced in Justice Scalia's majority decision. The *Bounds* Court determined that "the fundamental constitutional right of access to the courts requires prison authorities to assist inmates in the preparation and filing of meaningful legal papers by providing prisoners with adequate law libraries or adequate assistance from persons trained in the law." *Lewis* significantly altered the law as set forth in *Bounds*. First and foremost, *Lewis* held that "*Bounds* did not create an abstract, freestanding right to a law library or legal assistance." Another important area in which *Lewis* changed the landscape of prisoner access to the courts was by expressly holding that challenges to prison practices and policies on libraries, legal assistance, and other such things are to be reviewed under a rational basis test. Finally, *Lewis* changed the law under *Bounds* when it expressly disclaimed any statements in the *Bounds* opinion that suggest that the State "must enable the prisoner to discover grievances, and to litigate effectively once in court."

San Antonio Independent School District v. Rodriguez

(*School District*) v. (*Student's Parents*)
411 U.S. 1, 93 S.Ct. 1278 (1973)

THE RIGHT TO OBTAIN AN EDUCATION IS NOT A FUNDAMENTAL RIGHT

■ **INSTANT FACTS** A class of lower-income persons challenged Texas' system for financing public education.

■ **BLACK LETTER RULE** The right to acquire a public education is not a constitutionally guaranteed fundamental right; therefore, laws affecting that right are subject only to rational basis scrutiny.

■ PROCEDURAL BASIS

Appeal to the United States Supreme Court of a federal district court ruling striking down Texas' system for financing public education on equal protection grounds.

■ FACTS

During the 1940's, Texas imposed a public school financing scheme which required school districts to come up with a portion of their budget through local resources. To do so, the individual districts imposed property taxes on persons living within their respective boundaries. In Texas, as in all states, some of the school districts covered more affluent areas, and as a result received more money from the imposed property taxes than other school districts received. For example, after all available sources of funding were applied, the Edgewood Independent School District was able to spend approximately $356 per student. The Alamo Heights Independent School District, on the other hand, was able to spend $594 per student. The difference came primarily from the property tax revenue. Rodriguez (P), the parent of a student in the Edgewood District, headed up a class action lawsuit on behalf of all students in the less affluent districts, challenging the constitutionality of the Texas financing scheme.

■ ISSUE

Is the right to obtain an education a fundamental right?

■ DECISION AND RATIONALE

(Powell, J.) No. Rodriguez (P) asserts that the school financing system at issue impermissibly interferes with the exercise of what he deems to be a fundamental right—the right to obtain an education—and that accordingly our prior decisions require the application of strict scrutiny. Whether the right to obtain an education is a fundamental right has consumed the attention of courts and commentators in recent years. All agree that education is important, but the importance of a service performed by the State does not determine whether it must be regarded as fundamental for the purposes of the Equal Protection Clause. The key to discovering whether education is a fundamental right lies in assessing whether there is a right to education explicitly or implicitly guaranteed by the Constitution. Education is not afforded explicit protection under the Constitution. Nor is it implicitly protected. As we have said, the undisputed importance of education alone will not cause us to depart from the usual standard for reviewing a State's social and economic legislation. Rodriguez (P) contends, however, that education is distinguishable from other services provided by the State and is a fundamental personal right because it is essential to the effective exercise of First Amendment freedoms and to the intelligent utilization of the

San Antonio Independent School District v. Rodriguez (Continued)

right to vote. Even if it were conceded that some identifiable quantum of education is a constitutionally protected prerequisite to the meaningful exercise of either right, we have no indication that the present levels of educational expenditures in Texas provide an education that falls short. There is no evidence that the system fails to provide each child with an opportunity to acquire the basic skills necessary to enjoy the rights of speech and of full participation in the political process. As such, this is not a case in which the challenged state action must be subjected to strict judicial scrutiny. However, we need not rest our decision solely on the inappropriateness of the strict scrutiny test. A century of Supreme Court adjudication under the Equal Protection Clause supports the application of the traditional rational basis standard of review. We are urged to direct the States either to drastically alter the present system or to throw out the property tax altogether in favor of some other form of taxation. In such a complex arena in which no perfect alternatives exist, the Court does well not to impose too rigorous a standard of scrutiny lest all local fiscal schemes become subjects of criticism under the Equal Protection Clause. Furthermore, this Court's lack of specialized knowledge and experience in questions of education policy counsels against premature interference with the informed judgments made at the state and local levels. The judiciary is well advised to refrain from imposing on the States inflexible constitutional restraints that could handicap the continued research and experimentation vital to finding even partial solutions to educational problems and to keeping abreast of ever-changing conditions. Reversed.

■ DISSENT

(Brennan, J.) The statutory scheme at issue is devoid of any rational basis and therefore violates the Equal Protection Clause. I disagree with the Court's assertion that a right is fundamental for the purposes of equal protection analysis only if it is "explicitly or implicitly guaranteed by the Constitution." Our prior cases teach that fundamentality is a function of the right's importance in terms of the effectuation of those rights which are in fact constitutionally guaranteed. There can be no doubt that education is inextricably linked to the right to participate in the electoral process and to the rights of free speech and association. As such, any classification affecting education must be subjected to strict judicial scrutiny, and the statutory scheme now before us does not pass constitutional muster under this standard. Texas' school-financing scheme is unconstitutional.

■ DISSENT

(Marshall, J.) Today the Court, in an abrupt departure from the mainstream of recent state and federal court decisions on the unconstitutionality of education financing schemes dependent on taxable local wealth, decides that a State may constitutionally vary the quality of education which it offers to its children in accordance with the taxable wealth located in the school districts within which they reside. This holding is a retreat from our historic commitment to equality of educational opportunity and is not supported by any substantial justification. The determination of which interests are fundamental should be firmly rooted in the text of the Constitution. The task in every case should be to determine the extent to which constitutionally guaranteed rights are dependent on interests not mentioned in the Constitution. As the nexus between the specific constitutional guarantee and the non-constitutional interest draws closer, the non-constitutional interest becomes more fundamental and the degree of judicial scrutiny applied when the interest is infringed upon must be adjusted accordingly. Only if we closely protect these closely related interests from state discrimination do we ensure the integrity of the constitutional guarantee itself. It is true that this Court has never deemed the provision of free public education to be required by the Constitution. Nevertheless, the fundamental importance of education is amply indicated by our prior decisions, by the unique status society gives to public education, and by the close relationship between education and some of our most basic constitutional values. Education directly affects the ability of a child to exercise his or her First Amendment rights. Also important is the relationship between education and the political process—education instills in our young an understanding of and appreciation for the principles and operation of our governmental processes. But of most immediate and direct concern must be the demonstrated effect of education on the exercise of the franchise by the electorate. As we held in *Brown v. Board of Education* (1954), the opportunity of education "is a right which must be made available to all on equal terms." The factors just considered compel us to recognize the fundamentality of education and to scrutinize with appropriate care the bases for state discrimination affecting equality of educational opportunity in Texas. The Court seeks solace for its action in the possibility of legislative reform. The possibility of legislative action is no answer to this Court's duty under the Constitution to eliminate unjustified state discrimination. In this

San Antonio Independent School District v. Rodriguez (Continued)

case we have been presented with an instance of discrimination against an individual interest of large constitutional and practical importance. Because the States' justification for this discrimination is insufficient to support it, it should be adjudged unconstitutional.

Analysis:

San Antonio Independent School District v. Rodriguez is an important case because it provides a test for determining what constitutes a fundamental right for the purposes of Fourteenth Amendment protection. Whether something is a fundamental right is determined by looking at whether the right is explicitly or implicitly guaranteed by the Constitution. Thus, the rights included in the Bill of Rights, such as freedom of religion, freedom of the press, and due process in criminal trials, are considered fundamental rights. Also considered fundamental rights are rights that the Court has held are implicitly guaranteed by the Constitution, such as the right to privacy and the right to vote. Laws limiting these fundamental rights are subject to strict scrutiny analysis. All other interests are not considered fundamental and are subject only to the rational basis test. Accordingly, in the present case the Court applied minimal scrutiny and found it arguably reasonable that Texas (D) would use local property taxation to advance its goal of local control over schools.

Daniels v. Williams

(*Prisoner*) v. (*Correctional Officer*)
474 U.S. 327, 106 S.Ct. 662 (1986)

THE DUE PROCESS CLAUSE PROTECTS FAIRNESS IN GOVERNMENTAL DECISION-MAKING, NOT NEGLIGENCE WHICH RESULTS IN THE DEPRIVATION OF CITIZENS' LIFE, LIBERTY, OR PROPERTY

■ **INSTANT FACTS** A state prisoner who slipped and fell on a pillow filed an equal protection-based lawsuit against the correctional officer who had negligently left the pillow on the ground.

■ **BLACK LETTER RULE** The negligent act of a government official which causes unintended loss or injury to life, liberty, or property, while actionable at law, does not generally implicate the Due Process Clause.

■ **PROCEDURAL BASIS**

Not stated.

■ **FACTS**

While an inmate at the city jail in Richmond, Virginia, Daniels (P) slipped on a pillow negligently left on the stairs by Williams (D), a corrections officer. As a result of the fall, Daniels (P) suffered injuries to his back and ankle. Shortly thereafter, Daniels (P) filed a § 1983 civil rights action against Williams (D), arguing, among other things, that Williams' (D) negligence deprived him of his "liberty" interest in being free from bodily injury. Daniels (P) was not able to file a state tort suit because of issues involving sovereign immunity.

■ **ISSUE**

Can the Due Process Clause be used to prosecute what is essentially a tort lawsuit based on a theory of negligence of a government employee?

■ **DECISION AND RATIONALE**

(Rehnquist, J.) No. The Due Process Clause has historically been applied to deliberate decisions of government officials to deprive a person of life, liberty, or property. This history reflects the common-sense notion that the Due Process Clause was "intended to secure the individual from the arbitrary exercise of the powers of government." By requiring the government to follow appropriate procedures when its agents decide to effect any of the above-referenced deprivations, the Due Process Clause promotes fairness in such decisions. And by barring certain government actions regardless of the fairness of the procedures used to implement them, it serves to prevent governmental power from being used for purposes of oppression. The actions of prison custodians in leaving a pillow on the prison stairs are quite remote from the concerns just discussed. Lack of due care is a failure to measure up to the conduct of a reasonable person, not an abuse of power. To hold otherwise would trivialize the centuries-old principle of due process of law. The Constitution does not purport to supplant traditional tort law in laying down rules of conduct to regulate liability for injuries that attend living together in society. The Constitution and traditional tort law do not address the same concerns. As such, where a government official's act causing injury to life, liberty, or property is merely negligent, "no procedure for compensation is constitutionally required."

Daniels v. Williams (Continued)

Analysis:

The Fourteenth Amendment to the United States Constitution provides, in part, that no state shall "deprive any person of life, liberty, or property, without due process of law." *Daniels* is an important case because it addresses what constitutes a deprivation for the purposes of the Due Process Clause. Specifically, *Daniels* stands for the proposition that mere negligence on the part of a government employee that results in physical injury to another person is not a deprivation of liberty under the Fourteenth Amendment. There may be a common law tort claim in such a situation, but there is no violation of due process. Though *Daniels* provides some important information on the meaning of "deprive" as used in the Fourteenth Amendment, it does not address in any significant detail what kinds of government actions might actually constitute the type of constitutional violation Daniels (P) claimed he suffered in the present case.

■ CASE VOCABULARY

SOVEREIGN IMMUNITY: A principle of law which prevents a state from being sued unless it expressly consents to the lawsuit.

County of Sacramento v. Lewis

(*County Government*) v. (*Deceased Person*)
523 U.S. 833, 118 S.Ct. 1708 (1998)

THE PRINCIPLE OF DUE PROCESS EXISTS TO PROTECT AGAINST ARBITRARY GOVERNMENT ACTION BUT NOT RECKLESSNESS

■ **INSTANT FACTS** A lawsuit alleging a violation of due process was filed when a teenager was killed as a result of a high-speed chase with the police.

■ **BLACK LETTER RULE** In emergency situations involving law enforcement officials, negligence and recklessness will not create a constitutional deprivation; only conduct that "shocks the conscience" can create a due process deprivation, and to reach that level, there must be evidence of intent to harm.

■ **PROCEDURAL BASIS**

Not stated.

■ **FACTS**

On May 22, 1999, police officer James Smith (D) became involved in a high-speed chase involving his police car and a motorcycle. The motorcycle was driven by 18-year-old Brian Willard; Philip Lewis, age sixteen, was riding the motorcycle as a passenger. After reaching speeds in excess of 100 miles per hour and running two vehicles off the road, Willard crashed his motorcycle when attempting to make a sharp turn. The pursuing officer was unable to stop his vehicle in time to avoid hitting and killing Lewis (P), Willard's passenger. Lewis' (P) family filed suit against Smith's (D) employer, Sacramento County.

■ **ISSUE**

Does a police officer violate the Fourteenth Amendment's guarantee of due process when he causes death through deliberate or reckless indifference to life in a high-speed automobile chase aimed at apprehending a suspected offender?

■ **DECISION AND RATIONALE**

(Souter, J.) No. The core of the concept of due process is protection against arbitrary government action. Due process protection in the substantive sense limits what government may do in both its legislative and its executive capacities. Our cases dealing with abusive executive action have repeatedly emphasized that only the most egregious official conduct can be said to be arbitrary in the constitutional sense. To this end, we have spoken of the level of cognizable executive abuse or power as that which shocks the conscience and violates the decencies of civilized conduct. The constitutional concept of conscience-shocking is not the same as common law fault under tort law; it does not impose liability whenever someone cloaked with authority causes harm. We have accordingly rejected the lowest common denominator of customary tort liability as any mark of sufficiently shocking conduct, and have held that the Constitution does not guarantee due care on the part of state officials. It is, on the contrary, behavior at the other end of the culpability spectrum that would most probably support a substantive due process claim; conduct intended to injure in some way unjustifiable by any government interests is the sort of official action most likely to rise to the conscience-shocking level. On an occasion calling for fast action, the police have obligations that tend to tug against each other. A police officer deciding whether to give chase must balance the need to stop a suspect and the danger that a high-speed chase creates. To recognize a substantive due process violation when only mid-level fault has been shown would be to forget the principle of liability for deliberate indifference. When unforseen circumstances demand an officer's instant judgment, even precipitate recklessness fails to create the harmful purpose needed to spark the shock that implicates due process concerns. Accordingly, we hold that high-speech chases with no intent to harm suspects physically or to worsen their legal plight do not give rise to liability under the Fourteenth Amendment that is redressable by an action under § 1983. The police did nothing to cause Willard's high-speed driving, nothing to excuse his flouting of law enforcement authority to control traffic, and nothing beyond a refusal to call off the chase to encourage him to race through traffic at breakneck speed. Willard's outrageous behavior was practically instantaneous, and so was Smith's instinctive response. The officer's instinct was to do his job, not to induce lawlessness, or to terrorize, cause harm, or kill. Prudence was subject to countervailing enforcement considerations, and there is no reason to believe that they were tainted by an improper or malicious motive on his part. Smith's behavior does not shock the conscience.

Analysis:

In *Daniels v. Williams* (1986), the Supreme Court held that negligence on the part of a government official that results in an unintended loss of or injury to life, liberty, or property does not generally implicate the concept of due process. But what about a degree of culpability higher than mere negligence? What about recklessness or deliberate indifference? Some courts have held that when a government official acts recklessly and a loss of life, liberty, or property results, a constitutional deprivation can be found. The present case, however, teaches that at least in emergency situations involving law enforcement officials, not even recklessness will not create a constitutional deprivation; only conduct that "shocks the conscience" give rise to a due process deprivation in emergency situations, and to reach that level, there must be evidence of intent to harm.

DeShaney v. Winnebago County Department of Social Services

(Abused Child and his Mother) v. (Government Social Workers)
489 U.S. 189, 109 S.Ct. 998 (1989)

THE DUE PROCESS CLAUSE DOES NOT GUARANTEE THAT CITIZENS WILL BE PROVIDED WITH CERTAIN MINIMAL LEVELS OF SAFETY AND SECURITY

■ **INSTANT FACTS** An abused child and his mother filed suit against Winnebago County after it was discovered that a father who had been repeatedly beating his child was permitted by the County Department of Social Services to retain custody of the child despite warnings from hospitals and others that abuse was taking place.

■ **BLACK LETTER RULE** The Due Process Clause protects against deprivations of life, liberty, and property by arbitrary government action; nowhere does the language of the Clause require the State to protect the life, liberty, and property of its citizens against invasions by private actors.

■ PROCEDURAL BASIS

Appeal to the United States Supreme Court of a lower federal court decision in a § 1983 action.

■ FACTS

Between January of 1982 and March of 1984, Randy DeShaney frequently beat is young son, Joshua DeShaney (P). In 1984, things came to a head when Joshua (P), then five years old, was injured so badly that he fell into a life-threatening coma, suffering severe and likely life-long brain damage. Randy DeShaney was subsequently convicted of child abuse. After Joshua (P) was put into a coma, it came to light that over the years the Winnebago County Department of Social Services (D) had been given information about abuse against Joshua at least five separate times. It also came to light that on four of these five occasions the Department had continued to allow Joshua to reside with his father, and in the fifth they had only temporarily removed Joshua from the home. On at least two occasions Randy DeShaney would not allow the Department (D) to see Joshua, and in both instances no further action was taken. After Randy DeShaney's conviction, Joshua (P) and his mother (P) filed a § 1983 action against the Department (D) alleging that by failing to protect Joshua (P) against a risk of violence about which they knew or should have known, the Department (D) violated his right to liberty under the Fourteenth Amendment.

■ ISSUE

Does the Due Process Clause require the State to protect the life, liberty, and property of its citizens against invasions by private actors?

■ DECISION AND RATIONALE

(Rehnquist, J.) No. Joshua (P) contends that the State deprived him of his liberty interest in "free[dom] from . . . unjustified intrusions on personal security" by failing to provide him with adequate protection against his father's violence. But nothing in the language of the Due Process Clause requires the State to protect the life, liberty, and property of its citizens against invasion by private actors. The Clause is a limitation on the State's power to act, not a guarantee of certain minimal levels of safety and security. It cannot be read to include an affirmative obligation to ensure that life, liberty, and property do not come to harm through other means. Our prior cases show that the Due Process Clauses confer no affirmative right to governmental aid, even when it is necessary to secure life, liberty, or property, and that the State cannot be held liable for injuries that could have been averted had the requested aid been given. On this basis, we conclude that a State's failure to protect an individual against private violence does not constitute a due process violation. Joshua (P) contends, however, that even if the Due Process Clause imposes no affirmative obligation on the State to protect the general public, such a duty may arise out of certain "special relationships" assumed by the State with respect to particular individuals. Joshua (P) further argues that such a "special relationship" existed here because the State (D) knew of Joshua's (P) situation, and specifically proclaimed its intention to protect him. Having undertaken to protect Joshua (P), the State (D) acquired an affirmative duty to do so. Its failure to discharge that duty, Joshua (P) argues, was an abuse of governmental power that so "shocks the conscience" as to constitute a substantive due process violation. We disagree. In certain limited circumstances the Constitution imposes upon the State affirmative duties of care and protection with respect to particular individuals. But these cases stand only for the proposition that when the State takes a person into custody and holds him against his will, the Constitution imposes upon it a corresponding duty to assume some responsibility for his safety and general well-being. This affirmative duty to protect arises not from the State's knowledge of the person's predicament or from an expression of intent to help, but form the limitation which the State has imposed on his freedom. Joshua (P) did not suffer harm while in State custody, but while in his father's custody. The State (D) may have been aware of the dangers that Joshua (P) faced, but it played no part in their creation and did nothing to render him more vulnerable. That the State (D) once took temporary custody of Joshua (P) does not alter the analysis, for when it returned him he was in no worse position than before; the State does not become the permanent guarantor of an individual's safety by having once offered him shelter. Under these circumstances, the State (D) had no constitutional duty to protect Joshua (P), so its failure to do so does not constitute a violation of the Due Process Clause.

■ DISSENT

(Brennan, J.) I do not agree that the State did nothing to endanger Joshua (P). Through its child protection program, the State actively intervened in Joshua's (P) life and, by virtue of that intervention, acquired knowledge that Joshua (P) was in danger. "The State's knowledge of [an] individual's predicament [and] its expressions of intent to help him" can amount to a "limitation . . . on his freedom to act on his own behalf" or to obtain help from others. Wisconsin has established a child-welfare system designed to help children like Joshua (P). Wisconsin law places upon the local departments of social services a duty to investigate reported instances of child abuse. Wisconsin law also channels all reports of suspected child abuse to the local departments of social services for evaluation and, if necessary, further action. In these circumstances, a non-DSS employee would likely feel that her job was done as soon as she had reported her suspicions of child abuse to DSS (D). In other words, Wisconsin has relieved ordinary citizens and non-DSS governmental bodies of any obligation to do anything more than report their suspicions of child abuse. If DSS (D) ignores these suspicions, no one will step in to fill the gap. Wisconsin's child protection program thus effectively confined Joshua (P) to a violent home until such time as DSS (D) took action to remove him. The Due Process Clause "was intended to prevent government 'from abusing [its] power, or employing it as an instrument of oppression.'" Inaction on the part of the State can be just as oppressive as an affirmative abuse of power. Today's opinion construes the Clause to permit a State to displace private sources of protection and then, at the crucial movement, to shrug its shoulders and turn away from the harm it promised to prevent. I cannot agree that our Constitution is indifferent to such indifferences.

■ DISSENT

(Blackmun, J.) The facts here involve not mere passivity, but active state intervention in the life of Joshua DeShaney (P) that triggered a duty to aid him once it became clear that he was in danger. The Court fails to recognize this duty because it attempts to draw a sharp line between action and inaction. But such formalistic reasoning has no place in the interpretation of the Fourteenth Amendments. The Court also claims that its decision is compelled by existing legal doctrine. It does so because it too narrowly reads our Fourteenth Amendment precedents. A more sympathetic reading would compel a different result. Finally, it is a sad commentary upon American life and constitutional principles that this child is now assigned to live the remainder of his life profoundly retarded. Joshua (P) and his mother deserve the opportunity to have the facts of their case considered in the light of the constitutional protection that 42 U.S.C. § 1983 meant to provide.

Analysis:

DeShaney is another in the line of cases in which the Supreme Court addresses what is and is not a deprivation of life, liberty, or property in the constitutional due process sense. In this case, the Court held that governmental action or inaction that indirectly permits a citizen to be injured at the hands of a non-governmental actor does not rise to the level of a due process violation, and any loss of life, liberty, or property that results from that non-governmental action does not constitute a deprivation in the constitutional sense. In so holding, *DeShaney* aligns itself with *Daniels v. Williams* and *County of Sacramento v. Lewis* in reaffirming the principle that the Due Process Clause was written to prevent arbitrary and capricious, not negligent or inadvertent, deprivations of liberty. *DeShaney* also stands for the proposition that the state is not required to act to prevent private harms. Because the state lacks the resources to prevent all crimes, it cannot be required to compensate the victims of crimes that it does not and cannot prevent.

Town of Castle Rock v. Gonzales

(*Law Enforcement*) v. (*Crime Victim*)
545 U.S. 748, 125 S.Ct. 2796 (2005)

LANGUAGE STATING THAT POLICE "SHALL ARREST" RESTRAINING–ORDER VIOLATORS IS DISCRETIONARY, NOT MANDATORY

■ **INSTANT FACTS** Castle Rock (D) police officers did not enforce a restraining order against Gonzales's (P) estranged husband, and he murdered her three children.

■ **BLACK LETTER RULE** An individual who has obtained a restraining order against another does not have a constitutionally protected property interest in the enforcement of that order when there is probable cause to believe it was violated.

■ **PROCEDURAL BASIS**

Appeal from an order dismissing a complaint.

■ **FACTS**

Gonzales (P) obtained a restraining order against her estranged husband during their divorce proceedings. The order directed Gonzales's (P) husband not to disturb her or her children, and ordered him to stay at least 100 yards from the family home. The bottom of the order contained form language that told Gonzales's (P) husband that he could be arrested without notice if there was probable cause to believe that he had knowingly violated the order. The order also contained form language directing law enforcement officials to arrest or seek a warrant to arrest Gonzales's (P) husband if the official had probable cause to believe that the order was violated. After it was served, the order was modified to allow Gonzales's (P) husband to spend time with their three children.

On the day in question, Gonzales's (P) husband picked up the children from outside their home, without advance notice, between 5:00 and 5:30 p.m. Gonzales (P) called the police (D), but the officers who responded to the call said that there was nothing they could do. The officers suggested she call again at 10:00. Gonzales (P) called the police again after her husband called to say where he had the children, but the police again refused to do anything and told Gonzales (P) to wait until 10:00. Gonzales (P) called again shortly after 10:00, but was told to wait until midnight. She called at midnight, and then went to her husband's apartment. Gonzales (P) called the police from the apartment, and they told her to wait for an officer. No officer came, so around 12:50, she went to the police station. Gonzales (P) submitted an incident report, but the officer who took the report did nothing about it. At around 3:20 a.m., Gonzales's (P) husband was shot in a gunfight with the police outside the police station. Inside his truck were the bodies of all three children, whom Gonzales's (P) husband had murdered. Gonzales (P) brought a lawsuit claiming Castle Rock (D) violated the Due Process Clause because its police department had an official policy or custom of not responding to complaints of restraining order violations and tolerating non-enforcement of restraining orders.

■ **ISSUE**

Was the failure to respond to Gonzales's (P) complaints a due process violation?

Town of Castle Rock v. Gonzales (Continued)

■ DECISION AND RATIONALE

(Scalia, J.) No. An individual who has obtained a restraining order against another does not have a constitutionally protected property interest in the enforcement of that order when there is probable cause to believe it was violated. The Due Process Clause does not protect everything that can be described as a "benefit." To have a property interest in a benefit, a person must have a legitimate claim of entitlement to it. Such entitlements not created by the Constitution, but are created by an independent source, such as state law. A benefit is not a protected entitlement if it may be denied or granted in the discretion of government officials.

The critical language in the restraining order came from the preprinted notice to law-enforcement personnel on the back of the order. That notice restated the statute regarding a police officer's duties as to the violation of a restraining order. These provisions of Colorado law did not make enforcement of restraining orders mandatory. A well established tradition of police discretion has long coexisted with statutes that appear to call for mandatory arrest. A true mandate for arrest would require some stronger indication from the Colorado Legislature than is in the statute now. It is hard to imagine that an officer would not have some discretion to determine that circumstances counsel against enforcement in a particular situation

Even if an entitlement were created, it is by no means clear that an individual entitlement to enforcement of a restraining order would be a "property" interest for purposes of the Due Process Clause. Such a right would not resemble any traditional conception of property. The right to have a restraining order enforced does not "have some ascertainable monetary value." The alleged property interest here arises incidentally, out of a function that government actors have always performed. Reversed.

■ DISSENT

(Stevens, J.) The Court should certify the question of the existence of an entitlement to the Colorado Supreme Court. The majority gives undue weight to the various statutes that appear to mandate police enforcement but that are generally understood to preserve police discretion. The majority thus gives short shrift to the "mandatory arrest" statutes in the domestic violence context. The majority's formalistic analysis fails to take seriously the fact that the Colorado statute at issue here was enacted to benefit the narrow class of persons who are the beneficiaries of domestic abuse orders, and that the order here was issued to benefit Gonzales (P) and her children. Finally, the majority is wrong to assert that a citizen's interest in the government's commitment to provide law enforcement services in defined instances does not resemble any traditional conception of property.

Analysis:

The Colorado statute at issue in this case provided that a peace officer who had probable cause to believe that a restraining order was violated "shall arrest, or, if an arrest would be impractical under the circumstances, seek a warrant for the arrest of a restrained person." Colo. Rev. Stat. § 18-6-803.5 (3) (1999). It is difficult to see how the mandate for arrest could have been made much stronger. The majority placed some emphasis on the language that allows an officer to seek a warrant "if an arrest would be impractical." Although it appears to be up to the officer to determine the practicality of an arrest, that is not the same as saying that the officer has the discretion to ignore the information constituting probable cause.

■ CASE VOCABULARY

RESTRAINING ORDER: A court order prohibiting family violence; especially, an order restricting a person from harassing, threatening, and sometimes merely contacting or approaching another specified person.

Goldberg v. Kelly
(New York City Commissioner of Social Services) v. (Welfare Benefit Recipient)
397 U.S. 254, 90 S.Ct. 1011 (1970)

DUE PROCESS REQUIRES THAT AN EVIDENTIARY HEARING BE HELD BEFORE THE GOVERNMENT CAN TERMINATE A PERSON'S WELFARE BENEFITS

■ **INSTANT FACTS** A group of citizens facing the potential loss of financial aid without notice or a hearing filed suit seeking to have those procedures be provided.

■ **BLACK LETTER RULE** The extent to which procedural due process must be afforded in a particular situation is influenced by the extent of the loss suffered, and depends on whether the aggrieved party's interest in avoiding that loss outweighs the governmental interest in summary adjudication

■ PROCEDURAL BASIS
Appeal to the United States Supreme Court of New York federal district court.

■ FACTS
A group of New York City residents (P) became concerned that New York City and New York State officials (D) were going to cut off certain public assistance payments that they were receiving, and that it was going to be done without any prior notice or a hearing, so they filed a lawsuit seeking to preclude those two entities (D) from doing so. Their complaint alleged that to terminate financial assistance without a hearing was a violation of the recipients' right to procedural due process.

■ ISSUE
Does a State deny a person procedural due process when it terminates public assistance payments without giving the recipient the opportunity for an evidentiary hearing?

■ DECISION AND RATIONALE
(Brennan, J.) Yes. Goldberg (D) does not contend that procedural due process is inapplicable to the termination of welfare benefits. Such benefits are a matter of statutory entitlement for persons qualified to receive them; their termination involves state action that adjudicates important rights. The constitutional challenge cannot be answered by argument that public assistance benefits are a privilege and not a right. The extent to which procedural due process must be afforded to welfare benefits recipients is influenced by the extent to which one may suffer a loss, and depends on whether one's interest in avoiding that loss outweighs the governmental interest in summary adjudication. It is true that some governmental benefits may by administratively terminated without affording the recipient a pre-termination evidentiary hearing. But when welfare is discontinued, only a pre-termination evidentiary hearing provides the recipient with procedural due process. Termination of aid pending the resolution of a controversy over eligibility may deprive a recipient of the very means by which to live while he waits, meaning his need to concentrate on finding the means for daily subsistence may adversely affect his ability to seek redress from the welfare bureaucracy. Moreover, important governmental interests are promoted by affording recipients a pre-termination evidentiary hearing. Public assistance is a means to "promote the general Welfare, and secure the Blessings of Liberty to ourselves and our Posterity." The same governmental interests that counsel the provision of welfare, counsel its uninterrupted provision to those eligible to receive it; pre-termination evidentiary hearings are indispensable to that end. Goldberg

Goldberg v. Kelly (Continued)

(D) argues that these considerations are outweighed by countervailing governmental interests in conserving fiscal and administrative resources. The requirement of a prior hearing will involve some greater expense, and the benefits paid to ineligible recipients pending decision at the hearing probably cannot be recouped. But the State is not unable to minimize increased costs. By developing procedure for prompt pre-termination hearings and by skillful use of personnel and facilities, much of the drain on fiscal and administrative resources can be reduced. In short, the interest of the recipient in uninterrupted receipt of public assistance, coupled with the State's interest that his payments not be erroneously terminated, clearly outweighs the State's need to prevent an increase in its fiscal and administrative burdens. Pre-termination hearings need not take the form of a judicial or quasi-judicial trial. The pre-termination hearing has but one function: to produce an initial determination of the validity of the welfare department's grounds for discontinuance of payments. Thus, a complete record and a comprehensive opinion need not be provided at the pre-termination stage. What is required is a hearing held "at a meaningful time and in a meaningful manner." Furthermore, a recipient must have timely and adequate notice detailing the reasons for a proposed termination, and an effective opportunity to defend against it by confronting any adverse witnesses and by presenting his own arguments and evidence orally. Affirmed.

■ DISSENT

(Black, J.) Today more than nine million men, women, and children in the United States receive some kind of state or federal financial assistance. Since these gratuities are paid on the basis of need, the list of recipients is ever-changing. As such, there exists a constant administrative burden on government, and it certainly could not have anticipated that this burden would include the additional procedural expense imposed by the Court today. The Court holds that it would violate the Due Process Clause to stop paying any of these nine million people weekly or monthly allowances unless the government first affords them a full "evidentiary hearing," even though welfare officials are persuaded that the recipients are not rightfully entitled to receive a penny under the law. In other words, although some recipients might be on the list for payment wholly because of deliberate fraud, the Court holds that the government is helpless and must continue, until after an evidentiary hearing, to pay money that it does not owe, never has owed, and never could owe. There is no provision of the Constitution that thus paralyzes the government's efforts to protect itself against making payments to those who are not entitled to them. The Court states that this decision will benefit the poor and the needy. I think it will do the opposite. The end result of today's decision may well be that the government cannot reverse its decision to give welfare benefits until the recipient has had the benefits of full administrative and judicial review, including the opportunity to present his case to this Court. Since that process will usually entail a delay of several years, the inevitable result will be that the government will not put a claimant on the rolls until it has made an exhaustive investigation to determine eligibility. This will ensure that many will never get on the rolls, or at least that they will remain destitute during the lengthy determination of initial eligibility.

Analysis:

Prior to 1970 and the Court's decision in *Goldberg v. Kelly*, courts used what is known as the "rights-privileges distinction" to determine whether a party had a property interest protected by the Due Process Clause in a benefit received from the government. Under that test, due process upon deprivation was only required if receipt of the benefit was determined to be a right. If receipt was merely a privilege, then the government was permitted to deprive a person of the benefit without the requirement of a hearing. *Goldberg* changed the procedural due process landscape because it rejected the rights-privileges distinction in favor of a different test for determining whether the deprivation of a particular government payment or other benefit invoked the Due Process Clause. In holding that welfare payments could not be withdrawn without a hearing, the *Goldberg* Court focused not on whether receipt of such payments was a right, but on the importance of the benefit to the party receiving it: "The extent to which procedural due process must be afforded the recipient is influenced by the extent to which he may be 'condemned to suffer grievous loss,' and depends upon whether the recipient's interest in avoiding that loss outweighs the governmental interest in summary adjudication." This test did not remain in place for long, however. Two years later, in *Roth v. Board of Regents* (1972), the

Goldberg test was replaced with one that focused on expectations of entitlement (and arguably reinvigorated the rights-privileges distinction).

Board of Regents v. Roth

(*Employer*) v. (*Employee*)
408 U.S. 564, 92 S.Ct. 2701 (1972)

PROPERTY INTERESTS ARE NOT CREATED BY THE CONSTITUTION BUT BY INDEPENDENT SOURCES SUCH AS STATE LAW

■ **INSTANT FACTS** A government employee who had signed a one-year employment contract filed suit when his employer chose not to rehire him following the completion of the one year.

■ **BLACK LETTER RULE** A person is not deprived of liberty or property in violation of the Fourteenth Amendment when he is not hired or rehired for a government job but remains free to seek other employment.

■ **PROCEDURAL BASIS**

Appeal to the United States Supreme Court of a federal lawsuit filed by an individual challenging his employer's decision not to rehire him.

■ **FACTS**

In 1968, the University of Wisconsin-Oshkosh (D) hired David Roth (P) as an assistant professor of political science. Roth (P) was hired for a fixed term of one year, ending on June 30, 1969. Under Wisconsin law, a new teacher was entitled to nothing beyond a one-year appointment. Additionally, Wisconsin law gave the University (D) unfettered discretion with respect to offering a one-year professor continued employment. In February of 1969, the University (D) informed Roth (P) that he would not be rehired. It gave no reason for its decision and did not provide Roth (P) with the opportunity to challenge the decision. In response, Roth (P) filed suit against the University (D).

■ **ISSUE**

Does a government employee with a fixed term of employment have a Fourteenth Amendment liberty or property interest in continued employment after the fixed term expires such that a decision not to rehire the person must be accompanied by a hearing at which the person can challenge the decision?

■ **DECISION AND RATIONALE**

(Stewart, J.) No. The requirements of procedural due process apply only to the deprivation of interests encompassed by the Fourteenth Amendment's protection of liberty and property. When protected interests are implicated, the right to some kind of hearing is paramount. But the range of interests protected by procedural due process is not infinite. "Liberty" and "property" are very broad terms not defined in the Constitution. While this court has not attempted to define with exactness the liberty . . . guaranteed by the Fourteenth Amendment, it undoubtedly denotes not merely freedom from bodily restraint, but also the right of the individual to contract, to work, to marry and bring up children, to worship as one wishes, and generally to enjoy those privileges long recognized as essential to the orderly pursuit of happiness. There might be cases in which a State refused to re-employ a person under such circumstances that interests in liberty would be implicated, but this is not such a case. In declining to rehire Roth (P), the State (D) did not make any charge against him that might seriously damage his standing in his community. Similarly, there is no suggestion that the State (D) imposed on

Board of Regents v. Roth (Continued)

him a stigma that foreclosed his freedom to take advantage of other employment opportunities. Had it done either of these things, this would be a different case, but on the record before us, all that clearly appears is that Roth (P) was not rehired. It stretches the concept too far to suggest that a person is deprived of "liberty" when he simply is not rehired in one job but remains free to seek another. Roth (P) similarly does not have a property interest in a teaching position. This Court has held that the property interests protected by procedural due process extend well beyond actual ownership of real estate, chattels, or money. However, to have a property interest in a benefit, a person must have more than an abstract need or desire for it. He must have more than a unilateral expectation of it. He must have a legitimate claim of entitlement to it. Roth's (P) property interest in employment by the University (D) was created and defined by the terms of his appointment. Those terms secured his interest in employment up to June 30, 1969, at which time it was to terminate. They did not provide for contract renewal absent "sufficient cause." Indeed, they made no provision for renewal whatsoever. Thus, the terms of Roth's (P) appointment do not support a claim of entitlement to re-employment. In these circumstances. Roth (P) did not have a property interest sufficient to require a hearing when University officials (D) declined to renew his contract.

■ **DISSENT**

(Marshall, J.) This Court's prior decisions establish the principle that federal and state governments are prohibited from acting arbitrarily with respect to employment opportunities that they offer and control. In regard to these opportunities, the government may only act fairly and reasonably. This Court has also established that the fact that an employee has no contract guaranteeing work for a specific future period does not mean that he may be discharged at any time for any reason. In my view, every citizen who applies for a government job is entitled to it unless the government can establish some reason for denying the employment. This is a "property" right that I believe is protected by the Fourteenth Amendment. It is also liberty—liberty to work—which is the very essence of the personal freedom secured by the Due Process Clause. It is not burdensome for the government to give reasons for not employing someone when reasons exist. It can scarcely be argued that government would be crippled by a requirement that the reason be communicated to the person most directly affected by the government's action.

Analysis:

In the present case, the Court holds that in determining whether a property interest exists, the focus should be on whether there is a reasonable expectation of entitlement to the particular benefit. Because Roth (P) was given only a one-year appointment, he had no claim of entitlement to employment beyond that period and therefore did not, under the rule set forth in this case, have a property interest in future employment. The reason *Roth* can be said to resurrect the rights-privileges distinction is it allows the state to determine whether a benefit creates a property interest by articulating whether citizens are entitled to that benefit. If the state decides that there is entitlement to a certain benefit, it can make that benefit a property interest; if the state decides the contrary, however, it can preclude receipt of the benefit from being deemed a property interest. This particular rule has continued in effect and has been applied in a number of cases.

Goss v. Lopez

(*School Administrator*) v. (*Suspended Student*)
419 U.S. 565, 95 S.Ct. 729 (1975)

A STUDENT'S LEGITIMATE ENTITLEMENT TO A PUBLIC EDUCATION IS A PROPERTY INTEREST PROTECTED BY THE DUE PROCESS CLAUSE

■ **INSTANT FACTS** A group of high school students filed suit against their respective administrators for suspending them without the opportunity for a hearing on the issue.

■ **BLACK LETTER RULE** Having chosen to extend the right to an education to certain persons, a State cannot withdraw that right from a single person on grounds of misconduct absent fundamentally fair procedures to determine whether the misconduct has occurred.

■ **PROCEDURAL BASIS**

Appeal to the United States Supreme Court of a lower federal court decision holding that the Columbus Ohio Public School System violated the due process rights of a group of high school students.

■ **FACTS**

Lopez (P) and eight other named students were suspended for various reasons from public high school in Columbus, Ohio. Under Ohio law, a principal was permitted to suspend a student engaging in misconduct for up to ten days. Principals were also permitted to expel students if the need arose. When a student was expelled, Ohio law provided that student and his or her parents the opportunity to appeal the principal's decision to the Board of Education and attend a hearing to that effect. No such appeal was available for students who were suspended. When a hearing was denied to them, the nine students filed a federal civil rights action under 42 U.S.C. § 1983 claiming that the Columbus Ohio Public School System (D) had violated their constitutional right to due process.

■ **ISSUE**

Does the Due Process Clause apply to students suspended from public schools such that they have the right to request and have a hearing on the issue of suspension?

■ **DECISION AND RATIONALE**

(White, J.) Yes. The School (D) contends that because there is no constitutional right to public education, the Due Process Clause does not protect against expulsions from public school. This position misconceives the nature of the issue and is refuted by our prior decisions. The Fourteenth Amendment forbids the State to deprive any person of life, liberty, or property without due process of law. Protected property interests are not created nor their dimensions defined by the Constitution, but by independent sources such as state laws which entitle people to certain benefits. Here, on the basis of a state law which provides all persons of a certain age the right to a public education, Lopez (P) plainly has a legitimate claim of entitlement to a public education. State law also permits school principals to suspend students for up to ten days; but suspensions may not be imposed arbitrarily. Having chosen to extend the right to an education to certain persons, the State (D) cannot withdraw that right on grounds of misconduct absent fundamentally fair procedures to determine whether misconduct has occurred. The Due Process Clause also forbids arbitrary deprivations of liberty. "Where a person's

Goss v. Lopez (Continued)

good name [and] reputation ... is at stake because of what the government is doing to him," the minimal requirements of the Clause must be satisfied. *Wisconsin v. Constantineau* (1971). Charges of misconduct that have the potential of harming a student's reputation fall within this category. Once it is determined that due process applies, the question remains what process is due. The prospect of imposing elaborate hearing requirements in every suspension case is viewed with great concern by some school officials. But it would be a strange disciplinary system where the accused student is not permitted to tell his side of the story in order to make sure that an injustice is not done. We do not believe that school authorities must be totally free from notice and hearing requirements. Students facing temporary suspension have interests qualifying for protection of the Due Process Clause, and due process requires that the student be given notice of the charges against him and, if he denies them, an explanation of the evidence authorities have and an opportunity to present his side of the story. The Clause requires at least these rudimentary precautions against unfair or mistaken findings of misconduct and arbitrary exclusion from school.

■ DISSENT

(Powell, J.) In holding that the federal courts, rather than education officials and state legislatures, have the authority to determine the rules applicable to routine classroom discipline in public schools, the Court unnecessarily opens avenues for judicial intervention in the operation of our public schools that may adversely affect the quality of education. It justifies this unprecedented intrusion by identifying a new constitutional right: the right not to be suspended without notice and a due process hearing either before or promptly following the suspension. In my view, a student's interest in education is not infringed by a suspension of limited duration like that prescribed by Ohio law. Moreover, to the extent that there may be some infringement, it is too insubstantial to justify imposition of a constitutional rule.

Analysis:

Goss v. Lopez can be read to hold that citizens have a liberty interest in reputation in the sense that any injury to that reputation caused by governmental action is potentially a violation of the Fourteenth Amendment right to due process. This holding, however, is undermined by *Paul v. Davis* (1976), which was decided one year after *Goss*. *Paul* holds that governmental action that causes a mere tarnishing of a person's reputation, without more, is not a deprivation of liberty actionable under the Due Process Clause. This is not to say that *Goss* is useless to the student of constitutional law, however, because it does in fact address an issue of constitutional significance. Specifically, *Goss* reiterates the principle that life, liberty, and property interests are not generally created by the Constitution, but by other sources, such as state law. Furthermore, once a liberty or property interest is created, it cannot be arbitrarily taken away by the state. In this and prior cases, the Court held that there is no constitutional right to public education. However, in this case the Court also held that because Ohio law created a right to free education for all citizens of a certain age, a liberty interest exists in that right, meaning any deprivation of that state-created right is a deprivation of liberty actionable under the Fourteenth Amendment.

Paul v. Davis

(*Chief of Police*) v. (*Suspected Shoplifter*)
424 U.S. 693, 96 S.Ct. 1155 (1976)

REPUTATION IS NOT A LIBERTY OR PROPERTY INTEREST FOR THE PURPOSES OF THE FOURTEENTH AMENDMENT

■ **INSTANT FACTS** A suspected shoplifter filed suit when his face appeared on a law enforcement flier bearing the words "Active Shoplifters" and the mug shots of various persons known or believed to be shoplifters.

■ **BLACK LETTER RULE** The Fourteenth Amendment's guarantee against deprivations of liberty or property without due process does not apply to governmental actions which have the effect of harming a persons' reputation.

■ **PROCEDURAL BASIS**

Appeal to the United States Supreme Court of a federal civil rights action filed by an individual whose reputation was allegedly injured by the actions of two city and county officials.

■ **FACTS**

In an effort to protect local merchants during the Christmas Season of 1972, the Chief of Police of Louisville, Kentucky, (D) and the Sheriff of Jefferson County, Kentucky, (D) prepared a flier with the words "Active Shoplifters" at the top and the mug shots of suspected shoplifters underneath. The flier was circulated to all local merchants so that their security or other store personnel could watch out for the depicted individuals. One of the photographs on the poster was of Charles Davis III (P), who had been arrested for shoplifting in the summer of 1971. Davis (P) entered a plea of not guilty to the charge and shortly after the distribution of the flier, the charge against him was dismissed. Davis (P) filed suit against the Chief (D) and the Sheriff (D) alleging that their actions had violated his right to due process on the ground that the circulation of the flier inhibited his ability to enter businesses and seek employment.

■ **ISSUE**

Can the defamation of an individual that stems directly from some governmental act serve as the basis for a civil rights lawsuit against the government under 42 U.S.C. § 1983?

■ **DECISION AND RATIONALE**

(Rehnquist, J.) No. The words "liberty" and "property" as used in the Fourteenth Amendment do not single out reputation as a candidate for special protection. While we have in prior cases pointed out the drastic effect of the "stigma" which may result from defamation by the government, this line of cases does not establish the proposition that reputation alone, apart from some more tangible interests such as employment, is either "liberty" or "property" by itself sufficient to invoke the procedural protection of the Due Process Clause. This conclusion is quite consistent with our most recent holding in this area, *Goss v. Lopez*. While we noted in *Goss* that charges of misconduct could damage a student's reputation, we focused on the fact that Ohio law gives all children the right to attend school, and suspending the student there involved resulted in a deprivation of that right. Kentucky law does not provide Davis (P) with any legal guarantee of present enjoyment of reputation that has been violated in any way by Paul's (D) actions. Rather, his interest in reputation is simply one of a number of interests which the State may protect against injury by virtue of its tort law. And any harm or injury to that interest, even where inflicted by an officer of the State, does not result in a deprivation of any "liberty" or "property" interest. For these reasons we hold that the interest in reputation asserted in this case is neither "liberty" or "property" guaranteed against state deprivation without due process of law.

■ DISSENT

(Brennan, J.) I have always thought that one of this Court's most important roles is to provide against governmental violation of the constitutional safeguards that secure the legitimate expectations of every person to innate human dignity and a sense of worth. It is a regrettable abdication of that role, and a denigration of the Bill of Rights, when the Court tolerates arbitrary and capricious official conduct branding an individual a criminal without compliance with constitutional procedures designed to ensure the fair and impartial ascertainment of criminal culpability. I hope that today's decision, which repudiates a substantial body of case law, is a short-lived aberration.

Analysis:

Paul v. Davis (1976), the second of the reputation cases, effectively closes the door to reputation being a liberty interest, and makes it clear that governmental besmirchment of a person's reputation is not a deprivation of liberty in the due process sense. The Chief Justice believed that the government's actions in this case were, at best, a tort to be remedied under state law. In reaching the conclusion that it does, the majority decision distinguishes prior cases on the ground that those cases involved "more tangible interests such as employment," and focuses on the fact that reputation alone is not a liberty interest in the Fourteenth Amendment sense. In *Siegert v. Gilly* (1991), however, the decision in *Paul* was used to deny a reputation-based claim that involved not only damage to reputation, but also a tangible loss stemming from the defamation. Thus, even when there was more than a loss of reputation, the Court has, since the decision in *Paul*, refused to grant Fourteenth Amendment protections in this arena. Over the years *Paul* has been criticized as imposing an unduly narrow reading of liberty, but it still stands today as the rule to be applied when governmental action injures a person's reputation.

■ CASE VOCABULARY

CAPRICIOUS: Sudden, unpredictable, or impulsive.

Mathews v. Eldridge

(Secretary of Welfare) v. (Recipient of Disability Payments)
424 U.S. 319, 96 S.Ct. 893 (1976)

THE FUNDAMENTAL REQUIREMENT OF DUE PROCESS IS THE OPPORTUNITY TO BE HEARD AT A MEANINGFUL TIME AND IN A MEANINGFUL WAY

■ **INSTANT FACTS** A state disability benefit recipient filed suit when the state decided to stop providing him with the benefits he had been receiving.

■ **BLACK LETTER RULE** An identification of the specific dictates of due process generally requires consideration of three distinct factors: (1) the private interest that will be affected by the official action; (2) the risk of an erroneous deprivation of such interest through the procedures used, and the probable value, if any, of additional or substitute procedural safeguards; and (3) the Government's interest, including the function involved and the fiscal and administrative burdens that the additional or substitute procedural requirement would entail.

■ **PROCEDURAL BASIS**

Appeal to the United States Supreme Court of a lower court finding that a disability recipient had been denied due process in the termination of his disability benefits.

■ **FACTS**

In 1968, Eldridge (P) began receiving disability benefits from the state in which he lived. After just a few years, however, his benefits were revoked. The agency in charge of disability benefits terminated Eldridge's (P) benefits after considering his response to a questionnaire regarding his condition, reports from his physician and a psychiatric consultant, and Eldridge's (P) medical files. Eldridge (P) was informed of the termination, provided a statement of reasons for that termination, and given an opportunity to submit a written response to the State (D). Eldridge (P) provided the State (D) with a statement disputing the agency's decision, but the benefits were nonetheless terminated. Eldridge (P) filed suit, claiming that the procedure used by the state violated the due process clause.

■ **ISSUE**

Does the Due Process Clause of the Fifth Amendment require that, prior to the termination of Social Security disability benefit payments, the recipient be afforded an opportunity for an evidentiary hearing on the matter?

■ **DECISION AND RATIONALE**

(Powell, J.) No. Procedural due process imposes constraints on government decisions that deprive individuals of liberty or property interests that fall within the meaning of the Due Process Clause. The Secretary (D) does not contend that procedural due process is inapplicable to termination of Social Security Benefits. Rather, he contends that the existing procedures comport with the requirements of due process. Resolution of the issue requires analysis of the governmental and private interests that are affected. Our prior decisions indicate that identification of the specific dictates of due process generally requires consideration of three distinct factors: first, the private interest that will be affected by the official action; second, the risk of an erroneous deprivation of such interest, and the probable value, if any, of additional or substitute procedural safeguards; and finally, the Government's interest, including the function involved and the fiscal and administrative burdens that the additional or substitute procedural requirement would entail. Since a recipient whose benefits are terminated is awarded full retroactive relief if he ultimately prevails, his sole interest is in the uninterrupted receipt of income pending a final administrative decision. His potential injury is thus similar to that of the welfare recipient in *Goldberg*. Only in *Goldberg* has the Court held that due process requires an evidentiary hearing prior to a temporary deprivation. It was emphasized there that welfare assistance is given to those on the margin of subsistence. Eligibility for disability benefits, in contrast, is not based on financial need. The degree of potential deprivation that may be created by a particular decision is also a factor to be considered in assessing the validity of any administrative decision-making process. The potential deprivation here is likely to be less than in *Goldberg*. Although the hardship imposed on the erroneously terminated disability recipient may be significant, his need is still likely to be less than that of the welfare recipient. In addition, other forms of private and government assistance will become available where the termination of disability benefits places a worker or his family below the subsistence level. As such, there is less reason here than in *Goldberg* to depart from the ordinary principle that something less than an evidentiary hearing is sufficient prior to adverse administrative action. An additional factor to be considered is the fairness and reliability of the existing pre-termination procedures, and the probable value of additional procedural safeguards. In order to remain eligible for benefits, a medical assessment of a worker's physical or mental condition is required. This is a more focused and easily documented decision than the typical determination of welfare entitlement. In contrast to decisions regarding welfare benefits, in which a wide variety of information may be deemed relevant, the decision to discontinue disability benefits turns on standard and unbiased medical reports. This being the case, the potential value of an evidentiary hearing or oral presentation to the decision-maker is substantially less in this context than in *Goldberg*. A further safeguard against mistake is the policy of allowing the disability recipient's representative full access to all information relied upon by the State. In addition, prior to the cutoff of benefits, the agency informs the recipient of its tentative assessment and the reasons therefor, and provides a summary of the relevant evidence. The recipient then has the opportunity to submit additional evidence or arguments, enabling him to challenge the accuracy of the information in his file, as well as the correctness of the agency's conclusions. These procedures enable the recipient to mold his argument to respond to the precise issues which the decision-maker regards as crucial. The final factor to be assessed is public interest. This includes the administrative burden that would be associated with requiring an evidentiary hearing upon demand prior to the termination of disability benefits. The most visible burden would be the cost resulting from the increased number of hearings and the expense of providing benefits to ineligible recipients pending decision. Financial cost alone is not controlling, but the Government's interest in conserving scarce fiscal and administrative resources is a factor that must be weighed, as is the fact that at some point the benefit of an additional safeguard may be outweighed by the cost. We conclude that an evidentiary hearing is not required prior to the termination of disability benefits and that the present administrative procedures fully comport with due process. Reversed.

■ DISSENT

(Brennan, J.) The Court's determination that a discontinuance of disability benefits may cause the recipient to suffer only a limited deprivation is no argument, but is merely speculation. Moreover, the legislative determination to provide disability benefits presumes a need by the recipient which is not this Court's function to denigrate. Indeed, in the present case the termination resulted in a foreclosure on the Eldridge home and the repossession of their furniture. Finally, it is no argument that a worker who has been denied disability benefits may still seek other forms of public assistance.

Analysis:

Mathews is a significant constitutional case in that the three-part test adopted by the Court has since been used with regularity in reviewing claims that procedural due process was denied to a certain individual. The balancing test adopted in *Mathews* calls for a weighing of the costs of employing a particular set of procedural requirements against the potential benefits arising from the use of those procedures. *Mathews* demonstrates how this balancing test is employed. In *Mathews*, the Supreme Court found that the private interest at stake—disability payments—was not of great significance because the payments were either not likely to be a person's sole source of income, or alternative sources would arise upon termination of disability benefits. In addition, the Court also found that based on the nature of the evidence used to determine whether there should be a discontinuance of disability payments, there was no "risk of an erroneous deprivation" by not providing the recipient with a formal hearing. The Court also found that providing a hearing would involve significant "fiscal and administrative burdens." Thus, on the first side of the balancing scale, the Court did not find significant reason to hold that the procedures in place violated due process. On the other side, the Court found that the government's interest in conserving its resources and efficiently conducting its business were weighty enough to support the sufficiency of the procedures already in place.

■ CASE VOCABULARY

DENIGRATE: To belittle or make to appear unimportant.

PROCEDURAL DUE PROCESS: A constitutional guarantee that the process leading to a deprivation of a significant life, liberty, or property interest will be fair and equitable.

CHAPTER NINE

First Amendment: Freedom of Expression

Turner Broadcasting System, Inc. v. Federal Communications Commission

Instant Facts: Cable TV programmers challenged a federal statute requiring them to give channels to local TV broadcasters, contending it regulates them differently based on their programs' content.

Black Letter Rule: A federal law requiring cable TV providers to devote some channels to local, educational broadcasters is a content-neutral speech regulation, and thus subject to intermediate scrutiny.

Boos v. Barry

Instant Facts: Picketers challenged a statute which prohibited insulting anti-government signs in from of foreign embassies.

Black Letter Rule: A federal statute prohibiting anti-government signs near foreign embassies is a content-based speech regulation, and thus subject to strict scrutiny.

Republican Party of Minnesota v. White

Instant Facts: The Republican Party of Minnesota (P) challenged the constitutionality of a state rule prohibiting judicial candidates from expressing their political views.

Black Letter Rule: Government regulations that suppress speech on the basis of its content must be narrowly tailored to serve a compelling state interest.

City of Renton v. Playtime Theatres, Inc.

Instant Facts: When a city passed a zoning ordinance requiring porn theaters be far from houses, churches, schools, etc., a theater challenged its constitutionality.

Black Letter Rule: A zoning ordinance restricting pornographic theaters' placement must be analyzed as a content-neutral, "time, place, and manner" regulation.

National Endowment for the Arts v. Finley

Instant Facts: When Congress passed a statute instructing federal arts grantmakers to "consider" whether applicants' work is indecent or disrespectful, rejected applicants challenged.

Black Letter Rule: The Government may fund art based on its assessment of its artistic content, as long as it does not (A) abuse its discretion by penalizing disfavored viewpoints, or (B) violate other constitutional rights.

United States v. American Library Assn., Inc.

Instant Facts: The Children's Internet Protection Act conditions the receipt of federal funding on the installation of pornography filters on all public library computers.

Black Letter Rule: Congress may not pass legislation that induces individuals to engage in unconstitutional activities.

Near v. State of Minnesota ex rel. Olson

Instant Facts: When a newspaper editor was enjoined from publishing slanderous periodicals, he challenged the injunction as unconstitutional.

Black Letter Rule: Prior restraints against publication are invalid, unless they (A) protect national security during wartime, (B) restrict obscenity, or (C) protect against incitement to violence, or forcible overthrow of government.

New York Times Company v. United States

Instant Facts: During the Vietnam War, a newspaper which printed stolen military documents was enjoined, on national security grounds.

Black Letter Rule: If the government may impose prior restraints to protect national security, its proof burden is very high.

Nebraska Press Association v. Stuart

Instant Facts: When a court issued a gag order preventing media from reporting facts about a mass-murder, reporters challenged the order as unconstitutional.

Black Letter Rule: Court orders barring pretrial publicity by the media bear a "heavy presumption" of invalidity, which must be analyzed by considering (i) the extent and (prejudicial) nature of pretrial publicity, (ii) whether other means would mitigate that publicity's effects, (iii) how effective such an order would be, and (iv) the order's precise terms.

Alexander v. United States

Instant Facts: After a pornographer convicted of obscenity and racketeering had his entire business seized, he appealed the seizure as a "prior restraint."

Black Letter Rule: Government seizure of a business for criminal obscenity violations does not constitute a prior restraint.

Watchtower Bible and Tract Society of New York, Inc. v. Village of Stratton

Instant Facts: The Village of Stratton (D) adopted an ordinance requiring "canvassers" to obtain a free permit from the mayor's office before engaging in door-to-door activities.

Black Letter Rule: A law requiring a permit before engaging in door-to-door activities on private residential property violates the right of free speech.

Thomas and Windy City Hemp Development Board v. Chicago Park District

Instant Facts: A group advocating the legalization of marijuana challenged the constitutionality of a Chicago Park District (D) ordinance requiring a permit to conduct a public rally.

Black Letter Rule: A content-neutral regulation of access to public property is not unconstitutional so long as it provides adequate standards under which the regulation may be enforced.

City of Littleton, Colorado v. Z.J. Gifts D–4, L.L.C.

Instant Facts: Z.J. Gifts D–4, L.L.C. (P) sued the city of Littleton, Colorado (P), challenging the constitutionality of its adult business license ordinance.

Black Letter Rule: A licensing scheme implicating First Amendment interests must provide for "prompt judicial review" of any administrative denial of a license, which requires speedy access to the courts and a prompt judicial determination of any legal claims arising from the denial.

United States v. National Treasury Employees Union

Instant Facts: When Congress passed a law barring federal employees from being paid for speeches/writings, they challenged its constitutionality.

Black Letter Rule: Legislation which forbids payment for certain speech implicates the First Amendment.

West Virginia State Board of Education v. Barnette

Instant Facts: A state's mandatory flag salute was challenged by Jehovah's Witnesses.

Black Letter Rule: The government cannot compel silence or speech, whether verbal or symbolic, except to prevent "clear and present" danger of crime.

Rumsfeld v. Forum for Academic & Institutional Rights, Inc.

Instant Facts: The Solomon Amendment required colleges and universities that received federal funds to allow military recruiters access to campuses, and the Forum for Academic & Institutional Rights (P) claimed that the Amendment violated the First Amendment.

Black Letter Rule: Conditioning the receipt of federal funds on allowing military recruiters to have access to a college campus does not violate the First Amendment.

McIntyre v. Ohio Elections Commission

Instant Facts: An anonymous pamphleteer challenges a law banning anonymous electioneering.

Black Letter Rule: The government cannot compel anonymous speakers to reveal their identities.

Rust v. Sullivan

Instant Facts: Health care providers challenged regulations granting federal funding to family planning, on condition they not recommend abortion.

Black Letter Rule: It is constitutional for the government to selectively fund programs which encourage certain activities in the public interest, without also funding alternative approaches.

Legal Services Corp. v. Velazquez

Instant Facts: The plaintiff challenged the constitutionality of conditions placed on the use of federal funds distributed by Legal Services Corporation (D) to be used for indigent legal assistance.

Black Letter Rule: Private speech may not be restricted or controlled by limitations on the use of federal funds.

Schenck v. United States

Instant Facts: A wartime anti-draft pamphleteer challenged his conviction under the Espionage Act.

Black Letter Rule: The First Amendment does not protect speech which is used under such circumstances, and is of such a nature, that it creates a "clear and present danger" of inciting illegal activity.

Frohwerk v. United States

Instant Facts: During WWI, a pro-German newspaper writer, who advocated stopping the war against Germany, was convicted of obstructing the draft, under the Espionage Act.

Black Letter Rule: The First Amendment does not protect speech which is used under such circumstances, and is of such a nature, that it creates a "clear and present danger" of inciting illegal activity.

Debs v. United States

Instant Facts: A socialist who made an anti-draft speech to drafted men was convicted under the Espionage Act of obstructing the draft.

Black Letter Rule: The First Amendment does not protect speech which is used under such circumstances, and is of such a nature, that it creates a "clear and present danger" of inciting illegal activity.

Abrams v. United States

Instant Facts: Pro–Bolshevik anarchists, who urged munitions workers not to make weapons for use against Russians, were charged with hindering the war effort against Germany.

Black Letter Rule: The First Amendment does not protect speech which is used under such circumstances, and is of such a nature, that it creates a "clear and present danger" of inciting illegal activity.

Gitlow v. New York

Instant Facts: A communist radical, jailed for urging revolution, challenges a state law which criminalized advocating unlawful overthrow of government.

Black Letter Rule: State bans on advocacy of unlawful overthrow are valid exercises of police power, unless they are unreasonable.

Whitney v. California

Instant Facts: The organizer of a revolutionary communist organization was convicted for its advocacy of revolution and crime.

Black Letter Rule: A state may ban joining an organization which advocates overthrow by illegal means, as long as the ban is not unreasonable.

Dennis v. United States

Instant Facts: American Communist Party organizers, who taught revolutionary Communist doctrine, were convicted of conspiring to overthrow the government.

Black Letter Rule: The Government may restrict incitements to illegality, if the potential harms' severity, discounted by their improbability, justifies the degree of restriction.

Brandenburg v. Ohio

Instant Facts: A KKK speechmaker, jailed for advocating revenge against the government, challenged a state anti-syndicalism statute.

Black Letter Rule: The government cannot criminalize advocacy of crime, except where such advocacy is (i) intended to incite (ii) imminent lawless action, and (iii) is likely to produce such action.

Chaplinsky v. New Hampshire

Instant Facts: A provocative preacher was arrested for provoking a policeman with insults.

Black Letter Rule: The First Amendment does not protect "fighting words" which inflict emotional distress or tend to incite listeners to retaliatory violence.

Gooding v. Wilson

Instant Facts: A demonstrator, charged with using "abusive" language for cursing at arresting officers, challenges the statute as vague/overbroad.

Black Letter Rule: Speech restrictions are unconstitutionally overbroad if they are susceptible of application to protected speech, either (a) on their face or (b) as authoritatively construed by courts.

R.A.V. v. City of St. Paul, Minnesota

Instant Facts: A teen charged with burning a cross in a black neighbor's yard challenges the constitutionality of a statute banning bias-motivated speech.

Black Letter Rule: Government may not regulate speech, including "fighting words," based on its hostility or favoritism towards the message expressed.

Feiner v. New York

Instant Facts: A political speaker who stirred a crowd to threats and shoving was arrested for disorderly conduct.

Black Letter Rule: When a public speaker incites the audience to imminent riot, police may stop his speech.

Beauharnais v. Illinois

Instant Facts: A segregationalist was convicted for distributing leaflets libeling blacks.

Black Letter Rule: The government may punish racist speech as group libel, if such punishment is rationally related to preserving peace.

Virginia v. Black

Instant Facts: Three defendants were convicted of cross burning with intent to intimidate another person or group of persons and they appealed.

Black Letter Rule: A state statute banning cross burning with the intent to intimidate another person is not in itself an unconstitutional infringement on free expression, but the establishment of criminal intent from the prohibited act itself violates the First Amendment.

Roth v. United States

Instant Facts: A pornographer challenged a federal statute banning mailing "obscene" materials.

Black Letter Rule: Government may regulate "obscene" speech without implicating the First Amendment.

Paris Adult Theatre v. Slaton

Instant Facts: An adults-only pornographic theater challenged a state's restrictions on obscenity.

Black Letter Rule: States may restrict commercial obscenity, even that viewed by consenting adults, to further legitimate interests in maintaining order and morality.

Miller v. California

Instant Facts: A mail-order bookseller challenged his obscenity conviction for mailing unsolicited pornographic ads.

Black Letter Rule: The government may regulate "obscene" material which (i) depicts or describes sexual conduct, (ii) which conduct is defined specifically by state law, (iii) would be found to appeal to the "prurient interest" by "the average person, applying contemporary community standards," (iv) portrays sexual conduct in a "patently offensive" way, and (v) has no serious literary, artistic, political, or scientific value.

New York v. Ferber

Instant Facts: A state law banning distribution of child pornography is challenged.

Black Letter Rule: The state may regulate child pornography, if it (i) is a visual depiction (ii) of sexual conduct specifically described by the state, (iii) by children below a specified age, and (iv) is made with some scienter.

Ashcroft v. The Free Speech Coalition

Instant Facts: The facts of the case were not provided in the case excerpt.

Black Letter Rule: Speech restrictions prohibiting a substantial amount of protected speech are overbroad and unconstitutional.

Young v. American Mini Theatres, Inc.

Instant Facts: Detroit zoning ordinances dispersed pornographic theaters.

Black Letter Rule: The government may restrict zoning of pornography.

City of Erie v. Pap's A.M.

Instant Facts: When a city ordinance banned nude dancing based on "secondary effects," a nude bar challenged its constitutionality.

Black Letter Rule: The government may ban nude dancing, if (i) its intent is to prevent its secondary effects (rather than its content), and (ii) its regulation is "rationally related" to promoting "legitimate" state interests.

Stanley v. Georgia

Instant Facts: A man charged with criminal possession of obscene materials in his house challenged the ban's constitutionality.

Black Letter Rule: The government cannot criminalize private possession of obscene materials.

Cohen v. California

Instant Facts: A man arrested for disturbing the peace by wearing a jacket imprinted "Fuck the Draft" challenged the statute's constitutionality.

Black Letter Rule: The state cannot punish public use/display of expletives.

Federal Communications Commission v. Pacifica Foundation

Instant Facts: When the FCC reprimanded a radio station for broadcasting a monologue satirizing indecent words, the station challenged the order's constitutionality.

Black Letter Rule: The government may impose certain sanctions against radio/TV broadcasts containing patently-offensive language (involving sex or excretion) in certain circumstances, unless the sanctions target their social or political message.

Sable Communications of California, Inc. v. Federal Communications Commission

Instant Facts: The FCC banned a dial-up service which provided sexual phone messages.

Black Letter Rule: The government may regulate indecent dial-up telephone messages, but only (i) to promote "compelling" governmental interests, and (ii) by using the least-restrictive means possible.

Reno v. American Civil Liberties Union

Instant Facts: Activists challenged a statute criminalizing sexually-explicit, indecent communications sent/made available to minors over the Internet.

Black Letter Rule: The government may regulate the Internet to protect children from indecency, but only by using the least-restrictive method.

Ashcroft v. American Civil Liberties Union

Instant Facts: The American Civil Liberties Union (P) sought a preliminary injunction against the enforcement of the Child Online Protection Act, which prohibited the commercial dissemination of Internet content that is harmful to minors.

Black Letter Rule: A statute that suppresses a substantial amount of protected speech is unconstitutional if less restrictive alternatives exist to further the governmental objective.

Virginia State Board of Pharmacy v. Virginia Citizens Consumer Council, Inc.

Instant Facts: A state law barring pharmacists from advertising drug prices was challenged by consumers.

Black Letter Rule: Commercial speech is protected by the First Amendment.

Bolger v. Youngs Drug Products Corp.

Instant Facts: A drug company challenged a federal ban on ads for contraceptives.

Black Letter Rule: "Commercial speech" is a communication which (a) does no more than propose a commercial transaction, OR (b-i) is an advertisement, AND (ii) references specific products, AND (iii) is mailed for economic motivations.

Central Hudson Gas v. Public Service Commission of New York

Instant Facts: During an fuel shortage, an energy regulatory agency banned advertisements which might increase demand for electricity. When the agency continued the ban past the shortage, a utility sued.

Black Letter Rule: Non-deceptive/illegal advertising may be regulated if (i) the restriction is justified by "substantial" governmental interests, (ii) the restriction directly advances that interest, and (iii) the regulation is the least-restrictive method needed to achieve that interest.

Friedman v. Rogers

Instant Facts: When Texas forbade optometrists to practice under trade names, they challenged.

Black Letter Rule: The government may ban practicing under trade names.

Linmark Associates v. Township of Willingboro

Instant Facts: When a town bans house "For Sale" signs to prevent white flight, Realtors sue.

Black Letter Rule: The government cannot restrict commercial communications, unless false or misleading.

44 Liquormart, Inc. v. Rhode Island

Instant Facts: When a state banned liquor dealers from advertising prices, they sued.

Black Letter Rule: The government may regulate truthful, non-misleading commercial speech only if the regulation (i) directly furthers (ii) legitimate state interests.

Lorillard Tobacco Co. v. Reilly

Instant Facts: Lorillard Tobacco Company (P) challenged the constitutionality of Massachusetts regulations on the advertising of smokeless tobacco and cigar products near schools and playgrounds.

Black Letter Rule: Restrictions on commercial speech are invalid if the speech concerns lawful activity and they do not directly advance a substantial government interest in the narrowest manner possible.

New York Times Co. v. Sullivan

Instant Facts: When a police chief won a libel suit over false ads suggesting he harassed black activists, the defendants challenged the libel law as burdening speech.

Black Letter Rule: If tort law allows public officials to recover for defamation, it must require they (i) prove actual malice, (ii) prove the statement's falsity, and (iii) prove all elements with "clear and convincing" evidence.

Gertz v. Welch

Instant Facts: When a publisher slanders a civil litigator in a notorious case as a Communist and criminal, it claims privilege against defamation.

Black Letter Rule: States may enact defamation laws which allow non-"public" plaintiffs to recover compensatory damages upon proof of any level of fault, but cannot permit presumed or punitive damages without proof of knowing falsity or reckless disregard for truth.

Dun & Bradstreet, Inc. v. Greenmoss Builders, Inc.

Instant Facts: When a business sued its credit rater for defamatory inaccuracies and collected presumed and punitive damages, the rater claimed the award was unconstitutional under Gertz.

Black Letter Rule: For defamatory speech not involving "matters of public concern," defamation laws may allow plaintiffs to recover presumed and/or punitive damages without proving "actual malice."

Hustler Magazine v. Falwell

Instant Facts: After a porn magazine published a fake interview suggesting a televangelist is a drunken, incestuous hypocrite, he sued for intentional infliction of emotional distress.

Black Letter Rule: Public figures/public officials cannot recover for intentional infliction of emotional distress from defamatory publications, unless they prove (i) it contained false statements of fact, and (ii) was made with "actual malice."

Cox Broadcasting Corporation v. Cohn

Instant Facts: When TV reporters broadcast a rape victim's name, violating state criminal laws, the victim's parents sued for privacy violations.

Black Letter Rule: The government cannot impose civil or criminal liability for publicizing public documents' contents truthfully.

Florida Star v. B.J.F.

Instant Facts: When a newspaper uses public records to name a rape victim, against state law, the victim sues for public disclosure of private information.

Black Letter Rule: If a newspaper lawfully obtains truthful information about a matter of public significance, state law may not punish its publication, absent a need to further a state interest "of the highest order."

Bartnicki v. Vopper

Instant Facts: Bartnicki's (P) cell phone conversation with a union representative was intercepted and played on the radio by Vopper (D); Bartnicki (P) sued Vopper (D) for violation of a federal anti-wiretapping statute.

Black Letter Rule: If a media outlet lawfully obtains truthful information about a matter of public significance, publication of that information may not be sanctioned absent a need "of the highest order."

United States v. O'Brien

Instant Facts: An anti-draft protester who burned his Vietnam draft card claims privilege for "symbolic speech."

Black Letter Rule: When an act combines both "speech" and "nonspeech" elements, the government may impose regulations if they (i) are not otherwise unconstitutional, (ii) further "important" or "substantial" state interests (iii) which are unrelated to suppressing free expression, and (iv) their incidental restrictions on free speech are no greater than is essential to furthering the interest.

Texas v. Johnson

Instant Facts: A protester, jailed for burning an American flag, challenged the flag-desecration statute.

Black Letter Rule: The government may not ban flag-burning as a means of expression.

Buckley v. Valeo

Instant Facts: Opponents challenged a federal election-reform statute which limited campaign contributions and expenditures, claiming that money is political "expression."

Black Letter Rule: The government may limit campaign contributions, but not campaign expenditures.

Nixon v. Shrink Missouri Government PAC

Instant Facts: When a state imposed campaign contribution limits, lobbyists challenged.

Black Letter Rule: States may impose campaign contribution limits, at any amount which does not make contributions pointless.

Randall v. Sorrell

Instant Facts: Vermont (D) enacted a law that imposed limits on political contributions and on campaign expenditures, and Randall (P) claimed the limits were unconstitutional.

Black Letter Rule: Limits on campaign contributions may not be set so low as to magnify the advantages of incumbency and prevent a candidate from raising sufficient funds to mount an effective campaign.

First National Bank of Boston v. Bellotti

Instant Facts: When Massachusetts banned corporations from spending to influence referendums on individual tax policy, corporations challenged the ban as abridging corporate First Amendment rights.

Black Letter Rule: The government cannot ban corporations from spending to advocate their opinions publicly.

Hague v. Committee for Industrial Organization

Instant Facts: A city ordinance allowed the police chief to arbitrarily ban assembly in public streets and parks. When the chief ordered police to roust union pamphleteers and rallies from public places, they challenged the ordinance's constitutionality.

Black Letter Rule: The government must allow public places to be used for speech, and can regulate access only to ensure convenience and maintain order.

Schneider v. New Jersey

Instant Facts: Pamphleteers challenged several municipalities' ban on pamphleteering, to prevent litter.

Black Letter Rule: Governments may regulate pamphleteering to preserve public safety and permit car and pedestrian traffic, but may not ban it to prevent littering.

Perry Education Assn. v. Perry Local Educators' Assn.

Instant Facts: When a Board of Ed granted the official teachers' union exclusive access to its mail system, a rival group demanded equal access.

Black Letter Rule: In "public forums" (public spaces devoted to public speech, by traditional or government fiat) and "limited public forums" (public places the government voluntarily opens for expression), content-based speech restrictions are permitted only if (i) necessary to serve "compelling" governmental interests, and (ii) narrowly-tailored; "time, place, and manner" restrictions are allowed if they (i) are content-neutral, (ii) serve "significant" government interests, (iii) are narrowly-tailored, (iv) leave ample alternative channels of communication. Other public properties are "non-public forums," where the government may impose "time, place, and manner" restrictions, and may restrict speech if the restriction is (i) reasonable, and (ii) not intended to suppress certain viewpoints.

Police Department of Chicago v. Mosley

Instant Facts: When a city ordinance generally banned picketing schools, but exempted labor picketing, a non-labor school picketer challenged the ordinance as content-based.

Black Letter Rule: In "public forums," the government cannot selectively exclude certain speakers based on their content, issue, or viewpoint.

Hill et al. v. Colorado

Instant Facts: When Colorado passed a law obliquely aimed at preventing abortion clinic protesters from approaching entering patients, the protesters challenged it as content-based.

Black Letter Rule: A law banning speakers from approaching patients entering health care facilities is a content-neutral, valid, "time, place, and manner" restriction.

Ward v. Rock Against Racism

Instant Facts: When a city required park concerts to use city-approved amplifiers and sound technicians to reduce noise to surrounding areas and apartments, the concert organizer challenged the restriction as not narrowly-tailored/least-restrictive.

Black Letter Rule: "Time, place, and manner" restrictions are deemed sufficiently "narrowly-tailored" as long as they are more effective than no regulation at all, even if they are not the least-restrictive/intrusive method.

Adderley v. Florida

Instant Facts: Anti-discrimination protesters, arrested for trespassing on jail property, challenge their prosecution as unconstitutional.

Black Letter Rule: Jail property is a non-public forum, and the government may punish trespass there.

Greer v. Spock

Instant Facts: Political candidates, denied permission to speak at an Army training base, claim the base became a limited public forum when officials permitted other civilian speakers.

Black Letter Rule: Military bases are non-public forums, and the government need not permit speech there.

Lehman v. City of Shaker Heights

Instant Facts: When a public bus fleet allowed commercial ads but refused political ones, a candidate wishing to advertise claimed the ad space became a "public forum."

Black Letter Rule: When the government operates a commercial venture, it may accept commercial advertising but prohibit political ads.

United States v. Kokinda

Instant Facts: Campaign solicitors challenged a Post Office regulation banning solicitation on the sidewalks in front of its entrance.

Black Letter Rule: If the sidewalk outside a government property was constructed only to permit access (rather than for public convenience), then it is not a "public forum," and speech restrictions there are valid if "reasonable."

International Society for Krishna Consciousness, Inc. v. Lee

Instant Facts: When a state airport authority banned solicitation in terminals, Hare Krishnas challenged.

Black Letter Rule: Airports are non-public forums, and may ban solicitation.

Arkansas Educational Television Commission v. Forbes

Instant Facts: When a public TV station limited a debate to popular candidates, an unknown challenged his exclusion.

Black Letter Rule: Generally, the public has no right of access to state-owned TV, and publicly-televised candidate debates are "non-public forums."

Parker v. Levy

Instant Facts: When a black soldier was convicted under military law for urging blacks not to fight in Vietnam, he challenged military law as unconstitutionally overbroad.

Black Letter Rule: The Uniform Code of Military Justice's speech restrictions are not overbroad, considering the First Amendment offers military personnel lesser protection than civilians.

Thornburgh v. Abbott

Instant Facts: Prisoners and/or inmate-targeted journals challenged prison regulations giving wardens discretion to ban dangerous journals.

Black Letter Rule: Prisons' restrictions on speech are valid if (i) the government's objective is legitimate, and (ii) neutral, and (iii) the regulations are "rationally related" to that objective.

Shaw v. Murphy

Instant Facts: Murphy (D) was convicted of violating prison rules relating to inmate-to-inmate legal assistance.

Black Letter Rule: Restrictions on prisoners' communication must be "reasonably related to legitimate penological interests."

Tinker v. Des Moines Independent Community School District

Instant Facts: When a high school suspended students for wearing anti-Vietnam armbands, they claimed this violated their speech rights.

Black Letter Rule: Public schools cannot restrict students' expression, unless it would "materially and substantially interfere" with appropriate school discipline.

Bethel School District v. Fraser

Instant Facts: When a high school student laced a school speech with sexual innuendo, the school sanctioned him.

Black Letter Rule: Schools may sanction students' lewd speech.

Hazelwood School District v. Kuhlmeier

Instant Facts: When a school censored its newspaper, excising 6 articles to remove 2 about students' pregnancies and family problems, censored student-writers sued.

Black Letter Rule: When schools sponsor expressive activities, they may edit/censor the product if (i) their actions are "reasonably related" (ii) to "legitimate pedagogical concerns."

Morse v. Frederick

Instant Facts: Frederick (P) was suspended from high school for displaying a banner that was regarded as promoting drug use.

Black Letter Rule: Student speech that may reasonably be viewed as advocating illegal drug use may be restricted at school sponsored events.

Garcetti v. Ceballos

Instant Facts: Ceballos (P) raised concerns about possible deficiencies in a search warrant affidavit, and claimed he was subject to retaliation as a result.

Black Letter Rule: Public employees who speak as a part of their official duties are not protected from employer discipline by the First Amendment.

National Association for the Advancement of Colored People v. Alabama, ex rel. Patterson

Instant Facts: The controversial anti-discrimination group NAACP defied a court order compelling it to disclose all members, contending it violates their speech/assembly right by inviting retaliation.

Black Letter Rule: If disclosure of an expressive assembly's membership would chill its speech/assembly, then the state cannot compel it, absent a valid, controlling reason.

Board of Regents of the University of Wisconsin System v. Southworth

Instant Facts: When a public university charged a mandatory student activity fee used to fund various student groups' speech, dissenting students claimed "forced association."

Black Letter Rule: State-owned schools may condition their degree on students' funding others' possibly-objectionable speech, but students may insist on some viewpoint-neutral procedural safeguards to limit the speech their money supports.

Roberts v. United States Jaycees

Instant Facts: When a male-only civic organization's local chapter began admitting women to follow state anti-discrimination laws, the national organization threatened to dissolve them.

Black Letter Rule: The government may regulate to force expressive associations to admit other members non-discriminatorily, if that regulation (i) serves compelling state interests, (ii) which are unrelated to suppressing ideas, (iii) that cannot be achieved through means significantly less restrictive of association.

Hurley v. Irish–American Gay, Lesbian and Bisexual Group of Boston

Instant Facts: A private parade organizer banned a gay group from marching, claiming applying state anti-discrimination laws would compel them to make a pro-gay statement.

Black Letter Rule: State anti-discrimination law cannot require private parade organizers to admit certain groups, if admitting them would change the parade's message.

Boy Scouts of America v. Dale

Instant Facts: When the Boy Scouts expelled an openly-gay Scout leader as "forced expressive association," he claimed the expulsion violated state anti-discrimination law.

Black Letter Rule: "Expressive associations" need not accept members whose presence significantly impacts their ability to advocate their viewpoint, barring strong countervailing policy reasons.

Minneapolis Star and Tribune Company v. Minnesota Commissioner of Revenue

Instant Facts: When a state changed its state tax in a way which generally benefitted the press but gave greater benefits for small publications, a big newspaper challenged it.

Black Letter Rule: The government may not tax the press differently from other businesses, even to benefit it, unless (i) necessary (ii) to achieve "overriding" governmental interests (iii) which cannot be achieved through less-restrictive means.

Cohen v. Cowles Media Company

Instant Facts: A campaign aide, who dished dirt on a candidate for reporters' false promises of confidentiality, sued the reporters for promissory estoppel.

Black Letter Rule: When generally-applicable laws are applied to the media, the level of First Amendment scrutiny is no higher.

Branzburg v. Hayes

Instant Facts: Reporters challenged grand jury subpoenas requiring them to reveal confidential sources.

Black Letter Rule: Newsmen have no special privilege against grand jury subpoenas to identify confidential sources, except that available to the general public.

Red Lion Broadcasting Co. v. Federal Communications Commission

Instant Facts: A radio station challenged FCC regulations requiring it to give personally-attacked people a right to reply.

Black Letter Rule: The government may require broadcasters to give access to opposing views.

Miami Herald v. Tornillo

Instant Facts: A newspapers challenged a Florida law requiring it to give candidates it criticized the right to reply.

Black Letter Rule: The government cannot require newspapers to grant a "right of reply."

Richmond Newspapers, Inc. v. Virginia

Instant Facts: When a judge ordered a criminal trial closed to the public and media, by consent with the defendant and prosecutor, the media challenged.

Black Letter Rule: Criminal trials are presumptively open to the public and press, unless there are "overriding" interests.

Pell v. Procunier

Instant Facts: When a jail barred reporters from individual interviews with inmates, the reporters and inmates claimed a First Amendment right to conduct the interviews.

Black Letter Rule: Reporters have no special constitutional right to enter prisons or interview prisoners, beyond the rights granted to the general public.

Houchins v. KQED

Instant Facts: When a prison supervisor denied access to the prison except for restrictive tours without cameras and recorders, the media claimed a First Amendment right of access.

Black Letter Rule: The First Amendment gives the press no special right to enter government-controlled places, except that given to the public.

Turner Broadcasting System, Inc. v. Federal Communications Commission

(Cable TV Network) v. (Administrative Agency Enforcing Cable TV Laws)
512 U.S. 622, 114 S.Ct. 2445 (1994)

CONTENT-BASED SPEECH REGULATION IS STRICTLY SCRUTINIZED, WHILE CONTENT NEUTRAL LAWS ARE SUBJECT TO INTERMEDIATE SCRUTINY

■ **INSTANT FACTS** Cable TV programmers challenged a federal statute requiring them to give channels to local TV broadcasters, contending it regulates them differently based on their programs' content.

■ **BLACK LETTER RULE** A federal law requiring cable TV providers to devote some channels to local, educational broadcasters is a content-neutral speech regulation, and thus subject to intermediate scrutiny.

■ PROCEDURAL BASIS

In constitutional challenge to federal statute, appeal, on writ of certiorari.

■ FACTS

The federal *Cable Television Consumer Protection and Competition Act* ("*Act*") included a "must-carry" provision, requiring cable TV systems to devote one-third of their channels to local, "broadcast" TV stations. [This reduces the number of channels left available to cable "programmers" to air their own shows.] *Act*'s legislative findings justify this on the basis of a "substantial . . . interest in promoting . . . diversity of views," public (local) stations' provision of "educational and informational programming, . . . [thus] educating citizens," and *preserving localism in TV broadcasting.* Apparently, cable programmer Turner Broadcasting System, Inc. ("TBS") (P) sued the Federal Communications Commission ("FCC") (D), claiming *Act* constitutes unconstitutional content-based speech regulation, because it favors local, educational content. FCC (D) defended, claiming *Act* is content-neutral.

■ ISSUE

Is a federal law requiring cable TV providers to devote some channels to local, educational broadcasters a content-based speech regulation, thus subject to strict scrutiny?

■ DECISION AND RATIONALE

(Kennedy, J.) No. A federal law requiring cable TV providers to devote some channels to local, educational broadcasters is a content neutral speech regulation, and thus subject to intermediate scrutiny. The First Amendment generally forbids governmental controls over the content of private individuals' messages; any exceptions are few and narrow. If any governmental regulation imposes differential burdens upon speech because of its content, it is scrutinized strictly. (Similarly, laws compelling dissemination of speech bearing a particular message are subject to strict scrutiny.) In contrast, regulations unrelated to the speech's content are subject only to intermediate scrutiny, because they pose less risk of excising unpopular viewpoints from public discourse. In deciding whether particular regulations are content-based, the principal inquiry is whether the government adopted such regulation because of agreement or disagreement with the message conveyed. Often, a

Turner Broadcasting System, Inc. v. Federal Communications Commission (Continued)

regulation's purpose is evident on its face. But a facially-neutral regulation may be invalidated upon showing its purpose was to regulate based on content. Generally, "content-based" laws are those that distinguish favored speech from disfavored speech, on the basis of the ideas or views expressed. Here, the "must-carry" provisions are facially neutral; although they interfere with cable programming, the degree of interference does not depend on the programming's content, since it relates to all programmers. Remanded for determination under intermediate scrutiny.

■ CONCURRENCE AND DISSENT

(O'Connor, J.) I believe *Act* is effectively content-based, and should be scrutinized strictly. *Act* makes it easier for local broadcasters to secure on-air time, at cable programmers' expense. Here, *Act*'s legislative justifications express a preference for a diversity of viewpoints, for localism, for educational programming, and for programs featuring news and public affairs. Such preferences may be benignly-motivated, but they still prefer some content over other types. The First Amendment should not only bar government from suppressing speech it dislikes, but also from excepting *favored* speech from regulation.

Analysis:

Turner illustrates that content-based regulations are strictly scrutinized, while content-neutral laws require only intermediate scrutiny. Thus the way a court categorizes a particular law strongly impacts its chances of being found constitutional. Intermediate scrutiny will find content-neutral regulation constitutional if it (i) advances important governmental interests, (ii) which are unrelated to suppression of free speech, and (iii) does not burden more speech than is necessary to further those interests. After remand, this case was re-appealed to the Supreme Court, which reviewed the *Act*'s constitutionality under intermediate scrutiny and upheld it.

■ CASE VOCABULARY

CONTENT-BASED SPEECH REGULATION: Governmental regulations on speech which impose differing burdens on various types of communications, based on their content. Usually, this involves the government restricting messages it dislikes. Content-based regulation is subject to strict scrutiny.

CONTENT-NEUTRAL SPEECH REGULATION: Government regulations which affect all communications equally, regardless of the message being communicated. Such regulations' constitutionality is evaluated under intermediate scrutiny.

INTERMEDIATE SCRUTINY [OF CONTENT-NEUTRAL SPEECH RESTRICTIONS]: Standard whereby government regulation is deemed constitutional if it (i) advances important governmental interests, (ii) which is unrelated to prohibited interests (here, speech restrictions), and (iii) is no more restrictive than necessary to further legitimate interests.

STRICT SCRUTINY: Standard whereby government regulation will be upheld as constitutional only if found to further "compelling" state interests.

Boos v. Barry

(*Demonstrators*) v. (*Unknown, and Federal Government*)
485 U.S. 312, 108 S.Ct. 1157 (1988)

FOR SPEECH REGULATION TO BE DEEMED CONTENT-NEUTRAL, IT MUST BE BOTH VIEWPOINT-NEUTRAL AND SUBJECT-MATTER NEUTRAL

■ **INSTANT FACTS** Picketers challenged a statute which prohibited insulting anti-government signs in from of foreign embassies.

■ **BLACK LETTER RULE** A federal statute prohibiting anti-government signs near foreign embassies is a content-based speech regulation, and thus subject to strict scrutiny.

■ **PROCEDURAL BASIS**

In constitutional challenge to statute, seeking declaratory judgment, appeal to Supreme Court, on writ of certiorari.

■ **FACTS**

A "display" provision of the Washington, D.C. *Code* forbids displaying a sign within 500 feet of a foreign embassy if the sign brings the embassy's government into "public odium" or "public disrepute." Anti-Soviet demonstrator Boos (P) and other protestors (P) challenged the *Code* as an unconstitutional content-based speech restriction, claiming it differentiates between pro-government and anti-government messages. Defendants Barry (D) and Washington, D.C. (D) defended, contending *Code* is viewpoint-neutral and "necessary" to serve the "compelling" interest of protecting diplomats' dignity.

■ **ISSUE**

Is a federal statute prohibiting anti-government signs near foreign embassies a content-based speech regulation?

■ **DECISION AND RATIONALE**

(O'Connor, J.) Yes. A federal statute prohibiting anti-government signs near foreign embassies is a content-based speech regulation, and thus subject to strict scrutiny. Here, *Code*'s display provision is completely content-based, because whether individuals may picket before foreign embassies depends entirely on whether their signs criticize that government, or not. One subject of speech—criticism of foreign governments—is completely prohibited, while other subjects—such as favorable speech—is permitted. We agree the display provision is not viewpoint-based, because the clause determines which viewpoint is acceptable neutrally, by looking to the policies of the foreign government. But viewpoint-neutral speech regulation may still violate the First Amendment if it causes "prohibition of public discussion of an entire topic." Here, we find the clause is effectively content-based, because it prohibits an entire subject matter of speech—criticism of foreign governments. Thus, it must be strictly scrutinized to see if it is "necessary to serve a compelling state interest and ... narrowly drawn to achieve that end." Here, we find the display clause's stated purpose—to protect foreign diplomats' dignity—is insufficiently compelling. Generally, we previously held that American citizens must tolerate insulting and outrageous speech to enable the First Amendment to function. Further, a "dignity" standard is too subjective. We will not create different principles for foreign officials.

Boos v. Barry (Continued)

Analysis:

The basic holding here is that, for speech regulation to be deemed content-neutral, it must be both (i) subject-matter neutral (i.e., it cannot pre-empt discussion of specified topics), and also (ii) viewpoint-neutral (i.e., it cannot allow praise but forbid dissent). If it fails either of these tests, it is deemed content-based, and strictly scrutinized. The difficulty of this case is understanding why the Court considers the *Code*'s "display provision" to be viewpoint-neutral. After all, it seems to allow the viewpoint that the Soviet Union is a workers' paradise, but disallows the viewpoint that the U.S.S.R. is a dictatorship. The answer seems to be that the provision uses some kind of criteria to determine if the country's policies may be protested, but the excerpt doesn't explain how this works.

■ **CASE VOCABULARY**

SUBJECT-MATTER NEUTRAL: Speech regulation which does not forbid discussion of specified topics. For example, a statute which forbids all picketing except that connected to labor disputes is *not* subject-matter neutral, since it allows labor speech, but disallows other speech.

VIEWPOINT-NEUTRAL: Speech regulation which does not distinguish between various positions on an issue. For example, this would be violated if a law permitted pro-war rallies, but banned pacifist demonstrations.

Republican Party of Minnesota v. White

(Political Party) v. (Undisclosed Defendant)
536 U.S. 765, 122 S.Ct. 2528 (2002)

JUDICIAL IMPARTIALITY IS NOT A COMPELLING ENOUGH INTEREST TO JUSTIFY SUPPRESSING CANDIDATES' VIEWS

■ **INSTANT FACTS** The Republican Party of Minnesota (P) challenged the constitutionality of a state rule prohibiting judicial candidates from expressing their political views.

■ **BLACK LETTER RULE** Government regulations that supress speech on the basis of its content must be narrowly tailored to serve a compelling state interest.

■ **PROCEDURAL BASIS**

Certiorari to review a decision of the Eighth Circuit Court of Appeals affirming summary judgment for the defendant.

■ **FACTS**

In Minnesota, all state judges are elected by popular vote. The state's Code of Judicial Conduct includes an "announce clause" prohibiting candidates for judicial office from announcing their views on disputed or political issues. During his 1996 campaign for election as an associate justice of the Minnesota Supreme Court, Gregory Wersal distributed literature criticizing several of the court's positions on crime, welfare, and abortion. Facing a disciplinary investigation for violating the announce clause, Wersal withdrew his candidacy. Two years later, however, Wersal again ran for election to the Supreme Court and filed suit in federal court, challenging the constitutionality of the announce clause. The district court entered summary judgment against Wersal and the Republican Party (P), construing the clause to prohibit only expression concerning issues likely to be before the candidate if elected. The Eighth Circuit Court of Appeals affirmed, adding that the rule does not prohibit a general discussion of cases or political issues.

■ **ISSUE**

Does the First Amendment permit a state supreme court to prohibit candidates for judicial election in the state from announcing their views on disputed legal and political issues?

■ **DECISION AND RATIONALE**

(Scalia, J.) No. Because the announce clause suppresses speech on the basis of its content, it must be narrowly tailored to serve a compelling state interest to withstand constitutional scrutiny. White (D) contends that the announce rule furthers two compelling interests: "preserving the impartiality of the state judiciary and preserving the appearance of the impartiality of the state judiciary." The meaning of "impartiality" must be established to determine whether a compelling interest exists.

First, impartiality may mean "the lack of bias for or against either party to the proceeding," but the announce rule is not narrowly tailored to achieve impartiality in this sense. This understanding of impartiality means only that a judge will apply the law as he sees it to all parties. But, the judge's legal or political views do not change the outcome of cases or ensure equal application of the law anymore than his silence does. Whether the judge announces his views or not, he will apply the law the same.

A second possible meaning of impartiality may be the lack of preconception relating to a particular legal view. Such a definition, however, does not promote a compelling state interest. A lack of predisposition, if it is even possible, is not a prerequisite for justice. Justice demands a detailed familiarity with the law so that it may be applied correctly. Certainly, predisposition is a necessary consequence of legal experience.

Finally, impartiality may be seen to mean "open-mindedness." While such attributes are desirable of judicial officials, the announce clause does not appear to be adopted for this purpose. Understanding the term in this way, a judicial candidate who may have placed his well-known views on record in the past would be prohibited from reiterating them during his campaign, but would be free to once again express them when the election is over. There is nothing important or critical about the election process that justifies such a temporary infringement upon the freedom to express one's views. Thus, despite the meaning of the interest allegedly furthered, the interest is not sufficiently compelling to justify the infringement on candidates' First Amendment rights. Reversed and remanded.

■ CONCURRENCE

(O'Connor, J.) Judicial elections themselves undermine impartiality. By staking their position on the bench on popular votes, judges must be mindful not always of justice, but of popular opinion concerning the outcome of the case. Moreover, because contested elections involve campaigning, which in turn requires substantial campaign funds, judicial candidates must resist the temptation to favor the political interests of their contributors. By choosing to select its judges by popular vote, Minnesota has assumed the risk of judicial bias. Having assumed this risk, the state can hardly suppress speech to solve a problem it has caused.

■ CONCURRENCE

(Kennedy, J.) Content-based restrictions on speech that do not fall within a traditionally accepted exception should be invalidated without concern for the compelling state interest claimed or the narrow tailoring of the restriction. Because the speech at issue is "not obscene, not defamatory, not words tantamount to an act otherwise criminal, not an impairment of some other constitutional right, not an incitement to lawless action, and not calculated or likely to bring about imminent harm," it should be categorically protected.

■ DISSENT

(Stevens, J.) Judicial candidates should not enjoy the same freedom of expression as other political candidates. Unlike policy-making officials, judges often act alone rather than with majority approval. Minnesota has a compelling interest in ensuring that judges act impartiality, even in the most restricted sense offered by the Court. When interpreted as a lack of bias for or against one party or legal position, impartiality is furthered by prohibiting expressions in favor or opposition of a political or legal issue, which demonstrate the bias of the candidate. Campaign statements are intentionally made to convey the candidate's thoughts and beliefs and to demonstrate bias and closed-mindedness. Unlike other political offices, states ought not to tolerate such statements from judicial candidates.

■ DISSENT

(Ginsburg, J.) While executive and legislative officials represent the people, judges represent the law. They adjudicate cases and controversies to establish rights and liabilities among various parties. The critical distinction calls for similar differences in the manner in which they are selected. Because judges do not represent the people, their particular views on important political and legal issues are less important than they are with regard to their executive and legislative counterparts. The announce clause does not forbid judicial candidates to make their general views known, but rather prohibits comment on the outcome of specific cases over which they are likely to preside if elected. In the end, the announce clause ensures that judicial candidates are free to inform the electorate of their important views without demonstrating personal bias against a specific issue or legal position.

Analysis:

The wisdom of judicial elections notwithstanding, most states select some or all of their judges by popular vote. The Court's decision to treat judicial elections like elections for other political offices may give rise closer examination of the electoral policies of other states, but it also ensures judicial candidates greater protection to speak on important campaign issues.

■ CASE VOCABULARY

FIRST AMENDMENT: The constitutional amendment, ratified with the Bill of Rights of 1791, guaranteeing the freedoms of speech, religion, press, assembly, and petition.

City of Renton v. Playtime Theatres, Inc.

(City) v. (Pornographic Movie Theater)
475 U.S. 41, 106 S.Ct. 925 (1986)

LINE BETWEEN CONTENT-BASED AND CONTENT-NEUTRAL LAWS IS BLURRY

■ **INSTANT FACTS** When a city passed a zoning ordinance requiring porn theaters be far from houses, churches, schools, etc., a theater challenged its constitutionality.

■ **BLACK LETTER RULE** A zoning ordinance restricting pornographic theaters' placement must be analyzed as a content-neutral, "time, place, and manner" regulation.

■ **PROCEDURAL BASIS**

In constitutional challenge to municipal zoning ordinance, appeal from judgment for defendant city.

■ **FACTS**

The city of Renton, Washington ("City") (D) passed a zoning ordinance prohibiting "adult motion picture theaters" from locating within 1,000 feet of any residential zone, family dwelling, church, park, or school. One such establishment, Playtime Theatres, Inc. ("Theatres") (P), challenged the ordinance as an unconstitutional content-based speech restriction. City (D) defended, claiming the ordinance is a content neutral "time, place, and manner" restriction. At trial, the District Court held for City (D). Theatres (P) appeals.

■ **ISSUE**

Is a zoning ordinance restricting pornographic theaters' placement a content-based speech restriction?

■ **DECISION AND RATIONALE**

(Rehnquist, J.) No. A zoning ordinance restricting pornographic theaters' placement must be analyzed as a content-neutral, "time, place, and manner" regulation. This is because such ordinances do not ban adult theaters altogether, but merely specify a place for them. At first glance, City's (D) ordinance does not appear to fit neatly into either the category of "content neutral" or "content-based." While it treats specialty adult theaters differently from other kinds of theaters, it does so not because it objects to their films' content, but because of the "secondary effects" of such theaters on the surrounding community. "Time, place, and manner" regulations are acceptable if they (i) are designed to serve "substantial" governmental interests, and (ii) do not limit alternative avenues of communication unreasonably. Here, the District Court found City's (D) "predominant concern" was with adult theaters' "secondary effects," not their content. It is clear such concerns vindicate a city's respectable interest in preserving the quality of urban life. Affirmed.

■ **DISSENT**

(Brennan, J.) Ordinances which limit theaters' locations selectively, based exclusively on the content of the films shown there, are content-based restrictions, and should be analyzed accordingly. That such ordinances are based on "secondary" land-use effects does not make them content-neutral. Here, City's (D) ordinance discriminates on its face against adult theaters, without similarly restricting other movie theaters and adult entertainments. This suggests City (D) did not just intend to control

City of Renton v. Playtime Theatres, Inc. (Continued)

"secondary effects," but to discriminate against theaters showing pornography. Further, City (D) has not proven any undesirable secondary effects exist, or that they could not be addressed by less-intrusive restrictions.

Analysis:

Renton highlights the point that, sometimes, courts find it hard to draw a clear line between "content-based" and "content-neutral" speech restrictions. Here, the City's (D) restriction shares characteristics of both; it singles out theaters showing pornographic content, but it is not really intended to suppress the display of pornography, just to relocate it farther from children and residences. Many commentators criticized the Court's decision in *Renton*, suggesting it makes it too easy to pass content-based regulation by recasting it as content-neutral, or claiming it is intended to suppress vague "secondary effects" rather than the content itself. Even the Court itself applied *Renton* inconsistently in later cases, distinguishing it often.

■ CASE VOCABULARY

"TIME, PLACE, AND MANNER" REGULATION: Regulation which permits speech, but limits it to certain times, places, and manners. Ex. "Parades must be held during the day, away from private residences, etc." Such regulations' constitutionality is analyzed under much less-restrictive standards.

National Endowment for the Arts v. Finley

(Federal Artistic Grant Administrator) v. (Rejected Artists)
524 U.S. 569, 118 S.Ct. 2168 (1998)

GOVERNMENT MAY MAKE CONTENT-BASED DECISIONS WHEN AWARDING GRANTS FOR ARTISTIC MERIT

■ **INSTANT FACTS** When Congress passed a statute instructing federal arts grantmakers to "consider" whether applicants' work is indecent or disrespectful, rejected applicants challenged.

■ **BLACK LETTER RULE** The Government may fund art based on its assessment of its artistic content, as long as it does not (A) abuse its discretion by penalizing disfavored viewpoints, or (B) violate other constitutional rights.

■ **PROCEDURAL BASIS**

In facial First Amendment challenge to federal statute, appeal from judgment for plaintiffs.

■ **FACTS**

Congress created the National Endowment for the Arts ("NEA") (D) to encourage art by giving grants to promising artists. Under its enabling act, NEA (D) has vast discretion in deciding who gets funding, based only on its assessment of applicants' "artistic and cultural significance," "professional excellence," and encouraging "public knowledge, education, understanding, and appreciation of the arts." Later in 1989, there was a controversy over the work of 2 grant recipients: homo-erotic photographer Robert Mapplethorpe, and photographer Andres Serrano, whose photo "Piss Christ" showed a crucifix immersed in urine. Consequently, Congress amended NEA's (D) enabling act by inserting § 954(d)(1), directing its Chairperson, in establishing procedures to judge applicants' artistic merit, to "take into consideration general standards of decency and respect for the diverse beliefs and values of the American public." Several controversial artists (P), including Karen Finley (P), were considered for funding, but later rejected. These Artists (P) challenged § 954(d)(1) as facially violating the First Amendment, claiming it is viewpoint-discriminatory, because it rejects artistic speech which offends mainstream values or offends decency standards. NEA (D) defended, claiming § 954(d)(1) is hortatory rather than mandatory. Apparently, the District Court held for Artists (P), and NEA (D) appeals.

■ **ISSUE**

Is it a violation of the First Amendment for a statute to instruct a federal artistic grant programs to consider whether applicants' art offends public decency?

■ **DECISION AND RATIONALE**

(O'Connor, J.) No. The Government may fund art based on its assessment of its artistic content, as long as it does not (A) abuse its discretion by penalizing disfavored viewpoints, or (B) violate other constitutional rights. Plaintiffs claiming a law is facially violative of the First Amendment confront the heavy burden of demonstrating a "substantial" risk that applying the provision will lead to suppression of speech. Here, we find there is no such risk. We find § 954(d)(1) merely adds considerations to NEA's (D) grant-making process, but does not necessarily preclude awards to projects that are found "indecent" or "disrespectful." Whenever the Government establishes a program which awards grants based on artistic merit, it *must* make content-based judgments about the art's merit/content, but this is not discriminatory. It would become improper if the government were to use it to deny funding to disfavored viewpoints, to drive them from the marketplace. But this is not alleged here. Finally, we note the Government has wide latitude to set spending priorities. The Government may allocate competitive funding criteria "that would be impermissible [if] direct regulation of speech or a criminal penalty [were] at stake," as long as its legislation did not infringe on other constitutionally-protected rights. [Meaning its funding criteria can be "vague."] Reversed.

■ DISSENT

(Souter, J.) The majority is mistaken in concluding § 954(d)(1) is not viewpoint-based, that it is not a [binding] "regulation," and that NEA (D) may engage in viewpoint-based discrimination. The First Amendment's bedrock principle is that Congress generally cannot discriminate against otherwise-protected speech based on the offensiveness or unacceptableness of the views it expressed. This is exactly the purpose of a statute disfavoring any artistic expression that fails to respect America's popular beliefs.

Analysis:

Finley is another scenario where the distinction between "content-based" and "content-neutral" regulation becomes blurred. As the Court notes, anytime the government gives competitive, merit-based artistic grants, the government official who awards the grants must make a judgment favoring some content over others. But this content-based "discrimination" is permitted, because it is needed in order to enable arts funding. The majority opinion seems to rely strongly on the finding that § 954(d)(1) is non-binding, since it instructs NEA (D) to *consider* whether applicants' art is indecent/disrespectful, but does not automatically ban funding of even offensive art. However, the fact that this directive is optional does not make it viewpoint-neutral, and the circumstances surrounding § 954(d)(1)'s enactment evince a legislative intent to disfavor blasphemous, homoerotic, and otherwise "unpopular" art.

■ CASE VOCABULARY

HORTATORY: Encouraging, but not requiring.

VAGUENESS: Judicial doctrine whereby statutes are void if they are so vague that an average, reasonable person would not understand exactly what behavior it prohibits. Applied to speech regulation and criminal statutes.

United States v. American Library Assn., Inc.

(*Federal Government*) v. (*Library Association*)
539 U.S. 194, 123 S.Ct. 2297 (2003)

LIBRARIES DO NOT VIOLATE THE FIRST AMENDMENT BY BLOCKING PORNOGRAPHY

■ **INSTANT FACTS** The Children's Internet Protection Act conditions the receipt of federal funding on the installation of pornography filters on all public library computers.

■ **BLACK LETTER RULE** Congress may not pass legislation that induces individuals to engage in unconstitutional activities.

■ PROCEDURAL BASIS
Certiorari to review an undisclosed appellate decision.

■ FACTS
Under the Children's Internet Protection Act (CIPA), which was enacted to address problems relating to the availability of online pornography in public libraries, all public libraries must install software to block images of obscenity or child pornography in order to receive federal financial assistance. The American Library Association, Inc. (P) challenged the act as facially invalid because it induces libraries to violate their patrons' First Amendment rights. A federal district court agreed.

■ ISSUE
Does a statute conditioning the receipt of federal financial assistance on the installation of pornography-blocking computer software on public library computers violate the First Amendment?

■ DECISION AND RATIONALE
(Rehnquist, C.J.) No. While Congress may not use federal funding to induce individuals to engage in unconstitutional activities, it has wide latitude to establish conditions for federal financial assistance to achieve important policy objectives. The majority of libraries already refuse to carry pornographic materials in their print collections to protect minors from exposure to such content. The software required for CIPA compliance simply extends that policy to Internet materials as well. While the software threatens to block legitimate and worthwhile websites, adult patrons wishing to view that content can request a librarian to unblock the website or disable the software filter, as appropriate. The filters do not violate library patrons' First Amendment rights, and therefore CIPA does not induce public libraries to commit any constitutional violation. Reversed.

■ CONCURRENCE
(Kennedy, J.) As long as an adult user can access protected Internet content at his or her request, there is no facial constitutional problem. If an adult user was denied access to such content, however, constitutional problems may arise in application of the Act. Without any burden on the rights of adult users, the Government's (D) interest in protecting minors justifies the Act.

■ CONCURRENCE
(Breyer, J.) Because the statute implicates the public access to information through two "critically important sources"—the Internet through public libraries—the Court should employ a heightened

United States v. American Library Assn., Inc. (Continued)

scrutiny review to determine whether the First Amendment is offended. In other First Amendment matters, the Court has weighed the harm to speech-related interests against the justifications for governmental intrusions and any legitimate alternatives to the intrusion in question. Where the intrusion is disproportionate to the harm caused, the First Amendment is violated. Here, Congress maintains a legitimate objective of preventing access by minors to obscene or pornographic materials. In requiring software filters, the Act takes reasonable measures to further this legitimate objective without overburdening the First Amendment rights of adult users, who can ask to have the software disabled. Because the Act imposes a small burden on First Amendment interests, it withstands the heightened scrutiny analysis.

■ DISSENT

(Stevens, J.) While it is not unconstitutional for public libraries to filter pornographic content from their Internet terminals, Congress cannot insist on such measures as a condition of federal funding. In so doing, CIPA constitutes a nationwide restraint on Internet content without adequate concern for constitutionally protected speech. Because the software cannot distinguish between pornographic content and acceptable content (relying instead on the detection of key words), considerable lawful speech is suppressed in order to block out some unlawful speech. Because the software prevents patrons from viewing blocked content, adult patrons may not actually know what content is being blocked and cannot therefore request that the filter be disabled. The Court should not allow the receipt of federal funds to be conditioned on such a broad restriction on First Amendment rights.

■ DISSENT

(Souter, J.) Public libraries would violate the First Amendment if they voluntarily took the actions required by CIPA. Accordingly, any congressional rule conditioning the receipt of federal funds on such action is an unconstitutional exercise of the congressional spending power. First, the statute does not require libraries to disable the filtering software, but merely authorizes them to do so, and only for "bona fide research or other lawful purposes." Accordingly, patrons' First Amendment rights are limited by the discretion of library staff.

Absent the CIPA requirements, public libraries would not be justified in blocking Internet content from their adult patrons. "A library that chose to block an adult's Internet access to material harmful to children ... would be imposing a content-based restriction on communication of material in the library's control that an adult could otherwise lawfully see. This would simply be censorship." While a certain amount of censorship always exists in libraries due to limited financial budgets and shelf space, restrictions on Internet content are not the same as limiting library acquisitions. The decision not to acquire a specific book or publication is quite different from the decision to block access to Internet content already within the library's possession. Such censorship requires a strict scrutiny analysis to ensure it is narrowly tailored to further an important government objective. CIPA is not narrowly tailored to protecting children from harmful material.

Analysis:

Rather directly regulating speech, Congress used CIPA as an exercise of its spending power to achieve a similar result. While the Court upheld CIPA, it did not foreclose future constitutional challenges. The Court merely held that, on its face, CIPA was not an unconstitutional exercise of the spending power because it is capable of constitutional application. Potential constitutional challenges remain, however, if CIPA is in fact applied to suppress protected speech.

■ CASE VOCABULARY

CENSOR: To officially inspect (especially a book or film) and delete material considered offensive.

Near v. State of Minnesota ex rel. Olson

(*Enjoined Publisher*) v. (*State*)
283 U.S. 697, 51 S.Ct. 625 (1931)

COURT ORDERS ARE REGULATED AS "PRIOR RESTRAINTS"

■ **INSTANT FACTS** When a newspaper editor was enjoined from publishing slanderous periodicals, he challenged the injunction as unconstitutional.

■ **BLACK LETTER RULE** Prior restraints against publication are invalid, unless they (A) protect national security during wartime, (B) restrict obscenity, or (C) protect against incitement to violence, or forcible overthrow of government.

■ **PROCEDURAL BASIS**

After prosecution to enjoin publication, appeal challenging statute's constitutionality, on writ of certiorari.

■ **FACTS**

Minnesota's (P) statutes provide that "malicious, scandalous, and defamatory" periodicals may be abated, as a public nuisance. Once such periodicals are enjoined by court order, if they are re-issued, the court may impose contempt sanctions of $1,000 fine and 12 months' imprisonment. (It is a defense against enjoinment that the person charged can prove the story's truth and good faith motive.) A county prosecutor (P) sued to enjoin newspaper editor Near (D) from publishing *The Saturday Press*, which charged that a Jewish racketeer controlled Minnesota's (P) gambling, bootlegging, and racketeering, and that Minnesota's (P) police were not performing their duties energetically. At trial, the court found for Minnesota (P), and enjoined Near (D) from issuing "any publication whatsoever which is a malicious, scandalous or defamatory newspaper." Near (D) appeals, challenging the statute's constitutionality under the First Amendment. Minnesota (P) responds, saying the statute is necessary to suppress libel and scandal more effectively than is possible using prosecution.

■ **ISSUE**

Does a court order enjoining publication of defamatory speech violate the First Amendment?

■ **DECISION AND RATIONALE**

(Hughes, J.) Yes. Prior restraints against publication are invalid, unless they (a) protect national security during wartime, (b) restrict obscenity, or (c) protect against incitement to violence, or forcible overthrow of government. Historically, the First Amendment's chief purpose was to prevent prior restraints, as existed in monarchial England. Prior restraint is fundamentally different from after-the-fact punishment, because it seeks to suppress publication. This will result in impermissible censorship, of the kind the First Amendment was intended to stop. Reversed; statute voided as unconstitutional.

Analysis:

Near is notable for treating court orders as "prior restraints." While this case suggests they are not just presumed invalid, but rather, valid only in specified circumstances (to protect against violence or obscenity), later cases may allow some more discretion. The reason for courts' heightened distrust of

Near v. State of Minnesota ex rel. Olson (Continued)

prior restraints seems historical, because the British monarchy censored the press through licensing and prosecution. The reason that the court order at issue is a prior restraint is that it seeks to prohibit the publishing, in the future, of a defamatory newspaper, in general. It does not seek to prevent the future publication of the article that got Near (D) into trouble in the first place.

■ CASE VOCABULARY

ABATE: To stop something, e.g., a nuisance.

CONTEMPT: Violation of a court order. Usually punishable by fine and/or imprisonment.

PRIOR RESTRAINT: Speech restriction which is made in advance. Basically, it means a system which forbids all speech of certain types/topics.

New York Times Company v. United States

(*Newspapers*) v. (*Federal Government*)
403 U.S. 713, 91 S.Ct. 2140 (1971)

SUPREME COURT PERMITS NEWSPAPER TO PRINT MILITARY SECRETS

■ **INSTANT FACTS** During the Vietnam War, a newspaper which printed stolen military documents was enjoined, on national security grounds.

■ **BLACK LETTER RULE** If the government may impose prior restraints to protect national security, its proof burden is very high.

■ **PROCEDURAL BASIS**

In suit seeking injunction, appeal from appellate grant of injunction, reversing 2 lower courts' denial of injunction.

■ **FACTS**

The *New York Times* (D) obtained a stolen, classified Defense Department report on the Vietnam War, and published it. The *Washington Post* (D) also printed it. The United States (P) sued to enjoin publication, citing reasons of national security. The district court refused, and the D.C. Circuit affirmed, but the Second Circuit reversed and enjoined publication. *New York Times* (D) appeals.

■ **ISSUE**

May the government enjoin publication of classified information to protect national security?

■ **DECISION AND RATIONALE**

(Per Curiam) No. If the government may impose prior restraints to protect national security, its proof burden is very high. Prior restraints bear a heavy presumption of unconstitutionality. Thus, the government (P) carries a heavy burden of showing justification. Here, the lower courts found the United States (P) did not meet that burden. We agree. Injunction reversed.

■ **CONCURRENCE**

(Black, J.) The First Amendment should never allow injunctions against publication of news. I can imagine no greater perversion of the First Amendment's history and purpose.

■ **CONCURRENCE**

(Douglas, J.) The First Amendment's plain language forbids governmental restraints on the press. Its dominant purpose was to prevent governmental suppression of embarrassing information. Secrecy in government is fundamentally anti-democratic. Here, *New York Times'* (D) story is relevant to the national debate about Vietnam.

■ **CONCURRENCE**

(Brennan, J.) The First Amendment tolerates almost no prior restraints on the press. The only narrow exception is where the Nation is at war, during which the government may enjoin speech which actually

New York Times Company v. United States (Continued)

obstructs recruiting or reveals troop numbers/locations. Here, even if we concede the situation in Vietnam is tantamount to war, the United States (P) has not alleged that publication will have such effects.

■ **CONCURRENCE**

(Stewart, J.) The Executive should have sole power and vast discretion to wage war and conduct international relations, under the Constitution. But here, there is no proof that publication will surely result in direct, immediate, and irreparable damage to our Nation or people.

■ **CONCURRENCE**

(White, J.) The constitution offers extraordinary protection against prior restraints. Some circumstances may permit injunction for national security reasons. But here, the United States (P) has not met that heavy burden. To permit injunction would start courts down a long and hazardous road. But I believe some of these materials will harm the public interest, and that the *New York Times* (D) should not publish some of them.

■ **CONCURRENCE**

(Marshall, J.) A ban against publishing military secrets may be enacted only by Congress, not by the Executive (P) petitioning the Judiciary for injunctions.

■ **DISSENT**

(Burger, J.) The First Amendment is not absolute. But this Court is unable to decide this case competently, because we are not given the full facts, and are asked to review this case in frenetic haste. [The Court's opinion was written only 18 days after the papers were published.] The *New York Times* (D) should have tried to negotiate with the United States (P) on which papers could be published. I would affirm the decision below, preserving the injunction until the lower court completes this trial.

■ **DISSENT**

(Blackmun, J.) The First Amendment permits prior restraints in narrow circumstances. But such standards have not been developed yet. Yet I urge *New York Times* (D) not to publish these papers, because they will harm this Nation's war efforts.

Analysis:

This is the famous "Pentagon Papers" case, and is the main decision on whether courts can enjoin publication of news for reasons of national security. The opinion leaves several issues open. First, it is unclear whether the Court holds that prior restraint is never allowable to protect national security, though it is clear that the standard would be extremely high. Second, some of the Justices suggest that any prior restraint should come in the form of a Congressional statute, but it is unclear whether a majority would find such a statute constitutional.

Nebraska Press Association v. Stuart

(Media Industry Association) v. *(Judge)*
427 U.S. 539, 96 S.Ct. 2791 (1976)

COURTS' GAG ORDERS ARE RARELY CONSTITUTIONAL

■ **INSTANT FACTS** When a court issued a gag order preventing media from reporting facts about a mass-murder, reporters challenged the order as unconstitutional.

■ **BLACK LETTER RULE** Court orders barring pretrial publicity *by the media* bear a "heavy presumption" of invalidity, which must be analyzed by considering (i) the extent and (prejudicial) nature of pretrial publicity, (ii) whether other means would mitigate that publicity's effects, (iii) how effective such an order would be, and (iv) the order's precise terms.

■ **PROCEDURAL BASIS**

In prosecution for murder, motion to vacate court order restricting pretrial publicity.

■ **FACTS**

After the infamous murder of 6 in a small Nebraska town, police arrested local suspect Erwin Simants. The arrest attracted media coverage. Apparently, Simants confessed, and was found with incriminating evidence. Before trial, the prosecution and defense attorneys both petitioned for a restrictive order limiting what the media could report, to prevent pre-trial bias. (The media was unrepresented at this hearing.) Judge Stuart (D) granted an order prohibiting the media from reporting about Simants's confession, his statements to others, his written notes, etc., until a jury was impaneled. Industry association Nebraska Press Association (P) and other media members (P) sued Stuart (D), challenging the order's constitutionality and moving to intervene and vacate it.

■ **ISSUE**

Is a court order limiting the media's pretrial publicity a violation of the First Amendment?

■ **DECISION AND RATIONALE**

(Burger, J.) Yes. Court orders barring the media from pretrial publicity bear a "heavy presumption" of invalidity, which must be analyzed by considering (i) the extent and (prejudicial) nature of pretrial publicity, (ii) whether other means would mitigate that publicity's effects, (iii) how effective such an order would be, and (iv) the order's precise terms. The First Amendment sometimes creates publicity which interferes with the Sixth Amendment's guarantee of an impartial trial. But a court order barring pretrial publicity is a prior restraint, which bears a "heavy presumption" of invalidity. Courts, in determining such orders' validity, must examine (i) the extent and (prejudicial) nature of pretrial publicity, (ii) whether other means would mitigate that publicity's effects, (iii) how effective such an order would be, and (iv) the order's precise terms. Here, we find this order was unjustified. The trial judge (D) was correct in finding the extensive pretrial publicity might impair Simants's right to fair trial. We note that pretrial publicity, even if pervasive, cannot automatically be assumed to render the later trial unfair. Here, there is no evidence that other means to mitigate the publicity's effects were impossible. Such alternatives include: changing the trial's venue, postponing the trial until publicity subsides, questioning potential jurors more searchingly to screen out prejudice, clear jury instructions to disregard outside information, and sequestration. Finally, here, we find the order would be ineffective. These events happened in a

Nebraska Press Association v. Stuart (Continued)

small town, making rumors inevitable. This decision is limited to these facts, and we do not rule out the possibility that other situations may justify restraint. Motion to vacate granted.

Analysis:

While the Court says it may entertain the possibility of a valid gag order, commentators note that the requirements are so strict that no order could meet all of them. Lower courts treat *Nebraska Press* as an absolute ban on gag orders. There are no later Court cases approving prior restraints to stop pretrial publicity. But note that this case restricts gag orders against *the media*, not against participating attorneys and court personnel. Such gag orders are often issued and upheld.

■ CASE VOCABULARY

GAG ORDER: Court order against pretrial publicity, to prevent biasing prospective jurors.

SEQUESTRATION: Court-ordered isolation of jurors or witnesses, to prevent outside influences from swaying them.

Alexander v. United States

(Pornographer) v. (Federal Government)
509 U.S. 544, 113 S.Ct. 2766 (1993)

SEIZURES OF BUSINESSES' ASSETS FOR "OBSCENITY" VIOLATIONS ARE NOT "PRIOR RESTRAINTS"

■ **INSTANT FACTS** After a pornographer convicted of obscenity and racketeering had his entire business seized, he appealed the seizure as a "prior restraint."

■ **BLACK LETTER RULE** Government seizure of a business for criminal obscenity violations does not constitute a prior restraint.

■ PROCEDURAL BASIS

Following federal *RICO* conviction for obscenity and racketeering, appeal from judicial seizure of business assets.

■ FACTS

Pornographer Alexander (D), who sold pornographic magazines and sex toys and operated porn theaters, was charged by the United States (P) with obscenity, and with racketeering in violation of the *Racketeer Influenced and Corrupt Organizations Act (RICO)*. The obscenity violation was predicated on a finding that some of the videos he sold were legally "obscene." Alexander (D) was convicted of both charges, fined $100K and sentenced to 6 years' imprisonment. Under *RICO*, the United States (P) is also allowed to confiscate the assets of a business which engages in racketeering. Accordingly, United States (P) obtained forfeiture of Alexander's (D) entire porn business, worth $9M, upon proving it was engaged in racketeering. Alexander (D) appeals the forfeiture order, contending it is an unconstitutional prior restraint, because it prohibits future protected speech (pornography) based on past unprotected speech (obscenity). United States (P) defends, contending forfeiture is a permissible criminal punishment, since it punishes past racketeering rather than past speech.

■ ISSUE

Is seizure of businesses convicted of obscenity violations an unconstitutional prior restraint?

■ DECISION AND RATIONALE

(Rehnquist, J.) No. Government seizure of a business for criminal obscenity violations does not constitute a prior restraint. "Prior restraint" refers only to "administrative and judicial orders forbidding certain communications when issued in advance . . . ." Classic examples include temporary restraining orders and permanent injunctions which actually forbid speech activities. Here, the *RICO* statute does not prohibit engaging in expressive activities in the future, or require prior approval. *RICO*'s forfeiture statute calls for forfeiture of assets because of the financial role they play in the racketeering enterprise's operation. The statute seizes any such assets, oblivious to their expressive or non-expressive nature. Forfeiture does not prevent Alexander (D) from engaging in future expression, on penalty of contempt; it only deprives him of specific assets found to be related to his prior racketeering activities. This holding is necessitated by policy concerns; holding otherwise would enable racketeers to evade forfeiture by investing their criminal proceeds in businesses engaged in expressive activity. Affirmed.

Alexander v. United States (Continued)

■ DISSENT

(Kennedy, J.) The majority opinion chills free expression, because it allows seizure of a business's entire assets as punishment if even one of its products is found obscene.

Analysis:

Court orders seizing assets for past obscenity violations are classified as after-the-fact punishments, not "prior restraints." Thus, such seizures are exempt from the strict scrutiny imposed on prior restraints. In this case note that, while Alexander (D) ran a large pornography business for 30 years, only a few of his videocassettes were "obscene." Alexander (D) was convicted of racketeering, which may have been separate from his obscenity conviction. (For example, he may have used his video stores to launder drug profits). Alexander's (D) claim is that *RICO* effectively chills free speech, because it allows seizure of an entire pornographic business based on a few articles' obscenity. Justice Kennedy, dissenting, agrees that *RICO* could be used by the United States (P) to suppress pornographic businesses. But the majority opinion says the seizure was ordered to punish Alexander's (D) *racketeering*, not his obscenity.

■ CASE VOCABULARY

OBSCENITY: Under Supreme Court case law, sexually-explicit communications are deemed legally "obscene" if they (i) objectively arouse sexual excitement, AND (ii) depict sex in a patently offensive way, AND (iii) lack serious value. Communications deemed "obscene" are *not* protected by the First Amendment. Note that even porn is not necessarily always "obscene," because it need not depict sex in an *offensive* way.

RACKETEERING: Basically, one of several statutorily-specified crimes traditionally conducted by organized crime. Most often, this involves extortion, but also includes pimping, bookmaking, drug dealing, money laundering, etc. Under *RICO*, such "rackets" are punished more harshly, by seizure of all assets involved in the illegal business.

TEMPORARY RESTRAINING ORDER: Court order restricting a person from specified acts pending the outcome of a judicial proceeding, usually upon proof that allowing the act would cause irreparable harm to one party.

Watchtower Bible and Tract Society of New York, Inc. v. Village of Stratton

(Religious Group) v. (Local Municipality)
536 U.S. 150, 122 S.Ct. 2080 (2002)

FREEDOM OF SPEECH INCLUDES THE RIGHT TO DISSEMINATE RELIGIOUS VIEWS AT PRIVATE RESIDENCES

■ **INSTANT FACTS** The Village of Stratton (D) adopted an ordinance requiring "canvassers" to obtain a free permit from the mayor's office before engaging in door-to-door activities.

■ **BLACK LETTER RULE** A law requiring a permit before engaging in door-to-door activities on private residential property violates the right of free speech.

■ PROCEDURAL BASIS
Certiorari to review an undisclosed appellate decision.

■ FACTS
Watchtower Bible and Tract Society of New York, Inc. (P) publishes and distributes Bibles and coordinates the preaching activities of Jehovah's Witnesses nationwide. The Jehovah's Witnesses distribute religious literature door-to-door at no cost and do not solicit financial contributions, although they do accept donations. The Village of Stratton (D) enacted an ordinance prohibiting "canvassers" from "going in and upon" private property to promote any cause without first obtaining a permit from the mayor's office, which is available without charge upon completion of a registration form. The ordinance likewise permits Village (D) residents to complete a "No Solicitation Registration Form," which notifies permit holders of the resident's desire to be left alone. The Jehovah's Witnesses did not apply for a permit before engaging in door-to-door advocacy and challenge the constitutionality of the permit ordinance.

■ ISSUE
Does a town ordinance requiring a permit to engage in door-to-door activities violate the First Amendment?

■ DECISION AND RATIONALE
(Stevens, J.) Yes. Door-to-door pamphleteering and advocacy are historically important devices aiding in the dissemination of ideas and religious views. Towns and local municipalities, however, have a legitimate interest in regulating door-to-door activities, particularly when money is solicited, to ensure the safety of their residents. Here, the ordinance seeks to prevent fraud and crime against Village (D) residents and to protect their privacy. In so doing, the ordinance impinges the free speech of those disseminating their ideas, whether religious or otherwise. It is not narrowly tailored to monetary solicitations, but rather applies broadly to all door-to-door activities. "[A] law requiring a permit to engage in such speech constitutes a dramatic departure from our national heritage and constitutional tradition." Because the law infringes upon speech, it violates the First Amendment.

Watchtower Bible and Tract Society of New York, Inc. v. Village of Stratton (Continued)

■ DISSENT

(Rehnquist, C.J.) Door-to-door canvassers pose considerable threats to the peaceable enjoyment of private property and to the safety of those residing there. To allow some safeguard against the potential dangers of canvassers, the ordinance merely requires those wishing to engage in the door-to-door dissemination of information notify the mayor's office, which has no discretion to deny their permit. There is nothing unconstitutional or unreasonable about the ordinance's requirements. It is a valid measure to protect Village (D) residents with only a minor effect on free speech.

Analysis:

Because the ordinance vested no discretion in the government to deny the solicitation permit, the ordinance applies broadly to all regardless of the content of their speech. As such, one could argue that the ordinance has very little effect on First Amendment rights. Allowing the denial of a permit only upon a showing of a past crime related to canvassing enables the Village (D) to protect its residents only after a crime has occurred—a sever limitation, it could be argued, on its police power.

■ CASE VOCABULARY

FREEDOM OF SPEECH: The right to express one's thoughts and opinions without governmental restriction, as guaranteed by the First Amendment.

Thomas and Windy City Hemp Development Board v. Chicago Park District

(Permit Applicants) v. (Park District)
534 U.S. 316, 122 S.Ct. 775 (2002)

REQUIRING PERMITS FOR ALL PUBLIC ASSEMBLIES DOES NOT INFRINGE ON THE FREEDOM OF SPEECH

■ **INSTANT FACTS** A group advocating the legalization of marijuana challenged the constitutionality of a Chicago Park District (D) ordinance requiring a permit to conduct a public rally.

■ **BLACK LETTER RULE** A content-neutral regulation of access to public property is not unconstitutional so long as it provides adequate standards under which the regulation may be enforced.

■ PROCEDURAL BASIS

Certiorari to review an undisclosed decision.

■ FACTS

The Chicago Park District (D) operates public parks in Chicago. The District (D) adopted an ordinance requiring a permit before any person could "conduct a public assembly, parade, picnic, or other event involving more than fifty individuals" or involving amplified sound. The ordinance provides thirteen specified grounds for denial of a permit application and requires written notice of the reasons for denial. All denials are directly appealable to the General Superintendent of the Park District (D) and thereafter in state court. The plaintiffs had sought numerous permits to hold a public rally supporting the legalization of marijuana. Although some permits had been granted, the plaintiffs challenged the ordinance as facially unconstitutional.

■ ISSUE

Must a municipal park ordinance requiring individuals to obtain a permit before conducting large-scale events contain procedural safeguards against an invalid prior restraint?

■ DECISION AND RATIONALE

(Scalia, J.) No. In *Freedman v. Maryland*, the Court recognized that a statute or ordinance that conditions expression on the prior approval of content is particularly dangerous to the First Amendment. To safeguard against such dangers, the Court established three requirements to minimize the risk of an invalid prior restraint: "(1) any restraint prior to judicial review can be imposed only for a brief period during which the status quo must be maintained; (2) expeditious judicial review of that decision must be available; and (3) the censor must bear the burden of going to court to suppress the speech and must bear the burden of proof once in court."

These protections were necessary in *Freedman*, however, because the scheme involved related directly to the content of the expression concerned. The Park District's (D) ordinance is content-neutral and applies equally to all applicants. The ordinance does not authorize the approval or denial of applications based on the content of the expression, but rather the time, place, and manner in which the expression occurs. A content-neutral regulation of access to public property does not require such procedural safeguards. Such a regulation must, however, provide adequate standards to guide the decision-maker to minimize the danger of arbitrary denials. Here, the ordinance sets forth thirteen specific content-neutral reasons warranting denial of an application. It is not unconstitutional.

Analysis:

Compare the ordinance at issue here with that at issue in *Watchtower Bible and Tract Society of New York, Inc. v. Village of Stratton*. Whereas the Court approved regulations on the time, place, and manner of public rallies here because of thirteen clearly established bases for denying a permit, the Court disapproved of the Village of Stratton regulation that provided no bases for denial of a permit to solicit door to door. Can these two cases be reconciled?

■ CASE VOCABULARY

CONTENT–BASED RESTRICTION: A restraint on the substance of a particular type of speech. This type of restriction can survive a challenge only if it is based on a compelling state interest and its measures are narrowly drawn to accomplish that end.

PRIOR RESTRAINT: A governmental restriction on speech or publication before its actual expression. Prior restraints violate the First Amendment unless the speech is obscene, is defamatory, or creates a clear and present danger to society.

City of Littleton, Colorado v. Z.J. Gifts D–4, L.L.C.

(*Municipality*) v. (*Adult Business*)

541 U.S. 774, 124 S.Ct. 2219 (2004)

DENIAL OF AN "ADULT BUSINESS" LICENSE TRIGGERS "PROMPT" JUDICIAL REVIEW

■ **INSTANT FACTS** Z.J. Gifts D–4, L.L.C. (P) sued the city of Littleton, Colorado (P), challenging the constitutionality of its adult business license ordinance.

■ **BLACK LETTER RULE** A licensing scheme implicating First Amendment interests must provide for "prompt judicial review" of any administrative denial of a license, which requires speedy access to the courts and a prompt judicial determination of any legal claims arising from the denial.

■ PROCEDURAL BASIS

Certiorari to review an undisclosed appellate decision.

■ FACTS

The city of Littleton, Colorado (D) adopted an ordinance requiring all adult bookstores, novelty stores, and video stores to obtain a business license to do business in the city. The ordinance defines "adult business," provides eight explicit grounds for denial of the license, and allows for judicial review of any denial to a state district court. Z.J. Gifts D–4, L.L.C. (P) began a business selling adult books in an area not zoned for adult businesses. Rather than apply for a business license, Z.J. (P) sued to have the ordinance declared unconstitutional on its face.

■ ISSUE

Does the Littleton, Colorado, content-neutral adult business licensing ordinance satisfy the First Amendment requirement of prompt judicial review?

■ DECISION AND RATIONALE

(Breyer, J.) Yes. Constitutionally, any licensing scheme implicating First Amendment interests must provide for "prompt judicial review" of any administrative denial of a license. Prompt judicial review requires more than speedy access to the courts, and also includes a prompt judicial determination of any legal claims arising from the denial. Delay in rendering a judicial decision deprives the applicant of its license as much as delay in access to the courts.

However, Colorado law affords "prompt" judicial review. The First Amendment does not require special rules for judicial review of adult business licenses, for ordinary judicial review procedures may suffice. Colorado's general judicial review procedures arm judges with the means to avoid delays that will adversely affect a litigant's First Amendment interests and accelerate proceedings to minimize the harm. It is presumed, and there is no evidence to the contrary, that Colorado judges ably perform their duties when First Amendment interests are at stake. Likewise, the ordinance is content-neutral and the grounds for denying a license are explicit, objective, and nondiscriminatory. While Z.J. (P) may be denied a license, the ordinance does not censor content, for other qualified distributors may receive a license. Finally, the ordinance is not unconstitutional on its face for failure to provide for prompt judicial review. Local ordinances may permissibly rely on state laws governing judicial review without risking constitutional problems. "Where ... the regulation simply conditions the operation of an adult business on

City of Littleton, Colorado v. Z.J. Gifts D–4, L.L.C. (Continued)

compliance with neutral and nondiscretionary criteria, and does not seek to censor content, an adult business is not entitled to an unusually speedy judicial decision." The ordinance, on its face, is not unconstitutional.

Analysis:

Despite applying to businesses engaging in specific content, the ordinance here is content-neutral because the decision to grant or deny a license is not based on the content of the regulated speech. If the license were based on any content-related factor, however, the ordinance would invoke considerable First Amendment concerns.

■ CASE VOCABULARY

JUDICIAL REVIEW: A court's review of a lower court's or an administrative body's factual or legal findings.

United States v. National Treasury Employees Union

(Federal Government) v. (Federal Employees)
513 U.S. 454, 115 S.Ct. 1003 (1995)

BAN ON PAYMENT FOR CERTAIN COMMUNICATIONS IMPLICATES THE FIRST AMENDMENT

■ **INSTANT FACTS** When Congress passed a law barring federal employees from being paid for speeches/writings, they challenged its constitutionality.

■ **BLACK LETTER RULE** Legislation which forbids payment for certain speech implicates the First Amendment.

■ **PROCEDURAL BASIS**

In constitutional challenge to federal statute, appeal from judgment for plaintiffs.

■ **FACTS**

Congress enacted a law in 1989 that prohibited federal employees from accepting compensation for making speeches or writing articles. (The law was intended to discourage top officials from neglecting their official duties to make highly-paid speeches, and from granting favors to those that hire them.) The law applies even for communications unrelated to the employees' job. Some federal employees who moonlight as professional writers protested. On their behalf the National Treasury Employees Union ("Employees") (P) challenged the law as violating the First Amendment (by burdening their writing). The United States (D) defended, apparently claiming the honoraria ban was justified. The district court held for Employees (P). United States (D) appeals.

■ **ISSUE**

Does a law barring federal employees from being paid for speech violate the First Amendment?

■ **DECISION AND RATIONALE**

(Stevens, J.) Yes. Legislation which forbids payment for certain speech implicates the First Amendment. Federal employees, by working for the Government, do not relinquish the First Amendment rights to comment on matters of public interest that they would otherwise enjoy as citizens. Here, the ban, while not prohibiting speech outright or discriminating based on content or viewpoint, unquestionably imposes a significant burden on their expressive activity. This law, by not allowing federal employees compensation for their speech, effectively reduces its output. Further, the law is unjustified. Mostly, the Employees' (P) writing is unrelated to their jobs, and has no arguable adverse impact on their offices' efficiency. The ban is ineffective against its intended target—top officials whose fee is based on their high position—because they can still collect remuneration as a travel expense reimbursement. The ban's large-scale disincentive to Government workers' expression also imposes a significant burden on the public's right to hear them. We note that, in the past, federal employees like Nathaniel Hawthorne, Herman Melville, and Walt Whitman made significant contributions to the marketplace of ideas, and will not risk depriving the public of such benefits. Affirmed.

■ **DISSENT**

(Rehnquist, J.) I believe the law is justified, under intermediate scrutiny. The majority's analysis understates the weight that should be accorded to the government interest, and overstates the amount

United States v. National Treasury Employees Union (Continued)

of speech that actually will be deterred. Also, the majority finds the ban should not be extended to federal employees below rank GS-16, but we find that employees below this grade—such as tax/bank examiners—also have the power to confer favors on those who might pay to hear their speech.

Analysis:

This case reaffirms the principle that the denial of payment for speech implicates the First Amendment. Note that such denial is not automatically void, but is subject to intermediate scrutiny (as long as it is content- and viewpoint-neutral). So here, the Court balanced the competing interests and found that the Employees' (R) right to speak (and the public's right to hear them) outweighed the government's (D) interest in preventing abuse. Recall the earlier case of *Simon & Schuster* (Son of Sam Law), which held that criminals cannot be denied proceeds from their memoirs. The policy reasons were similar to those in this case: denying payment for writings may deprive the public of valuable information.

■ CASE VOCABULARY

HONORARIUM (plural "honoraria"): Fee paid to a public speaker. Here, top government officials often command high prices for making speeches to the private sector.

West Virginia State Board of Education v. Barnette

(State Board of Education) v. (Jehovah's Witnesses)
319 U.S. 624, 63 S.Ct. 1178 (1943)

GOVERNMENT CANNOT COMPEL SPEECH

■ **INSTANT FACTS** A state's mandatory flag salute was challenged by Jehovah's Witnesses.

■ **BLACK LETTER RULE** The government cannot compel silence or speech, whether verbal or symbolic, except to prevent "clear and present" danger of crime.

■ **PROCEDURAL BASIS**

In First Amendment challenge to state resolution, appeal from judgment for plaintiffs.

■ **FACTS**

In 1942, the West Virginia State Board of Education ("West Virginia") (D) adopted a resolution ordering that a flag salute become mandatory in public schools, and that all teachers and students "shall be required to participate ...; ... refusal to salute ... [shall] be regarded as ... insubordination." (The flag salute is non-verbal; it requires only that participants raise their hand while the Pledge of Allegiance is read.) Insubordination is punished by expulsion, which lasts until compliance. If a child is thus expelled, he is deemed an "unlawfully absent" delinquent; he may be sent to a juvenile reformatory, and his parents are punishable by fine ($50) and imprisonment (30 days). Several Jehovah's Witnesses (P) refused the flag salute, on religious grounds. Under their interpretation of the Bible's command, "Thou shalt not make ... any graven image," they consider the flag an "image." These Jehovah's Witnesses (P) were expelled and their parents prosecuted, or threatened with prosecution. The Jehovah's Witnesses (P), including Barnette (P), challenged the resolution, contending it was state-compelled speech. At trial, the court held for Jehovah's Witnesses (P). West Virginia (D) appeals.

■ **ISSUE**

May a state require school personnel to salute the American flag?

■ **DECISION AND RATIONALE**

(Jackson, J.) No. The government cannot compel silence or speech, whether verbal or symbolic, except to prevent "clear and present" danger of crime. The flag salute is a form of utterance, because symbolism is deemed a communication. It is unclear whether West Virginia (D) intends students to believe the Pledge of Allegiance and suppress contrary sentiments, or just pretend assent. If the aim is to suppress sentiments, our case law holds that censorship or suppression of expression is constitutional only when the speech would create a "clear and present danger" of some type of action which the State is empowered to prevent and punish [i.e., crime]. If the aim is to command involuntary affirmation, it could be commanded only on even more immediate and urgent grounds. Here, West Virginia (D) has not proven any such danger. To claim that patriotism will not flourish without involuntary ceremonies demeans our populace's commitment to free thought. The purpose of the Bill of Rights' Fourteenth Amendment is to protect certain rights from politics and majorities; one such right is freedom of religion. If there is any fixed star in our constitutional constellation, it is that no official ...

can prescribe what shall be orthodox in politics, nationalism, religion, or other matters of opinion, or force citizens to profess their faith therein, by word or deed. If there are any circumstances which permit an exception, they do not now occur to us. Affirmed.

■ DISSENT

(Frankfurter, J.) It is my personal opinion that the flag salute is unwise. But I believe we Justices should put aside personal opinions about this law's wisdom. Accordingly, I do not believe the Due Process Clause's right to "liberty" would extend to deny West Virginia (D) the right to promote the legitimate goal of good citizenship by means of a flag salute.

Analysis:

This is the Supreme Court's classic pronouncement on Government-compelled expression, or forced silence—it is unconstitutional, except to prevent immediate crime. (For example, the State can forbid incitements to crime.) Also, note that compelled "speech" includes non-verbal symbols or gestures.

Rumsfeld v. Forum for Academic & Institutional Rights, Inc.

(Secretary of Defense) v. (Organization of Law Schools)
547 U.S. 47, 126 S.Ct. 1297 (2006)

LAW SCHOOLS MUST ALLOW MILITARY RECRUITERS ON CAMPUS IF THEY WANT FEDERAL FUNDS

■ **INSTANT FACTS** The Solomon Amendment required colleges and universities that received federal funds to allow military recruiters access to campuses, and the Forum for Academic & Institutional Rights (P) claimed that the Amendment violated the First Amendment.

■ **BLACK LETTER RULE** Conditioning the receipt of federal funds on allowing military recruiters to have access to a college campus does not violate the First Amendment.

■ **PROCEDURAL BASIS**

Appeal from an order of the Third Circuit directing an injunction against enforcement of the Solomon Amendment.

■ **FACTS**

Several law schools restricted military recruiters' access to their students because the government's (D) ban on homosexuals in the military violated school anti-discrimination policies. The Solomon Amendment, 10 U.S.C. § 983 (b), was enacted in response. The Amendment provides that any institution of higher learning that receives any federal funds must allow military recruiters the same access to students as provided to any other employer. The Forum for Academic & Institutional Rights (P) (FAIR), an organization of law schools and law faculties, brought an action to enjoin enforcement of the Amendment. FAIR (P) claimed that the Amendment violated its members' First Amendment rights of Freedom of Speech and Freedom of Association. The Third Circuit Court of Appeals ordered that an injunction against enforcement be issued.

■ **ISSUE**

Does the law requiring access to law schools by military recruiters violate the First Amendment?

■ **DECISION AND RATIONALE**

(Roberts, C.J.) No. Conditioning the receipt of federal funds on allowing military recruiters to have access to a college campus does not violate the First Amendment. The Forum (P) and its members are free to express disagreement with the policy and still receive federal funds. The Forum (P) argues that, pursuant to the Solomon Amendment, it is required to provide assistance to military recruiters, and that this conduct has elements of expression to it. The First Amendment prohibits the government from telling people what they must say, the Forum (P) argues. But the recruiting assistance mandated by the Amendment does not amount to the sort of compelled speech that has been found unconstitutional in the past. The compelled speech is plainly incidental to the Amendment's regulation of conduct.

Compelled-speech cases have often limited the government's ability to force a speaker to host or accommodate another speaker's message. In those cases, the complaining speaker's own message was affected by the speech that would be accommodated. Accommodating the military's (D) message does not affect FAIR's (P) message, because schools are not speaking when they host recruiters.

Rumsfeld v. Forum for Academic & Institutional Rights, Inc. (Continued)

Allowing recruiters on campus is not inherently expressive. Treating military (D) and non-military recruiters alike does not suggest that FAIR (P) agrees with any speech by recruiters. The expressive component of allowing recruiters on campus is not created by the conduct, but by any speech that accompanies that conduct.

The Solomon Amendment does not violate FAIR's (P) freedom of expressive association. Recruiters are not part of a law school. They are outsiders who come on campus for a limited purpose. They do not become members of the school's expressive association. Students and faculty are free to associate to express their disapproval of the military's (D) message. Reversed.

Analysis:

The Solomon Amendment applies to all parts of a college or university, not just law schools. The law schools' objections to military recruiters on campus might be lessened if new policies regarding gays in the military were adopted. In May 2010, gay rights groups, congressional leaders, and the White House worked out a deal to pass a repeal of the "don't ask, don't tell" policy that prohibits gays and lesbians from serving openly in the military. At the time of this writing, it is uncertain whether the deal will go through, and what the final terms will be.

■ CASE VOCABULARY

FREEDOM OF ASSOCIATION: The right to join with others in a common undertaking that would be lawful if pursued individually. This right is protected by the First Amendment to the U.S. Constitution. The government may not prohibit outsiders from joining an association, but the insiders do no necessarily have a ride to exclude others.

McIntyre v. Ohio Elections Commission

(*Anonymous Pamphleteer*) v. (*State Agency*)
514 U.S. 334, 115 S.Ct. 1511 (1995)

GOVERNMENT CANNOT COMPEL ANONYMOUS SPEAKERS TO DISCLOSE IDENTITY

■ **INSTANT FACTS** An anonymous pamphleteer challenges a law banning anonymous electioneering.

■ **BLACK LETTER RULE** The government cannot compel anonymous speakers to reveal their identities.

■ PROCEDURAL BASIS
In First Amendment challenge to state law, appeal.

■ FACTS
The *Ohio Code* forbids distributing anonymous materials in connection with any election. Pamphleteer Ms. McIntyre (P) distributed anonymous leaflets opposing a school tax levy, at a pre-referendum meeting. The Ohio Elections Commission (D) learned of this, and fined McIntyre (P) $100. McIntyre (P) challenged the *Code* provision as unconstitutional compelled speech. Ohio (D) defended, contending *Code* was justified to prevent fraud and libel, and to provide full information to the electorate.

■ ISSUE
May a law ban anonymous communications in connection with elections?

■ DECISION AND RATIONALE
(Stevens, J.) No. The government cannot compel anonymous speakers to reveal their identities. Here, the speech in question—handing out leaflets advocating a politically controversial viewpoint—is a "core" political communication protected by the First Amendment. When a law burdens core political speech, we apply "exacting scrutiny," meaning we uphold it only if it is (i) narrowly-tailored (ii) to serve an "overriding" state interest. Throughout history anonymous writing had an honorable tradition of advocacy and dissent, and a role in aiding the progress of mankind. In literature, great works were often produced anonymously. There are legitimate reasons for writing anonymously: fear of economic or official retaliation, concern for social ostracism, or desire for privacy. In literature, the interest in having anonymous works enter the marketplace outweighs the public interest in disclosure. This freedom to publish anonymously extends beyond the literary realm. Anonymity serves the function of letting personally unpopular speakers ensure that hearers will not prejudge their message. Here, Ohio (D)'s interests are not overriding, and its laws are not narrowly tailored. Its stated purpose of informing the electorate fully is not strong; revealing the speaker's identity is no more important than revealing other facts, which pamphleteers are free to omit. True, the state's interest in preventing falsehoods is heightened during elections, when lies' effects may be especially harmful to the public. But the *Code* provision here is overbroad; it encompasses documents which are not false or misleading. Also, current laws on fraud and libel can be enforced effectively against even anonymous speakers, as here. Judgment for plaintiff.

McIntyre v. Ohio Elections Commission (Continued)

■ **CONCURRENCE**

(Thomas, J.) I agree that this *Code* provision violates the First Amendment. But I would reach this result by interpreting the First Amendment historically, giving it the meaning it had when adopted. There is no record of the Bill of Rights' drafters discussing anonymous political expression. Thus, our analysis must focus on the Founders' beliefs concerning them. There is little doubt the framers themselves wrote political articles anonymously. For example, the *Federalist Papers* were published under the pseudonym "Publius." Thus, anonymous communications should be permitted, but only because the framers so intended.

■ **DISSENT**

(Scalia, J.) Currently, laws like Ohio's (D) exist in 49 states. Further, such state initiatives are supported by Congress and the President, as well as both political parties. Such laws have existed since the 19th century. They are useful to promote accountability. Thus, they should be retained.

Analysis:

The holding in this case is classified in the text as demonstrating compelled speech. Namely, compelling anonymous speakers to disclose their identity is deemed to implicate the First Amendment. However, in formulating policy, consider whether anonymous publications are more likely to be legitimate, or false and manipulative. Note that this case is not the first to articulate this holding, but merely one of the most recent.

Rust v. Sullivan

(Federal Grant Recipients) v. (Secretary of Health and Human Services)
500 U.S. 173, 111 S.Ct. 1759 (1991)

SUPREME COURT APPLIES "UNCONSTITUTIONAL CONDITION" RULE INCONSISTENTLY

■ **INSTANT FACTS** Health care providers challenged regulations granting federal funding to family planning, on condition they not recommend abortion.

■ **BLACK LETTER RULE** It is constitutional for the government to selectively fund programs which encourage certain activities in the public interest, without also funding alternative approaches.

■ PROCEDURAL BASIS

In First Amendment challenge to federal agency regulations, appeal from judgment for agency.

■ FACTS

In 1970, Congress enacted *Public Health Service Act's* (*Act*) *Title X*, which provides federal funding for family-planning services, by authorizing the Department of Health and Human Services (HHS) (D) to give grants to health care facilities to offer family planning care. Under *Title X*, all such grants are subject to HHS' (D) Secretary's (D) regulations. But *Act* also provides, "none of the funds ... shall be used in programs where abortion is a method of family planning." This was intended to ensure *Title X* funds are used only to support contraception, population research, infertility treatment, etc. Later, HHS Secretary Rust (D) promulgated regulations about how to keep *Title X* programs separate from abortion services. Under these regulations, *Title X*-funded organizations must (i) not provide abortion counseling, or referrals to abortionists, (ii) not encourage abortion, or lobby/litigate to make it available, and (iii) keep their funded projects "physically and financially separate" from abortion providers. Several grant recipients, including Rust (P), (collectively, "Grantees" (P)) challenged the regulations' constitutionality, contending they (i) constitute viewpoint-based discrimination, because they allow only anti-abortion speech, and (ii) violate the "unconstitutional conditions" doctrine, by conditioning government funding on recipients foregoing their constitutional speech rights. At trial, the court held for HHS (D). Grantees (P) appeal.

■ ISSUE

Can the government fund a program providing family planning services, but disallow recipients from making abortion-related speech?

■ DECISION AND RATIONALE

(Rehnquist, J.) Yes. It is constitutional for the government to selectively fund programs which encourage certain activities in the public interest, without also funding alternative approaches. The statutory prohibition here is constitutional. First, the regulations here do not constitute viewpoint-based discrimination. When the Government decides to fund a program to encourage activities it believes to be in the public interest, the constitution does not require it to also fund alternative approaches. For example, when Congress funded the National Endowment for Democracy, it was not required to also encourage fascism. In funding one such program, the Government has not discriminated, but merely chosen to

Rust v. Sullivan (Continued)

fund one to the exclusion of the others. The legislature's decision not to subsidize a fundamental right is not deemed to infringe that right, and cannot be equated with a "penalty." *Title X* was originally intended to encourage (non-abortive) family planning, not to fund all prenatal care. Thus, when the Government appropriates funds to establish a program, it may make regulations which ensure the funding is restricted to activities within the statute's scope. To hold otherwise would render many Government-funded programs suspect. Second, these regulations do not implicate the "unconstitutional condition" doctrine. [That doctrine says the government cannot (A) condition a benefit on giving up a constitutional right, nor (B) deny benefits for exercising one's constitutional rights.] Our "unconstitutional conditions" cases involve situations where the Government has placed a condition on receipt of the subsidy, rather than a condition on a particular program/service. Here, the regulations do not deny benefits, but merely ensure public funds are spent for the purposes authorized. The regulations do not force Grantees (P) to give up pro-abortion speech; they merely require Grantees (P) to keep such activities separate from *Title X* activities. Affirmed.

■ DISSENT

(Blackmun, J.) This *Title X* regulation effectively upholds viewpoint-based suppression of speech, because it is imposed on those dependent on Government grants. It has the purpose and effect of manipulating pregnant women to carry their babies to term. This case is irreconcilable with our past cases.

Analysis:

The Court recognized here that while employees were actually working on the Title X project, their freedom of expression was limited, but this "limitation was a consequence of their decision to accept employment in a project, the scope of which was permissibly restricted by the funding authority." Perhaps in this case the dissent is correct; the Supreme Court has applied the "unconstitutional condition" doctrine haphazardly. When the Court seeks to void a governmental funding preference, it finds that adopting the government's viewpoint is a condition to receiving funding. But when the Court approves of the program, it announces that the government is subsidizing the activity, but not others. There apears to be no predictable, dominant approach in the caselaw.

■ CASE VOCABULARY

"UNCONSTITUTIONAL CONDITIONS": Doctrine whereby the government cannot condition a benefit on giving up a constitutional right. Similarly, the government cannot deny benefits for exercising one's constitutional rights.

Legal Services Corp. v. Velazquez

(Non–Profit Corporation) v. (Undisclosed Plaintiff)
531 U.S. 533, 121 S.Ct. 1043 (2001)

RESTRICTIONS ON FEDERAL FUNDING TO INDIGENT LITIGANTS VIOLATE THE FIRST AMENDMENT

■ **INSTANT FACTS** The plaintiff challenged the constitutionality of conditions placed on the use of federal funds distributed by Legal Services Corporation (D) to be used for indigent legal assistance.

■ **BLACK LETTER RULE** Private speech may not be restricted or controlled by limitations on the use of federal funds.

■ **PROCEDURAL BASIS**

Certiorari to review an undisclosed appellate decision.

■ **FACTS**

Legal Services Corporation (LSC) (D) is a congressionally created non-profit District of Columbia corporation formed to distribute federal funds to local organizations "for the purpose of providing financial support for legal assistance in noncriminal proceedings or matters to persons financially unable to afford legal assistance." As a condition for federal funding, Congress prohibited the use of LSC (D) funds for the purpose of *amending* or *challenging* existing welfare laws. However, LSC (D) grantees may use funds to *challenge agency interpretations or applications* of existing welfare laws.

■ **ISSUE**

Do restrictions on the use of federal funds to challenge existing federal law violate the First Amendment?

■ **DECISION AND RATIONALE**

(Kennedy, J.) Yes. "When the government disburses public funds to private entities to convey a governmental message, it may take legitimate and appropriate steps to ensure that its message is neither garbled nor distorted by the grantee." The LSC program, however, does not promote a governmental message, but rather was formed to promote private speech. LSC (D) funds are disbursed to further the legal rights of indigent recipients, not to further some governmental agenda. There is no government speech implicated, and the program presumes that private speech is necessary. Yet, the limitations on the use of funds place a substantial restriction on that private speech. In so doing, the program prevents attorneys from advocating for their clients' rights and deprives the courts of the candor and independence they demand from attorney advocates. Having chosen to fund legal assistance for the indigent, Congress may not selectively restrict the scope of legal positions taken. Such restrictions on private speech suppress the dissemination of ideas in violation of the First Amendment.

■ **DISSENT**

(Scalia, J.) The LSC Act grants federal subsidies, which are incapable of regulating speech absent some coercive effect on the recipient. It does not create a public forum for speech nor prevent one from advocating a legal position. Instead, the Act defines the scope of federal spending. In *Rust v. Sullivan*,

Legal Services Corp. v. Velazquez (Continued)

the Court approved a federal spending program that prohibited recipient doctors from counseling patients on abortion as a family planning method. There, the Court rejected the First Amendment argument, reasoning that the "decision not to subsidize the exercise of a fundamental right does not infringe the right." Just as in *Rust*, the decision not to subsidize an assault on federal welfare laws does not violate the First Amendment. The recipient doctors in Rust had a confidential obligation to their patients, and LSC fund recipients have a confidential obligation to their clients. To justify one as government speech and dismiss the other as private speech "is so unpersuasive it hardly needs response." The program does not prevent anybody from speaking nor coerce anyone to speak differently. It merely limits what private speech the government will subsidize, just as in *Rust*.

Analysis:

Because the LSC Act is itself federal welfare legislation, the use of LSC funds to challenge existing welfare laws could be considered ironic. There is no constitutional right to receive the government benefits the LSC Act provides, as the right to access to the courts does not include the duty of the government to pay for that access in non-criminal matters. Query whether it is ever appropriate to require the limited relinquishment of important rights in exchange for important government assistance.

Schenck v. United States

(Anti-Draft Pamphleteer) v. *(Federal Prosecution)*
249 U.S. 47, 39 S.Ct. 247 (1919)

SUPREME COURT ADOPTS "CLEAR AND PRESENT DANGER" TEST DURING WWI

■ **INSTANT FACTS** A wartime anti-draft pamphleteer challenged his conviction under the *Espionage Act.*

■ **BLACK LETTER RULE** The First Amendment does not protect speech which is used under such circumstances, and is of such a nature, that it creates a "clear and present danger" of inciting illegal activity.

■ **PROCEDURAL BASIS**

In *Espionage Act of 1917* prosecution for obstructing draft, appeal from conviction.

■ **FACTS**

During World War I, Congress passed the *Espionage Act of 1917 (Act),* [which makes it a crime, during wartime, to "obstruct the recruiting or enlistment service of the United States," among other activities which hinder the war effort. The penalty was imprisonment up to 20 years, plus fines of up to $10K.] Anti-draft protesters (D), including Schenck (D), circulated anti-conscription leaflets. These leaflets said conscription violated the Thirteenth Amendment, that conscripts were little better than convicts, that conscription was despotic and monstrous, that the draft served Wall Street's elite, etc.. They said, "Do not submit to intimidation," but urged only peaceful measures, like petitioning for repeal of conscription laws. The United States (P) charged Schenck (D) with conspiring to violate *Act* by causing/attempting to cause insubordination in the armed services. Schenck (D) was convicted, and now appeals, contending his speech was protected by the First Amendment.

■ **ISSUE**

Is anti-draft speech, made during wartime, protected by the First Amendment?

■ **DECISION AND RATIONALE**

(Holmes, J.) No. The First Amendment does not protect speech which is used under such circumstances, and is of such a nature, that it creates a "clear and present danger" of inciting illegal activity. Though the First Amendment was intended primarily to prevent prior restraints, it well may be that its protections extend further. [Remember, this case is ancient.] The character of every act depends on its circumstances. In such [incitement] cases, the question is whether the words used are used in such circumstances, and are of such a nature, as to create a "clear and present danger" that they will bring about the substantive evils that Congress has a right to prevent [i.e., illegal acts]. When a nation is at war, many things that might be said in peacetime are such a hindrance to its war effort that they cannot be endured. We admit that, in ordinary times, the defendants would have been within their rights to say what they said. If it were proven that the words produced actual obstruction of recruiting, these words would carry liability. *Act* punishes not only actual obstruction, but also conspiracies to obstruct. We find Schenck's (D) intent in circulating the pamphlet was to obstruct the draft; we do not see what other effect it could be expected to have, and it would not have been mailed unless intended to have some effect. Thus, it is punishable as conspiracy, whether effective or not. Affirmed.

Schenck v. United States (Continued)

Analysis:

This case introduces the "clear and present danger" test. This test was used for a few years, then abandoned. Note that the "clear and present danger" test is a balancing test; while it recognizes that Schenck's (D) opinion has some value deserving some degree of protection, it accords greater weight to the government's interest in maintaining its war effort. However, while this case articulates the "clear and present danger" test, the Court never reaches the issue of whether Schenck's (D) words were actually likely to cause immediate interference, finding instead that his intent was sufficient to charge him with conspiracy.

Frohwerk v. United States

(Pro-German Publisher) v. (Federal Prosecution)
249 U.S. 204, 39 S.Ct. 249 (1919)

SUPREME COURT RE-AFFIRMS "CLEAR AND PRESENT DANGER" TEST

■ **INSTANT FACTS** During WWI, a pro-German newspaper writer, who advocated stopping the war against Germany, was convicted of obstructing the draft, under the *Espionage Act*.

■ **BLACK LETTER RULE** The First Amendment does not protect speech which is used under such circumstances, and is of such a nature, that it creates a "clear and present danger" of inciting illegal activity.

■ PROCEDURAL BASIS

In *Espionage Act of 1917* prosecution for obstructing the draft, post-conviction appeal.

■ FACTS

[During World War I, Congress passed the *Espionage Act of 1917* (Act), which makes it a crime, during wartime, to "obstruct the recruiting or enlistment service of the United States," among other activities which hinder the war effort.] Frohwerk (D) and Gleeser (D) published a pro-German newspaper, the *Missouri Staats Zeitung*, which criticized America's involvement in the war. Frohwerk (D) wrote 12 articles, which said it was a mistake to send American soldiers to France, that the order came from corporate trusts and was intended to benefit Wall Street, that the German nation was strong and unconquerable, and that readers should "cease firing." The United States (P) charged Frohwerk (D) with conspiracy to violate *Act*. Frohwerk (D) was convicted, sentenced to 10 years' imprisonment, and fined. Frohwerk (D) appeals, apparently contending he wrote the articles for money, without actually intending that it have any results.

■ ISSUE

During wartime, may a newspaper urge readers to stop fighting?

■ DECISION AND RATIONALE

(Holmes, J.) No. [The First Amendment does not protect speech which is used under such circumstances, and is of such a nature, that it creates a "clear and present danger" of inciting illegal activity.] Criticisms of the war effort may be protected under the First Amendment, even in wartime. Americans do not lose their right to condemn either measures or men because the country is at war. On the record before us, we cannot hold that the trial court erred in finding that Frohwerk's (D) paper was circulated in quarters where a little breath would kindle a flame, and that this was known to Frohwerk (D), and relied upon. This is true even though there is no evidence Frohwerk (D) made any special effort to reach men subject to the draft. Even if Frohwerk's (D) chief intent was compensation, this would not exonerate him. Affirmed.

Analysis:

This case re-affirms *Schenck*'s "clear and present danger" test, without mentioning it by name. Interestingly, this opinion, by Justice Holmes, was written only a week after his opinion in *Schenck*. This

Frohwerk v. United States (Continued)

test is necessarily fact-specific, focusing on the speaker's intent and circumstances. Unfortunately, neither of these cases really gives us a detailed analysis of the circumstances that are deemed dangerous, and neither considers whether there is any real danger the speech will have its intended effects.

■ CASE VOCABULARY

PLAINTIFF IN ERROR: Archaic term for "appellant."

TRUST: Here, a large, monopolistic corporation.

Debs v. United States

(Pro-Socialist Speaker) v. *(Federal Prosecution)*
249 U.S. 211, 39 S.Ct. 252 (1919)

COURT AGAIN UPHOLDS *ESPIONAGE ACT OF 1917*

■ **INSTANT FACTS** A socialist who made an anti-draft speech to drafted men was convicted under the *Espionage Act* of obstructing the draft.

■ **BLACK LETTER RULE** The First Amendment does not protect speech which is used under such circumstances, and is of such a nature, that it creates a "clear and present danger" of inciting illegal activity.

■ PROCEDURAL BASIS
In *Espionage Act* prosecution, appeal from conviction.

■ FACTS
Socialist speaker Debs (D) gave a pro-socialist speech to a crowd, apparently composed of men who had been drafted. In his speech, Debs (D) praised 3 socialists who were jailed for helping others evade the draft, suggesting they were imprisoned for their efforts to better mankind. Then, Debs (D) condemned Prussian militarism, apparently in a way which suggested the United States (P) was similar. Then, Debs (D) advocated socialism and predicted it would succeed internationally. Finally, Debs (D) told the draftees "you need to know that you are fit for something better than slavery and cannon fodder." Debs (D) was charged under the *Espionage Act of 1917* with (i) obstruction/attempting to obstruct the draft, and (ii) inciting/attempting to incite mutiny. After trial, Debs (D) was convicted on both charges, and sentenced to 10 years' imprisonment. Debs (D) appeals, apparently contending that, because his particular audience members—men who were drafted, but not yet on active duty—were not part of the military yet, inciting them could not be considered as hampering the "military."

■ ISSUE
Is an anti-draft speech, made to recently-drafted men, punishable under the *Espionage Act of 1917*?

■ DECISION AND RATIONALE
(Holmes, J.) Yes. [The First Amendment does not protect speech which is used under such circumstances, and is of such a nature, that it creates a "clear and present danger" of inciting illegal activity.] First, we find the verdict for obstructing recruitment must be sustained. The United States (P) presented strong arguments about *Act*'s legislative history, showing that under it, persons registered and enrolled in the draft, and the draft, and thus subject to be called into active service, were part of the "military forces." We see no sufficient reason to discuss the question in detail. Second, it is less important to consider whether the verdict upon the other count—for causing/attempting to cause insubordination—is equally impregnable. [It is moot because any sentence under this count would run concurrently with the first.] Conviction affirmed.

Analysis:
The defendant in this case was Eugene V. Debs, leader of the American Socialist Party and a vocal pro-socialist and pro-labor speaker. In *Debs* (decided near the time that *Schenck* was written), Justice

Debs v. United States (Continued)

Holmes affirmed Debs' conviction for merely encouraging listeners to obstruct the recruiting service. But, in this case, he spoke more in common law speech terms, which were adopted later by the Court (but not Holmes) in the *Abrams* and *Gitlow* cases, which appear next.

■ **CASE VOCABULARY**

WORKHOUSE: Jail for minor offenders serving short sentences.

Abrams v. United States

(Pro-Russian Pamphleteers) v. *(Federal Prosecution)*
250 U.S. 616, 40 S.Ct. 17 (1919)

HOLMES' FAMOUS DISSENT CALLS FOR "CLEAR AND PRESENT DANGER" TEST TO CONSIDER ACTUAL IMMEDIACY

■ **INSTANT FACTS** Pro-Bolshevik anarchists, who urged munitions workers not to make weapons for use against Russians, were charged with hindering the war effort against Germany.

■ **BLACK LETTER RULE** The First Amendment does not protect speech which is used under such circumstances, and is of such a nature, that it creates a "clear and present danger" of inciting illegal activity.

■ **PROCEDURAL BASIS**

In *Espionage Act* prosecution, post-conviction appeal.

■ **FACTS**

The *Espionage Act*, as amended in 1918 (*1918 Act*) makes it illegal, during wartime, to (A) "to ... utter ... disloyal ... and abusive language about the form of government of the United States," (B) "to unlawfully utter ... [words] intended to bring the form of government of the United States into contempt," (C) utter language "intended to incite ... resistance to the United States in said war," and (D) "when the United States [is] at war with the Imperial German Government, ... willfully, by utterance ... to urge ... curtailment of production of ... products necessary ... to the prosecution of the war ... with the intent by such curtailment to cripple or hinder the United States in the prosecution of the war." [In 1918, Russia's American-allied Czarist government was overthrown by the anti-American Bolsheviks. The new Russian government signed a peace treaty with Germany. In response, the U.S. sent a small group of Marines into Siberia.] 5 Russian-born anarchists, including Abrams (D) (collectively, "Anarchists" (D)), feared the U.S. (P) intended to intervene against the Bolsheviks. Anarchists (D) produced and circulated a leaflet, which said American capitalists intended to ally with German militarists to crush Russian workers, that the Allies would intervene against the Bolsheviks in Czechoslovakia, etc. The leaflet encouraged munitions plant workers not to aid this intervention, saying, "Workers in the ammunition factories, you are producing bullets ... to murder not only the Germans, but also your dearest, best, who are in Russia fighting for freedom." However, the leaflet was also anti-German, saying, "It is absurd to call us pro-German. We have more reason for denouncing German militarism than has the coward of the White House." Anarchists (D) were charged with violating the *1918 Act*, as excerpted above. At trial, Anarchists (D) defended, contending the *1918 Act* punished the intent to impede the American war effort (against Germany) or criticize American government, whereas they did not care about the U.S.'s government and intended only to prevent American intervention against Russia. Anarchists (D) were convicted, and now appeal, contending their speech is protected by the First Amendment, and that *1918 Act* is unconstitutional.

■ **ISSUE**

Does the First Amendment protect wartime speech which urges workers not to produce munitions?

Abrams v. United States (Continued)

■ DECISION AND RATIONALE

(Clarke, J.) No. The First Amendment does not protect speech which is used under such circumstances, and is of such a nature, that it creates a "clear and present danger" of inciting illegal activity. The *1918 Act* is constitutional, as discussed in *Schenck* and *Frohwerk.* Affirmed.

■ DISSENT

(Holmes, J.) The United States (P) constitutionally may punish speech that produces, or is intended to produce, a "clear and imminent danger" that it will bring about forthwith substantive evils that the United States constitutionally may prevent. This power is greater in wartime, which adds new dangers. This holding was stated in *Schenck, Frohwerk*, and *Debs*, which were correctly decided. But the government may prevent only *present* danger of *immediate* evil, or an intent to bring it. Here, no one can suppose Anarchists' (D) surreptitious publication of silly anonymous leaflets, without more, would present any immediate danger of hindering the success of government arms. Anarchists' (D) leaflet does not attack the United States' (P) form of government. Some of the leaflets do urge curtailment of munitions. But to make such conduct criminal, the statute requires it be "with the intent by such curtailment to cripple or hinder the United States in the prosecution of the war." Here, no such intent is proved. Anarchists' (D) only object is to help Russia and stop American intervention there, not to impede the United States (P) in its war being against Germany. The policy is this: it is natural for people sure of their ideals to persecute opposing expression. But over time, as men have seen many disputed creeds upset, they came to believe that the ultimate good is better reached by free trade in ideas. The best test of ideas' truth is their power to become accepted in the competition of the market. That experiment is the theory of our Constitution. We should be eternally vigilant against attempts to check opinions we loathe, unless they so imminently threaten immediate interference with the law's pressing purpose that immediate check is required to save the country.

Analysis:

Abrams is famous for Holmes' spirited "marketplace of ideas" dissent, which suggests that the "clear and present danger" test be applied truly, by examining the actual likelihood of danger created by the speech. Note that this is a reversal for Holmes, who wrote the majority opinions in *Schenck, Frohwerk*, and *Debs.* In contrast to the other Espionage Act cases, Holmes's application of the clear and present danger test promoted the protection of speech to the extent that a genuine immediacy of a danger or an intent to bring it about must be present. Here, Holmes concluded that despite wartime tensions, the Abrams (D) defendants' circular did not present an immediate danger. A possible cause of Holmes' instilling a genuine immediacy element into the clear and present danger test is criticism by Justice Learned Hand. Documented correspondence indicates that Hand believed the clear and present danger test to be unworkable, and that freedom of speech should not rest on guesses about the future impact of words. Instead, Hand believed the determination of punishable speech should rest on a more feasible and concrete analysis, particularly that Congress may punish speech only where the words are directly an incitement. Hand's test is exemplified in the next case.

■ CASE VOCABULARY

CONTUMELY: Insolence, contempt. [Don't see that one much on the SAT anymore.]

PLUTOCRACY: Government by the rich.

Gitlow v. New York

(*Communist Revolutionary*) v. (*State*)
268 U.S. 652, 45 S.Ct. 625 (1925)

SUPREME COURT SUPERSEDES "CLEAR AND PRESENT DANGER" TEST WITH "REASONABLENESS" STANDARD

■ **INSTANT FACTS** A communist radical, jailed for urging revolution, challenges a state law which criminalized advocating unlawful overthrow of government.

■ **BLACK LETTER RULE** State bans on advocacy of unlawful overthrow are valid exercises of police power, unless they are unreasonable.

■ PROCEDURAL BASIS
In criminal prosecution for criminal anarchy, post-conviction appeal.

■ FACTS
In 1919, Socialist Party extremists formed the radical Left Wing Section, which advocated revolution. Left Wing Section member Gitlow (D) published its newspaper, *The Revolutionary Age*, which condemned "moderate Socialism" for accepting the parliamentary state, repudiated introducing Socialism by legislative means, and advocated "Communitst Revolution," "class struggle," mass revolts and strikes, destroying the parliamentary state to found a "revolutionary dictatorship of the proletariat," etc. New York State (P) prosecuted Gitlow (D) for statutory criminal anarchy. The statute says, "Criminal anarchy is the doctrine that organized government should be overthrown by force or violence ... or ... assassination ... or by any unlawful means. The advocacy of such doctrine ... is a felony." Gitlow (D) was convicted; he now appeals, contending the statute violates the Fourteenth Amendment Due Process Clause.

■ ISSUE
Does a statute which bans advocating the overthrow of government by unlawful means violate the Fourteenth Amendment Due Process Clause?

■ DECISION AND RATIONALE
(Sanford, J.) No. State bans on advocacy of unlawful overthrow are valid exercises of police power, unless they are unreasonable. We assume the Fourteenth Amendment's Due Process Clause extends to protect against states' infringement of free speech. A State may exercise its police power to punish utterances which: threaten the public welfare, corrupt public morals, incite crime, or disturb public peace. Such a policy is needed to allow the State to preserve itself. Police statutes may be declared unconstitutional only if arbitrary or unreasonable. In determining the statute's validity, every presumpiton is to be indulged in favor of the statute's validity. It is clear that utterances inciting overthrow of government by unlawful means present sufficient danger of substantive evil that the state may punish them. The State need not prove the utterance would necessarily cause violence, and need not wait until actual disturbances are imminent. A single revolutionary spark may kindle a fire that, smoldering, may burst into sweeping conflagration. We sustain the statute here, since it was neither arbitrary nor unreasonable to prevent such incitement. Affirmed.

Gitlow v. New York (Continued)

■ **DISSENT**

(Holmes, J.) I would apply the "clear and present danger" test. Under it, I find there was no present danger of the government being overthrown by Gitlow's (D) few supporters. The principle of free speech requires allowing ideas of communist dictatorship, even if they are destined to be accepted by the majority.

Analysis:

The *Gitlow* court opted to defer to the state legislatures in not applying the clear and present danger test. A great disadvantage to the Court's decision was a lack of uniformity in the protection of U.S. citizens' freedom of speech. Circumstances surrounding an individual's speech would be viewed according to the local statute instead of one federal clear and present danger test. Thus, a speaker in New York may find less protection than a writer in California. According to the Court, only when the statute prohibits certain acts and not speech directly would the clear and present danger test apply. Procedurally, this case is the first to apply the First Amendment to state laws, by finding the Fourteenth Amendment Due Process Clause (which is applicable to states) also incorporates the First Amendment. Also, this is the first case to move away from the prior "clear and present danger" test, in favor of a "reasonableness" standard.

■ **CASE VOCABULARY**

CRIMINAL ANARCHY: Urging the overthrow of government or business by violence or other unlawful means. a.k.a. "criminal syndicalism."

CRIMINAL SYNDICALISM: Urging the overthrow of government or business by violence or other unlawful means.

FOURTEENTH AMENDMENT DUE PROCESS CLAUSE: Constitutional provision requiring that, before the government can fine, imprison, or execute a person, it must follow a fair procedure. Supreme Court case law holds that this applies to *states'* laws, so it can be used to challenge state law as unconstitutional.

POLICE POWER: States' right to regulate in the interests of public safety, health, morality, etc.

Whitney v. California
(Communist Organizer) v. (State)
274 U.S. 357, 47 S.Ct. 641 (1927)

JUSTICE BRANDEIS, CONCURRING, URGES TOLERANCE OF FREE SPEECH, EVEN AT THE RISK OF VIOLENCE

■ **INSTANT FACTS** The organizer of a revolutionary communist organization was convicted for its advocacy of revolution and crime.

■ **BLACK LETTER RULE** A state may ban joining an organization which advocates overthrow by illegal means, as long as the ban is not unreasonable.

■ PROCEDURAL BASIS
In prosecution for criminal syndicalism, post-conviction appeal.

■ FACTS
California (P) enacted a *Criminal Syndicalism Act*, which criminalized "any doctrine ... advocating ... crime, sabotage ..., unlawful violence ... or terrorism ... as a means of accomplishing a change in industrial ownership ... or political change." [Basically making it illegal to join any organization which advocates revolution.] Ms. Whitney (D) was active in organizing the radical Communist Labor Party. This Party advocated communist revolution. Apparently, some of its members also conspired to commit more immediate crimes. California (P) prosecuted Whitney (D) for criminal syndicalism. Whitney (D) defended, contending she never intended the Party to violate any law or support violence. Whitney (D) was convicted, and now appeals.

■ ISSUE
May a state criminalize joining an organization which advocates overthrow of business or government by illegal means?

■ DECISION AND RATIONALE
(Sanford, J.) Yes. A state may ban joining an organization which advocates overthrow by illegal means, as long as the ban is not unreasonable. The State, in exercising its police power, may punish utterances which threaten the public welfare, incite crime, disturb the peace, or endanger the foundation of organized government. Syndicalism laws are constitutional, unless proven arbitrary or unreasonable. In deciding, the state legislature's decision—that associations which advocate overthrow through unlawful means endanger public peace, and should be banned—deserves great weight. Every presumption is to be indulged in favor of the statute's validity. Here, *Act* essentially bans joining with others in an association which advocates unlawful methods to accomplish its ends. This is akin to conspiracy. It is reasonable for the state to find that such united action is more dangerous to public peace than isolated, individual action. We cannot find California (P) was unreasonable in adopting *Act*. Affirmed.

■ CONCURRENCE
(Brandeis, J.) Free speech is a critical, fundamental right. It should not be restricted unless (i) there is reasonable likelihood (ii) of violence serious enough to threaten the State itself, (iii) which is so

Whitney v. California (Continued)

imminent that there is no time for full discussion. The constitution's framers did not fear political change. Political order should not be maintained by coerced silence. For the sake of free speech, the state should be prepared to tolerate small risks, mild fears, and even some violence and property damage. I cannot agree with the majority's finding that assembling a political party which advocates mass action far in the future is so immediate, conspiratorial, and dangerous that it should be prohibited. But here, I would uphold Whitney's (D) conviction, because there is evidence the Party was furthering present, serious crimes.

Analysis:

Whitney's majority opinion affirms the "reasonableness" test originated in *Gitlow* and affirms the syndicalism statute's constitutionality. The case is better known for Justice Brandeis' concurrence, which advocates a return to the "clear and present danger" standard and urges extreme tolerance for free speech, even in the face of violence. Academics view Brandeis's dissent as similar to Justice Holmes' dissent in *Schenck v. United States*, a brilliantly written opinion expounding the value of free speech as essential to our democratic government. The clear and present danger test was kept alive by strong and well-drafted dissents, or in this case a concurrence, by Justices Holmes and Brandeis. In this concurrence, Justice Brandeis was essentially praising Holmes's theory of the free market of ideas as a means to combat bad and immoral ideas as opposed to fear and enforced silence. In comparison to Justice Holmes's test, Justice Brandeis clarifies what type of circumstances constitute a clear and present danger. He states that speech may be imminently dangerous if its existence poses a threat before it can be combated with opposing debate. Justice Brandeis also declares that the danger must be serious and not trivial.

■ CASE VOCABULARY

SYNDICALISM: Urging overthrow of business or government by unlawful means.

Dennis v. United States

(Communist Organizers) v. (Federal Prosecution)
341 U.S. 494, 71 S.Ct. 857 (1951)

SUPREME COURT ANALYZES INCITEMENT ACCORDING TO ITS RISK OF HARM

■ **INSTANT FACTS** American Communist Party organizers, who taught revolutionary Communist doctrine, were convicted of conspiring to overthrow the government.

■ **BLACK LETTER RULE** The Government may restrict incitements to illegality, if the potential harms' severity, discounted by their improbability, justifies the degree of restriction.

■ **PROCEDURAL BASIS**

In prosecution for conspiracy to overthrow government, post-conviction appeal.

■ **FACTS**

Under the *Smith Act* (*Act*), it is illegal... to (i) "knowingly or willfully advocate [or] abet ... the ... desirability ... of overthrowing any government in the United States by ... violence, or (ii) with intent to cause ... [such] overthrow, ... to print ... any written ... matter advocating ... the desirability ... of overthrowing ... government ... by violence, ... or affiliate with any such ... group ... knowing the purposes thereof." Also, (iii) it is "unlawful ... to attempt ... or ... conspire to commit ... any [such] acts." Several Communists (D), including Dennis (D) (collectively, "Communists" (D)), organized the Communist Party of the U.S.A. ("Party"). Neither Party nor Communists (D) directly advocated immediate violence or revolution. However, Communists (D) and Party taught from Marxist-Leninist texts, which say the proletariat should eventually seize power. The United States (P) charged Communists (D) with conspiring to violate *Act*. Communists (D) defended, apparently contending they never advocated (immediate) overthrow. Communists (D) were convicted, and now appeal, contending *Act* violates the First Amendment and Bill of Rights.

■ **ISSUE**

Is it unconstitutional to criminalize membership in a group which advocates *abstractly* the overthrow of government?

■ **DECISION AND RATIONALE**

(Vinson, J.) No. The Government may restrict incitements to illegality, if the potential harms' severity, discounted by their improbability, justifies the degree of restriction. Government may restrict speech which poses a "clear and present danger" of evils. Now, we must decide what "clear and present danger" means. In the court below, Chief Judge Learned Hand said courts "must ask whether the gravity of the evil, discounted by its improbability, justifies such invasion of free speech." We adopt this statement. This evil—overthrow by violence and terror—is sufficiently grave that the government must fight it. Holding otherwise would leave the government powerless to protect itself against anarchy. Under this standard, the government may prevent attempted revolutions, even those doomed to fail. Also, if the government is aware a revolutionary group intends to strike as soon as circumstances permit, it may stop the group immediately, without waiting until the putsch is about to be executed. There is no difference between advocating overthrow, and a conspiracy to advocate overthrow. The

Dennis v. United States (Continued)

conspiracy itself is the danger, and may be banned. Thus, *Act* is constitutionally justified. Here, there is evidence Communists (D) organized Party as a conspiracy to eventually overthrow the U.S. government. Their imprisonment is justified under the circumstances, including the inflammable nature of world conditions, similar uprisings elsewhere, and Party's ideological connections with hostile Communist nations. Convictions affirmed.

■ CONCURRENCE

(Frankfurter, J.) This case involves a conflict of interests vital to our society—the government's right to safeguard the nation via anti-conspiracy laws, versus the right to advocate political theory. These interests are best resolved by Congress, which is representative and democratically-elected. The Supreme Court can set aside Congress' decision only if it has no reasonable basis. But we should remember that venomous speech may be constitutional, but still unwise.

■ DISSENT

(Black, J.) Here, Communists (D) were charged not with attempted overthrow or any overt act, but merely for assembling to discuss and publish certain ideas at a later date. To prevent this is prior restraint, which is forbidden by the First Amendment. Even if *Act* were constitutional, Communists (D) cannot be convicted under the "clear and present danger" test, since they pose no immediate risk. While a policy of unfettered communication of ideas entails dangers, the Founders believed its benefits were worth the risk.

■ DISSENT

(Douglas, J.) Communists's (D) pathetic Party cannot be found to pose a "clear and present danger" to American government. Communists (D) did not teach techniques of terrorism and warfare. They taught only Marxist-Leninist doctrine, from texts which are not banned. I believe these texts reveal Communism's ugliness, and make it less attractive. We can take judicial notice of the fact that in the U.S., Communists are inconsequential as a political faction. They are miserable merchants of unwanted ideas, who are no longer threatening. We should not sacrifice free speech to punish non-dangerous ideas just because we find them abhorrent.

Analysis:

This case represents a reformulation of the "clear and present danger" test. As such, this opinion represents a major change in First Amendment jurisprudence. Additionally, this case is important in that it provided lower courts with a concrete definition of "clear and present danger," and an admonition that the judge, not the jury, would decide whether a clear and present danger existed. Finally, this case signaled the end of the imminency requirement set forth in *Whitney*, meaning, in this case, that the government did not have to wait until an uprising in search of overthrow of the government was imminent before acting to subvert actions, including speech. In his dissent Justice Douglas vehemently opposed the decision for this very reason—he did not see the sense in restricting speech that, in his opinion, had no possibility of action behind it.

■ CASE VOCABULARY

PUTSCH: Revolution by violence.

Brandenburg v. Ohio
(Ku Klux Klan Speechmaker) v. *(State Prosecution)*
395 U.S. 444, 89 S.Ct. 1827 (1969)

SUPREME COURT OFFERS GREATER CONSTITUTIONAL PROTECTION TO ADVOCACY OF VIOLENCE

■ **INSTANT FACTS** A KKK speechmaker, jailed for advocating revenge against the government, challenged a state anti-syndicalism statute.

■ **BLACK LETTER RULE** The government cannot criminalize advocacy of crime, except where such advocacy is (i) *intended* to incite (ii) *imminent* lawless action, and (iii) is *likely to produce* such action.

■ **PROCEDURAL BASIS**

In prosecution for criminal syndicalism, post-conviction appeal.

■ **FACTS**

Ohio's (P) *Criminal Syndicalism* statute (*Statute*) bans "advocating ... the ... propriety of crime, ... violence, or unlawful ... terrorism as a means of accomplishing industrial or political reform," and also "voluntarily assembling with any ... group ... formed to teach or advocate the doctrines of criminal syndicalism." Ku Klux Klansman Brandenburg (D) spoke at a KKK rally. At the rally, about 12 men gathered wearing hoods and carrying guns, burned a cross, and made speeches. Brandenburg (D) denounced Blacks and Jews, advocated their deportation, and apparently called for "revengeance" [against the government, for not upholding white supremacy]. Brandenburg (D) was prosecuted for syndicalism. (As evidence, Ohio (P) introduced film of the rally, taken by a TV reporter Brandenburg (D) had invited.) Brandenburg (D) was convicted, and sentenced to 1–10 years' imprisonment. Brandenburg (D) appeals, contending *Statute* violates the First Amendment by punishing abstract teachings which do not urge immediate illegality.

■ **ISSUE**

May the government ban advocacy of illegality?

■ **DECISION AND RATIONALE**

(Per Curiam) No. The government cannot criminalize advocacy of crime, except where such advocacy is (i) *intended* to incite (ii) *imminent* lawless action, and (iii) is *likely to produce* such action. 22 states adopted criminal syndicalism laws in 1917–1920. The Supreme Court sustained the constitutionality of California's, which resembles Ohio's (P). *Whitney*. But later decisions discredited *Whitney*. *See Dennis*. Our later decisions fashioned the principle that the First Amendment does not permit the State to forbid advocacy of using force or crime, except where such advocacy is (i) *intended* to incite (ii) *imminent* lawless action, and (iii) is *likely to produce* such action. Previously, we held, "mere abstract teaching ... of the moral propriety ... or even ... necessity for ... violence, is not the same as preparing a group for violent action, and steeling it ...." Thus, any statute which fails to draw a distinction between (punishable) incitement to imminent lawlessness and (protected) abstract advocacy would violate the First Amendment and Fourteenth Amendment [Due Process Clause]. Here, *Statute* draws no such

Brandenburg v. Ohio (Continued)

distinction, because it punishes mere advocacy, and assembly for the purpose of advocacy. Conviction reversed; statute void.

Analysis:

Since its publication, *Brandenburg* has been interpreted as requiring three elements in order for speech advocating criminal conduct to be suppressed: (1) Express advocacy of law violation; (2) Advocacy that calls for immediate violation of the law, and (3) The immediate violation of the law must be likely to occur. This is a change from the prior law under *Dennis*, in that an immediacy and imminency requirement is re-read into the law. Thus, the focus is placed on the likelihood that the words will produce immediate lawless action. This case also changes First Amendment law in that it expressly overrules *Whitney* and does not apply, or even mention, the "clear and present danger" test that Justices Black and Douglas obviously despised so much. Finally, this case makes a clear distinction between teaching or advocating the use of force to overthrow the government, and inciting or producing imminent lawless action. The Court made clear that statutes that do not make the distinction are unconstitutional, and as the majority opinion points out, approximately twenty states, at the time the opinion was handed down, had nonconforming statutes.

■ CASE VOCABULARY

PER CURIAM: [Judicial opinion] written by the court as a whole, without identifying any individual judge as the author.

Chaplinsky v. New Hampshire
(*Insulting Speaker*) v. (*State Prosecution*)
315 U.S. 568, 62 S.Ct. 766 (1942)

"FIGHTING WORDS" ARE UNPROTECTED BY FIRST AMENDMENT

■ **INSTANT FACTS** A provocative preacher was arrested for provoking a policeman with insults.

■ **BLACK LETTER RULE** The First Amendment does not protect "fighting words" which inflict emotional distress or tend to incite listeners to retaliatory violence.

■ **PROCEDURAL BASIS**

In prosecution under "fighting words" statute, post-conviction appeal challenging statute's constitutionality.

■ **FACTS**

New Hampshire's (P) public laws ban provocative taunts: "No person shall address any offensive, derisive or annoying word to any other person who is lawfully in any ... public place, nor call him by any offensive ... name, nor make any noise ... in his presence ... with intent to ... offend ... him, or to prevent him from pursuing his ... occupation." New Hampshire's (P) courts interpret this law as forbidding only face-to-face words which "have a direct tendency to cause ... violence by" hearers, and find the statute's purpose was to prevent retaliatory violence. Jehovah's Witness Chaplinsky (D) preached and distributed literature on a street in Rochester, NH, denouncing religion as a "racket." This angered bystanders, and apparently caused an incident. Policemen, including Police Marshal Bowering (P), led Chaplinsky (D) away, intending to arrest him. Chaplinsky (D) insulted the Marshal (P), saying, "You are a God damned racketeer" and "a damned Fascist and the whole government of Rochester are Fascists or agents of Fascists." Chaplinsky (D) was charged with violating the statute cited above, and convicted. Chaplinsky (D) appeals, contending the statute violates the First/Fourteenth Amendment, facially and as applied.

■ **ISSUE**

Does a statute punishing "fighting words" violate the First/Fourteenth Amendment?

■ **DECISION AND RATIONALE**

(Judge Not Stated) No. The First Amendment does not protect "fighting words" which inflict emotional distress or tend to incite listeners to retaliatory violence. Even under the broadest interpretation of the First/Fourteenth Amendment, it is understood the right to free speech is not absolute under all circumstances. There are certain narrowly-defined classes of speech which may be prohibited and punished without Constitutional problem. These include obscenity, profanity, and libel. Also unprotected are "fighting words"—those which, by their utterance, inflict [emotional] injury or tend to incite immediate breach of the peace. It is understood that such utterances are not essential to any exposition of ideas, and are of such slight social value as a step to truth that any benefit is clearly outweighed by the social interest in maintaining order and morality. Here, the statute is constitutional. It is applied narrowly, to include only face-to-face utterance of "classical fighting words," newer words equally likely

Chaplinsky v. New Hampshire (Continued)

to cause violence, and other disorderly words, including profanity, obscenity, and threats. This application is also constitutional. It is not necessary to prove Chaplinsky's (D) words were likely to provoke average persons to retaliate, thus breaching the peace. Conviction affirmed.

Analysis:

Chaplinsky is important for two major reasons. The first is as the seminal case establishing the "fighting words" doctrine. The case is also heavily cited for the proposition that some speech is unprotected by the Constitution and for its listing of classes of unprotected speech. But note that the doctrine has evolved even though *Chaplinsky* was never expressly overruled. In this case, fighting words were defined as taunts that provoke violence, as well as insults that inflict emotional distress. Today, the latter insults are protected from prosecution, as long as they fall short of defamation or the "extreme and outrageous" standard of tortious emotional distress. In other cases, the Court often overruled "fighting words" bans by finding them vague/overbroad, or declaring anti-hate-speech laws to be unconstitutionally content-based.

■ CASE VOCABULARY

"FIGHTING WORDS": Words likely to provoke hearers into retaliatory violence.

OBSCENITY: Basically, depictions of sex in a way which disgusts the average person.

Gooding v. Wilson
(*State Official*) v. (*Cursing Demonstrator*)
405 U.S. 518, 92 S.Ct. 1103 (1972)

GOVERNMENT CANNOT PROHIBIT "ABUSIVE" LANGUAGE, EXCEPT FOR "FIGHTING WORDS"

■ **INSTANT FACTS** A demonstrator, charged with using "abusive" language for cursing at arresting officers, challenges the statute as vague/overbroad.

■ **BLACK LETTER RULE** Speech restrictions are unconstitutionally overbroad if they are susceptible of application to protected speech, either (a) on their face or (b) as authoritatively construed by courts.

■ **PROCEDURAL BASIS**

In prosecution for using "opprobrious words" and "abusive language," appeal from appellate reversal of conviction.

■ **FACTS**

Georgia's (P) *Code § 26-6303* prohibits using abusive language: "Any person who shall, without provocation, use to ... another, and in his presence ... opprobrious words or abusive language, tending to cause a breach of the peace ... shall be guilty of a misdemeanor." [At an anti-war protest which was broken up by police, demonstrator] Wilson (D) said to two officers, "White son of a bitch, I'll kill you.... You son of a bitch, I'll choke you to death.... You son of a bitch, if you ever put your hands on me again, I'll cut you all to pieces." Wilson (D) was arrested and charged with violating *§ 26-6303*. Wilson (D) defended, apparently contending *§ 26-6303* is unconstitutionally vague and overbroad because it *could* be interpreted to apply to protected speech. [Remember, a constitutional "vagueness"/"overbreadth" challenge to a statute need allege only that the statute, on its face, *could* be applied to curtail Constitutionally-protected rights. It need not allege the statute actually was applied incorrectly in this instance.] Court held for Wilson (D). Georgia (P) appeals, contending *§ 26-6303* is narrowly-drawn on its face, and also has been interpreted by state courts to apply only to unprotected "fighting words."

■ **ISSUE**

May a statute punish "opprobrious words and abusive language ... tending to cause a breach of the peace?"

■ **DECISION AND RATIONALE**

(Brennan, J.) No. Speech restrictions are unconstitutionally overbroad if they are susceptible of application to protected speech, either (a) on their face or (b) as authoritatively construed by courts. *§ 26-6303* punished only spoken words. Therefore, it can survive facial constitutional challenge only if it, as construed authoritatively by Georgia's (P) courts, is not susceptible of application to speech which is protected by the First/Fourteenth Amendment. If the statute is itself is on its face narrowly-drawn and constitutional, but is interpreted by state courts to infringe on protected speech, then the statute must be found unconstitutional. Here, *§ 26-6303* could be applied to punish more than unprotected "fighting words." The dictionary defines "opprobrious" as "intended to convey disgrace," and "abusive" as

Gooding v. Wilson (Continued)

including "harsh insulting language." Also, Georgia's (P) courts have construed § 26–6303 to apply to utterances which are not "fighting words." Thus, § 26–6303 has potential to be applied overbroadly. § 26–6303 is distinguishable from *Chaplinsky*'s "fighting words" statute, which passed constitutional muster because it was narrowly limited to "fighting words," and construed similarly by New Hampshire's courts. Conviction reversal affirmed; statute void.

■ DISSENT

(Burger, J.) I join Blackmun's dissent fully. The majority opinion is bizarre, because it inexplicably finds a statute unconstitutional, not based on its facial wording, but based on the way state courts have applied it in a few isolated cases. There is no evidence demonstrating § 26–6303 has significance potential for sweeping application to suppress important protected speech.

■ DISSENT

(Blackmun, J.) *§ 26–6303* is not vague. It punishes abusive language clearly, and Wilson (D) had full notice his language was punishable as abusive.

Analysis:

This case illustrates one tactic used by the Court after *Chaplinsky* to limit "fighting words" prohibitions— the Court finds such bans vague and/or overbroad. The First Amendment overbreadth doctrine tests the constitutionality of legislation in terms of its *potential* applications. Additionally, since the Court can invalidate a statute for overbreadth without explaining precisely how the statute should have been drafted to pass constitutional muster, it leaves legislatures with no guidance on how to avoid the Court's objections in the future. Basically, this case means statutes cannot criminalize angry, abusive, vulgar speech, unless it is likely to provoke imminent retaliation. Blackmun, dissenting, reaches his conclusion by addressing the vagueness issue, but ignoring the more pressing claim of overbreadth.

■ CASE VOCABULARY

OPPROBRIOUS: "intended to convey disgrace;" abusive; derogatory.

R.A.V. v. City of St. Paul, Minnesota

(*Cross-Burning Teen*) v. (*City Government*)
505 U.S. 377, 112 S.Ct. 2538 (1992)

GOVERNMENT MAY NOT BAN HATE-BASED SPEECH

■ **INSTANT FACTS** A teen charged with burning a cross in a black neighbor's yard challenges the constitutionality of a statute banning bias-motivated speech.

■ **BLACK LETTER RULE** Government may not regulate speech, including "fighting words," based on its hostility or favoritism towards the message expressed.

■ **PROCEDURAL BASIS**

In prosecution for disorderly conduct, appeal from appellate judgement declaring statute constitutional.

■ **FACTS**

Under St. Paul, Minnesota's (P) *Bias-Motivated Crime Ordinance,* "Whoever places on public or private property a symbol ..., including ... a burning cross or ... swastika, which one knows or has reasonable grounds to know arouses anger, alarm or resentment in others on the basis of race, color, creed, religion or gender commits [misdemeanor] disorderly conduct." R.A.V., a teen, burned a cross in a black family's yard, and was prosecuted under the *Ordinance.* R.A.V. (D) moved to dismiss, contending the *Ordinance* was unconstitutionally overbroad and facially content-based. The trial court dismissed. St. Paul (P) appealed. On appeal, the Minnesota Supreme Court reversed, finding (i) the *Ordinance* is not overbroad, because Minnesota courts construe it as limited to "fighting words," and (ii) the *Ordinance* is justified as a narrowly-tailored means of accomplishing the compelling governmental interest in protecting against bias threats. R.A.V. (D) appeals.

■ **ISSUE**

May the government ban speech motivated by bias?

■ **DECISION AND RATIONALE**

(Scalia, J.) No. Government may not regulate speech, including "fighting words," based on its hostility or favoritism towards the message expressed. In construing the *Ordinance*, we are bound to accept the Minnesota Supreme Court's authoritative interpretation: that the *Ordinance* reaches only "fighting words," as defined in *Chaplinsky.* Under the First Amendment, content-based regulations are presumed invalid. However, we permit restrictions on speech content in a few limited areas, which are "of such slight social value [in reaching] truth that any benefit ... is clearly outweighed by the social interest in order." Our cases mean such low-value speech (e.g., obscenity, defamation, "fighting words") can be regulated [*to limit their harm*]. But this does not mean they are entirely unprotected by the First Amendment. Even low-value speech, like "fighting words," cannot be made vehicles for content discrimination, which is unrelated to their proscribable harm (i.e., violence). While "fighting words" constitute "no *essential* part of any exposition of ideas," they retain some expressive content, which merits constitutional protection. Thus, while "fighting words" may be proscribed on the basis of their violent effects, they cannot be proscribed based on the government's hostility or favoritism towards their message. Thus, it is permissible to ban all "fighting words" as a class based on their effects, because

R.A.V. v. City of St. Paul, Minnesota (Continued)

this does not risk governmental viewpoint discrimination. Or, the government may impose content-based restrictions where such content is associated with secondary effects. *Renton v. Playtime Theatres* [government may zone porn purveyors because of porn's effects on neighborhood]. Or, government may regulate against certain *conduct*, even if this incidentally burdens speech. (For example, anti-treason laws may interfere with telling national secrets to enemies.) There may be other bases as well. Indeed, when regulating totally-proscribable speech, it may not even be necessary to identify any specific (neutral) basis, as long as the content discrimination presents no realistic possibility of official suppression of ideas. Here, we find the *Ordinance* is facially unconstitutional, even as (narrowly) construed. It targets only those "fighting words" that insult, or provoke violence, on the basis of race, color, etc. But it allows "fighting words" which use other bases. Also, the *Ordinance's* practical operation entails actual viewpoint discrimination, since it would allow those arguing in favor of racial tolerance to use "fighting words," but not allows racists to use similar words. (Pro-tolerance speakers could say, "All anti-Catholic bigots are bastards," but the bigots could not respond that, "All papists are.") [A blow to bigoted tolerance advocates everywhere.] This has the effect of allowing one side to use all tactics, while restricting the other side. We believe that burning crosses in others' yards is reprehensible. But St. Paul (P) should use other means to prevent such behavior, without adding the First Amendment to the fire. We need not consider whether *Ordinance* is also overbroad. Reversed; statute void.

■ CONCURRENCE

(White, J.) I agree the *Ordinance* is unconstitutional. But this result should be reached under existing caselaw, by finding the *Ordinance* fatally overbroad. Here, the majority departs from our prior cases, by denying we had held that some speech is unprotected categorically because it is deemed near-worthless. Also, this case fails to apply strict scrutiny, as required by precedent.

■ CONCURRENCE

(Blackmun, J.) I concur in the judgement, because I find the *Ordinance* reaches beyond "fighting words." But I disagree with the majority's decision that a State cannot regulate harmful speech unless it also regulates harmless speech. If this case is followed, then all expression will have to be given the same protection. I believe that protection will inevitably be low for all speech, since this Court will never provide child pornography or cigarette advertising with the same protection customarily granted to political speech. If this case is not followed, it will stand as a manipulation of doctrine to decide issues of "political correctness," which are not before it. I see no values compromised by laws prohibiting hoodlums from driving minorities out of their homes.

Analysis:

R.A.V. is a very significant doctrinal development for "fighting words" laws. After *R.A.V.*, such laws will be valid only if they do not draw content-based distinctions. Effectively, this means all anti-bias speech laws are void. But it also effectively threatens all fighting words laws, since a law banning all conceivable fighting words is likely to be so vague or overbroad that it is void on those grounds. Also, note the majority's controversial position that even unprotected speech cannot be subject to content-based regulation. Traditionally, fighting words were considered unprotected by the First Amendment. However, Justice Scalia's opinion asserts that even when the government seeks to regulate a traditionally unprotected category of speech, it may not do so in a content-based manner. Thus, the law of fighting words was changed in this case. The decision also holds that even when government is regulating a previously unprotected category of speech, it may not do so in a manner based on content.

■ CASE VOCABULARY

AD LIBITUM: At will; at pleasure.

CONTENT DISCRIMINATION: Speech regulation which depends on the speech's subject matter, effectively banning all expression on a specific issue (both pro or con).

INVECTIVE: Angry abuse.

MARQUIS OF QUEENSBERRY RULES: "Gentlemanly" rules of fistfighting, developed by this [oft-trounced] Marquis. They were so restrictive that no one using them could win the fight against someone who did not.

VIEWPOINT DISCRIMINATION: Speech regulation which varies depending on the viewpoint advocated (i.e., regulating pro differently from con).

Feiner v. New York

(Public Speaker) v. (State)
340 U.S. 315, 71 S.Ct. 303 (1951)

WHEN SPEECH ENGENDERS HOSTILE AUDIENCE REACTION, IT MAY BE STOPPED IF IT CREATES "CLEAR AND PRESENT DANGER"

■ **INSTANT FACTS** A political speaker who stirred a crowd to threats and shoving was arrested for disorderly conduct.

■ **BLACK LETTER RULE** When a public speaker incites the audience to imminent riot, police may stop his speech.

■ **PROCEDURAL BASIS**

In prosecution for disorderly conduct, appeal from appellate affirmation of conviction.

■ **FACTS**

Feiner (D) stood on a street and made a political speech to a crowd of 75 whites and blacks. In the course of speaking, Feiner (D) derogated politicians, including Truman, Syracuse's mayor, the American Legion, etc. Apparently, Feiner (D) also urged blacks to rise up in arms against whites to fight for equal rights. Within the crowd, some threatened Feiner (D), while others supported him. There was shoving, muttering, threats, and restlessness. New York's (P) police arrived. At first, they tolerated Feiner's (D) speech, and only tried to keep the crowd from blocking traffic. Later, the police, fearing riot, asked Feiner (D) to stop talking, twice. Feiner (D) refused. Finally, the police arrested Feiner (D), and charged him with disorderly conduct. After trial, Feiner (D) was convicted, on a finding his speech created imminent danger of disorder. Feiner (D) appealed, but lost. Feiner (D) appeals again.

■ **ISSUE**

May police punish a public speaker whose speech causes audience unrest?

■ **DECISION AND RATIONALE**

(Vinson, J.) Yes. When a public speaker incites the audience to imminent riot, police may stop his speech. Normally, a hostile audience's objections cannot be allowed to silence speakers. Nor can police have complete discretion to disperse otherwise-lawful public speeches, since this would make police an instrument for suppressing unpopular views. But when speakers go beyond persuasion, and undertake to incite riot, police may prevent imminent breach of the peace. We affirm the lower courts' findings that Feiner's (D) speech and circumstances created imminent danger of disorder. Conviction affirmed.

■ **DISSENT**

(Black, J.) Here, the facts do not show Feiner's (D) speech involved any imminent danger of disorder. It is not unusual that controversial speeches should cause the audience to mutter, shove, threaten the speaker, and disagree, even violently. Also, before police can interfere with lawful public speech for breaching the peace, they must make all reasonable efforts to protect him and his constitutional right to

Feiner v. New York (Continued)

speak. I believe the majority's contrary holding effectively allows the state and police to censor speech with impunity. Also, I believe Feiner (D) was imprisoned for his views' unpopularity.

Analysis:

This case is important in that it raises the issue of the hostility of the audience, and holds that, in some situations, the possibility of a hostile response by an audience can justify a suppression of speech (so long as the suppression is unrelated to the ideas inherent in the message). The decision of the majority in this case was a very fact-driven decision. Not all cases in which there is a possibly hostile audience will end up with a similar result. In fact, in subsequent cases, *Feiner* has been distinguished on its facts, and the court has not held that in every instance of a street demonstration, suppression of the speech is permissible. Overall, subsequent cases have shown that when it is clear that police can handle the crowd without suppressing speech, any suppression is a violation of the First Amendment.

Beauharnais v. Illinois

(Racist Pamphleteer) v. (State)
343 U.S. 250, 72 S.Ct. 725 (1952)

RACIST SPEECH MAY BE PUNISHED AS "GROUP LIBEL"

■ **INSTANT FACTS** A segregationalist was convicted for distributing leaflets libeling blacks.

■ **BLACK LETTER RULE** The government may punish racist speech as group libel, if such punishment is rationally related to preserving peace.

■ **PROCEDURAL BASIS**

In prosecution for criminal libel, appeal from affirmation of conviction.

■ **FACTS**

The *Illinois Criminal Code* provides, "It shall be unlawful ... to ... exhibit in any public place ... any ... picture [or] drama which portrays depravity, criminality, unchastity, or lack of virtue of a class of citizens, of any race, color, creed or religion which ... exposes [them] to contempt, derision, or obloquy or which is productive of breach of the peace." White supremacist Beauharnais (D), president of a segregationist group, distributed anti-black leaflets. Beauharnais's (D) leaflets called for Chicago politicians "to halt the further encroachment, harassment and invasion of white people, their property, neighborhoods and persons, by the Negro," urged "one million self respecting white people in Chicago to unite," and added, "if persuasion and the need to prevent the white race from becoming mongrelized by the negro will not unite us, then the aggressions, ... rapes, robberies, knives, guns and marijuana of the negro, surely will," etc. Beauharnais (D) was convicted of violating the *Code*. Beauharnais (D) appeals, challenging the *Code's* constitutionality as vague and overbroad, and alleging his pamphlets created no "clear and present danger."

■ **ISSUE**

May a state criminalize group libel?

■ **DECISION AND RATIONALE**

(Frankfurter, J.) Yes. The government may punish racist speech as group libel, if such punishment is rationally related to preserving peace. The state's power to punish criminal libel has always been recognized. If the state can punish libel of individuals, it cannot be denied the right to also punish similar libel of defined groups, unless this punishment is purposeless or unrelated to maintaining the peace. Here, we find Illinois (P) was reasonable in restricting malicious defamation calculated to provoke, especially considering Illinois' (P) history of racial violence. We find *Code*, as construed by Illinois' (P) courts, is neither vague nor overbroad. It is unnecessary to consider whether the "clear and present danger" standard was met, since libel is not constitutionally protected. Conviction affirmed.

■ **DISSENT**

(Black, J.) The majority degrades the First Amendment's protections to the "rational basis" level. Also, the majority overstates the historic permissibility of libel statutes. Effectively, by banning "libel" of huge

Beauharnais v. Illinois (Continued)

groups, the state discourages people from saying anything critical of those groups. I reject this notion that government can punish people for having their say about public concerns.

Analysis:

Beauharnais espouses a very strong right to regulate hate speech. While this case was never overruled, later cases signal the Court's retreat from its holding. Defamation liability was later held to be limited by the First Amendment in *New York Times v. Sullivan.* Also, *R.A.V.* suggests hate speech enjoys some constitutional protection. Further, the provision in this case would today likely be voided for vagueness and overbreadth.

■ CASE VOCABULARY

CRIMINAL LIBEL: Written defamation which is criminalized, usually because it incites treason or disorder.

GROUP LIBEL: Libel of an entire class (e.g., race, religion, nationality), rather than an individual.

INFORMATION: Indictment.

OBLOQUY: Disgrace.

STAR CHAMBER: Special court created by King Charles to persecute his enemies through unfair trials. Today, "Star Chamber" refers to any court biased for the state.

Virginia v. Black
(*Prosecuting Authority*) v. (*Ku Klux Klan Member*)
538 U.S. 343, 123 S.Ct. 1536 (2003)

A STATUTE ESTABLISHING INTENT TO INTIMIDATE FROM THE ACT OF BURNING A CROSS VIOLATES THE FIRST AMENDMENT

■ **INSTANT FACTS** Three defendants were convicted of cross burning with intent to intimidate another person or group of persons and they appealed.

■ **BLACK LETTER RULE** A state statute banning cross burning with the intent to intimidate another person is not in itself an unconstitutional infringement on free expression, but the establishment of criminal intent from the prohibited act itself violates the First Amendment.

■ PROCEDURAL BASIS
Certiorari to review a decision of the Virginia Supreme Court.

■ FACTS
Three defendants, including Black (D), were separately convicted under a Virginia statute prohibiting the burning of a cross in public or on another's property "with the intent of intimidating any person or group of persons." The statute provides that the act of cross burning itself constitutes prime facie evidence of an intent to intimidate. Black (D) was convicted of burning a cross as part of a Ku Klux Klan rally on another's property, with his consent. At his trial, the jury was instructed that Black's (D) motivations demonstrated his intent. The jury was further instructed that it may infer Black's (D) intent from the act of burning. In a separate trial, two other defendants, who were not Klan members, were convicted under the statute of burning a cross in a black neighbor's yard as retaliation for complaints of gunshots near the home. The jury was instructed in that trial that guilt could be supported by evidence that "the defendant did a direct act toward the commission of the cross burning" with "the intent of intimidating any person or group of persons." After one defendant pleaded guilty, the other was convicted of attempted cross burning. The three cases were consolidated to challenge the constitutionality of the cross-burning statute. The Virginia Supreme Court declared the statute unconstitutional on its face because it discriminated against expression on the basis of content and allowed an inference of intent based on the commission of the act.

■ ISSUE
May a state criminally ban cross burning with the intent to intimidate a person or group of persons without violating the First Amendment?

■ DECISION AND RATIONALE
(O'Connor, J.) Yes. While the First Amendment protects the right of free expression, it does not prevent a state from punishing content of slight social value that is outweighed by the social interest in order and morality, such as a "true threat." Statements made "to communicate a serious expression of an intent to commit an act of unlawful violence to a particular individual or group of individuals" are not protected, even if the speaker never intends to carry out the violence. While cross burning has not always been used for the purpose of intimidation, the Ku Klux Klan's practice of cross burning as a

Virginia v. Black (Continued)

symbol of white supremacy and minority hatred has created a sense of fear of violence in targeted victims. The Klan uses the burning cross to symbolically communicate its message, which historically has involved violence and the threat of violence against others. While the Klan may have a targeted class of victims, however, the statute does not. The statute does not penalize expressions of intimidation motivated only by racial or religious animosity, but targets intimidation of any kind. It does not regulate the content of a particular expression differently than that of another. "The First Amendment permits Virginia to outlaw cross burning done with the intent to intimidate because burning a cross is a particularly virulent form of intimidation."

While the Constitution permits a state cross-burning statute, the Virginia statute is unconstitutional on its face because it allows for prima facie evidence of intent based on the commission of the act, which strips away the very reasons the First Amendment permits such a statute. A burning cross does not always indicate the intent to intimidate. It may represent other expressions of the actor's views. The prima facie evidence provision necessarily convicts a defendant who burns a cross. Because freedom of expression is important, and the statute makes no distinction between expression with and without social value, the statute is unconstitutional on its face. Affirmed in part, vacated in part and remanded.

■ CONCURRENCE IN PART

(Souter, J.) Under *R.A.V. v. St. Paul*, the government may not prohibit the use of symbols that are provocative "on the basis of race, color, creed, religion or gender." An exception was created for those government regulations involving content that "consist[] entirely of the very reason the entire class of speech at issue is proscribable." The Court uses this exception to justify the Virginia statute's constitutionality. The exception, however, does not apply to the cross-burning statute. First, while cross burning may have been legislatively targeted because of its special power to threaten, it may also have been targeted because of legislative disapproval of the white supremacy doctrine. Also, the cross-burning statute is not like laws prohibiting threats to the President. Threats against the President are prohibited regardless of the message, focusing instead on the special risks and costs associated with the victim. The cross-burning statute, however, suppresses not only intended intimidation, but also the message of white supremacy, even when such a message was unintended by the burner. The prima facie evidence provision threatens any finding of a high probability that valid expression is suppressed by diverting the jury's attention away from evidence of intent and allowing deliberation to be consumed by ideological discussion of the Klan's message, not the defendant's.

■ DISSENT

(Thomas, J.) Cross burning "almost invariably" means lawlessness and the threat of physical violence. For those not easily intimidated by the threat of violence, the Klan historically and systematically resorted to physical violence to serve its purposes. Those who enacted the statute clearly understood the distinction between terrorist threats and racial expression, for the statute does not target all racist expression, but rather merely the conduct of cross burning directly associated with threats of violence. Because the statute does not prohibit racist expression, the First Amendment is not implicated. Even under a First Amendment analysis, however, the permissible inference of intent does not present a constitutional problem. The inference is rebuttable and the "innocent cross-burner" has the opportunity to demonstrate his intentions to the jury. Moreover, the jury must still find the existence of each element of the offense beyond a reasonable doubt to support a conviction.

Analysis:

If the state's objective in enacting the cross burning statute was the protection of others from the threat of violence, there appear to be alternatives that are less intrusive on the First Amendment. Simple trespass statutes, for example, may criminalize the conduct of persons who enter another's property, regardless of the content of their message while there. But Black (D) was punished for burning a cross on another's property with the landowner's *consent*. The landowner was not the target of a threat of violence, yet the statute permissibly punishes Black (D) nonetheless.

■ CASE VOCABULARY

PRIMA FACIE EVIDENCE: Evidence that will establish a fact or sustain a judgment unless contradictory evidence is produced.

Roth v. United States

(Pornography Mailer) v. (Federal Prosecution)
354 U.S. 476, 77 S.Ct. 1304 (1957)

"OBSCENITY" IS NOT PROTECTED BY THE FIRST AMENDMENT

■ **INSTANT FACTS** A pornographer challenged a federal statute banning mailing "obscene" materials.

■ **BLACK LETTER RULE** Government may regulate "obscene" speech without implicating the First Amendment.

■ **PROCEDURAL BASIS**

In federal prosecution for criminal obscenity, post-conviction appeal.

■ **FACTS**

A federal obscenity statute prohibits mailing of "Every obscene, lewd, lascivious, or filthy ... picture, writing, ... or other publication of an indecent character." [Roth (D), a pornographic bookseller, was charged when he mailed a pornographic book and advertisement.] At trial, the court instructed the jury that the statutory word "obscene" means "immorality which has relation to sexual impurity and has a tendency to excite lustful thoughts." Roth (D) was convicted. Roth (D) appeals, contending the statutory definition of "obscenity" is vague and overbroad.

■ **ISSUE**

May the government ban mailing of "obscene" materials?

■ **DECISION AND RATIONALE**

(Brennan, J.) Yes. Government may regulate "obscene" speech without implicating the First Amendment. This is the first time this Court is faced with the question of whether obscenity is covered by the First or Fourteenth Amendment. But prior opinions' dicta indicates this Court always assumed obscenity is not protected by free speech ideas. The First Amendment's drafters did not intend it to protect obscenity, since at the time it was drafted, most states punished obscenity. The First Amendment was intended to protect ideas which have even the slightest redeeming social importance. But we recognize that obscenity is utterly without redeeming social importance. This view is supported by many local and foreign legislatures. However, "obscenity" is not synonymous with sex. "Obscene" material is that which deals with sex in a manner appealing to prurient interest. But sex portrayed in artistic, literary, or scientific works is protected, because sex is a matter of human interest and public concern. We recognize that obscenity statutes' terms are imprecise. But we hold such imprecision does not violate due process. We find such statutes are not overbroad or vague. Conviction affirmed.

■ **DISSENT**

(Douglas, J.) The majority's definition of obscenity turns on the effect a book instills in readers' minds, not for any overt acts or harmful conduct. This vague standard permits unfettered censorship, in violation of First Amendment principles.

Roth v. United States (Continued)

Analysis:

This case is significant in that it was the first time the Supreme Court directly encountered the constitutionality of obscenity under the First Amendment. In making its ruling, the Court narrowed the test for obscenity, rejecting the prior standard that defined obscenity as anything that would raise prurient desires in the most susceptible person. Because the Court felt that material which dealt with sex in a legitimate, non-prurient way should be protected, the court adopted a different, less-restrictive standard that looked to the effect that the material would have not on a susceptible person, but on the average person holding contemporary community standards. Thus, the test became a more objective one. The Court held that if a reasonable person found that the material created prurient desires, then the government could constitutionally ban it.

■ **CASE VOCABULARY**

OBSCENITY: Sexually-oriented expression which appeals to prurient interests.

PRURIENT: Exciting lustful desires.

Paris Adult Theatre v. Slaton

(*Pornographic Theatre*) v. (*Civil Complainant and State*)
413 U.S. 49, 93 S.Ct. 2628 (1973)

STATES CAN RESTRICT ADULTS' VIEWING OF OBSCENITY, TO PRESERVE MORALITY

■ **INSTANT FACTS** An adults-only pornographic theater challenged a state's restrictions on obscenity.

■ **BLACK LETTER RULE** States may restrict commercial obscenity, even that viewed by consenting adults, to further legitimate interests in maintaining order and morality.

■ **PROCEDURAL BASIS**

In civil complaint for obscenity seeking injunction, appeal from appellate reversal of the Ordinance for defendant.

■ **FACTS**

Georgia's (P) *Code* bans or restricts obscene movies. Paris Adult Theatre ("Theater") (D) showed pornographic films. It restricted access to adults only, posting this sign: "Adult Theatre—You must be 21 and able to prove it. If viewing the nude body offends you, Please Do Not Enter." Apparently, a citizen named Slaton (P) filed a civil complaint charging the Theatre (D) violated the *Code*; this complaint was prosecuted by Georgia's (P) district attorney and solicitor. [The civil complaint was punishable by injunction against showing obscene pictures.] The Theatre (D) challenged the *Code*'s constitutionality, alleging the state cannot restrict obscenity viewed only by consenting adults, because this violates their right to privacy. At trial, the court held for the Theatre (D). Georgia (P) appealed. On appeal, the court reversed, holding obscenity is totally unprotected. Theatre (D) appeals.

■ **ISSUE**

Does a ban on exhibiting obscenity to consenting adults violate their constitutional right to privacy?

■ **DECISION AND RATIONALE**

(Burger, C.J.) No. States may restrict commercial obscenity, even that viewed by consenting adults, to further legitimate interests in maintaining order and morality. This Court has consistently held obscene material unprotected by the First Amendment. *Roth*. This is true even when it is exhibited only to consenting adults. While most cases usually involve regulation to prevent exposure to juveniles and unconsenting adults, these are not the only legitimate reasons for restricting obscenity. Other legitimate interests which justify state regulation of commercial obscenity include maintaining the quality of life, preserving the community environment, setting the tone of commerce, preserving public safety, and maintaining decency. Arguably, there is a correlation between obscenity and crime. Commercial obscenity is unprotected by any constitutional doctrine of privacy. Affirmed.

■ **DISSENT**

(Brennan, J.) *Roth*'s denial of protection to obscenity, affirmed here, infringes on the First Amendment. This Court's decisions have not articulated a clear way to distinguish (unprotected) "obscenity" from sexually-oriented but protected speech. Thus, people who distribute sexually-oriented materials lack fair

Paris Adult Theatre v. Slaton (Continued)

notice of whether their product will be found "obscene." I do not believe there is any standard which can reduce such vagueness without violating the First Amendment, so I would protect all sex speech. The effort to suppress obscenity is predicated on unprovable assumptions about sex, behavior, morality, and religion.

■ DISSENT

(Douglas, J.) I always felt obscenity should be protected by the First Amendment. What constitutes "obscenity" is a matter of individual taste. Under the First Amendment, judges should not be censors.

Analysis:

One important aspect of this decision is the Court's refusal to grant an unlimited exception under the First Amendment to displays of material for consenting adults only. *Paris* is also significant in that the Court sets forth a number of state interests that justify restrictions or bans on the sale or display of obscene material to consenting adults. These interests include: limiting crime, which the Court stated can be linked to obscenity; maintaining a high quality of life in the community, including regulating the tone of commerce in city centers; and maintaining a high moral tone of the society. In sum, the decision seems to say that states can ban obscenity based on the secondary effects that the obscenity will have on the community, and provides a roadmap to states and communities for drafting anti-obscenity regulations. Banning obscenity based on secondary effects was, at the time of this decision, a relatively new idea, and in so holding the Court changed the law of obscenity significantly.

■ CASE VOCABULARY

SOLICITOR: Representative; agent. Here, the Georgia solicitor is apparently the official who acts on private *civil* complaints, bringing suit on behalf of the state.

Miller v. California

(Mail-Order Pornographer) v. (State Prosecution)
413 U.S. 15, 93 S.Ct. 2607 (1973)

SUPREME COURT ARTICULATES MODERN DEFINITION OF "OBSCENITY"

■ **INSTANT FACTS** A mail-order bookseller challenged his obscenity conviction for mailing unsolicited pornographic ads.

■ **BLACK LETTER RULE** The government may regulate "obscene" material which (i) depicts or describes sexual conduct, (ii) which conduct is defined specifically by state law, (iii) would be found to appeal to the "prurient interest" by "the average person, applying contemporary community standards," (iv) portrays sexual conduct in a "patently offensive" way, and (v) has no serious literary, artistic, political, or scientific value.

■ **PROCEDURAL BASIS**

In prosecution for obscenity, post-conviction appeal.

■ **FACTS**

California (P) *Penal Code* bans knowingly distributing obscene matter. Mail order pornographer Miller (D) was convicted for mailing unsolicited ads for pornographic books. Miller (D) appeals, claiming the *Code* violates the First Amendment.

■ **ISSUE**

May the state restrict obscenity?

■ **DECISION AND RATIONALE**

(Burger, C.J.) Yes. The government may regulate "obscene" material which (i) depicts or describes sexual conduct, (ii) which conduct is defined specifically by state law, (iii) would be found to appeal to the "prurient interest" by "the average person, applying contemporary community standards," (iv) portrays sexual conduct in a "patently offensive" way, and (v) has no serious literary, artistic, political, or scientific value. Previously, we held "obscene" material is unprotected by the First Amendment. Now, we must clearly define "obscene," to limit what the state may regulate. "Obscene" material is that which (i) depicts or describes sexual conduct, (ii) which conduct is defined specifically by state law, (iii) would be found to appeal to the "prurient interest" by "the average person, applying contemporary community standards," (iv) portrays sexual conduct in a "patently offensive" way, and (v) has no serious literary, artistic, political, or scientific value. It need not be "utterly without redeeming social value." This standard allows the state to limit commercial exploitation of sex, and pursuing its legitimate interest in preventing exhibition to juveniles and unwilling recipients, while providing fair notice to possible offenders.

Analysis:

Miller was the first obscenity case since *Roth* in which a majority of the justices agreed on a test for determining what is obscenity. The Court instituted a requirement that the material be without literary, artistic, political, or scientific value. In a sense, the Court did nothing more than alter the burden of proof that must be met; the government does not specifically have to prove a lack of redeeming social value,

Miller v. California (Continued)

but it likely cannot win its case without a showing that the material does lack literary or artistic value. This case is also important in that it sets forth a requirement that anti-obscenity statutes be sufficiently detailed to inform producers of pornography and possibly obscene material what they can and cannot do. The Court also holds that states can only ban as obscene depictions or descriptions of hard core sexual acts. Finally, this case also clarifies the meaning of the phrase "contemporary community standards" in that the Court makes it clear that these standards are not national standards, but are local and can change depending on the locality.

■ CASE VOCABULARY

PRURIENT: Sexually arousing.

New York v. Ferber

(*State Prosecution*) v. (*Not Stated*)
458 U.S. 747, 102 S.Ct. 3348 (1982)

CHILD PORNOGRAPHY IS UNPROTECTED BY FIRST AMENDMENT, OBSCENE OR NOT

■ **INSTANT FACTS** A state law banning distribution of child pornography is challenged.

■ **BLACK LETTER RULE** The state may regulate child pornography, if it (i) is a *visual* depiction (ii) of sexual conduct specifically described by the state, (iii) by children below a specified age, and (iv) is made with some scienter.

■ PROCEDURAL BASIS

Constitutional challenge to statute.

■ FACTS

New York's (P) statutes criminalized knowing promotion of sexual performances by children under 16 by distributing such materials. Ferber (D) challenged the statute's constitutionality.

■ ISSUE

May a state regulate child pornography?

■ DECISION AND RATIONALE

(White, J.) Yes. The state may regulate child pornography, if it (i) is a *visual* depiction (ii) of sexual conduct specifically described by the state, (iii) by children below a specified age, and (iv) is made with some scienter. Recently, pornographic child exploitation has become a serious problem, which has been combated by many state and federal laws. States are entitled to greater constitutional leeway in regulating pornographic depictions of children, beyond *Miller*'s adult "obscenity" standard. The state has a compelling interest in protecting minors. Child pornography is related to child sex abuse, since recording exacerbates harm to the child, and because producing child porn requires such abuse. The value of child pornography is exceedingly modest, if not de minimis. Regulating child porn is consistent with earlier decisions. Child pornography is unprotected by the First Amendment. But there are laxer limits on what the state may regulate as "child pornography." Such regulation must be limited to (i) *visual* depictions (ii) of sexual conduct specifically described by the state, (iii) by children below a specified age, and (iv) be made with some scienter. It need not be found prurient to the average person, "patently offensive," or without social value when considered as a whole.

■ CONCURRENCE

(Brennan, J.) I agree the state has greater leeway to regulate child pornography, due to its special interest in protecting youth. But the First Amendment forbids regulation of child pornography that has serious literary, artistic, scientific, or medical value.

New York v. Ferber (Continued)

Analysis:

The Court here explained how the *Miller* test must be modified when dealing with child pornography: A trier of fact need not find that the material appeals to the prurient interest of the average person; it is not required that sexual conduct be portrayed in a patently offensive manner; and the material at issue need not be considered as a whole. *Ferber* dealt with the New York law as if it were a type of obscenity legislation, but the *Ferber* statute was really quite different. The purpose of obscenity legislation is to protect consumers or viewers of obscenity. The purpose of the New York law is *not* to protect the consumers who watch a child's sexual performance; it is to *protect the young children* from being used and abused as performers in a sexual performance.

■ CASE VOCABULARY

OBSCENITY: Material which (i) depicts or describes sexual conduct, (ii) which conduct is defined specifically by state law, (iii) would be found to appeal to the "prurient interest" by "the average person, applying contemporary community standards," (iv) portrays sexual conduct in a "patently offensive" way, and (v) has no serious literary, artistic, political, or scientific value. *Miller v. California*

SCIENTER: In criminal law, a "knowing" violation.

Ashcroft v. The Free Speech Coalition
(*Attorney General*) v. (*Business Association*)
535 U.S. 234, 122 S.Ct. 1389 (2002)

CONGRESS MAY NOT SUPPRESS SEXUALLY EXPLICIT IMAGES THAT "APPEAR TO BE" CHILD PORNOGRAPHY

■ **INSTANT FACTS** The facts of the case were not provided in the case excerpt.

■ **BLACK LETTER RULE** Speech restrictions prohibiting a substantial amount of protected speech are overbroad and unconstitutional.

■ **PROCEDURAL BASIS**
Certiorari to review an undisclosed appellate decision.

■ **FACTS**
The facts of the case were not provided in the case excerpt.

■ **ISSUE**
Does the Child Pornography Prevention Act of 1996 violate the First Amendment?

■ **DECISION AND RATIONALE**
(Kennedy, J.) Yes. Under *Miller v. California*, obscene materials lacking serious literary, artistic, political, or scientific value are not protected speech under the First Amendment. In *New York v. Ferber*, however, the Court distinguished between ordinary pornography and child pornography, recognizing that, although certain sexually explicit speech may not meet *Miller's* definition of obscenity, the government nonetheless maintains an important interest in protecting children from participation in such content. Accordingly, pornography can be constitutionally banned only if it is obscene or if it involves the use of children in its creation. The Child Pornography Prevention Act of 1996 (CPPA) extends this ban further to reach not only pornographic speech in which children are depicted, but also speech in which children "appear to be" depicted, whether minors are actually used or not. As a result, the CPPA prohibits speech that is neither obscene under *Miller* nor child pornography under *Ferber*.

Under the CPPA, child pornography is defined not only as images made using real children, but also as including "any visual depiction, including any photograph, film, video, picture, or computer or computer-generated image picture [that] is, or appears to be, of a minor engaging in sexually explicit conduct." It also prohibits any sexually explicit image that is "advertised, promoted, presented, described, or distributed in such a manner that conveys the impression [of] a minor engaging in sexually explicit conduct." Through this broad language, the CPPA is unconstitutional on its face as prohibiting a substantial amount of protected speech. The CPPA makes no exception for speech possessing substantial literary, artistic, political, or scientific value. Countless literary and cinematic works depict sexual activities of minor, whether minors are in fact used in their creation. Under the CPPA, works of William Shakespeare and Academy Award-winning films would be illegal speech, with criminal penalties applicable to their creators and audiences alike. Unlike *Ferber*, which targeted the means in which child pornography is produced, the CPPA targets the content of the production, without proper respect for the value of its message.

The Government (D) argues that the CPPA is necessary nonetheless because pedophiles may use virtual child pornography to seduce children. Yet, the Court has continually held that speech fit for adults may not be banned merely because it may fall into the hands of children or be used for an improper purpose. Nor can speech be banned because of its potential to incite lawlessness in those unable to control their private thoughts. Without a strong connection between the content of the speech and the harm to be prevented, the Government (D) may not ban otherwise protected speech. Despite the similarities between child pornography and virtual child pornography, the Government may not ban the latter in order to suppress the former. Because the CPPA extends beyond *Miller* and *Ferber*, it is overbroad and unconstitutional on its face.

■ DISSENT IN PART

(O'Connor, J.) The Government (D) has a compelling interest in protecting the Nation's children from sex offenders and child pornography. A ban on virtual child pornography supports these objectives. To reconcile the "appears to be" language of the statute and the protection of legitimate speech, the language should be interpreted narrowly, as "virtually indistinguishable from." Under this meaning, the statute would properly include any computer-generated images that, if real children were involved, would amount to child pornography, while excepting cartoons and other works that depict children engaging in sexually suggestive behavior. This understanding of the statute would be narrowly tailored to reaching the Government's (D) compelling interest and comply with the First Amendment.

■ DISSENT

(Rehnquist, C.J.) Congress has a compelling interest in protecting the safety of America's youth and should be given broad deference in dealing with any technological advances that threaten this interest. The statute should not be invalidated because a limiting instruction can be given to exclude works of literary and artistic value and properly enforce Congress's intent. In this way, the statute can be limited to "the sordid business of pandering."

Analysis:

If virtual child pornography remains protected speech, many fear the end of the exception of child pornography itself as unprotected speech. As technology continues to advance, life-like child pornography may in fact be produced without the use of live children. Yet, government agents may not be able to distinguish between computer-generated child pornography and live child pornography. If one is protected, while the other is not, such proof becomes crucial, not to mention time-consuming and expensive.

■ CASE VOCABULARY

CHILD PORNOGRAPHY: Material depicting a person under the age of 18 engaged in sexual activity. Child pornography is not protected by the First Amendment—even if it falls short of the legal standard for obscenity—and those directly involved in its distribution can be criminally punished.

OBSCENITY: Extremely offensive under contemporary community standards of morality and decency; grossly repugnant to the generally accepted notions of what is appropriate. Under the Supreme Court's three-part test, material is legally obscene—and therefore not protected under the First Amendment—if, taken as a whole, the material (1) appeals to the prurient interest in sex, as determined by the average person applying contemporary community standards; (2) portrays sexual conduct, as specifically defined by the applicable state law, in a patently offensive way; and (3) lacks serious literary, artistic, political, or scientific value. *Miller v. California*, 413 U.S. 15, 93 S. Ct. 2607 (1973).

OVERBREADTH DOCTRINE: The doctrine holding that if a statute is so broadly written that it deters free expression, then it can be struck down on its face because of its chilling effect—even if it also prohibits acts that may legitimately be forbidden. The Supreme Court has used this doctrine to invalidate a number of laws, including those that would disallow peaceful picketing or require loyalty oaths.

Young v. American Mini Theatres, Inc.

(*Detroit City Official*) v. (*Porn Theater*)
427 U.S. 50, 96 S.Ct. 2440 (1976)

GOVERNMENT MAY ZONE THE LOCATION OF PORNOGRAPHIC THEATRES

■ **INSTANT FACTS** Detroit zoning ordinances dispersed pornographic theaters.

■ **BLACK LETTER RULE** The government may restrict zoning of pornography.

■ PROCEDURAL BASIS

First Amendment challenge to city zoning ordinance.

■ FACTS

Detroit (D) instituted a zoning ordinance dispersing "adult" theaters (and other "seedy" businesses), to 1,000 feet from each other and 500 feet of residences. Its legislature found this would disperse "Skid Rows," which concentrate pornography, poverty, and crime. Porn theater American Mini Theatres, Inc. ("Theatre") (P) challenged the ordinance's constitutionality, claiming (i) it is discriminatory, content-based regulation, and (ii) it is unjustified.

■ ISSUE

Is it constitutional for a zoning ordinance to disperse pornographic businesses?

■ DECISION AND RATIONALE

(Stevens, J.) Yes. The government may restrict zoning of pornography. First, the ordinance's classification *is* content-based, covering only specified, pornographic films. But the First Amendment protection accorded to various speech often varies based on its content. True, the First Amendment forbids total suppression of erotica, because it arguably has artistic value. But society's interest in protecting erotica is of a different, and lesser, magnitude than its interest in protecting social/political speech. Few would march their sons to war to preserve citizens' rights to see pornography. Here, this ordinance will not limit the total number of pornographic theaters significantly, nor deny either exhibitors nor viewers access to the market. Second, we find Detroit's (D) ordinance was reasonably justified by its strong interest in preserving its neighborhoods' character. The ordinance was based on a factual finding, which we cannot second-guess. Also, cities must have reasonable opportunities to experiment with solutions.

■ DISSENT

(Stewart, J.) The majority improperly denies pornography its full constitutional protection, just because porn is objectionable to some. The Bill of Rights was designed to protect against precisely such majoritarian limitations.

Analysis:

Here, the Court admits the zoning is content-based, but upholds it, explicitly saying pornography enjoys *limited* protection under the First Amendment because it is *low-value* expression. The Court placed great emphasis on the continual availability of these movies and the fact that the restrictions were unrelated to the suppression of ideas. Nevertheless, the regulation describes the theatres in terms of the content of their films. It should be noted that the restriction in *American Mini* Theatres did not ban all adult theatres or even affect the number of adult movie theatres in the city. It just dispersed them, and the city had presented evidence that a concentration of adult theatres led to a deterioration of surrounding neighborhoods.

City of Erie v. Pap's A.M.

(*City*) v. (*Nude Dancing Bar*)
529 U.S. 277, 120 S.Ct. 1382 (2000)

GOVERNMENT MAY RESTRICT NUDE DANCING'S SECONDARY EFFECTS

■ **INSTANT FACTS** When a city ordinance banned nude dancing based on "secondary effects," a nude bar challenged its constitutionality.

■ **BLACK LETTER RULE** The government may ban nude dancing, if (i) its intent is to prevent its secondary effects (rather than its content), and (ii) its regulation is "rationally related" to promoting "legitimate" state interests.

■ PROCEDURAL BASIS
First Amendment challenge to city ordinance, seeking declaration and injunction against enforcement.

■ FACTS
The City of Erie, PA (D) enacted an ordinance banning public nudity, claiming such displays promote "secondary effects" like prostitution, sexually-transmitted disease, crime, etc. Nude-dancing club Pap's A.M. (P) challenged the ordinance under the First Amendment, claiming that compliance would violate dancers' free expression by forcing them to dance wearing pasties and G-strings. After trial, the Pennsylvania Supreme Court held for Pap's (P). Erie (D) appeals.

■ ISSUE
May a city ordinance ban nude dancing?

■ DECISION AND RATIONALE
(O'Connor, J.) Yes. The government may ban nude dancing, if (i) its intent is to prevent its secondary effects (rather than its content), and (ii) its regulation is "rationally related" to promoting "legitimate" state interests. Nudity is not inherently expressive. But we think that nude dancing is marginally expressive, thus deserving limited First Amendment protection. If government regulation involves interests related to the expression's content, then it must pass intermediate scrutiny. But if the government's purpose is unrelated to suppressing expression, then it need meet only "less stringent" standards. *Barnes* held the governmental interest in combating prostitution and other crime is not inherently related to suppressing expression. Put another way, ordinances which regulate "secondary effects"—expressions' impact of public health, safety, welfare, etc.—are scrutinized less strictly than those regulating "primary effects"—the expression's effects on audiences. Here, Erie's (D) ordinance is content-neutral; it does not facially restrict nude dancing, and its legislative history shows a purpose to combat secondary effects. Regulating secondary effects is an important, justified state interest. Further, this ordinance's impact on the dancing's overall expressiveness is de minimis, since the dancers can still perform in pasties and g-strings. Reversed.

■ CONCURRENCE
(Scalia, J.) When the government regulates non-speech "expressive" conduct, the First Amendment applies only where the government prohibits the conduct's communicative attributes. Here, the ordinance targets the secondary effects, not the communication. But the government is empowered to

City of Erie v. Pap's A.M. (Continued)

ban nude dancing completely, based on its historic power to foster morals, and the traditional judgement that nude dancing itself is immoral.

■ DISSENT

(Souter, J.) While this Court never articulated clear definitions of "intermediate scrutiny," it should require at least some factual justification. Here, Erie (D) presents no evidence that nude dancing has secondary effects, nor that banning it will have beneficial effects.

■ DISSENT

(Stevens, J.) The majority expands the secondary effects doctrine impermissibly. Previously, secondary effects could justify only zoning restrictions, which are minimal impositions on expression. Under the majority opinion, it can justify a total ban, which is effectively censorship.

Analysis:

This case shows that the Court views nude dancing as "low-value" speech, which merits lesser constitutional protection, just like commercial pornography. Here, the Court holds that nude dancing cannot be regulated simply because of its "objectionable" / "immoral" message, but it can effectively be restricted (though not banned) by the government's unsubstantiated assertion that it causes others harm.

■ CASE VOCABULARY

SECONDARY EFFECTS: Doctrine that government may regulate speech when that speech produces harmful "secondary effects," like immorality, crime, prostitution, etc. Previously, this doctrine was applied to uphold zoning restrictions on pornographic businesses.

Stanley v. Georgia
(*Porn Viewer*) v. (*State Prosecution*)
394 U.S. 557, 89 S.Ct. 1243 (1969)

GOVERNMENT CANNOT PUNISH PRIVATE POSSESSION OF OBSCENITY

■ **INSTANT FACTS** A man charged with criminal possession of obscene materials in his house challenged the ban's constitutionality.

■ **BLACK LETTER RULE** The government cannot criminalize private possession of obscene materials.

■ **PROCEDURAL BASIS**

In prosecution for criminal possession of obscenity, post-conviction appeal.

■ **FACTS**

Georgia's (P) laws forbid "knowingly having possession of obscene matter." Georgia's (P) police, executing a search warrant, raided the house of suspected bookmaker Stanley (D). They found little evidence of bookmaking, but found obscene film reels. Stanley (D) was convicted for possessing obscenity. Stanley (D) challenged the statute's constitutionality, claiming punishing private possession of obscene materials violates the First/Fourteenth Amendment. Georgia (P) defended contending *Roth* [state may ban obscene porn advertisements] allows the state to combat obscenity, and that obscene materials tend to promote rape and deviance.

■ **ISSUE**

Can a state ban possession of obscene materials?

■ **DECISION AND RATIONALE**

(Marshall, J.) No. The government cannot criminalize private possession of obscene materials. *Roth* recognized the government's valid interest in dealing with obscenity. But *Roth* does not mean that all such regulations are constitutional. The First and Fourteenth Amendments prohibit criminalizing mere private possession of obscene material. The Constitution protects people's right to receive information, regardless of their social worth. Also, prosecution for having obscenity in one's home threatens the fundamental right against governmental intrusions into one's privacy. Whatever the justification for other anti-obscenity statutes, they do not allow the State to tell a man, sitting alone in his house, what he may read or watch; that would be mind control. Here, Georgia's (D) claims of secondary effects have little empirical basis. Conviction reversed.

Analysis:

Stanley must be read quite narrowly. The crucial fifth vote in *Stanley* was Justice Harlan's; in spite of the broad language of the opinion, the *Stanley* Court's own summary of its decision emphasized that "the States retain broad power to regulate obscenity; that power simply does not extend to mere possession by the individual in the privacy of his own home." The Court itself had previously emphasized. In other

Stanley v. Georgia (Continued)

contexts, the privacy of the home and Justice Harlan in particular had been concerned with the sanctity of the home, although he repeatedly emphasized the broad power of the state over obscenity outside of the home. While the Court has refused to expand *Stanley*, it has also not explained why a seller of obscenity may not raise the third-party right of persons to keep the obscenity in the home. As the Court later admitted: "*Stanley* should not be read too broadly." *Osborne v. Ohio*, 495 U.S. 103, 107.

Cohen v. California

(*Draft Objector*) v. (*State*)
403 U.S. 15, 91 S.Ct. 1780 (1971)

GOVERNMENT CANNOT PUNISH PUBLIC DISPLAY OF EXPLETIVES

■ **INSTANT FACTS** A man arrested for disturbing the peace by wearing a jacket imprinted "Fuck the Draft" challenged the statute's constitutionality.

■ **BLACK LETTER RULE** The state cannot punish public use/display of expletives.

■ **PROCEDURAL BASIS**

In prosecution for breach of peace, post-conviction appeal.

■ **FACTS**

California's (P) *Penal Code* forbids disturbing the peace ("maliciously and willfully disturbing the peace or quiet of any neighborhood or person ... by ... offensive conduct"). Anti-Vietnam draft objector Cohen (D) appeared in a California courthouse corridor wearing a jacket which said: "Fuck the Draft." Cohen (D) did not say anything to anyone, and no one objected, except the police. Cohen (D) was convicted of violating the *Code*. Cohen (D) appeals, contending *Code* is unconstitutional.

■ **ISSUE**

Can a state punish breaching the peace by offensive words?

■ **DECISION AND RATIONALE**

(Harlan, J.) No. The state cannot punish the public use/display of expletives. Previously, we held the government may restrict certain forms of expression, including obscenity, fighting words, incitement to violence, and speech forced on unwilling viewers [i.e., obscene mailings]. Here, Cohen's (D) acts do not fall into any such category. They are not obscene, because his words were not significantly erotic. They are not fighting words, since they were not directed as a personal insult against any hearer. They are not incitements, since there is no showing that Cohen (D) intended to arouse anyone violently, or succeeded. For it to be regulable to protect hearers from harm, it must be proven that substantial privacy interests were invaded in an essentially intolerable manner. Any broader authority would empower the government to silence dissidents based on personal predilections. Here, bystanders' brief exposure to Cohen's (D) speech is insufficient invasion. Further, there are policy reasons why the government should not be able to excise epithets from public discourse. Public discussion is a powerful social force, which must tolerate offensive utterances. If the state began punishing every word it deems offensive, its power to regulate would be boundless and arbitrary, especially since the decision on what is "offensive" is individualistic. "One man's vulgarity is another man's lyric." Also, expletives convey emotive force in addition to a cognitive meaning, and thus contribute to speech's overall message. Finally, forbidding certain words runs substantial risk of suppressing certain unpopular ideas. Conviction reversed.

Cohen v. California (Continued)

■ DISSENT

(Blackmun, J.) Under *Chaplinsky* [fighting words doctrine], expression which is mainly conduct rather than speech is regulable. Here, that was the case.

Analysis:

As this decision shows, the Supreme Court feels that public debate and discussion of ideas is healthy, which is why Cohen's (D) speech was held to be protected by the First Amendment. Indeed, the Court writes that the constitutional right to free expression is powerful medicine in a society such as ours, as it will ultimately produce a more informed and capable citizenry. The Court points out that sometimes this free discussion may appear to create discord and offensive utterance, but in the end, society will be better off because of it. Indeed, it is held, the First Amendment removes potential governmental restraints on the arena of public discussion, allowing the people to voice their views and be better for it. Though the Court stresses the importance of governmental fostering of free debate. It does place limits on that freedom to speak—the Court makes it clear that people cannot say anything they want anywhere they want. The Court states that in our homes, we have a right to restrict what we hear— freedom of speech does not allow one person to invade the sanctity of another's home for the purpose of spreading an offensive or unwanted message. The Court also points out the fact that when people go into public, they assume a risk of hearing unwanted and possibly offensive speech. Though that is a concern, the Court feels that suppressing speech would raise greater concerns.

Federal Communications Commission v. Pacifica Foundation

(Federal Broadcast-Regulating Agency) v. *(Radio Station)*
438 U.S. 726, 98 S.Ct. 3026 (1978)

GOVERNMENT MAY RESTRICT TV/RADIO BROADCAST OF INDECENT LANGUAGE

■ **INSTANT FACTS** When the FCC reprimanded a radio station for broadcasting a monologue satirizing indecent words, the station challenged the order's constitutionality.

■ **BLACK LETTER RULE** The government may impose certain sanctions against radio/TV broadcasts containing patently-offensive language (involving sex or excretion) in certain circumstances, unless the sanctions target their social or political message.

■ **PROCEDURAL BASIS**

Appeal from agency order reprimanding broadcaster.

■ **FACTS**

The Federal Communications Commission (FCC) (D) is empowered to regulate TV/radio broadcasting. Its federal enabling statutes forbid "any obscene, indecent, or profane ... radio communications," and empower The FCC (D) to "encourage ... more effective use of radio in the public interest." Radio station owner Pacifica Foundation (P) decided to broadcast satirist George Carlin's vulgar monologue "Filthy Words," which listed words people found indecent and unfit to say on public airwaves. The monologue was included in a radio program about attitudes toward language, aired at 2 PM, and started with a warning the broadcast would include "sensitive language which might be regarded as offensive." A man who tuned into the broadcast while driving with his boy complained to The FCC (D). When The FCC (D) forwarded the complaint to Pacifica (P) for comment, Pacifica (P) responded that it was part of a social commentary, was preceded by warnings, was not "obscene," and was socially-relevant satire. The FCC (D) issued a declaratory order, holding Pacifica (P) "could have been ... subject [to] administrative sanctions." (While The FCC (D) imposed no sanctions against Pacifica (P), the order was added to Pacifica's (P) license file, and could be sanctionable later, if more complaints against Pacifica (P) were received.) Pacifica (P) sued to challenge The FCC's (D) order's constitutionality, contending (i) The FCC's (D) construction of the statute is potentially overbroad, and (ii) non-obscene profanity cannot be abridged.

■ **ISSUE**

Can the FCC reprimand a radio station's airing of indecent language?

■ **DECISION AND RATIONALE**

(Stevens, J.) Yes. The government may impose certain sanctions against radio/TV broadcasts containing patently-offensive language (involving sex or excretion) in certain circumstances, unless the sanctions target their social or political message.... First, we cannot consider whether The FCC's (D) general interpretation is overbroad. Our review is limited to whether The FCC (D) may proscribe this particular broadcast. While The FCC's (D) order may lead some broadcasters to censor themselves, at most it will deter patently offensive references to excretion and sex. Such references enjoy only peripheral protection under the First Amendment. Second, we find the government may regulate radio

Federal Communications Commission v. Pacifica Foundation (Continued)

and TV broadcasts containing patently offensive words about excretion or sex. While their regulation is content-based, this may be permissible. Generally, offensive words enjoy limited protection under the First Amendment, because their low value is less than society's interest in morality. Nevertheless, offensive words enjoy constitutional protection *in certain contexts*, even if they lack social value. Government cannot restrict them because of their political content or viewpoint. But prior cases recognize that they are less-protected when transmitted over broadcast media [TV and radio]. This is because broadcast media confronts the citizen, not only in public, but also in the privacy of their homes, where their right to be left alone outweighs intruders' First Amendment rights. This problem cannot be rectified by broadcasting warnings, because the audience may tune in after the warning. It is irrelevant that hearers may avoid further offense by turning off the radio/TV, since some damage is already done. Also, radio/TV broadcasting is uniquely accessible to children, and cannot effectively be withheld from them. We find The FCC's (D) action here was reasonable to prevent nuisance *under these circumstances*, considering the content, time of day, etc. We do not hold that occasional expletives in commercial or artistic conversations would justify a sanction, or that such broadcasts justify criminal prosecution. The FCC order affirmed.

■ **CONCURRENCE**

[Omitted.]

■ **DISSENT**

[Omitted.]

Analysis:

The majority held, despite the pleadings of Pacifica (D), that content-based restriction can, in some cases, be enforced and upheld. It is also important to note that, as the Court points out, the language sanctioned in this case might be protected if used in another context. Thus, the Court makes it clear that context matters when it comes to regulation of speech. The Court focuses on the importance of privacy in the home; a major reason behind the Court's holding is the fact that people should be able to control what enters the home, and when indecent language is used on the radio, that control becomes severely limited. This provides a very far-reaching result, in that it is possible that, if the case had come out the other way, there would be no restriction on what could be said or done on the radio or television. Thus, the decision can be seen as a protector of that segment of the public that does not want to be unwittingly exposed to indecent language.

Sable Communications of California, Inc. v. Federal Communications Commission

(Dial-Up Phone Porn Provider) v. (Federal Telephone Regulatory Agency)
492 U.S. 115, 109 S.Ct. 2829 (1989)

GOVERNMENT CANNOT BAN "INDECENT" DIAL-UP PORN

■ **INSTANT FACTS** The FCC banned a dial-up service which provided sexual phone messages.

■ **BLACK LETTER RULE** The government may regulate indecent dial-up telephone messages, but only (i) to promote "compelling" governmental interests, and (ii) by using the least-restrictive means possible.

■ PROCEDURAL BASIS

In agency enforcement action, appeal from judgment for defendant.

■ FACTS

The *Communications Act of 1934 § 223(b)* bars commercial, interstate phone messages from containing both "indecent" and "obscene" messages. "Dial-a-porn" provider Sable Communications (D) offered prerecorded, sex-oriented messages, which could be accessed by calling its phone number. Apparently, it blocked children from accessing it, by requiring a credit card number and access code, and using some type of scrambling. The Federal Communications Commission (P) sued to enforce § 223(b) against Sable (D), alleging Sable (D) does not do enough to block minors' access, and that applying § 223(b) is justified to serve the compelling state interest in protecting minors. Sable (D) defended, contending § 223(b) is unconstitutional, because it bans both "obscene" and (protected) "indecent" speech. At trial, the District Court held (i) § 223(b)'s ban on "obscene" speech was valid, but (ii) its restrictions on "indecent" communications were unconstitutional, because not narrowly-tailored. FCC (P) appeals.

■ ISSUE

May the government ban indecent telephone messages?

■ DECISION AND RATIONALE

(White, J.) No. The government may regulate indecent dial-up telephone messages, but only (i) to promote "compelling" governmental interests, and (ii) by using the least-restrictive means possible. First, we agree § 223(b) may restrict "obscene" messages, because obscenity is unprotected by the First Amendment. Second, we find § 223(b) is unconstitutional, because not narrowly-tailored. Sexual expression which is indecent but not obscene is protected. The government may regulate it to promote compelling interests, but only if it chooses the least-restrictive means available to further that interest. Here, the government's interest in shielding minors from indecent speech is compelling, even if the speech is not obscene. But we find the FCC's (P) method—banning Sable's (D) messages altogether—is not narrowly-tailored. Sable (D) uses safeguards against minors (e.g., credit cards, access codes, scrambling), and FCC's (P) claim that enterprising youngsters could evade them are unproven. FCC (P) cannot rely on *Pacifica* [radio station may be reprimanded for airing George Carlin's "Filthy Words"] for

Sable Communications of California, Inc. v. Federal Communications Commission (Continued)

a broad mandate to regulate, because *Pacifica* is distinguishable. *Pacifica* was fact-specific. Also, it did not involve a total ban on indecent communications. In addition, it relied on broadcasting's "unique" attributes: it is uniquely pervasive, can intrude into the home's privacy without warning, and is "uniquely accessible to children, even those too young to read." Private commercial telephone communications, such as Sable's (D), are substantially different, since the dial-it medium requires listeners to take affirmative steps to receive communications, so there is no "captive audience" of unwilling listeners. Affirmed.

Analysis:

Sable Communications illustrates that the Court's protection of "indecent" communication is decided on a medium-by-medium basis. However, for "dial-a-porn" providers, there is one important hindrance. While *Sable* protects dial-up indecency, it does not protect dial-up *obscenity*. This case holds that Congress can constitutionally impose an outright ban on "obscene" interstate, pre-recorded, commercial telephone messages ("dial-a-porn"). The First Amendment does not protect obscenity. However, the Court invalidated the portion of the statute at issue that imposed an outright ban on "indecent" dial-a-porn messages. The Government does have a compelling interest in protecting minors, but the law at issue was not narrowly tailored for that purpose.

■ CASE VOCABULARY

OBSCENITY: Material which: (i) depicts or describes sexual conduct, (ii) which conduct is defined specifically by state law, (iii) *would be found to appeal to the "prurient interest" by "the average person*, applying contemporary community standards," (iv) portrays sexual conduct *in a "patently offensive" way*, and (v) has no serious literary, artistic, political, or scientific value.

Reno v. American Civil Liberties Union

(U.S. Attorney General) v. *(Activist Organizations)*
521 U.S. 844, 117 S.Ct. 2329 (1997)

GOVERNMENT MAY REGULATE INTERNET INDECENCY ONLY BY LEAST-RESTRICTIVE MEANS

■ **INSTANT FACTS** Activists challenged a statute criminalizing sexually-explicit, indecent communications sent/made available to minors over the Internet.

■ **BLACK LETTER RULE** The government may regulate the Internet to protect children from indecency, but only by using the least-restrictive method.

■ PROCEDURAL BASIS

In First Amendment challenge to federal statute, appeal from declaration of unconstitutionality.

■ FACTS

Congress enacted the *Telecommunications Act of 1996* to deregulate and encourage growth/competition of telecoms (e.g., local telephone, video, broadcasting). That legislation also contains the *Communications Decency Act (CDA)*. *CDA § 223(a)* criminalizes knowing transmission of "obscene" or "indecent" messages to recipients under 18, and *§ 223(d)* criminalizes knowingly sending or displaying "patently offensive" messages in a manner that is available to them. The Internet is used by about 40 million people, which is estimated to grow to 200 million by 1999. It contains sexually-explicit text, pictures, and chat. Almost all pornography sites are preceded by warnings about content, so the chance of children viewing them accidentally is "slim." The methods for blocking minors' access include: requiring a credit card number or password, or parental control software which blocks specified porn sites and/or screens for specified sexual words. But there is no way to screen out pornographic pictures, or detect minors' use of sexual chat/email. Apparently, the activist American Civil Liberties Union (ACLU) challenged *CDA § 223(a)* and *§ 223(d)* as unconstitutionally overbroad. ACLU (P) apparently claimed *CDA* suppressed non-pornographic sexually-explicit information, and claimed that requiring credit card numbers to access such information would require non-commercial sites to obtain prohibitively-expensive software and bar adults without credit cards. U.S. Attorney General Janet Reno (D) defended, contending *CDA* was a "time, place, and manner" restriction, and/or justified by the government's compelling interest in protecting minors. After trial, the District Court found *CDA* violates the First Amendment. Reno (D) appeals.

■ ISSUE

May the government criminalize the sending/display of "indecent" and "patently offensive" materials to minors over the Internet?

■ DECISION AND RATIONALE

(Stevens, J.) No. The government may regulate the Internet to protect children from indecency, but only by using the least-restrictive method. *CDA* is not a "time, place, and manner" restriction, since it applies to the entire Internet, and is intended to regulate the primary effects of speech rather than secondary effects. Instead, *CDA* is a content-based blanket restriction. Content-based regulations of constitutionally-protected speech must (i) serve compelling governmental interests, and (ii) *have no less-restrictive*

Reno v. American Civil Liberties Union (Continued)

alternatives which would be at least as effective in achieving that purpose. Prior cases recognized that each medium may present its own problems, and not every medium can be analyzed under *Pacifica* [FCC may reprimand radio broadcast of indecent words]. Here, *Pacifica* is distinguishable, since the Internet has no history of being the least-protected medium, and because *CDA* is a criminal statute. Here, we find § 223(a) § 223(d) void for vagueness. They use the vague terms "indecent" and "patently offensive," without defining or distinguishing them. This effectively suppresses much valuable, non-pornographic sexual speech that adults have a constitutional right to receive, and to send to each other. Further, *CDA*'s severe criminal sanctions will chill speakers. The Government, in protecting children, may not reduce the adult population to only what is fit for children. Affirmed.

Analysis:

This case does not formulate new rules of law, as many First Amendment cases do. In fact, the bases of the opinion rely on traditional arguments gleaned from prior cases. What is significant about this case is the fact that it is the application of established First Amendment law to a new medium heretofore unrestricted—it takes the First Amendment into virgin territory. The internet presents a problem for content-based restrictions because, unlike the physical world (as the dissent points out), physical zoning of the internet is not possible such that minors can be wholly restricted from certain areas. Until technology can advance to the point that minors can be physically restricted from "adult zones," meaning they will have as much difficulty entering an adult website as they would entering an adult movie theater, the fact that minors may be subjected to indecent and pornographic material on the Internet is not enough to persuade the Court to permit restrictions on speech.

■ CASE VOCABULARY

PRIMARY EFFECTS: A communication's contents' effects on the audience.

SECONDARY EFFECTS: The effects a communication tends to create which are unrelated to its content. Usually, this is applied to let the government zone pornographic businesses, to prevent concentrations of prostitution and crime.

Ashcroft v. American Civil Liberties Union

(Attorney General) v. *(Public Advocate)*
542 U.S. 656, 124 S.Ct. 2783 (2004)

PREVENTING THE DISSEMINATION OF HARMFUL INTERNET CONTENT IS NOT THE LEAST RESTRICTIVE ALTERNATIVE TO PROTECT MINORS

■ **INSTANT FACTS** The American Civil Liberties Union (P) sought a preliminary injunction against the enforcement of the Child Online Protection Act, which prohibited the commercial dissemination of Internet content that is harmful to minors.

■ **BLACK LETTER RULE** A statute that suppresses a substantial amount of protected speech is unconstitutional if less restrictive alternatives exist to further the governmental objective.

■ **PROCEDURAL BASIS**

Certiorari to review a federal appellate decision affirming a preliminary injunction.

■ **FACTS**

The Child Online Protection Act (COPA) imposes criminal penalties for knowingly posting Internet content that is "harmful to minors" for a "commercial purpose." No person may be convicted, however, if he or she restricts access to such content by requiring a credit card or other method of age verification before granting access. The American Civil Liberties Union (P) sought a preliminary injunction in federal court, claiming that the statute violates the First Amendment. The district court agreed, finding that the Government (D) had not proven that alternatives less restrictive on First Amendment rights do not exist. A federal court of appeals affirmed.

■ **ISSUE**

Does the Child Online Protection Act violate the First Amendment?

■ **DECISION AND RATIONALE**

(Kennedy, J.) Yes. A statute that suppresses a substantial amount of protected speech is unconstitutional if less restrictive alternatives exist to further the governmental objective. The burden of proving no such alternatives exist lies with the Government (D). Under this test, the Court ensures that the Government (D) is able to further its important objectives, but with as little infringement upon the Constitution as possible.

Here, COPA targets Internet producers who place material unsuitable for minors on the Web for profit to reduce "opportunities for minors to access materials through the World Wide Web in a manner that can frustrate parental supervision or control." By targeting the source, however, COPA prohibits content that, while unsuitable for minors, is protected by the First Amendment. It prevents adults from viewing protected speech by preventing its dissemination regardless of the audience. Blocking and filtering software provide a less restrictive alternative. While filters may block some protected speech and fail to detect some harmful speech, the impact on the First Amendment is significantly reduced. In fact, because COPA is limited to content on American websites, filters may be more successful in protecting minors by blocking overseas content as well. Because less restrictive alternatives exist to further the Government's (D) objective, COPA is unconstitutional.

■ DISSENT

(Scalia, J.) Because "the sordid business of pandering" does not involve protected speech, COPA does not raise any constitutional concerns.

■ DISSENT

(Breyer, J.) Congress could not have achieved its objective in a less restrictive manner. In enacting COPA, Congress sought to protect minors from commercial pornography on the Internet. COPA is limited to content that is legally obscene, and does not prohibit any protected speech. Instead, the statute merely requires sufficient evidence of the user's age before access is granted. The Government (D) has a compelling interest in protecting minors from exposure to commercial pornography. Filtering software does not serve this interest. It inadequately blocks all pornographic content, and it costs private citizens money they may choose not to spend. Moreover, blocking software is limited to the computer on which it is installed, leaving Internet access in other locations susceptible to pornographic content. While COPA may not prevent minors' exposure to overseas content, it blocks a considerable amount of pornographic content, which furthers the Government's (D) compelling interest.

Analysis:

The decision in this case illustrates just how difficult it is to regulate Internet pornography. By striking down COPA, the Court invalidates sweeping attempts to regulate the production of online pornography as too restrictive on First Amendment rights. Yet, as illustrated in *United States v. American Library Association*, 539 U.S. 194 (2001), restricted access to online pornography raises different First Amendment concerns in other contexts.

■ CASE VOCABULARY

PRELIMINARY INJUNCTION: A temporary injunction issued before or during trial to prevent an irreparable injury from occurring before the court has a chance to decide the case.

Virginia State Board of Pharmacy v. Virginia Citizens Consumer Council, Inc.

(*Pharmacists' Self-Regulatory Association*) v. (*Consumer Group*)
425 U.S. 748, 96 S.Ct. 1817 (1976)

FIRST AMENDMENT PROTECTS COMMERCIAL SPEECH

■ **INSTANT FACTS** A state law barring pharmacists from advertising drug prices was challenged by consumers.

■ **BLACK LETTER RULE** Commercial speech is protected by the First Amendment.

■ **PROCEDURAL BASIS**

In First Amendment challenge to state law, appeal from invalidation of law.

■ **FACTS**

Virginia law made it unethical for licensed pharmacists to advertise prescription drug prices (a pharmacist shall be guilty of unprofessional conduct if he "publishes, advertises or promoted, directly or indirectly, in any manner whatsoever, any amount price, ... discount ... or credit ... for any [prescription] drug.") This law, apparently urged by the Virginia State Board of Pharmacy (Board) (D), was ostensibly intended to prevent pharmacists from lowering quality to slash prices, and from over-prescribing unneeded drugs. [But as a result, drug prices varied up to 650%.] Consumer advocate Virginia Citizens Consumer Council, Inc. (Consumers) (P) challenged the advertising ban as violating the First Amendment right to commercial speech. After trial, the court invalidated the law. Board (D) appeals.

■ **ISSUE**

Does the First Amendment protect commercial speech?

■ **DECISION AND RATIONALE**

(Blackmun, J.) Yes. Commercial speech is protected by the First Amendment. Early decisions suggested commercial speech was unprotected. *Valentine v. Christensen* (1942). But more recent decisions held "commercial speech" is protected. *Bigelow v. Virginia* (1975) [ads for abortions protected]. Policy supports protecting commercial speech. Speech does not lose its protection just because money is spent to project it. If speech is to be denied protection, the reason must be based on its content. Yet such distinctions cannot be made for commercial contents. It is irrelevant that the advertiser's interest in speaking is purely economic. Individual consumers may have very keen interests in receiving commercial information, especially poor prescription drug users. Generally, society may have a strong public interest in the free flow of commercial information. Advertising, however tasteless, still disseminates information about who is selling what product, at what price. This helps consumers make well-informed buying decisions, which is necessary for free-market economies. Board's (D) arguments supporting the ban are unpersuasive. True, Virginia has a strong interest in maintaining pharmacists' professionalism. But these high standards are maintained by Virginia's close regulation of them, not by prices. Thus, we hold commercial speech is protected. But the state may still regulate it, e.g., to suppress commercial falsehoods, deceptive or misleading advertisements, advertisements for illegal transactions, etc. Affirmed.

■ DISSENT

(Rehnquist, J.) The majority opinion has undesirable consequences. It will keep states from discouraging undesirable products, such as prescription drugs, liquor, and cigarettes. Traditionally, the First Amendment was intended to protect sociopolitical speech, not consumers' crass purchasing decisions. Here, the majority overturns Virginia's legislative decision that advertising drug prices will encourage wider use of unnecessary drugs, which is reasonable. Also, Consumers (P) lack standing, because they are not disadvantaged directly by the statute.

Analysis:

In 1942, the Supreme Court stated in *Valentine v. Chrestensen* the rule that speech that was purely commercial advertising was not entitled to any protection under the First Amendment. In this case, that rule was wholly abandoned, as the Court held that even purely commercial speech is entitled to First Amendment protection. Thus, this case represents an about-face in the law. This case is also important in that it recognizes that while there is clearly a right given to speakers to speak, the hearer of speech has a First Amendment right to receive information—the people of Virginia had a right to hear how much drugs should cost. The majority of prior First Amendment cases had dealt strictly with the right to speak—this is one of the first cases to address the right to be spoken to, and as such it is significant.

Bolger v. Youngs Drug Products Corp.
(*Federal Official*) v. (*Contraceptives Advertiser*)
463 U.S. 60, 103 S.Ct. 2875 (1983)

SUPREME COURT ANNOUNCES TEST OF "COMMERCIAL" SPEECH

■ **INSTANT FACTS** A drug company challenged a federal ban on ads for contraceptives.

■ **BLACK LETTER RULE** "Commercial speech" is a communication which (a) does no more than propose a commercial transaction, OR (b-i) is an advertisement, AND (ii) references specific products, AND (iii) is mailed for economic motivations.

■ **PROCEDURAL BASIS**
In First Amendment challenge of federal statute, appeal from finding of constitutionality.

■ **FACTS**
A federal statute prohibited mailing unsolicited ads for contraceptives. Contraceptive marketer Youngs Drug Products Corp. (Youngs) (P) wished to mail several unsolicited pamphlets: multi-item flyers promoting drugstore products (including contraceptives), flyers especially advertising prophylactics, and informational pamphlets recommending contraception. Apparently, Youngs (P) sued to declare the statute unconstitutionally restrictive of free speech. At trial, the District Court apparently found Youngs' (P) ads were "commercial speech," and denied them protection. Youngs (P) appeals.

■ **ISSUE**
May the government regulate informational advertising as "commercial speech"?

■ **DECISION AND RATIONALE**
(Marshall, J.) Yes. "Commercial speech" is a communication which (a) does no more than propose a commercial transaction, OR (b-i) is an advertisement, AND (ii) references specific products, AND (iii) is mailed for economic motivations. The degree of First Amendment protection varies for "commercial" and non-commercial speech. Core "commercial speech" is that which does "no more than propose a commercial transaction." Here, Youngs' (P) flyers are such core commercial speech. But speech can also be (non-core) "commercial" if (i) it is an advertisement, (ii) it refers to specific products, AND (iii) the distributor has economic motivations to mail it. These elements combined provide strong evidence that speech is "commercial." But any single one does not. That advertisements discuss important public issues does not make them non-commercial. This is because companies already have the right to make direct comments on public issues, and immunizing "issue"-oriented advertising from government regulation would immunize false/misleading product misinformation. Here, we find Youngs' (P) flyers were "commercial." "Commercial speech" enjoys qualified, but substantial, First Amendment protection. [Here, we find the Government's (D) justification for the statute are insufficient to warrant its sweeping prohibitions.] Reversed.

Analysis:
Virginia State Board of Pharmacy held that "commercial speech" enjoys less First Amendment protection than non-commercial speech. This case examined the Court's definition of "commercial"

Bolger v. Youngs Drug Products Corp. (Continued)

speech. Advertisements that merely offer something for sale, presumably without also advocating the item's benefits, are classic commercial speech. Problems begin to arise when the speech or advertisement does more than merely offer something for sale, but instead may advocate the use of the product.

Central Hudson Gas v. Public Service Commission of New York

(Regulated Utility) v. (Regulatory Agency)
447 U.S. 557, 100 S.Ct. 2343 (1980)

COMMERCIAL SPEECH SUBJECT TO INTERMEDIATE SCRUTINY

■ **INSTANT FACTS** During an fuel shortage, an energy regulatory agency banned advertisements which might increase demand for electricity. When the agency continued the ban past the shortage, a utility sued.

■ **BLACK LETTER RULE** Non-deceptive / non-illegal advertising may be regulated if (i) the restriction is justified by "substantial" governmental interests, (ii) the restriction *directly* advances that interest, and (iii) the regulation is the least-restrictive method needed to achieve that interest.

■ **PROCEDURAL BASIS**

In First Amendment challenge to agency regulation, appeal from judgment for agency.

■ **FACTS**

During a fuel shortage, energy regulatory agency Public Service Commission of New York (Commission) (D) ordered regulated energy utilities to cease all advertising that "promotes the use of electricity." After the shortage passed, Commission (D) decided to continue the ban. Electric utility Central Hudson Gas (P) challenged the ban on First Amendment grounds. At trial, the court found the ban constitutional. Central Hudson (P) appeals.

■ **ISSUE**

May the government ban advertising by electricity utilities, to conserve energy?

■ **DECISION AND RATIONALE**

(Powell, J.) No. Non-deceptive/non-illegal advertising may be regulated if (i) the restriction is justified by "substantial" governmental interests, (ii) the restriction *directly* advances that interest, and (iii) the regulation is the least-restrictive method needed to achieve that interest. (There is no constitutional impediment to suppressing commercial messages which either advertise unlawful activities, or are more likely to deceive the public than inform it.) The government bears the burden of proving these elements. Here, there is no allegation of illegality or deception. Commission's (D) interest—energy conservation—is substantial, considering America's dependence on Arab oil. The ban advances Commission's (D) interest in conservation directly, since there is an immediate connection between advertising and demand for electricity. But the ban here is not narrowly-tailored. It reaches all promotional advertising, regardless of its impact on overall energy use. For example, it would suppress info about electrical devices/services that would cause no net increase in energy usage. Also, Commission (D) has not proven that more limited restrictions would be ineffective. Reversed.

Analysis:

Central Hudson's test remains the standard used to decide whether government may regulate commercial speech. Essentially, it is intermediate scrutiny. The extra prong is merely that, if the speech

Central Hudson Gas v. Public Service Commission of New York (Continued)

advertises illegal activities or is false/misleading, the government may impose any restriction, including a ban. This is because false advertising, and solicitation to illegality, is unprotected. Note that later cases no longer require that the regulatory method be the *least* restrictive; modern cases require it be sufficiently narrowly-tailored.

■ CASE VOCABULARY

INTERMEDIATE SCRUTINY: Standard whereby government regulations are constitutional only if they are (i) "substantially" related to (ii) "significant" governmental interests, and (iii) use the least-restrictive means available to achieve that interest.

Friedman v. Rogers
(Other Five Members of Texas Optometry Board) v. (Member of Optometry Board)
440 U.S. 1, 99 S.Ct. 887 (1979)

GOVERNMENT MAY REGULATE TRADE NAMES, AS INHERENTLY DECEPTIVE

■ **INSTANT FACTS** When Texas forbade optometrists to practice under trade names, they challenged.

■ **BLACK LETTER RULE** The government may ban practicing under trade names.

■ **PROCEDURAL BASIS**

First/Fourteenth Amendment challenge to state statute.

■ **FACTS**

Texas's (D) legislature prohibited practicing optometry under a trade name, finding trade names could deceive the public. [For reasons, see analysis below.] Apparently, some Optometrists (P) challenged the ban as unconstitutional, probably contending trade names are not inherently misleading.

■ **ISSUE**

May a state ban the use of trade names?

■ **DECISION AND RATIONALE**

(Powell, J.) Yes. The government may ban practicing under trade names. Trade names are a form of commercial speech, and nothing more. They convey no additional information about the services offered, or their price. Over time, the public wrongly tends to associate a trade name with a certain level of price and quality. Since trade-name users can change and manipulate their trade names at will, there is significance possibility that trade names will be used to mislead the public. The possibilities for deception are numerous. Since trade names may remain unchanged despite changes in the optometric staff, trade names may capitalize on the reputation of an optometrist no longer associated with that practice. Also, trade names free optometrists from relying on their personal reputations, and even allows them to change names to escape a reputation for negligence or misconduct. An optometrist owning several shops can give a false impression of competition by using different trade names. Texas's (D) legislature's concerns were based on their actual experience. Clearly, Texas' (D) interest in protecting the public from trade names' deceptive and misleading use is substantial and well-demonstrated, and the statute is a constitutionally-permissible regulation in furtherance of that interest.

Analysis:

Friedman differentiated "commercially motivated" speech, which appears entitled to full First Amendment protection, from "commercial speech," which is subject to the *ad hoc* approach. It is now clear that cases such as *New York Times Co. v. Sullivan* did not involve "commercial speech" in the sense of speech designed to sell a product or solicit patronage for profit. Instead such cases involved speech concerning non-commercial issues, even though the speech might have been motivated by commercial

Friedman v. Rogers (Continued)

and monetary desires of the speakers. This commercially motivated speech is not "commercial speech," and it is protected by all First Amendment principles. The majority opinion in *Friedman* indicated that commercial speech is speech connected to the selling of a product or service. Such speech has more limited First Amendment protection than does non-commercial speech.

■ CASE VOCABULARY

TRADE NAME: A business name, used by a professional to designate his practice. For example, an optometrist might call his practice by the trade name "Thrifty Optometry" rather than "Dr. Friedman, M.D., Optometry."

Linmark Associates v. Township of Willingboro

(Seller of Property) v. (Town Governmen)
431 U.S. 85, 97 S.Ct. 1614 (1977)

GOVERNMENT CAN'T BAN "FOR SALE" SIGNS

■ **INSTANT FACTS** When a town bans house "For Sale" signs to prevent white flight, Realtors sue.

■ **BLACK LETTER RULE** The government cannot restrict commercial communications, unless false or misleading.

■ **PROCEDURAL BASIS**

In First Amendment challenge to town ordinance, appeal from voiding.

■ **FACTS**

The Township of Willingboro (D), concerned that white homeowners were leaving racially-mixed neighborhoods, prohibited posting house signs saying "For Sale" or "Sold." Apparently, realtor Linmark Associates (P) challenged the law's constitutionality, under *Virginia Pharmacy Board* [commercial speech merits First Amendment protection], and won when the District Court found Township (D) failed to prove any panic selling was occurring. Township (D) appeals, claiming it is necessary for the important goal of promoting stable, racially-integrated housing.

■ **ISSUE**

Can a town government ban house "for sale" signs to prevent panic selling?

■ **DECISION AND RATIONALE**

(Marshall, J.) No. The government cannot restrict commercial communications, unless false or misleading. This case is similar to *Virginia Pharmacy Board*. Here, house sellers are just as interested in communicating their sale, and buyers are just as interested in receiving such communications. The societal interest in the free flow of information is not less than for drug sales. This information is vitally important to homebuyers, since it impacts on one of their most important decisions. Township's (D) claimed necessity is unconvincing. True, its interest in promoting racially-integrated housing is vital; this Court previously recognized integration's benefits for blacks and whites, and Congress promotes it. But Township (D) never proved this ordinance is necessary or effective. Township (D) never proved it experienced substantial panic selling by whites. There is no proof any panic selling was caused by "For Sale" signs, which were displayed in only 2% of homes. Also, it is unproven that proscribing signs will reduce public awareness of sales, thus decreasing public panic. More fundamentally, *Virginia Pharmacy Board* stands for the proposition that the First Amendment requires governments to let people obtain full information, to make their own, informed decisions. Under *Virginia Pharmacy Board*, government can restrict commercial information only if it is false or misleading. Holding otherwise would let any locality suppress facts which reflect poorly on it, on the pretext that disclosure would make residents act "irrationally." Affirmed; ordinance void.

Analysis:

The Court emphasized that the Township's (D) ordinance, by its own terms, made clear that it was not concerned with the time, place, or manner of the speech but its content. It did not prohibit all lawn signs, or all lawn signs of a particular size, in order, perhaps, to promote aesthetic values or other goals unrelated to the suppression of free expression. Rather, it banned signs that said, "For Sale." The Court also found the defect in the ordinance "basic" because if "dissemination of this information can be restricted, then every locality in the country can suppress any facts that reflect poorly on the locality, so long as a plausible claim can be made that disclosure would cause the recipients of the information to act 'irrationally.'"

■ CASE VOCABULARY

A FORTIORARI: Even more strongly; even more so.

WHITE FLIGHT: White residents' leaving their racially-mixed neighborhoods.

44 Liquormart, Inc. v. Rhode Island

(*Liquor Dealers*) v. (*State Government*)
517 U.S. 484, 116 S.Ct. 1495 (1996)

GOVERNMENT CAN'T STOP LIQUOR DEALERS FROM ADVERTISING

■ **INSTANT FACTS** When a state banned liquor dealers from advertising prices, they sued.

■ **BLACK LETTER RULE** The government may regulate truthful, non-misleading commercial speech only if the regulation (i) directly furthers (ii) legitimate state interests.

■ PROCEDURAL BASIS

In First Amendment challenge to state statute, appeal from voiding.

■ FACTS

Rhode Island (D) banned all advertisements which "make reference to the price of any alcoholic beverages," to promote "temperance." [This effectively prevents price competition among booze sellers, keeping prices high.] Liquor dealer 44 Liquormart, Inc. (P) challenged the statute on First Amendment grounds. At trial, the District Court held the statute unconstitutional, finding insufficient evidence the statute would meet its aim of reducing consumption. Rhode Island (D) appeals, claiming the statute is justified by its substantial interest in promoting temperance, and narrowly tailored.

■ ISSUE

May the government ban advertisements of liquor prices?

■ DECISION AND RATIONALE

(Stevens, J.) No. The government may regulate truthful, non-misleading commercial speech only if the regulation (i) directly furthers (ii) legitimate state interests. Generally, the First Amendment requires courts be skeptical of statutes that keep people from receiving accurate information, for what the government perceives is their own good. This applies equally to commercial speech. We tolerate greater regulation of commercial speech because governments have interests in protecting consumers from "commercial harms." But we note that bans on truthful, non-misleading information usually are enacted not to prevent commercial harms; rather, they often hide underlying governmental policies, which often could be implemented without restricting speech. The government must prove the statute (i) directly advances (ii) a substantial state interest. "Direct advancing" requires statutes be voided if they provide only "ineffectual or remote support for the government's purpose." Thus, the state bears the burden of proving its statute will advance its interest "to a material degree." If the state wishes to take drastic measures, like suppressing accurate advertising completely, it must make stronger showings. Here, Rhode Island (D) has substantial interests in reducing alcohol consumption. But this law does not directly advance them. Even if we assume that a price-advertising ban will mitigate competition and maintain higher prices, and that higher prices will tend to reduce demand and consumption somewhat, still we have seen no evidence this effect will be significant. The record suggests the ban may encourage some poor, low-volume drinkers to refrain. But there is no evidence that other types of drinkers will be deterred substantially. At trial, the District Court found they would not. Also, the statute is

44 Liquormart, Inc. v. Rhode Island (Continued)

not narrowly tailored; other regulations not involving speech would be more likely to promote tolerance (e.g., minimum prices, increased alcohol taxes). Affirmed; statute void.

■ CONCURRENCE

(Thomas, J.) When the government's interest is to keep the consumer of permissible goods ignorant, to manipulate their marketplace choices, this should be illegal per se. Such interests are illegitimate. I would not apply *Central Hudson Gas'* balancing test.

■ CONCURRENCE

(O'Connor, J.) I would decide this case more narrowly, based on *Hudson Central.* Under its test, Rhode Island's (D) statute is not sufficiently narrowly tailored to reducing consumption; liquor taxes would be more direct and efficient.

Analysis:

In the majority opinion, though referencing *Central Hudson.* Justice Stevens asserts that strict scrutiny should be applied to at least some regulations of commercial speech (in this case restrictions on non-misleading speech). He stated that, "when a State entirely prohibits the dissemination of truthful, non-misleading commercial messages for reasons unrelated to the preservation of a fair bargaining process, there is far less reason to depart from the rigorous review that the First Amendment generally demands." *Central Hudson* does not apply strict scrutiny, but instead applies a lesser-degree of scrutiny. However, because the opinion in this case is a plurality opinion, and not enough justices expressly agreed to alter or abandon the *Central Hudson* test, it still stands today as the proper test for reviewing restrictions on commercial speech.

Lorillard Tobacco Co. v. Reilly

(*Tobacco Company*) v. (*State Official*)
533 U.S. 525, 121 S.Ct. 2404 (2001)

RESTRICTIONS ON COMMERCIAL SPEECH ARE NOT SUBJECT TO STRICT SCRUTINY

■ **INSTANT FACTS** Lorillard Tobacco Company (P) challenged the constitutionality of Massachusetts regulations on the advertising of smokeless tobacco and cigar products near schools and playgrounds.

■ **BLACK LETTER RULE** Restrictions on commercial speech are invalid if the speech concerns lawful activity and they do not directly advance a substantial government interest in the narrowest manner possible.

■ **PROCEDURAL BASIS**

Certiorari to review an undisclosed appellate decision.

■ **FACTS**

The Massachusetts Attorney General promulgated state regulations to eliminate deception and unfairness in the marketing, sale, and distribution of tobacco products targeting child-users. In part, the state regulations prohibited the outdoor advertising of smokeless tobacco and cigar products within 1,000 feet of any school or playground. Likewise, the state regulations forbade indoor, point-of-sale advertising of smokeless tobacco and cigar products lower than five feet from the floor in establishments located within 1,000 feet of a school or playground. Although the Federal Cigarette Labeling and Advertising Act (FCLAA) established a federal scheme to regulate all advertising of cigarettes, it did not expressly preempt state and local regulation relating to smokeless tobacco and cigar products. Lorillard Tobacco Company (P) challenged the advertising regulations as violating the First Amendment.

■ **ISSUE**

Do the Massachusetts regulations on outdoor and indoor advertising of smokeless tobacco and cigar products violate the First Amendment?

■ **DECISION AND RATIONALE**

(O'Connor, J.) Yes. To determine the measure of protection afforded to commercial speech, four elements must be considered. First, the speech "at least must concern lawful activity and not be misleading." Second, the governmental interest at stake must be substantial. If these elements are satisfied, a restriction on commercial speech must directly advance the substantial government interest asserted and, finally, be no more extensive than necessary to do so. Only the last two elements are in question here.

With respect to the outdoor advertising regulations, the Attorney General (D) has provided ample evidence that advertisement of smokeless tobacco and cigar products stimulates sales and consumption, and that the suppression of such advertisement has the opposite effect. Accordingly, the regulations directly advance the substantial government interest of regulating minor consumption of tobacco products. The regulations are not, however, the least extensive means available to do so. Because of the number of schools and playgrounds in Massachusetts's major metropolitan areas, the

Lorillard Tobacco Co. v. Reilly (Continued)

outdoor advertising regulations effectively ban tobacco advertisements in almost all of these areas. Assuming that the tobacco advertisements disseminate truthful information, the scope and breadth of the regulations are, therefore, not a reasonable means to the ends sought. Manufacturers and retailers in these areas will be unable to inform paying customers that tobacco products are for sale within their stores. Such a burden on speech is too onerous considering the interests the regulations seek to further.

The indoor, point-of-sale restrictions likewise violate the First Amendment. Although seeking to prevent tobacco use by minors, not all minors are less than five feet tall, and those who are can certainly look up and see the advertisement. Accordingly, the indoor regulations do not directly further a substantial government interest and are not a reasonably fit to such a goal either.

■ CONCURRENCE IN PART

(Thomas, J.) When the government seeks to restrict truthful speech because of the message it conveys, strict scrutiny should apply. However, the advertising ban is not narrowly tailored to further a compelling government interest. The regulations seek to protect children from the health risks associated with tobacco use. But health risks are posed by fast food and alcohol consumption as well. Yet, children consistently view advertisements for these products in many different media. The state may not create an exception to commercial speech without a stronger interest asserted.

■ CONCURRENCE IN PART

(Stevens, J.) Although protection of minors from tobacco use before they reach an age to make a mature, informed decision is a compelling government interest, the regulations are not tailored appropriately to reach this end. By prohibiting advertisement within 1,000 feet of schools and playgrounds, the regulations restrict advertising not only as to the children they seek to protect, but also in regard to adults to whom manufacturers and retailers may wish to advertise. The government may not suppress speech to adult consumers merely because it is not fit for children. Accordingly, the regulations do not employ the least restrictive means of reaching their objective.

Analysis:

The challenged regulations ban advertisements in specified locations only because of the content of the messages conveyed. Under traditional First Amendment jurisprudence, such content-based restrictions call for the strictest of scrutiny. Yet, in the arena of commercial speech, the Court does not apply the same analysis. Should the protection of speech be different merely because it is uttered for profit?

■ CASE VOCABULARY

COMMERCIAL SPEECH: Communication (such as advertising and marketing) that involves only the commercial interests of the speaker and the audience, and is therefore afforded lesser First Amendment protection than social, political, or religious speech.

New York Times Co. v. Sullivan

(*Newspaper and Advertisers*) v. (*Public Official*)
376 U.S. 254, 84 S.Ct. 710 (1964)

SUPREME COURT ARTICULATES REQUIREMENTS FOR SLANDERED PUBLIC OFFICIALS TO SUE

■ **INSTANT FACTS** When a police chief won a libel suit over false ads suggesting he harassed black activists, the defendants challenged the libel law as burdening speech.

■ **BLACK LETTER RULE** If tort law allows public officials to recover for defamation, it must require they (i) prove actual malice, (ii) prove the statement's falsity, and (iii) prove all elements with "clear and convincing" evidence.

■ **PROCEDURAL BASIS**

In civil libel suit, appeal of appellate affirmation of verdict for defendant.

■ **FACTS**

In the early 1960s, several black Clergymen (D) ran a full-page ad in the *New York Times*, criticizing Montgomery, Alabama's police chief (with others) of intimidating black student-protesters with weapons, padlocking their dining hall, and expelling them. The ad also implied the police (with others) assaulted Martin Luther King, bombed his house, and arrested him falsely seven times. Some of these statements were false and/or misleading. Montgomery, Alabama's police chief Sullivan (P) sued *Times* (D) and Clergymen (D) civilly for libel, claiming the comments were understood to be addressed against him personally. Under Alabama's civil libel law, if writings are found "libelous per se," the jury need only find that the defendants actually published them, and that the writings were "of or concerning" (i.e., about) the plaintiff. (Notably, plaintiffs did not need to prove any actual malice, or specific monetary damages.) Defendants could claim their statements' truth as an affirmative defense, if *they* could prove them true. At trial, the judge instructed the jury accordingly, and told them Clergymen's (D) statements were not privileged. The jury found *Times* (D) and Clergymen (D) liable, and awarded the full $500,000 sought. *Times* (D) and Clergymen (D) appealed, but Alabama's Supreme Court affirmed. Defendants appeal again, claiming their writings were protected under the First/Fourteenth Amendments.

■ **ISSUE**

May state tort law allow a public official to recover for libel for inaccurate political commentary without proving intent to slander?

■ **DECISION AND RATIONALE**

(Brennan) No. If tort law allows public officials to recover for defamation, it must require they (i) prove actual malice, (ii) prove the statement's falsity, and (iii) prove all elements with "clear and convincing" evidence. Holding otherwise would allow the government to chill criticism of its officials through lax pleading requirements, violating First Amendment policy. The Founders recognized that debate on public issues should be uninhibited, and may well include attacks on government officials which are vehement, caustic, and unpleasantly sharp. The First Amendment's protections have never depended on the speech's truth, nor their popularity or social utility. It is especially onerous to assign defendants the burden of proving truth. This is because some erroneous statement is inevitable in free debate, and

New York Times Co. v. Sullivan (Continued)

should be tolerated. Similarly, even defamatory speech is protected. [That is, protected from excessive sanctions, but not fully immune from liability, of course.] That criticism of officials' conduct impacts these officials' professional reputations is irrelevant. Also, that the defamation law allows a defense of truth is insufficient, since requiring critics to guarantee their statements' truth on pain of unlimited libel judgments encourages self-censorship. It would also chill legitimate criticism, because critics might doubt they could prove their statements' truth in court, or pay legal expenses. Here, the proof presented is insufficient to prove actual malice, since there is no evidence that Clergymen (D) authorized use of their names in the ad, or were aware of its falsity. Thus, the judgment cannot constitutionally be sustained. Reversed.

Analysis:

This is a very important case because it is the first to set forth the actual malice standard for judging commentary made about the conduct of public officials, a standard that significantly changed libel law. In essence, the Court requires that public officials, in order to recover damages for libel, must prove that the speaker of the defamatory words spoke or printed with actual malice, i.e., with knowledge that the statement was false or with reckless disregard as to whether it was false. This is significant because it places a difficult burden upon public officials—they cannot simply prove that defamatory statements were made and have damages inferred. The Court also makes it clear that state libel laws must protect free speech as required by the First Amendment. Since its publication, this decision has been clarified in a large number of subsequent cases, as the doctrine of actual malice and public officials, and it has been crafted and refined.

■ CASE VOCABULARY

[ACTUAL] MALICE: Knowledge that a (defamatory) statement was actually false, or reckless disregard for its truth/falsity.

DEFAMATION: Falsehoods which injure someone's reputation and/or cause economic losses.

LIBEL: Defamation (damaging falsehood) in writing or print.

LIBEL PER SE: Libel (written slander) that is automatically deemed defamatory, without the need to prove it was harmful. Certain falsehoods are so widely understood to be harmful that they are deemed libelous as a matter of law.

RECKLESS [DISREGARD]: To do an act without caring about the consequences. Here, "reckless disregard for truth" means saying something without bothering to find out whether it's true.

SEDITION: Treasonous or anti-government speech. The *Sedition Act of 1798* imposed harsh fines and sentences for anti-government activism.

SPECIAL DAMAGES: Actual, quantifiable monetary loss caused by a tort. Required to be pleaded for some torts.

Gertz v. Welch

(*Lawyer*) v. (*Publisher*)
418 U.S. 323, 94 S.Ct. 2997 (1974)

NEW YORK TIMES INAPPLICABLE TO NON-"PUBLIC" PLAINTIFFS

■ **INSTANT FACTS** When a publisher slanders a civil litigator in a notorious case as a Communist and criminal, it claims privilege against defamation.

■ **BLACK LETTER RULE** States may enact defamation laws which allow non-"public" plaintiffs to recover compensatory damages upon proof of any level of fault, but cannot permit presumed or punitive damages without proof of knowing falsity or reckless disregard for truth.

■ FACTS

Policeman Nuccio shot a youth named Nelson fatally, for which he was prosecuted, and ultimately convicted of murder. Later, Nelson's family hired attorney and bar activist Gertz (P) to sue Nuccio civilly. The right-wing paper *American Opinion*, edited by Welch (D), published an article claiming Nuccio was framed by a Communist conspiracy to weaken American police departments. The article claimed Gertz (P) was the architect of a "frame-up," "Leninist," "Communist-fronter," and member of the "Marxist League for Industrial Democracy" and "Intercollegiate Socialist Society," and implied Gertz (P) has a criminal record. While Gertz (P) was active in the leftist National Lawyers Guild, the article claimed the Guild "probably did more than any other outfit to plan the Communist attack on the Chicago police during the 1968 Democratic Convention." The article contained falsehoods and inaccuracies, which Welch (D) never checked or substantiated. Gertz (P) sued Welch (D) for defamation. Welch (D) defended, claiming privilege under *New York Times* and alleging Gertz's (P) civic involvement made him a "public figure."

■ ISSUE

May defamation laws allow non-public plaintiffs to recover for negligent or reckless defamation?

■ DECISION AND RATIONALE

(Powell) Yes. States may enact defamation laws which allow non-"public" plaintiffs to recover compensatory damages upon proof of any level of fault, but cannot permit presumed or punitive damages without proof of knowing falsity or reckless disregard for truth. The Constitution should protect erroneous statements of fact. Though they themselves are not important enough to protect, making publishers strictly liable for factual inaccuracies promotes intolerable self-censorship. But no protection extends to intentional lies and careless errors, which are worthless as steps to truth. Also, states have legitimate interests in enacting laws against defamation, to protect the dignity of public officials, public figures, and private figures. For public officials and public figures, states may allow recovery for reputational injuries only on "clear and convincing" proof that the defamatory falsehood was made with knowledge of its falsity or reckless disregard for its truth. *New York Times.* "Public officials" are those holding office. "Public figures" are those who actively seek and obtain public attention based on their notoriety. The government's interest in protecting public officials and public figures reputation is less than its interest in protecting private individuals, since public officials/figures usually have access to media and realistic opportunities to counteract false statements, and since they voluntarily risk public

Gertz v. Welch (Continued)

scrutiny by thrusting themselves into public controversies. Even if some public officials/figures lack such opportunities/motivations, the media has the right to assume they do. However, the government may enact stronger defamation laws to protect *private* individuals, because they lack such qualities. States may enact defamation laws which allow non-"public" plaintiffs to recover compensatory damages upon proof of any level of fault, but cannot permit presumed or punitive damages without proof of knowing falsity or reckless disregard for truth. We overrule *Rosenbloom v. Metromedia, Inc.* (1971), whose plurality suggested the *New York Times* standard applies to all subjects of "public or general interest," even if the plaintiff is a private person; its holding abridges the state's legitimate interest unacceptably, and judges should not have discretion to decide which matters concern the "public interest." Next, we find Gertz (P) is not a "public figure." While Gertz (P) was prominent in the legal community, his fame did not extend to either the jury or the general public. Judgment for plaintiff affirmed.

■ DISSENT

(Brennan, J.) Allowing the state to impose all but strict liability does not permit adequate "breathing room" for free debate. Instead, we should follow *Rosenbloom.*

■ DISSENT

(White, J.) Traditionally, states were allowed to set their defamation laws freely, because the Court consistently recognized that libel is unprotected. The majority opinion effectively federalizes libel laws and overturns the laws of 50 states. While this sweeping change is legitimate under judicial review, it is ill-considered.

Analysis:

This case is significant in several ways. First, it overrules *Rosenbloom*, which had applied the *New York Times* standard to even non-public plaintiffs, when they were involved in matters concerning the "general interest" or "public interest." Second, it sets some new limits on state libel laws, albeit laxer ones. Note that under *Gertz*, to recover general or punitive damages, plaintiffs must still prove "actual malice." However, they can recover specific damages (actual, provable economic losses) upon showing merely negligent misstatements. Finally, *Gertz* offers some more information on the Court's definition of "public" plaintiffs, though there is still no precise definition. If the Court's principal concern is to protect the communications industry from large libel judgments, the dissent is correct that the new requirements with respect to general and punitive damages would be ample protection.

■ **CASE VOCABULARY**

AD HOC: For this particular purpose.

PLURALITY: Decision where there is no opinion joined by a majority of judges; the concurrence in the most judges join is the "plurality."

Dun & Bradstreet, Inc. v. Greenmoss Builders, Inc.
(*Credit Rater*) v. (*Rated Business*)
472 U.S. 749, 105 S.Ct. 2939 (1985)

GERTZ INAPPLICABLE TO PRIVATE FIGURES, SLANDERED ABOUT NON-PUBLIC MATTERS

■ **INSTANT FACTS** When a business sued its credit rater for defamatory inaccuracies and collected presumed and punitive damages, the rater claimed the award was unconstitutional under *Gertz*.

■ **BLACK LETTER RULE** For defamatory speech not involving "matters of public concern," defamation laws may allow plaintiffs to recover presumed and/or punitive damages without proving "actual malice."

■ **PROCEDURAL BASIS**

In defamation suit, appeal from judgment for plaintiff and award of punitive damages.

■ **FACTS**

Dun & Bradstreet, Inc. ("D&B") (D) reports credit and financial information about businesses. In compiling its report on Greenmoss Builders, Inc. (P), D&B (D) miscalculated its assets and liabilities grossly, and mistakenly reported Greenmoss (P) filed for bankruptcy. (The mistake happened because one of Greenmoss's (P) employees, not the company itself, filed for *personal* bankruptcy.) D&B (D) misreported on Greenmoss (P) to five subscribers. Under D&B's (D) terms, information recipients cannot reveal the information to others. Greenmoss (P) learned of the error, requested a correction, and requested the names of the receiving subscribers, to contact them. D&B (D) issued a correction and sent it to the 5 subscribers, but would not disclose their names. Greenmoss (P) sued D&B (D) for defamation, recovering $50K in presumed compensatory damages and $300K in punitive damages. D&B (D) appeals, contending credit reporting involves public issues, and presumed and punitive damages cannot be awarded without proof of malice, under *Gertz*. Greenmoss (P) responds, contending *Gertz* is inapplicable, because its credit report is not a public issue.

■ **ISSUE**

May a defamation plaintiff recover presumed and punitive damages for inaccurate credit reporting?

■ **DECISION AND RATIONALE**

(Powell, J.) Yes. For defamatory speech not involving "matters of public concern," defamation laws may allow plaintiffs to recover presumed and/or punitive damages without proving "actual malice." First, *Gertz* is inapplicable if the defamatory statement involved no issue of public concern. [Remember, *Gertz* held state defamation laws may not allow non-"public" plaintiffs to recover *presumed or punitive* damages without proof of knowing falsity/reckless disregard.] For speech other than "matters of public concern," the constitutional protection is less, and the state interest in protecting slandered individuals substantially outweighs it. States properly allow recovery for defamation for presumed damages, without requiring proof of "actual malice." This is because, in practice, proving actual damages from defamation is often impossible, even though it is obvious serious harm occurred. Traditionally, courts allowed presumed damages for 200 years. Second, individuals' credit reports are not matters of public concern;

Dun & Bradstreet, Inc. v. Greenmoss Builders, Inc. (Continued)

they interest only the speaker and its business audience. Here, this is especially true, since D&B's (D) reports were confidential. Judgment for plaintiff affirmed.

■ **DISSENT**

(Brennan, J.) This case's narrow issue is whether jury awards of presumed and punitive damages based on less than "actual malice" are constitutional. *Gertz* says, "no." The majority opinion is flawed. Even if judges can, and should, distinguish between "public" and "private concerns," the majority's definition of "public concerns" is too narrow. Credit reporting surely involves public concerns.

Analysis:

Dun & Bradstreet effectively modifies *Gertz*, limiting it to "matters of public concern" (and "public officials" and "figures"). Thus, defamation laws may permit non-public plaintiffs, slandered on matters of non-public concern, to recover on proving mere negligence and/or pleading presumed damages. But remember, if even non-public plaintiffs are slandered *on matters of public concern, Gertz* still applies.

■ **CASE VOCABULARY**

ACTUAL MALICE: Making defamatory statements either (a) knowing they're false, or (b) making reckless claims (i.e., realizing there's a strong chance they're false). Actual malice requires more than mere negligent misstatements.

PRESUMED DAMAGES: In defamation, damages awarded for defamatory statements *without* a showing of actual, quantifiable economic losses. In jurisdictions which allow presumed damages, plaintiffs can collect even if they cannot plead specific, actual losses. (a.k.a. general damages).

Hustler Magazine v. Falwell

(*Satirical Magazine*) v. (*Televangelist*)
485 U.S. 46, 108 S.Ct. 876 (1988)

NEW YORK TIMES EXTENDS TO INTENTIONAL INFLICTION OF EMOTIONAL DISTRESS SUITS BY "PUBLIC" PLAINTIFFS

■ **INSTANT FACTS** After a porn magazine published a fake interview suggesting a televangelist is a drunken, incestuous hypocrite, he sued for intentional infliction of emotional distress.

■ **BLACK LETTER RULE** Public figures / public officials cannot recover for intentional infliction of emotional distress from defamatory publications, unless they prove (i) it contained false statements of *fact*, and (ii) was made with "actual malice."

■ PROCEDURAL BASIS

In suit for intentional infliction of emotional distress and other torts, appeal from judgment for plaintiff.

■ FACTS

Porn magazine Hustler (D) ran a liquor ad parody libeling televangelist and sociopolitical commentator Jerry Falwell (P). The ad, a fake "interview," features Falwell (P) saying his "first time" was during a drunken, incestuous rendezvous with his mother in an outhouse. The ad suggested Falwell (P) was an immoral, drunken hypocrite who preached only when drunk. Hustler's (D) ad disclaimed itself as parody. Falwell (P) sued Hustler (D) and its publisher Larry Flynt (D) for invasion of privacy, libel, and intentional infliction of emotional distress. After trial, the jury found Hustler's (D) ad was not libelous, because it could not reasonably be understood as factual. But the jury found the defendants liable for intentional infliction of emotional distress, awarding $100K in compensatory damages and $100K in punitive damages. Hustler (D) appeals, claiming *New York Times* applies to intentional infliction of emotional distress. Falwell (P) responds, contending it does not, and that this ad is not sociopolitical commentary meriting protection.

■ ISSUE

May a public figure recover compensatory and punitive damages for intentional infliction of emotional distress from speech?

■ DECISION AND RATIONALE

(Rehnquist, C.J.) No. Public figures/public officials cannot recover for intentional infliction of emotional distress from defamatory publications, unless they prove (i) it contained false statements of *fact*, and (ii) was made with "actual malice." Generally, the law may impose tort liability for intentional infliction of emotional distress, because of its bad motives; most jurisdictions do. This is permissible in most circumstances. But public figures and public officials should not be allowed to sue for intentional infliction of emotional distress for defamatory publications unless they prove (i) it contained false statements of *fact*, and (ii) was made with "actual malice." Our policy is to preserve Americans' right to criticize men and measures. To do so, we must tolerate unreasoned or immoderate parodies. Parody, by definition, involves exaggerating people's physical features and embarrassments, often to offend the target. Allowing liability would subject political cartoonists and satirists to penalties, on flimsy evidence.

Hustler Magazine v. Falwell (Continued)

We cannot judge whether any specific caricature is so "outrageous" that it is no longer a legitimate political cartoon; there is no clear distinction, and giving discretion to judges and juries to apply their subjective standards would offend freedom of speech. Award for plaintiff reversed.

Analysis:

Hustler basically extends *New York Times* from defamation suits to the often-unrelated tort of intentional infliction of emotional distress. This tort only sometimes involves speech. It is usually used to prosecute harassment, obscene calls, offensive pranks, etc. However, in practice, it is rarely used, because the requirement of "extreme and outrageous" behavior is so high that it's rarely met. This extension of the law to one tort sets the stage for expanding it to other torts, which is illustrated by later cases. Here the Court held that public figures—and also public officials—cannot recover damages for intentional infliction of emotional distress without also showing that the publication contains a false statement "of fact" made with actual knowledge that the statement was false or with reckless disregard as to whether or not it was true. In this case, the parody was not reasonably believable, so no damages could be awarded.

■ CASE VOCABULARY

ACTUAL MALICE: Making defamatory statements while either (i) knowing they're false, or (ii) making them recklessly, disregarding a significant chance they're false.

INTENTIONAL INFLICTION OF EMOTIONAL DISTRESS: Tort whereby a person intentionally performs "extreme" and/or "outrageous" acts which are intended to, and do, cause extreme emotional distress.

INVASION OF PRIVACY: Torts whereby one subjects another to embarrassing publicity. Unlike defamation, invasion of privacy may involve revealing information which is true, but private. "Privacy" torts include unauthorized commercial appropriation of one's name/likeness and disclosing offensive, unimportant private info.

LIBEL: Written defamation, in print or picture.

Cox Broadcasting Corporation v. Cohn

(TV Station) v. (Rape Victim's Parents)
420 U.S. 469, 95 S.Ct. 1029 (1975)

NO LIABILITY EXISTS FOR PUBLICIZING PUBLIC DOCUMENTS

■ **INSTANT FACTS** When TV reporters broadcast a rape victim's name, violating state criminal laws, the victim's parents sued for privacy violations.

■ **BLACK LETTER RULE** The government cannot impose civil or criminal liability for publicizing public documents' contents truthfully.

■ PROCEDURAL BASIS

In suit for public disclosure of private facts, appeal from appellate reversal of judgment for plaintiff.

■ FACTS

Georgia statutes prohibit publishing/broadcasting rape victims' names. The Cohns' (P) daughter was raped and killed, and several men were prosecuted. Late in the trial, the court made available indictments containing the daughter's name. TV station owner Cox Broadcasting Corporation ("Broadcaster") (D) aired her name on TV. Cohn (P) sued Broadcaster (D), essentially for the common-law tort of public disclosure of private facts, citing the statute as evidence his daughter's privacy was violated impermissibly. Apparently, Cohn (P) won money damages. Broadcaster (D) appeals, claiming publication of public court documents is privileged. Cohn (P) responded that the statute and common law are justified by the state's interest in protecting victims' privacy.

■ ISSUE

May the government impose sanctions for publicizing court documents' contents?

■ DECISION AND RATIONALE

(White, J.) No. The government cannot impose civil or criminal liability for publicizing public documents' contents truthfully. We consider only the narrow issue of whether the government may impose sanctions for publishing the name of rape victims, obtained from public, judicial records opened for inspection. We do not address the broader question of whether the First/Fourteenth Amendment ever permits civil or criminal liability of truthful publications. There are powerful arguments for suggesting that there is some zone of privacy surrounding individuals, which the government may protect from intrusion by the press. But we do not believe the government can prohibit media from publishing public records' contents, for policy reasons. People rely on media to report news they couldn't investigate themselves, especially for reporting of government affairs. The media, in reporting on government workings, relies heavily on official records and government documents made open to the public. Media coverage improves judicial proceedings through public scrutiny. Trials are public events, and what transpires in courtrooms is public property. Presumably, the state itself concluded that making the records public would serve the public interest. Making such information available to the media, but sanctioning them for printing it for being "offensive," would encourage timidity and self-censorship, suppressing newsworthy items. Reversed.

Analysis:

In this case, both litigants' interests are strong. People generally do not enjoy having their private lives exposed to the public; this seems especially exploitative when the media peddles embarrassing scandals in which the public has no (legitimate) interest except rumor-mongering. However, public information is often an important source for legitimate media investigation. Even more strikingly, it seems hypocritical for the state to let people know this information if they come to the courthouse in person, but then say this information is not suitable for broadcast to other, equally situated members of the public.

■ CASE VOCABULARY

PUBLIC DISCLOSURE OF PRIVATE FACTS: Tort of publishing non-public information, which is not "of legitimate concern to the public," and whose publication would offend reasonable people.

ZONE OF PRIVACY: Idea that individuals deserve certain privacy rights, which the government should protect by civil/criminal law. (It does not necessarily imply a *physical* radius, into which reporters can't enter.)

Florida Star v. B.J.F.

(Newspaper) v. *(Rape Victim)*
491 U.S. 524, 109 S.Ct. 2603 (1989)

COURT REAFFIRMS NO LIABILITY FOR PEOPLE PUBLISHING LAWFULLY-OBTAINED, TRUTHFUL INFORMATION

■ **INSTANT FACTS** When a newspaper uses public records to name a rape victim, against state law, the victim sues for public disclosure of private information.

■ **BLACK LETTER RULE** If a newspaper *lawfully* obtains *truthful* information about a matter of public significance, state law may not punish its publication, absent a need to further a state interest "of the highest order."

■ **PROCEDURAL BASIS**

In civil suit for public disclosure of private information, appeal from judgment for plaintiff.

■ **FACTS**

Florida statutes make it unlawful to "print, publish, or broadcast [sex assault victims' names] in any instrument of mass communication." A woman, identified as B.J.F. (P), was raped, and reported it to police. The Florida police prepared a report, including B.J.F.'s (P) full name. Following police policy, they placed the report in their pressroom, which offers unrestricted access. A reporter from *The Florida Star* (D) copied the report and published an article, including B.J.F.'s (P) name. Consequently, B.J.F. (P) received harassing calls and rape threats, and was forced to move and seek therapy. B.J.F. (P) sued for civil invasion of privacy, apparently claiming Florida Star (D) was negligent per se in violating the statute. At trial, B.J.F. (P) prevailed, receiving $75K compensation and $25K in punitive damages. Florida Star (D) appeals, claiming publication of publicly-available information is protected, under *Cox Broadcasting*.

■ **ISSUE**

May a newspaper be found liable for publishing lawfully-obtained, truthful information?

■ **DECISION AND RATIONALE**

(Marshall, J.) No. If a newspaper *lawfully* obtains *truthful* information about a matter of public significance, state law may not punish its publication, absent a need to further a state interest "of the highest order." *Cox Broadcasting* is not necessarily controlling here; Cox involved media reports which aided the judiciary by publicizing trials, which is not present here. We hold someone publishing truthful, lawfully-obtained information may be liable only when the punishment (i) is narrowly-tailored (ii) to "a state interest of the highest order." Here, the statute does not meet those requirements. First, because the statute only protects legally-obtained information, the government has ample means to restrict the information which may be obtained legally. Second, since the information is already publicly available, punishing disseminators is unlikely to advance state interests. This is especially true where the government itself made the information available; it would be anomalous to sanction persons other than those who released it. Third, punishing media for publishing truthful information encourages excessive "timidity and self-censorship." We do not hold that truthful publication is automatically constitutionality

Florida Star v. B.J.F. (Continued)

protected, or that there is no zone of personal privacy within which the government may prevent the press's intrusion. Reversed.

■ DISSENT

(White, J.) The majority undermines the tort of publication of private facts, one of the 20th century's most noteworthy laws. This tort recognizes, properly, that some truthful information about people should not be published, because of its consequences. Here, B.J.F.'s (P) continued harassment deserves compensation.

Analysis:

This case essentially reiterates the principle first articulated in *Cox Broadcasting*: states usually cannot bar disclosure of already-public information. Again, the Court reaches its decision by an ostensible interest-balancing test. Objectively, there is no policy reason why newspaper readers need to know B.J.F.'s (P) name, or even initials. While the public has legitimate interests in knowing about local crime rates and investigations, they are no better off knowing victims' names than reading. "An unidentified local woman was raped; police are investigating." Still, it would be perverse to punish *The Florida Star* (D) for publishing information disseminated rather carelessly by the police. The better policy may be for police to stop leaving sensitive information lying around in public view.

■ CASE VOCABULARY

NEGLIGENCE PER SE: Negligence presumed, without need for proof, when a defendant's acts violated statutory law.

Bartnicki v. Vopper

(*Union's Chief Negotiator*) v. (*Radio Show Host*)
532 U.S. 514, 121 S.Ct. 1753 (2001)

ILLEGALLY OBTAINED INFORMATION MAY BE PUBLISHED BY A THIRD-PARTY WHO OBTAINS IT THROUGH PROPER MEANS

■ **INSTANT FACTS** Bartnicki's (P) cell phone conversation with a union representative was intercepted and played on the radio by Vopper (D); Bartnicki (P) sued Vopper (D) for violation of a federal anti-wiretapping statute.

■ **BLACK LETTER RULE** If a media outlet lawfully obtains truthful information about a matter of public significance, publication of that information may not be sanctioned absent a need "of the highest order."

■ **PROCEDURAL BASIS**

Certiorari to review an undisclosed appellate decision.

■ **FACTS**

Bartnicki (P) was the lead negotiator for a teacher's union. During a cell phone call with the union's president, Bartnicki (P) stated that, unless negotiations started progressing, the union would have to "blow off [the school district negotiators'] front porches." After the school district and teachers settled, Vopper (D) played a tape of the conversation between Bartnicki (P) and the union president on his local radio talk show. Bartnicki (P) sued Vopper (D) for the unlawful disclosure of the contents of the intercepted call. During discovery, it was learned that Vopper (D) received the recording from a union opponent, who claimed to have received the unsolicited recording in his mailbox. In defense of the action, Vopper (D) claimed he did not himself intercept the call and does not know who did, that the radio station legally obtained a tape of the call, and that the subject matter of the conversation was a matter of public concern.

■ **ISSUE**

May a third party publish unlawfully obtained information if the third party himself obtains the information legally?

■ **DECISION AND RATIONALE**

(Stevens, J.) Yes. In an effort to protect individual privacy interests, Congress passed Title III of the Omnibus Crime Control and Safe Streets Act, punishing under subsection (c) any person who "willfully discloses, or endeavors to disclose, to any other person the contents of any wire or oral communication, knowing or having reason to know that the information was obtained through the interception of a [protected] wire or oral communication." Since its adoption, Title III has been expanded beyond wire and oral communications to include electronic and cordless telephone communications. As it exists, the statute is content neutral, protecting all wire, oral, or electronic communications regardless of their content. Yet, subsection (c) does not regulate conduct, but rather prohibits one from revealing the content of a particular truthful message.

Bartnicki v. Vopper (Continued)

The government, as intervenor, identified two interests served by the federal statute. First, the statute removes the incentive to intercept private conversations; second, it minimizes the harm to those whose conversations have been unlawfully intercepted. The desire to deter privacy violations is a worthy goal, but punishing a disclosure of information related to the public interest by one not involved in the initial illegality does not properly serve that goal. Moreover, the fear of disclosure of private conversations may have a chilling effect on private speech. The Court cannot accept one interest as superior to the other; instead, it must balance the competing interests.

It is clear that some violations of privacy are worse than others and, while interception alone is embarrassing, public disclosure can be even worse. Notwithstanding the legitimate access to an illegally intercepted message, there is justification for preventing disclosure. This case presents a different scenario, however. The information that was intercepted is related to an important public issue. "One of the costs associated with participation in public affairs is an attendant loss of privacy." Accordingly, the broadcast was not illegal.

■ CONCURRENCE

(Breyer, J.) The holding of this case is strictly limited to the facts presented here: the lawful conduct on the part of the broadcasters and the fact the subject matter was of public concern. Because the statute presents the competing constitutional issues of the right of privacy and the freedom of speech, the statute must reasonably balance its speech-restricting and speech-enhancing consequences. The statute encourages private speech by protecting it from interception and future disclosure, but discourages public speech by protecting private communications from disclosure. Yet, here, the statute acts to disproportionately infringe upon the freedom of the press. Bartnicki (P) had no legitimate interest in the privacy of his inflammatory statements, and Vopper (D) acted lawfully in receiving the tape. Likewise, the speakers on the tape were limited public figures, voluntarily speaking of matters of public concern, eroding away their interests in the privacy of their communication. In cases such as this, involving a low privacy interest relating to a matter of public concern, the rights of the press must prevail.

■ DISSENT

(Rehnquist, C.J.) Technology facilitates countless important and confidential conversations, raising concerns over privacy. To prevent at least some of these violations of privacy, laws have been enacted prohibiting the intentional interception of communications. The majority holds that these statutes all violate the First Amendment, at least in those cases where the content of the calls involves a matters a public concern. As a result, the majority must see that this holding, rather than encouraging freedom of speech, impedes it. Under the prior rulings of this Court, the statute should withstand constitutional challenge. It is narrowly drafted, content-neutral, and affects only information obtained illegally. Since the law furthers a substantial government interest, it should be enforced. Broadcasting conversations of public figures ignores the fact that even they have the right to engage in private conversations without fear of interception.

Analysis:

Just as in *Sullivan v. New York Times*, the Court here forced those that choose to venture into the public arena to suffer a certain loss of privacy. In Chief Justice Rehnquist's dissent, he reminds the Court that even public figures have the right to engage in private conversations. While the Court makes every effort to describe the radio station's access to the taped conversation as "legal," it would be difficult for the radio station to claim a belief that the conversation was lawfully intercepted.

■ CASE VOCABULARY

CHILLING EFFECT: The result of a law or practice that seriously discourages the exercise of a constitutional right, such as the right to appeal or the right of free speech.

INTERVENOR: One who voluntarily enters a pending lawsuit because of a personal stake in it.

United States v. O'Brien

(Federal Prosecution) v. *(Anti-Draft Protester)*
391 U.S. 367, 88 S.Ct. 1673 (1968)

COURT ARTICULATES TEST FOR WHEN "SYMBOLIC" ACTIONS ARE PROTECTED

■ **INSTANT FACTS** An anti-draft protester who burned his Vietnam draft card claims privilege for "symbolic speech."

■ **BLACK LETTER RULE** When an act combines both "speech" and "nonspeech" elements, the government may impose regulations if they (i) are not otherwise unconstitutional, (ii) further "important" or "substantial" state interests (iii) which are unrelated to suppressing free expression, and (iv) their incidental restrictions on free speech are no greater than is essential to furthering the interest.

■ **PROCEDURAL BASIS**

In prosecution under *Universal Military Training and Service Act* (for mutilating draft certificate-cards), appeal from conviction.

■ **FACTS**

Under the federal *Universal Military Training and Service Act of 1948*, men over 18 must register for the draft, and carry their registration certificates with them. The certificates state the bearer's name, registration status, residence, draft eligibility, contact information for his local draft board, and a reminder to update the board about status changes. Congress' *1965 Amendment* makes it illegal to "forge, alter, or in any manner change" or "knowingly destroy or ... mutilate" these certificates. During the Vietnam War, anti-draft protester O'Brien (D) burned his certificate in front of a crowd before a courthouse. O'Brien (D) was convicted of violating the *1965 Amendment*. O'Brien (D) appeals, claiming the *1965 Amendment* is unconstitutional (i) as applied to him, because his act was protected "symbolic speech," and (ii) on its face, because Congress' purpose in enacting it was to suppress freedom of speech.

■ **ISSUE**

May the government regulate "symbolic," expressive actions?

■ **DECISION AND RATIONALE**

(Warren, J.) Yes. When an act combines both "speech" and "nonspeech" elements, the government may impose regulations if they (i) are not otherwise unconstitutional, (ii) further "important" or "substantial" state interests (iii) which are unrelated to suppressing free expression, and (iv) their incidental restrictions on free speech are no greater than is essential to furthering the interest. First, we find O'Brien's (D) act was not protected as "symbolic speech." We cannot accept that all types of conduct can be labeled "speech," just because the actor intends to express ideas. Previously, we held that, when acts combine both "speech" and "nonspeech" elements, the government may impose regulations if they (i) are not otherwise unconstitutional, (ii) further "important" or "substantial" state interests (iii) which are unrelated to suppressing free expression, and (iv) their incidental restrictions on free speech are no greater than is essential to furthering the interest. Here, we find the *1965 Amendments* are justified. Congress' power to draft is beyond question, and issuing certificates to administer the draft serves legitimate, substantial interests. Requiring draft certificates, and preventing their alteration, is necessary for many reasons. Requiring certificates allows instant verification of

United States v. O'Brien (Continued)

whether bearers registered. The certificates' printed information facilitates communication with draft boards. They remind registrants to report necessary status changes to draft boards. Also, prohibitions on alteration are needed to prevent forgery and deception. Thus, the *1965 Amendments* are valid as applied to O'Brien (D). Second, we reject O'Brien's (D) arguments that the *1965 Amendments'* "purpose" was "to suppress freedom of speech." Under settled principles, this Court will not strike down facially-constitutional statutes based on alleged, illicit legislative motives. When this Court interprets statutes, it looks to legislators' statements for guidance. But this does not justify voiding facially-valid statutes. Even if some legislators' remarks suggest illicit motives, they are not presumed to speak for the whole Congress. Conviction affirmed.

Analysis:

Under *O'Brien*, those laws that will pass constitutional muster must further an important or substantial governmental interest, involve an incidental restriction on alleged First Amendment freedoms, and be tailored in such a way that restrictions on speech are no greater than necessary to further the governmental interest. Though *O'Brien* was decided in 1968, the rule still applies today. *O'Brien* is also significant in that it distinguishes between content-based and content-neutral laws, and the level of scrutiny that should be applied when reviewing each. Under the *O'Brien* test, when the governmental interest behind the law is related to the suppression of free expression, the law is content-based. In these situations, *O'Brien* requires that strict scrutiny be applied. However, when the governmental interest behind the law is unrelated to freedom of expression, the law is content-neutral. In these cases, less than strict scrutiny is applied in determining the constutionality of the law.

■ **CASE VOCABULARY**

SYMBOLIC SPEECH: Non-verbal conduct, done to express an idea, e.g., demonstrating, black-power salute, burning draft cards. As this case shows, symbolic speech receives *some* First Amendment protection.

Texas v. Johnson

(State) v. (Flag-Burner)
491 U.S. 397, 109 S.Ct. 2533 (1989)

EXPRESSIVE FLAG-BURNING IS PROTECTED

■ **INSTANT FACTS** A protester, jailed for burning an American flag, challenged the flag-desecration statute.

■ **BLACK LETTER RULE** The government may not ban flag-burning as a means of expression.

■ **PROCEDURAL BASIS**

In criminal prosecution for flag desecration, post-conviction appeal.

■ **FACTS**

Texas's (D) law criminalizes desecrating venerated objects. At an anti-Republican/anti-corporate rally there, protester Johnson (D) burned the American flag, while others chanted: "America, the red, white, and blue, we spit on you." Johnson (D) was convicted of desecration. Johnson (D) appeals, claiming flag-burning is symbolic speech, protected by the First Amendment. Texas (P) defends, claiming its statute is justified by its need to (i) prevent breach of peace, and (ii) preserve the flag as a symbol of nationhood and national unity.

■ **ISSUE**

May a state ban public flag-burning, to preserve the peace and national symbol?

■ **DECISION AND RATIONALE**

(Brennan, J.) No. The government may not ban flag-burning as a means of expression. First, we must determine whether flag-burning constitutes expressive conduct, meriting First Amendment protection. If so, we must decide whether the government's regulation is related to suppressing speech. If not, we apply the *O'Brien* standard. If it is, we must ask whether the governmental interest is justified, under "the most exacting scrutiny." [Here, we hold Johnson's (D) flag-burning was expressive.] Texas (P) offers 2 interests: preventing breach of peace, and preserving the flag as a symbol. A. [Texas's (P) interest in preserving peace is unrelated to suppressing expression.] But Texas's (P) statute is not justified by its interest in preventing breach of peace, since Johnson's (D) actions neither threatened nor caused disturbance. B. Texas's (P) other claimed interest—preserving the flag as symbolizing national unity—is aimed at suppressing expression whose content is anti-America. Thus, we subject it to "the most exacting scrutiny." Here, we find it unjustified. The First Amendment's bedrock principle is that government may not prohibit expression because it disagrees with its message. This principle is not dependent on the mode of expression, and applies equally to the expressive act of flag-burning. We cannot allow the government to ban desecration of certain "special" symbols; this would require courts to decide which symbols warrant special status, which would allow judges to impose their political preferences on the citizenry. We are convinced that forbidding punishment of flag-burning will not endanger most people's respect for the flag. We should not consecrate the flag by punishing its

Texas v. Johnson (Continued)

desecration, for in doing so we dilute the freedom that this cherished emblem represents. Conviction reversed.

■ DISSENT

(Rehnquist, C.J.) America's flag occupies a unique position as our national symbol of unity, and its burning does not represent any "point of view." Public flag-burning is no essential part of any exposition of ideas. Also, it tends to incite breach of peace. Banning it would not restrict expression much; people could still burn flags in private, or burn many other national symbols.

■ DISSENT

(Stevens, J.) The American flag is a unique, cherished symbol. Sanctioning its public desecration will tarnish its value. This tarnish is unjustified by the ban's trivial burden on expression; protesters would still be able to use any alternative words/actions to criticize the flag.

Analysis:

At the time this case was decided, almost all of the fifty states, as well as the federal government, had laws that made mutilation or desecration of the American flag a crime. The ruling in this case, for the most part, made these statutes unconstitutional. This decision also reiterates the heightened level of scrutiny given to symbolic expression. Because the majority felt that Johnson's (D) prosecution was directly related to expression, heightened scrutiny applied. On a political level, this decision elicited considerable negative reaction. Congress reacted to the decision by drafting a statute that it thought would pass Constitutional muster, but in *United States v. Eichman* that statute was similarly held unconstitutional. It is generally thought that the only way Congress could prohibit the burning of the flag without violating the First Amendment is to pass a Flag Burning Amendment.

Buckley v. Valeo
(Campaign Act Opponents) v. *(Senate Officia)*
424 U.S. 1, 96 S.Ct. 612 (1976)

CAMPAIGN SPENDING IS PROTECTED AS "SPEECH"

■ **INSTANT FACTS** Opponents challenged a federal election-reform statute which limited campaign contributions and expenditures, claiming that money is political "expression."

■ **BLACK LETTER RULE** The government may limit campaign contributions, but not campaign expenditures.

■ **PROCEDURAL BASIS**
In First Amendment challenge to federal statute, appeal from finding of constitutionality.

■ **FACTS**
The *Federal Election Campaign Act of 1971* ("*Act*") sought to limit campaign contributions and spending, curb candidate's obligations to donors, level the playing field between big and small contributors, keep independently-rich candidates from out-spending poor ones, and curb rising campaign costs. § 608(b) limits campaign contributions for federal candidates to $1,000, with the stated aim of preventing corrupt *quid pro quo* influence-peddling, the appearance of corruption, and freeze skyrocketing campaign spending. § 608(e)(1) limits [electioneering-related] expenditures "relative to [for/against] a clearly specified candidate" to $1,000. The stated aim is to keep special interests from evading § 608(b)'s contribution limits by directly campaigning for the candidate independently. § 608(c) caps overall spending on federal campaigns, to reduce campaigns' costs' inflation. § 608(a)(1) caps candidates' private expenditure from personal/family fortunes; this prevents independently-rich candidates from gaining advantage, and limits overall campaign spending. Other provisions required disclosure of contributions, and provided for public funding of presidential elections. Several candidates, incumbents, and political organizations, including Buckley (P) (collectively, "Challengers"), sued Senate Secretary Valeo (D), challenging *Act* as burdening contributors' and candidates' "core" First Amendment right to speak effectively, through paid mass media. Valeo (D) defended, claiming *Act* regulates conduct rather than speech, and is justified by strong government interests. At trial, the Court of Appeals found *Act* regulated conduct rather than speech, applied *O'Brien* [speech plus conduct analyzed under intermediate scrutiny], and upheld *Act*. Challengers (P) appeal.

■ **ISSUE**
Can the government limit campaign contributions and expenditures?

■ **DECISION AND RATIONALE**
(Per Curiam) No. The government may limit campaign contributions, but not campaign expenditures. I.A. General Principles: Political contributions and expenditures are "speech," not conduct. Thus, *O'Brien* [acts combining speech with conduct are regulable, under intermediate scrutiny] is inapplicable. This Court never suggested that certain communications' dependence on the expenditure of money introduces a non-speech element, or reduces the "exacting scrutiny" required by the First Amendment. Thus, communications involving the spending of money may be deemed speech, or conduct, or both.

Buckley v. Valeo (Continued)

Further, *Act's* governmental interests—reducing the voices of monied people and interest groups, reducing federal campaigns' overall scope, and equalizing all voters' relative political influence—involve "suppressing communication," because *Act* is predicated on the assumption that the communication integral to contributing/spending is harmful [i.e., buying influence]. II.B. Contribution Limitations: § 608(b)'s contribution limits are justified, under the government's strong interest in preventing large contributors from obtaining corrupt political *quid pro quo* from candidates and incumbents, and the strong interest of preventing the appearance of corruption. 608(b)'s contribution limit is narrowly-tailored against large contributions, and does not undermine materially the potential for effective discussion of candidates and campaign issues. II.C. But *Act's* limits on expenditures are unjustified. II.C.1. § 608(e)(1)'s limits on independent electioneering for/against candidates is unjustified. Its effects are to prevent anyone except candidates, media owners, and political organizations from spending money to voice views about candidates. But the governmental interest is weak. First, it is easily evaded; supporters can promote favored candidates/issues indirectly and independently, without identifying any candidates. Second, there is less danger of indirect tactics causing real/apparent corruption, since § 608(b)'s contribution limits prevent prearranged/coordinated expenditures, and independent ads may prove ineffective or even harmful to candidates. But § 608(e)(1) burdens "core" expression heavily; since the First Amendment includes the right to vigorous advocacy, including effective mass media. II.C.2. *Act* § 608(a)(1)'s limits on personal spending are substantial, unjustified restraints; the First Amendment allows people, including candidates, unfettered opportunity to advocate their own election tirelessly. [Finally, a legal victory for downtrodden tycoons everywhere.] II.C.3. Similarly, § 608(c)'s limits on overall campaign spending are unjustified. Campaign spending limits necessarily limit the number of issues discussed, their depth, and the audience reached, because all mass communication costs money. In practice, these limits cause substantial restriction. There is no countervailing governmental interest suggested; if the evil is candidates' dependence on big contributions, this is addressed by § 608(c)'s contribution limits. Any governmental alm of reducing allegedly-skyrocketing campaign costs is illegitimate; the First Amendment denies government the power to determine that spending to promote one's political views is excessive or wasteful. Also, we uphold the provisions requiring disclosure of contributions; they inform the public, deter actual/apparent corruption, and allow enforcement of contribution limits. There may be some situations, like minor/dissident parties, where the burden of disclosure is so much greater than the reduced governmental interest in disclosure that disclosure becomes unjustified. But this is not present here. Finally, the provision providing public funds for presidential elections is valid; it increases expression, facilitates more electoral participation, and is voluntary. Reversed; statute constitutional in part.

Analysis:

Buckley v. Valeo was extremely influential on political campaigns. Despite later challenges, the Court upheld this case's distinction; capping contributions is legal, but expenditure limits are not. Consequently, much campaign contribution and spending was taken over indirectly by political action committees. Today, election spending keeps rising. Critics charge that, with the spending "bar" constantly rising, third party candidates cannot afford to campaign effectively, unless they are independently wealthy. Of course, the Court's reasoning is subject to criticism. Some say political spending is not "pure" speech. Critics point out that interest groups *can* buy influence indirectly, by spending on independent ads that promote favored candidates and issues.

■ CASE VOCABULARY

AMICI [CURIAE]: ("Friends [of the court]") Non-litigants who submit briefs supporting one litigant, usually because the case's broader outcome affects them.

PER CURIAM: Judicial opinion not ascribed to any one judge. Effectively. It is authored by the court as a whole.

QUID PRO QUO: ("This for that.") Exchange of favors of equal value.

Nixon v. Shrink Missouri Government PAC

(*Missouri Official*) v. (*Political Action Committee*)
528 U.S. 377, 120 S.Ct. 897 (2000)

BUCKLEY APPLIES TO STATES' CAMPAIGN CONTRIBUTION LIMITS

■ **INSTANT FACTS** When a *state* imposed campaign contribution limits, lobbyists challenged.

■ **BLACK LETTER RULE** States may impose campaign contribution limits, at any amount which does not make contributions pointless.

■ PROCEDURAL BASIS

In constitutional challenge to state statute, appeal from voiding.

■ FACTS

Missouri (D) statutes implemented limits on campaign contributions, with the aim of reducing campaign corruption, and the appearance of it. The limits were the same $1,000 as in *Buckley*, but inflation-adjusted. Political action committee Shrink Missouri Government PAC ("PAC") (P) challenged the state law's constitutionality, contending that (i) the contribution amounts permitted were so small they restricted effective campaign "speech," and (ii) the statute was unjustified, absent proof of actual corruption or voter apathy. At trial, the Court of Appeals invalidated the statute, finding Missouri (D) failed to prove corruption actually existed, or was perceived by voters. Missouri (D) appeals, contending contribution limits are valid under *Buckley* to serve the interests of preventing corruption and voter disillusionment.

■ ISSUE

May states impose campaign contribution limits?

■ DECISION AND RATIONALE

(Souter, J.) Yes. States may impose campaign contribution limits, at any amount which does not make contributions pointless. PAC (P) claims Missouri (D) failed to present sufficient evidence that its statute was warranted to prevent actual corruption and voter apathy, and the Court of Appeals agreed. We hold the statute is not void for lack of evidence. The amount of empirical evidence needed to satisfy heightened scrutiny of statutes will vary, depending on the claimed justification's novelty and plausibility. Missouri's (D) cited justification—the dangers of large, corrupt contributions, and public perception of it discouraging voter turnout—is neither novel nor implausible; we stated in *Buckley* that these interests were legitimate. While the record does not show Missouri's (D) legislature relied on *Buckley*'s findings, we find its evidence sufficient. *Buckley* rejected the contention that government could not constitutionally limit campaign contributions to below any *fixed* amount. That the amount is not fixed, but rather inflation-adjusted, is irrelevant; First Amendment concerns cannot be determined by deciding whether these dollar limits match inflation. Instead, we ask whether the contribution limitation is so radical that it effectively renders political associations ineffective, mutes candidates' messages, and renders contribution pointless. Here, Missouri's (D) limits are not insufficient; they need not be pegged to *Buckley*'s $1,000 limit, or even inflation-adjusted. Reversed; statute constitutional.

Nixon v. Shrink Missouri Government PAC (Continued)

■ CONCURRENCE

(Stevens, J.) Money is property, not speech. The First Amendment need not provide spending the same protection as the right to speak freely.

■ DISSENT

(Kennedy, J.) We should repeal *Buckley*; it caused bad consequences, *Buckley's* requirements created "covert speech"—contributors' increasingly-elaborate methods to evade fixed spending limits, which are not inflation-adjusted. The preferred method is to conceal pro-candidate advertising as "advocacy." Thus, unregulated "soft money" is contributed in unlimited amounts, masquerading as "issue advocacy" which promote/attack candidates' positions without specifically urging their election/defeat. While unregulated "soft money" is unrestricted, honest disclosed campaign contributions are limited, and their purchasing power decreases. Worse, this Court's decision in *Buckley* makes this situation self-perpetuating. Under *Buckley*, candidates cannot limit "soft money" unless they raise enough of it to get elected.

■ DISSENT

(Thomas, J.) *Buckley* was analytically flawed. In this decision, the majority further weakens campaign contributions' protection. [Presumably, by holding they may be limited to less than $1,000.] I would overrule *Buckley*, instead examining campaign contribution limits under strict scrutiny. Under that standard, Missouri's (D) limits are unconstitutional.

Analysis:

PAC (P) claimed that, before Missouri (D) could adopt laws aimed at curbing corruption, it needed to present empirical evidence that such corruption exists. The Court says no; it can be presumed, from *Buckley*. Next, someone apparently suggested that contribution limits must be fixed at a certain minimally effective dollar amount and must be inflation-indexed (that is, Increase at the level of general nationwide inflation) to maintain that minimum level's buying power. Again, the Court said no. But the Court does suggest that there may be a point at which limits are so low that following them would not allow effective campaigns, and that such limits would be unconstitutional. *Nixon* is notable for the strong dissents condemning *Buckley*, suggesting that the Court might be amenable to reversing it later.

■ CASE VOCABULARY

BASELINE: A minimum dollar amount, to be adjusted (upward) for inflation.

GRATUITY: Usually, something given for free; a tip. Here, it means "bribe."

ISSUE ADVOCACY: Pro-candidate ad veiled as an ad unrelated to the campaign. By not specifically urging voters to vote for/against a candidate, "issue" ads evade regulation as "campaign contributions."

SOFT MONEY: Campaign contributions which evade federal limits. The limits apply only to contributions "relative to a clearly identified candidate." i.e., they only apply when a paid ad tells voters to ballot for/against a candidate. Thus, "issue advocacy" ads evade this restriction, and thus can spend any amount.

SUI GENERIS: "Of its own kind." Peculiar; concocted.

Randall v. Sorrell

(Campaign Contributor) v. (Vermont Attorney General)
548 U.S. 230, 126 S.Ct. 2479 (2006)

CAMPAIGN CONTRIBUTION LIMITS MUST BE REASONABLE TO BE CONSTITUTIONAL

■ **INSTANT FACTS** Vermont (D) enacted a law that imposed limits on political contributions and on campaign expenditures, and Randall (P) claimed the limits were unconstitutional.

■ **BLACK LETTER RULE** Limits on campaign contributions may not be set so low as to magnify the advantages of incumbency and prevent a candidate from raising sufficient funds to mount an effective campaign.

■ PROCEDURAL BASIS

Appeal from an order of the court of appeals remanding the case for factual findings.

■ FACTS

A law enacted in Vermont (D) imposed limits on campaign expenditures and on campaign contributions. The expenditure limits restricted the amount a candidate for state office could spend during a two-year election cycle. The limits on contributions limited the amounts an individual could give to a candidate in a two-year cycle. Political parties and committees were subject to the same contribution limits. "Expenditure" and "contribution" were both defined broadly. Randall (P) claimed that the limits violated the First Amendment.

■ ISSUE

Were the limits on expenditures and fundraising unconstitutional?

■ DECISION AND RATIONALE

(Breyer, J.) Yes. Limits on campaign contributions may not be set so low as to magnify the advantages of incumbency and prevent a candidate from raising sufficient funds to mount an effective campaign. The limits on campaign expenditures are clearly unconstitutional under *Buckley v. Valeo,* 424 U.S. 1 (1976). Sorrell (D) asks the Court to overrule *Buckley* because subsequent experience has shown that contribution limits and disclosure requirements alone cannot effectively deter corruption. Alternately, Sorrell (D) argues that *Buckley* can be distinguished because Vermont (D) raises a new justification for its law; namely, that expenditure limits free candidates from the need to spend time raising money. These arguments are not persuasive. There is no good reason to overrule *Buckley,* and there is no basis for distinguishing it from this case.

Ordinarily, legislators are the ones best equipped to determine whether campaign contribution limits are too low. The courts will usually defer to their judgment. There are, however, lower bounds to contribution limits, and judicial scrutiny is appropriate when the limits approach those lower bounds. It cannot simply be said that "the lower the limit, the better." The limits in the Vermont (D) statute are low enough to generate suspicion that they are not closely drawn to match Vermont's (D) interests. They are substantially lower than the limits previously upheld by the Court, and the limits in other states.

Randall v. Sorrell (Continued)

The Court's independent examination of the record leads to the conclusion that the limits are set unconstitutionally low. There are five factors that lead to this conclusion. The first factor is that the record suggests, without proving conclusively, that the limits will significantly restrict the amounts available for challengers to run competitive campaigns. Second, application of the limits to political parties threatens harm to the important right to associate in a political party. Third, the law seems to count volunteer expenses against a volunteer's contribution limit. Fourth, the contribution limits are not indexed for inflation so that the real value of the limits declines every year. Fifth, Vermont (D) has not advanced any special interest that might warrant such a low limit on contributions. The justifications advanced are the same as those present in *Buckley*. Reversed

■ CONCURRENCE

(Alito, J.) Sorrell (D) has not made a case for reexamining *Buckley*. It is unnecessary to reach that issue.

■ CONCURRENCE

(Kennedy, J.) Court precedent has created and permitted the present new order of campaign finance. It is appropriate to concur only in the judgment.

■ CONCURRENCE

(Thomas, J.) The result reached by the plurality is correct; however, *Buckley* provides insufficient protection for political speech and should be overruled.

■ DISSENT

(Stevens, J.) *Buckley* should be overruled. The interest in freeing candidates from the burden of fundraising is a compelling one. There is no convincing evidence that expenditure limits are fronts for incumbent protection.

■ DISSENT

(Souter, J.) The Court is asked to use the framework in *Buckley* to determine whether there is evidence of a need to limit campaign fundraising. The contribution limits set by Vermont law are not so low as to make political association ineffective, or to make the contributions meaningless.

Analysis:

The order appealed from in this case was an order remanding the case for factual findings on whether there were less restrictive means of achieving Vermont's (D) goals. The plurality opinion engages in its own fact-finding. Note in particular the first of the five factors relied upon to find the contribution limits unconstitutional: that the record "suggests, but does not conclusively prove, that [the] contribution limits will significantly restrict the amount of funding available."

■ CASE VOCABULARY

STARE DECISIS: The doctrine of precedent, under which it is necessary for a court to follow earlier judicial decisions when the same points arise again in litigation.

First National Bank of Boston v. Bellotti

(*Corporations*) v. (*Massachusetts Official*)
435 U.S. 765, 98 S.Ct. 1407 (1978)

COURT REAFFIRMS CORPORATIONS' FIRST AMENDMENT RIGHTS TO ADVOCATE POLITICAL VIEWS

■ **INSTANT FACTS** When Massachusetts banned corporations from spending to influence referendums on *individual* tax policy, corporations challenged the ban as abridging corporate First Amendment rights.

■ **BLACK LETTER RULE** The government cannot ban corporations from spending to advocate their opinions publicly.

■ **PROCEDURAL BASIS**

In constitutional challenge to state statute, appeal from finding of constitutionality.

■ **FACTS**

Massachusetts (D) enacted a criminal statute banning banks and business corporations from spending to influence referendum votes, unless the referendum's issue materially affected their property, business, or assets. Further, the statute banned such banks and corporations from contributions/expenditures on any referendum involving *individuals'* tax issues, by automatically deeming personal tax issues unrelated to corporations' business. Several banks and corporations, including First National Bank of Boston (P) (collectively, "Corporations" (P)), wished to publicize their views on a referendum to authorize the legislature to impose graduated income taxes on individuals. [Presumably, this would increase the maximum taxable rate for high-income individuals. Like Corporations' (P) managers, who promptly voted to use (shareholders') corporate money to lobby to reduce their own, personal taxes.] Corporations (P) challenged the statute's constitutionality, claiming it violates their First Amendment rights to publicize their "speech." Massachusetts (D) defended, apparently contending (i) corporations should not have First Amendment rights, (ii) the statute is justified to prevent corporations' undue influence on referendums and the (demoralizing) perception of it, and (iii) this statute protects corporate shareholders from having their assets squandered on issues not affecting their corporation. At trial, the court held for Massachusetts (D), holding corporations' speech is unprotected, unless it pertains directly to their business interests. Corporations (P) appeal, contending this holding is unprecedented.

■ **ISSUE**

May a state deny corporations the right to advertise their views on referendums about individuals' tax issues?

■ **DECISION AND RATIONALE**

(Powell, J.) No. The government cannot ban corporations from spending to advocate their opinions publicly. The court below framed the issue wrongly; at issue is not whether corporations enjoy First Amendment rights, but rather whether this statute abridges expression protected by the First Amendment. It does. Here, Corporations' (P) speech would be considered "core" speech, since it discusses governmental affairs. If the speakers were not corporations, no one would suggest the government could silence such speech. We make no distinction between speech made by individuals, and that

First National Bank of Boston v. Bellotti (Continued)

made by corporations. Speech's inherent worth doesn't depend on its source's organizational structure; truth is no less true when spoken by corporations. There is no precedent for deciding that corporations' speech is unprotected if it doesn't concern their direct business interests. In fact, proclaiming that corporations may speak only on business issues would be an impermissible restriction; the government is constitutionally disqualified from dictating which issues speakers may address, or which speakers are qualified to discuss public issues. Massachusetts's (D) argument that the statute addresses problems of undue influence and voter disillusionment may be valid, but Massachusetts (D) never proved that these theoretical problems actually exist. We find these risks are less for referendums than they would be in public elections, since there are no candidates to bribe, and the public perceives this. If this statute is meant to protect shareholders against having their invested resources channeled into speech which they oppose, it is not tailored to do so. It is under-inclusive; corporations may still lobby to influence everything except referendums, e.g., legislation, elections. It is also over-inclusive; it would ban the corporation from speaking on referendum issues even if all shareholders supported its position. Reversed; statute void.

■ DISSENT

(White, J.) This statute is justified, under states' traditional power to regulate corporate decision-making. Such statutes are widespread, and have been accepted for many years. They involve a necessary, permissible balance between what are essentially two competing First Amendment rights. Also, this Court should not second-guess the legislature on laws involving political process, since the legislature has more expertise.

Analysis:

Consider what's at issue here. Massachusetts (D) apparently had a flat state income tax, meaning all individuals paid the same rate, regardless of income. It wanted to switch to the modern, progressive "graduated" income tax, where low-income people would pay a lower rate, and the rich would pay higher rates. This graduated tax policy recognizes that the rich are better able to pay more, because more of their income is disposable (i.e., surplus over and above basic living expenses). To institute this, Massachusetts (D) needs a referendum. Corporate *managers* oppose the graduated tax; they're all rich, so they would pay higher rates. Note that the issue doesn't affect the *corporation*'s profitability itself; it just determines how much pay its *employees* get to keep for themselves. So, the corporation itself should have no legitimate business spending shareholders' capital on lobbying for laws that don't even affect it. But here's the conflict of interest the statute was designed to prevent: the corporation's *managers*, who control its purse strings, are perfectly happy to spend *the shareholders'* money to advance their own *personal* agendas. Worse, most shareholders may support the graduated tax—especially if they're in low tax brackets—so that their managers are effectively using their own money against them.

■ CASE VOCABULARY

GRADUATED INCOME TAX: Tax where higher-income people pay tax at a higher percentage rate than lower-income people.

REFERENDUM: Procedure for enacting law by a popular vote on the issue. In some states, certain types of laws can be passed only by popular referendum, not by the legislature itself.

Hague v. Committee for Industrial Organization

(*City Police Chief*) v. (*Union Activists*)
307 U.S. 496, 59 S.Ct. 954 (1939)

PUBLIC MAY USE GOVERNMENTAL PROPERTY FOR ORDERLY SPEECH

■ **INSTANT FACTS** A city ordinance allowed the police chief to arbitrarily ban assembly in public streets and parks. When the chief ordered police to roust union pamphleteers and rallies from public places, they challenged the ordinance's constitutionality.

■ **BLACK LETTER RULE** The government must allow public places to be used for speech, and can regulate access only to ensure convenience and maintain order.

■ PROCEDURAL BASIS

In facial First Amendment challenge to city ordinance, appeal from voiding of ordinance.

■ FACTS

Jersey City, NJ's (D) ordinance allows its Director of Safety to refuse summarily to issue demonstrators a permit to assemble in streets and parks, based on his mere opinion that refusing would prevent "riots, disturbances or disorderly assemblage." A union organizer, Committee for Industrial Organization ("Union") (P), urged workers to assemble into unions, by distributing handbills, giving out placards, and holding rallies in parks and streets. Union's (P) handbills, signs, and rallies were peaceful and legal. Nevertheless, Safety Director Hague (D) instructed the police to disperse Union's (P) rallies and roust its pamphleteers, often violently. Union (P) challenged the ordinance as facially restricting First Amendment speech/assembly rights. At trial, the court found the ordinance facially invalid, finding Union's (P) activists were not disturbing the peace, and that Hague's (D) police acted arbitrarily and illegally. Hague (D) appeals, apparently claiming the City (D) owns "title" to public streets and parks, and can restrict their use.

■ ISSUE

May a city ordinance give officials discretion to prevent speech and assembly in public streets and parks?

■ DECISION AND RATIONALE

(Roberts, J.) No. The government must allow public places to be used for speech, and can regulate access only to ensure convenience and maintain order. Regardless of who "owns" streets and parks, traditionally they have been deemed to be held in trust by the government, for the people. Historically, streets and parks were always used to assemble, communicate thoughts, and discuss public questions. Since ancient times, use of streets and public places has been recognized as one of citizens' privileges, immunities, rights, and liberties. That right is not absolute; public speech cannot disturb the general comfort, convenience, peace, and order. The government may regulate speech in public places, but only to preserve convenience and order. Further, the government cannot deny use of public places altogether. Here, the ordinance is unconstitutional on its face. It gives the Director of Safety arbitrary discretion to restrict or even deny speech in public spaces, even for reasons unrelated to maintaining order. Police may not maintain order in public places by simply closing them to speech and assembly. Affirmed; ordinance void.

Analysis:

It was not until *Hague v. C.I.O.* that the Supreme Court recognized that states may not abridge the rights of assembly and petition. The justices used two different lines of reasoning. Justice Roberts found protection for the right of assembly as a privilege and immunity of a United States citizen, within the meaning of the Fourteenth Amendment. The opinion of Justice Stone (not reproduced in the casebook) found protection for the right of assembly in the Due Process Clause of the Fourteenth Amendment. The due process theory has prevailed, and it is into that broad clause that the Supreme Court has breathed an expansive interpretation of civil rights.

■ **CASE VOCABULARY**

COLLECTIVE BARGAINING: Union's negotiation for wages/benefits on behalf of all members, to increase bargaining power.

TITLE: Legal ownership.

TRUST: Property, held by an administrator, which belongs to another.

Schneider v. New Jersey

(*Pamphleteers*) v. (*Municipalities*)
308 U.S. 147, 60 S.Ct. 146 (1939)

GOVERNMENT CANNOT BAN PAMPHLETEERING TO PREVENT LITTER

■ **INSTANT FACTS** Pamphleteers challenged several municipalities' ban on pamphleteering, to prevent litter.

■ **BLACK LETTER RULE** Governments may regulate pamphleteering to preserve public safety and permit car and pedestrian traffic, but may not ban it to prevent littering.

■ PROCEDURAL BASIS
In three consolidated misdemeanor prosecutions for illegal pamphleteering, post-conviction appeals.

■ FACTS
Several Pamphleteers (D), including Jehovah's Witness Schneider (D), were convicted under various municipal ordinances which banned pamphleteering, to prevent litter. Generally, the ordinances banned distributing hand-bills to pedestrians/motorists, putting leaflets on cars, throwing leaflets on the ground, and/or canvassing without a prior permit. Apparently, though the Pamphleteers (D) were not littering, they were arrested for distributing pamphlets illegally, on the theory they were responsible for the litter. Pamphleteers (D) appeal, claiming the ordinance restricts speech.

■ ISSUE
May municipalities ban pamphleteering to prevent littering?

■ DECISION AND RATIONALE
(Roberts, J.) No. Governments may regulate pamphleteering to preserve public safety and permit car and pedestrian traffic, but may not ban it to prevent littering. The government's interest in keeping streets clean and neat is insufficient to justify banning pamphleteering to willing recipients. Free speech is a fundamental right which deserves great weight. The state may not curtail it to avoid litter, even if this imposes extra burdens on its sanitation department. If a government wishes to prevent littering, it must use other means, such as punishing the litterers themselves. Municipal authorities, as public trustees, are empowered to perform their duty of keeping the streets open from auto and pedestrian traffic, and may regulate pedestrians' conduct on those streets to prevent congestion. E.g., pamphleteers can be stopped from blocking cars, or blocking pedestrians. Also, the government may ban littering directly. We do not hold that government can ban commercial soliciting/canvassing, or set reasonable hours for canvassing. Convictions reversed; statutes void.

Analysis:
This case, along with the simultaneous decision in *Hague*, signals the Court's transition from the theory that government has absolute control over (government-owned) public places, to the view that it may regulate access for public safety and convenience, but cannot ban speech on them altogether.

■ CASE VOCABULARY

TRUSTEES: Representatives who manage property on behalf of its owner. Under the "public trust doctrine," governmental controls public lands, but only as a trustee for the people.

Perry Education Assn. v. Perry Local Educators' Assn.

(Teachers' Official Union) v. (Rival Teachers' Association)
460 U.S. 37, 103 S.Ct. 948 (1983)

SUPREME COURT SUMMARIZES HOW VARIOUS FORUMS—"PUBLIC," "LIMITED PUBLIC," AND "NON-PUBLIC"—MAY BE REGULATED

■ **INSTANT FACTS** When a Board of Ed granted the official teachers' union exclusive access to its mail system, a rival group demanded equal access.

■ **BLACK LETTER RULE** In "public forums" (public spaces devoted to public speech, by traditional or government fiat) and "limited public forums" (public places the government voluntarily opens for expression), content-based speech restrictions are permitted only if (i) necessary to serve "compelling" governmental interests, and (ii) narrowly-tailored; "time, place, and manner" restrictions are allowed if they (i) are content-neutral, (ii) serve "significant" government interests, (iii) are narrowly-tailored, (iv) leave ample alternative channels of communication. Other public properties are "non-public forums," where the government may impose "time, place, and manner" restrictions, and may restrict speech if the restriction is (i) reasonable, and (ii) not intended to suppress certain viewpoints.

■ **PROCEDURAL BASIS**

In constitutional challenge to governmental contract/policy, appeal from appellate affirmation of judgment against challenger.

■ **FACTS**

A township teachers' union, Perry Education Assn. (PEA, or "Union") (D), was elected as local teachers' exclusive representative for collective bargaining. Under Union's (D) collective bargaining agreement with the Board of Education, Union (D) was the only union that could use the townships' interschool mail system and teacher mailboxes. A rival union, Perry Local Educators' Assn. (PLEA, or "Rival") (P) was formed, and wanted access to school mail and mailboxes. Rival (P) challenged the collective bargaining agreement's exclusivity provision, claiming that once the (governmental) Board of Education had opened school mail to Union (D) and various non-school groups, it had made school mail a "limited public forum," which could not be closed to dissenters like Rival (P). Apparently, Rival (P) lost in court and on appeal, and now appeals again.

■ **ISSUE**

If a school board lets its internal mail system be used by a union and others, may it deny use by a rival union?

■ **DECISION AND RATIONALE**

(White, J.) Yes. The issue of whether public property may be accessed, and the constitutional standard by which restrictions are judged, depends on the disputed property's character, as either a "public forum," "limited public forum," or "non-public forum." "Public forums" are those properties which have been devoted to assembly and debate, by traditional or government fiat (pronouncement), e.g., streets, parks. In public forums, excluding speech based on its content is permitted only if necessary (i) to serve "compelling" governmental interests, and (ii) narrowly-tailored to achieve that end. Also, the govern-

Perry Education Assn. v. Perry Local Educators' Assn. (Continued)

ment may enforce restrictions on the "time, place, and manner" of expression, if they (i) are content-neutral, (ii) serve "significant" government interests, (iii) are narrowly-tailored, and (iv) leave open ample alternative channels of communication. "Limited public forums" are those public properties which the government voluntarily opened for public communication. The government was not required to open them, and is not required to keep them open indefinitely. But as long as the government keeps such places open for expressive activities, it can regulate them only as if they were "public forums." For example, content-based restrictions are strictly scrutinized, and content-neutral "time, place, and manner" restrictions are permissible. Other public properties, which are reserved for public communication by tradition or designation, are classified as "non-public forums." There, the government may impose "time, place, and manner" restrictions. Also, the government may limit the place to its intended purpose (which may include banning speech), if the anti-speech restriction (i) is reasonable, and (ii) is not an effort by officials to suppress a speaker's views. This is because the government, like private owners, has the power to use its property exclusively for its intended purposes. Here, the Board of Education's school mail system is a *non*-public forum. Traditionally, it was never public. Nor is it a limited public forum, since its normal, intended function was to communicate *the school's* messages to teachers, not the views of outsiders. Thus, the Board of Education has no constitutional obligation to let any organization use its mail system. Affirmed; exclusive contract valid.

Analysis:

This case, while it did not create the "public/limited/non-public forum" distinction, summarizes it succinctly. Thus, the basic issue concerning speech in public places is, was this place opened for public speech, either by tradition, by proclamation, or by temporary/permanent government policy? If so, any speech restrictions must survive strict scrutiny. Also, this case introduces "time, place, and manner" restrictions and the standard for evaluating them. Finally, this case suggests the rule for speech on *private* property: owners may restrict speech and access at will, because private property usage doesn't implicate the Constitution.

■ CASE VOCABULARY

COLLECTIVE BARGAINING: Union's practice of negotiating on behalf of all member-employees.

FIAT: Rule made by proclamation, often without any authority or reason.

PUBLIC FORUM: Public property which was used for public speaking/communication/assembly, by traditional or government tolerance.

LIMITED PUBLIC FORUM: Public property which the government at some point affirmatively permitted to be used for public communication, e.g., a public university's square.

NON-PUBLIC FORUM: Any public property which was never open for public speech, by either tradition, toleration, or consent, such as courthouses and airports.

Police Department of Chicago v. Mosley

(City) v. (Protestor)
408 U.S. 92, 92 S.Ct. 2286 (1972)

IN PUBLIC FORUMS, GOVERNMENT CANNOT SELECTIVELY EXCLUDE SOME CONTENT OR ISSUES

■ **INSTANT FACTS** When a city ordinance generally banned picketing schools, but exempted labor picketing, a non-labor school picketer challenged the ordinance as content-based.

■ **BLACK LETTER RULE** In "public forums," the government cannot selectively exclude certain speakers based on their content, issue, or viewpoint.

■ PROCEDURAL BASIS

First Amendment/Fourteenth Amendment Equal Protection Clause challenge to city ordinance.

■ FACTS

Chicago's (D) ordinance prohibits picketing near schools, but allows an exception for peaceful labor picketing. Anti-discrimination activist Mosley (P) picketed a high school to protest its discriminatory racial quotas, a grievance unrelated to labor. Mosley (P) sued Police Department of Chicago (D), challenging the ordinance as violating Fourteenth Amendment equal protection, and the First Amendment, by being content-based, i.e., allowing labor-related contents, but not others. Chicago (D) claimed it was a valid "time, place, and manner" restriction.

■ ISSUE

May a city generally ban picketing in certain places, but allow exceptions for labor picketing?

■ DECISION AND RATIONALE

(Marshall, J.) No. In "public forums," the government cannot selectively exclude certain speakers based on their content, issue, or viewpoint. We analyze this ordinance under the Fourteenth Amendment's Equal Protection Clause, because it treats some picketing differently from others. But this analysis is intertwined with the First Amendment claim, since picketing is "expressive" conduct, and this ordinance is content-based. Generally, the First Amendment means government cannot restrict expression based on its message, ideas, topic, or content. Under the First Amendment and Equal Protection Clause, government may not grant use of forums to people whose views it finds acceptable, but deny use to those expressing disfavored views. Once the government opens a forum for speech/assembly by some groups, it may not selectively prohibit others from using it, based on their speech's content. There, speech may be regulated by valid "time, place, and manner" restrictions, but these must be content-neutral. Here, they are content-based, since labor content is allowed, but other content is not. Under an equal protection analysis, there may be sufficient regulatory interests justifying selective exclusions or distinctions among picketers, but these must withstand careful scrutiny. Examples would include conflicting demands on the same space, pickets which risk creating disorder. Here, this is not the case. Judgment for plaintiff; ordinance void.

Analysis:

Once a forum is open to the public, the government cannot admit some speakers but bar others. Generally, striking workers are allowed to picket their place of employment. The government may prohibit all picketing near schools, probably to reduce disruption to students' learning. This rule would be valid. But it would mean that striking *school* employees could not picket their workplace. Thus, Chicago's (D) exception was carved out to let school employees have labor rights *comparable to others'*. However, the Court's rule is absolute, and doesn't tolerate the government's good motives any more than bad ones.

■ CASE VOCABULARY

EQUAL PROTECTION CLAUSE: Fourteenth Amendment clause requiring the Constitution be applied equally to all people in similar circumstances.

Hill et al. v. Colorado

(Abortion-Clinic Protesters) v. *(State Legislature)*
530 U.S. 703, 120 S.Ct. 2480 (2000)

SUPREME COURT SAYS OBLIQUE LAW AIMED AT ABORTION PROTESTERS IS TECHNICALLY "CONTENT-NEUTRAL"

■ **INSTANT FACTS** When Colorado passed a law obliquely aimed at preventing abortion clinic protesters from approaching entering patients, the protesters challenged it as content-based.

■ **BLACK LETTER RULE** A law banning speakers from approaching patients entering health care facilities is a content-neutral, valid, "time, place, and manner" restriction.

■ **PROCEDURAL BASIS**

In First Amendment facial challenge to state statute, appeal from appellate finding of constitutionality.

■ **FACTS**

Colorado (D) enacted a statute which basically restricted pro-lifers' "sidewalk counseling" (standing in front of abortion clinics, carrying anti-abortion signs, distributing pamphlets, and trying to talk women out of aborting). Specifically, the statute makes it illegal, within 100 feet of any "health care facility"'s entrance, to "knowingly approach" within 8 feet of a person "for the purpose of passing a leaflet or handbill to, displaying a sign to, or engaging in oral protest, education, or counseling," without consent. [Note that it is nominally content-neutral; it doesn't explicitly single out anti-abortion messages.] Also, the statute allows already-present pro-lifers to stand their ground and talk, show signs, and offer handbills as women pass by; they need not move 8 feet away. Several activist Pro-Lifers (P), including Hill (P), challenged the statute as facially unconstitutional, and sued to enjoin enforcement. Colorado (D) defended, apparently claiming the law was (i) content-neutral, (ii) justified by its interest in protecting patients from intrusive speech, and (iii) valid as a "time, place, and manner" restriction. At trial, the court upheld the statute, finding it was content-neutral, and a permissible "time, place, and manner" restriction. Pro-Lifers (P) appealed several times, and lost. Pro-Lifers (P) appeal again.

■ **ISSUE**

May a state law ban people from approaching patients entering medical facilities?

■ **DECISION AND RATIONALE**

(Stevens, J.) Yes. A law banning speakers from approaching patients entering health care facilities is a content-neutral, valid, "time, place, and manner" restriction. This case involves conflicting rights. On one hand, the First Amendment protects advocacy, especially on public sidewalks, even if hearers are offended. On the other, states traditionally have police power to protect citizens' health/safety. Prior cases recognized that speakers generally are entitled to advocate positions that are offensive to listeners. But some unwanted, offensive speech is recognized as so intrusive it violates people's "right to be let alone." Content-neutral speech restrictions are valid if (i) they do not discriminate based on the message's content, and (ii) are justified by sufficient government interests, (iii) which are unrelated to suppressing speech. "Content neutral" means the regulation was not adopted "because of disagreement with the message it conveys." Here, the statute is content-neutral, for several reasons. It does not

Hill et al. v. Colorado (Continued)

regulate *speech* itself, but only the places where some speech can occur. It applies equally to all demonstrators, regardless of viewpoint. It makes no reference to the speech's content. It imposes some minor restrictions, but still allows protesters to educate unwilling listeners in other ways. Next, we note "time, place, and manner" restrictions are valid if they (i) are content-neutral, (ii) serve "significant" government interests, (iii) are narrowly-tailored, and (iv) leave ample alternative channels of communication. We find the statute is a valid "time, place, and manner" restriction. [We already found the statute is content-neutral, and supported by legitimate government interests.] The 8-foot distance doesn't preclude most communications. It doesn't affect displaying signs. It keeps speakers from approaching to speak or offer pamphlets, but they can do this to passers-by by standing near the entrance and not moving away. We find the statute narrowly-tailored, imposing no more burden than necessary. We note precedents saying the government has special interests in controlling activities around certain public/private places, e.g., schools, courthouses, polls, private homes. Also, states have special interests around health care facilities; patients entering for any purpose are often particularly vulnerable, physically and emotionally. Affirmed; statute valid.

■ DISSENT

(Scalia, J.) The majority subverts precedent to restrict unpopular anti-abortion views. In [*Roe v. Wade*], this Court wrongly deprived anti-abortionists of the political right to support anti-abortion legislation. Now, it continues its assault on anti-abortionists, restricting their First Amendment rights to advocate women against abortion. If this statute involved anyone but anti-abortionists, it would be deemed content-based. The Court says any restriction is content-neutral if it merely (i) does not discriminate among viewpoints, and (ii) doesn't restrict the subject matter that may be discussed. But this is insufficient to define content-neutral restrictions. For example, a false "manner" restriction saying people could make only "happy" speech would pass the test. [No, it wouldn't; happiness is a viewpoint, as opposed to dissatisfaction. Nice try, though.] Further, it is obvious this statute takes aim specifically at anti-abortion protesters; the statute's careful language suggests this. This statute should be required to meet strict scrutiny. If, as the majority suggests, protecting people from unwelcome communications is a compelling state interest, then the First Amendment is a dead letter. And this statute is as "narrowly-tailored" as a tent. [Most people don't realize Scalia has a sense of humor . . . .] In sum, this decision is a blatant attack against pro-lifers.

■ DISSENT

(Kennedy, J.) I agree with Scalia's dissent. Also, the statute is content-based, because it restricts speech on particular topics. One in particular.

Analysis:

This case is included to illustrate what is deemed a "content-neutral" restriction. It is a recent case and viewed by many as important. According to this case, a statute that does not *explicitly* ban certain viewpoints or topics is content-neutral. That this statute is obliquely targeted directly, and only, at anti-abortion demonstrators in front of abortion clinics, is ignored by the Court. The majority says it would be equally applicable to "used car salesmen, animal rights activists, fundraisers, environmentalists, and missionaries." True, but in practice, how many of these groups regularly lurk outside of health care facilities? Consider whether, the Court would follow this precedent in cases involving topics less unpopular than abortion.

■ CASE VOCABULARY

ET AL.: "And others."

POLICE POWER: A state's right to enact laws which protect its citizens' health and safety. It has nothing to do with police.

"TIME, PLACE, AND MANNER" RESTRICTION: Government's limit on the permissible form of speech on public/semi-public property, usually to minimize disruption/inconvenience to the property's ordinary functions.

Ward v. Rock Against Racism
(City Official) v. (Concert Organizer)
491 U.S. 781, 109 S.Ct. 2746 (1989)

FOR "TIME, PLACE, AND MANNER" RESTRICTIONS, "NARROWLY-TAILORED" DOESN'T MEAN "LEAST RESTRICTIVE"

■ **INSTANT FACTS** When a city required park concerts to use city-approved amplifiers and sound technicians to reduce noise to surrounding areas and apartments, the concert organizer challenged the restriction as not narrowly-tailored/least-restrictive.

■ **BLACK LETTER RULE** "Time, place, and manner" restrictions are deemed sufficiently "narrowly-tailored" as long as they are more effective than no regulation at all, even if they are not the least-restrictive/intrusive method.

■ **PROCEDURAL BASIS**

In First Amendment challenge to city regulation, appeal from finding of constitutionality.

■ **FACTS**

New York's Central Park contains a concert stage and amphitheater, within earshot of apartments and the Park's Sheep Meadow, a place devote to passive recreation, e.g., reading, resting, walking. Concert organizer Rock Against Racism (P) repeatedly staged noisy concerts, prompting noise complaints from residents and Meadow users. Thus, New York City (D) instituted a regulation requiring performers to use only amplifiers and sound technicians provided by New York City (D). Rock Against Racism (P) challenged the regulation's constitutionality, apparently claiming New York City (D) had no interest in reducing noise, and that its regulation was more restrictive than necessary. New York City (D) defended, contending the regulation is a "time, place, and manner" restriction necessary to avoid intrusive noise and protect the Meadow's character, and need not be the least-restrictive method. At trial, the court upheld the regulation. Rock Against Racism (P) appeals.

■ **ISSUE**

In imposing "time, place, and manner" restrictions, must the government use the least-restrictive method?

■ **DECISION AND RATIONALE**

(Kennedy, J.) No. "Time, place, and manner" restrictions are deemed sufficiently "narrowly-tailored" as long as they are more effective than no regulation at all, even if they are not the least-restrictive/intrusive method. Music is traditionally recognized as "expression." "Time, place, and manner" restrictions are valid if they (i) are content-neutral, (ii) serve "significant" government interests, (iii) leave ample alternative channels of communication , and (iv) *are "narrowly-tailored." In the context of "time, place, and manner" restrictions, "narrowly-tailored" means the regulation must "promote a substantial government interest that would be achieved less effectively absent the regulation." It need not be the least-restrictive or least-intrusive method.* It cannot burden substantially more speech than necessary to further those interests. The reason is that we have never applied strict scrutiny to "time, place, and manner" restrictions; it is inappropriate. Here, this regulation is content-neutral. Government has substantial interests in protecting citizens from unwelcome noise. Here, the regulation is sufficiently

Ward v. Rock Against Racism (Continued)

narrow; it promotes New York City's (D) substantial interest in reducing noise, and is more effective than having no such policy. Also, the regulation leaves open other channels. Affirmed; statute valid.

■ DISSENT

(Marshall, J.) Previously, "time, place, and manner" restrictions' "narrowly-tailored" element required using the least-restrictive method. The majority's redefinition gives officials too much discretion, and power to damage speech rights.

Analysis:

Prior cases held that "time, place, and manner" restrictions must be "narrowly tailored," among other things. This case is important for its watered-down definition of "narrowly tailored." Basically, this definition has nothing to do with being narrowly tailored, in either its literal definition or its historic requirement of being least-restrictive. Apparently, this test is satisfied if the regulation is even minimally effective; that is, it must be more effective than no regulation at all. It's hard to imagine a regulation that won't pass this test. But remember, this definition of "narrowly tailored" applies only to "time, place, and manner" restrictions. For other speech restraints, "narrowly tailored" continues to mean "least-restrictive."

Adderley v. Florida

(*Demonstrators*) v. (*State*)
385 U.S. 39, 87 S.Ct. 242 (1966)

JAILS ARE NON-PUBLIC FORUMS

■ **INSTANT FACTS** Anti-discrimination protesters, arrested for trespassing on jail property, challenge their prosecution as unconstitutional.

■ **BLACK LETTER RULE** Jail property is a non-public forum, and the government may punish trespass there.

■ **PROCEDURAL BASIS**

In prosecution for criminal trespass, appeal from appellate affirmation of conviction.

■ **FACTS**

Florida's (P) statutes criminalize "trespass with malicious and mischievous intent." Many student Demonstrators (D), including Adderley (D), went to a nearby state jail, and on its grounds demonstrated against racist and segregationalist policies by Florida's (P) officials, and its arrest of other demonstrators. The jail's sheriff asked them to leave, then ordered it, and threatening to arrest them. When many Demonstrators (D) refused, they were arrested, charged with trespass, and convicted. On appeal, Demonstrators' (D) convictions were affirmed. Demonstrators (D) appeal again, claiming Florida's (P) enforcement of trespass laws against them violates First Amendment freedom of speech, press, and assembly, and the right to petition government for redress of grievances, largely because jails are "reasonable" and "appropriate" places to allow civil rights protests.

■ **ISSUE**

May the government enforce trespass laws against speakers on jailhouse grounds?

■ **DECISION AND RATIONALE**

(Black, J.) Yes. Jail property is a non-public forum, and the government may punish trespass there. Nothing in the Constitution forbids states' even-handed enforcement of generally-applicable trespass statutes against speakers on jailhouse grounds. The state has the power to preserve the property it controls for its intended use, just like private owners. Here, Florida's (P) enforcement was even-handed; there is no evidence Florida's (P) sheriff arrested Demonstrators (D) because he objected to their speech or objective, rather than to clear the jail grounds for jail uses. Demonstrators' (D) claim of a Constitutional right to conduct civil rights protests in jails violates precedent. It amounts to a claim that speakers wishing to propagandize protest views have a constitutional right to demonstrate whenever, however, and wherever they wish. Prior cases rejected that argument. Affirmed; convictions affirmed.

■ **DISSENT**

(Douglas, J.) Historically, jailhouses are governmental seats, and obvious places to assemble to protest unjust imprisonment and petition for redress, e.g., Tower of London, Bastille.

Adderley v. Florida (Continued)

Analysis:

This case illustrates the narrow point that jails are non-public forums. Consequently, speakers there can be ousted or arrested. While this case does not discuss why jails are non-public, other cases involving jails show the Court is reluctant to permit any speech that might disrupt security.

■ CASE VOCABULARY

TRESPASS: Unauthorized entry onto another's land.

Greer v. Spock

(*Army Official*) v. (*Political Candidate*)
424 U.S. 828, 96 S.Ct. 1211 (1976)

MILITARY BASES ARE NON-PUBLIC

■ **INSTANT FACTS** Political candidates, denied permission to speak at an Army training base, claim the base became a limited public forum when officials permitted other civilian speakers.

■ **BLACK LETTER RULE** Military bases are non-public forums, and the government need not permit speech there.

■ **PROCEDURAL BASIS**

In First Amendment challenge to military regulations, appeal from invalidation.

■ **FACTS**

Fort Dix is a federally-owned Army (D) post used to train soldiers. Civilians are permitted to visit unrestricted areas freely. Previously, the Army (D) invited various civilian speakers, clergy, actors, and musicians to speak/perform there. But Army's (D) regulations ban partisan political speeches and demonstrations. Candidates from the People's Party and Socialist Workers' Party, including Spock (P) [no, not that Spock!], requested permission to speak and pamphleteer there, but were denied. Spock (P) challenged the Army (D) regulations, probably claiming the Army (D) had made Fort Dix a limited public forum by previously opening it to speakers. At trial, the court held for Spock (P). Army (D) appeals.

■ **ISSUE**

May the government forbid political speech at army training posts?

■ **DECISION AND RATIONALE**

(Stewart, J.) Yes. Military bases are non-public forums, and the government need not permit speech there. The First Amendment never meant that people who want to propagandize views have a constitutional right to do so whenever, however, and wherever they please. The government has power to preserve the property it controls for the use to which it is lawfully dedicated. Maintaining an army is an indispensable function, which the Constitution itself provides for. Consequently, it is the business of military installations, like Fort Dix, to train soldiers, not provide public forums. Reversed; regulation valid.

■ **DISSENT**

(Brennan, J.) The majority completely subverts First Amendment concerns to national security. The inquiry should instead balance these competing interests. Here, there is no reason why training soldiers effectively requires excluding political speakers, except the Army's (D) wish to suppress certain ideologies.

Analysis:

Here, the majority assumes that permitting speech would disrupt military preparedness, without explanation. But this is not necessarily true. Possible disruptions include: speakers snooping around restricted areas, demonstrations disrupting actual training exercises, and speakers talking recruits out of militarism. But here, the first two concerns are absent, since the speakers are requesting permission, presumably in a public place, during off hours. That leaves only the third risk, which, some argue, is one the First Amendment should require the Army to bear.

Lehman v. City of Shaker Heights

(Politician) v. *(City, as Owner of Public Transportation)*
418 U.S. 298, 94 S.Ct. 2714 (1974)

PUBLIC TRANSPORTATION'S AD SPACE IS NOT A "PUBLIC FORUM"

■ **INSTANT FACTS** When a public bus fleet allowed commercial ads but refused political ones, a candidate wishing to advertise claimed the ad space became a "public forum."

■ **BLACK LETTER RULE** When the government operates a commercial venture, it may accept commercial advertising but prohibit political ads.

■ **PROCEDURAL BASIS**

First Amendment challenge to public transportation system's policy.

■ **FACTS**

The City of Shaker Heights (D) operated a public bus service. City (D) allowed advertising inside its buses, in the form of "car cards" (posters). But City (D) allowed only commercial advertisements, and rejected political ads, possibly because it did not want captive riders forced to view political propaganda. Candidate Lehman (P) asked to put his paid ads in buses, but City (D) refused. Lehman (P) sued, claiming City (D) created a public forum by allowing advertising, and was discriminating impermissibly by rejecting political content.

■ **ISSUE**

Is advertising space in public transportation a public forum?

■ **DECISION AND RATIONALE**

(Blackmun, J.) No. When the government operates a commercial venture, it may accept commercial advertising but prohibit political ads. Public transportation ads are not traditional public forums, like open space, parks, meeting halls, streets, etc. Instead, public transportation is a commercial venture, which must be allowed to earn profits and please customers. Like private commercial ventures, governmental ventures need not accept every proffered ad. Such public utilities limit the advertising it allows, as long as its policy is not arbitrary, capricious, or invidious. Here, City's (D) decision was reasonable. It allows any commercial ad, regardless of content. But it may reject non-commercial, political/advocacy ads because, e.g., such ads are shorter term than commercial ones, riders would be exposed to controversial/offensive propaganda, this might create suspicions of favoritism, there might be administrative problems in parceling limited space to many candidates. Holding otherwise would require all government facilities' display cases to be opened to all pamphleteers and politicians, which the Constitution does not require. Judgment for defendant; policy valid.

■ **CONCURRENCE**

(Douglas, J.) I concur, but for the reason that bus passengers getting to/from work are effectively a captive audience; the First Amendment does not allow people to force their views on captive listeners incapable of declining to receive it.

Lehman v. City of Shaker Heights (Continued)

■ DISSENT

(Brennan, J.) Once City (D) began accepting commercial and public service advertising, it voluntarily established a public forum, and waived any claim that advertising is incompatible with its buses' primary function of providing transportation. Once City (D) created this public forum, it cannot discriminate solely on subject matter or content. Here, a ban on only political advertising is suspicious; the line between "ideological" and "non-ideological" speech is unclear. Further, by accepting possibly-objectionable/controversial commercial and public service ads, City (D) waived the argument that it is rejecting political ads because they may offend riders.

Analysis:

This case demonstrates yet another *non*-public forum: a "public utility," or for-profit commercial venture run by the government. Evidently, when the city operates as a private business, it is held to a lower standard of scrutiny: But note that this standard is still higher than that applied to *private* businesses. This interesting case highlights some factors the Court will consider when reviewing speech restrictions. Is there a captive audience that is forced to see or hear the message? If so, subject matter regulation is more likely to be allowed. Is the speech political or commercial? Commercial speech is generally afforded "less" First Amendment protection than political speech. Is the dissent correct in claiming that this case reverses this traditional priority? It seems odd that the city allows advertising that promotes cigarette use, but forbids a politician from campaigning for tougher smoking laws.

■ CASE VOCABULARY

CHAUTAUQUA: Recreational excursion.

HYDE PARK: British park, traditionally used for public speeches.

INVIDIOUS: Objectionable; improperly discriminatory.

PROFFER: Offer.

United States v. Kokinda
(*Postal Service*) v. (*Campaign Solicitors*)
497 U.S. 720, 110 S.Ct. 3115 (1990)

SOME GOVERNMENT FACILITIES' SIDEWALKS MAY NOT BE "PUBLIC"

■ **INSTANT FACTS** Campaign solicitors challenged a Post Office regulation banning solicitation on the sidewalks in front of its entrance.

■ **BLACK LETTER RULE** If the sidewalk outside a government property was constructed only to permit access (rather than for public convenience), then it is not a "public forum," and speech restrictions there are valid if "reasonable."

■ **PROCEDURAL BASIS**
In First Amendment challenge to federal regulation, appeal from invalidation.

■ **FACTS**
The Postal Service's (D) regulations prohibit "soliciting alms and contribution" on postal premises. This policy was adopted because Postal Service (D) found it received so many requests that postal managers were distracted from their duties. Democratic Party fundraiser Kokinda (P) wished to solicit near a post office entrance, in a road connecting the post office's door to its parking lot. Previously, that post office allowed its sidewalks to be used for speeches, pamphleteering, and picketing, as long as it did not disrupt postal operations. Kokinda (P) challenged Postal Service's (D) regulation, apparently contending (i) the area in front of its entrance is a sidewalk, and thus a "public forum," and (ii) the post office had made its premises into a "limited public forum" by allowing other speakers. Apparently, Kokinda (P) won at trial. Postal Service (D) appeals.

■ **ISSUE**
May a government regulate speech in the sidewalks outside its property?

■ **DECISION AND RATIONALE**
(O'Connor, J.) Yes. If the sidewalk outside a government property was constructed only to permit access (rather than for public convenience), then it is not a "public forum," and speech restrictions there are valid if "reasonable." Solicitation is a form of expression protected by the First Amendment. Government-owned property is not automatically open to the public. When the government acts as a proprietor managing its internal operations, its restrictions are subject to lesser scrutiny than when acting as a lawmaker in regulating/licensing others. While the government acting as proprietor doesn't enjoy absolute immunity from the First Amendment, its restrictions are valid unless "arbitrary, capricious, or invidious." This means its restrictions are valid if reasonable. First, we find the entrance path to the post office is not equivalent to a public sidewalk, and thus is not open to speech. This is because the path here, which connects the post office's entrance to its parking lot, was constructed solely to allow passage for postal workers and business, not for the public's benefit. Next, we find the Postal Service (D) never expressly dedicated its sidewalks as a limited public forum open to speech. No Postal Service (D) regulation does this. Further, the government's mere permission of limited discourse does not create a limited public forum; for that, it must intentionally open a non-traditional forum for public

United States v. Kokinda (Continued)

discourse. Here, that Postal Service (D) permitted some speech on its property does not mean it dedicated its premises to speech activities. Further, we find Postal Service's (D) restriction was reasonable. It was based on Postal Service's (D) long, actual experience that permitting solicitation actually distracted postal managers. This is not unreasonable. Reversed; regulation valid.

■ CONCURRENCE

(Kennedy, J.) I agree Postal Service's (D) regulation comports with the First Amendment, but for different reasons. I believe the postal property here became a limited public forum, because of the varied activities Postal Service (D) permitted on postal sidewalks. But, I find Postal Service's (D) regulation was a valid "time, place, and manner" restriction.

■ DISSENT

(Brennan, J.) The sidewalk here is a public sidewalk. Even if it were not, Postal Service's (D) regulation is not valid as a "time, place, and manner" restriction, because it is content-based. Even under the majority's standard—reasonableness—I find Postal Service's (D) distinction between solicitation and other speech unreasonable.

Analysis:

Kokinda is viewed as tightening the "limited public forum" doctrine. In considering whether the sidewalk here is a traditionally-public sidewalk, the Court does not consider all sidewalks as a whole, but the specific history of *this* postal walkway in particular. This analysis suggests a narrowing of the "limited public forum" doctrine, since it allows the conclusion that some sidewalks are not the "public" sidewalks that *Perry* suggests all streets are.

■ CASE VOCABULARY

ALMS: Contributions for charity, especially for the poor or beggars.

INVIDIOUS: Objectionably prejudicial; discriminatory.

SOLICITATION: Asking for various things. Here, contributions and political donations.

International Society for Krishna Consciousness, Inc. v. Lee

(*Airport Solicitors*) v. (*State Airport Authority*)
505 U.S. 672, 112 S.Ct. 2701 (1992)

AIRPORTS ARE NONPUBLIC, AND MUST PERMIT PAMPHLETS BUT NOT SOLICITATION

■ **INSTANT FACTS** When a state airport authority banned solicitation in terminals, Hare Krishnas challenged.

■ **BLACK LETTER RULE** Airports are non-public forums, and may ban solicitation.

■ **PROCEDURAL BASIS**

In First Amendment challenge to state agency regulations, appeal from validation.

■ **FACTS**

In New York/New Jersey, airports are managed by the Port Authority (D). Port Authority's (D) regulations banned repeatedly soliciting money or distributing pamphlets in airport terminals. The Hare Krishna cult organization, International Society for Krishna Consciousness, Inc. ("ISKCON") (P), encourages members to disseminate religious books and solicit funds, in public places including airports. ISKCON (P) challenged the regulation, claiming (i) "transportation nodes" like airports are traditional "public forums," and (ii) the regulation is unreasonable. At trial, the court upheld the regulation. ISKCON (P) appeals.

■ **ISSUE**

May airports ban solicitation?

■ **DECISION AND RATIONALE**

(Rehnquist, C.J.) Yes. Airports are non-public forums, and may ban solicitation. Our precedents provide guidance on what constitutes public forums. Traditional "public property" is that whose "principal purpose [is] free exchange of ideas." [No, that's not parks' and streets' *primary* purpose.] Government property does not become a "public forum" by government inaction, or just because the government permits people to visit freely a place it owns/operates. The decision to create a public forum must be made "by *intentionally* opening a *nontraditional* forum for *public discourse*." Finally, the property's location may be relevant; if property is separate from an acknowledged public area, this may indicate it is non-public. Under these precedents, airports are not traditionally-public forums. Airports are not old enough to qualify as "time immemorial." Further, they have not been used as speech forums until recently. Authorities have never opened airports/terminals for speech; in fact, they frequently litigate against it. We cannot hold they are part of "transportation nodes;" the relevant analytical unit is airports, and we need not treat all transport nodes similarly. Generally, businesses are reasonable in restricting solicitation on their premises; we recognized it disrupts pedestrian traffic, and risks face-to-face duress. These risks are especially relevant here, where impeded traffic may cause passengers to miss flights, and where passengers are too rushed to complain to terminal authorities. Affirmed; regulation valid.

International Society for Krishna Consciousness, Inc. v. Lee (Continued)

Analysis:

This case surprised many observers by holding that a government-owned airport open to the public is *not* a public forum. The majority readily agreed that the Krishnas were engaging in a form of speech, but rejected the argument that airport terminals, like the sidewalks and streets, are public forums. The majority also rejected the comparison of airports with bus or rail terminals, even though all may be regarded as transportation centers. The majority emphasized that state-owned airports are like privately owned airports in that they are *commercial* establishments funded by user fees and designed to make a regulated profit. The Court also held that prohibiting the solicitation of funds in an airport terminal (a non-public forum) is constitutional because it is "*reasonable.*"

■ CASE VOCABULARY

DURESS: Pressure to agree, whether psychological or physical threats. Here, the Court concludes people who cannot avoid the Krishnas (P), because they are late, disabled, or encumbered by bags/children may be forced to give money to avoid having to walk around them.

Arkansas Educational Television Commission v. Forbes

(*Public TV Station*) v. (*Unknown Candidate for Congress*)
523 U.S. 666, 118 S.Ct. 1633 (1998)

PUBLIC TV GENERALLY IS NOT A "FORUM," BUT PUBLICLY-TELEVISED CANDIDATE DEBATES ARE "NON-PUBLIC FORUMS"

■ **INSTANT FACTS** When a public TV station limited a debate to popular candidates, an unknown challenged his exclusion.

■ **BLACK LETTER RULE** Generally, the public has no right of access to state-owned TV, and publicly-televised candidate debates are "non-public forums."

■ PROCEDURAL BASIS

In First Amendment challenge to state-owned broadcaster's decision, appeal from appellate reversal of judgment for defendant.

■ FACTS

Arkansas owns the Arkansas Educational Television Commission (AETC) (D), which owns/operates non-commercial public TV stations. AETC (D) planned a televised debate among candidates for federal office, but limited participation to major party candidates, or others with strong popular support. Unknown candidate Ralph Forbes (P), a perennial candidate for various offices, was running for election to Congress, and requested permission to debate. AETC (D) refused, because Forbes (P) had no following. Forbes (P) sued for injunction and damages, claiming (i) public TV's debates are "public forums," and (ii) his exclusion was viewpoint-based. AETC (D) defended, claiming (i) televised debates are not public forums, (ii) his exclusion was based on his lack of public support, and (iii) journalistic discretion allowed/required them to exclude some candidates. At trial, the jury found for AETC (D), finding Forbes' (P) exclusion was viewpoint-neutral. But on appeal, the Court of Appeals held for Forbes (P). AETC (D) appeals.

■ ISSUE

May publicly-televised debates deny access to some candidates?

■ DECISION AND RATIONALE

(Kennedy, J.) Yes. Generally, the public has no right of access to state-owned TV, but publicly-televised candidate debates are "non-public forums." The "public forum" doctrine arose in parks/streets, and should not be extended mechanically to public TV broadcasting. Exercises of editorial discretion are "speech." Generally, giving public access would undermine broadcasters' staffs' journalistic purpose and statutory obligations. Congress rejected the theory that broadcast facilities should be open to all, on a non-selective basis. Instead, broadcasters are statutorily required to exercise discretion in selecting their programming. Protecting editorial discretion requires their immunity from claims of viewpoint discrimination, since the two often appear similar. Holding otherwise would require courts to formulate criteria for access, whereas this decision is best left to journalistic discretion. Thus, no Congressional law or policy requires open access. Further, we are reluctant to extend First Amendment doctrine to compel public broadcasters to allow access to *public broadcasting in general.* However, *publicly-*

Arkansas Educational Television Commission v. Forbes (Continued)

televised candidate debates are "non-public forums," because they are designed as forums for political speech, and are historically vital to the election process. They are not a traditional public forum, because TV is too recent. Nor are they designated "limited public forums;" these are created when the government designates public property available to an entire class of speakers ("general access"), not when it reserves eligibility for access to a particular class, whose members must then individually obtain permission to use it ("selective access"). This rule's policy is to encourage some debate, where a contrary rule might force public TV stations to refrain from broadcasting such debates. Also, forced inclusion of all candidates would undermine their educational value, by creating a cacophony. However, even in non-public forums, speakers' exclusion is valid only if it (i) is not viewpoint-based, and (ii) is reasonable. Here, the jury found Forbes' (P) exclusion was based not on his viewpoint, but on his objective lack of popular support. Thus, AETC's (D) decision was a reasonable exercise of journalistic discretion. Reversed; judgment for AETC (D).

■ DISSENT

(Stevens, J.) Publicly-televised electoral debates should be public forums, because they are designed as political forums, and important to the electoral process. Thus, access cannot be arbitrary. Here, it is, since AETC (D) has no clear standards, and thus must make subjective, ad hoc judgements.

Analysis:

This decision concludes the book's summary of cases setting criteria for whether various forums are public, limited public, or non-public. Generally, as the text notes, the Court's decisions on the topic are case-by-case, and often inconsistent. Here, the Court says TV is too new to be *traditionally* public. But it makes policy exceptions for publicly televised debates, because of their significance. But note this decision does not affect *private* TV stations televising debates; the First Amendment does not apply to private property.

■ CASE VOCABULARY

AD HOC: ("For this" [purpose]) Something formed for one particular purpose; individualistic.

CACOPHONY: Noise caused by many discordant voices. Here, the Court means that, if too many candidates debate, they might all try to out-talk each other, and/or each would have too little time to articulate his platform.

Parker v. Levy
(Army Official) v. (Dismissed Soldier)
417 U.S. 733, 94 S.Ct. 2547 (1974)

SOLDIERS RECEIVE *LESS* PROTECTION FROM THE FIRST AMENDMENT

■ **INSTANT FACTS** When a black soldier was convicted under military law for urging blacks not to fight in Vietnam, he challenged military law as unconstitutionally overbroad.

■ **BLACK LETTER RULE** The *Uniform Code of Military Justice*'s speech restrictions are not overbroad, considering the First Amendment offers military personnel lesser protection than civilians.

■ **PROCEDURAL BASIS**

In court-martial under *Uniform Code of Military Justice*, post-conviction appeal, challenging statutory provisions as overbroad.

■ **FACTS**

Apparently, the *Uniform Code of Military Justice* includes several articles restricting what enlisted men may say and read, and how they may assemble. Penalties range from minor administrative sanctions to severe criminal penalties. Apparently, these articles are broad and somewhat vague. During the Vietnam War, Army captain-physician Levy (D), apparently black, publicly denounced the Army's (P) racism and role in Vietnam to other soldiers, apparently at a bar. Levy's (D) statements included, "The United States is wrong in being involved in the Viet Nam War.... I don't see why any colored soldier should go to Viet Nam; they should refuse ... and if sent should refuse to fight because they are discriminated against and denied freedom in the United States, and ... sacrificed and discriminated against ... by being given all the hazardous duty and suffering the majority of casualties.... Special Forces personnel are liars and thieves and killers of peasants and ... women and children." Army (P) used its discretion to decide these words justified court-martialing Levy (D); he was dismissed, deprived of pay/benefits, and sentenced to 3 years' hard labor. Levy (D) appeals, contending those sections of the *Code* are so overbroad they violate the First Amendment, by not giving sufficient warning of what words are prohibited. Apparently, on appeal, the court reversed Levy's (D) conviction. Army (P) appeals.

■ **ISSUE**

Are the *Uniform Code of Military Justice*'s speech restrictions overbroad?

■ **DECISION AND RATIONALE**

(Rehnquist, J.) No. The *Uniform Code of Military Justice*'s speech restrictions are not overbroad, considering the First Amendment offers military personnel lesser protection than civilians. This Court recognized that the military, by necessity, may develop laws different from those of civilian society, because its mission is to be prepared to fight. While members of the military are not excluded from the First Amendment's protection, including "overbreadth" doctrine, the First Amendment is applied differently to military personnel. This is permissible because for the military, obedience is fundament, and the weighty countervailing interests present in civilian society must be accorded a good deal less weight. Generally, we find the *Code*'s restriction of specified speech is not overbroad enough to violate the First Amendment. While it may ultimately be applied in a way that violates the fringes of speech protected by the First Amendment, we find this probability is insufficient to invalidate those provisions. Here, Levy's (D) speech—a commissioned officer publicly urging enlisted men to refuse orders—was unprotected by even expansive notions of the First Amendment. Reversed; conviction reinstated.

■ DISSENT

(Douglas, J.) The First Amendment, on its face, does not exempt military personnel. True, the military requires discipline, which requires obeying valid orders. But other speech may be permissible. Congress cannot assume the power to curtail which books military personnel may read, nor suppress conversations at a bar, ban discussion of public affairs, or prevent assembly, as long as it does not interfere with military duties.

■ DISSENT

(Stewart, J.) Here, the statutory provisions at issue are unconstitutionally vague, so as to be incomprehensible to servicemen. They did not sufficiently warn Levy (D) that his speech was illegal. Such vague laws' capacity for arbitrary and discriminatory enforcement are improper, and even demoralizing.

Analysis:

This case signals the Court's general tolerance of greater speech restrictions in the military than are permissible in civilian society. The reasons are obvious: the army is an authoritarian institution, which relies on obedience rather than free discourse. Unfortunately, this case does not really articulate how much less protection the First Amendment offers to soldiers, so the only lesson is, "somewhat less."

■ CASE VOCABULARY

COURT-MARTIAL: Military trial for punishing soldiers' violations of the *Uniform Code of Military Justice.*

OVERBREADTH DOCTRINE: Law is deemed unconstitutionally "overbroad" if they (i) restrict "significantly"/"substantially" more speech than the Constitution allows, and (ii) plaintiff can demonstrate a "significant number" of situations where it *could* be applied to restrict protected speech. Note the plaintiff can prevail even if his own act was clearly prohibited, if he proves the law has the *potential* to be misapplied in *other* situations.

PENUMBRA: Hazy area; shadow.

Thornburgh v. Abbott

(*Prisoners and/or Journals*) v. (*Federal Bureau of Prisons*)
490 U.S. 401, 109 S.Ct. 1874 (1989)

PRISONERS FORFEIT SOME FIRST AMENDMENT RIGHTS

■ **INSTANT FACTS** Prisoners and / or inmate-targeted journals challenged prison regulations giving wardens discretion to ban dangerous journals.

■ **BLACK LETTER RULE** Prisons' restrictions on speech are valid if (i) the government's objective is legitimate, and (ii) neutral, and (iii) the regulations are "rationally related" to that objective.

■ **PROCEDURAL BASIS**

In First Amendment challenge to federal agency regulation, appeal from validation.

■ **FACTS**

The Federal Bureau of Prisons' ("Prisons") (D) regulations generally let inmates receive outside publications, but allow the warden to bar some publications. By regulation, wardens may ban a publication "only if it is determined detrimental to the security, good order, or discipline of the institution or . . . might facilitate criminal activity," but not "solely because its content is religious, philosophical, political, social, or sexual, or because its content is unpopular or repugnant." Prisons (D) banned, among other publications, one issue of prisoner-oriented magazine *Labyrinth*, whose article "Medical Murder" claimed guards let asthmatic inmates die through inadequate medical facilities, malpractice, and neglect. Prisons (D) based its decision on concerns it would cause hostility toward prison doctors. Apparently, several inmates and/or magazines (collectively, "Inmates") (P) challenged the regulation as facially unconstitutional, probably claiming it gave wardens arbitrary authority to violate the First Amendment. At trial, the District Court upheld the regulation. Inmates (P) appeal.

■ **ISSUE**

May prison regulations allow wardens to bar publications which threaten jails' security or discipline?

■ **DECISION AND RATIONALE**

(Blackmun, J.) Yes. Prisons' restrictions on speech are valid if (i) the government's objective is legitimate, and (ii) neutral, and (iii) the regulations are "rationally related" to that objective. Generally, prisoners are not entirely deprived of First Amendment protections. Also, outsiders have First Amendment rights to communicate with prisoners. But these protections are lessened, because of the paramount need to maintain prisons' security. Courts should give considerable deference to prison administrators' reasonable, expert judgment. Prisons' restrictions on speech are valid if (i) the government's objective is legitimate, and (ii) neutral, and (iii) the regulations are "rationally related" to that objective. Here, the censorship allowed by Prisons' (D) regulations would, outside the prison, raise First Amendment concerns. But in jails, we find it reasonable. Publications pose the risks of inciting riots. Also, if other inmates see someone reading certain publications, they may draw inferences about the reader's beliefs, sexuality, gang affiliation, etc., and attack him. Here, Prisons' (D) regulations further the important, legitimate goal of protecting security, and do not permit wholesale exclusion without cause. Affirmed, regulation valid.

Thornburgh v. Abbott (Continued)

■ CONCURRENCE

(Stevens, J.) Prisons (D) used this regulation to suppress 46 publications, despite testimony that officials believed they posed no threat. Prison officials should not be allowed to impose censorship upon a mere showing of "reasonableness." This excessively deprives inmates of First Amendment protections.

Analysis:

Like the army, jail is a place where First Amendment protections are reduced, because the Court recognizes a greater need to maintain safety, discipline, and security. Not surprisingly, under the permissive "rational basis" standard, most jailhouse regulations are upheld. But one exceptional case held that prisons could not censor inmates' grievance letters to those outside.

Shaw v. Murphy

(*Prison Official*) v. (*Inmate*)
532 U.S. 223, 121 S.Ct. 1475 (2001)

PRISON OFFICIALS HAVE DISCRETION TO RESTRICT PRISONERS' SPEECH

■ **INSTANT FACTS** Murphy (D) was convicted of violating prison rules relating to inmate-to-inmate legal assistance.

■ **BLACK LETTER RULE** Restrictions on prisoners' communication must be "reasonably related to legitimate penological interests."

■ PROCEDURAL BASIS

Certiorari to review a decision of a federal court of appeals.

■ FACTS

While incarcerated, Murphy (D) served as an "inmate law clerk," giving legal advice to fellow inmates. Upon learning that a fellow inmate had been charged with assaulting a prison guard, Murphy (D) sent him a letter containing legal advice. Prison rules prohibited his assignment to the case. After Murphy's (D) letter was intercepted, he was charged with insolence, interference with a due process hearing, and disruption of orderly prison operation. Murphy (D) was convicted of the first two charges and punished. On appeal, the court reversed the conviction, holding that inmate-to-inmate legal assistance is entitled to more protection under the First Amendment than other correspondence.

■ ISSUE

Is inmate-to-inmate legal assistance entitled to heightened First Amendment protection?

■ DECISION AND RATIONALE

(Thomas, J.) No. Under *Turner v. Safley*, restrictions on prisoners' communication must be "reasonably related to legitimate penological interests." This test does not consider the value of the content of the communication, but rather leaves within the discretion of prison officials when such communications need to be restricted. To increase First Amendment protection based on the content of prisoner communications, federal courts would intrude upon prison management. Moreover, even if heightened First Amendment protection were warranted in some cases, legal assistance would not be one of them. Inmate-to-inmate legal assistance threatens to disrupt the prison system as much as it may protect an inmate's legal rights. The First Amendment provides no additional protection to prisoners' conversations involving legal assistance than it does to other prisoner communications.

Analysis:

Although incarcerated criminals retain those constitutional rights consistent with their incarceration, such as due process and equal protection, the Court acknowledges that not all fundamental rights are retained. However, giving the government discretion over criminals' First Amendment rights contrasts significantly with the majority of the Supreme Court's First Amendment jurisprudence.

Tinker v. Des Moines Independent Community School District

(Student Protesters) v. (Public High School)
393 U.S. 503, 89 S.Ct. 733 (1969)

SCHOOLS CANNOT BAN STUDENTS' EXPRESSIVE CONDUCT, UNLESS DISRUPTIVE

■ **INSTANT FACTS** When a high school suspended students for wearing anti-Vietnam armbands, they claimed this violated their speech rights.

■ **BLACK LETTER RULE** Public schools cannot restrict students' expression, unless it would "materially and substantially interfere" with appropriate school discipline.

■ PROCEDURAL BASIS
In First Amendment challenge to public school's action, appeal from judgement for defendant.

■ FACTS
During the Vietnam War, several high school students (P), including Tinker (P) (collectively, "Protesters" (P)), protested American involvement by wearing black armbands to school. The Des Moines Independent Community School District ("School") (D) suspended Protesters (P) until they removed the armbands, claiming they provoked hostility in other students and distracted students from schoolwork. Protesters (P) challenged School's (D) policy, claiming it suppresses speech unreasonably. School (D) defended, claiming it was necessary to prevent disturbances, avoid distracting other students from learning, and prevent classes from turning into political debates. At trial, the District Court held for School (D), finding its action reasonably based on fear of disturbances. Protesters (P) appeal.

■ ISSUE
May a public school suspend students for wearing expressive symbols?

■ DECISION AND RATIONALE
(Fortas, J.) No. Public schools cannot restrict students' expression, unless it would "materially and substantially interfere" with appropriate school discipline. Teachers and students retain First Amendment rights, albeit modified to accomodate some need for discipline. Generally, school officials have authority to set educational policy and maintain discipline, but with constitutional safeguards. This case does not relate to schools' right to control disruptive clothing, hair styles, attitudes, agressive action, or demonstrations. Here, School (D) essentially restricts "pure speech" by banning/punishing passive wearing of protest symbols. For school officials to ban expressing certain opinions, they must show it would "materially and substantially interfere with the requirements of appropriate discipline in the operation of the school." It is not enough to claim unsubstantiated fear of disturbance; the Constitution requires us to take that risk in order to promote children's' independence. This is especially true if the school prohibits one particular viewpoint. Here, School (D) never proved any reasonable belief that Protesters' (P) armbands threatened disruption. State-operated schools cannot suppress all risk of disturbance through authoritarianism; they do not have sufficient authority over students to deprive them of fundamental First Amendment rights. Reversed; judgment for plaintiffs.

Tinker v. Des Moines Independent Community School District (Continued)

■ DISSENT

(Black, J.) This Court should defer to school officials' decisions on educational policy and school discipline. Students are too immature to make such decisions, and other students should not be distracted from their learning and forced to hear their immature speech. Here, there is sufficient evidence for School (D) to decide that Protesters' (P) armbands were disruptive and distracting.

Analysis:

Tinker is included as an illustration of "early" Court caselaw on school discipline. Early cases were more permissive, affording greater weight to students' First Amendment rights than to teachers' right to impose discipline. The next case contrasts this with an example of later, more restrictive caselaw. Throughout, the Court recognizes that schools require *some* level of authoritarianism, somewhere between that found in jails and the army and that permitted in general society. However, these cases wrestle with finding where on that spectrum schools belong.

■ CASE VOCABULARY

DEPORTMENT: The way a person carries himself; "attitude."

NASCENT: Developing.

UNDIFFERENTIATED: Inexplicable in concrete terms; i.e., speculative.

Bethel School District v. Fraser

(*School*) v. (*Student Speaker*)
478 U.S. 675, 106 S.Ct. 3159 (1986)

LATER SCHOOL-SPEECH CASES ARE LESS TOLERANT OF STUDENTS' SPEECH RIGHTS

■ **INSTANT FACTS** When a high school student laced a school speech with sexual innuendo, the school sanctioned him.

■ **BLACK LETTER RULE** Schools may sanction students' lewd speech.

■ **PROCEDURAL BASIS**

In First Amendment challenge to public school's sanction, appeal from appellate affirmation of judgement for plaintiff.

■ **FACTS**

Bethel High School (D) has a policy agaist obscene language. High school student Fraser (P), at a mandatory school assembly, delievered a sexaully-metaphoric speech to 14-year-old boys and girls, nominating another student for office. Fraser (P) said, "I know a man who is firm—he's firm in his pants, he's firm in his shirt, his character is firm—but most . . . of all, his belief in you, the students of Bethel, is firm. [He] is a man who takes his point and pounds it in. If necessary, he'll take an issue and nail it to the wall. He doesn't attack things in spurts—he drives hard, pushing and pushing until finally—he succeeds. [He] is a man who will go to the very end—even the climax, for each and every one of you. So vote for [him] for A.S.B. vice-president—he'll never come between you and the best our high school can be." In response, School (D) suspended Fraser (P) for 3 days, and made him ineligible to speak at graduation. Fraser (P) sued, claiming School's (D) action violated *Tinker*'s guarantee of student speech. At trial, the District Court found for Fraser (P), citing *Tinker* and finding School (D) failed to prove the speech was disruptive. The Court of Appeals affirmed. School (D) appeals.

■ **ISSUE**

Can a school sanction a student's lewd speech?

■ **DECISION AND RATIONALE**

(Burger, J.) Yes. Schools may sanction students' lewd speech. *Tinker* held schools cannot ban non-disruptive, passive expression of political viewpoints, which did not intrude upon schoolwork or other students' rights. Here, Fraser's (P) speech is distinguishable; it is non-political, not passive, and disruptive. Schools are justified in prohibiting vulgar, offensive terms in public discourse, as a lesson on what kind of speech is not tolerated in society. In schools, teachers and older students are role models for younger students; Fraser (P) sets a bad example. Fraser's (P) innuendo was offensive to adults, and could be seriously damaging to young girls, who are just discovering sexuality. School (D) acted permissibly in sanctioning Fraser (P). Reversed; judgment for defendant.

■ **CONCURRENCE**

(Brennan, J.) I concur, but on narrower grounds. School officials have discretion in teaching students how to conduct civil, effective public discourse, and to prevent disruption of educational assemblies. School's (D) action was permissible.

Bethel School District v. Fraser (Continued)

■ DISSENT

(Marshall, J.) Under *Tinker*, the school must prove the prohibited speech was disruptive. Here, both lower courts found School (D) failed to show this about Fraser's (P) speech, and I see no reason to find otherwise.

Analysis:

This case illustrates the Court's "later" school-speech cases, which apply *Tinker*'s interest-balancing test, but tend to give greater weight to the school's interests. Here, the majority reaches its decision by distinguishing *Tinker*'s passive, political protest. Still, the defendant school here may be criticized for the same reasons as *Tinker*'s; it fails to prove actual disruption or harm to students.

Hazelwood School District v. Kuhlmeier

(School) v. (Student Journalists)
484 U.S. 260, 108 S.Ct. 562 (1988)

SCHOOL-SPONSORED STUDENT ACTIVITIES MAY BE CENSORED

■ **INSTANT FACTS** When a school censored its newspaper, excising six articles to remove two about students' pregnancies and family problems, censored student-writers sued.

■ **BLACK LETTER RULE** When schools *sponsor* expressive activities, they may edit/censor the product if (i) their actions are "reasonably related" (ii) to "legitimate pedagogical concerns."

■ **PROCEDURAL BASIS**

In First Amendment challenge to state school's censorship, appeal from appellate judgment for plaintiffs.

■ **FACTS**

Hazelwood School District (D) printed a newspaper in conjunction with its journalism class. The paper was distributed to students, families, and community members. School's (D) policy was for its principal to approve page proofs before publication. The (female) principal objected to two articles. One dealt with School's (D) schoolgirls' pregnancies, using false names; the principal feared the girls' identities were identifiable from the text, and felt the article's references to sex and birth control were inappropriate for younger readers. Another article quoted a named student's complaint that his father spent little time at home; she felt the student's family should have an opportunity to respond. (The principal was unaware that the author's final draft omitted the student's name.) To remove the articles, the principal ordered that two entire pages be deleted (even though they also contained four other, non-objectionable articles) to meet the printing deadline. Several student-authors (P) whose articles were deleted, including Kuhlmeier (P), sued, claiming (i) the newspaper was a "public forum," and (ii) its censorship violated their First Amendment rights. The Court of Appeals held for Students (P). School (D) appeals.

■ **ISSUE**

May schools censor student's writings in school-funded publications?

■ **DECISION AND RATIONALE**

(White, J.) Yes. When schools *sponsor* expressive activities, they may edit/censor the product if (i) their actions are "reasonably related" (ii) to "legitimate pedagogical concerns." Public school students retain some First Amendment protections, but these may be less than those of adults in society. Schools need not tolerate expression in schools which is inconsistent with its "basic educational mission." The decision of whether certain speech is inconsistent generally should rest with school officials, not judges. (I) Public schools, and their publications, are not public forums. Here, the newspaper was recognized as part of School's (D) regular journalism curriculum. (II) When schools *sponsor* expressive activities, they may edit/censor the product if (i) their actions are "reasonably related" (ii) to "legitimate pedagogical concerns." This is distinguishable from *Tinker*, which dealt with whether schools must tolerate students' *personal* speech. With school-sponsored expression, schools may take steps to, e.g., assure participants learn the intended lesson, ensure readers are not exposed to material inappropriate for their maturity, prevent students' views from being misattributed to the school, and dissociate themselves from poor-quality work, speech that interferes with other students' rights, work that is biased or vulgar, expression which appears to promote socially-unacceptable acts, or speech which associates the school with one side of a controversy. This standard recognizes that educational policy should be set by school officials, not judges. Here, we find the principal acted reasonably in deleting the articles, for the reasons she cited. Reversed; judgment for defendant.

■ DISSENT

(Brennan, J.) School (D) broke its promise to its journalism Students (P) that it would not censor free expression and diverse viewpoints. Also, School (D) violated the First Amendment. Under *Tinker*, censorship was not allowed, because Students' (P) articles were not disruptive, and did not violate other students' rights. School's (D) censorship had no valid pedagogical purpose. Further, even if it did, the principal should have chosen less drastic means than excising 6 articles completely.

Analysis:

Again, the Court retreats from *Tinker* and cracks down on students' expression by distinguishing *Tinker* and creating a more restrictive rule for school-sponsored activities. This rule often hits student expression disproportionately hard, since high school students usually lack the money to fund their expression (e.g., newspapers, plays) without school support.

■ CASE VOCABULARY

IMPRIMATUR: Mark indicating ownership or authorship.

Morse v. Frederick

(*Principal*) v. (*Student*)
551 U.S. 393, 127 S.Ct. 2618 (2007)

SCHOOLS MAY PROPERLY RESTRICT SOME STUDENT SPEECH

■ **INSTANT FACTS** Frederick (P) was suspended from high school for displaying a banner that was regarded as promoting drug use.

■ **BLACK LETTER RULE** Student speech that may reasonably be viewed as advocating illegal drug use may be restricted at school sponsored events.

■ **PROCEDURAL BASIS**

Appeal from an order reversing a grant of summary judgment.

■ **FACTS**

Morse (D), the principal of a high school, permitted students and staff members to leave class to watch the Olympic Torch Relay as it passed by the school. Watching the relay was a school-approved social event or class trip. Teachers and staff members monitored the students. Frederick (P) stood with friends across the street from the school to watch the relay. When the torchbearers and television camera crews covering the event passed by, Frederick (P) and his friends unveiled a fourteen foot banner that read "BONG HiTS 4 JESUS." The banner was readable by students across the street. Morse (D) told the students to take the banner down, but Frederick (P) refused. Morse (D) confiscated the banner and suspended Frederick (P) for ten days. Morse (D) said that she confiscated the banner because she thought it encouraged illegal drug use. Frederick's (P) suspension was sustained. The school superintendent (D) determined that Frederick's (P) conduct that led to his suspension was in the midst of students, during school hours, and during a school-sanctioned activity. The superintendent (D) further explained that Frederick (P) was not disciplined because Morse (D) disagreed with his message, but because the banner appeared to advocate the use of illegal drugs. Frederick (P) claimed that the banner was just nonsense, meant to attract television cameras.

■ **ISSUE**

Did Frederick's (P) suspension violate the First Amendment?

■ **DECISION AND RATIONALE**

(Roberts, C.J.) No. Student speech that may reasonably be viewed as advocating illegal drug use may be restricted at school sponsored events. The message of Frederick's (P) banner is cryptic, but Morse's (D) interpretation of the banner as promoting drug use is a reasonable one. This is not a case about political debate over the legalization of drug use or possession.

The constitutional rights of students in public schools are not automatically coextensive with the rights of adults in other settings. Still, student expression may not be suppressed unless school officials reasonably conclude that the expression will be materially and substantially disruptive. Student speech in school-sponsored activities may be controlled as long as the control is reasonably related to legitimate educational concerns.

Morse v. Frederick (Continued)

Frederick's (P) banner could not be taken as sponsored by the school, but schools may regulate some speech that could not otherwise be censored. The special characteristics of the school environment, coupled with the governmental interest in stopping student drug abuse, allow schools to restrict student expression that they reasonably regard as promoting illegal drug use. Reversed.

■ CONCURRENCE

(Thomas, J.) The history of the First Amendment suggests that student speech in public schools is not protected. Courts upheld the rights of schools to maintain order through the doctrine of *in loco parentis*.

■ CONCURRENCE

(Alito, J.) The Court's opinion is based on the understanding that it goes no further than holding that a school may restrict speech that advocates illegal drug use, but that does not comment on any political or social issue, including the legalization of drugs.

■ CONCURRENCE IN PART, DISSENT IN PART

(Breyer, J.) Morse (D) was protected by qualified immunity, and so could not be sued for money damages.

■ DISSENT

(Stevens, J.) Frederick (P) was not sending a message to other students, he was trying to attract the attention of television cameras. The school's (D) interest in protecting students from speech that is regarded as promoting illegal drug use does not justify disciplining Frederick (P) for his ambiguous statement. It is a gross non sequitur to conclude that the school (D) could suppress student speech that was never meant to persuade anyone to do anything. The Court invited viewpoint discrimination. Any student speech that mentions drugs is now subject to censorship.

Analysis:

Justice Alito's concurrence states that he would not allow restriction of speech that advocates legalization of drugs. The majority is careful to note that this type of advocacy is not an issue in this case. The line between the two types of speech could be a fine one. School administrators could be put in the position of parsing student speech to make sure that "legalization" does not turn into "advocating use."

■ CASE VOCABULARY

IN LOCO PARENTIS: Of, relating to, or acting as a temporary guardian or caretaker of a child, taking on all or some of the responsibilities of a parent.

Garcetti v. Ceballos

(*District Attorney*) v. (*Deputy*)
547 U.S. 410, 126 S.Ct. 1951 (2006)

PUBLIC EMPLOYEES' WORK–RELATED SPEECH IS UNPROTECTED

■ **INSTANT FACTS** Ceballos (P) raised concerns about possible deficiencies in a search warrant affidavit, and claimed he was subject to retaliation as a result.

■ **BLACK LETTER RULE** Public employees who speak as a part of their official duties are not protected from employer discipline by the First Amendment.

■ **PROCEDURAL BASIS**

Appeal from an order of the court of appeals reversing a grant of summary judgment.

■ **FACTS**

Ceballos (P) was a deputy district attorney. A defense attorney contacted him and expressed concern about possible inaccuracies in a search warrant affidavit. Ceballos (P) investigated, and concluded that there were inaccuracies. He brought these inaccuracies to the attention of his superiors (D), but they decided to proceed with the prosecution. Ceballos (P) was called to testify at a hearing to challenge the warrant. The court rejected the challenge. Ceballos (P) claimed that after he testified, he was subject to retaliation. The retaliation included reassignment to another position, transfer to another courthouse, and denial of a promotion.

■ **ISSUE**

Was Ceballos's (P) speech protected by the First Amendment?

■ **DECISION AND RATIONALE**

(Kennedy, J.) No. Public employees who speak as a part of their official duties are not protected from employer discipline by the First Amendment. Public employees do not surrender all of their First Amendment rights. A governmental employer has a broader discretion to limit speech, but those limitations must be directed at speech that has some potential to affect the entity's operations. A government employee who speaks as a citizen on a matter of public concern may face only those restrictions on his or her speech that are necessary for their employers to operate efficiently and effectively.

Ceballos (P) spoke inside his office, about the subject matter of his employment, but this is not dispositive. The dispositive factor is that Ceballos's (P) speech was a part of his duty to advise his superiors about how to proceed with a pending case. Restricting speech that owes its existence to a public employee's official responsibilities does not infringe any liberties the employee had as a private citizen. Ceballos's (P) superiors (D) were not prohibited from evaluating his performance.

■ **DISSENT**

(Stevens, J.) It is senseless to let constitutional protection for speech hinge on whether it falls within a job description. It also seems perverse to make a new rule that encourages employees to air their concerns publicly before speaking with their superiors.

Garcetti v. Ceballos (Continued)

■ DISSENT

(Souter, J.) The interests in addressing official wrongdoing and threats to health and safety can outweigh the government's interest in the efficient implementation of policy. There is no good reason to categorically discount a speaker's interest in commenting on a matter of public concern just because the speaker is a government employee. First Amendment protection also rests on the value to the public of receiving the information and opinions that may be disclosed by a public employee. A public employee who speaks out on work-related issues has the potential to disrupt the workplace, but that disruption may sometimes be necessary.

■ DISSENT

(Breyer, J.) The majority's view is too absolute. There may be circumstances where the governmental justification for suppressing speech may be limited. This is such a case. Ceballos (P) claims that he was retaliated against, in part, on the basis of speech that he claims fell within his obligations under *Brady v. Maryland,* 373 U.S. 83 (1963). The speech at issue here is professional speech, and the obligation to speak is imposed by the Constitution.

Analysis:

The dissents of Justices Souter and Breyer raise two important points that seem to have been overlooked by the majority. Justice Souter remarks that, not only does Ceballos (P) have an interest in being able to speak freely, but the public has an interest in hearing what he has to say. Justice Breyer notes that what Ceballos (P) said was required by *Brady v. Maryland.* A failure to speak out about the defective search warrant affidavit could have led to a conviction in the case being overturned. But perhaps the plaintiff's redress does not lie in a constitutional claim, but in a tort-based retaliation or "whistleblower" claim.

■ CASE VOCABULARY

BRADY MATERIAL: Information or evidence that is favorable to a defendant's case and that the prosecution has a duty to disclose. The prosecution's withholding of such information violates the defendant's due process rights.

National Association for the Advancement of Colored People v. Alabama, ex rel. Patterson

(Anti-Discrimination Advocacy Group) v. (State Government)
357 U.S. 449, 78 S.Ct. 1163 (1958)

IF DISCLOSURE OF MEMBERS WOULD CHILL GROUP SPEECH, IT IS NOT REQUIRED

■ **INSTANT FACTS** The controversial anti-discrimination group NAACP defied a court order compelling it to disclose all members, contending it violates their speech/assembly right by inviting retaliation.

■ **BLACK LETTER RULE** If disclosure of an expressive assembly's membership would chill its speech/assembly, then the state cannot compel it, absent a valid, controlling reason.

■ PROCEDURAL BASIS
In civil suit, appeal from contempt judgment against plaintiff.

■ FACTS
In the course of litigation between them, Alabama (D) obtained a court order compelling the anti-discrimination activist organization NAACP (P) to disclose membership lists revealing all members in state, including officers, employees, and rank-and-file members. NAACP (P) refused to disclose its rank-and-filers, fearing disclosure would expose them to harassment, as happened previously. Consequently, the court entered a civil contempt judgment against NAACP (P). NAACP (P) appeals the contempt judgment, claiming compelled production of the list violates Fourteenth Amendment due process, and is unjustified because Alabama (D) has little need to identify rank-and-filers.

■ ISSUE
May the government compel disclosure of political assemblies' members?

■ DECISION AND RATIONALE
(Harlan, J.) No. If disclosure of an expressive assembly's membership would chill its speech/assembly, then the state cannot compel it, absent a valid, controlling reason. Fourteenth Amendment due process includes speech and association, which are both necessary for effective advocacy. If state action has the effect of curtailing either, it is subject to "closest" scrutiny. Compelled disclosure of advocacy groups' membership may chill speech and assembly by the group and individual members, by exposing members to reprisals for their beliefs. Here, NAACP (P) proved that when it previously revealed members' names, they were blacklisted, fired, threatened, etc. Under these circumstances, compelling NAACP (P) to produce would chill members' expression. Here, Alabama (D) has not demonstrated an interest sufficient to justify this chilling effect. NAACP (P) is willing to disclose its officers and paid agents. Further, NAACP (P) is not using this tactic to gain immunity from government investigation. Order void; judgment for plaintiff.

Analysis:
This case illustrates the process the Supreme Court uses to analyze government actions that implicate fundamental rights. This process usually involves application of the highest level of scrutiny in the

Nat'l Ass'n for the Advancement of Colored People v. Alabama (Continued)

Court's arsenal—strict scrutiny. Under strict scrutiny analysis there must be a compelling governmental interest, and the means of achieving that interest must be narrowly tailored to meet or achieve the desired end. To be compelling, the governmental interest must be of sufficient importance to outweigh the rights being subsumed. Narrow tailoring means that the governmental interest must not be achievable through less restrictive means. One of the cases Alabama (D) relied on to buttress its position is *Bryant v. Zimmerman*, a 1926 Supreme Court case upholding a New York law requiring disclosure of membership lists of organizations requiring loyalty oaths. Justice Harlan distinguished *Bryant* by relying on the fact that it focused on the violent and unlawful nature of the Ku Klux Klan's activities and the organization's refusal to provide New York with any information about its local activities. Presumably, had the activities of the NAACP (P) presented concerns similar to those raised by the activities of the Ku Klux Klan, and had disclosure of the organization's membership lists been necessary to quell those concerns, the Court would have enforced the trial court's judgment. This case shows the Court's willingness to permit some organizations to resist laws requiring disclosure of members, and the policy justifications for it.

■ CASE VOCABULARY

EX REL.: On behalf of.

CONTEMPT [OF COURT]: Refusal to obey a (civil) court order; punishable by various sanctions.

DUE PROCESS CLAUSE: Constitutional provision requiring that people not be deprived of "life, liberty, or property" without a fair trial or similar procedural safeguard. Here, NAACP (P) probably claimed the contempt judgment, which carried a large fine, deprived it of money (property) unconstitutionally.

Board of Regents of the University of Wisconsin System v. Southworth

(*Public University*) v. (*Dissenting Students*)

529 U.S. 217, 120 S.Ct. 1346 (2000)

PUBLIC SCHOOLS MAY COMPEL DUES BE SPENT ON OTHERS' SPEECH, IF FUNDING IS VIEW-POINT-NEUTRAL

■ **INSTANT FACTS** When a public university charged a mandatory student activity fee used to fund various student groups' speech, dissenting students claimed "forced association."

■ **BLACK LETTER RULE** State-owned schools may condition their degree on students' funding others' possibly-objectionable speech, but students may insist on some *viewpoint-neutral* procedural safeguards to limit the speech their money supports.

■ **PROCEDURAL BASIS**

In First Amendment/freedom of association challenge to state-owned university's policy, appeal from appellate affirmation of judgment for plaintiffs.

■ **FACTS**

The Board of Regents of the University of Wisconsin ("Regents") (D) require University's students to pay a mandatory student activities fee of $331, which is used partly to fund various "registered student organizations'" (RSOs) advocacy of varied politics, ideologies, etc. Some student Dissenters (P), including Southworth (P), challenged the fee, claiming it was unconstitutional for the (state-owned) University to force them to spend money to subsidize speech they may oppose. Regents (D) defended, claiming the activities promote University's educational mission, by enhancing the college experience, promoting extracurricular activities, stimulating advocacy, debate, and political participation, developing social skills, etc. At trial, the District Court invalidated the policy. On appeal, the Court of Appeals affirmed. Regents (D) appeal again.

■ **ISSUE**

May a state university require students to pay fees used to subsidize various speech?

■ **DECISION AND RATIONALE**

(Kennedy, J.) Yes. State-owned schools may condition their degree on students' funding others' possibly-objectionable speech, but students may insist on some *viewpoint-neutral* procedural safeguards to limit the speech their money supports. This case is somewhat analogous to our "compelled association" decisions in *Abood v. Detroit Board of Education* (1977) [government employees may be required to pay union's collective bargaining costs, but not its ideological or political causes] and *Keller v. State Bar of California* (1990) [compulsory bar dues can be collected to regulate lawyers and improve legal services, but not anti-gun or anti-nuke initiatives], but also somewhat distinguishable. Also somewhat analogous are our "public forum" cases; while student activities funds are not traditionally-public forums, such funds should be similarly viewpoint-neutral. If a state-owned school conditions its degree on agreeing to fund others' possibly-objectionable speech, then students may insist on some

Board of Regents of the University of Wisconsin System v. Southworth (Continued)

viewpoint-neutral procedural safeguards to limit the speech their money supports. However, we cannot dictate the exact type of safeguard; while *it must allocate funding viewpoint-neutrally*, the no-advocacy rule applicable in *Abood* and *Keller* is unworkable here, and the school itself has more expertise to find one. In so holding, we recognize public universities' important, substantial purposes in promoting speech and educational experience, as well as students' right not to have to subsidize objectionable speech. Here, Regents (D) may require student activity fees to contribute to speech. But it is unclear whether Regents' (D) current procedural safeguard—a student referendum, allowing any student organization to be funded/de-funded by majority vote—is viewpoint-neutral; it may allow the majority to silence minorities' viewpoints. We remand to determine whether the referendum is a sufficient safeguard. This holding does not suggest government may not use tax revenues to advance *its own* policies/messages, even though they may be objectionable to some taxpayers; such conflict is inevitable. Affirmed in part; remanded in part.

Analysis:

This case is a useful summary of previous caselaw on "compelled association," and also applies it to analogous situations. The issue arises when people are forced to join an association—usually a union/professional association, but not always—and to contribute dues, which are then used to support policies they oppose. For unions and bar associations, the rule is that they may collect dues and use them for essential functions (e.g., collective bargaining, maintaining professional standards), but may not spend them on viewpoint advocacy.

Roberts v. United States Jaycees

(Organization's State Chapters) v. (National Males' Organization)
468 U.S. 609, 104 S.Ct. 3244 (1984)

"FREE ASSOCIATION" INCLUDES RIGHTS TO DISCRIMINATE ONLY IN INTIMATE OR NECESSARILY-EXCLUSIVE ASSOCIATIONS

■ **INSTANT FACTS** When a male-only civic organization's local chapter began admitting women to follow state anti-discrimination laws, the national organization threatened to dissolve them.

■ **BLACK LETTER RULE** The government may regulate to force expressive associations to admit other members non-discriminatorily, if that regulation (i) serves compelling state interests, (ii) which are unrelated to suppressing ideas, (iii) that cannot be achieved through means significantly less restrictive of association.

■ FACTS

The national chapter of the Junior Chamber of Commerce, a.k.a. United States "Jaycees" (D), is an educational/civic organization. Its "regular," voting membership is open only to men aged 18–35. Membership is non-selective otherwise. Others—women and old men—may only join as non-voting "associate" members; they can't vote, hold internal office, or participate in some training/award ceremonies. Jaycees' (D) Minnesota Chapters (P), headed by Roberts (P), have admitted women as full members for years, to follow Minnesota anti-discrimination laws. Minnesota's *Human Rights Act* provided, "It is unfair [and] discriminatory practice . . . to deny any person the full and equal enjoyment of the . . . privileges . . . of a place of public accommodation [including such organizations] because of . . . sex" and other categories. The national Jaycees (D) sanctioned the Minnesota Chapters (P) by invalidating their votes, and finally threatened to revoke their charters. Minnesota Chapters (P) sued, claiming Jaycees (D) were forcing them to violate *Act*. Jaycees (D) defended, contending that government laws forcing them to admit women as full members violated their First Amendment "freedom *not* to associate." The Eighth Circuit held for Jaycees (D), contending *Act* violates their First/Fourteenth Amendment rights. Minnesota Chapters (P) appeal.

■ ISSUE

May a state force private associations to stop discriminating in admitting members?

■ DECISION AND RATIONALE

(Brennan, J.) Yes. The government may regulate to force expressive associations to admit other members non-discriminatorily, if that regulation (i) serves compelling state interests, (ii) which are unrelated to suppressing ideas, (iii) that cannot be achieved through means significantly less restrictive of association. Our cases affirming "freedom of association" contain two components: (i) the right to enter certain intimate, human relationships without governmental interference, and (ii) the right to associate with others to collectively pursue First Amendment speech. We analyze these separately. Component II.A. "Freedom of association" includes the right to form and maintain certain highly-personal relationships, without interference by the state. Such relationships usually involve family: marriage, childbirth, raising/educating children, cohabiting with relatives, etc. Such relationships tend to include these characteristics: small size, high selectivity, secluded activities, congeniality, purpose, policies, and others. Here, Jaycees' (D) organization is not such a close personal one; it is large, basically non-selective, and requires admitting strangers. Component II.B. "Freedom of association" also includes the right to associate with others, to collectively pursue First Amendment activities, e.g., speaking, worshiping, petitioning government for redress. To be effective, such associations often must be allowed to consist of only members of a certain background; admitting everyone would dilute their opinions. Thus, "freedom of association" also includes the right *not* to associate with some. This freedom is implicated when the government imposes penalties/withholds benefits to punish membership, requires disclosure of members seeking anonymity, interferes with the group's internal organization or affairs, etc. Interference with the group's affairs includes forcing it to admit new members. Here, the last one is implicated. However, the right to associate/not associate is not absolute. The government may regulate the right to associate for expression, if that regulation (i) serves compelling state interests, (ii) which are unrelated to suppressing ideas, (iii) that cannot be achieved through means significantly less restrictive of association. Here, we find *Act* may require Jaycees (D) to admit women. *Act* serves the compelling interest of eradicating gender discrimination, which cannot be achieved through other means. Further, Jaycees (D) have not demonstrated that admitting women would impose serious, actual burdens on men; it already admits women as partial members, and the risk that women will skew Jaycees' (D) manly policies is unproven. Reversed.

Analysis:

Private establishments, confined to people of certain races, genders, backgrounds, etc., are often popular groups for meeting others with similar interests, and possibly uniting with them. But historically, they have also been used to justify discrimination. So, the Court's test balances both interests. Most often, the interest in preventing discrimination will tip the scale, except for rare highly personal groups, and probably also for groups whose message is based on discrimination, e.g., the KKK.

Hurley v. Irish-American Gay, Lesbian and Bisexual Group of Boston

(*Private Parade Organizers*) v. (*Gay Marchers*)
515 U.S. 557, 115 S.Ct. 2338 (1995)

PARADE ORGANIZERS NEED NOT ADMIT GAYS AS GROUP

■ **INSTANT FACTS** A private parade organizer banned a gay group from marching, claiming applying state anti-discrimination laws would compel them to make a pro-gay statement.

■ **BLACK LETTER RULE** State anti-discrimination law cannot require private parade organizers to admit certain groups, if admitting them would change the parade's message.

■ **PROCEDURAL BASIS**
In state/federal equal rights challenge to private association's policy, appeal from state court's compromise decision.

■ **FACTS**
The city of Boston (D) gave authority to organize its annual St. Patrick's Day parade to the South Boston Allied War Veterans Council ("Council") (D), including authority to accept/reject certain marchers. One applicant was the Irish-American Gay, Lesbian and Bisexual Group of Boston ("GLIB") (P), which applied to march publicly, as a group, under its own pro-gay banner. Council (D) rejected GLIB's (P) application. GLIB (P) sued Boston (D), Council (D), and organizer John "Wacko" Hurley (D), contending the denial violates Massachusetts' public accommodations law, which prohibits "any distinction, discrimination or restriction on account of . . . sexual orientation . . . relative to the admission of any person to, or treatment in any place of public accommodation." [GLIB (P) did not claim violations of its own First Amendment speech rights, or Fourteenth Amendment equal protection.] Council (D) defended, claiming that applying the public accommodations law would violate Council's (D) First Amendment rights by effectively dictating that their private parade must include visible support for gays. At trial, the state court fashioned a compromise: GLIB (P) members could participate individually, but not as a discrete unit, and without a banner. GLIB (P) appeals, apparently contending this compromise is illegal because it effectively forces them to alter their message's content.

■ **ISSUE**
May state anti-discrimination law require private parade organizers to admit certain groups?

■ **DECISION AND RATIONALE**
(Souter, J.) No. State anti-discrimination law cannot require private parade organizers to admit certain groups, if admitting them would change the parade's message. Parades are deemed a form of expression, since banding together, and marching, makes a statement to marchers and onlookers. Further, the act of marching in a parade is itself "expression," even absent banners, singing, etc. Here, the St. Patrick's Day Parade is expressive. First, we find the state court's compromise—allowing GLIB's (P) members to participate, but only as individuals—would be unconstitutional. Under the First Amendment, speakers retain full autonomy to choose their message's content, without state interfer-

Hurley v. Irish-American Gay, Lesbian and Bisexual Group of Boston (Continued)

ence. But requiring GLIB (P) members to march individually would alter their expressive conduct's meaning. Next, the First Amendment also requires that one who chooses to speak also may decide "what not to say," including certain viewpoints. Here, Council's (D) decision to exclude a pro-gay message it did not like was a valid exercise of the right against compelled speech. That GLIB (P) was rather unselective in admitting other marchers is irrelevant; private speakers do not forfeit constitutional protection simply by admitting other, varied messages, or having no single, exclusive message of their own. We do not say we support Council's (D) anti-gay viewpoint, but only that it has the right to maintain it. Reversed; judgment for defendants.

Analysis:

After the Court expounded its interest-balancing test in *Jaycees* for determining whether freedom of association justified discrimination, it ignored that test here, instead finding the parade's organizers had an absolute right to control the message "their" parade conveys. In *Hurley*, the Court refuses to consider the strong state interest in combating long-standing anti-gay discrimination and does not consider whether excluding gays is a central component of the Council's (D) message. Maybe this case is distinguishable from *Jaycees* because the Council's (D) claim is not that admitting gays amounts to "compelled *association*," but that including pro-gay banners, etc. amounts to "compelled *speech*" effectively supporting gays.

Boy Scouts of America v. Dale

(Youth Civil Organization) v. (Gay Scout Leader)
530 U.S. 640, 120 S.Ct. 2446 (2000)

BOY SCOUTS MAY EXCLUDE GAY LEADERS

■ **INSTANT FACTS** When the Boy Scouts expelled an openly-gay Scout leader as "forced expressive association," he claimed the expulsion violated state anti-discrimination law.

■ **BLACK LETTER RULE** "Expressive associations" need not accept members whose presence significantly impacts their ability to advocate their viewpoint, barring strong countervailing policy reasons.

■ **PROCEDURAL BASIS**

In state constitutional challenge to private organization's policy, appeal from judgment for plaintiff.

■ **FACTS**

Boy Scouts of America (D) is an organization which strives to teach boys about civics, patriotism, morals, and athleticism. Longtime scout and New Jersey adult scout leader Dale (P) later admitted his homosexuality, and was publicized as a gay rights activist. Afterwards, Boy Scouts (D) revoked Dale's (P) membership, on the grounds its policy "specifically forbid[s] membership to homosexuals." New Jersey's public accommodation statute prohibits discrimination based on sexual orientation in places of public accommodation. Dale (P) sued Boy Scouts (D), contending it violated New Jersey's statute. The state court held for Dale (P), finding Boy Scouts (D) was a place of public accommodation subject to the statute, and violated the statute. Boy Scouts (D) appeal, claiming (i) it is an expressive association (ii) whose message includes rejecting homosexuality, and (iii) this message would be altered by compulsion if it had to include known homosexuals, in violation of First Amendment "freedom of association."

■ **ISSUE**

May the Boy Scouts expel gay Scout leaders?

■ **DECISION AND RATIONALE**

(Rehnquist, C.J.) Yes. "Expressive associations" need not accept members whose presence significantly impacts their ability to advocate their viewpoint, barring strong countervailing policy reasons. Generally, forced inclusion of unwanted persons in a group infringes its freedom of expressive association if their presence significantly affects the group's ability to advocate public/private viewpoints. But freedom of expressive association can be overridden by government regulations (i) adopted to serve "compelling" state interests, (ii) unrelated to suppressing ideas, (iii) that cannot be achieved through means significantly less restrictive of associational freedoms. To qualify for "freedom of expressive association," the group must engage in some expression, public or private, advocacy or not. Here, we find Boy Scouts' (D) general mission—"to instill values in young people" is clear, and constitutes expression. Next, we find forced inclusion of gays would impede Boy Scouts' (D) ability to advocate this viewpoint. Boy Scouts' (D) Oath and Law include the values of being "morally straight" and "clean," which can be understood to be anti-gay. Also, Boy Scouts (D) publicly expressed this

Boy Scouts of America v. Dale (Continued)

interpretation in prior litigation. Forcing Boy Scouts (D) to keep Dale (P) on as a leader would effectively compel it to send the message that it accepts gays. Applying New Jersey's statute would compel this result, in violation of the First Amendment. Reversed, judgment for defendant.

■ DISSENT

(Stevens, J.) Boy Scouts (D) should be required to retain Dale (P), since it has no effective anti-gay "message" that would be impaired, under *Jaycees*. Boy Scouts' (D) Handbook does not explicitly mention homosexuality, and leaves any teaching of sexuality to boys' guardians. Its references to "morally straight" and "clean" say nothing about homosexuality. Further, Boy Scouts (D) purports to represent all boys and exclude none, suggesting it should include gays. Also, Boy Scouts (D) renounces sectarianism. Even if its message is religious, some religions accept homosexuality. Further, policy should promote New Jersey's eradication of anti-gay bias, not legitimize it.

Analysis:

Unlike *Hurley*, this case does actually apply the *Jaycee* balancing test of expressive interests versus anti-discrimination policy. But query how seriously the Court takes this latter policy, since this decision gives it short shrift, discounting these worthwhile policies while making the questionable inference that Boy Scouts' (D) vague reference to "morally straight" and "clean" are "obvious" condemnations of homosexuality.

■ CASE VOCABULARY

ECUMENISM: Piety.

EXPRESSIVE ASSOCIATION: Right to form groups to do communicative/religious activities collectively. Distinguished from the associational right to maintain family relationships free of governmental interference.

Minneapolis Star and Tribune Company v. Minnesota Commissioner of Revenue

(Newspaper) v. *(State Tax Collector)*
460 U.S. 575, 103 S.Ct. 1365 (1983)

THE PRESS CANNOT BE TAXED DIFFERENTLY FROM OTHER BUSINESSES, EVEN TO BENEFIT IT

■ **INSTANT FACTS** When a state changed its state tax in a way which generally benefitted the press but gave greater benefits for small publications, a big newspaper challenged it.

■ **BLACK LETTER RULE** The government may not tax the press differently from other businesses, even to benefit it, unless (i) necessary (ii) to achieve "overriding" governmental interests (iii) which cannot be achieved through less-restrictive means.

■ **PROCEDURAL BASIS**

First Amendment challenge to state tax statute's amendment.

■ **FACTS**

Minnesota (D) changed its tax laws to tax periodicals differently than general businesses. Previously, Minnesota (D) charged a sales tax on most goods, but exempted periodicals from sales tax and use taxes. Later, Minnesota (D) changed its law, keeping the press' sales tax exemption, but charging it to a use tax on the cost of paper and ink used, *over the first $100K/year.* [This advantaged small presses, which spent less than $100K per year on supplies, and thus paid no tax.] One large newspaper-taxpayer, Minneapolis Star and Tribune Company ("Star Tribune") (P) sued, (i) challenging any tax which treated the press differently is unconstitutional, under *Grosjean v. American Press Co.* (1936) [Gov. Huey Long cannot impose punitive newspaper-ad tax on his critics], and (ii) protesting the fact that under the tax, Star Tribune (P) and other large newspapers pay almost all of the use tax, since small papers are exempt. Minnesota (D) defended, claiming (i) the use tax is just a substitute for the generally-applicable sales tax, and (ii) the tax actually benefits the press instead of "abridging" it. Evidently, at trial, the court held for Minnesota (D). Star Tribune (P) appeals.

■ **ISSUE**

May the government tax the press differently than others businesses?

■ **DECISION AND RATIONALE**

(O'Connor, J.) No. The government may not tax the press differently from other businesses, even to benefit it, unless (i) necessary (ii) to achieve "overriding" governmental interests (iii) which cannot be achieved through less-restrictive means. II. *Grosjean* is distinguishable; it involved Gov. Huey Long's imposition of a tax to punish newspapers which criticized him. Here, there is no evidence Minnesota's (D) motives are improper. Thus, we must consider this case under general First Amendment principles. III. The First Amendment permits government to subject the press to generally-applicable taxes and economic regulations. But a tax that affects the press differentially is invalid, unless (i) necessary (ii) to achieve an "overriding" governmental interest. This is because the Framers would have objected to differential taxes, which have potential to chill the press's vigor through punitive taxation, thus denying

Minneapolis Star and Tribune Company v. Minnesota Commissioner of Revenue (Continued)

the public much information. We note that legislatures can pass such differential taxes with little resistance, since other industries unaffected by it will not protest. Further, differential taxes are presumed unconstitutional, because their goal is usually improper. Here, Minnesota's (D) justification is inadequate. Minnesota (D) claims its use tax is merely a substitute for a generally-applicable sales tax, but this argument has two flaws. First, it offers no reason why it did not use the less-restrictive sales tax. Also, even if a tax policy *favors* the press, we still reject it for policy reasons; precedents allowing differential, beneficial treatment may later justify differential punitive taxes, or the chilling threat of them. [Only on the Slippery Slopes.] Also, since Minnesota's (D) use tax is paid by only the few largest newspapers, it resembles a penalty on big businesses. Courts are poorly equipped to evaluate different tax methods precisely. [Because if lawyer-judges could do math, they'd have been bankers.] Reversed; statute void.

■ DISSENT

(Rehnquist, J.) Minnesota's (D) law does not violate the First Amendment, since it favors the press rather than "abridging" or burdening it. Simple math calculations show Star Tribune (P) pays less tax under Minnesota's (D) use tax than it would under a sales tax.

Analysis:

This case extends *Grosjean*'s basic rule that the state cannot tax the press differently—even if that difference benefits the press. An interesting observation is that, if the $100,000 exemption had not been added to the law, under the rationale used by the court, the tax may have been valid. This is so because all newspapers would be taxed equally. Justice Rehnquist's dissent takes the Court to task on its assertion that assessing the relative economic impacts of different tax schemes is too difficult a task for courts to perform. He doesn't seem to have any problem at all in figuring the different burdens. This suggests that the Court may have been reaching a little in order to buttress what it viewed as a weak ratio decidendi. What the Court recognized, and the main reason for it deciding the way it did, is that a separate and distinct method of taxing newspapers has the potential to be used by the government in a somewhat clandestine manner to choke off the voice of the press. This is because even though the tax is currently less burdensome than an alternative scheme, because it is imposed on a small segment of the population, very few people will know when the tax becomes more and more burdensome to the point where it is suppressing First Amendment freedoms. Without knowledge of the problem in the general public, it will most likely go unchecked. Even with knowledge it may still go unchecked because those who do know won't care since they don't see the tax as affecting them.

■ CASE VOCABULARY

A FORTIORI: Even more so.

SALES TAX: State tax levied as a percentage of the cost of final goods bought, collected from the buyer.

USE TAX: State tax which is levied on goods that are not bought in the state, but are brought into the state and used there. Usually, states impose use taxes to avoid giving in-state users incentives to avoid sales taxes by importing goods from out of state.

Cohen v. Cowles Media Company

(Campaign Aide) v. *(Newspaper)*
501 U.S. 663, 111 S.Ct. 2513 (1991)

FIRST AMENDMENT DOES NOT SHIELD PRESS FROM GENERALLY-APPLICABLE LAWS

■ **INSTANT FACTS** A campaign aide, who dished dirt on a candidate for reporters' false promises of confidentiality, sued the reporters for promissory estoppel.

■ **BLACK LETTER RULE** When generally-applicable laws are applied to the media, the level of First Amendment scrutiny is no higher.

■ **PROCEDURAL BASIS**

In tortious promissory estoppel action, appeal from judgment for defendants.

■ **FACTS**

During Minnesota's gubernatorial elections, the Republican candidate's advisor Cohen offered information to several reporters from various Newspapers (D), some owned by Cowles Media Company (D). Cohen (P) promised the information only on promise of confidentiality; Newspapers (D) promised. Then, Cohen (P) gave Newspapers (D) public court documents showing his candidate's Democratic opponent had been arrested for unlawful assembly and petit theft. However, it turned out the arrest for unlawful assembly was for protesting against minority hiring discrimination, and was later dismissed. The theft conviction was for leaving a store without paying for $6 of goods, possibly by mistake, and was also dismissed. Newspapers (D) published the story, but identified Cohen (P) as the source. Cohen (P) was fired. Cohen (P) sued Newspapers (D) for promissory estoppel. Newspapers (D) defended, claiming the government cannot punish the press for publishing truthful, lawfully-obtained information, absent state interests of the highest order. Apparently, the trial court held for Newspapers (D). Cohen (P) appeals, claiming the press is not immune from generally-applicable laws.

■ **ISSUE**

May the media be sued for promissory estoppel for revealing confidential sources?

■ **DECISION AND RATIONALE**

(White, J.) Yes. When generally-applicable laws are applied to the media, the level of First Amendment scrutiny is no higher. Cases involving other circumstances hold the government cannot punish media for publishing truthful, lawfully-obtained information about matters of public significance. But these cases are not controlling here. Rather, what is controlling is the equally well-established doctrine that enforcing generally-applicable laws against the media does not violate the First Amendment merely because it incidentally affects media's ability to gather/report news. The press has no special First Amendment rights. It cannot acquire information illegally, e.g., break into houses/offices with impunity. Similarly, reporters are not immune from the common duty to answer grand jury subpoenas, even if this requires them to reveal their sources. When laws of general applicability are enforced against media, the First Amendment standard of scrutiny is no higher than for others. Here, Minnesota's doctrine of promissory estoppel is generally-applicable; it does not single out the press, and is applied to all. That

Cohen v. Cowles Media Company (Continued)

this rule may inhibit truthful news reporting is irrelevant, such burdens are incidental and permissible. Reversed.

■ DISSENT

(Souter, J.) There is nothing talismanic about generally-applicable laws to require they always be validated when applied to media. Instead, we must balance the competing interests of press and privacy. Freedom of the press is valuable in informing citizenry and allowing informed self-government. Here, Newspapers (D) performed a public service by revealing Cohen (P); this added information was relevant to voters, because it showed his character, which might reflect on his candidate's character. However, promises of confidentiality can sometimes create media liability, if the plaintiffs are private individuals whose identity is not a public concern.

Analysis:

This case stands for the proposition that the press enjoys no special immunity from laws that are otherwise generally applicable. While this principle has been articulated since 1945. *Cohen* is a particularly strong restatement. However, this doctrine conflicts with the policy behind *Cox Broadcasting Corporation* (1975) [state law cannot punish TV station for revealing rape victim's name, *obtained from court records*] and *Florida Star v. B.J.F.* (1989) [if media *lawfully* obtains *truthful* information about matter of public significance, state law may not punish publication, absent state interest "of the highest order"].

■ CASE VOCABULARY

AMICI [CURIAE]: ("Friends [of the court]"). In a lawsuit, non-parties who write briefs on one party's behalf, usually because the case's outcome will affect their interests.

GRAND JURY: Jury which decides whether there is sufficient evidence to indict (charge) someone with a crime.

GUBERNATORIAL: Having to do with the Governor.

PETIT THEFT: Stealing property whose worth is below a statutory minimum, usually $100.

PROMISSORY ESTOPPEL: Quasi-contract doctrine allowing plaintiffs to recover for damages caused by their reasonable reliance on defendants' promises.

Branzburg v. Hayes

(*Reporters*) v. (*Prosecutors*)
408 U.S. 665, 92 S.Ct. 2646 (1972)

SUBPOENAED REPORTERS MUST REVEAL CONFIDENTIAL SOURCES

■ **INSTANT FACTS** Reporters challenged grand jury subpoenas requiring them to reveal confidential sources.

■ **BLACK LETTER RULE** Newsmen have no special privilege against grand jury subpoenas to identify confidential sources, except that available to the general public.

■ PROCEDURAL BASIS

In consolidated cases, constitutional challenge to grand jury subpoenas.

■ FACTS

Several crime Reporters (D), including Branzburg (D), printed stories containing information obtained from criminals, on condition of anonymity. (Branzburg (D) himself interviewed hashish manufacturer-dealers and reported the process.) Later, Reporters (D) were subpoenaed by Prosecutors (P) to testify before a grand jury and reveal their sources. Reporters (D) refused, and were held in contempt. Reporters (D) challenge the Prosecutors' (P) subpoena and/or court's order to testify, claiming the First Amendment's freedom of the press guarantees them the right not to testify before grand juries, at least until there is proof the testimony in relevant to the crimes being considered, and not easily obtainable from other sources.

■ ISSUE

Do newsmen have a privilege against grand jury subpoenas asking them to reveal confidential sources?

■ DECISION AND RATIONALE

(White, J.) No. Newsmen have no special privilege against grand jury subpoenas to identify confidential sources, except that available to the general public. Free press and speech is necessary in informing the public, and news gathering should enjoy some protection to seek out news. But generally, the press is not immune from laws generally applicable to the public. Generally, the public is not immune from grand juries' subpoenas. Under this precedent, neither are reporters. While applying generally-applicable laws to reporters may burden news-gathering incidentally, these burdens are tolerable. Subpoenas do not restrict the press excessively; reporters may still obtain and publish confidential information. Some states' statutes give newsmen statutory privilege against testifying. We believe that requiring disclosure of confidential sources restricts news-gathering justifiably, to promote the government's stronger interest in identifying criminals. There is no evidence that many of reporters' sources are criminals, who would be deterred from talking. We are not convinced that other informers—those who are not themselves criminals, but merely reporting on others' crimes—will be deterred significantly; often they want to speak anyway, and are protected by grand juries' secrecy and the police's witness protection. Holding otherwise would create a system of informers constitutionally accountable only to reporters, not the public or police. If Congress wants this result, it must legislate it. Judgment for prosecutors; subpoenas valid.

Branzburg v. Hayes (Continued)

■ CONCURRENCE

(Powell, J.) I understand the Court's decision to have limited scope. It holds that generally, newsmen have no automatic privilege against grand juries' subpoenas. But newsmen still retain procedural remedies if they believe the grand jury is conducted in bad faith, is investigating matters unrelated to his source, or should not hear their testimony for other reasons. In such circumstances, the newsmen may move to quash and obtain a protective order. Newsmen's claim to privilege should be judged case-by-case, weighing the press' freedom against the general duty to testify.

■ DISSENT

(Stewart, J.) The majority eviscerates the press' ability to gather news for the public. Obviously, sources will be more reluctant to give confidential information knowing it may be revealed to grand juries. While this cannot be proven empirically with scientific precision, this Court has never required impossibly-precise proof before.

Analysis:

Here, the Court shot down claims of First Amendment privilege for reporters, as it did consistently in other contexts. The Court later followed *Branzburg*, expanding the no-privilege rule to other types of court proceedings, for similar reasons. However, Congress protected the press somewhat through the later *Privacy Protection Act of 1980*, which forbade police investigators to search newsrooms for evidence. Also, note that some states have statutes immunizing reporters from having to testify, though these are exceptional. In his dissent, Justice Stewart sounds the alarm that journalists will be co-opted by the government as an additional investigative arm. Is this a rational fear? It is rare to hear of a reporter being compelled to give up sources in the name of law enforcement. In contrast, the majority seems to say that because ordinary citizens are not exempt from relaying information gained in confidence, neither should the press be. Is this a logical conclusion?

■ CASE VOCABULARY

GRAND JURY: Jury which decides whether the prosecutor has sufficient evidence to charge a person with a crime. It is empowered to subpoena witnesses.

IMPRIMATUR: Mark indicating ownership. Here, it means experts' stamp of approval.

PROTECTIVE ORDER: Court order protecting a witness from abusive/harassing discovery or trial tactics.

QUASH: To void, e.g., a subpoena.

SUBPOENA DUCES TECUM: Subpoena requesting documents rather than live testimony.

Red Lion Broadcasting Co. v. Federal Communications Commission

(Radio Broadcaster) v. (Broadcasting Regulatory Agency)
395 U.S. 367, 89 S.Ct. 1794 (1969)

GOVERNMENT MAY REQUIRE TV/RADIO BROADCASTERS TO GIVE "EQUAL ACCESS"

■ **INSTANT FACTS** A radio station challenged FCC regulations requiring it to give personally-attacked people a right to reply.

■ **BLACK LETTER RULE** The government may require broadcasters to give access to opposing views.

■ **PROCEDURAL BASIS**

In consolidated cases, First Amendment challenge to federal agency regulations.

■ **FACTS**

The Federal Communications Commission ("FCC") (D) regulates TV/radio broadcasting. FCC (D) adopted a "fairness policy," which it later codified into regulations. Under its "personal attack" component, if a broadcaster airs a personal attack against a person, that person may demand free air time to rebut. Similarly, its "political editorial" rule apparently requires that, when broadcasters present a controversial topic, they must give access to opposing viewpoints. These policies were adopted to ensure that broadcasters present even-handed coverage to the public. Radio broadcaster Red Lion Broadcasting Co. (P) aired one broadcast, involving author Cook's biography of Barry Goldwater. In Red Lion's (P) broadcast, the guest speaker attacked Cook's credibility, saying he was fired for making false charges against officials, supported Communist organizations, opposed Edgar Hoover and the CIA, and had written his "book to smear and destroy" Goldwater. Cook demanded free reply time, under the "personal attack" rule. Red Lion (P) refused. Cook complained to FCC (D), which ordered Red Lion (P) to give free reply time. Red Lion (P) challenged FCC's (D) "personal attack" rule, claiming it violates the First Amendment to restrict broadcasters' editorial discretion to require equal coverage. [In a consolidated case, another plaintiff, RTNDA (P), challenged the "political editorial" rule.]

■ **ISSUE**

May the FCC require broadcasters to give access to opposing views?

■ **DECISION AND RATIONALE**

(White, J.) Yes. The government may require broadcasters to give access to opposing views: (1) First, we note FCC's (D) "fairness doctrine" was within Congress' grant of authority to FCC (D). Legislative history shows Congress intervened to allocate broadcast frequencies among competing viewpoints. (2). Broadcasting is protected by the First Amendment, but the level of protection varies for each medium, according to its characteristics. Broadcasting's main characteristic is the limited number of frequencies. It is different from speech or writing, where anyone can participate. Congress could have rationed the limited frequencies to competing parties to share. Instead, Congress assigned each frequency to one party. But those chosen were not given an exclusive monopoly to air only their views. The First

Red Lion Broadcasting Co. v. Federal Communications Commission (Continued)

Amendment does not forbid requiring licensees to share their frequency with others, and to represent balanced viewpoints for the public good. In broadcasting, the public's right to receive diverse programming is paramount over broadcasters' speech/editorial rights. It is not inconsistent with the First Amendment's goal of informing the public for FCC (D) to adopt "personal attack" and "editorial opinion" rules. Holding otherwise would allow a few broadcasters to make time available to the highest bidders, communicate only their own views, and permit commentary only by those they agree with. Arguments that requiring equal access would encourage broadcasters to self-censor are speculative and unproven. Judgment for defendant; regulation valid.

Analysis:

Note that the Court analyzes these kinds of claims on a medium-by-medium basis. This "equal time" rule is applicable only to *broadcast* media, i.e., TV and radio. It seems inconsistent with the Court's usual championing of editorial discretion and the right against government-compelled speech. The next case disclaims the same rule for print media. The Court's rather unique decision here is predicated on the assumption that, since the government "created" broadcast frequencies, it retains power to regulate them for the public interest. Note also that the Court dismisses the "chilling effect" argument without consideration here, but will later take it much more seriously in the context of other media.

■ CASE VOCABULARY

FIDUCIARY: Person who acts as an agent for another, in his best interest.

NOTICE OF PROPOSED RULE MAKING: Notice required before a government agency creates certain types of regulations. The public must be given notice, and allowed to send comments to the agency.

PROXY: Representative for another person.

Miami Herald v. Tornillo

(Newspaper) v. (Political Candidate)
418 U.S. 241, 94 S.Ct. 2831 (1974)

LAW CANNOT REQUIRE NEWSPAPERS TO GRANT "RIGHT OF REPLY"

■ **INSTANT FACTS** A newspapers challenged a Florida law requiring it to give candidates it criticized the right to reply.

■ **BLACK LETTER RULE** The government cannot require newspapers to grant a "right of reply."

■ **PROCEDURAL BASIS**

Not stated.

■ **FACTS**

Florida's "right of access" statute provided that, if a *newspaper* attacked a candidate's personal character or official record, he could demand it print his reply (up to the original article's length), free. Non-compliance is a criminal misdemeanor. When candidate Tornillo ran for state Representative, the newspaper *Miami Herald* (D) ran editorials criticizing him. When Tornillo (P) demanded *Miami Herald* (D) print his reply, it refused. Tornillo (P) sued for injunction and actual and punitive damages, and apparently won. *Miami Herald* (D) appeals, claiming governmental dictation on what newspapers must print violates the First Amendment. Tornillo (P) responds, claiming (i) the statute is justified by the need to present varied viewpoints in today's monopolistic, one-sided news industry, and (ii) the statute does not restrict newspapers' right to print their own opinions.

ISSUE

May the government require newspapers to give criticized people a "right of access"?

■ **DECISION AND RATIONALE**

(Burger, C.J.) No. The government cannot require newspapers to grant a "right of reply." Any governmental compulsion for newspapers to publish that which they do not want to publish is unconstitutional. It may be true that today's media is much more concentrated and monopolistic that the press of 1776, due to consolidation of smaller newspapers into a few large ones, and joint ownership of both newspapers and TV. True, this gives a few owners power to shape public opinion. For these reasons, dissidents cannot just print rival publications, as they could in 1776. It may be that the public would be better served by giving equal access, or by better journalistic discretion. But the Constitution merely protects freedom of the press; it does require the press to be responsible. "Right of reply" statutes penalize the press based on content; printing others' replies takes up editorial time and newspaper space, which is not unlimited. Further, it might chill political coverage by inducing editors to avoid controversy. Even if this were not true, forced publication would intrude upon editorial discretion: the choice of content, size, and opinion. This violates the First Amendment. Judgment for defendant; statute void.

Miami Herald v. Tornillo (Continued)

Analysis:

While *Red Lion* upheld "right to reply" rules in the context of *broadcast* media, *Miami Herald* invalidates them when applied to print. Even if a compulsory law did not create economic problems or cause the newspaper to have to forego printing something else to give space to a reply, the reply law's great evil was that it intruded on the rights and functions of the newspaper and its editors and reporters. *Miami Herald* firmly established that the right of newspaper editors to choose what they wish to print or not to print cannot be abridged to allow the public access to the newspaper media. There is a "virtually insurmountable barrier" that the freedom of the press erects between governmental regulation and the print media. An important distinction between the fairness doctrine as applied to electronic media and the fairness doctrine that cannot be applied to the print media is that the former enjoys a legal monopoly, which serves to justify FCC regulations requiring "fairness." There is no *legal* monopoly of—and no technological justification for a legal monopoly of—newspapers.

■ CASE VOCABULARY

"RIGHT OF REPLY": Statutory right of a public person criticized by media to require them to similarly publish/broadcast his rebuttal, for free.

Richmond Newspapers, Inc. v. Virginia

(Media) v. (State)
448 U.S. 555, 100 S.Ct. 2814 (1980)

CRIMINAL TRIALS ARE PRESUMED OPEN TO PUBLIC/PRESS

■ **INSTANT FACTS** When a judge ordered a criminal trial closed to the public and media, by consent with the defendant and prosecutor, the media challenged.

■ **BLACK LETTER RULE** Criminal trials are presumptively open to the public and press, unless there are "overriding" interests.

■ **PROCEDURAL BASIS**

First Amendment challenge to court order and/or state trial-procedure law.

■ **FACTS**

Virginia (D) law apparently gives judges discretion to close trials to the public. A murder defendant was retried there for the fourth time, after three mistrials, of which one was caused by press publicity. The defendant moved to close the fourth trial to the public and press. The prosecutor didn't object. Accordingly, the judge closed the trial. Richmond Newspapers, Inc. (P) challenged the decision as violating various First Amendment rights of the press and public. Virginia (D) defended, claiming the Constitution never explicitly guarantees the public the right to attend trials, and citing *Gannet Co. v. DePasquale* [press/public may be barred from pretrial motion hearings].

■ **ISSUE**

May the public and press be barred from attending criminal trials?

■ **DECISION AND RATIONALE**

(Burger, C.J.) No. Criminal trials are presumptively open to the public and press, unless there are "overriding" interests. This is a case of first impression. *Gannet* [Sixth Amendment's guarantee that accused is entitled to public trial does not confer rights of access on public/press] is not controlling; it covered pretrial proceedings, not trials. Traditionally in both England and colonial America, criminal trials were presumptively open. This openness also has real benefits. It assures the public that crimes are being punished, ensures procedural fairness, and discourages perjury, misconduct, and biased decisions. Having public trials also quells community resentment. When shocking crimes occur, the public is often outraged. Having an open trial is an outlet which assures the public that justice is being done, thus preventing vigilantism. If trial procedures are kept secret, an unexpected decision may cause the public to believe the system is flawed or corrupt. Further, this Court's holdings consistently support the presumption that criminal trials are public. Further, the First Amendment guarantees the press and public some right to receive information, and prohibits government from impeding this information summarily. Further, closing criminal trials implicates First Amendment rights of speech, press, and even assembly. That the Constitution's text includes no explicit right of the public to attend trials is irrelevant; certain unarticulated rights are implicit. One such right implied in the First Amendment is the public's right to attend criminal trials, absent compelling reasons. Order reversed.

Richmond Newspapers, Inc. v. Virginia (Continued)

■ **CONCURRENCE**

(Brennan, J.) I concur, to the extent that mere agreement by a judge and the parties cannot close a trial to the public, *without more justification.* This is because of the public criminal trial's long tradition, acceptance, and role in furthering the appearance of justice. Also, publicizing trials is important politically, because it exposes judges' law-making to public scrutiny.

■ **DISSENT**

(Rehnquist, J.) The Constitution does not contain any guarantee that the public may observe criminal trials.

Analysis:

As noted, *Gannet* held the public/press has no right to access pre-trial evidentiary hearings. However, after *Richmond Newspapers*, the Court later opened other aspects of criminal trials, e.g., witness testimony, jury selection, etc. Thus, *Gannet* may no longer be good law. Note that the Court has not recognized a *special* right for the press, beyond that available to the general public. Also, *Richmond Newspapers* does not apply to *civil* trials.

■ **CASE VOCABULARY**

AMALGAM: Combination.

CATHARSIS: An emotional change or reconciliation.

CHUSE: "Choose." (Archaic spelling.)

RIGHT OF VISITATION: Here, a right to attend criminal trials.

Pell v. Procunier

(*Reporters and Inmates*) v. (*State Prison Official*)
417 U.S. 817, 94 S.Ct. 2800 (1974)

REPORTERS HAVE NO CONSTITUTIONAL RIGHT TO ENTER JAILS OR INTERVIEW PRISONERS

■ **INSTANT FACTS** When a jail barred reporters from individual interviews with inmates, the reporters and inmates claimed a First Amendment right to conduct the interviews.

■ **BLACK LETTER RULE** Reporters have no special constitutional right to enter prisons or interview prisoners, beyond the rights granted to the general public.

■ **PROCEDURAL BASIS**
In First Amendment challenge to state agency's regulations, cross-appeal.

■ **FACTS**
California's Department of Corrections' (D) regulations prohibit "press and other media interviews with specific individual inmates." This is because Department of Corrections (D) previously found that, when reporters interviewed individual prisoners, these inmates gained notoriety and influence among prisoners, and became disciplinary problems. Department of Corrections (D) allows the media, and often also the public, other means of access. The public (and media) may participate in regular public tours. Newsmen may visit all prison areas. In so doing, they may stop and interview any inmates encountered; if safe, guards will leave to allow a private interview. Or, newsmen may interview inmates selected at random about topics including prison conditions. Also, newsmen covering a specific prison program may sit in on group meetings and interview individual participants. Inmates may write letters, and receive them. Department of Corrections (D) allows in-person visitation by only limited people—family, clergy, attorneys, and prior acquaintances—because it decided these people would be most rehabilitative, and admitting others would compromise security. Several Reporters (P), including Pell (P), who wished to interview specific prisoners joined with those Prisoners (P) in suing to enjoin enforcement of Department of Corrections' (D) regulations. Prisoners (P) claim their First Amendment rights include the right to meet with media, e.g., to discuss prison conditions or having their writings published. Reporters (P) claim First Amendment freedom of the press should give them a right to interview prisoners, as long as this does not threaten security or other substantial, correctional interests.

■ **ISSUE**
Do reporters have a First Amendment right to gain access to prisons and interview inmates?

■ **DECISION AND RATIONALE**
(Stewart, J.) No. Reporters have no special constitutional right to enter prisons or interview prisoners, beyond the rights granted to the general public. First, we consider Prisoners' (P) claim of a First Amendment right to talk to media. We assume the First Amendment would generally include a right to talk to willing media. But we recognize that inmates enjoy fewer First Amendment protections, by necessity. When prison officials make decisions, we defer to their expertise and jurisdiction, absent substantial evidence they are unreasonable. For inmates, the government may restrict one of their avenues of communication with outsiders, if (i) the restriction is content-neutral, and (ii) alternative

Pell v. Procunier (Continued)

means are sufficient. Here, they are. Inmates can write letters outside, meet with certain visitors, including reporters who they knew before incarceration, etc. While such government restrictions would be inappropriate for the general public, they are appropriate for inmates. Next, we consider Reporters' (P) claimed First Amendment right to interview willing inmates. No such right exists, either under the Constitution's text or Court precedent. The First Amendment bars government from interfering with a free press, but does not require government to provide special access. Generally, we held the First Amendment does not guarantee the press special access to information not available to the general public. E.g., reporters are regularly excluded from grand jury proceedings, Supreme Court conferences, official bodies' executive sessions, and private organizations' meetings. Similarly, Reporters (P) are not entitled to more access than the general public. We note Department of Corrections (D) allows extraordinary access to the general public and even more to newsmen, including tours, random interviews, group meetings, etc. There is no danger that Department of Corrections' (D) regulation is intended to conceal prison conditions or frustrate Reporters' (P) investigation of them. Judgment for defendant; regulation valid.

■ DISSENT

(Powell, J.) An absolute ban against prisoner-press interviews impermissibly keeps the press from performing its constitutionally-established function of informing the people about their government's conduct.

Analysis:

Starting from the proposition that "[l]awful incarceration brings about the necessary withdrawal or limitation of many privileges and rights, a retraction justified by the considerations underlying our penal system," the Court proceeded to balance the rights of inmates against the state's legitimate interests in security and rehabilitation of prisoners. The Court placed great emphasis on the fact that the prisoners had alternative means of communication with the press, including uncensored mailing privileges and a visitation policy allowing face-to-face conversation with family, attorneys, the clergy and longstanding friends. These alternative channels are sufficient to ensure that reasonable and effective means of communication with the outside remain open to the prisoner. *Pell* may not have much precedential value outside the restricted environment of a prison, for it does not apply usual First Amendment standards. However, the case does firmly reject a right of access by the press greater than that of the general public, a holding that goes beyond prison cases.

■ CASE VOCABULARY

CROSS-APPEAL: An appeal by the appellee (i.e., the winner), usually heard simultaneously with the regulation (appellant's/loser's) appeal. Apparently, this case is a cross-appeal, but the excerpt doesn't explain it further.

EXECUTIVE SESSION: A group's meeting, to carry out its powers/duties, without general members present.

Houchins v. KQED

(*Prison Supervisor*) v. (*Media Organization*)
438 U.S. 1, 98 S.Ct. 2588 (1978)

REPORTERS HAVE NO SPECIAL RIGHT OF ACCESS TO JAILS

■ **INSTANT FACTS** When a prison supervisor denied access to the prison except for restrictive tours without cameras and recorders, the media claimed a First Amendment right of access.

■ **BLACK LETTER RULE** The First Amendment gives the press no special right to enter government-controlled places, except that given to the public.

■ PROCEDURAL BASIS

First Amendment challenge to state agency's regulations.

■ FACTS

TV and radio broadcaster KQED (P) was a news organization that previously reported on various jails' conditions. After an inmate's suicide at Santa Rita jail, KQED (P) investigated, finding a prison psychologist there who said the facility's poor conditions caused many inmates' illnesses, and apparently reported prisoners were beaten and raped, and have their grievance letters censored. When KQED (P) asked Santa Rita's supervisor Sheriff Houchins (D) for permission to enter and film conditions, Houchins (D) refused. Instead, Houchins (D) hastily organized highly-restricted public tours, which entered limited portions of the jail, avoided the scenes of alleged abuses, forbade interviews, banned cameras and tape recorders, and did not let reporters see any prisoners. KQED (P) sued, contending the importance of publicizing prison conditions justified a special right of access with recording equipment, under the First Amendment.

■ ISSUE

Does the First Amendment require jails to allow reporters to enter with recording equipment?

■ DECISION AND RATIONALE

(Houchins, J.) No. The First Amendment gives the press no special right to enter government-controlled places, except that given to the public. It is true that prison conditions are matters of public importance, that reporting them allows the public to make informed judgments, and that the media is important in informing the public. But prison administrators are the ones authorized, and better equipped, to administer prisons. In *Pell*, we clearly held the First Amendment does not imply the media has a special right of access to prisons, or other facilities controlled by government. Also, the decision whether to open jails to public view is a political decision for Congress, not this Court. Even under our rule, the media can still inform the public about prison conditions, using indirect methods. E.g., it can recruit people to visit jails and report, receive inmates' letters, and interview prisoners' attorneys, former inmates, visitors, public officials, and employees. Judgment for defendant.

■ CONCURRENCE

(Stewart, J.) The First Amendment does not guarantee the media special access, only "equal access" comparable to the public's. But "equal access," when applied to reporters, should include the means

Houchins v. KQED (Continued)

for reporters to convey the prison's sights and sounds to the public. This requires allowing them cameras and recorders.

■ DISSENT

(Stevens, J.) The First Amendment's core objective is to allow the public to receive full information. To enable this, the Constitution must offer some protection to information-gathering, for the public's benefit. The public's right is violated by Houchins' (D) no-access policy, which is unjustified because KQED's (P) previous reports from other jails caused no danger.

Analysis:

The seven-member, fragmented court in this case could produce no majority opinion. The plurality found that there is no First or Fourteenth Amendment right of access to government information or sources of information within the government's control. Further, the press has no greater right of access than that of the public generally. Because there was no majority opinion and two Justices—Marshall and Blackmun—did not participate, the *Houchins* decision probably will not end litigation over public access to prisons in cases where there is only limited access to parts of the jail. However, the seven justices did agree that the press has no greater right of access to prisons than the public generally. The Court, once again, rejected the notion that the institutional press has greater First Amendment rights than the public generally.

■ CASE VOCABULARY

ADJUNCT: Assistant.

CHAPTER TEN

First Amendment: Religion

United States v. Seeger

Instant Facts: Seeger (D) was convicted for refusing to serve in the military after his exemption as a conscientious objector was denied.

Black Letter Rule: The test of whether a belief "in a relation to a Supreme Being" is a religion is whether it is sincere and meaningful and occupies a place in the life of its possessor parallel to that filled by the orthodox belief in God.

United States v. Ballard

Instant Facts: Three relatives are convicted for mail fraud after falsely representing a miraculous communication with the spirit world that gave them the ability to heal the sick, and soliciting funds and memberships in the "I Am" movement.

Black Letter Rule: Finders of fact may only determine if a religious belief is sincere, but may not determine whether the beliefs themselves are true or false.

Employment Division, Department of Human Resources of Oregon v. Smith

Instant Facts: Two former employees, after losing their jobs for using peyote as part of their religious ceremony, were denied unemployment benefits and challenged the denial under the Free Exercise clause of the First Amendment.

Black Letter Rule: Generally applicable, religion-neutral laws that have the effect of burdening a particular religious practice need not be justified by a compelling interest, unless another constitutional protection is burdened in conjunction, or the government has provided for individualized treatment in an unemployment compensation scheme.

Sherbert v. Verner

Instant Facts: The State unconstitutionally denied Sherbert (P) the right to receive unemployment benefits, because Sherbert (P) could not work on Saturdays, the Sabbath Day of her religion, and therefore could not find employment.

Black Letter Rule: A denial of government funded benefits to those who are otherwise eligible, but leave their place of employment because of religious reasons, unconstitutionally infringes on their right to free exercise of religion.

Church of the Lukumi Babalu Aye v. City of Hialeah

Instant Facts: Followers of the Santeria religion brought a Free Exercise Clause challenge against the city in which they planned to establish a church, after the city passed ordinances prohibiting animal sacrifices in response to the members' religious practice of such sacrifices.

Black Letter Rule: If a law that burdens the free exercise of religion fails to satisfy the requirements of neutrality and general applicability, it must be justified by a compelling governmental interest, and must be narrowly tailored to advance that interest.

Cutter v. Wilkinson

Instant Facts: Cutter (P) claimed that the prison's (D) refusal to allow him to practice a "non-traditional" religion violated his rights under the Religious Land Use and Institutionalized Persons Act (RLUIPA), and Wilkinson (D) claimed the portion of the Act that related to prison inmates was unconstitutional.

Black Letter Rule: The Religious Land Use and Institutionalized Persons Act is a permissible accommodation of religion that does not violate the Establishment Clause.

Locke v. Davey

Instant Facts: Davey (D) sought to use state scholarship funds for a degree in pastoral ministries.

Black Letter Rule: The Free Exercise Clause does not ensure the right to state-financed religious instruction.

County of Allegheny v. American Civil Liberties Union Greater Pittsburgh Chapter

Instant Facts: A county's holiday displays were challenged on the ground that they violated the Establishment Clause.

Black Letter Rule: A government's act is unconstitutional under the Establishment Clause if, being evaluated in its context, the act has the effect of endorsing religion or could be understood by viewers to be an endorsement of religion.

Larson v. Valente

Instant Facts: A church challenged the constitutionality of an act that required some religious charity organizations to participate in a system of registration and disclosure.

Black Letter Rule: Denominational preferences must be invalidated unless justified by a compelling governmental interest, and closely fitted to further that interest.

Lemon v. Kurtzman

Instant Facts: The constitutionality of two statutes that provided financial support to private schools, including church-related educational institutions, were challenged under the Establish Clause.

Black Letter Rule: In order to be constitutional under the Establishment Clause, a non-discriminatory regulation must: 1) have a secular legislative purpose; 2) have a principal or primary effect that neither advances nor inhibits religion and 3) not foster an excessive government entanglement with religion.

Rosenberger v. Rector and Visitors of the University of Virginia

Instant Facts: A University's student organization funding program is charged with violating freedom of speech, after denying benefits to religious student groups in fear of violating the establishment clause.

Black Letter Rule: The Establishment Clause is not violated by a university's financial support of a religious organization's activities as part of a viewpoint neutral "student activities" funding program.

Santa Fe Independent School District v. Doe

Instant Facts: The constitutionality of a school district's policy which allowed invocations to be given prior to football games, was challenged under the Establishment Clause by school students and their families.

Black Letter Rule: Allowing invocations during high school football will constitute excessive entanglement between the government and religion in violation of the Establishment Clause.

McCreary County v. American Civil Liberties Union of Kentucky

Instant Facts: Two counties displayed the Ten Commandments in their courthouses, and the ACLU objected.

Black Letter Rule: The manifest objective of governmental action may be dispositive in an Establishment Clause inquiry, and the development of that action should be considered when determining its purpose.

Van Orden v. Perry

Instant Facts: Van Orden (P) claimed that a monument on the grounds of the Texas Capitol that displayed the Ten Commandments violated the Establishment Clause.

Black Letter Rule: Displaying religious content or a message consistent with religious doctrine is not necessarily an Establishment Clause violation.

Engel v. Vitale

Instant Facts: The Board of Education of Union Free School District in Hyde Park, New York, adopted a policy of student recitation of a prayer at the beginning of each school day.

Black Letter Rule: The Establishment Clause of the First Amendment forbids any part of the business of government to compose official prayers for any group of the American people to recite as a part of a religious program carried on by the government.

Lee v. Weisman

Instant Facts: An Establishment Clause challenge to the practice of prayers at public school ceremonies is raised, after a public school principal invited a rabbi to deliver an invocation and benediction at a graduation.

Black Letter Rule: Government coercion to participate in religious activities violates the Establishment Clause.

Mitchell v. Helms

Instant Facts: Federal law that authorized the government to distribute funds to state and local agencies, which in turn loaned educational materials and equipment to public and private schools, was challenged as violating the Establishment Clause.

Black Letter Rule: A federal student-aid funding program used to loan educational materials and equipment to public and private schools, including religious schools, which does not result in religious indoctrination by the government, define its recipients by reference to religion, and cannot be viewed as an endorsement of religion, will not violate the establishment clause.

Zelman v. Simmons–Harris

Instant Facts: To offer its students better educational opportunities, the Ohio Pilot Project Scholarship Program provided, inter alia, tuition assistance to private, religiously affiliated schools.

Black Letter Rule: By not endorsing a specific religion or limiting parental choices to religious-affiliated schools when offering vouchers to parents of students in the Cleveland School District, Ohio's Pilot Project Scholarship Program does not violate the Establishment Clause of the First Amendment.

United States v. Seeger

(*Federal Government*) v. (*Conscientious Objector*)
380 U.S. 163, 85 S.Ct. 850 (1965)

"RELIGION" IS ANY SINCERE BELIEF AKIN TO A BELIEF IN GOD

■ **INSTANT FACTS** Seeger (D) was convicted for refusing to serve in the military after his exemption as a conscientious objector was denied.

■ **BLACK LETTER RULE** The test of whether a belief "in a relation to a Supreme Being" is a religion is whether it is sincere and meaningful and occupies a place in the life of its possessor parallel to that filled by the orthodox belief in God.

■ PROCEDURAL BASIS

Certiorari to review an undisclosed appellate decision.

■ FACTS

Under § 6(j) of the Universal Military Training and Service Act, persons may be exempted from military services if their "religious training and belief" renders them conscientiously opposed to war and military conflict. The Act defined "religious training and belief" as "an individual's belief in a relation to a Supreme Being involving duties superior to those arising from any human relation." In 1957, Seeger (D) claimed an exemption as a conscientious objector because of his "belief in and devotion to goodness and virtue for their own sakes, and a religious faith in a purely ethical creed." Because Seeger's (D) exemption application did not acknowledge his belief in God, his exemption was denied as not "in a relation to a Supreme Being," and he was subsequently convicted for his refusal to serve in the armed forces.

■ ISSUE

Within the meaning of the Universal Military Training and Service Act, is a belief in goodness and virtue "in a relation to a Supreme Being," absent a belief in God?

■ DECISION AND RATIONALE

(Clark, J.) Yes. As a country comprised of numerous religious sects, the concept of "Supreme Being" takes on differing meanings. Congress's use of the phrase "Supreme Being" rather than "God" acknowledges its intent to apply the statutory exemption to persons of all religions and their various concepts of a "Supreme Being," as opposed to political, sociological, or philosophical beliefs. "[T]he test of belief 'in a relation to a Supreme Being' is whether a given belief that is sincere and meaningful occupies a place in the life of its possessor parallel to that filled by the orthodox belief in God of one who clearly qualifies for the exemption." Seeger's (D) good-faith beliefs satisfy this test.

Analysis:

The test established in *Seeger* applies in the context of a federal statute, without consideration of the First Amendment. In later years, the Court rejected the "functional equivalence" test as constitutional doctrine. In *Wisconsin v. Yoder*, the Court recognized the longtime organizational practices of the Amish in lending a definition to religion. These standards, however, seem to have arisen more from the facts of the cases than from constitutional interpretation.

United States v. Ballard

(*Criminal Prosecutors*) v. (*Cult*)
322 U.S. 78, 64 S.Ct. 882 (1944)

TRUTH OR FALSITY DETERMINATIONS OF A RELIGIOUS MOVEMENT'S BELIEFS HELD IMPERMISSIBLE

■ **INSTANT FACTS** Three relatives are convicted for mail fraud after falsely representing a miraculous communication with the spirit world that gave them the ability to heal the sick, and soliciting funds and memberships in the "I Am" movement.

■ **BLACK LETTER RULE** Finders of fact may only determine if a religious belief is sincere, but may not determine whether the beliefs themselves are true or false.

■ **PROCEDURAL BASIS**

Certification to the United States Supreme Court, of a conviction by trial court for the use of mail to defraud.

■ **FACTS**

Guy W. Ballard, Edna W Ballard, and Donald Ballard (the Ballards) (D), were indicted for using and conspiring to use the mails to defraud. The twelve count indictment indicated that the Ballards (D) formed designated corporations, distributed and sold literature, solicited funds, and sought memberships into the "I Am" movement through false and fraudulent representations, pretenses and promises. The Ballards (D) allegedly made knowingly false claims and representations to others with the intent to defraud, that by reason of supernatural attainment, they had the power to heal those afflicted with any disease, injuries, or ailments. They further represented that they had in fact cured hundreds of persons afflicted with diseases and ailments. The district court found the Ballards (D) guilty and they now appeal.

■ **ISSUE**

May jury consider questions concerning the truth or falsity of religious beliefs?

■ **DECISION AND RATIONALE**

(Douglas, J.) No. The truth or verity of the Ballards' (D) religious doctrines or beliefs should not have been submitted to the jury. The First Amendment's dual aspect not only prohibits compulsion by the law of the acceptance of any creed or the practice of any form of worship, it also safeguards the free exercise of the chosen form of religion. Therefore, the two concepts embraced by the Amendment are the freedom to believe and the freedom to act. While the first is absolute, the second cannot be. Freedom of thought, which includes freedom of religious beliefs, is basic in a society of free men. Men believe what they cannot prove, and they cannot be put to the proof of their religious doctrines or beliefs. The fact that religious experiences, which are as real as life to some and incomprehensible to others, may be beyond the understanding of mortals does not mean that they can be made suspect before the law. Indeed, little would be left of religious freedom, if those who take their gospel from the New Testament, were tried before a jury charged with the duty of determining whether its teachings were false. The Fathers of the Constitution were aware of the varied and extreme views of religious

United States v. Ballard (Continued)

sects, of the violent disagreements among them, and of the lack of any one religious creed on which all would agree. Accordingly, they fashioned a government which envisaged the widest possible toleration of conflicting views, making man's relation to his God no concern of the state. The religious views of the Ballard's (D) in the instant case may seem incredible to most, but if those doctrines are subject to trial before a jury charged with finding their truth or falsity, then the same can be done with all religious beliefs. When triers of fact undertake such a task, they enter a forbidden domain. Accordingly, we conclude that the District Court ruled properly when it withheld from the jury, all questions concerning the truth or falsity of the religious beliefs or doctrines of the Ballard's (D). Finders of fact may only determine if a religious belief is sincere, but may not determine whether the beliefs itself are true or false.

■ **DISSENT**

(Jackson, J.) The Ballard's (D) were brought to trial for mail fraud on an indictment charging them with "knowingly" false representations. The trial judged ruled that the court could not try whether the statements were untrue, but could inquire whether the Ballards (D) knew them to be untrue. First, I cannot see how we can separate an issue as to what is believed from considerations as to what is believable. Similarly, that one knowingly falsified is best proved by showing that what he said happened never happened. How can the Government prove these persons knew something to be false when it cannot prove it to be false? If we try religious sincerity severed from religious verity, we isolate the dispute from the very considerations which provide its most reliable answer. Second, any inquiry into intellectual honesty in religion raises profound psychological problems. William James reminds us that the vitality of religion is in the experiences of its followers, including those with the unseen, voices and visions, and responses to prayer. If religious liberty is to include the right to communicate such experiences to others, it seems an impossible task for juries to separate fancied ones from real ones. Like some tones and colors, such experiences have existence for one but not the other. When one comes to a trial which turns on any aspect of religious belief or representation, unbelievers among his judges are likely not to understand and are almost certain not to believe him. If the members of the I Am cult get comfort from the celestial guidance of their "Saint Germain," however doubtful it seems to me, it is hard to say that they do not get what they pay for. Prosecutions of this character could easily turn into religious prosecution. Religious leaders may be convicted of fraud for making false claims on matters other than faith, by for instance representing that funds will be used to build a new church but instead are being used for personal purposes. But that is not the case here. I would dismiss the indictment and have no more to do with the examination of others' faiths.

Analysis:

While the courts have never propounded an exact definition of "religion," any determination is limited to the subjective view of the follower. That is, it is not the court's job to judge the religion itself, but instead its function is limited to a consideration of the sincerity of one's views. With this mind, Justice Jackson makes a seemingly good point in his dissent. The interests of the general public are greatly furthered by the government's ability to protect the nation from fraud hidden in the cloak of faith. Put simply, the Ballards (D) were charged with actual "knowledge" of falsehood. This would seem to require a finding that the views or claims of a religion were in fact false. But the dissent may have read the charge too literally. It can be inferred from the majority opinion that the finder of fact is to assume that the beliefs are true. Thus the determination of "actual knowledge of falsehood" would be based on a consideration of whether a follower of the belief actually believes it to be true.

■ **CASE VOCABULARY**

RELIGION: A sincere, honest, meaningful, and good faith belief in something, that occupies a place in the life of its possessor parallel to that filled by the orthodox belief in God, and that is not essentially political, sociological, or philosophical.

Employment Division, Department of Human Resources of Oregon v. Smith

(*Unemployment Services*) v. (*Peyote-Ingesting Employees*)
494 U.S. 872, 110 S.Ct. 1595 (1990)

A DENIAL OF UNEMPLOYMENT BENEFITS TO PERSONS DISCHARGED FOR VIOLATING A CRIMINAL STATUTE WITH RELIGIOUS CONDUCT IS CONSTITUTIONAL

■ **INSTANT FACTS** Two former employees, after losing their jobs for using peyote as part of their religious ceremony, were denied unemployment benefits and challenged the denial under the Free Exercise clause of the First Amendment.

■ **BLACK LETTER RULE** Generally applicable, religion-neutral laws that have the effect of burdening a particular religious practice need not be justified by a compelling interest, unless another constitutional protection is burdened in conjunction, or the government has provided for individualized treatment in an unemployment compensation scheme.

■ **PROCEDURAL BASIS**

Review by United States Supreme Court of an action challenging the constitutionality of a state's denial of unemployment benefits.

■ **FACTS**

Alfred Smith (Smith) (P1) and Galen Black (Black) (P2), were fired from their jobs with a private drug rehabilitation organization because of their ingestion of peyote for sacramental purposes at a ceremony of the Native American Church of which both are members. Oregon law criminally prohibits the knowing or intentional possession of controlled substances unless prescribed by a medical practitioner. Peyote, an hallucinogen derived from the plant Lophophora Williamsii Lemaire, is listed as a controlled substance. After being fired, Smith (P1) and Black (P2) applied to the Employment Division (D) for unemployment compensation, but were determined to be ineligible for benefits because the cause of their discharge was work-related misconduct. The Oregon Supreme Court held the use of peyote was protected by the Free Exercise Clause. Employment Division (D) appeals.

■ **ISSUE**

Can a state constitutionally deny unemployment benefits to persons discharged for work-related misconduct, when the work-related misconduct was religiously motivated?

■ **DECISION AND RATIONALE**

(Scalia, J.) Yes. The free exercise of religion entails the right to believe and profess whatever religious doctrine one desires. Thus, the First Amendment obviously excludes all government regulation of religious beliefs. However, the "exercise of religion" often involves not only belief, but the performance of physical acts. It would be true that a State would be prohibiting the free exercise of religion if it sought to ban such acts or abstentions only when they are engaged in for religious purposes. Here however, Smith (P1) and Black (P2), seek to carry the meaning of "free exercise" one large step further, in their contention that their religious motivation for using peyote places them beyond the reach of a criminal law that is not directed at their religious practice, and is of general applicability. We disagree. Our decisions have consistently held that the right of free exercise does not relieve an individual of the obligation to comply with a valid and neutral law of general applicability on the grounds that the law

Employment Division, Department of Human Resources of Oregon v. Smith (Continued)

proscribes religious conduct. Our most recent decision involving a neutral, generally applicable law that compelled religiously forbidden activity was *United States v. Lee* [where an Amish employee sought exemption from collection and payment of Social Security taxes, claiming that his faith prohibited participation in government support programs]. There, we rejected that an exemption was constitutionally required. Indeed, the tax system would not function if denominations were allowed to challenge the tax system because the funds were spent in a manner that violates their religious beliefs. The only decision in which we have held that the First Amendment bars application of a neutral, generally applicable law to religiously motivated action involved a violation of the Free Exercise Clause in conjunction with other constitutional protections, such as freedom of speech or press. The instant case does not present such a hybrid situation. Smith (P1) and Black (P2) urge us to hold that when otherwise prohibitible conduct is accompanied by religious convictions, not only the convictions but the conduct itself must be free from governmental regulation. We have never held that, and decline to do so now to a content-neutral regulation. Smith (P1) and Black (P2) further contend that even though exemption from generally applicable criminal laws need not automatically be extended to religiously motivated actors, and the claim for a religious exemption must be evaluated under the balancing test set forth in *Sherbert v. Verner*. Under the *Sherbert* test, a governmental action that substantially burdens a religious practice must be justified by a compelling government interest. Although we have applied this test on three occasions to invalidate state unemployment compensation rules that conditioned the availability of benefits upon an applicant's willingness to work under religiously prohibited conditions, we have never invalidated governmental action on the basis of *Sherbert* outside the context of unemployment compensation. In recent years we have abstained from applying the *Sherbert* test outside the employment compensation field altogether. Even if we were inclined to apply *Sherbert* outside the unemployment compensation field, we would not apply it to a generally applicable criminal law. Unlike an across the board criminal prohibition, a distinct feature of unemployment compensation programs is that their eligibility criteria invite consideration of the particular circumstances behind an applicant's unemployment. The government's ability to enforce generally applicable prohibitions of socially harmful conduct cannot depend on measuring the effects of a governmental action on a religious objector's spiritual development. To make an individual's obligation to obey such a law contingent upon the law's coincidence with his religious beliefs, except where the State's interest is "compelling", would permit him by virtue of his beliefs to become a law unto himself, contradicting both constitutional tradition and common sense. The "compelling government interest" standard as used in the context of, for example, racial discrimination and free speech is not remotely comparable to using it for the purposes of the instant case. In those other fields, it produces equality of treatment and an unrestricted flow of contending speech.

Here, it would produce a private right to ignore generally applicable laws. Nor is it possible to limit the test, as Smith (P1) and Black (P2) contend, to situations where the prohibited conduct is "central" to the individual's religion. It is not appropriate for judges to determine the "centrality" of religious beliefs. This would be akin to the unacceptable business of evaluating the relative merits of differing religious claims. If the "compelling interest" test is to be applied at all, then, it must be applied across the board, and many laws will fail. Any society adopting such a system would be courting anarchy, with that danger increasing in direct proportion to the society's diversity of religious beliefs. The rule Smith (P1) and Black (P2) favor would open the prospect of constitutionally required religious exemptions from civic obligations of almost every conceivable kind, which the First Amendment's protection of religious liberty does not require. Values that are protected against government interference through enshrinement in the Bill of Rights are not thereby banished from the political process, as States can be expected to be solicitous of that value in its legislation. Therefore it is no surprise that many States have made an exception to their drug laws for sacramental peyote use. But this is not to say that it is constitutionally required, or that appropriate occasions for its creation can be discerned by the courts. Generally applicable, religion-neutral laws that have the effect of burdening a particular religious practice need not be justified by a compelling interest, unless another constitutional protection is burdened in conjunction, or the government has provided for individualized treatment in an unemployment compensation scheme. Here, because the ingestion of peyote was prohibited under Oregon law, and because the prohibition is constitutional, Oregon may, consistent with the Free Exercise Clause, deny unemployment compensation when the dismissal results from the use of the drug. Reversed.

Employment Division, Department of Human Resources of Oregon v. Smith (Continued)

■ CONCURRENCE

(O'Connor, J.) The Court today holds that where the law is a generally applicable criminal prohibition, our usual free exercise jurisprudence does not even apply. However, to reach this result, the Court not only gives a strained reading of the First Amendment, but also disregards our consistent application of free exercise doctrine to cases involving generally applicable regulations that burden religious conduct. A person who is barred from engaging in religiously motivated conduct is barred from freely exercising his religious. It is difficult to deny that a law that prohibits religiously motivated conduct, even if the law is generally applicable, does not at least implicate First Amendment concerns. Although the Court responds that generally applicable laws are "one large step" removed from laws aimed at specific religious practices, the first amendment does not distinguish between laws that are generally applicable and laws that target particular religious practices. Our free exercise cases have all concerned generally applicable laws that had the effect of significantly burdening a religious practice. If the First Amendment is to have any vitality it ought not be construed to cover only the extreme and hypothetical case where a religion is directly targeted. To say that person's right to free exercise has been burdened, of course, does not mean that he has an absolute right to engage in the conduct. We have recognized that the freedom to act, unlike the freedom to believe, cannot be absolute. We have respected both the First Amendment's express textual mandate and the governmental interest involved by requiring the government to justify any substantial burden on religiously motivated conduct by a compelling state interest and by means narrowly tailored to achieve that interest. The Court attempts to support its narrow reading of the Clause by claiming that we have never found that a person's religious beliefs excuse him from compliance with an otherwise valid law. But as the court notes, we have in fact interpreted the Clause to forbid application of a generally applicable prohibition to religiously motivated conduct.

In cases where we rejected the particular constitutional claims, the compelling interests were carefully weighed. Where a government regulation burdens free exercise of religion, we have consistently asked the government to demonstrate that unbending application of its regulation to the religious objector is essential to accomplish an overriding governmental interest, or represents the least restrictive means of achieving some compelling state interest. In my view, the sounder approach is to apply this test in each case to determine whether the burden is constitutionally significant and whether the particular criminal interest asserted by the State before us compelling. Although the Court suggests that the compelling interest test, as applied to generally applicable laws, would result in a constitutional anomaly, the First Amendment unequivocally makes freedom of religion, like freedom of speech, a constitutional norm. A law that makes criminal such an activity therefore triggers constitutional concern and heightened judicial scrutiny, even if it does not target the particular religious conduct at issue. Finally, The Court today suggests that the disfavoring of minority religions is an unavoidable consequence under our system, and that accommodation of such religions must be left to the political process. In my view, however, the First Amendment was enacted precisely to protect the rights of those whose religious practices are not shared by the majority and may be viewed with hostility. The compelling interest test reflects the First Amendment's mandate of preserving religious liberty to the fullest extent possible in a pluralistic society. Nevertheless, I would reach the same result here, applying our established free exercise jurisprudence. There is no dispute that Oregon's criminal prohibition places a severe burden on the ability of Smith (P1) and Black (P2) to freely exercise their religion. There is also no dispute that Oregon has a significant interest in enforcing laws that control the possession and use of controlled substances by its citizens. Although the question is close, I would conclude that uniform application of Oregon's criminal prohibition is "essential" to accomplish its overriding interest in preventing the physical harm caused by the use of a Schedule I controlled substance. Since the health effects caused by the use of controlled substances exist regardless of the motivation of the user, the use of such substances, even for religious purposes, violates the very purpose of the laws that prohibit them. Furthermore, uniform application is essential to the effectiveness of Oregon's stated interest in preventing any possession of peyote, in view of the societal interest in preventing drug trafficking.

■ DISSENT

(Blackmun, J.) Until today, I thought that such a statute may stand only if the law in general, and the State's refusal to allow a religious exemption in particular, were justified by a compelling interest that cannot be served by less restrictive means. The majority however, dismisses it as a "constitutional

Employment Division, Department of Human Resources of Oregon v. Smith (Continued)

anomaly," mischaracterizing this Court's precedents. This distorted view of our precedents lead the majority to conclude that strict scrutiny of a state law burdening the free exercise of religion is a "luxury" that a well-ordered society cannot afford, and that the repression of minority religions is an "unavoidable consequence of democratic government." I do not believe the Founders thought their dearly bought freedom from religious persecution a "luxury," but an essential element of liberty. They could not have thought religious intolerance "unavoidable," for they drafted the Religion Clauses precisely in order to avoid that intolerance. Although the State proclaims an interest in protecting the health and safety of its citizens, it offers no evidence that religious use of peyote has ever harmed anyone. The carefully circumscribed ritual context in which respondents used peyote is far removed from the irresponsible and unrestricted recreational use of unlawful drugs. The Native American Church's internal restrictions on, and supervision of, its members' use of peyote substantially obviate the State's health and safety concerns. Thus, I conclude that Oregon's interest is not sufficiently compelling to outweigh respondents' right to the free exercise of their religion, and cannot justify its denial of unemployment benefits.

Analysis:

As you will see later in this chapter, the Court applied the strict scrutiny standard in *Sherbert v. Verner*, and overturned a denial of unemployment compensation based on individualized treatment of a person who could not find employment because she could not work on Saturday, which was the Sabbath Day of her religion. The Court in the instant case limited the holding of *Sherbert* to cases involving such individualized treatment. Accordingly, the denial in this case was not overturned because the denial was based on a violation of a generally applicable criminal law. Thus, when determining the constitutionality of a generally applicable, religion-neutral law under the Free Exercise Clause, rational basis scrutiny is to be used except when: (1) the Free Exercise claim is brought in conjunction with another constitutional protection, such as free speech or (2) the government has provided for individualized treatment, such as in the unemployment compensation scheme in *Sherbert*.

■ CASE VOCABULARY

FREE EXERCISE CLAUSE: A constitutional guarantee provided in the First Amendment, which prohibits governmental abridgement of the right to freely exercise one's religion.

PEYOTE: A hallucinatory drug derived from the mescal cactus plant.

Sherbert v. Verner

(Seventh-day Adventist) v. (Government Representative)
374 U.S. 398, 83 S.Ct. 1790 (1963)

THE STATE MAY NOT DENY THE RECEIPT OF UNEMPLOYMENT BENEFITS TO AN ELIGIBLE PERSON IF SHE REFUSES TO WORK ON HER SABBATH

■ **INSTANT FACTS** The State unconstitutionally denied Sherbert (P) the right to receive unemployment benefits, because Sherbert (P) could not work on Saturdays, the Sabbath Day of her religion, and therefore could not find employment.

■ **BLACK LETTER RULE** A denial of government funded benefits to those who are otherwise eligible, but leave their place of employment because of religious reasons, unconstitutionally infringes on their right to free exercise of religion.

■ **PROCEDURAL BASIS**

Certification to the United States Supreme Court after the State's highest court denied relief to petitioner.

■ **FACTS**

Sherbert (P), a member of the Seventh-day Aventist Church, was discharged by her employer because she refused to work on Saturday due to her religious beliefs. After being unable to obtain other employment for the same reason, she filed a claim for unemployment compensation benefits. However she was denied benefits by the Employment Security Commission (Commission) (D), who found that Sherbert's (P) restriction upon her availability to work on Saturday, brought her within the provision disqualifying for benefits insured workers who fail, without good cause, to accept other suitable work when offered. The Supreme Court of South Carolina found in favor of the Commission (D), and Sherbert (P) appealed to the U.S. Supreme Court.

■ **ISSUE**

Does the state's refusal to grant unemployment benefits to those who refuse to work on Saturday for religious reasons, unconstitutionally infringe on the right to the free exercise of religion?

■ **DECISION AND RATIONALE**

(Brennan, J.) Yes. A denial of government funded benefits to those who are otherwise eligible, but leave their place of employment because of religious reasons, unconstitutionally infringes on their right to free exercise of religion. The Free Exercise Clause prohibits the government from either compelling affirmation of a repugnant belief, nor penalizing or discriminating against individuals or groups because of their religious beliefs, nor employing the taxing power to inhibit the dissemination of particular religious views. However, the Court has rejected challenges to government regulation of certain acts prompted by religious beliefs or principles, which have invariably posed some substantial threat to public safety, peace, or order. Here, Sherbert's (P) objection to Saturday work constitutes no conduct prompted by religious principles of a kind within the reach of state legislation. Therefore, if the decision of the South Carolina Supreme Court is to withstand appellant's constitutional challenge, it must be either because her disqualification represents no infringement by the State of her rights of free exercise, or because any incidental burden on the free exercise of Sherbert's (P) religion is of a subject within the State's constitutional power to regulate, and justified by a compelling state interest. First, it is dear that

Sherbert v. Verner (Continued)

the disqualification for benefits imposes a burden on the free exercise of Sherbert's (P) religion. On the one hand, the consequences of such a disqualification to religious principles and practices may be only an indirect result of welfare legislation within the State's general competence to enact. Furthermore, it is true that no criminal sanctions directly compel appellant to work a six-day week. But that does not end our inquiry. Here, it is apparent that Sherbert's (P) declared ineligibility for benefits derives solely from the practice of her religion, and that there is pressure upon her to forego that practice. The ruling forces her to choose between following the precepts of her religion, thereby forgoing her benefits, and abandoning one of the precepts of her religion in order to accept work. Imposition of such a choice is analogous to a fine imposed against Sherbert (P) for her Saturday worship. We must next consider whether some compelling state interest enforced in the eligibility provision of the statute, justifies the substantial infringement of Sherbert's (P) First Amendment right. A showing of a mere rational relationship will not suffice here, as this is a highly sensitive constitutional area. Thus, even if the possibility of spurious claims did threaten to dilute the fund and disrupt the scheduling of work, it would plainly be incumbent upon the Commission (D) to demonstrate that no alternative forms of regulation would combat such abuses without infringing First Amendment rights. Reversed.

■ DISSENT

(Harlan, J.) The implication of the present decision are far more troublesome than its apparently narrow dimensions would indicate. The meaning of today's holding is that the State must furnish unemployment benefits to one who is unavailable for work because of religious convictions. Thus, the State must single out those whose behavior is religiously motivated, even though it denies such assistance to others whose identical behavior is not religiously motivated. I cannot subscribe to the conclusion that the State is constitutionally compelled to carve out an exception to its general rule of eligibility in the present case. Those situations in which the Constitution may require special treatment on account of religion are few and far between, and this view is amply supported by the course of constitutional litigation in this area. Here, such compulsion is particularly inappropriate in light of the indirect, remote, and insubstantial effect of the decision on the exercise of Sherbert's (P) religion and in light of the direct financial assistance to religion that today's decision requires.

Analysis:

The holding of this case was narrowed by the later opinion in *Employment Division v. Smith*, where it was held that a generally applicable, religion-neutral criminal law that substantially burdened particular religious practices did not have to be justified by a compelling interest in order to form the basis for a denial of unemployment compensation benefits. As it stands today, the situation faced by *Sherbert* seems to be one of two situations in which the Court will apply strict scrutiny to a generally applicable, religion-neutral law that burdens the free exercise of religion. More specifically, the Court will apply strict scrutiny when the government provides for individualized treatment, as is the practice in unemployment compensation schemes. In all other Free Exercise Clause situations, the Court will most likely apply rational basis scrutiny.

■ CASE VOCABULARY

SABBATH DAY: A religiously commanded day of rest and worship, in recognition of God's blessing of the seventh day as the day he finished his accomplishments and rested. The "seventh day", if recognized, may vary between different religions, depending on whether the religion regards Sunday or Monday as the first day of the week.

Church of the Lukumi Babalu Aye v. City of Hialeah

(Santeria Adherents) v. (The City)
508 U.S. 520, 113 S.Ct. 2217 (1993)

LAWS THAT RESTRICT FREEDOM OF RELIGIOUS PRACTICE THAT ARE NOT OF GENERAL APPLICABILITY MUST BE NARROWLY TAILORED TO ACHIEVE A COMPELLING GOVERNMENT INTEREST

■ **INSTANT FACTS** Followers of the Santeria religion brought a Free Exercise Clause challenge against the city in which they planned to establish a church, after the city passed ordinances prohibiting animal sacrifices in response to the members' religious practice of such sacrifices.

■ **BLACK LETTER RULE** If a law that burdens the free exercise of religion fails to satisfy the requirements of neutrality and general applicability, it must be justified by a compelling governmental interest, and must be narrowly tailored to advance that interest.

■ **PROCEDURAL BASIS**

Grant of review by the United States Supreme Court, of state ordinances which substantially burdened a religion's practices.

■ **FACTS**

In April of 1987, the Church of Lukumi Babalu Aye, Inc. (Church) (P) leased land in the City of Hialeah, Florida, and announced plans to establish a house of worship, school, cultural center, and museum. The Church (P) practices the Santeria religion, which teaches that every individual has a destiny from God that is fulfilled with the aid and energy of spirits called orishas. One of the principal forms of devotion to the orishas is animal sacrifices, which include the sacrifice of chickens, pigeons, doves, ducks, guinea pigs, goats, sheep, and turtles. According to Santeria teachings, the orishas are powerful but not immortal, and they depend on sacrifices for survival. These sacrifices are performed at birth, marriage, and death rites, for the cure of sick, the initiation of new members and priests, and during annual celebrations. The sacrificed animals are cooked and eaten, except after healing and death rituals. In response to the Church's (P) announcement, the City of Hialeah (Hialeah) (D) adopted three ordinances addressing the issue of animal sacrifice. Ordinance 87-52 defined "sacrifice" as, "to unnecessarily...kill an animal in a public or private ritual or ceremony not for the primary purpose of food consumption." It also prohibited owning animals "intending to use such animal for food purposes." The application of 87-52 was restricted to those who kill, slaughter, or sacrifice any animal for any type of ritual, regardless of whether the animal was to be consumed. Moreover, it made an exemption for the slaughtering of animals raised for food purposes by licensed establishments. Ordinance 87-71 prohibited animal sacrifices within city limits. Ordinance 87-72 defined "slaughter" as "the killing of animals for food" and barred it outside areas zoned for slaughterhouses. It exempted the slaughtering or processing of "small numbers of hogs and/or cattle per week in accordance with state law." The Church (P) challenges these ordinances.

■ **ISSUE**

Must laws that are not generally applicable or neutral be justified by a compelling governmental interest?

■ **DECISION AND RATIONALE**

(Kennedy, J.) Yes. Generally, laws that are neutral and of generally applicability need not be justified by a compelling interest, even if the law has the incidental effect of burdening a particular religious

Church of the Lukumi Babalu Aye v. City of Hialeah (Continued)

practice. However, if a law that burdens the free exercise of religion fails to satisfy the requirements of neutrality and general applicability, it must be justified by a compelling governmental interest, and must be narrowly tailored to advance that interest. First, a law targeting religious "beliefs" is never permissible. However, if the object of a law is to infringe upon or restrict "practices" because of their religious motivation, the law is not neutral and is invalid unless it is justified by a compelling interest and is narrowly tailored to advance that interest. To determine the object of a law, we must begin with its text, for the minimum requirement that the law does not discriminate on its face. A law lacks facial neutrality if it refers to a religious practice without some discernible secular meaning. While the words "sacrifice" and "ritual" have strong religious connotations and are consistent with the Church's (P) claim of facial discrimination, these words also have a secular meaning. So while the contention of facial discrimination has support, the argument is not conclusive. However, facial neutrality is not determinative. The Free Exercise Clause also protects against governmental hostility which is masked as well as overt. After viewing the record, there is sufficient support for the conclusion that the suppression of Santeria worship was the object of the ordinances. The effect of a law in its real operation is strong evidence of its object. Although the subject at hand does implicate multiple concerns unrelated to religious animosity, the ordinances, when considered together, disclose an object remote from these legitimate concerns. It is a necessary conclusion that almost the only conduct subject to these ordinances is the religious exercise of Santeria church members. Ordinance 87–71 excludes almost all killings of animals except for religious sacrifice, and the primary purpose requirement narrows the proscribed category even further, in particular by exempting kosher slaughter. The net result is that few if any killings of animals are prohibited other than for Santeria Sacrifice. Furthermore, the ordinances proscribe more religious conduct than is necessary to achieve its stated ends. The legitimate governmental interest in protecting the public health and preventing cruelty to animals could be addressed by a restriction stopping far short of a flat prohibition. For instance, if improper disposal is the harm to be prevented, the city could have imposed a general regulation on the disposal of organic garbage. Therefore, these ordinances had as their object the suppression of religion and are not neutral. Next, we turn to the second requirement of general applicability. Here, we need not define with precision the standard used to evaluate whether a prohibition is of general applicability, for these ordinances fall well below the minimum standard necessary to protect First Amendment rights. Although Hialeah (D) argues that the ordinances advance interest in protecting the public health and preventing animal cruelty, the ordinances fail to prohibit nonreligious conduct that endangers these interests in a similar or greater degree than Santeria sacrifice does. Thus, we conclude that these ordinances pursue the city's governmental interest only against conduct motivated by religious beliefs. This precise evil is what the requirement of generally applicability is designed to prevent. Accordingly, these laws must undergo application of the most rigorous scrutiny, which is almost always fatal. While there are legitimate ends cited by Hialeah (D), the means of reaching these ends are either overbroad or underinclusive. From what we have already stated, it follows that these ordinances cannot withstand scrutiny.

Analysis:

This case summarizes the laws and required standards of review with respect to an evaluation of government regulations under the Free Exercise Clause. As stated by the Court, any law that targets religious "beliefs" will automatically be struck down. However, religious "conduct" or "actions" that are religiously motivated cannot be given the same type of absolute protection. Strict scrutiny, though, is probably the next best thing. Accordingly, any law that is not of general applicability or religion-neutral, or, in other words, any law that targets religious practices on its face or as applied, must be justified by a compelling government interest and narrowly tailored to advance that interest. In situations where the law is neutral and generally applicable, only rational basis review is required, except in the two types of situations mentioned earlier in this chapter.

■ CASE VOCABULARY

SANTERIA: A religion which teaches that every individual has a destiny from God that is fulfilled with the aid and energy of powerful but not immortal spirits that rely on animal sacrifice for survival.

Cutter v. Wilkinson

(*Inmate*) v. (*Director of Corrections*)
544 U.S. 709, 125 S.Ct. 2113 (2005)

ACCOMODATING RELIGIOUS PRACTICES IN A PRISON IS NOT "ESTABLISHMENT" OF A RELIGION

■ **INSTANT FACTS** Cutter (P) claimed that the prison's (D) refusal to allow him to practice a "non-traditional" religion violated his rights under the Religious Land Use and Institutionalized Persons Act (RLUIPA), and Wilkinson (D) claimed the portion of the Act that related to prison inmates was unconstitutional.

■ **BLACK LETTER RULE** The Religious Land Use and Institutionalized Persons Act is a permissible accommodation of religion that does not violate the Establishment Clause.

■ **PROCEDURAL BASIS**

Appeal from an order of the Sixth Circuit Court of Appeals ordering dismissal of Cutter's (P) complaints.

■ **FACTS**

Cutter (P) was an inmate at an Ohio correctional institution (D). He was an adherent of a "non-mainstream" religion. Cutter (P) claimed that prison officials (D) did not allow him the same right to practice his religion as provided to inmates who practiced other religions. Cutter (P) alleged that the officials (D) violated section 3 of the Religious Land Use and Institutionalized Persons Act (RLUIPA), 42 U.S.C. § 2000cc–1. That section provides that the government may not "impose a substantial burden on the religious exercise of a person residing in or confined to an institution." A burden on religious practice may be justified if it furthers a compelling governmental interest, and it is the least restrictive means of furthering that interest. Prison officials (D) responded by arguing that § 3 improperly advanced religion in violation of the Establishment Clause. The court of appeals reversed the district court's refusal to dismiss Cutter's (P) complaint.

■ **ISSUE**

Does section 3 of the RLUIPA violate the Establishment Clause?

■ **DECISION AND RATIONALE**

(Ginsburg, J.) No. The Religious Land Use and Institutionalized Persons Act is a permissible accommodation of religion that does not violate the Establishment Clause. Section 3 of the RLUIPA eases exceptional government-created burdens on private religious exercise. When applying the law, courts must take into account the burden that a requested religious accommodation may place on non-beneficiaries. Courts must also be satisfied that the requirements of the Act are and will be administered neutrally among different faiths. The Act thus protects institutionalized persons who are unable to attend to their religious needs freely and who are dependent on the government's permission and accommodation.

The RLUIPA does not elevate religious accommodation over the need to maintain order and safety in an institution. When the compelling governmental interest standard in the Act is applied, context matters. Deference will be given to the expertise of correctional officials in making the necessary accommodations.

Precedent does not require invalidation of a law that gives "greater protection to religious rights than to other constitutionally protected rights." If that were so, no religious accommodation would be allowed for any faith. Reversed.

Analysis:

The RLUIPA was passed in 2000 to correct part of the holding in *City of Boerne v. Flores,* 521 U.S. 507 (1997). In that case, the Court held that the Religious Freedom Restoration Act, 42 U.S.C. 2000bb *et seq.,* was unconstitutional as applied to the states. In a concurring opinion not reprinted in the casebook, Justice Thomas noted that Congress conditioned states' receipt of federal funds on compliance with the RLIUPA. In his view, a state could avoid the requirements of the Act by refusing to accept federal funds for its correctional institutions, making this case like *Rumsfeld v. Forum for Academic & Institutional Rights, Inc.*

■ CASE VOCABULARY

ESTABLISHMENT CLAUSE: The First Amendment provision that prohibits the government from creating or favoring a particular religion.

FREE EXERCISE CLAUSE: The constitutional provision prohibiting the government from interfering in people's religious practices or forms of worship.

Locke v. Davey
(*Governor*) v. (*Scholarship Recipient*)
540 U.S. 712, 124 S.Ct. 1307 (2004)

PREVENTING PUBLIC FUNDING OF RELIGIOUS INSTRUCTION JUSTIFIES SCHOLARSHIP RESTRICTIONS

■ **INSTANT FACTS** Davey (D) sought to use state scholarship funds for a degree in pastoral ministries.

■ **BLACK LETTER RULE** The Free Exercise Clause does not ensure the right to state-financed religious instruction.

■ **PROCEDURAL BASIS**

Certiorari to review an undisclosed appellate decision.

■ **FACTS**

The State of Washington established a scholarship program to assist gifted students achieve a post-secondary education. To be eligible for the scholarship, a student had to be enrolled in an eligible Washington post-secondary educational institution, including private religiously affiliated institutions, but could not pursue a degree in theology while receiving the scholarship. This restriction followed the state constitution prohibition on the use of state funds for educational degrees that are "devotional in nature or designed to induce religious faith." Davey (P) received a scholarship and attended an eligible Christian college, where he sought a double major in business management/administration and pastoral ministries. The school insisted that Davey (P) agree in writing that he would not pursue the theology degree, and when he refused his scholarship was rescinded.

■ **ISSUE**

Is a scholarship program that restricts the use of the funds to non-religious majors invalid under the Free Exercise Clause?

■ **DECISION AND RATIONALE**

(Rehnquist, C.J.) No. The state scholarship program involves the "play in the joints" between the Establishment Clause and the Free Exercise Clause. The scholarship program itself does not violate the Establishment Clause, even if state funds were eligible for devotional studies, because the link between government funds and religious training is broken by the recipients' voluntary actions. Under the more expansive state constitution, however, such voluntary actions are unconstitutional expenditures of public money. These more stringent state limitations seek to prevent the use of taxpayer dollars, directly or indirectly, in furtherance of any religious purpose. The limitations are not hostile to religion, for scholarship funds may be used for a secular education at accredited religious institutions. Instead, they seek to further the historic state interest in preventing public financing of religious instruction. The scholarship program is not "inherently constitutionally suspect."

■ **DISSENT**

(Scalia, J.) The scholarship program patently discriminates against religion in favor of secular uses of public funds. The state makes funds generally available for higher education, but withdraws such

Locke v. Davey (Continued)

benefits when the recipient chooses to use them for religious exercise. Religion is the only field of study excepted by the program, although the recipient is otherwise eligible for the benefits. By depriving Davey (P) of the benefits of others similarly situated solely because of his religious exercise, the state's scholarship program violates the Free Exercise Clause.

Analysis:

It is difficult to understand how a limitation on the use of generally available public scholarship funds satisfies the Free Exercise Clause when their use is restricted to non-religious purposes. The apparent philosophical differences between the Washington Constitution and the U.S. Constitution may help explain. The federal Free Exercise Clause is generally concerned with governmental neutrality, ensuring that each individual's right to religious expression is preserved. The Washington Constitution, however, seeks not neutrality, but governmental abstention from public expenditures for any religious cause.

■ CASE VOCABULARY

ESTABLISHMENT CLAUSE: The First Amendment provision that prohibits the government from creating or favoring a particular religion.

FREE EXERCISE CLAUSE: The constitutional provision (U.S. Const. amend. I) prohibiting the government from interfering in people's religious practices or forms of worship.

County of Allegheny v. American Civil Liberties Union Greater Pittsburgh Chapter

(Holiday Displayers) v. *(ACLU)*
492 U.S. 573, 109 S.Ct. 3086 (1989)

HOLIDAY DISPLAYS CAN VIOLATE THE ESTABLISHMENT CLAUSE IF THEY ENDORSE A PATENTLY RELIGIOUS MESSAGE

■ **INSTANT FACTS** A county's holiday displays were challenged on the ground that they violated the Establishment Clause.

■ **BLACK LETTER RULE** A government's act is unconstitutional under the Establishment Clause if, being evaluated in its context, the act has the effect of endorsing religion or could be understood by viewers to be an endorsement of religion.

■ PROCEDURAL BASIS

Review by the United States Supreme Court of an action challenging the constitutionality of local government's holiday displays.

■ FACTS

The County of Allegheny (Allegheny) (D) consistently placed two holiday displays on public property. The first was a crèche placed on the Grand Staircase of the County Courthouse, and the second was a Chanukah menorah placed outside the City-County Building, next to a Christmas tree and a sign saluting liberty. The American Civil Liberties Union (ACLU) (P) brought an action challenging the constitutionality of displays. The Court of Appeals ruled that each display violated the Establishment Clause of the First Amendment, concluding that the displays had the impermissible effect of endorsing religion. Allegheny (D) appeals to the U.S. Supreme Court.

■ ISSUE

In determining whether the government's use of an object with religious meaning has the effect of endorsing religion in violation of the Establishment Clause, must it be considered by what viewers may fairly understand to be the purpose of the display?

■ DECISION AND RATIONALE

(Blackmun, J.) Yes. We have come to understand the Establishment Clause to mean that government may not promote or affiliate itself with any religion, may not discriminate among persons on the basis of their religious beliefs and practices, may not delegate a governmental power to a religious institution, and may not involve itself too deeply in such an institution's affairs. In recent years, we have paid closer attention to whether a challenged governmental practice has the purpose or effect of "endorsing" religion. Although the word "endorsement" is not self-defining, it derives its meaning from other words that we have found useful over the years. Thus, it has been noted that the prohibition against governmental endorsement of religion precludes governmental conveyance or attempts to convey a message that religion or a particular religious belief is favored or preferred. In *Lynch v. Donnelly*, we considered whether including a crèche in an annual Christmas display, located in a private park, violated the Establishment Clause. In a 5–4 decision, we upheld the inclusion of the crèche, holding that the inclusion did not have the effect of advancing or promoting religion. Since *Lynch*, we have made clear that when evaluating the effect of government conduct under the Establishment Clause, we must ascertain whether the challenged action is sufficiently likely to be perceived by adherents of the controlling denominations as an endorsement, and by the non-adherents as a disapproval, of their individual religious choices. A government's act is unconstitutional under the Establishment Clause if, being evaluated in its context, the act has the effect of endorsing religion or could be understood by viewers to be an endorsement of religion. In the instant case, there is no doubt that the crèche itself is capable of communicating a religious message. Under our holding in *Lynch*, the effect of a creche display turns on its setting. Here, unlike in *Lynch*, nothing in the context of the display detracts from the crèche's religious message. The *Lynch* display composed a series of figures and objects, such as a Santa house and a talking well, each of which had its own focal point. Here however, the crèche stands alone as a single element of the display. The menorah display presents a closer constitutional question, because it is a primary symbol for a holiday that, like Christmas, has both religious and secular dimensions. In considering the setting of the display, the necessary result of placing the menorah next to the Christmas tree is to create an overall "holiday setting," that represents both Christmas and Chanukah. But this does not end our inquiry. The simultaneous endorsement of Judaism and Christianity is no less constitutionally infirm than the endorsement of just one. Thus, the relevant question is whether the combined display of the tree, sign, and menorah has the effect of endorsing two religious faiths, or rather simply recognizes that both are part of the same winter-holiday season, which has attained a secular status in our society. The latter seems far more plausible. The judgment of the court of appeal is affirmed with regards to the creche, but reversed with regards to the menorah.

■ CONCURRENCE

(O'Connor, J.) I agree with Court's analysis of the constitutionality of the crèche. The display of religious symbols in public areas of core government buildings runs a special risk of making religion relevant, in reality or public perception, to status in the political community. However, with regard to the menorah, although I agree with the decision, I believe the relevant question for Establishment Clause purposes is whether the city display sends a message of government endorsement of Judaism or whether it sends a message of pluralism and freedom to choose one's own beliefs. The message of pluralism by the city's combined holiday display is not a message that endorses religion over nonreligion.

■ CONCURRENCE AND DISSENT

(Brennan, J.) An object that retains a specifically Christian or other religious meaning is incompatible with the separation of church and state demanded by our constitution. Accordingly, I agree with the Court that the display of the crèche is unconstitutional. I cannot agree, however, that the Christmas tree and menorah shows no favoritism toward Christianity, Judaism, or both. Indeed, I should have thought that the answer as to the first display supplied the answer to the second.

■ CONCURRENCE AND DISSENT

(Stevens, J.) The Establishment Clause should be construed to create a strong presumption against the display of religious symbols on public property. Displays of this kind inevitably have a greater tendency to emphasize sincere and deeply felt differences among individuals than to achieve an ecumenical goal. The Establishment Clause does not allow public bodies to foment such disagreement.

■ CONCURRENCE AND DISSENT

(Kennedy, J.) The majority's view of the Establishment Clause is inconsistent with our history and precedents. The Establishment Clause permits government some latitude in recognizing and accommodating the central role religion plays in our society. Any approach less sensitive to our heritage would border on latent hostility toward religion, as it would require government in all its multifaceted roles to acknowledge only the secular, to the exclusion and so to the detriments of the religious. Our cases disclose two limiting principles. First, the government may not coerce support for or participation in any religion or its exercise. Second, it may not give direct benefits to religion in such a degree that it in fact "establishes" a religion, or tends to do so. These principles are not difficult to apply to the facts of this case. Here, the government sought to do no more than "celebrate the season" and acknowledge the historical background and nature of the Chanukah and Christmas holidays. This interest falls well within the tradition of government accommodation and acknowledgment of religion that has marked our history from the beginning. If government is to participate in its citizen's celebration of a holiday that contains both a secular and a religious component, enforced recognition of only the secular aspect would signify the callous indifference toward religious faith that our cases and traditions do not require. Although the Religion Clauses do not require government to acknowledge these holidays or their religious component, our strong tradition of government accommodation and acknowledgments permits government to do so. The crèche and the menorah are purely passive symbols of religious holidays. There is no evidence of government coercion, or that the government's power was used to further the interests of religion. Those who disagree with the message conveyed by these displays are free to ignore them, just like with any other form of government speech.

Analysis:

The relatively specific standard of review that was applied by the Court without serious debate from 1971 until 1987 was, as you will read later in this chapter, the three-part *Lemon* test, which required a law to have a secular purpose, neither advance or inhibit religion, and not cause excessive government entanglement with religion in order to be valid. Although this test has not been overruled, it has been losing support in the Court and has been consistently modified in its application over recent decades. The test applied in the instant case was the "endorsement test" advanced by Justice O'Connor in *Lynch v. Donnelly*. The endorsement test is sometimes used in the application of the second prong of the *Lemon* test and, as illustrated in this case, seems to control for the purposes of evaluating the government's display of religious symbols on public property.

■ CASE VOCABULARY

CRECHE: A visual representation of the scene in the manger in Bethlehem shortly after the birth of Jesus Christ.

ECUMENICAL: Representing the whole worldwide Christian church.

ESTABLISHMENT CLAUSE: The First Amendment prohibition that proscribes government acts that establish or may tend to establish religion.

Larson v. Valente

(Department of Commerce) v. (Religious Charity Organization)
456 U.S. 228, 102 S.Ct. 1673 (1982)

GOVERNMENT DISCRIMINATION AMONG RELIGIOUS GROUPS WILL VIOLATE THE ESTABLISHMENT CLAUSE

■ **INSTANT FACTS** A church challenged the constitutionality of an act that required some religious charity organizations to participate in a system of registration and disclosure.

■ **BLACK LETTER RULE** Denominational preferences must be invalidated unless justified by a compelling governmental interest, and closely fitted to further that interest.

■ **PROCEDURAL BASIS**

Certification to the United States Supreme Court of a constitutional challenge to a charity registration act.

■ **FACTS**

In 1961, John R. Larson, Commissioner of Securities, and Warren Spannaus, Attorney General of Minnesota, implemented the Minnesota Charitable Solicitation Act (MCSA), which provided for a system of registration and disclosure respecting charitable organizations. The MCSA was designed to protect the public from fraudulent practices in the solicitation of contributions for charitable purposes, by requiring charitable organizations registering, to file an extensive annual report with the Minnesota Department of Commerce (Department) (D), detailing their total receipts and income from all sources, their costs of management, fundraising, and public education, and their transfers of any property or funds out of the State, along with a description of the recipients and purposes for those transfers. Although "religious organizations" were originally exempted from the MCSA, in 1978, the MCSA was amended to include a "fifty per cent" rule. This rule provided that only those religious organizations that received more than half of their total contributions from members or affiliated organizations would remain exempt from the MCSA. Shortly after the amendment, the Department (D) notified Holy Spirit Association for the Unification of World Christianity (Unification Church) (P) that it was required to register under the amended MCSA. Valente, Barber, Haft, and Korman, followers of the Unification Church (P), brought suit against the Department (D).

■ **ISSUE**

Must a government act or regulation that discriminates among religious groups, be justified by a compelling interest, and narrowly tailored to advance that interest, in order to be upheld under the Establishment Clause?

■ **DECISION AND RATIONALE**

(Brennan, J.) Yes. Denominational preferences must be invalidated unless justified by a compelling governmental interest, and closely fitted to further that interest. The clearest command of the Establishment Clause is that one religious denomination cannot be officially preferred over another. This constitutional prohibition of denominational preferences is inextricably connected with the continuing vitality of the Free Exercise Clause. It was Madison's vision that every denomination would be equally at

Larson v. Valente (Continued)

liberty to exercise and propagate its beliefs. Such equality would be impossible in an atmosphere of official denominational preference. Free exercise can only be guaranteed when legislators and voters are required to accord to their own religions the very same treatment given to small, new, or unpopular denominations. Here, the fifty per cent rule clearly grants denominational preferences of the sort consistently and firmly denounced in our precedents. Thus, the rule must be invalidated unless it is justified by a compelling governmental interest, and closely fitted to further that interest. The Department (D) asserts that the State has a significant interest in protecting its citizens from abusive practices in the solicitation of funds for charity, and that this interest retains importance when the solicitation is conducted by a religious organization. Assuming the MCSA addresses a sufficiently "compelling" governmental interest, the Department (D) must still demonstrate that the fifty per cent rule is closely fitted to further the interest that it assuredly serves. The Department (D) argues that the distinction between contributions solicited from members and nonmembers is eminently sensible. They urge that members are reasonably assumed to have significant control over the solicitation of contributions from themselves to their organization, and over the expenditure of the funds that they contribute as well. Furthermore, the Department (D) notes that as a matter of Minnesota law, members of organizations have greater access than nonmembers to the financial records of the organization. The Department's (D) argument is thus based on three distinct premises: 1) That members of a religious organization can and will exercise supervision and control over the organization's solicitation activities when membership contributions exceed fifty per cent; 2) that membership control is an adequate safeguard against abusive solicitations of the public by the organization; and 3) that the need for public disclosure rises in proportion with the percentage of nonmember contributions. Acceptance of these premises are necessary to the Department's (D) argument, but we find no substantial support for any of them in the record. Accordingly, we find that the Department (D) has failed to demonstrate that the fifty per cent rule is "closely fitted" to further a "compelling governmental interest."

Analysis:

This case illustrates a firmly established requirement of not only the Establishment Clause, but of the Free Exercise Clause as well. That is, the government may not prefer one religion or sect over others or, for that matter, religion over non-religion. Any such discrimination will only be upheld if the strict scrutiny standard is satisfied. This "neutrality test" is the first step to be applied in any evaluation of a government regulation. More specifically, the initial inquiry is whether the law facially differentiates among religions. If the law does not discriminate on its face, the inquiry should proceed to the government "coercion test" (whether the government is coercing participation in religion), if applicable, and then to the *Lemon* test (purpose-effect-entanglement).

Lemon v. Kurtzman

(Not Stated) v. (Not Stated)
403 U.S. 602, 91 S.Ct. 2105 (1971)

PRIVATE SCHOOL FINANCIAL ASSISTANCE PROGRAMS THAT RESULT IN AID BEING GIVEN TO CHURCH-RELATED INSTITUTIONS VIOLATE THE ESTABLISHMENT CLAUSE

■ **INSTANT FACTS** The constitutionality of two statutes that provided financial support to private schools, including church-related educational institutions, were challenged under the Establish Clause.

■ **BLACK LETTER RULE** In order to be constitutional under the Establishment Clause, a non-discriminatory regulation must: 1) have a secular legislative purpose; 2) have a principal or primary effect that neither advances nor inhibits religion and 3) not foster an excessive government entanglement with religion.

■ **PROCEDURAL BASIS**

Grant of review by the United States Supreme Court of the constitutionality of two statutory financial support programs.

■ **FACTS**

Pennsylvania adopted a statutory program that provides financial support to nonpublic elementary and secondary schools by way of reimbursement for the cost of teachers' salaries, textbook, and instructional materials in specified secular subjects. Similarly, Rhode Island has adopted a statute under which the State pays directly to teachers in nonpublic elementary schools a supplement of 15% of their annual salary. Under each statute state aid has been given to church-related educational institutions. The U.S. Supreme Court grants review of the constitutionality of each statute.

■ **ISSUE**

Will a State program that provides financial assistance to private schools, including church-related institutions, violate the Establishment Clause of the First Amendment?

■ **DECISION AND RATIONALE**

(Burger, J.) Yes. The authors of the Religion Clauses did not simply prohibit the establishment of a state church or state religion, but instead commanded that there should be "no law respecting an establishment of religion." Although a given law might not establish a state religion, it may nevertheless be one "respecting" that end in the sense of being a step that could lead to such establishment, and hence offend the First Amendment. Any lines drawn must be with reference to the three main evils against which the Establishment Clause was intended to afford protection. Those are sponsorship, financial support, and active involvement of the sovereign in religious activity. Every analysis in this area must begin with consideration of the cumulative criteria developed by the Court over many years. In order to be constitutional under the Establishment Clause, a non-discriminatory regulation must: 1) have a secular legislative purpose; 2) have a principal or primary effect that neither advances nor inhibits religion and 3) not foster an excessive government entanglement with religion. With respect to the two statutes at issue here, there is no basis to conclude that the legislative intent was to advance religion. The statutes themselves clearly state that they are intended to enhance the quality of the secular education in all schools covered by the compulsory attendance laws. However, we find that the cumulative impact of the entire relationship arising under the statutes in each State involves excessive

Lemon v. Kurtzman (Continued)

entanglement between government and religion. This determination requires an examination of the character and purpose of the institutions that are benefited, the nature of the aid that the State provides, and the resulting relationship between the government and the religious authority. Here we find that both statutes foster an impermissible entanglement, and conclude that both statutes are unconstitutional.

Analysis:

While conservatives believe that the *Lemon* test has resulted in too many Establishment Clause violations, liberals tend to believe that the test has not provided a sufficient safeguard against accommodation of religion, resulting in breaches in the wall of separation between church and state. Although the test has not been formally overruled and has been invoked in recent years, the current and future role of the *Lemon* test is uncertain. The Court has "tweaked" its application in some cases, and has decided many cases without using the *Lemon* evaluation altogether.

■ **CASE VOCABULARY**

SECULAR: Having nothing to do with "religion" or being "religion neutral."

Rosenberger v. Rector and Visitors of the University of Virginia

(Christian Student Group) v. (University)
515 U.S. 819, 115 S.Ct. 2510 (1995)

A SCHOOL PROGRAM'S REFUSAL TO ASSIST STUDENT GROUPS THAT DEAL WITH RELIGIOUS SUBJECT MATTER HELD TO VIOLATE FREEDOM OF SPEECH

■ **INSTANT FACTS** A University's student organization funding program is charged with violating freedom of speech, after denying benefits to religious student groups in fear of violating the establishment clause.

■ **BLACK LETTER RULE** The Establishment Clause is not violated by a university's financial support of a religious organization's activities as part of a viewpoint neutral "student activities" funding program.

■ **PROCEDURAL BASIS**

Certification to the United States Supreme Court of a constitutional challenge against a University's refusal to provide financial assistance to religious.

■ **FACTS**

The Rector and Visitors of the University of Virginia (University) (D) authorizes the payment of outside contractors for the printing costs of a variety of student publications. Before a student group is eligible to submit from its outside contractors for payment by the school's Student Activities Fund (SAF), it must become a Contracted Independent Organization (CIO). This status is available to any group whose members are students, whose managing officers are fulltime students, and who complies with certain procedural requirements. The purpose of the SAF is to support a broad range of extracurricular student activities that are related to the educational purpose of the University (D). The Guidelines require that the SAF be administered in a manner consistent with the educational purpose of the University as well as with state and federal law. It receives its money from mandatory student fees. The student activities that are excluded from SAF support are, among others, religious activities, which are defined as any activity that primarily promotes or manifests a particular belief in or about a deity or an ultimate reality. In 1990 Wide Awake Productions (WAP) (P), formed by Ronald Rosenberger and other undergraduates, was established to publish a magazine of philosophical and religious expression, to facilitate discussion which fosters an atmosphere of sensitivity to and tolerance of Christian viewpoints, and to provide a unifying focus for Christians of multicultural backgrounds. WAP (P) publishes Wide Awake: A Christian Perspective at the University of Virginia. Soon after it was organized WAP (P) acquired CIO status. WAP (P) was not considered a religious organization because according to the Guidelines, a religious organization is, "an organization whose purpose is to practice a devotion to an acknowledged ultimate reality of deity." A few months later, WAP (P) requested the SAF to pay its printer for the cost of printing the newspaper. The Appropriations Committee of the Student Council denied the request on the grounds that Wide Awake was a "religious activity." WAP (P) appealed to the full Student Council arguing that denial of SAF support on the basis of the magazine's religious perspective violated the Constitution. The appeal was denied and WAP (P) appealed to the next level, the Student Activities Committee, ultimately to be denied once more. WAP (P) then filed suit in the United States District.

Rosenberger v. Rector and Visitors of the University of Virginia (Continued)

■ ISSUE

Will a University violate the Establishment Clause by providing financial support to a religious organization's activities as part of a viewpoint neutral "student activities" funding program?

■ DECISION AND RATIONALE

(Kennedy, J.) No. It goes without saying that the government may not regulate speech based on its substantive content or the message it conveys. Discrimination against speech because of its message is presumed to be unconstitutional. When the government targets not subject matter, but particular views taken by speakers on a subject the violation of the First Amendment is more blatant. These principles provide the framework prohibiting the State to exercise view-point discrimination, even when the limited public forum is one of its own creation. Once a state opens a limited forum, it must respect the lawful boundaries it has itself set. In determining whether the State is acting to preserve the limits of the forum it has created so that exclusion of a class of speech is legitimate, we have observed a distinction between content discrimination which may be permissible if it preserves the purposes of that limited forum, and viewpoint discrimination which is presumed impermissible when directed against speech otherwise within the forum's limitations. These same principles apply to the SAF. The University (D) insists that this case does not involve viewpoint discrimination, because the Guidelines set limits based on content and not viewpoint. We disagree, and conclude that viewpoint discrimination is the proper way to interpret the University's (D) objections to Wide Awake. The University (D) does not exclude religion as a subject matter but selects for disfavored treatment those student journalistic efforts with religious editorial viewpoints. Religion may be a vast area of inquiry, but it also provides a perspective and standpoint from which a variety of subjects may be discussed and considered. The prohibited perspective, not the general subject matter, resulted in the refusal to make third-party payments, for the subjects discussed were otherwise within the approved category of publications. The University (D) argues that the State must have substantial discretion in determining how to allocate scarce resources to accomplish its educational mission, and that content-based funding decisions are both inevitable and lawful. However, it does not follow that viewpoint based restrictions are proper when the University (D) does not itself speak or subsidize transmittal of a message it favors, but instead expends funds to encourage a diversity of views from private speakers. A holding that the University (D) may not discriminate based on the viewpoint of private persons whose speech it facilitates, does not restrict the University's (D) own speech or ability to accomplish its educational mission, which is controlled by different principles. Furthermore, there would be no Establishment Clause violation in the University's honoring of its duties under the Free Speech Clause by providing funds to the religious groups. The program here is neutral toward religion, and is acting with the purpose and effect of helping student groups and fostering a wide array of activities and viewpoints on campus. There is absolutely no significant difference between a school using its funds to operate a facility to which students have access, and a school paying a third-party contractor to operate the facility on its behalf. The Establishment Clause is not violated by a university's financial support of a religious organization's activities as part of a viewpoint neutral "student activities" funding program.

■ DISSENT

(Souter, J.) This is the first time that the Court has allowed direct government financial subsidies to a religious organization. Using public funds for the direct subsidization of preaching the word is categorically forbidden under the Establishment Clause, and if the Clause was meant to accomplish nothing else, it was meant to bar this use of public money.

Analysis:

The situation here deals with whether allowing religious speech on government property, or assisting religious speech with government funds, violates the Establishment Clause. There was no Establishment Clause violation because the program was religion-neutral and had the secular purpose and effect of helping foster a wide array of activities and view points on campus. In a similar case, *Board of Education of Westside Community School v. Mergens*, the Court upheld the Federal Equal Access Act, which prohibited schools that opened their facilities to student groups from denying equal access to any student group based on the content of their speech, even if certain groups dealt with religious subject matter. The Court reasoned that preventing discrimination of speech was a legitimate secular purpose, that secondary school students were not likely to perceive that their school endorses religious speech, and that there was no excessive entanglement with religion where faculty sponsors were not allowed to participate in the religious group's meetings. As the Court in the instant case points out, there is no difference between the situation faced here and the one faced in *Mergens*.

■ CASE VOCABULARY

CONTENT BASED REGULATION: A regulation that discriminates based on broad categories or topics.

VIEWPOINT BASED REGULATION: A regulation that discriminates based on viewpoints within specific categories or topics.

Santa Fe Independent School District v. Doe

(*Pregame Prayer Policy*) v. (*Students and Parents*)
530 U.S. 290, 120 S.Ct. 2266 (2000)

PUBLIC INVOCATIONS GIVEN BEFORE HIGH SCHOOL FOOTBALL GAMES ARE HELD UNCONSTITUTIONAL

■ **INSTANT FACTS** The constitutionality of a school district's policy which allowed invocations to be given prior to football games, was challenged under the Establishment Clause by school students and their families.

■ **BLACK LETTER RULE** Allowing invocations during high school football will constitute excessive entanglement between the government and religion in violation of the Establishment Clause.

■ **PROCEDURAL BASIS**

Certification to the United States Supreme Court of an action challenging a school district's policy of allowing prayers before football games.

■ **FACTS**

Prior to 1994, Santa Fe High School's student council chaplain delivered a prayer over the public address system before each varsity football game. Two sets of current or former students and their mothers (Does) (P), consisting of Mormon and Catholic families, challenged this practice in District Court, and were allowed to litigate anonymously to protect them from intimidation or harassment. While the proceedings were pending in the District Court, the Santa Fe School District (District) (D) adopted a different policy that permitted but did not require, prayer initiated and led by a student at all home games. The policy, titled "Prayer at Football Games," authorized one student to determine whether "invocations" should be delivered, and another student to select the spokesperson to deliver them. The policy omitted any requirement that the content of the invocation be nonsectarian and nonproselytising, and a fallback provision that automatically added that limitation if the preferred policy should be enjoined. On august 31, 1995, the District's (D) high school students voted to determine whether a student would deliver prayer at varsity football games and chose to allow the prayer. A week later, they selected a student to deliver the prayer. In October, the District (D) adopted its final policy which was essentially the same as the August policy, but omitted the word "prayer" from its title, and referred to "messages" and "statements" as well as "invocations." The District Court entered an order modifying the policy to permit only nonsectarian, nonproselytizing prayer. The Court of Appeals held that even as modified, the football prayer was invalid. The District (D) appeals.

■ **ISSUE**

Does a policy permitting student-led, student-initiated prayer at football games violate the Establishment Clause?

■ **DECISION AND RATIONALE**

(Stevens, J.) Yes. Allowing invocations during high school football will constitute excessive entanglement between the government and religion in violation of the Establishment Clause. This case is properly guided by the principles we endorsed in *Lee v. Weisman*, where we held that a prayer

Santa Fe Independent School District v. Doe (Continued)

delivered by a rabbi at a middle school graduation ceremony violated the Clause. The District (D) argues that the principles are inapplicable to its policy, because the messages are private student speech and because there is a crucial difference between "government speech" endorsing religion, which is prohibited by the Establishment Clause, and "private speech" endorsing religion which the Free Speech and Free Exercise Clauses protect. Although we agree with this distinction, we are not persuaded that the pre-game invocation is "private speech," because they are authorized by a government policy and take place on government property at a government-sponsored school-related events. Of course, not every message delivered under such circumstances is the government's own. However, the pre-game ceremony here is not the type of forum discussed in *Rosenberger v. Rector and Visitors of the University of Virginia* [were it was held that financial support for student religious groups as part of a student activities funding program, did not violate the Establishment Clause] and similar cases. Unlike in those cases, the District's (D) officials do not evince any intent to open the pre-game ceremony to indiscriminate use by the student body generally. Instead, the school allows only one student to give the invocation or statement, which is subject to particular content and topic regulations. Moreover, although granting only one student access to the stage does not necessarily preclude a finding that the school has created a limited public forum, here the student election system ensures that only those messages deemed "appropriate" under the District's (D) policy may be delivered. This guarantees the effective silencing of minority candidate views, and does nothing to protect the minority. Furthermore, the District (D) has failed to divorce itself from the religious content in the invocations. The reality of the situation plainly reveals that its policy involves both perceived and actual endorsement of religion, because the school's involvement makes it clear that the pregame prayers bear the imprint of the State and thus put school-age children who objected in an untenable position. The text of the October policy exposes the extent of the school's entanglement. The elections take place because the school board allows it, are conducted by the high schools student council upon advice and direction by the principal, and the statement or invocation is to be consistent with the goals and purposes of this policy, which are to solemnize the event, to promote good sportsmanship and student safety, and to establish the appropriate environment for competition. In addition, the policy encourages and invites religious messages, since religious messages are the most obvious method of "solemnizing" the event, and because the stated purposes of the policy further narrow the types of messages deemed appropriate, suggesting that a solemn, yet nonreligious message, would be prohibited. Indeed, the only type of message that is expressly endorsed in the text is an "invocation,"—a term that primarily describes an appeal for divine assistance. In fact, it is clear that the students understood that the central question before them during the elections was whether a prayer should be a part of the pre-game ceremony. Surely, regardless of the listener's support for, or objection to the message, an objective high school student will perceive the inevitable pregame prayer as stamped with her school's seal of approval.

The delivery of a religious message over the school's public address system, by a speaker representing the student body, under the supervision of school faculty, and pursuant to a school policy that explicitly and implicitly encourages public prayer, cannot be properly characterized as "private" speech. The District (D) next argues that its football policy is distinguishable from *Lee*, because it does not coerce students to participate in religious observances. While it is true that attendance at these games is distinguishable from the need to show up for class or the desire to attend one's graduation, there are some students such as cheerleaders or the players themselves, who have committed to mandatory seasonal attendance, sometimes for class credit. In addition, to many, attendance and participation in extracurricular activities is part of a complete educational experience. The choice between whether to attend these games or to risk facing a personally offensive religious ritual is in no practical sense an easy one for many. The Constitution demands that the school may not force this difficult choice upon these students. The First Amendment prohibits a state from requiring one of its citizens to forfeit his rights and benefits as the price of resisting conformance to a state sponsored religious practice. Even if the decision to attend was seen as purely voluntary, the delivery of a pregame prayer had the improper effect of coercing those present to participate in an act of religious worship.

■ DISSENT

(Rehnquist, C.J.) The Court distorts existing precedent to conclude that the District's (D) student-message program is invalid on its face. To do so, it applies the most rigid version of the test of *Lemon v. Kurtzman* [where the Court held that a regulation, in order to be constitutional, must have a secular

Santa Fe Independent School District v. Doe (Continued)

purpose, cannot have the effect of advancing or inhibiting religion, and must not excessively entangle the government with religion]. Even if it were appropriate to apply the *Lemon* test here, this program should not be invalidated on its face. The District's (D) policy has plausible secular purposes. Where a government body expresses a plausible secular purpose for enactment, courts should generally defer to that stated intent. Although the Court apparently believes that solemnizing football games is an illegitimate purpose, the voters in the school district seem to disagree, and nothing in the Establishment Clause prevents them form making this choice.

Analysis:

Although this case deals with religious speech in a school setting, there are significant differences between the situation here and the situations faced in *Rosenberger* and similar cases. Unlike in those cases, allowing a pregame prayer or invocation does not involve the right to free speech, because the school has not opened some limited forum for expression. This same result would have been reached had school officials participated in the after-school religious organizations in previous cases. It is also possible that the District's (D) policy could have been struck down without an evaluation under the *Lemon* test, as unconstitutionally coercing religious participation. It is impermissible for the government to coerce participation in religious activities.

■ CASE VOCABULARY

PROSELYTIZE: To encourage or persuade an individual to convert from an untrue faith to a true one.

McCreary County v. American Civil Liberties Union of Kentucky

(County Government) v. (Civil Rights Organization)
545 U.S. 844, 125 S.Ct. 2722 (2005)

TEN COMMANDMENTS DISPLAYS IN COUNTY COURTHOUSES VIOLATE THE ESTABLISHMENT CLAUSE

■ **INSTANT FACTS** Two counties displayed the Ten Commandments in their courthouses, and the ACLU objected.

■ **BLACK LETTER RULE** The manifest objective of governmental action may be dispositive in an Establishment Clause inquiry, and the development of that action should be considered when determining its purpose.

■ PROCEDURAL BASIS
Appeal from an order affirming the grant of a preliminary injunction.

■ FACTS
McCreary County (D) and Pulaski County (D) each put up in their courthouses displays of copies of the Ten Commandments. The displays contained an abridged text of the King James Version of the Commandments, and included a citation to the Book of Exodus. The American Civil Liberties Union (P) sought an injunction against the displays. Before the court ruled on the request, the Counties (P) authorized second, expanded displays. The resolutions expanding the displays referred to the Ten Commandments as the "precedent legal code" on which the laws of Kentucky were based, along with grounds for that assertion. The expanded exhibits added other items that had either a religious theme or that were excerpted to highlight a religious element. A third display, without a resolution authorizing or directing it, was put up later. That exhibit was called the "Foundations of American Law and Government," and it showed the Commandments along with other documents deemed important to the historical foundation of American government.

■ ISSUE
Did the displays violate the Establishment Clause?

■ DECISION AND RATIONALE
(Souter, J.) Yes. The manifest objective of governmental action may be dispositive in an Establishment Clause inquiry, and the development of that action should be considered when determining its purpose. The purpose needs to be understood in light of the context of the action. When a government acts with the predominant purpose of advancing religion, the Establishment Clause's central value of religious neutrality is violated. When a government shows a purpose to favor religion, it sends a message to nonbelievers that they are not full members of the political community. Adherents are told that they are favored members. The apparent purpose can have an impact greater than the intent expressly decreed.

The Counties (D) argue that consideration of the purpose should be truncated because the purpose is unknowable. Examining the purpose of a law is a staple of statutory interpretation. It also makes practical sense when the official objective can be understood from readily discoverable facts. The

McCreary County v. American Civil Liberties Union of Kentucky (Continued)

inquiry is not rigged to find a dominant religious purpose in every case. If a motive to advance religion is hidden so well that no one can see it, the government has not made a divisive announcement that it is taking religious sides. The Counties (D) also propose an alternate inquiry that would essentially accept any proffered claim to a secular purpose. There is no precedent for such an inquiry. A legislature's stated reasons for an action will be given deference but the secular purpose must be genuine. The context of a government's action is relevant evidence that will not be ignored.

The Ten Commandments are an instrument of religion. The first display by the Counties (D) emphasized the religious message. The second exhibit, which placed the Commandments with other documents, also had an impermissible religious purpose. The focus of the second displays was on the religious parts of the documents, which showed that the Commandments were being displayed precisely because of their sectarian content. The second displays are called "dead and buried," but the reasonable observer cannot forget them. The third display quoted more of the explicitly religious language of the Commandments than the first two did. No reasonable observer could believe that the objective behind the first two displays had changed.

The dissent states that the Framers of the Constitution believed that government could endorse monotheism, the core belief of one religion. The dissent is correct in saying that there is evidence that some of the Framers of the Constitution thought that some endorsement of religion was compatible with the Establishment Clause. There is, however, also evidence that the Framers intended to establish government neutrality in matters of religion. The fair inference is that there was no common understanding of the limits of the Establishment Clause. Affirmed.

■ CONCURRENCE

(O'Connor, J.) The goal of the Religion Clauses in the First Amendment is to preserve religious liberty to the fullest extent possible in a pluralistic society. Voluntary religious belief and expression may be threatened as much by government sponsorship of religious expression as it is by government action that threatens or impedes expression. The Religion Clauses protect adherents of all religions, as well as those who believe in no religion at all.

■ DISSENT

(Scalia, J.) Government invocation of religion has a long tradition in America. Those who wrote the Constitution believed that morality was essential to the well-being of society and that encouraging religion was the best way to foster morality. History and tradition do not support the idea of neutrality between religion and nonreligion. Strict neutrality would permit no public religious expression at all. Governmental invocation of God is not an establishment of religion.

Analysis:

Justice Souter suggests that there may be a way in which the counties could "undo" the religious taint attributed to the earlier displays by coming up with some new, non-religious way to display the Ten Commandments in their courthouses. But this speculation seems a bit improbable, when the Court basically characterizes the third display as an ineffective attempt to cover up the counties' original purpose. Perhaps, as the dissent asserts, the original intent should not taint the counties' later efforts, and each display should be considered in its own right.

Van Orden v. Perry

(Texas Resident) v. *(Governor)*
545 U.S. 677, 125 S.Ct. 2854 (2005)

DISPLAYING THE TEN COMMANDMENTS DID *NOT* VIOLATE THE ESTABLISHMENT CLAUSE IN THIS CASE

■ **INSTANT FACTS** Van Orden (P) claimed that a monument on the grounds of the Texas Capitol that displayed the Ten Commandments violated the Establishment Clause.

■ **BLACK LETTER RULE** Displaying religious content or a message consistent with religious doctrine is not necessarily an Establishment Clause violation.

■ **PROCEDURAL BASIS**

Appeal from an order affirming denial of an injunction.

■ **FACTS**

Seventeen monuments and twenty-one historical markers were located on the grounds of the Texas Capitol. One of those monuments was a granite monolith with the text of the Ten Commandments. The monument was donated by the Fraternal Order of Eagles in 1961. Van Orden (P) objected to seeing the monument when he went to the Capitol. He brought an action for a declaration that the monument violated the Establishment Clause, and for an injunction directing the removal of the monument.

■ **ISSUE**

Did the placement of the monument on the Capitol grounds violate the Establishment Clause?

■ **DECISION AND RATIONALE**

(Rehnquist, C.J.) No. Displaying religious content or a message consistent with religious doctrine is not necessarily an Establishment Clause violation. Our institutions presuppose a supreme being, but those institutions must not force religious observation on the people. Courts must neither abdicate the responsibility to maintain a separation between church and state nor evince hostility towards religion by disabling government from recognizing our religious heritage. There is a long history of official acknowledgement of religion by all three branches of American government. The Ten Commandments are certainly religious, but they have undeniable historical meaning as well.

The display of the Ten Commandments here is a passive one. Texas (D) has treated the Capitol grounds monuments as representing several strands in Texas political and legal history. The Ten Commandments monument has a dual religious and political significance. It does not violate the Establishment Clause. Affirmed.

■ **CONCURRENCE**

(Thomas, J.) The text and history of the Establishment Clause resist incorporation against the states. Even if the Clause is incorporated, the monument here is not the establishment of religion. The Framers understood establishment to involve actual legal coercion.

Van Orden v. Perry (Continued)

■ CONCURRENCE

(Breyer, J.) This is a borderline case. The monument was used to convey a secular message as well as a religious one. The group that donated the monument had to highlight the Commandments' role in shaping civic morality. In addition, the physical setting of the monument does not suggest a religious purpose. The monument has sat on the Capitol grounds for over forty years with no objections.

■ DISSENT

(Stevens, J.) The sole function of the monument is to display the Ten Commandments. The Establishment Clause creates a strong presumption against the display of religious symbols on public property. The issue is obfuscated rather than clarified by simplistic commentary on the various ways in which religion has played a role in American life, and by the recitation of the many governmental "acknowledgments" of the role the Ten Commandments played. The plurality relies heavily on the religious rhetoric used by the nation's leaders. These leaders, however, are expressing their views as individual members of the polity, not as an official policy. The plurality also refers to religious statements made by the framers of the Constitution, but those statements were not incorporated into the text of the Constitution. In addition, the framers had a much narrower view of the term "religion" than the plurality would be willing to accept.

■ DISSENT

(Souter, J.) The Religion Clauses are not absolute, but neutrality is required as a general rule. The monument's presentation, which includes religious text and symbols, is in contrast to the constitutional depictions of the monument. If neutrality towards religion is to mean anything, any citizen should be able to visit the state Capitol without having to confront religious expressions clearly meant as an official religious position.

Analysis:

It is difficult to distinguish this case from *McCreary County v. American Civil Liberties Union of Kentucky*, 545 U.S. 844 (2005), decided on the same day as this case. The *McCreary County* case held the displays of the Ten Commandments in county courthouses to be unconstitutional. The critical distinction seems to be that, in *McCreary County*, there were detailed legislative findings supporting the claim that the purpose of the display was to support religion. In this case, the stated purpose for placing the monument was to provide moral guidance. The Court draws a very fine line.

■ CASE VOCABULARY

INCORPORATION: The process of applying the provisions of the Bill of Rights to the states by interpreting the 14th Amendment's Due Process Clause as encompassing those provisions.

Engel v. Vitale

(Parent) v. *(School Official)*
370 U.S. 421, 82 S.Ct. 1261 (1962)

ORGANIZED PRAYERS IN PUBLIC SCHOOLS ARE UNCONSTITUTIONAL

■ **INSTANT FACTS** The Board of Education of Union Free School District in Hyde Park, New York, adopted a policy of student recitation of a prayer at the beginning of each school day.

■ **BLACK LETTER RULE** The Establishment Clause of the First Amendment forbids any part of the business of government to compose official prayers for any group of the American people to recite as a part of a religious program carried on by the government.

■ PROCEDURAL BASIS

Certiorari to review an undisclosed appellate decision.

■ FACTS

The Board of Education of Union Free School District in Hyde Park, New York, adopted a policy of student recitation of a prayer at the beginning of each school day.

■ ISSUE

May a public school district constitutionally require its students to recite a prayer at the beginning of each school day?

■ DECISION AND RATIONALE

(Black, J.) No. The Establishment Clause of the First Amendment forbids any "part of the business of government to compose official prayers for any group of the American people to recite as a part of a religious program carried on by the government." A prohibition on government-imposed prayer was a primary reason for the Establishment Clause and cannot be sanctioned in public schools. Although students need not verbally recite the prayer, and regardless of any nondenominational language, no public school may endorse any practice respecting religious exercise.

■ DISSENT

(Stewart, J.) The First Amendment was adopted to ensure freedom of religion and prohibit the establishment of an official government religion. America was founded on deeply entrenched spiritual ideals that should not be ignored or discouraged. A non-denominational public school prayer, in which students may silently refrain from participation, is not unconstitutional.

Analysis:

School prayer may be the most recognizable context of Establishment Clause challenges. Yet, despite the separation of church and state, many public schools throughout the United States formerly opened their days with a prayer recitation. Today, few would question the impropriety of such a policy.

Lee v. Weisman

(Student) v. (Principal)
505 U.S. 577, 112 S.Ct. 2649 (1992)

INCLUDING RELIGIOUS OR RELIGION RELATED TOPICS IN OFFICIAL PUBLIC SCHOOL CEREMONIES VIOLATES THE ESTABLISHMENT CLAUSE

■ **INSTANT FACTS** An Establishment Clause challenge to the practice of prayers at public school ceremonies is raised, after a public school principal invited a rabbi to deliver an invocation and benediction at a graduation.

■ **BLACK LETTER RULE** Government coercion to participate in religious activities violates the Establishment Clause.

■ PROCEDURAL BASIS

Certification to the United States Supreme Court of an Establishment Clause challenge to a public school's practice of saying a prayer at graduation.

■ FACTS

For many years, it had been the policy of the Providence Rhode Island School Committee and the Superintendent of School to permit principals to invite members of the clergy to give invocations and benediction at middle school and high school graduations. Accordingly, the principal of Nathan Bishop Middle School, Robert E. Lee (D) invited a rabbi to deliver prayers at the graduation exercises and the rabbi accepted. As part of another custom of Providence school officials, Lee (D) provided the rabbi with a pamphlet entitled "Guidelines for Civic Occasions," prepared by the National Conference of Christians and Jews, which recommends that public prayers at nonsectarian civic ceremonies be composed with "inclusiveness and sensitivity," though it acknowledges that prayer in general may be inappropriate on some civic occasions. Lee (D) also advised the rabbi that the invocation and benediction should be nonsectarian. During the invocation and benediction, the rabbi referred to "God" and the "Lord" while asking blessings of the graduates, parents, and school officials among others. Daniel Weisman (Weisman) (P), acting on behalf of his fourteen-year-old daughter Deborah Weisman, who graduated from Nathan Bishop Middle School, raised an Establishment Clause challenge to this practice.

■ ISSUE

Does the inclusion of general religious content in an official public school function violate the Establishment Clause?

■ DECISION AND RATIONALE

(Kennedy, J.) Yes. The government involvement with religious activity here, is pervasive to the point of creating a state-sponsored and state-directed religious exercise in a public school. State officials are directing the performance of a formal religious exercise at promotional and graduation ceremonies for secondary schools. Even for those students who object to the religious exercise, their attendance and participation in the religious activity are in a fair and real sense obligatory, though the school district does not require attendance as a condition for receipt of the diploma. Conducting this formal religious observance conflicts with settled rules pertaining to prayer exercises for students, and that suffices to

Lee v. Weisman (Continued)

determine the question before us. There is no need here, to reconsider our decision in *Lemon v. Kurtzman* [where the Court held that in order to be constitutional, a government act or regulation must have a secular purpose, must not advance nor inhibit religion, and must not cause excessive governmental entanglement with religion]. It is beyond dispute that the Constitution guarantees that government may not coerce anyone to support or participate in religion or religious faith. The State's involvement in the school prayers challenged today violates this central principle. First, both the decision to give an invocation and benediction, and the choice of religious participant, here a rabbi, is attributable to the state as actions by school principal Lee (D). Second, Lee (D) directed and controlled the content of the prayers, by providing the rabbi with "Guidelines for Civic Occasions," and advising him that his prayers should be nonsectarian. It is a cornerstone principle of our Establishment Clause jurisprudence that the government take no part in composing official prayer for anyone to recite as part of a religious program carried on by the government. That is exactly what the school officials attempt to do here. With respect to the students, we have observed before that there are heightened concerns with protecting freedom of conscience from subtle coercive pressure in elementary and secondary public schools. It is undeniable that the school district's supervision and control of a high school graduation ceremony places public pressure, as well as peer pressure, on attending students to stand as a group or maintain respectful silence during the invocation and benediction. This pressure, though subtle and indirect, can be as real as any overt compulsion. While most people would not view their standing or remaining silent as being equivalent to approval or participation in prayer, for the dissenter of young age there may be a reasonable perception that she is being forced to pray in a manner her conscience does not allow. There can be no doubt that for many of the students, the act of standing or remaining silent was an expression of participation in the rabbi's prayer. Thus a reasonable dissenter could believe that the group exercise signified her own participation or approval of it. The argument that graduation is purely voluntary lacks all persuasion. To say that a teenage student has a real choice not to attend her high school graduation is formalistic in the extreme, as everyone knows that high school graduation is one of life's most significant occasions. A student is not free to absent herself from the graduation exercise in any real sense of the term "voluntary," for absence would require forfeiture of those intangible benefits which have motivated the student through youth and all her high school years. The Government's argument gives insufficient recognition to the real conflict of conscience faced by the young student. The essence of the Government's position is that for a social occasion of this importance, it is the objector, not the majority, who must take a unilateral and private action to avoid compromising religious scruples, hereby electing to miss the graduation exercise. However, it is a tenet of the First Amendment that the State cannot require one of its citizens to forfeit his or her rights and benefits as the price of resisting conformance to state-sponsored religious practice. We have never suggested that a school can persuade or compel a student to participate in a religious exercise. Government coercion to participate in religious activities violates the Establishment Clause.

■ CONCURRENCE

(Blackmun, J.) The Court today holds that the graduation prayer is unconstitutional because the State in effect required participation in a religious exercise. Although our precedents make clear that proof of government coercion is not necessary to prove an Establishment Clause violation, it is an obvious indication that the government is endorsing or promoting religion. But it is not enough that the government restrain from compelling religious practices. It must not engage in them either. We have believed that religious freedom cannot exist in the absence of a free democratic government, and that such government cannot endure when there is fusion between religion and the political regime. To that end, our cases have prohibited government endorsement of religion, its sponsorship, and active involvement in religion, whether or not citizens were coerced to conform.

■ DISSENT

(Scalia, J.) In holding that the Establishment Clause prohibits invocations and benedictions at public-school graduation ceremonies, the Court lays waste to a tradition that is as old as public-school graduation ceremonies themselves. The history and tradition of our Nation are replete with public ceremonies featuring prayers of thanksgiving and petition. The Court's argument that state officials have "coerced" students to take part in the invocation and benediction at graduation ceremonies is incoherent. The Court does not say for example, that students are psychologically coerced to bow their heads, place there hands in a Durer-like prayer position, pay attention to the prayers, utter "Amen", or in fact pray. Instead, it claims only that students are coerced to stand or maintain respectful silence. The Court's notion that a student who simply sits in "respectful silence" during the invocation and benediction has somehow joined, or would, somehow be perceived as having joined is nothing short of ludicrous. Surely our society is not one in which anyone who does not stand on his chair and shout obscenities can reasonably be deemed to have assented to everything said in his presence. Since the Court does not dispute that students exposed to prayer at graduation ceremonies retain the free will to sit, there is absolutely no basis for the Court's decision. Even the subtle coercion to stand does not remotely establish "participation" or the appearance of it. I also find it odd that the Court concludes that high school graduates may not be subjected to this supposed psychological coercion, yet refrains from addressing whether "mature adults" may. Since many graduating seniors are old enough to vote, why does the Court treat them like first-graders? While I have no quarrel with the Court's general proposition that the Establishment Clause prohibits government coercion to support or participate in religion of its exercise, I see no warrant for expanding the concept of coercion beyond acts backed by threat of penalty. Furthermore, the personal interests of those other than Weisman (P) are not inconsequential. The longstanding American tradition of prayer at official ceremonies displays with unmistakable clarity that the Establishment Clause does not forbid the government to accommodate it. The real issue before us today is whether a mandatory choice in favor of frustrating the desires of a religious majority has been imposed by the Constitution. As the age-old practices of our people show, the answer to that question is not at all in doubt. To deprive our society of that important unifying mechanism, in order to spare the non-believer what seems to me the minimal inconvenience of standing or even in respectful nonparticipation, is as senseless in policy as it is unsupported in law.

Analysis:

Everyone attends countless ceremonies in their lives where prayers are said as a matter of course. Are they endorsing the religion of the speaker when they stand and bow along with the others in attendance? Probably not. Justice Scalia has a point when he states that a mere showing of respect is all such actions entail. Why, then, does the Court hold that such prayers in the public school violate the Constitution? The reason is that young people are more impressionable and susceptible to peer pressure than adults. They feel the need to conform to what the larger group is doing, wearing, saying, etc. Children are effectively forced to attend a graduation ceremony. They are forced to listen to prayers that may be wholly at odds with their personal beliefs. Do they rise and bow as the bulk of their peers will do, or do they remain seated as everyone around them stands, all the while noticing the one or two lone individuals who rebel? It is this pressure to conform, this coercion as the Court calls it, that is key.

Mitchell v. Helms
(Not Stated) v. (Not Stated)
530 U.S. 793, 120 S.Ct. 2530 (2000)

FEDERAL PROGRAMS THAT AID PUBLIC AND PRIVATE SCHOOLS BY LOANING EDUCATION MATERIALS AND EQUIPMENT DO NOT VIOLATE THE ESTABLISHMENT CLAUSE

■ **INSTANT FACTS** Federal law that authorized the government to distribute funds to state and local agencies, which in turn loaned educational materials and equipment to public and private schools, was challenged as violating the Establishment Clause.

■ **BLACK LETTER RULE** A federal student-aid funding program used to loan educational materials and equipment to public and private schools, including religious schools, which does not result in religious indoctrination by the government, define its recipients by reference to religion, and cannot be viewed as an endorsement of religion, will not violate the establishment clause.

■ **PROCEDURAL BASIS**

Certification to the United States Supreme Court of an action challenging the constitutionality of a federal student-aid funding program.

■ **FACTS**

Chapter 2 of the Education and Improvement Act of 1981, channels federal funds to local educational agencies (LEA's), which are usually public school districts, through state educational agencies (SEA's), to implement programs to assist children in elementary and secondary schools. Chapter 2, among other things, provides aid for the acquisition and use of instructional aid and educational material. The most significant of Chapter 2's restrictions is that the "services, material, and equipment" provided to private schools must be "secular, neutral, and nonideological." Private schools may not acquire control of Chapter 2 funds or title to Chapter 2 materials, equipment, or property, but instead these schools receive the material and equipment by submitting to the LEA an application detailing which items they seek and how it will be used. Upon approval, LEA purchases those items from the school's allocation of funds, and then lends them to that school. In Jefferson Parish, Louisiana, private schools have primarily used their allocations for non-recurring expenses, usually materials and equipment including library books, computers, projectors, television sets, tape recorders, laboratory equipment, maps, globes, filmstrips, and cassette recordings. On average, about 30% of Chapter 2 funds spent per year are allocated for private schools, and roughly 46 private schools have participated since 1987. Of these 46, 34 are Roman Catholic, 7 are otherwise religiously affiliated, and 5 were not religiously affiliated. What is challenged is the constitutionality of Chapter 2 as applied in Jefferson Parish.

■ **ISSUE**

Is a federal program, whose funds are used to loan educational material and equipment to public and private schools, including religious schools, a law respecting an establishment of religion in violation of the Establishment Clause?

■ **DECISION AND RATIONALE**

(Thomas, J.) No. The Establishment Clause dictates that "Congress shall make no law respecting an establishment of religion." Although we have consistently struggled to apply these simple words in the

Mitchell v. Helms (Continued)

context of governmental aid to religious schools, we brought some clarity to our case law in *Agostini v. Felton* [where the Court allowed remedial education teachers to provide instruction in private schools], by consolidating some of our previously disparate considerations under a revised test. In *Lemon* we had considered whether a statute: 1) has a secular purpose, 2) has a primary effect of advancing or inhibiting religion, or 3) creates excessive entanglement between government and religion. In *Agostini* we examined only the first two factors in evaluating aid to schools. We acknowledge that our cases discussing excessive entanglement had applied many of the same considerations as had our cases discussing primary effect, and we therefore recast *Lemon's* entanglement inquiry as simply one criterion relevant to determining a statute's effect. In determining the effect of a statute, we then considered whether the statute: 1) results in governmental indoctrination, 2) defines its recipients by reference to religion, or 3) creates an excessive entanglement. Because respondents do not challenge the District Court's holding that Chapter 2 has a secular purpose and does not create excessive entanglement, we will only consider the effect of Chapter 2, using the first two *Agostini* criteria. First, the question of whether governmental aid to religious school results in indoctrination is ultimately a question of whether any religious indoctrination that occurs, could reasonably be attributed to governmental action. This consistently turns upon the principle of neutrality, upholding aid that is offered to a broad range of groups or persons without regard to their religion. If the government is offering assistance to recipients who provide a broad range of indoctrination, the government itself is not thought responsible for any particular indoctrination. As a way of assuring neutrality, we have repeatedly considered whether any governmental aid that goes to a religious institution does so as a result of the genuinely independent and private choices of individuals. If numerous private choices, rather than the single choice of a government, determine the distribution of aid pursuant to neutral eligibility criteria, then a government cannot grant special favors that might lead to a religious establishment. In *Witters*, we held that the Establishment Clause did not bar a State from including within a neutral program, tuition payments for vocational rehabilitation of a blind person studying at a Christian college to become a pastor, missionary, or youth director. Similarly, in *Mueller*, we upheld a tax deduction for educational expenses because it neutrally provides state assistance to a broad spectrum of school-age children, and because numerous private choices of individual parents determined which schools would benefit from the deductions. As here, any aid to parochial schools was available only as a result of decisions of individual parents. Thus no "state approval" could have been deemed to been conferred on any particular religion, or on religion generally. Furthermore, just because an aid program offers private and religious schools a benefit, does not mean that the program, by reducing the cost of religious education, creates, under *Agostini's* second criterion, an incentive for parents to choose such an education for their children. Any aid will have some such effect. Respondents argue that direct, nonincidental aid to the primary educational mission of religious schools is always impermissible, and that provision to religious schools of aid that is divertible to religious use is similarly impermissible.

These arguments are inconsistent with our more recent case law. First, although some of our earlier cases did emphasize the distinction between direct and indirect aid, the purpose of this distinction was merely to prevent "subsidization" of religion. Our more recent cases address this purpose not through the direct / indirect distinction, but through the principle of private choice, as incorporated in the first *Agostini* criteria. If aid to any religious school, first passes through the hands (literally or figuratively) of numerous private individuals who are free to direct the aid elsewhere, the government has not provided any "support of religion." Although the presence of private choice is easier to see when aid literally passes through the hands of individuals, there is no reason to require such a form. Of course, we have seen special dangers when money is given to religious schools directly rather than indirectly. But direct payments of money are not at issue in this case, and we refuse to allow a "special" case to create a rule for all cases. Second, although we agree with respondents that aid to religious schools may not be religious in nature, we do not agree that aid may not be divertible to religious use. So long as the governmental aid is not itself unsuitable for use in the public schools because of religious content, and eligibility for aid is determined in a constitutionally permissible manner, any use of that aid to indoctrinate cannot be attributed to the government and is thus not of constitutional concern. A concern for divertibility is misplaced not only because it fails to explain why the sort of aid that we have allowed is permissible, but also because it envelops all aid, no matter how trivial, and thus has the most attenuated link to any realistic concern for preventing an "establishment of religion." One of the dissents factors is whether a school that receives aid is pervasively sectarian. The dissent is correct that there was a period when this factor mattered, particularly if the school was a primary or secondary school. But that period is one that the Court should regret. There are numerous reasons to dispense with this factor. First, its relevance in our precedents is in sharp decline. Second, the religious nature of a recipient should not matter to the constitutional analysis, so long as the recipient furthers the government's secular purpose. The pervasively sectarian recipient has not received any special favor, and it is most bizarre that the Court would reserve special hostility for those who take their religion seriously, or who make the mistake of being effective in transmitting their views to children. Third, courts should refrain from inquiring into the recipient's religious views, which is required by a focus on whether a school is pervasively sectarian. Finally, hostility to aid to pervasively sectarian schools has a shameful pedigree that we do not hesitate to disavow. Although the dissent professes concern for "the implied exclusion of the less favored," the exclusion of "pervasively sectarian" schools from government-aid programs is just that. In sum, a federal student-aid funding program used to loan educational materials and equipment to public and private schools, including religious schools, which does not result in religious indoctrination by the government, define its recipients by reference to religion, and cannot be viewed as an endorsement of religion, will not violate the establishment clause. In applying the two relevant *Agostini* criteria, we find that Chapter 2 does not result in governmental indoctrination because it determines eligibility for aid neutrally, allocates that aid based on the private choices of the parents of schoolchildren, and does not provide aid that has an impermissible content. Nor does Chapter 2 define its recipients by reference to religion.

■ CONCURRENCE

(O'Connor, J.) Two specific aspects of the opinion compel me to write separately. First, the plurality's treatment of neutrality comes dose to assigning that factor singular importance in the future adjudication of Establishment Clause challenges to government school-aid programs. We have never held that a government-aid program passes constitutional muster solely because of the neutral criteria it employs as a basis for distributing aid. Neutrality is but one of several factors. Second, the plurality's approval of actual diversion of government aid to religious indoctrination is in tension with our precedents, and unnecessary to decide the instant case. I do not believe that we should treat a per-capita-aid program the same as the true private choice programs. When the government provides aid directly to the student, that student can attend a religious school and yet retain control over whether the secular government aid will be applied toward religious education. A government program of direct aid to religious schools based on the number of students attending differs in that if the religious school uses the aid to inculcate religion in its students, it is reasonable to say that the government has communicated a message of endorsement, and a perception of government support for the advancement of religion. If a per-capita-aid program is identical in relevant constitutional respects, as the plurality contends, to a true private-choice program, then there is no reason that the government should be precluded from providing direct money payments to religious organizations based on the number of persons belonging to each organization. I would adhere to the rule that we have applied in the context of textbook lending programs. That is, to establish a First Amendment violation, plaintiffs must prove that the aid in question actually is, or has been used, for religious purposes. The evidence proffered by respondents concerning actual diversion of Chapter 2 aid is de minimis.

■ DISSENT

(Souter, J.) When evenhandedness refers to distribution to limited groups within society, like groups of schools of schoolchildren, it does not make sense to regard the benefit as aid to the recipients. Hence, if we looked no further than neutrality, and failed to ask what activities the aid might support or did support, religious schools could be blessed with government funding as massive as expenditures made for the benefit of their public school counterparts, and religious missions would thrive on public money. This is why consideration of less than universal neutrality had never been recognized as dispositive and has always been teamed with attention to other facts bearing on the substantive prohibition of support for a school's religious objective. The facts most obviously relevant to the Chapter 2 scheme here, are those showing divertibility and actual diversion in the circumstances of pervasively sectarian religious schools and the lack of effective safeguards. The aid that the government provided was highly susceptible to unconstitutional use. Among other things, the record shows that nonpublic schools requested and the government purchased at least 191 religious books with taxpayer funds. The evidence pervasively suggests that other aid was actually diverted as well. The Chapter 2 fund computers took over the support of the computing network system whenever there was a breakdown of

Mitchell v. Helms (Continued)

the master computer purchased with the religious school's own funds. So too were film projectors and videotape machines bought and used in religious indoctrination over a period of years. The Court has no choice but to hold that the program as applied violated the Establishment Clause.

Analysis:

This case illustrates the Court's likely shift in its approach to the Establishment Clause with respect to aid-to-school programs. It gives a good historical overview of this shift during the 15 years that it took for this case to be litigated. Initially, in 1985, the District Court found that the aid-to-school program had the primary effect of advancing religion because the materials lent to the Catholic schools were direct aid, relying upon two previous Supreme Court decisions that held similar programs unconstitutional. However, six years later, and after the first district court judge had retired, another district court judge upheld the program, relying upon three Supreme Court decisions, which had been decided since the initial District Court's holding. While the matter was on appeal, the Supreme Court decided *Agostini*, which approved a program that provided public employees to teach remedial classes at private schools (thereby overruling two previous Supreme Court decisions to the contrary). In *Agostini* the Court seemed to articulate a new approach in determining the effect of a statute, looking to whether the aid program: (1) resulted in governmental indoctrination, (2) defined its recipients by reference to religion, and (3) created an excessive entanglement.

Zelman v. Simmons–Harris

(Superintendent of Public Instruction) v. (Taxpayers and Others)
536 U.S. 639, 122 S.Ct. 2460 (2002)

A SCHOOL VOUCHER PROGRAM IS CONSTITUTIONAL

■ **INSTANT FACTS** To offer its students better educational opportunities, the Ohio Pilot Project Scholarship Program provided, inter alia, tuition assistance to private, religiously affiliated schools.

■ **BLACK LETTER RULE** By not endorsing a specific religion or limiting parental choices to religious-affiliated schools when offering vouchers to parents of students in the Cleveland School District, Ohio's Pilot Project Scholarship Program does not violate the Establishment Clause of the First Amendment.

■ **PROCEDURAL BASIS**

Certiorari to review an undisclosed appellate decision.

■ **FACTS**

As part of a plan to improve education in Cleveland, Ohio's Pilot Project Scholarship Program (the "Program") was designed to provide financial aid to students to be able to attend a private school or another school of the student's parent's choosing. The Program also provided financial assistance to obtain tutoring. Both religious and nonreligious schools were part of the program, as were urban and suburban schools. The financial aid was granted on the basis of need and parents were given sole authority to decide which schools to select. In the 1999–2000 school year, eighty-two percent of the private schools that were in the program had a religious affiliation. Sixty percent of the participating families were below the poverty line. The school district also offered two other educational alternatives: students could attend community schools that receive double the per-student funding or a magnet school that offered the students the ability to emphasize certain subject areas.

■ **ISSUE**

Does Ohio's Pilot Project Scholarship Program have the effect of advancing or inhibiting religion in violation of the Establishment Clause?

■ **DECISION AND RATIONALE**

(Rehnquist, C.J.) No. The First Amendment's Establishment Clause prohibits a state from enacting laws with the purpose or effect advancing or inhibiting religion through its laws. The purpose of the Program here was unquestionably to provide educational alternatives to poor students in light of the public school system's failures. In deciding whether an unintended side effect of a law has been the advancement or inhibition of religion, courts have previously distinguished between programs that provide funds directly to religious institutions and those in which government funds reach them as the result of the independent choices of individuals. This is a program of true choice. Participants in the Program are not chosen by race, religion, or any other designation. All residents in the district are equally able to participate. The only preference in the program is for low-income families to receive a greater amount of financial assistance and receive priority for admissions. There are no financial incentives that encourage students to attend religion-backed schools. "The incidental advancement of a religious mission, or the perceived endorsement of a religious message, is reasonably attributable to the individual recipient, not to the government, whose role ends with the disbursement of benefits."

Zelman v. Simmons–Harris (Continued)

If anything, there is a disincentive to choose those schools based on the financial aid given to non-religious schools. The respondents in this case argue that a constitutional violation exists based simply on the perception that the Program is endorsing religious schools. In the absence of a real endorsement, the Court cannot find a violation. The program provides sufficient secular opportunities for Cleveland parents of school-age children. It cannot be said that the Program is coercing parents to send their children to schools with religious affiliations. The Ohio Program is religion-neutral. Aid is distributed evenly based on need.

■ CONCURRENCE

(O'Connor, J.) While 82% of the schools participating in the voucher program are religious, the total amount of public expenditures to religious schools is minimal compared to the dollars spent in non-religious community and magnet schools under the program, demonstrating the relatively minor effect the program has on the advancement of religion. Furthermore, the Cleveland voucher program is religion-neutral. Parents are not required to select parochial schools for their children, and it is not essential that the secular schools be superior to the parochial schools in all respects in order for them to provide a reasonable alternative for the parents. Indeed, many of the parents in the area chose to send their children to non-religious, non-private schools, and no evidence was offered to establish that any student who did not want to attend a nonreligious school was forced to do so.

■ CONCURRENCE

(Thomas, J.) The Establishment Clause provides, "Congress shall make no law respecting an establishment of religion." It says nothing to address the authority of the States to make such laws. If this right is to be incorporated by the Fourteenth Amendment to apply to the States, it should advance, not constrain, individual liberty, and therefore allow States greater latitude to experiment with programs that touch upon religious matters so long as they do not infringe upon the free exercise of religion. The Fourteenth Amendment guarantees liberty. It should not be used to invalidate a neutral State program that seeks to afford greater educational liberty merely because it touches upon the subject of religion.

■ DISSENT

(Stevens, J.) The use of government funds for the religious indoctrination of Cleveland's grammar school students cannot be legitimized merely because of an educational crisis. The fact that those students receiving an insufficient public education receive state funds for their choice to attend a religious school renders the program one "respecting an establishment of religion." Likewise, whether the choice to attend parochial school is voluntarily made by parents does not justify such a use of public funds.

■ DISSENT

(Souter, J.) Under the Program, Ohio is providing private tax money to citizens to be used to pay tuition at religious elementary and middle schools. The religious schools will use some of that money to support the advancement of religious objectives. Doing so violates the Establishment Clause whether it is done for a noble cause or a malevolent one.

The program is not neutral. The voucher program itself applies only to private schools, without consideration of public schools, which can receive no voucher payments. Seen in this light, it matters not whether a majority of students attend public schools or whether none do at all. The voucher program provides tuition payments directly to parents for private schools, without regard to whether those schools are secular or not.

Likewise, the voucher program does not involve free choice. Choice is a nebulous concept that can be manipulated in many fashions to establish the freedom of its exercise. The majority finds free choice because it calculates that only 20% of voucher recipients attend religious schools. Justice O'Connor finds free choice because the total funds spent at religious schools under the program is small in comparison. However, nearly all of the schools in the district that in fact received vouchers were religious. This unexplained fact indicates that some component of the voucher program negates free choice and urges voucher payments toward parochial schools. Evidence shows that two-thirds of the parents who enrolled their children in parochial schools did not agree with the schools' religious doctrine. Their decisions are not a product of free choice, but rather a choice of the best educational opportunity available to their children under the program.

Even if the program were neutral and a product of free choice, the Establishment Clause forbids such a use of public tax dollars. The Establishment Clause demands that no taxpayer be compelled to fund the religious instruction of the nation's children. The Court's decision renders the Establishment Clause meaningless in matters of educational aid, for it provides the blueprint for future educational plans to survive constitutional scrutiny.

■ DISSENT

(Breyer, J.) Although well-intentioned, the voucher program poses the serious risk of religious conflict the Establishment Clause seeks to prevent. When public money is used for religious purposes, religious sects battle to gain the most funding they can. Religious tension emerges when one sect benefits more than another. The Establishment Clause combats this tension not by equal entitlement of public funds, but by separating church and state through the complete prohibition against the use of public funds for religious purposes. In a diverse religious culture as ours, religious equality cannot be achieved under any funding program. Because the Establishment Clause, in part, sought to eliminate such conflict, the program is unconstitutional.

Analysis:

Justice Souter complains that supporting the religious schools through this system violates the spirit of the Constitution, even if pursued for a good cause. In the absence of a reasonable alternative, Justice Souter would appear to prefer that the students endure a poor education. Query whether the decision the Court reached here would have been the same or different if the Constitution included a provision similar to Texas's that required an "efficient" system of education, as described in *Edgewood Independent School District v. Kirby*, 777 S.W.2d 391 (Texas 1989).